GARDNER'S
ART through the AGES

GARDNER'S
ART through the AGES
A CONCISE GLOBAL HISTORY

FRED S. KLEINER

THIRD EDITION

WADSWORTH
CENGAGE Learning

Australia • Brazil • Japan • Korea • Mexico • Singapore • Spain • United Kingdom • United States

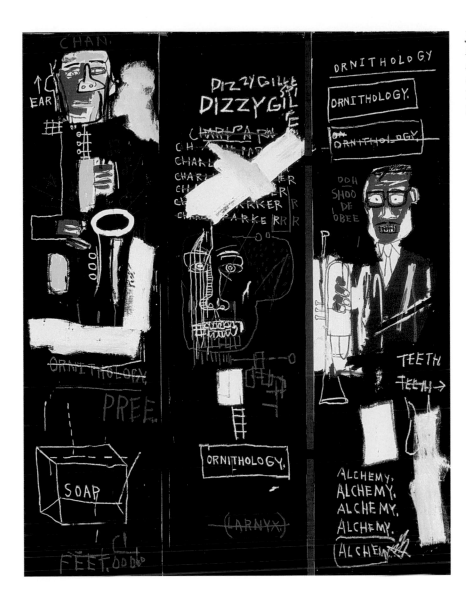

JEAN-MICHEL BASQUIAT, *Horn Players*, 1983. Acrylic and oil paintstick on three canvas panels, 8′ × 6′ 3″. Broad Art Foundation, Santa Monica.

In recent decades, many of the most innovative artists worldwide have addressed social and political issues in their work. This focus on the content and meaning of art represents these artists' rejection of the postwar abstract art movement in order once again to embrace the persuasive powers of art to communicate.

During his tragically brief career, JEAN-MICHEL BASQUIAT (1960–1988) recorded in his paintings the minority cultural experience in America. Born in Brooklyn in a comfortable home—his father was an accountant from Haiti and his mother a black Puerto Rican—Basquiat rebelled against middle-class values, dropped out of school at 17, and took to the streets. He first drew attention as an artist when he participated in a 1980 group show—the "Times Square Show"—in an abandoned 42nd Street building. Eight years later, after a meteoric rise to fame, he died of a heroin overdose at age 27.

Many of Basquiat's paintings celebrate black heroes, for example, the legendary jazz musicians Charlie "Bird" Parker and Dizzy Gillespie, whom he memorialized in *Horn Players*. The fractured figures, the bold colors against a black background, and the deliberately scrawled, crossed-out, and misspelled graffiti ("ornithology"—the study of birds—is a pun on Parker's nickname) create a dynamic composition suggesting the rhythms of jazz music and the excitement of the streets of New York, "the city that never sleeps."

Basquiat's intensely personal approach to painting characterizes the art of the modern era in general, but it is not typical of many periods of the history of art when artists toiled in anonymity to fulfill the wishes of their patrons, whether Egyptian pharaohs, Roman emperors, medieval monks, or African kings. *Art through the Ages* surveys the art of all periods from prehistory to the present worldwide, and it examines how artworks of all kinds have always reflected the historical contexts in which they were created.

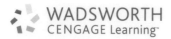

Gardner's Art through the Ages: A Concise Global History,
Third Edition

Fred S. Kleiner

Publisher: Clark Baxter

Senior Development Editor: Sharon Adams Poore

Assistant Editor: Ashley Bargende

Associate Media Editor: Kimberly Apfelbaum

Marketing Manager: Jeanne Heston

Marketing Coordinator: Klaira Markenzon

Senior Marketing Communications Manager: Heather Baxley

Senior Content Project Manager: Lianne Ames

Senior Art Director: Cate Rickard Barr

Senior Print Buyer: Mary Beth Hennebury

Rights Acquisition Specialist: Mandy Groszko

Production Service: Joan Keyes, Dovetail Publishing Services

Text and Cover Designer: tani hasegawa

Cover Image: © 2011 Estate of Jean-Michel Basquiat/ADAGP, Paris/Artists Rights Society (ARS), New York. Photography: Douglas M. Parker Studio, Los Angeles. Image courtesy of The Broad Art Foundation, Santa Monica.

Compositor: Thompson Type, Inc.

For product information and technology assistance, contact us at
Cengage Learning Customer & Sales Support, 1-800-354-9706

For permission to use material from this text or product, submit all requests online at **www.cengage.com/permissions.** Further permissions questions can be emailed to **permissionrequest@cengage.com.**

Library of Congress Control Number: 2011941009

ISBN-13: 978-1-111-84072-3

ISBN-10: 1-111-84072-5

Wadsworth
20 Channel Center Street
Boston, MA 02210
USA

Cengage Learning is a leading provider of customized learning solutions with office locations around the globe, including Singapore, the United Kingdom, Australia, Mexico, Brazil and Japan. Locate your local office at **international.cengage.com/region.**

Cengage Learning products are represented in Canada by Nelson Education, Ltd.

For your course and learning solutions, visit **www.cengage.com.** Purchase any of our products at your local college store or at our preferred online store **www.cengagebrain.com.**

Instructors: Please visit **login.cengage.com** and log in to access instructor-specific resources.

Printed in the United States of America

1 2 3 4 5 6 7 15 14 13 12

Brief Contents

Contents

Preface

THE GARDNER LEGACY IN THE 21ST CENTURY

I take great pleasure in introducing the extensively revised and expanded third edition of *Gardner's Art through the Ages: A Concise Global History.* When Helen Gardner published the first edition of *Art through the Ages* in 1926, she could not have imagined that more than 85 years later instructors all over the world would still be using her textbook in their classrooms. Nor could she have foreseen that a new publisher would make her text available in special editions corresponding to a wide variety of introductory art history courses ranging from yearlong global surveys to Western- and non-Western-only surveys to the one-semester course for which this concise edition was designed. Indeed, if Professor Gardner were alive today, she would not recognize the book that long ago became— and remains—the most widely read introduction to the history of art and architecture in the English language. During the past half-century, successive authors have constantly reinvented Helen Gardner's groundbreaking global survey, always keeping it fresh and current, and setting an ever-higher standard with each new edition. I am deeply gratified that both professors and students seem to agree that the second edition, released in 2009, lived up to that venerable tradition, for they made it the number-one choice for one-semester art history survey courses. I hope they will find the third edition of this best-selling book exceeds the high expectations they have for each new Gardner.

KEY FEATURES OF THE THIRD EDITION

For the third concise edition of *Art through the Ages,* I have added several important new features while retaining the basic format and scope of the previous edition. The new edition boasts more photographs, plans, and drawings than the previous two versions of the book, and nearly all of them are in color and have been reproduced according to the highest standards of clarity and color fidelity. The hundreds of new images in the third edition include dozens of superb photographs taken by Jonathan Poore exclusively for the Gardner series during three photographic campaigns in France and Italy in 2009, 2010, and 2011. The accompanying online resources also include custom videos made at each site by Sharon Adams Poore. This extraordinary new archive of visual material ranges from ancient Roman ruins in southern France to Romanesque and Gothic churches in France and Tuscany to Le Corbusier's modernist chapel at Ronchamp and the postmodern Pompidou Center in Paris. The third edition also features the highly acclaimed architectural drawings of John Burge. Together, these exclusive photographs, videos, and drawings provide readers with a visual feast unavailable anywhere else.

The captions accompanying those illustrations contain, as before, a wealth of information, including the name of the artist or architect, if known; the formal title (printed in italics), if assigned, description of the work, or name of the building; the provenance or place of production of the object or location of the building; the date; the material(s) used; the size; and the present location if the work is in a museum or private collection. Scales accompany not only all architectural plans, as is the norm, but also appear next to each photograph of a painting, statue, or other artwork—another unique feature of the Gardner books. The works discussed in the new concise edition of *Art through the Ages* vary enormously in size, from colossal sculptures carved into mountain cliffs and paintings that cover entire walls or ceilings to tiny figurines and coins that one can hold in the hand. Although the captions contain the pertinent dimensions, it is difficult for students who have never seen the paintings or statues in person to translate those dimensions into an appreciation of the real size of the objects. The scales provide an effective and direct way to visualize how big or how small a given artwork is and its relative size compared with other objects in the same chapter and throughout the book.

Also retained in this edition are the Quick-Review Captions introduced in the first edition. Students have overwhelmingly reported that they found these brief synopses of the most significant aspects of each artwork or building illustrated invaluable when preparing for examinations. Another popular tool, introduced in the second edition to aid students in reviewing and mastering the material, reappears in the third edition. Each chapter ends with a full-page feature called *The Big Picture,* which sets forth in bullet-point format the most important characteristics of each period or artistic movement discussed in the chapter. Small illustrations of characteristic works accompany the summary of major points. This edition, however, introduces two new features in every chapter: a timeline summarizing the major developments during the era treated (again in bullet-point format for easy review) and a chapter-opening essay on a characteristic painting, sculpture, or building. Called *Framing the Era,* these in-depth essays are accompanied by a general view and four enlarged details of the work discussed.

Boxed essays also appear throughout the rest of the book. In this edition the essays are more closely tied to the main text than ever before. Consistent with that greater integration, almost all boxes now incorporate photographs of important artworks discussed in the text proper that also illustrate the theme treated in the boxed essays. These essays fall under five broad categories:

Architectural Basics boxes provide students with a sound foundation for the understanding of architecture. These discussions are concise explanations, with drawings and diagrams, of the major aspects of design and construction. The information included is essential to an understanding of architectural technology and terminology. The boxes address questions of how and why various forms developed, the problems architects confronted, and the solutions they used to resolve them. Topics discussed include how the Egyptians built the pyramids; the orders of classical architecture; Roman concrete construction; and the design and terminology of mosques, stupas, and Gothic cathedrals.

Materials and Techniques essays explain the various media artists employed from prehistoric to modern times. Because materials and techniques often influence the character of artworks, these discussions contain essential information on why many monuments appear as they do. Hollow-casting bronze statues; fresco painting; Renaissance drawings; engravings, etchings, and lithographs; and daguerreotype and calotype photography are among the many subjects treated.

Religion and Mythology boxes introduce students to the principal elements of the world's great religions, past and present, and to the representation of religious and mythological themes in painting and sculpture of all periods and places. These discussions of belief systems and iconography give readers a richer understanding of some of the greatest artworks ever created. The topics include the gods and goddesses of Mount Olympus; the life of Jesus in art; Muhammad and Islam; Buddhism and Buddhist iconography; and Aztec religion.

Art and Society essays treat the historical, social, political, cultural, and religious context of art and architecture. Topics include Egyptian mummification; Byzantine icons and iconoclasm; pilgrimages and the cult of relics; primitivism and colonialism; public funding of controversial art; the Mesoamerican ball game; and African masquerades.

Finally, in the *Artists on Art* boxes, artists and architects throughout history discuss both their theories and individual works. Examples include Leonardo da Vinci discussing the art of painting; Artemisia Gentileschi talking about the special problems she confronted as a woman artist; Jacques-Louis David on Neoclassicism; Gustave Courbet on Realism; Henri Matisse on color; Diego Rivera on art for the people; and Judy Chicago on her seminal work *The Dinner Party.*

For every new edition of *Art through the Ages,* I also re-evaluate the basic organization of the book. In this new concise edition, the treatment of the art of the later 20th century and the opening decade of the 21st century has been significantly reconfigured. There are now separate chapters on the art and architecture of the period from 1945 to 1980 and from 1980 to the present. Moreover, the second of these chapters (Chapter 16, "Contemporary Art Worldwide") is no longer confined to Western art but presents the art and architecture of the past three decades as a multifaceted global phenomenon.

Rounding out the features in the book itself is an expanded Bibliography of books in English, including both general works and a chapter-by-chapter list of more focused studies, and a Glossary containing definitions of all italicized terms introduced in the text. The third edition of *Art through the Ages: A Concise Global History* also features a host of state-of-the-art online resources (see Resources, page xviii).

WRITING AND TEACHING THE HISTORY OF ART

Nonetheless, some things have not changed in this new edition, including the fundamental belief that guided Helen Gardner so many years ago—that the primary goal of an introductory art history textbook should be to foster an appreciation and understanding of historically significant works of art of all kinds from all periods and from all parts of the globe. Because of the longevity and diversity of the history of art, it is tempting to assign responsibility for telling its story to a large team of specialists. The original publisher of *Art through the Ages* took this approach for the first edition prepared after Helen Gardner's death, and it has now become the norm for introductory art history surveys. But students overwhelmingly say the very complexity of the global history of art makes it all the more important for the story to be told with a consistent voice if they are to master so much diverse material. I think Helen Gardner would be pleased to know that *Art through the Ages* once again has a single storyteller—aided in no small part by invaluable advice from well over a hundred reviewers and other consultants whose assistance I gratefully acknowledge at the end of this Preface.

I continue to believe that the most effective way to tell the story of art through the ages, especially to anyone studying art history for the first time, is to organize the vast array of artistic monuments according to the civilizations that produced them and to consider each work in roughly chronological order. This approach has not merely stood the test of time. It is the most appropriate way to narrate the *history* of art. The principle underlying my approach to every period of art history is that the enormous variation in the form and meaning of the paintings, sculptures, buildings, and other artworks men and women have produced over the past 30,000 years is largely the result of the constantly changing contexts in which artists and architects have worked. A historically based narrative is therefore best suited for a global history of art because it enables the author to situate each work discussed in its historical, social, economic, religious, and cultural context. That is, after all, what distinguishes art history from art appreciation.

In the 1926 edition of *Art through the Ages*, Helen Gardner discussed Henri Matisse and Pablo Picasso in a chapter entitled "Contemporary Art in Europe and America." Since then many other artists have emerged on the international scene, and the story of art through the ages has grown longer and even more complex. As already noted, that is reflected in the addition of a new chapter at the end of the book on contemporary art in which developments on all continents are treated together for the first time. Perhaps even more important than the new directions artists and architects have taken during the past several decades is that the discipline of art history has also changed markedly—and so too has Helen Gardner's book. The third concise edition fully reflects the latest art historical research emphases while maintaining the traditional strengths that have made previous editions of *Art through the Ages* so popular. While sustaining attention to style, chronology, iconography, and technique, I also ensure that issues of patronage, function, and context loom large in every chapter. I treat artworks not as isolated objects in sterile 21st-century museum settings but with a view toward their purpose and meaning in the society that produced them at the time they were produced. I examine not only the role of the artist or architect in the creation of a work of art or a building, but also the role of the individuals or groups who paid the artists and influenced the shape the monuments took. Further, in this new concise edition, I devote more space than ever before to the role of women and women artists in societies worldwide over time. In every chapter, I have tried to choose artworks and buildings that reflect the increasingly wide range of interests of scholars today, while not rejecting the traditional list of "great" works or the very notion of a "canon."

CHAPTER-BY-CHAPTER CHANGES IN THE THIRD EDITION

All chapters include changes in the text reflecting new research and discoveries. A chapter-by-chapter enumeration of primary revisions follows.

Introduction: What Is Art History?: New chapter opener features a bronze relief from Benin. Added Joan Mitchell; portrait bust of the Roman emperor Augustus; and Ogata Korin's *Waves at Matsushima*.

1: Prehistory and the First Civilizations: New Framing the Era essay ("The Cradle of Civilization") and new timeline. New photographs of the Standard of Ur; head of an Akkadian ruler; stele with law code of Hammurabi; Ishtar Gate; mortuary temple of Hatshepsut; temple of Ramses II at Abu Simbel; temple of Amen-Re at Karnak; and portrait of Nefertiti. New drawing of Egyptian mastaba tombs. Added Palace of Ashurnasirpal II at Kalhu.

2: Ancient Greece: New Framing the Era essay ("The Perfect Temple") and new timeline. New photographs of *Spring Fresco,* Thera; palace at Tiryns; temple of Hera at Paestum; Athena Nike parapet relief; Praxiteles's *Hermes and Dionysos;* theater at Epidauros; and *Nike of Samothrace.*

3: The Roman Empire: New Framing the Era essay ("The Ancient World's Greatest Empire") and new timeline. New photographs of Etruscan temple model; Tomb of the Leopards; Pompeii amphitheater; cubiculum of the Boscoreale villa; Pont-du-Gard; Arch of Titus; Pantheon; and Arch of Constantine. Added painted portrait of family of Septimius Severus and portrait bust of Caracalla.

4: Early Christianity and Byzantium: New Framing the Era essay ("Romans, Jews, and Christians") and new timeline. Added *Harbaville Triptych.*

5: The Islamic World: New Framing the Era essay ("The Rise and Spread of Islam") and new timeline. New photographs of the Córdoba Great Mosque and the Palace of the Lions in the Alhambra.

6: Early Medieval and Romanesque Europe: New Framing the Era essay ("Missionaries Spread Christian Art") and new timeline. New photographs of the interior of Saint-Sernin, Toulouse; the cloister and south portal of Saint-Pierre, Moissac; the tympana of Saint-Lazare, Autun, and La Madeleine, Vézelay; the cathedral complex at Pisa; and the west facade and interior of Saint-Étienne, Caen.

7: Gothic and Late Medieval Europe: New Framing the Era essay ("The Age of the Great Cathedrals") and new timeline. New photographs of Chartres Cathedral west facade and Royal Portal sculptures, flying buttresses, stained-glass rose window and lancets, and Saint Theodore; Saint-Denis ambulatory; exterior of Notre-Dame, Paris; Amiens Cathedral nave; Reims Cathedral *Annunciation* and *Visitation;* the *Virgin of Paris;* Salisbury and Cologne Cathedral naves; Nicola Pisano's Pisa Baptistery pulpit; Sala della Pace frescoes, Siena; and Orvieto and Florence Cathedrals. Added rear panels of Duccio's *Maestà.*

8: The Early Renaissance in Europe: New Framing the Era essay ("Medici Patronage and Classical Learning") and new timeline. New photographs of Donatello's *Saint Mark;* exterior and courtyard of the Palazzo Medici-Riccardi; and the facade of Santa Maria Novella. Added Botticelli's *Primavera;* Piero della Francesca's

Resurrection and double-portrait of *Battista Sforza and Federico da Montefeltro*; Brunelleschi's Ospedale degli Innocenti; and a new diagram of linear perspective.

9: High Renaissance and Mannerism in Europe: New Framing the Era essay ("Earthly Delights in the Netherlands") and new timeline. New photographs of the west end of Saint Peter's by Michelangelo; Palladio's Villa Rotonda; the Chateau de Chambord; and El Escorial, near Madrid. Added Giorgione's *Tempest;* Giulio Romano's Palazzo del Tè, Mantua; Dürer's *Melencolia I.* Reattributed *Pastoral Symphony* to Titian.

10: Baroque Europe: New Framing the Era essay ("Baroque Art and Spectacle") and new timeline. New photographs of Saint Peter's from the air and of the exterior of Borromini's San Carlo alle Quattro Fontane. Added Bernini's Four Rivers Fountain and Gentileschi's *Self-Portrait as the Allegory of Painting.*

11: Rococo to Neoclassicism in Europe and America: New Framing the Era essay ("Art and Science in the Era of Enlightenment") and new timeline. New photograph of Soufflot's Panthéon. Added Boffrand's Salon de la Princesse; Clodion's *Nymph and Satyr Carousing;* Reynolds's *Lord Heathfield;* and Jefferson's University of Virginia.

12: Romanticism, Realism, and Photography, 1800 to 1870: New Framing the Era essay ("Napoleon at Jaffa") and new timeline. New photograph of Daumier's *Rue Transnonain* and O'Sullivan's *Harvest of Death, Gettysburg.* Added Friedrich's *Wanderer above a Sea of Mist* and Nash's Royal Pavilion, Brighton.

13: Impressionism, Post-Impressionism, and Symbolism, 1870 to 1900: New Framing the Era essay ("Impressions of Modern Life") and new timeline. New photograph of the Eiffel Tower. Added James Abbott McNeill Whistler; Auguste Rodin's *The Gates of Hell;* and Victor Horta and Art Nouveau.

14: Modernism in Europe and America, 1900 to 1945: New Framing the Era essay ("Global War, Anarchy, and Dada") and new timeline. New map of Europe at the end of World War I. New photograph of Frank Lloyd Wright's Fallingwater. Added Aaron Douglas and the Harlem Renaissance; Edward Weston's *Pepper No. 30;* Giorgio de Chirico's *The Song of Love;* Margaret Bourke-White; and the Chrysler Building.

15: Modernism and Postmodernism in Europe and America, 1945 to 1980: Chapter 15 in the second edition expanded and divided into two chapters in this edition (15 and 16). New Framing the Era essay ("Art and Consumer Culture") and new timeline. Added Arshile Gorky; Bridget Riley; David Smith's *Cubi XII;* Jasper Johns's *Three Flags;* Andy Warhol's *Green Coca-Cola Bottles;* Claes Oldenburg; Audrey Flack; and Diane Arbus. New photographs of Solomon R. Guggenheim

Museum, New York; Notre-Dame-du-Haut, Ronchamp; Seagram Building, New York; Georges Pompidou National Center of Art and Culture, Paris; and Robert Smithson's *Spiral Jetty.*

16: Contemporary Art Worldwide: New chapter integrating art in and outside Europe and America from 1980 to the present. New Framing the Era essay ("Art as Sociopolitical Message") and new timeline. Added Robert Mapplethorpe; Shahzia Sikander; Jean-Michel Basquiat; Willie Bester; Shirin Neshat; Xu Bing; Jenny Saville; Norman Foster's Hong Kong and Shanghai Bank; Renzo Piano's Tjibaou Cultural Centre and green architecture; Rachel Whiteread; and Andreas Gursky. New photographs of Gehry's Guggenheim Bilbao Museo and Christo and Jeanne-Claude's *Surrounded Islands.*

17: South and Southeast Asia: New Framing the Era essay ("The Life of the Buddha") and new timeline. Added *Parinirvana,* Gal Vihara. New photographs of the east torana of the Great Stupa, Sanchi; cave 1, Ajanta; cave 1, Badami; cave 1, Elephanta; Vishnu Temple, Deogarh; Rajarajeshvara Temple, Thanjavur; Vishvanatha Temple, Khajuraho; and Great Temple, Madurai.

18: China and Korea: New Framing the Era essay ("The Forbidden City") and new timeline. Added flying horse of Governor-General Zhang and Silla gold-and-jade crown. New photographs of terracotta army of the First Emperor of Qin; Vairocana Buddha, Longmen Caves; Garden of the Master of the Fishing Nets, Suzhou; and Namdaemun, Seoul.

19: Japan: New Framing the Era essay ("Famous Views of Edo") and new timeline. Added Hiroshige's *Plum Estate, Kameido;* Kano Eitoku's *Chinese Lions;* Koetsu's *Boat Bridge.* New photographs of Phoenix Hall, Uji; Taian teahouse, Kyoto; Katsura Imperial Villa; and Kenzo's Olympic stadiums, Tokyo.

20: Native America: New Framing the Era essay ("The Founding of Tenochtitlán") and new timeline. Added *Codex Mendoza;* Tetitla apartment mural painting, Teotihuacán; Temple of the Sun, Cuzco; Adena pipe; and Bodmer's *Hidatsa Warrior.* New photographs of Olmec head, La Venta; Nasca Lines hummingbird; Machu Picchu; and Cliff Palace.

21: Africa: New Framing the Era essay ("Kalabari Ijaw Ancestral Screens") and new timeline. Added Djenne terracotta archer; Chokwe Chibinda Ilunga; and Olowe of Ise's Ikere palace doors.

ACKNOWLEDGMENTS

A work as extensive as a global history of art could not be undertaken or completed without the counsel of experts in all areas of world art. As with previous editions, Cengage/Wadsworth has enlisted more than a hundred art historians to review every chapter of *Art through the Ages* in order to ensure that the text lives up to the Gardner reputation for accuracy as well as readability. I take great pleasure in acknowledging here those individuals who made important contributions to the third concise edition and to the unabridged fourteenth edition on which the shorter version is based: Michael Jay Adamek, Ozarks Technical Community College; Charles M. Adelman, University of Northern Iowa; Christine Zitrides Atiyeh, Kutztown University; Gisele Atterberry, Joliet Junior College; Roann Barris, Radford University; Philip Betancourt, Temple University; Karen Blough, SUNY Plattsburgh; Elena N. Boeck, DePaul University; Betty Ann Brown, California State University–Northridge; Alexandra A. Carpino, Northern Arizona University; Anne Walke Cassidy, Carthage College; Harold D. Cole, Baldwin Wallace College; Sarah Cormack, Webster University, Vienna; Jodi Cranston, Boston University; Nancy de Grummond, Florida State University; Kelley Helmstutler Di Dio, University of Vermont; Owen Doonan, California State University–Northridge; Marilyn Dunn, Loyola University Chicago; Tom Estlack, Pittsburgh Cultural Trust; Lois Fichner-Rathus, The College of New Jersey; Arne R. Flaten, Coastal Carolina University; Ken Friedman, Swinburne University of Technology; Rosemary Gallick, Northern Virginia Community College; William V. Ganis, Wells College; Marc Gerstein, University of Toledo; Clive F. Getty, Miami University; Michael Grillo, University of Maine; Amanda Hamilton, Northwest Nazarene University; Martina Hesser, Grossmont College; Heather Jensen, Brigham Young University; Mark Johnson, Brigham Young University; Jacqueline E. Jung, Yale University; John F. Kenfield, Rutgers University; Asen Kirin, University of Georgia; Joanne Klein, Boise State University; Yu Bong Ko, Tappan Zee High School, Rob Leith, Buckingham Browne & Nichols School; Adele H. Lewis, Arizona State University; Kate Alexandra Lingley, University of Hawaii–Manoa; Ellen Longsworth, Merrimack College; Matthew Looper, California State University–Chico; Nuria Lledó Tarradell, Universidad Complutense, Madrid; Anne McClanan, Portland State University; Mark Magleby, Brigham Young University; Gina Miceli-Hoffman, Moraine Valley Community College; William Mierse, University of Vermont; Amy Morris, Southeastern Louisiana University; Charles R. Morscheck, Drexel University; Johanna D. Movassat, San Jose State University; Carola Naumer, Truckee Meadows Community College; Irene Nero, Southeastern Louisiana University; Robin O'Bryan, Harrisburg Area Community College; Laurent Odde, Kutztown University of Pennsylvania; E. Suzanne Owens, Lorain County Community College; Catherine Pagani, The University of Alabama; Martha Peacock, Brigham Young University; Mabi Ponce de Leon, Bexley High School; Curtis Runnels, Boston University; Malia E. F. Serrano, Grossmont College; Molly Skjei, Normandale Community College; Fred T. Smith, Kent State University; Thomas F. Strasser, Providence College; James Swensen, Brigham Young University; John Szostak, University of Hawaii–Manoa; Katherine H. Tachau, University of Iowa; Debra Thompson, Glendale Community College; Alice Y. Tseng, Boston University; Carol Ventura, Tennessee Technological University; Marc Vincent, Baldwin Wallace College; Deborah Waite, University of Hawaii–Manoa; Lawrence Waldron, Saint John's University; Victoria Weaver, Millersville University; Margaret Ann Zaho, University of Central Florida.

I am also happy to have this opportunity to express my gratitude to the extraordinary group of people at Cengage/Wadsworth involved with the editing, production, and distribution of *Art through the Ages*. Some of them I have now worked with on various projects for nearly two decades and feel privileged to count among my friends. The success of the Gardner series in all of its various permutations depends in no small part on the expertise and unflagging commitment of these dedicated professionals, especially Clark Baxter, publisher; Sharon Adams Poore, senior development editor (as well as videographer extraordinaire); Lianne Ames, senior content project manager; Mandy Groszko, rights acquisition specialist; Kimberley Apfelbaum, associate media editor; Ashley Bargende, assistant editor; Elizabeth Newell, editorial assistant; Cate Rickard Barr, senior art director; and Jeanne M. Heston, senior marketing manager; Heather Baxley, senior marketing communications manager; and the incomparable group of local sales representatives who have passed on to me the welcome advice offered by the hundreds of instructors they speak to daily during their visits to college campuses throughout North America.

I am also deeply grateful to the following out-of-house contributors to the third concise edition: the peerless and tireless Joan Keyes, Dovetail Publishing Services; tani hasegawa, designer; Susan Gall, copy editor; Catherine Schnurr, Mary-Lise Nazaire, Lauren McFalls, and Corey Geissler, PreMediaGlobal, photo researchers; Pat Lewis, proofreader; Alma Bell, Scott Paul, John Pierce, and Lori Shranko, Thompson Type; Jay and John Crowley, Jay's Publishing Services; and, of course, Jonathan Poore and John Burge, for their superb photos and architectural drawings.

Finally, I owe thanks to my former co-author, Christin J. Mamiya of the University of Nebraska–Lincoln, for her friendship and advice, especially with regard to the expanded contemporary art section of the third edition, as well as to my colleagues at Boston University and to the thousands of students and the scores of teaching fellows in my art history courses since I began teaching in 1975. From them I have learned much that has helped determine the form and content of *Art through the Ages* and made it a much better book than it otherwise might have been.

Fred S. Kleiner

Resources

FOR FACULTY

PowerLecture with Digital Image Library

This flashdrive is an all-in-one lecture and class presentation tool that makes it easy to assemble, edit, and present customized lectures for your course using Microsoft® Power-Point®. The Digital Image Library provides high-resolution images (maps, diagrams, and the fine art images from the text) for lecture presentations, either in PowerPoint® presentation format, or in individual file formats compatible with other image-viewing software. A zoom feature allows you to magnify selected portions of an image for more detailed display in class, or you can display images side by side for comparison. You can easily add your own images to those from the text. The Google Earth™ application allows you to zoom in on an entire city, as well as key monuments and buildings. There are links to specific figures for every chapter in the book. PowerLecture also includes an Image Transition Guide, an electronic Instructor's Manual, a Test Bank with multiple-choice, matching, short-answer, and essay questions in ExamView® computerized format and text-specific Microsoft® PowerPoint® slides.

WebTutor™ with eBook on WebCT® and Blackboard®

WebTutor™ enables you to assign pre-formatted, text-specific content that is available as soon as you log on. You can also customize the WebTutor™ environment in any way you choose. Content includes the Interactive ebook, Test Bank, Practice Quizzes, Video Study Tools, Google Earth™ Activities, Virtual Museum Tours and Audio Lectures.

To order, contact your Cengage Learning representative.

FOR STUDENTS

CourseMate™ with eBook

Make the most of your study time by accessing everything you need to succeed in one place. Open the interactive eBook, take notes, review image and audio flashcards, watch videos, and take practice quizzes online with CourseMate™. You will find zoomable, high-resolution images along with videos created specifically to enhance your reading comprehension, audio chapter summaries, compare and contrast activities, Guide to Studying, and more.

To get access, visit CengageBrain.com

Slide Guide

The Slide Guide is a lecture companion that allows you to take notes alongside thumbnails of the same art images that are shown in class. This handy booklet includes reproductions of the images from the book, with full captions, page numbers, space for note taking, as well as Google Earth™ exercises for key cities, monuments, and buildings that will take you to these locations to better understand the works that you are studying. The Slide Guide is also available as downloadable Word® documents in CourseMate™.

To order, go to **www.cengagebrain.com**

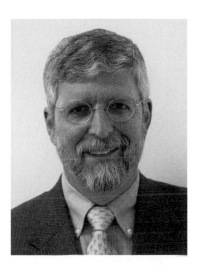

FRED S. KLEINER (Ph.D., Columbia University) is the author or co-author of the 10th, 11th, 12th, 13th, and 14th editions of *Gardner's Art through the Ages,* as well as all editions of *Gardner's Art through the Ages: A Concise Global History,* and more than a hundred publications on Greek and Roman art and architecture, including *A History of Roman Art,* also published by Wadsworth. He has taught the art history survey course for more than three decades, first at the University of Virginia and, since 1978, at Boston University, where he is currently Professor of Art History and Archaeology and Chair of the Department of the History of Art and Architecture. From 1985 to 1998, he was Editor-in-Chief of the *American Journal of Archaeology.*

Long acclaimed for his inspiring lectures and dedication to students, Professor Kleiner won Boston University's Metcalf Award for Excellence in Teaching as well as the College Prize for Undergraduate Advising in the Humanities in 2002, and he is a two-time winner of the Distinguished Teaching Prize in the College of Arts and Sciences Honors Program. In 2007, he was elected a Fellow of the Society of Antiquaries of London, and, in 2009, in recognition of lifetime achievement in publication and teaching, a Fellow of the Text and Academic Authors Association.

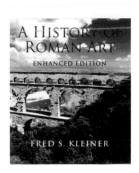

Also by Fred Kleiner: *A History of Roman Art, Enhanced Edition* (Wadsworth/Cengage Learning 2010; ISBN 9780495909873), winner of the 2007 Texty Prize as the best new college textbook in the humanities and social sciences. In this authoritative and lavishly illustrated volume, Professor Kleiner traces the development of Roman art and architecture from Romulus' foundation of Rome in the eighth century BCE to the death of Constantine in the fourth century CE, with special chapters devoted to Pompeii and Herculaneum, Ostia, funerary and provincial art and architecture, and the earliest Christian art.

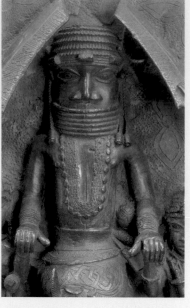

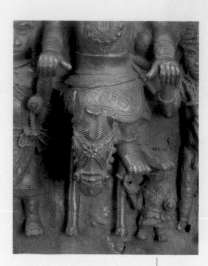

Why did this Benin kingdom sculptor vary the sizes of the figures? Why is the central equestrian figure much larger than his horse? How did the artist inform the viewer the rider is a king?

Art historians seek to understand not only why individual artworks appear as they do but also why those works exist at all. Who paid this African artist to make this bronze plaque? Why?

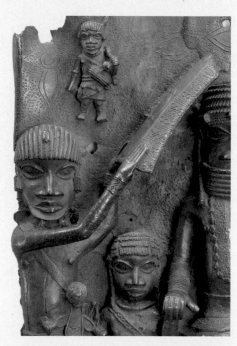

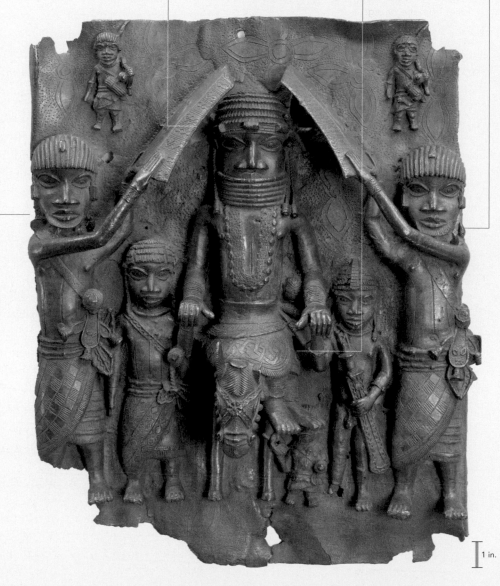

Dating and signing artworks are relatively recent practices. How can art historians determine when an unlabeled work such as this one was made, and by whom? Style, technique, and subject are clues.

1 in.

I-1 King on horseback with attendants, from Benin, Nigeria, ca. 1550–1680. Bronze, 1′ 7½″ high. Metropolitan Museum of Art, New York (Michael C. Rockefeller Memorial Collection, gift of Nelson A. Rockefeller).

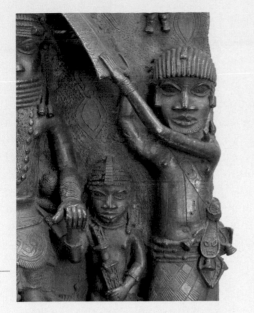

Introduction

What Is Art History?

What tools and techniques did the African sculptor employ to transform molten bronze into this plaque representing a king and his attendants projecting in high relief from the background plane?

What is art history? Except when referring to the modern academic discipline, people do not often juxtapose the words *art* and *history*. They tend to think of history as the record and interpretation of past human actions, particularly social and political actions. In contrast, most think of art, quite correctly, as part of the present—as something people can see and touch. Of course, people cannot see or touch history's vanished human events, but a visible, tangible artwork is a kind of persisting event. One or more artists made it at a certain time and in a specific place, even if no one now knows who, when, where, or why. Although created in the past, an artwork continues to exist in the present, long surviving its times. The first painters and sculptors died 30,000 years ago, but their works remain, some of them exhibited in glass cases in museums built only a few years ago.

Modern museum visitors can admire these objects from the remote past—and countless others humankind has produced over the millennia, whether bronze sculptures from Africa (FIG. I-1) or paintings on canvas by American artists (FIG. I-2)—without any knowledge of the circumstances leading to the creation of those works. The beauty or sheer size of an object can impress people, the artist's virtuosity in the handling of ordinary or costly materials can dazzle them, or the subject depicted can move them emotionally. Viewers can react to what they see, interpret the work in the light of their own experience, and judge it a success or a failure. These are all valid responses to a work of art. But the enjoyment and appreciation of artworks in museum settings are relatively recent phenomena, as is the creation of artworks solely for museum-going audiences to view.

Today, it is common for artists to work in private studios and to create paintings, sculptures, and other objects that commercial art galleries will offer for sale, as the American painter JOAN MITCHELL (1925–1992) did when she created large untitled canvases of pure color (FIG. I-2). Usually, someone the artist has never met will purchase the artwork and display it in a setting the artist has never seen. This practice is not a new phenomenon in the history of art—an ancient potter decorating a vase for sale at a village market stall probably did not know who would buy the pot or where it would be housed—but it is not at all typical. In fact, it is exceptional. Throughout history, most artists created paintings, sculptures, and other objects for specific patrons and settings and to fulfill a specific purpose, even if today no one knows the original contexts of those artworks. Museum visitors can appreciate the visual and tactile qualities of these objects, but cannot understand why they were made or why they appear as they do without knowing the circumstances of their creation. Art *appreciation* does not require knowledge of the historical context of an artwork (or a building). Art *history* does.

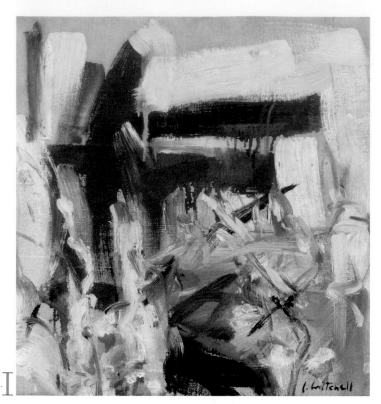

1 in.

I-2 JOAN MITCHELL, *Untitled*, ca. 1953–1954. Oil on canvas, 1′ 5″ × 1′ 4″. Butler Institute of American Art, Youngstown (gift of Marilynn Meeker, 1986).

Mitchell painted this untitled abstract composition without knowing who would buy it or where it would be displayed, but throughout history, most artists created works for specific patrons and settings.

ART HISTORY IN THE 21ST CENTURY

Art historians study the visual and tangible objects humans make and the structures humans build. Beginning with the earliest Greco-Roman art critics on, scholars have studied objects their makers consciously manufactured as "art" and to which the artists assigned formal titles. But today's art historians also study a multitude of objects their creators and owners almost certainly did not consider to be "works of art." Few ancient Romans, for example, would have regarded a coin bearing their emperor's portrait as anything but money. Today, an art museum may exhibit that coin in a locked case in a climate-controlled room, and scholars may subject it to the same kind of art historical analysis as a portrait by an acclaimed Renaissance or modern sculptor or painter.

The range of objects art historians study is constantly expanding and now includes, for example, computer-generated images, whereas in the past almost anything produced using a machine would not have been regarded as art. Most people still consider the performing arts—music, drama, and dance—as outside art history's realm because these arts are fleeting, impermanent media. But during the past few decades even this distinction between "fine art" and "performance art" has become blurred. Art historians, however, generally ask the same kinds of questions about what they study, whether they employ a restrictive or expansive definition of *art*.

The Questions Art Historians Ask

How Old Is It? Before art historians can write a history of art, they must be sure they know the date of each work they study. Thus, an indispensable subject of art historical inquiry is *chronology*, the dating of art objects and buildings. If researchers cannot determine a monument's age, they cannot place the work in its historical context. Art historians have developed many ways to establish, or at least approximate, the date of an artwork.

Physical evidence often reliably indicates an object's age. The material used for a statue or painting—bronze, plastic, or oil-based pigment, to name only a few—may not have been invented before a certain time, indicating the earliest possible date someone could have fashioned the work. Or artists may have ceased using certain materials—such as specific kinds of inks and papers for drawings—at a known time, providing the latest possible date for objects made of those materials. Sometimes the material (or the manufacturing technique) of an object or a building can establish a very precise date of production or construction. The study of tree rings, for instance, usually can determine within a narrow range the date of a wood statue or a timber roof beam.

Documentary evidence can help pinpoint the date of an object or building when a dated written document mentions the work. For example, financial records may note when church officials commissioned a new altarpiece for a church—and how much they paid to which artist.

Thus, a central aim of art history is to determine the original context of artworks. Art historians seek to achieve a full understanding not only of why these "persisting events" of human history look the way they do but also of why the artistic events happened at all. What unique set of circumstances gave rise to the construction of a particular building or led a specific patron to commission a certain artist to fashion a singular artwork for a particular place? The study of history is therefore vital to art history. And art history is often indispensable for a thorough understanding of history. Art objects and buildings are historical documents that can shed light on the peoples who made them and on the times of their creation in ways other historical documents may not. Furthermore, artists and architects can affect history by reinforcing or challenging cultural values and practices through the objects they create and the structures they build. Thus, the history of art and architecture is inseparable from the study of history, although the two disciplines are not the same.

The following pages introduce some of the distinctive subjects art historians address and the kinds of questions they ask, and explain some of the basic terminology they use when answering these questions. Readers armed with this arsenal of questions and terms will be ready to explore the multifaceted world of art through the ages.

Internal evidence can play a significant role in dating an artwork. A painter might have depicted an identifiable person or a kind of hairstyle, clothing, or furniture fashionable only at a certain time. If so, the art historian can assign a more accurate date to that painting.

Stylistic evidence is also very important. The analysis of *style*—an artist's distinctive manner of producing an object—is the art historian's special sphere. Unfortunately, because it is a subjective assessment, stylistic evidence is by far the most unreliable chronological criterion. Still, art historians sometimes find style a very useful tool for establishing chronology.

What Is Its Style? Defining artistic style is one of the key elements of art historical inquiry, although the analysis of artworks solely in terms of style no longer dominates the field the way it once did. Art historians speak of several different kinds of artistic styles.

Period style refers to the characteristic artistic manner of a specific time, usually within a distinct culture, such as "Archaic Greek." But many periods do not display any stylistic unity at all. How would someone define the artistic style of the second decade of the new millennium in North America? Far too many crosscurrents exist in contemporary art for anyone to describe a period style of the early 21st century—even in a single city such as New York.

Regional style is the term art historians use to describe variations in style tied to geography. Like an object's date, its *provenance,* or place of origin, can significantly determine its character. Very often two artworks from the same place made centuries apart are more similar than contemporaneous works from two different regions. To cite one example, usually only an expert can distinguish between an Egyptian statue carved in 2500 BCE and one made in 500 BCE. But no one would mistake an Egyptian statue of 500 BCE for one of the same date made in Greece or Mexico.

Considerable variations in a given area's style are possible, however, even during a single historical period. In late medieval Europe, French architecture differed significantly from Italian architecture. The interiors of Beauvais Cathedral (FIG. I-3) and the church of Santa Croce (FIG. I-4) in Florence typify the architectural styles of France and Italy, respectively, at the end of the 13th century. The rebuilding of the east end of Beauvais Cathedral began in 1284.

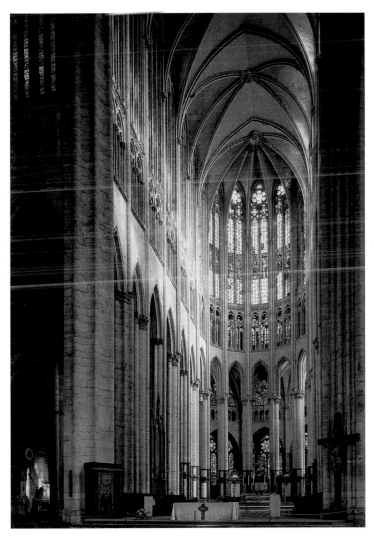

I-3 Choir of Beauvais Cathedral (looking east), Beauvais, France, rebuilt after 1284.

The style of an object or building often varies from region to region. This cathedral has towering stone vaults and large stained-glass windows typical of 13th-century French architecture.

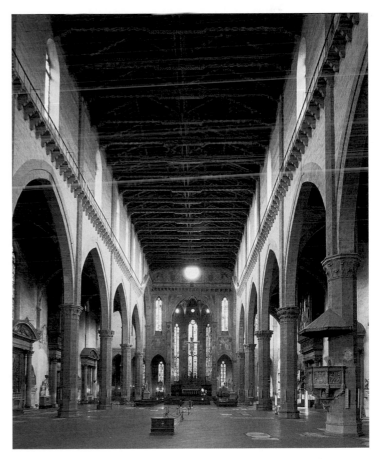

I-4 Interior of Santa Croce (looking east), Florence, Italy, begun 1294.

In contrast to Beauvais Cathedral (FIG. I-3), this contemporaneous Florentine church conforms to the quite different regional style of Italy. The building has a low timber roof and small windows.

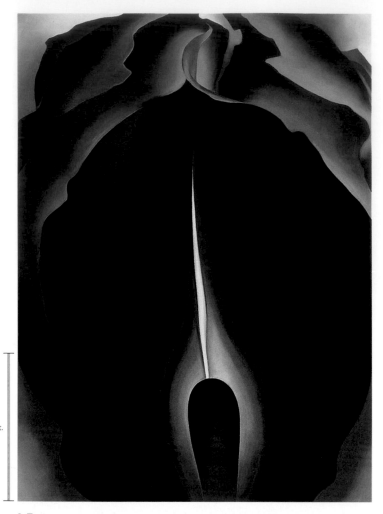

1 ft.

I-5 GEORGIA O'KEEFFE, *Jack-in-the-Pulpit No. 4,* 1930. Oil on canvas, 3′ 4″ × 2′ 6″. National Gallery of Art, Washington, D.C. (Alfred Stieglitz Collection, bequest of Georgia O'Keeffe).

O'Keeffe's paintings feature close-up views of petals and leaves in which the organic forms become powerful abstract compositions. This approach to painting typifies the artist's distinctive personal style.

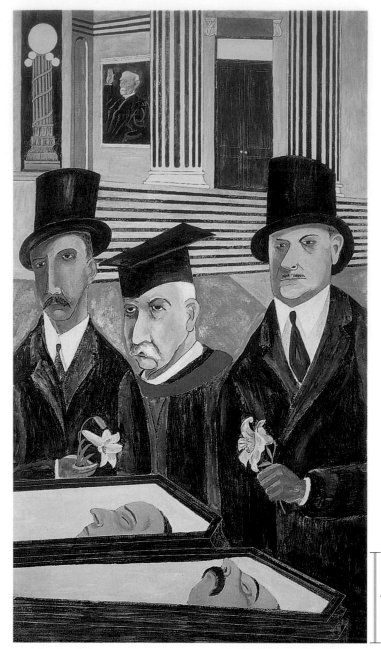

1 ft.

I-6 BEN SHAHN, *The Passion of Sacco and Vanzetti,* 1931–1932. Tempera on canvas, 7′ ½″ × 4′. Whitney Museum of American Art, New York (gift of Edith and Milton Lowenthal in memory of Juliana Force).

O'Keeffe's contemporary, Shahn developed a style markedly different from hers. His paintings are often social commentaries on recent events and incorporate readily identifiable people.

Construction commenced on Santa Croce only 10 years later. Both structures employ the *pointed arch* characteristic of this era, yet the two churches differ strikingly. The French church has towering stone ceilings and large expanses of colored-glass windows, whereas the Italian building has a low timber roof and small, widely separated windows. Because the two contemporaneous churches served similar purposes, regional style mainly explains their differing appearance.

Personal style, the distinctive manner of individual artists or architects, often decisively explains stylistic discrepancies among monuments of the same time and place. In 1930, GEORGIA O'KEEFFE (1887–1986) painted *Jack-in-the-Pulpit No. 4* (FIG. I-5), a sharply focused close-up view of petals and leaves. O'Keeffe captured the growing plant's slow, controlled motion while converting the plant into a powerful abstract composition of lines, shapes, and colors (see the discussion of art historical vocabulary in the next section). Only a year later, another American artist, BEN SHAHN (1898–1969), painted *The Passion of Sacco and Vanzetti* (FIG. I-6), a stinging commen-

tary on social injustice inspired by the trial and execution of two Italian anarchists, Nicola Sacco and Bartolomeo Vanzetti. Many people believed Sacco and Vanzetti had been unjustly convicted of killing two men in a robbery in 1920. Shahn's painting compresses time in a symbolic representation of the trial and its aftermath. The two executed men lie in their coffins. Presiding over them are the three members of the commission (headed by a college president wearing academic cap and gown) who declared the original trial fair and cleared the way for the executions. Behind, on the wall

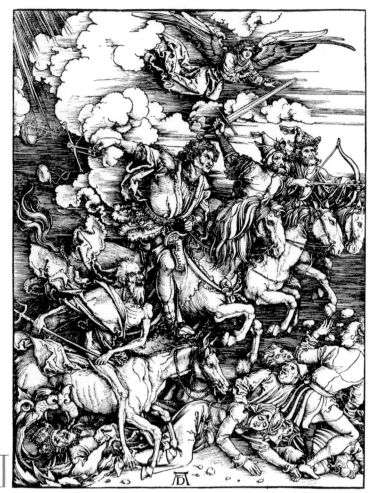

I-7 ALBRECHT DÜRER, *The Four Horsemen of the Apocalypse,* ca. 1498. Woodcut, 1' 3¼" × 11". Metropolitan Museum of Art, New York (gift of Junius S. Morgan, 1919).

Personifications are abstract ideas codified in human form. Here, Albrecht Dürer represented Death, Famine, War, and Pestilence as four men on charging horses, each man carrying an identifying attribute.

of a stately government building, hangs the framed portrait of the judge who pronounced the initial sentence. Personal style, not period or regional style, sets Shahn's canvas apart from O'Keeffe's. The contrast is extreme here because of the very different subjects the artists chose. But even when two artists depict the same subject, the results can vary widely. The *way* O'Keeffe painted flowers and the *way* Shahn painted faces are distinctive and unlike the styles of their contemporaries. (See the "Who Made It?" discussion.)

The different kinds of artistic styles are not mutually exclusive. For example, an artist's personal style may change dramatically during a long career. Art historians then must distinguish among the different period styles of a particular artist, such as the "Blue Period" and the "Cubist Period" of the prolific 20th-century artist Pablo Picasso.

What Is Its Subject? Another major concern of art historians is, of course, subject matter. Some artworks, such as modern *abstract* paintings (FIG. I-2), have no subject, not even

a setting. But when artists represent people, places, or actions, viewers must identify these features to achieve complete understanding of the work. Art historians traditionally separate pictorial subjects into various categories, such as religious, historical, mythological, *genre* (daily life), portraiture, *landscape* (a depiction of a place), *still life* (an arrangement of inanimate objects), and their numerous subdivisions and combinations.

Iconography—literally, the "writing of images"—refers both to the content, or subject of an artwork, and to the study of content in art. By extension, it also includes the study of *symbols,* images that stand for other images or encapsulate ideas. In Christian art, two intersecting lines of unequal length or a simple geometric cross can serve as an emblem of the religion as a whole, symbolizing the cross of Jesus Christ's crucifixion. A symbol also can be a familiar object the artist imbued with greater meaning. A balance or scale, for example, may symbolize justice or the weighing of souls on judgment day.

Artists may depict figures with unique *attributes* identifying them. In Christian art, for example, each of the authors of the biblical gospel books, the four evangelists, has a distinctive attribute. People can recognize Saint John by the eagle associated with him, Luke by the ox, Mark by the lion, and Matthew by the winged man.

Throughout the history of art, artists have also used *personifications*—abstract ideas codified in human form. Worldwide, people visualize Liberty as a robed woman wearing a rayed crown and holding a torch because of the fame of the colossal statue set up in New York City's harbor in 1886. *The Four Horsemen of the Apocalypse* (FIG. I-7) is a terrifying late-15th-century depiction of the fateful day at the end of time when, according to the Bible's last book, Death, Famine, War, and Pestilence will annihilate the human race. German artist ALBRECHT DÜRER (1471–1528) personified Death as an emaciated old man with a pitchfork. Dürer's Famine swings the scales for weighing human souls, War wields a sword, and Pestilence draws a bow.

Even without considering style and without knowing a work's maker, informed viewers can determine much about the work's period and provenance by iconographical and subject analysis alone. In *The Passion of Sacco and Vanzetti* (FIG. I-6), for example, the two coffins, the trio headed by an academic, and the robed judge in the background are all pictorial clues revealing the painting's subject. The work's date must be after the trial and execution, probably while the event was still newsworthy. And because the two men's deaths caused the greatest outrage in the United States, the painter–social critic was probably American.

Who Made It? If Ben Shahn had not signed his painting of Sacco and Vanzetti, an art historian could still assign, or *attribute,* the work to him based on knowledge of the artist's personal style. Although signing (and dating) works is quite common (but by no means universal) today, in the history of art countless works exist whose artists remain unknown.

Because personal style can play a major role in determining the character of an artwork, art historians often try to attribute anonymous works to known artists. Sometimes they assemble a group of works all thought to be by the same person, even though none of the objects in the group is the known work of an artist with a recorded name. Art historians thus reconstruct the careers of artists such as "the Achilles Painter," the anonymous ancient Greek artist whose masterwork is a depiction of the hero Achilles. Scholars base their *attributions* on internal evidence, such as the distinctive way an artist draws or carves drapery folds, earlobes, or flowers. It requires a keen, highly trained eye and long experience to become a *connoisseur,* an expert in assigning artworks to "the hand" of one artist rather than another.

Sometimes a group of artists works in the same style at the same time and place. Art historians designate such a group as a school. *School* does not mean an educational institution. The term connotes only chronological, stylistic, and geographic similarity. Art historians speak, for example, of the Dutch school of the 17th century and, within it, of subschools such as those of the cities of Haarlem, Utrecht, and Leyden.

Who Paid For It? The interest many art historians show in attribution reflects their conviction that the identity of an artwork's maker is the major reason the object looks the way it does. For them, personal style is of paramount importance. But in many times and places, artists had little to say about what form their work would take. They toiled in obscurity, doing the bidding of their *patrons,* those who paid them to make individual works or employed them on a continuing basis. The role of patrons in dictating the content and shaping the form of artworks is also an important subject of art historical inquiry.

In the art of portraiture, to name only one category of painting and sculpture, the patron has often played a dominant role in deciding how the artist represented the subject, whether that patron or another person, such as a spouse, son, or mother. Many Egyptian pharaohs and some Roman emperors insisted artists depict them with unlined faces and perfect youthful bodies no matter how old they were when portrayed. In these cases, the state employed the sculptors and painters, and the artists had no choice but to depict their patrons in the officially approved manner. This is why Augustus, who lived to age 76, looks so young in his portraits (FIG. I-8). Although Roman emperor for more than 40 years, Augustus demanded artists always represent him as a young, godlike head of state.

All modes of artistic production reveal the impact of patronage. Learned monks provided the themes for the sculptural decoration of medieval church portals. Renaissance princes and popes dictated the subject, size, and materials of artworks destined for display in buildings also constructed according to their specifications. An art historian could make a very long list of commissioned works, and it would indicate patrons have had diverse tastes and needs throughout the history of art and consequently demanded

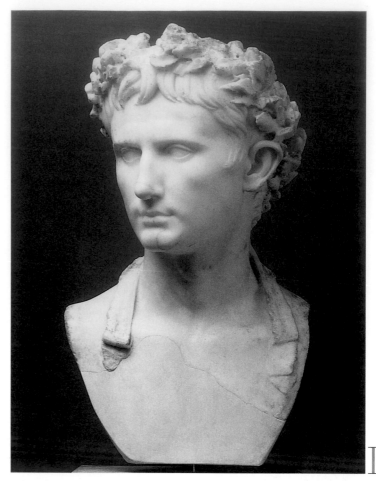

I-8 Bust of Augustus wearing the corona civica, early first century CE. Marble, 1' 5" high. Glyptothek, Munich.

Patrons frequently dictate the form their portraits will take. The Roman emperor Augustus demanded he always be portrayed as a young, godlike head of state even though he lived to age 76.

different kinds of art. Whenever a patron contracts an artist or architect to paint, sculpt, or build in a prescribed manner, personal style often becomes a very minor factor in the ultimate appearance of the painting, statue, or building. In these cases, the identity of the patron reveals more to art historians than does the identity of the artist or school.

The Words Art Historians Use

As in all fields of study, art history has its own specialized vocabulary consisting of hundreds of words, but certain basic terms are indispensable for describing artworks and buildings of any time and place. They make up the essential vocabulary of *formal analysis,* the visual analysis of artistic form. Definitions and discussions of the most important art historical terms follow.

Form and Composition *Form* refers to an object's shape and structure, either in two dimensions (for example, a figure painted on a canvas) or in three dimensions (such as a statue carved from a marble block). Two forms may take the same shape but differ in their color, texture, and other qualities. *Composition* refers to how an artist organizes (*composes*) forms in an artwork, either by placing shapes on a flat surface or by arranging forms in space.

Material and Technique To create art forms, artists shape materials (pigment, clay, marble, gold, and many more) with tools (pens, brushes, chisels, and so forth). Each of the materials and tools available has its own potentialities and limitations. Part of all artists' creative activity is to select the *medium* and instrument most suitable to the purpose—or to develop new media and tools, such as bronze and concrete in antiquity and cameras and computers in modern times. The processes artists employ, such as applying paint to canvas with a brush, and the distinctive, personal ways they handle materials constitute their *technique*. Form, material, and technique interrelate and are central to analyzing any work of art.

Line Among the most important elements defining an artwork's shape or form is *line*. A line can be understood as the path of a point moving in space, an invisible line of sight. More commonly, however, artists and architects make a line visible by drawing (or chiseling) it on a *plane,* a flat surface. A line may be very thin, wirelike, and delicate. It may be thick and heavy. Or it may alternate quickly from broad to narrow, the strokes jagged or the outline broken. When a continuous line defines an object's outer shape, art historians call it a *contour line.* All of these line qualities are present in Dürer's *Four Horsemen of the Apocalypse* (FIG. I-7). Contour lines define the basic shapes of clouds, human and animal limbs, and weapons. Within the forms, series of short broken lines create shadows and textures. An overall pattern of long parallel strokes suggests the dark sky on the frightening day when the world is about to end.

Color Light reveals all colors. Light in the world of the painter and other artists differs from natural light. Natural light, or sunlight, is whole or *additive light.* As the sum of all the wavelengths composing the visible *spectrum,* it may be disassembled or fragmented into the individual colors of the spectral band. The painter's light in art—the light reflected from pigments and objects—is *subtractive light.* Paint pigments produce their individual colors by reflecting a segment of the spectrum while absorbing all the rest. Green pigment, for example, subtracts or absorbs all the light in the spectrum except that seen as green, which it reflects to the eyes.

Artists call the three basic colors—red, yellow, and blue—the *primary colors.* The *secondary colors* result from mixing pairs of primaries: orange (red and yellow), purple (red and blue), and green (yellow and blue). *Complementary colors*—red and green, yellow and purple, and blue and orange—complete, or "complement," each other, one absorbing colors the other reflects.

Painters can manipulate the appearance of colors, however. One artist who made a systematic investigation of the formal aspects of art, especially color, was JOSEF ALBERS (1888–1976), a German-born artist who immigrated to the United States in 1933. In *Homage to the Square: "Ascending"* (FIG. I-9)—one of hundreds of color variations on the same

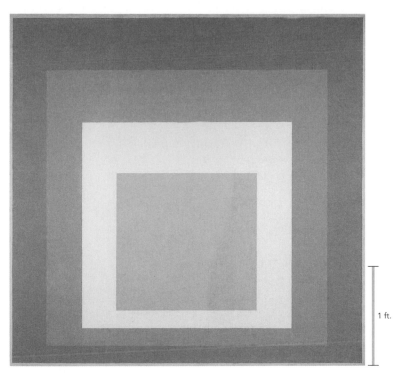

I-9 JOSEF ALBERS, *Homage to the Square: "Ascending,"* 1953. Oil on composition board, 3' 7½" × 3' 7½". Whitney Museum of American Art, New York.

Albers painted hundreds of canvases using the same composition but employing variations in color saturation and tonality in order to reveal the relativity and instability of color perception.

composition of concentric squares—Albers demonstrated "the discrepancy between physical fact and psychic effect."[1] Because the composition remains constant, the *Homage* series succeeds in revealing the relativity and instability of color perception. Albers varied the *saturation* (a color's brightness or dullness) and *tonality* (lightness or darkness) of each square in each painting. As a result, the sizes of the squares from painting to painting appear to vary (although they remain the same), and the sensations emanating from the paintings range from clashing dissonance to delicate serenity. In this way Albers proved "we see colors almost never unrelated to each other."[2] Artists' comments on their own works are often invaluable to art historians.

Texture The term *texture* refers to the quality of a surface, such as rough or shiny. Art historians distinguish between true texture, that is, the tactile quality of the surface, and represented texture, as when painters depict an object as having a certain texture, even though the pigment is the true texture. Texture is, of course, a key determinant of any sculpture's character. People's first impulse is usually to handle a piece of sculpture—even though museum signs often warn "Do not touch!" Sculptors plan for this natural human response, using surfaces varying in texture from rugged coarseness to polished smoothness. Textures are often intrinsic to a material, influencing the type of stone, wood, plastic, clay, or metal sculptors select.

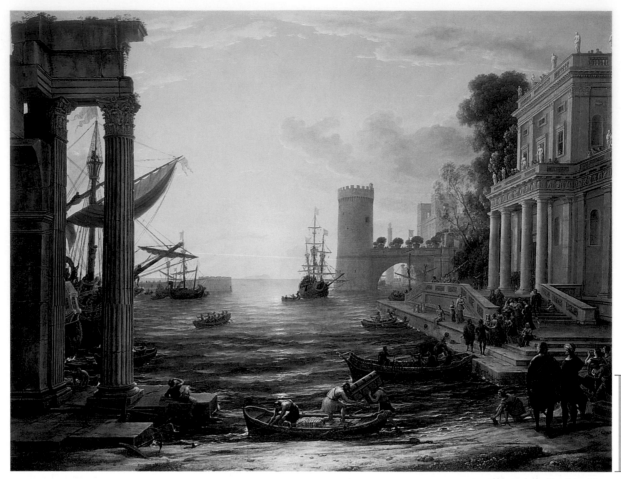

I-10 CLAUDE LORRAIN, *Embarkation of the Queen of Sheba,* 1648. Oil on canvas, 4′ 10″ × 6′ 4″. National Gallery, London.

To create the illusion of a deep landscape, Claude Lorrain employed perspective, reducing the size of and blurring the most distant forms. Also, all diagonal lines converge on a single point.

1 ft.

Space and Perspective *Space* is the bounded or boundless "container" of objects. For art historians, space can be the real three-dimensional space occupied by a statue or a vase or contained within a room or courtyard. Or space can be *illusionistic,* as when painters depict an image (or illusion) of the three-dimensional spatial world on a two-dimensional surface.

Perspective is one of the most important pictorial devices for organizing forms in space. Throughout history, artists have used various types of perspective to create an illusion of depth or space on a two-dimensional surface. The French painter CLAUDE LORRAIN (1600–1682) employed several perspective devices in *Embarkation of the Queen of Sheba* (FIG. **I-10**), a painting of a biblical episode set in a 17th-century European harbor with a Roman ruin in the left foreground. For example, the figures and boats on the shoreline are much larger than those in the distance. Decreasing an object's size makes it appear farther away from the viewer. Also, the top and bottom of the port building at the painting's right side are not parallel horizontal lines, as they are in a real building. Instead, the lines converge beyond the structure, leading the viewer's eye toward the hazy, indistinct sun on the horizon. These perspective devices—the reduction of figure size, the convergence of diagonal lines, and the blurring of distant forms—have been familiar features of Western art since the ancient Greeks. But it is important to note at the outset that all kinds of perspective are only pictorial conventions, even when one or more types of perspective may be so common in a given culture that people accept them as "natural" or as "true" means of representing the natural world.

In *Waves at Matsushima* (FIG. **I-11**), a Japanese seascape painting on a six-part folding screen, OGATA KORIN (1658–1716) ignored these Western perspective conventions. A Western viewer might interpret the left half of Korin's composition as depicting the distant horizon, as in Claude's painting, but the sky is a flat, unnatural gold, and in five of the six sections of the composition, waves fill the full height of the screen. The rocky outcroppings decrease in size with distance, but all are in sharp focus, and there are no shadows. The Japanese artist was less concerned with locating the boulders and waves in space than with composing shapes on a surface, playing the water's swelling curves against the jagged contours of the rocks. Neither the French nor the Japanese painting can be said to project "correctly" what viewers "in fact" see. One painting is not a "better" picture of the world than the other. The European and Asian artists simply approached the problem of picture-making differently.

Foreshortening Artists also represent single figures in space in varying ways. When the Flemish artist PETER PAUL RUBENS (1577–1640) painted *Lion Hunt* (FIG. **I-12**), he used *foreshortening* for all the hunters and animals—that is, he represented their bodies at angles to the picture plane. When in

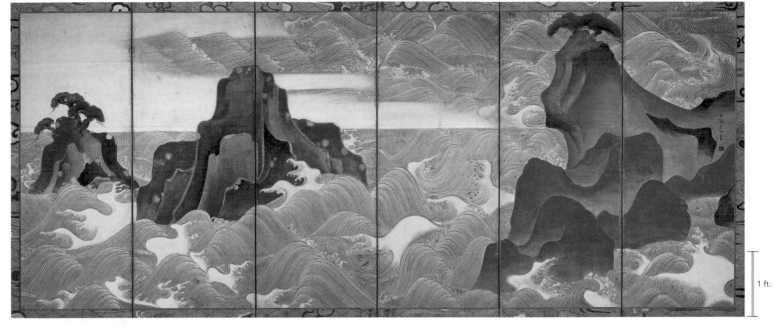

1 ft.

I-11 OGATA KORIN, *Waves at Matsushima*, Edo period, ca. 1700–1716. Six-panel folding screen, ink, color, and gold leaf on paper, 4′ 11⅛″ × 12′ ⅞″. Museum of Fine Arts, Boston (Fenollosa-Weld Collection).

Korin was more concerned with creating an intriguing composition of shapes on a surface than with locating boulders and waves in space. Asian artists rarely employed Western perspective.

life one views a figure at an angle, the body appears to contract as it extends back in space. Foreshortening is a kind of perspective. It produces the illusion that one part of the body is farther away than another, even though all the forms are on the same surface. Especially noteworthy in *Lion Hunt* are the gray horse at the left, seen from behind with the bottom of its left rear hoof facing viewers and most of its head hidden by its rider's shield, and the fallen hunter at the painting's lower right corner, whose barely visible legs and feet recede into the distance.

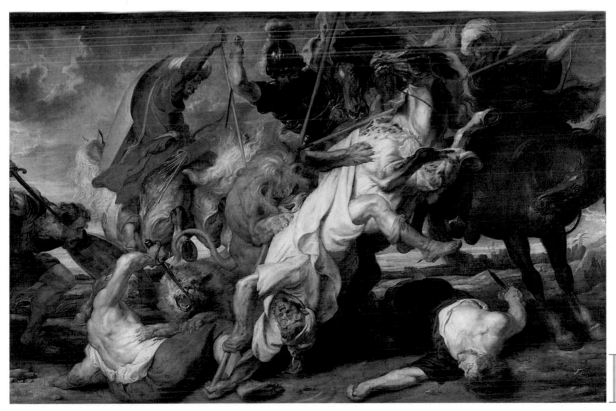

I-12 PETER PAUL RUBENS, *Lion Hunt*, 1617–1618. Oil on canvas, 8′ 2″ × 12′ 5″. Alte Pinakothek, Munich.

Foreshortening—the representation of a figure or object at an angle to the picture plane—is a common device in Western art for creating the illusion of depth. Foreshortening is a kind of perspective.

1 ft.

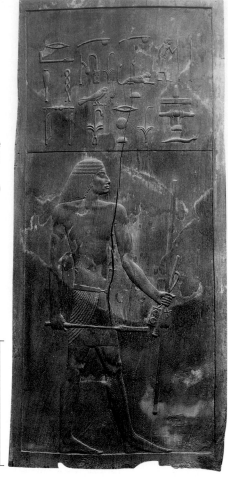

I-13 Hesire, relief from his tomb at Saqqara, Egypt, Dynasty III, ca. 2650 BCE. Wood, 3′ 9″ high. Egyptian Museum, Cairo.

Egyptian artists combined frontal and profile views to give a precise picture of the parts of the human body, as opposed to depicting how an individual body appears from a specific viewpoint.

1 ft.

The artist who carved the portrait of the ancient Egyptian official Hesire (FIG. **I-13**) did not employ foreshortening. That artist's purpose was to present the various human body parts as clearly as possible, without overlapping. The lower part of Hesire's body is in profile to give the most complete view of the legs, with both the heels and toes of the feet visible. The frontal torso, however, allows viewers to see its full shape, including both shoulders, equal in size, as in nature. (Compare the shoulders of the hunter on the gray horse or those of the fallen hunter in *Lion Hunt*'s left foreground.) The result, an "unnatural" 90-degree twist at the waist, provides a precise picture of human body parts. Rubens and the Egyptian sculptor used very different means of depicting forms in space. Once again, neither is the "correct" manner.

Proportion and Scale *Proportion* concerns the relationships (in terms of size) of the parts of persons, buildings, or objects. People can judge "correct proportions" intuitively ("That statue's head seems the right size for the body."). Or proportion can be a mathematical relationship between the size of one part of an artwork or building and the other parts within the work. Proportion in art implies using a *module,* or basic unit of measure. When an artist or architect uses a formal system of proportions, all parts of a building, body, or other entity will be fractions or multiples of the module. A module might be the diameter of a *column,* the height of a human head, or any other component whose dimensions can

be multiplied or divided to determine the size of the work's other parts.

In certain times and places, artists have used *canons,* or systems, of "correct" or "ideal" proportions for representing human figures, constituent parts of buildings, and so forth. In ancient Greece, many sculptors formulated canons of proportions so strict and all-encompassing that they calculated the size of every body part in advance, even the fingers and toes, according to mathematical ratios.

Proportional systems can differ sharply from period to period, culture to culture, and artist to artist. Part of the task art history students face is to perceive and adjust to these differences. In fact, many artists have used disproportion and distortion deliberately for expressive effect. Dürer's Death (FIG. I-7) has hardly any flesh on his bones, and his limbs are distorted and stretched. Disproportion and distortion distinguish him from all the other figures in the work, precisely as the artist intended.

In other cases, artists have used disproportion to focus attention on one body part (often the head) or to single out a group member (usually the leader). These intentional "unnatural" discrepancies in proportion constitute what art historians call *hierarchy of scale,* the enlarging of elements considered the most important. On the bronze plaque from Benin, Nigeria, illustrated here (FIG. I-1), the sculptor enlarged all the heads for emphasis and also varied the size of each figure according to the person's social status. Central, largest, and therefore most important is the Benin king, mounted on horseback. The horse has been a symbol of power and wealth in many societies from prehistory to the present. That the Benin king is disproportionately larger than his horse, contrary to nature, further aggrandizes him. Two large attendants fan the king. Other figures of smaller size and lower status at the Benin court stand on the king's left and right and in the plaque's upper corners. One tiny figure next to the horse is almost hidden from view beneath the king's feet.

One problem students of art history—and professional art historians too—confront when studying illustrations in art history books is that although the relative sizes of figures and objects in a painting or sculpture are easy to discern, it is impossible to determine the absolute size of the work reproduced because they all appear at approximately the same size on the page. Readers of *Art through the Ages* can learn the exact size of all artworks from the dimensions given in the captions and, more intuitively, from the scales positioned at the lower left or right corner of each illustration.

Carving and Casting Sculptural technique falls into two basic categories, *subtractive* and *additive. Carving* is a subtractive technique. The final form is a reduction of the original mass of a block of stone, a piece of wood, or another material. Wood statues were once tree trunks, and stone statues began as blocks pried from mountains. The unfinished marble statue illustrated here (FIG. I-14) by renowned Italian artist MICHELANGELO BUONARROTI (1475–1564) clearly reveals the original shape of the stone block. Michelangelo thought

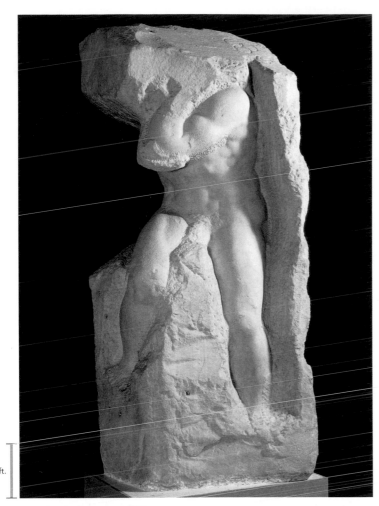

I-14 Michelangelo Buonarroti, *unfinished captive*, 1527–1528. Marble, 8' 7½" high. Galleria dell'Accademia, Florence.

Carving a freestanding figure from stone or wood is a subtractive process. Italian master sculptor Michelangelo thought of sculpture as a process of "liberating" the statue within the block of marble.

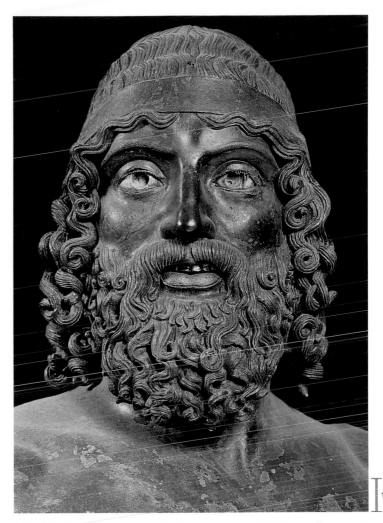

I-15 Head of a warrior, detail of a statue (FIG. 2-32) from the sea off Riace, Italy, ca. 460–450 BCE. Bronze, full statue 6' 6" high. Museo Archeologico Nazionale, Reggio Calabria.

The sculptor of this life-size statue of a bearded Greek warrior cast the head, limbs, torso, hands, and feet in separate molds, then welded the pieces together and added the eyes in a different material.

of sculpture as a process of "liberating" the statue within the block. All sculptors of stone or wood cut away (subtract) "excess material." When they finish, they "leave behind" the statue—in this example, a twisting nude male form whose head Michelangelo never freed from the stone block.

In additive sculpture, the artist builds up the forms, usually in clay around a framework, or *armature*. Or a sculptor may fashion a *mold,* a hollow form for shaping, or *casting,* a fluid substance such as bronze. The ancient Greek sculptor who made the bronze statue of a warrior found in the sea near Riace, Italy, cast the head (FIG. **I-15**) as well as the limbs, torso, hands, and feet (FIG. 2-32) in separate molds, and then *welded* them together (joined them by heating). Finally, the artist added features, such as the pupils of the eyes (now missing) in other materials. The warrior's teeth are silver, and his lower lip is copper.

Relief Sculpture *Statues* and *busts* (head, shoulders, and chest) that exist independent of any architectural frame or setting and that viewers can walk around are *freestanding sculptures,* or *sculptures in the round.* In *relief* sculpture, the subjects project from the background but remain part of it.

In *high-relief* sculpture, the images project boldly. In some cases (FIG. I-1), the relief is so high that not only do the forms cast shadows on the background, but some parts are in the round. In *low relief,* or *bas-relief* sculpture (FIG. I-13), the projection is slight. Artists can produce relief sculptures, as they do sculptures in the round, either by carving or casting.

Architectural Drawings People experience buildings both visually and by moving through and around them, so they perceive architectural space and mass together. Architects can represent these spaces and masses graphically in several ways, including as plans, sections, elevations, and cutaway drawings.

A *plan,* essentially a map of a floor, shows the placement of a structure's masses and, therefore, the spaces they circumscribe and enclose. A *section,* a kind of vertical plan, depicts the placement of the masses as if the building were cut through along a plane. Drawings showing a theoretical slice across a structure's width are *lateral sections.* Those cutting

Art History in the 21st Century   **11**

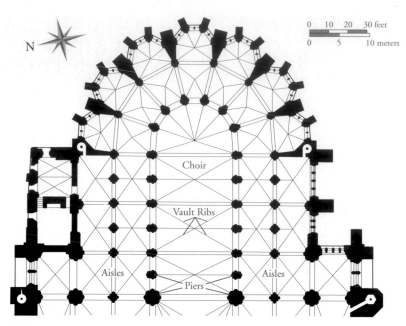

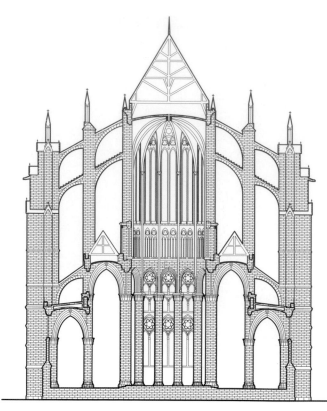

I-16 Plan (*left*) and lateral section (*right*) of Beauvais Cathedral (FIG. I-3), Beauvais, France, rebuilt after 1284.

Architectural drawings are indispensable aids for the analysis of buildings. Plans are maps of floors, recording the structure's masses. Sections are vertical "slices," across either a building's width or length.

through a building's length are *longitudinal sections*. Illustrated here are the plan and lateral section (FIG. **I-16**) of Beauvais Cathedral, which may be compared with the photograph of the church's *choir* (FIG. I-3). The plan shows the choir's shape and the location of the *piers* dividing the *aisles* and supporting the *vaults* above, as well as the pattern of the crisscrossing vault *ribs*. The lateral section shows not only the interior of the choir with its vaults and *stained-glass* windows, but also the structure of the roof and the form of the exterior *flying buttresses* holding the vaults in place.

Other types of architectural drawings appear throughout this book. An *elevation* drawing is a head-on view of an external or internal wall. A *cutaway* combines in a single drawing an exterior view with an interior view of part of a building.

This overview of the art historian's vocabulary is not exhaustive, nor have artists used only painting, drawing, sculpture, and architecture as media over the millennia. Ceramics, jewelry, textiles, photography, and computer graphics are just some of the numerous other arts. All of them involve highly specialized techniques described in distinct vocabularies. As in this introductory chapter, new terms appear in *italics,* accompanied by their definition, when they first appear. The comprehensive Glossary at the end of the book contains definitions of all italicized terms.

Art History and Other Disciplines

By its very nature, the work of art historians intersects with the work of others in many fields of knowledge, not only in the humanities but also in the social and natural sciences. Today, art historians must go beyond the boundaries of what the public and even professional art historians of previous

generations considered the specialized discipline of art history. Art historical research in the 21st century is typically interdisciplinary in nature. To cite one example, in an effort to unlock the secrets of a particular statue, an art historian might conduct archival research hoping to uncover new documents shedding light on who paid for the work and why, who made it and when, where it originally stood, how contemporaries viewed it, and a host of other questions. Realizing, however, that the authors of the written documents often were not objective recorders of fact but observers with their own biases and agendas, the art historian may also use methodologies developed in fields such as literary criticism, philosophy, sociology, and gender studies to weigh the evidence the documents provide.

At other times, rather than attempting to master many disciplines at once, art historians band together with other specialists in multidisciplinary inquiries. Art historians might call in chemists to date an artwork based on the composition of the materials used or might ask geologists to determine which quarry furnished the stone for a particular statue. X-ray technicians might be enlisted in an attempt to establish whether a painting is a forgery. Of course, art historians often reciprocate by contributing their expertise to the solution of problems in other disciplines. A historian, for example, might ask an art historian to determine—based on style, material, iconography, and other criteria—if any of the portraits of a certain king date after his death. Such information would help establish the ruler's continuing prestige during the reigns of his successors. (Some portraits of Augustus [FIG. I-8], the founder of the Roman Empire, postdate his death by decades, even centuries.)

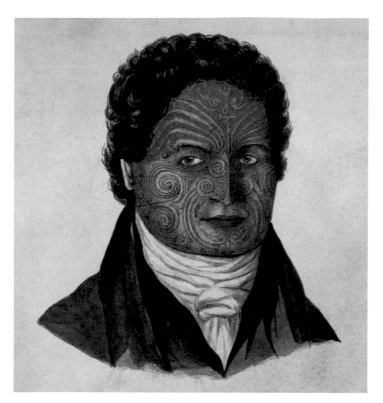 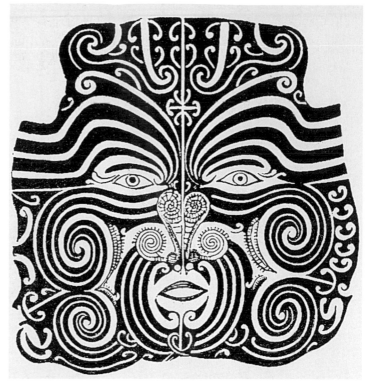

I-17 *Left:* JOHN HENRY SYLVESTER, *Portrait of Te Pehi Kupe,* 1826. Watercolor, 8¼″ × 6¼″. National Library of Australia, Canberra (Rex Nan Kivell Collection). *Right:* TE PEHI KUPE, *Self-Portrait,* 1826. From Leo Frobenius, *The Childhood of Man* (New York: J. B. Lippincott, 1909).

These strikingly different portraits of the same Maori chief reveal the different ways of seeing of a European artist and an Oceanic one. Understanding the cultural context of artworks is vital to art history.

DIFFERENT WAYS OF SEEING

The history of art can be a history of artists and their works, of styles and stylistic change, of materials and techniques, of images and themes and their meanings, and of contexts and cultures and patrons. The best art historians analyze artworks from many viewpoints. But no art historian (or scholar in any other field), no matter how broad-minded in approach and no matter how experienced, can be truly objective. As were the artists who made the works illustrated and discussed in this book, art historians are members of a society, participants in its culture. How can scholars (and museum visitors and travelers to foreign locales) comprehend cultures unlike their own? They can try to reconstruct the original cultural contexts of artworks, but they are limited by their distance from the thought patterns of the cultures they study and by the obstructions to understanding—the assumptions, presuppositions, and prejudices peculiar to their own culture—their own thought patterns raise. Art historians may reconstruct a distorted picture of the past because of culture-bound blindness.

A single instance underscores how differently people of diverse cultures view the world and how various ways of seeing can cause sharp differences in how artists depict the world. Illustrated here are two contemporaneous portraits of a 19th-century Maori chieftain (FIG. **I-17**)—one by an Englishman, JOHN SYLVESTER (active early 19th century), and the other by the New Zealand chieftain himself, TE PEHI KUPE (d. 1829). Both reproduce the chieftain's facial tattooing. The European artist (FIG. I-17, *left*) included the head and shoulders and downplayed the tattooing. The tattoo pattern is one aspect of the likeness among many, no more or less important than the chieftain's European attire. Sylvester also recorded his subject's momentary glance toward the right and the play of light on his hair, fleeting aspects having nothing to do with the figure's identity.

In contrast, Te Pehi Kupe's self-portrait (FIG. I-17, *right*)—made during a trip to Liverpool, England, to obtain European arms to take back to New Zealand—is not a picture of a man situated in space and bathed in light. Rather, it is the chieftain's statement of the supreme importance of the tattoo design announcing his rank among his people. Remarkably, Te Pehi Kupe created the tattoo patterns from memory, without the aid of a mirror. The splendidly composed insignia, presented as a flat design separated from the body and even from the head, is the Maori chieftain's image of himself. Only by understanding the cultural context of each portrait can viewers hope to understand why either representation appears as it does.

As noted at the outset, the study of the context of artworks and buildings is one of the central concerns of art historians. *Art through the Ages* seeks to present a history of art and architecture that will help readers understand not only the subjects, styles, and techniques of paintings, sculptures, buildings, and other art forms created in all parts of the world during 30 millennia but also their cultural and historical contexts. That story now begins.

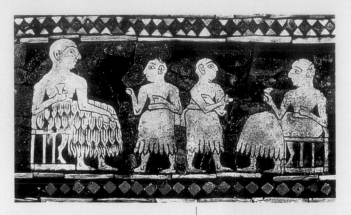

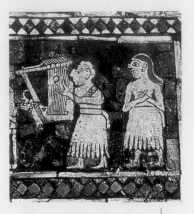

The human figures in Sumerian art are a composite of frontal and profile views. Artists used hierarchy of scale to distinguish the most important (largest) figures from those of lesser rank in society.

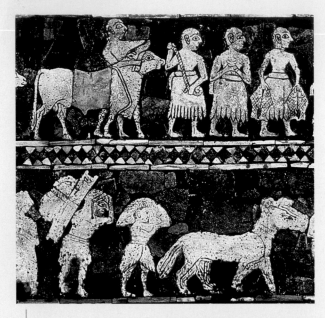

The entertainers at this banquet of Sumerian nobility include a musician playing a bull-headed harp of a type found in royal graves at Ur. The long-haired bare-chested singer is a court eunuch.

The Sumerians may have been the first culture to use pictures to tell coherent stories. Sumerian artists divided the pictorial field into a series of registers with figures on a common ground line.

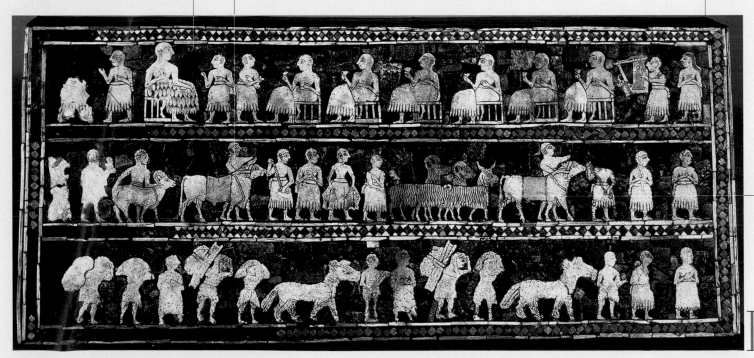

1-1 Peace side of the *Standard of Ur,* from tomb 779, Royal Cemetery, Ur (modern Tell Muqayyar), Iraq, ca. 2600–2400 BCE. Wood, lapis lazuli, shell, and red limestone, 8″ × 1′ 7″. British Museum, London. ◼◣

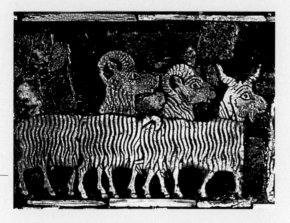

As in prehistoric art, representations of animals in Mesopotamian art are always strict profile views, save for the animals' eyes, which are seen from the front, as are also sometimes an animal's two horns.

Prehistory and the First Civilizations

THE CRADLE OF CIVILIZATION

Mesopotamia—a Greek word meaning "the land between the [Tigris and Euphrates] rivers"—is the core of the region often called the Fertile Crescent and the presumed locale of the biblical Garden of Eden (Gen. 2:10–15), where humans first learned how to use the wheel and plow and how to control floods and construct irrigation canals. In the fourth millennium BCE, the inhabitants of ancient Sumer, the world's first civilization, also established the earliest complex urban societies, called *city-states,* and invented writing. They may also have been the first culture to use pictures to tell coherent stories, far surpassing the tentative efforts at pictorial narration that survive on the walls of prehistoric caves in western Europe (FIG. 1-6) and in early shrines in Turkey (FIG. 1-7).

The so-called *Standard of Ur* (FIG. **1-1**), a rectangular box of uncertain function found in a tomb in the Sumerian city that was home to the biblical Abraham, is one of the earliest extant works incorporating all of the pictorial conventions that would dominate ancient narrative art for more than 2,000 years. Using shell, red limestone, and lapis lazuli (a rich azure-blue stone imported from Afghanistan), the artist divided the pictorial field into three successive bands (called *registers* or *friezes*) and placed all the figures on a common *ground line* (here, the horizontal base of the register). This compositional format marked a significant break with the haphazard figure placement of prehistoric art. The Sumerians also pioneered the use of *hierarchy of scale,* a highly effective way of distinguishing the most important (largest) figure from those of lesser rank. This pictorial convention would also have a long future in the history of art.

In FIG. 1-1, the narrative reads from left to right and bottom to top. In the lowest band, men carry provisions on their backs. Above, attendants transport a variety of animals and fish for the great banquet depicted in the uppermost register. There, seated dignitaries and a larger-than-life personage—probably a king (third from the left)—feast, while a harp player and singer entertain the group. Some art historians have interpreted the scene as a celebration after the victory in warfare represented on the other side of the wooden box (FIG. 1-14). But the two sides may be independent narratives illustrating the two principal roles of a Sumerian ruler—the mighty warrior who defeats enemies of his city-state, and the chief administrator who, with the blessing of the gods, assures the bountifulness of the land in peacetime. The absence of an inscription prevents connecting the scenes with a specific occasion or person, but the *Standard of Ur* is undoubtedly among the world's oldest depictions of contemporaneous events—another of the many seminal innovations of the Sumerians.

PREHISTORY

Humankind originated in Africa in the very remote past. Yet it was not until millions of years later that ancient hunters began to represent (literally, "to present again"—in different and substitute form) the world around them and to fashion the first examples of what people generally call "art." The immensity of this intellectual achievement cannot be exaggerated.

Paleolithic Age

The earliest preserved art objects date to around 30,000 BCE, during the Old Stone Age or *Paleolithic* period (from the Greek *paleo,* "old," and *lithos,* "stone"). Paleolithic artworks are of an astonishing variety. They range from simple shell necklaces to human and animal forms in ivory, clay, and stone to monumental paintings, engravings, and relief sculptures covering the huge wall surfaces of caves.

Venus of Willendorf One of the oldest sculptures discovered to date, carved using simple stone tools, is the tiny limestone figurine (FIG. **1-2**) of a woman nicknamed the *Venus of Willendorf* after its *findspot* in Austria (MAP **1-1**). Art historians can only speculate on the function and meaning of this and similar objects because they date to a time before writing, before (or *pre-*) history. Yet the preponderance of female over male figures in the Old Stone Age seems to indicate a preoccupation with women, whose child-bearing capabilities ensured the survival of the species. The anatomical exaggeration of the Willendorf figurine has suggested to many scholars that this and other prehistoric statuettes of women served as fertility images. The breasts of the Willendorf woman are enormous, far larger in proportion than the tiny forearms and hands resting on them. The sculptor also used a stone *burin* to *incise* (scratch) into the stone the outline of the pubic triangle. Sculptors often omitted this detail in other Paleolithic female figurines, however, and many of the

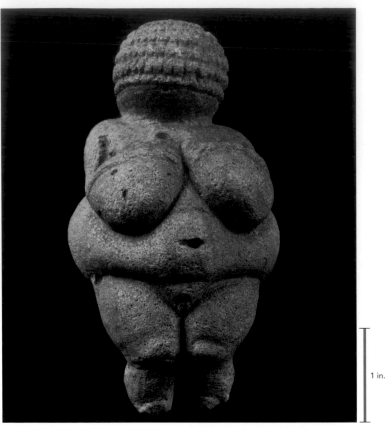

1 in.

1-2 Nude woman (*Venus of Willendorf*), from Willendorf, Austria, ca. 28,000–25,000 BCE. Limestone, 4¼" high. Naturhistorisches Museum, Vienna. ◼◀

One of the oldest sculptures known, this tiny figurine, with its anatomical exaggeration, typifies Paleolithic representations of women, whose child-bearing capabilities ensured the survival of the species.

women also have far more slender proportions than the Willendorf woman, leading some scholars to question the nature of these figures as fertility images. In any case, the makers' intent seems to have been to represent not a specific woman but the female form.

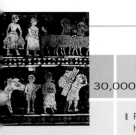

Prehistory and the First Civilizations

			BCE
Stone Age	Sumer, Akkad, **Old Kingdom**	Babylonia, **New Kingdom**	Assyria, **Achaemenid Persia**
30,000 ⎯⎯⎯⎯⎯⎯ 3500	3500 ⎯⎯⎯⎯⎯⎯ 2150	2150 ⎯⎯⎯ 1070	900 ⎯⎯⎯⎯⎯⎯ 330

▌ Paleolithic (30,000–9000 BCE) humans create the first sculptures and paintings. The works range in scale from tiny figurines to life-size paintings on walls ▌ In the Neolithic (8000–3500 BCE) age, the first settled communities appear in Anatolia and Mesopotamia. Artists produce the first monumental sculptures and earliest paintings with coherent narratives	▌ Sumerians (3500–2332 BCE) establish the first city-states, construct temples on ziggurats, and adopt the register format for narrative art ▌ Akkadians (2332–2150 BCE) produce the earliest known monumental hollow-cast bronze sculptures ▌ Old Kingdom (2575–2134 BCE) Egyptian sculptors create statuary types expressing the eternal nature of pharaonic kingship. The Fourth Dynasty pharaohs build the Great Pyramids at Gizeh	▌ Hammurabi, the greatest Babylonian king (r. 1792–1750 BCE), sets up a stele recording his comprehensive laws ▌ Egyptian New Kingdom (1550–1070 BCE) architects construct grandiose pylon temples. Akhenaton introduces a new religion and new art forms	▌ Assyrians (900–612 BCE) construct fortified citadels guarded by lamassu and carve monumental reliefs celebrating their prowess in warfare and hunting ▌ Achaemenid Persians (559–330 BCE) build an immense palace complex at Persepolis featuring an audience hall that could accommodate 10,000 guests

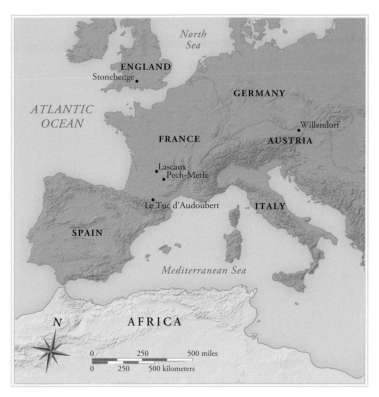

MAP 1-1 Prehistoric sites in western Europe.

After using both hands to form the overall shape of the animals, the artist smoothed the surfaces with a spatula-like tool and used fingers to shape the eyes, nostrils, mouths, and manes. Like nearly every other Paleolithic representation of animals, these bison are in strict profile. The profile is the only view of an animal wherein the head, body, tail, and all four legs can be seen. A frontal view would conceal most of the body, and a three-quarter view would not show either the front or side fully. Only the profile view is completely informative about the animal's shape, and this is why it was the almost universal choice during the Stone Age and for thousands of years thereafter (compare FIG. 1-1). Placing a premium on "variety" or "originality" either in subject choice or representational manner is a quite modern notion in the history of art. The aim of the earliest sculptors and painters was to create a convincing image of the subject, a kind of pictorial definition of the animal capturing its very essence, and only the profile view met their needs.

Le Tuc d'Audoubert Far more common than Paleolithic representations of humans are sculptures and paintings of animals. An early example of animal sculpture is the pair of clay bison reliefs (FIG. **1-3**) in the cave at Le Tuc d'Audoubert, France. The sculptor modeled the forms by pressing the clay against the surface of a large boulder at the back of the cave.

Cave Painting The bison of Le Tuc d'Audoubert are among the largest sculptures of the Paleolithic period, but they are dwarfed by the "herds" of painted animals that roam the cave walls of southern France and northern Spain. Examples of Paleolithic painting now have been found at more than 200 European sites. Nonetheless, archaeologists still regard painted caves as rare occurrences, because even though the cave images number in the hundreds, prehistoric artists created them over a period of some 10,000 to 20,000 years. Paleolithic painters drew their subjects using chunks of red and yellow ocher. For painting, they ground these same ochers into powders they mixed with water before applying. Large flat stones served as *palettes* to hold the pigment. The

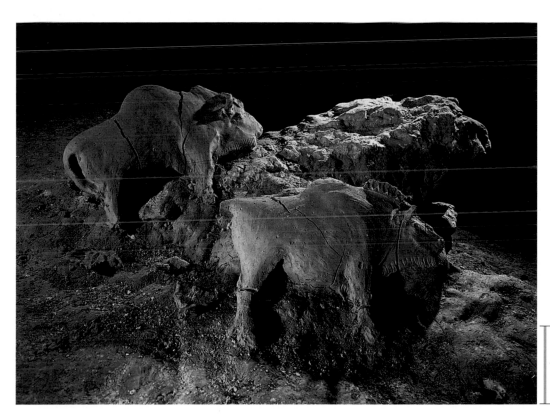

1-3 Two bison, reliefs in the cave at Le Tuc d'Audoubert, France, ca. 15,000–10,000 BCE. Clay, right bison 2' $\frac{7}{8}$" long.

Animals are far more common than humans in Old Stone Age art. In both relief sculpture and painting, they always appear in profile, the only view completely informative about the animals' shape.

1 ft.

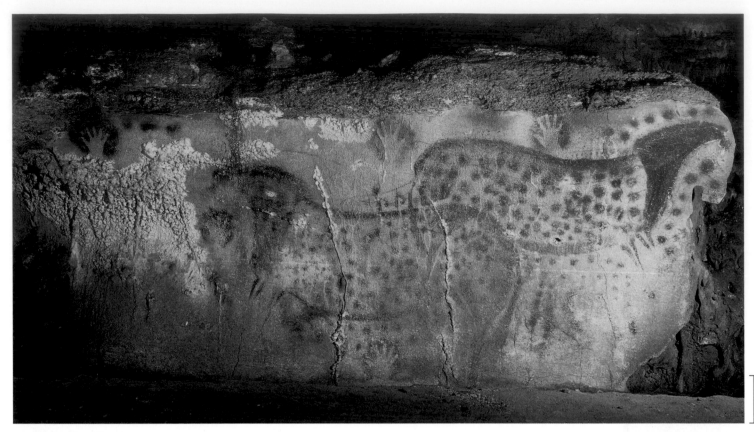

1 ft.

1-4 Spotted horses and negative hand imprints, wall painting in the cave at Pech-Merle, France, ca. 23,000–22,000 BCE. 11′ 2″ long.

Many Paleolithic paintings include abstract signs and handprints. Some scholars think the Pech-Merle painted hands are "signatures" of cult or community members or, less likely, of individual painters.

painters made brushes from reeds, bristles, or twigs, and may have used a blowpipe of reeds or hollow bones to spray pigments on out-of-reach surfaces. Some caves have natural ledges on the rock walls upon which the painters could have stood in order to reach the upper surfaces of the naturally formed "rooms" and corridors. To illuminate their work, the painters used stone lamps filled with marrow or fat, perhaps with a wick of moss. Despite the difficulty of making the tools and pigments, modern attempts at replicating the techniques of Paleolithic painting have demonstrated that skilled workers could cover large surfaces with images in less than a day.

Pech-Merle A *mural* (wall) painting (FIG. **1-4**) at Pech-Merle, France, provides some insight into the reason Stone Age artists chose certain subjects for specific locations. One of the horses (at the right in the illustration) may have been inspired by the rock formation in the wall surface resembling a horse's head and neck. Like the clay bison at Le Tuc d'Audoubert, the Pech-Merle horses are in strict profile. Here, however, painted hands accompany them. These and the majority of painted hands at other sites are "negative"— that is, the painter placed one hand against the wall and then brushed or blew or spat pigment around it. Occasionally, the painter dipped a hand in the pigment and then pressed it against the wall, leaving a "positive" imprint. These handprints must have had a purpose. Some scholars have considered them "signatures" of cult or community members

or, less likely, of individual painters. Checks, dots, squares, and other abstract signs appear near the painted animals in other Paleolithic caves. Several observers think these signs are a primitive form of writing, but like the hands—and everything else in Paleolithic art—their meaning is unknown (see "Art in the Old Stone Age," page 19).

Lascaux Perhaps the best-known Paleolithic cave is that at Lascaux, near Montignac, France, which features a large circular gallery called the Hall of the Bulls (FIG. **1-5**). Not all of the painted animals are bulls, despite the modern nickname, and the several species depicted vary in size. The artists represented many of the animals, such as the great bull at the right in the illustration, using outline alone, but others are colored silhouettes. On the walls of the Lascaux cave the two basic approaches to drawing and painting in the history of art appear side by side. These differences in style and technique alone suggest that different artists painted the animals at various times. The modern impression of a rapidly moving herd of beasts was unlikely the original intent. In any case, the "herd" consists of several kinds of animals of disparate sizes moving in different directions. Although most share a common ground line, some, for example, those in the upper right corner of FIG. **1-5**, seem to float above the viewer's head, like clouds in the sky. The painting has no setting, no background, no indication of place. The Paleolithic painter's sole concern was representing the animals, not locating them in a specific place.

Art in the Old Stone Age

Since the discovery of the first cave paintings in the late 19th century, scholars have wondered why the hunters of the Old Stone Age decided to cover the walls of dark caverns with animal images (FIGS. 1-3 to 1-6). Various theories have been proposed.

Some scholars have argued that the animals were mere decoration, but this explanation cannot account for the narrow range of subjects or the inaccessibility of many of the representations. In fact, the remoteness and difficulty of access to many of the images, and indications the caves were in use for centuries, are precisely why many other scholars have suggested that the prehistoric hunters attributed magical properties to the images they painted and sculpted. According to this argument, by confining animals to the surfaces of their cave walls, the Paleolithic artists believed they were bringing the wild beasts under their control. Some have even hypothesized that the hunters of the Old Stone Age performed rituals or dances in front of the images and that these rites served to improve their luck in tracking and killing the animals. Some researchers have speculated that the animal representations may have served as teaching tools to instruct new hunters about the character of the various species they would encounter or even to serve as targets for spears.

In contrast, some prehistorians have argued that the magical purpose of the paintings and reliefs was not to facilitate the *destruction* of animal species. Instead, they believe the first painters and sculptors created animal images to ensure the *survival* of the herds on which Paleolithic peoples depended for their food supply and for their clothing. A central problem for both the hunting-magic and food-creation theories is that the animals that seem to have been diet staples of Old Stone Age peoples are not those most frequently portrayed.

Other researchers have sought to reconstruct an elaborate mythology based on the cave paintings and sculptures, suggesting that Paleolithic humans believed they had animal ancestors. Still others have equated certain species with men and others with women and postulated various meanings for the abstract signs that sometimes accompany the images. Almost all of these theories have been discredited over time, and most prehistorians admit that no one knows the intent of the representations. In fact, a single explanation for all Paleolithic animal images, even ones similar in subject, style, and composition, is unlikely to apply universally. The works remain an enigma—and always will, because before the invention of writing, no contemporary explanations could be recorded.

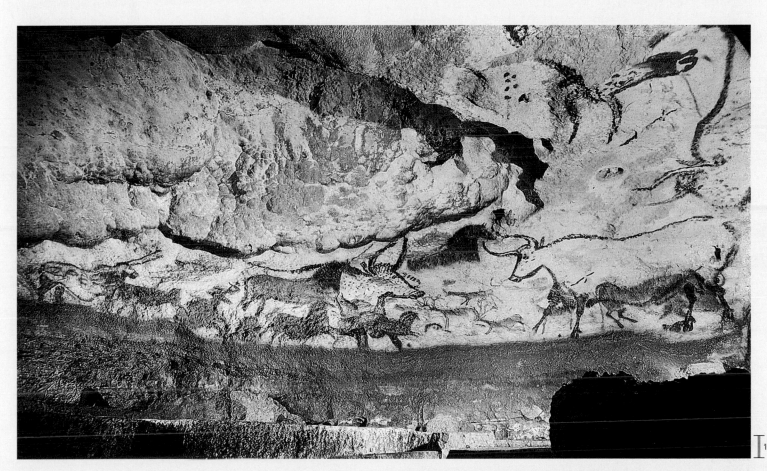

1-5 Left wall of the Hall of the Bulls in the cave at Lascaux, France, ca. 16,000–14,000 BCE. Largest bull 11′ 6″ long.

The purpose and meaning of Paleolithic cave paintings are unknown, but it is clear that the painters' sole concern was representing the animals, not locating them in a specific place or on a common ground line.

Another feature of the Lascaux paintings deserves attention. The bulls show a convention of representing horns art historians call *twisted perspective,* or *composite view,* because viewers see the heads in profile but the horns from the front.

Thus, the painter's approach is not consistently optical (seen from a fixed viewpoint). Rather, the approach is descriptive of the fact that cattle have two horns. Two horns are part of the concept "bull." In strict profile, only one horn would be

If these paintings of two animals and a bird-faced (masked?) man, deep in a well shaft in the Lascaux cave, depict a hunting scene, they constitute the earliest example of narrative art ever discovered.

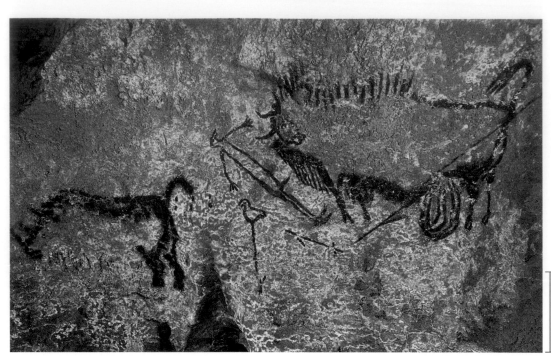

1 ft.

visible, but to paint the animal in that way would amount to an incomplete definition of it.

Perhaps the most perplexing painting in any Paleolithic cave is the one deep in the well shaft (FIG. **1-6**) at Lascaux, where man (as opposed to woman) makes one of his earliest appearances in prehistoric art. At the left, and moving to the left, is a rhinoceros. Beneath its tail are two rows of three dots of uncertain significance. At the right is a bison, with less realistic proportions, probably the work of someone else. The second painter nonetheless successfully suggested the bristling rage of the animal, whose bowels hang from its belly in a heavy coil. Between the two beasts is a bird-faced (masked?) man with outstretched arms and hands having only four fingers. The man is depicted with far less care and detail than either animal, but the painter made the hunter's gender explicit by the prominent penis. The position of the man is ambiguous. Is he wounded or dead or merely tilted back and unharmed? Do the staff(?) with the bird on top and the spear belong to him? Is it he or the rhinoceros that has gravely wounded the bison—or neither? Which animal, if either, has knocked the man down, if indeed he is on the ground? Are these three images related at all? Modern viewers can be sure of nothing, but if the painters placed the figures beside each other to tell a story, then this is evidence for the creation of narrative compositions involving humans and animals at a much earlier date than anyone had imagined only a few generations ago. Yet it is important to remember that even if the artists intended to tell a story, very few people would have been able to "read" it. The painting, in a deep shaft, is very difficult to reach and could have been viewed only in flickering lamplight. Like all Paleolithic art, the scene in the Lascaux well shaft remains enigmatic.

Neolithic Age

Around 9000 BCE, the ice covering much of northern Europe during the Paleolithic period melted as the climate grew warmer. The reindeer migrated north, and the woolly mammoth and rhinoceros disappeared. The Paleolithic gave way to a transitional period, the *Mesolithic*, or Middle Stone Age, when Europe became climatically, geographically, and bio-

logically much as it is today. Then, for several thousand years at different times in different parts of the globe, a great new age, the *Neolithic* (New Stone Age), dawned. Humans began to domesticate plants and animals and settle in fixed abodes. Their food supply assured, many groups changed from hunters to herders, to farmers, and finally to townspeople. Wandering hunters settled down to organized community living in villages surrounded by cultivated fields. The new sedentary societies of the Neolithic age originated systematic agriculture, weaving, metalworking, pottery, and counting and recording with tokens, and constructed religious shrines as well as homes. Recent excavations at Göbekli Tepe in southeastern Turkey may already have overturned this traditional sequence, however. German archaeologists discovered that prehistoric hunter-gatherers built a stone temple with animal reliefs at that site around 9000 BCE, long before sedentary farmers established permanent village communities at sites such as Çatal Höyük.

Çatal Höyük The Neolithic settlement at Çatal Höyük on the central Anatolian plateau flourished between 6500 and 5700 BCE and was one of the world's first experiments in urban living. The regularity of the town's plan suggests the inhabitants built the settlement to some predetermined scheme. The houses, constructed of mud brick strengthened by sturdy timber frames, varied in size but repeated the same basic plan. The rooms have plastered and painted floors and walls with platforms along the walls that served as sites for sleeping, working, and eating. The living buried the dead beneath the floors.

The excavators have found many rooms decorated with mural paintings and plaster reliefs. These "shrines" had an uncertain function, but their number indicates the rooms played an important role in the life of the Neolithic settlement. On the wall of one room, archaeologists discovered a

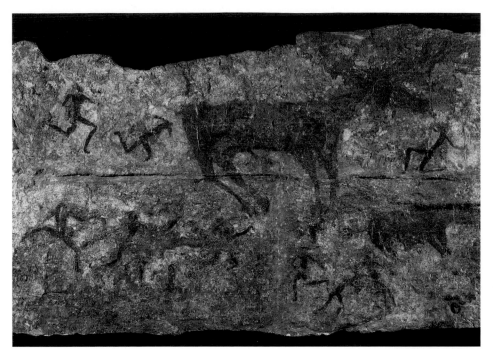

Ain Ghazal A second well-excavated Neolithic settlement is Ain Ghazal, near Amman, Jordan. Occupied from around 7200 to 5000 BCE, Ain Ghazal has produced striking finds, including two caches containing three dozen plaster statuettes (FIG. **1-8**) datable to the mid-seventh millennium BCE. The sculptures, which appear to have been ritually buried, are white plaster built up over a core of reeds and twine, with black bitumen, a tarlike substance, for the pupils of the eyes. Some of the figures have painted clothing. Only rarely did the sculptors indicate the gender of the figures. Whatever their purpose, by their size (a few exceed three feet in height) and sophisticated technique, the Ain Ghazal statuettes differ fundamentally from Paleolithic figurines such as the four-inch-tall Willendorf

painted representation of a deer hunt (FIG. **1-7**). The mural is worlds apart from the cave paintings the hunters of the Paleolithic period produced. Perhaps what is most strikingly new about the Çatal Höyük painting and others like it is the regular appearance of the human figure—not only singly but also in large, coherent groups with a wide variety of poses, subjects, and settings. As noted earlier, humans were unusual in Paleolithic painting, and pictorial narratives are almost unknown. Even the "hunting scene" (FIG. 1-6) in the well at Lascaux is doubtful as a narrative. In Neolithic paintings, scenes with humans dominating animals are central subjects.

In the Çatal Höyük hunt, the group of hunters—and no one doubts it is, indeed, an organized hunting party, not a series of individual figures—is a rhythmic repetition of basic shapes, but the painter took care to distinguish important descriptive details (for example, bows, arrows, and garments) and the heads have clearly defined noses, mouths, chins, and hair. The Neolithic painter placed all the heads in profile for the same reason Paleolithic painters universally chose the profile view for representations of animals. Only the side view of the human head shows all its shapes clearly. However, at Çatal Höyük the torsos are frontal—again, the most informative viewpoint—whereas the painter chose the profile view for the legs and arms. This composite view of the human body is as artificial as the twisted horns of the Lascaux bulls (FIG. 1-5) because the human body cannot make an abrupt 90-degree shift at the hips. But it well describes what a human body is, as opposed to how it appears from a particular viewpoint. The technique of painting also changed dramatically since Paleolithic times. The Çatal Höyük painters used brushes to apply their pigments to a ground of dry white plaster. The careful preparation of the wall surface is in striking contrast to the direct application of pigment to the rock surfaces of Old Stone Age caves.

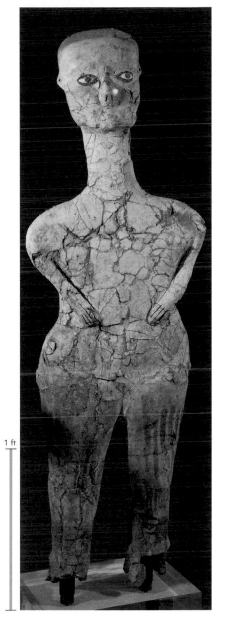

1 ft

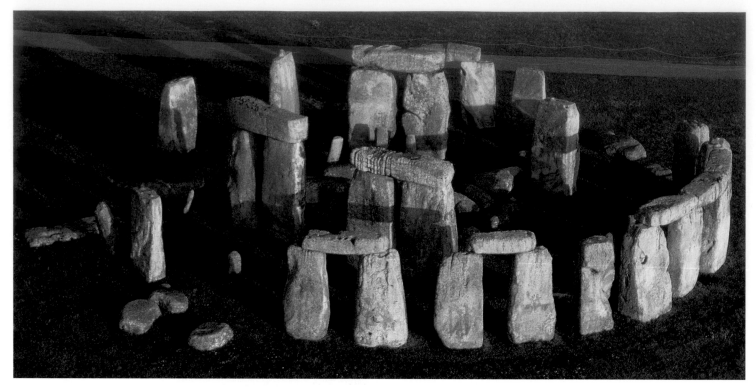

1-9 Aerial view of Stonehenge (looking northwest), Salisbury Plain, Wiltshire, England, ca. 2550–1600 BCE.

One of the earliest examples of monumental architecture in Neolithic Europe, the circle of 24-foot-tall trilithons at Stonehenge probably functioned as an astronomical observatory and solar calendar.

woman (FIG. 1-2). They mark the beginning of monumental sculpture in the ancient world.

Stonehenge In western Europe, where Paleolithic paintings and sculptures abound, no comparably developed towns of the time of Çatal Höyük or Ain Ghazal have been found. However, in succeeding millennia, perhaps as early as 4000 BCE, the local Neolithic populations in several areas developed a monumental architecture employing massive rough-cut stones. The very dimensions of the stones, some as tall as 17 feet and weighing as much as 50 tons, have prompted historians to call them *megaliths* (great stones) and to designate the culture that produced them *megalithic*.

Although megalithic monuments are plentiful throughout Europe, the arrangement of huge stones in a circle (called a *henge*), often surrounded by a ditch, is almost entirely limited to Britain. The most imposing example is Stonehenge (FIG. **1-9**) near Salisbury, a complex of rough-cut sarsen (a form of sandstone) stones and smaller "bluestones" (various volcanic rocks). Outermost is a ring, 97 feet in diameter, of 24-foot-tall sarsen *monoliths* supporting *lintels* (horizontal stone blocks used to span an opening). This simple *post-and-lintel system* of construction is still in use today. Next is a ring of bluestones, which in turn encircles a horseshoe (open end facing east) of *trilithons* (three-stone constructions)—five lintel-topped pairs of the largest sarsens, each weighing 45 to 50 tons. Standing apart and to the east (outside the photograph) is the "heel-stone," which, for a person looking outward from the center of the complex, would have marked the point where the sun rose at the summer solstice. Construction of Stonehenge probably occurred in several phases in the centuries before and after 2000 BCE. It seems to have been a kind of astronomical observatory. During the Middle Ages, the Britons believed the mysterious structures were the work of the magician Merlin of the King Arthur legend, who spirited them from Ireland. Most archaeologists now consider Stonehenge a remarkably accurate solar calendar. This achievement is testimony to the rapidly developing intellectual powers of Neolithic humans as well as to their capacity for heroic physical effort.

ANCIENT MESOPOTAMIA AND PERSIA

The fundamental change in human society from the dangerous and uncertain life of the hunter and gatherer to the more predictable and stable life of the farmer and herder first occurred in the "fertile crescent" of Mesopotamia, the land mass that forms a huge arc from the mountainous border between Turkey and Syria through Iraq to Iran's Zagros Mountain range (MAP **1-2**). There, in present-day southern Iraq, the world's first great civilization—Sumer (FIG. 1-1)—arose in the valley between the Tigris and Euphrates Rivers.

Sumer

Ancient Sumer was not a unified nation. Rather, it comprised a dozen or so independent city-states under the protection of different Mesopotamian deities. The Sumerian rulers were the gods' representatives on earth and the stewards of their earthly treasure. The rulers and priests directed all commu-

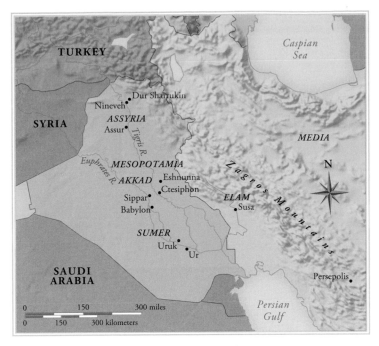

MAP 1-2 Ancient Mesopotamia and Persia.

munities gained permanent identities as discrete cities. The city-state was one of the great Sumerian inventions.

White Temple, Uruk The layout of Sumerian cities reflected the central role of the gods in daily life. The temple honoring each state's chief god formed the city's monumental nucleus. In fact, the vast temple complex was a kind of city within a city, where priests and scribes carried on official administrative and commercial business as well as oversaw all religious functions.

The outstanding preserved example of early Sumerian temple architecture is the 5,000-year-old White Temple (FIG. **1-10**) at Uruk, the home of the legendary Gilgamesh. Sumerian builders did not have access to stone quarries and instead formed mud bricks for the superstructures of their temples and other buildings. The fragile nature of the building materials did not, however, prevent the Sumerians from erecting towering works, such as the Uruk temple, several centuries before the Egyptians built their stone pyramids (FIGS. 1-25 and 1-26). This says a great deal about the Sumerians' desire to provide grandiose settings for the worship of their deities.

The Uruk temple (whose whitewashed walls suggested its modern nickname) stands atop a high platform, or *ziggurat*, 40 feet above street level. A stairway leads to the temple at the top. As in other Sumerian temples, the corners of the White Temple are oriented to the cardinal points of the compass. The building, probably dedicated to Anu, the sky god, is of modest proportions (61 by 16 feet). By design, it did not accommodate large throngs of worshipers but only a select few, the priests and perhaps the leading community members. The temple had several chambers. The central hall, or *cella*, was the divinity's room and housed a stepped altar. The Sumerians referred to their temples as "waiting rooms," a reflection of their belief that the deity would descend from the

nal activities, including canal construction, crop collection, and food distribution. Because the Sumerians developed agriculture to such an extent that only a portion of the population had to produce food, some members of the community were free to specialize in other activities, including manufacturing, trade, and administration. Labor specialization is the hallmark of the first complex urban societies. In the Sumerian city-states of the fourth millennium BCE, activities that once had been individually initiated became institutionalized for the first time. The community, rather than the family, assumed responsibility for defense against enemies and the caprices of nature. Whether ruled by a single person or a council chosen from among the leading families, these com-

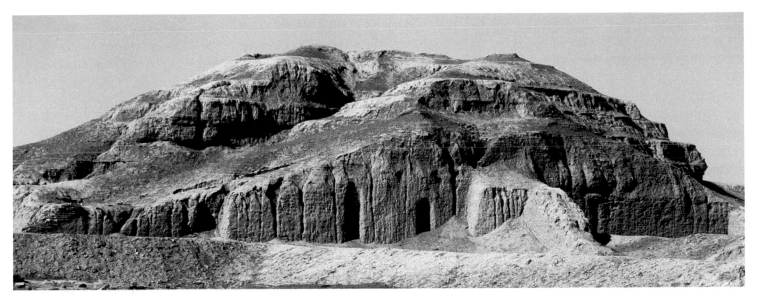

1-10 White Temple and ziggurat, Uruk (modern Warka), Iraq, ca. 3200–3000 BCE.

Using only mud bricks, the Sumerians erected temples on high platforms called ziggurats several centuries before the Egyptians built stone pyramids. The most famous ziggurat was the biblical Tower of Babel.

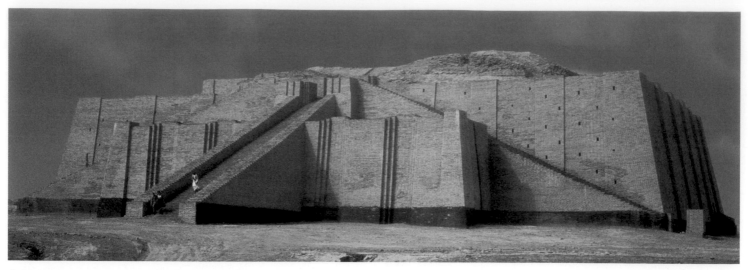

1-11 Ziggurat (looking southwest), Ur (modern Tell Muqayyar), Iraq, ca. 2100 BCE.

The Ur ziggurat, one of the largest in Mesopotamia, is 50 feet high. It has three (restored) ramplike stairways of a hundred steps each that originally ended at a gateway to a brick temple, which does not survive.

heavens to appear before the priests in the cella. Whether the Uruk temple had a roof is uncertain.

Ziggurat, Ur Eroded ziggurats still dominate most of the ruined cities of Sumer. The best preserved is that at Ur (FIG. **1-11**), built about a millennium later than the Uruk ziggurat and much grander. The base is a solid mass of mud brick 50 feet high. The builders used baked bricks laid in bitumen for the facing of the entire monument. Three (restored) ramplike stairways of a hundred steps each converge on a tower-flanked gateway. From there another flight of steps probably led to the temple proper, which does not survive. The loftiness of the great ziggurats of Mesopotamia made a profound impression on the peoples of ancient Mesopotamia. The tallest ziggurat of all—at Babylon—was about 270 feet high. Known to the Hebrews as the Tower of Babel, it became the centerpiece of a biblical tale about insolent pride. Humankind's desire to build a tower to Heaven angered God. Therefore, the Lord caused the workers to speak different languages, preventing them from communicating with one another and bringing construction of the ziggurat to a halt.

Warka Vase As noted in the opening discussion of the *Standard of Ur* (FIG. 1-1), the Sumerians, pioneers in so many areas, were the first masters of pictorial narration. Several hundred years older than the *Standard of Ur* is the so-called *Warka Vase* (FIG. **1-12**) from Uruk (modern Warka), the first great work of narrative relief sculpture known. Found within the temple complex dedicated to Inanna, the goddess of love and war, it depicts a religious festival in her honor. The *Warka Vase* is the earliest known instance of the adoption of the register format for telling a story, which artists still employ today in modified form in comic books.

The lowest band on the *Warka Vase* shows ewes and rams—in strict profile, as in Stone Age art—above crops and

a wavy line representing water. The animals and plants underscore that Inanna has blessed Uruk's inhabitants with good crops and increased herds. Above, naked men carry baskets and jars overflowing with earth's abundance. They will present their bounty to the goddess as a *votive offering* (gift of gratitude to a deity usually made in fulfillment of a vow) and will deposit it in her temple. The spacing of each figure involves no overlapping. The Uruk men, like the Çatal Höyük deer hunters (FIG. 1-7), are a composite of frontal and profile views, with large staring frontal eyes in profile heads. (If the eyes were in profile, they would not "read" as eyes at all because they would not have their distinctive oval shape.)

In the uppermost (and tallest) band is a female figure with a tall horned headdress, probably Inanna but perhaps her priestess. A nude male figure brings a large vessel brimming with offerings to be deposited in the goddess's shrine. At the far right is an only partially preserved clothed man usually, if ambiguously, referred to as a "priest-king," that is, both a religious and secular leader. The greater height of the priest-king and Inanna compared to the offering bearers indicates their greater importance (hierarchy of scale). Some scholars interpret the scene as a symbolic marriage between the priest-king and the goddess, ensuring her continued goodwill—and reaffirming the leader's exalted position in society.

Eshnunna Statuettes Further insight into Sumerian religion comes from a cache of gypsum statuettes inlaid with shell and black limestone found in a temple at Eshnunna (modern Tell Asmar). The two largest figures (FIG. **1-13**), like all the others, represent mortals, rather than deities. They hold the small beakers the Sumerians used in religious rites. The men wear belts and fringed skirts. Most have beards and shoulder-length hair. The women wear long robes, with the right shoulder bare. Similar figurines from other sites bear inscriptions with the name of the donor and the god or even

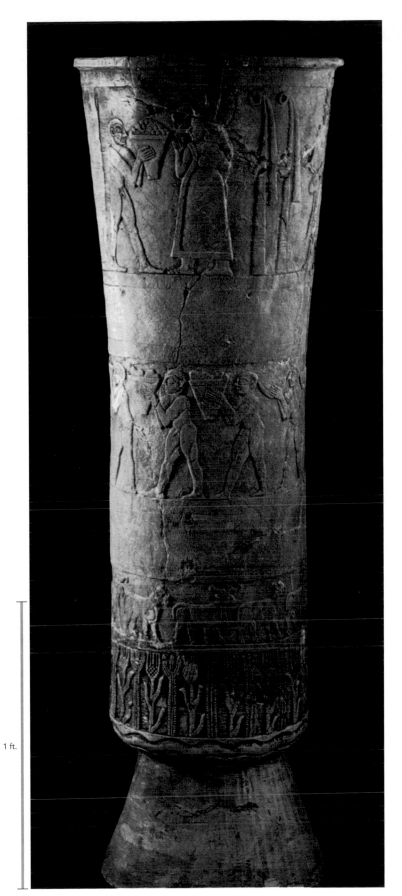

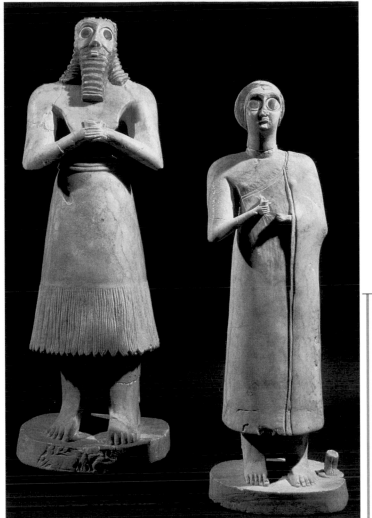

1-13 Statuettes of two worshipers, from the Square Temple at Eshnunna (modern Tell Asmar), Iraq, ca. 2700 BCE. Gypsum, shell, and black limestone, man 2' 4¼" high, woman 1' 11¼" high. National Museum of Iraq, Baghdad.

The oversized eyes probably symbolized the perpetual wakefulness of these substitute worshipers offering prayers to the deity. The beakers the figures hold were used to pour libations for the gods.

1-12 Presentation of offerings to Inanna (*Warka Vase*), from Uruk (modern Warka), Iraq, ca. 3200–3000 BCE. Alabaster, 3' ¼" high. National Museum of Iraq, Baghdad.

In this oldest known example of Sumerian narrative art, the sculptor divided the tall stone vase's reliefs into registers, a significant break with the haphazard figure placement found in earlier art.

specific prayers to the deity on the owner's behalf. With their heads tilted upward, they wait in the Sumerian "waiting room" for the divinity to appear. Most striking is the disproportionate relationship between the inlaid oversized eyes and the tiny hands. Scholars have explained the exaggeration of the eye size in various ways. Because the purpose of these votive figures was to offer constant prayers to the gods on their donors' behalf, the open-eyed stares most likely symbolize the eternal wakefulness necessary to fulfill their duty.

Standard of Ur The spoils of war, as well as success in farming and trade, brought considerable wealth to some of the city-states of ancient Sumer. Nowhere is this clearer than in the so-called Royal Cemetery at Ur. Archaeologists debate whether those buried in this cemetery were true kings and queens or simply aristocrats, priests, and priestesses, but their tombs were regal in character. They contained

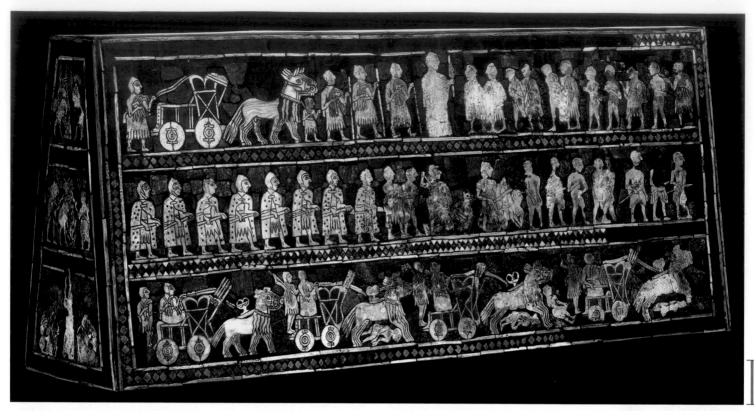

1-14 War side of the *Standard of Ur,* from tomb 779, Royal Cemetery, Ur (modern Tell Muqayyar), Iraq, ca. 2600–2400 BCE. Wood, shell, lapis lazuli, and red limestone, 8″ × 1′ 7″. British Museum, London. ◼◀

Using a mosaic-like technique, this Sumerian artist depicted a battlefield victory in three registers. The narrative reads from bottom to top, and the size of the figures varies with their importance in society.

gold helmets and daggers with handles of lapis lazuli, golden beakers and bowls, jewelry of gold and lapis, musical instruments, chariots, other luxurious items, and the *Standard of Ur* (FIGS. 1-1 and **1-14**), the sloping sides of which are inlaid with shell, lapis lazuli, and red limestone. The excavator who discovered this box-shaped object thought the Sumerians mounted it on a pole as a kind of military standard, hence its nickname. Art historians usually refer to the two long sides of the box as the "war side" (FIG. 1-14) and "peace side" (FIG. 1-1).

On the war side, four ass-drawn four-wheeled war chariots crush enemies, whose bodies appear on the ground in front of and beneath the animals. Above, foot soldiers gather up and lead away captured foes. In the uppermost register, soldiers present bound captives (whom the victors have stripped naked to degrade them) to a kinglike figure, who has stepped out of his chariot. His central place in the composition and his greater stature (his head breaks through the border at the top) set him apart from all the other figures.

Akkad

In 2334 BCE, the loosely linked group of cities known as Sumer came under the domination of a great ruler, Sargon of Akkad (r. 2332–2279 BCE). Archaeologists have yet to locate the specific site of the city of Akkad, but it was in the vicinity of Babylon. Under Sargon (whose name means "true king") and his successors, the Akkadians introduced a new concept of royal power based on unswerving loyalty to the king rather than to the city-state. Naram-Sin (r. 2254–2218 BCE),

Sargon's grandson, regarded the governors of his cities as mere servants, and called himself "King of the Four Quarters"— in effect, ruler of the earth, akin to a god.

Akkadian Portraiture A magnificent copper head (FIG. **1-15**) portraying an Akkadian king embodies this new concept of absolute monarchy. The head is all that survives of a statue knocked over in antiquity, perhaps during the sack of Nineveh in 612 BCE. To make a political statement, the enemy not only toppled the Akkadian royal portrait but gouged out the eyes (once inlaid with precious or semiprecious stones), broke off the lower part of the beard, and slashed the ears. Nonetheless, the king's majestic serenity, dignity, and authority are evident. So, too, is the masterful way the sculptor balanced *naturalism* and *abstract* patterning. The artist carefully observed and recorded the distinctive profile of the nose and long, curly beard, and brilliantly communicated the differing textures of flesh and hair, even the contrasting textures of the mustache, beard, and the braided hair on the top of the head. The coiffure's triangles, lozenges, and overlapping disks of hair and the great arching eyebrows that give such character to the portrait reveal the artist was also sensitive to formal pattern. No less remarkable is the fact that this is a life-size, hollow-cast metal sculpture (see "Hollow-Casting Life-Size Bronze Statues," Chapter 2, page 67), one of the earliest known. The head demonstrates the sculptor's skill in casting and polishing copper and in engraving the details.

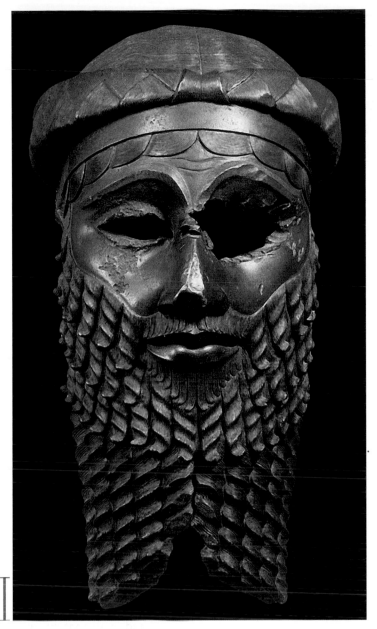

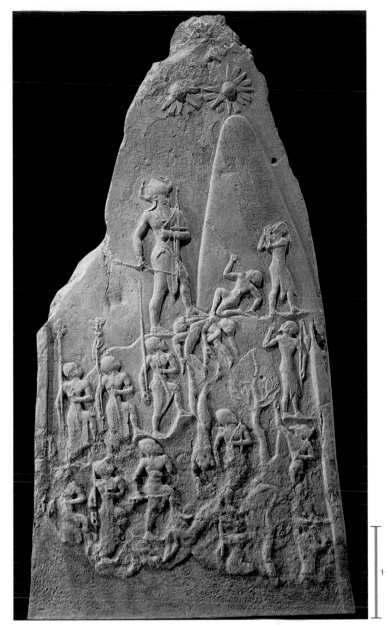

1-15 Head of an Akkadian ruler, from Nineveh (modern Kuyunjik), Iraq, ca. 2250–2200 BCE. Copper, 1' 2⅜" high. National Museum of Iraq, Baghdad.

The sculptor of this oldest known life-size hollow-cast head captured the distinctive features of the ruler while also displaying a keen sense of abstract pattern. Vandals defaced the head in antiquity.

1-16 Victory stele of Naram-Sin, from Susa, Iran, ca. 2254–2218 BCE. Pink sandstone, 6' 7" high. Musée du Louvre, Paris.

To commemorate his conquest of the Lullubi, Naram-Sin set up this stele showing him leading his army up a mountain. The sculptor staggered the figures, abandoning the traditional register format.

Naram-Sin The godlike sovereignty the kings of Akkad claimed is also evident in the victory stele (FIG. **1-16**) Naram-Sin set up at Sippar. A *stele* is a carved stone slab erected to commemorate a historical event or, in some other cultures, to mark a grave (FIG. **2-45**). Naram-Sin's stele commemorates his defeat of the Lullubi, a people of the Iranian mountains to the east. On the stele, the grandson of Sargon leads his victorious army up the slopes of a wooded mountain. His routed enemies fall, flee, die, or beg for mercy. The king stands alone, far taller than his men, treading on the bodies of two of the fallen Lullubi. He wears the horned helmet signifying divinity—the first time a king appears as a god in Mesopotamian art. At least three favorable stars (the stele is damaged at the top) shine on his triumph.

By storming the mountain, Naram-Sin seems also to be scaling the ladder to the heavens, the same conceit that lies behind Mesopotamian ziggurat towers. His troops march up the slope behind him in orderly files, suggesting the discipline and organization of the king's forces. In contrast, the enemy is in disarray, which the artist communicated by depicting the Lullubi in a great variety of postures. (One falls head first down the mountainside.) The Akkadian artist adhered to older conventions in many details, especially by portraying the king and his soldiers in composite views and by placing a frontal two-horned helmet on Naram-Sin's profile head. But the sculptor showed daring innovation in creating one of the first landscapes in the history of art and setting the figures on successive tiers within that landscape.

Ancient Mesopotamia and Persia **27**

This was a bold rejection of the standard compositional formula of telling a story in a series of horizontal registers.

Babylon

Around 2150 BCE, a mountain people, the Gutians, brought an end to Akkadian power. The cities of Sumer, however, soon united in response to the alien presence, drove the Gutians out of Mesopotamia, and established a Neo-Sumerian state ruled by the kings of Ur. This age, which historians call the Third Dynasty of Ur, saw the construction of the Ur ziggurat (FIG. 1-11). Sumer's resurgence was short-lived, however. The last of the Ur kings fell at the hands of the Elamites, who ruled the territory east of the Tigris River. In the next two centuries the traditional Mesopotamian political pattern of several independent city-states existing side by side reemerged and persisted until one of those cities, Babylon, succeeded in establishing a centralized government that ruled southern Mesopotamia in the 18th and 17th centuries BCE.

Hammurabi Babylon's most powerful king was Hammurabi (r. 1792–1750 BCE). Famous in his own time for his conquests, he is best known today for his comprehensive laws, which prescribed penalties for everything from adultery and murder to the cutting down of a neighbor's trees. Hammurabi's laws are inscribed in 3,500 lines of *cuneiform* (wedge-shaped) characters on a tall black-basalt stele (FIG. **1-17**) discovered at Susa in Iran. At the top, Hammurabi stands before Shamash, the flame-shouldered sun god. The king raises his hand in

1-17 Stele with the laws of Hammurabi, from Susa, Iran, ca. 1780 BCE. Basalt, 7′ 4″ high. Musée du Louvre, Paris. ■◀

The stele recording Hammurabi's remarkably early comprehensive laws also is one of the first examples of an artist employing foreshortening—the representation of a figure or object at an angle.

1 ft.

respect. The god extends to Hammurabi the rod and ring that symbolize authority. The symbols are builders' tools—measuring rods and coiled rope—and connote Hammurabi's capacity to build the social order and to measure people's lives, that is, to render judgments and enforce laws. The sculptor depicted Shamash in the familiar convention of combined front and side views, but with two important exceptions. The god's great headdress with its four pairs of horns is in true profile so that only four, not all eight, of the horns are visible. Also, the artist seems to have tentatively explored the notion of *foreshortening*—a device for suggesting depth by representing a figure or object at an angle, instead of frontally or in profile. Shamash's beard is a series of diagonal rather than horizontal lines, suggesting its recession from the picture plane. The sculptor also depicted the god's throne at an angle. Innovations such as these and the bold abandonment of the register format in favor of a tiered landscape on the Naram-Sin stele were exceptional in early eras of the history of art. These occasional departures from normal representational modes testify to the creativity of Mesopotamian artists.

Assyria

The Babylonian Empire toppled in the face of an onslaught by the Hittites, an Anatolian people who conquered and sacked Babylon around 1595 BCE. They then retired to their homeland, leaving Babylon in the hands of the Kassites. By around 900 BCE, however, the Assyrians had overtaken Mesopotamia. The new conquerors took their name from Assur, the city of the god Ashur on the Tigris River. At the height of their power, the Assyrians ruled an empire that extended from the Tigris to the Nile and from the Persian Gulf to Asia Minor.

Dur Sharrukin The royal citadel of Sargon II (r. 721–705 BCE) at Dur Sharrukin is the most completely excavated of the many Assyrian palaces. Its ambitious layout reveals the confidence of the Assyrian kings in their all-conquering might, but its strong defensive walls also reflect a society ever fearful of attack during a period of almost constant warfare. The city measured about a square mile in area and included a great ziggurat and six sanctuaries for six different gods. The palace, elevated on a mound 50 feet high, covered some 25 acres and had more than 200 courtyards and timber-roofed rooms. Sargon II regarded his city and palace as an expression of his grandeur. In one inscription, he boasted, "I built a city with [the labors of] the peoples subdued by my hand, whom [the gods] Ashur, Nabu, and Marduk had caused to lay themselves at my feet and bear my yoke." And in another text, he proclaimed, "Sargon, King of the World, has built a city. Dur Sharrukin he has named it. A peerless palace he has built within it."

Guarding the gate to Sargon's palace were colossal limestone monsters (FIG. **1-18**), which the Assyrians probably called *lamassu*. These winged, man-headed bulls served to ward off the king's enemies. The task of moving and installing these immense stone sculptures was so daunting that several reliefs in the palace of Sargon's successor celebrate the feat, showing scores of men dragging lamassu figures with the aid of ropes and sledges. The Assyrian lamassu sculptures are partly in the round, but the sculptor nonetheless conceived them as high reliefs on adjacent sides of a corner. They combine the front view of the animal at rest with the side view of it in motion. Seeking to present a complete picture of the lamassu from both the front and the side, the sculptor gave the monster five legs—two seen from the front, four seen from the side. This sculpture, then, is yet another case of early artists' providing a conceptual picture of an animal or person and of all its important parts, as opposed to an optical view of the lamassu as it really would stand in space.

Kalhu For their palace walls the Assyrian kings commissioned extensive series of narrative reliefs exalting royal power and piety. The sculptures record official ceremonies, religious rituals, battlefield victories, and the slaying of wild animals. (The Assyrians, like many other societies before and after, regarded prowess in hunting as a manly virtue on a par with success in warfare.) One of the most extensive cycles of Assyrian narrative reliefs comes from the northwest palace of Ashurnasirpal II (r. 883–859 BCE) at Kalhu. Throughout the palace, painted gypsum reliefs sheathed the lower parts of the mud-brick walls below brightly colored plaster. Rich textiles on the floors contributed to the luxurious ambience.

The relief illustrated here (FIG. **1-19**) depicts a battle in 878 BCE when the Assyrians drove the enemy's forces into the Euphrates River. Two archers shoot arrows at three foes trying to escape. One swims with an arrow in his back. The other two attempt to float to safety by inflating animal skins. Their destination is a fort where three compatriots await them. Represented as if in the river, it must, of course, have been on land, perhaps at some distance from the battle. Ancient artists often compressed distances and enlarged the

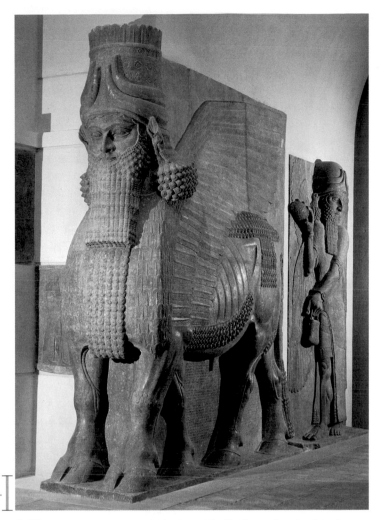

1 ft.

1-18 Lamassu (man-headed winged bull), from the citadel of Sargon II, Dur Sharrukin (modern Khorsabad), Iraq, ca. 720–705 BCE. Limestone, 13' 10" high, Musée du Louvre, Paris.

Ancient sculptors insisted on showing complete views of animals. This four-legged composite monster that guarded an Assyrian palace has five legs—two when seen from the front and four in profile view.

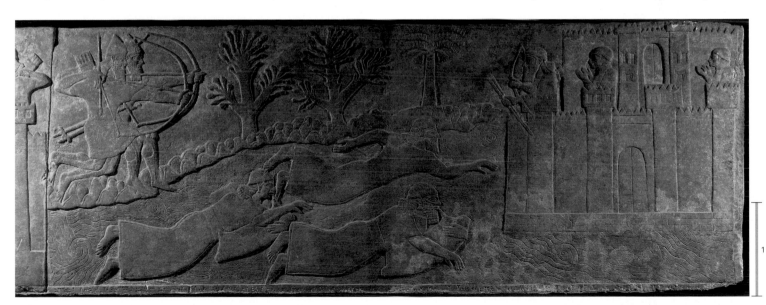

1 ft.

1-19 Assyrian archers pursuing enemies, relief from the northwest palace of Ashurnasirpal II, Kalhu (modern Nimrud), Iraq, ca. 875–860 BCE. Gypsum, 2' 10⅝" high. British Museum, London.

Extensive series of narrative stone reliefs exalting royal power adorned the walls of Assyrian palaces. This one in Kalhu shows Ashurnasirpal II's archers driving the enemy into the Euphrates River.

human actors so they would stand out from their environment (compare FIG. 1-16). The Assyrian sculptor also combined different viewpoints in the same composition. The spectator views the water from above, and the men, trees, and fort from the side. The artist made other adjustments for clarity. The archers' bowstrings are in front of their bodies but behind their heads in order not to hide their faces. (The men will snare their heads in their bows when they launch their arrows.) All these liberties with optical reality result, however, in a vivid and easily legible narrative.

Neo-Babylonia

The Assyrian Empire was never very secure, and in the mid-seventh century BCE it began to disintegrate, eventually collapsing from the simultaneous onslaught of the Medes from the east and the resurgent Babylonians from the south. For almost a century beginning in 612 BCE, Neo-Babylonian kings held sway over the former Assyrian Empire.

Ishtar Gate The most renowned Neo-Babylonian king was Nebuchadnezzar II (r. 604–562 BCE), who restored Babylon to its rank as one of the great cities of antiquity. The city's famous hanging gardens were among the Seven Wonders of the ancient world, and, as noted previously, the Bible (Gen. 11:1–9) immortalized its enormous ziggurat dedicated to Marduk,

the chief god of the Babylonians, as the Tower of Babel. Nebuchadnezzar's Babylon was a mud-brick city, but dazzling blue *glazed* bricks sheathed the most important monuments. Some of the buildings, such as the Ishtar Gate (FIG. **1-20**), with its imposing *arcuated* (*arch*-shaped) opening flanked by towers, featured glazed bricks with molded reliefs of animals, real and imaginary. The Babylonian artists molded and glazed each brick separately, then set the bricks in proper sequence on the wall. On the Ishtar Gate, profile figures of Marduk's dragon and Adad's bull alternate. (Ishtar was the Babylonian equivalent of Inanna; Adad was the Babylonian god of storms.) Lining the processional way leading up to the gate were reliefs of Ishtar's sacred lion, glazed in yellow, brown, and red against a blue ground.

Achaemenid Persia

Although Nebuchadnezzar—the "king of kings" in the book of Daniel (2:37)—had boasted he "caused a mighty wall to circumscribe Babylon . . . so that the enemy who would do evil would not threaten," Cyrus of Persia (r. 559–529 BCE) captured the city in the sixth century BCE. Cyrus was the founder of the Achaemenid dynasty and traced his ancestry back to a mythical King Achaemenes. Babylon was but one of the Persians' conquests. Egypt fell to them in 525 BCE, and by 480 BCE the Persian Empire was the largest the world had yet

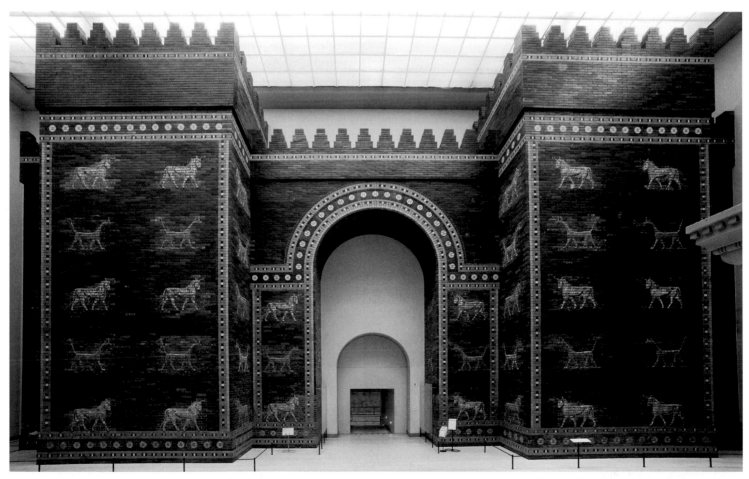

1-20 Ishtar Gate (restored), Babylon, Iraq, ca. 575 BCE. Vorderasiatisches Museum, Staatliche Museen zu Berlin, Berlin.

Babylon under King Nebuchadnezzar II was one of the greatest cities of the ancient world. Its monumental arcuated Ishtar Gate featured glazed brick reliefs of Marduk's dragon and Adad's bull.

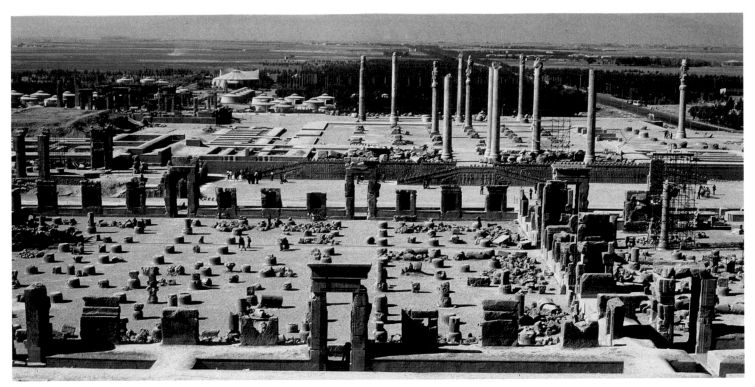

1-21 Aerial view of Persepolis (looking west with the apadana in the background), Iran, ca. 521–465 BCE.

The imperial Persian capital at Persepolis contained a grandiose royal audience hall with 36 colossal columns. The terraces leading up to it feature reliefs of subject nations bringing tribute to the king.

known, extending from the Indus River in South Asia to the Danube River in northeastern Europe. If the Greeks had not turned back the Persians in 479 BCE, the Achaemenids would have taken control of southeastern Europe as well (see Chapter 2). The Achaemenid line ended with the death of Darius III in 330 BCE, after his defeat at the hands of Alexander the Great (FIG. 2-50).

Persepolis The most important source of knowledge about Persian art and architecture is the ceremonial and administrative complex on the citadel at Persepolis (FIG. **1-21**), which the successors of Cyrus, Darius I (r. 522–486 BCE) and Xerxes (r. 486–465 BCE), built between 521 and 465 BCE. Situated on a high plateau, the heavily fortified complex of royal buildings stood on a wide platform overlooking the plain. Alexander the Great razed the site in a gesture symbolizing the destruction of Persian imperial power. Even in ruins, the Persepolis citadel is impressive. The approach to the citadel led through a monumental gateway called the Gate of All Lands, a reference to the harmony among the peoples of the vast Persian Empire. Assyrian-inspired colossal man-headed winged bulls flanked the great entrance. Broad ceremonial stairways provided access to the platform and the huge royal audience hall, or *apadana,* in which 10,000 guests could stand at one time amid 36 colossal *columns* with 57-foot *shafts* topped by sculpted animals.

The reliefs decorating the walls of the terrace and staircases leading to the apadana represent processions of royal guards, Persian nobles and dignitaries, and representatives from 23 subject nations bringing tribute to the king. Every emissary wears a characteristic costume and carries a typical regional gift for the conqueror. Traces of paint prove the reliefs were brightly colored. Although Assyrian palace reliefs may have inspired those at Persepolis, the Persian sculptures differ in style. The forms are more rounded, and they project more from the background. Some of the details, notably the treatment of drapery folds, echo forms characteristic of Archaic Greek sculpture (see Chapter 2), and Greek style was one of the many ingredients of Achaemenid art. Persian art testifies to the active exchange of ideas and artists among Mediterranean, Mesopotamian, and Persian civilizations at this date. A building inscription at Susa, for example, names Ionian Greeks, Medes (who occupied the land north of Persia), Egyptians, and Babylonians among those who built and decorated the palace.

The Sasanians Alexander the Great's conquest of Persia in 330 BCE marked the beginning of a long period of first Greek and then Roman rule in western Asia. In the third century CE, however, a new power rose up in Persia that challenged the Romans and sought to force them out of the region. The new rulers called themselves Sasanians. They traced their lineage to a legendary figure named Sasan, said to be a direct descendant of the Achaemenid kings. The first Sasanian king, Artaxerxes I (r. 211–241), founded the New Persian Empire in 224 CE after he defeated the Parthians (another of Rome's eastern enemies). The son and successor of Artaxerxes, Shapur I (r. 241–272), succeeded in further extending Sasanian territory. So powerful was the Sasanian army that in 260 CE Shapur I was able to capture the Roman emperor Valerian near Edessa (in modern Turkey). The New Persian Empire endured more than 400 years, until the Arabs drove the Sasanians out of Mesopotamia in 636, just four years after the death of Muhammad. Thereafter, the greatest artists and architects of Mesopotamia worked in the service of Islam (see Chapter 5).

EGYPT UNDER THE PHARAOHS

Blessed with ample sources of stone of different hues suitable for carving statues and fashioning building blocks, the ancient Egyptians left to posterity a profusion of spectacular monuments spanning three millennia. Many of them glorify the kings whom they called *pharaohs* and believed to be divine. Indeed, the Egyptians devoted enormous resources to erecting countless monuments and statues to honor the pharaohs during their lifetimes and to constructing and furnishing magnificent tombs to serve as their god-kings' eternal homes in the afterlife.

The backbone of Egypt was, and still is, the Nile River, which, through annual floods supported all life in that ancient land (MAP **1-3**). Even more than the Tigris and the Euphrates Rivers of Mesopotamia, the Nile defined the cultures that developed along its banks. Originating deep in Africa, the world's longest river flows through regions that may not receive a single drop of rainfall in a decade. Yet crops thrive from the rich soil that the Nile brings thousands of miles

from the African hills. In antiquity, the land bordering the Nile consisted of marshes dotted with island ridges. Amphibious animals swarmed in the marshes and were hunted through tall forests of *papyrus* and rushes (FIG. 1-29). Egypt's fertility was famous. When the Kingdom of the Nile became a province of the Roman Empire after the death of Queen Cleopatra (r. 51–30 BCE), it served as the granary of the Mediterranean world.

Predynastic and Early Dynastic Periods

The Predynastic, or prehistoric, beginnings of Egyptian civilization are obscure. Nevertheless, tantalizing remains of tombs, paintings, pottery, and other artifacts attest to the existence of a sophisticated culture on the banks of the Nile around 3500 BCE. In Predynastic times, Egypt was divided geographically and politically into Upper Egypt (the southern, upstream part of the Nile Valley) and Lower (northern) Egypt. The ancient Egyptians began the history of their kingdom with the unification of the two lands, an event which until recently historians had thought occurred during the rule of the First Dynasty pharaoh Menes.

Palette of King Narmer Many scholars have identified Menes with King Narmer, whose image and name appear on both sides of a ceremonial *palette* (stone slab with a circular depression) found at Hierakonpolis. The palette (FIG. **1-22**) is an elaborate, formalized version of a utilitarian object commonly used in the Predynastic period to prepare eye makeup. (Egyptians used makeup to protect their eyes against irritation and the glare of the sun.) Narmer's palette is the earliest extant labeled work of historical art. Although historians no longer believe it commemorates the foundation of the first of Egypt's 31 dynasties around 2920 BCE (the last ended in 332 BCE),[1] it does record the unification of Upper and Lower Egypt at the end of the Predynastic period. Scholars now think this unification occurred over several centuries, but the palette reflects the ancient Egyptian belief that the creation of the "Kingdom of the Two Lands" was a single great event.

King Narmer's palette is important not only as a document marking the transition from the prehistorical to the historical period in ancient Egypt but also as a kind of early blueprint of the formula for figure representation that characterized most Egyptian art for 3,000 years. At the top of each side of the palette are two heads of a goddess usually identified as Hathor, the divine mother of all pharaohs, who here takes the form of a cow with a woman's face. Between the Hathor heads is a *hieroglyph* giving Narmer's name (catfish = *nar*; chisel = *mer*) within a frame representing the pharaoh's palace. Below, the story of the unification of Egypt unfolds in registers.

On the back of the palette (FIG. 1-22, *left*), the king, wearing the high, white, bowling-pin-shaped crown of

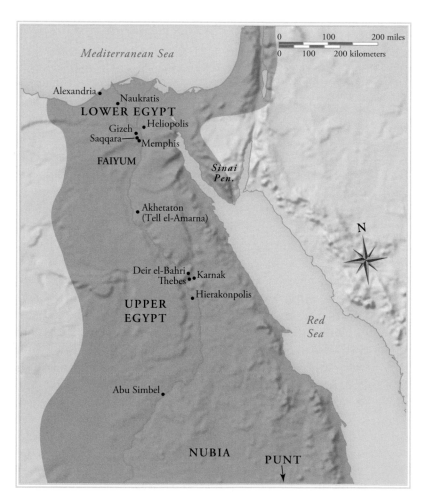

MAP 1-3 Ancient Egypt.

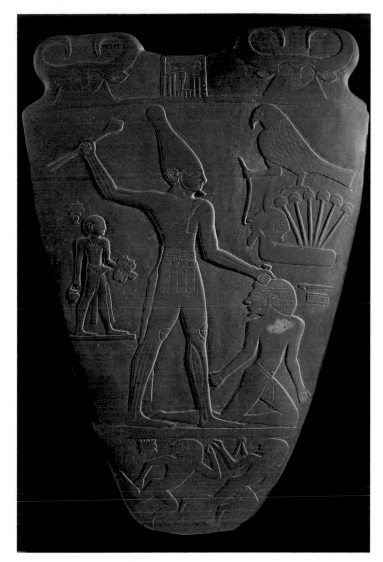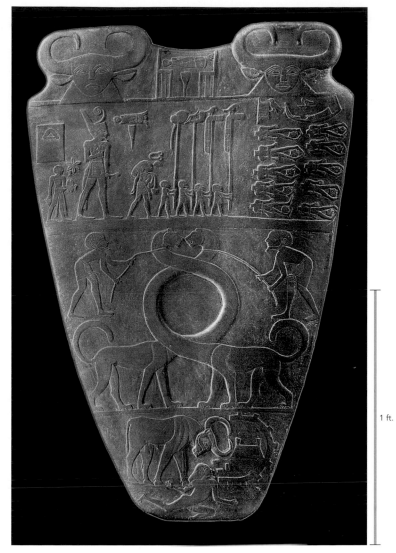

1-22 Palette of King Narmer (*left,* back; *right,* front), from Hierakonpolis, Egypt, Predynastic, ca. 3000–2920 BCE. Slate, 2′ 1″ high. Egyptian Museum, Cairo.

These oldest preserved labeled historical reliefs commemorate the unification of Upper and Lower Egypt. Narmer, the largest figure, effortlessly defeats a foe on one side, and on the other surveys the beheaded enemy.

Upper Egypt and accompanied by a much smaller attendant carrying his sandals, slays an enemy. Above and to the right, the falcon with human arms is Horus, the Egyptian god who was the special protector of the pharaohs. The falcon-god takes captive a man-headed hieroglyph with a papyrus plant growing from it that stands for the land of Lower Egypt. Below the king are two fallen enemies. On the front (FIG. 1-22, *right*), the elongated necks of two felines form the circular depression that would have held eye makeup in an ordinary palette not made for display. The intertwined necks of the animals may be another pictorial reference to Egypt's unification. In the uppermost register, Narmer, wearing the red crown of Lower Egypt, reviews the beheaded bodies of the enemy. The artist depicted each body with its severed head neatly placed between its legs. On both sides of the palette, the god-king performs his ritual task alone and, by virtue of his superior rank,

towers over his own men and the enemy. In the lowest band a great bull knocks down a rebellious city whose fortress walls are seen from above. The bull symbolizes the king's superhuman strength. Specific historical narrative was not the artist's goal in this work. What was important was the characterization of the king as supreme, isolated from and larger than all ordinary men and solely responsible for the triumph over the enemy. Here, at the very beginning of Egyptian history, is evidence of the Egyptian convention of thought, of art, and of state policy that established the pharaoh as a divine ruler.

Tombs and the Afterlife Narmer's palette is exceptional among surviving Egyptian artworks because it is commemorative rather than funerary in nature. In fact, Egyptian tombs provide the principal, if not the exclusive, evidence for the historical reconstruction of Egyptian civilization. The

Mummification and Immortality

The Egyptians did not make the sharp distinction between body and soul that is basic to many religions. Rather, they believed that from birth a person had a kind of other self, the *ka* or life force, which, on the death of the body, could inhabit the corpse and live on. For the ka to live securely, however, the body had to remain as nearly intact as possible. To ensure that it did, the Egyptians developed the technique of embalming (*mummification*) to a high art.

Embalming generally lasted 70 days. The first step was the surgical removal of the lungs, liver, stomach, and intestines through an incision in the left flank. The Egyptians thought these organs were most subject to decay, so wrapped them individually and placed them in four jars for eventual deposit in the burial chamber with the corpse. Egyptian surgeons extracted the brain through the nostrils and discarded it because they did not attach any special significance to that organ. But they left in place the heart, necessary for life and also regarded as the seat of intelligence.

Next, the body was treated for 40 days with natron, a naturally occurring salt compound that dehydrated the body. Then the embalmers filled the corpse with resin-soaked linens, and closed and covered the incision with a representation of Horus's eye, a powerful *amulet* (a device to ward off evil and promote rebirth). Finally, they treated the body with lotions and resins, and wrapped it tightly with hundreds of yards of linen bandages to maintain its shape. The Egyptians often placed other amulets within or on the resulting *mummy*. Masks (FIG. 1-37) covered the linen-wrapped faces of the wealthy.

Preserving the deceased's body by mummification was only the first requirement for immortality. Food and drink also had to be provided, as did clothing, utensils, and furniture. Nothing that had been enjoyed on earth was to be lacking in the tomb (FIG. 1-23). Statuettes called *ushabtis* (answerers) performed any labor the deceased required in the afterlife, answering whenever his or her name was called. The Egyptians also set up portrait statues of the dead in their tombs. The statues guaranteed the permanence of the person's identity by providing substitute dwelling places for the ka in case the mummy disintegrated. Wall paintings and reliefs recorded the recurring round of human activities. The Egyptians hoped and expected that the images and inventory of life, collected and set up within the tomb's protective stone walls, would ensure immortality.

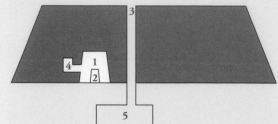

1. Chapel
2. False door
3. Shaft into burial chamber
4. Serdab (chamber for statue of deceased)
5. Burial chamber

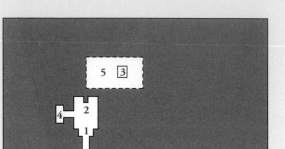

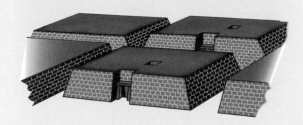

1-23 Section (*top*), plan (*center*), and restored view (*bottom*) of typical Egyptian mastaba tombs.

The standard early form of Egyptian tomb had an underground burial chamber and rooms to house a portrait statue and offerings to the deceased. Scenes of daily life often decorated the interior walls.

overriding concern in this life was to ensure safety and happiness in the next life. The majority of monuments the Egyptians left behind reflect this preoccupation (see "Mummification and Immortality," above).

The standard tomb type in early Egypt was the *mastaba* (Arabic, "bench"), a rectangular brick or stone structure with sloping sides erected over an underground burial chamber (FIG. 1-23). The form probably developed from earthen mounds that had covered even earlier tombs. Although mastabas originally housed single burials, as in FIG. 1-23, they later became increasingly complex in order to accommodate multiple family burials. The main feature of these tombs, other than the burial chamber itself, was the chapel, which had a false door through which the ka could join the world of the living and partake in the meals placed on an offering table. Some mastabas also had a *serdab,* a small concealed chamber housing a statue of the deceased. Adorning the chapel's interior walls and the ancillary rooms were colored relief carvings and paintings of scenes from daily life intended magically to provide the deceased with food and entertainment.

Imhotep and Djoser One of the most renowned figures in Egyptian history was IMHOTEP, master builder for King Djoser (r. 2630–2611 BCE) of the Third Dynasty. Imhotep's is the first recorded name of an artist. A man of legendary talent, he also served as the pharaoh's official seal bearer and as high priest of the sun god Re. After his death, the Egyptians deified Imhotep and in time probably inflated the list of his achievements, but he undoubtedly designed Djoser's stepped pyramid (FIG. **1-24**) at Saqqara, near Memphis, Egypt's capital at the time. The pyramid was the centerpiece

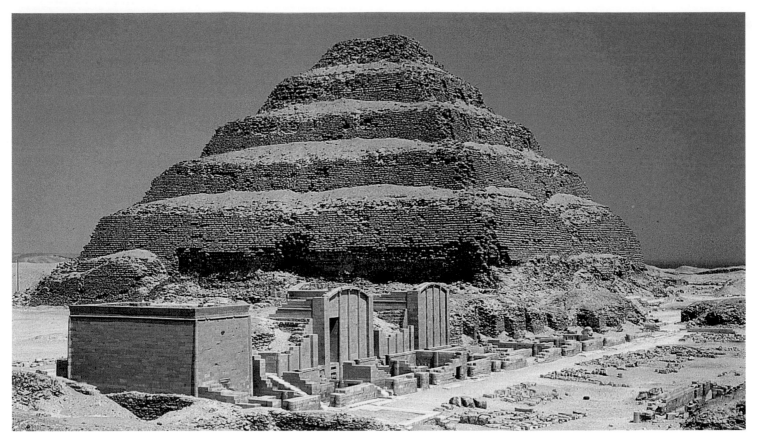

1-24 IMHOTEP, stepped pyramid (looking northeast) of Djoser, Saqqara, Egypt, Third Dynasty, ca. 2630–2611 BCE. ◼◀

The first pyramid took the form of a series of stacked mastabas. Djoser's stepped pyramid was the centerpiece of an immense funerary complex glorifying the god-king and his eternal existence in the hereafter.

of an immense (37-acre) rectangular enclosure surrounded by a monumental (34 feet high and 5,400 feet long) wall of white limestone. The huge precinct also enclosed a funerary temple, where priests performed daily rituals in celebration of the divine pharaoh, and several structures connected with the Jubilee Festival, the event that perpetually reaffirmed the royal existence in the hereafter.

Built before 2600 BCE, Djoser's pyramid is one of the oldest stone structures in Egypt and, in its final form, the first truly grandiose royal tomb. Begun as a large mastaba with each of its faces oriented toward one of the cardinal points of the compass, the tomb was enlarged at least twice before assuming its ultimate shape. About 200 feet high, the stepped pyramid seems to be composed of a series of mastabas of diminishing size, stacked one atop another. The tomb's dual function was to protect the mummified king and his possessions and to symbolize, by its gigantic presence, his absolute and godlike power. Beneath the pyramid was a network of several hundred underground rooms and galleries, resembling a palace. It was to be Djoser's new home in the afterlife.

Old Kingdom

The Old Kingdom is the first of the three great periods of Egyptian history, called the Old, Middle, and New Kingdoms, respectively. Many Egyptologists now begin the Old Kingdom with the first pharaoh of the Fourth Dynasty, Sneferu (r. 2575–2551 BCE), although the traditional division of kingdoms places Djoser and the Third Dynasty in the Old Kingdom. It ended with the demise of the Eighth Dynasty around 2134 BCE.

Great Pyramids At Gizeh stand the three Great Pyramids (FIG. **1-25**), the oldest of the Seven Wonders of the ancient world. The prerequisites for membership in this elite club were colossal size and enormous cost. The Gizeh pyramids testify to the wealth and pretensions of the Fourth Dynasty pharaohs Khufu (r. 2551–2528 BCE), Khafre (r. 2520–2494 BCE), and Menkaure (r. 2490–2472 BCE). The three pyramids, built in the course of about 75 years, represent the culmination of an architectural evolution that began with the mastaba, but the classic pyramid form is not simply a refinement of the stepped pyramid (FIG. **1-24**). The new tomb shape probably reflects the influence of Heliopolis, the seat of the powerful cult of Re, whose emblem was a pyramidal stone, the *ben-ben*. The Great Pyramids are symbols of the sun. The Pyramid Texts, inscribed on the burial chamber walls of many royal tombs, refer to the sun's rays as the ramp the pharaoh uses to ascend to the heavens. Djoser's stepped pyramid may also have been conceived as a giant stairway. The pyramids were where Egyptian kings were reborn in the afterlife, just as the sun is reborn each day at dawn. As with Djoser's stepped

Building the Great Pyramids

The Great Pyramids (FIG. 1-25) across the Nile from modern Cairo attest to Egyptian builders' mastery of masonry construction and ability to mobilize, direct, house, and feed a huge workforce engaged in one of the most labor-intensive enterprises ever undertaken. Like all building projects of this type, the process of erecting the pyramids began with the quarrying of stone, in this case primarily the limestone of the Gizeh plateau itself. Teams of skilled workers had to cut into the rock and remove large blocks of roughly equal size using stone or copper chisels and wooden mallets and wedges. Often, the artisans had to cut deep tunnels to find high-quality stone free of cracks and other flaws. To remove a block, the workers cut channels on all sides and partly underneath. Then they pried the stones free from the bedrock with wooden levers.

After workers liberated the stones, the rough blocks had to be transported to the building site and *dressed* (shaped to the exact dimensions required, with smooth faces for a perfect fit). The Egyptians moved the massive blocks for the Great Pyramids using wooden rollers and sleds. Stonemasons dressed the blocks by chiseling and pounding the surfaces and, in the last stage, by rubbing and grinding the surfaces with fine polishing stones. Architectural historians call this kind of construction *ashlar masonry*—carefully cut and regularly shaped blocks of stone piled in successive rows, or *courses*.

To set the ashlar blocks in place, workers erected great rubble ramps against the core of the pyramid. They adjusted the ramps' size and slope as work progressed and the tomb grew in height. Scholars debate whether the Egyptians used simple linear ramps inclined at a right angle to one face of the pyramid or zigzag or spiral ramps akin to staircases. Linear ramps would have had the advantage of simplicity and would have left three sides of the pyramid unobstructed. But zigzag ramps placed against one side of the structure or spiral ramps winding around the pyramid would have greatly reduced the slope of the incline and would have made the dragging of the blocks easier. Some scholars also have suggested a combination of straight and spiral ramps.

The Egyptians used ropes, pulleys, and levers both to lift and to lower the stones, guiding each block into its designated place. Finally, the pyramid received a facing of white limestone cut so precisely that the eye could scarcely detect the joints. Some casing stones remain at the apex of the pyramid of Khafre (FIGS. 1-25, *center*, and 1-26, *left*).

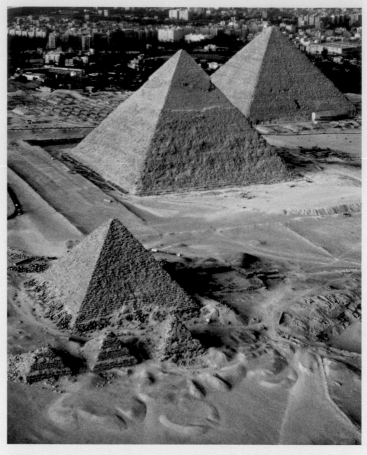

1-25 Great Pyramids, Gizeh, Egypt, Fourth Dynasty. *From bottom:* pyramids of Menkaure, ca. 2490–2472 BCE; Khafre, ca. 2520–2494 BCE; and Khufu, ca. 2551–2528 BCE. ◼◀

The Great Pyramids of Gizeh took the shape of the ben-ben, the emblem of the sun, Re. The sun's rays were the ramp the Egyptian pharaohs used to ascend to the heavens after their death and rebirth.

---

pyramid, the four sides of each of the Great Pyramids are oriented to the cardinal points of the compass. But the funerary temples associated with the three Gizeh pyramids are not on the north side, facing the stars of the northern sky, as was Djoser's temple. The temples are on the east side, facing the rising sun and underscoring their connection with Re.

Of the three Fourth Dynasty pyramids at Gizeh, the tomb of Khufu is the oldest and largest. Except for the internal galleries and burial chamber, it is an almost solid mass of limestone masonry (see "Building the Great Pyramids," above), a veritable stone mountain. When its original stone facing was intact, the sunlight it reflected would have been dazzling, underscoring the pyramid's role as a solar symbol. The Gizeh pyramids are immense. At the base, the length of one side of Khufu's tomb is approximately 775 feet, and

its area is some 13 acres. Its present height is about 450 feet (originally 480 feet). The structure contains roughly 2.3 million blocks of stone, each weighing an average of 2.5 tons. During Napoleon's campaign in Egypt, the scholars he brought with him calculated that the blocks in the three Great Pyramids were sufficient to build a wall 1 foot wide and 10 feet high around France.

From the remains surrounding the pyramid of Khafre, archaeologists have been able to reconstruct an entire funerary complex consisting of the pyramid itself with the pharaoh's burial chamber; the *mortuary temple* adjoining the pyramid on the east side, where priests made offerings to the god-king; the roofed causeway leading to the mortuary temple; and the *valley temple* at the edge of the floodplain. Many Egyptologists believe the complex served not only as the king's tomb and temple but also as his palace in the afterlife.

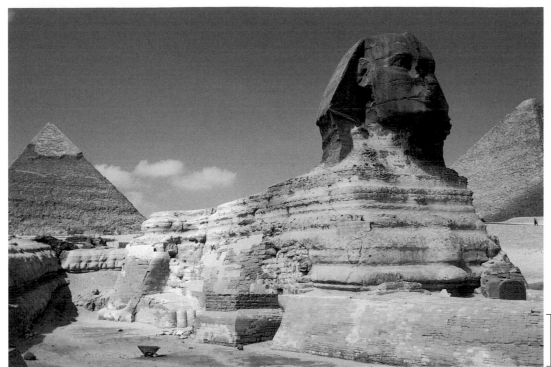

Carved out of the Gizeh stone quarry, the Great Sphinx is of colossal size. The sphinx has the body of a lion and the head of a pharaoh (probably Khafre) and is associated with the sun god.

10 ft.

Great Sphinx Beside the causeway and dominating the valley temple of Khafre rises the Great Sphinx (FIG. **1-26**). Carved from a spur of rock in an ancient quarry, the colossal statue is probably an image of Khafre (originally complete with the pharaoh's ceremonial beard and *uraeus* cobra head-dress), although some scholars believe it portrays Khufu and antedates Khafre's complex. Whichever king it portrays, the *sphinx*—a lion with a human head—was associated with the sun god and therefore was an appropriate image for a pha-raoh. The composite form suggests the pharaoh combines human intelligence with the fearsome strength and authority of the king of beasts.

Khafre Enthroned Although the Egyptians used wood, clay, and other materials, mostly for images of those not of the royal or noble classes, the primary material for funer-ary statuary was stone to ensure a permanent substitute home for the ka if the deceased's mummy was destroyed (see "Mummification and Immortality," page 34). The seated statue of Khafre illustrated here (FIG. **1-27**) comes from the pharaoh's valley temple near the Great Sphinx. The stone is dio-rite, an exceptionally hard dark stone brought some 400 miles down the Nile from royal quarries in the south. Khafre wears a simple kilt and sits rigidly upright on a throne formed of two stylized lions' bodies. Between the legs of the throne are intertwined lotus and papyrus plants— symbolic of the united Egypt. The falcon-god Horus extends his protective wings to shelter the pharaoh's head. Khafre has the royal false beard fastened to his chin

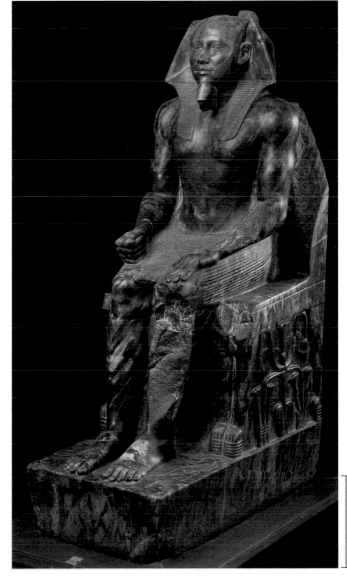

1-27 Khafre enthroned, from Gizeh, Egypt, Fourth Dynasty, ca. 2520–2494 BCE. Diorite, 5′ 6″ high. Egyptian Museum, Cairo. ■◀

This portrait from his pyramid complex depicts Khafre as an enthroned divine ruler with a perfect body. The rigidity of the pose creates an aura of eternal stillness, appro-priate for the timeless afterlife.

1 ft.

and wears the royal linen *nemes* headdress with uraeus cobra. The headdress covers his forehead and falls in pleated folds over his shoulders. As befitting a divine ruler, the sculptor portrayed Khafre with a well-developed, flawless body and a perfect face, regardless of his real age and appearance. Because Egyptians considered ideal proportions appropriate for representing their god-kings, the statue of Khafre is not a true likeness and was not intended to be. The purpose of pharaonic portraiture was not to record individual features or the distinctive shapes of bodies, but rather to proclaim the divine nature of Egyptian kingship.

The enthroned Khafre radiates serenity. The sculptor created this effect, common to Egyptian royal statues, in part by giving the figure great compactness and solidity, with few projecting, breakable parts. The form manifests the purpose: to last for eternity. Khafre's body is one with the unarticulated slab that forms the back of the king's throne. His arms follow the bend of his body and rest on his thighs, and his legs are close together. Part of the original stone block still connects the king's legs to his the chair. Khafre's pose is frontal, rigid, and *bilaterally symmetrical* (the same on either side of an axis, in this case the vertical axis). The sculptor suppressed all movement and with it the notion of time, creating an aura of eternal stillness.

To produce the statue, the artist first drew the front, back, and two profile views of the pharaoh on the four vertical faces of the stone block. Next, apprentices *chiseled* away the excess stone on each side, working inward until the planes met at right angles. Finally, the master sculpted the parts of Khafre's body, the falcon, and so forth. The polished surface was achieved by *abrasion* (rubbing or grinding). This subtractive method accounts in large part for the blocklike look of the standard Egyptian statue. Nevertheless, other sculptors, both ancient and modern, with different aims, have transformed stone blocks into dynamic, twisting human forms (for example, FIGS. I-14 and 2-57).

Menkaure and Khamerernebty The seated statue is one of only a small number of basic formulaic types the Egyptians employed to represent the human figure. Another is the image of a person or deity standing, either alone or in a group, for example, the double portrait (FIG. **1-28**) of Menkaure and one of his wives, probably Queen Khamerernebty. The statue once stood in Menkaure's valley temple at Gizeh. Here, too, the figures remain wedded to the stone block. Menkaure's pose—duplicated in countless other Egyptian statues—is rigidly frontal with the arms hanging straight down and close to his well-built body. He clenches his hands into fists with the thumbs forward and advances his left leg slightly, but no shift occurs in the angle of the hips to correspond to the uneven distribution of weight. Khamerernebty stands in a similar position. Her right arm, however, circles around the king's waist, and her left hand gently rests on his left arm. This frozen stereotypical gesture indicates their marital status. The husband and wife show no other sign of affection or emotion and look not at each other but out into space.

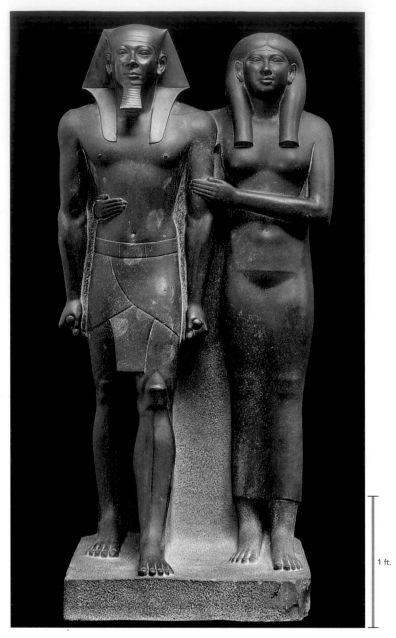

1-28 Menkaure and Khamerernebty(?), from Gizeh, Egypt, Fourth Dynasty, ca. 2490–2472 BCE. Graywacke, 4′ 6½″ high. Museum of Fine Arts, Boston. ◼◀

This double portrait displays the conventional postures used for Egyptian statues designed as substitute homes for the ka. The frozen gestures signify the man and woman are husband and wife.

Tomb of Ti Egyptian artists also depicted the dead in relief sculpture and in mural painting, sometimes singly (FIG. I-13) and sometimes in a narrative context. The painted limestone relief scenes decorating the walls of the Saqqara mastaba of a Fifth Dynasty official named Ti typify the subjects Old Kingdom patrons favored for the adornment of their final resting places. Depictions of agriculture and hunting fill Ti's tomb. The Egyptians associated these activities with the provisioning of the ka in the hereafter, but the subjects also had powerful symbolic overtones. In ancient Egypt, success in the hunt, for example, was a metaphor for triumph over the forces of evil.

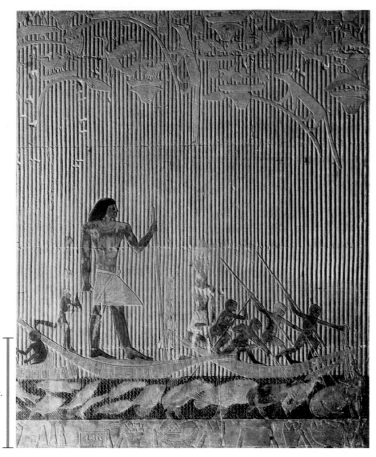

1 ft.

1-29 Ti watching a hippopotamus hunt, relief in the mastaba of Ti, Saqqara, Egypt, Fifth Dynasty, ca. 2450–2350 BCE. Painted limestone, 4' high.

In Egypt, a successful hunt was a metaphor for triumph over evil. In this painted tomb relief, the deceased stands aloof from the hunters busily spearing hippopotami. Ti's size reflects his high rank.

In the relief illustrated here (FIG. **1-29**), Ti, his men, and his boats move slowly through the marshes, hunting hippopotami and birds in a dense growth of towering papyrus. The sculptor delineated the reedy stems of the plants with repeated fine grooves that fan out gracefully at the top into a commotion of frightened birds and stalking foxes. The water beneath the boats, signified by a pattern of wavy lines, is crowded with hippopotami and fish. Ti's men are frantically busy with their spears, whereas Ti, depicted twice their size, stands aloof. The basic conventions of Egyptian figure representation—used a half millennium earlier for King Narmer's palette (FIG. 1-22)—appear again here. As in the Predynastic relief, the artist exaggerated the size of Ti to announce his rank, and combined frontal and profile views of Ti's body to show its characteristic parts clearly. This conceptual (as opposed to optical) approach to representation was well suited for Egyptian funerary art because it emphasizes the essential nature of the deceased, not his accidental appearance. Ti's conventional pose contrasts with the realistically rendered activities of his tiny servants and with the naturalistically carved and painted birds and animals among the papyrus buds. Ti's immobility implies he is not an actor in the hunt.

He does not *do* anything. He simply *is,* a figure apart from time and an impassive observer of life, like his ka. Scenes such as this demonstrate that Egyptian artists could be close observers of daily life. The absence of the anecdotal (that is, of the time-bound) from their representations of the deceased both in relief and in the round was a deliberate choice. The artists' primary purpose was to suggest the deceased's eternal existence in the afterlife, not to portray nature.

The idealized and stiff image of Ti is typical of Egyptian relief sculpture. Egyptian artists regularly ignored the endless variations in body types of real human beings. Painters and sculptors did not sketch their subjects from life but applied a strict *canon,* or system of proportions, to the human figure. They first drew a grid on the wall. Then they placed various human body parts at specific points on the network of squares. The height of a figure, for example, was a fixed number of squares, and the head, shoulders, waist, knees, and other parts of the body also had a predetermined size and place within the scheme. This approach to design lasted for more than 2,500 years. Specific proportions might vary from workshop to workshop and change over time, but the principle of the canon persisted.

New Kingdom

About 2150 BCE, the Egyptians challenged the pharaohs' power, and for more than a century the land was in a state of civil unrest and near anarchy. But in 2040 BCE the pharaoh of Upper Egypt, Mentuhotep II (r. 2050–1998 BCE), managed to unite Egypt again under the rule of a single king and established the Middle Kingdom (11th to 14th Dynasties), which brought stability to Egypt for four centuries. In the 17th century, it too disintegrated. Power passed to the Hyksos, or shepherd kings, who descended on Egypt from the Syrian and Mesopotamian uplands. But around 1600–1550 BCE native Egyptian kings rose up in revolt, and Ahmose I (r. 1550–1525 BCE), final conqueror of the Hyksos and first king of the 18th Dynasty, ushered in the New Kingdom, the most glorious period in Egypt's long history. At this time, Egypt extended its borders by conquest from the Euphrates River in the east deep into Nubia (the Sudan) to the south (MAP 1-3). A new capital—Thebes, in Upper Egypt—became a great metropolis with magnificent palaces, tombs, and temples along both banks of the Nile.

Hatshepsut One of the most intriguing figures in ancient history was the New Kingdom pharaoh Hatshepsut (r. 1473–1458 BCE). In 1479 BCE, Thutmose II (r. 1492–1479 BCE), the fourth pharaoh of the 18th Dynasty, died. Hatshepsut, his principal wife (and half sister), had not given birth to any sons who survived, so the title of king went to the 12-year-old Thutmose III, son of Thutmose II by a minor wife. Hatshepsut became regent for the boy-king. Within a few years, however, the queen proclaimed herself pharaoh and insisted her father Thutmose I had chosen her as his successor during his lifetime. Hatshepsut is the first great female monarch whose name has been recorded. For two decades she ruled what was then the most powerful and prosperous empire in

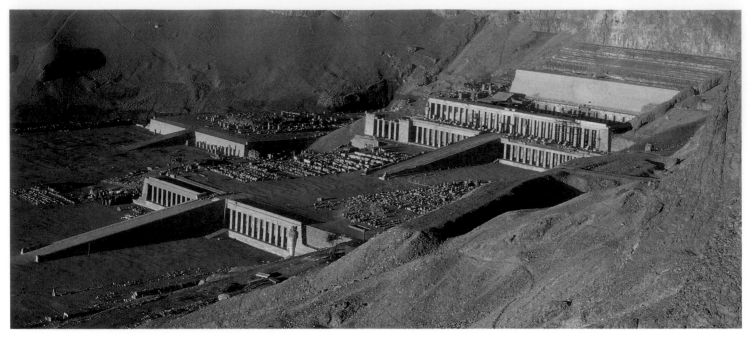

1-30 Mortuary temple of Hatshepsut (looking southwest), Deir el-Bahri, Egypt, 18th Dynasty, ca. 1473–1458 BCE.

Hatshepsut was the first great female monarch in history. Her immense terraced funerary temple featured an extensive series of painted reliefs recounting her divine birth, coronation, and great deeds.

the world. As always, Egyptian sculptors produced statues of their pharaoh in great numbers for display throughout the kingdom. Hatshepsut uniformly wears the costume of the male pharaohs, with royal headdress and kilt, and in some cases even a false ceremonial beard. Many inscriptions refer to Hatshepsut as "*His* Majesty."

One of the most impressive of the many grandiose monuments the New Kingdom pharaohs built is Hatshepsut's mortuary temple (FIG. **1-30**) on the Nile at Deir el-Bahri. The temple rises from the valley floor in three terraces connected by ramps on the central axis. It is striking how visually well suited the structure is to its natural setting. The long

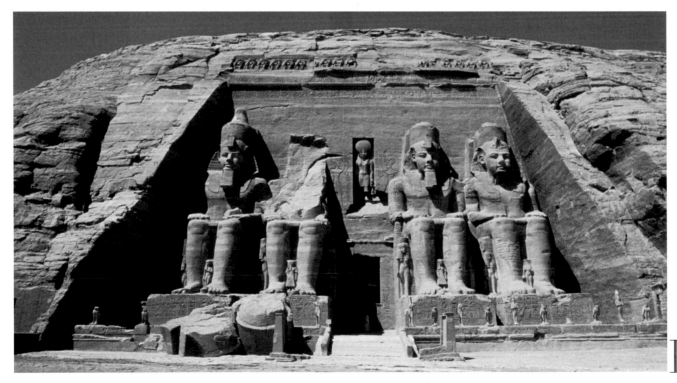

10 ft.

1-31 Facade of the temple of Ramses II, Abu Simbel, Egypt, 19th Dynasty, ca. 1290–1224 BCE. Sandstone, colossi 65′ high.

Four rock-cut colossal images of Ramses II dominate the facade of his mortuary temple. Inside, more gigantic figures of the long-reigning king depict him as Osiris, god of the dead and giver of eternal life.

horizontals and verticals of the *colonnades* of the terraces repeat the pattern of the limestone cliffs above. In Hatshepsut's day, the terraces were not the barren places they are now but gardens with frankincense trees and rare plants the pharaoh brought from the faraway "land of Punt" on the Red Sea. Her expedition to Punt figures prominently in the once brightly painted low reliefs that cover many walls of the complex. In addition to representing great deeds, the reliefs also show Hatshepsut's divine birth and coronation. She was said to be the daughter of the sun god, whose sanctuary was on the temple's uppermost level. The reliefs of Hatshepsut's mortuary temple, unfortunately defaced after her death, constitute the first great tribute to a woman's achievements in the history of art.

Ramses II Perhaps the greatest pharaoh of the New Kingdom was Ramses II (r. 1290–1224 BCE), who ruled Egypt for two-thirds of a century, an extraordinary accomplishment in an era when life expectancy was far less than it is today. Four colossal images of Ramses never fail to impress visitors to the pharaoh's mortuary temple (FIG. **1-31**) at Abu Simbel. The 65-foot-tall portraits, carved directly into the cliff face, are almost a dozen times an ancient Egyptian's height, even though the pharaoh is seated. The grand scale of the *facade* statues extends inside the temple also, where giant (32-foot-tall) figures of the king, carved as one with the *pillars,* face each another across the narrow corridor. Ramses appears in his *atlantids* (statue-columns) in the guise of Osiris, god of the dead and king of the underworld, as well as giver of eternal life.

Temple of Amen-Re, Karnak Colossal scale also characterizes the temples the New Kingdom pharaohs built to honor one or more of the gods. Successive kings often added to them until they reached gigantic size. The temple of Amen-Re (FIG. **1-32**) at Karnak, for example, was largely the work of the 18th Dynasty pharaohs, including Hatshepsut, but Ramses II (19th Dynasty) and others also contributed sections. Parts of the complex date as late as the 26th Dynasty.

The Karnak temple has an artificial sacred lake within its precinct, a reference to the primeval waters before creation. The temple rises from the earth as the original sacred mound rose from the waters at the beginning of time. In other respects, however, the temple is a typical, if especially

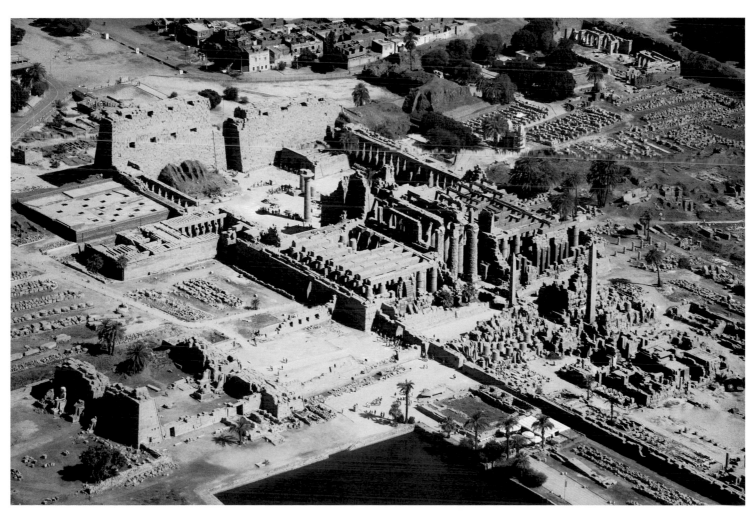

1-32 Aerial view of the temple of Amen-Re (looking north), Karnak, Egypt, begun 15th century BCE.

The vast Karnak temple complex contains an artificial lake associated with the primeval waters of the Egyptian creation myth and a pylon temple with a bilaterally symmetrical axial plan.

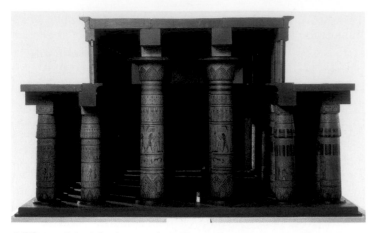

1-33 Model of the hypostyle hall, temple of Amen-Re, Karnak, Egypt, 19th Dynasty, ca. 1290–1224 BCE. Metropolitan Museum of Art, New York.

The two central rows of columns of Karnak's hypostyle hall are 70 feet high, with capitals 22 feet in diameter. The columns support a clerestory that admitted sunlight to illuminate the hall's interior.

large, New Kingdom *pylon temple.* The name derives from the simple and massive *pylons* (gateways with sloping walls) that are characteristic features of New Kingdom temple design. A typical pylon temple is bilaterally symmetrical along a single axis that runs from an approaching avenue through a colonnaded court and hall into a dimly lit sanctuary. Only the pharaohs and the priests could enter the sanctuary. A chosen few were admitted to the great columnar hall. The majority of the people could proceed only as far as the open court. The central feature of the New Kingdom pylon temple plan— a narrow axial passageway through the complex—characterizes much of Egyptian architecture. The approaches to the Old Kingdom pyramids (FIG. 1-25) of Gizeh and to the multilevel mortuary temple of Hatshepsut (FIG. 1-30) at Deir el-Bahri also conform to the Egyptian preference for *axial plans.*

In the Karnak plan, the hall (FIG. **1-33**) between the court and sanctuary has its long axis placed at right angles to the corridor of the entire building complex. Inside this *hypostyle hall* (one in which columns support the roof) are 134 massive sandstone columns, which supported a roof of stone slabs carried on stone lintels. The lintels rest on cubical blocks that in turn rest on giant bud-cluster or bell-shaped *capitals* (heads) resembling lotus or papyrus (the plants of Upper and Lower Egypt). The 12 central columns are 70 feet tall, and the capitals are 22 feet in diameter at the top, large enough to hold a hundred people. The Egyptians, who used no cement, depended on precise cutting of the joints and the weight of the huge stone blocks to hold the columns in place.

In the Amen-Re temple at Karnak and in many other Egyptian hypostyle halls, the two central rows of columns are taller than those at the sides. Raising the roof's central section created a *clerestory.* Openings in the clerestory permitted sunlight to filter into the interior, although the stone grilles would have blocked much of the light. This method of construction appeared in primitive form in the Old Kingdom valley temple of Khafre at Gizeh. The clerestory is

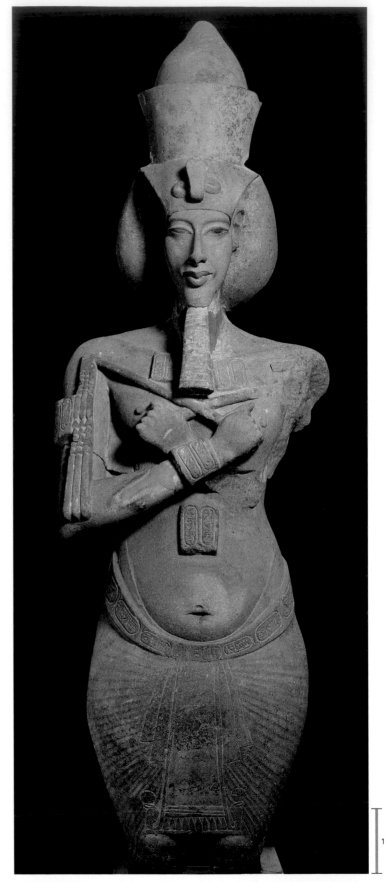

1 ft.

1-34 Akhenaton, from the temple of Aton, Karnak, Egypt, 18th Dynasty, ca. 1353–1335 BCE. Sandstone, 13' high. Egyptian Museum, Cairo.

Akhenaton initiated both religious and artistic revolutions. This androgynous figure is a deliberate reaction against tradition. It may be an attempt to portray the pharaoh as Aton, the sexless sun disk.

evidently an Egyptian innovation, and its significance cannot be overstated. Before the invention of the electric light bulb, illuminating a building's interior was always a challenge for architects. The clerestory played a key role in the history of architecture until very recently.

Akhenaton The Karnak sanctuary also provides evidence for a period of religious upheaval during the New Kingdom and for a corresponding revolution in Egyptian art. In the mid-14th century BCE, Amenhotep IV, later known as Akhenaton (r. 1353–1335 BCE), abandoned the worship of most of the Egyptian gods in favor of the sun disk Aton, whom the pharaoh declared to be the universal and only god. Akhenaton deleted the name of Amen from all inscriptions and even from his own name and that of his father, Amenhotep III. He emptied the great temples, enraged the priests, and moved his capital downriver from Thebes to present-day Amarna, a site he named Akhetaton (after his new god). The pharaoh claimed to be both the son and sole prophet of Aton. Moreover, in stark contrast to earlier practice, artists represented Akhenaton's god neither in animal nor in human form but simply as the sun disk emitting life-giving rays. The pharaohs who followed Akhenaton reestablished the cult and priesthood of Amen and restored the temples and the inscriptions. Akhenaton's religious revolution was soon undone, and his new city largely abandoned.

During the brief heretical episode of Akhenaton, profound changes also occurred in Egyptian art. A colossal statue (FIG. **1-34**) of Akhenaton from Karnak, toppled and buried after his death, retains the standard frontal pose of pharaonic portraits. But the effeminate body, with its curving contours, and the long face with full lips and heavy-lidded eyes are a far cry indeed from the idealized faces and heroically proportioned bodies (FIG. 1-28) of Akhenaton's predecessors. Akhenaton's body is curiously misshapen, with weak arms, a narrow waist, protruding belly, wide hips, and fatty thighs. Modern physicians have tried to explain his physique by attributing a variety of illnesses to the pharaoh. They cannot agree on a diagnosis, and their premise—that the statue is an accurate depiction of a physical deformity—is probably faulty. Some art historians think Akhenaton's portrait is a deliberate artistic reaction against the established style, paralleling the suppression of traditional religion. They argue that Akhenaton's artists tried to formulate a new androgynous image of the pharaoh as the manifestation of Aton, the sexless sun disk. But no consensus exists other than that the style was revolutionary and short-lived.

Nefertiti A painted limestone bust (FIG. **1-35**) of Akhenaton's queen, Nefertiti (her name means "the beautiful one has come"), also breaks with the past. The portrait exhibits an expression of entranced musing and an almost mannered sensitivity and delicacy of curving contour. Nefertiti was an influential woman during her husband's kingship. She frequently appears in the decoration of the Aton temple at Karnak, and not only is she equal in size to her husband, but she

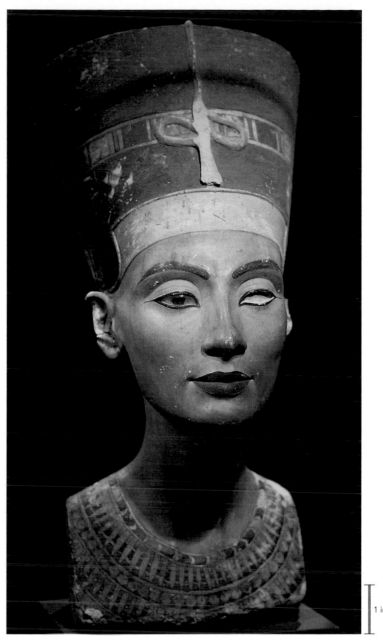

1 in.

1-35 THUTMOSE, *Nefertiti*, from Amarna, Egypt, 18th Dynasty, ca. 1353–1335 BCE. Painted limestone, 1′ ¼″ high. Ägyptisches Museum, Staatliche Museen zu Berlin, Berlin.

Found in the workshop of the master sculptor Thutmose, this unfinished bust portrait of Nefertiti depicts Akhenaton's influential wife with a pensive expression and a long, delicately curved neck.

sometimes wears pharaonic headgear. Excavators discovered the portrait illustrated here in the workshop of the sculptor THUTMOSE. It is a deliberately unfinished model very likely by the master's own hand. The left eye socket still lacks the inlaid eyeball, making the portrait a kind of before-and-after demonstration piece. With this elegant bust, Thutmose may have been alluding to a heavy flower on its slender stalk by exaggerating the weight of the crowned head and the length of the almost serpentine neck. The sculptor seems to have adjusted the likeness of his subject to meet the era's standard of spiritual beauty.

1-36 Innermost coffin of Tutankhamen, from his tomb at Thebes, Egypt, 18th Dynasty, ca. 1323 BCE. Gold with inlay of enamel and semiprecious stones, 6' 1" long. Egyptian Museum, Cairo.

Tutankhamen was a boy-king who owes his fame to the discovery of his treasure-laden tomb. His mummy was encased in three nested coffins. The innermost one, the costliest, portrays the pharaoh as Osiris.

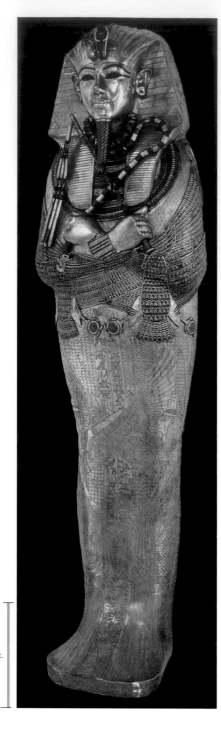

1 ft.

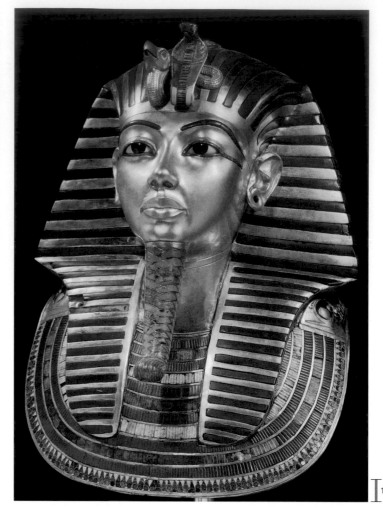

1 in.

1-37 Death mask of Tutankhamen, from the innermost coffin (FIG. 1-36) in his tomb at Thebes, Egypt, 18th Dynasty, ca. 1323 BCE. Gold with inlay of semiprecious stones, 1' 9¼" high. Egyptian Museum, Cairo.

The gold mask that covered Tutankhamen's mummy radiates grandeur and richness. It is a sensitive portrayal of the adolescent king dressed in his official regalia, including nemes headdress and false beard.

Tutankhamen Probably Akhenaton's son by a minor wife, Tutankhamen (r. 1333–1323 BCE) ruled Egypt for a decade and died at age 18. Although a minor figure in Egyptian history, Tutankhamen is famous today because of the fabulously rich treasure of sculpture, furniture, and jewelry discovered in 1922 in his tomb at Thebes. The principal find was the enshrined body of the pharaoh himself. The royal mummy reposed in the innermost of three coffins, nested one within the other. The innermost coffin (FIG. **1-36**) was the most luxurious of the three. It shows Tutankhamen in the guise of Osiris. Made of beaten gold (about a quarter ton of it) and inlaid with such semiprecious stones as lapis lazuli, turquoise, and carnelian, it is a supreme monument to the sculptor's and goldsmith's crafts. The portrait mask (FIG. **1-37**), which covered the king's face, is also made of gold

with inlaid semiprecious stones. It is a sensitive portrayal of the serene adolescent king dressed in his official regalia, including the nemes headdress and false beard. The general effect of the mask and of the tomb treasures as a whole is of grandeur and richness expressive of Egyptian power, pride, and affluence.

Egypt in Decline During the first millennium BCE, Egypt lost the commanding role it once had played in the ancient world. The empire dwindled away, and foreign powers invaded, occupied, and ruled the land, until Alexander the Great of Macedon and his Greek successors and, eventually, the Romans, took control of the land of the Nile. But even after Egypt became a province of the Roman Empire, its prestige remained high. Visitors to Rome today who enter the city on the road from the airport encounter the tomb of a Roman nobleman who died around 12 BCE. His memorial takes the form of a pyramid, 2,500 years after the Old Kingdom pharaohs erected the Great Pyramids of Gizeh.

Prehistory and the First Civilizations

Prehistory

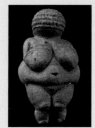

I The first sculptures and paintings antedate the invention of writing by tens of thousands of years. No one knows why humans began to paint and carve images or what role those images played in the lives of Paleolithic hunters. Women were far more common subjects than men, but animals, not humans, dominate Paleolithic art (ca. 30,000–9000 BCE). Surviving works range in size from tiny figurines to painted walls and ceilings covered with over-life-size animals. Animals always appear in profile in order to show clearly the head, body, tail, and all four legs.

I The Neolithic age (ca. 8000–3500 BCE) revolutionized human life with the beginning of agriculture and the formation of the first settled communities. The earliest known monumental sculptures date to the seventh millennium BCE. In painting, coherent narratives became common, and artists began to represent human figures as composites of frontal and profile views.

Venus of Willendorf,
ca. 28,000–25,000 BCE

Ancient Mesopotamia and Persia

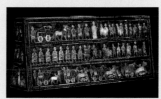

I The Sumerians (ca. 3500–2332 BCE) founded the world's first city-states and invented writing in the fourth millennium BCE. They were also the first to build towering temple platforms, called ziggurats, and to place figures in registers to tell coherent stories.

I The Akkadians (ca. 2332–2150 BCE) were the first Mesopotamian rulers to call themselves kings of the world and to assume divine attributes. Akkadian artists may have been the first to cast hollow life-size bronze sculptures and to place figures at different levels in a landscape setting.

Standard of Ur, ca. 2600–2400 BCE

I During the Third Dynasty of Ur (ca. 2150–1800 BCE) and under the kings of Babylon (ca. 1800–1600 BCE), the Neo-Sumerians constructed one of the largest Mesopotamian ziggurats at Ur. Babylonian artists were among the first to experiment with foreshortening.

I At the height of their power, the Assyrians (ca. 900–612 BCE) ruled an empire extending from the Persian Gulf to the Nile and Asia Minor. Assyrian palaces were fortified citadels with gates guarded by monstrous lamassu. Painted reliefs glorifying the king decorated the ceremonial halls.

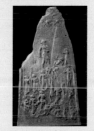

I The Neo-Babylonian kings (612–559 BCE) erected the biblical Tower of Babel and the Ishtar Gate.

I The capital of the Achaemenid Empire (559–330 BCE) was Persepolis, where the Persians built a huge palace complex with an audience hall that could accommodate 10,000 people.

Victory stele of Naram-Sin,
ca. 2254–2218 BCE

Egypt under the Pharaohs

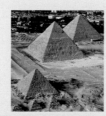

I The palette of King Narmer, which commemorates the unification of Upper and Lower Egypt around 3000–2920 BCE, established the basic principles of Egyptian representational art for 3,000 years.

I Imhotep, architect of the funerary complex of King Djoser (r. 2630–2611 BCE) at Saqqara, is the first known artist in history.

I During the Old Kingdom (ca. 2575–2134 BCE), the Egyptians built the Great Pyramids at Gizeh, emblems of the sun on whose rays the pharaohs ascended to the heavens after their death. Old Kingdom artists established the statuary types that would dominate Egyptian art for 2,000 years, suppressing all movement in order to express the eternal nature of pharaonic kingship.

Great Pyramids, Gizeh,
ca. 2551–2472 BCE

I During the New Kingdom (ca. 1550–1070 BCE), the most significant architectural innovation was the axially planned pylon temple incorporating an immense gateway, columnar courtyards, and a hypostyle hall with clerestory windows. Powerful pharaohs such as Hatshepsut (r. 1473–1458 BCE) and Ramses II (r. 1290–1224 BCE) constructed gigantic temples in honor of their patron gods and, after their deaths, for their own worship. Akhenaton (r. 1353–1335 BCE) abandoned the traditional Egyptian religion in favor of Aton, the sun disk, and initiated a short-lived artistic revolution in which physical deformities and undulating curves replaced the idealized physiques and cubic forms of earlier Egyptian art.

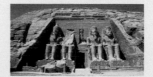

Temple of Ramses II, Abu Simbel,
ca. 1290–1224 BCE

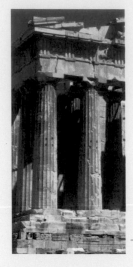

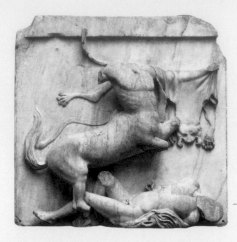

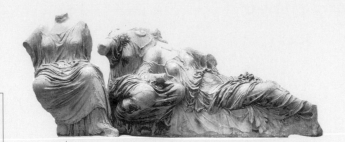

The reliefs depicting Greeks battling semihuman centaurs are allegories of the triumph of civilization and rational order over barbarism and chaos—and of the Greek defeat of the Persians in 479 BCE.

The statues in the two pediments of the Parthenon depicted important events in the life of Athena, the patron goddess of Athens. The east pediment represented Athena's birth from the head of Zeus.

The architects of the Parthenon calculated the dimensions of every part of the temple using harmonic numerical ratios, which determined, for example, the height and diameter of each column.

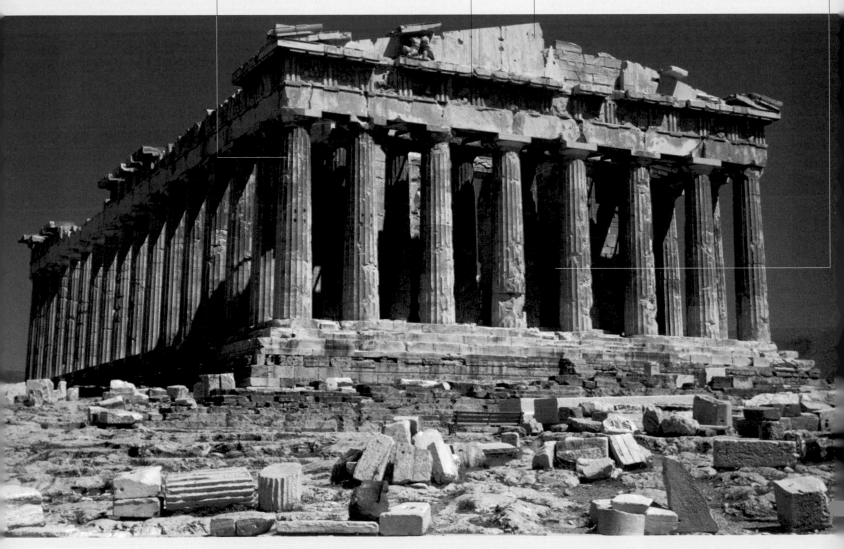

2-1 IKTINOS and KALLIKRATES, Parthenon (temple of Athena Parthenos; looking southeast), Acropolis, Athens, Greece, 447–438 BCE. ◼◀

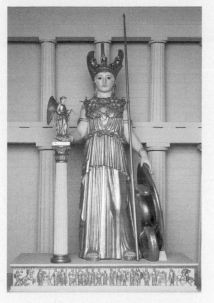

The costliest part of the Parthenon's lavish sculptural program was inside the temple—Phidias's colossal gold-and-ivory statue of Athena presenting the personification of Victory to Athens.

2

Ancient Greece

THE PERFECT TEMPLE

Although the Greeks borrowed many ideas from Egypt and Mesopotamia, they quickly developed an independent artistic identity. Their innovations in painting, sculpture, and architecture are the foundation of the Western tradition. Indeed, no building type has ever had a longer and more profound impact on the later history of architecture than the Greek temple, which was itself a multimedia monument, richly adorned with painted statues and reliefs.

The greatest Greek temple was the Parthenon (FIG. **2-1**), erected on the Acropolis of Athens in the mid-fifth century BCE. It represents the culmination of a century-long effort by Greek architects to build a temple having perfect proportions. Consistent with the thinking of the influential philosopher Pythagoras of Samos, who believed beauty resided in harmonic numerical ratios, the architect IKTINOS calculated the dimensions of every part of the Parthenon in terms of a fixed proportional scheme. Thus, the ratio of the length to the width of the building, the number of columns on the long versus the short sides, even the relationship between the diameter of a column and the space between neighboring columns, conformed to an all-encompassing mathematical formula. The result was a "perfect temple."

The Athenians did not, however, construct the Parthenon to solve a purely formal problem of architectural design. Nor was this perfect temple, dedicated to Athena Parthenos (the Virgin), a shrine honoring the goddess alone. The temple also celebrated the Athenian people, who a generation earlier had led the Greeks in their successful effort to defeat the Persians after they had sacked the Acropolis in 480 BCE. Under the direction of PHIDIAS, a team of gifted sculptors lavishly decorated the building with statues and reliefs that in many cases alluded to the victory over the Persians. For example, the sculptural program included a series of reliefs depicting nude Greek warriors battling with the part-horse part-human *centaurs*—an allegory of the triumph of civilization (that is, Greek civilization) over barbarism (in this case, the Persians). The statues in one of the *pediments* (the triangular area above the columns beneath the gabled roof) told the story of the birth of Athena, who emerged from the head of her father Zeus, king of the gods, fully armed and ready to protect her people. The costliest sculpture, and most prestigious of all, however, Phidias reserved for himself: the colossal gold-and-ivory statue of Athena inside the temple in which the warrior goddess presented the Athenians with the winged personification of Victory—an unmistakable reference to the Greek victory over the Persians.

THE GREEKS AND THEIR GODS

Ancient Greek art occupies a special place in the history of art through the ages. Many of the cultural values of the Greeks, especially the exaltation of humanity as "the measure of all things," remain today fundamental tenets of Western civilization. In fact, these ideas are so completely part of modern Western habits of mind that most people are scarcely aware the concepts originated in Greece 2,500 years ago.

The Greeks, or *Hellenes,* as they called themselves, never formed a single nation but instead established independent city-states on the Greek mainland, on the islands of the Aegean Sea, and on the western coast of Asia Minor (MAP **2-1**). In 776 BCE, the separate Greek states held their first athletic games in common at Olympia. From then on, despite their differences and rivalries, the Greeks regarded themselves as sharing a common culture, distinct from the surrounding "barbarians" who did not speak Greek.

Even the gods of the Greeks (see "The Gods and Goddesses of Mount Olympus," page 49) differed in kind from those of neighboring civilizations. Unlike Egyptian and Mesopotamian deities (see Chapter 1), the Greek gods and goddesses differed from humans only in being immortal. The

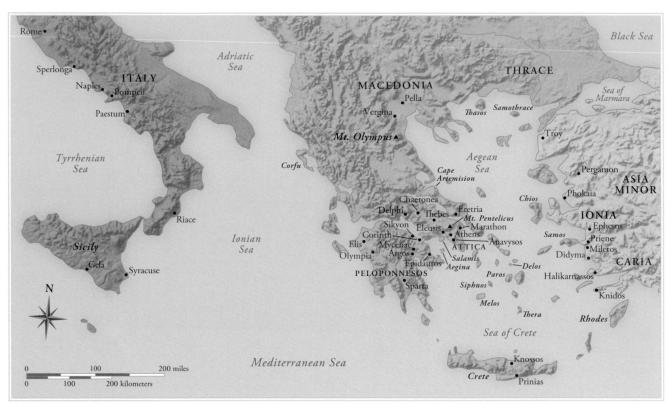

MAP 2-1 The Greek world.

Ancient Greece

	Early Cycladic		Minoan and Mycenaean		Geometric and Archaic		Classical		Hellenistic	BCE
3000		2000		1200		900		480	323	30

- Early Cycladic sculptors create marble figurines for graves to accompany the dead into the afterlife

- Minoans construct major palaces on Crete and adorn the walls with frescoes
- Volcanic eruption destroys Thera, ca. 1628 BCE
- Mycenaeans bury their dead in deep shaft graves with gold funerary masks
- Mycenaeans construct fortified citadels at Mycenae and Tiryns and build tombs featuring corbeled domes

- Revival of figure painting in Greece during the Geometric period
- Construction of the oldest peripteral Doric and Ionic temples
- First Greek life-size stone statues with "Archaic smiles"
- Innovations in black- and red-figure vase painting

- Contrapposto introduced in Greek statuary
- Polykleitos formulates his canon of proportions
- Pericles rebuilds the Athenian Acropolis after the Persian sack
- Praxiteles humanizes the Greek gods and goddesses

- Hellenistic kingdoms replace Athens as leading cultural centers
- Artists explore new subjects in sculpture and painting

The Gods and Goddesses of Mount Olympus

The Greek deities most often represented in art—not only in antiquity but also in the Middle Ages, the Renaissance, and up to the present—are the 12 gods and goddesses of Mount Olympus. Listed here are the Olympian gods (and their Roman equivalents).

- **Zeus (Jupiter)** was king of the gods and ruled the sky. His weapon was the thunderbolt, and with it he led the other gods to victory over the giants, who had challenged the Olympians for control of the world.
- **Hera (Juno),** the wife and sister of Zeus, was the goddess of marriage.
- **Poseidon (Neptune),** Zeus's brother, was lord of the sea. He controlled waves, storms, and earthquakes with his three-pronged pitchfork (*trident*).
- **Hestia (Vesta),** sister of Zeus, Poseidon, and Hera, was goddess of the hearth.
- **Demeter (Ceres),** Zeus's third sister, was the goddess of grain and agriculture.
- **Ares (Mars),** the god of war, was the son of Zeus and Hera and the lover of Aphrodite. As father of the twin founders of Rome, Romulus and Remus, Mars looms much larger in Roman mythology and religion than Ares does in Greek.
- **Athena (Minerva),** the goddess of wisdom and warfare, was a virgin (*parthenos* in Greek). She was also born not from a woman's womb but from the head of her father, Zeus.
- **Hephaistos (Vulcan),** the son of Zeus and Hera, was the god of fire and of metalworking. He provided Zeus his scepter and Poseidon his trident, and fashioned the armor Achilles wore in battle against Troy. He was also the "surgeon" who split open Zeus's head when he gave birth to Athena. Hephaistos was lame and, uncharacteristically for a god, ugly. His wife, Aphrodite, was unfaithful to him.

- **Apollo (Apollo)** was the god of light and music, and a great archer. He was the son of Zeus with **Leto (Latona),** daughter of one of the Titans who preceded the Olympians. His epithet *Phoibos* means "radiant," and the Greeks and Romans sometimes identified the young, beautiful Apollo with the sun (**Helios/Sol**).
- **Artemis (Diana),** the sister of Apollo, was the goddess of the hunt and of wild animals. Because she was Apollo's twin, the Greeks and Romans occasionally regarded Artemis as the moon (**Selene/Luna**).
- **Aphrodite (Venus),** the daughter of Zeus and Dione (one of the *nymphs*—the goddesses of springs, caves, and woods), was the goddess of love and beauty. She was the mother of the Trojan hero Aeneas by Anchises.
- **Hermes (Mercury),** the son of Zeus and another nymph, was the fleet-footed messenger of the gods and possessed winged sandals. He was also the guide of travelers and carried the *caduceus*, a magical herald's rod.

Several non-Olympian deities also appear frequently in ancient and later art.

- **Hades (Pluto),** Zeus's other brother, was equal in stature to the Olympian deities but never resided on Mount Olympus. Zeus allotted him lordship over the Underworld when he gave the realm of the sea to Poseidon. Hades was the god of the dead.
- **Dionysos (Bacchus)** was the god of wine and the son of Zeus and a mortal woman.
- **Eros (Amor or Cupid)** was the winged child-god of love and the son of Aphrodite and Ares.
- **Asklepios (Aesculapius),** the son of Apollo and a mortal woman, was the healing god whose serpent-entwined staff is the emblem of modern medicine.

Greeks made their gods into humans and their humans into gods. This humanistic worldview led the Greeks to create the concept of democracy (rule by the *demos,* the people) and to make seminal contributions in the fields of art, literature, and science.

The distinctiveness and originality of Greek civilization should not, however, obscure the enormous debt the Greeks owed to the cultures of Mesopotamia and Egypt. The ancient Greeks themselves readily acknowledged borrowing ideas, motifs, conventions, and skills from these older civilizations. Nor should a high estimation of Greek art and culture blind anyone to the realities of Hellenic life and society. Even "democracy" was a political reality for only one segment of the Greek demos. Slavery was a universal institution among the Greeks, and Greek women were in no way the equals of Greek men. Women normally remained secluded in their homes, emerging usually only for weddings, funerals, and religious festivals. They played little part in public or political life. Nonetheless, the importance of the Greek contribution to the later development of Western civilization and Western art can hardly be overstated.

The story of art in Greece does not begin with the Greeks, however, but with their prehistoric predecessors in the Aegean world—the people who would later become the heroes and heroines of Greek mythology.

PREHISTORIC AEGEAN

Historians, art historians, and archaeologists alike divide the prehistoric Aegean into three geographic areas. Each has a distinctive artistic identity. *Cycladic* art is the art of the Cycladic Islands (so named because they "circle" around Delos), as well as of the adjacent islands in the Aegean, excluding Crete. *Minoan* art, named for the legendary King Minos, encompasses the art of Crete. *Mycenaean* art, which takes its name from the great citadel of Mycenae celebrated in Homer's *Iliad,* the epic tale of the Trojan War, is the art of the Greek mainland (*Hellas* in Greek).

Cycladic Art

Although the heyday of the prehistoric Aegean was not until the second millennium BCE, humans inhabited Greece as far back as the Paleolithic period. Village life was firmly established in Greece in Neolithic times. However, the earliest distinctive Aegean artworks date to the third millennium BCE and come from the Cyclades.

2-2 Figurine of a woman, from Syros (Cyclades), Greece, ca. 2600–2300 BCE. Marble, 1′ 6″ high. National Archaeological Museum, Athens.

Most Cycladic statuettes come from graves and depict nude women, but whether they represent the deceased is uncertain. The sculptor rendered the female body schematically as a series of triangles.

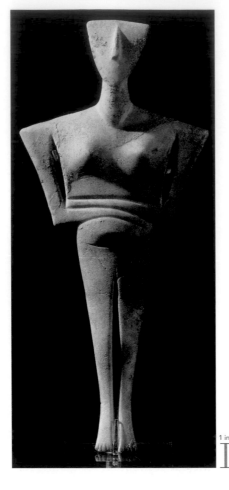

Cycladic Statuettes Marble was abundantly available in the Aegean Islands, and many Cycladic marble sculptures survive. Most of these, like many of their Stone Age predecessors (FIG. 1-2), represent nude women with their arms folded across their abdomens. One example (FIG. 2-2), about a foot and a half tall—but only about a half inch thick—comes from a grave on Syros. The sculptor rendered the human body in a highly schematic manner. Large simple triangles dominate the form—the head, the body itself (which tapers from exceptionally broad shoulders to tiny feet), and the incised triangular pubis. The feet have the toes

pointed downward, so the figurine cannot stand upright and must have been placed on its back in the grave—lying down, like the deceased. Archaeologists debate whether the Syros and other Cycladic statuettes represent fertility figures or goddesses. In any case, the artist took pains to emphasize the breasts as well as the pubic area. The slight swelling of the belly may suggest pregnancy. Traces of paint found on some of the Cycladic figurines indicate that at least parts of these sculptures were colored. The now almost featureless faces would have had painted eyes and mouths in addition to the sculpted noses. Red and blue necklaces and bracelets, as well as painted dots on the cheeks and necks, characterize a number of the surviving figurines.

Minoan Art

During the third millennium BCE, on both the Aegean Islands and the Greek mainland, most settlements were small and consisted only of simple buildings. Graves containing costly offerings such as the Syros statuette were rare. In contrast, the hallmark of the second millennium BCE is the construction of large palaces on Crete. This was the golden age of the prehistoric Aegean, the era when the first great Western civilization emerged. The Cretan palaces were large, comfortable, and handsome, with residential suites for the king and his family and courtyards for pageants, ceremonies, and games. They also had storerooms, offices, and shrines, enabling these huge complexes to serve as the key administrative, commercial, and religious centers of Minoan life. The size and number of the palaces, as well as the rich finds they have yielded, attest to the power and prosperity of the Minoans.

Knossos The largest Cretan palace—at Knossos (FIG. 2-3)—was the legendary home of King Minos and of the *minotaur*, a creature half bull and half man. According to the myth, the minotaur inhabited a vast labyrinth, and when the Athenian king Theseus defeated the monster, he was able to find

2-3 Aerial view (looking northeast) of the palace at Knossos (Crete), Greece, ca. 1700–1370 BCE. ◼◀

The largest palace on Crete, this was the legendary home of King Minos. Scores of rooms surround a large rectangular court. The palace's mazelike plan gave rise to the myth of the Minotaur in the labyrinth.

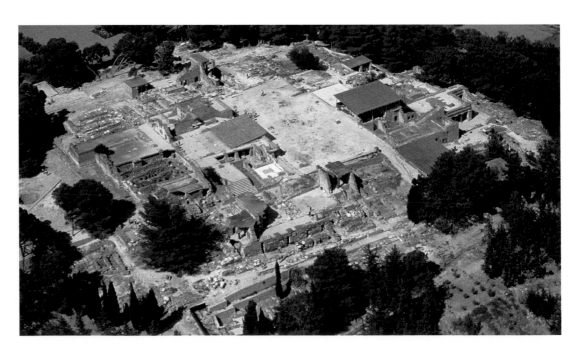

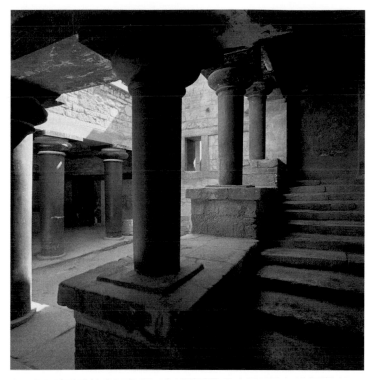

2-4 Stairwell in the residential quarter of the palace at Knossos (Crete), Greece, ca. 1700–1370 BCE. ■◀

The Knossos palace was complex in elevation as well as plan. It had at least three stories on all sides of the courtyard. Minoan columns taper from top to bottom, the opposite of Egyptian and Greek columns.

in elevation as well as plan. It had as many as three stories around the central court and even more on the south and east sides where the terrain sloped off sharply. Interior staircases (FIG. 2-4) built around light and air wells provided necessary illumination and ventilation. The Minoans fashioned their columns of wood and usually painted the shafts red. The columns had black, bulbous, cushionlike capitals resembling those of the later Greek Doric order (FIG. 2-20, *left*) but the shafts taper from a wide top to a narrower base, the opposite of both Egyptian and later Greek columns.

Mural paintings liberally adorned the Knossos palace, constituting one of its most striking features. The paintings depict many aspects of Minoan life (bull-leaping, processions, and ceremonies) and of nature (birds, animals, flowers, and marine life). Unlike the Egyptians, who painted in *fresco secco* (*dry fresco*), the Minoans coated the rough fabric of their rubble walls with a fine white lime plaster and used a *true* (*wet*) *fresco* method (see "Fresco Painting," Chapter 7, page 213). The Minoan frescoes required rapid execution and great skill.

The most famous fresco (FIG. **2-5**) from the palace at Knossos depicts the Minoan ceremony of bull-leaping, in which a young man grasped the horns of a bull and vaulted onto its back—a perilous and extremely difficult acrobatic maneuver. The young women have fair skin and the leaping youth has dark skin in accord with the widely accepted ancient convention for distinguishing male and female. The painter brilliantly suggested the powerful charge of the bull by elongating the animal's shape and using sweeping lines to form a funnel of energy, beginning at the very narrow hindquarters of the bull and culminating in its large, sharp horns and galloping forelegs. The human figures also have stylized shapes, with typically Minoan pinched waists. The elegant, elastic, highly animated Cretan figures, with their long curly hair and proud and self-confident bearing, are easy to distinguish from Mesopotamian and Egyptian figures.

his way out of the maze only with the aid of Minos's daughter Ariadne. She had given Theseus a spindle of thread to mark his path through the labyrinth and help him safely find his way out again. The aerial view reveals that the Knossos palace was indeed mazelike in plan. Its central feature was a large rectangular court. The builders arranged the other palace units—living quarters, ceremonial rooms, and storerooms—around this primary space. The palace was complex

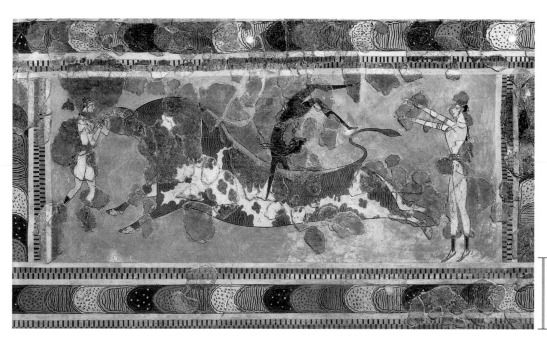

2-5 Bull-leaping, from the palace at Knossos (Crete), Greece, ca. 1400–1370 BCE. Fresco, 2′ 8″ high, including border. Archaeological Museum, Herakleion. ■◀

Frescoes decorated the Knossos palace walls. The Minoan men and women have stylized bodies with narrow waists. The skin color varies with gender, a common convention in ancient paintings.

1 ft.

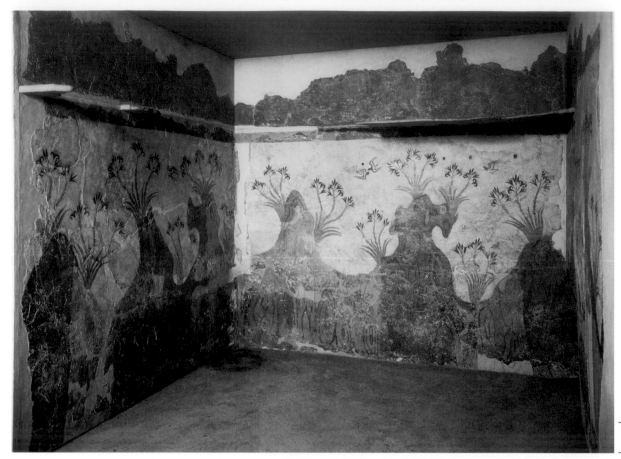

2-6 Landscape with swallows (*Spring Fresco*), from room Delta 2, Akrotiri, Thera (Cyclades), Greece, ca. 1650–1625 BCE. Fresco, 7′ 6″ high. National Archaeological Museum, Athens.

Aegean muralists painted in wet fresco, which required rapid execution. In this wraparound landscape, the painter used vivid colors and undulating lines to capture the essence of nature.

1 ft.

Thera Much better preserved than the Knossos frescoes are the mural paintings uncovered in the excavations of Akrotiri on the volcanic island of Thera in the Cyclades, some 60 miles north of Crete. The excellent condition of the Theran paintings is due to an enormous seismic explosion on the island that buried Akrotiri in volcanic pumice and ash around 1628 BCE. One almost perfectly preserved Theran mural painting, known as the *Spring Fresco* (FIG. **2-6**), is the largest prehistoric example of a pure landscape—a picture of a place without humans or animals. The artist's aim, however, was not to render the rocky island terrain realistically but to capture its essence. The irrationally undulating and vividly colored rocks, the graceful lilies swaying in the cool island breezes, and the darting swallows express the vigor of growth, the delicacy of flowering, and the lightness of birdsong and flight. In the lyrical language of curving line, the Theran artist celebrated the rhythms of nature. The *Spring Fresco* represents the polar opposite of the first efforts at mural painting in the caves of Paleolithic Europe, where animals (and occasionally humans) appeared as isolated figures with no indication of setting.

Minoan Pottery Minoan painters also decorated small objects, especially ceramic pots, usually employing dark silhouettes against a cream-colored ground. On a flask (FIG. **2-7**) found at Palaikastro on Crete the tentacles of an octopus reach out over the curving surfaces of the vessel, embracing the piece and emphasizing its volume. The vase is a masterful realization of the relationship between the vessel's decoration and its shape, always a problem for the ceramist.

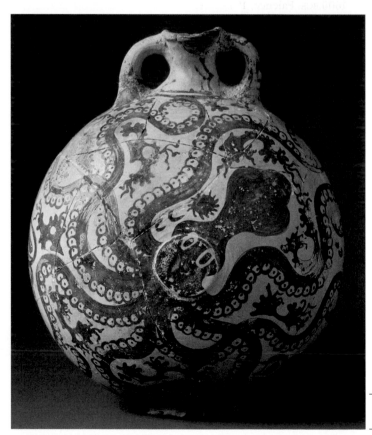

1 in.

2-7 Octopus flask, from Palaikastro (Crete), Greece, ca. 1450 BCE. 11″ high. Archaeological Museum, Herakleion.

The sea figures prominently in Minoan art. This painter perfectly matched the octopus motif to the shape of the vase. The sea creature's tentacles reach out to fill the curving surfaces of the vessel.

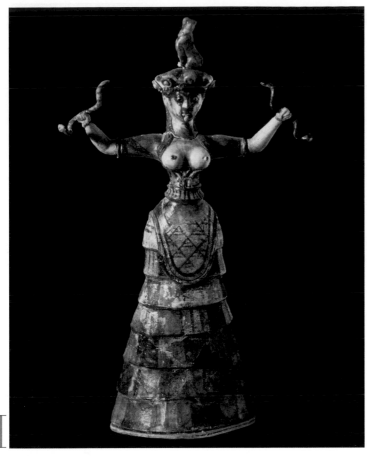

1 in.

2-8 *Snake Goddess*, from the palace at Knossos (Crete), Greece, ca. 1600 BCE. Faience, 1' 1¼" high. Archaeological Museum, Herakleion.

This Minoan figurine may represent a priestess, but it is more likely a bare-breasted goddess. The snakes in her hands and the feline on her head imply she wields power over the animal world.

Snake Goddess In contrast to Mesopotamia and Egypt, Minoan Crete has yielded no trace of temples or monumental statues of gods, kings, or monsters, although large wooden images may once have existed. What remains of Minoan sculpture is uniformly small in scale, such as the *faience* (low-fired glasslike silicate) statuette known as the *Snake Goddess* (FIG. **2-8**), found in the palace at Knossos. It is one of several similar figurines that some scholars believe may represent mortal priestesses rather than a deity, although the promi-

nently exposed breasts suggest these figurines stand in the long line of prehistoric fertility images usually considered divinities. The Knossos woman holds snakes in her hands and supports a tamed leopardlike feline peacefully on her head. This implied power over the animal world also seems appropriate for a deity. The frontality of the figure is reminiscent of Egyptian and Mesopotamian statuary, but the costume, with its open bodice and flounced skirt, is distinctly Minoan.

Minoan Decline Scholars dispute the circumstances ending the Minoan civilization, although most now believe Mycenaeans had already moved onto Crete and established themselves at Knossos in the 15th century BCE. Parts of the palace continued to be occupied until its final destruction around 1200 BCE, but its importance as a cultural center faded soon after 1400 BCE, as the focus of Aegean civilization shifted to the Greek mainland.

Mycenaean Art

The origin of the Mycenaeans is also the subject of continuing debate. The only certainty is the presence of these forerunners of the Greeks on the mainland at the beginning of the second millennium BCE. Some scholars believe the mainland was a Minoan economic dependency for a long time, but by 1500 BCE a distinctive Mycenaean culture was flourishing in Greece.

Tiryns The destruction of the Cretan palaces left the mainland culture supreme. Although historians refer to this civilization as Mycenaean, Mycenae was but one of several large palace complexes. The best-preserved and most impressive Mycenaean remains are those of the fortified palaces at Tiryns and Mycenae. Construction of both citadels began about 1400 BCE. Homer, writing in the mid-eighth century BCE, called the citadel of Tiryns (FIG. **2-9**), located about 10 miles from Mycenae, "Tiryns of the Great Walls." In the second century CE, when Pausanias, author of an invaluable guidebook to Greece, visited the site, he marveled at the towering fortifications and considered the walls of Tiryns as spectacular as the pyramids of Egypt. Indeed, the Greeks of the historical age believed mere humans could not have built a fortress this large and attributed the construction of

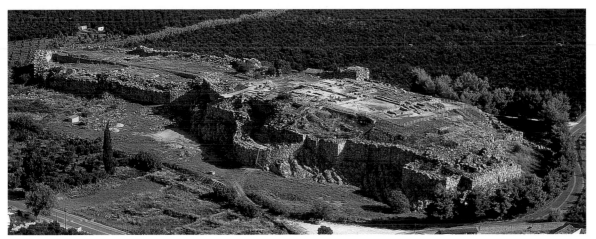

2-9 Aerial view of the citadel (looking northeast), Tiryns, Greece, ca. 1400–1200 BCE.

In the *Iliad*, Homer called the fortified citadel of Tiryns the city "of the great walls." The huge roughly cut stone blocks are examples of Cyclopean masonry, named after the mythical one-eyed giants.

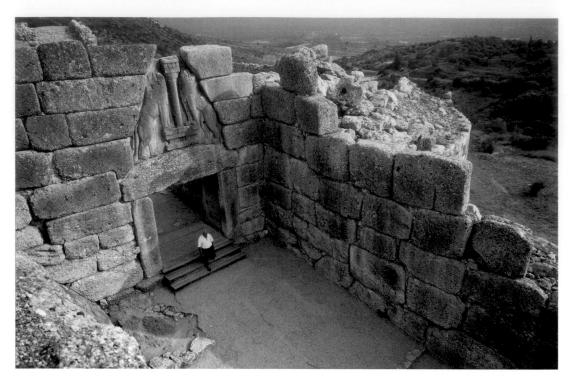

2-10 Lion Gate (looking southeast), Mycenae, Greece, ca. 1300–1250 BCE. Limestone, relief panel 9′ 6″ high. ◼◀

The largest sculpture in the pre-historic Aegean is the relief of confronting lions that fills the relieving triangle of Mycenae's main gate. The gate itself consists of two great monoliths and a huge lintel.

Tiryns and the other Mycenaean citadels to the mythical *Cyclopes,* a race of one-eyed giants. Architectural historians still employ the term *Cyclopean masonry* to refer to the huge, roughly cut stone blocks forming the massive Mycenaean fortification walls. The walls of Tiryns average about 20 feet in thickness and incorporate blocks often weighing several tons each. The heavily fortified Mycenaean palaces contrast sharply with the open Cretan palaces (FIG. 2-3) and clearly reveal their defensive character.

Lion Gate, Mycenae The entrance to the citadel at Mycenae was the so-called Lion Gate (FIG. **2-10**), protected on the left by a wall built on a natural rock outcropping and on the right by a projecting bastion of large blocks. Any approaching enemies would have had to enter this 20-foot-wide channel and face Mycenaean defenders above them on both sides. The gate itself consists of two great monolithic posts capped with a huge lintel. Above the lintel, the masonry courses form a *corbeled arch,* constructed by placing the blocks in horizontal courses and then cantilevering them inward until they meet, leaving an opening that lightens the weight the lintel carries. Filling this *relieving triangle* is a great limestone slab with two lions in high relief facing a central Minoan-type column.

The whole design admirably matches its triangular shape, harmonizing in dignity, strength, and scale with the massive stones that form the walls and gate. Similar groups appear in miniature on Cretan seals, but the concept of placing monstrous guardian figures at the entrances to palaces, tombs, and sacred places has its origin in Mesopotamia and Egypt (FIGS. 1-18 and 1-26). At Mycenae, the sculptors fashioned the animals' heads separately. Some scholars have suggested the lost heads may have been human and the Mycenaean guardians sphinxes instead of lions.

Treasury of Atreus The Mycenaeans erected the Lion Gate and the towering fortification wall circuit of which it formed a part a few generations before the presumed date

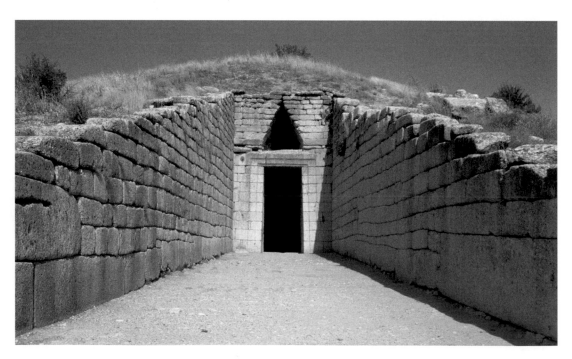

2-11 Treasury of Atreus, Mycenae, Greece, ca. 1300–1250 BCE. ◼◀

The best-preserved Mycenaean tholos tomb is named after Homer's King Atreus. An earthen mound covers the burial chamber, entered through a doorway at the end of a long passageway.

of the Trojan War. At that time, elite families buried their dead outside the citadel walls in tombs covered by enormous earthen mounds. The best preserved of these *tholos tombs* is the so-called Treasury of Atreus (FIG. **2-11**), which the later Greeks already mistakenly believed was the repository of the treasure of Atreus, father of King Agamemnon, who waged war against Troy. A long passageway leads to a doorway surmounted by a relieving triangle similar to that in the roughly contemporaneous Lion Gate and to the beehive-shaped burial chamber (*tholos*). Composed of a series of stone-corbeled courses laid on a circular base, the tholos (FIG. **2-12**) has a lofty pointed *dome* in the form of a *corbeled vault*. The principle involved is no different from a corbeled arch. The builders probably constructed the vault using cantilevered rough-hewn blocks. After the masons set the stones of the dome in place, they had to finish the surfaces with great precision to make them conform to both the horizontal and vertical curvature of the wall. About 43 feet high, this Mycenaean

domed chamber was the largest vaulted space without interior supports ever built before the Roman Empire.

Royal Shaft Graves The Treasury of Atreus was thoroughly looted long before its modern rediscovery, but archaeologists have unearthed spectacular grave goods elsewhere at Mycenae. Just inside the Lion Gate, but predating it by some three centuries, is the burial area designated as Grave Circle A. Here, at a site protected within the circuit of the later walls, six deep shafts served as tombs for kings and their families. The excavation of the royal shaft graves yielded many gold artifacts, including beaten (*repoussé*) gold masks. (Homer described the Mycenaeans as "rich in gold.") Art historians have often compared the Mycenaean mask illustrated here (FIG. **2-13**) to Tutankhamen's gold mummy mask (FIG. 1-37). The treatment of the human face is, of course, more primitive in the Mycenaean mask. But this is one of the first known attempts in Greece to render the human face at life-size, whereas the Egyptian mask stands in a long line of monumental sculptures going back more than a millennium. It is not known whether the Mycenaean masks were intended as portraits, but the goldsmiths recorded different physical types with care. The illustrated mask, with its full beard, must depict a mature man, perhaps a king—although not Agamemnon, as its 19th-century discoverer wished. If Agamemnon was a real king, he lived some 300 years after the manufacture of this mask.

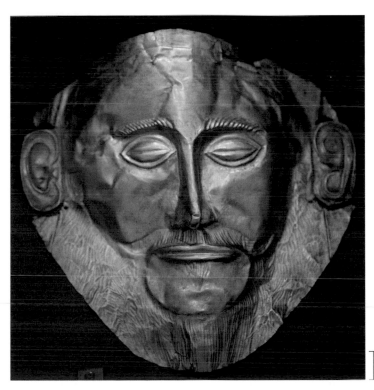

1 in.

2-12 Interior of the Treasury of Atreus, Mycenae, Greece, ca. 1300–1250 BCE. ◼◀

The beehive-shaped tholos of the Treasury of Atreus consists of corbeled courses of stone blocks laid on a circular base. The 43-foot-high dome was the largest in the ancient world for almost 1,500 years.

2-13 Funerary mask, from Grave Circle A, Mycenae, Greece, ca. 1600–1500 BCE. Gold, 1' high. National Archaeological Museum, Athens. ◼◀

Homer described the Mycenaeans as "rich in gold." This beaten (repoussé) gold mask of a bearded man comes from a royal shaft grave. It is one of the first attempts at life-size sculpture in Greece.

The End of Mycenae Despite their mighty walls, the citadels of Mycenae and Tiryns were burned between 1250 and 1200 BCE, when the Mycenaeans seem to have been overrun by northern invaders or to have fallen victim to internal warfare. By Homer's time, the apogee of Aegean civilization was but a distant memory, and the men and women of Crete and Mycenae had assumed the stature of heroes from a lost golden age.

GREECE

The destruction of the Mycenaean palaces brought with it the disintegration of the Bronze Age social order. The disappearance of powerful kings and their retinues led to the loss of the knowledge of how to construct fortified citadels and vaulted tombs, to paint frescoes, and to sculpt in stone. Depopulation, poverty, and an almost total loss of contact with the outside world characterized the succeeding centuries, sometimes called the Dark Age of Greece.

Geometric and Archaic Art

Only in the eighth century BCE did economic conditions improve and the population begin to grow again. This era was in its own way a heroic age, a time when the Greeks established the Olympic Games, wrote down Homer's epic poems (formerly passed orally from bard to bard), began to trade with their neighbors in both the east and the west, and returned the human figure to Greek art.

Geometric Krater Art historians call the art of this formative period *Geometric* because Greek vase painting of the time consisted primarily of abstract motifs. One of the earliest instances of the introduction of narrative scenes among the Geometric patterns is a huge *krater* (FIG. **2-14**), or bowl for mixing wine and water, that marked the grave of a man buried in the Dipylon cemetery in Athens around 740 BCE. At well over three feet tall, this vase is a considerable technical achievement. The artist covered much of the krater's surface with precisely painted abstract angular motifs in horizontal bands. Especially prominent is the *meander,* or key, pattern around the rim. But the Geometric painter reserved the widest part of the krater for two bands of human figures and horse-drawn chariots. Befitting the vase's function as a grave marker, the scenes depict the mourning for a man laid out on his bier and the grand chariot procession in his honor. The painter filled every empty space with circles and M-shapes, negating any sense that the mourners and soldiers inhabit open space. The human figures, animals, and furniture are as two-dimensional as the geometric shapes elsewhere on the vessel. In the upper band, the shroud, raised to reveal the corpse, is an abstract checkerboard-like backdrop. The figures are silhouettes constructed of triangular (frontal) torsos with attached profile arms, legs, and heads (with a single large frontal eye in the center), following the age-old convention. To distinguish male from female, the painter added a penis growing out of one of the deceased's thighs. The mourning women, who tear their hair out in grief, have

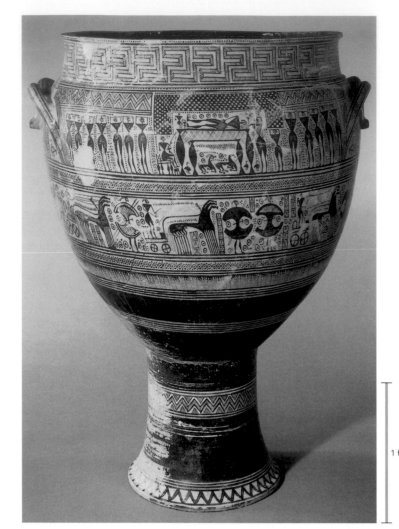

2-14 Geometric krater, from the Dipylon cemetery, Athens, Greece, ca. 740 BCE. 3′ 4½″ high. Metropolitan Museum of Art, New York.

Figure painting returned to Greek art in the Geometric period, named for the abstract motifs on vessels such as this funerary krater featuring a mourning scene and a procession in honor of the deceased.

breasts emerging beneath their armpits. In both cases the artist's concern was specifying gender, not anatomical accuracy. Below, the warriors look like walking shields, and the two wheels of the chariots appear side by side. The horses have the correct number of heads and legs but seem to share a common body, so there is no sense of depth. Despite the highly stylized and conventional manner of representation, this vessel marks a significant turning point in the history of Greek art. Not only did the human figure reenter the painter's repertoire, but Geometric artists also revived the art of storytelling in pictures.

Lady of Auxerre During the seventh century BCE, the first Greek stone sculptures since the Mycenaean Lion Gate (FIG. 2-10) began to appear. One of the earliest, probably originally from Crete, is a limestone statuette of a goddess or maiden (*kore;* plural, *korai*) popularly known as the *Lady of Auxerre* (FIG. **2-15**) after the French town that is her oldest recorded location. Because she does not wear a headdress, as early Greek goddesses frequently do, and the gesture of her right hand probably signifies prayer, the *Lady of Auxerre* is most likely a kore. The style is characteristic of the early *Archaic* period. The flat-topped head takes the form of a triangle framed by complementary triangles of four long strands of hair each. Also typical are the small belted waist and a fondness for pattern, seen, for example, in the almost Geometric treatment of the long skirt with its incised concentric squares, once brightly painted.

Art historians refer to this early Greek style as *Daedalic,* after the legendary artist Daedalus, whose name means "the skillful one." In addition to having been a great sculptor, Daedalus reputedly built the labyrinth of Knossos (FIG. 2-3) and designed a temple at Memphis in Egypt. The historical Greeks attributed to him almost all the great achievements in early sculpture and architecture. The story that Daedalus worked in Egypt reflects the enormous influence of Egyptian art and architecture on the Greeks.

New York Kouros One of the earliest Greek examples of life-size statuary (FIG **2-16**) is the marble *kouros* ("youth"; plural, *kouroi*) now in New York, which emulates the stance of Egyptian statues (FIG. 1-28). In both Egypt and Greece, the figure is rigidly frontal with the left foot advanced slightly. The arms are held beside the body, and the fists are clenched with the thumbs forward. Nevertheless, Greek kouros statues differ from

their Egyptian models in two important ways. First, the Greek sculptors liberated the figures from the stone block. The Egyptian obsession with permanence was alien to the Greeks, who were preoccupied with finding ways to represent motion rather than stability in their sculpted figures. Second, the kouroi are nude. Greek athletes competed nude in the Olympic Games, and, in the absence of identifying attributes, Greek youths as well as maidens are formally indistinguishable from Greek statues of deities.

The New York kouros shares many traits with the *Lady of Auxerre* (FIG. 2-15), especially the triangular shape of head and hair and the flatness of the face—the hallmarks of the Daedalic style. Eyes, nose, and mouth all sit on the front of the head, and ears on the sides. The long hair forms a flat backdrop behind the head. This is the result of the sculptor's having drawn these features on four independent sides of the marble block, following the same workshop procedure used in Egypt for millennia. The kouros also has the slim waist of earlier Greek statues and exhibits the same love of pattern. The pointed arch of the rib cage, for example, echoes the V-shaped ridge of the hips, which suggests but does not accurately reproduce the rounded flesh and muscle of the human body.

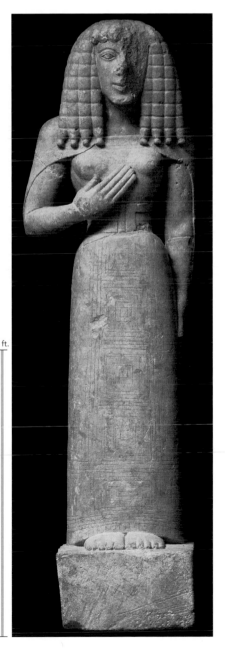

2-15 *Lady of Auxerre,* ca. 650–625 BCE. Limestone, 2′ 1½″ high. Musée du Louvre, Paris.

One of the earliest Greek stone sculptures, this kore (maiden) typifies the Daedalic style of the seventh century BCE with its triangular face and hair and lingering Geometric fondness for abstract pattern.

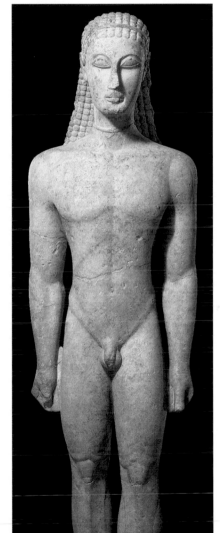

2-16 Kouros, from Attica, Greece, ca. 600 BCE. Marble, 6′ ½″ high. Metropolitan Museum of Art, New York. ■◀

The sculptors of the earliest life-size statues of kouroi (young men) adopted the Egyptian pose for standing figures (FIG. 1-28), but the kouroi are nude and freestanding, liberated from the stone block.

2-17 Kroisos, from Anavysos, Greece, ca. 530 BCE. Marble, 6' 4" high. National Archaeological Museum, Athens. ◼◀

This later kouros displays increased naturalism in its proportions and more rounded modeling of face, torso, and limbs. Kroisos also smiles—the Archaic Greek sculptor's way of indicating life.

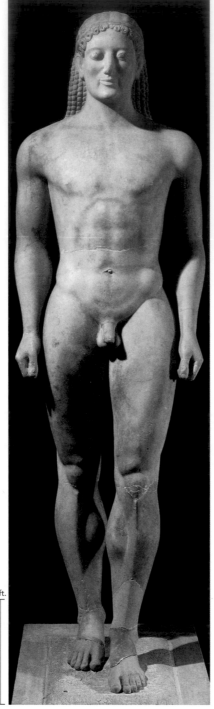

2-18 *Peplos Kore*, from the Acropolis, Athens, Greece, ca. 530 BCE. Marble, 4' high. Acropolis Museum, Athens.

Unlike men, women are always clothed in Archaic statuary. This smiling kore is a votive statue of a goddess wearing four garments. She held her identifying attribute in her missing left hand.

Kroisos Sometime around 530 BCE, a young man named Kroisos died a hero's death in battle, and his family erected a kouros statue (FIG. **2-17**) over his grave at Anavysos, not far from Athens. Although the stance is the same as in the earlier New York kouros, this sculptor rendered human anatomy in a far more naturalistic manner. The head is no longer too large for the body, and the face is more rounded, with swelling cheeks replacing the flat planes of the earlier work. The long hair does not form a stiff backdrop to the head but falls naturally over the back. The V-shaped ridges of the New York kouros have become rounded, fleshy hips. Also new is that Kroisos smiles—or seems to. From this time on, Archaic Greek statues always smile—even in the most inappropriate contexts (FIG. 2-29). Art historians have proposed various interpretations of this so-called *Archaic smile,* but the smile should not be taken literally. Rather, it is the Archaic sculptor's way of indicating that the person portrayed is alive. By adopting this convention, the Greek artist signaled a very different intention from that of Egyptian sculptors.

Some original paint survives on the Kroisos statue, enhancing the sense of life. Greek artists painted all their stone statues. The modern notion that Greek statuary was pure white is mistaken. The Greeks did not color their statues garishly, however. They left the flesh in the natural color of the stone, which they waxed and polished. Artists painted the

eyes, lips, hair, and drapery in *encaustic,* a technique in which the pigment is mixed with hot wax before applying it to the statue.

Peplos Kore A stylistic "sister" to Kroisos, also with paint preserved, is the smiling *Peplos Kore* (FIG. **2-18**), so called because until recently scholars thought she wore a *peplos,* a simple, long, woolen belted garment. She wears four garments, however, one of which only goddesses wore. The attribute the goddess held in her missing left hand would have identified her. Whichever goddess the *Peplos Kore* portrays, the contrast with the *Lady of Auxerre* (FIG. 2-15) is striking. Although in both cases the drapery conceals the entire body save for head, arms, and feet, the sixth-century BCE sculptor rendered the soft female form much more naturally. This softer treatment of the flesh also sharply differentiates later korai from kouroi, which have hard, muscular bodies.

Greek Temples Egypt also had a profound influence on Greek architecture. Shortly after the foundation of a Greek trading colony at Naukratis (MAP 1-3) around 650–630 BCE, the Greeks began constructing the first stone buildings since the fall of the Mycenaean kingdoms. Although Greek temples cannot be confused with Egyptian buildings, columnar halls such as that at Karnak (FIG. 1-32) clearly inspired Greek architects.

Doric and Ionic Temples

The plan and elevation of Greek temples varied with date, geography, and the requirements of individual projects, but Greek temples have common defining elements that set them apart from both the religious edifices of other civilizations and other kinds of Greek buildings.

▌ **Plan** (FIG. 2-19) The temple core was the *naos*, or *cella*, which housed the cult statue of the deity. In front was a *pronaos*, or porch, often with two columns between the *antae*, or extended walls (columns *in antis*, that is, between the antae). A smaller second room might be placed behind the cella, but more frequently the Greek temple had a porch at the rear (*opisthodomos*) set against the blank back wall of the cella. The second porch served only a decorative purpose, satisfying the Greek passion for balance and symmetry. Around this core, Greek builders might erect a colonnade across the front of the temple

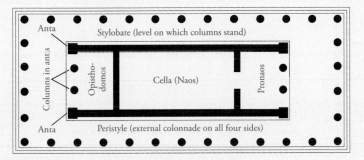

2-19 Plan of a typical Greek peripteral temple.

Greek temples had peripteral colonnades and housed cult statues of the gods in the central room, or cella. Worshipers gathered outside the temples, where priests made offerings at open-air altars.

(*prostyle*; FIG. 2-42), across both front and back (*amphiprostyle*; FIG. 2-43), or, more commonly, all around the cella and its porch(es) to form the *peristyle* of a *peripteral* temple (FIGS. 2-19, 2-21, and 2-36).

▌ **Elevation** (FIG. 2-20) The elevation of a Greek temple consists of the platform, the colonnade, and the superstructure (*entablature*). In the Archaic period, two basic systems, or *orders*, evolved for articulating the three units. The Greek architectural orders differ both in the nature of the details and in the relative proportions of the parts. The names of the orders derive from the Greek regions where they were most commonly employed. The *Doric*, formulated on the mainland, remained the preferred manner there and in the Greeks' western colonies. The *Ionic* was the order of choice in the Aegean Islands and on the western coast of Asia Minor. The geographical distinctions are by no means absolute. The Ionic order, for example, was often used in Athens.

In both orders, the columns rest on the *stylobate*, the uppermost course of the platform. The columns have two or three parts, depending on the order: the *shaft*, usually adorned with vertical channels (*flutes*); the *capital*; and, in the Ionic order, the *base*. Greek column shafts, in contrast to their Minoan and Mycenaean forebears, taper gradually from bottom to top. Greek capitals have two elements. The lower part (the *echinus*) varies with the order. In the Doric, it is convex and cushionlike, similar to the echinus of Minoan (FIG. 2-4) and Mycenaean (FIG. 2-10) capitals. In the Ionic, it is small and supports a bolster ending in spirals (the *volutes*). The upper element, present in both orders, is a flat square block (the *abacus*) that provides the immediate support for the entablature.

The entablature has three parts: the *architrave* or *epistyle*, the main weight-bearing and weight-distributing element; the *frieze*; and the *cornice*, a molded horizontal projection that together with two sloping (*raking*) cornices forms a triangle that frames the *pediment*. In the Ionic order, the architrave is usually subdivided into three horizontal bands (*fasciae*). Doric order architects subdivided the frieze into *triglyphs* and *metopes*, whereas Ionic builders left the frieze open to provide a continuous field for relief sculpture.

The Doric order is massive in appearance, its sturdy columns firmly planted on the stylobate. Compared with the weighty and severe Doric, the Ionic order seems light, airy, and much more decorative. Its columns are more slender and rise from molded bases. The most obvious differences between the two orders are, of course, in the capitals—the Doric, severely plain, and the Ionic, highly ornamental.

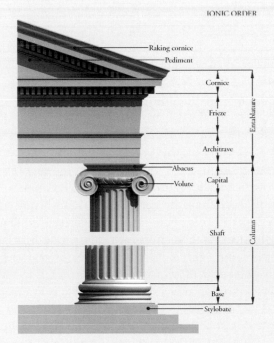

2-20 Elevations of the Doric and Ionic orders (John Burge).

The major orders of Greek architecture were the Doric and Ionic. They differ primarily in the form of the capitals and the treatment of the frieze. The Doric frieze is subdivided into triglyphs and metopes.

The basic plan of all Greek temples (see "Doric and Ionic Temples," above, and FIGS. **2-19** and **2-20**) reveals an order, compactness, and symmetry that reflect the Greeks' sense of proportion and their effort to achieve ideal forms in terms of regular numerical relationships and geometric rules (see "The Perfect Temple," page 47). The earliest temples tended

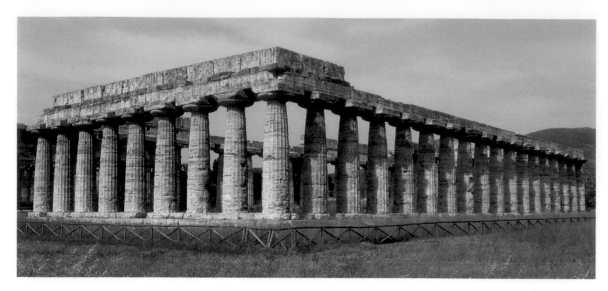

2-21 Temple of Hera ("Basilica," looking northeast), Paestum, Italy, ca. 550 BCE. ◼◀

The peristyle of this huge early Doric temple consists of heavy, closely spaced cigar-shaped columns with bulky, pancakelike capitals, characteristic features of Archaic Greek architecture.

to be long and narrow, with the proportion of the ends to the sides roughly expressible as 1:3. From the sixth century BCE on, temples tended to be a little longer than twice their width. To the Greek mind, proportion in architecture and sculpture was much the same as harmony in music, reflecting and embodying the cosmic order. The history of Greek temple architecture is the history of Greek architects' unflagging efforts to find the most satisfactory (that is, what they believed were perfect) proportions for each part of the building and for the structure as a whole.

The Greeks gathered to worship outside, not inside, their temples. The altar was always in the open air at the east end of the temple, facing the rising sun. The temple contained the *cult statue* of the deity, the grandest of all votive offerings. Both in its early and mature manifestations, the Greek temple was the house of the god or goddess, not of his or her followers.

Figural sculpture played a major role in the exterior program of the Greek temple from early times. The Greeks painted their architectural sculptures and usually placed statues and reliefs only in the building parts that had no structural function. This is true particularly of the Doric order, where decorative sculpture appears only in the metope and pediment "voids." Ionic builders, less severe in this respect as well, were willing to decorate the entire frieze. Occasionally, they replaced their columns with female figures (*caryatids;* FIG. 2-42). The Greeks also often painted the capitals, decorative moldings, and other architectural elements, which enabled architects to bring out more clearly the relationships of the structural parts and soften the stone's glitter at specific points, as well as provide a background to set off the figures.

Temple of Hera, Paestum The premier example of early Greek efforts at Doric temple design is not in Greece but in Italy, at Paestum. The huge (80 by 170 feet) Archaic temple (FIG. **2-21**) erected there around 550 BCE retains its entire peripteral colonnade, but most of the entablature, including the frieze, pediment, and roof, has vanished. Called the "Basilica" after the Roman columnar hall building type

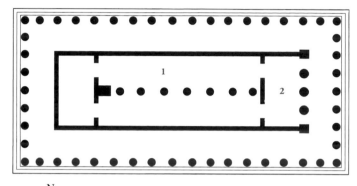

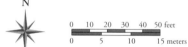

N

| 0 | 10 | 20 | 30 | 40 | 50 feet |
| 0 | | 5 | | 10 | 15 meters |

1. Cella with central row of columns
2. Pronaos with three columns in antis

2-22 Plan of the Temple of Hera, Paestum, Italy, ca. 550 BCE.

The Hera temple's plan reveals its early date. The building has an odd number of columns on the facade and a single row of columns in the cella, leaving no place for a central statue of the goddess.

(see Chapter 3) that early investigators felt it resembled, the structure was a shrine to the goddess Hera. The misnomer is partly due to the building's plan (FIG. **2-22**), which differs from that of most other Greek temples. The unusual feature, found only in early Archaic temples, is the central row of columns dividing the cella into two aisles. Placing columns underneath the *ridgepole* (the timber beam running the length of the building below the peak of the gabled roof) might seem the logical way to provide internal support for the roof structure, but it had several disadvantages. The placement of the cella columns precluded a central *cult statue*. Further, in order to correspond with the interior, the temple's facade required an odd number of columns (nine in this case). At Paestum, the builders also set three columns in antis instead of the standard two, which in turn ruled out a central doorway for viewing the statue. However, the architect still achieved a simple 1:2 ratio of facade and flank columns by erecting 18 columns on each side of the temple.

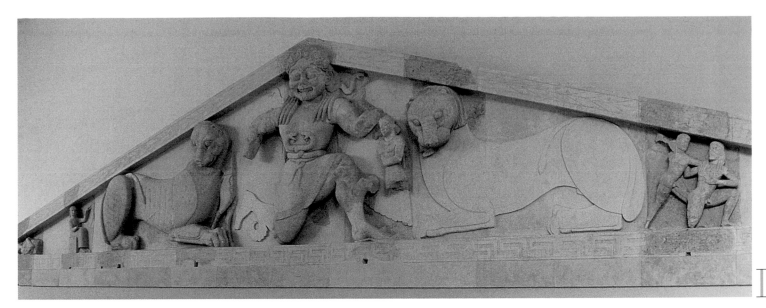

2-23 West pediment, Temple of Artemis, Corfu, Greece, ca. 600–580 BCE. Limestone, greatest height 9′ 4″. Archaeological Museum, Corfu.

The hideous Medusa and two panthers at the center of this early pediment served as temple guardians. To either side, and much smaller, are scenes from the Trojan War and the battle of gods and giants.

Another early aspect of the Paestum temple is the shape of its heavy, closely spaced columns with their large, bulky, pancakelike Doric capitals, which seem compressed by the overbearing weight of a high, massive entablature. The columns have a pronounced swelling (*entasis*) at the middle of the shafts, giving them a profile akin to that of a cigar. The columns and capitals thus express in a vivid manner their weight-bearing function. The heaviness of the design and the narrowness of the spans between the columns probably reflect the Archaic builders' fear that thinner and more widely spaced columns would result in the superstructure's collapse. In later Doric temples, the builders placed the columns farther apart, and the shafts became more slender, the entasis subtler, the capitals smaller, and the entablature lighter.

Temple of Artemis, Corfu Even older than the Paestum temple is the Doric temple of Artemis at Corfu, which dates to the early sixth century BCE. The building is unfortunately in ruins, but most of the sculpture that embellished its west pediment (FIG. **2-23**) survives. Designing figural decoration for a pediment was never an easy task for the Greek sculptor because of the pediment's awkward triangular shape. The central figures had to be of great size (more than nine feet tall at Corfu), but as the pediment tapered toward the corners, the available area became increasingly cramped.

At the center of the Corfu pediment is the *gorgon* Medusa, a demon with a woman's body and a bird's wings. Medusa also had a hideous face and snake hair, and anyone who gazed at her turned into stone. The sculptor depicted her in the conventional Archaic bent-leg, bent-arm, pinwheel-like posture that signifies running or, for a winged creature, flying. To her left and right are two great felines. Together

they serve as temple guardians, repulsing all enemies from the sanctuary of the goddess. Between Medusa and the great beasts are two smaller figures—the human Chrysaor at her left and the winged horse Pegasus at her right (only the rear legs remain). Chrysaor and Pegasus were Medusa's children. They sprang from her head when the Greek hero Perseus severed it with his sword. Their presence here with the living Medusa is therefore a chronological impossibility. The Archaic artist was not interested in telling a coherent story but in identifying the central figure by depicting her offspring. Narration was, however, the purpose of the much smaller groups situated in the pediment's corners. To the viewer's right is Zeus, brandishing his thunderbolt and slaying a kneeling giant. In the extreme corner was a dead giant. The *gigantomachy* (battle of gods and giants) was a popular Greek theme that was a metaphor for the triumph of reason and order over chaos. In the pediment's left corner is one of the Trojan War's climactic events: Achilles's son Neoptolemos kills the enthroned King Priam. The fallen figure to the left of this group may be a dead Trojan.

The master responsible for the Corfu pediments was a pioneer, and the figures' composition shows all the signs of experimentation. The lack of narrative unity in the Corfu pediment and the figures' extraordinary diversity of scale eventually gave way to pediment designs featuring figures all acting out a single event and appearing the same size. But the Corfu designer already had shown the way by realizing, for example, that the area beneath the raking cornice could be filled with gods and heroes of similar size by employing a combination of standing, leaning, kneeling, seated, and prostrate figures. The Corfu master also discovered that animals could be very useful space fillers because, unlike humans, they have one end taller than the other.

Black-Figure Painting Greek artists also pioneered a new ceramic painting technique during the Archaic period. Invented in Corinth, *black-figure painting* quickly replaced the simpler silhouette painting favored in the Geometric period. The black-figure painter also put down black silhouettes on the clay surface, but then used a *graver* (a sharp, pointed instrument) to incise linear details in the black-*glaze* forms, usually adding highlights in purplish red or white over the black figures before firing the vessel. The combination of the weighty black silhouettes with the delicate detailing and the bright polychrome overlay proved to be irresistible, and painters in other Greek cities soon copied the technique from the Corinthians.

Exekias The acknowledged master of the black-figure technique was an Athenian named EXEKIAS. An *amphora,* or two-handled storage jar (FIG. **2-24**), bears his signature as both painter and potter. Such signatures, common on Greek vases, reveal both pride and a sense of self-identity as an "artist." They also served as "brand names" because the vases of Athens and Corinth were widely exported. (The Exekias amphora was found in a tomb at Vulci, an Etruscan city in central Italy.) Unlike his Geometric predecessors, Exekias used figures of monumental stature and placed them in a single large framed panel. At the left is Achilles, fully armed. He plays a dice game with his comrade Ajax. Ajax has taken off his helmet, but both men hold their spears. Their shields are nearby, and each man is ready for action at a moment's notice. The gravity and tension that characterize this composition are rare in Archaic art.

Exekias had no equal as a black-figure painter. This is evident in details such as the extraordinarily intricate engraving of the patterns on the heroes' cloaks (highlighted with delicate touches of white) and in the masterful composition. The arch formed by the backs of the two warriors echoes the shape of the rounded shoulders of the amphora. The shape of the vessel (compare FIG. 2-26) is echoed again in the void between the heads and spears of Achilles and Ajax. Exekias also used the spears to lead viewers' eyes toward the thrown dice, where the heroes' eyes are fixed. Of course, those eyes do not really look down at the table but stare out from the profile heads in the old manner. For all

his brilliance, Exekias was still wedded to many of the old conventions. Real innovation in figure drawing would have to await the invention of a new ceramic painting technique of greater versatility than black-figure.

Red-Figure Painting The birth of this new technique, called *red-figure painting,* occurred around 530 BCE. Red-figure is the opposite of black-figure. What was previously black became red, and vice versa. The artist used the same black glaze for the figures, but instead of creating silhouettes the painter outlined the figures and then colored the background black, reserving the red clay for the figures themselves. For the interior details, the artist used a soft brush in place of a metal graver, enabling the painter to vary the glaze thickness, building it up to give relief to hair curls or diluting it to create brown shades, thereby expanding the chromatic range of the Greek vase painter's craft.

Euphronios One of the most admired red-figure painters was EUPHRONIOS, whose krater depicting the struggle between Herakles (Roman Hercules), the greatest Greek hero, and the giant Antaios (FIG. **2-25**) reveals the exciting possibilities of the new technique. Antaios was a son of Earth, and he derived his power from contact with the ground. To defeat him, Herakles had to lift him up into the air and strangle him while no part of the giant's body touched the earth. Here, the two wrestle on the ground, and Antaios still possesses enormous strength. Nonetheless, Herakles has the upper hand. The giant's face is a mask of pain. His eyes roll and he bares his teeth. His right arm is paralyzed, with the fingers limp.

Euphronios used diluted glaze to delineate the muscles of both figures and to produce a golden brown hue for Antaios's unkempt hair—an intentional contrast with the emotionless Herakles's neat coiffure and carefully trimmed beard. But rendering human anatomy and hair convincingly was not his only interest. Euphronios also wished to show

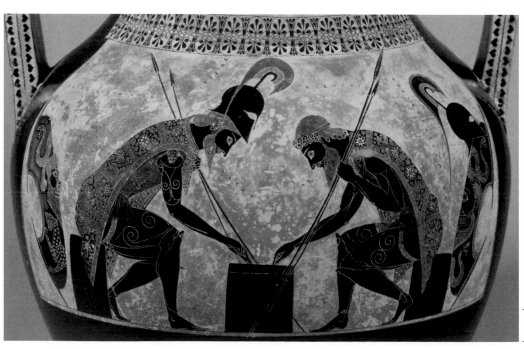

2-24 EXEKIAS, Achilles and Ajax playing a dice game (detail of a black-figure amphora), from Vulci, Italy, ca. 540–530 BCE. Amphora 2' high; detail 8½" high. Musei Vaticani, Rome. ◼◣

The dramatic tension, coordination of figural poses and vase shape, and intricacy of the engraved patterns of the cloaks are hallmarks of Exekias, the greatest master of black-figure painting.

1 in.

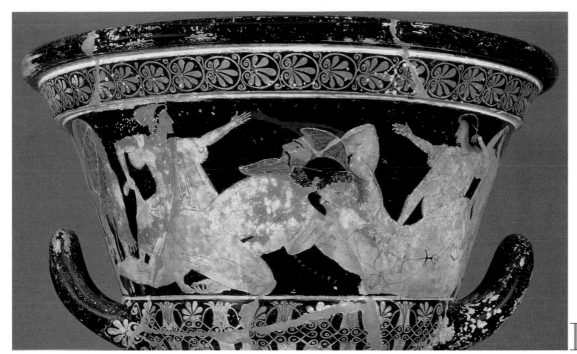

2-25 Euphronios, Herakles wrestling Antaios (detail of a red-figure calyx krater), from Cerveteri, Italy, ca. 510 BCE. Krater 1' 7" high; detail 7¾" high. Musée du Louvre, Paris.

The early red-figure master Euphronios rejected the age-old composite view for painted figures and instead attempted to reproduce the way the human body appears from a specific viewpoint.

1 in.

that his figures occupy space. He deliberately rejected the conventional composite posture for the human figure and attempted to reproduce how a particular human body is *seen*. He presented, for example, not only Antaios's torso but also his right thigh from the front. The lower leg disappears behind the giant, and only part of the right foot is visible. The viewer must mentally make the connection between the upper leg and the foot. Euphronios's panel is a window onto a mythological world with protagonists moving in three-dimensional space—a revolutionary new conception of what a picture is supposed to be.

Euthymides A preoccupation with the art of drawing per se is evident in a remarkable amphora (FIG. **2-26**) painted by EUTHYMIDES, a rival of Euphronios's. The subject is appropriate for a wine storage jar—three tipsy revelers. But the theme was little more than an excuse for the artist to experiment with the representation of unusual positions of the human form. It is no coincidence that the bodies do not overlap, for each is an independent figure study. Euthymides cast aside the conventional frontal and profile composite views. Instead, he painted torsos that are not two-dimensional surface patterns but are *foreshortened*, that is, drawn in a three-quarter view. Most noteworthy is the central figure, shown from the rear with a twisting spinal column and buttocks in three-quarter view. Earlier artists had no interest in attempting to depict figures seen from behind or at an angle because those postures not only are incomplete but also do not show the "main" side of the human body. For Euthymides, however, the challenge of drawing figures seen from unusual viewpoints was a reward in itself. With understandable pride he proclaimed his achievement by adding to the formulaic signature "Euthymides painted me" the phrase "as never Euphronios [could do!]"

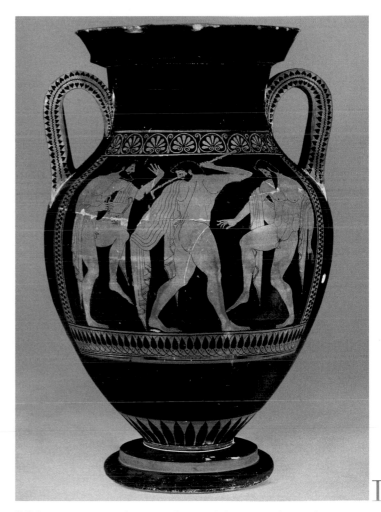

1 in.

2-26 EUTHYMIDES, Three revelers (red-figure amphora), from Vulci, Italy, ca. 510 BCE. 2' high. Staatliche Antikensammlungen, Munich. ◼◀

Euthymides chose this theme as an excuse to represent bodies in unusual positions, including a foreshortened three-quarter rear view. He claimed to have surpassed Euphronios as a draftsman.

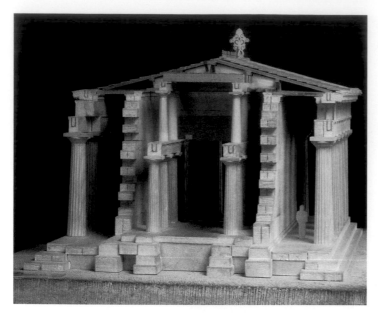

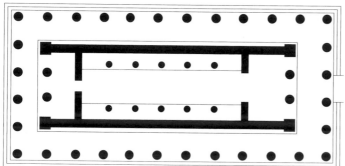

2-27 Model showing internal elevation (*top*) and plan (*bottom*) of the Temple of Aphaia, Aegina, Greece, ca. 500–490 BCE. Model: Glyptothek, Munich.

In this refined Doric design, the columns are more slender and widely spaced, there are only six columns on the facade, and the cella has two colonnades, each of two stories, framing the cult statue.

Temple of Aphaia, Aegina The years just before and after 500 BCE were also a time of dynamic transition in architecture and architectural sculpture. The key monument is the temple (FIG. **2-27**) dedicated to Aphaia, a local nymph, at Aegina. The colonnade consists of six Doric columns on the facade and 12 on the flanks, resulting in a much more compact structure than the impressive but ungainly Archaic temple (FIGS. 2-21 and 2-22) at Paestum, even though the ratio of width to length is similar. Doric architects had learned a great deal in the half-century that elapsed between construction of the two temples. The columns of the Aegina temple are more widely spaced and more slender. The capitals create a smooth transition from the vertical shafts below to the horizontal architrave above. Gone are the Archaic flattened echinuses and bulging shafts of the Paestum columns. The Aegina architect also refined the internal elevation and plan. In place of a single row of columns down the cella's center is a double colonnade—and each row has two stories. This arrangement enabled a statue to be placed on the central axis and also gave those gathered in front of the building an unobstructed view through the pair of columns in the pronaos.

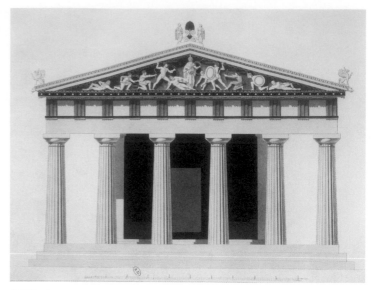

2-28 GUILLAUME-ABEL BLOUET, restored view (1828) of the facade of the Temple of Aphaia, Aegina, Greece, ca. 500–490 BCE.

The Aegina sculptors solved the problem of placing figures in a triangular pediment by using the whole range of body postures from upright to leaning, falling, kneeling, and lying. Only Athena is larger than the rest.

Painted life-size statuary filled the Aegina temple's pediments (FIG. **2-28**). Both depicted the same subject and had similar compositions. The theme was the war between the Greeks and Trojans. Athena stands at the center. She is larger than all the other figures because she is superhuman, but all the mortal heroes are the same size, regardless of their position in the pediment. Unlike the experimental design at Corfu (FIG. 2-23), the Aegina pediments feature a unified theme and consistent scale. The designer achieved the latter by using the whole range of body postures from upright (Athena) to leaning, falling, kneeling, and lying (Greeks and Trojans).

The sculptures of the west pediment were set in place upon completion of the building around 490 BCE. The eastern statues are a decade or two later. It is instructive to compare the earlier and later figures. The sculptor of the west pediment's dying warrior (FIG. **2-29**) still conceived the statue in the Archaic mode. The warrior's torso is rigidly frontal, and he looks out directly at the spectator—and smiles, despite the bronze arrow puncturing his chest. He resembles a mannequin in a store window whose arms and legs have been arranged by someone else for effective display. The comparable figure (FIG. **2-30**) in the east pediment is radically different. This warrior's posture is more natural and more complex, with the torso placed at an angle to the viewer (compare FIG. 2-25). Moreover, the man reacts to his wound. He knows death is inevitable, but still struggles to rise once again, using his shield for support. He does not look out at the viewer. This dying warrior is concerned with his plight, not with the viewer. The two statues belong to different eras. The eastern warrior is not a creation of the Archaic world, when sculptors imposed anatomical patterns (and smiles) on

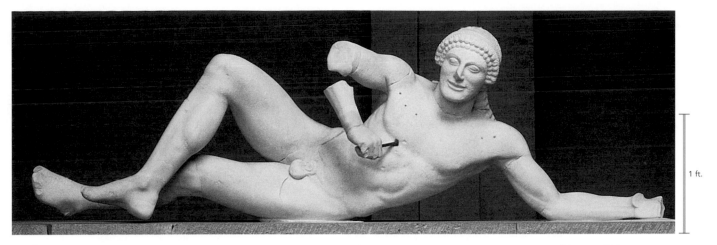

2-29 Dying warrior, from the west pediment of the Temple of Aphaia, Aegina, Greece, ca. 490 BCE. Marble, 5′ 2½″ long. Glyptothek, Munich.

Sculptors installed the two sets of Aegina pediment statues 10 to 20 years apart. The earlier statues exhibit Archaic features. This fallen warrior still has a rigidly frontal torso and an Archaic smile.

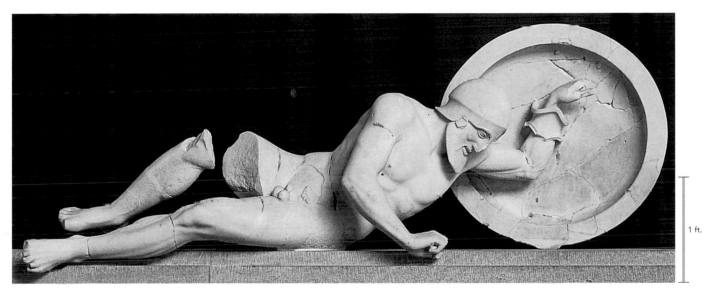

2-30 Dying warrior, from the east pediment of the Temple of Aphaia, Aegina, Greece, ca. 480 BCE. Marble, 6′ 1″ long. Glyptothek, Munich.

This later dying warrior already belongs to the Classical era. His posture is more natural, and he exhibits a new self-consciousness. Concerned with his own pain, he does not face the viewer.

statues from without. This statue belongs to the Classical world, where statues move as humans move and possess the self-consciousness of real men and women. This constitutes a radical change in the conception of the nature of statuary. In sculpture, as in painting, the Classical revolution had occurred.

Early and High Classical Art

Art historians mark the beginning of the *Classical** age from a historical event: the defeat of the Persian invaders of Greece by the allied Hellenic city-states. Shortly after the sack of Athens in 480 BCE, the Greeks won a decisive naval victory over the Persians at Salamis. It had been a difficult war, and at times it appeared Asia would swallow up Greece and the Persian king Xerxes (see Chapter 1) would rule over all. The narrow escape of the Greeks from domination by Asian "barbarians" nurtured a sense of Hellenic identity so strong that from then on European civilization would be distinct from Asian civilization. Historians universally consider the decades following the removal of the Persian threat as the high point of Greek civilization. This is the era of the dramatists Aeschylus, Sophocles, and Euripides, as well as Herodotus, the "father of history," the statesman Pericles, the philosopher Socrates, and many of the most famous Greek architects, sculptors, and painters.

---

* In *Art through the Ages*, the adjective *Classical*, with uppercase *C*, refers specifically to the Classical period of ancient Greece, 480–323 BCE. Lowercase *classical* refers to Greco-Roman antiquity in general, that is, the period treated in Chapters 2 and 3.

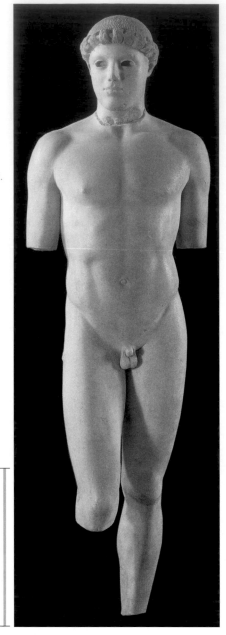

2-31 *Kritios Boy,* from the Acropolis, Athens, Greece, ca. 480 BCE. Marble, 3' 10" high. Acropolis Museum, Athens.

This is the first statue to show how a person naturally stands. The sculptor depicted the weight shift from one leg to the other (contrapposto). The head also turns slightly—and the Archaic smile is gone.

1 ft.

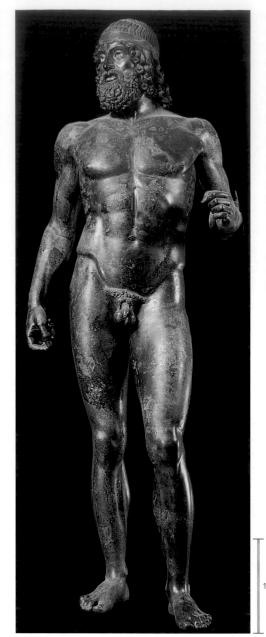

2-32 Warrior, from the sea off Riace, Italy, ca. 460–450 BCE. Bronze, 6' 6" high. Museo Archeologico Nazionale, Reggio Calabria.

One of the few surviving Classical bronze statues, the Riace warrior has inlaid eyes, silver teeth and eyelashes, and copper lips and nipples. The sculptor cast the various body parts in individual molds.

1 ft.

Kritios Boy The sculptures of the Early Classical period (ca. 480–450 BCE) display a seriousness that contrasts sharply with the smiling figures of the Archaic period. But a more fundamental and significant break from the Archaic style was the abandonment of the rigid and unnatural Egyptian-inspired pose of Archaic statuary, as in the marble statue known as the *Kritios Boy* (FIG. **2-31**)—because art historians once thought it was the work of the sculptor Kritios. Never before had a sculptor been concerned with portraying how a human being (as opposed to a stone image) truly stands. Real people do not stand in the stiff-legged pose of the kouroi and korai or their Egyptian predecessors. Humans shift their weight and the position of the torso around the vertical (but flexible) axis of the spine. The sculptor of the *Kritios Boy* was among the first to grasp this anatomical fact and to represent it in statuary. The youth has a slight dip to the right hip, indicating the shifting of weight onto his left leg. His right leg is bent, at ease. The head also turns slightly to the right and tilts, breaking the unwrit-ten rule of frontality dictating the form of virtually all earlier statues. This weight shift, called *contrapposto* (counterbalance), separates Classical from Archaic Greek statuary.

Riace Warrior An unknown sculptor carried the innovations of the *Kritios Boy* even further in the bronze statue (FIG. **2-32**) of a warrior found in the sea near Riace, Italy. It is one of a pair of nearly perfectly preserved statues discovered in a ship that sank in antiquity on its way from Greece probably to Rome. The statue lacks only its shield, spear, and helmet. It is a masterpiece of hollow-casting (see "Hollow-Casting Life-Size Bronze Statues," page 67, and FIG. **2-33**), with inlaid eyes, silver teeth and eyelashes, and copper lips and nipples. The weight shift is more pronounced than in the *Kritios Boy.* The warrior's head turns more forcefully to the right, his shoulders tilt, his hips swing more markedly, and his arms have been freed from the body. Natural motion in space has replaced Archaic frontality and rigidity.

Hollow-Casting Life-Size Bronze Statues

Monumental bronze statues such as the Riace warrior (FIG. 2-32) could not be manufactured using a single simple mold, as could small-scale figures. Weight, cost, and the tendency of large masses of bronze to distort when cooling made life-size castings in solid bronze impractical. Instead, the Greeks hollow-cast large statues by the *cire perdue* (lost-wax) method. The process entailed several steps and had to be repeated many times because bronze workers typically cast monumental statues such as the Riace warrior (FIG. 2-32) in parts—head, arms, hands, torso, and so forth.

First, the sculptor fashioned a full-size clay model of the intended statue. Then an assistant formed a clay master mold around the model and removed the mold in sections. When dry, the various pieces of the master mold were reassembled for each separate body part. Next, assistants applied a layer of beeswax to the inside of each mold. When the wax cooled, the sculptor removed the mold, revealing a hollow wax model in the shape of the original clay model. The artist could then correct or refine details—for example, engrave fingernails on the wax hands, or individual locks of hair on the head.

In the next stage, an assistant applied a final clay mold (*investment*) to the exterior of the wax model, and poured liquid clay inside the model. Apprentices then hammered metal pins (*chaplets*) through the new mold to connect the investment with the clay core (FIG. 2-33a). Next, the wax was melted out ("lost") and molten bronze poured into the mold in its place (FIG. 2-33b). When the bronze hardened and assumed the shape of the wax model, the sculptor removed the investment and as much of the core as possible. The last step was to fit together and solder the individually cast pieces, smooth the joins and any surface imperfections, inlay the eyes, and add teeth, eyelashes, and accessories such as spears and wreaths.

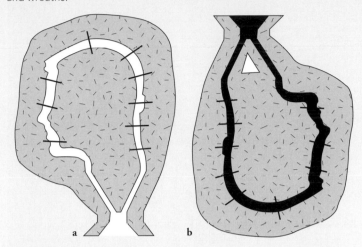

2-33 Two stages of the lost-wax method of bronze-casting (after Sean A. Hemingway).

Drawing **a** shows a clay mold (investment), wax model, and clay core connected by chaplets. Drawing **b** shows the wax melted out and the molten bronze poured into the mold to form the cast bronze head.

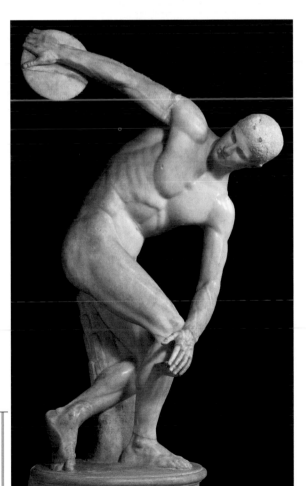

2-34 MYRON, *Diskobolos* (*Discus Thrower*). Roman copy of a bronze statue of ca. 450 BCE. Marble, 5′ 1″ high. Museo Nazionale Romano—Palazzo Massimo, Rome.

This marble copy of Myron's lost bronze statue captures how the sculptor froze the action of discus throwing and arranged the nude athlete's body and limbs so they form two intersecting arcs.

1 ft.

Myron, *Diskobolos* The *Kritios Boy* and the Riace warrior are at rest, but Early Classical Greek sculptors also explored the problem of representing figures engaged in vigorous action. The famous *Diskobolos* (*Discus Thrower*) by MYRON (FIG. **2-34**), with its arms boldly extended, body twisted, and right heel raised off the ground, is such a statue. Nothing comparable survives from the Archaic period. The pose suggests the motion of a pendulum clock. The athlete's right arm has reached the apex of its arc but has not yet begun to swing down again. Myron froze the action and arranged the body and limbs to form two intersecting arcs, creating the impression of a tightly stretched bow a moment before the archer releases the string.

The illustrated marble statue, however, is not Myron's, which was bronze. It is a copy made in Roman times. Roman demand so far exceeded the supply of famous Greek statues that a veritable industry was born to meet the call for copies to display in public places and private villas alike. Usually, the copies were of less costly painted marble, which presented a different appearance than shiny bronze. In most cases, the copyist also had to add an intrusive tree trunk to support the great weight of the stone statue and place struts between arms and body to strengthen weak points. The copies rarely approach the quality of the originals, but they are indispensable today. Without them it would be impossible to reconstruct the history of Greek sculpture after the Archaic period.

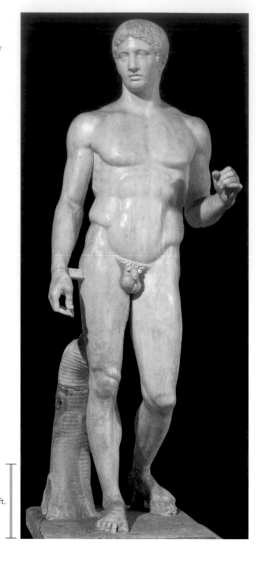

2-35 POLYKLEITOS, *Doryphoros* (*Spear Bearer*). Roman copy from the palaestra, Pompeii, Italy, of a bronze statue of ca. 450–440 BCE. Marble, 6′ 11″ high. Museo Archeologico Nazionale, Naples. ▪◀

Polykleitos sought to portray the perfect man and to impose order on human movement. He achieved his goals through harmonic proportions and a system of cross balance for all parts of the body.

1 ft.

Polykleitos, *Doryphoros* One of the most frequently copied Greek statues was the *Doryphoros* (FIG. **2-35**) or *Spear Bearer* by POLYKLEITOS, a work that epitomizes the intellectual rigor of High Classical (ca. 450–400 BCE) statuary design. The *Doryphoros* is the culmination of the evolution in Greek statuary from the Archaic kouros to the *Kritios Boy* to the Riace warrior. The contrapposto is more pronounced than ever before in a standing statue, but Polykleitos was not content with simply rendering a figure that stands naturally. His aim was to impose order on human movement, to make it "beautiful," to "perfect" it. He achieved this through a system of cross balance of the figure's various parts. Note, for instance, how the straight-hanging arm echoes the rigid supporting leg, providing the figure's right side with the columnar stability needed to anchor the left side's dynamically flexed limbs. The tensed and relaxed limbs oppose each other diagonally. The right arm and the left leg are relaxed, and the tensed supporting leg opposes the flexed arm, which held a spear. In like manner, the head turns to the right while the hips twist slightly to the left. And although the *Doryphoros* seems to take a step forward, he does not move. This dynamic asymmetrical balance, this motion while at rest, and the resulting harmony of opposites are the essence of the Polykleitan style.

Polykleitos made the *Doryphoros* as a demonstration piece to accompany his treatise on the ideal statue of a nude man. *Spear Bearer* is but a modern descriptive name for the work. The title the artist assigned to the statue was *Canon*. Polykleitos was greatly influenced by the philosopher Pythagoras of Samos, who lived during the latter part of the sixth century BCE. A famous geometric theorem still bears his name. Pythagoras also discovered that harmonic chords in music are produced on the strings of a lyre at regular intervals that may be expressed as ratios of whole numbers—2:1, 3:2, 4:3. He and his followers, the Pythagoreans, believed more generally that underlying harmonic proportions could be found in all of nature, determining the form of the cosmos as well as of things on earth, and that beauty resided in harmonious numerical ratios. By this reasoning, a perfect statue would be one constructed according to an all-encompassing mathematical formula. That is what Polykleitos achieved in his *Doryphoros*—as did Iktinos in his design for the Parthenon (FIG. 2-1). Galen, a physician who lived during the second century CE, summarized Polykleitos's philosophy as follows:

> [Beauty arises from] the commensurability [*symmetria*] of the parts, such as that of finger to finger, and of all the fingers to the palm and the wrist, and of these to the forearm, and of the forearm to the upper arm, and, in fact, of everything to everything else, just as it is written in the *Canon* of Polykleitos. . . . Polykleitos supported his treatise [by making] a statue according to the tenets of his treatise, and called the statue, like the work, the *Canon*.[1]

This is why Pliny the Elder, writing in the first century CE, maintained that Polykleitos "alone of men is deemed to have rendered art itself [that is, the theoretical basis of art] in a work of art."[2]

Athenian Acropolis While Polykleitos was working out his prescription for the perfect statue, the Athenians, under the leadership of Pericles, initiated one of the most ambitious building projects ever undertaken—the reconstruction of the Acropolis (*acropolis* means "high city") after the Persian sack. In 478 BCE, in the aftermath of the Persian defeat, the Greeks formed an alliance for mutual protection against any renewed threat from the East. The new confederacy came to be known as the Delian League because its headquarters were on the Cycladic island of Delos. Although at the outset each league member had an equal vote, Athens was "first among equals," providing the allied fleet commander and determining which cities were to furnish ships and which were instead to pay an annual tribute to the treasury at Delos. Continued fighting against the Persians kept the alliance intact, but Athens gradually assumed a dominant role. In 454 BCE, the league transferred the Delian treasury to Athens, ostensibly for security reasons. Tribute continued to be paid, but Pericles did not expend the surplus reserves for the common good of the allied Greek states. Instead, he expropriated the funds to resurrect the Acropolis (FIG. **2-36**). Thus, the Periclean building program was not the glorious fruit of Athenian democracy, as commonly thought, but the

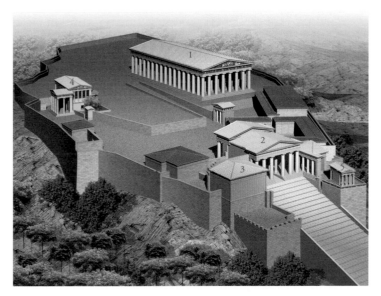

2-36 Restored view of the Acropolis, Athens, Greece (John Burge). (1) Parthenon, (2) Propylaia, (3) Erechtheion, (4) Temple of Athena Nike.

Under Pericles, the Athenians undertook one of history's most ambitious building projects—the reconstruction of the Acropolis after the Persian sack. The funds came from the Delian League treasury.

by-product of tyranny and the abuse of power. Too often art and architectural historians do not ask how a monument was financed. The answer can be very revealing.

The centerpiece of the Periclean Acropolis was the Parthenon (FIGS. 2-1 and 2-36, no. 1), erected in the remarkably short period between 447 and 438 BCE. (Work on the temple's ambitious sculptural ornamentation continued until 432 BCE.) In 437 BCE, construction commenced on a grand new gateway to the Acropolis, the Propylaia (FIG. 2-36, no. 2). Two later temples, the Erechtheion (FIG. 2-36, no. 3) and the Temple of Athena Nike (FIG. 2-36, no. 4), built after Pericles died, were probably also part of the original project.

Parthenon: Architecture Most of the peripteral colonnade of the Parthenon (FIG. 2-1) still stands (or has been reerected), and art historians know a great deal about the building and its sculptural program. The architect was Iktinos, assisted, according to some sources, by KALLIKRATES. The statue of Athena in the cella (page 47, *top*) was the work of Phidias, who was also the overseer of the temple's sculptural decoration. In fact, Plutarch stated Phidias was in charge of the entire Periclean building program. Just as the contemporaneous *Doryphoros* may be seen as the culmination of nearly two centuries of searching for the ideal proportions of the human body, so, too, the Parthenon may be viewed as the ideal solution to the Greek architect's quest for perfect proportions in Doric temple design (see "The Perfect Temple," page 47). The Parthenon architects and Polykleitos were kindred spirits in their belief that strict adherence to harmonious numerical ratios resulted in beautiful proportions. For the Parthenon, the controlling ratio for the *symmetria* of the parts may be expressed algebraically as $x = 2y + 1$. Thus, for example, the temple's plan (FIG. **2-37**) called for 8 columns on the short ends and 17 on the long sides because $17 = (2 \times 8) + 1$. The stylobate's ratio of length to width is 9:4, because $9 = (2 \times 4) + 1$.

The Parthenon's harmonious design and the mathematical precision of the sizes of its constituent elements obscure the fact that throughout the building are pronounced deviations from the strictly horizontal and vertical lines assumed to be the basis of all Greek temples. The stylobate, for example, curves upward at the center on all four sides, forming a kind of shallow dome, and this curvature carries up into the entablature. Moreover, the peristyle columns lean inward slightly. Those at the corners have a diagonal inclination and are also about two inches thicker than the rest. If their lines continued, they would meet about 1.5 miles above the temple. These deviations from the norm meant virtually every Parthenon block had to be carved according to the special

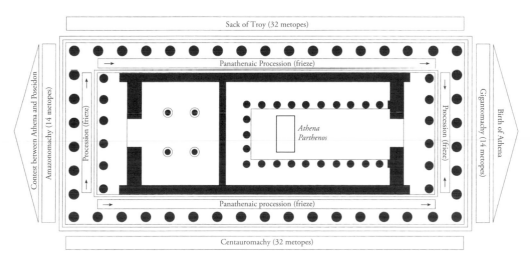

2-37 Plan of the Parthenon, Acropolis, Athens, Greece, with diagram of the sculptural program (after Andrew Stewart), 447–432 BCE.

The Parthenon was lavishly decorated. Statues filled both pediments, and reliefs adorned all 92 Doric metopes as well as the 524-foot Ionic frieze. In the cella was Phidias's colossal gold-and-ivory Athena.

set of specifications dictated by its unique place in the structure. Vitruvius, a Roman architect of the late first century BCE, explained these adjustments as compensations for optical illusions. Vitruvius noted, for example, that if a stylobate is laid out on a level surface, it will appear to sag at the center. He also recommended that the corner columns of a building should be thicker because they are surrounded by light and would otherwise appear thinner than their neighbors.

One of the ironies of the Parthenon, the world's most famous Doric temple, is that it is "contaminated" by Ionic elements. Although the cella (FIG. 2-37) had a two-story Doric colonnade, the back room (which housed the goddess's treasury and the tribute collected from the Delian League) had four tall and slender Ionic columns as sole supports for the superstructure. And whereas the temple's exterior had a Doric frieze, the inner frieze running around the top of the cella wall was Ionic. Perhaps this fusion of Doric and Ionic elements reflected the Athenians' belief that the Ionians of the Cycladic Islands and Asia Minor were descendants of Athenian settlers and were therefore their kin. Or it may be Pericles's and Iktinos's way of suggesting Athens was the leader of *all* the Greeks. In any case, a mix of Doric and Ionic features characterizes the fifth-century buildings of the Acropolis as a whole.

Athena Parthenos The Parthenon was more lavishly decorated than any Greek temple before it, Doric or Ionic. Every one of the 92 Doric metopes was decorated with relief sculpture (FIG. 2-37). So, too, was entire length of the 524-foot Ionic frieze. Dozens of larger-than-life-size statues filled both pediments. And inside was the most expensive item of all—Phidias's gold-and-ivory 38-foot-tall *chryselephantine Athena Parthenos* (page 47, *top*). Fully armed, the goddess held Nike (the winged female personification of victory) in her extended right hand. No one doubts this Nike referred to the victory of 479 BCE. The memory of the Persian sack of the Acropolis was still vivid, and the Athenians were intensely conscious that, by driving back the Persians, they were saving their civilization from the "barbarians" who had committed atrocities against the Greeks of Asia Minor. In fact, the *Athena Parthenos* incorporated multiple allusions to the Persian defeat. On the thick soles of Athena's sandals was a representation of a *centauromachy* and emblazoned on the exterior of her shield were high reliefs depicting the battle of Greeks and Amazons (*Amazonomachy*), in which Theseus drove the Amazons (female warriors) out of Athens. On the shield's interior, Phidias painted a gigantomachy. Each of these mythological contests was a metaphor for the triumph of order over chaos, of civilization over barbarism, and of Athens over Persia.

Parthenon: Metopes Phidias took up these same themes again in the Parthenon's metopes (FIG. 2-37). The south metopes, for example, depicted the battle of Lapiths and centaurs, a combat in which Theseus of Athens played a major role. On one extraordinary slab (FIG. **2-38**), a triumphant centaur rises up on its hind legs, exulting over the crum-

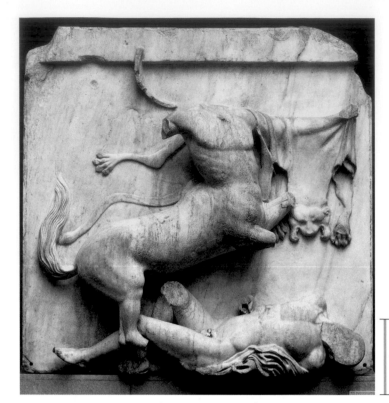

2-38 *Centauromachy,* metope from the south frieze of the Parthenon, Acropolis, Athens, Greece, ca. 447–438 BCE. Marble, 4′ 8″ high. British Museum, London. ◼◁

The Parthenon's centauromachy metopes allude to the Greek defeat of the Persians. Here, the High Classical sculptor brilliantly distinguished the vibrant living centaur from the lifeless Greek corpse.

pled body of the Greek it has defeated. The relief is so high that parts are fully in the round. Some have broken off. The sculptor brilliantly distinguished the vibrant, powerful form of the living beast from the lifeless corpse on the ground. In other metopes the Greeks have the upper hand, but the full set suggests that the battle was a difficult one against a dangerous enemy and that losses as well as victories occurred. The same was true of the war against the Persians.

Parthenon: Pediments The subjects of the two pediments were especially appropriate for a temple celebrating Athena—and the Athenians. The east pediment depicted the birth of the goddess. At the west was the contest between Athena and Poseidon to determine which one would become the city's patron deity. Athena won, giving her name to the city and its people. It is significant that in the story and in the pediment the Athenians are the judges of the relative merits of the two gods. This reflects the same arrogance that led to the use of Delian League funds to adorn the Acropolis.

All that remains of the east pediment's statues are the spectators to the left and the right who witnessed Athena's birth on Mount Olympus. At the far left are the head and arms of Helios (the sun) and his chariot horses rising from the pediment floor (FIG. 2-39). Next to them is a powerful male figure usually identified as Dionysos or possibly Herakles,

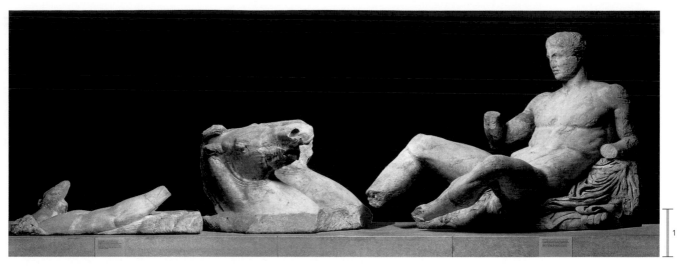

1 ft.

2-39 Helios and his horses, and Dionysos (Herakles?), from the east pediment of the Parthenon, Acropolis, Athens, Greece, ca. 438–432 BCE. Marble, greatest height 4′ 3″. British Museum, London.

The east pediment of the Parthenon depicts the birth of Athena. At the left, Helios and his horses energetically emerge from the pediment's floor, suggesting the sun rising above the horizon at dawn.

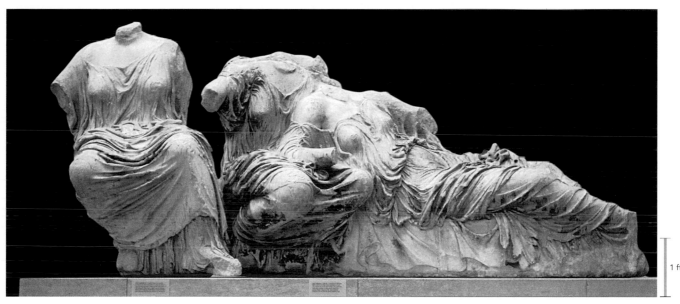

1 ft.

2-40 Three goddesses (Hestia, Dione, and Aphrodite?), from the east pediment of the Parthenon, Acropolis, Athens, Greece, ca. 438–432 BCE. Marble, greatest height 4′ 5″. British Museum, London.

These statues representing three goddesses conform perfectly to the sloping right side of the Parthenon's east pediment. The thin and heavy folds of the garments alternately reveal and conceal the body forms.

who entered the realm of the gods after he completed 12 impossible labors. At the right (FIG. **2-40**) are three goddesses, probably Hestia, Dione, and Aphrodite, and either Selene (Moon) or Nyx (Night) and more horses, this time sinking below the pediment's floor. Here, Phidias discovered an entirely new way to deal with the awkward triangular frame of the pediment. Its floor is the horizon line, and charioteers and their horses move through it effortlessly.

Phidias and his assistants were master sculptors. They fully understood not only the surface appearance of human anatomy, both male and female, but also the mechanics of how muscles and bones make the body move. They mastered the rendition of clothed forms as well. In the Dione-Aphrodite group (FIG. **2-40**), the thin and heavy folds of the garments alternately reveal and conceal the main and lesser body masses while swirling in a compositional tide that subtly unifies the figures. The articulation and integration of the bodies produce a wonderful variation of surface and play of light and shade. Moreover, all the figures, even the animals, are brilliantly characterized. The horses of the sun, at the beginning of the day, are energetic. Those of the moon or night, having labored until dawn, are weary.

2-41 Two details of the Panathenaic Festival procession frieze, from the Parthenon, Acropolis, Athens, Greece, ca. 447–438 BCE. Marble, 3′ 6″ high. *Top:* horsemen (north frieze), British Museum, London. *Bottom:* elders and maidens (east frieze), Musée du Louvre, Paris. ◀

The Parthenon's Ionic frieze represents the festival procession of citizens on horseback and on foot that took place every four years. The temple celebrated the Athenians as much as the goddess Athena.

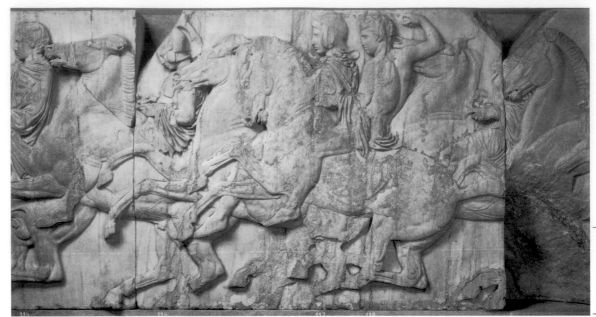

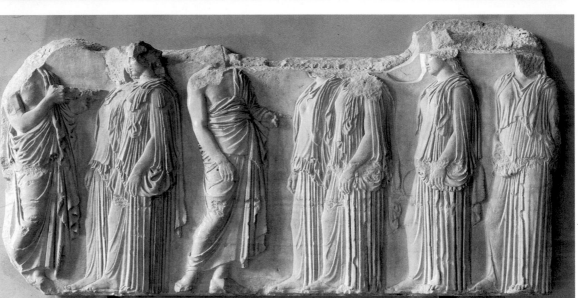

Parthenon: Ionic Frieze In many ways the most remarkable part of the Parthenon's sculptural program is the inner Ionic frieze (FIG. **2-41**). Scholars still debate its subject, but most agree it represents the Panathenaic Festival procession that took place every four years in Athens. The procession began at the Dipylon Gate to the city and ended on the Acropolis, where the Athenians placed a new peplos on an ancient wooden statue of Athena. That statue (probably similar in general appearance to the *Lady of Auxerre,* FIG. 2-15) had been housed in the Archaic temple the Persians razed, but the Athenians removed it on the eve of the Persian attack. On the Parthenon frieze, the procession begins on the west, that is, at the temple's rear, the side facing the gateway to the Acropolis. It then moves in parallel lines down the long north and south sides of the building and ends at the center of the east frieze, over the doorway to the cella housing Phidias's statue (FIG. 2-37). The upper part of the frieze is in higher relief than the lower part so that the more distant and more shaded upper zone is as legible from the ground as

the lower part of the frieze. This is another instance of taking optical effects into consideration.

The frieze vividly communicates the procession's acceleration and deceleration. At the outset, on the west side, marshals gather and youths mount their horses. On the north (FIG. 2-41, *top*) and south, the momentum of the cavalcade picks up. On the east, the procession slows to a halt (FIG. 2-41, *bottom*) in the presence of seated gods and goddesses, the invited guests. The role assigned to the Olympian deities is extraordinary. They do not take part in the festival or determine its outcome but are merely spectators. They watch the Athenian people, the new masters of a new Aegean empire who considered themselves worthy of depiction on a temple. The Parthenon celebrated the greatness of Athens and the Athenians as much as it honored Athena.

Erechtheion In 421 BCE, work finally began on the temple that was to replace the Archaic Athena temple the Persians had destroyed. The new structure, the Erechtheion

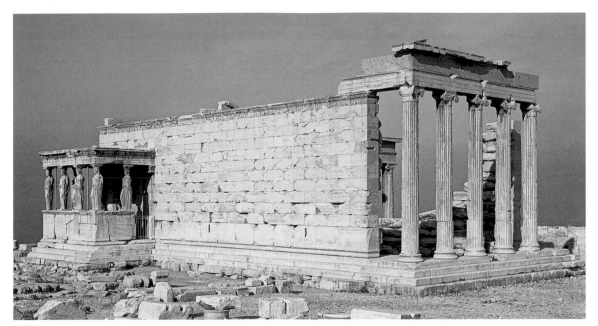

2-42 Erechtheion (looking northwest), Acropolis, Athens, Greece, ca. 421–405 BCE.

The asymmetrical form of the Erechtheion is unique for a Greek temple. It reflects the need to incorporate preexisting shrines into the plan. The decorative details are perhaps the finest in Greek architecture.

(FIG. **2-42**), built to the north of the old temple's remains, was to be a multiple shrine, however. It honored Athena and became the new home of the ancient wooden image of the goddess that was the goal of the Panathenaic Festival procession. But it also incorporated shrines to a host of other gods and demigods who loomed large in the city's legendary past. Among these were Erechtheus, an early king of Athens, during whose reign the Athena idol fell from the heavens, and Kekrops, another king of Athens, who served as judge of the contest between Athena and Poseidon. In fact, the site chosen for the new temple was the very spot where that contest occurred. Poseidon had staked his claim to Athens by striking the Acropolis rock with his trident and producing a salt-water spring. Athena had miraculously caused an olive tree to grow.

The asymmetrical plan of the Ionic Erechtheion is unique for a Greek temple and the antithesis of the simple and harmoniously balanced plan of the Doric Parthenon across the way. Its irregular form reflected the need to incorporate the tomb of Kekrops and other preexisting shrines, the trident mark, and the olive tree into a single complex. The unknown architect responsible for the building also had to struggle with the problem of uneven terrain. The area could not be made level by terracing because that would disturb the sacred sites. As a result, the Erechtheion has four sides of very different character, and each side also rests on a different ground level.

Perhaps to compensate for the awkward character of the building as a whole, the architect took great care with the Erechtheion's decorative details. The Ionic capitals were inlaid with gold, rock crystal, and colored glass, and the frieze received special treatment. The stone chosen was dark-blue limestone to contrast with the white marble relief figures attached to the blue frieze and the white walls and columns. The temple's most striking and famous feature is its south porch, where caryatids replaced Ionic columns. Although the cary-

atids exhibit the weight shift standard for the era, the flute-like drapery folds concealing their stiff, weight-bearing legs underscores their role as architectural supports. The figures have enough rigidity to suggest the structural column and just the degree of flexibility needed to suggest the living body.

Temple of Athena Nike Another Ionic building on the Athenian Acropolis is the small Temple of Athena Nike (FIG. **2-43**), designed by Kallikrates, who may have been responsible for the Parthenon's Ionic elements. The temple stands on what was once a Mycenaean bastion and greets

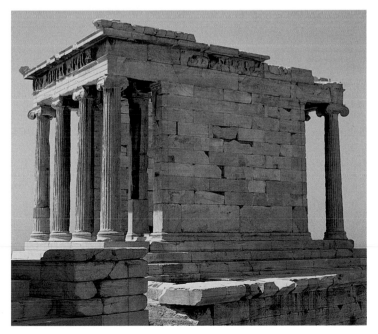

2-43 KALLIKRATES, Temple of Athena Nike (looking southwest), Acropolis, Athens, Greece, ca. 427–424 BCE.

The small Ionic temple at the entrance to the Acropolis celebrates Athena as bringer of victory, and one of the friezes depicts the Greek defeat of the Persians at Marathon.

adorned the balustrade, always in different attitudes. Sometimes she erects trophies bedecked with Persian spoils. Other times she brings forward sacrificial bulls for Athena. One relief (FIG. 2-44) shows Nike adjusting her sandal—an awkward posture rendered elegant and graceful by a sculptor who carried the style of the Parthenon pediments (FIG. 2-40) even further and created a figure whose garments cling so tightly to the body they seem almost transparent, as if drenched with water. The drapery folds form intricate linear patterns unrelated to the body's anatomical structure and have a life of their own as abstract designs.

Hegeso Stele Decorating temples was not the only job available to sculptors in fifth-century BCE Athens. Around 400 BCE, the family of a young woman named Hegeso, daughter of Proxenos, set up a grave stele (FIG. 2-45) in her memory in the Dipylon cemetery, where, centuries earlier, Athenians had marked graves with enormous vases (FIG. 2-14). Hegeso is the well-dressed woman seated on an elegant chair (with footstool). She examines a piece of jewelry (once rendered in paint, not now visible) selected from a box a servant girl brings to her. The maid's simple unbelted *chiton* contrasts sharply with the more elaborate attire of her mistress. The garments of both women reveal the body forms beneath them, as on the parapet reliefs of the Athena Nike temple. The faces are serene, without a trace of sadness. Indeed, the sculptor depicted both mistress and maid in a characteristic shared moment out of daily life. Only the epitaph reveals Hegeso is the one who has departed.

The simplicity of the scene on the Hegeso stele is deceptive, however. This is not merely a bittersweet scene of tranquil domestic life before an untimely death. The setting itself is significant—the secluded women's quarters of a Greek house, from which Hegeso rarely would have emerged. Contemporaneous grave stelae of men regularly show them in the public domain, often as warriors. The servant girl is not so much the faithful companion of the deceased in life as she is Hegeso's possession, like the jewelry box. The slave girl may look solicitously at her mistress, but Hegeso has eyes only for her ornaments. Both slave and jewelry attest to the wealth of Hegeso's father, unseen but prominently cited in the epitaph. (It is noteworthy that there is no mention of the mother's name.) Indeed, even the jewelry box carries a deeper significance, for it probably represents the dowry Proxenos would have provided to his daughter's husband when she left her father's home to enter her husband's home. In the patriarchal society of ancient Greece, the dominant position of men is manifest even when only women are depicted.

White-Ground Painting All the masterpieces of Classical painting have vanished because they were on wooden panels, but ancient authors describe them as polychrome. The anonymous artist known as the ACHILLES PAINTER was able to emulate the polychromy of monumental panels by using the *white-ground painting* technique for a *lekythos* (flask containing perfumed oil; FIG. 2-46) he painted about 440 BCE. White-

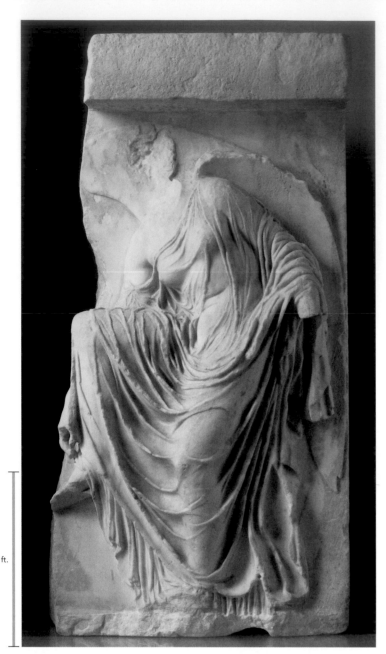

1 ft.

2-44 Nike adjusting her sandal, from the south side of the parapet of the Temple of Athena Nike, Acropolis, Athens, Greece, ca. 410 BCE. Marble, 3′ 6″ high. Acropolis Museum, Athens.

Dozens of images of winged Victory adorned the parapet on three sides of the Athena Nike temple. The sculptor carved this Nike with garments that appear almost transparent.

all visitors entering Athena's great sanctuary. Like the Parthenon, the Athena Nike temple commemorated the victory over the Persians—and not just in its name. Part of the frieze represented the battle of Marathon, which turned the tide against the Persians—a human event, as in the Parthenon's Panathenaic Festival procession frieze. But on the later temple the sculptors chronicled a specific occasion, not a recurring event involving anonymous citizens.

Around the building, at the bastion's edge, was a *parapet* decorated with exquisite reliefs. The theme matched that of the temple proper—victory. Dozens of images of Nike

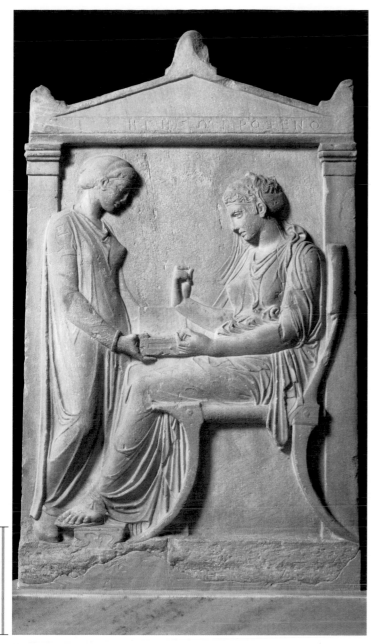

2-45 Grave stele of Hegeso, from the Dipylon cemetery, Athens, Greece, ca. 400 BCE. Marble, 5′ 2″ high. National Archaeological Museum, Athens.

On her tombstone, Hegeso examines jewelry from a box her servant girl holds. Mistress and maid share a serene moment out of daily life. Only the epitaph reveals Hegeso is the one who died.

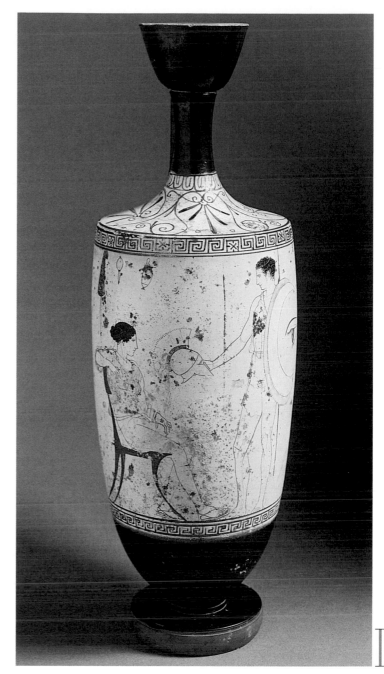

2-46 ACHILLES PAINTER, Warrior taking leave of his wife (white-ground lekythos), from Eretria, Greece, ca. 440 BCE. 1′ 5″ high. National Archaeological Museum, Athens.

White-ground painters applied the colors after firing because most colored glazes could not withstand the kiln's heat. The Achilles Painter here displayed his mastery at drawing an eye in profile. ◼◀

ground painting takes its name from the chalky-white *slip* (liquefied clay) used to provide a background for the figures. Early experiments with white-ground painting date to the late sixth century BCE, but the method became popular only toward the middle of the fifth century BCE. White-ground is essentially a variation of the red-figure technique. First, the painter covered the pot with a slip of very fine white clay, then applied black glaze to outline the figures, and diluted brown, purple, red, and white to color them. The artist could use other colors—for example, the yellow chosen for the garments of both figures on this lekythos—but these had to be applied after firing because the Greeks did not know how to

make them withstand the intense heat of the kiln. Despite the obvious attractions of the technique, the impermanence of the expanded range of colors discouraged white-ground painting on everyday vessels, such as amphoras and kraters. In fact, Greek painters explored the full polychrome possibilities of the white-ground technique almost exclusively on lekythoi, which families commonly placed in graves as offerings to the deceased. For vessels designed for short-term use, the fragile nature of white-ground painting was of little concern.

The subject of the Achilles Painter's lekythos is appropriate for its funerary purpose. A youthful warrior takes leave of his wife. The red scarf, mirror, and jug hanging on the wall behind the woman indicate the setting is the interior of their home. The motif of the seated woman is strikingly similar to that of Hegeso on her grave stele (FIG. 2-45), but here the woman is the survivor. It is her husband, preparing to go to war, who will depart, never to return. On his shield is a large painted eye, roughly life-size. Greek shields often bore decorative devices such as the horrific face of Medusa, intended to ward off evil spirits and frighten the enemy. This eye recalls this tradition, but for the Achilles Painter it was little more than an excuse to display superior drawing skills. Since the late sixth century BCE, Greek painters had abandoned the Archaic habit of placing frontal eyes on profile faces and attempted to render the eyes in profile. The Achilles Painter's mastery of this difficult problem in foreshortening is on exhibit here.

Late Classical Art

The Peloponnesian War, which began in 431 BCE, ended in 404 BCE with the complete defeat of a plague-weakened Athens. The victor, Sparta, and then Thebes undertook the leadership of Greece, both unsuccessfully. In the middle of the fourth century BCE, a threat from without caused the rival Greek states to put aside their animosities and unite for their common defense, as they had earlier against the Persians. But at the battle of Chaeronea in 338 BCE, the Greek cities suffered a devastating loss and had to relinquish their independence to the Macedonian king, Philip II (r. 359–336 BCE). After Philip's assassination, his son Alexander III, better known as Alexander the Great (r. 336–323 BCE), succeeded him. Alexander led a powerful army on an extraordinary campaign that overthrew the Persian Empire (the ultimate revenge for the Persian invasion of Greece), wrested control of Egypt, and even reached India.

The fourth century BCE was thus a time of political upheaval, which had a profound impact on the psyche of the Greeks and on the art they produced. In the fifth century BCE, Greeks had generally believed that rational human beings could impose order on their environment, create "perfect" statues such as Polykleitos's *Canon* (FIG. 2-35), and discover the "correct" mathematical formulas for constructing temples such as the Parthenon (FIG. 2-1). The Parthenon frieze (FIG. 2-41) celebrated the Athenians as a community of citizens with shared values. The Peloponnesian War and the unceasing strife of the fourth century BCE brought an end to the serene idealism of the previous century. Disillusionment and alienation followed. Greek thought and Greek art began to focus more on the individual and on the real world of appearances instead of on the community and the ideal world of perfect beings and perfect buildings.

Praxiteles The new approach to art is immediately apparent in the work of PRAXITELES, one of the great masters of the Late Classical period (ca. 400–323 BCE). Praxiteles did not

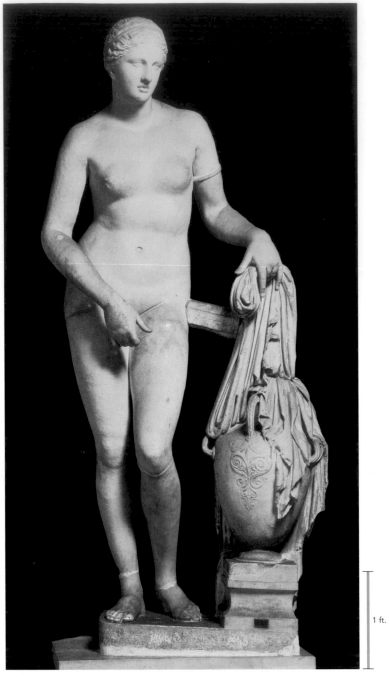

1 ft.

2-47 PRAXITELES, *Aphrodite of Knidos*. Roman copy of a marble statue of ca. 350–340 BCE. Marble, 6′ 8″ high. Musei Vaticani, Rome. ◼◂

The first nude statue of a Greek goddess caused a sensation. But Praxiteles was also famous for his ability to transform marble into soft and radiant flesh. His Aphrodite had "dewy eyes."

reject the favored sculptural themes of the High Classical period, and his Olympian gods and goddesses retained their superhuman beauty. But in his hand, the Greek deities lost some of their solemn grandeur and took on a worldly sensuousness. Nowhere is this new humanizing spirit plainer than in the statue of Aphrodite (FIG. 2-47) Praxiteles sold to the Knidians after another city had rejected it. The lost marble original is known only through copies of Roman date, but Pliny considered it "superior to all the works, not only of Praxiteles, but indeed in the whole world."[3] The statue made

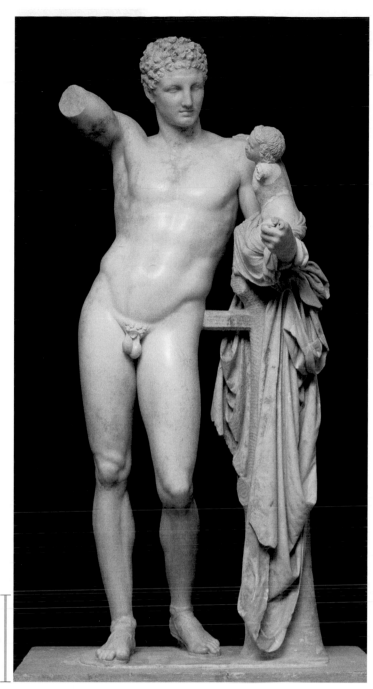

2-48 PRAXITELES, Hermes and the infant Dionysos, from the Temple of Hera, Olympia, Greece. Copy of a marble statue of ca. 340 BCE. Marble, 7′ 1″ high. Archaeological Museum, Olympia.

Praxiteles humanized the Olympian deities. This Hermes is as sensuous as his Aphrodite. The god gazes dreamily into space while he dangles a bunch of grapes as temptation for the infant wine god.

image. In fact, the goddess engages in a trivial act out of everyday life. She has removed her garment, draped it over a large *hydria* (water pitcher), and is about to step into the bath.

Although shocking in its day, the *Aphrodite of Knidos* is not openly erotic (the goddess modestly shields her pelvis with her right hand), but she is quite sensuous. Lucian, writing in the second century CE, noted that she had a "welcoming look," a "slight smile," and "dewy eyes,"[4] and that Praxiteles was renowned for his ability to transform marble into soft and radiant flesh.

Unfortunately, the rather mechanical Roman copies do not capture the quality of Praxiteles's modeling of the stone, but the statue of Hermes and the infant Dionysos (FIG. **2-48**) found in the Temple of Hera at Olympia provides a good idea of the "look" of the *Aphrodite of Knidos*. Once thought to be by the hand of the master himself but now generally considered a copy of the highest quality, the statue depicts Hermes resting in a forest during his journey to deliver Dionysos to Papposilenos and the nymphs, who assumed responsibility for raising the child. Hermes leans on a tree trunk (here it is an integral part of the composition and not the copyist's addition), and his slender body forms a sinuous, shallow S-curve that is the hallmark of many of Praxiteles's statues. He gazes dreamily into space while he dangles a bunch of grapes (now missing) as a temptation for the infant who is to become the Greek god of the vine. This is the kind of tender and very human interaction between an adult and a child that one encounters frequently in real life but that had been absent from Greek statuary before the fourth century BCE.

The quality of the carving is superb. The modeling is deliberately smooth and subtle, producing soft shadows that follow the planes as they flow almost imperceptibly one into another. The delicacy of the marble facial features stands in sharp contrast to the metallic precision of Polykleitos's bronze *Doryphoros* (FIG. 2-35). The High Classical sculptor even subjected the *Spear Bearer*'s locks of hair to the laws of symmetry, and the hair does not violate the skull's perfect curve. The comparison of these two statues reveals the sweeping change in artistic attitude and intent that took place from the fifth to the fourth century BCE. In the statues of Praxiteles, the Olympian deities still possess a beauty mortals can aspire to, although not achieve, but they are no longer aloof. Praxiteles's gods have stepped off their pedestals and entered the world of human experience.

Lysippos As renowned in his day as Praxiteles was LYSIPPOS, whom Alexander the Great selected to create his official portrait. (Alexander could afford to employ the best. His father, Philip II, hired the leading thinker of his age, Aristotle, as the young Alexander's tutor.) Lysippos introduced a new canon of proportions in which the bodies were more slender than those of Polykleitos and the heads roughly one-eighth the height of the body rather than one-seventh, as in the previous century. One of Lysippos's most famous works, *Apoxyomenos,* a bronze statue of an athlete scraping oil from his body after exercising—known, as usual, only from

Knidos famous, and Pliny reported that many people sailed there just to see it. The *Aphrodite of Knidos* caused such a sensation in its time because Praxiteles took the unprecedented step of representing the goddess of love undressed. Female nudity had been rare in earlier Greek art and confined almost exclusively to paintings on vases designed for household use. The women so depicted also were usually not noblewomen or goddesses but courtesans or slave girls, and no one had ever dared fashion a life-size statue of an undressed goddess. Moreover, Praxiteles's Aphrodite is not a cold and remote

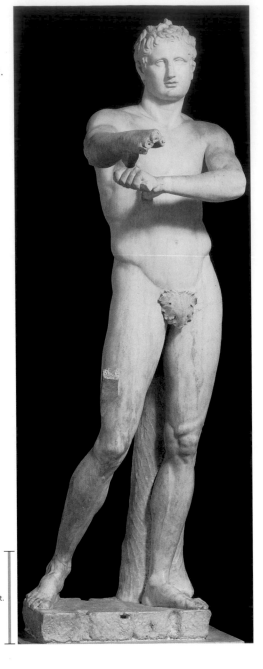

2-49 LYSIPPOS, *Apoxyomenos* (*Scraper*). Roman copy of a bronze statue of ca. 330 BCE. Marble, 6′ 9″ high. Musei Vaticani, Rome. ◼◂

Lysippos introduced a new canon of proportions and a nervous energy to his statues. He also broke down the dominance of the frontal view and encouraged viewing his statues from multiple angles.

1 ft.

Roman copies in marble (FIG. **2-49**)—exhibits the new proportions. A comparison with Polykleitos's *Doryphoros* (FIG. 2-35) reveals more than a change in physique, however. A nervous energy, lacking in the balanced form of the *Doryphoros,* runs through the Lysippan statue. The *strigil* (scraper) is about to reach the end of the right arm, and at any moment the athlete will switch it to the other hand so that he can scrape his left arm. At the same time, he will shift his weight and reverse the positions of his legs. Lysippos also began to break down the dominance of the frontal view in statuary and encouraged the observer to view his athlete from multiple angles. Because Lysippos represented the apoxyomenos with his right arm boldly thrust forward, the figure breaks out of the shallow rectangular box that defined the boundaries of earlier statues. To comprehend the action, the observer must move to the side and view Lysippos's work at a three-quarter angle or in full profile.

Battle of Issus The life of Alexander the Great very much resembled an epic saga, full of heroic battles, exotic locales, and unceasing drama. Alexander was a man of singular character, an inspired leader with boundless energy and an almost foolhardy courage, who always personally led his army into battle. A Roman *mosaic* (see "Mosaics," Chapter 4, page 129) captures the extraordinary character of the Macedonian king. It also provides a welcome glimpse at the lost art of Greek monumental painting during Alexander's time. In the so-called *Alexander Mosaic* (FIG. **2-50**), the mosaicist employed *tesserae* (cubical pieces of glass or tiny stones cut to the desired size and shape) to "paint" what art historians believe is a reasonably faithful copy of a famous panel painting dating around 310 BCE by PHILOXENOS OF ERETRIA. The subject is a great battle between Alexander the Great and the Persian king Darius III, probably the battle of Issus in southeastern Turkey, which Darius fled in humiliating defeat.

Battle of Issus is notable for the artist's technical mastery of problems that had long fascinated Greek painters. Even Euthymides (FIG. 2-26) would have marveled at Philoxenos's depiction of the rearing horse seen in a three-quarter rear view below Darius. The subtle modulation of the horse's rump through shading in browns and yellows goes far beyond anything even a white-ground vase painter (FIG. 2-46) ever attempted. Other details are even more impressive. The Persian to the right of the rearing horse has fallen to the ground and raises, backward, a dropped Macedonian shield to protect himself from being trampled. Philoxenos recorded the reflection of the man's terrified face on the polished surface of the shield. Everywhere in the scene men, animals, and weapons cast shadows on the ground. This interest in the reflection of insubstantial light on a shiny surface, and in the absence of light (shadows), stands in marked contrast to earlier painters' preoccupation with the clear presentation of weighty figures seen against a blank background. Philoxenos here truly opened a window into a world filled not only with figures, trees, and sky but also with light.

Most impressive about *Battle of Issus,* however, is the psychological intensity of the drama unfolding before the viewer's eyes. Alexander leads his army into battle without even a helmet to protect him. He drives his spear through one of Darius's bodyguards while the Persian's horse collapses beneath him. Alexander is only a few yards away from Darius, and he directs his gaze at the king, not at the man impaled on his now-useless spear. Darius has called for retreat. In fact, his charioteer is already whipping the horses and speeding the king to safety. Before he escapes, Darius looks back at Alexander and in a pathetic gesture reaches out toward his brash foe. But the victory has slipped from his hands. In Pliny's opinion, Philoxenos's painting of the battle between Alexander and Darius was "inferior to none."[5]

Theater of Epidauros In ancient Greece, actors did not perform plays repeatedly over months or years as they do today, but only during sacred festivals. Greek drama was closely associated with religious rites and was not pure entertainment. In the fifth century BCE, for example, the Athenians

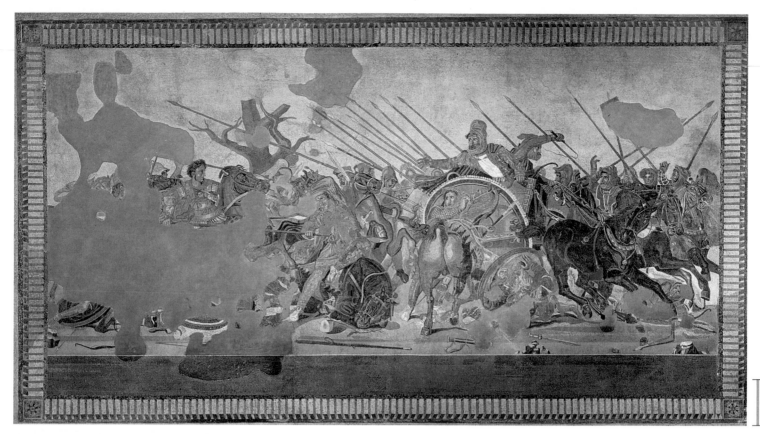

2-50 PHILOXENOS OF ERETRIA, *Battle of Issus,* ca. 310 BCE. Roman copy (*Alexander Mosaic*) from the House of the Faun, Pompeii, Italy, late second or early first century BCE. Tessera mosaic, 8′ 10″ × 16′ 9″. Museo Archeologico Nazionale, Naples. ◼◀

Battle of Issus reveals Philoxenos's mastery of foreshortening, of modeling figures in color, and of depicting reflections and shadows, as well as his ability to capture the psychological intensity of warfare.

staged the great tragedies of Aeschylus, Sophocles, and Euripides during the Dionysos festival in the theater dedicated to the god on the southern slope of the Acropolis. Yet it is Epidauros that boasts the finest theater (FIG. **2-51**) in Greece. The architect was POLYKLEITOS THE YOUNGER.

The precursor of the formal Greek theater was a circular piece of earth where actors performed sacred rites, songs, and dances. This area later became the orchestra of the theater. *Orchestra* literally means "dancing place." At Epidauros an altar to Dionysos stood at the center of the circle. The specta-

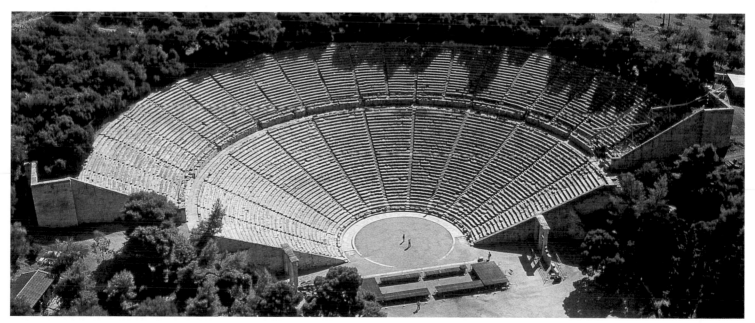

2-51 POLYKLEITOS THE YOUNGER, aerial view of the theater (looking northeast), Epidauros, Greece, ca. 350 BCE.

The Greeks always situated theaters on hillsides to support the cavea of stone seats overlooking the circular orchestra. The Epidauros theater is the finest in Greece. It accommodated 12,000 spectators.

tors sat on a slope overlooking the orchestra—the *theatron*, or "place for seeing," and watched the actors and chorus in the orchestra. When the Greek theater took architectural shape, the builders always situated the auditorium (*cavea*, Latin for "hollow place," "cavity") on a hillside. The cavea at Epidauros, composed of wedge-shaped sections of stone benches separated by stairs, is somewhat greater than a semicircle in plan. The auditorium is 387 feet in diameter, and its 55 rows of seats accommodated about 12,000 spectators. They entered the theater via a passageway between the seating area and the scene building (*skene*), which housed dressing rooms for the actors and also formed a backdrop for the plays. The design is simple but perfectly suited to its function. Even in antiquity the Epidauros theater was famous for the harmony of its proportions. Although spectators sitting in some of the seats would have had a poor view of the skene, all had unobstructed views of the orchestra. Because of the excellent acoustics of the open-air cavea, everyone could hear the actors and chorus.

Hellenistic Art

Alexander the Great's conquest of Persia and Egypt ushered in a new cultural age that historians and art historians alike call *Hellenistic*. The Hellenistic period opened with the death of Alexander in 323 BCE and lasted nearly three centuries, until the double suicide of Queen Cleopatra of Egypt and her Roman consort Mark Antony in 30 BCE, after their decisive defeat at the battle of Actium by Antony's rival Augustus (FIG. 3-24). A year later, Augustus made Egypt a province of the Roman Empire.

The cultural centers of the Hellenistic period were the court cities of the Greek kings who succeeded Alexander and divided his far-flung empire among themselves. Chief among them were Antioch in Syria, Alexandria in Egypt, and Pergamon in Asia Minor. An international culture united the Hellenistic world, and its language was Greek. Hellenistic kings became enormously rich on the spoils of the East, priding themselves on their libraries, art collections, and scientific enterprises, as well as on the learned men they could assemble at their courts. The world of the small, austere, and heroic city-state passed away, as did the power and prestige of its center, Athens. A cosmopolitan ("citizen of the world" in Greek) civilization, much like today's, replaced it.

Altar of Zeus, Pergamon The kingdom of Pergamon, founded in the early third century BCE after the breakup of Alexander's empire, embraced almost all of western and southern Asia Minor. The Pergamene kings enjoyed immense wealth and expended much of it on embellishing their capital city. The Altar of Zeus, erected about 175 BCE, is the most famous Hellenistic sculptural ensemble. The monument's west front (FIG. 2-52) has been reconstructed in Berlin. The altar proper was on an elevated platform, framed by an Ionic colonnade with projecting wings on either side of a broad central staircase.

All around the altar platform was a sculpted frieze almost 400 feet long, populated by about a hundred larger-than-life-size figures. The subject is the battle of Zeus and the gods against the giants. The Pergamene frieze is the most extensive representation Greek artists ever attempted of that epic conflict for control of the world. The gigantomachy also appeared on the shield of Phidias's *Athena Parthenos* and on some of the Parthenon metopes because the Athenians wished to draw a parallel between the defeat of the giants and the defeat of the Persians. The Pergamene king Attalos I (r. 241–197 BCE) had successfully turned back an invasion of the Gauls in Asia Minor. The gigantomachy of the Altar of Zeus alluded to his victory over those barbarians—and also established a connection with Athens, whose earlier defeat of the Persians was by then legendary, and with the Parthenon, which the Hellenistic Greeks already recognized as a Classical monument—in both senses of the word. The figure

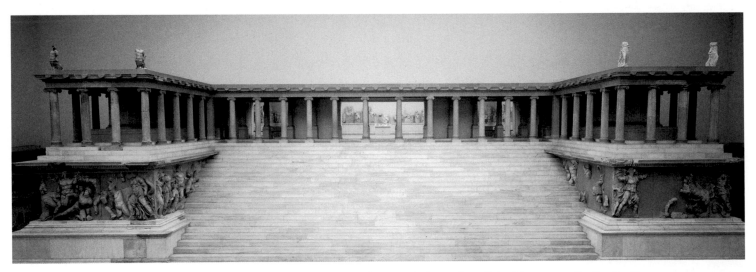

2-52 Reconstructed west front of the Altar of Zeus, Pergamon, Turkey, ca. 175 BCE. Staatliche Museen zu Berlin, Berlin.

The gigantomachy frieze of Pergamon's monumental Altar of Zeus is almost 400 feet long. The battle of gods and giants alluded to the victory of King Attalos I over the Gauls of Asia Minor.

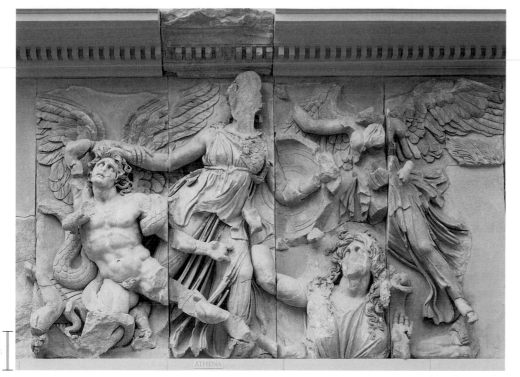

2-53 Athena battling Alkyoneos, detail of the gigantomachy frieze of the Altar of Zeus, Pergamon, Turkey, ca. 175 BCE. Marble, 7' 6" high. Staatliche Museen zu Berlin, Berlin.

The tumultuous gigantomachy of the Pergamon altar has an emotional power unparalleled in earlier Greek art. Violent movement, swirling draperies, and vivid depictions of suffering fill the frieze.

of Athena (FIG. **2-53**), for example, who grabs the hair of the giant Alkyoneos as Nike flies in to crown her, resembles Athena in the Parthenon's east pediment.

The Pergamene frieze, however, is not a dry series of borrowed motifs. On the contrary, its tumultuous narrative has an emotional intensity that has no parallel in earlier sculpture. The battle rages everywhere, even up and down the steps leading to Zeus's altar (FIG. 2-52). Violent movement, swirling draperies, and vivid depictions of death and suffering fill the frieze. Wounded figures writhe in pain, and their faces reveal their anguish. Deep carving creates dark shadows. The figures project from the background like bursts of light.

Dying Gaul The Altar of Zeus was not the only Pergamene monument to celebrate the victory of Attalos I over the Gauls. An earlier Pergamene statuary group had explicitly represented the defeat of the barbarians, instead of cloaking it in mythological disguise. The Pergamene victors were apparently not part of this group, however. The viewer saw only their Gallic foes and their noble and moving response to defeat. Roman copies of some of these figures survive, including a trumpeter (FIG. **2-54**) who collapses on his large oval shield as blood pours out of the gash in his chest. If this figure is the *tubicen* (trumpeter) Pliny mentions in his *Natural History,* then the sculptor's name was EPIGONOS. In any case, the sculptor carefully studied and reproduced the distinctive features of the foreign Gauls, most notably their long, bushy hair and mustaches and the *torques* (neck bands) they frequently wore. The artist also closely observed male anatomy. Note the tautness of the fallen Gaul's chest and the bulging veins of his left leg—implying the unseen Greek hero who struck down this noble and savage foe must have been an extraordinarily powerful man. The Hellenistic figure is reminiscent of the dying warrior from the east pediment of the Temple of Aphaia at Aegina (FIG. 2-30), but the pathos and drama of the suffering Gaul are far more pronounced.

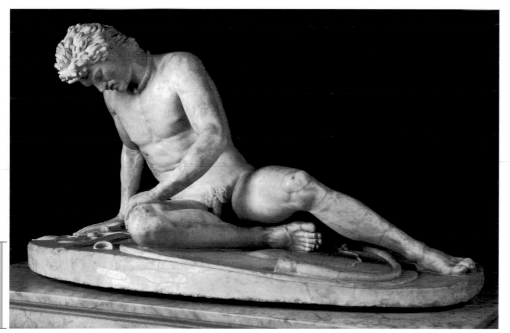

2-54 EPIGONOS (?), Dying Gaul. Roman copy of a bronze statue from Pergamon, Turkey, ca. 230–220 BCE. Marble, 3' $\frac{1}{2}$" high. Museo Capitolino, Rome.

The defeat of the Gauls was also the subject of Pergamene statuary groups. The barbaric Gauls have bushy hair, mustaches, and neck bands, but the sculptor portrayed them as noble foes.

Nike of Samothrace Another masterpiece of Hellenistic sculpture is the statue of winged Victory set up in the Sanctuary of the Great Gods on the island of Samothrace. The *Nike of Samothrace* (FIG. **2-55**) has just alighted on the prow of a Greek warship. She raises her (missing) right arm to crown the naval victor, just as Nike placed a wreath on Athena's head on the Altar of Zeus (FIG. 2-52). But the Pergamene relief figure seems calm by comparison. The Samothracian Nike's wings still beat, and the wind sweeps her drapery. Her *himation* (woolen mantle) bunches in thick folds around her right leg, and her linen chiton is pulled tightly across her abdomen and left leg.

The statue's setting amplified this theatrical effect. The sculptor set the war galley in the upper basin of a two-tiered fountain. In the lower basin were large boulders. The fountain's flowing water created the illusion of rushing waves hitting the prow of the ship. The statue's reflection in the shimmering water below accentuated the sense of lightness and movement. The sound of splashing water added an aural dimension to the visual drama. Here, the Hellenistic sculp-tor combined art and nature, and resoundingly rejected the Polykleitan conception of a statue as an ideally proportioned, self-contained entity on a bare pedestal. The Hellenistic statue interacts with its environment and appears as a living, breathing, and intensely emotive presence.

Venus de Milo In the Hellenistic period, sculptors regularly followed Praxiteles's lead in undressing Aphrodite, but they also openly explored the eroticism of the nude female form. The *Venus de Milo* (FIG. **2-56**) is a larger-than-life-size marble statue of Aphrodite found on Melos together with its inscribed base (now lost) signed by the sculptor ALEXANDROS OF ANTIOCH-ON-THE-MEANDER. In this statue, the goddess of love is more modestly draped than the *Aphrodite of Knidos* (FIG. 2-47) but is more overtly sexual. Her left hand (separately preserved) holds the apple the Trojan hero Paris awarded her when he judged her the most beautiful goddess. Her right hand may have lightly grasped the edge of her drapery near the left hip in a halfhearted attempt to keep it from slipping

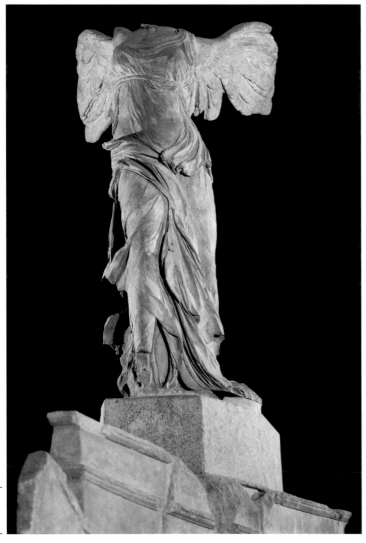

2-55 Nike alighting on a warship (*Nike of Samothrace*), from Samothrace, Greece, ca. 190 BCE. Marble, figure 8′ 1″ high. Musée du Louvre, Paris. ◼◀

Victory lands on a ship's prow to crown a naval victor. Her wings still beat, and the wind sweeps her drapery. The statue's placement in a fountain of splashing water heightened the dramatic visual effect.

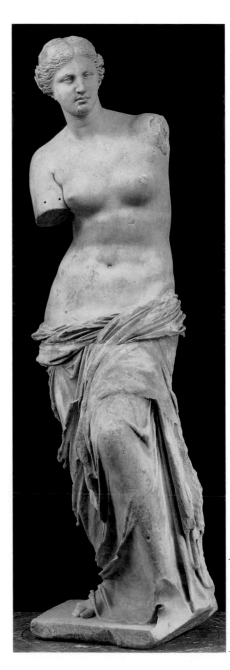

2-56 ALEXANDROS OF ANTIOCH-ON-THE-MEANDER, Aphrodite (*Venus de Milo*), from Melos, Greece, ca. 150–125 BCE. Marble, 6′ 7″ high. Musée du Louvre, Paris.

Displaying the eroticism of many Hellenistic statues, this Aphrodite is more overtly sexual than the Knidian Aphrodite (FIG. 2-47). The goddess's slipping garment teases the spectator.

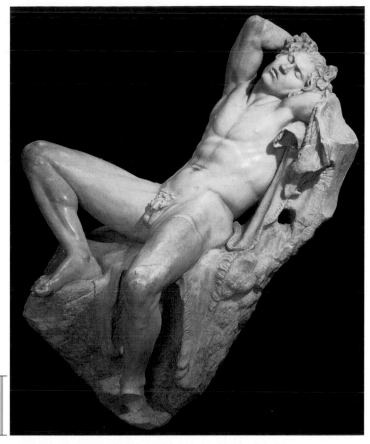

1 ft.

2-57 Sleeping satyr (*Barberini Faun*), from Rome, Italy, ca. 230–200 BCE. Marble, 7′ 1″ high. Glyptothek, Munich.

Here, a Hellenistic sculptor represented a restlessly sleeping, drunken satyr, a semihuman in a suspended state of consciousness—the antithesis of the Classical ideals of rationality and discipline.

farther down her body. The sculptor intentionally designed the work to tease the spectator, instilling this partially draped Aphrodite with a sexuality absent from Praxiteles's entirely nude image of the goddess.

Barberini Faun Archaic statues smile at the viewer, and even when Classical statues look away, they are always awake and alert. Hellenistic sculptors often portrayed sleep. The suspension of consciousness and the entrance into the fantasy world of dreams—the antithesis of the Classical ideals of rationality and discipline—had great appeal for them. This newfound interest is evident in a marble statue (FIG. **2-57**) of a drunken, restlessly sleeping *satyr* (a semihuman follower of Dionysos) known as the *Barberini Faun* after the Italian cardinal who once owned it. The satyr has consumed too much wine and has thrown down his panther skin on a convenient rock, then fallen into a disturbed, intoxicated sleep. His brows are furrowed, and one can almost hear him snore.

Eroticism also comes to the fore in this statue. Although men had been represented naked in Greek art for hundreds of years, Archaic kouroi and Classical athletes and gods do not exude sexuality. Sensuality surfaced in the works of Praxiteles and his followers in the fourth century BCE. But the dreamy and supremely beautiful Hermes playfully dangling grapes before the infant Dionysos (FIG. **2-48**) has nothing of

the blatant sexuality of the *Barberini Faun,* whose wantonly spread legs focus attention on his genitals. Homosexuality was common in the man's world of ancient Greece. It is not surprising that when Hellenistic sculptors began to explore the sexuality of the human body, they turned their attention to both men and women.

Old Market Woman Hellenistic sculpture stands in contrast to Classical sculpture in other ways too. Many Hellenistic sculptors had a deep interest in exploring realism—the very opposite of the Classical period's idealism. This realistic mode is evident above all in Hellenistic statues of old men and women from the lowest rungs of the social order. Shepherds, fishermen, and drunken beggars are common—the kinds of people pictured earlier on red-figure vases but never before thought worthy of monumental statuary. One statue of this type (FIG. **2-58**) depicts a haggard old woman bringing chickens and a basket of fruits and vegetables to sell in the market. Her face is wrinkled, her body bent with age, and her spirit broken by a lifetime of poverty. She carries on because she must, not because she derives any pleasure from life. No one knows the purpose of statues like this one, but they attest to an interest in social realism absent in earlier Greek statuary.

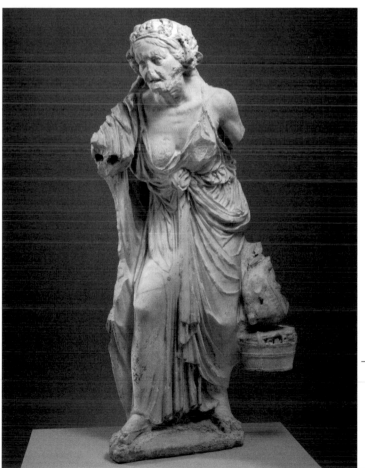

1 ft.

2-58 Old market woman. Roman copy(?) of a marble statue of ca. 150–100 BCE. Marble, 4′ ½″ high. Metropolitan Museum of Art, New York.

Hellenistic art is sometimes brutally realistic. Many statues portray old men and women from the lowest rungs of society—subjects Archaic and Classical artists never considered suitable for monumental sculpture.

2-59 ATHANADOROS, HAGESANDROS, and POLYDOROS OF RHODES, Laocoön and his sons, from Rome, Italy, early first century CE. Marble, 7′ 10½″ high. Musei Vaticani, Rome.

Hellenistic style lived on in Rome. Although stylistically akin to Pergamene sculpture (FIG. 2-53), this statue of sea serpents attacking Laocoön and his two sons matches the account given only in the *Aeneid*.

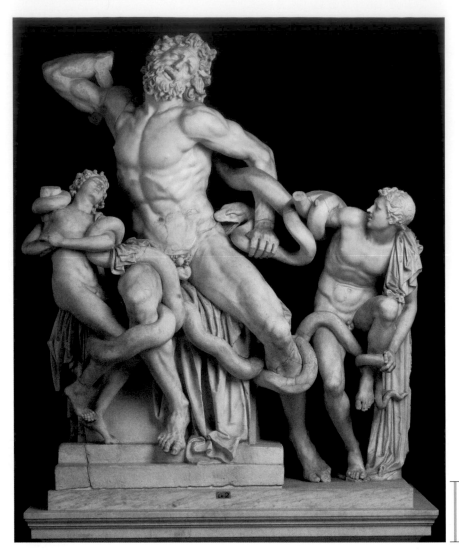

1 ft.

Laocoön In the opening years of the second century BCE, the Roman general Flamininus defeated the Macedonian army and declared the old city-states of Classical Greece free once again. The Greek cities never regained their former glory, however. Greece became a Roman province in 146 BCE. When Athens, 60 years later, sided with King Mithridates VI of Pontus (r. 120–63 BCE) in his war against Rome, the general Sulla crushed the Athenians. Thereafter, although Athens retained some of its earlier prestige as a center of culture and learning, politically it was merely another city in the ever-expanding Roman Empire. Nonetheless, Greek artists continued to be in great demand, both to furnish the Romans with an endless stream of copies of Classical and Hellenistic masterpieces and to create new statues in Greek style for Roman patrons.

The most famous work of this type is the statue of the Trojan priest Laocoön and his sons (FIG. **2-59**). Long believed to be an original of the second century BCE, the marble group was found in the palace of the emperor Titus (r. 79–81 CE). Pliny attributed the statue to three sculptors—ATHANADOROS, HAGESANDROS, and POLYDOROS OF RHODES—who art historians now generally think worked in the early first century CE. These artists probably based their group on a Hellenistic masterpiece depicting Laocoön and only one son. Their variation on the original added the son at Laocoön's left (note the greater compositional integration of the other two figures) to conform with the Roman poet Vergil's account in the *Aeneid*. Vergil vividly described the strangling of Laocoön and his *two* sons by sea serpents while sacrificing at an altar. The gods who favored the Greeks in the war against Troy had sent the serpents to punish Laocoön, who had tried to warn his compatriots about the danger of bringing the Greeks' wooden horse within the walls of their city. In Vergil's graphic account, Laocoön suffered in terrible agony. The Rhodian sculptors communicated the torment of the priest and his sons in a spectacular fashion in this marble group. The three Trojans writhe in pain as they struggle to free themselves from the death grip of the serpents. One

bites into Laocoön's left hip as the priest lets out a ferocious cry. The serpent-entwined figures recall the suffering giants of the frieze of the Altar of Zeus at Pergamon, and Laocoön himself is strikingly similar to Alkyoneos (FIG. 2-53), Athena's opponent. In fact, many scholars believe a Pergamene statuary group of the second century BCE was the inspiration for the three Rhodian sculptors.

That the work seen by Pliny and displayed in the Vatican Museums today was made for Romans rather than Greeks was confirmed in 1957 by the discovery of fragments of several Hellenistic-style groups illustrating scenes from Homer's *Odyssey* in a grotto that served as the picturesque summer banquet hall of the seaside villa of the Roman emperor Tiberius (r. 14–37 CE) at Sperlonga, some 60 miles south of Rome. The same three sculptors Pliny cited as the creators of the Laocoön group signed one of the Sperlonga groups. At Tiberius's villa and in Titus's palace, Hellenistic sculpture lived on long after Greece ceased to be a political force. When Rome inherited the Pergamene kingdom in 133 BCE, it also became heir to the Greek artistic legacy. What Rome adopted from Greece it passed on to the medieval and modern worlds. If Greece was peculiarly the inventor of the European spirit, Rome was its propagator and amplifier.

Ancient Greece

Prehistoric Aegean

I The major surviving artworks of the third millennium BCE in Greece are Cycladic marble statuettes. Most come from graves and may represent the deceased.

I The golden age of Crete was the Late Minoan period (ca. 1600–1200 BCE). The palace at Knossos was a vast multistory structure so complex in plan it gave rise to the myth of the minotaur in the labyrinth of King Minos. Large fresco paintings adorned the walls, but all surviving Minoan sculptures are of small scale.

I The Mycenaeans (ca. 1600–1200 BCE) constructed great citadels at Mycenae, Tiryns, and elsewhere with "Cyclopean" walls of huge irregularly shaped stone blocks. Masters of corbel vaulting, the Mycenaeans also built beehive-shaped tholos tombs such as the Treasury of Atreus, which boasted the largest dome before the Roman Empire. The graves of the kings of Mycenae have yielded gold masks and other luxury items.

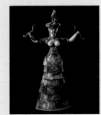

Snake Goddess, Knossos, ca. 1600 BCE

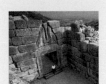

Lion Gate, Mycenae, ca. 1300–1250 BCE

Geometric and Archaic Art

I The human figure returned to Greek art during the Geometric period (ca. 900–700 BCE) in the form of simple silhouettes amid other abstract motifs on vases.

I Around 600 BCE, during the Archaic period (ca. 700–480 BCE), the first life-size stone statues appeared in Greece. The earliest kouroi emulated the frontal poses of Egyptian statues, but artists depicted the young men nude, the way Greek athletes competed in the Olympic Games. During the course of the sixth century, Greek sculptors refined the proportions and added "Archaic smiles" to the faces of their statues to make them seem more lifelike. The Archaic age also saw the construction of the first stone temples with peripteral colonnades and the codification of the Doric and Ionic orders. Vase painters developed in turn the black- and red-figure techniques. Euphronios and Euthymides rejected the age-old composite view for the human figure and experimented with foreshortening.

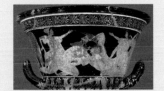

Euphronios, Herakles and Antaios wrestling, ca. 510 BCE

Classical Art

I The fifth century BCE was the golden age of Greece, when Aeschylus, Sophocles, and Euripides wrote their plays, and Herodotus, the "father of history," lived. During the Early Classical period (480–450 BCE), which opened with the Greek victory over the Persians, sculptors revolutionized statuary by introducing contrapposto (weight shift) to their figures.

I In the High Classical period (450–400 BCE), under the patronage of Pericles and the artistic directorship of Phidias, the Athenians rebuilt the Acropolis after 447 BCE. Polykleitos developed a canon of proportions for the perfect statue, and Iktinos and Kallikrates applied mathematical formulas to temple design in the belief beauty resulted from the use of harmonic numbers.

I In the aftermath of the Peloponnesian War, which ended in 404 BCE, Greek artists began to focus more on the real world of appearances than on the ideal world of perfect beings. During the Late Classical period (400–323 BCE), sculptors humanized the remote deities and athletes of the fifth century. Praxiteles, for example, caused a sensation when he portrayed Aphrodite undressed.

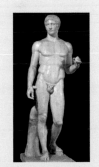

Polykleitos, *Doryphoros*, ca. 450–440 BCE

Hellenistic Art

I The Hellenistic age (323–30 BCE) extends from the death of Alexander the Great until the death of Cleopatra, when Egypt became a province of the Roman Empire. The great cultural centers of the era were no longer the city-states of Archaic and Classical Greece, but royal capitals such as Pergamon in Asia Minor. Hellenistic sculptors explored new subjects—Gauls with mustaches and necklaces, impoverished old women—and treated traditional subjects in new ways. Hellenistic artists delighted in depicting violent movement and unbridled emotion.

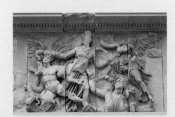

Altar of Zeus, Pergamon, ca. 175 BCE

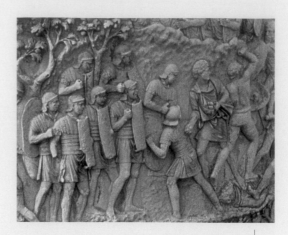

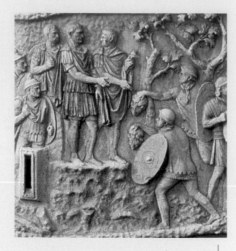

The spiral frieze of the Column of Trajan recounts the emperor's two military campaigns in Dacia (present-day Romania). Here, Roman soldiers present severed Dacian heads to Trajan.

The campaign against the Dacians had few interludes. As soon as one skirmish ended, the Romans moved on and launched another attack. On Trajan's Column, each scene merges with the next.

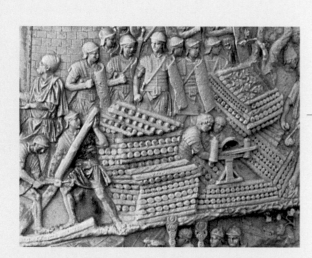

The sculptors of the frieze of Trajan's Column depicted not only combat but all aspects of warfare. Here, Roman soldiers pile up logs to be transported for use at the next battle site.

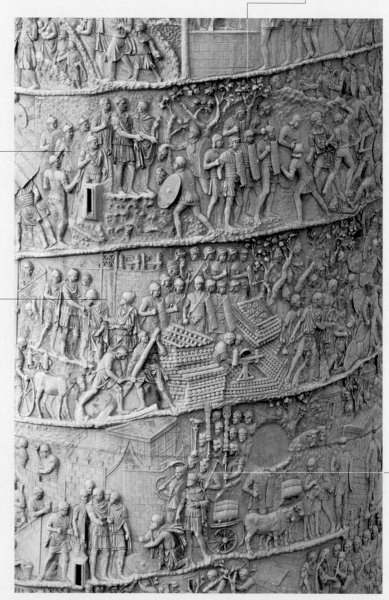

3-1 Detail of three bands of the spiral frieze of the Column of Trajan (FIG. 3-36), Forum of Trajan, Rome, Italy, dedicated 112 CE. ◼◀

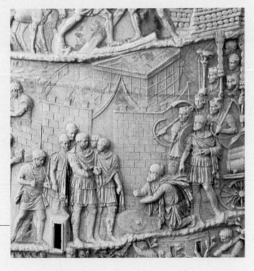

After losing a battle, a Dacian chieftain kneels before Trajan and seeks mercy. The war does not end, however, until, at the end of the frieze, the Dacian king Decebalus commits suicide.

The Roman Empire

THE ANCIENT WORLD'S GREATEST EMPIRE

At the death of the emperor Trajan in 117 CE, for the first time in history a single government ruled an empire extending from the Nile to the Strait of Gibraltar, from the Tigris and Euphrates to the Rhone, Danube, Thames, and beyond (MAP 3-1). No government, before or after, ever used art more effectively as a political tool.

Trajan, perhaps Rome's greatest general, had led the imperial army to victory in both the East and West, bringing vast new territories under Roman dominion. To celebrate his successes in Dacia (roughly equivalent to present-day Romania), Trajan erected a 128-foot-tall column (FIG. 3-36) in Rome. Although frequently imitated, the Column of Trajan was the first of its kind. Its distinguishing new feature was the 625-foot frieze winding around the shaft 23 times from bottom to top. It recounts the emperor's two campaigns against the Dacians.

Illustrated here (FIG. 3-1) are three of the bands midway up the column. Carving the frieze was a complex process. First, the stonemasons had to fashion enormous marble column drums, hollowed out to accommodate the internal spiral staircase running the entire length of the column shaft. The sculptors carved the figures and buildings after the drums were in place to ensure they lined up perfectly. (Note the horizontal line through the lowest frieze in the photograph corresponding to the junction between two column drums.) The sculptors carved the last scenes in the narrative first, working from the top to the bottom of the shaft so that falling marble chips or a dropped chisel would not damage the reliefs below.

At the top left of the section shown, a group of Roman soldiers storms a Dacian fortress with their shields raised and joined to form a protective turtle-shell. To the right, the battle won, Trajan, flanked by two lieutenants, views the severed Dacian heads that his soldiers have brought to him as evidence of the successful completion of their mission. Farther to the right, another battle begins. In the middle band, Trajan, again with an officer at each side, accepts the surrender of two Dacians. But, as before, there are still more enemies to pursue and conquer, so the Roman army cuts down more trees and piles up the logs to be transported for use at the next battle site. Another scene of surrender, this time with a Dacian kneeling before the emperor, is the subject of the lowest band, coupled with the loading of carts as the army moves on.

The repetition of standard motifs such as these characterizes the frieze as a whole. From every vantage point, Trajan could be seen directing the military operation. His personal involvement in all aspects of the Dacian campaigns—and in expanding Rome's empire on all fronts—was one of the central messages of the Column of Trajan.

ROME, CAPUT MUNDI

The Roman Empire spanned three continents, and Roman monuments of art and architecture are the most conspicuous and numerous of any ancient civilization. In Europe, the Middle East, and North Africa today, Roman temples and basilicas have an afterlife as churches. The powerful concrete vaults of ancient Roman buildings form the cores of modern houses, stores, restaurants, factories, and museums. Bullfights, sporting events, operas, and rock concerts take place in Roman amphitheaters. Ships dock in what were once Roman ports, and western Europe's highway system still closely follows the routes of Roman roads.

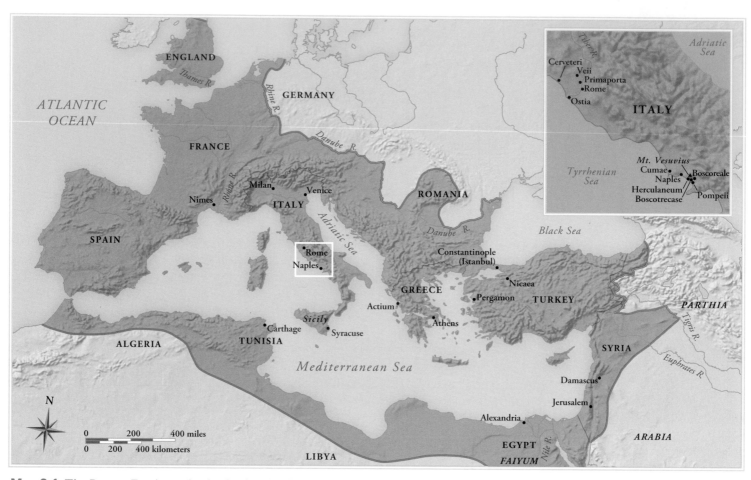

Map 3-1 The Roman Empire at the death of Trajan in 117 CE.

The Roman Empire

	Etruscan and Republican	BCE / CE	Early Empire		High Empire		Late Empire	
700		27		96		192		337

Etruscan and Republican

- The Etruscans construct temples of mud brick and wood with columns and stairs only on the front and terracotta statuary on the roof
- At Cerveteri, the Etruscans bury their dead beneath huge earthen tumuli in multichambered tombs resembling houses. Tarquinian tombs feature fresco paintings depicting funerary banquets
- Republican builders Hellenize Etruscan architecture and decorate walls in the First and Second Styles
- Republican sculptors produce veristic (superrealistic) portraits

Early Empire

- Augustan artists revive the Classical style in art and architecture
- Architects realize the full potential of concrete construction
- Roman painters introduce the Third and Fourth Styles

High Empire

- Trajan extends the Empire and builds a new forum in Rome
- Hadrian builds the Pantheon, a triumph of concrete technology
- The domination of the Classical style begins to erode under the Antonines

Late Empire

- A new non-Classical Late Imperial style takes root under the Severans
- Portraits of the soldier emperors reveal the insecurity of the age
- Diocletian establishes the tetrarchy
- Constantine founds a New Rome at Constantinople

Ancient Rome also lives on in the Western world in concepts of law and government, in languages, in the calendar—even in the coins used daily. Roman art speaks in a language almost every Western viewer can readily understand. Its diversity and eclecticism foreshadowed the modern world. The Roman use of art, especially portraits and narrative reliefs (FIG. 3-1), to manipulate public opinion is similar to the carefully crafted imagery of contemporary political campaigns. And the Roman mastery of concrete construction began an architectural revolution still felt today. But in 753 BCE, when according to legend, Romulus founded what would become the *caput mundi*—the "head (capital) of the world"—Rome was neither the most powerful nor the most sophisticated city even in central Italy. In fact, in the sixth century BCE, the rulers of Rome were Etruscan kings.

ETRUSCAN ART

The heartland of the Etruscans was the territory between the Arno and Tiber Rivers of central Italy. During the eighth and seventh centuries BCE, the Etruscans, as highly skilled seafarers, enriched themselves through trade abroad. By the sixth century BCE, they controlled most of northern and central Italy. Their most powerful cities included Tarquinia, Cerveteri, Vulci, and Veii. The Etruscan cities never united to form a state, however. Any semblance of unity among the independent cities was based primarily on common linguistic ties and religious beliefs and practices. This lack of political cohesion eventually made the Etruscans relatively easy prey for the Romans.

Etruscan Temples In the sixth century BCE, the most innovative artists and architects in the Mediterranean were the Greeks (see Chapter 2). Still, however eager Etruscan artists may have been to emulate Greek works, the distinctive Etruscan temperament always manifested itself. In religious architecture, for example, the differences between Etruscan

temples and their Greek prototypes far outweigh the similarities. Because of the materials Etruscan architects employed, usually only the foundations of their temples have survived. Supplementing the archaeological record is the Roman architect Vitruvius's treatise on architecture written near the end of the first century BCE. In it, Vitruvius provided an invaluable chapter on Etruscan temple design.

The typical Archaic Etruscan temple (FIG. **3-2**) resembled Greek stone gable-roofed temples (FIGS. 2-27, *left,* and 2-36), but it had wood columns and a tile-covered wood roof, and sun-dried mud-brick walls. Entrance was via a narrow staircase at the center of the front of the temple, which sat on a high podium, the only part of the building made of stone. Columns were only at the front of the building, creating a deep porch occupying roughly half the podium and setting off one side of the structure as the main side. In contrast, the front and rear of Greek temples were indistinguishable, and builders placed steps and columns on all sides. Furthermore, although the columns of Etruscan temples resembled Greek Doric columns (FIG. 2-20, *left*), *Tuscan columns* were made of wood, were unfluted, and had bases. Also, because of the lightness of the superstructure they had to support, fewer, more widely spaced columns were the rule in Etruscan temple design. Unlike their Greek counterparts, Etruscan temples also frequently had three cellas—one for each of their chief gods, Tinia (Roman Jupiter/Greek Zeus), Uni (Juno/Hera), and Menrva (Minerva/Athena). Pedimental statuary was also rare in Etruria. The Etruscans normally placed narrative statuary—in *terracotta* instead of stone—on the roofs of their temples.

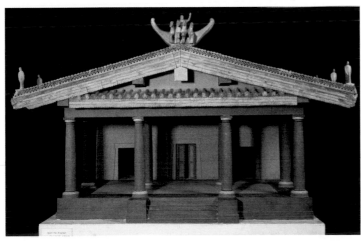

3-2 Model of a typical Etruscan temple of the sixth century BCE, as described by Vitruvius. Istituto di Etruscologia e di Antichità Italiche, Università di Roma, Rome. ◼◀

Etruscan temples resembled Greek temples but had widely spaced unfluted wood columns only at the front, sun-dried mud-brick walls, and a narrow staircase at the center of the façade.

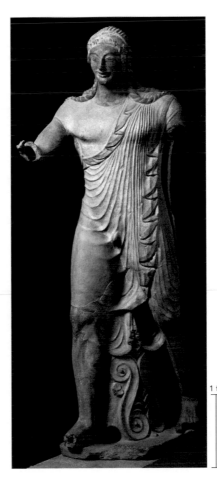

Apollo of Veii The finest surviving Archaic Etruscan temple statue is the life-size image of Apulu (FIG. **3-3**)—the Greco-Roman Apollo—from the Portonaccio sanctuary at Veii. It displays the energy and excitement that characterize Archaic Etruscan art

3-3 Apulu (*Apollo of Veii*), from the roof of the Portonaccio temple, Veii, Italy, ca. 510–500 BCE. Painted terracotta, 5' 11" high. Museo Nazionale di Villa Giulia, Rome.

This statue of Apulu was part of a group depicting a Greek myth. Distinctly Etruscan, however, are the god's vigorous motion and gesticulating arms and the placement of the statue on a temple roof.

1 ft.

in general. The *Apollo of Veii* was one of a group of at least four painted terracotta figures that adorned the rooftop of the Portonaccio temple. Apulu confronted Hercle (Hercules/Herakles) for possession of the Ceryneian hind, a wondrous gold-horned beast sacred to the god's sister Artumes (Diana/Artemis). The bright paint and the rippling folds of Apulu's garment immediately distinguish the statue from the nude images of the Greek gods. Apulu's vigorous striding motion, gesticulating arms, fanlike calf muscles, and animated face are also distinctly Etruscan.

Cerveteri Sarcophagus Also made of terracotta, the favored medium for life-size statuary in Etruria, is a *sarcophagus* (FIG. **3-4**) in the form of a husband and wife reclining on a banqueting couch, from a tomb at Cerveteri. *Sarcophagus* literally means "flesh-eater," and most ancient sarcophagi contained the bodies of the deceased, but this one contained only ashes. Cremation was the most common means of disposing of the dead in Etruscan Italy. This kind of funerary monument had no parallel at this date in Greece, where there were no monumental tombs that could house large sarcophagi. The Greeks buried their dead in simple graves marked by a vase (FIG. 2-14), statue (FIG. 2-17), or stele (FIG. 2-45). Moreover, only men dined at Greek banquets. Their wives remained at home, excluded from most aspects of public life. The image of a husband and wife sharing the same banqueting couch is uniquely Etruscan.

The man and woman on the Cerveteri sarcophagus are as animated as the *Apollo of Veii* (FIG. 3-3), even though they are at rest. They are the antithesis of the stiff and formal figures encountered in Egyptian funerary sculpture (FIG. 1-28). Also typically Etruscan, and in sharp contrast to contemporaneous Greek statues with their emphasis on proportion and balance, is the manner in which the Cerveteri sculptor rendered the upper and lower parts of each body. The artist only summarily modeled the legs, and the transition to the torso at the waist is unnatural. The sculptor's interest focused on the upper half of the figures, especially on the vibrant faces and gesticulating arms. The Cerveteri banqueters and the *Apollo of Veii* speak to the viewer in a way Greek statues of similar date never do.

Banditaccia Necropolis The exact findspot of the Cerveteri sarcophagus is not known, but the kind of tomb that housed Etruscan sarcophagi is well documented. The typical tomb in Cerveteri's Banditaccia necropolis took the form of a mound, or *tumulus,* not unlike the Mycenaean Treasury of Atreus (FIG. 2-11). But whereas the Mycenaeans constructed their tholos tombs with masonry blocks and then encased them in earthen mounds, each Etruscan tumulus covered one or more subterranean multichambered tombs cut out of the dark local limestone called tufa. The largest Banditaccia mounds are truly of colossal size, exceeding 130 feet in diameter and reaching nearly 50 feet in height. Arranged in an orderly manner along a network of streets, the Cerveteri cemetery was a veritable city of the dead (the literal meaning of the Greek word *necropolis*). The Cerveteri tumuli highlight the very different values of the Etruscans and the Greeks. The Etruscans' temples no longer stand because they constructed them of wood and mud brick, but their grand underground tombs are as permanent as the bedrock itself. The Greeks employed stone for the shrines of their gods but only rarely built monumental tombs for their dead.

The most elaborately decorated Cerveteri tomb is the so-called Tomb of the Reliefs (FIG. **3-5**), which accommodated the remains of several generations of a single family. The walls, ceiling beams, piers, and funerary couches of this tomb were, as in other Cerveteri tombs, gouged out of the tufa bedrock, but in this instance brightly painted stucco reliefs cover the stone. The stools, mirrors, drinking cups, pitchers, and knives effectively suggest a domestic context, underscoring the visual and conceptual connection between Etruscan houses of the dead and those of the living.

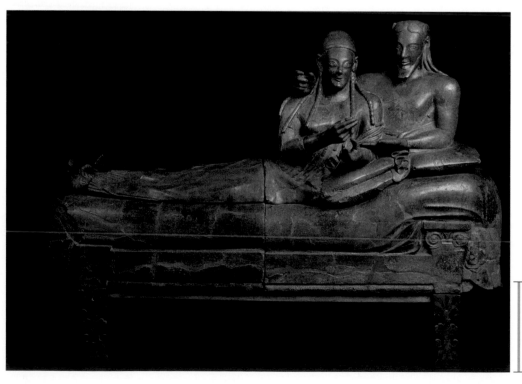

3-4 Sarcophagus with reclining couple, from the Banditaccia necropolis, Cerveteri, Italy, ca. 520 BCE. Painted terracotta, 3′ 9½″ × 6′ 7″. Museo Nazionale di Villa Giulia, Rome. ◼◀

Sarcophagi in the form of a husband and wife on a dining couch have no parallels in Greece. The artist's focus on the upper half of the figures and the emphatic gestures are Etruscan hallmarks.

1 ft.

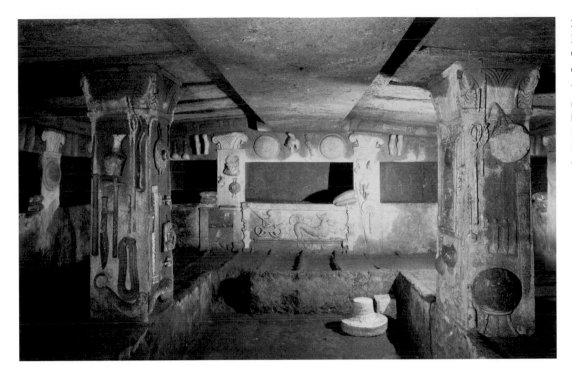

Tomb of the Leopards The Etruscans also decorated their underground burial chambers with mural paintings. Painted tombs are statistically rare, the privilege of only the wealthiest Etruscan families. Most have been found in the Monterozzi necropolis at Tarquinia. A well-preserved example, dating to the early fifth century BCE, is the Tomb of the Leopards (FIG. **3-6**), named for the beasts guarding the tomb from their perch within the pediment of the rear wall. The leopards recall the panthers on each side of Medusa in the pediment (FIG. 2-23) of the Artemis temple at Corfu. But mythological figures, whether Greek or Etruscan, are uncommon in Tarquinian murals. Indeed, the Tomb of the Leopards features murals depicting banqueting couples (the men with dark skin, the women with light skin, in conformity with the age-old convention)—painted versions of the terracotta sarcophagus (FIG. 3-4) from Cerveteri. Pitcher- and cup-bearers serve the guests, and musicians entertain them. The banquet takes place in the open air or perhaps in a tent set up for the occasion. In characteristic Etruscan fashion, the banqueters, servants, and entertainers all make exaggerated gestures with unnaturally enlarged hands. The man on the couch at the far right on the rear wall holds up an egg, the symbol of regeneration. The tone is joyful—a celebration of the good life of the Etruscan elite, rather than a somber contemplation of death.

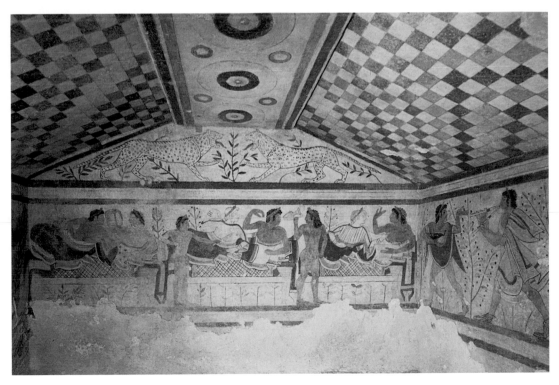

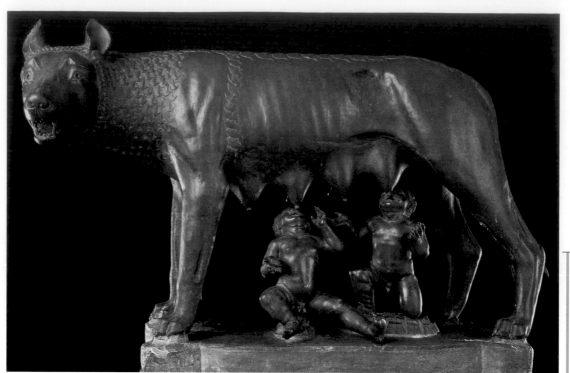

3-7 *Capitoline Wolf*, from Rome, Italy, ca. 500–480 BCE. Bronze, 2' 7½" high. Musei Capitolini—Palazzo dei Conservatori, Rome.

An Etruscan sculptor cast this statue of the she-wolf that nursed the infants Romulus and Remus, founders of Rome. The animal has a tense, gaunt body and an unforgettable psychic intensity.

1 ft.

Capitoline Wolf The fifth century BCE was a golden age in Greece but not in Etruria. In 509 BCE, the Romans expelled the last of their Etruscan kings and replaced the monarchy with a republican form of government. In 474 BCE, the allied Greek forces of Cumae and Syracuse defeated the Etruscan fleet off Cumae, effectively ending Etruscan dominance of the seas—and with it Etruscan prosperity. These events had important consequences in the world of art and architecture. The number of Etruscan tombs, for example, decreased sharply, and the quality of the furnishings declined markedly. No longer did the Etruscan elite fill their tombs with gold jewelry and imported Greek vases or decorate the walls with mural paintings of the first rank. But art did not cease in Etruria.

The best-known Etruscan statue of the Classical period is the *Capitoline Wolf* (FIG. **3-7**), one of the most memorable portrayals of an animal in the history of world art. The statue is a somewhat larger than life-size hollow-cast bronze image of the legendary she-wolf that nursed Romulus and Remus after they were abandoned as infants. When the twins grew to adulthood, they quarreled, and Romulus killed his brother. On April 23, 753 BCE, he founded Rome and became the city's first king. The *Capitoline Wolf* is not, however, a work of Roman art, which had not yet developed a distinct identity, but the product of an Etruscan workshop. (The suckling infants are Renaissance additions.) The sculptor brilliantly characterized the she-wolf physically and psychologically. The body is tense, with spare flanks, gaunt ribs, and taut, powerful legs. The lowered neck and head, alert ears, glaring eyes, and ferocious muzzle capture the psychic intensity of the fierce and protective beast as danger approaches.

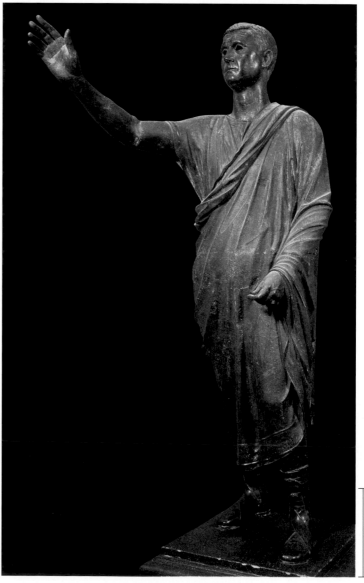

1 ft.

3-8 Aule Metele (*Arringatore*), from Cortona, Italy, early first century BCE. Bronze, 5' 7" high. Museo Archeologico Nazionale, Florence.

Inscribed in Etruscan, this bronze statue of an orator is Etruscan in name only. Aule Metele wears the short toga and high boots of a Roman magistrate, and the portrait style is Roman as well.

An Outline of Roman History

MONARCHY (753–509 BCE)

Latin and Etruscan kings ruled Rome from the city's founding by Romulus until the revolt against Rome's last king, Tarquinius Superbus (exact dates of rule unreliable).

REPUBLIC (509–27 BCE)

The Republic lasted almost 500 years, until the Senate bestowed the title of Augustus on Octavian, the grandnephew of Julius Caesar and victor over Mark Antony in the civil war that ended the Republic. Some major figures were

- Marcellus, b. 268(?), d. 208 BCE, consul
- Sulla, b. 138, d. 79 BCE, consul and dictator
- Julius Caesar, b. 100, d. 44 BCE, consul and dictator
- Mark Antony, b. 83, d. 30 BCE, consul

EARLY EMPIRE (27 BCE–96 CE)

The Early Empire began with the rule of Augustus and his Julio-Claudian successors and continued until the end of the Flavian dynasty. The emperors discussed in this chapter were

- Augustus, r. 27 BCE–14 CE
- Nero, r. 54–68
- Vespasian, r. 69–79

- Titus, r. 79–81
- Domitian, r. 81–96

HIGH EMPIRE (96–192 CE)

The High Empire began with the death of Domitian and the rule of the Spanish emperors, Trajan and Hadrian, and ended with the last emperor of the Antonine dynasty. The major rulers of this period were

- Trajan, r. 98–117
- Hadrian, r. 117–138
- Marcus Aurelius, r. 161–180

LATE EMPIRE (192–337 CE)

The Late Empire began with the Severan dynasty and included the so-called soldier emperors of the third century, the tetrarchs, and Constantine, the first Christian emperor. Among these emperors were

- Septimius Severus, r. 193–211
- Caracalla, r. 211–217
- Trajan Decius, r. 249–251
- Diocletian, r. 284–305
- Constantine I, r. 306–337

Aule Metele Veii fell to the Romans in 396 BCE, after a terrible 10-year siege. Rome concluded peace with Tarquinia in 351, but by the beginning of the next century, the Romans had annexed Tarquinia too, and they conquered Cerveteri in 273. By the first century BCE, Roman hegemony over the Etruscans became total. A life-size bronze portrait statue (FIG. **3-8**) dating to this period is an eloquent symbol of the Roman absorption of the Etruscans. Known as the *Arringatore* (*Orator*), the statue portrays Aule Metele raising his arm to address an assembly. Although the sculptor inscribed the man's Etruscan name and the names of both of his Etruscan parents on the hem of his garment, the orator wears the short toga and high laced boots of a Roman magistrate. His head also resembles contemporaneous Roman portraits. Aule Metele is Etruscan in name only. If the origin of the Etruscans remains the subject of debate, the question of their demise has a ready answer. Aule Metele and his compatriots became Romans, and Etruscan art became Roman art.

ROMAN ART

The Rome of Romulus in the eighth century BCE comprised only small huts of wood, wattle, and daub clustered together on the Palatine Hill overlooking what was then uninhabited marshland. In the Archaic period, Rome was essentially an Etruscan city, both politically and culturally. Its greatest shrine, the late-sixth-century BCE Temple of Jupiter on the Capitoline Hill, was built by an Etruscan king, designed by an Etruscan architect, made of wood and mud brick in the Etruscan manner, and decorated with terracotta statuary fashioned by an Etruscan sculptor. When the Romans expelled the last of Rome's Etruscan kings in 509 BCE, they established a constitutional government, or republic (see "An Outline of Roman History," above), and the she-wolf (FIG. 3-7) became its emblem.

The Republic

The new Roman Republic vested power mainly in a *senate* (literally, "a council of elders," "senior citizens") and in two elected *consuls*. Under extraordinary circumstances, a *dictator* could be appointed for a limited term and a specific purpose, such as commanding the army during a crisis. Before long, the descendants of Romulus conquered Rome's neighbors one by one: the Etruscans to the north, the Samnites and the Greek colonists to the south. Even the Carthaginians of North Africa, who under Hannibal's dynamic leadership had annihilated some of Rome's legions and almost brought down the Republic, fell before the mighty Roman armies.

The year 211 BCE was a turning point both for Rome and for Roman art. Breaking with precedent, Marcellus, conqueror of the fabulously wealthy Sicilian Greek city of Syracuse, brought back to Rome not only the usual spoils of war—captured arms and armor, gold and silver coins, and

3-9 Model of the city of Rome during the early fourth century CE. Museo della Civiltà Romana, Rome. (1) Temple of Portunus, (2) Palatine Hill, (3) Capitoline Hill, (4) Pantheon, (5) Forum of Trajan, (6) Markets of Trajan, (7) Forum Romanum, (8) Basilica Nova, (9) Arch of Titus, (10) Arch of Constantine, (11) Colossus of Nero, (12) Colosseum.

At the height of its power, Rome was the capital of the greatest empire in the ancient world. The Romans ruled from the Tigris and Euphrates to the Thames and beyond, from the Nile to the Rhine and Danube.

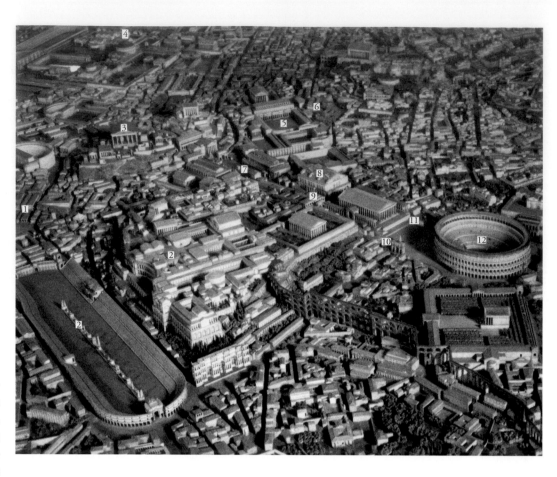

the like—but also the city's artistic patrimony. Thus began, in the words of the historian Livy, "the craze for works of Greek art."[1] Exposure to Greek sculpture and painting and to the splendid marble temples of the Greek gods increased as the Romans expanded their conquests beyond Italy. Greece became a Roman province in 146 BCE, and in 133 BCE the last king of Pergamon willed his kingdom to Rome (see page 84). Nevertheless, although the Romans developed a virtually insatiable taste for Greek "antiques," the influence of Etruscan art and architecture persisted. The artists and architects of the Roman Republic drew on both Greek and Etruscan traditions.

Temple of Portunus, Rome The mixing of Greek and Etruscan forms is the primary characteristic of the temple of Portunus (FIGS. **3-9**, no. 1, and **3-10**), the Roman god of harbors. Popularly known as the Temple of Fortuna Virilis, its plan follows the Etruscan pattern with a high podium and a wide flight of steps only at the front. The six freestanding columns are all in the deep porch. But the builders constructed the temple of stone (local tufa and travertine), overlaid originally with *stucco* in imitation of Greek marble. The columns are not Tuscan but Ionic, complete with flutes and bases, and there is a matching Ionic frieze. Moreover, in an effort to approximate a peripteral Greek temple yet maintain the basic Etruscan plan, the architect added a series of Ionic *engaged columns* (attached half-columns) to the sides and back of the cella. Although the design combines Etruscan and Greek elements, the resultant mix—a *pseudoperipteral* temple—is uniquely Roman.

Verism The patrons of Republican religious and civic buildings were in almost all cases men of old and distinguished families, often victorious generals who used the spoils of war

to finance public works. These *patricians* were fiercely proud of their lineage. They kept likenesses (*imagines*) of their ancestors in wooden cupboards in their homes and paraded them at the funerals of prominent relatives. Ancestral portraiture

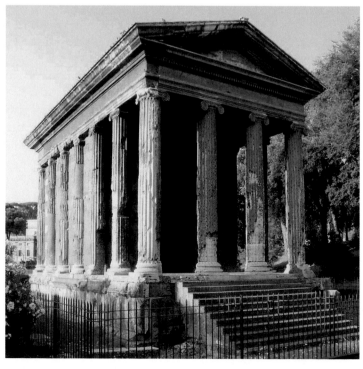

3-10 Temple of Portunus (Temple of Fortuna Virilis), Rome, Italy, ca. 75 BCE (James E. Packer). ◼◀

Republican temples combined Etruscan plans and Greek elevations. This stone pseudoperipteral temple employs the Ionic order, but it has a staircase and freestanding columns only at the front.

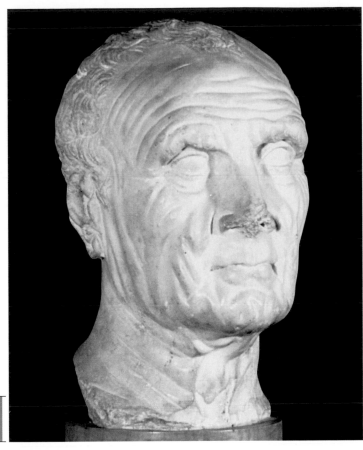

was one way the patrician class celebrated its elevated position in society. The subjects of these portraits were almost exclusively men of advanced age, for generally only elders held power in the Republic. These patricians did not ask sculptors to idealize them. Instead, they requested brutally realistic images with their distinctive features, in the tradition of the treasured household imagines.

One of the most striking of these so-called *veristic* (superrealistic) portraits is the head of an unidentified patrician (FIG. **3-11**) from Osimo. The sculptor painstakingly recorded each rise and fall, each bulge and fold, of the facial surface, like a map maker who did not want to miss the slightest detail of surface change. Scholars debate whether Republican veristic portraits are truly blunt records of individual features or exaggerated types designed to make a statement about personality: serious, experienced, determined, loyal to family and state—the most admired virtues during the Republic.

Pompeii and the Cities of Vesuvius

On August 24, 79 CE, Mount Vesuvius, a long-dormant volcano, suddenly erupted, burying many prosperous towns around the Bay of Naples, among them Pompeii (FIG. **3-12**). The eruption was a catastrophe for the Romans but a boon for archaeologists, enabling them to reconstruct the art and life of the Vesuvian towns to a degree impossible anywhere else.

The Oscans, one of the many Italic population groups occupying Italy during the peak of Etruscan power, were the first to settle at Pompeii. Toward the end of the fifth century BCE, the Samnites, another Italic people, took over the town. Under the influence of their Greek neighbors, the

1 in.

3-11 Head of an old man, from Osimo, mid-first century BCE. Marble, life-size. Palazzo del Municipio, Osimo.

Veristic (superrealistic) portraits of old men from distinguished families were the norm during the Republic. The sculptor of this head painstakingly recorded every detail of the elderly man's face.

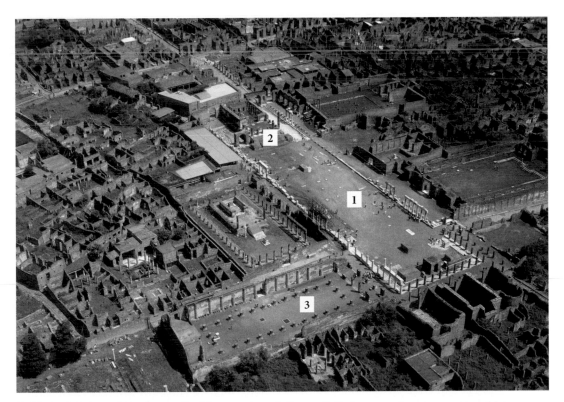

3-12 Aerial view of the forum (looking northeast), Pompeii, Italy, second century BCE and later. (1) forum, (2) Temple of Jupiter (Capitolium), (3) basilica.

The center of Roman civic life was the forum. At Pompeii, colonnades frame a rectangular plaza with the city's main temple at the north end and the basilica (law court) at the southwest corner.

Samnites greatly expanded the original settlement and gave monumental shape to the city center. Pompeii fought with other Italian cities on the losing side against Rome in the so-called Social War that ended in 89 BCE, and in 80 BCE, Sulla founded a new Roman colony on the site, with Latin as its official language. The colony's population had grown to between 10,000 and 20,000 when Mount Vesuvius buried Pompeii in volcanic ash.

Forum The center of civic life in any Roman town was its *forum* (public square). Pompeii's forum (FIG. 3-12, no. 1) lies in the southwest corner of the expanded Roman city but at the heart of the original town. The forum probably took on monumental form in the second century BCE when the Samnites, inspired by Hellenistic architecture, constructed two-story *porticos* (colonnades) on three sides of the long and narrow plaza. At the north end they built the Temple of Jupiter (FIG. 3-12, no. 2). When Pompeii became a Roman colony, the Romans converted the temple into a *Capitolium*—a triple shrine to Jupiter, Juno, and Minerva. The temple is of standard Republican type, constructed of tufa covered with fine white stucco and combining an Etruscan plan with Greek columns. It faces into the civic square, dominating the area. This contrasts with the siting of Greek temples (FIG. 2-36), which stood in isolation and could be approached and viewed from all sides, like colossal statues on giant stepped pedestals. The Roman forum, like the Etrusco-Roman temple, has a chief side, a focus of attention.

All around the square, behind the colonnades, were secular and religious structures, including the town's adminis-

trative offices. Most important was the *basilica* at the southwest corner (FIG. 3-12, no. 3). It is the earliest well-preserved example of its kind. Constructed during the late second century BCE, the basilica was Pompeii's law court and administrative center. In plan it resembled the forum itself: long and narrow, with two stories of columns dividing the interior into a central *nave* and flanking *aisles*.

Amphitheater Shortly after the Romans took control of Pompeii, two of the town's wealthiest officials used their own funds to build the earliest known *amphitheater* (FIG. **3-13**) at the southeastern end of town. The word *amphitheater* means "double theater," and Roman amphitheaters resemble two Greek theaters put together. Greek theaters were always situated on natural hillsides (FIG. 2-51), but supporting an amphitheater's continuous elliptical *cavea* (seating area) required building an artificial mountain. Only concrete, unknown to the Greeks, could easily meet that requirement (see "Roman Concrete Construction," page 97). In the Pompeii amphitheater, shallow concrete barrel vaults (FIG. **3-14a**) form a giant retaining wall holding up the earthen mound and stone seats. Barrel vaults running all the way through the elliptical mountain form the tunnels leading to the *arena*, the central area where the Pompeians staged bloody *gladiator* combats and wild animal hunts. (*Arena* is Latin for "sand," which soaked up the blood of the wounded and killed.) Roman amphitheaters stand in sharp contrast, both architecturally and functionally, to Greek theaters, where actors performed comedies and tragedies.

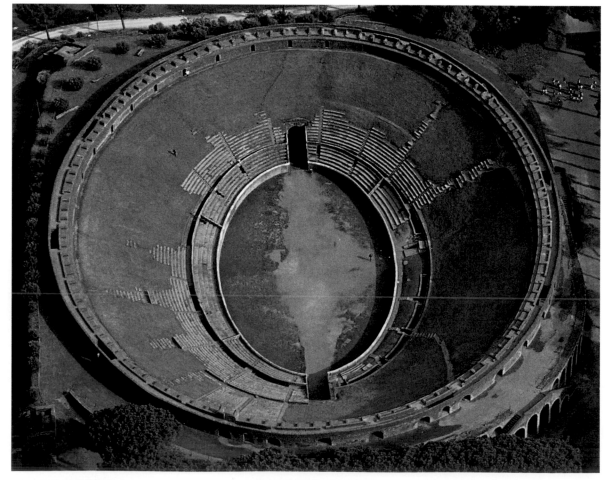

3-13 Aerial view of the amphitheater (looking southeast), Pompeii, Italy, ca. 70 BCE.

Pompeii boasts the earliest known amphitheater. Roman concrete technology made its elliptical cavea possible. The Pompeians staged bloody gladiatorial combats and wild animal hunts in the arena.

Roman Concrete Construction

The history of Roman architecture would be very different had the Romans been content to use the same building materials the Greeks, Etruscans, and other ancient peoples did. Instead, the Romans developed concrete construction, which revolutionized architectural design. Roman builders mixed *concrete* according to a changing recipe of lime mortar, volcanic sand, water, and small stones (*caementa*, from which the English word *cement* derives). Workers poured the mixture into wooden frames and left it to dry. When the concrete hardened completely, they removed the wooden molds, revealing a solid mass of great strength, though rough in appearance. The Romans often covered the rough concrete with stucco or with marble *revetment* (facing). Despite this lengthy procedure, concrete walls were much less costly to construct than walls of imported Greek marble or even local tufa and travertine.

The advantages of concrete went well beyond cost, however. It was possible to fashion concrete shapes unachievable in masonry construction, especially huge vaulted and domed rooms without internal supports. The new medium became a vehicle for shaping architectural space and enabled Roman architects to design buildings in revolutionary ways.

The most common types of Roman concrete vaults and domes are

Barrel vaults Also called the *tunnel vault,* the *barrel vault* (FIG. 3-14a) is an extension of a simple *arch,* creating a semicylindrical ceiling over parallel walls. Pre-Roman builders constructed barrel vaults using traditional ashlar masonry (FIG. 1-20), but those earlier vaults were less stable than concrete barrel vaults. If even a single block of a cut-stone vault comes loose, the whole vault may collapse. Also, masonry barrel vaults can be illuminated only by light entering at either end of the tunnel. Using concrete, Roman builders could place windows at any point in a barrel vault, because once the concrete hardened, it formed a seamless sheet of "artificial stone" in which the openings did not lessen the vault's structural integrity. Whether made of stone or concrete, barrel vaults require *buttressing* (lateral support) of the walls below the vaults to counteract their downward and outward *thrust.*

Groin vaults A *groin* (or *cross*) *vault* (FIG. 3-14b) is formed by the intersection at right angles of two barrel vaults of equal size. Besides appearing lighter than the barrel vault, the groin vault needs less buttressing. Whereas the barrel vault's thrust is continuous along the entire length of the supporting wall, the groin vault's thrust is concentrated along the groins, the lines at the juncture of the two barrel vaults. Buttressing is needed only at the points where the groins meet the vault's vertical supports, usually *piers.* The system leaves the area between the piers open, enabling light to enter. Builders can construct groin vaults as well as barrel vaults using stone blocks, but masonry groin vaults have the same structural limitations when compared to concrete vaults.

When a series of groin vaults covers an interior hall (FIG. 3-14c; compare FIGS. 3-37, 3-46, and 3-51), the open lateral arches of the vaults form the equivalent of a *clerestory* of a traditional timber-roofed structure (FIGS. 4-3 and 4-4). A *fenestrated* (with openings or windows) sequence of groin vaults has a major advantage over a wooden clerestory. Concrete vaults are relatively fireproof.

Hemispherical domes If a barrel vault is a round arch extended in a line, then a hemispherical *dome* (FIG. 3-14d) is a round arch rotated around the full circumference of a circle. Masonry domes (FIG. 2-12), like masonry vaults, cannot accommodate windows without threat to their stability. Concrete domes can be opened up even at their apex with a circular "eye" (*oculus*), enabling light to reach the often vast spaces beneath (FIG. 3-40). Hemispherical domes usually rest on concrete cylindrical *drums.*

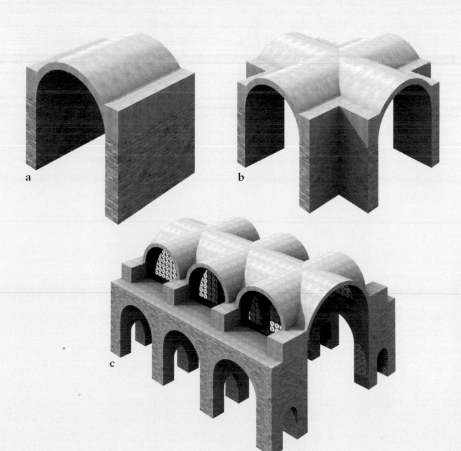

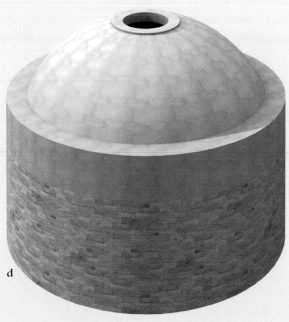

3-14 Roman concrete construction (John Burge). (**a**) barrel vault, (**b**) groin vault, (**c**) fenestrated sequence of groin vaults, (**d**) hemispherical dome with oculus.

Concrete domes and vaults of varying designs enabled Roman builders to revolutionize the history of architecture by shaping interior spaces in novel ways.

The Roman House

The entrance to a typical Roman *domus* (private house) was through a narrow foyer (*fauces*), which led to a large central reception area, the *atrium*. The rooms flanking the fauces could open onto the atrium, as in FIG. 3-16, or onto the street, in which case the family could use or rent them as shops. The roof over the atrium was partially open to the sky, not only to admit light but also to channel rainwater into a basin (*impluvium*) to be stored in cisterns for household use. Opening onto the sides of the atrium were small bedrooms called *cubicula* (cubicles). At the back were two recessed areas (*alae*, "wings") and the owner's *tablinum* (home office), a dining room (*triclinium*), kitchen, and sometimes a small garden. Extant houses display endless variations of the same basic plan, but all Roman houses of this type were inward-looking in nature. The design shut off the street's noise and dust, and all internal activity focused on the brightly illuminated atrium at the center of the residence.

During the second century BCE, the Roman house took on Greek airs. Builders added a *peristyle* (colonnaded) garden at the rear, as in FIG. 3-16, providing a second internal source of illumination as well as a pleasant setting for meals served in a summer triclinium. The axial symmetry of the plan meant that on entering the fauces of the house, a visitor had a view through the atrium directly into the peristyle garden (as in FIG. 3-15), which often boasted a fountain or pool, marble statuary, mural paintings, and mosaic floors.

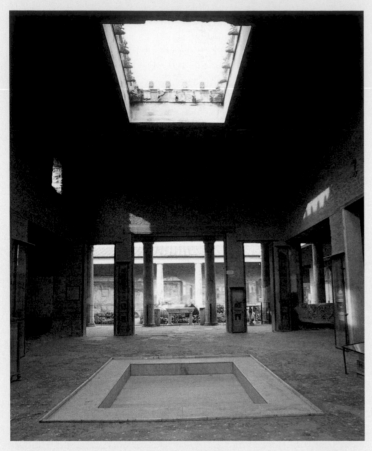

3-15 Atrium of the House of the Vettii, Pompeii, Italy, second century BCE, rebuilt 62–79 CE.

Older Roman houses had a small garden behind the atrium, but beginning in the second century BCE, builders added peristyles with Greek columns at the rear, as in the House of the Vettii.

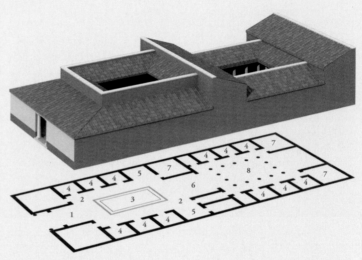

3-16 Restored view and plan of a typical Roman house of the Late Republic and Early Empire (John Burge). (1) fauces, (2) atrium, (3) impluvium, (4) cubiculum, (5) ala, (6) tablinum, (7) triclinium, (8) peristyle.

Roman houses were inward-looking with a central atrium open to the sky and an impluvium to collect rainwater. A visitor standing in the fauces had an axial view through to the peristyle garden.

House of the Vettii The evidence from Pompeii regarding Roman domestic architecture (see "The Roman House," above) is unparalleled anywhere else. One of the best-preserved houses at Pompeii is the House of the Vettii. A photograph (FIG. 3-15) taken in the *fauces* shows the *impluvium* in the center of the *atrium*, the opening in the roof above, and, in the background, the *peristyle* garden (FIG. 3-16). Of course, only the wealthy—whether patricians or former slaves like the Vettius brothers, who made their fortune as merchants—could own large private houses. The masses, especially in expensive cities like Rome, lived in multistory apartment houses.

Samnite House The houses and villas around Mount Vesuvius have also yielded the most complete record of the changing fashions in mural painting anywhere in the ancient world. Art historians divide the various Roman mural types into four so-called Pompeian Styles. In the *First Style,* the decorator's aim was to imitate costly marble panels (compare FIG. 3-40) using painted stucco relief. The fauces (FIG. 3-17) of the so-called Samnite House at Herculaneum greets visitors with a stunning illusion of walls faced with marbles imported from quarries throughout the Mediterranean. This approach to wall decoration is comparable to the modern practice of using cheaper manufactured materials to approximate the

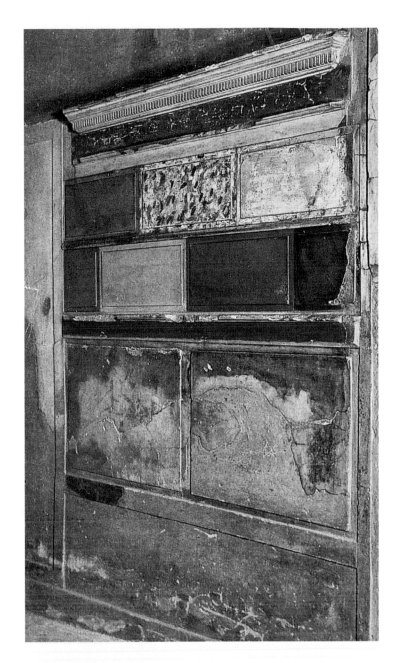

In First Style murals, the aim was to imitate costly marble panels using painted stucco relief. The style is Greek in origin and another example of the Hellenization of Republican architecture.

look and shape of genuine wood paneling. The First Style is not, however, uniquely Roman. Similar mural schemes are well documented in Greece from the late fourth century BCE on. The use of the First Style in Italian houses is yet another example of the Hellenization of Republican architecture.

Villa of the Mysteries In contrast, the *Second Style,* introduced around 80 BCE, seems to be a Roman innovation and is in most respects the antithesis of the First Style. Second Style painters aimed to dissolve a room's confining walls and replace them with the illusion of an imaginary three-dimensional world. An early example of the new style is the room (FIG. **3-18**) that gives its name to the Villa of the Mysteries at Pompeii. Many archaeologists believe this chamber was used to celebrate, in private, the rites of the Greek god Dionysos (Roman Bacchus). Dionysos was the focus of an unofficial mystery religion popular among Italian women at this time. The precise nature of the Dionysiac rites is unknown, but the figural cycle in the Villa of the Mysteries, illustrating mortals (all female save for one boy) interacting with mythological figures, probably provides some evidence for the cult's initiation rites. In these rites, young women united in marriage with Dionysos. The Second Style painter created the illusion of a shallow ledge on which human and divine actors move around the room. Especially striking is the way some of the figures interact across the corners of the room. For example, a seminude winged woman at the far right of the rear wall lashes out with her whip across the space of the room at a kneeling woman with a bare back (the initiate and bride-to-be of Dionysos) on the left end of the right wall.

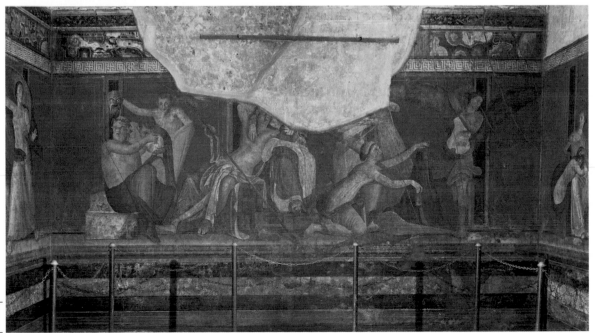

3-18 Dionysiac mystery frieze, Second Style wall paintings in room 5 of the Villa of the Mysteries, Pompeii, Italy, ca. 60–50 BCE. Frieze, 5' 4" high.

Second Style painters created the illusion of an imaginary three-dimensional world on the walls of Roman houses. The figures in this room act out the initiation rites of the mystery religion of Dionysos.

1 ft.

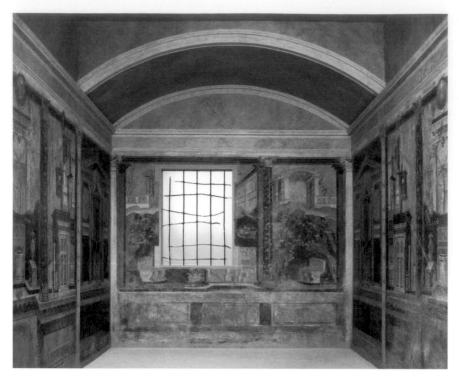
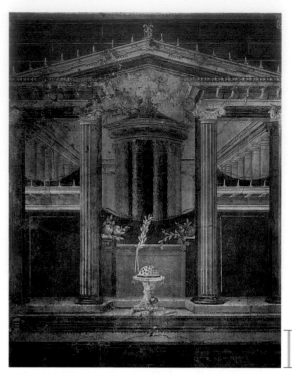

1 ft.

3-19 Second Style wall paintings (general view, *left,* and detail of tholos, *right*) from cubiculum M of the Villa of Publius Fannius Synistor, Boscoreale, Italy, ca. 50–40 BCE. Fresco, 8′ 9″ high. Metropolitan Museum of Art, New York.

In this Second Style bedroom, the painter opened up the walls with vistas of towns, temples, and colonnaded courtyards. The convincing illusionism is due in part to the artist's use of linear perspective.

Boscoreale In later Second Style designs, painters created a three-dimensional setting that also extends beyond the wall, as in cubiculum M (FIG. **3-19**) from the Villa of Publius Fannius Synistor at Boscoreale. All around the room the painter opened up the walls with vistas of Italian towns, marble tem-

ples, and colonnaded courtyards. Painted doors and gates invite the viewer to walk through the wall into the magnificent world the painter created. Familiarity with *linear perspective* (see "Linear and Atmospheric Perspective," Chapter 8, page 237) explains in large part the Boscoreale painter's success in

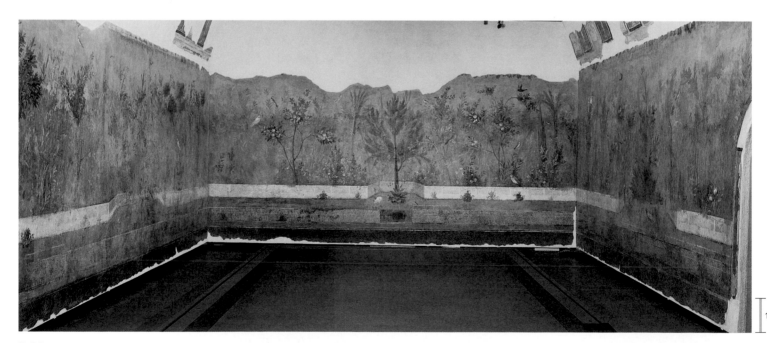

1 ft.

3-20 Gardenscape, Second Style wall paintings, from the Villa of Livia, Primaporta, Italy, ca. 30–20 BCE. Fresco, 6′ 7″ high. Museo Nazionale Romano—Palazzo Massimo alle Terme, Rome.

The ultimate example of a Second Style "picture window" wall is Livia's gardenscape. To suggest recession, the painter used atmospheric perspective, intentionally blurring the most distant forms.

suggesting depth. In this kind of perspective, all the receding lines in a composition converge on a single point along the painting's central axis. Ancient writers state that Greek painters of the fifth century BCE first used linear perspective for the design of Athenian stage sets (hence its Greek name, *skenographia*, "scene painting"). In the Boscoreale cubiculum, the painter most successfully used linear perspective in the far corners, where a low gate leads to a peristyle framing a round temple (FIG. 3-19, *right*).

Primaporta The ultimate example of a Second Style picture-window mural is the gardenscape (FIG. **3-20**) in the Villa of Livia, wife of the emperor Augustus, at Primaporta, just north of Rome. To suggest recession, the painter mastered another kind of perspective, *atmospheric perspective*, indicating depth by the increasingly blurred appearance of objects in the distance. At Primaporta, the artist precisely painted the fence, trees, and birds in the foreground, whereas the details of the dense foliage in the background are indistinct.

Boscotrecase The Primaporta gardenscape is the polar opposite of First Style designs, which reinforce, rather than deny, the heavy presence of confining walls. But tastes changed rapidly in the Roman world, as in society today. Not long after Livia decorated her villa, Roman patrons began to favor mural designs that reasserted the primacy of the wall surface. In the *Third Style* of Pompeian painting, popular from about 15 BCE to 60 CE, artists no longer attempted to replace the walls with three-dimensional worlds of their own creation. Nor did they seek to imitate the appearance of the marble walls of Hellenistic kings. Instead they adorned walls with delicate linear fantasies sketched on predominantly *monochromatic* (one-color) backgrounds. One of the earliest examples of the new style is cubiculum 15 (FIG. **3-21**) in the Villa of Agrippa Postumus at Boscotrecase. Nowhere did the artist use illusionistic painting to penetrate the wall. In place of the stately columns of the Second Style are insubstantial and impossibly thin *colonnettes* supporting featherweight canopies barely reminiscent of pediments. In the center of this delicate and elegant architectural frame is a tiny floating landscape painted directly on the jet black ground. It is hard to imagine a sharper contrast with the panoramic gardenscape at Livia's villa.

1 ft.

3-21 Detail of a Third Style wall painting, from cubiculum 15 of the Villa of Agrippa Postumus, Boscotrecase, Italy, ca. 10 BCE. Fresco, 7′ 8″ high. Metropolitan Museum of Art, New York.

In the Third Style, Roman painters decorated walls with delicate linear fantasies sketched on monochromatic backgrounds. Here, a tiny floating landscape on a black ground is the central motif.

3-22 Fourth Style wall paintings in the Ixion Room (triclinium P) of the House of the Vettii (FIG. 3-15), Pompeii, Italy, ca. 70–79 CE.

Fourth Style murals are often garishly colored, crowded, and confused compositions mixing fragmentary architectural views, mythological paintings, and First and Third Style motifs.

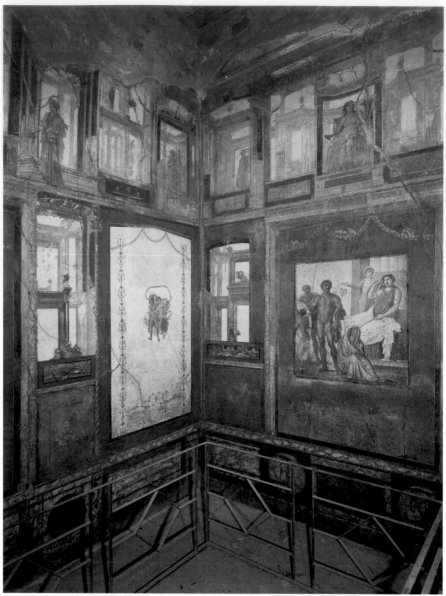

Ixion Room In the *Fourth Style,* a taste for illusionism returned once again. This style was fashionable in the two decades before the Vesuvian eruption of 79 CE and is characterized by crowded and confused compositions mixing fragmentary architectural vistas, framed panel paintings, and motifs favored in the First and Third Styles. The Ixion Room (FIG. **3-22**), a triclinium opening onto the peristyle in the House of the Vettii, is a characteristic example of the late Fourth Style. Dating just before the eruption of 79 CE, the mural scheme is a kind of summation of all the previous styles. The lowest zone, for example, is one of the most successful imitations anywhere of costly multicolored imported marbles. The large white panels in the corners of the room, with their delicate floral frames and floating central motifs, would fit naturally into the most elegant Third Style design. Unmistakably Fourth Style, however, are the fragmentary architectural vistas of the central and upper zones. They are unrelated to one another, do not constitute a unified cityscape beyond the wall, and the painted figures would tumble into the room if they took a single step forward.

The Ixion Room takes its name from the mythological painting at the center of the rear wall. Ixion had attempted to seduce Hera, and Zeus punished him by binding him to a perpetually spinning wheel. The panels on the two side walls also have Greek myths as subjects. The Ixion Room is a kind of private art gallery. Many art historians believe lost Greek panel paintings were the models for the many mythological paintings on Third and Fourth Style walls. Although few, if any, of the Pompeiian paintings can be described as true copies of famous Greek works, they attest to the Romans' continuing admiration for Greek art.

Still Life Another important genre of Roman mural painting was the *still life* (a painting of inanimate objects, artfully arranged). A still life with peaches and a carafe (FIG. **3-23**),

3-23 Still life with peaches, detail of a Fourth Style wall painting, from Herculaneum, Italy, ca. 62–79 CE. Fresco, 1′ 2″ × 1′ 1½″. Museo Archeologico Nazionale, Naples.

The Roman interest in illusionism explains the popularity of still-life paintings. This painter paid scrupulous attention to the play of light and shadow on different shapes and textures.

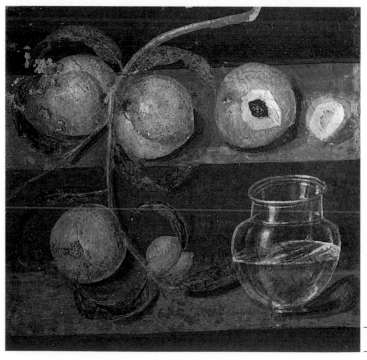

1 in.

a detail of a Fourth Style wall from Herculaneum, is one of the finest extant examples. The painter was a master of illusionism who devoted as much attention to the shadows and highlights on the fruit, the stem and leaves, and the glass jar as to the objects themselves.

The Early Empire

The murder of Julius Caesar on the Ides of March, 44 BCE, plunged the Roman world into a bloody civil war. The fighting lasted until 31 BCE when Octavian, Caesar's grandnephew and adopted son, crushed the naval forces of Mark Antony and Queen Cleopatra of Egypt at Actium in northwestern Greece. Antony and Cleopatra committed suicide, and in 30 BCE, Egypt, once the wealthiest and most powerful kingdom of the ancient world, became another province in the ever-expanding Roman Empire.

Augustus Historians mark the passage from the Roman Republic to the Roman Empire from the day in 27 BCE when the Senate conferred the majestic title of Augustus (the Majestic, or Exalted, One; r. 27 BCE–14 CE) on Octavian. The Empire was ostensibly a continuation of the Republic, with the same constitutional offices, but in fact Augustus, as *princeps* (first citizen), occupied all the key positions. He was consul and *imperator* ("commander in chief"; root of the word *emperor*) and even, after 12 BCE, *pontifex maximus* (chief priest of the state religion). These offices gave Augustus control of all aspects of Roman public life.

With powerful armies keeping order on the Empire's frontiers and no opposition at home, Augustus brought peace and prosperity to a war-weary Mediterranean world. Known in his day as the *Pax Augusta* (Augustan Peace), the peace Augustus established prevailed for two centuries. It came to be called simply the *Pax Romana*. During this time the emperors commissioned a huge number of public works throughout the Empire, all on an unprecedented scale. Imperial portraits and monuments covered with reliefs recounting the emperors' great deeds reminded people everywhere of the source of peace and prosperity. These portraits and reliefs, however, often presented a picture of the emperors and their achievements bearing little resemblance to historical fact. Their purpose was not to provide an objective record but to mold public opinion.

When Augustus vanquished Antony and Cleopatra and became undisputed master of the Mediterranean world, he was not yet 32 years old. The rule by elders that had characterized the Roman Republic for nearly 500 years came to an abrupt end. Suddenly, Roman portraitists had to produce images of a youthful head of state. But Augustus was not merely young. The Senate had declared Caesar a god after his death, and Augustus, though never claiming to be a god himself, widely advertised himself as the son of a god. His portraits were designed to present the image of a godlike leader who miraculously never aged.

The models for Augustus's idealized portraits were Classical Greek statues. The portrait of Augustus (FIG. **3-24**)

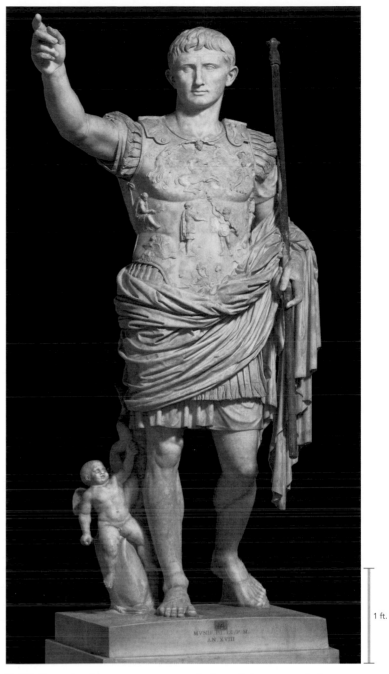

3-24 Portrait of Augustus as general, from Primaporta, Italy, early-first-century CE copy of a bronze original of ca. 20 BCE. Marble, 6′ 8″ high. Musei Vaticani, Rome. ◼◀

The models for Augustus's idealized portraits, which depict him as a never-aging god, were Classical Greek statues (FIG. 2-35). This statue portrays the emperor as commander in chief.

from Primaporta depicts the emperor as general, standing like Polykleitos's *Doryphoros* (FIG. 2-35) but with his right arm raised to address his troops in the manner of the orator Aule Metele (FIG. 3-8). Augustus's head, although depicting a recognizable individual, also emulates the Polykleitan youth's head in its overall shape, the sharp ridges of the brows, and the tight cap of layered hair. The reliefs on his breastplate celebrate a victory over the Parthians. The Cupid at Augustus's feet refers to his divine descent from Venus through Julius Caesar.

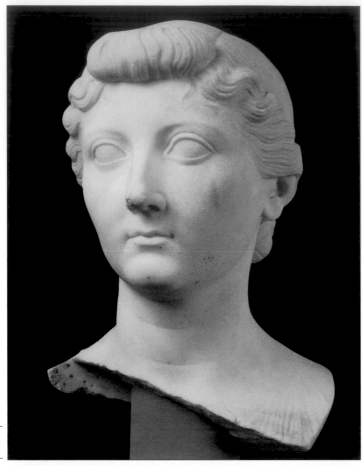

3-25 Portrait bust of Livia, from Arsinoe, Egypt, early first century CE. Marble, 1′ 1½″ high. Ny Carlsberg Glyptotek, Copenhagen.

Although Livia sports the latest Roman coiffure, her youthful appearance and sharply defined features derive from images of Greek goddesses. She died at 87, but, like Augustus, never aged in her portraits.

Livia A marble portrait (FIG. **3-25**) of Livia shows that the imperial women of the Augustan age shared the emperor's eternal youthfulness. Although the empress sports the latest Roman coiffure, with the hair rolled over the forehead and knotted at the nape of the neck, her blemish-free skin and sharply defined features derive from images of Classical Greek goddesses. Livia outlived Augustus by 15 years, dying at age 87. In her portraits, the coiffure changed with the introduction of each new fashion, but her face remained ever young, befitting her exalted position in the Roman state.

Ara Pacis Augustae On Livia's birthday in 9 BCE, Augustus dedicated the Ara Pacis Augustae (Altar of Augustan Peace; FIG. **3-26**), the monument celebrating his most important achievement, the establishment of peace. Acanthus tendrils adorn the lower zone of the altar's marble precinct walls, which have Corinthian *pilasters* at the corners. The *Corinthian capital* was a Greek innovation of the fifth century BCE, but it did not become popular until Hellenistic and especially Roman times. More ornate then either the Doric or Ionic capital, the Corinthian capital consists of a double row of acanthus leaves, from which tendrils and flowers emerge, wrapped around a bell-shaped echinus. The rich floral and vegetal ornament of the altar's exterior alludes to the prosperity that peace brings.

Four panels on the east and west ends of the Ara Pacis depict carefully selected mythological subjects, including (at the right in FIG. 3-26) a relief of Aeneas making a sacrifice. Aeneas was the son of Venus and one of Augustus's forefathers. The connection between the emperor and Aeneas was a key element of Augustus's political ideology for his new Golden Age. It is no coincidence Vergil wrote the *Aeneid*

3-26 Ara Pacis Augustae (Altar of Augustan Peace, looking northeast), Rome, Italy, 13–9 BCE. ■◀

Augustus sought to present his new order as a Golden Age equaling that of Athens under Pericles. The Ara Pacis celebrates the emperor's most important achievement, the establishment of peace.

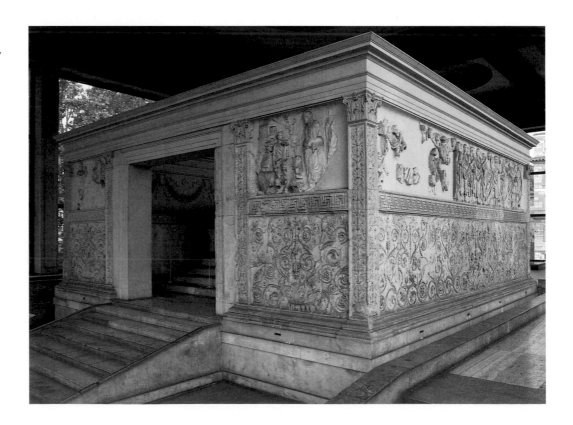

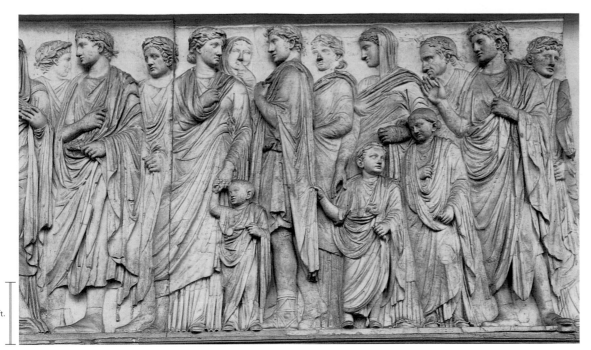

3-27 Procession of the imperial family, detail of the south frieze of the Ara Pacis Augustae, Rome, Italy, 13–9 BCE. Marble, 5′ 3″ high. ◼◀

Although inspired by the Ionic frieze (FIG. 2-41) of the Parthenon, the Ara Pacis procession depicts recognizable individuals, including children. Augustus promoted marriage and childbearing.

1 ft.

during the rule of Augustus. The epic poem glorified the young emperor by celebrating the founder of the Julian line.

Processions of the imperial family (FIG. **3-27**) and other important dignitaries appear on the long north and south sides of the Ara Pacis. The inspiration for these parallel friezes was very likely the Panathenaic procession frieze (FIG. 2-41, *bottom*) of the Parthenon. Augustus sought to present his new order as a Golden Age equaling that of Athens under Pericles. The emulation of Classical models thus made a political statement, as well as an artistic one. Even so, the Roman and Greek processions are very different in character. On the Parthenon, anonymous figures act out an event that recurred every four years. The frieze stands for all Panathenaic Festival processions. The Ara Pacis depicts a specific event—probably the inaugural ceremony of 13 BCE—and recognizable historical figures. Among those portrayed

are children, who restlessly tug on their elders' garments and talk to one another when they should be quiet on a solemn occasion. Augustus was concerned about a decline in the birthrate among the Roman nobility, and he enacted a series of laws designed to promote marriage, marital fidelity, and raising children. The portrayal of men with their families on the Altar of Peace served as a moral exemplar.

Pont-du-Gard During the Pax Romana, Rome sent engineers to construct aqueducts, roads, and bridges throughout its far-flung empire. In southern France, outside Nîmes, the aqueduct-bridge known as the Pont-du-Gard still stands (FIG. **3-28**). The aqueduct provided about 100 gallons of water a day for each inhabitant of Nîmes from a mountain spring some 30 miles away. The water flowed over the considerable distance by gravity alone in channels built with a continuous

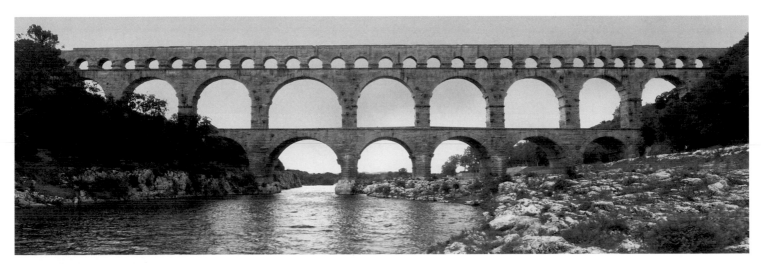

3-28 Pont-du-Gard, Nîmes, France, ca. 16 BCE. ◼◀

Roman engineers constructed roads, bridges, and aqueducts throughout the empire. This aqueduct bridge brought water from a distant mountain spring to Nîmes—about 100 gallons a day for each inhabitant.

gradual decline over the entire route from source to city. The three-story Pont-du-Gard maintained the height of the water channel where the water crossed the Gard River. Each large arch spans some 82 feet and consists of blocks weighing up to two tons each. The bridge's uppermost level is a row of smaller arches, three above each of the large openings below. They carry the water channel itself. The harmonious proportional relationship between the larger and smaller arches reveals that the Roman hydraulic engineer who designed the aqueduct also had a keen aesthetic sense.

The Flavians For a half century after Augustus's death, Rome's emperors all came from his family, the Julians, or his wife Livia's, the Claudians. But the outrageous behavior of Nero (r. 54–68 CE) produced a powerful backlash. Facing assassination, Nero commited suicide in 68 CE, bringing the Julio-Claudian dynasty to an end. A year of renewed civil strife followed. The man who emerged triumphant in this brief but bloody conflict was Vespasian (r. 69–79 CE), a general who had served under Nero. Vespasian, whose family name was Flavius, had two sons, Titus (r. 79–81 CE) and Domitian (r. 81–96 CE). The Flavian dynasty ruled Rome for more than a quarter century.

Colosseum The Flavian Amphitheater, or Colosseum (FIGS. **3-29** and 3-9, no. 12), was one of Vespasian's first undertakings after becoming emperor. The decision to build the Colosseum was very shrewd politically. The site chosen was on the property Nero had confiscated from the Roman people after a great fire in 64 CE in order to build a private villa for himself. By constructing the new amphitheater there, Vespasian reclaimed the land for the public and also provided Romans with the largest arena for gladiatorial combats and other lavish spectacles ever constructed. The Colosseum could hold more than 50,000 spectators, but it takes its name from its location beside the Colossus of Nero (FIG. 3-9, no. 11). The 120-foot-tall statue at the entrance to his urban villa portrayed the emperor as the sun god. To mark the opening of the Colosseum, the Flavians staged games for 100 days. The highlight was the flooding of the arena to stage a complete naval battle with more than 3,000 participants.

The Colosseum, like the much earlier Pompeian amphitheater (FIG. 3-13), could not have been built without concrete. A complex system of barrel-vaulted corridors holds up

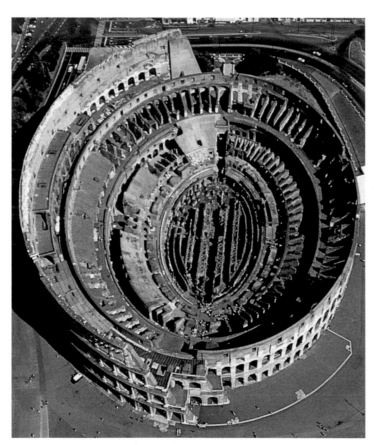

3-29 Aerial view of the Colosseum (Flavian Amphitheater, looking east), Rome, Italy, ca. 70–80 CE. ◼◀

Vespasian built the Colosseum, the world's largest amphitheater, on land Nero had confiscated from the public. A complex system of concrete barrel vaults once held up the seats for 50,000 spectators.

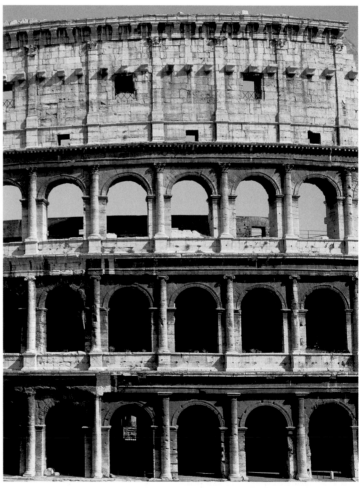

3-30 Detail of the facade of the Colosseum (Flavian Amphitheater), Rome, Italy, ca. 70–80 CE. ◼◀

Engaged Tuscan, Ionic, and Corinthian columns frame the arcuated openings of the Colosseum's facade. This mix of Greek and Roman elements masked the amphitheater's skeleton of concrete vaults.

the enormous oval seating area. This concrete "skeleton" is exposed today because the amphitheater's marble seats were hauled away during the Middle Ages and Renaissance. Also visible now are the arena substructures, which housed waiting rooms for the gladiators, animal cages, and machinery for raising and lowering stage sets as well as animals and humans. Ingenious lifting devices brought beasts from their dark dens into the arena's bright light.

The exterior travertine shell (FIG. **3-30**) is approximately 160 feet high, the height of a modern 16-story building. The architect divided the facade into four bands, with large arched openings piercing the lower three. Ornamental Greek orders frame the arches in the standard Roman sequence for multistoried buildings: from the ground up, Tuscan, Ionic,

and then Corinthian. The use of engaged columns and a lintel to frame the openings in the Colosseum's facade is a common motif on Roman buildings. Like the pseudoperipteral temple (FIG. 3-10), which combines Greek orders and Etruscan plan, this way of decorating a building's facade mixed Greek orders with an architectural form foreign to Greek post-and-lintel architecture, namely the arch. The Roman practice of framing an arch with Greek engaged columns had no structural purpose, but it added variety to the surface and unified the multistoried facade by casting a net of verticals and horizontals over it.

Flavian Portraiture Flavian portraits survive in large numbers, but a marble bust (FIG. **3-31**) of a young woman, probably a Flavian princess, is of special interest. The portrait is notable for its elegance and delicacy and for the virtuoso way the sculptor rendered the differing textures of hair and flesh. The elaborate Flavian coiffure, with its corkscrew curls picked out using a drill instead of a chisel, is a dense mass of light and shadow set off boldly from the softly modeled and highly polished skin of the face and swanlike neck.

Arch of Titus When Titus died in 81 CE, his younger brother Domitian succeeded him. The new emperor set up a *triumphal arch* (FIGS. **3-32** and 3-9, no. 9) in Titus's honor on

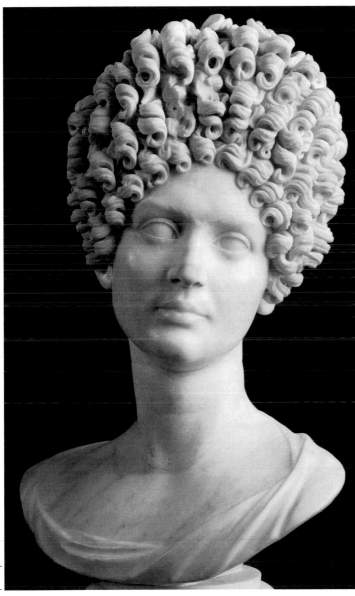

1 in.

3-31 Portrait bust of a Flavian woman, from Rome, Italy, ca. 90 CE. Marble, 2′ 1″ high. Musei Capitolini—Museo Capitolino, Rome.

The Flavian sculptor reproduced the elaborate coiffure of this elegant woman by drilling deep holes for the corkscrew curls, and carved the rest of the hair and the face with hammer and chisel.

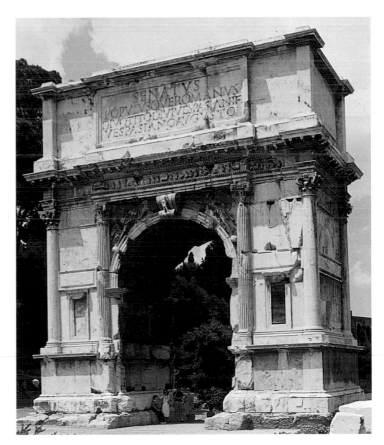

3-32 West facade of the Arch of Titus, Rome, Italy, after 81 CE. ◼️

Domitian set up this arch on the road leading into the Roman Forum to honor his brother, the emperor Titus, who became a god after his death. Victories fill the spandrels of the arcuated passageway.

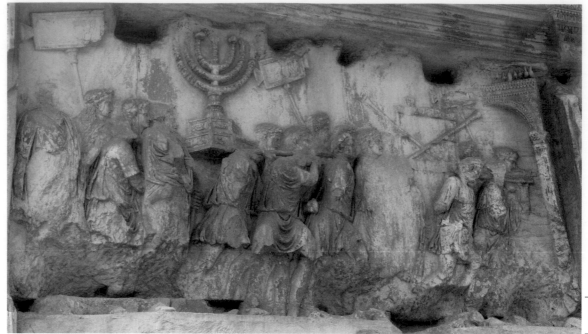

3-33 Spoils of Jerusalem, relief panel in the passageway of the Arch of Titus (FIG. 3-32), Rome, Italy, after 81 CE. Marble, 7' 10" high.

The relief panels of the Arch of Titus commemorate the emperor's greatest achievement—the conquest of Judaea. Here, Roman soldiers carry in triumph the spoils of the Jewish temple in Jerusalem.

1 ft.

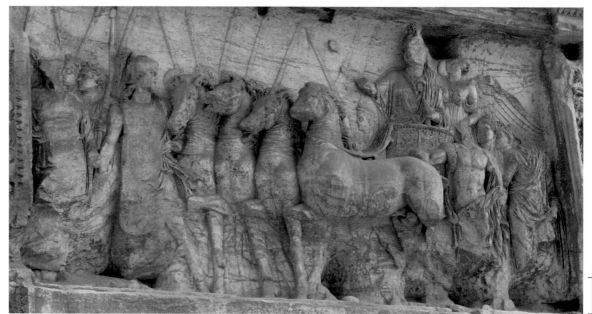

3-34 Triumph of Titus, relief panel in the passageway of the Arch of Titus (FIG. 3-32), Rome, Italy, after 81 CE. Marble, 7' 10" high.

Victory crowns Titus in his triumphal chariot. Also present are personifications of Honor and Valor in this first known instance of the intermingling of human and divine figures in a Roman historical relief.

1 ft.

the road leading into the Roman Forum (FIG. 3-9, no. 7). The Arch of Titus is a typical early triumphal arch in having only one passageway. As on the Colosseum, engaged columns frame the *arcuated* (curved or arched) opening. Reliefs depicting personified Victories fill the *spandrels* (the area between the arch's curve and the framing columns and entablature). A dedicatory inscription stating the Senate erected the arch to honor the god Titus, son of the god Vespasian, dominates the *attic*. The Senate normally proclaimed Roman emperors gods after they died, unless they ran afoul of the senators and were damned. The statues of those who suffered *damnatio memoriae* were toppled, and their names erased from public inscriptions. This was Nero's fate.

Inside the passageway of the Arch of Titus are two great relief panels. They represent the triumphal parade of Titus after his return from the conquest of Judaea at the end of

the Jewish wars in 70 CE. One of the reliefs (FIG. **3-33**) depicts Roman soldiers carrying the spoils from the temple in Jerusalem. Despite considerable damage to the relief, the illusion of movement is convincing. The parade emerges from the left background into the center foreground and disappears through the obliquely placed arch in the right background. The energy and swing of the column of soldiers suggest a rapid march. The sculptor rejected the low relief style of the Ara Pacis (FIG. 3-27) in favor of extremely deep carving, which produces strong shadows. The heads of the forward figures have broken off because they stood free from the block. Their high relief emphasized their different placement in space compared with the heads in low relief, which are intact. The play of light and shade across the protruding foreground and receding background figures enhances the sense of movement.

On the other side of the passageway, the panel (FIG. **3-34**) shows Titus in his triumphal chariot. Victory rides with the emperor and places a wreath on his head. Below her is a bare-chested youth who is probably a personification of Honor (*Honos*). A female personification of Valor (*Virtus*) leads the horses. These allegorical figures transform the relief from a record of Titus's battlefield success into a celebration of imperial virtues. A comparable intermingling of divine and human figures characterized the Mysteries frieze (FIG. 3-18) at Pompeii, but the Arch of Titus panel is the first known instance of divine beings interacting with humans on an official Roman historical relief. (On the Ara Pacis, FIG. 3-26, the gods, heroes, and personifications appear in separate framed panels, carefully segregated from the procession of living Romans.) The Arch of Titus, however, honors the god Titus, not the living emperor. Soon afterward, however, this kind of interaction between mortals and immortals became a staple of Roman narrative relief sculpture, even on monuments set up while the emperor was alive.

The High Empire

Domitian's extravagant lifestyle and ego resembled Nero's. He so angered the senators that he was assassinated in 96 CE. The first emperor of the second century, chosen with the consent of the Senate, was Trajan (r. 98–117 CE), a capable and popular general. Born in Spain, Trajan was the first non-Italian to rule Rome. During his reign, the Roman Empire reached its greatest extent, and the imperial government took on ever greater responsibility for its people's welfare by instituting a number of farsighted social programs.

Forum of Trajan Trajan's major building project in Rome was a huge new forum (FIGS. **3-35** and 3-9, no. 5), which glorified his victories in two wars in Dacia (see page 87). The architect was APOLLODORUS OF DAMASCUS, Trajan's chief military engineer, who during the Dacian campaign had constructed a world-famous bridge across the Danube River. Apollodorus's plan incorporated the main features of most early forums (FIG. 3-12), except a huge basilica, not a temple, dominated the colonnaded open square. The temple (completed after the emperor's death and dedicated to the newest god in the Roman pantheon, Trajan himself) stood instead behind the basilica. Entry to Trajan's forum was through an impressive gateway resembling a triumphal arch. Inside the forum were other reminders of Trajan's military prowess. A larger-than-life-size gilded-bronze equestrian statue of the emperor stood at the center of the great court in front of the basilica. Statues of captive Dacians stood above the columns of the forum porticos.

The Basilica Ulpia (Trajan's family name was Ulpius) was a much larger and far more ornate version of the basilica in the forum of Pompeii (FIG. 3-12, no. 3). As shown in FIG. 3-35, no. 4, it had *apses,* or semicircular recesses, on each short end. Two aisles flanked the nave on each side. The building was vast: about 400 feet long (without the apses) and 200 feet wide. Light entered through clerestory windows, made possible by elevating the timber-roofed nave above the colonnaded aisles. In the Republican basilica at Pompeii, light reached the nave only indirectly through aisle windows. The clerestory (used already at Karnak in New Kingdom Egypt; FIG. 1-33) was a much better solution.

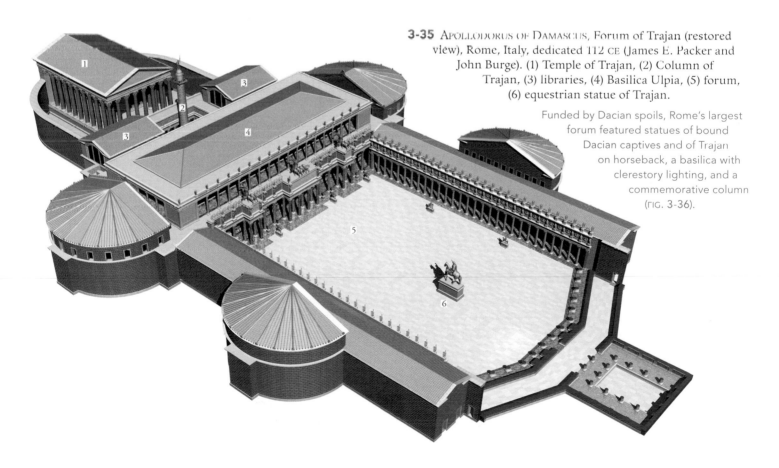

3-35 APOLLODORUS OF DAMASCUS, Forum of Trajan (restored view), Rome, Italy, dedicated 112 CE (James E. Packer and John Burge). (1) Temple of Trajan, (2) Column of Trajan, (3) libraries, (4) Basilica Ulpia, (5) forum, (6) equestrian statue of Trajan.

Funded by Dacian spoils, Rome's largest forum featured statues of bound Dacian captives and of Trajan on horseback, a basilica with clerestory lighting, and a commemorative column (FIG. 3-36).

3-36 Column of Trajan, Forum of Trajan, Rome, Italy, dedicated 112 CE. ◼◼

The spiral frieze (FIG. 3-1) of Trajan's Column tells the story of the Dacian wars in more than 150 episodes. The reliefs depict all aspects of the campaigns, from battles to sacrifices to road and fort construction.

Column of Trajan The Column of Trajan (FIG. **3-36**), erected between the Basilica Ulpia and the Temple of Trajan, still stands. Its monumental base pictures captured Dacian arms and armor. A heroically nude statue of the emperor once topped the column. The spiral frieze winding around the shaft (FIG. 3-1) recounts Trajan's two Dacian campaigns in more than 150 episodes in which some 2,500 figures appear. The relief is very low so as not to distort the contours of the column. Paint enhanced the legibility of the figures, but it is still very difficult for anyone to follow the narrative from beginning to end. Consequently, much of the frieze consists of easily recognizable compositions: Trajan addressing his troops, sacrificing to the gods, and so on. The narrative is not a reliable chronological account of the Dacian wars, as once thought. The sculptors nonetheless accurately recorded the general character of the campaigns. Notably, battle scenes take up only about a quarter of the frieze. The Romans spent more time constructing forts, transporting men and equipment, and preparing for battle than they did fighting. The focus is always on the emperor, who appears repeatedly in the frieze, but the enemy is not belittled. The Romans won because of their superior organization and more powerful army, not because they were inherently superior beings.

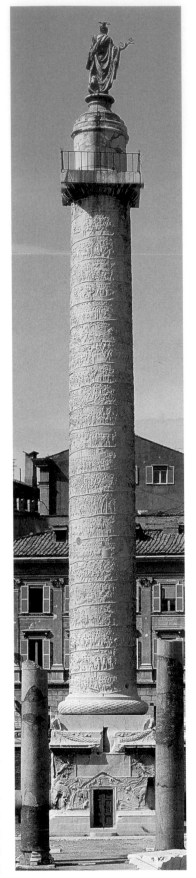

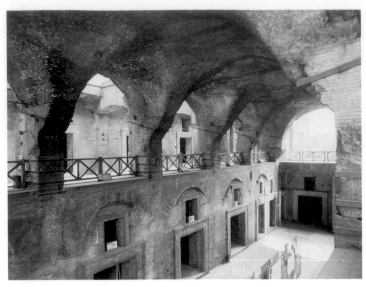

3-37 APOLLODORUS OF DAMASCUS, interior of the great hall, Markets of Trajan, Rome, Italy, ca. 100–112 CE.

The great hall of the Markets of Trajan resembles a modern shopping mall. It housed two floors of shops, with the upper ones set back and lit by skylights. Concrete groin vaults cover the central space.

Markets of Trajan On the Quirinal Hill overlooking the forum, Apollodorus built the Markets of Trajan (FIG. 3-9, no. 6) to house both shops and administrative offices. Concrete made possible the transformation of the hill into a multilevel complex. The basic unit was the *taberna*, a single-room shop covered by a barrel vault. The shops were on several levels. They opened either onto a hemicyclical facade winding around one of the great *exedras* (semicircular recessed areas) of Trajan's forum, onto a paved street higher up the hill, or onto a great indoor market hall (FIG. **3-37**) resembling a modern shopping mall. The hall housed two floors of shops, with the upper shops set back on each side and lit by skylights. Light from the same sources reached the ground-floor shops through arches beneath the great umbrella-like groin vaults (FIG. 3-14c) covering the hall.

Pantheon Upon Trajan's death, Hadrian (r. 117–138 CE), also a Spaniard and a relative of Trajan's, succeeded him as emperor. Almost immediately, he began work on the Pantheon (FIG. **3-38** and 3-9, no. 4), the "temple of all gods." The Pantheon reveals the full potential of concrete, both as a building material and as a means for shaping architectural space. The approach to the temple was from a columnar courtyard (FIG. **3-39**, *left*), and, like temples in Roman forums, the Pantheon stood at one narrow end of the enclosure. Its facade of eight Corinthian columns—almost all that could be seen from ground level in antiquity—was a bow to tradition. Everything else about the Pantheon was revolutionary. Behind the columnar porch is an immense concrete drum covered by a huge hemispherical dome (FIGS. 3-14d and 3-40) 142 feet in diameter. The dome's top is also 142 feet from the floor (FIG. **3-39**, *right*). The design is thus based on the intersection of two circles (one horizontal, the other vertical). The interior space can be imagined as the orb of the earth and the dome as the vault of the heavens.

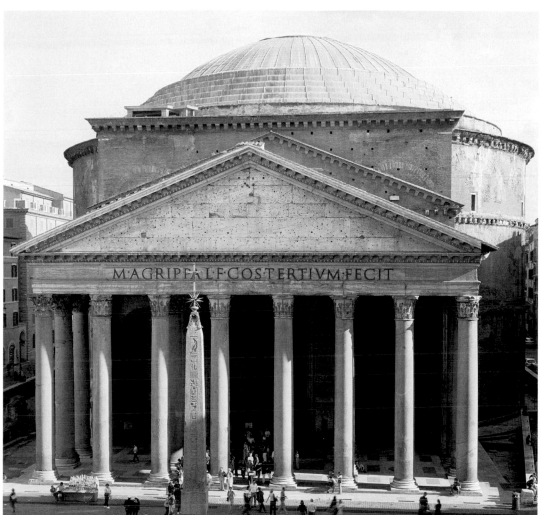

The Pantheon's traditional facade masked its revolutionary cylindrical drum and its huge hemispherical dome. The interior symbolized both the orb of the earth and the vault of the heavens.

rable basalt went into the mix for the foundations, and the recipe gradually changed until, at the top, featherweight pumice replaced stones to lighten the load. The dome's thickness also decreases as it nears the oculus, the circular opening 30 feet in diameter that is the only light source for the interior. The use of *coffers* (sunken decorative panels) lessened the dome's weight, without weakening its structure, and also provided a handsome pattern of squares within the vast circle. Renaissance drawings suggest each coffer once had a glistening gilded-bronze rosette at its center, enhancing the symbolism of the dome as the starry heavens.

If the Pantheon's design is simplicity itself, executing that design took all the ingenuity of Hadrian's engineers. The builders constructed the cylindrical drum level by level using concrete of varied composition. Extremely hard and durable

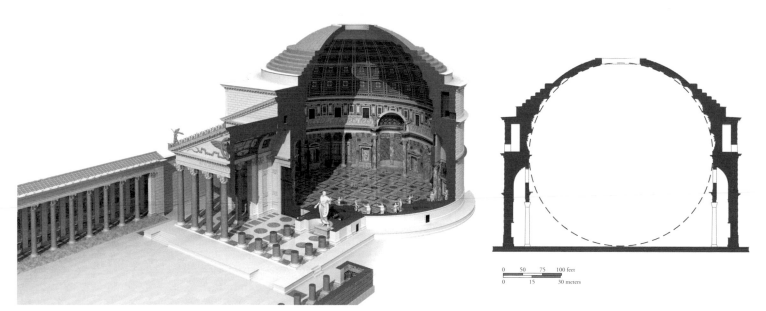

3-39 Restored cutaway view (*left*) and lateral section (*right*) of the Pantheon, Rome, Italy, 118–125 CE (John Burge).

Originally, the approach to Hadrian's "temple of all gods" was from a columnar courtyard. Like a temple in a Roman forum (FIG. 3-12), the Pantheon stood at one narrow end of the enclosure.

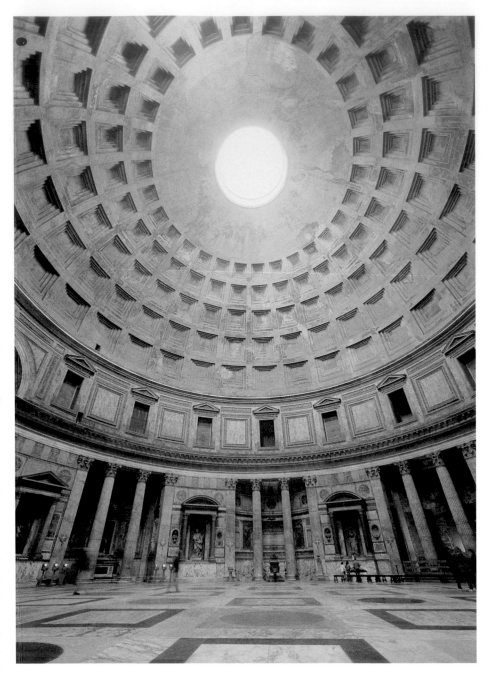

3-40 Interior of the Pantheon (looking south), Rome, Italy, 118–125 CE.

The coffered dome of the Pantheon is 142 feet in diameter and 142 feet high. The light entering through its oculus forms a circular beam that moves across the dome as the sun moves across the sky.

Below the dome, much of the original marble veneer of the walls, niches, and floor has survived (FIG. **3-40**). In the Pantheon, visitors can appreciate, as almost nowhere else (compare FIG. 3-46), how magnificent the interiors of Roman concrete buildings could be. But despite the luxurious skin of the Pantheon's interior, on first entering the structure, visitors do not sense the weight of the enclosing walls but the vastness of the space they enclose. In pre-Roman architecture, the form of the enclosed space was determined by the placement of the solids, which did not so much shape space as interrupt it. Roman architects were the first to conceive of architecture in terms of units of space that could be shaped by the enclosures. The Pantheon's interior is a single unified, self-sufficient whole, uninterrupted by supporting solids. Through the oculus, the space opens to the drifting clouds, the blue sky, the sun, and the gods. Inside the Pantheon, the architect used light not merely to illuminate the darkness but to create drama and underscore the symbolism of the interior shape. On a sunny day, the light passing through the oculus forms a circular beam, a disk of light that moves across the coffered dome in the course of the day as the sun moves across the sky itself. Escaping from the noise and heat of a Roman summer day into the Pantheon's cool, calm, and mystical immensity is an experience not to be missed.

Marcus Aurelius Perhaps the most majestic surviving portrait of a Roman emperor is the larger-than-life-size gilded-bronze equestrian statue (FIG. **3-41**) of Marcus Aurelius (r. 161–180 CE), one of the Antonine emperors who followed Hadrian. Marcus possesses a superhuman grandeur and is much larger than any normal human would be in relation to his horse. He stretches out his right arm in a gesture that is both a greeting and an offer of clemency. Beneath the horse's raised right foreleg, an enemy once cowered, begging the emperor for mercy. The statue expresses the majestic power of the Roman emperor as ruler of the whole world. This mes-

sage of supreme confidence is not, however, conveyed by the emperor's head, with its long, curly hair and full beard, consistent with the latest fashion. Marcus's forehead is lined, and he seems weary, saddened, and even worried. For the first time, the strain of constant warfare on the frontiers and the burden of ruling a worldwide empire show in the emperor's face. The Antonine sculptor ventured beyond Republican verism, exposing the ruler's character, his thoughts, and his soul for all to see, as Marcus revealed them himself in his *Meditations,* a deeply moving philosophical treatise setting forth the emperor's personal worldview. This kind of introspective verism was a profound change from classical idealism. It marks a major turning point in the history of ancient art.

Mummy Portraits Painted portraits were common in the Roman Empire, but most have perished. In Roman Egypt, however, large numbers have been found because the Egyp-

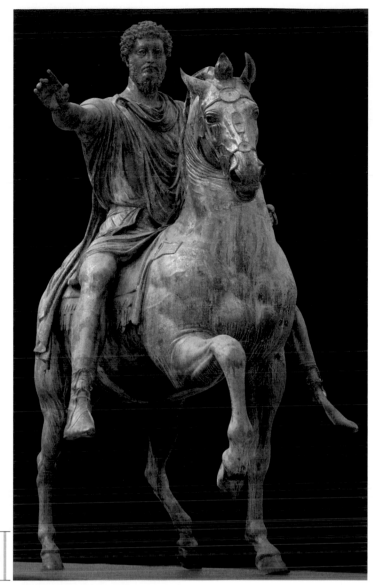

3-41 Equestrian statue of Marcus Aurelius, from Rome, Italy, ca. 175 CE. Bronze, 11′ 6″ high. Musei Capitolini—Palazzo dei Conservatori, Rome. ◼◀

In this portrait on horseback, which conveys the power of the Roman emperor, Marcus Aurelius stretches out his arm in a gesture of clemency. An enemy once cowered beneath the horse's raised foreleg.

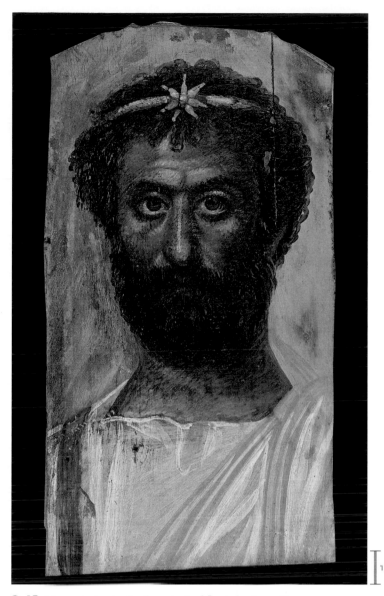

3-42 Mummy portrait of a priest of Serapis, from Hawara (Faiyum), Egypt, ca. 140–160 CE. Encaustic on wood, 1′ 4¾″ × 8¾″. British Museum, London.

In Roman times, the Egyptians continued to bury their dead in mummy cases, but painted portraits replaced the traditional masks. The painting medium is encaustic—colors mixed with hot wax.

tians continued to bury their dead in mummy cases (see "Mummification," Chapter 1, page 34), with painted portraits on wood replacing the traditional stylized portrait masks. One example (FIG. **3-42**) depicts a priest of the Egyptian god Serapis. The technique is *encaustic,* in which the painter mixes colors with hot wax and then uses a spatula to apply the wax pigment. The priest's portrait exhibits the painter's refined use of the brush and spatula, mastery of the depiction of varied textures and of the play of light over the soft and delicately modeled face, and sensitive portrayal of the deceased's calm demeanor. Artists also applied encaustic to stone, and the mummy portraits give some idea of the original appearance of Roman marble portraits. According to Pliny, when Praxiteles (FIGS. 2-47 and 2-48), perhaps the

greatest marble sculptor of the ancient world, was asked which of his statues he preferred, the master replied, "Those that Nikias painted."[2] This anecdote underscores the importance of coloration in ancient statuary.

The Late Empire

By the time of Marcus Aurelius, two centuries after Augustus established the Pax Romana, Roman power was beginning to erode. It was increasingly difficult to keep order on the frontiers, and even within the Empire many challenged the authority of Rome. The assassination of Marcus's son Commodus (r. 180–192 CE) brought the Antonine dynasty to an end. The economy was in decline, and the efficient imperial bureaucracy was disintegrating. Even the official state

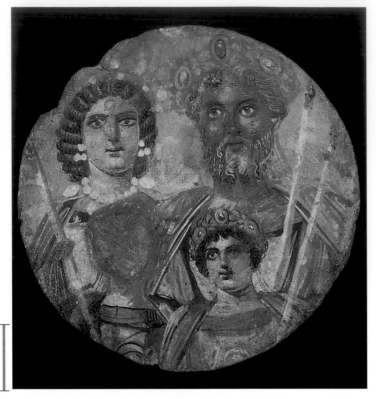

3-43 Painted portrait of Septimius Severus and his family, from Egypt, ca. 200 CE. Tempera on wood, 1' 2" diameter. Antikensammlung, Staatliche Museen zu Berlin, Berlin.

This unique painted imperial portrait shows Septimius Severus with gray hair. With him are his wife, Julia Domna, and their two sons, but Geta's head was removed after his damnatio memoriae.

1 in.

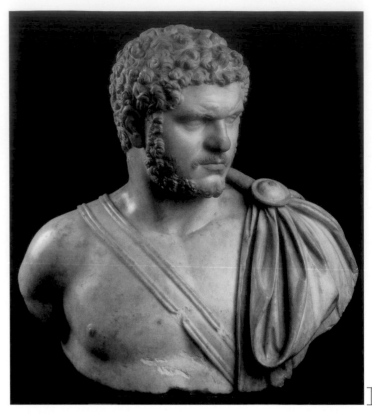

3-44 Portrait bust of Caracalla, ca. 211–217 CE. Marble, 1' 10¾" high. Antikensammlung, Staatliche Museen zu Berlin, Berlin.

Caracalla's portraits introduced a new fashion in male coiffure but are more remarkable for the dramatic turn of the emperor's head and the moving characterization of his personality.

1 in.

religion was losing ground to Eastern cults, Christianity among them. The Late Empire was a pivotal era in world history during which the *polytheistic* (belief in multiple gods) ancient world gradually gave way to the Christian Middle Ages.

The Severans Civil conflict followed Commodus's death. When it ended, an African-born general named Septimius Severus (r. 193–211 CE) was master of the Roman world. A unique painted portrait (FIG. **3-43**) found in Egypt depicts the emperor and his family—his wife, Julia Domna, and their two sons, Caracalla and Geta. The *tondo* (circular) portrait is of special interest for two reasons beyond its survival. Severus's hair is tinged with gray, suggesting his marble portraits also may have revealed his advancing age in this way. Also noteworthy is the erasure of Geta's face. When Caracalla (r. 211–217 CE) succeeded his father as emperor, he had his younger brother murdered and ordered the Senate to damn Geta's memory. The Severan family portrait is an eloquent testimony to that damnatio memoriae and to the long arm of Roman authority, which reached all the way to Egypt in this case. This kind of defacement of a rival's image is not unknown in other societies, but the Roman government employed damnatio memoriae as a political tool more often and more systematically than any other civilization.

Caracalla In the Severan *roundel,* the artist portrayed Caracalla as a boy with long, curly Antonine hair. The portraits of Caracalla as emperor are very different. In a bust (FIG. **3-44**) in Berlin, Caracalla appears in heroic nudity save for a mantle over one shoulder and a sword sheath across his chest. His hair and beard are much shorter than his father's—initiating a new fashion in male coiffure during the third century CE. More remarkable, however, is the moving characterization of Caracalla's personality, a further development from the groundbreaking introspection of Marcus Aurelius. Caracalla's brow is knotted, and he abruptly turns his head over his left shoulder. The sculptor probably intended the facial expression and the dramatic movement to suggest energy and strength, but it appears to the viewer as if the emperor suspects danger from behind. Caracalla had reason to be fearful. An assassin's dagger felled him in the sixth year of his rule.

Baths of Caracalla The Severans were active builders in the capital, and even during his short reign Caracalla built the greatest in a long line of bathing and recreational complexes constructed with imperial funds to win the public's favor. The Baths of Caracalla (FIG. **3-45**) covered an area of almost 50 acres. All the rooms had thick brick-faced concrete

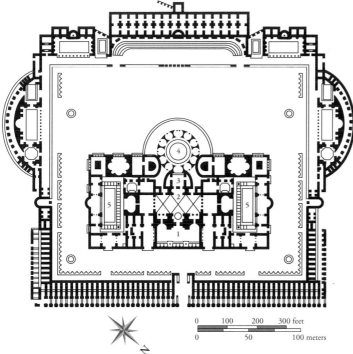

3-45 Plan of the Baths of Caracalla, Rome, Italy, 212–216 CE. (1) natatio, (2) frigidarium, (3) tepidarium, (4) caldarium, (5) palaestra.

Caracalla's baths could accommodate 1,600 bathers. They resembled a modern health spa and included libraries, lecture halls, and exercise courts in addition to bathing rooms and a swimming pool.

walls up to 140 feet high covered by enormous concrete vaults. The design was symmetrical along a central axis, facilitating the Roman custom of taking sequential plunges in warm-, hot-, and cold-water baths in, respectively, the *tepidarium, caldarium,* and *frigidarium.* There were stuccoed vaults, mosaic floors, marble-faced walls, and colossal statuary throughout the complex, which also had landscaped gardens, lecture halls, libraries, colonnaded exercise courts (*palaestras*), and a giant swimming pool (*natatio*). Archaeologists estimate that up to 1,600 bathers at a time could enjoy this Roman equivalent of a modern health spa. A branch of one of the city's major aqueducts supplied water, and furnaces circulated hot air through hollow floors and walls throughout the bathing rooms.

The concrete vaults of the Baths of Caracalla collapsed long ago, but visitors can approximate the original appearance of the central bathing hall from the nave (FIG. **3-46**) of the church of Santa Maria degli Angeli in Rome, which was once the frigidarium of the later Baths of Diocletian. Although the Renaissance interior has many new elements foreign to a Roman bath, its rich wall treatment, colossal columns, immense groin vaults, and clerestory lighting provide a better sense of what it was like to be in a Roman imperial bathing complex than does any other building in the world.

Trajan Decius The assassination of Caracalla opened a half century of almost continuous civil war. The Roman legions declared one general after another emperor, only to have each murdered in turn by another general a few years or even a few months later. The unstable times of the so-called soldier emperors nonetheless produced some of the most moving portraits in the history of art. Following the lead of the sculptors of the Marcus Aurelius and Caracalla

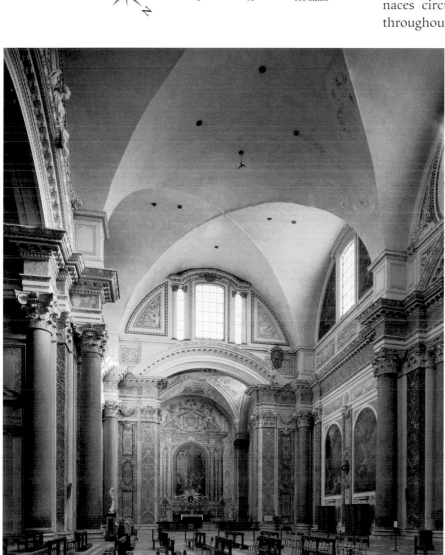

3-46 Frigidarium, Baths of Diocletian, Rome, Italy, ca. 298–306 CE (remodeled by MICHELANGELO BUONARROTI as the nave of Santa Maria degli Angeli, 1563).

The groin-vaulted nave of the church of Santa Maria degli Angeli in Rome was once the frigidarium of the Baths of Diocletian. It gives an idea of the lavish adornment of imperial Roman baths.

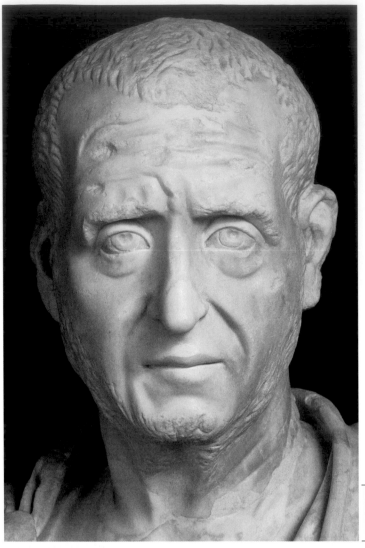

portraits, artists fashioned likenesses of the soldier emperors that are as notable for their emotional content as they are for their technical virtuosity. Portraits (FIG. **3-47**) of Trajan Decius (r. 249–251), for example, show the emperor—best known for persecuting Christians—as an old man with bags under his eyes and a sad expression. The eyes glance away nervously rather than engage the viewer directly, revealing the anxiety of a man who knows he can do little to restore order to an out-of-control world. The sculptor modeled the marble as if it were pliant clay, compressing the sides of the head at the level of the eyes, incising the hair and beard into the stone, and chiseling deep lines in the forehead and around the mouth. The portrait exposes the anguished soul of the man—and of the times.

Ludovisi Battle Sarcophagus Beginning under Trajan and Hadrian and especially during the rule of the Antonines, the Romans began to favor burial over cremation. This reversal of funerary practices may reflect the influence of Christianity and other Eastern religions, whose adherents believed in an afterlife for the human body. Whatever the explanation, the shift to burial led to a sudden demand for sarcophagi. By the third century CE, burial had become so widespread even the imperial family practiced it in place of cremation. An

1 in.

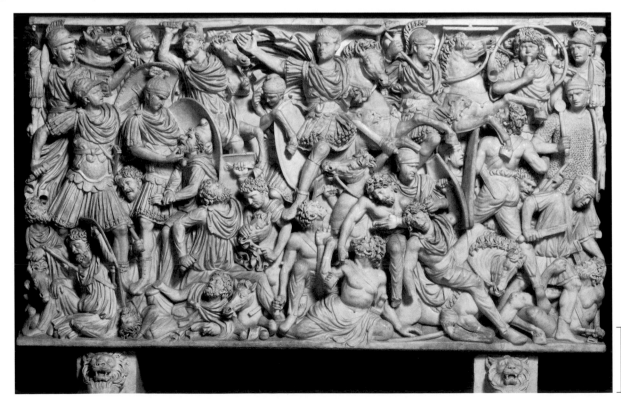

3-48 Sarcophagus with battle of Romans and barbarians (*Ludovisi Battle Sarcophaus*), from Rome, Italy, ca. 250–260 CE. Marble, 5′ high. Museo Nazionale Romano—Palazzo Altemps, Rome.

A chaotic scene of battle between Romans and barbarians decorates the front of this unusually large sarcophagus. The sculptor piled up the writhing, emotive figures in an emphatic rejection of classical perspective.

1 ft.

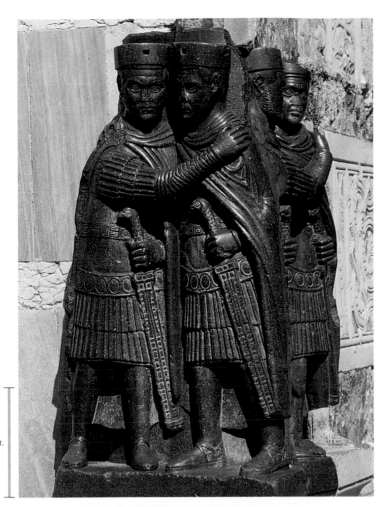

3-49 Portraits of the four tetrarchs, from Constantinople (Istanbul), Turkey, ca. 305 CE. Porphyry, 4′ 3″ high. Saint Mark's, Venice.

Diocletian established the tetrarchy to bring order to the Roman world. Whenever the four rulers appeared together, artists did not portray them as individuals but as nearly identical partners in power.

religions. On the youth's forehead is the emblem of Mithras, the Persian god of light, truth, and victory over death.

Tetrarchy In an attempt to restore order to the Roman Empire, Diocletian (r. 284–305 CE), whose troops proclaimed him emperor, decided to share power with his potential rivals. In 293 CE, he established the *tetrarchy* (rule by four) and adopted the title of Augustus of the East. The other three *tetrarchs* were a corresponding Augustus of the West, and Eastern and Western Caesars (whose allegiance to the two Augusti was cemented by marriage to their daughters). In art, if not in life, the four tetrarchs often appeared together. Artists did not try to capture their individual appearances and personalities but sought instead to represent the nature of the tetrarchy itself—that is, to portray four equal partners in power. In two pairs of porphyry (purple marble) tetrarchic portraits (FIG. **3-49**) in Venice, it is impossible to name the rulers. Each emperor has lost his identity as an individual and been subsumed into the larger entity of the tetrarchy. Each wears an identical breastplate and cloak and grasps a sheathed sword in the left hand. With their right arms they embrace one another in an overt display of concord. The figures have large cubical heads and squat, shapeless bodies. The faces are emotionless masks, distinguished only by the beard on two of the figures (probably the older Augusti, differentiating them from the younger Caesars). Nonetheless, each pair is as alike as freehand carving can achieve. In this group portrait, carved eight centuries after Greek sculptors first freed the human form from the rigidity of the Egyptian-inspired kouros stance, an artist once again conceived the human figure in iconic terms. Idealism, naturalism, individuality, and personality have disappeared.

Constantine and Christianity The short-lived concord among the tetrarchs ended with Diocletian's abdication in 305 CE. An all-too-familiar period of conflict among rival Roman armies followed. The eventual victor was Constantine (r. 306–337 CE), son of Constantius Chlorus, Diocletian's Caesar of the West. After the death of his father, Constantine invaded Italy in 312 and took control of Rome. Constantine attributed his decisive victory at the Milvian Bridge, the gateway to the capital, to the aid of the Christian god. The next year, he and Licinius, Constantine's coemperor in the East, issued the Edict of Milan, ending persecution of Christians. In time, Constantine and Licinius became foes, and in 324 Constantine defeated and executed Licinius near Byzantium (modern Istanbul, Turkey). Constantine, now the unchallenged ruler of the whole Roman Empire, founded a "New Rome" at the site of Byzantium and named it Constantinople (City of Constantine). In 325, at the Council of Nicaea, Christianity became the de facto official religion of the Roman Empire. From this point on, the ancient cults declined rapidly. Constantine dedicated Constantinople on May 11, 330, "by the commandment of God," and in 337, the emperor was baptized on his deathbed.

unusually large sarcophagus—the *Ludovisi Battle Sarcophagus* (FIG. **3-48**)—dating to the mid-third century is decorated on the front with a chaotic scene of battle between Romans and one of their northern foes, probably the Goths. The sculptor spread the writhing and highly emotive figures evenly across the entire relief, with no illusion of space behind them. This piling of figures is an emphatic rejection of classical perspective. Like the realistic and emotive portraits of the soldier emperors, it underscores the increasing dissatisfaction of third-century CE artists with the Classical style.

Within the dense mass of intertwined bodies, the central horseman stands out vividly. He is bareheaded and thrusts out his open right hand to demonstrate he holds no weapon. Several scholars have identified him as one of the sons of Trajan Decius. In an age when the Roman army was far from invincible and emperors were constantly felled by other Romans, this young general boasts that he is a fearless commander assured of victory. His self-assurance may stem from his having embraced one of the increasingly popular Eastern mystery

Colossus of Constantine The most impressive by far of Constantine's preserved portraits is an eight-and-one-half-foot-tall head (FIG. **3-50**), one of several fragments of a colossal enthroned statue of the emperor composed of a brick core, a wood torso covered with bronze, and a head and limbs of marble. Constantine's artist modeled the seminude seated portrait on Roman images of Jupiter, but also resuscitated the Augustan image of an eternally youthful head of state. The emperor held an orb (possibly surmounted by the cross of Christ), the symbol of global power, in his extended left hand. Constantine's personality is lost in this immense image of eternal authority. The colossal size, the likening of the emperor to Jupiter, the eyes directed at no person or thing of this world—all combine to produce a formula of overwhelming power appropriate to Constantine's exalted position as absolute ruler.

Basilica Nova Constantine's gigantic portrait sat in the western apse of the Basilica Nova (New Basilica; FIGS. **3-51** and 3-9, no. 8) in Rome. From its position in the apse, the emperor's image dominated the interior of the basilica in much the same way enthroned statues of divinities loomed over awestruck mortals who entered the cellas of Greco-Roman temples. The Basilica Nova ruins never fail to impress tourists with their size and mass. The original structure was 300 feet long and 215 feet wide. Brick-faced concrete walls 20 feet thick supported coffered barrel vaults in the aisles. These vaults also buttressed the groin vaults of the nave, which was 115 feet high. Marble slabs and stuccos covered the walls and floors. The restored view in FIG. 3-51 effectively suggests the immensity of the interior, where the great vaults dwarf even the emperor's colossal portrait. The drawing also clearly reveals the fenestrated groin vaults, a lighting system akin to the clerestory of a traditional stone-and-timber basilica (FIG. 3-35, no. 4). The architect here applied to basilica design the lessons learned in the design and construction of buildings such as Trajan's great market hall (FIG. 3-37) and the Baths of Caracalla and Diocletian (FIG. 3-46).

Arch of Constantine Also grandiose is the triple-passageway arch (FIGS. **3-52** and 3-9, no. 10) Constantine erected next to the Colosseum. The arch was the largest in Rome since the end of the Severan dynasty. The builders, however, took much of the sculptural decoration from earlier monuments of Trajan, Hadrian, and Marcus Aurelius. Constantine's sculptors refashioned the second-century reliefs to honor him by recutting the heads of the earlier emperors with his features. Some art historians have cited the Arch of Constantine as evidence of a decline in creativity and technical skill in the waning years of the Late Roman Empire. Although such a judgment is in part deserved, it ignores the fact the reused sculptures were carefully selected to associate Constantine with famous emperors of the second century. One of the arch's few Constantinian reliefs underscores that message. It shows Constantine on the speaker's platform in

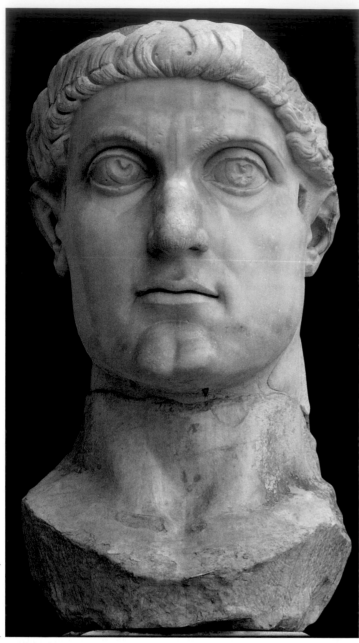

3-50 Portrait of Constantine, from the Basilica Nova, Rome, Italy, ca. 315–330 CE. Marble, 8′ 6″ high. Musei Capitolini—Palazzo dei Conservatori, Rome. ◼◀

Constantine's portraits revive the Augustan image of an eternally youthful ruler. This colossal head is one fragment of an enthroned Jupiter-like statue of the emperor holding the orb of world power.

1 ft.

For many scholars, the transfer of the seat of power from Rome to Constantinople and the recognition of Christianity mark the beginning of the Middle Ages. Constantinian art is a mirror of this transition from the classical to the medieval world. In Rome, for example, Constantine was a builder in the grand tradition of the emperors of the first, second, and early third centuries, constructing public baths, a basilica in the Roman Forum, and a triumphal arch. But he was also the patron of the city's first churches (see Chapter 4).

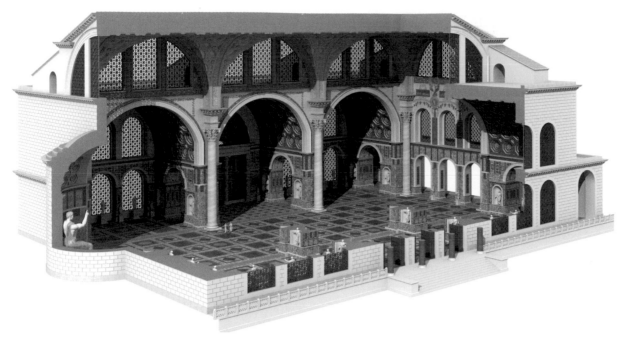

Roman builders applied the lessons learned constructing baths and market halls to the Basilica Nova, in which fenestrated concrete groin vaults replaced the clerestory of a stone-and-timber basilica.

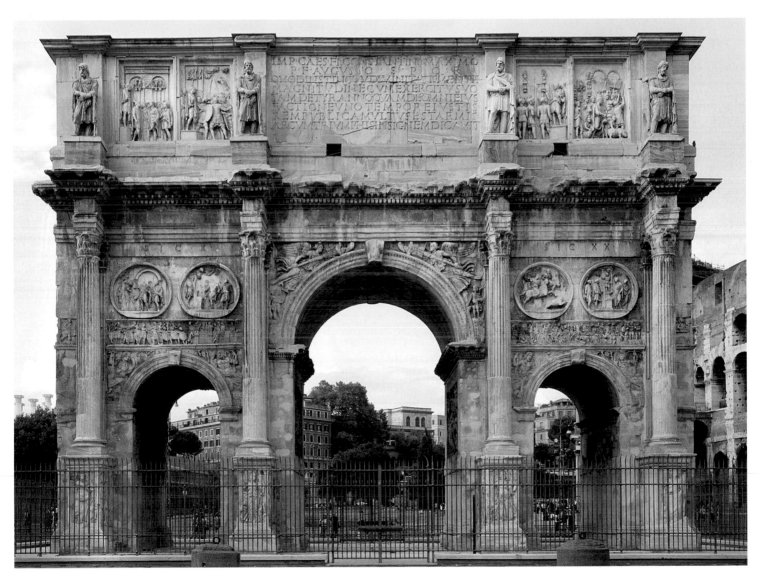

3-52 South facade of the Arch of Constantine, Rome, Italy, 312–315 CE. ◼️📹

Much of the sculptural decoration of Constantine's arch came from monuments of Trajan, Hadrian, and Marcus Aurelius. Sculptors recut the heads of the earlier emperors to substitute Constantine's features.

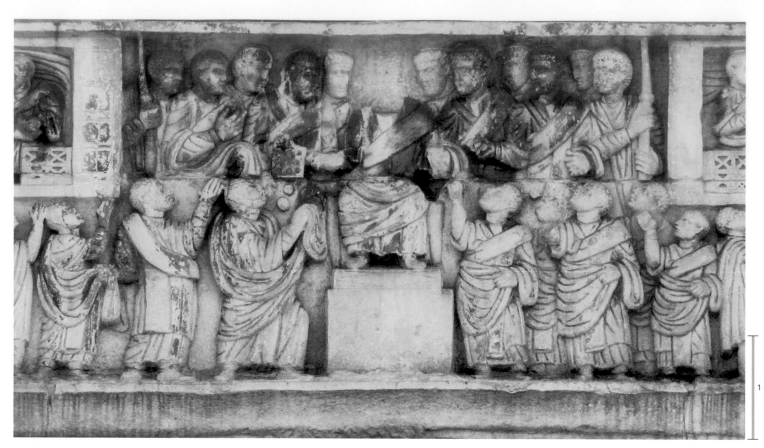

3-53 Distribution of largesse, detail of the north frieze of the Arch of Constantine, Rome, Italy, 312–315 CE. Marble, 3' 4" high.

This Constantinian frieze is less a narrative of action than a picture of actors frozen in time. The composition's rigid formality reflects the new values that would come to dominate medieval art.

the Roman Forum between statues of Hadrian and Marcus Aurelius.

In another Constantinian relief (FIG. **3-53**), the emperor distributes largesse to grateful citizens who approach him from right and left. Constantine is a frontal and majestic presence, elevated on a throne above the recipients of his munificence. The figures are squat in proportion, like the tetrarchs (FIG. 3-49). They do not move according to any Classical principle of naturalistic movement but, rather, with the mechanical and repeated stances and gestures of puppets. The relief is very shallow, the forms are not fully modeled, and the details are incised. The frieze is less a narrative of action than a picture of actors frozen in time so the viewer can distinguish instantly the all-important imperial donor (at the center on a throne) from his attendants (to the left and right above) and the recipients of the largesse (below and of smaller stature).

An eminent art historian once characterized this approach to pictorial narrative as a "decline of form," and when judged by the standards of Classical art, it was. But the composition's rigid formality, determined by the rank of those portrayed, was consistent with a new set of values. It soon became the preferred mode, supplanting the Classical notion that a picture is a window onto a world of anecdotal action. Comparing this Constantinian relief with a Byzantine icon (FIG. 4-19) reveals that the new compositional principles are those of medieval art. They are very different from, but not necessarily "better" or "worse" than, those of Greco-Roman art. The Arch of Constantine is the quintessential monument of its era, exhibiting a respect for the past in the reuse of second-century sculptures while at the same time rejecting the norms of Classical design in the fourth-century frieze and thereby paving the way for the iconic art of the Middle Ages.

The Roman Empire

Etruscan Art

▌ The Etruscans admired Greek art and architecture but did not copy Greek works. They constructed their temples of wood and mud brick instead of stone and placed the columns and stairs only at the front. Terracotta statuary decorated the roof. Most surviving Etruscan artworks come from underground tomb chambers. At Cerveteri, earthen mounds (tumuli) covered tombs with interiors sculptured to imitate the houses of the living. At Tarquinia, painters adorned tomb walls with frescoes, usually depicting funerary banquets.

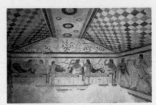

Tomb of the Leopards, Tarquinia, ca. 480–470 BCE

Republican Art

▌ In the centuries following the establishment of the Republic (509–27 BCE), Rome conquered its neighbors in Italy and then moved into Greece, bringing exposure to Greek art and architecture. Republican temples combined Etruscan plans with the Greek orders, and houses boasted peristyles with Greek columns. The Romans, however, pioneered the use of concrete as a building material. The First Style of mural painting derived from Greece, but the illusionism of the Second Style is distinctly Roman. Republican portraits were usually superrealistic likenesses of elderly patricians.

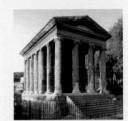

Temple of Portunus, Rome, ca. 75 BCE

Early Imperial Art

▌ Augustus (r. 27 BCE–14 CE) established the Roman Empire after defeating Antony and Cleopatra. The Early Empire (27 BCE–96 CE) extends from Augustus to the Flavian emperors (r. 68–96 CE).

▌ Augustan art revived the Classical style with frequent references to Periclean Athens, and Augustus's portraits always depict him as an idealized youth. Under the Flavians, architects exploited the full potential of concrete in buildings such as the Colosseum, Rome's largest amphitheater. The Arch of Titus celebrates the Flavian victory in Judaea. The eruption of Mount Vesuvius in 79 CE buried Pompeii and Herculaneum. During the quarter century before the disaster, painters decorated the walls of houses in the Third and Fourth Styles.

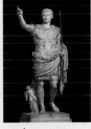

Augustus as general, ca. 20 BCE

High Imperial Art

▌ During the High Empire (96–192 CE), beginning with Trajan (r. 98–117 CE), the Roman Empire reached its greatest extent.

▌ Trajan's new forum and markets transformed the center of Rome. The Column of Trajan commemorated his Dacian campaigns in a spiral frieze with thousands of figures. Hadrian (r. 117–138 CE) built the Pantheon, the temple to all the gods, incorporating in its design the forms of the orb of the earth and the dome of the heavens. Under the Antonines (r. 138–192 CE), imperial artists introduced a psychological element in portraiture.

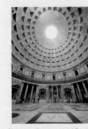

Pantheon, Rome, 118–125 CE

Late Imperial Art

▌ The Late Empire (192–337 CE) opened with the Severans (r. 193–235 CE) and closed with Constantine (r. 306–337 CE), who ended persecution of the Christians and transferred the imperial capital from Rome to Constantinople in 330.

▌ During the chaotic era of the soldier emperors (r. 235–284 CE), artists revealed the anxiety and insecurity of the emperors in moving portraits. Diocletian (r. 284–305 CE) reestablished order by sharing power. Statues of the tetrarchs portray the four emperors as identical and equal rulers, not as individuals. Constantine restored one-man rule. The abstract formality of Constantinian art paved the way for the iconic art of the Middle Ages.

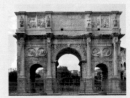

Arch of Constantine, Rome, 312–315 CE

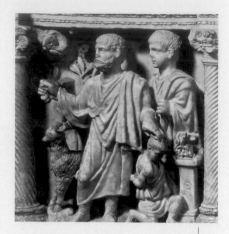

Episodes from Hebrew scripture, including Abraham sacrificing Isaac, appear side by side with scenes from the life of Jesus on this sarcophagus of a recent convert to Christianity.

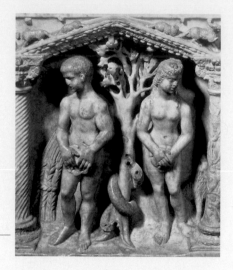

The Jewish scenes on Junius Bassus's sarcophagus had special significance for Christians. Adam and Eve's original sin of eating the apple in the Garden of Eden necessitated Christ's sacrifice.

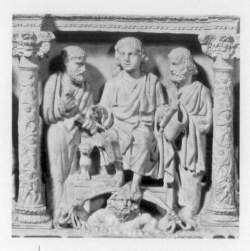

Christ, long-haired and youthful in the Early Christian tradition, sits above a personification of the Roman sky god. Flanking the new ruler of the universe are Saints Peter and Paul.

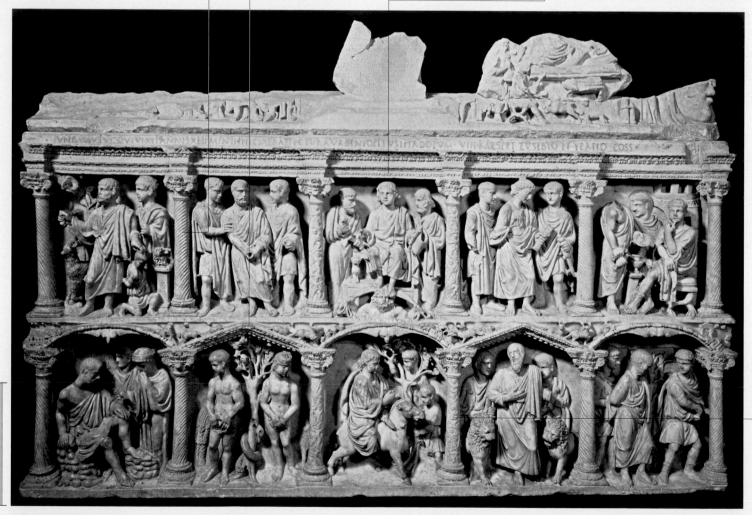

1 ft.

4-1 Sarcophagus of Junius Bassus, from Rome, Italy, ca. 359. Marble, 3′ 10½″ × 8′. Museo Storico del Tesoro della Basilica di San Pietro, Rome.

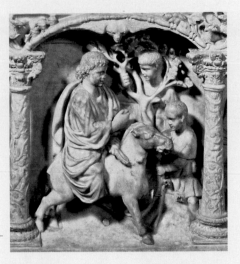

The compositions of many Early Christian reliefs derive from Greco-Roman art. The scene of Jesus entering Jerusalem on a donkey recalls portrayals of Roman emperors entering conquered cities.

Early Christianity and Byzantium

ROMANS, JEWS, AND CHRISTIANS

During the third and fourth centuries, a rapidly growing number of Romans rejected polytheism (belief in multiple gods) in favor of monotheism (the worship of a single all-powerful god)—but they did not stop commissioning works of art. A prominent example is Junius Bassus, the mid-fourth-century city prefect of Rome who converted to Christianity and, according to the inscription on his sarcophagus (FIG. 4-1), was baptized just before his death in 359. He grew up immersed in traditional Roman culture and initially paid homage to the old Roman gods, but when he died, he chose to be buried in a sarcophagus decorated with episodes from Hebrew scripture and the life of Jesus.

The sculptor decorated the front of Junius Bassus's sarcophagus with 10 figural scenes in relief, organized in two registers of five compartments, each framed by columns, a well-established format for Roman sarcophagi. The deceased does not appear in any of the compartments, however. Instead, Jewish and Christian biblical stories fill the niches. Jesus has pride of place and appears in the central compartment of each register: as a teacher enthroned between Saints Peter and Paul (above), and entering Jerusalem on a donkey (below). Both compositions owe a great deal to official Roman art. In the upper zone, Jesus, like an enthroned Roman emperor, sits above a personification of the sky god holding a billowing mantle over his head, indicating the Savior is ruler of the universe. The scene below derives in part from portrayals of Roman emperors entering conquered cities on horseback, but Jesus's steed and the absence of imperial attributes contrast sharply with the imperial models the sculptor used as compositional sources.

The Jewish scenes on the Junius Bassus sarcophagus include the stories of Adam and Eve and Abraham and Isaac, which took on added significance for Christians as foretelling events in the life of their Savior. Christians believe Adam and Eve's original sin of eating the apple in the Garden of Eden ultimately necessitated Christ's sacrifice for the salvation of humankind. At the upper left, Abraham, father of the Hebrew nation, is about to sacrifice his son, Isaac. Christians view this Genesis story as a *prefiguration* (prophetic forerunner) of God's sacrifice of his son, Jesus.

The crucifixion, however, does not appear on the sarcophagus and was rarely depicted in Early Christian art. Artists emphasized Jesus's divinity and exemplary life as teacher and miracle worker, not his suffering and death at the hands of the Romans (see "The Life of Jesus in Art," pages 130–131). This sculptor, however, alluded to the crucifixion in the scenes in the two compartments at the upper right showing Jesus led before Pontius Pilate for judgment. The Romans condemned Jesus to death, but he triumphantly overcame it. Junius Bassus hoped for a similar salvation.

EARLY CHRISTIANITY

Very little is known about the art of the first Christians. When art historians speak about "Early Christian art," they are referring to the earliest preserved artworks having Christian subjects, not the art of Christians at the time of Jesus. Few Christian artworks can be dated before the late third and early fourth centuries,* that is, to the time when Christians were a persecuted minority in the Roman Empire. For example, the emperor Diocletian (r. 284–305) became so concerned by the growing popularity of Christianity in the Roman army ranks that he ordered a fresh round of persecutions in 303 to 305, a half century after the last great persecutions under Trajan Decius (FIG. 3-47). As Christianity's appeal grew, so too did the Roman state's fear of weakening imperial authority because the Christians refused to pay even token homage to the official gods of the Roman state, which included deified emperors as well as the traditional pantheon of gods and goddesses. Persecution finally ended only when Constantine came to believe the Christian god was the source of his power rather than a threat to it (see page 117). In 313, he issued the Edict of Milan, which established Christianity as a legal religion with equal or superior standing to the traditional Roman cults.

Catacombs

Most Early Christian art in the city of Rome is found in the *catacombs*—vast subterranean networks of passageways and chambers that served as cemeteries. The name derives from the Latin *ad catacumbas,* which means "in the hollows." The Christian community tunneled the catacombs out of the tufa bedrock, much as the Etruscans fashioned the underground tomb chambers (FIG. 3-5) at Cerveteri. The catacombs are less elaborate than the Etruscan tombs, but much more extensive. The known catacombs in Rome run for 60 to 90 miles and housed as many as four million bodies.

Peter and Marcellinus Often, the Christians carved out small rooms, called *cubicula* (as in Roman houses), to serve as

*From this point on, all dates are CE unless otherwise indicated.

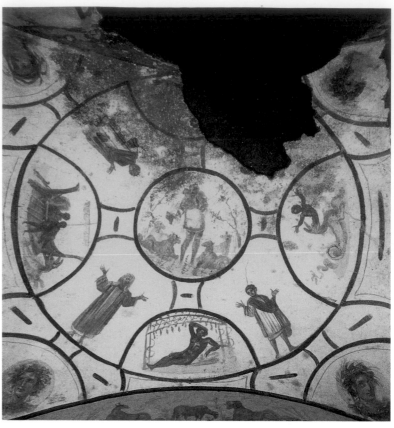

4-2 The Good Shepherd, the story of Jonah, and orants, painted ceiling of a cubiculum in the Catacomb of Saints Peter and Marcellinus, Rome, Italy, early fourth century.

Christian catacomb paintings often mixed Old and New Testament themes. Jonah was a popular subject because he emerged safely from a sea monster after three days, prefiguring Christ's resurrection.

mortuary chapels within the catacombs. The painted ceiling (FIG. 4-2) of a cubiculum in the Catacomb of Saints Peter and Marcellinus in Rome features a large circle circumscribing the symbol of the Christian faith, the cross. The arms of the cross terminate in four *lunettes* (semicircular frames) illustrating the key episodes from the biblical story of Jonah. Sailors throw Jonah from his ship on the left. On the right, he emerges from the sea dragon (usually translated as "whale" in English) that swallowed him. At the bottom, safe on land, Jonah contemplates the miracle of his salvation and the mercy of God.

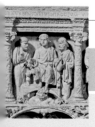

Early Christianity and Byzantium

CE						
0	Early Christian	527	Justinian to Iconoclasm	726 Iconoclasm 843	Middle and Late Byzantine	1453
	▮ Earliest Christian sarcophagi and catacomb paintings (third century)		▮ Justinian (r. 527–565) builds Hagia Sophia with a 180-foot-high dome resting on pendentives		▮ Theodora repeals iconoclasm, 843	
	▮ Constantine (r. 306–337) constructs the first churches in Rome and founds Constantinople as the New Rome		▮ Dedication of San Vitale at Ravenna with its rich mosaic program, 547		▮ Churches feature exterior walls with decorative patterning, Greek-cross plans, and domes on drums	
	▮ Mosaics become the primary medium for church decoration		▮ Icon painting flourishes at Mount Sinai until Leo III bans picturing the divine in 726		▮ Ivory triptychs for personal prayer become popular	
	▮ Earliest preserved illustrated manuscripts with biblical themes (early sixth century)				▮ Michael VIII recaptures Constantinople after the Crusader sack of 1204	
					▮ Fall of Constantinople to the Ottoman Turks, 1453	

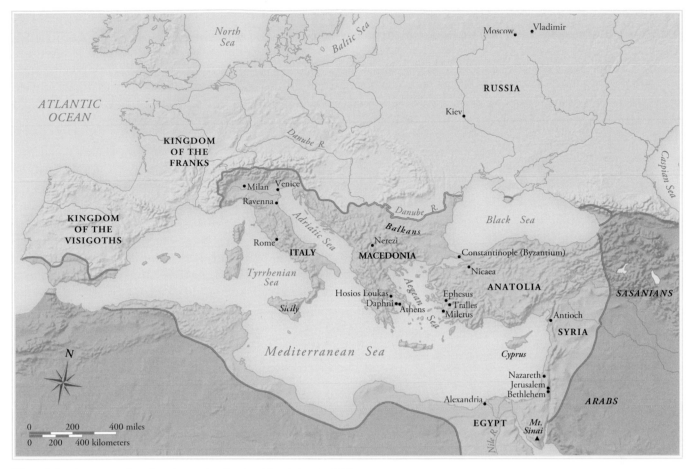

MAP 4-1 The Byzantine Empire at the death of Justinian in 565.

From the beginning, the Old Testament (Hebrew scripture) played an important role in Christian life and Christian art, in part because Jesus was a Jew and so many of the first Christians were converted Jews, but also because Christians came to view many of the persons and events of the Old Testament as prefigurations of persons and events in the New Testament (the Gospel books and other writings). Jesus himself established the pattern for this kind of biblical interpretation when he compared Jonah's spending three days in the belly of the sea monster to the comparable time he would be entombed in the earth before his resurrection (Matt. 12:40). In the fourth century, Saint Augustine (354–430) confirmed the validity of this approach to the Old Testament when he stated that "the New Testament is hidden in the Old; the Old is clarified by the New."[1]

A man, a woman, and at least one child occupy the compartments between the Jonah lunettes. They are *orants* (praying figures), raising their arms in the ancient attitude of prayer. Together they make up a cross-section of the Christian family seeking a heavenly afterlife. The central medallion shows Christ as the Good Shepherd, whose powers of salvation the painter underscored by placing the four episodes of the Jonah story around him. In Early Christian art, Jesus often appears as the youthful and loyal protector of the Christian flock who said to his disciples, "I am the good shepherd; the good shepherd gives his life for the sheep" (John 10:11). Only after Christianity became the Roman Empire's official religion in 380 did Christ take on in art such imperial attributes as the halo, the purple robe, and the throne, which denoted rulership.

Architecture and Mosaics

The earliest Christian places of worship were usually remodeled private houses that could accommodate only a small community. Once Christianity achieved imperial sponsorship under Constantine, an urgent need suddenly arose to construct churches. The new buildings had to meet the requirements of Christian *liturgy* (the ritual of public worship), provide a suitably monumental setting for the celebration of the Christian faith, and accommodate the rapidly growing numbers of worshipers. Constantine believed the Christian god had guided him to victory, and in lifelong gratitude he protected and advanced Christianity throughout the Empire. As emperor, he was, of course, obliged to safeguard the ancient Roman religion, traditions, and monuments, and he was (for his time) a builder on a grand scale in the heart of the city (FIGS. 3-51 and 3-52). But Constantine, eager to provide buildings to house the Christian rituals and venerated burial places, especially the memorials of founding saints, also was the first major patron of Christian architecture. He constructed elaborate basilicas, memorials, and *mausoleums* not only in Rome but also in Constantinople, his "New Rome" in the East, and at sites sacred to Christianity, most notably Bethlehem, the birthplace of Jesus, and Jerusalem, the site of his crucifixion (MAP 4-1).

Early Christianity 125

Old Saint Peter's The greatest of Constantine's churches in Rome was Old Saint Peter's (FIG. **4-3**), probably begun as early as 319. The present-day church (FIGS. 10-2 and 10-3) is a replacement for the Constantinian structure. Old Saint Peter's stood on the spot where the emperor and Pope Sylvester (r. 314–335) believed Peter, the founder of the Christian community in Rome, had been buried. Excavations in the Roman cemetery beneath the church have in fact revealed a second-century memorial erected in honor of the Christian *martyr* at his reputed grave. Old Saint Peter's therefore fulfilled Jesus's prophecy when he said, "Thou art Peter, and upon this rock [in Greek, *petra*] I will build my church" (Matt. 16:18).

The plan and elevation of the immense church, capable of housing 3,000 to 4,000 worshipers at one time, resemble those of Roman basilicas, such as Trajan's Basilica Ulpia (FIG. 3-35, no. 4), rather than the design of any Greco-Roman temple. The Christians, understandably, did not want their houses of worship to mimic the form of polytheistic shrines, but practical considerations also contributed to their shunning the classical temple type. The Greco-Roman temple housed only the cult statue of the deity. All rituals took place outside at open-air altars. Therefore, architects would have found it difficult to adapt the classical temple as a building accommodating large numbers of people within it. The Roman basilica, in contrast, was ideally suited as a place for congregation.

Like Roman basilicas, Old Saint Peter's had a wide central *nave* with flanking *aisles* and an *apse* at the end (FIG. 4-3, *bottom*). Worshipers entered the 300-foot-long nave through a *narthex,* or vestibule, whereupon they had an uninterrupted view of the altar in the apse. In front of the building proper was an open colonnaded courtyard, very much like the forum proper in the Forum of Trajan (FIG. 3-35, no. 5) but called an *atrium,* like the central room in a private house. A special feature of the Constantinian basilica was the *transept,* or transverse aisle, an area perpendicular to the nave between the nave and apse. It housed Saint Peter's *relics* (the body parts, clothing, or any object associated with a saint or Christ himself; see "Pilgrimages and the Cult of Relics," Chapter 6, page 173), which hordes of pilgrims came to see. The transept became a standard element of church design in the West only much later, when it also took on, with the nave and apse, the symbolism of the Christian cross.

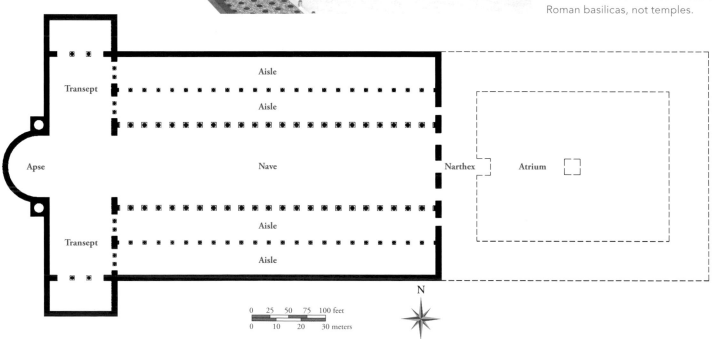

4-3 Restored cutaway view (*top*) and plan (*bottom*) of Old Saint Peter's, Rome, Italy, begun ca. 319 (John Burge).

Built by Constantine, the first imperial patron of Christianity, this huge church stood over Saint Peter's grave. The building's plan and elevation derive from those of Roman basilicas, not temples.

Aisle

Transept

Aisle

Apse Nave Narthex Atrium

Aisle

Transept

Aisle

N

0 25 50 75 100 feet
0 10 20 30 meters

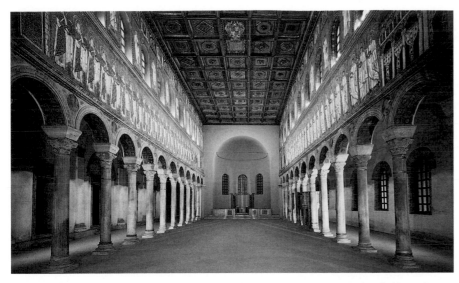

4-4 Interior of Sant'Apollinare Nuovo (looking east), Ravenna, Italy, dedicated 504. ◼◀

Early Christian basilican churches were timber-roofed and illuminated by clerestory windows. The steady rhythm of the nave arcade focused attention on the apse, which framed the altar.

Compared with Roman temples, which usually displayed statuary in pediments on their facades, most Early Christian basilicas were quite austere on the exterior. Inside, however, were frescoes and mosaics, marble columns, grandiose chandeliers, and gold and silver vessels on jeweled altar cloths for use in the Mass. In Saint Peter's, a huge marble *baldacchino* (domical canopy over an altar), supported by four spiral porphyry columns, stood at the crossing of the nave and transept, marking the location of Saint Peter's tomb. Some idea of the character of the interior of Old Saint Peter's can be gleaned from the restored view (FIG. 4-3, *top*) of the church and from a photograph (FIG. 4-4) of the nave of Sant'Apollinare Nuovo, an Early Christian basilica

in Ravenna. The columns of both nave *arcades* produce a steady rhythm that focuses all attention on the apse, which frames the altar. In the Ravenna church, as in Old Saint Peter's, light drenches the nave from the *clerestory* windows piercing the thin upper wall beneath the timber roof. The same light illuminates the mosaics in Sant'Apollinare Nuovo's nave. Mosaics and frescoes commonly adorned the nave and apse of Early Christian churches.

Santa Costanza The rectangular basilican church design featuring a *longitudinal plan* was long the favorite of the Western Christian world. But Early Christian architects also adopted another classical architectural type: the *central-plan* building, a structure in which the parts are of equal or almost equal dimensions around the center. Roman central-plan buildings were usually round or polygonal domed structures. Byzantine architects developed this form to monumental proportions and amplified its theme in numerous ingenious variations (FIGS. 4-12 and 4-23). In the West, builders generally used the central plan for structures adjacent to the main basilicas, such as mausoleums, *baptisteries,* and private chapels, rather than for churches, as in the East.

A highly refined example of the central-plan design is Santa Costanza (FIGS. 4-5 and 4-6) in Rome, built in the mid-fourth century, possibly as the mausoleum for Constantina, the emperor Constantine's daughter. Recent excavations have called the traditional identification into question, but the building housed Constantina's monumental porphyry sarcophagus, even if the structure was not originally

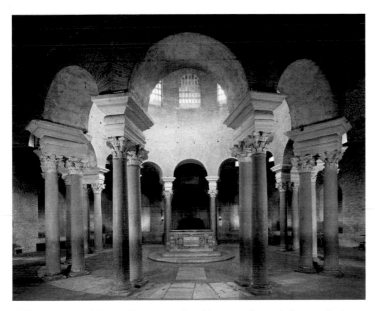

4-5 Interior of Santa Costanza (looking southwest), Rome, Italy, ca. 337–351. ◼◀

Possibly built as the mausoleum of Constantine's daughter, Santa Costanza later became a church. Its central plan, featuring a domed interior, would become the preferred form for Byzantine churches.

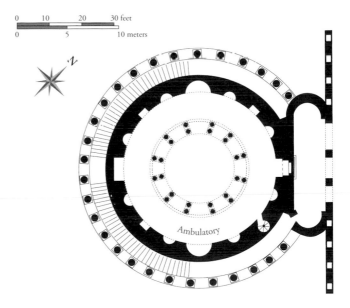

4-6 Plan of Santa Costanza, Rome, Italy, ca. 337–351.

Santa Costanza has antecedents in the domed temples (FIG. 3-40) and mausoleums of the Romans, but its plan, with 12 pairs of columns and a vaulted ambulatory, is unique.

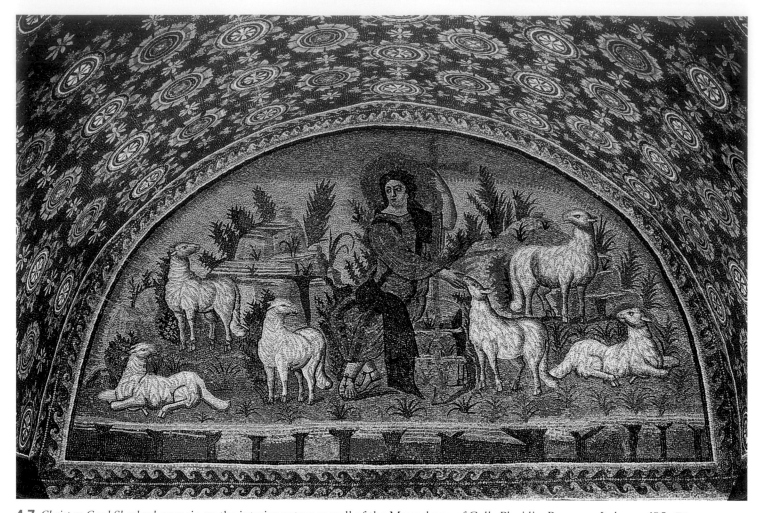

4-7 *Christ as Good Shepherd,* mosaic on the interior entrance wall of the Mausoleum of Galla Placidia, Ravenna, Italy, ca. 425. ▰◀

Jesus sits among his flock, haloed and robed in gold and purple. The landscape and the figures, with their cast shadows, are the work of a mosaicist still deeply rooted in the naturalistic classical tradition.

her tomb. The mausoleum, later converted into a church, stood next to the basilica of Saint Agnes, who was buried in a nearby catacomb. Santa Costanza's design derives from the domed structures of the Romans, such as the Pantheon (FIGS. 3-38 to 3-40), but the architect introduced a ringlike barrel-vaulted corridor called an *ambulatory,* separated from the central domed cylinder by 12 pairs of columns. Like most Early Christian basilicas, Santa Costanza has a severe brick exterior, but its interior was very richly adorned with mosaics, although most are lost.

Mausoleum of Galla Placidia Mosaic decoration (see "Mosaics," page 129) played an important role in the interiors of Early Christian buildings of all types. Mosaics not only provided a beautiful setting for Christian rituals but also were vehicles for instructing the faithful, many of them recent converts, about biblical stories and Christian dogma. The so-called Mausoleum of Galla Placidia in Ravenna is a rare example of a virtually intact Early Christian mosaic program. Galla Placidia was the half sister of the emperor Honorius (r. 395–423), who had moved the capital of his crumbling Western Roman Empire from Milan to Ravenna in 404. Built shortly after 425, almost a quarter century before

Galla Placidia's death in 450, the "mausoleum" was probably originally a chapel honoring the martyred Saint Lawrence. The building has a characteristically unadorned brick exterior. Inside, however, mosaics cover every square inch above the marble-faced walls.

Christ as Good Shepherd (FIG. **4-7**) is the subject of the lunette above the entrance. No earlier version of the Good Shepherd is as regal as this one. Instead of carrying a lamb on his shoulders, Jesus sits among his flock, haloed and robed in gold and purple. To his left and right, the sheep are distributed evenly in groups of three. But their arrangement is rather loose and informal, and they occupy a carefully described landscape extending from foreground to background beneath a blue sky. All the forms have three-dimensional bulk and cast shadows and are still deeply rooted in the classical tradition.

Sant'Apollinare Nuovo In 476, Ravenna fell to Odoacer, the first Germanic king of Italy, whom Theodoric, king of the Ostrogoths, overthrew in turn. Theodoric established his capital at Ravenna in 493. The mosaics in his palace church, Sant'Apollinare Nuovo (FIG. **4-4**), date from different periods, but those Theodoric commissioned already reveal a new,

Mosaics

As an art form, *mosaic* had a rather simple and utilitarian beginning, seemingly invented primarily to provide an inexpensive and durable flooring. Originally, mosaicists set small beach pebbles, unaltered from their natural form and color, into a thick coat of cement. Artisans soon discovered, however, that the stones could be arranged in decorative patterns. At first, these *pebble mosaics* were uncomplicated and confined to geometric shapes. Generally, the artists used only black and white stones. The earliest examples of this type date to the eighth century BCE. Eventually, mosaicists arranged the stones to form more complex pictorial designs, and by the fourth century BCE, artists depicted elaborate figural scenes using a broad range of colors—red, yellow, and brown, in addition to black, white, and gray—and shaded the figures, clothing, and setting to suggest volume.

By the middle of the third century BCE, Greek artists had invented a new kind of mosaic employing *tesserae* (Latin, "cubes" or "dice"). These tiny cut stones gave mosaicists much greater flexibility because they could adjust the size and shape of the tesserae. More nuanced gradations of color also became possible (FIG. 2-50), and mosaicists finally could aspire to rival the achievements of panel painters. In Early Christian mosaics (FIGS. 4-7 and 4-8), the tesserae are usually made of glass, which reflects light and makes the surfaces sparkle. Ancient mosaicists occasionally used glass tesserae, but the Romans preferred opaque marble pieces.

Mosaics quickly became the standard means of decorating walls and vaults in Early Christian buildings, although mural paintings were also popular. The mosaics caught the light flooding through the windows in vibrant reflection, producing sharp contrasts and concentrations of color that could focus attention on a composition's central, most relevant features. Early Christian mosaics were not meant to incorporate the subtle tonal changes a naturalistic painter's approach would require. Artists "placed," rather than blended, colors. Bright, hard, glittering texture, set within a rigorously simplified pattern, became the rule. For mosaics situated high in an apse or ambulatory vault or over the nave colonnade, far above the observer's head, the painstaking use of tiny tesserae seen in Roman floor mosaics would be pointless. Early Christian mosaics, designed to be seen from a distance, employed larger tesserae. The mosaicists also set the pieces unevenly so that their surfaces could catch and reflect the light.

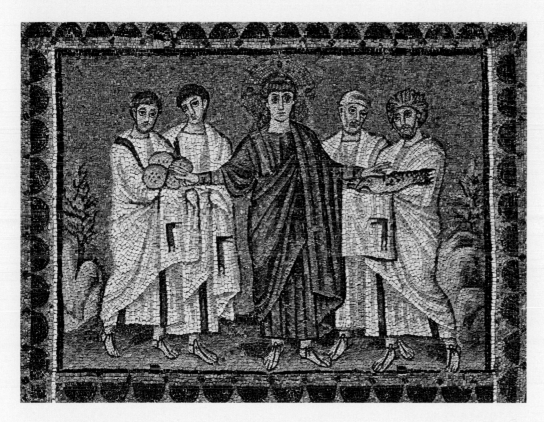

4-8 *Miracle of the Loaves and Fishes,* mosaic in the top register of the nave wall (above the clerestory windows in FIG. 4-4) of Sant'Apollinare Nuovo, Ravenna, Italy, ca. 504.

In contrast to FIG. 4-7, Jesus here faces directly toward the viewer. Blue sky has given way to the otherworldly splendor of heavenly gold, the standard background color for medieval mosaics.

much more abstract and formal, style. They depict scenes from Jesus's life (see "The Life of Jesus in Art," pages 130–131), for example, *Miracle of the Loaves and Fishes* (FIG. **4-8**). Beardless, in the imperial dress of gold and purple, and now distinguished by the cross-inscribed *nimbus* (halo) that signifies his divinity, the Savior faces directly toward the viewer. With extended arms he directs his disciples to distribute to the great crowd the miraculously increased supply of bread and fish he has produced. The mosaicist told the story with the least number of figures necessary to make its meaning explicit, aligning the figures laterally, moving them close to the foreground, and placing them in a shallow picture box. The landscape setting, which the artist who worked for Galla Placidia so explicitly described, is here merely a few rocks and bushes enclosing the figure group like parentheses. The blue sky of the physical world has given way to the otherworldly splendor of heavenly gold, which lifts the mosaic out of time and space and emphasizes the spiritual over the physical.

The Life of Jesus in Art

Christians believe Jesus of Nazareth is the son of God, the *Messiah* (Savior, *Christ*) of the Jews prophesied in the Old Testament. His life—his miraculous birth from the womb of a virgin mother, his preaching and miracle working, his execution by the Romans and subsequent ascent to Heaven—has been the subject of countless artworks from Roman times through the present day. Although during certain periods artists rarely, if ever, depicted many of the events of Jesus's life, it is useful to summarize here the entire cycle of events as they usually appear in artworks.

INCARNATION AND CHILDHOOD

The first "cycle" of the life of Jesus consists of the events of his conception (Incarnation), birth, infancy, and childhood.

▍ **Annunciation to Mary** The archangel Gabriel announces to the Virgin Mary that she will miraculously conceive and give birth to God's son, Jesus. Artists sometimes indicated God's presence at the Incarnation by a dove, the symbol of the Holy Spirit, the third "person" of the *Trinity* with God the Father and Jesus.

▍ **Visitation** The pregnant Mary visits Elizabeth, her older cousin, who is pregnant with the future John the Baptist. Elizabeth is the first to recognize that the baby Mary is bearing is the son of God.

▍ **Nativity, Annunciation to the Shepherds,** and **Adoration of the Shepherds** Jesus is born at night in Bethlehem and placed in a basket. Mary and her husband, Joseph, marvel at the newborn, while an angel announces the birth of the Savior to shepherds in the field.

▍ **Adoration of the Magi** A bright star alerts three wise men (*magi*) in the East that the King of the Jews has been born. They travel 12 days to find the holy family and present precious gifts to the infant Jesus.

▍ **Presentation in the Temple** Mary and Joseph bring their son to the temple in Jerusalem, where the aged Simeon, who God said would not die until he had seen the Messiah, recognizes Jesus as the prophesied Savior of humankind.

▍ **Massacre of the Innocents** and **Flight into Egypt** King Herod, fearful that a rival king has been born, orders the massacre of all infants in Bethlehem, but an angel warns the holy family, and they escape to Egypt.

▍ **Dispute in the Temple** Joseph and Mary travel to Jerusalem for the feast of *Passover* (the celebration of the release of the Jews from bondage to the pharaohs of Egypt). Jesus, only 12 years old at the time, engages in learned debate with astonished Jewish scholars in the temple, foretelling his ministry.

PUBLIC MINISTRY

The public ministry cycle comprises the teachings of Jesus and the miracles he performed.

▍ **Baptism** Jesus's public ministry begins with his *baptism* at age 30 by John the Baptist in the Jordan River. God's voice proclaims Jesus is his son.

▍ **Calling of Matthew** Jesus summons Matthew, a tax collector, to follow him, and Matthew becomes one of his 12 disciples, or *apostles*.

▍ **Miracles** In the course of his teaching and travels, Jesus performs many miracles, revealing his divine nature. These include acts of healing and raising the dead, turning water into wine, and walking on water. In the miracle of loaves and fishes, for example, Jesus transforms a few loaves of bread and a handful of fishes into enough food to feed several thousand people.

▍ **Delivery of the Keys to Peter** The fisherman Peter was one of the first men Jesus summoned as a disciple. Jesus chooses Peter (whose name means "rock") as his successor, and declares Peter is the rock on which his church will be built. Jesus symbolically delivers to Peter the keys to the Kingdom of Heaven.

▍ **Transfiguration** Jesus scales a high mountain and, in the presence of Peter and two other disciples, James and John the Evangelist, transforms himself into radiant light. God, speaking from a cloud, discloses Jesus is his son.

▍ **Cleansing of the Temple** Jesus returns to Jerusalem, where he finds money changers and merchants conducting business in the temple. He rebukes them and drives them out of the sacred precinct.

PASSION

The passion (from Latin *passio*, "suffering") cycle includes the episodes leading to Jesus's death, resurrection, and ascent to Heaven.

▍ **Entry into Jerusalem** On the Sunday before his crucifixion (Palm Sunday), Jesus rides triumphantly into Jerusalem on a donkey, accompanied by disciples.

▍ **Last Supper** and **Washing of the Disciples' Feet** In Jerusalem, Jesus celebrates Passover with his disciples. During this last supper, Jesus foretells his imminent betrayal, arrest, and death and invites the disciples to remember him when they eat bread (symbol of his body) and drink wine (his blood). This ritual became the celebration of *Mass* (*Eucharist*) in the Christian Church. At the same meal, Jesus sets an example of humility for his apostles by washing their feet.

▍ **Agony in the Garden** Jesus goes to the Mount of Olives in the Garden of Gethsemane, where he struggles to overcome his human fear of death by praying for divine strength.

▍ **Betrayal** and **Arrest** One of the disciples, Judas Iscariot, agrees to betray Jesus to the Jewish authorities in return for 30 pieces of silver. Judas identifies Jesus to the soldiers by kissing him, whereupon the soldiers arrest Jesus.

▍ **Trials of Jesus** and **Denial of Peter** The soldiers bring Jesus before Caiaphas, the Jewish high priest, who interrogates Jesus about his claim to be the Messiah. Meanwhile, the disciple Peter thrice denies knowing Jesus, as Jesus predicted he would. Jesus is then brought before the Roman governor of Judaea, Pontius Pilate, on the charge of treason because he had proclaimed himself as King of the Jews. Pilate asks the crowd to choose between freeing Jesus or Barabbas, a murderer. The

Manuscript Illumination

The long tradition of placing pictures in manuscripts began in Egypt. Illustrated ancient books, however, are rare. An important invention during the Early Roman Empire was the *codex,* which greatly aided the dissemination of manuscripts as well as their preservation. *Codices* are much like modern books, composed of separate leaves (*folios*) enclosed within a cover and bound together at one side. The new format superseded the long manuscript scroll (*rotulus*) used by the Egyptians, Greeks, Etruscans, and Romans. (Jesus holds a rotulus in his left hand in FIG. 4-1, *top right.*) Much more durable *vellum* (calfskin) and *parchment* (lambskin), which provided better surfaces for painting, also replaced the comparatively brittle *papyrus* (an Egyptian plant) used for ancient scrolls. As a result, luxuriousness of people choose Barabbas, and the judge condemns Jesus to death. Pilate washes his hands, symbolically relieving himself of responsibility for the mob's decision.

- **Flagellation** and **Mocking** The Roman soldiers who hold Jesus captive whip (flagellate) him and mock him by dressing him as King of the Jews and placing a crown of thorns on his head.

- **Carrying of the Cross, Raising of the Cross,** and **Crucifixion** The Romans force Jesus to carry the cross on which he will be crucified from Jerusalem to Mount Calvary (Golgotha, the "place of the skull," Adam's burial place). Jesus falls three times, and his robe is stripped along the way. Soldiers erect the cross and nail his hands and feet to it. Jesus's mother, John the Evangelist, and Mary Magdalene mourn at the foot of the cross, while soldiers torment Jesus. One of them (Longinus) stabs Jesus in the side with a spear. After suffering great pain, Jesus dies. The crucifixion occurred on a Friday, and Christians celebrate the day each year as Good Friday.

- **Deposition, Lamentation,** and **Entombment** Two disciples, Joseph of Arimathea and Nicodemus, remove Jesus's body from the cross (the deposition) and take him to the tomb Joseph had purchased for himself. Joseph, Nicodemus, the Virgin Mary, John the Evangelist, and Mary Magdalene mourn over the dead Jesus (the lamentation). (When in art the isolated figure of the Virgin Mary cradles her dead son in her lap, it is called a *Pietà*—Italian for "pity.") In portrayals of the entombment, Jesus's followers lower his body into a sarcophagus in the tomb.

- **Descent into Limbo** During the three days he spends in the tomb, Jesus (after death, Christ) descends into Hell, or Limbo, and triumphantly frees the souls of the righteous, including Adam, Eve, Moses, David, Solomon, and John the Baptist.

- **Resurrection** and **Three Marys at the Tomb** On the third day (Easter Sunday), Christ rises from the dead and leaves the tomb while the Roman guards sleep. The Virgin Mary, Mary Magdalene, and Mary, the mother of James, visit the tomb but find it empty. An angel informs them Christ has been resurrected.

- **Noli Me Tangere, Supper at Emmaus,** and **Doubting of Thomas** During the 40 days between Christ's resurrection and his ascent to Heaven, he appears on several occasions to his followers. Christ warns Mary Magdalene, weeping at his tomb, with the words "Don't touch me" (*Noli me tangere* in Latin), but he tells her to inform the apostles of his return. At Emmaus he eats supper with two of his astonished disciples. Later, Christ invites Thomas, who cannot believe Jesus has risen, to touch the wound in his side that he received at his crucifixion.

- **Ascension** On the 40th day, on the Mount of Olives, with his mother and apostles as witnesses, Christ gloriously ascends to Heaven in a cloud.

ornament became increasingly typical. Art historians refer to the painted books produced before the invention of the printing press as *illuminated manuscripts,* from the Latin *illuminare,* meaning "to adorn, ornament, or brighten," and *manu scriptus* (handwritten).

Vienna Genesis The oldest well-preserved painted manuscript containing biblical scenes is the early-sixth-century

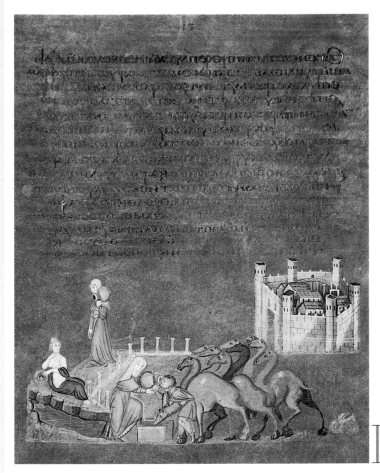

1 in.

4-9 *Rebecca and Eliezer at the Well,* folio 7 recto of the *Vienna Genesis,* early sixth century. Tempera, gold, and silver on purple vellum, $1' \frac{1}{4}'' \times 9\frac{1}{4}''$. Österreichische Nationalbibliothek, Vienna.

This sumptuously painted book is the oldest well-preserved manuscript containing biblical scenes. Two episodes of the Rebecca story appear in a single setting filled with classical motifs.

Vienna Genesis, so called because of its present location. The book is sumptuous. The pages are fine calfskin dyed with rich purple, the same dye used to give imperial cloth its distinctive color. The Greek text is in silver ink. Folio 7 (FIG. **4-9**) illustrates *Rebecca and Eliezer at the Well* (Gen. 24:15–61). When Isaac, Abraham's son, was 40 years old, his parents sent their servant Eliezer to find a wife for him. Eliezer chose Rebecca, because when he stopped at a well, she was the first woman to draw water for him and his camels. The *Vienna Genesis* illustration presents two episodes of the story within a single frame. In the first episode, at the left, Rebecca leaves the city of Nahor to fetch water from the well. In the second episode, she offers water to Eliezer and 10 camels, while one of them already laps water from the well. The artist painted Nahor as a walled city seen from above, like the cityscapes of the Column of Trajan frieze (FIG. 3-1). Rebecca walks to the well along the colonnaded avenue of a Roman city. A seminude female personification of a spring is the source of the well water. These are further reminders of the persistence of classical motifs and stylistic modes in Early Christian art even while other artists (FIG. 4-8) were rejecting classical norms in favor of a style better suited for a focus on the spiritual instead of the natural world.

BYZANTIUM

In the decades following the foundation in 324 of Constantinople—the New Rome in the East, on the site of the Greek city of Byzantium—the pace of Christianization of the Roman Empire quickened. In 380, Theodosius I (r. 379–395) issued an edict finally establishing Christianity as the state religion. In 391, he enacted a ban against worshiping the old gods, and in 394, the emperor abolished the Olympic Games, the enduring symbol of the classical world and its values. Theodosius died in 395, and imperial power passed to his two sons, Arcadius, who became Emperor of the East, and Honorius, Emperor of the West. Though not formally codified, the division of the Roman Empire became permanent. In the western half, the Visigoths, under their king Alaric, sacked Rome in 410. The Western Empire soon collapsed, replaced by warring kingdoms that, during the Middle Ages, formed the foundations of the modern nations of Europe (see Chapter 6). The eastern half of the Roman Empire, only loosely connected by religion to the West and with only minor territorial holdings there, had a long and complex history of its own. Centered at New Rome, the Eastern Christian Empire remained a cultural and political entity for a millennium, until the last of a long line of Eastern Roman emperors, ironically named Constantine XI, died at Constantinople in 1453, defending it in vain against the Muslim armies of the Ottoman Turks (see Chapter 5).

Historians refer to that Eastern Christian Roman Empire as Byzantium (MAP 4-1), employing Constantinople's original name, and use the term *Byzantine* to identify whatever pertains to Byzantium—its territory, its history, and its culture.

The Byzantine emperors, however, did not use the term to define themselves. They called their empire Rome and themselves Romans. Though they spoke Greek and not Latin, the Eastern Roman emperors never relinquished their claim as the legitimate successors to the ancient Roman emperors.

The Byzantine emperors considered themselves the earthly vicars of Jesus Christ. Their will was God's will. They exercised the ultimate spiritual as well as temporal authority. As sole executives for Church and state, the emperors shared power with neither senate nor Church council. They reigned supreme, combining the functions of both pope and Caesar, which the Christian West would keep strictly separate. The Byzantine emperors' exalted position made them quasi-divine. The imperial court was an image of the Kingdom of Heaven.

Art historians divide the history of Byzantine art into three periods. The first, Early Byzantine, extends from the founding of Constantinople in 324 to the onset of *iconoclasm* (the destruction of images used in religious worship) in 726 under Leo III. The Middle Byzantine period begins with the renunciation of iconoclasm in 843 and ends with the occupation of Constantinople in 1204 by Crusaders from the West. Late Byzantine corresponds to the two centuries after the Byzantines recaptured Constantinople in 1261 until its final loss in 1453 to the Ottoman Turks.

Early Byzantine Art

The first golden age of Byzantine art is the reign of Justinian (r. 527–565). At this time Byzantine art emerged as a recognizably novel and distinctive style, leaving behind the uncertainties and hesitations of Early Christian artistic experiment.

4-10 ANTHEMIUS OF TRALLES and ISIDORUS OF MILETUS, aerial view of Hagia Sophia (looking north), Constantinople (Istanbul), Turkey, 532–537. ◼◂

Justinian's reign was the first golden age of Byzantine art and architecture. Hagia Sophia was the most magnificent of the more than 30 churches Justinian built or restored in Constantinople alone.

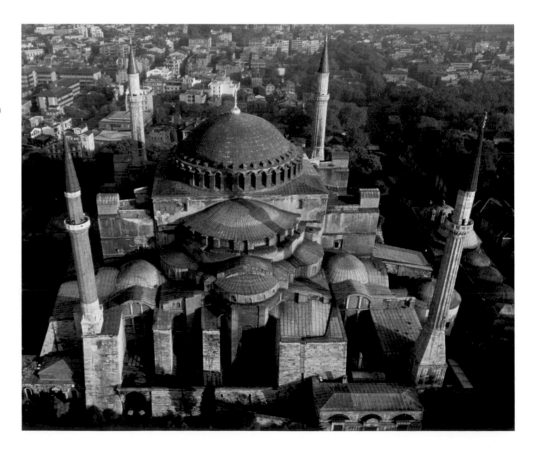

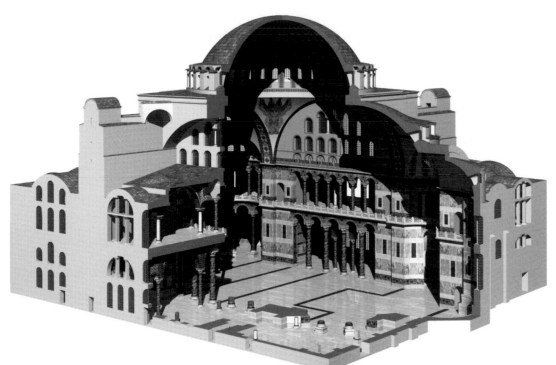

4-11 ANTHEMIUS OF TRALLES and ISIDORUS OF MILETUS, restored cutaway view (*top*) and plan (*bottom*) of Hagia Sophia, Constantinople (Istanbul), Turkey, 532–537 (John Burge). ◼

In Hagia Sophia, Justinian's architects succeeded in fusing two previously independent architectural traditions: the vertically oriented central-plan building and the longitudinally oriented basilica.

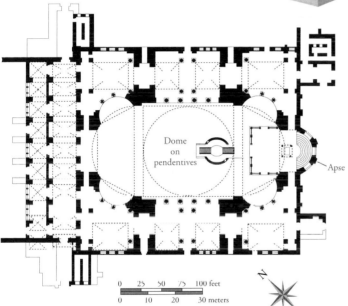

grandest building and one of the supreme accomplishments of world architecture. Hagia Sophia's dimensions are formidable: about 270 feet long and 240 feet wide. Its dome is 108 feet in diameter, and its crown rises some 180 feet above the pavement. In exterior view, the great dome dominates the structure, but the building's external aspects today are much changed from their original appearance. The huge buttresses are later additions to the Justinianic design, as are the four towering *minarets* the Turks constructed after their conquest of 1453, when Hagia Sophia became a *mosque* (see Chapter 5).

The characteristic Byzantine plainness and unpretentiousness of the exterior (FIG. 4-10) scarcely prepare visitors for the building's interior (FIG. 4-12), which was once richly appointed. Colored stones from throughout the known world sheathed the walls and floors. But the feature that distinguishes Hagia Sophia from equally lavishly revetted Roman buildings such as the Pantheon (FIG. 3-40) is the special mystical quality of the light flooding the interior. The soaring canopy-like dome that dominates the inside as well as the outside of the church rides on a halo of light from 40 windows in the dome's base, which creates the illusion the dome rests on light, not masonry. Procopius observed that the dome looked as if it were suspended by "a golden chain from Heaven" and that "the space is not illuminated by the sun from the outside, but the radiance is generated within, so great an abundance of light bathes this shrine all around."[2]

A Justinianic poet and *silentiary* (an usher responsible for maintaining silence), Paul Silentiarius, compared the dome to "the firmament which rests on air" and described the vaulting as covered with "gilded tesserae from which a glittering stream of golden rays pours abundantly and strikes men's eyes with irresistible force. It is as if one were gazing at the midday sun in spring."[3] Thus, Hagia Sophia has a vastness of space shot through with light, and a central dome

Justinianic art and architecture definitively expressed, with a new independence and power of invention, the unique character of the Eastern Christian culture centered at Constantinople. In the capital alone, Justinian built or restored more than 30 churches, and his activities as builder extended throughout the Byzantine Empire. The historian Procopius of Caesarea (ca. 500–565) declared the emperor's ambitious building program was an obsession that cost his subjects dearly in taxation. But Justinian's monuments defined the Byzantine style in architecture forever after.

Hagia Sophia The emperor's most important project was the construction of Hagia Sophia (FIGS. **4-10** and **4-11**), the Church of Holy Wisdom, in Constantinople. ANTHEMIUS OF TRALLES and ISIDORUS OF MILETUS designed and built the church for Justinian between 532 and 537. It is Byzantium's

Pendentives

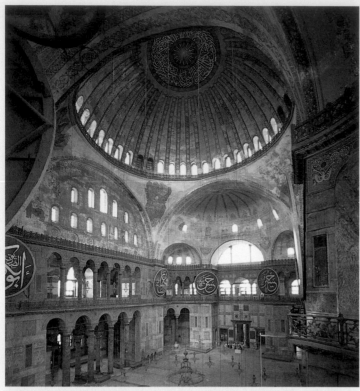

4-12 ANTHEMIUS OF TRALLES AND ISIDORUS OF MILETUS, interior of Hagia Sophia (looking southwest), Constantinople (Istanbul), Turkey, 532–537. ◼◣

Pendentive construction made possible Hagia Sophia's lofty dome, which seems to ride on a halo of light. A contemporary said the dome seemed to be suspended by "a golden chain from Heaven."

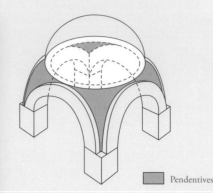

4-13 Dome on pendentives.

Roman domes rested on cylindrical drums (FIG. 3-14,d). Byzantine architects used pendentives (triangular sections of a sphere) to place a dome on a ring over a square, as in Hagia Sophia (FIG. 4-12).

▢ Pendentives

Perhaps the most characteristic feature of Byzantine architecture is the placement of a dome, which is circular at its base, over a square, as at Hagia Sophia (FIGS. 4-11 and 4-12) in Constantinople and Saint Mark's (FIG. 4-23) in Venice. The structural device that made this feat possible was the *pendentive* (FIG. 4-13).

In pendentive construction (from the Latin *pendere*, "to hang"), a dome rests on what is, in effect, a second, larger dome. The builders omit the top portion and four segments around the rim of the larger dome, producing four curved triangles, or pendentives. The pendentives join to form a ring and four arches whose planes bound a square. The pendentives and arches transfer the weight of the dome to the four piers from which the arches spring. The first use of pendentives on a monumental scale was in Hagia Sophia in the mid-sixth century. In Roman and Early Christian central-plan buildings, such as the Pantheon (FIGS. 3-39 and 3-40) and Santa Costanza (FIG. 4-5), the domes spring directly from the circular top of a cylinder (FIG. 3-14d).

that appears to be supported by the light it admits. Light is the mystic element—light that glitters in the mosaics, shines forth from the marbles, and pervades and defines spaces that escape definition. Light seems to dissolve material substance and transform it into an abstract spiritual vision.

Pendentives To achieve this illusion of a floating "dome of Heaven," Anthemius and Isidorus used *pendentives* (see "Pendentives," above, and FIGS. **4-12** and **4-13**) to transfer the weight from the great dome to the piers beneath rather than to the walls. With pendentives, not only could the space beneath the dome be unobstructed but scores of windows also could puncture the walls. The pendentives created the impression of a dome suspended above, not held up by, walls. Experts today can explain the technical virtuosity of Justinian's builders, but it remained a mystery to their contemporaries. Procopius communicated the sense of wonderment experienced by those who entered Hagia Sophia: "No

matter how much they concentrate . . . they are unable to understand the craftsmanship and always depart from there amazed by the perplexing spectacle."[4]

By placing a hemispherical dome on a square base instead of on a circular base, as in the Pantheon, Anthemius and Isidorus succeeded in fusing two previously independent and seemingly mutually exclusive architectural traditions: the vertically oriented central-plan building and the longitudinally oriented basilica. Hagia Sophia is, in essence, a domed basilica (FIG. 4-11)—a uniquely successful conclusion to several centuries of experimentation in Christian church architecture. However, the thrusts of the pendentive construction at Hagia Sophia made external buttresses necessary, as well as huge internal northern and southern wall piers and eastern and western half-domes. The semidomes' thrusts descend, in turn, into still smaller half-domes surmounting columned *exedrae* that give a curving flow to the design.

The diverse vistas and screenlike ornamented surfaces mask the structural lines. The columnar arcades of the nave and second-story galleries have no real structural function. Like the walls they pierce, they are only part of a fragile "fill" between the huge piers. Structurally, although Hagia Sophia may seem Roman in its great scale and majesty, the organization of its masses is not Roman. The very fact the "walls" in Hagia Sophia are concealed (and barely adequate) piers indicates the architects sought Roman monumentality as an effect and did not design the building according to Roman principles. Using brick in place of concrete was a further departure from Roman practice and marks Byzantine architecture as a distinctive structural style. Hagia Sophia's eight great supporting piers are ashlar masonry, but the screen walls are brick, as are the vaults of the aisles and galleries and the dome and semicircular half-domes.

The ingenious design of Hagia Sophia provided the illumination and the setting for the solemn liturgy of the Greek Orthodox faith. The large windows along the rim of the great dome poured light down upon the interior's jeweled splendor, where priests staged the sacred spectacle. Sung by clerical choirs, the Orthodox equivalent of the Latin Mass celebrated the sacrament of the Eucharist at the altar in the *apsidal* sanctuary, in spiritual reenactment of Jesus's crucifixion. Processions of chanting priests, accompanying the *patriarch* (archbishop) of Constantinople, moved slowly to and from the sanctuary and the vast nave. The gorgeous array of their vestments rivaled the interior's polychrome marbles and mosaics, all glowing in shafts of light from the dome.

The nave of Hagia Sophia was reserved for the clergy, not the congregation. The laity, segregated by sex, had only partial views of the brilliant ceremony from the shadows of the aisles and galleries, restrained in most places by marble parapets. The emperor was the only lay person privileged to enter the sanctuary. When he participated with the patriarch in the liturgical drama, standing at the pulpit beneath the great dome, his rule was sanctified and his person exalted. Church and state were symbolically made one, as in fact they were. The church building was then the earthly image of the court of Heaven, its light the image of God and God's holy wisdom. At Hagia Sophia, the ambitious scale of imperial Rome and the religious mysticism of the Eastern Christian Empire combined to create a monument that is at once a summation of antiquity and a positive assertion of the triumph of Christian faith.

San Vitale In 539, Justinian's general Belisarius captured Ravenna from the Ostrogoths. As the Eastern Empire's foothold in Italy, Ravenna enjoyed great prosperity, and its culture became an extension of Constantinople's. Its art, even more than that of the Byzantine capital (where relatively little outside of architecture has survived), clearly reveals the transition from the Early Christian to the Byzantine style.

San Vitale (FIGS. **4-14** and **4-15**), dedicated by Bishop Maximianus (r. 546–556) in 547 in honor of Saint Vitalis, who died a martyr at the hands of the Romans in the second century, is the most spectacular building in Ravenna. Construction began under Bishop Ecclesius (r. 522–532) shortly after Theodoric's death in 526. Julianus Argentarius (Julian

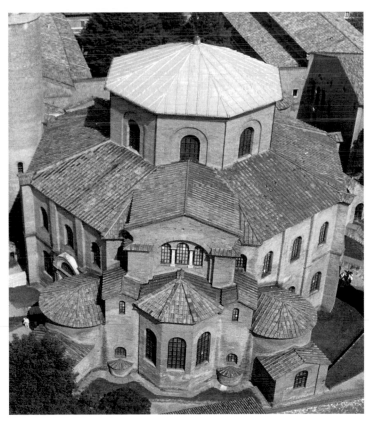

4-14 Aerial view of San Vitale (looking northwest), Ravenna, Italy, 526–547. ◾◀

Justinian's general Belisarius captured Ravenna from the Ostrogoths. The city became the seat of Byzantine dominion in Italy. San Vitale honored Saint Vitalis, a second-century Ravenna martyr.

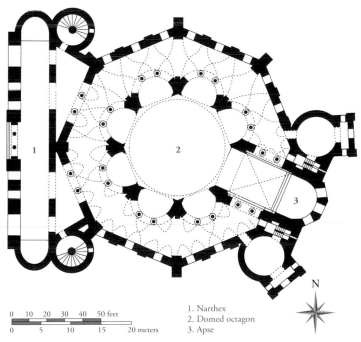

0 10 20 30 40 50 feet
0   5   10   15   20 meters

1. Narthex
2. Domed octagon
3. Apse

4-15 Plan of San Vitale, Ravenna, Italy, 526–547.

Centrally planned like Justinian's churches in Constantinople, San Vitale is unlike any other church in Italy. The design features two concentric octagons. A dome crowns the taller, inner octagon.

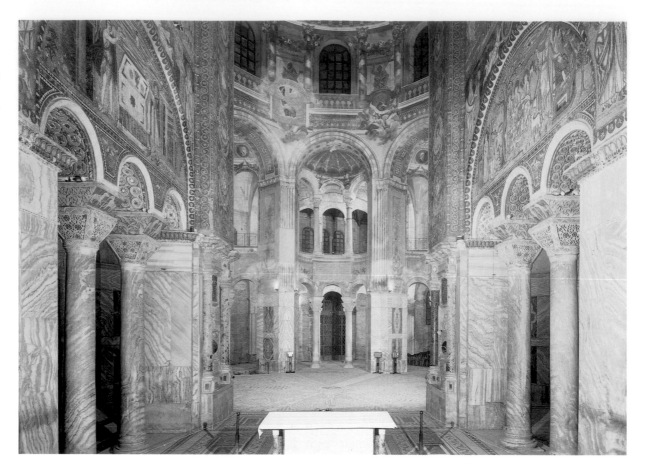

4-16 Interior of San Vitale (looking from the apse into the choir), Ravenna, Italy, 526–547. ▶️

Light filtered through alabaster-paned windows plays over the glittering mosaics and glowing marbles sheathing San Vitale's complex wall and vault shapes, producing a sumptuous effect.

the Banker) provided the enormous sum of 26,000 *solidi* (gold coins) weighing in excess of 350 pounds required to proceed with the work. San Vitale is unlike any of the Early Christian churches (FIG. 4-4) of Ravenna. It is not a basilica. Rather, it is centrally planned, like Justinian's churches in Constantinople.

The design features two concentric octagons. The dome-covered inner octagon rises above the surrounding octagon to provide the interior (FIG. **4-16**) with clerestory lighting. Eight large rectilinear piers alternate with curved, columned exedrae, pushing outward into the surrounding two-story ambulatory and creating an intricate eight-leafed plan (FIG. 4-15). The exedrae closely integrate the inner and outer spaces that otherwise would have existed simply side by side as independent units. A cross-vaulted *choir* preceding the apse interrupts the ambulatory and gives the plan some axial stability. Weakening this effect, however, is the off-axis placement of the narthex, whose odd angle never has been explained. (The atrium, which no longer exists, may have paralleled a street running in the same direction as the angle of the narthex.)

San Vitale's intricate plan and elevation combine to produce an effect of great complexity. The exterior's octagonal regularity is not readily apparent inside. A rich diversity of ever-changing perspectives greets visitors walking through the building. Arches looping over arches, curving and flattened spaces, and wall and vault shapes seem to change constantly with the viewer's position. Light filtered through

alabaster-paned windows plays over the glittering mosaics and glowing marbles that cover the building's complex surfaces, producing a sumptuous effect.

The mosaics (FIGS. **4-17** and **4-18**) in San Vitale's choir and apse, like the building itself, must be regarded as one of the greatest achievements of Byzantine art. Completed less than a decade after the Ostrogoths surrendered Ravenna, the apse and choir decorations form a unified composition, whose theme is the holy ratification of Justinian's right to rule. In the apse vault are Christ, who extends the golden martyr's wreath to Saint Vitalis, the patron saint of the church, and Bishop Ecclesius, who offers a model of San Vitale to Christ. On the choir wall to the left of the apse mosaic appears Justinian (FIG. 4-17). He stands on the Savior's right side. Uniting the two visually and symbolically are the imperial purple they wear and their halos. A dozen attendants accompany Justinian, paralleling Christ's 12 apostles. Thus, the mosaic program underscores the dual political and religious role of the Byzantine emperor.

The positions of the figures are all-important. They express the formulas of precedence and rank. Justinian is at the center, distinguished from the other dignitaries by his purple robe and halo. At his left is Bishop Maximianus. The mosaicist stressed the bishop's importance by labeling his figure with the only identifying inscription in the composition. The artist divided the figures into three groups: the emperor and his staff; the clergy; and the imperial guard, bearing a shield with the *Christogram,* the monogram made up of chi

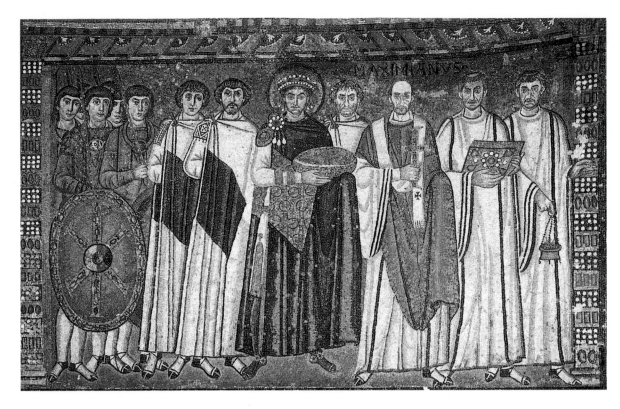

4-17 Justinian, Bishop Maximianus, and attendants, mosaic on the north wall of the apse, San Vitale, Ravenna, Italy, ca. 547. ◼◀

San Vitale's mosaics reveal the new Byzantine aesthetic. Justinian is foremost among the weightless and speechless frontal figures hovering before the viewer, their positions in space uncertain.

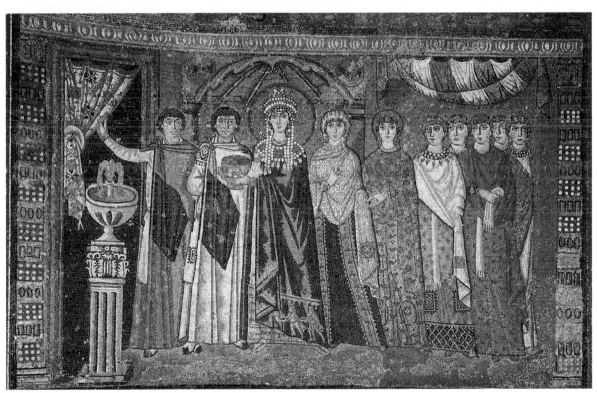

4-18 Theodora and attendants, mosaic on the south wall of the apse, San Vitale, Ravenna, Italy, ca. 547. ◼◀

Justinian's counterpart on the opposite wall is the powerful Empress Theodora. Neither she nor Justinian ever visited Ravenna. San Vitale's mosaics are proxies for the absent sovereigns.

(X), rho (P), and iota (I), the initial letters of Christ's name in Greek. Each group has a leader whose feet precede (by one foot overlapping) the feet of those who follow. The positions of Justinian and Maximianus are curiously ambiguous. Although the emperor appears to be slightly behind the bishop, the golden *paten* (large shallow bowl for the Eucharist bread) he carries overlaps the bishop's arm. Thus, symbolized by place and gesture, the imperial and churchly powers are in balance. The emperor's paten, the bishop's cross, and the attendant clerics' book and censer produce a slow forward movement that strikingly modifies the scene's rigid formality. The artist placed nothing in the background, wishing the observer to understand the procession as taking place in this very sanctuary. Thus, the emperor appears forever as a participant in the sacred rites and as the proprietor of this royal church and the ruler of the Western Empire.

The procession at San Vitale recalls but contrasts with that of Augustus and his entourage on the Ara Pacis

(FIG. 3-27), built more than a half millennium earlier in Rome. There the fully modeled marble figures have their feet planted firmly on the ground. The Romans talk among themselves, unaware of the viewer's presence. All is anecdote, all very human and of this world, even if the figures themselves conform to a classical ideal of beauty that cannot be achieved in reality. The frontal figures of the Byzantine mosaic hover before viewers, weightless and speechless, their positions in space uncertain. Tall, spare, angular, and elegant, the figures have lost the rather squat proportions characteristic of much Early Christian figural art. The garments fall straight, stiff, and thin from the narrow shoulders. The organic body has dematerialized, and, except for the heads, some of which seem to be true portraits, viewers see a procession of solemn spirits gliding silently in the presence of the sacrament. Indeed, the theological basis for this approach to representation was the idea that the divine was invisible and that the purpose of religious art was to stimulate spiritual seeing. Theodulf of Orleans summed up this idea around 790, when he wrote "God is beheld not with the eyes of the flesh but only with the eye of the mind."[5] The mosaics of San Vitale reveal this new Byzantine aesthetic, one very different from that of the classical world but equally compelling. Byzantine art disparages matter and material values. It is an art in which blue sky has given way to heavenly gold, an art without solid bodies or cast shadows, and with the perspective of Paradise, which is nowhere and everywhere.

Justinian's counterpart on the opposite wall of the apse is his empress, Theodora (FIG. 4-18), who was Justinian's most trusted adviser as well as his spouse. She too is accompanied by her retinue. Both processions move into the apse, Justinian proceeding from left to right and Theodora from right to left, in order to take part in the Eucharist. Justinian carries the paten containing the bread, Theodora the golden cup with the wine. The portraits in the Theodora mosaic exhibit the same stylistic traits as those in the Justinian mosaic, but the mosaicist represented the women within a definite architecture, perhaps the atrium of San Vitale. The empress stands in state beneath an imperial canopy, waiting to follow the emperor's procession. An attendant beckons her to pass through the curtained doorway. The fact she is outside the sanctuary in a courtyard with a fountain and only about to enter attests that, in the ceremonial protocol, her rank was not quite equal to her consort's. But the very presence of Theodora at San Vitale is significant. Neither she nor Justinian ever visited Ravenna. Their participation in the liturgy at San Vitale is pictorial fiction. The mosaics are proxies for the absent sovereigns. Justinian is present because he was the head of the Byzantine state, and his inclusion in the mosaic underscores that his authority extends over his territories in Italy. But Theodora's portrayal is more surprising and testifies to her unique position in Justinian's court. Theodora's prominent role in the mosaic program of San Vitale is proof of the power she wielded at Constantinople and, by extension, at Ravenna. In fact, the representation of the three magi on the border of her robe suggests the empress belongs in the elevated company of the three monarchs bearing gifts who approached the newborn Jesus.

Mount Sinai During Justinian's reign, almost continuous building took place, not only in Constantinople and Ravenna but throughout the Byzantine Empire. Between 548 and 565, Justinian rebuilt an important early *monastery* (monks' compound) at Mount Sinai in Egypt where Moses received the Ten Commandments from God. Now called Saint Catherine's, the monastery marked the spot at the foot of the mountain where the Bible says God first spoke to the Hebrew prophet from a burning bush.

Monasticism began in Egypt in the third century and spread rapidly to Palestine and Syria in the East and as far as Ireland in the West (see Chapter 6). It began as a migration to the wilderness by those who sought a more spiritual way of life, far from the burdens, distractions, and temptations of town and city. In desert places, these refuge seekers lived austerely as hermits, in contemplative isolation, cultivating the soul's perfection. So many thousands fled the cities that the authorities became alarmed—noting the effect on the tax base, military recruitment, and business in general. The origins of the monastic movement are associated with Saint Anthony and Saint Pachomius in Egypt in the fourth century. By the fifth century, many of the formerly isolated monks had begun to live together within a common enclosure and to formulate regulations governing communal life under the direction of an *abbot* (see "Medieval Monasteries and Benedictine Rule," Chapter 6, page 168). The monks typically lived in a walled monastery, an architectural complex that included the monks' residence (an alignment of single cells), an *oratory* (monastic church), a *refectory* (dining hall), a kitchen, storage and service quarters, and a guest house for pilgrims (FIG. 6-9). The monastery at Mount Sinai had been an important pilgrimage destination since the fourth century, and Justinian's fortress protected not only the monks but also the lay pilgrims during their visits. The Mount Sinai church was dedicated to the Virgin Mary, whom the Orthodox Church had officially recognized in the mid-fifth century as the Mother of God (*Theotokos,* "she who bore God" in Greek).

Icons Illuminated manuscripts and *icons* (see "Icons and Iconoclasm," page 139) played important roles in monastic life. Unfortunately, few early icons survive because of the wholesale destruction of images that occurred in the eighth century. One of the finest early examples (FIG. **4-19**) comes from Mount Sinai. The medium is encaustic on wood, continuing a tradition of panel painting in Egypt that, like so much else in the Byzantine world, goes back to the Roman Empire (FIGS. 3-42 and 3-43). The icon depicts the enthroned Theotokos and Child with Saints Theodore and George. The two guardian saints intercede with the Virgin on the worshiper's behalf. Behind them, two angels gaze upward at a shaft of light where the hand of God appears. The foreground figures are strictly frontal and have a solemn demeanor. Background details are few and suppressed. The shallow

Icons and Iconoclasm

Icons (Greek, "images") are small portable paintings depicting Christ, the Virgin, or saints (or a combination of all three, as in FIG. 4-19). Icons survive from as early as the fourth century. From the sixth century on, they became enormously popular in Byzantine worship, both public and private. Eastern Christians considered icons a personal, intimate, and indispensable medium for spiritual transaction with holy figures. Some icons (for example, FIG. 4-26) came to be regarded as wonder-working, and believers ascribed miracles and healing powers to them.

Icons, however, were by no means universally accepted. From the beginning, many Christians were deeply suspicious of the practice of imaging the divine, whether on portable panels, on the walls of churches, or especially as statues that reminded them of ancient idols. The opponents of Christian figural art had in mind the prohibition of images the Lord dictated to Moses in the Second Commandment: "Thou shalt not make unto thee any graven image or any likeness of anything that is in heaven above, or that is in the earth beneath, or that is in the water under the earth. Thou shalt not bow down thyself to them, nor serve them" (Exod. 20:4, 5).

Opposition to icons became especially strong in the eighth century, when the faithful often burned incense and knelt before the icons in prayer to seek protection or a cure for illness. Although the purpose of icons was only to evoke the presence of the holy figures addressed in prayer, in the minds of many, icons became identified with the personages represented. Icon veneration became confused with idol worship, and this brought about an imperial ban on *all* sacred images and edicts ordering the destruction of holy pictures (*iconoclasm*).

The consequences of iconoclasm for the early history of Byzantine art are difficult to overstate. For more than a century, not only did the portrayal of Christ, the Virgin, and the saints cease, but the *iconoclasts* (breakers of images) also systematically destroyed countless works from the first several centuries of Christendom.

4-19 Virgin (Theotokos) and Child between Saints Theodore and George, icon, sixth or early seventh century. Encaustic on wood, 2' 3" × 1' 7¾". Monastery of Saint Catherine, Mount Sinai, Egypt.

Byzantine icons are the heirs to the Roman tradition of portrait painting on small wood panels (FIG. 3-42), but their Christian subjects and function as devotional objects broke sharply from classical models.

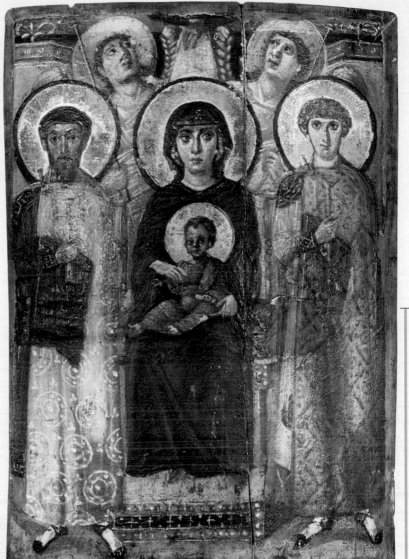

1 ft.

---

forward plane of the picture dominates; space is squeezed out. Traces of Greco-Roman illusionism remain in the Virgin's rather personalized features, in her sideways glance, and in the posing of the angels' heads. But the painter rendered the saints in the new Byzantine manner.

Iconoclasm The preservation of Early Byzantine icons at the Mount Sinai monastery is fortuitous but ironic, for opposition to icon worship was especially prominent in Syria and Egypt. There, in the seventh century, a series of calamities erupted, indirectly causing the imperial ban on images. The Sasanians, chronically at war with Rome, swept into the eastern provinces, and between 611 and 617 they captured the great cities of Antioch, Jerusalem, and Alexandria. The Byzantine emperor Heraclius (r. 610–641) had hardly defeated them in 627 when a new and overwhelming power appeared unexpectedly on the stage of history. The Arabs, under the banner of the new Islamic religion, conquered not only Byzantium's eastern provinces but also Persia itself, replacing the Sasanians in the age-old balance of power with the Christian West (see Chapter 5). In a few years the Arabs launched attacks on Constantinople, and Byzantium was fighting for its life.

These were catastrophic years for the Eastern Roman Empire. They terminated once and for all the long story of imperial Rome, closed the Early Byzantine period, and inaugurated the medieval era of Byzantine history. The Byzantine Empire lost almost two-thirds of its territory—many cities and much of its population, wealth, and material resources. The shock of these events persuaded Emperor Leo III (r. 717–741) that God was punishing the Christian Roman Empire for its idolatrous worship of icons by setting upon it the merciless armies of the infidel—an enemy that, moreover, shunned the representation not only of God but of all living things in holy places (see Chapter 5). In 726, he formally prohibited the use of images, and for more than a century Byzantine artists produced little new religious figurative art.

Middle Byzantine Art

In the ninth century, a powerful reaction against iconoclasm set in. New *iconophile* (image-loving) emperors condemned the destruction of images as a heresy, and restoration of the images began in 843 under Empress Theodora. Shortly thereafter, under the Macedonian dynasty, the emperors once again became lavish patrons of religious art. Basil I (r. 867–886), head of the new line of emperors, regarded himself as the restorer of the Roman Empire. He denounced as usurpers the Carolingian monarchs of the West (see Chapter 6) who, since 800, had claimed the title "Roman Empire" for their realm. Basil bluntly reminded their emissary that the only true emperor of Rome reigned in Constantinople. They were not Roman emperors but merely "kings of the Germans."

Hosios Loukas Although the new emperors did not wait long to redecorate the churches of their predecessors, they undertook little new church construction in the decades after the renunciation of iconoclasm. But in the 10th century and through the 12th, a number of monastic churches arose that are the flowers of Middle Byzantine architecture. They feature a brilliant series of variations on the domed central plan. From the exterior, the typical later Byzantine church building is a domed cube, with the dome rising above the square on a kind of cylinder or *drum*. The churches are small, vertical, high-shouldered, and, unlike earlier Byzantine buildings, have exterior wall surfaces decorated with vivid patterns, probably reflecting Islamic architecture.

The Katholikon (FIG. **4-20**) at Hosios Loukas (Saint Luke) in Greece, dates to the early 11th century and exemplifies church design during this second golden age of Byzantine art and architecture. Light stones framed by dark red bricks make up the walls. The interplay of arcuated windows, projecting apses, and varying roof lines further enhances this surface dynamism. The plan is in the form of a domed cross in square with four equal-length, vaulted cross arms (the *Greek cross*).

Daphni Mosaics covered the walls, vaults, and domes of Middle Byzantine churches. Some of the best-preserved examples are in the monastic church of the Dormition (from the Latin for "sleep," referring to the ascension of the Virgin Mary to Heaven at the moment of her death), at Daphni, near Athens. The main elements of the late-11th-century pictorial program are intact, although the mosaics underwent restoration in the 19th century. Gazing down from on high in the dome (FIG. **4-21**) is the fearsome image of *Christ as Pantokrator* (literally "ruler of all" in Greek but usually applied to Christ in his role as last judge of humankind). The dome mosaic is

4-20 Katholikon (looking northeast), Hosios Loukas, Greece, first quarter of 11th century.

Middle Byzantine churches typically are small and high-shouldered, with a central dome on a drum and exterior wall surfaces with decorative patterns, probably reflecting Islamic architecture.

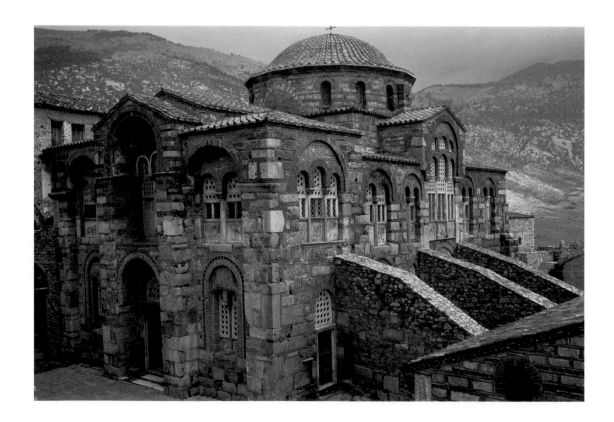

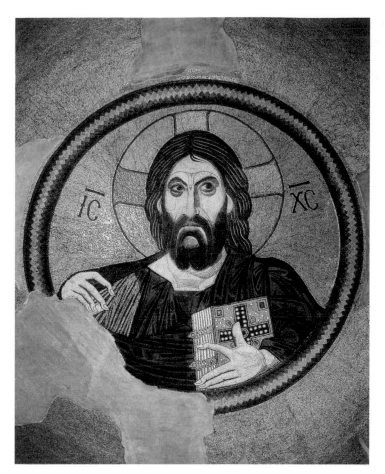

4-21 *Christ as Pantokrator,* mosaic in the dome of the Church of the Dormition, Daphni, Greece, ca. 1090–1100.

The fearsome image of Christ as *pantokrator* (ruler of all) is like a gigantic icon hovering dramatically in space, connecting the awestruck worshiper below with Heaven through Christ.

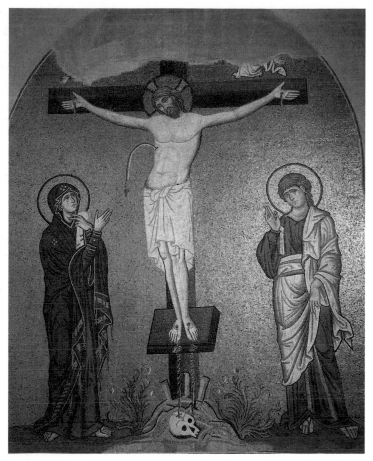

4-22 *Crucifixion,* mosaic in the north arm of the east wall of the Church of the Dormition, Daphni, Greece, ca. 1090–1100.

The Daphni *Crucifixion* is a subtle blend of Hellenistic style and the more abstract Byzantine manner. The Virgin Mary and Saint John point to Christ on the cross as if to a devotional object.

the climax of an elaborate hierarchical mosaic program including several New Testament episodes below. The Daphni pantokrator is like a gigantic icon hovering dramatically in space. The image serves to connect the awestruck worshiper in the church below with Heaven through Christ.

Below the dome, on the wall beneath the barrel vault of one arm of the Greek cross, is the *Crucifixion* (FIG. **4-22**). Like the pantokrator mosaic in the dome, the Daphni *Crucifixion* is a subtle blend of the painterly, naturalistic style of Early Christian art and the later, more abstract and formalistic Byzantine style. The Byzantine artist fully assimilated classicism's simplicity, dignity, and grace into a perfect synthesis with Byzantine piety and pathos. The figures have regained the classical organic structure to a surprising degree, particularly compared to figures from the Justinianic period (compare FIGS. **4-17** and **4-18**). The style is a masterful adaptation of classical statuesque qualities to the linear Byzantine manner.

In quiet sorrow and resignation, the Virgin and Saint John flank the crucified Christ. A skull at the foot of the cross indicates Golgotha, the "place of skulls." The artist needed nothing else to set the scene. The picture is not a narrative of the historical event of Jesus's execution, although it contains anecdotal details. Christ has a tilted head and sagging body, and although the Savior is not overtly in pain, blood and water spurt from the wound Longinus inflicted on him, as recounted in Saint John's Gospel. The Virgin and John point to the figure on the cross as if to a devotional object. They act as intercessors between the viewer below and Christ, who, in the dome, appears as the last judge of all humans.

Saint Mark's, Venice The revival on a grand scale of church building and of figural mosaics extended beyond the Greek-speaking Byzantine East in the 10th to 12th centuries, especially in areas of the former Western Roman Empire where the ties with Constantinople were the strongest. In the Early Byzantine period, Venice, about 80 miles north of Ravenna on the eastern coast of Italy, was a dependency of that Byzantine stronghold. In 751, Ravenna fell to the Lombards, who wrested control of most of northern Italy from Constantinople. Venice, however, became an independent power. Its *doges* (dukes) enriched themselves and the city through seaborne commerce, serving as the crucial link between Byzantium and the West.

4-23 Interior of Saint Mark's (looking east), Venice, Italy, begun 1063.

Modeled on a church in Constantinople, Saint Mark's has a dome over the crossing, four other domes over the arms of the Greek cross, and 40,000 square feet of Byzantine-style mosaics.

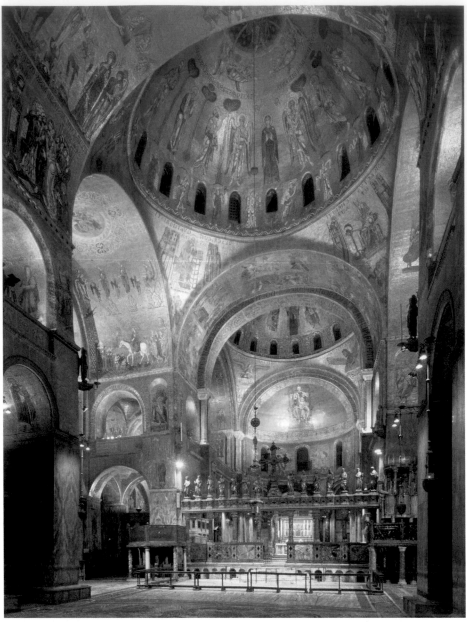

Venice had obtained the relics of Saint Mark from Alexandria in Egypt in 829, and the doges constructed the first Venetian shrine dedicated to the evangelist shortly thereafter. In 1063, Doge Domenico Contarini (r. 1043–1071) began construction of the present Saint Mark's, modeled on the Church of the Holy Apostles at Constantinople, built in Justinian's time. That shrine no longer exists, but its key elements were a *cruciform* (cross-shaped) plan with a central dome over the crossing and four other domes over the four equal arms of the Greek cross, as at Saint Mark's.

The interior (FIG. **4-23**) of Saint Mark's is, like its plan, Byzantine in effect. Light enters through a row of windows at the bases of all five domes, vividly illuminating a rich cycle of mosaics. Both Byzantine and local artists worked on the project over the course of several centuries. Most of the mosaics date to the 12th and 13th centuries. Cleaning and restoration on a grand scale have enabled visitors to experience the full radiance of 40,000 square feet of mosaics covering all the walls, arches, vaults, and domes, like a gold-brocaded and figured fabric.

In the vast central dome, 80 feet above the floor and 42 feet in diameter, Christ ascends to Heaven in the presence of the Virgin Mary and the 12 apostles. In the great arch framing the crossing are the *Crucifixion* and *Resurrection* and Christ's liberation from death of Adam and Eve, John the Baptist, and other biblical figures. The mosaics have explanatory labels in both Latin and Greek, reflecting Venice's position as the key link between Eastern and Western Christendom in the later Middle Ages. The insubstantial figures on the walls, vaults, and domes appear weightless, and they project no farther from their flat field than the elegant Latin and Greek letters above them. Nothing here reflects on the world of matter, of solids, of light and shade, of perspective space. Rather, the mosaics reveal the mysteries of the Christian faith.

Harbaville Triptych Middle Byzantine artists also excelled in the production of sumptuous small-scale artworks, including bejeweled icons, illuminated manuscripts, and carved ivories. A masterpiece of ivory carving is the *Harbaville Triptych* (FIG. **4-24**), a portable shrine with hinged wings used for private devotion. Ivory *triptychs* were very popular—among those who could afford such luxurious items—and they often replaced icons for use in personal prayer. Carved on the wings of the *Harbaville Triptych,* both inside and out, are four pairs of full-length figures and two pairs of medallions depicting saints. A cross dominates the central panel on the back of the triptych (not illustrated). On the inside is a scene of *Deësis* (supplication). John the Baptist and the Theotokos appear as intercessors, praying on behalf of the viewer to the enthroned Savior. Below them are five apostles.

The formality and solemnity usually associated with Byzantine art yielded here to a softer, more fluid technique. The figures may lack true classical contrapposto, but the looser stances (most stand on bases, like freestanding statues) and three-quarter views of many of the heads relieve the hard austerity of the customary frontal pose. This more natural, classical spirit was a second, equally important, stylistic current of the Middle Byzantine period. It also surfaced in mural painting and book illumination.

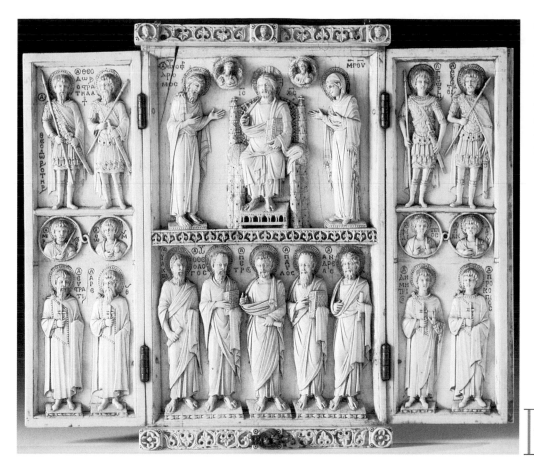

Christ enthroned with saints (*Harbaville Triptych*), ca. 950. Ivory, central panel 9½″ × 5½″. Musée du Louvre, Paris.

In this small three-part shrine with hinged wings used for private devotion, the ivory carver depicted the figures with looser classical stances, in contrast to the frontal poses of most Byzantine figures.

1 in.

Paris Psalter The so-called *Paris Psalter* (FIG. 4-25)—a *psalter* is a book containing King David's Psalms—also reasserts the artistic values of the Greco-Roman past with astonishing authority. Art historians believe the manuscript dates from the mid-10th century—the Macedonian Renaissance, a time of enthusiastic and careful study of the language and literature of ancient Greece, and of humanistic reverence for the classical past. On the manuscript's first folio, David, the psalmist, surrounded by sheep, goats, and his faithful dog, plays his harp in a rocky landscape with a town in the background. Similar settings appeared frequently in Pompeian murals. Befitting an ancient depiction of Orpheus, the Greek hero who could charm even inanimate objects with his music, allegorical figures accompany the biblical harpist. Melody looks over his shoulder, while Echo peers from behind a column. A reclining male figure points to a Greek inscription identifying him as representing the mountain of Bethlehem. These allegorical figures do not appear in the Bible. They are the stock population of Greco-Roman painting. Apparently, the artist translated a classical model into a Byzantine pictorial idiom. In works such as this, Byzantine artists kept the classical style alive in the Middle Ages.

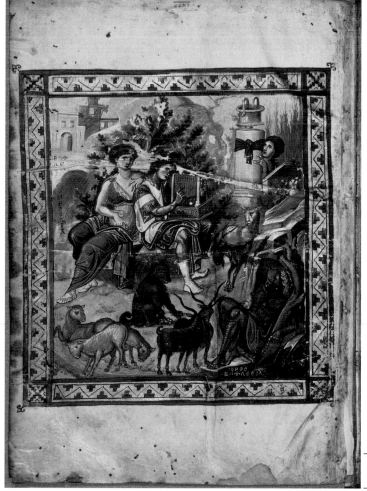

4-25 *David Composing the Psalms,* folio 1 verso of the *Paris Psalter,* ca. 950–970. Tempera on vellum, 1′ 2⅛″ × 10¼″. Bibliothèque Nationale, Paris.

During the Macedonian Renaissance, Byzantine artists revived the classical style. This painter portrayed David as if a Greek hero, accompanied by personifications of Melody, Echo, and Bethlehem.

1 in.

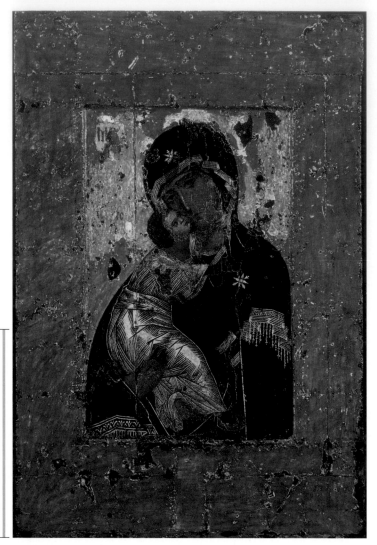

4-26 Virgin of Compassion icon (*Vladimir Virgin*), late 11th or early 12th century, with later repainting. Tempera on wood, 2′ 6½″ × 1′ 9″. Tretyakov Gallery, Moscow.

In this Middle Byzantine icon, the painter depicted Mary as the Virgin of Compassion, who presses her cheek against her son's as she contemplates his future. The reverse side shows the instruments of Christ's passion.

Vladimir Virgin Nothing in Middle Byzantine art better demonstrates the rejection of the iconoclastic viewpoint than the painted icon's return to prominence. After the restoration of images, such icons multiplied by the thousands to meet public and private demand. In the 11th century, the clergy began to display icons in hierarchical order (Christ, the Theotokos, John the Baptist, and then other saints, as on the *Harbaville Triptych*) in tiers on the *templon,* the columnar screen separating the sanctuary from the main body of a Byzantine church.

One example is the renowned *Vladimir Virgin* (FIG. **4-26**). Descended from works such as the Mount Sinai icon (FIG. 4-19), the *Vladimir Virgin* clearly reveals the stylized abstraction resulting from centuries of working and reworking the conventional image. Probably the work of a Constantinopolitan painter, the *Vladimir Virgin* displays all the characteristic traits of Byzantine Virgin and Child icons: the

Virgin's long, straight nose and small mouth; the golden rays in the infant's drapery; the sweep of the unbroken contour that encloses the two figures; and the flat silhouette against the golden ground. But this is a much more tender and personalized image of the Virgin than that in the Mount Sinai icon. Here Mary is depicted as the Virgin of Compassion, who presses her cheek against her son's in an intimate portrayal of Mother and Child. A deep pathos infuses the image as Mary contemplates the future sacrifice of her son. (The back of the icon bears images of the instruments of Christ's passion.)

The icon of Vladimir, like most icons, has seen hard service. Placed before or above altars in churches or private chapels, the icon became blackened by the incense and the smoke from candles that burned before or below it. It was taken to Kiev (Ukraine) in 1131, then to Vladimir (Russia) in 1155 (hence its name), and in 1395, as a wonder-working image, to Moscow to protect that city from the Mongols. The Russians believed the sacred picture saved the city of Kazan from later Tartar invasions and all of Russia from the Poles in the 17th century. The *Vladimir Virgin* is a historical symbol of Byzantium's religious and cultural mission to the Slavic world.

Byzantium after 1204

When rule passed from the Macedonian to the Comnenian dynasty in the later 11th and the 12th centuries, three events of fateful significance changed Byzantium's fortunes for the worse. The Seljuk Turks conquered most of Anatolia. The Byzantine Orthodox Church broke finally from the Church of Rome. And the Crusades brought the Latins (a generic term for the peoples of the West) into Byzantine lands on their way to fight for the Christian cross against the Saracens (Muslims) in the Holy Land (see page 179).

Crusaders had passed through Constantinople many times en route to "smite the infidel" and had marveled at its wealth and magnificence. Envy, greed, religious fanaticism (the Latins called the Greeks "heretics"), and even ethnic enmity motivated the Crusaders when, during the Fourth Crusade in 1203 and 1204, the Venetians persuaded them to divert their expedition against the Muslims in Palestine and to attack Constantinople instead. They took the city and sacked it.

The Latins set up kingdoms within Byzantium, notably in Constantinople itself. What remained of Byzantium split into three small states. The Palaeologans ruled one of these, the kingdom of Nicaea. In 1261, Michael VIII Palaeologus (r. 1259–1282) succeeded in recapturing Constantinople. But his empire was no more than a fragment, and even that disintegrated during the next two centuries. Isolated from the Christian West by Muslim conquests in the Balkans and besieged by Muslim Turks to the East, Byzantium sought help from the West. It was not forthcoming. In 1453, the Ottoman Turks, then a formidable power, took Constantinople and brought to an end the long history of Byzantium (see Chapter 5).

Early Christianity and Byzantium

Early Christianity

I Very little Christian art or architecture survives from the first centuries of Christianity. "Early Christian art" means the earliest art having Christian subjects, not the art of Christians at the time of Jesus. The major surviving examples are frescoes in the catacombs of Rome and marble sarcophagi depicting Old and New Testament stories.

I Constantine (r. 306–337) issued the Edict of Milan in 313 granting Christianity legal status equal or superior to the traditional Roman cults. The emperor was the first great patron of Christian art and built the first churches in Rome, including Old Saint Peter's. In 330, he moved the capital of the Roman Empire to Constantinople (Greek Byzantium).

I The emperor Theodosius I (r. 379–395) proclaimed Christianity the official religion of the Roman Empire in 380 and banned worship of the old Roman gods in 391. Honorius (r. 395–423) moved the capital of his Western Roman Empire to Ravenna in 404. Rome fell to the Visigoth king Alaric in 410.

I Mosaics became a major vehicle for the depiction of Christian themes in the naves and apses of churches, which closely resembled Roman basilicas in both plan and elevation. The first manuscripts with biblical illustrations date to the early sixth century.

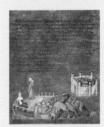
Sarcophagus of
Junius Bassus, ca. 359

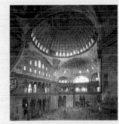
Vienna Genesis,
early sixth century

Byzantium

I The reign of Justinian (r. 527–565) opened the first golden age of Byzantine art (527–726). Justinian was a great patron of the arts, and in Constantinople alone he built or restored more than 30 churches, including Hagia Sophia (Church of Holy Wisdom). A brilliant fusion of central and longitudinal plans, the church featured a 180-foot-high dome resting on pendentives, rivaling the architectural wonders of Rome.

I The seat of Byzantine power in Italy was Ravenna, which also prospered under Justinian. San Vitale is Ravenna's greatest church. Its mosaics, with their weightless, hovering, frontal figures against a gold background, reveal the new Byzantine aesthetic.

I Justinian also rebuilt the monastery at Mount Sinai in Egypt, which boasts the finest surviving Early Byzantine icons. In 726, however, Leo III (r. 717–741) enacted a ban against picturing the divine, initiating the era of iconoclasm (726–843).

I Middle Byzantine (843–1204) churches, such as those at Hosios Loukas and Daphni have highly decorative exterior walls and feature domes resting on drums above the center of a Greek cross. The climax of the interior mosaic programs was often an image of *Christ as Pantokrator* in the dome.

I Middle Byzantine artists also excelled in ivory carving and manuscript illumination. The *Paris Psalter* is noteworthy for its revival of classical naturalism.

I In 1204, Latin Crusaders sacked Constantinople, bringing to an end the second golden age of Byzantine art. In 1261, Emperor Michael VIII Palaeologus (r. 1259–1282) succeeded in recapturing the city. Constantinople remained in Byzantine hands until it was taken in 1453 by the Ottoman Turks.

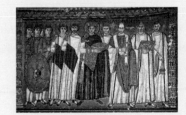
Hagia Sophia,
Constantinople, 532–537

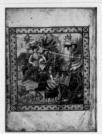
San Vitale, Ravenna, 526–547

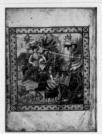
Paris Psalter,
ca. 950–970

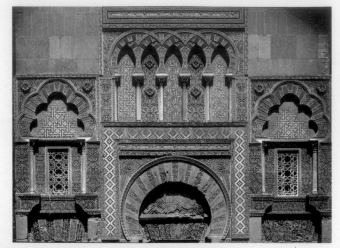

The horseshoe-shaped and multilobed arches of the gates to the Mezquita at Córdoba were part of the expansion and remodeling of the mosque carried out by the Umayyad caliph al-Hakam II.

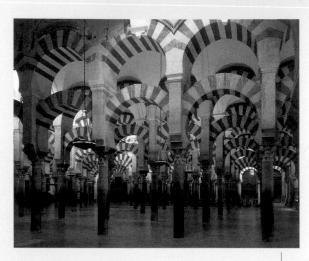

Islamic architecture draws on diverse sources. The horseshoe-shaped arches of the Córdoba mosque may derive from Visigothic architecture. The Arabs overthrew that Christian kingdom in 711.

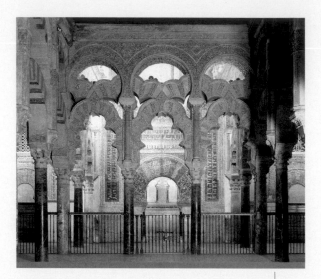

In the 10th century, al-Hakam II also added a maqsura to the Córdoba Mezquita. The hall highlights Muslim architects' bold experimentation with curvilinear shapes and different kinds of arches.

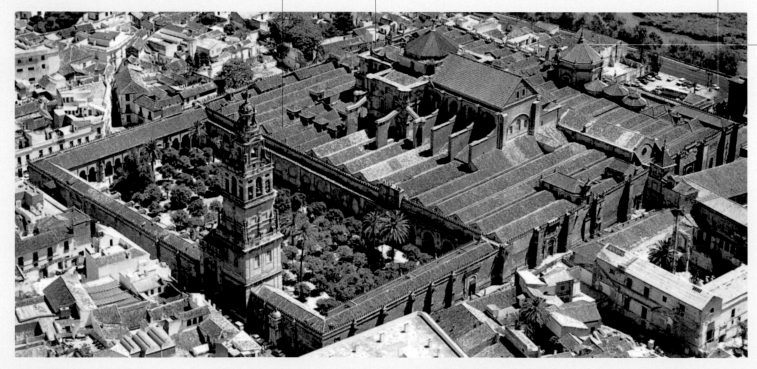

5-1 Aerial view of the Mezquita (Great Mosque; looking east), Córdoba, Spain, 8th to 10th centuries; rededicated as the Cathedral of Saint Mary, 1236.

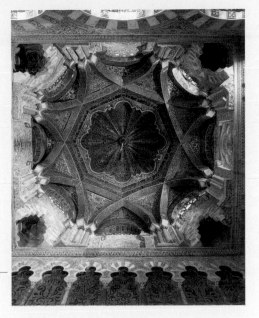

Byzantine artists installed the mosaics in the mihrab dome in the Córdoba mosque, but the decorative patterns formed by the crisscrossing ribs and the multilobed arches are distinctly Islamic.

The Islamic World

THE RISE AND SPREAD OF ISLAM

At the time of Muhammad's birth around 570, the Arabian peninsula was peripheral to the Byzantine and Sasanian Empires. The Arabs, nomadic herders and caravan merchants who worshiped many gods, resisted the Prophet's teachings of Islam, an Arabic word meaning "submission to the one God (*Allah* in Arabic)." Within a decade of Muhammad's death in 632, however, Muslims (those who submit) ruled Arabia, Palestine, Syria, Iraq, and northern Egypt. From there, the new religion spread rapidly both eastward and westward.

With the rise of Islam also came the birth of a compelling new worldwide tradition of art and architecture. In the Middle East and North Africa, Islamic art largely replaced Late Roman, Early Christian, and Byzantine art. In India, the establishment of Muslim rule at Delhi in the early 13th century brought Islamic art and architecture to South Asia (see Chapter 17). In fact, perhaps the most famous building in Asia, the Taj Mahal (FIG. 17-16) at Agra, is an Islamic mausoleum. At the opposite end of the then-known world, Abd al-Rahman I (r. 756–788) founded a Spanish Muslim dynasty at Córdoba, which became the center of a brilliant court culture that profoundly influenced medieval Europe.

The jewel of the capital at Córdoba was its Great Mosque (FIG. **5-1**), begun in 784 and enlarged several times during the 9th and 10th centuries until it eventually became one of the largest mosques in the Islamic West. In 1236, the Christians rededicated and remodeled the shrine as a church (the tallest part of the complex, at the center of the aerial view, is Córdoba's cathedral) after they recaptured the city from the Muslims.

A visual feast greets all visitors to the mosque. Its Muslim designers used overlapping horseshoe-shaped arches (which became synonymous with Islamic architecture in Europe) in the uppermost zone of the eastern and western gates to the complex. Double rows of arches surmount the more than 500 columns in the mosque's huge prayer hall. Even more elaborate multilobed arches on slender columns form dazzling frames for other areas of the mosque, especially in the maqsura, the hall reserved for the ruler, which at Córdoba connects the mosque to the palace. Crisscrossing ribs form intricate decorative patterns in the complex's largest dome.

The Córdoba Mezquita (Spanish, "mosque") typifies Islamic architecture both in its conformity to the basic principles of mosque design and in its incorporation of distinctive regional forms.

MUHAMMAD AND ISLAM

The religion of Islam arose in Arabia early in the seventh century (see "Muhammad and Islam," page 149). At the time, the Arabs were not major players on the world stage. Yet within little more than a century, Muslim armies had subdued the Middle East, and the followers of Muhammad controlled much of the Mediterranean (MAP 5-1). The swiftness of the Islamic advance is among the wonders of history. By 640, Muslims ruled Syria, Palestine, and Iraq. In 642, the Byzantine army abandoned Alexandria, marking the Muslim conquest of northern Egypt. In 651, Islamic forces ended more than 400 years of Sasanian rule in Iran. All of North Africa was under Muslim control by 710. A victory in southern Spain in 711 seemed to open all of western Europe to the Muslims. By 732, they had advanced north to Poitiers in France. There, however, the Franks turned them back. In Spain, in contrast, the Muslim rulers of Córdoba (FIG. 5-1) flourished until 1031, and not until 1492 did Islamic influence and power end in Iberia. In the East, the Muslims reached the Indus River by 751. In Anatolia, relentless Muslim pressure against the shrinking Byzantine Empire eventually caused its collapse in 1453.

ARCHITECTURE

During the early centuries of Islamic history, the Muslim world's political and cultural center was the Fertile Crescent of ancient Mesopotamia. The caliphs of Damascus (capital of modern Syria) and Baghdad (capital of Iraq) appointed provincial governors to rule the vast territories they controlled. These governors eventually gained relative independence by

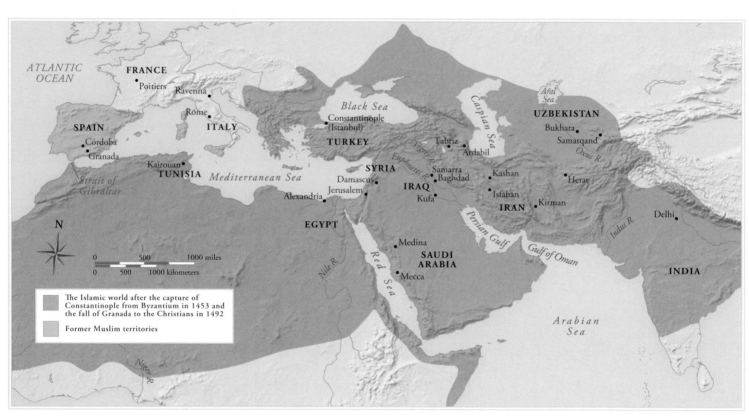

MAP 5-1 The Islamic world around 1500.

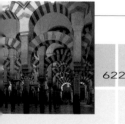

The Islamic World

622	756	1453	1924
▪ The Umayyads, the first Islamic dynasty, build the Dome of the Rock to celebrate the triumph of Islam in Jerusalem ▪ The Abbasids produce the earliest Korans with Kufic calligraphy	▪ The Spanish Umayyad dynasty builds the Great Mosque in their capital at Córdoba ▪ The Nasrids embellish the Alhambra with magnificent palaces ▪ Book illumination flourishes at the Timurid court ▪ Safavid artisans perfect the manufacture of mosaic tiles	▪ The Ottomans capture Byzantine Constantinople in 1453	

Muhammad and Islam

Muhammad, founder of Islam and revered by Muslims as the Final Prophet in the line including Abraham, Moses, and Jesus, was a native of Mecca on the west coast of Arabia. Born around 570 into a family of merchants, Muhammad was critical of the polytheistic religion of his fellow Arabs. In 610, he began to receive the revelations of God through the archangel Gabriel. Opposition to Muhammad's message among the Arabs was strong, and in 622, the Prophet and his followers abandoned Mecca for a desert oasis eventually called Medina (City of the Prophet). Muslims mark the beginning of Islam and date events from this flight—known as the *Hijra* (emigration)—in the same way the Christian calendar begins with Christ's birth. Barely eight years later, in 630, Muhammad returned to Mecca with 10,000 soldiers. He took control of the city, converted the population to Islam, and destroyed all the idols. But he preserved as the Islamic world's symbolic center the small cubical building that had housed the idols. The Arabs associated the *Kaaba* (from the Arabic for "cube") with the era of Abraham and Ishmael, the common ancestors of Jews and Arabs. Muhammad died in Medina in 632.

The essential tenet of Islam is acceptance of and submission to Allah's will. Muslims must live according to the rules laid down in the collected revelations communicated through Muhammad during his lifetime and recorded in the *Koran,* Islam's sacred book. The word *Koran* means "recitations"—a reference to Gabriel's instructions to Muhammad in 610 to "recite in the name of Allah."

The profession of faith in the one God is the first of five obligations binding all Muslims. In addition, the faithful must worship five times daily, facing Mecca, give alms to the poor, fast during the month of Ramadan, and once in a lifetime—if possible—make a pilgrimage to Mecca. The revelations in the Koran are not the only guide for Muslims. Muhammad's words and exemplary ways and customs, the *Hadith,* recorded in the *Sunnah,* offer models to all Muslims on ethical problems of everyday life. The reward for the faithful is Paradise.

Islam has much in common with Judaism and Christianity. Muslims think of their religion as a continuation, completion, and in some sense a reformation of those other great monotheisms. Islam incorporates many teachings of Hebrew scripture, with their sober ethical standards and rejection of idol worship. But, unlike Jesus in the New Testament Gospels, Muhammad did not claim to be divine. Rather, he was God's messenger, the Final Prophet, who purified and perfected the common faith of Jews, Christians, and Muslims in one God. Islam also differs from Judaism and Christianity in its simpler organization. Muslims worship God directly, without a hierarchy of rabbis, priests, or saints acting as intermediaries.

In Islam, as Muhammad defined it, the union of religious and secular authority was even more complete than in Byzantium. Muhammad established a new social order and took complete charge of his community's temporal as well as spiritual affairs. After Muhammad's death, the *caliphs* (from the Arabic for "successor") continued this practice of uniting religious and political leadership in one ruler.

setting up dynasties in various territories and provinces, most notably the Umayyads in Syria (661–750) and in Spain (756–1031) and the Abbasids in Iraq (750–1258). Like other potentates before and after, the Muslim caliphs were builders on a grand scale.

Dome of the Rock The first great Islamic building was the Dome of the Rock (FIG. **5-2**) in Jerusalem. The Muslims had taken the city from the Byzantines in 638, and the Umayyad caliph Abd al-Malik (r. 685–705) erected the monumental shrine between 687 and 692 as an architectural tribute to the triumph of Islam. The Dome of the Rock marked the coming of the new religion to the city that had been, and still is, sacred to both Jews and Christians. The structure stands on

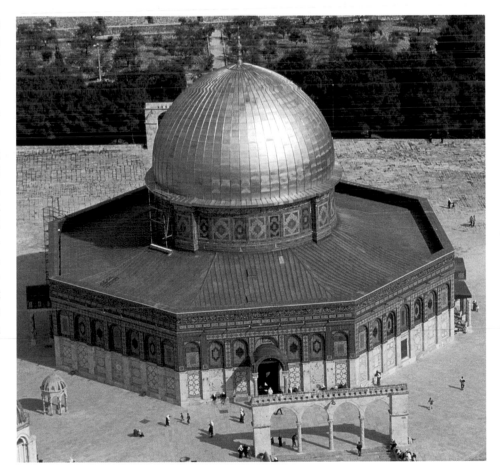

5-2 Aerial view (looking southwest) of the Dome of the Rock, Jerusalem, 687–692.

Abd al-Malik built the Dome of the Rock to commemorate the triumph of Islam in Jerusalem on a site sacred to Muslims, Christians, and Jews. The shrine takes the form of an octagon with a towering dome.

5-3 Interior of the Dome of the Rock, Jerusalem, 687–692.

On the interior of the Dome of the Rock, the original mosaics are largely intact. At the center of the rotunda is the rocky outcropping later associated with Adam, Abraham, and Muhammad.

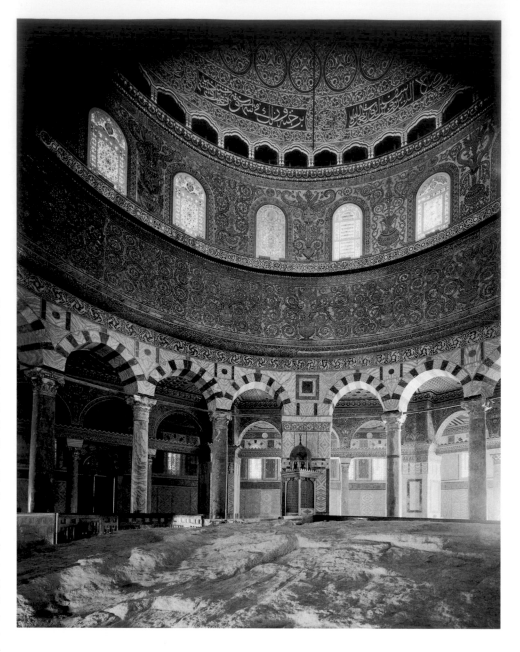

the spot where the Hebrews built the Temple of Solomon that the Roman emperor Titus destroyed in the year 70 (see page 108). In time, the site acquired additional significance as the reputed location of Adam's grave and the place where Abraham prepared to sacrifice Isaac. It houses the rock (FIG. **5-3**) that later came to be identified with the spot Muhammad began his miraculous journey to Heaven (the *Miraj*), and then, in the same night, returned to his home in Mecca.

In its form, construction, and decoration, the Dome of the Rock is firmly in the Late Roman-Byzantine tradition. It is a domed octagon resembling San Vitale (FIG. 4-14) in Ravenna in its basic design. In all likelihood, a neighboring Christian monument, Constantine's Church of the Holy Sepulcher inspired the Dome of the Rock's designers. That fourth-century domed *rotunda* also bore a family resemblance to the roughly contemporaneous Santa Costanza (FIG. 4-5) in Rome. Crowning the Islamic shrine is a 75-foot-tall double-shelled wooden dome, which so dominates the elevation as to reduce the octagon to function merely as its base. This soaring, majestic unit creates a decidedly more commanding effect than do Late Roman and Byzantine domical structures (for example, FIG. 4-10). The silhouettes of those domes are comparatively insignificant when seen from the outside.

The building's exterior has been much restored. Tiling from the 16th century and later has replaced the original mosaic. Yet the vivid, colorful patterning wrapping the walls like a textile is typical of Islamic ornamentation. It contrasts markedly with Byzantine brickwork and Greco-Roman sculptured decoration. The interior's mosaic ornament (FIG. **5-3**) is largely intact and suggests the original appearance of the exterior walls. Against a lush vegetal background, Abd al-Malik's mosaicists depicted crowns, jewels, chalices, and other royal motifs—probably a reference to the triumph of Islam over the Byzantine and Persian Empires. Inscriptions, mostly from the Koran, underscore Islam as the superior new monotheism, superseding both Judaism and Christianity in Jerusalem.

Kairouan The Dome of the Rock is a unique monument. Throughout the Islamic world, the most important buildings were usually mosques (see "The Mosque," page 151). Of all the variations, the hypostyle mosque most closely reflects the mosque's supposed precursor, Muhammad's house in Medina. One of the oldest well-preserved hypostyle mosques is the mid-eighth-century Great Mosque (FIG. **5-4**) at Kairouan in Tunisia. Like the Dome of the Rock, the Kairouan mosque owes much to Greco-Roman and Early Christian architecture. The precinct takes the form of a slightly askew parallelogram of huge scale, some 450 by 260 feet. Lateral entrances on the east and west lead to an arcaded forecourt (FIG. 5-4, no. 7), resembling a Roman forum (FIG. 3-35) and the atrium

The Mosque

Islamic religious architecture is closely related to Muslim prayer. In Islam, worshiping can be a private act and requires neither prescribed ceremony nor a special locale. Only the *qibla*—the direction (toward Mecca) Muslims face while praying—is important. But worship also became a communal act when the first Muslim community established a simple ritual for it. To celebrate the Muslim sabbath, which occurs on Friday, the community convened each Friday at noon, probably in the Prophet's house in Medina. The main feature of Muhammad's house was a large square court with rows of palm trunks supporting thatched roofs along the north and south sides. The southern side, which faced Mecca, was wider and had a double row of trunks. The *imam*, or leader of collective worship, stood on a stepped pulpit, or *minbar*, set up in front of the southern (qibla) wall.

These features became standard in the Islamic house of worship, the *mosque* (from Arabic *masjid*, "a place of prostration"), where the faithful gather for the five daily prayers. The *congregational mosque* (also called the *Friday mosque* or *great mosque*) was ideally large enough to accommodate a community's entire population for the Friday noon prayer. An important feature of both ordinary and congregational mosques is the *mihrab* (FIGS. 5-4, no. 2, and 5-11), a semicircular niche set into the qibla wall. Often a dome over the bay in front of the mihrab marked its position (FIGS. 5-4, no. 3, and 5-7). The niche may honor the place where the Prophet stood in his house at Medina when he led communal worship.

In some mosques, a *maqsura* precedes the mihrab. The maqsura is the area reserved for the ruler or his representative. Mosques may also have one or more *minarets* (FIGS. 5-4, no. 8, and 5-5), towers used to call the faithful to worship. Early mosques were generally *hypostyle halls*, communal worship halls with roofs held up by a multitude of columns (FIGS. 5-4, no. 4, and 5-6). An important later variation is the mosque with four *iwans* (vaulted rectangular recesses), one on each side of a courtyard (FIG. 5-10).

Today, despite many variations in design and detail and the employment of building techniques and materials unknown in Muhammad's day, the mosque's essential features remain unchanged. The orientation of all mosques everywhere, whatever their plan, is Mecca, and the faithful worship facing the qibla wall.

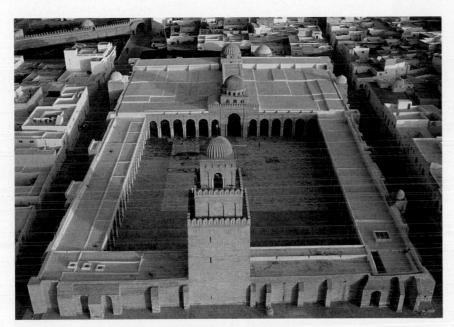

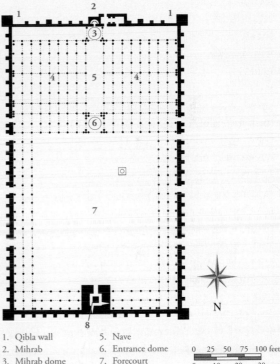

5-4 Aerial view (looking south; *left*) and plan (*right*) of the Great Mosque, Kairouan, Tunisia, ca. 836–875. ◼◀

Kairouan's Great Mosque is an early hypostyle mosque with forecourt and columnar prayer hall. The hypostyle plan most closely resembles the layout of Muhammad's house in Medina.

1. Qibla wall	5. Nave
2. Mihrab	6. Entrance dome
3. Mihrab dome	7. Forecourt
4. Hypostyle prayer hall	8. Minaret

of an Early Christian basilica (FIG. 4-3). The courtyard is oriented north-south on axis with the mosque's minaret (no. 8) and the two domes (nos. 3 and 6) of the hypostyle prayer hall (no. 4). The first dome (no. 6) is over the entrance bay, the second (no. 3) over the bay that fronts the mihrab (no. 2) set into the qibla wall (no. 1). A raised nave (no. 5) connects the domed spaces and prolongs the north-south axis of the minaret and courtyard. Eight columned aisles flank the nave on either side, providing space for a large congregation. The hypostyle mosque synthesizes elements received from other cultures into a novel architectural unity.

Samarra The three-story minaret of the Kairouan mosque is square in plan and believed to be a near copy of a Roman lighthouse, but minarets can take a variety of forms. Perhaps the most striking and novel is the minaret of the immense (more than 45,000 square yards) Great Mosque at Samarra, Iraq, the capital of the Abbasid caliph al-Mutawakkil

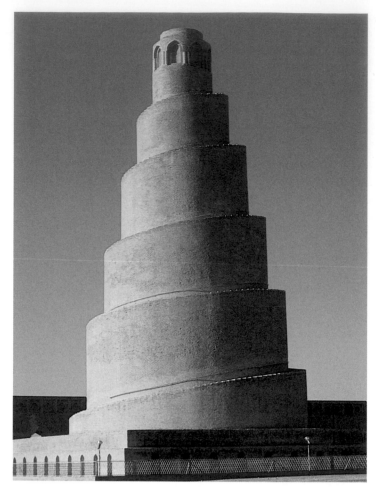

5-5 Malwiya Minaret, Great Mosque, Samarra, Iraq, 848–852.

The unique spiral Malwiya (snail shell) Minaret of Samarra's Great Mosque is more than 165 feet tall and can be seen from afar. It served to announce the presence of Islam in the Tigris Valley.

intended the Malwiya Minaret, visible from a considerable distance in the flat plain around Samarra, to announce the presence of Islam in the Tigris Valley. Unfortunately, since 2005 the minaret has suffered damage during the continuing unrest in Iraq.

Córdoba At the time the Umayyads built the Kairouan mosque (FIG. 5-4), the Abbasids ruled much of North Africa. In 750, they had overthrown the Umayyad caliphs and moved the capital from Damascus to Baghdad. Abd-al-Rahman I (r. 756–788), the only Umayyad notable to escape the Abbasid massacre of his clan in Syria, fled to Spain in 750. There, the Arabs, who had overthrown the Christian kingdom of the Visigoths in 711, accepted the fugitive as their overlord, and he founded the Spanish Umayyad dynasty. Their capital was Córdoba, which became the center of a brilliant culture rivaling that of the Abbasids at Baghdad and exerting major influence on the civilization of the Christian West.

The centerpiece of Umayyad Córdoba was its Great Mosque (FIG. 5-1), begun in 784 by Abd al-Rahman I. The hypostyle prayer hall (FIG. 5-6) has 36 piers and 514 columns topped by a unique system of double-tiered arches that carried a wooden roof (later replaced by vaults). The two-story system was the builders' response to the need to raise the roof to an acceptable height using short columns that had been employed earlier in other structures. The lower arches are horseshoe shaped, a form perhaps adapted from earlier Mesopotamian architecture or of *Visigothic* (Spanish Christian) origin. In the West, the horseshoe-shaped arch quickly became closely associated with Muslim architecture. Visually, these arches seem to billow out like windblown sails,

(r. 847–861), who built the mosque between 848 and 852. At the time of its construction the Samarra mosque was the largest in the world. Known as the Malwiya ("snail shell" in Arabic) Minaret (FIG. **5-5**), it is more than 165 feet tall. Although it now stands alone, originally a bridge linked the minaret to the mosque. The distinguishing feature of the brick tower is its stepped spiral ramp, which increases in slope from bottom to top. Because it is too tall to have been used to call Muslims to prayer, the Abbasids probably

5-6 Prayer hall of the Mezquita (Great Mosque), Córdoba, Spain, 8th to 10th centuries.

Córdoba was the capital of the Spanish Umayyad dynasty. In the Great Mosque's hypostyle prayer hall, 36 piers and 514 columns support a unique series of double-tiered horseshoe-shaped arches.

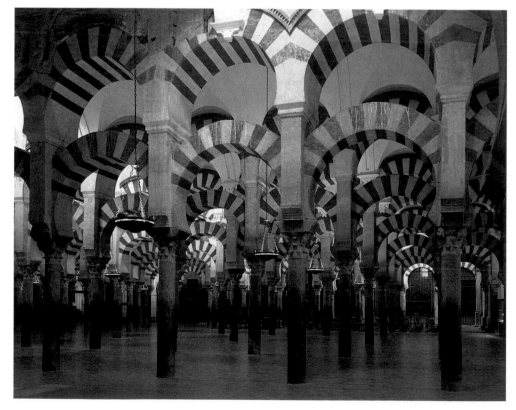

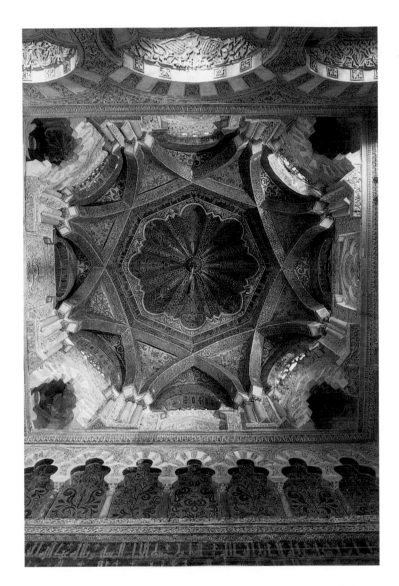

and they contribute greatly to the light and airy effect of the Córdoba mosque's interior.

In 961, al-Hakam II (r. 961–976) became caliph and immediately undertook major renovations to Córdoba's Mezquita, including the addition of a series of domes to emphasize the axis leading to the mihrab. The dome (FIG. **5-7**) covering the area in front of the mihrab rests on an octagonal base crisscrossed by ribs that form an intricate pattern centered on two squares set at 45-degree angles to each other. It is a prime example of Islamic experimentation with highly decorative multilobed arches. The Muslim builders created rich and varied abstract patterns and further enhanced the magnificent effect of the complex arches by sheathing the surfaces with mosaics. Al-Hakam II brought the mosaicists and even the tesserae to Spain from Constantinople.

Alhambra In the early years of the 11th century, the Umayyad caliphs' power in Spain unraveled, and their palaces fell prey to Berber soldiers from North Africa. The Berbers ruled southern Spain for several generations but could not resist the pressure of Christian forces from the north. Córdoba fell to the Christians in 1236. From then until the final Christian triumph in 1492, the Nasrids, an Arab dynasty that had established its capital at Granada in 1232, ruled the remaining Muslim territories in Spain. On a rocky spur at Granada, the Nasrids constructed a huge palace-fortress called the Alhambra ("the Red" in Arabic), named for the rose color of the stone used for its walls and 23 towers. By the end of the 14th century, the complex, a veritable city with a population of 40,000, included at least a half dozen royal residences.

The Palace of the Lions takes its name from its courtyard (FIG. **5-8**), which contains

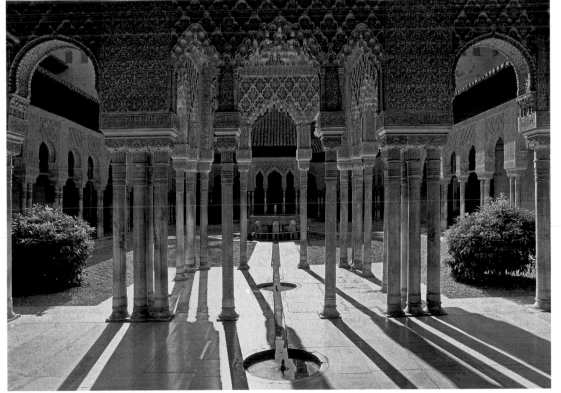

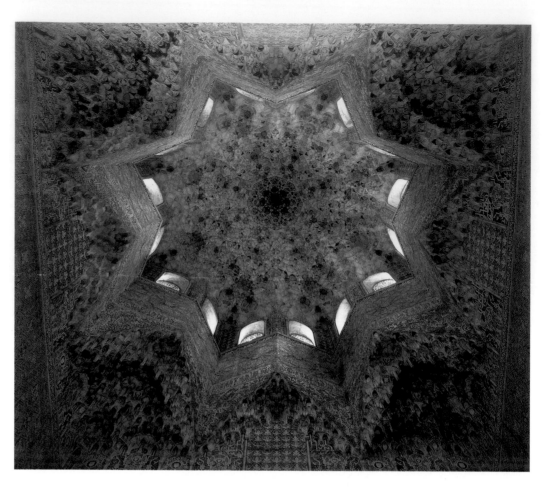

5-9 Muqarnas dome, Hall of the Abencerrajes, Palace of the Lions, Alhambra, Granada, Spain, 1354–1391.

The structure of this dome on an octagonal drum is difficult to discern because of the intricately carved stucco muqarnas. The prismatic forms reflect sunlight, creating the effect of a starry sky.

a fountain with 12 marble lions carrying a water basin on their backs. The Alhambra's lion fountain is an unusual instance of freestanding stone sculpture in the Islamic world, unthinkable in a sacred setting. But the design of the courtyard is distinctly Islamic and features many multilobed pointed arches and lavish stuccoed walls with interwoven abstract motifs and Arabic *calligraphy* (ornamental writing). The palace was the residence of Muhammad V (r. 1354–1391), and its courtyards, lush gardens, and luxurious carpets and other furnishings served to conjure the image of Paradise.

The Palace of the Lions is noteworthy also for its elaborate stucco ceilings. A spectacular example is the dome (FIG. **5-9**) of the so-called Hall of the Abencerrajes. The dome rests on an octagonal drum pierced by eight pairs of windows, but its structure is difficult to discern because of the intricate carved stucco decoration. The builders covered the ceiling with some 5,000 *muqarnas*—tier after tier of stalactite-like prismatic forms that seem aimed at denying the structure's solidity. The purpose of the muqarnas ceiling was to catch and reflect sunlight as well as to form beautiful abstract patterns. The lofty vault in this hall and others in the palace symbolized the dome of Heaven. The flickering light and shadows create the effect of a starry sky as the sun's rays move from window to window during the day. To underscore the symbolism, the palace walls were inscribed with verses by the court poet Ibn Zamrak, who compared the Alhambra's lacelike muqarnas ceilings to "the heavenly spheres whose orbits revolve."

Isfahan At the opposite end of the Islamic world, in Iran, successive dynasties erected a series of mosques at Isfahan. The largest is the Friday Mosque (FIG. **5-10**), constructed by the Abbasids during the eighth century. In the late 11th century, the Seljuk *sultan* (ruler) Malik Shah I (r. 1072–1092) transformed the Abbasid hypostyle structure into a distinctly Iranian mosque with a large courtyard bordered by a two-

story arcade on each side. Four vaulted iwans open onto the courtyard, one at the center of each side. The southwestern iwan leads into a dome-covered room in front of the mihrab that functioned as a maqsura reserved for the sultan and his attendants. It is uncertain whether Isfahan's Friday Mosque is the earliest example of a four-iwan mosque, but that plan became standard in Iranian religious architecture. In this type of mosque, the qibla iwan is always the largest. Its size (and the dome that often accompanied it) immediately indicated to worshipers the proper direction for prayer.

Madrasa Imami The iwans of the Isfahan mosque feature soaring pointed arches framing tile-sheathed muqarnas vaults. The muqarnas ceilings probably date to the 14th century. The ceramic-tile revetment on the walls and vaults is the work of the 17th-century Safavid dynasty (r. 1501–1732) of Iran. The use of glazed tiles has a long history in Mesopotamia (FIG. 1-20) and Persia. The golden age of Islamic ceramic tilework was the 16th and 17th centuries in Iran and Turkey. Employed as a veneer over a brick core, tiles could sheathe entire buildings (FIG. 5-2), including domes and minarets.

One of the masterworks of Iranian tilework is the 14th-century mihrab (FIG. **5-11**) from the Madrasa Imami in Isfahan. (A *madrasa* is an Islamic theological college, often incorporating a mosque.) It is also a splendid example of Arabic calligraphy. The Islamic world held the art of calligraphy in high esteem, and the walls of buildings often displayed the sacred words of the Koran. Quotations from the Koran appear, for example, in a mosaic band above the outer ring of

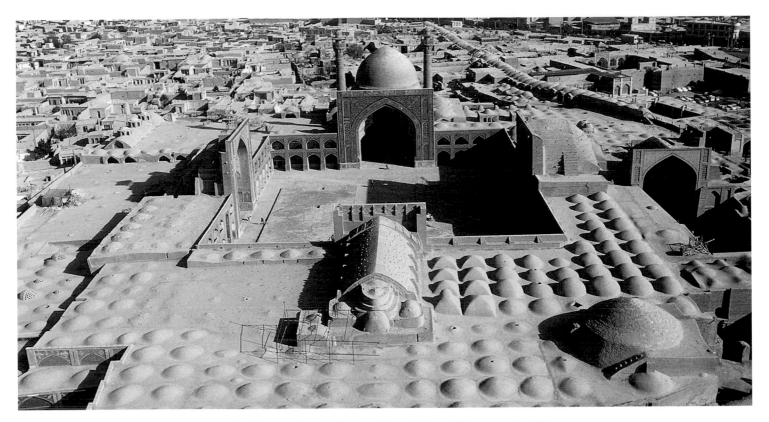

5-10 Aerial view of the Friday Mosque (looking southwest), Isfahan, Iran, 11th to 17th centuries. ■◀

Mosques take a variety of forms. In Iran, the standard type of mosque has four iwans opening onto a courtyard. The largest (qibla) iwan leads into a dome-covered maqsura in front of the mihrab.

columns inside the Dome of the Rock (FIG. 5-3). The Isfahan mihrab exemplifies the perfect aesthetic union between calligraphy and abstract ornament. The pointed arch framing the mihrab niche bears an inscription from the Koran in an early stately rectilinear script called *Kufic*, after the city of Kufah, one of the renowned centers of Arabic calligraphy. A cursive style, *Muhaqqaq*, fills the mihrab's outer rectangular frame. The tile ornament on the curving surface of the niche and the area above the pointed arch consists of tighter and looser networks of geometric and abstract floral motifs. The technique used here is the most difficult of all the varieties Islamic artisans practiced: *mosaic tilework*. Every piece had to be chiseled and cut to fit its specific place in the mihrab—even the tile inscriptions. The ceramist smoothly integrated the subtly varied decorative patterns with the framed inscription in the center of the niche, which proclaims the mosque is the domicile of the pious believer. The mihrab's outermost inscription—detailing the five pillars of Islamic faith—serves as a fringelike extension, as well as a boundary, for the entire design. The unification of calligraphic and geometric elements is so complete that only the practiced eye can distinguish them.

5-11 Mihrab from the Madrasa Imami, Isfahan, Iran, ca. 1354. Glazed mosaic tilework, 11′ 3″ × 7′ 6″. Metropolitan Museum of Art, New York. ■◀

This Iranian mihrab is a masterpiece of Iranian tilework, but it is also a splendid example of Arabic calligraphy. In the Islamic world, the walls of buildings often displayed the sacred words of the Koran.

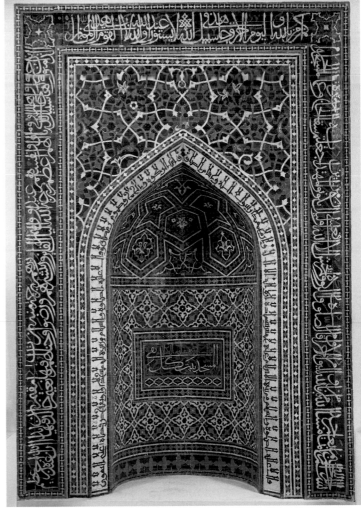

1 ft.

Architecture   155

LUXURY ARTS

In the smaller-scale, and often private, realm of the luxury arts, Muslim artists also excelled. Indeed, in the Islamic world, the term *minor arts* is especially inappropriate. Although of modest size, the books, textiles, ceramics, and metalwork Muslim artists produced in great quantities are among the finest works of any age. From the vast array of Islamic luxury arts, a few masterpieces may serve to suggest both the range and quality of small-scale Islamic art.

The Koran The earliest preserved Korans date to the ninth century, and the finest of them are masterpieces of Arabic calligraphy. Muslim scribes wanted to reproduce the Koran's sacred words in a script as beautiful as human hands could contrive. Koran pages were either bound into books or stored as loose sheets in boxes. Most of the early examples feature the angular Kufic script used in the central panel of the mihrab in FIG. 5-11. Arabic is written from right to left with certain characters connected by a baseline. In Kufic script, the uprights usually form right angles with the baseline. As with Hebrew and other Semitic languages, the usual practice was to write in consonants only. But to facilitate recitation of the Koran, scribes often indicated vowels by red or yellow symbols above or below the line.

All of these features are present in a 9th- or early 10th-century Koran page (FIG. 5-12) now in Dublin that carries the heading and opening five text lines of *surah* (chapter) 18. The Arabic *calligrapher* recorded the passage using black ink. Vowels appear in red below a decorative band incorporating the chapter title in gold and ending in a palm-tree *finial* (a crowning ornament). This approach to page design has parallels at the extreme northwestern corner of the then-known world—in the early medieval manuscripts of the British Isles, where text and ornamentation are similarly united (FIG. 6-1). But the stylized human and animal forms that populate those Christian books never appear in Korans. Islamic tradition shuns the representation of fauna of any kind in sacred contexts. This also explains the total absence of figural ornament in mosques, setting the Islamic world sharply apart from both the classical world and Christian Europe and Byzantium.

Mosque Lamps Well-endowed mosques possessed luxurious furnishings, including highly decorated glass lamps. Islamic artists perfected this art form, and fortunately, despite their exceptionally fragile nature, many examples survive, in large part because those who handled the lamps did so with reverence and care. One of the finest is the mosque lamp (FIG. 5-13) made for Sayf al-Din Tuquztimur (d. 1345), an official in the court of the Mamluk sultan al-Nasir Muhammad, whose capital was Cairo, Egypt—the largest Muslim city of the late Middle Ages. The glass lamps hung on chains from mosque ceilings. The shape of Tuquztimur's lamp is

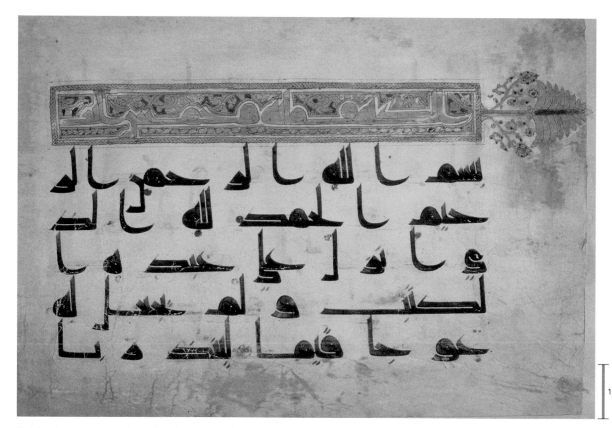

1 in.

5-12 Koran page with beginning of surah 18, 9th or early 10th century. Ink and gold on vellum, 7¼″ × 10¼″. Chester Beatty Library and Oriental Art Gallery, Dublin. ◼️◀

The script used in the oldest-known Korans is the stately rectilinear Kufic. This page has five text lines and a palm tree finial but characteristically does not include depictions of animals or humans.

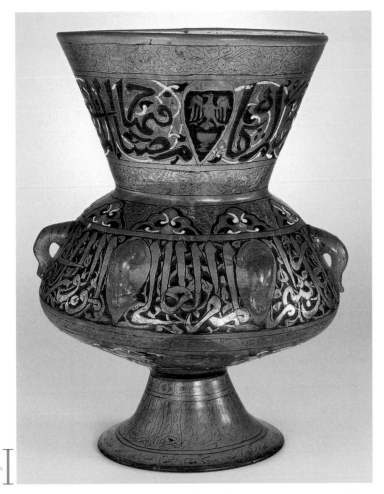

5-13 Mosque lamp of Sayf al-Din Tuquztimur, from Egypt, 1340. Glass with enamel decoration, 1' 1" high. British Museum, London.

The enamel decoration of this glass mosque lamp includes a quotation from the Koran comparing God's light with the light in a lamp. The burning wick dramatically illuminated the sacred verse.

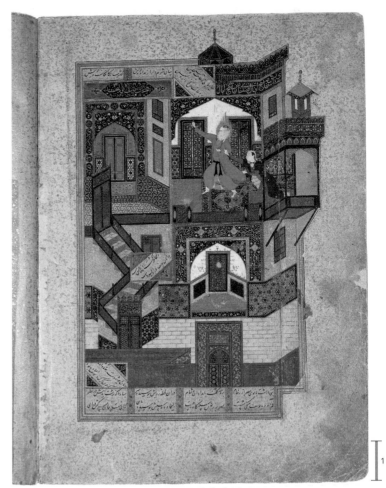

5-14 BIHZAD, *Seduction of Yusuf*, folio 52 verso of the *Bustan* of Sultan Husayn Mayqara, from Herat, Afghanistan, 1488. Ink and color on paper, $11\frac{7}{8}" \times 8\frac{5}{8}"$. National Library, Cairo.

This vividly colored manuscript page depicts human figures, which never appear in Islamic religious art. Bihzad's intricate decorative detailing is a brilliant balance between pattern and perspective.

typical of the period, consisting of a conical neck, a wide body with six vertical handles, and a tall foot. Inside, a small glass container held the oil and wick. The *enamel* ornament enlivens the surfaces. The decoration includes Tuquztimur's emblem—an eagle over a cup (Tuquztimur served as the sultan's cup-bearer)—and cursive Arabic calligraphy giving the official's name and titles as well as a quotation of the Koranic verse (24:35) comparing God's light to the light in a lamp. When the lamp was lit, the verse (and Tuquztimur's name) would have been dramatically illuminated.

Timurid *Bustan* In the late 14th century, a new Islamic empire arose in Central Asia under the leadership of Timur (r. 1370–1405), known in the Western world as Tamerlane. Timur, a successor of the Mongol conqueror Genghis Khan, quickly extended his dominions to include Iran and parts of Anatolia. The Timurids, who ruled until 1501, were great patrons of art and architecture in Herat, Bukhara, Samarqand, and other cities. Herat in particular became a leading center for the production of luxurious books under the patronage of the Timurid sultan Husayn Mayqara (r. 1470–1506).

In contrast to Korans, Timurid secular books often featured full-page narrative paintings with human and animal figures.

The most famous Persian painter of his age was BIHZAD, who worked at the Herat court and illustrated the sultan's copy of the *Bustan* (*Orchard*) by the Persian poet Sadi (ca. 1209–1292). One page (FIG. **5-14**) represents a story in both the Bible and the Koran—the seduction of Yusuf (Joseph) by Potiphar's wife, Zulaykha. Bihzad dispersed Sadi's text throughout the page in elegant Arabic script in a series of beige panels. According to the tale as told by Jami (1414–1492), an influential mystic theologian and poet whose Persian text appears in blue in the white pointed arch at the composition's lower center, Zulaykha lured Yusuf into her palace and led him through seven rooms, locking each door behind him. In the last room she threw herself at Yusuf, but he resisted and was able to flee when the seven doors opened miraculously. Bihzad's painting of the story features vivid color, intricate decorative detailing suggesting luxurious textiles and tiled walls, and a brilliant balance between two-dimensional patterning and perspective depictions of balconies and staircases.

5-15 MAQSUD OF KASHAN, carpet from the funerary mosque of Shaykh Safi al-Din, Ardabil, Iran, 1540. Knotted pile of wool and silk, 34′ 6″ × 17′ 7″. Victoria & Albert Museum, London.

Textiles are among the glories of Islamic art. This carpet required roughly 25 million knots. It presents the illusion of a heavenly dome with mosque lamps reflected in a lotus-blossom-filled pool of water.

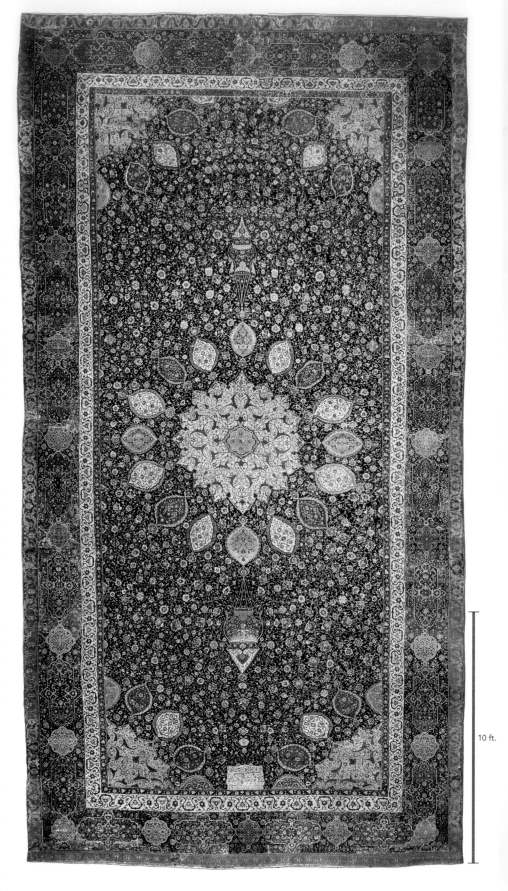

10 ft.

Ardabil Carpet Because wood is scarce in most of the Islamic world, the kinds of furniture used in the West—beds, tables, and chairs—are rare in Muslim buildings. A room's function (eating or sleeping, for example) can change simply by rearranging the carpets and cushions. Textiles are among the glories of Islamic art. Unfortunately, because of their fragile nature and the heavy wear carpets endure, only a few fragmentary early Islamic textiles have been preserved. Perhaps the best later example of the weaver's art is a pair of carpets from the funerary mosque in Ardabil, Iran, of Shaykh Safi al-Din (1252–1334), but they date to 1540, two centuries after the construction of the mosque, during the reign of Shah Tahmasp (r. 1524–1576). Tahmasp elevated carpet weaving to a national industry and set up royal factories at Isfahan, Kashan, Kirman, and Tabriz. The name of MAQSUD OF KASHAN is woven into the fabric of the Ardabil carpet illustrated here (FIG. **5-15**). Maqsud must have been the artist who supplied the master pattern to two teams of royal weavers (one for each of the two carpets). The carpet, almost 35 by 18 feet, consists of roughly 25 million knots, some 340 to the square inch. (Its twin has even more knots.)

The design consists of a central sunburst medallion, representing the inside of a dome, surrounded by 16 pendants. Mosque lamps (appropriate motifs for the Ardabil funerary mosque) hang from two pendants on the long axis of the carpet. The lamps are of different sizes. This may be an optical device to make the two appear equal in size when viewed from the end of the carpet at the room's threshold (the bottom end in FIG. 5-15). Covering the rich blue background are leaves and flowers attached to delicate stems spreading over the whole field. The entire composition presents the illusion of a heavenly dome with lamps reflected in a pool of water full of floating lotus blossoms.

Islam in Asia Islamic artists and architects also brought their distinctive style to South Asia, where a Muslim sultanate was established at Delhi in India in the early 13th century. These important Islamic works are an integral part of the history of Asian art and are treated in Chapter 17.

The Islamic World

Architecture

▌ The Umayyads (r. 661–750) were the first Islamic dynasty. They ruled from their capital at Damascus (Syria) until the Abbasids (r. 750–1258) overthrew them and established a new capital at Baghdad (Iraq).

▌ The first great Islamic building was the Dome of the Rock, a domed octagon commemorating the triumph of Islam in Jerusalem, which the Muslims captured from the Byzantines in 638.

▌ The earliest mosques, for example, the Abbasid Great Mosque at Kairouan (Tunisia), were of the hypostyle hall type and incorporated arcaded courtyards and minarets.

▌ The Umayyad capital in Spain was at Córdoba, where the caliphs (r. 756–1031) built and expanded the Great Mosque between the 8th and 10th centuries. The mosque features horseshoe-shaped and multilobed arches and mosaic-clad domes.

▌ The last Spanish Muslim dynasty was the Nasrid (r. 1230–1492), whose capital was at Granada. The Alhambra is the best surviving example of Islamic palace architecture. It is famous for its stuccoed walls and arches and its muqarnas decoration on vaults and domes.

▌ The Timurid (r. 1370–1501) and Safavid (r. 1501–1732) dynasties ruled Iran and Central Asia for almost four centuries and were great patrons of art and architecture. The art of tilework reached its peak under the patronage of the Safavid dynasty. Builders of the time frequently used mosaic tiles to cover the walls and vaults of mosques and madrasas.

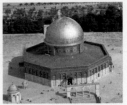

Dome of the Rock, Jerusalem, 687–692

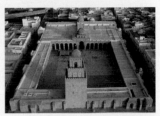

Great Mosque, Kairouan, ca. 836–875

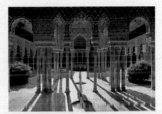

Palace of the Lions, Granada, 1354–1391

Luxury Arts

▌ The earliest preserved Korans date to the ninth century and feature Kufic calligraphy and decorative motifs but no figural illustrations. Islamic tradition shuns the representation of fauna of any kind in sacred contexts.

▌ The Timurid court at Herat (Afghanistan) employed the most skilled painters of the day, who specialized in illustrating secular books with narrative scenes incorporating people and animals. The most famous Persian painter of his age was Bihzad, who illustrated books for Sultan Husayn Mayqara (r. 1470–1506).

▌ Muslim artists also excelled in the art of enamel-decorated glass lamps, which illuminated mosque interiors. They hung on chains from the ceiling and often bore elegant calligraphic inscriptions with quotations from the Koran.

▌ Textiles are among the glories of Islamic art. Some carpets, for example, the pair designed by Maqsud of Kashan for a 16th-century funerary mosque at Ardabil (Iran), were woven with at least 25 million knots each.

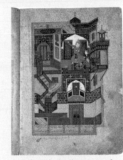

Bihzad, *Seduction of Yusuf*, 1488

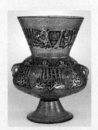

Mosque lamp of Sayf al-Din Tuquztimur, 1340

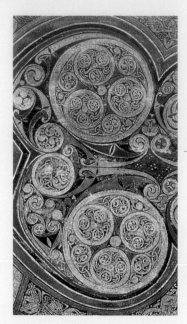

In this opening page to the Gospel of Saint Matthew, the painter transformed the biblical text into abstract pattern, literally making God's words beautiful. The intricate design recalls early medieval metalwork.

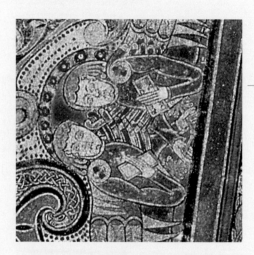

The chi-rho-iota (XPI) page is not purely embellished script and abstract pattern. Half-figures of winged angels appear to the left of *chi*, accompanying the monogram as if accompanying Christ himself.

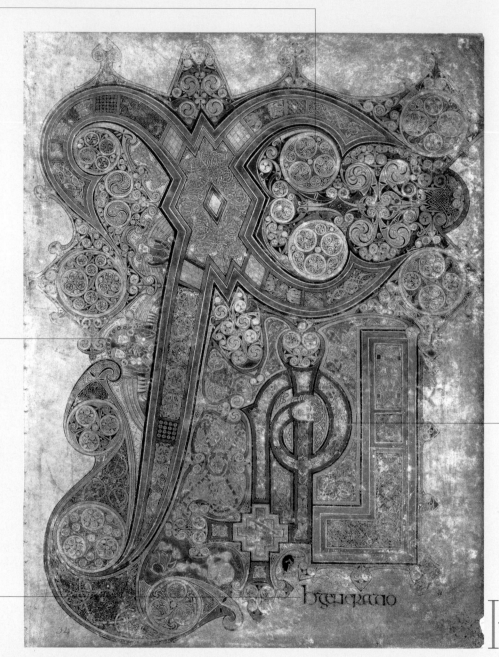

1 in.

6-1 Chi-rho-iota (XPI) page, folio 34 recto of the *Book of Kells*, probably from Iona, Scotland, late eighth or early ninth century. Tempera on vellum, 1' 1" × 9½". Trinity College Library, Dublin.

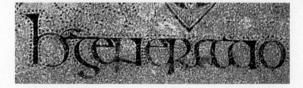

The only unadorned letters in the opening of the passage read on Christmas Eve are the two words *autem* (abbreviated simply as *h*) and *generatio:* "Now this is how the birth of Christ came about."

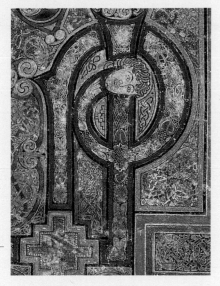

6

Early Medieval and Romanesque Europe

The other figural elements on this page of the *Book of Kells* include a male head growing out of the end of the curve in the letter *rho*. Animals are at the base of *rho* to the left of *h generatio*.

MISSIONARIES SPREAD CHRISTIAN ART

The half millennium between 500 and 1000 was the great formative period of western medieval art, a time of great innovation. The patrons of many of these works were Christian missionaries, who brought to the non-Christian peoples of the former northwestern provinces of the Roman Empire not only the Gospel, but the culture of the Early Christian Mediterranean world as well.

In Ireland, the most distant European outpost, the Christianization of the Celts began in the fifth century. By the end of the seventh century, monks at several Irish monasteries were producing magnificent illuminated books for use by the clergy and to impress the illiterate with the beauty of God's words. The greatest early medieval Irish book is the *Book of Kells*, which one commentator described in the *Annals of Ulster* for the year 1003 as "the chief relic of the western world." The manuscript was probably the work of scribes and illuminators at the monastery at Iona. The monks kept the book in an elaborate metalwork box, as befits a greatly revered "relic," and likely displayed it on the church altar.

The page reproduced here (FIG. **6-1**) opens the account of the nativity of Jesus in the Gospel of Saint Matthew. The initial letters of Christ in Greek (XPI, *chi-rho-iota*) occupy nearly the entire page, although two words—*autem* (abbreviated simply as *h*) and *generatio*—appear at the lower right. Together they read: "Now this is how the birth of Christ came about." The page corresponds to the opening of Matthew's Gospel, the passage read in church on Christmas Eve. The illuminator transformed the holy words into extraordinarily intricate abstract designs recalling metalwork (FIG. 6-2), but the page is not purely embellished script and abstract pattern. The letter *rho*, for example, ends in a male head, and animals are at its base to the left of *h generatio*. Half figures of winged angels appear to the left of *chi*. Close observation reveals many other figures, human and animal. When the priest Giraldus Cambrensis visited Ireland in 1185, he described a manuscript he saw that, if not the *Book of Kells* itself, must have been very much like it:

> Fine craftsmanship is all about you, but you might not notice it. Look more keenly at it and you . . . will make out intricacies, so delicate and subtle, so exact and compact, so full of knots and links, with colors so fresh and vivid, that you might say that all this was the work of an angel, and not of a man. For my part, the oftener I see the book, the more carefully I study it, the more I am lost in ever fresh amazement, and I see more and more wonders in the book.[1]

In the early Middle Ages, the monasteries of northern Europe were both the repositories of knowledge in the midst of an almost wholly illiterate population and the greatest centers of art production.

EARLY MEDIEVAL EUROPE

Historians once referred to the thousand years (roughly 400 to 1400) between the dying Roman Empire's official adoption of Christianity and the rebirth (Renaissance) of interest in classical art as the Dark Ages. They viewed this period as a blank between classical antiquity and the beginning of modern Europe. This negative assessment, a legacy of the humanist scholars of Renaissance Italy, persists today in the retention of the noun *Middle Ages* and the adjective *medieval* to describe this "era in between" and its art. Modern scholars, however, long ago ceased to regard the art of medieval Europe as unsophisticated or inferior. On the contrary, medieval artists produced some of the world's most innovative and beautiful artworks.

Early medieval (ca. 500–1000) art in western Europe (MAP 6-1) was a unique fusion of the classical heritage of Rome's northwestern provinces, the cultures of the non-Roman peoples north of the Alps, and Christianity. Over the centuries, the various population groups merged, and a new order gradually replaced what had been the Roman Empire, resulting eventually in today's European nations.

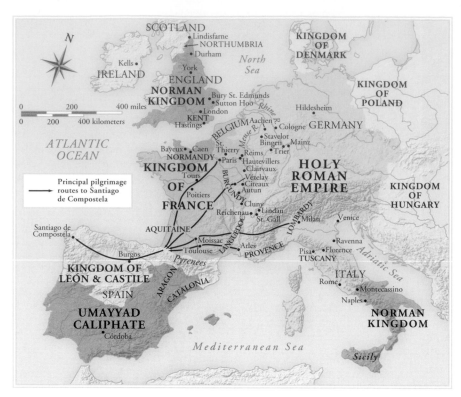

MAP 6-1 Western Europe around 1100.

Art of the Warrior Lords

Art historians do not know the full range of art and architecture these non-Roman cultures produced. What has survived is probably not fully representative and consists almost exclusively of small "status symbols"—weapons and items of personal adornment such as bracelets, pendants, and belt buckles discovered in lavish burials. Earlier scholars, who viewed medieval art through a Renaissance lens, ignored these "minor arts" because of their small scale, seeming utilitarian nature, and abstract ornamentation, and because their makers rejected the classical idea that naturalistic representation should be the focus of artistic endeavor. In the early Middle Ages, people regarded these objects as treasures. The artworks enhanced their owners' prestige

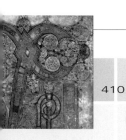

Early Medieval and Romanesque Europe

410	Warrior Lords	768	Hiberno-Saxon and Carolingian	919	Ottonian	1024	Romanesque	1200

Warrior Lords	Hiberno-Saxon and Carolingian	Ottonian	Romanesque
▪ After the fall of Rome, artists produce portable items of personal adornment featuring cloisonné ornamentation and intertwined animal and interlace patterns	▪ Christian missionaries commission sumptuous illuminated manuscripts featuring full pages devoted to embellishing the word of God ▪ Charlemagne and his Carolingian successors (768–877) initiate a conscious revival of the art and culture of Early Christian Rome ▪ Carolingian architects introduce the twin-tower westwork and modular plans for basilican churches	▪ Ottonian architects introduce the alternate-support system and galleries into the naves of churches ▪ Ottonian metalworkers cast the huge historiated bronze doors of Saint Michael's at Hildesheim. An Ottonian sculptor revives the art of freestanding statuary in the *Gero Crucifix*	▪ Early Romanesque architects replace the timber roofs of churches with barrel vaults in the nave and groin vaults in the aisles, and add radiating chapels to ambulatories for the display of relics ▪ In the 12th century, builders introduce groin vaulting in church naves in conjunction with a three-story elevation (arcade-tribune-clerestory) ▪ Relief sculpture becomes commonplace in church portals, usually greeting worshipers with a vision of Christ as last judge ▪ Manuscript illumination flourishes in the scriptoria of Cluniac monasteries

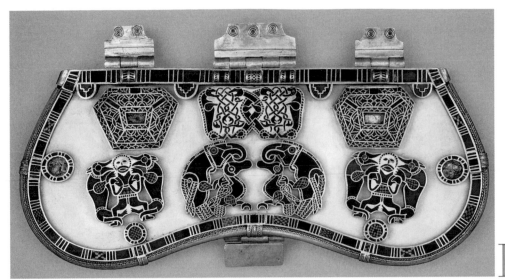

6-2 Purse cover, from the Sutton Hoo ship burial in Suffolk, England, ca. 625. Gold, glass, and enamel cloisonné with garnets and emeralds, 7½" long. British Museum, London (gift of Mrs. E. M. Pretty). ▪◀

This purse cover comes from a treasure-laden royal burial ship. The combination of abstract interlace ornamentation with animal figures is the hallmark of the early Middle Ages in western Europe.

1 in.

and testified to the stature of those buried with them. In the great Anglo-Saxon epic *Beowulf*, Beowulf's comrades cremate the hero's body and place his ashes in a huge *tumulus* (burial mound) overlooking the sea. As an everlasting tribute, they "buried rings and brooches in the barrow, all those adornments that brave men had brought out from the hoard after Beowulf died. They bequeathed the gleaming gold, treasure of men, to the earth."[2]

Sutton Hoo Ship Burial The *Beowulf* saga also recounts the funeral of the warrior lord Scyld, whom his companions laid to rest in a ship overflowing with arms and armor and costly adornments set adrift in the North Sea. In 1939, archaeologists uncovered a treasure-laden ship in a burial mound at Sutton Hoo, England. It epitomizes the early medieval tradition of burying great lords with rich furnishings. Among the many precious finds were a gold belt buckle, 10 silver bowls, 40 gold coins, and 2 silver spoons inscribed SAULOS and PAULOS (Saint Paul's names in Greek before and after his baptism). The spoons may allude to a conversion to Christianity. Some historians have associated the site with the East Anglian king Raedwald (r. 599?–625), who was baptized a Christian before his death in 625.

The most extraordinary Sutton Hoo find was a purse cover (FIG. **6-2**) decorated with seven *cloisonné* plaques. Early medieval metalworkers produced cloisonné jewelry by soldering small metal strips, or *cloisons* (French, "partitions"), edge-up, to a metal background, and then filling the compartments with semiprecious stones, pieces of colored glass, or glass paste fired to resemble sparkling jewels. On the Sutton Hoo purse cover, four symmetrically arranged groups of cloisonné figures make up the lower row. The end groups consist of a facing man standing between two profile beasts. The trio is a pictorial parallel to the epic sagas of the era in which heroes such as Beowulf battle and conquer horrific monsters. The two center groups represent eagles attacking ducks. The convex beaks of the eagles fit against the concave beaks of the ducks. The two figures fit together so snugly

they seem at first to be a single dense abstract design. This is true also of the man-animals motif.

Above these figures are three geometric designs. The outer ones are purely linear. The central design is an interlace pattern in which the interlacements evolve into writhing animal figures. Elaborate intertwining linear patterns are characteristic of many times and places, but the combination of interlace with animal figures was uncommon outside the realm of the early medieval warlords. In fact, metalcraft with interlace patterns and other motifs beautifully integrated with the animal form was, without doubt, the premier art of the early Middle Ages in northwestern Europe.

Hiberno-Saxon Art

The Christianization of the British Isles, which began in the fifth century, accelerated in the sixth. In 563, for example, Saint Columba founded an important monastery on the Scottish island of Iona, where he successfully converted the native Picts to Christianity. Iona monks established the monastery at Lindisfarne off the northern coast of Britain in 635 and around 800 produced the extraordinary *Book of Kells* (FIG. 6-1), named after the abbey in central Ireland that once owned it. The manuscript is the most outstanding example of the style art historians have named *Hiberno-Saxon* to denote the monastic art of Ireland, England, and Scotland.

The most distinctive products of the Hiberno-Saxon monasteries were Christian books, which brought the word of God to a predominantly illiterate populace who regarded the monks' sumptuous volumes with awe. Books were scarce and jealously guarded treasures of the libraries and *scriptoria* (writing studios) of monasteries or major churches. One of the most characteristic features of Hiberno-Saxon book illumination is the inclusion of full pages devoted neither to text nor to illustration but to pure embellishment. Interspersed between the text pages are so-called *carpet pages* (FIG. 6-3), resembling textiles, made up of decorative panels of abstract and zoomorphic forms. Many books also contain pages where the illuminator enormously enlarged the initial

The cross-inscribed carpet page of the *Lindisfarne Gospels* exemplifies the way Hiberno-Saxon illuminators married Christian imagery and the animal-interlace style of the early medieval warlords.

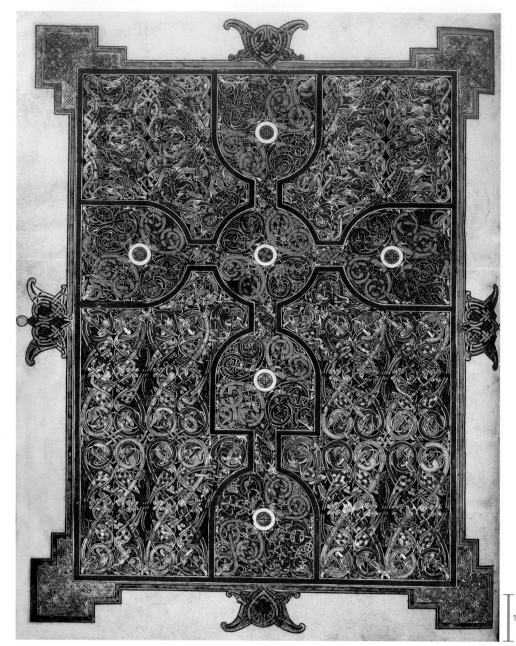

letters of an important passage of sacred text and transformed those letters into elaborate decorative patterns (FIG. 6-1). Such manuscript pages, which merged the abstraction of early medieval personal adornment with the pictorial tradition of Early Christian art, have no precedents in Greco-Roman books.

Lindisfarne Gospels The marriage between Christian imagery and the animal-interlace style of the northern warlords is evident in the cross-inscribed carpet page (FIG. **6-3**) of the *Lindisfarne Gospels.* The *Gospels* (good news), the opening four books of the New Testament, tell the story of the life of Christ, but the painter of the *Lindisfarne Gospels* had little interest in narrative. On the page illustrated here, serpentine interlacements of fantastic animals devour one another, curling over and returning on their writhing, elastic shapes. The rhythm of expanding and contracting forms produces a vivid effect of motion and change, but the painter held it in check by the regularity of the design and by the dominating motif of the inscribed cross. The cross—the all-important symbol of the imported religion—stabilizes the rhythms of the serpentines and, perhaps by contrast with its heavy immobility, seems to heighten the effect of motion. The illuminator placed the motifs in detailed symmetries, with inversions, reversals, and repetitions the viewer must study closely to appreciate not only their variety but also their mazelike complexity. The zoomorphic forms intermingle with clusters and knots of line, and the whole design vibrates with energy. The color is rich yet cool. The painter adroitly adjusted shape and color to achieve a smooth and perfectly even surface.

Carolingian Art

On Christmas Day of the year 800 in Saint Peter's (FIG. 4-3), Pope Leo III (r. 795–816) crowned Charles the Great (Charlemagne), king of the Franks since 768, as emperor of Rome (r. 800–814). In time, Charlemagne came to be seen as the first Holy (that is, Christian) Roman Emperor, a title his successors in the West did not formally adopt until the 12th century. Born in 742, when northern Europe was still in chaos, Charlemagne consolidated the Frankish kingdom his father and grandfather bequeathed him and defeated the Lombards in Italy. He thus united Europe and laid claim to reviving the glory of the Roman Empire. (His official seal bore the words *renovatio imperii Romani*—renewal of the Roman Empire.) Charlemagne gave his name (*Carolus Magnus* in Latin) to an entire era, the *Carolingian* period.

Charlemagne was a sincere admirer of learning, the arts, and classical culture. He invited to his court at Aachen, Germany, the best minds of his age, among them Alcuin (d. 804), master of the *cathedral* (bishop's church) school at York, the center of Northumbrian learning. One of Charlemagne's dearest projects was the recovery of the true text of the Bible, which, through centuries of errors in copying, had become quite corrupted. Alcuin of York's revision of the Bible became the most widely used. Charlemagne himself could read and speak Latin fluently, in addition to Frankish, his native tongue. He also could understand Greek, and held books, both sacred and secular, in especially high esteem, importing many and producing far more.

Coronation Gospels The most famous of Charlemagne's books is the *Coronation Gospels*. The text is in handsome gold letters on purple vellum. The major full-page illuminations show the four Gospel authors at work—Saints Matthew, Mark, Luke, and John, the four *evangelists* (from the Greek word for "one who announces good news"). The page (FIG. **6-4**) depicting Saint Matthew follows the venerable tradition of author portraits, which were familiar features of Greek and Latin books. Similar representations of seated philosophers or poets writing or reading abound in ancient art. The Matthew of the *Coronation Gospels* also reveals the legacy of classical art. Deft, illusionistic brushwork defines the massive drapery folds wrapped around the evangelist's body. The Carolingian painter used color and modulation of light and shade to create the illusion of three-dimensional form.

The cross-legged chair, the lectern, and the saint's toga are familiar Roman accessories, and the placement of the book and lectern top at an angle suggests a Mediterranean model employing classical perspective. The landscape background is also a classical feature, and the frame consists of the kind of acanthus leaves commonly found in Roman art. Almost nothing is known in the Hiberno-Saxon or Frankish world that could have prepared the way for this portrayal of Saint Matthew. If a Frankish, rather than an Italian or a Byzantine, artist painted the evangelist portraits of the *Coronation Gospels,* the Carolingian artist had fully absorbed the classical manner. Classical painting style was one of the many components of Charlemagne's program to establish Aachen as the capital of a renewed Christian Roman Empire.

Ebbo Gospels Another Saint Matthew (FIG. **6-5**), in a Gospel book made for Archbishop Ebbo of Reims, France, may be an interpretation of an author portrait very similar to the one the *Coronation Gospels* master used as a model. The *Ebbo Gospels* illuminator, however, replaced the classical calm and solidity of the *Coronation Gospels* evangelist with an energy

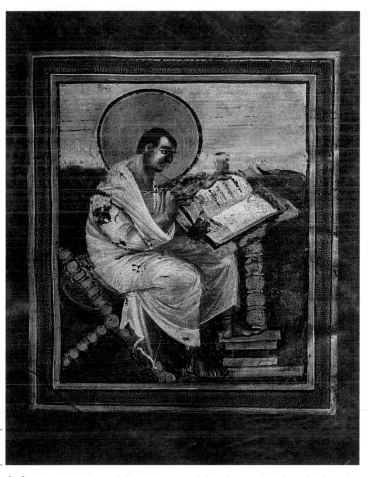

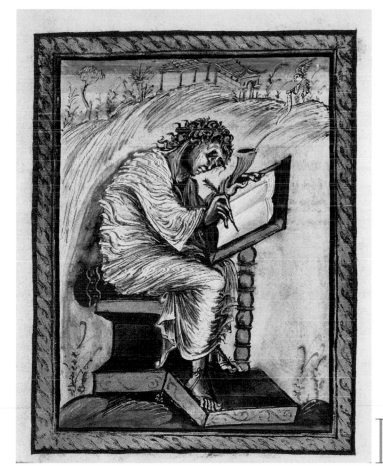

6-4 Saint Matthew, folio 15 recto of the *Coronation Gospels* (*Gospel Book of Charlemagne*), from Aachen, Germany, ca. 800–810. Ink and tempera on vellum, 1' ¾" × 10". Schatzkammer, Kunsthistorisches Museum, Vienna. ◼◢

The books produced for Charlemagne's court reveal the legacy of classical art. The Carolingian painter used light, shade, and perspective to create the illusion of three-dimensional form.

6-5 Saint Matthew, folio 18 verso of the *Ebbo Gospels* (*Gospel Book of Archbishop Ebbo of Reims*), from Hautvillers, France, ca. 816–835. Ink and tempera on vellum, 10¼" × 8¾". Bibliothèque Municipale, Épernay. ◼◢

Saint Matthew writes frantically, and the folds of his drapery writhe and vibrate. Even the landscape rears up alive. This painter merged classical illusionism with the northern European linear tradition.

6-6 *Crucifixion,* front cover of the *Lindau Gospels,* from Saint Gall, Switzerland, ca. 870. Gold, precious stones, and pearls, 1' 1⅜" × 10⅜". Pierpont Morgan Library, New York. ◼◀

Sacred books with covers of gold and jewels were among the most costly and revered Romanesque art objects. This Carolingian cover revives the Early Christian imagery of the youthful Jesus.

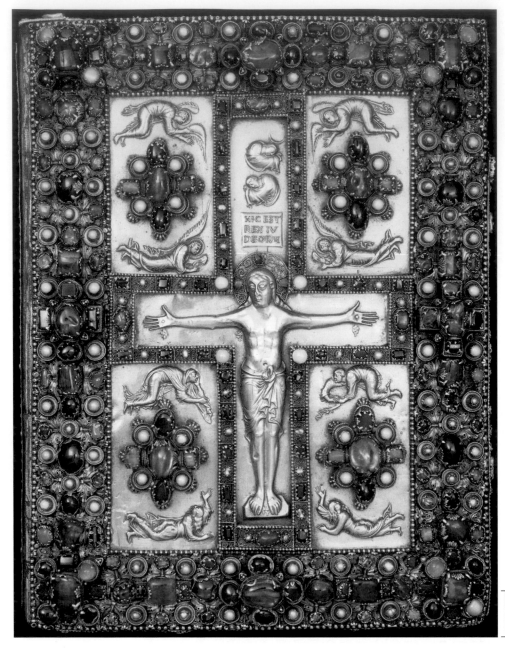

1 in.

approaching frenzy. Matthew writes in frantic haste. His hair stands on end, his eyes open wide, the folds of his drapery writhe and vibrate, and the landscape behind him rears up alive. The painter even set the page's leaf border in motion. The *Ebbo Gospels* painter translated a classical prototype into a new Carolingian style, merging classical illusionism and the northern linear tradition.

Lindau Gospels The taste for luxurious portable objects, the hallmark of the art of the early medieval warlords, persisted under Charlemagne and his successors. The Carolingians commissioned numerous works employing costly materials, including book covers made of gold and jewels and sometimes also ivory or pearls. Gold and gems not only glorified the word of God but also evoked the heavenly Jerusalem. One of the most sumptuous Carolingian book covers (FIG. 6-6) is the one later added to the *Lindau Gospels.* The gold cover, fashioned in one of the royal workshops of Char-

lemagne's grandson, Charles the Bald (r. 840–875), presents a youthful Christ in the Early Christian tradition, nailed to the cross but oblivious to pain. Surrounding Christ are pearls and jewels (raised on golden claw feet so that they can catch and reflect the light even more brilliantly and protect the delicate metal relief from denting). The statuesque open-eyed figure, rendered in hammered relief, is classical both in conception and in execution. In contrast, the four angels and the personifications of the Moon and the Sun above and the crouching figures of the Virgin Mary and Saint John (and two other figures of uncertain identity) in the quadrants below display the vivacity and nervous energy of the *Ebbo Gospels* Saint Matthew (FIG. 6-5). The *Lindau Gospels* cover highlights the stylistic diversity of early medieval art in Europe. Here, however, the translated figural style of the Mediterranean prevailed, in keeping with the classical tastes and imperial aspirations of the Frankish emperors of Rome.

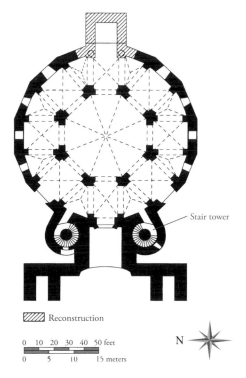

6-7 Restored plan of the Palatine Chapel of Charlemagne, Aachen, Germany, 792–805.

Charlemagne sought to emulate Byzantine splendor in Germany. The plan of his Aachen palace chapel is based on that of San Vitale (FIG. 4-15), but the Carolingian plan is simpler.

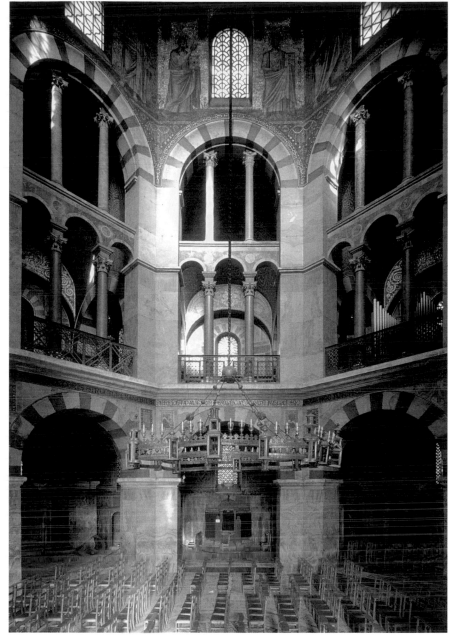

6-8 Interior of the Palatine Chapel of Charlemagne (looking east), Aachen, Germany, 792–805.

Charlemagne's chapel is the first vaulted medieval structure north of the Alps. The architect transformed the complex, glittering interior of San Vitale (FIG. 4-16) into simple, massive geometric form.

Aachen In his eagerness to reestablish the imperial past, Charlemagne looked to Rome and Ravenna for architectural models. One was the former heart of the Roman Empire, which he wanted to renew. The other was the western outpost of Byzantine might and splendor (see Chapter 4), which he wanted to emulate at Aachen. Charlemagne often visited Ravenna, and once brought from there porphyry columns to adorn his Palatine (palace) Chapel. The plan (FIG. **6-7**) of the Aachen chapel resembles that of Ravenna's San Vitale (FIG. 4-15), and a direct relationship very likely exists between the two.

A comparison between the Carolingian chapel, the first vaulted structure of the Middle Ages north of the Alps, and its southern counterpart is instructive. The Aachen plan is simpler. The architect omitted San Vitale's apselike extensions reaching from the central octagon into the ambulatory. At Aachen, the two main units stand in greater independence of each other. This solution may lack the subtle sophistication of the Byzantine building, but the Palatine Chapel gains geometric clarity. A view of its interior (FIG. **6-8**) shows that Charlemagne's builders converted the "floating" quality of San Vitale (FIG. 4-16) into massive geometric form.

On the exterior, two cylindrical towers with spiral staircases flank the entrance portal. This was a first step toward the great dual-tower facades of western European churches from the 10th century to the present. Above the portal, Charlemagne could appear in a large framing arch and be seen by those gathered in the atrium in front of the chapel. (The plan includes only part of the atrium.) Directly behind that second-story arch was Charlemagne's marble throne. From there he could peer down at the altar in the apse. Charlemagne's imperial gallery followed the model of the imperial gallery at Hagia Sophia (FIGS. 4-11 and 4-12) in Constantinople, even if the design of the facade broke sharply from Byzantine tradition.

Medieval Monasteries and Benedictine Rule

Since Early Christian times, the monks who established monasteries also made the rules that governed communal life. The most significant of these monks was Benedict of Nursia (Saint Benedict, ca. 480–547), who founded the Benedictine Order in 529. By the ninth century, the "Rule" Benedict wrote (*Regula Sancti Benedicti*) had become standard for all western European monastic communities, in part because Charlemagne had encouraged its adoption throughout the Frankish territories.

Saint Benedict believed the corruption of the clergy that accompanied the increasing worldliness of the Church had its roots in the lack of firm organization and regulation. As he saw it, idleness and selfishness had led to neglect of the commandments of God and of the Church. The cure for this was communal association in an *abbey* under the absolute rule of an *abbot* the monks elected (or an *abbess* the nuns chose), who would ensure the clergy spent each hour of the day in useful work and in sacred reading. The emphasis on work and study and not on meditation and austerity is of great historical significance. Since antiquity, manual labor had been considered demeaning, the business of the lowborn or of slaves. Benedict raised it to the dignity of religion. By thus exalting the virtue of manual labor, Benedict not only rescued it from its age-old association with slavery but also recognized it as the way to self-sufficiency for the entire religious community.

Whereas some of Saint Benedict's followers emphasized spiritual "work" over manual labor, others, most notably the Cistercians (see page 176), put Benedict's teachings about the value of physical work into practice. These monks reached into their surroundings and helped reduce the vast areas of daunting wilderness of early medieval Europe. They cleared dense forest teeming with wolves, bear, and wild boar, drained swamps, cultivated wastelands, and built roads, bridges, and dams as well as monastic churches and their associated living and service quarters.

The ideal monastery (FIG. 6-9) provided all the facilities necessary for the conduct of daily life—a mill, bakery, infirmary, vegetable garden, and even a brewery—so the monks felt no need to wander outside its protective walls. These religious communities were centrally important to the revival of learning. The clergy, who were also often scribes and scholars, had a monopoly on the skills of reading and writing in an age of almost universal illiteracy. The monastic libraries and scriptoria, where the monks and nuns read, copied, illuminated, and bound books with ornamented covers, became centers of study. Monasteries were almost the sole repositories of what remained of the literary culture of the Greco-Roman world and early Christianity. Saint Benedict's require-

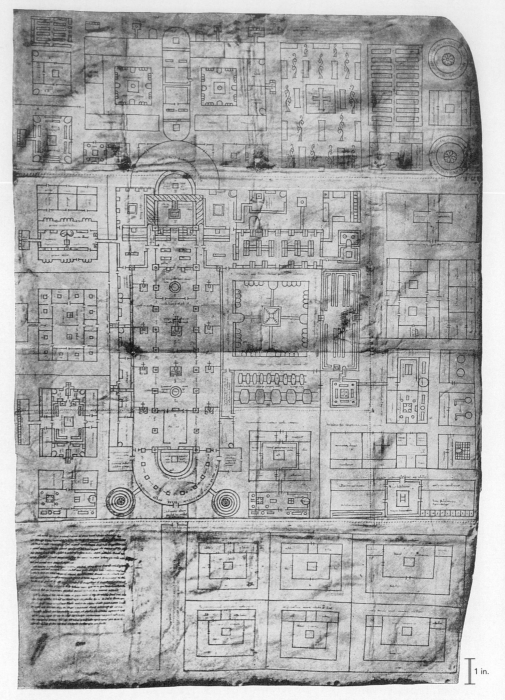

6-9 Schematic plan for a monastery, from Saint Gall, Switzerland, ca. 819. Red ink on parchment, 2' 4" × 3' 8⅛". Stiftsbibliothek, Saint Gall.

The purpose of this plan for an ideal, self-sufficient Benedictine monastery was to separate the monks from the laity. Near the center is the oratory (church) with its cloister, the monks' earthly paradise.

ments of manual labor and sacred reading came to include writing and copying books, studying music for chanting daily prayers, and—of great significance—teaching. The monasteries were also the schools of the early Middle Ages.

Saint Gall A major initiative of the Carolingian period was the construction and expansion of monasteries. About 819, Haito, the abbot of Reichenau and bishop of Basel, commissioned a schematic plan (FIG. **6-9**) for a Benedictine monastic community (see "Medieval Monasteries and Benedictine Rule," page 168) and sent it to the abbot of Saint Gall in Switzerland as a guide for the rebuilding of the Saint Gall monastery. The plan provides precious information about Carolingian monastic communities. The design's fundamental purpose was to separate the monks from the laity (nonclergy) who also inhabited the community. Variations of the scheme may be seen in later monasteries all across western Europe.

Near the center, dominating everything, was the *oratory* (monastic church) with its *cloister*, a colonnaded courtyard (compare FIG. 6-17, *left*) not unlike the Early Christian atrium (FIG. 4-3) but situated to the side of the church rather than in front of its main portal. Reserved for the monks alone, the cloister was a kind of earthly paradise removed from the world at large. Clustered around the cloister were the most essential buildings: dormitory, *refectory* (dining hall), kitchen, and storage rooms. Other structures, including an infirmary, school, guest house, bakery, brewery, and workshops, filled the areas around this central core of church and cloister.

Haito invited the abbot of Saint Gall to adapt the plan as he saw fit, and indeed, the Saint Gall builders did not follow the Reichenau model precisely. Nonetheless, had the abbot wished, Haito's plan could have served as a practical guide for the Saint Gall masons because it was laid out using a *module* (standard unit) of 2.5 feet. The designer consistently employed that module, or multiples or fractions of it, for all elements of the plan. For example, the nave's width, indicated on the plan as 40 feet, is equal to 16 modules. Each monk's bed is 2.5 modules long.

The prototypes carrying the greatest authority for Charlemagne and his builders were those from the time of Constantine. The widespread adoption of the Early Christian basilica, at Saint Gall and elsewhere, rather than the domed central plan of Byzantine churches, was crucial to the subsequent development of western European church architecture. Unfortunately, no Carolingian basilica has survived in its original form. Nevertheless, it is possible to reconstruct the appearance of some of them with fair accuracy. The monastery church at Saint Gall, for example, was essentially a traditional basilica, but it had features not found in any Early Christian church. Most obvious is the addition of a second apse on the west end of the building.

Not quite as evident but much more important to the subsequent development of church architecture in northern Europe was the presence of a transept at Saint Gall, a rare feature, but one that characterized the two greatest Early Christian basilicas in Rome, Saint Peter's (FIG. 4-3) and Saint Paul's. The Saint Gall transept is as wide as the nave on the plan and was probably the same height. Early Christian builders had not been concerned with proportional relationships. On the Saint Gall plan, however, the various parts of the building relate to one another by a geometric scheme that ties them together into a tight and cohesive unit. Equalizing the widths of nave and transept automatically makes the area where they cross (the *crossing*) a square. Most Carolingian churches shared this feature. But Haito's planner also used the *crossing square* as the unit of measurement for the remainder of the church plan. The transept arms are equal to one crossing square, the distance between transept and apse is one crossing square, and the nave is 4.5 crossing squares long. In addition, the two aisles are half as wide as the nave, integrating all parts of the church in a rational and orderly plan.

The Saint Gall plan also reveals another important feature of many Carolingian basilicas: towers framing the end(s) of the church. Haito's plan shows only two towers, both cylindrical and on the west side of the church, as at the Palatine Chapel (FIG. 6-7) at Aachen, but they stand apart from the church facade. If a tower existed above the crossing, the silhouette of Saint Gall would have shown three towers, altering the horizontal profile of the traditional basilica and identifying the church even from afar. Other Carolingian basilicas had towers incorporated in the fabric of the west end of the building, thereby creating a unified monumental facade greeting all those entering the church. Architectural historians call this feature of Carolingian and some later churches the *westwork* (from the German *Westwerck*, "western entrance structure").

Ottonian Art

Charlemagne was buried in the Palatine Chapel at Aachen. His empire survived him by fewer than 30 years. When his son Louis the Pious (r. 814–840) died, Louis's sons—Charles the Bald, Lothair, and Louis the German—divided the Carolingian Empire among themselves. In 843, after bloody conflicts, the brothers signed a treaty partitioning the Frankish lands into western, central, and eastern areas, very roughly foreshadowing the later nations of France and Germany and a third realm corresponding to a long strip of land stretching from the Netherlands and Belgium to Rome. In the mid-10th century, the eastern part of the former empire consolidated under the rule of a new Saxon line of German emperors called, after the names of the three most illustrious family members, the *Ottonians*. The pope crowned the first Otto (r. 936–973) in Rome in 962. The three Ottos not only preserved but enriched the culture and tradition of the Carolingian period.

Hildesheim A great patron of Ottonian art and architecture was Bishop Bernward (r. 993–1022) of Hildesheim, Germany. He was the tutor of Otto III (r. 983–1002) and builder of the abbey church of Saint Michael at Hildesheim. Bernward was a scholar who made Hildesheim a center of learning. He was also an expert craftsman and bronze-caster. In 1001, he traveled to Rome as the guest of Otto III. During this stay, Bernward studied at first hand the ancient monuments the Carolingian and Ottonian emperors revered.

6-10 Saint Michael's (looking northwest), Hildesheim, Germany, 1001–1031.

Built by Bishop Bernward, a great art patron, Saint Michael's is a masterpiece of Ottonian basilica design. The church's two apses, two transepts, and multiple towers give it a distinctive profile.

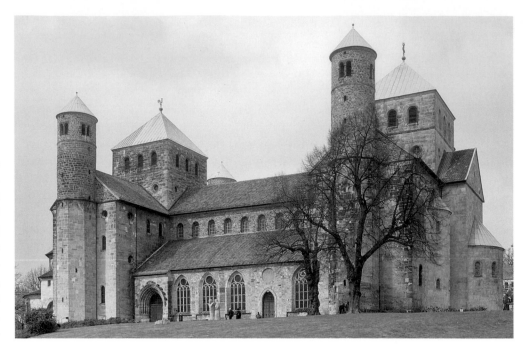

Constructed between 1001 and 1031 (and rebuilt after a bombing raid during World War II), Saint Michael's has a double-transept plan (FIGS. **6-10** and **6-11**), two apses, six towers, and a westwork. The two transepts create eastern and western centers of gravity. The nave merely seems to be a hall connecting them. Lateral entrances leading into the aisles from the north and south additionally make for an almost complete loss of the traditional basilican orientation toward the east. Some ancient Roman basilicas, such as the Basilica Ulpia (FIG. 3-35, no. 4) in Trajan's Forum, also had two apses and entrances on the side, and Bernward probably was familiar with this variant basilican plan.

At Hildesheim, as in the Saint Gall monastery plan (FIG. 6-9), the builders adopted a modular approach. The crossing squares, for example, are the basis for the nave's dimensions—three crossing squares long and one square wide. The placement of heavy piers at the corners of each square gives visual emphasis to the three units. These piers alternate with pairs of columns to form what architectural historians call the *alternate-support system*. The alternating piers and columns divide the nave into vertical units, mitigating the tunnel-like horizontality of the Early Christian basilica.

Bernward's Doors In 1001, when Bishop Bernward was in Rome, he resided in Otto III's palace on the Aventine hill in the neighborhood of Santa Sabina, an Early Christian church renowned for its carved wooden doors. Those doors, decorated with episodes from both the Old and New Testaments, may have inspired the remarkable 16-feet-tall bronze doors (FIG. **6-12**) the bishop had cast for Saint Michael's. They are technological marvels because the Ottonian metalworkers cast each giant door in a single

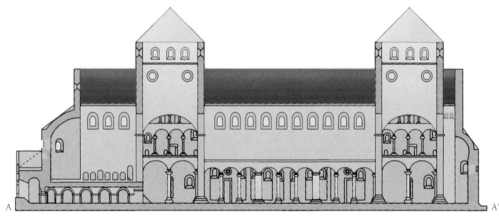

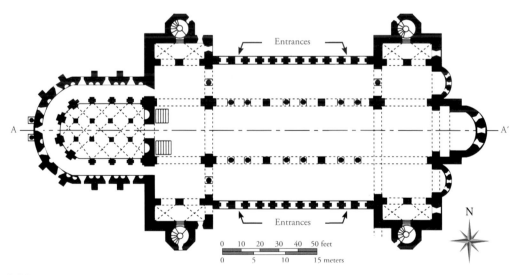

6-11 Longitudinal section (*top*) and plan (*bottom*) of the abbey church of Saint Michael's, Hildesheim, Germany, 1001–1031. ◼◂

Saint Michael's entrances are on the side. Alternating piers and columns divide the space in the nave into vertical units. These features transformed the tunnel-like horizontality of Early Christian basilicas.

piece with the figural sculpture. Carolingian sculpture, like most sculpture since the fall of Rome, consisted primarily of small-scale art executed in ivory and precious metals, often

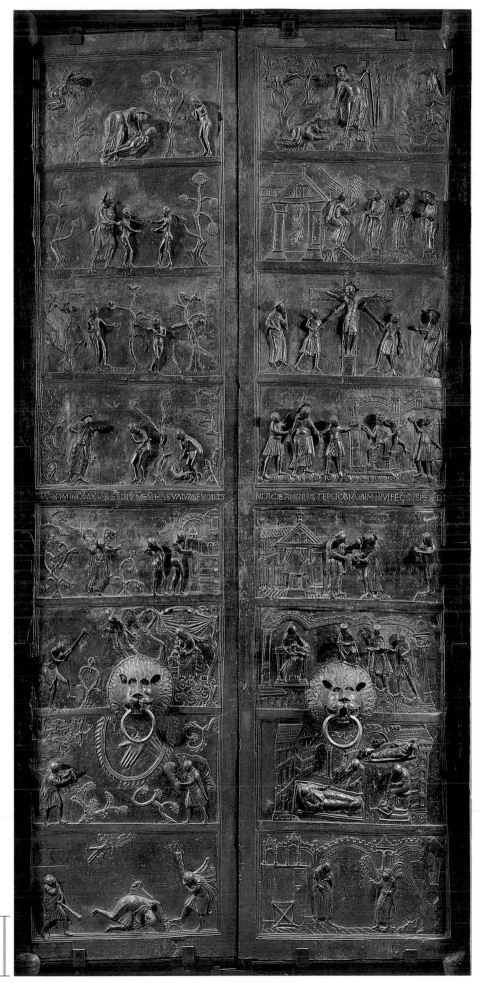

1 ft.

for book covers (FIG. 6-6). The Hildesheim doors are huge in comparison, but the 16 individual panels stem from this tradition.

The panels of the left door illustrate highlights from Genesis, beginning with the creation of Eve (at the top) and ending with the murder of Adam and Eve's son Abel by his brother Cain (at the bottom). The right door recounts the life of Jesus (reading from the bottom up), starting with the annunciation to the Virgin and terminating with the appearance to Mary Magdalene of Christ after his resurrection. Together, the doors tell the story of original sin and ultimate redemption, showing the expulsion from the Garden of Eden and the path back to Paradise through the Church. As in Early Christian times, the Ottonian clergy interpreted Hebrew scripture as prefiguring the New Testament. For example, the panel depicting the fall of Adam and Eve is juxtaposed with the crucifixion. Eve nursing the infant Cain is opposite Mary with the Christ Child in her lap. The figures show a vivid animation that recalls the *Ebbo Gospels* Saint Matthew (FIG. 6-5), but the narrative compositions also reveal the Hildesheim artist's genius for anecdotal detail. For example, in the fourth panel from the top on the left door, God, portrayed as a man, accuses Adam and Eve after their fall from grace. He jabs his finger at them with the force of his whole body. The frightened pair crouches, not only to hide their shame but also to escape the lightning bolt of divine wrath. Each passes the blame—Adam pointing backward to Eve and Eve pointing downward to the deceitful serpent. Adam and Eve both struggle to point with one arm while attempting to shield their bodies from view with the other. With an instinct for expressive pose and gesture, the artist brilliantly communicated their newfound embarrassment at their nakedness and their unconvincing denials of wrongdoing.

6-12 Doors with relief panels (Genesis, left door; life of Christ, right door), commissioned by Bishop Bernward for Saint Michael's, Hildesheim, Germany, 1015. Bronze, 15' 5¾" high. Dom-Museum, Hildesheim. ◼️◄

Bernward's doors tell the story of original sin and redemption, and draw parallels between the Old and New Testaments, as in the expulsion from Paradise and the infancy and suffering of Christ.

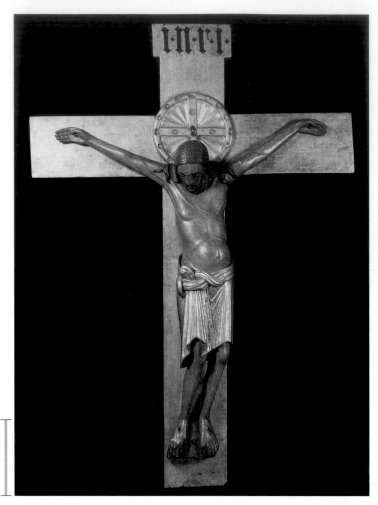

6-13 Crucifix commissioned by Archbishop Gero for Cologne Cathedral, Germany, ca. 970. Painted wood, height of figure, 6′ 2″. Cathedral, Cologne. ◼◀

In this early example of the revival of monumental sculpture in the Middle Ages, an Ottonian sculptor depicted with unprecedented emotional power the intense agony of Christ's ordeal on the cross.

Gero Crucifix The Ottonian period also witnessed a revival of interest in freestanding statuary. The outstanding example is the crucifix (FIG. **6-13**) Archbishop Gero (r. 969–976) commissioned in 970 for display in Cologne Cathedral. Carved in oak, then painted and gilded, the six-foot-tall image of Christ nailed to the cross presents a dramatically different conception of the savior than that seen on the *Lindau Gospels* cover (FIG. 6-6), with its Early Christian imagery of the youthful Christ triumphant over death. The bearded Christ of the Cologne crucifix is more akin to Byzantine representations (FIG. 4-22) of the suffering Jesus, but the emotional power of the Ottonian work is greater still. The sculptor depicted the Savior as an all-too-human martyr. Blood streaks down his forehead from the (missing) crown of thorns. His eyelids are closed, his face is contorted in pain, and his body sags under its weight. The muscles stretch to their limit—those of his right shoulder and chest seem almost to rip apart. The halo behind Christ's head may foretell his subsequent resurrection, but the worshiper can sense only his pain. Gero's crucifix is the most powerful characterization of intense agony of the early Middle Ages.

ROMANESQUE EUROPE

The Romanesque era is the first since Archaic and Classical Greece to take its name from an artistic style rather than from politics or geography. Unlike Carolingian and Ottonian art, named for emperors, or Hiberno-Saxon art, a regional term, *Romanesque* is a title art historians invented to describe medieval art and architecture that appeared "Roman-like." Architectural historians first employed the adjective in the early 19th century to describe European architecture of the 11th and 12th centuries. They noted that certain architectural elements of this period, principally barrel and groin vaults based on the round arch, resembled those of ancient Roman architecture. Thus, the word distinguished most Romanesque buildings from earlier medieval timber-roofed structures, as well as from later Gothic churches with vaults resting on pointed arches (see Chapter 7). Scholars in other fields quickly borrowed the term. Today, *Romanesque* broadly designates the history and culture of western Europe between about 1050 and 1200.

During the 11th and 12th centuries, thousands of ecclesiastical buildings were remodeled or newly constructed. This immense building enterprise was in part a natural byproduct of the rise of independent towns and the prosperity they enjoyed. But it also was an expression of the widely felt relief and thanksgiving that the conclusion of the first Christian millennium in the year 1000 had not brought an end to the world, as many had feared. In the Romanesque age, the construction of churches became almost an obsession. As the monk Raoul Glaber (ca. 985–ca. 1046) observed in 1003, "It was as if the whole earth . . . were clothing itself everywhere in the white robe of the church."³

The enormous investment in ecclesiastical buildings and furnishings also reflected a significant increase in pilgrimage traffic in Romanesque Europe (see "Pilgrimages and the Cult of Relics," page 173). Pilgrims were important sources of funding for those monasteries possessing the *relics* of venerated saints. The clergy of the various monasteries vied with one another to provide the most magnificent settings for the display of their relics. They found justification for their lavish expenditures on buildings and furnishing in the Bible itself, for example, in Psalm 26:8, "Lord, I have loved the beauty of your house, and the place where your glory dwells." Traveling pilgrims fostered the growth of towns as well as monasteries. Pilgrimages were a major economic as well as conceptual catalyst for the art and architecture of the Romanesque period.

Although art historians use the adjective *Romanesque* to describe 11th- and 12th-century art and architecture throughout Europe, pronounced regional differences exist. To a certain extent, Romanesque art and architecture can be compared to European Romance languages, which vary regionally but have a common core in Latin, the language of the Romans.

France

Some of the most innovative developments in Romanesque architecture and architectural sculpture occurred in France.

Pilgrimages and the Cult of Relics

The cult of *relics* was not new in the Romanesque era. For centuries, Christians had traveled to sacred shrines housing the body parts of, or objects associated with, the holy family or the saints. The faithful had long believed bones, clothing, instruments of martyrdom, and the like had the power to heal body and soul. The veneration of relics, however, reached a high point in the 11th and 12th centuries.

In the Romanesque era, pilgrimage was the most conspicuous feature of public religious devotion, proclaiming pilgrims' faith in the power of saints and hope for their special favor. The major shrines—Saint Peter's and Saint Paul's in Rome and the Church of the Holy Sepulcher in Jerusalem—drew pilgrims from throughout Europe. Christians braved bad roads and hostile wildernesses infested with robbers who preyed on innocent travelers—all for the sake of salvation. The journeys could take more than a year to complete—when they were successful. People often undertook pilgrimage as an act of repentance or as a last resort in their search for a cure for some physical disability. Hardship and austerity were means of increasing pilgrims' chances for the remission of sin or of dis-

ease. The distance and peril of the pilgrimage were measures of pilgrims' sincerity of repentance or of the reward they sought.

For those with insufficient time or money to make a pilgrimage to Rome or Jerusalem, holy destinations could be found closer to home. In France, for example, the church at Vézelay (FIG. 6-22) housed the bones of Mary Magdalene. Pilgrims could also view Saint Lazarus's remains at Autun (FIG. 6-21) and Saint Saturninus's at Toulouse (FIG. 6-14). Each of these great shrines was also an important way station en route to the most venerated Christian shrine in western Europe, the tomb of Saint James at Santiago de Compostela in northwestern Spain (MAP 6-1).

Large crowds of pilgrims paying homage to saints placed a great burden on the churches housing their relics, but they also provided significant revenues, making possible the construction of ever grander and more luxuriously appointed shrines. The popularity of pilgrimages led to changes in church design, principally longer and wider naves and aisles, transepts and ambulatories with additional chapels (FIG. 6-15), and second-story galleries (FIG. 6-16).

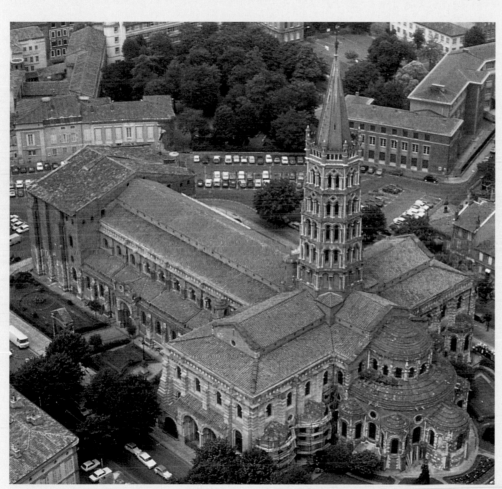

6-14 Aerial view of Saint-Sernin (looking northwest), Toulouse, France, ca. 1070–1120. ■◀

Pilgrimages were a major economic catalyst for the art and architecture of the Romanesque period. The clergy vied with one another to provide magnificent settings for the display of holy relics.

Toulouse Around 1070, construction of a great new church began in honor of Toulouse's first bishop, Saint Saturninus (Saint Sernin in French). Large congregations gathered at the southwestern French shrines along the pilgrimage routes to Santiago de Compostela, and the unknown architect designed Saint-Sernin to accommodate them. The grand scale

of the building is apparent in the aerial view (FIG. **6-14**), which includes automobiles, trucks, and nearly invisible pedestrians. The church's 12th-century exterior is still largely intact, although the two towers of the western facade (at the left in FIG. **6-14**) were never completed, and the prominent *crossing tower* dates to the Gothic and later periods.

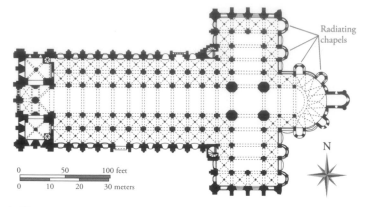

6-15 Plan of Saint-Sernin, Toulouse, France, ca. 1070–1120 (after Kenneth John Conant).

Increased traffic led to changes in church design. "Pilgrimage churches" have longer and wider naves and aisles, as well as transepts and ambulatories with radiating chapels for viewing relics.

Saint-Sernin's plan (FIG. **6-15**) is extremely regular and geometrically precise. The crossing square, flanked by massive piers and marked off by heavy arches, served as the module for the entire church. Each nave *bay,* for example, measures exactly one-half of the crossing square, and each aisle bay measures exactly one-quarter. The Toulouse design is a highly refined realization of the planning scheme first seen at Saint Gall (FIG. 6-9). But the Toulouse plan differs in significant ways from those of earlier monastic churches. It exem-

plifies what has come to be called the "pilgrimage church" type. At Toulouse, the builders provided additional space for curious pilgrims, worshipers, and liturgical processions by increasing the length of the nave, doubling the side aisles, and adding a transept and ambulatory with *radiating chapels* housing the church's relics so the faithful could view them without having to enter the choir where the main altar stood.

Saint-Sernin also has upper galleries, or *tribunes,* over the inner aisles opening onto the nave (FIG. **6-16**), which housed overflow crowds on special occasions. The tribunes played an important role in buttressing the continuous semicircular cut-stone *barrel vault* that covers Saint-Sernin's nave. *Groin vaults* (indicated by Xs on the plan, FIG. **6-15**; compare FIG. 3-14) in the tribunes as well as in the ground-floor aisles absorbed the pressure (*thrust*) exerted by the barrel vault along the entire length of the nave and transferred the main thrust to the thick outer walls.

The builders of Saint-Sernin were not content merely to buttress the massive nave vault. They also carefully coordinated the vault's design with that of the nave arcade below and with the modular plan of the building as a whole. The nave elevation, which features *engaged columns* embellishing the piers marking the corners of the bays, fully reflects the church's geometric floor plan (FIG. **6-15**). Architectural historians refer to piers with columns or pilasters attached to their rectangular cores as *compound piers.* At Saint-Sernin, the engaged columns rise from the bottom of the compound piers to the vault's *springing* (the lowest stone of an arch) and continue across the

6-16 Interior of Saint-Sernin (looking east), Toulouse, France, ca. 1070–1120. ◼◀

Saint-Sernin's groin-vaulted tribune galleries housed overflow crowds and buttressed the nave's stone barrel vault whose transverse arches continue the lines of the compound piers.

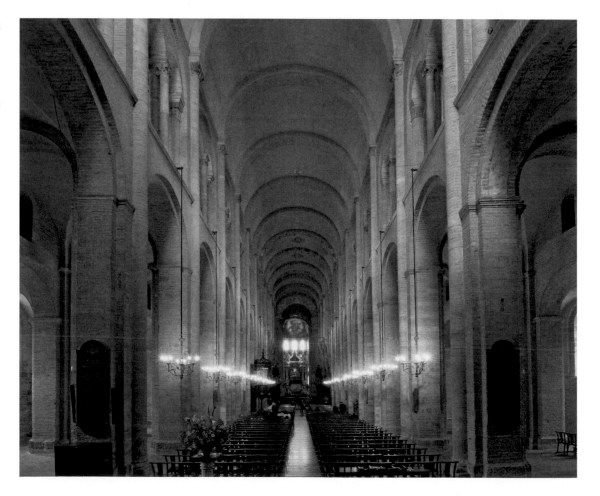

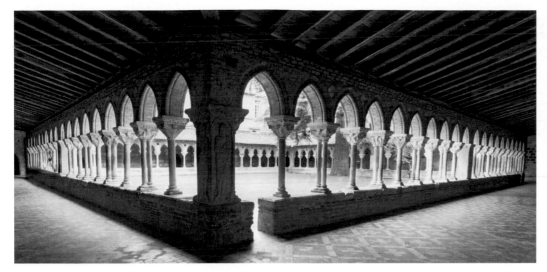

6-17 General view of the cloister (*left;* looking southeast) and detail of the pier with the relief of Abbot Durandus (*right*), Saint-Pierre, Moissac, France, ca. 1100–1115. Relief: limestone, 6' high. ■◀

The revived tradition of stonecarving probably began with historiated capitals. The most extensive preserved ensemble of sculptured early Romanesque capitals is in the Moissac cloister.

1 ft.

nave as *transverse arches.* As a result, the Saint-Sernin nave gives the impression of being numerous identical vertical volumes of space placed one behind the other, marching down the building's length in orderly procession. Saint-Sernin's spatial organization corresponds to and renders visually the plan's geometric organization. This rationally integrated scheme, with repeated units decorated and separated by moldings, would have a long future in later European church architecture.

Saint-Sernin's stone vaults provided protection from the devastating conflagrations that regularly destroyed traditional timber-roofed basilicas. But although fireproofing was no doubt one of the attractions of vaulted naves and aisles in an age when candles and lamps provided interior illumination, other factors probably played a greater role in the decision to make the enormous investment of time and funds required. The rapid spread of stone vaulting throughout Romanesque Europe was most likely the result of a desire to provide a suitably majestic setting for the display of relics as well as enhanced acoustics for the Christian liturgy and the music accompanying it. Some contemporaneous texts, in fact, comment on the "wondrous" visual impact of costly stone vaults.

Moissac Saint-Sernin also features a group of seven marble slabs representing angels, apostles, and Christ. Dated to the year 1096, they are among the earliest known examples of large-scale Romanesque sculpture. Stone sculpture had almost disappeared from the art of western Europe during the early Middle Ages. The revival of stone carving is a hallmark of the Romanesque age—and one of the reasons the period is aptly named. The revived tradition of stone carving seems to have begun with decorating column and pier capitals with reliefs. The most extensive preserved ensemble of sculptured early Romanesque capitals is in the cloister (FIG. **6-17**, *left*) of Saint-Pierre at Moissac in southwestern France. The monks of the Moissac abbey joined the Cluniac order in 1047, and

Moissac quickly became an important stop along the pilgrimage route to Santiago de Compostela. Enriched by the gifts of pilgrims and noble benefactors, they adorned their church with an elaborate series of relief sculptures.

At Moissac, as elsewhere, the cloister and its garden provided the monks (and nuns) with a foretaste of Paradise. In the cloister, they could read their devotions, pray, meditate, and carry on other activities secluded from the outside world. Moissac's cloister sculpture program consists of large figural reliefs on the piers as well as *historiated* (ornamented with figures) capitals on the columns. The pier reliefs (FIG. 6-17, *right*) portray the 12 apostles and the monastery's first Cluniac abbot, Durandus (r. 1047–1072), whom the monks buried in the cloister. The 76 capitals alternately crown single and paired column shafts. They are variously decorated, some with abstract patterns, many with biblical scenes or the lives of saints, others with fantastic monsters of all sorts. *Bestiaries*—collections of illustrations of real and imaginary animals—became very popular in the Romanesque age. The monstrous forms were reminders of the chaos and deformity of a world without God's order. Medieval artists delighted in inventing composite multiheaded beasts and other fantastic creations.

Bernard of Clairvaux Historiated capitals were common in Cluniac monasteries. Many medieval monks, especially those of the Cluniac order, equated piety with the construction of beautiful churches with elegant carvings. But one of the founding principles of monasticism was the rejection of worldly pleasures in favor of the *vita contemplativa* (life of contemplation, as opposed to the active life of the lay population).

The Romanesque Church Portal

Sculpture in a variety of materials adorned different areas of Romanesque churches, but the primary location was the grand stone portal through which the faithful had to pass. Sculpture had decorated church doorways before. For example, Ottonian bronze doors featuring Old and New Testament scenes marked the entrance from the cloister to Saint Michael's at Hildesheim (FIG. 6-12). In the Romanesque era (and during the Gothic period that followed), sculpture usually appeared in the area *around*, rather than *on*, the doors.

Shown in FIG. 6-18 are the parts of church portals Romanesque sculptors regularly decorated with figural reliefs:

I *Tympanum* (FIGS. 6-19, 6-21, and 6-22), the prominent semicircular *lunette* above the doorway proper, comparable in importance to the triangular pediment of a Greco-Roman temple.

I *Voussoirs* (FIG. 6-22), the wedge-shaped blocks that together form the *archivolts* of the arch framing the tympanum.

I *Lintel* (FIGS. 6-21 and 6-22), the horizontal beam above the doorway.

I *Trumeau* (FIGS. 6-19 and 6-20), the center post supporting the lintel in the middle of the doorway.

I *Jambs* (FIG. 6-19), the side posts of the doorway.

6-18 The Romanesque church portal (John Burge).

The clergy considered the church doorway the beginning of the path to salvation through Christ. Many Romanesque churches feature didactic sculptural reliefs above and beside the entrance portals.

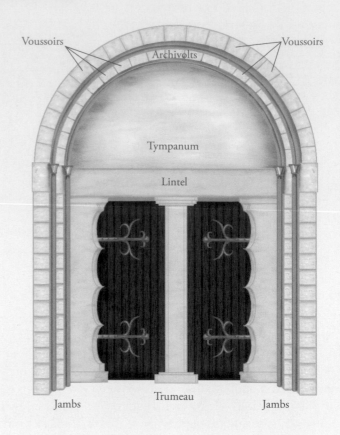

Some monks were appalled by sumptuous churches and their costly furnishings. One group of Benedictine monks founded a new order at Cîteaux in eastern France in 1098. The Cistercians (from the Latin name for Cîteaux) split from the Cluniac order to return to the strict observance of the Rule of Saint Benedict. The Cistercian movement expanded with astonishing rapidity. Within a half century, more than 500 Cistercian monasteries had been established. The Cistercians rejected figural sculpture as a distraction from their devotions. The most outspoken Cistercian critic was Abbot Bernard of Clairvaux (1090–1153). In a letter Bernard wrote in 1127 to William, abbot of Saint-Thierry, he complained about the rich outfitting of non-Cistercian churches: "[I]n the cloisters . . . so plentiful and astonishing a variety of [monstrous] forms is seen that one would rather read in the marble than in books, and spend the whole day wondering at every single one of them than in meditating on the law of God."[4]

During the Romanesque period, stone sculpture also spread to other areas of the church, both inside and out. The proliferation of sculpture reflects the changing role of many churches in western Europe. In the early Middle Ages, most churches served small monastic communities, and the worshipers were primarily or exclusively clergy. With the rise of towns in the Romanesque period, churches, especially those on the major pilgrimage routes, increasingly served the lay public. To reach this new, largely illiterate audience and to draw a wider population into their places of worship, the clergy decided to display Christian symbols and stories throughout their churches, especially in the portals (see "The Romanesque Portal," above, and FIG. 6-18) facing onto the town squares. Stone, rather than painting or mosaic, was the most suitable durable medium for exterior decorative programs.

The tympanum of the south portal (FIG. 6-19) of Saint-Pierre at Moissac depicts the second coming of Christ as king and judge of the world in its last days. The pictorial programs of Romanesque church facades reflect the idea, dating to Early Christian times, that Christ is the door to salvation ("I am the door; who enters through me will be saved"—John 10:9). As befits his majesty, the enthroned Christ is at the center of the Moissac tympanum. Flanking him are the signs of the four evangelists—Matthew's winged man, Mark's lion, John's eagle, and Luke's ox. To the left and right are attendant angels holding scrolls to record human deeds for judgment. The figures of crowned musicians, which complete the design, are the 24 elders who accompany Christ as the kings of this world and make music in his praise. Two courses of wavy lines symbolizing the clouds of Heaven divide the elders into three tiers.

Many variations exist within the general style of Romanesque sculpture, as within Romanesque architecture. The

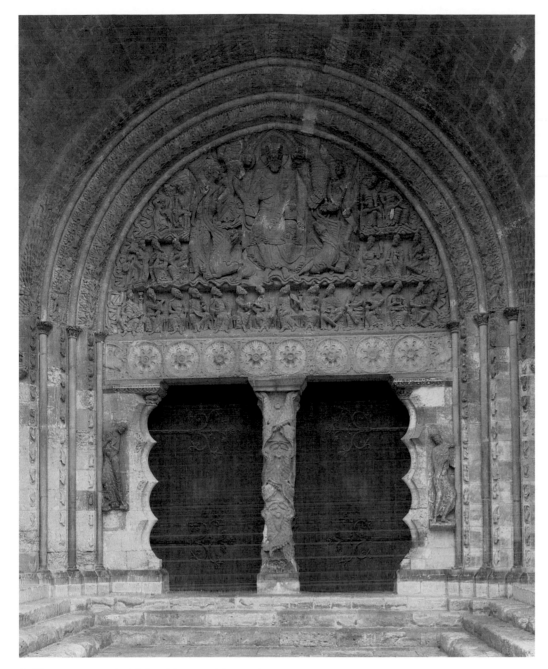

6-19 South portal of Saint-Pierre, Moissac, France, ca. 1115–1135. ■◀

A vision of the second coming of Christ on judgment day greets worshipers entering Saint-Pierre at Moissac. The sculptural program reflects the belief that Christ is the door to salvation.

6-20 Old Testament prophet (Jeremiah or Isaiah?), right side of the trumeau of the south portal of Saint-Pierre, Moissac, France, ca. 1115–1130. ■◀

This animated prophet displays the scroll recounting his vision. His position below the apparition of Christ as last judge is in keeping with the tradition of pairing Old and New Testament themes.

extremely elongated bodies of the scroll-carrying angels, the cross-legged dancing pose of Saint Matthew's angel, the jerky movement of the elders' heads, the zigzag and dovetail lines of the draperies, the bandlike folds of the torsos, and the bending back of the hands against the body are all characteristic of the anonymous Moissac master's distinctive style. The animation of the individual figures, however, contrasts with the stately monumentality of the composition as a whole, producing a dynamic tension in the tympanum.

Below the tympanum are a richly decorated trumeau and elaborate door jambs with scalloped contours, the latter a borrowing from Islamic Spain (FIG. 5-7). Six roaring interlaced lions adorn the front of the trumeau. Lions were the church's ideal protectors. In the Middle Ages, people believed lions slept with their eyes open. On the trumeau's right face is a prophet (FIG. **6-20**) displaying the scroll bearing his prophetic vision. The prophet is tall and thin and he executes a cross-legged step. The animation of the body reveals the passionate nature of the soul within. The long, serpentine locks of hair and beard frame an arresting image of the dreaming mystic. The prophet seems entranced by his vision of what is to come.

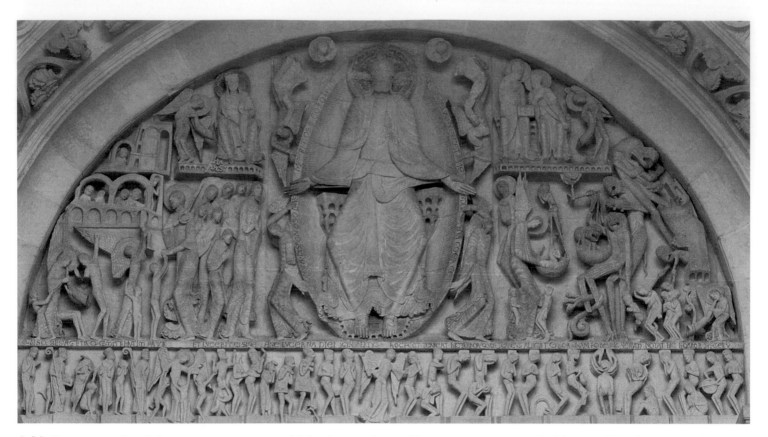

6-21 GISLEBERTUS, *Last Judgment,* west tympanum of Saint-Lazare, Autun, France, ca. 1120–1135. Marble, 21' wide at base. ◼◂

Christ, enthroned in a mandorla, presides over the separation of the blessed from the damned in this dramatic vision of the last judgment, designed to terrify those guilty of sin and beckon them into the church.

Autun In 1132, the Cluniac bishop Étienne de Bage consecrated the Burgundian cathedral of Saint-Lazare (Saint Lazarus) at Autun. For its tympanum (FIG. **6-21**) he commissioned the sculptor GISLEBERTUS to carve a dramatic vision of the *Last Judgment.* Four trumpet-blowing angels announce the second coming of Christ. Enthroned in a *mandorla* at the center, Christ is far larger than any other figure. He dispassionately presides over the separation of the saved from the damned. At the left, an obliging angel boosts one of the blessed into the heavenly city. Below, the souls of the dead line up to await their fate. Two of the men near the middle of the lintel carry bags emblazoned with a cross and a shell. These are the symbols of pilgrims to Jerusalem and Santiago de Compostela, respectively. Those who had made the difficult journey would be judged favorably. To their right, three small figures beg an angel to intercede on their behalf. The angel responds by pointing to the judge above. On the right side are those who will be condemned to Hell. Giant hands pluck one poor soul from the earth. Directly above is Gislebertus's unforgettable vision of the weighing of souls. Angels and the Devil's agents try to manipulate the balance for or against a soul. Hideous demons guffaw and roar. Their gaunt, lined bodies, with legs ending in sharp claws, writhe and bend like long, loathsome insects. A devilish creature, leaning from the dragon mouth of Hell, drags souls in, while above him a howling demon crams souls headfirst into a furnace.

The Autun tympanum must have inspired terror in the believers who passed beneath it as they entered the cathedral. Even those who could not read could, in the words of Bernard of Clairvaux, "read in the marble." For the literate, the Autun clergy composed explicit written warnings to reinforce the pictorial message, and had the words engraved in Latin on the tympanum. For example, beneath the weighing of souls, the inscription reads, "May this terror terrify those whom earthly error binds, for the horror of these images here in this manner truly depicts what will be."[5]

Vézelay Another large tympanum (FIG. **6-22**)—at the Church of La Madeleine (Mary Magdalene) at Vézelay—depicts the *Pentecost* and the *Mission of the Apostles.* As related in Acts 1:4–9, Christ foretold the 12 apostles would receive the power of the Holy Spirit and become the witnesses of the truth of the Gospels throughout the world. The light rays emanating from Christ's hands represent the instilling of the Holy Spirit in the apostles (Acts 2:1–42) at the Pentecost (the seventh Sunday after Easter). The apostles, holding the Gospel books, receive their spiritual assignment to preach the Gospel to all nations. The Christ figure is a splendid essay in calligraphic design. The drapery lines shoot out in rays, break into quick zigzag rhythms, and spin into whorls, wonderfully conveying the spiritual light and energy flowing from Christ over and into the equally animated apostles. The

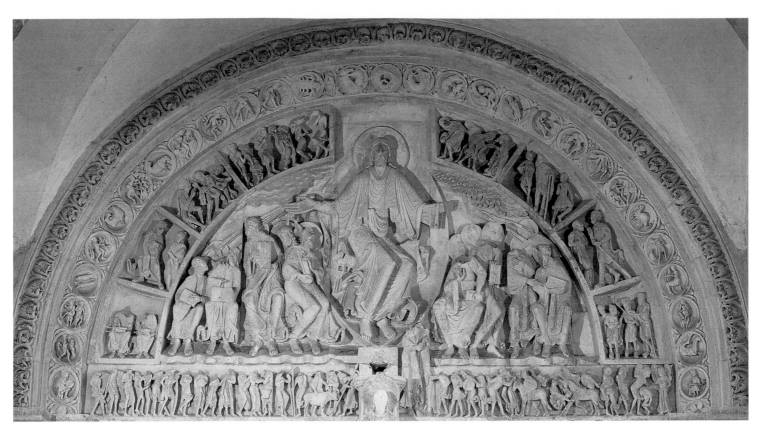

6-22 *Pentecost* and *Mission of the Apostles,* tympanum of the center portal of the narthex of La Madeleine, Vézelay, France, 1120–1132. ◼◀

In the tympanum of the church most closely associated with the Crusades, light rays emanating from Christ's hands instill the Holy Spirit in the apostles, whose mission is to convert the world's heathens.

overall composition, as well as the detailed treatment of the figures, contrast with the much more sedate representation of the second coming (FIG. 6-19) at Moissac, where a grid of horizontal and vertical lines contains almost all the figures. The sharp differences between the two tympana highlight the regional diversity of Romanesque art.

The world's heathen, the objects of the apostles' mission, appear on the lintel below and in eight compartments around the tympanum. The portrayals of the yet-to-be-converted constitute a medieval anthropological encyclopedia. Present are the legendary giant-eared Panotii of India, Pygmies (who require ladders to mount horses), and a host of other races, some characterized by a dog's head, others by a pig's snout, and still others by flaming hair. The assembly of agitated figures also includes hunchbacks, mutes, blind men, and lame men. Humanity, still suffering, awaits the salvation to come. As at Moissac and Autun, as worshipers passed through the portal, the tympanum established God's omnipotence and presented the Church as the road to salvation.

Crusades *Mission of the Apostles* was an ideal choice for the Vézelay tympanum. Vézelay is more closely associated with the Crusades than any other church in Europe. The *Crusades* (taking of the Cross) were mass armed pilgrimages, whose stated purpose was to wrest the Christian shrines of the Holy Land from Muslim control. Similar vows bound Crusaders

and pilgrims. They hoped not only to atone for sins and win salvation but also to glorify God and extend the power of the Church. Pope Urban II (r. 1088–1099) had intended to preach the launching of the First Crusade at Vézelay in 1095. In 1147, Bernard of Clairvaux called for the Second Crusade at Vézelay, and King Louis VII of France took up the cross there. In 1190, it was from Vézelay that King Richard the Lionhearted of England and King Philip Augustus of France set out on the Third Crusade. The spirit of the Crusades determined in part the iconography of the Vézelay tympanum. The Crusades were a kind of "second mission of the apostles" to convert the infidel.

Moralia in Job Unlike monumental stone sculpture, the art of painting needed no "revival" in the Romanesque period. Monasteries had been producing large numbers of illuminated manuscripts for centuries. One of the major Romanesque scriptoria was at the abbey of Cîteaux, mother church of the Cistercian order. Just before Bernard of Clairveaux joined the monastery in 1112, the monks completed work on an illuminated copy of Saint Gregory's (Pope Gregory the Great, r. 590–604) *Moralia in Job.* It is an example of Cistercian illumination before Bernard's passionate opposition to monastic figural art led in 1134 to a Cistercian ban on elaborate paintings in manuscripts. After 1134, the Cistercian order prohibited full-page illustrations, and even initial letters

6-23 Initial *R* with knight fighting a dragon, folio 4 verso of the *Moralia in Job,* from Cîteaux, France, ca. 1115–1125. Ink and tempera on vellum, 1′ 1¾″ × 9¼″. Bibliothèque Municipale, Dijon.

Ornamented initials date to the Hiberno-Saxon era (FIG. 6-1), but this artist translated the theme into Romanesque terms. The duel between knight and dragons symbolized a monk's spiritual struggle.

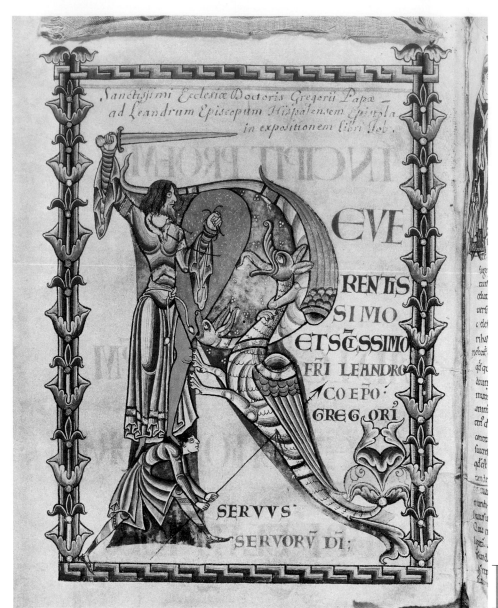

had to be nonfigurative and of a single color. The historiated initial reproduced here (FIG. **6-23**) clearly would have been in violation of Bernard's ban if it had not been painted before his prohibition took effect. A knight, his squire, and two roaring dragons form an intricate letter *R,* the initial letter of the salutation *Reverentissimo.* This page is the opening of Gregory's letter to "the most revered" Leander, bishop of Seville, Spain. The knight is a slender, regal figure who raises his shield and sword against the dragons while the squire, crouching beneath him, runs a lance through one of the monsters.

Ornamented initials date to the Hiberno-Saxon period (FIG. 6-1), but in the *Moralia in Job,* the artist translated the theme into Romanesque terms. The Leander page may be a reliable picture of a medieval baron's costume. The typically French Romanesque banding of the torso and partitioning of the folds are evident, but the master painter deftly avoided stiffness and angularity. The partitioning here accentuates the knight's verticality and elegance and the thrusting action of his servant. The flowing sleeves add a spirited flourish to the swordsman's gesture. The knight, handsomely garbed, cavalierly wears no armor and calmly aims a single stroke, unmoved by the ferocious dragons lunging at him. The duel between knight and dragons may be an allegory of the spiritual struggle of monks against the Devil for the salvation of souls.

Holy Roman Empire and Italy

The Romanesque successors of the Ottonians were the Salians (r. 1027–1125), a dynasty of Franks. They ruled an empire corresponding roughly to present-day Germany and the Lombard region of northern Italy (MAP 6-1). Like their predecessors, the Salian emperors were important patrons of art and architecture, although, as elsewhere in Romanesque Europe, the monasteries remained great centers of artistic production.

Hildegard of Bingen The most prominent nun of the 12th century and one of the greatest religious figures of the Middle Ages was Hildegard of Bingen (1098–1179). Born into an aristocratic family that owned large estates in the German Rhineland, Hildegard began to have visions at a very early age, and her parents had her study to become a nun. In 1141, God instructed Hildegard to disclose her visions to the world. Bernard of Clairvaux certified in 1147 that those visions were authentic. Archbishop Heinrich of Mainz joined in the endorsement, and in 1148, the Cistercian pope Eugenius III (r. 1145–1153) formally authorized Hildegard "in the name of Christ and Saint Peter to publish all that she had learned from the Holy Spirit." At this time Hildegard became the abbess of a new convent built for her near Bingen. As reports of Hildegard's visions spread, kings, popes, barons, and prelates sought her counsel.

One of the most interesting Romanesque books is Hildegard's *Scivias* (*Know the Ways* [*Scite vias*] *of God*). On the opening page (FIG. **6-24**), Hildegard sits within a monastery experiencing her divine vision. Five long tongues of fire emanating from above enter her brain, just as she describes the

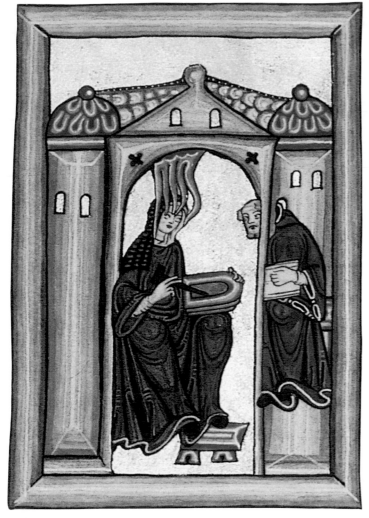

6-24 Hildegard receives her visions, detail of a facsimile of a lost folio in the Rupertsberger *Scivias* by Hildegard of Bingen, from Trier or Bingen, Germany, ca. 1150–1179. Abbey of St. Hildegard, Rüdesheim/Eibingen.

Hildegard of Bingen was one of the great religious figures of the Middle Ages. Here, she experiences a divine vision, shown as five tongues of fire emanating from above and entering her brain.

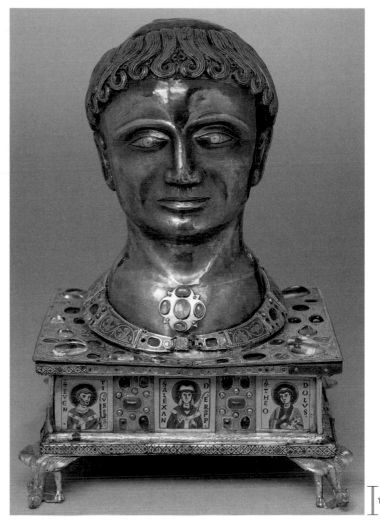

1 in.

6-25 Head reliquary of Saint Alexander, from the abbey church, Stavelot, Belgium, 1145. Silver repoussé (partly gilt), gilt bronze, gems, pearls, and enamel. 1' 5¼" high. Musées Royaux d'Art et d'Histoire, Brussels.

This reliquary is typical in the use of costly materials to house saints' relics. The combination of an idealized classical head with Byzantine-style enamels underscores the stylistic diversity of Romanesque art.

experience in the accompanying text. Hildegard immediately sets down what has been revealed to her on a wax tablet resting on her left knee. Nearby, the monk Volmar, Hildegard's confessor, copies into a book all she has written. Here, in a singularly dramatic context, is a picture of the essential nature of ancient and medieval book manufacture—individual scribes copying and recopying texts by hand.

Reliquary of Saint Alexander As noted, Romanesque church officials competed with one another in the display of relics and often expended large sums on elaborate containers to house them. The *reliquary* of Saint Alexander (FIG. **6-25**), made in 1145 for Abbot Wibald of Stavelot in Belgium to house the relics of Pope Alexander II (r. 1061–1073), is one of the finest examples. The idealized head, fashioned in beaten (*repoussé*) silver with bronze gilding for the hair, resembles portraits of youthful Roman emperors such as Augustus (FIG. I-8) and Constantine (FIG. 3-50). The saint wears a col-

lar of jewels and enamel plaques around his neck. Enamels and gems also adorn the box on which the head is mounted. The three plaques on the front depict Saints Eventius, Alexander, and Theodolus. The nine plaques on the other three sides represent female allegorical figures—Wisdom, Piety, and Humility among them. Although a local artist produced these enamels in the Meuse River region, the models were surely Byzantine. Saint Alexander's reliquary underscores the multiple sources of Romanesque art, as well as its stylistic diversity. Not since antiquity had people journeyed as extensively as they did in the Romanesque period, and artists regularly saw works of wide geographic origin. Abbot Wibald himself epitomizes the well-traveled 12th-century clergyman. He was abbot of Montecassino in southern Italy and participated in the Second Crusade. Frederick Barbarossa (Holy Roman Emperor, r. 1152–1190) sent him to Constantinople to arrange Frederick's wedding to the niece of the Byzantine emperor Manuel Comnenus.

6-26 Interior of Sant'Ambrogio (looking east), Milan, Italy, late 11th to early 12th century.

The architect of this Milanese church was one of the first to use groin vaults in the nave. Each nave bay corresponds to two aisle bays. The alternate-support system complements this modular plan.

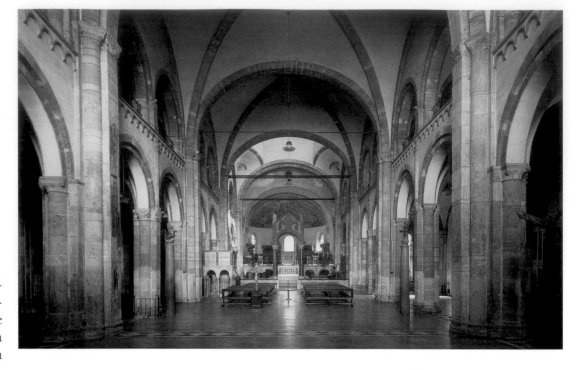

Milan Nowhere is the regional diversity of Romanesque art and architecture more readily apparent than in Italy. Developments in Lombardy parallel those elsewhere in the Holy Roman Empire, but in central Italy the Early Christian tradition remained very strong. The Lombard church of Sant'Ambrogio (FIG. **6-26**), erected in Milan in the late 11th or early 12th century in honor of Saint Ambrose, the city's first bishop (d. 397), is an example of the experimentation with different kinds of vaulting that characterizes Romanesque architecture north of the Alps. Sant'Ambrogio has a nave and two aisles but no transept. Above each inner aisle is a tribune gallery. Each nave bay consists of a full square flanked by two small squares in each aisle, all covered with groin vaults.

The technical problems of building groin vaults of cut stone (as opposed to concrete, knowledge of which did not survive the fall of Rome) at first limited their use to the covering of small areas, such as the individual bays of the aisles of Saint-Sernin (FIGS. 6-15 and 6-16) at Toulouse. In Sant'Ambrogio, the nave vaults are slightly domical, rising higher than the transverse arches. The windows in the octagonal dome over the last bay provide the major light source for the otherwise

6-27 Cathedral complex (looking northeast), Pisa, Italy; cathedral begun 1063; baptistery begun 1153; campanile begun 1174. ◼◢

Pisa's cathedral more closely resembles Early Christian basilicas than structurally more experimental French and German Romanesque churches. Separate bell towers and baptisteries are Italian features.

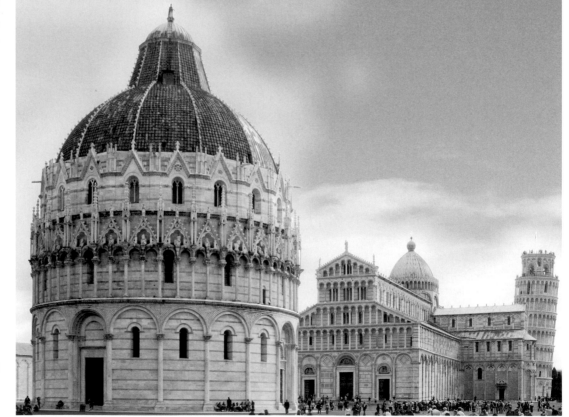

rather dark interior. (The building lacks a clerestory.) The emphatic alternate-support system perfectly reflects the geometric regularity of the plan. The lightest pier moldings stop at the gallery level, and the heavier ones rise to support the nave vaults. The compound piers even continue into the ponderous vaults, which have supporting arches, or *ribs,* along their groins. This is one of the first instances of *rib vaulting,* a salient characteristic of mature Romanesque and of later Gothic architecture (see "The Gothic Rib Vault," Chapter 7, page 194).

Pisa Although the widespread use of stone vaults in 11th- and 12th-century churches inspired the term *Romanesque,* Italian Romanesque churches outside Lombardy usually retained the wooden roofs of their Early Christian predecessors. The cathedral complex (FIG. **6-27**) at Pisa dramatically testifies to the regional diversity of Romanesque architecture. The cathedral, its freestanding *campanile* (bell tower), and the baptistery, where infants and converts were initiated into the Christian community, present a rare opportunity to study a coherent group of three Romanesque buildings. Save for the upper portion of the baptistery, with its remodeled Gothic exterior, the three structures are stylistically homogeneous.

Construction of Pisa Cathedral began first—in 1063, the same year work began on Saint Mark's (FIG. 4-23) in Venice, another prosperous maritime city. The spoils of a naval victory over the Muslims off Palermo in Sicily in 1062 funded the Pisan project. Pisa Cathedral is large, with a nave and four aisles, and is one of the most impressive and majestic Romanesque churches. At first glance, the cathedral resembles an Early Christian basilica, but its broadly projecting transept with apses, the crossing dome, and the facade's multiple arcade galleries distinguish it as Romanesque. So too does the rich marble *incrustation* (wall decoration consisting of bright panels of different colors, as in the Pantheon's interior; FIG. 3-40). The cathedral's campanile is Pisa's famous Leaning Tower (FIG. 6-27, *right*). Graceful arcaded galleries mark the tower's stages and repeat the cathedral's facade motif, effectively relating the round campanile to its mother building. The tilted vertical axis of the tower is the result of a settling foundation. The tower began to "lean" even while under construction, and now inclines some 5.5 degrees out of plumb at the top.

Normandy and England

After their conversion to Christianity in the early 10th century, the Vikings—Scandinavian traders and pirates named after the *viks* ("coves" or "trading places" of the Norwegian coastline)—settled on the northern French coast in present-day Normandy, the home of the Norsemen, or Normans. The Normans quickly developed a distinctive Romanesque architectural style that became the major source of French Gothic architecture.

Caen Most critics consider the abbey church of Saint-Étienne at Caen the masterpiece of Norman Romanesque architecture. Begun by William of Normandy (William the Conqueror; see pages 186–188) in 1067, work must have advanced rapidly because the Normans buried him in the church in 1087. Saint-Étienne's west facade (FIG. **6-28**) is a striking design rooted in the tradition of Carolingian and Ottonian westworks, but it reveals a new unified organizational scheme. Four large buttresses divide the facade into three bays that correspond to the nave and aisles. Above the buttresses, the towers also display a triple division and a progressively greater piercing of their walls from lower to upper stages. (The culminating spires are a Gothic addition.) The tripartite division extends throughout the facade, both vertically and horizontally, organizing it into a close-knit, well-integrated design consistent with the careful and methodical planning of the entire structure.

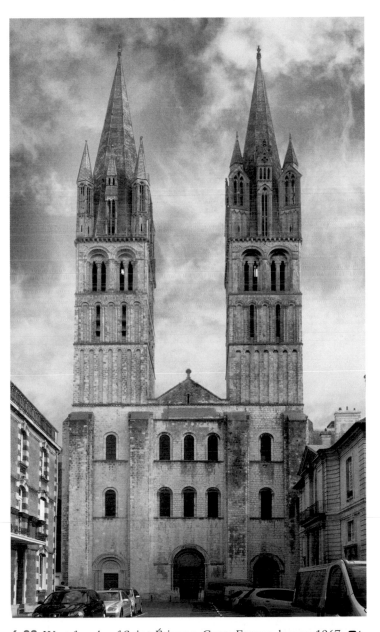

6-28 West facade of Saint-Étienne, Caen, France, begun 1067. ◼◀

The division of Saint-Étienne's facade into three parts corresponding to the nave and aisles reflects the methodical planning of the entire structure. The towers also have a tripartite design.

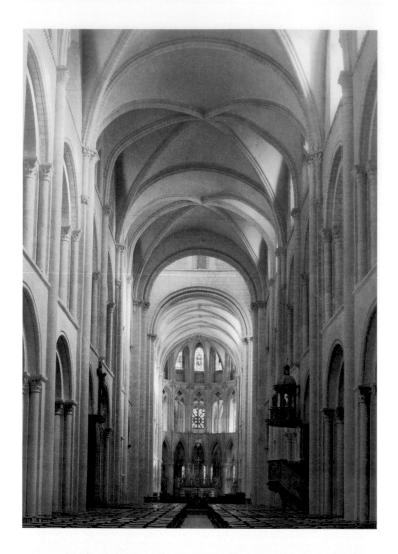

6-29 Interior of Saint-Étienne (looking east), Caen, France, vaulted ca. 1115–1120. ■◀

The six-part groin vaults of Saint-Étienne made clerestory windows possible. The three-story elevation with its large arched openings provides ample light and makes the nave appear taller than it is.

The original design of Saint-Étienne called for a timber roof, but the Caen nave (FIG. **6-29**) had compound piers with simple engaged half columns alternating with piers with half columns attached to pilasters. When the Normans decided to install groin vaults around 1115, the existing alternating compound piers proved a good match. Those piers soar all the way to the vaults' springing. Their branching ribs divide the large square-vault compartments into six sections—a *sexpartite vault*. The vaults rise high enough to provide room for clerestory windows. The resulting three-story elevation, with its large arched openings, allows ample light to reach the interior. It also makes the nave appear taller than it is. As in Sant'Ambrogio (FIG. 6-26), the Norman building has rib vaults. The diagonal and transverse ribs form a structural skeleton that partially supports the still fairly massive paneling between them. But despite the heavy masonry, the large windows and reduced interior wall surface give Saint-Étienne's nave a light and airy quality unusual in the Romanesque period.

Durham Cathedral William of Normandy's conquest of Anglo-Saxon England in 1066 began a new epoch in English history. In architecture, it signaled the importation of

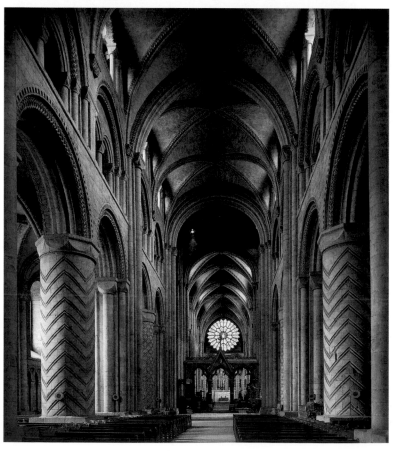

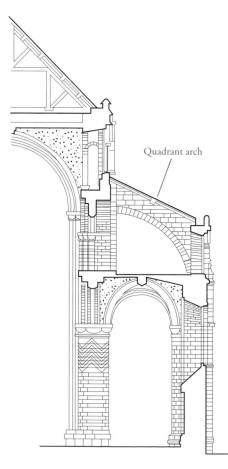

Quadrant arch

6-30 Interior (*left;* looking east) and lateral section (*right*) of Durham Cathedral, Durham, England, begun ca. 1093.

Durham Cathedral is the first example of a rib groin vault placed over a three-story nave. The architect used quadrant arches in place of groin vaults in the tribune as buttresses of the nave vaults.

Norman Romanesque building and design methods. Construction of Durham Cathedral (FIG. **6-30**), on the Scottish frontier of northern England, began around 1093—before the remodeling of the Caen church. Durham Cathedral, however, was a vaulted structure from the beginning. Consequently, the pattern of the ribs of the nave's groin vaults corresponds perfectly to the design of the arcade below. Each seven-part nave vault covers two bays. Large, simple pillars ornamented with abstract designs (diamond, chevron, and cable patterns, all originally painted) alternate with compound piers that carry the transverse arches of the vaults. The pier-vault relationship scarcely could be more visible or the building's structural rationale better expressed.

The bold surface patterning of the pillars in the Durham nave is a reminder that the raising of imposing stone edifices such as the Romanesque churches of England and Normandy required more than just the talents of master designers. A corps of expert masons had to transform rough stone blocks into the precise shapes necessary for their specific place in the church's fabric. Although thousands of simple quadrangular blocks make up the great walls of these buildings, the stone-cutters also had to produce large numbers of blocks of far more complex shapes. To cover the nave and aisles, the masons had to carve blocks with concave faces to conform to the curve of the vault. Also required were blocks with projecting moldings for the ribs, blocks with convex surfaces for the pillars or with multiple profiles for the compound piers, and so forth. It was an immense undertaking, and it is no wonder medieval building campaigns often lasted for decades.

Durham Cathedral is the earliest example known of a rib groin vault placed over a three-story nave. In the nave's western parts, completed before 1130, the rib vaults have slightly pointed arches, bringing together for the first time two key elements that determined the structural evolution of Gothic architecture. Also of great significance is the way the English builders buttressed the nave vaults. The lateral section (FIG. **6-30**, *right*) exposes the simple *quadrant arches* (arches whose curve extends for one-quarter of a circle's circumference) that take the place of groin vaults in the Durham tribune. The structural descendants of these quadrant arches are the flying buttresses that epitomize the mature Gothic solution to church construction (see "The Gothic Cathedral," Chapter 7, page 197).

Bury Bible Many of the finest illustrated manuscripts of the Romanesque age were the work of monks in English scriptoria, following in the tradition of Hiberno-Saxon books. The *Bury Bible,* produced at the Bury Saint Edmunds abbey in England around 1135, exemplifies the sumptuous illumination common to the large Bibles used in wealthy Romanesque abbeys not subject to the Cistercian restrictions on painted manuscripts. One page (FIG. **6-31**) shows two scenes

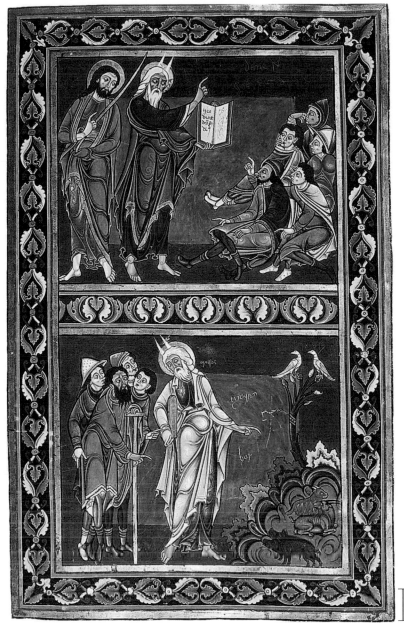

1 in.

6-31 MASTER HUGO, *Moses Expounding the Law,* folio 94 recto of the *Bury Bible,* from Bury Saint Edmunds, England, ca. 1135. Ink and tempera on vellum, 1′ 8″ × 1′ 2″. Corpus Christi College, Cambridge.

Master Hugo was a rare Romanesque lay artist, one of the emerging class of professional artists and artisans who depended for their livelihood on commissions from wealthy monasteries.

from Deuteronomy framed by symmetrical leaf motifs in softly glowing harmonized colors. The upper register depicts *Moses Expounding the Law.* The prophet has horns, consistent with Saint Jerome's translation of the Hebrew word that also means "rays." The lower panel portrays Moses pointing out the clean and unclean beasts. The gestures are slow and gentle and have quiet dignity. The figures of Moses and Aaron seem to glide. This presentation is quite different from the abrupt emphasis and spastic movement of contemporaneous Romanesque relief sculptures. Yet patterning remains in the multiple divisions of the draped limbs, the lightly shaded volumes connected with sinuous lines and ladderlike folds.

The artist responsible for the *Bury Bible* is known: MASTER HUGO, who was also a sculptor and metalworker. With Gislebertus (FIG. 6-21), Hugo was one of the small but growing number of Romanesque artists who signed their works or whose names were recorded. In the 12th century, artists, illuminators as well as sculptors, increasingly began to identify themselves. Although most medieval artists remained anonymous, the contrast of the Romanesque period with the early Middle Ages is striking. Hugo apparently was a secular artist, one of the emerging class of professional artists and artisans who depended for their livelihood on commissions from well-endowed monasteries. These artists resided in towns rather than within secluded abbey walls, and they traveled frequently to find work. They were the exception, however, and most Romanesque scribes and illuminators continued to be monks and nuns working anonymously in the service of God.

Eadwine Psalter Named for the English monk EADWINE THE SCRIBE, the *Eadwine Psalter* contains 166 illustrations. The last page (FIG. **6-32**), however, presents a rare picture of a Romanesque artist at work. The style of the Eadwine portrait resembles that of the *Bury Bible,* but although the patterning is still firm (notably in the cowl and the thigh), the drapery falls more softly and follows the movements of the body beneath it. Here, the abstract patterning of many Romanesque painted and sculpted garments yielded slightly, but clearly, to the requirements of more naturalistic representation. The Romanesque artist's instinct for decorating the surface remained, as is apparent in the gown's whorls and spirals. Significantly, the artist painted those interior lines very lightly so they would not conflict with the functional lines containing them.

The "portrait" of Eadwine—it is probably a generic type and not a specific likeness—is in the long tradition of author portraits in ancient and medieval manuscripts, although the true author of the *Eadwine Psalter* is King David. Eadwine exaggerated his importance by likening himself to an evangelist writing his Gospel (FIGS. 6-4 and 6-5) and by including an inscription within the inner frame giving his name and proclaiming he is a "prince among scribes." He declares the excellence of his work will cause his fame to endure forever, and consequently he can offer his book as an acceptable gift to God. Eadwine, like other Romanesque sculptors and painters who signed their works, may have been concerned for his fame, but these artists, whether clergy or laity, were as yet unaware of the concepts of fine art and fine artist. To them, their work existed not for its own sake but for God's. Nonetheless, works such as this one are an early sign of a new attitude toward the role of the artist

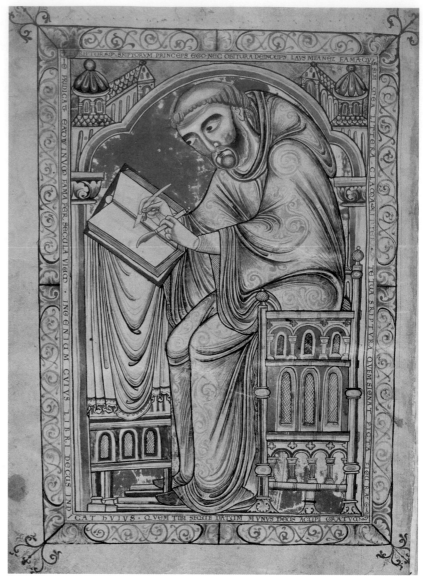

6-32 EADWINE THE SCRIBE, Eadwine the scribe at work, folio 283 verso of the *Eadwine Psalter,* ca. 1160–1170. Ink and tempera on vellum. Trinity College, Cambridge. ◼◀

Although he humbly offered his book as a gift to God, the English monk Eadwine added an inscription to his portrait declaring that he was a "prince among scribes" whose fame would endure forever.

in society that presages the reemergence in the Renaissance of the classical notion of individual artistic genius.

Bayeux Tapestry The most famous work of English Romanesque art is neither a book nor Christian in subject. The so-called *Bayeux Tapestry* (FIGS. **6-33** and **6-34**) is unique in medieval art. It is not a woven *tapestry,* but rather an *embroidery* made of wool sewn on linen. Closely related to Romanesque manuscript illumination, its borders contain the kinds of real and imaginary animals found in contemporaneous books, and an explanatory Latin text sewn in thread accompanies many of the pictures. Some 20 inches high and about 230 feet long, the *Bayeux Tapestry* is a continuous, friezelike, pictorial narrative of

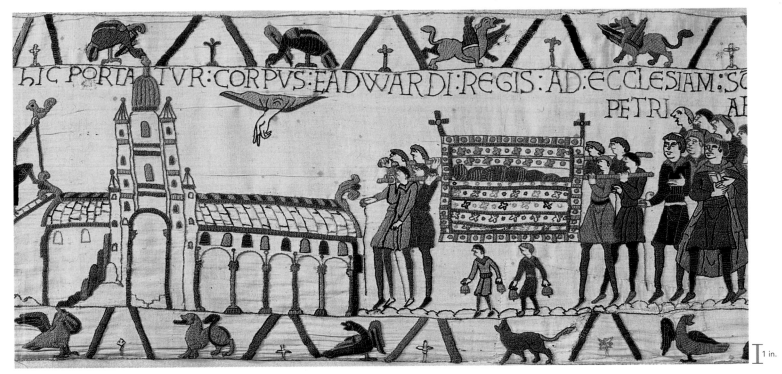

6-33 Funeral procession to Westminster Abbey, detail of the *Bayeux Tapestry*, from Bayeux Cathedral, Bayeux, France, ca. 1070–1080. Embroidered wool on linen, 1′ 8″ high (entire length of fabric, 229′ 8″ long). Centre Guillaume le Conquérant, Bayeux. ◼◀

The *Bayeux Tapestry* is not a tapestry but rather an embroidery. The women needleworkers employed eight colors of dyed wool yarn and sewed the threads onto the linen fabric.

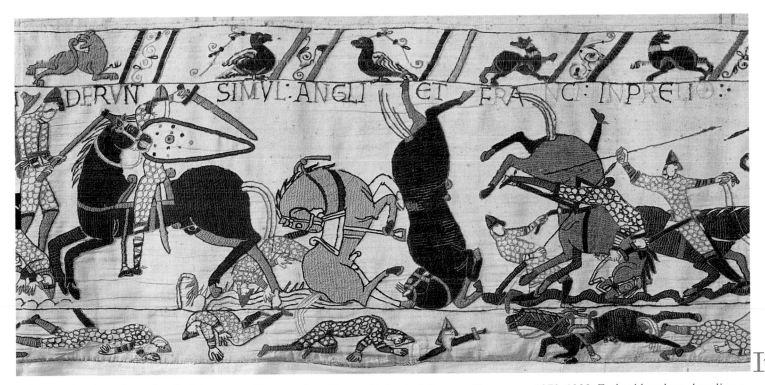

6-34 Battle of Hastings, detail of the *Bayeux Tapestry*, from Bayeux Cathedral, Bayeux, France, ca. 1070–1080. Embroidered wool on linen, 1′ 8″ high (entire length of fabric, 229′ 8″ long). Centre Guillaume le Conquérant, Bayeux. ◼◀

The *Bayeux Tapestry* is unique in medieval art. Like historical narratives in Roman art, it depicts contemporaneous events in full detail, as in the scroll-like frieze of Trajan's Column (FIG. 3-1).

a crucial moment in England's history and of the events leading up to it. The Norman defeat of the Anglo-Saxons at Hastings in 1066 brought England under the control of the Normans, uniting all of England and much of France under one rule. The dukes of Normandy became the kings of England. Commissioned by Bishop Odo, the half brother of the conquering Duke William, the embroidery may have been sewn by women at the Norman court. Many art historians, however, believe it was the work of English stitchers in Kent, where Odo was earl after the Norman conquest. Odo donated the work to Bayeux Cathedral (hence its nickname), but it is uncertain whether it was originally intended for display in the church's nave, where the theme would have been a curious choice.

The events that precipitated the Norman invasion of England are well documented. In 1066, Edward the Confessor (r. 1042–1066), the Anglo-Saxon king of England, died. The Normans believed Edward had recognized William of Normandy as his rightful heir. But the crown went to Harold, earl of Wessex, the king's Anglo-Saxon brother-in-law, who had sworn an oath of allegiance to William. The betrayed Normans, descendants of the seafaring Vikings, boarded their ships, crossed the English Channel, and crushed Harold's forces.

Illustrated here are two episodes of the epic tale as represented in the *Bayeux Tapestry*. The first detail (FIG. 6-33) depicts King Edward's funeral procession. The hand of God points the way to the church in London where he was buried—Westminster Abbey, consecrated on December 28, 1065, just a few days before Edward's death. The church was one of the first Romanesque buildings erected in England, and the embroiderers took pains to record its main features, including the imposing crossing tower and the long nave with tribunes. Here William was crowned king of England on Christmas Day, 1066. The second detail (FIG. 6-34) shows the Battle of Hastings in progress. The Norman cavalry cuts down the English defenders. Filling the lower border are the dead and wounded, although the upper register continues the animal motifs of the rest of the embroidery. The Romanesque artist co-opted some of the characteristic motifs of Greco-Roman battle scenes, for example, the horses with twisted necks and contorted bodies (compare FIG. 2-50), but rendered the figures in the Romanesque manner. Linear patterning and flat color replaced classical three-dimensional volume and modeling in light and dark hues.

The *Bayeux Tapestry* stands apart from all other Romanesque artworks in depicting in full detail an event at a time shortly after it occurred, recalling the historical narratives of ancient Roman art. Art historians have often likened the Norman embroidery to the scroll-like frieze of the Column of Trajan (FIGS. 3-1 and 3-36). Like the Roman account, the story told on the textile is the conqueror's version of history, a proclamation of national pride. As in the ancient frieze, the narrative is not confined to battlefield successes. It is a complete chronicle of events. Included are the preparations for war, with scenes depicting the felling and splitting of trees for ship construction, the loading of equipment onto the vessels, the cooking and serving of meals, and so forth. In this respect, the *Bayeux Tapestry* is the most *Roman*-esque work of Romanesque art.

Early Medieval and Romanesque Europe

Early Medieval Art

▌ The surviving artworks of the period following the fall of Rome in 410 are almost exclusively small-scale status symbols, especially items of personal adornment featuring cloisonné decoration consisting of abstract and zoomorphic motifs. Especially characteristic are intertwined animal and interlace patterns.

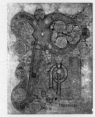

Book of Kells, late eighth or early ninth century

▌ Art historians call the Christian art of early medieval Ireland and Britain Hiberno-Saxon. The most important extant artworks are the illuminated manuscripts produced in the monastic scriptoria of Ireland and Northumbria. The most distinctive features of these books are the full pages devoted neither to text nor to illustration but to pure embellishment. Some text pages present the initial letters of important passages enlarged and transformed into elaborate decorative patterns.

▌ In 800, Pope Leo III crowned Charlemagne, king of the Franks since 768, emperor of Rome (r. 800–814). Charlemagne reunited much of western Europe and initiated a conscious revival of the art and culture of Early Christian Rome during the Carolingian period (768–877). Carolingian illuminators merged the illusionism of classical painting with the northern linear tradition. Carolingian sculptors revived the Early Christian tradition of depicting Christ as a statuesque youth. Carolingian architects looked to Ravenna and Early Christian Rome for models but transformed their sources, introducing, for example, the twin-tower western facade for basilicas and employing strict modular plans for entire monasteries as well as individual buildings.

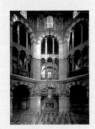

Palatine Chapel, Aachen, 792–805

▌ In the 10th century, a new line of emperors, the Ottonians (r. 919–1024), consolidated the eastern part of Charlemagne's former empire and sought to preserve and enrich the culture and tradition of the Carolingian period. Ottonian architects built basilican churches incorporating the towers and westworks of their Carolingian models but introduced the alternate-support system and tribune galleries into the nave elevation. Ottonian sculptors revived the art of monumental sculpture in works such as the *Gero Crucifix* and the colossal bronze doors of Saint Michael's at Hildesheim.

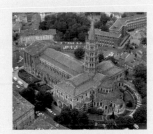

Saint Michael's, Hildesheim, 1001–1031

Romanesque Art

▌ *Romanesque* takes its name from the Romanlike barrel and groin vaults based on round arches employed in many European churches built between 1050 and 1200. Romanesque vaults, however, are made of stone, not concrete. Numerous churches sprang up along the French pilgrimage roads leading to the shrine of Saint James at Santiago de Compostela. These churches were large enough to accommodate crowds of pilgrims who came to view the relics displayed in radiating chapels off the ambulatory and transept. Elsewhere, especially in the Holy Roman Empire and in Normandy and England, innovative architects began to use groin vaults in naves and introduced the three-story elevation of nave arcade, tribune, and clerestory.

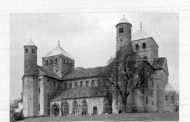

Saint-Sernin, Toulouse, ca. 1070–1120

▌ The Romanesque period also brought the revival of monumental stone relief sculpture in cloisters and especially in church portals, where scenes of Christ as last judge often greeted the faithful as they entered the doorway to the road to salvation. The sculptor Gislebertus was one of a growing number of Romanesque artists who signed their works. The names of some Romanesque manuscript painters are also known, including Master Hugo, a rare instance of a professional lay artist during the early Middle Ages.

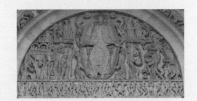

Gislebertus, *Last Judgment*, Autun, ca. 1120–1135

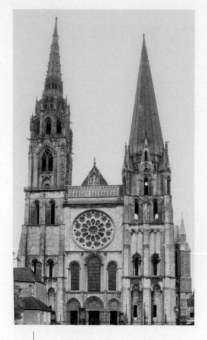

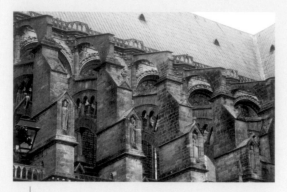

Architectural historians consider the rebuilt Chartres Cathedral the first great monument of High Gothic architecture. It is the first church to have been planned from the beginning with flying buttresses.

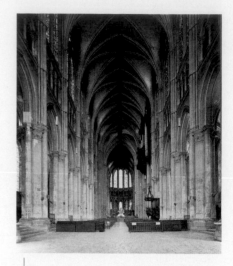

Chartres Cathedral is the key monument of both Early and High Gothic architecture. The west facade still has much in common with Romanesque designs, but features statues on the door jambs.

Chartres set the pattern for High Gothic cathedrals in the use of four-part rib vaults springing from pointed arches and in the introduction of a three-story nave elevation (arcade, triforium, clerestory).

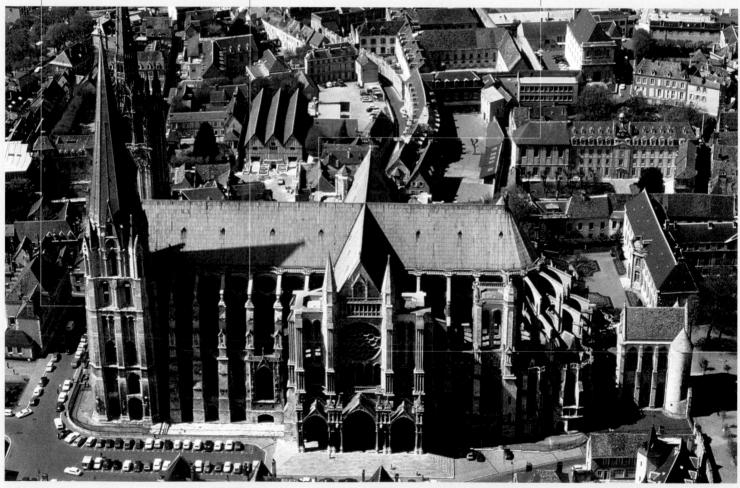

7-1 Aerial view of Chartres Cathedral (looking north), Chartres, France, as rebuilt after 1194. ▣◀

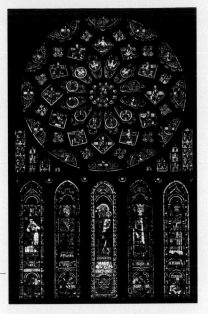

Flying buttresses made possible the replacement of heavy masonry walls with immense stained-glass windows, which transformed natural sunlight into divine light of various hues.

7

Gothic and Late Medieval Europe

THE AGE OF THE GREAT CATHEDRALS

In 1550, Giorgio Vasari (1511–1574) first used *Gothic* as a term of ridicule to describe late medieval art and architecture, which he attributed to the Goths and regarded as "monstrous and barbarous."[1] With the publication that year of his influential *Introduction to the Three Arts of Design*, Vasari codified for all time the notion the early Renaissance artist Lorenzo Ghiberti (1378–1455) had already advanced in his *Commentarii*, namely that the Middle Ages was a period of decline. The Italian humanists, who regarded Greco-Roman art as the standard of excellence, believed the uncouth Goths were responsible both for the downfall of Rome and for the decline of the classical style in art and architecture. They regarded "Gothic" art with contempt and considered it ugly and crude.

In the 13th and 14th centuries, however, Chartres Cathedral (FIG. **7-1**) and similar French buildings set the standard throughout most of Europe. For the clergy and the lay public alike, the great cathedrals towering over their towns were not distortions of the classical style but *opus modernum* (modern work), glorious images of the City of God, the Heavenly Jerusalem, which they were privileged to build on earth.

The Gothic cathedral was the unique product of an era of peace and widespread economic prosperity, deep spirituality, and extraordinary technological innovation. The essential ingredients of these towering shrines were lofty masonry rib vaults on pointed arches invisibly held in place by external (flying) buttresses, and interiors illuminated with mystical light coming through huge colored-glass windows (see "The Gothic Cathedral," page 197).

The key monument of this exciting new style is Chartres Cathedral, discussed in detail later. Begun around 1145, the church dedicated to Our Lady (Notre Dame), the Virgin Mary, housed her mantle, a precious relic. The lower parts of the massive west towers and the portals between them are all that remain of that Early Gothic cathedral destroyed by fire in 1194 before it had been completed. Reconstruction of the church began immediately, but in the High Gothic style with flying buttresses, rib vaults on pointed arches, and immense stained-glass windows. Chartres Cathedral is therefore a singularly instructive composite of a 12th-century facade and a 13th-century nave and transept, and documents the early and mature stages of the development of Gothic architecture in the place of its birth, the region around Paris called the Île-de-France.

LATE MEDIEVAL EUROPE

The 12th through 14th centuries were a time of profound change in European society. The focus of both intellectual and religious life shifted definitively from monasteries in the countryside and pilgrimage churches to rapidly expanding cities with enormous cathedrals reaching to the sky. In these new urban centers, prosperous merchants made their homes and formed *guilds* (professional associations), and scholars founded the first universities. Although the papacy was at the height of its power, and Christian knights still waged Cru-sades against the Muslims, the independent secular nations of modern Europe were beginning to take shape (MAP 7-1).

By the 13th century, the architectural style of Chartres Cathedral and other buildings in Paris and its environs had spread throughout western Europe. In fact, some late medieval writers referred to Gothic buildings as *opus francigenum* (French work). Nevertheless, many regional variants existed within European Gothic, just as distinct regional styles characterized the Romanesque period. Therefore, this chapter deals with contemporaneous developments in the major regions—France, England, the Holy Roman Empire, and Italy—in separate sections.

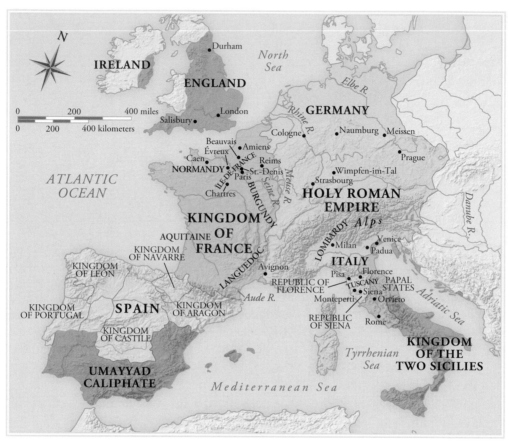

MAP 7-1 Europe around 1200.

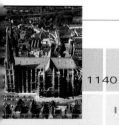

Gothic and Late Medieval Europe

1140	Early Gothic	1194	High Gothic	1300	Late Gothic	1400

Early Gothic

▌ Abbot Suger begins rebuilding the French royal abbey church at Saint-Denis with rib vaults on pointed arches and stained-glass windows

▌ Introduced at Saint-Denis, sculpted jamb figures also adorn all three portals of the west facade of Chartres Cathedral

High Gothic

▌ The rebuilt Chartres Cathedral sets the pattern for High Gothic churches: four-part nave vaults braced by external flying buttresses, three-story elevation (arcade, triforium, clerestory), and stained-glass windows in place of heavy masonry

▌ At Chartres and Reims in France, at Naumburg in Germany, and elsewhere, statues become more independent of their architectural setting

▌ Manuscript illumination moves from monastic scriptoria to urban lay workshops, especially in Paris

Late Gothic

▌ The Perpendicular style in England emphasizes surface embellishment over structural clarity

▌ In Florence, Giotto, considered the first Renaissance artist, pioneers a naturalistic approach to painting based on observation

▌ In Siena, Duccio softens the Byzantine-inspired maniera greca and humanizes religious subject matter

▌ Secular themes emerge as important subjects in civic commissions, as in the frescoes of Siena's Palazzo Pubblico

FRANCE

About 1130, King Louis VI (r. 1108–1137) moved his official residence to Paris, spurring much commercial activity and a great building boom. Paris soon became the leading city of France, indeed of northern Europe. Although Rome remained the religious center of Western Christendom, Paris became its intellectual capital. The University of Paris attracted the best minds from all over Europe. Virtually every thinker of note in the Gothic world at some point studied or taught at Paris. Even in the Romanesque period, Paris was a center of learning. Its Cathedral School professors, known as Schoolmen, developed the philosophy called *Scholasticism*. Until the 12th century, both clergy and laymen considered truth the exclusive property of divine revelation as given in holy scripture. But the Schoolmen sought to demonstrate reason alone could lead to certain truths. Their goal was to prove the central articles of Christian faith by argument (*disputatio*). By the 13th century, the Schoolmen of Paris already had organized as a professional guild of master scholars, separate from the numerous Church schools the bishop of Paris oversaw. The structure of the Parisian guild served as the model for many other European universities.

Architecture and Architectural Decoration

Architectural historians generally agree Saint-Denis, a few miles north of Paris, was the birthplace of Gothic architecture. Dionysius (*Denis* in French) was the legendary saint who brought Christianity to Roman Gaul.

Suger and Saint-Denis On June 11, 1144, King Louis VII of France (r. 1137–1180), Queen Eleanor of Aquitaine, and an entourage of court members, together with five French archbishops and other distinguished clergy, converged on the Benedictine abbey church of Saint-Denis for the dedication of its new east end. The original Carolingian basilica housed the tomb of Saint Denis and those of nearly all the French kings. The basilica was France's royal church, the very symbol of the monarchy. By the early 12th century, however, the church was in disrepair and had become too small to accommodate the growing number of pilgrims. Its abbot, Suger (ca. 1081–1151), also believed the Carolingian shrine was of insufficient grandeur to serve as the official church of the French kings. In 1135, Suger began to rebuild Saint-Denis by erecting a new west facade with sculptured portals. Work began on the east end (FIGS. **7-2** and **7-3**) in 1140. Suger died before he could remodel the nave, but he attended the 1144 dedication of the new choir, ambulatory, and radiating chapels.

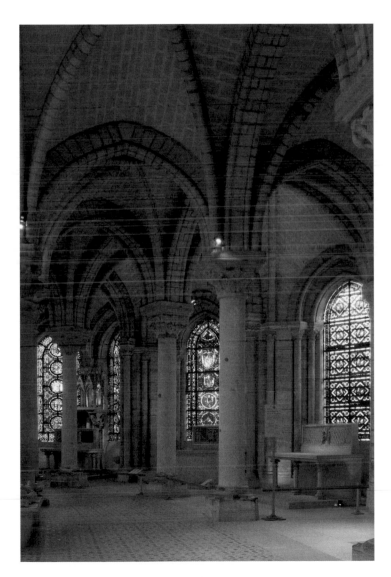

7-2 Ambulatory and radiating chapels (looking northeast), abbey church, Saint-Denis, France, 1140–1144. ▮◀

Abbot Suger's remodeling of Saint-Denis marked the beginning of Gothic architecture. Rib vaults with pointed arches spring from slender columns. The radiating chapels have stained-glass windows.

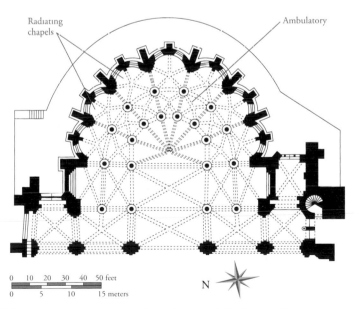

7-3 Plan of the east end, abbey church, Saint-Denis, France, 1140–1144 (after Sumner Crosby).

The innovative plan of the east end of Saint-Denis dates to Abbot Suger's lifetime. By using very light rib vaults, the builders were able to eliminate the walls between the radiating chapels.

The Gothic Rib Vault

The ancestors of the Gothic *rib vault* are the Romanesque vaults found at Caen (FIG. 6-29), Durham (FIG. 6-30), and elsewhere. The rib vault's distinguishing feature is the crossed, or diagonal, *ribs* (arches) under its groins, as seen in the Saint-Denis ambulatory and chapels (FIG. 7-2). The ribs form the *armature*, or skeletal framework, for constructing the vault. Gothic vaults generally have more thinly vaulted *webs* (the masonry between the ribs) than found in Romanesque vaults. But the chief difference between the two styles of rib vaults is the *pointed arch*, an integral part of the Gothic skeletal armature. French Romanesque architects (FIG. 6-18) borrowed the form from Muslim Spain and passed it to their Gothic successors. Pointed arches enabled Gothic builders to make the crowns of all the vault's arches approximately the same level, regardless of the space to be vaulted. The Romanesque architects could not achieve this with their semicircular arches.

The drawings in FIG. 7-4 illustrate this key difference. In FIG. 7-4a, the rectangle *ABCD* is an oblong nave bay to be vaulted. *AC* and *DB* are the diagonal ribs; *AB* and *DC*, the transverse arches; and *AD* and *BC*, the nave arcade's arches. If the architect uses semicircular arches (*AFB*, *BJC*, and *DHC*), their radii and, therefore, their heights (*EF*, *IJ*, and *GH*) will be different because the width of a semicircular arch determines its height. The result will be a vault (FIG. 7-4b) with higher transverse arches (*DHC*) than the arcade's arches (*CJB*). The vault's crown (*F*) will be still higher. If the builder uses pointed arches, the transverse (*DLC*) and arcade (*BKC*) arches can have the same heights (*GL* and *IK* in FIG. 7-4a). The result will be a Gothic rib vault (FIG. 7-4c) where the points of the arches (*L* and *K*) are at the same level as the vault's crown (*F*).

A major advantage of the Gothic vault is its flexibility, which enables the vaulting of compartments of varying shapes, as at Saint-Denis (FIG. 7-3). Pointed arches also channel the weight of the vaults more directly downward than do semicircular arches. The vaults therefore require less buttressing to hold them in place, in turn enabling the stonemasons to open up the walls and insert large windows beneath the arches. Because pointed arches also lead the eye upward, they make the vaults appear taller than they are. In FIG. 7-4, the crown (*F*) of both the Romanesque (b) and Gothic (c) vaults is the same height from the pavement, but the Gothic vault seems taller. Both the physical and visual properties of rib vaults with pointed arches aided Gothic builders in their quest for soaring height in church interiors.

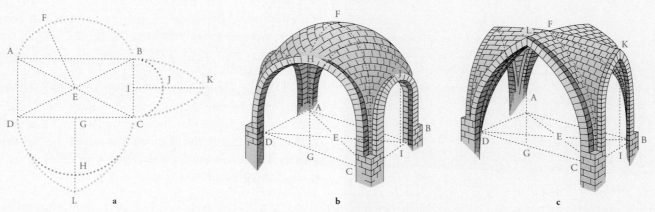

7-4 Diagram (**a**) and drawings of rib vaults with semicircular (**b**) and pointed (**c**) arches.

Pointed arches channel the weight of the rib vaults more directly downward than do semicircular arches, requiring less buttressing. Pointed arches also make the vaults appear taller than they are.

The remodeled portion of Saint-Denis represented a sharp break from past practice. Innovative rib vaults resting on pointed, or *ogival,* arches (see "The Gothic Rib Vault," above, and FIG. **7-4c**) cover the ambulatory and chapels (FIG. 7-2). These pioneering, exceptionally lightweight vaults spring from slender columns in the ambulatory and from the thin masonry walls framing the chapels. The lightness of the vaults enabled the builders to eliminate the walls between the chapels and open up the outer walls and fill them with stained-glass windows (see "Stained-Glass Windows," page 199). Suger and his contemporaries marveled at the "wonderful and uninterrupted light" that poured in through these "most sacred windows."[2] The abbot called the colored light *lux nova,* "new light." The polychrome rays coming through the windows shone on the walls and columns, almost dissolving them. The light-filled space made Suger feel as if he were "dwelling . . . in some strange region of the universe which neither exists entirely in the slime of the earth nor entirely in the purity of Heaven." In Suger's eyes, his splendid new church was a way station on the road to Paradise, which "transported [him] from this inferior to that higher world."[3] Both the new type of vaulting and the use of stained glass became hallmarks of French Gothic architecture.

Royal Portal, Chartres Saint-Denis is also the key monument of Early Gothic sculpture. Little of the sculpture Suger commissioned for the west facade of the abbey church survived the French Revolution of the late 18th century, but originally, statues of Old Testament kings, queens, and prophets attached to columns screened the jambs of all three doorways. This innovative design appeared immediately afterward at Chartres Cathedral (FIG. 7-1). Work on the west facade

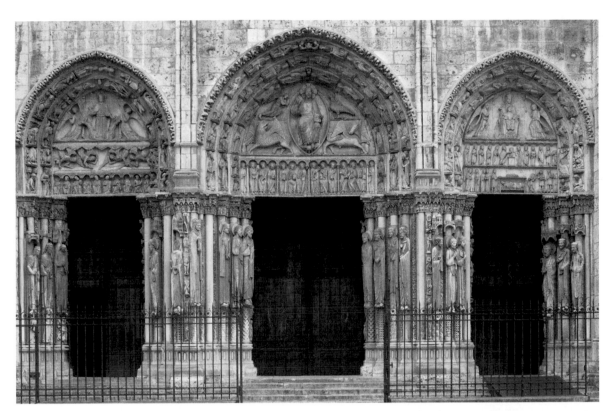

7-5 Royal Portal, west facade, Chartres Cathedral, Chartres, France, ca. 1145–1155. ■◀

The sculptures of the Royal Portal proclaim the majesty and power of Christ. The tympana depict, from left to right, Christ's ascension, the second coming, and Jesus in the lap of the Virgin Mary.

began around 1145. The west entrance or "Royal Portal" (FIG. **7-5**)—so named because of the figures of kings and queens (FIG. 7-6) flanking its three doorways—constitutes the most complete surviving ensemble of Early Gothic sculpture.

The iconographic program of the Royal Portal proclaims the majesty and power of Christ. Christ's ascension into Heaven appears in the tympanum of the left doorway. The second coming is the subject of the center tympanum, as at Moissac (FIG. 6-19). The tympanum in the right portal depicts Jesus in the lap of the Virgin Mary. Mary's prominence on the Chartres facade has no parallel in the sculptural programs of Romanesque church portals. At Chartres, the Virgin (Notre Dame) assumed a central role, a position she maintained throughout the Gothic period. As the Mother of the Savior, Mary stood compassionately between the last judge and the horrors of Hell, interceding for all her faithful. Worshipers in the later 12th and 13th centuries sang hymns to the Virgin and dedicated great cathedrals to her. Soldiers carried her image into battle on banners, and Mary's name joined Saint Denis's as part of the French king's battle cry. The Virgin became the spiritual lady of chivalry, and the Christian knight dedicated his life to her. The severity of Romanesque themes stressing the last judgment yielded to the gentleness of Gothic art, in which Mary is the kindly queen of Heaven.

Statues of Old Testament kings and queens (FIG. **7-6**) occupy the jambs flanking each doorway of the Royal Portal. They are the royal ancestors of Christ and, both figuratively and literally, support the New Testament figures above the doorways. They wear 12th-century clothes, and medieval observers may have regarded them as images of the kings and queens of France. (This was the motivation for vandalizing

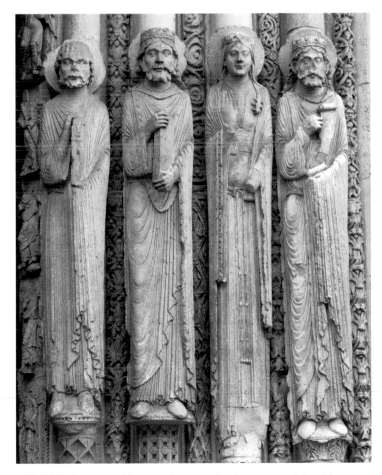

7-6 Old Testament kings and queen, jamb statues, right side of the central doorway of the Royal Portal, Chartres Cathedral, Chartres, France, ca. 1145–1155. ■◀

The biblical kings and queens of the Royal Portal are the royal ancestors of Christ. These Early Gothic jamb figures display the first signs of a new naturalism in European sculpture.

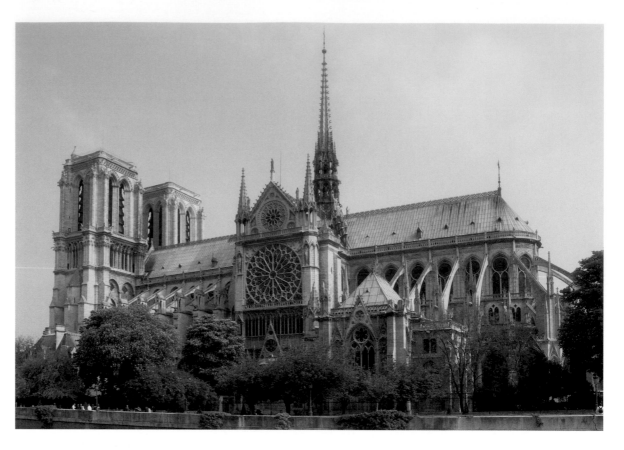

7-7 Notre-Dame (looking northwest), Paris, France, begun 1163; nave and flying buttresses, ca. 1180–1200; remodeled after 1225. ◼◀

Architects first used flying buttresses on a grand scale at the Cathedral of Notre-Dame in Paris. The buttresses countered the outward thrust of the nave vaults and held up the towering nave walls.

the comparable figures at Saint-Denis during the French Revolution.) The figures stand rigidly upright with their elbows held close against their hips. The linear folds of their garments—inherited from the Romanesque style, along with the elongated proportions—generally echo the vertical lines of the columns behind them. (In this respect, Gothic jamb statues differ significantly from classical caryatids; FIG. 2-42. The Gothic figures are *attached* to columns. The classical statues *replaced* the columns.) Yet, within and despite this architectural straitjacket, the statues display the first signs of a new naturalism. Although technically high reliefs, the kings and queens stand out from the plane of the wall. The new naturalism—enhanced by painting, as was the norm for medieval as well as ancient stone sculpture—is noticeable particularly in the statues' heads, where kindly human faces replace the masklike features of most Romanesque figures. The sculptors of the Royal Portal figures initiated an era of artistic concern with personality and individuality.

Notre-Dame, Paris Because of the rapid urbanization of Paris under Louis VI and his successors and the accompanying population boom, a new cathedral became a necessity. Notre-Dame (FIG. **7-7**) occupies a picturesque site on an island in the Seine River called the Île-de-la-Cité. The Gothic church, which replaced an earlier timber-roofed basilica, has a complicated building history. The choir and transept were completed by 1182, the nave by about 1225, and the facade not until about 1250 to 1260. The original nave elevation had four stories, with a stained-glass *oculus* (small round window) inserted between the vaulted tribune and clerestory typical

of Norman Romanesque churches, such as Saint-Étienne (FIG. 6-29) at Caen. As a result, windows filled two of the four stories, further reducing the masonry area.

To hold the much thinner—and taller—walls of Notre-Dame in place, the unknown architect introduced exterior arches (*flying buttresses*) that spring from the lower roofs over the aisles and ambulatory (FIG. 7-7) and counter the outward thrust of the nave vaults. Gothic builders introduced flying buttresses as early as 1150 in a few smaller churches, but at Notre-Dame in Paris they circle a great urban cathedral. The internal quadrant arches (FIG. 6-30, *right*) beneath the aisle roofs at Durham Cathedral perform a similar function and may be regarded as precedents for exposed Gothic flying buttresses. The combination of precisely positioned flying buttresses and rib vaults with pointed arches was the ideal solution to the problem of constructing lofty naves with huge windows. The flying buttresses, which function as extended fingers holding up the walls, are key components of the distinctive "look" of Gothic cathedrals (see "The Gothic Cathedral," page 197, and FIG. **7-8**).

Chartres after 1194 Churches burned frequently in the Middle Ages, and the clergy often had to raise money unexpectedly for new building campaigns. In contrast to monastic churches, which usually were small and often could be completed fairly quickly, the construction of urban cathedrals frequently extended over decades and sometimes over centuries. The rebuilding of Chartres Cathedral (FIG. 7-1) after the devastating fire of 1194 took a relatively short 27 years. Architectural historians generally consider the

The Gothic Cathedral

Most of the architectural components of Gothic cathedrals appeared in earlier structures, but Gothic architects combined the elements in new ways. The essential ingredients of their formula for constructing churches in the *opus modernum* style were rib vaults with pointed arches, flying buttresses, and huge colored-glass windows. The cutaway view of a typical Gothic cathedral in FIG. 7-8 illustrates how these and other important Gothic architectural devices worked together.

I **Pinnacle** (FIG. 7-8, no. 1) A sharply pointed ornament capping the piers or flying buttresses; also used on cathedral facades.

I **Flying buttresses** (2) Masonry struts that transfer the thrust of the nave vaults across the roofs of the side aisles and ambulatory to a tall pier rising above the church's exterior wall.

I **Vaulting web** (3) The masonry blocks that fill the area between the ribs of a groin vault.

I **Diagonal rib** (4) In plan, one of the ribs forming the X of a groin vault. In FIG. 7-4, the diagonal ribs are the lines *AC* and *DB*.

I **Transverse rib** (5) A rib crossing the nave or aisle at a 90-degree angle (lines *AB* and *DC* in FIG. 7-4).

I **Springing** (6) The lowest stone of an arch; in Gothic vaulting, the lowest stone of a diagonal or transverse rib.

I **Clerestory** (7) The windows below the vaults in the nave elevation's uppermost level. By using flying buttresses and rib vaults on pointed arches, Gothic architects could build huge clerestory windows and fill them with *stained glass* held in place by ornamental stonework called *tracery*.

I **Oculus** (8) A small round window.

I **Lancet** (9) A tall, narrow window crowned by a pointed arch.

I **Triforium** (10) The story in the nave elevation consisting of arcades, usually *blind*, but occasionally filled with stained glass.

I **Nave arcade** (11) The series of arches supported by piers separating the nave from the side aisles.

I **Compound pier (cluster pier) with shafts (responds)** (12) A pier with a group, or cluster, of attached shafts, or responds, extending to the springing of the vaults.

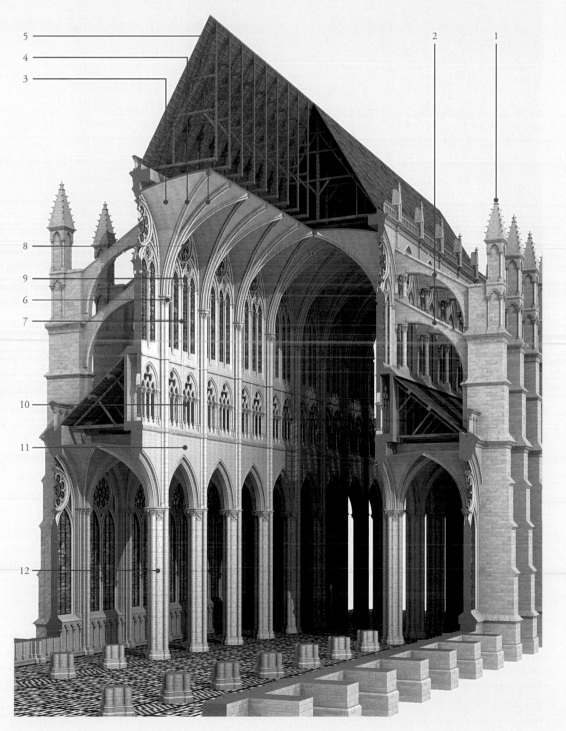

7-8 Cutaway view of a typical French Gothic cathedral (John Burge). ◼▸

The major elements of the Gothic formula for constructing a church in the *opus modernum* style were rib vaults with pointed arches, flying buttresses, and stained-glass windows.

the space corresponding to the exterior strip of wall covered by the sloping timber roof above the galleries. The new High Gothic tripartite nave elevation consisted of arcade, triforium, and clerestory with greatly enlarged windows. The Chartres windows are almost as tall as the main arcade and consist of double lancets with a single crowning oculus. The strategic placement of flying buttresses made possible the construction of nave walls with so many voids that heavy masonry played merely a minor role.

Chartres Stained Glass Despite the vastly increased size of its clerestory windows, the Chartres nave (FIG. 7-9) is relatively dark. This seeming contradiction is the result of using light-muffling colored glass for the windows. The purpose of the Chartres windows was not to illuminate the interior with bright sunlight but to transform natural light into Suger's mystical *lux nova* (see "Stained-Glass Windows," page 199). Chartres Cathedral retains almost the full complement of its original stained glass. Although the windows have a dimming effect, they transform the character of the church's interior in dramatic fashion. The immense (approximately 43 feet in diameter) *rose window* (circular stained-glass window) and tall lancets of the north transept (FIG. 7-10) were the gift of Queen Blanche of Castile around 1220. Yellow castles on a red ground and yellow *fleurs-de-lis* (three-petaled iris flowers; the French monarchy's floral emblem) on a blue ground fill

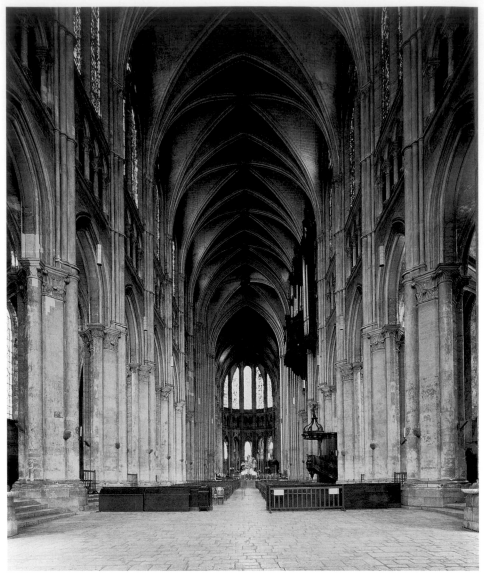

7-9 Interior of Chartres Cathedral (looking east), Chartres, France, begun 1194. ◼◀

Chartres Cathedral set the High Gothic standard with its four-part nave vaults and tripartite elevation consisting of nave arcade, triforium, and clerestory with tall stained-glass windows.

post-1194 Chartres Cathedral the first High Gothic building. At Chartres (FIG. 7-9), rectangular nave bays with four-part vaults replaced the square bays with six-part vaults and the alternate-support system used at Saint-Étienne (FIG. 6-29) at Caen and in Early Gothic churches. The new system, in which a single square in each aisle (rather than two, as before) flanks a single rectangular unit in the nave, became the High Gothic norm. The High Gothic nave vault covered only one bay and therefore could be braced more easily than its Early Gothic predecessor, making taller naves more practical to build.

The 1194 Chartres Cathedral was also the first church planned from its inception to have flying buttresses, another key High Gothic feature. The flying buttresses enabled the builders to eliminate the tribune above the aisle, which had partially braced Romanesque and Early Gothic naves. Taking its place was the *triforium,* the band of arcades between the clerestory and the nave arcade. The triforium occupies

the eight narrow windows in the rose's lower spandrels. The iconography is also fitting for a queen. The enthroned Virgin and Child appear in the roundel at the center of the rose, which resembles a gem-studded book cover or cloisonné brooch. Around her are four doves of the Holy Spirit and eight angels. Twelve square panels contain images of Old Testament kings, including David and Solomon (at the 12 and 1 o'clock positions, respectively). These are the royal ancestors of Christ. Isaiah (11:1–3) had prophesized the Messiah would come from the family of the patriarch Jesse, father of David. The genealogical "tree of Jesse" is a familiar motif in medieval art. Below, in the lancets, are Saint Anne and the baby Virgin. Flanking them are four of Christ's Old Testament ancestors—Melchizedek, David, Solomon, and Aaron—echoing the royal genealogy of the rose, but at a larger scale.

The rose and lancets change in hue and intensity with the hours, turning solid architecture into a floating vision of

Stained-Glass Windows

Stained-glass windows are almost synonymous with Gothic architecture. They differ from the mural paintings and mosaics that adorned earlier churches in one all-important respect. They do not conceal walls. They replace them. Moreover, they transmit rather than reflect light, filtering and transforming the natural sunlight. Abbot Suger called this colored light *lux nova*. Suger's contemporary, Hugh of Saint-Victor (1096–1142), a prominent Parisian theologian, believed "stained-glass windows are the Holy Scriptures . . . and since their brilliance lets the splendor of the True Light pass into the church, they enlighten those inside."* William Durandus (ca. 1237–1296), bishop of Mende, expressed a similar sentiment at the end of the 13th century: "The glass windows in a church are Holy Scriptures, which expel the wind and the rain, that is, all things hurtful, but transmit the light of the True sun, that is, God, into the hearts of the faithful."†

The manufacture of stained-glass windows was costly and labor-intensive. A German monk named Theophilus recorded the full process around 1100. First, the master designer drew the exact composition of the planned window on a wood panel, indicating all the linear details and noting the colors for each section. Glassblowers provided flat sheets of glass of different colors to *glaziers* (glassworkers), who cut the windowpanes to the required size and shape with special iron shears. Glaziers produced an even greater range of colors by *flashing* (fusing one layer of colored glass to another). Next, painters added details such as faces, hands, hair, and clothing in enamel by tracing the master design on the wood panel through the colored glass. Then they heated the painted glass to fuse the enamel to the surface. At that point, the glaziers "leaded" the various fragments of glass—that is, they joined them by strips of lead called *cames*. The *leading* not only held the pieces together but also separated the colors to heighten the design's effect as a whole. The distinctive character of Gothic stained-glass windows is largely the result of this combination of fine linear details with broad flat expanses of color framed by black lead. Finally, the glassworkers strengthened the completed window with an armature of iron bands (FIG. 7-10).

The form of the stone frames for the stained-glass windows also evolved. Early rose windows have stained glass held in place by *plate tracery* (FIG. 7-1, *top left*). The glass fills only the "punched holes" in the heavy ornamental stonework. *Bar tracery* (FIG. 7-10), a later development, is much more slender. The stained-glass windows fill almost the entire opening, and the stonework is unobtrusive, more like delicate leading than masonry wall.

* Hugh of Saint-Victor, *Speculum de mysteriis ecclesiae*, sermon 2.
†William Durandus, *Rationale divinorum officiorum*, 1.1.24. Translated by John Mason Neale and Benjamin Webb, *The Symbolism of Churches and Church Ornaments* (Leeds: Green, 1843), 28.

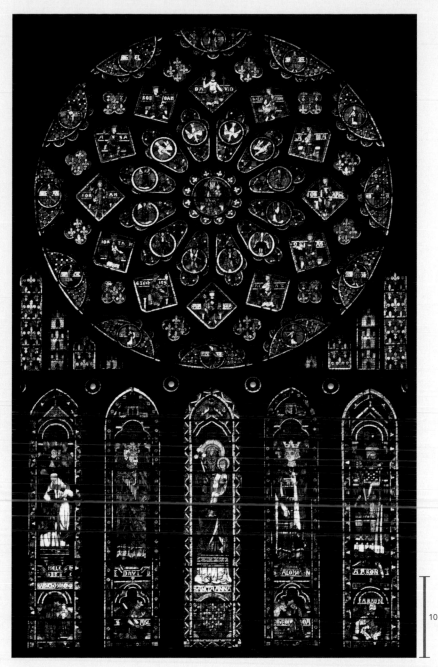

10 ft.

7-10 Rose window and lancets, north transept, Chartres Cathedral, Chartres, France, ca. 1220. Stained glass, rose window 43' in diameter. ◼◂

Stained-glass windows transformed natural light into Suger's lux nova. This immense rose window with tall lancets was the gift of Blanche of Castile, queen of France, to Chartres Cathedral.

the celestial heavens. Almost the entire mass of wall opens up into stained glass held in place by an intricate stone armature of bar tracery. Here, the Gothic passion for luminous colored light led to a most daring and successful attempt to subtract all superfluous material bulk just short of destabilizing the structure. That this vast, complex fabric of stone-set glass has maintained its structural integrity for almost 800 years attests to the Gothic builders' engineering genius.

Although the statue of Theodore is still attached to a column, the setting no longer determines its pose. The High Gothic sculptor portrayed the saint in a contrapposto stance, as in classical statuary.

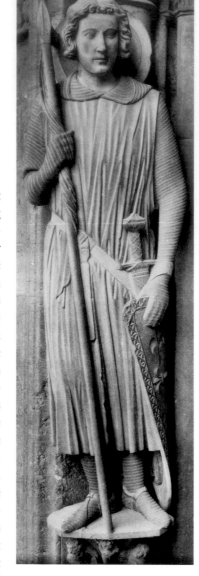

Chartres South Transept

The sculptures adorning the portals of the two Chartres transepts erected after the 1194 fire are also prime examples of the new High Gothic spirit. The Chartres transept portals (FIG. 7-1) project more forcefully from the church than do the Early Gothic portals of its west facade (FIG. 7-5). Similarly, the statues of saints on the portal jambs are more independent from the architectural framework. Saint Theodore (FIG. **7-11**), placed in the Porch of the Martyrs in the south transept around 1230, reveals the great changes Gothic sculpture had undergone since the Royal Portal statues (FIG. 7-6) of the mid-12th century. The High Gothic sculptor portrayed Theodore as the ideal Christian knight, clothing him in the cloak and chain-mail armor of 13th-century Crusaders. The handsome, long-haired youth holds his spear firmly in his right hand and rests his left hand on his shield. He turns his head to the left and swings out his hip to the right. The body's resulting torsion and pronounced sway recall ancient Greek statuary, especially the contrapposto stance of Polykleitos's *Spear Bearer* (FIG. 2-35). The changes that occurred in 13th-century Gothic sculpture echo the revolutionary developments in Greek sculpture during the transition from the Archaic to the Classical style (see Chapter 2) and could appropriately be described as a second "Classical revolution."

Amiens Cathedral

The builders of Chartres Cathedral set a pattern many other Gothic architects followed, even if they refined the details. Construction of Amiens Cathedral began in 1220, while work was still in progress at Chartres. The architects were ROBERT DE LUZARCHES, THOMAS DE CORMONT, and RENAUD DE CORMONT. The nave (FIG. **7-12**) was ready by 1236 and the radiating chapels by 1247, but work

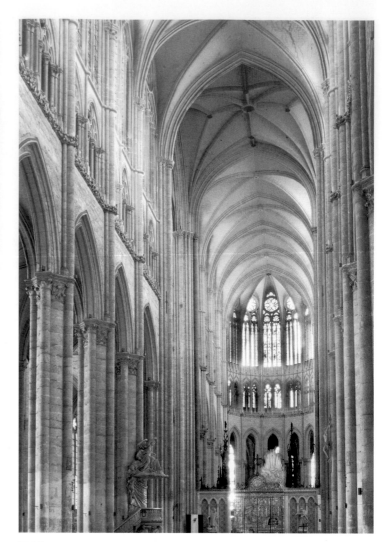

7-12 ROBERT DE LUZARCHES, THOMAS DE CORMONT, and RENAUD DE CORMONT, interior of Amiens Cathedral (looking east), Amiens, France, begun 1220. ◼◀

The concept of a self-sustaining skeletal architecture reached full maturity at Amiens Cathedral. The four-part vaults on pointed arches rise an astounding 144 feet above the nave floor.

on the choir continued until almost 1270. The Amiens elevation derived from the High Gothic formula of Chartres (FIG. 7-9), but Amiens Cathedral's proportions are more slender, and the number and complexity of the lancet windows in both its clerestory and triforium are greater. The whole design reflects the builders' confident use of the complete High Gothic structural vocabulary: the rectangular-bay system, the four-part rib vault, and a buttressing system that made possible the almost complete dissolution of heavy masses and thick weight-bearing walls. At Amiens, the concept of a self-sustaining skeletal architecture reached full maturity.

The nave vaults of Chartres Cathedral rise to a height of 120 feet. Those at Amiens are 144 feet above the floor, reflecting the French Gothic obsession with constructing ever taller cathedrals. At Amiens, the vault ribs converge to the colonnettes and speed down the shell-like walls to the compound piers. Almost every part of the superstructure has its corresponding element below. The overall effect is of effortless strength, of a buoyant lightness not normally associated with stone architecture. The light flooding in from the

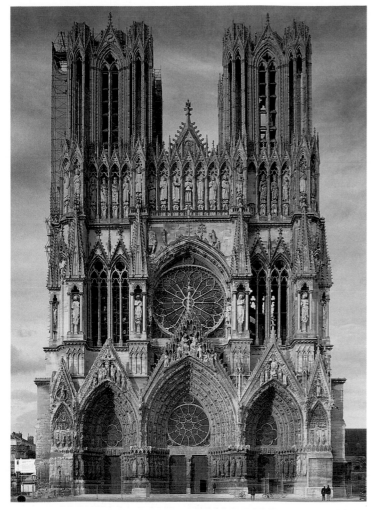

7-13 GAUCHER DE REIMS and BERNARD DE SOISSONS, west facade of Reims Cathedral, Reims, France, ca. 1225–1290.

Reims Cathedral's facade reveals High Gothic architects' desire to replace heavy masonry with intricately framed voids. Stained-glass windows, not stone reliefs, fill the three tympana.

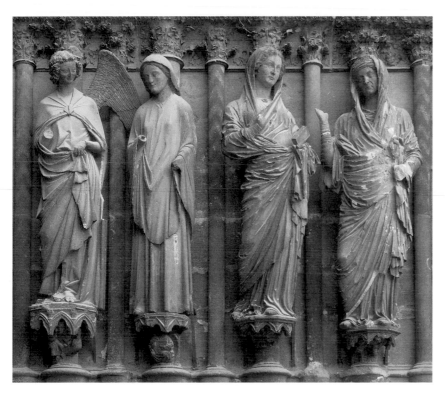

7-14 *Annunciation* and *Visitation,* jamb statues on the right side of the central doorway of the west facade, Reims Cathedral, Reims, France, ca. 1230–1255. ◼️◀

Several sculptors working in diverse styles carved the Reims jamb statues, but all the figures resemble freestanding statues with bodies and arms in motion. The biblical figures converse through gestures.

clerestory—and, in the choir, also from the triforium—makes the vaults seem even more insubstantial. The effect recalls another great building, one utterly different from Amiens but where light also plays a defining role: Hagia Sophia (FIG. 4-12) in Constantinople. At Amiens, the designers also reduced the building's physical mass by structural ingenuity and daring, and light further dematerializes what remains. If Hagia Sophia is the perfect expression of Byzantine spirituality in architecture, Amiens, with its soaring vaults and giant windows admitting divine colored light, is its Gothic counterpart.

Reims Cathedral Construction of Reims Cathedral (FIG. **7-13**) began only a few years after work commenced at Amiens. Its west facade, designed by GAUCHER DE REIMS and BERNARD DE SOISSONS, displays the Gothic desire to reduce sheer mass and replace it with intricately framed voids. The builders punctured almost the entire stone skin of the building. The deep piercing of walls and towers left few areas for decoration, but sculptors covered the remaining surfaces with a network of colonnettes, arches, pinnacles, rosettes, and other decorative stonework that visually screens and nearly dissolves the structure's solid core. Sculpture also extends to the areas above the portals, especially the band of statues (the so-called *kings' gallery*) running the full width of the facade directly above the rose window. Especially striking is the treatment of the tympana over the doorways, where stained-glass windows replaced the stone relief sculpture of earlier facades. The contrast with Romanesque heavy masonry construction (FIG. 6-28) is extreme. No less noteworthy, however, is the rapid transformation of the Gothic facade since Saint-Denis and Chartres (FIG. 7-1, *top left*).

Reims Cathedral is also a prime example of the High Gothic style in sculpture. Four of the most prominent statues (FIG. **7-14**) represent the *Annunciation* and *Visitation*. They are further testimony to the Virgin's central role in Gothic iconography. The statues appear completely detached from their architectural background because the sculptors shrank the supporting columns into insignificance. The columns in no way restrict the free and easy movements of the full-bodied figures. Compare the Reims jamb statues with those of the Chartres Royal Portal (FIG. 7-6), where the background columns occupy a volume equal to that of the figures.

The Reims statues also vividly illustrate how long it frequently took to complete the sculptured ornamentation of a large Gothic cathedral. Sculptural projects of this magnitude normally required decades to complete and entailed hiring many sculptors often working in diverse styles. Art historians believe three different sculptors carved the plify the wall-dissolving High Gothic architectural style. The architect of Sainte-Chapelle (FIG. **7-15**) in Paris extended this approach to an entire building. Louis IX (Saint Louis, r. 1226–1270) built Sainte-Chapelle, joined to the royal palace, as a repository for the crown of thorns and other relics of Christ's passion he had purchased in 1239. The chapel is a masterpiece of the so-called *Rayonnant* (radiant) style of the High Gothic age, which was the preferred style of the royal Parisian court of Saint Louis. In Sainte-Chapelle, 6,450 square feet of stained glass make up more than three-quarters of the structure. The supporting elements are hardly more than large *mullions,* or vertical stone bars. The emphasis is on the extreme slenderness of the architectural forms and on linearity in general. Sainte-Chapelle's enormous windows filter the light and fill the interior with an unearthly rose-violet atmosphere. Approximately 49 feet high and 15 feet wide, they were the largest stained-glass windows up to their time.

Virgin of Paris The "court style" of Sainte-Chapelle has its pictorial parallel in the mannered elegance of the Reims Gabriel statue (FIG. **7-14**, *left*), but the style long outlived Saint Louis. An example of the court style in Late Gothic sculpture is the statue nicknamed the *Virgin of Paris* (FIG. **7-16**) because of its location in the Parisian Cathedral of Notre-Dame (FIG. **7-7**). The sculptor portrayed Mary in an exaggerated S-curve posture. She is a worldly queen and wears

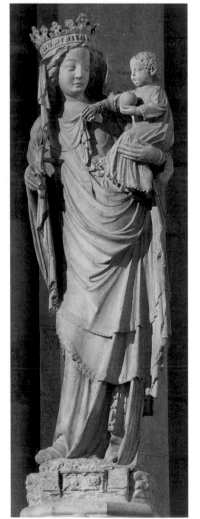

a heavy gem-encrusted crown. The princely Christ Child reaches toward his young mother. The tender, anecdotal characterization of mother and son seen here is a later manifestation of the humanization of the portrayal of religious figures in Gothic sculpture. Late Gothic statuary is very different in tone from the solemnity of most High Gothic figures, just as Late Classical Greek statues of the Olympian gods (FIG. **2-48**) differ from High Classical depictions.

7-16 Virgin and Child (*Virgin of Paris*), Notre-Dame, Paris, France, early 14th century. ◼◀

Late Gothic sculpture is elegant and mannered. Here, the solemnity of Early and High Gothic religious figures gave way to a tender, anecdotal portrayal of Mary and Jesus as royal mother and son.

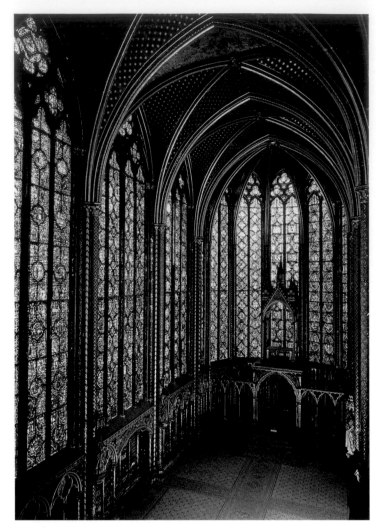

7-15 Interior of the upper chapel (looking northeast), Sainte-Chapelle, Paris, France, 1243–1248. ◼◀

At Louis IX's Sainte-Chapelle, the architect succeeded in dissolving the walls to such an extent that 6,450 square feet of stained glass account for more than three-quarters of the Rayonnant Gothic structure.

four statues in FIG. **7-14** at different times during the quarter century from 1230 to 1255. The *Visitation* group (FIG. **7-14**, *right*) is the work of an artist who probably studied classical statuary. Reims was an ancient Roman city. The heads of both Mary and Elizabeth resemble Roman portraits, and the rich folds of the garments also recall ancient statuary. The Gothic statues closely approximate the classical naturalistic style and feature contrapposto postures in which the swaying of the hips is much more pronounced than in the Chartres Saint Theodore (FIG. **7-11**). (It is even more exaggerated in the elegant elongated body of the angel Gabriel in the *Annunciation* group, FIG. **7-14**, *left*.) The right legs of the *Visitation* figures bend, and the knees press through the rippling folds of the garments. The sculptor also set the figures' arms in motion. Mary and Elizabeth turn their faces toward each other, and they converse through gestures. In the Reims *Visitation* group, the formerly isolated Gothic jamb statues became actors in a biblical narrative.

Sainte-Chapelle, Paris The stained-glass windows inserted into the portal tympana of Reims Cathedral exem-

Book Illumination and Luxury Arts

Paris's claim as the intellectual center of Gothic Europe did not rest solely on the stature of its university faculty and on the reputation of its architects, masons, sculptors, and stained-glass makers. The city was also a renowned center for the production of fine books. Dante Alighieri (1265–1321), the great Florentine poet, in fact, referred to Paris in his *Divine Comedy* (ca. 1310–1320) as the city famed for the art of illumination.[4] During the Gothic period, bookmaking shifted from monastic scriptoria shut off from the world to urban workshops of professional artists. The owners of these for-profit secular businesses sold their products to the royal family, scholars, and prosperous merchants. The Parisian workshops were the forerunners of modern publishing houses.

God as Creator One of the finest examples of French Gothic book illustration is the frontispiece (FIG. **7-17**) of a moralized Bible produced in Paris during the 1220s. *Moralized Bibles* are heavily illustrated, each page pairing paintings of Old and New Testament episodes with explanations of their moral significance. The page reproduced here does not conform to this formula because it is the introduction to all that follows. Above the illustration, the scribe wrote (in French rather than Latin): "Here God creates heaven and earth, the sun and moon, and all the elements." The painter depicted God in the process of creating the world, shaping the universe with the aid of a compass. Within the perfect circle already created are the spherical sun and moon and the unformed matter that will become the earth once God applies the same geometric principles to it. In contrast to the biblical account of creation, in which God created the sun, moon, and stars after the earth had been formed, and made the world by sheer force of will and a simple "Let there be" command, the Gothic artist portrayed God systematically creating the universe by applying geometrical principles and using some of the same tools mortal builders use.

Blanche of Castile Not surprisingly, most of the finest Gothic books known today belonged to the French monarchy. One of these is a moralized Bible now in the Pierpont Morgan Library that Blanche of Castile ordered during her regency (1226–1234) for her teenage son. The dedication page (FIG. **7-18**) has a costly gold background and depicts

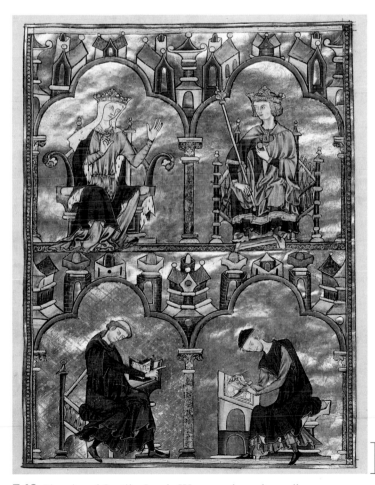

7-17 *God as Creator of the World,* folio 1 verso of a moralized Bible, from Paris, France, ca. 1220–1230. Ink, tempera, and gold leaf on vellum, 1' 1½" × 8¼". Österreichische Nationalbibliothek, Vienna.

Paris boasted renowned workshops for the production of illuminated manuscripts. In this book, the artist portrayed God in the process of creating the universe using a Gothic builder's compass.

7-18 Blanche of Castile, Louis IX, a monk, and a scribe, dedication page (folio 8 recto) of a moralized Bible, from Paris, France, 1226–1234. Ink, tempera, and gold leaf on vellum, 1' 3" × 10½". Pierpont Morgan Library, New York.

The dedication page of this royal book depicts Saint Louis, his mother and French regent Blanche of Castile, a monk, and a lay scribe at work on the paired illustrations of a moralized Bible.

Blanche and Louis enthroned beneath triple-lobed arches and miniature cityscapes. Below, in similar architectural frames, are a monk and a scribe. The older clergyman instructs the scribe, who already has divided his page into two columns of four roundels each, a format often used for the paired illustrations of moralized Bibles. The inspirations for such pages were probably the roundels of Gothic stained-glass windows (compare the windows of Louis's own Sainte-Chapelle, FIG. 7-15).

The picture of Gothic book production on the dedication page of Blanche of Castile's moralized Bible is a very abbreviated one. The manufacturing process used in the workshops of 13th-century Paris involved many steps and numerous specialized artists, scribes, and assistants of varying skill levels. The Benedictine abbot Johannes Trithemius (1462–1516) described the way books were still made in his day in his treatise *In Praise of Scribes:*

> If you do not know how to write, you still can assist the scribes in various ways. One of you can correct what another has written. Another can add the rubrics [headings] to the corrected text. A third can add initials and signs of division. Still another can arrange the leaves and attach the binding. Another of you can prepare the covers, the leather, the buckles and clasps. All sorts of assistance can be offered the scribe to help him pursue his work without interruption. He needs many things which can be prepared by others: parchment cut, flattened and ruled for script, ready ink and pens. You will always find something with which to help the scribe.[5]

Preparation of the illuminated pages also involved several hands. Some artists, for example, specialized in painting borders or initials. Only the workshop head or one of the most advanced assistants would paint the main figural scenes. Given this division of labor and the assembly-line nature of Gothic book production, it is astonishing how uniform the style is on a single page, as well as from page to page, in most illuminated manuscripts. Inscriptions in some Gothic books state the production costs—the prices paid for materials, especially gold, and for the execution of initials, figures, flowery script, and other embellishments. By this time, illuminators were professional guild members, and their personal reputation guaranteed the quality of their work. Although the cost of materials was still the major factor determining a book's price, individual skill and "brand name" increasingly decided the value of the illuminator's services. The centuries-old monopoly of the Church in book production had ended.

Virgin of Jeanne d'Evreux The royal family also patronized goldsmiths, silversmiths, and other artists specializing in the production of luxury works in metal and enamel for churches, palaces, and private homes. Especially popular were statuettes of sacred figures, which the wealthy purchased either for private devotion or as gifts to churches. The Virgin Mary was a favored subject. Perhaps the finest of these costly statuettes is the large silver-gilt figurine known

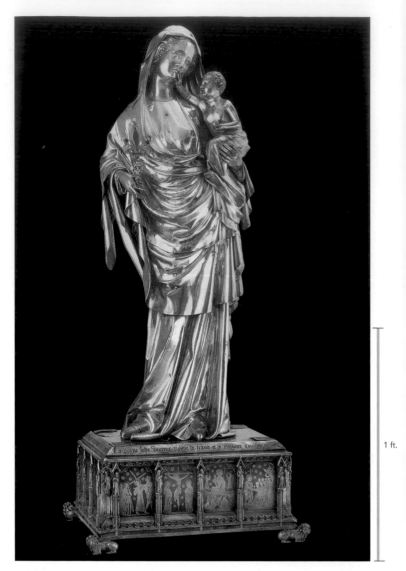

1 ft.

7-19 *Virgin of Jeanne d'Evreux,* from the abbey church, Saint-Denis, France, 1339. Silver gilt and enamel, 2' 3½" high. Musée du Louvre, Paris. ◼◀

Queen Jeanne d'Evreux donated this sumptuous reliquary-statuette to the royal abbey of Saint-Denis. It shares with the *Virgin of Paris* (FIG. 7-16) the intimate human characterization of the holy figures.

as the *Virgin of Jeanne d'Evreux* (FIG. **7-19**). The queen, wife of Charles IV (r. 1322–1328), donated the image of the Virgin and Child to the royal abbey church of Saint-Denis (FIG. 7-2) in 1339. Mary stands on a rectangular base decorated with enamel scenes of Christ's passion. But no hint of grief appears in the beautiful young Mary's face. The Christ Child, also without a care in the world, playfully reaches for his mother. The elegant proportions of the two figures, Mary's swaying posture, the heavy drapery folds, and the intimate human characterization of mother and son are also features of the roughly contemporaneous *Virgin of Paris* (FIG. 7-16). In both instances, Mary appears not only as Christ's mother but as queen of Heaven. The Saint-Denis Mary originally had a crown on her head, and the scepter she holds is in the form of the fleur-de-lis. The statuette also served as a reliquary. The Virgin's scepter contained hairs believed to come from Mary's head.

ENGLAND

In 1269, the prior (deputy abbot) of the church of Saint Peter at Wimpfen-im-Tal in the German Rhineland hired "a very experienced architect who had recently come from the city of Paris" to rebuild his monastery church.[6] The architect reconstructed the church *opere francigeno* (in the French manner)—that is, in the *opus modernum* style of the Île-de-France, which by the second half of the 13th century became dominant throughout Europe. European architecture did not, however, turn Gothic all at once or even uniformly. Almost everywhere, patrons and builders modified the Parisian court style according to local preferences.

Salisbury Cathedral Salisbury Cathedral (FIG. **7-20**) embodies the essential characteristics of English Gothic architecture. Begun in 1220, the English church is contemporaneous to the cathedrals of Amiens and Reims, but the differences between the French and English buildings are striking. Although Salisbury's facade has lancet windows and blind arcades with pointed arches and statuary, it reveals a very different sensibility. The English architect did not seek to match the soaring height of the Amiens and Reims (FIG. 7-13) facades or try to make the facade correspond to the three-part division of the interior (nave and aisles). Instead, the Salisbury facade is a squat screen in front of the nave, wider than the building behind it. Different, too, is the emphasis on the great crossing tower (added about 1320 to 1330), which dominates the silhouette. Salisbury's height is modest compared with that of Amiens and Reims. Because height is not a decisive factor in the English building, the architect used the flying buttress sparingly. In short, the English builders adopted some of the superficial motifs of French Gothic architecture but did not embrace its structural logic or emphasis on height.

Salisbury's interior (FIG. **7-21**), although Gothic in its three-story elevation, pointed arches, four-part rib vaults, compound piers, and triforium tracery, conspicuously departs from the French Gothic style of Amiens (FIG. 7-12). The pier colonnettes stop at the springing of the nave arches and do not connect with the vault ribs. Instead, the vault ribs rise from corbels in the triforium, producing a strong horizontal emphasis. Underscoring this horizontality is the rich color

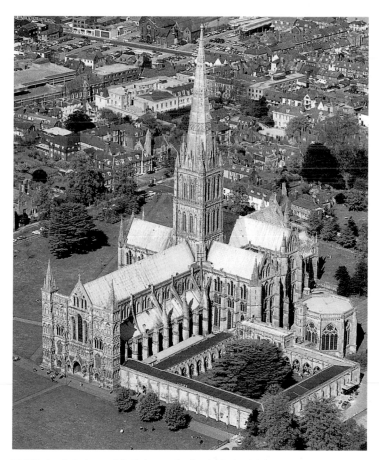

7-20 Aerial view of Salisbury Cathedral (looking northeast), Salisbury, England, 1220–1258; west facade completed 1265; spire ca. 1320–1330. ◼◀

Exhibiting the distinctive regional features of English Gothic architecture, Salisbury Cathedral has a squat facade that is wider than the building behind it. The architects used flying buttresses sparingly.

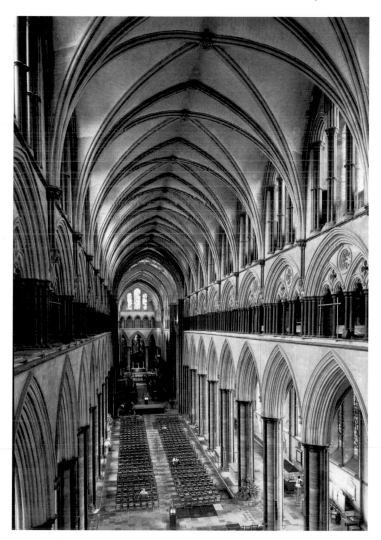

7-21 Interior of Salisbury Cathedral (looking east), Salisbury, England, 1220–1258.

Salisbury Cathedral's interior also differs from contemporaneous French Gothic designs in the strong horizontal emphasis of its three-story elevation and the use of dark Purbeck marble for moldings.

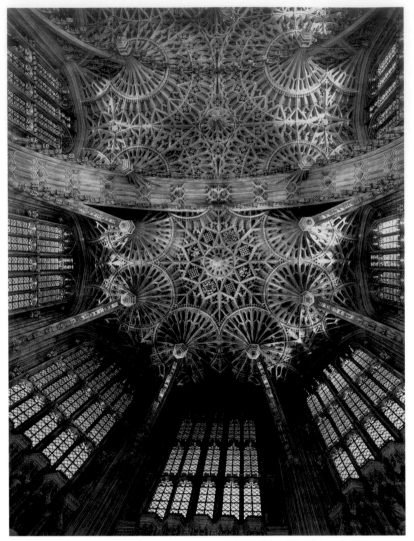

7-22 ROBERT and WILLIAM VERTUE, fan vaults of the chapel of Henry VII, Westminster Abbey, London, England, 1503–1519. ■◀

Two hallmarks of the Perpendicular style of English Late Gothic architecture are the multiplication of vault ribs and the use of fan vaults with lacelike tracery pendants resembling stalactites.

contrast between the light stone of the walls and vaults and the dark marble (from the Isle of Purbeck in southeastern England) used for the triforium moldings and corbels, compound pier responds, and other details.

Chapel of Henry VII English Gothic architecture found its native language in the elaboration of architectural pattern for its own sake. The pier, wall, and vault elements, still relatively simple at Salisbury, became increasingly complex and decorative in the 14th century and later. In the early-16th-century chapel of Henry VII adjoining Westminster Abbey in London, the so-called *Perpendicular* style of late English Gothic is on display. The style takes its name from the pronounced verticality of its decorative details, in contrast to the horizontal emphasis of Salisbury and Early English Gothic. In Henry's chapel, ROBERT and WILLIAM VERTUE multiplied the vault ribs (FIG. **7-22**) and pulled them into uniquely English *fan vaults* (vaults with radiating ribs forming a fanlike pattern) with large hanging *pendants* resembling stalactites. Intricate tracery recalling lace overwhelms the cones hang-

ing from the ceiling. The chapel represents the dissolution of structural Gothic into decorative fancy. The architects released the French Gothic style's original lines from their function and multiplied them into the uninhibited architectural virtuosity and theatrics of the English Perpendicular style.

HOLY ROMAN EMPIRE

The architecture of the Holy Roman Empire remained conservatively Romanesque well into the 13th century. In many German churches, the only Gothic feature was the rib vault, buttressed solely by the heavy masonry of the walls. By mid-century, though, the French Gothic style began to make a profound influence.

Cologne Cathedral Begun in 1248 under the direction of GERHARD OF COLOGNE, Cologne Cathedral was not completed until more than 600 years later. It is the largest cathedral in northern Europe and boasts a giant (422-foot-long) nave (FIG. **7-23**) with two aisles on each side. The 150-foot-high 14th-century choir is a skillful variation of the Amiens Cathedral choir (FIG. 7-12) design, with double lancets in the triforium and tall, slender single windows in the clerestory above and choir arcade below. The Cologne choir expresses the Gothic quest for height even more emphatically than do many French Gothic buildings.

Strasbourg Cathedral As did French Gothic architects, French sculptors also often set the standard for their counterparts in other countries. In the German Rhineland, work began in 1176 on a new cathedral for Strasbourg in present-day France. The apse, choir, and transepts were in place by around 1240. Stylistically, these sections of Strasbourg Cathedral are Romanesque. But the reliefs of the two south-transept portals are fully Gothic and reflect developments in contemporaneous French sculpture.

The left tympanum (FIG. **7-24**) presents *Death of the Virgin*. A comparison of the Strasbourg Mary on her deathbed with the Mary of the Reims *Visitation* group (FIG. 7-14, *right*) shows the stylistic kinship of the Strasbourg and Reims masters. The 12 apostles gather around the Virgin, forming an arc of mourners well suited to the semicircular frame. At the center, Christ receives his mother's soul (the doll-like figure he holds in his left hand). Mary Magdalene, wringing her hands in grief, crouches beside the deathbed. The sorrowing figures express emotion in varying degrees of intensity, from serene resignation to gesturing agitation. The sculptor organized the group by dramatic pose and gesture and by the rippling flow of deeply incised drapery that passes among them like a rhythmic electric pulse. The sculptor's objective was to imbue the sacred figures with human emotions and to stir emotional responses in observers. In Gothic France, as already noted, art became increasingly humanized and natural. In the Holy Roman Empire, artists carried this humanizing trend even further by emphasizing passionate drama.

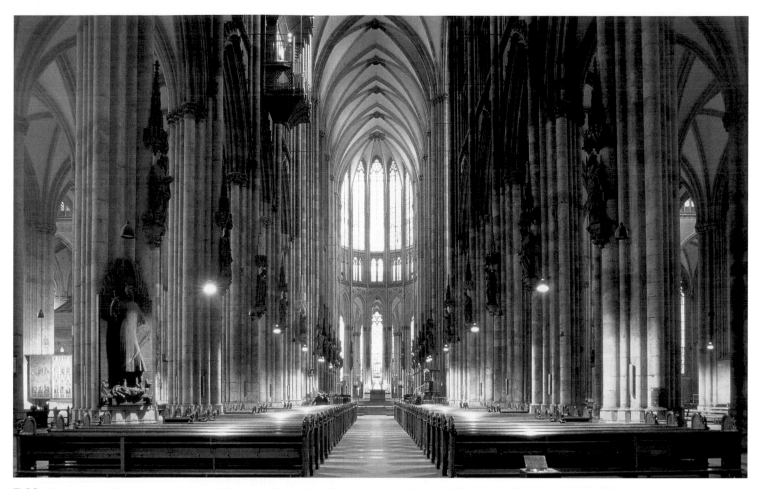

7-23 GERHARD OF COLOGNE, interior of Cologne Cathedral (looking east), Cologne, Germany. Choir completed 1322.

Cologne Cathedral's nave is 422 feet long. The 150-foot-high choir, a taller variation on the Amiens Cathedral choir (FIG. 7-12), is a prime example of Gothic architects' quest for height.

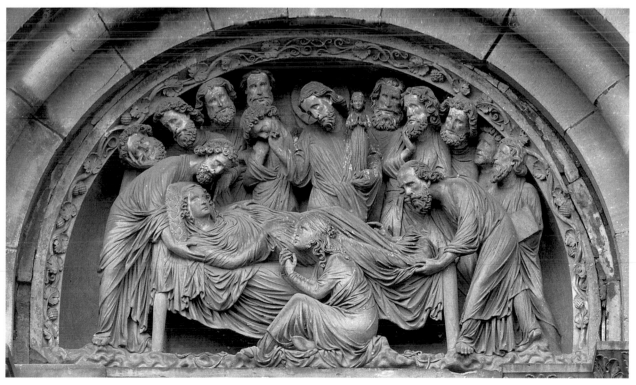

7-24 *Death of the Virgin,* tympanum of the left doorway of the south transept, Strasbourg Cathedral, Strasbourg, France, ca. 1230.

Stylistically akin to the *Visitation* group (FIG. 7-14, *right*) of Reims Cathedral, the figures in Strasbourg's south-transept tympanum express profound sorrow through dramatic poses and gestures.

of the Naumburg statues. Two of the figures (FIG. **7-25**) stand out from the group because of their exceptional quality. They represent the margrave (German military governor) Ekkehard II of Meissen and his wife, Uta. The statues are attached to columns and stand beneath architectural canopies, following the pattern of French Gothic portal statuary, but they project from the architecture more forcefully and move more freely than contemporaneous French jamb figures. Their location indoors accounts for the preservation of much of the original paint. Ekkehard and Uta give modern viewers an excellent idea of the appearance of the portal sculptures of medieval churches before exposure to sun and rain for centuries.

The period costumes and the individualized features and personalities of the margrave and his wife give the impression they posed for their portraits, although the subjects lived well before the Naumburg Master's time. Ekkehard, the intense knight, contrasts with the beautiful and aloof Uta. With a wonderfully graceful gesture, she draws the collar of her cloak partly across her face while she gathers up a soft fold of drapery with a jeweled, delicate hand. The sculptor

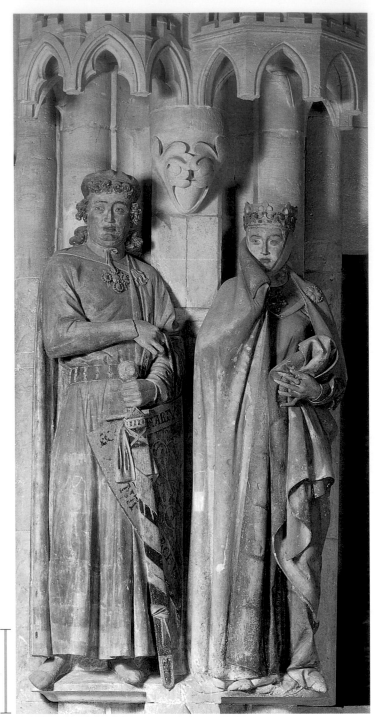

1 ft.

7-25 NAUMBURG MASTER, *Ekkehard and Uta,* statues in the west choir, Naumburg Cathedral, Naumburg, Germany, ca. 1249–1255. Painted limestone, Ekkehard 6′ 2″ high.

The period costumes and individualized features of these donor portraits give the impression Ekkehard and Uta posed for their statues, but they lived long before the Naumburg Master's time.

Naumburg Cathedral The Strasbourg style, with its feverish emotionalism, was particularly appropriate for narrating dramatic events in relief. The sculptor entrusted with the decoration of the west choir of Naumburg Cathedral— the NAUMBURG MASTER—faced a very different challenge. The commission was to carve statues of the 12 benefactors of the original 11th-century church. The vivid gestures and agitated faces of the Strasbourg portal contrast with the quiet solemnity

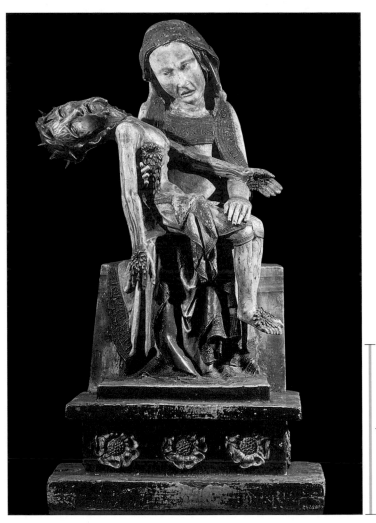

1 ft.

7-26 *Röttgen Pietà,* from the Rhineland, Germany, ca. 1300–1325. Painted wood, 2′ 10½″ high. Rheinisches Landesmuseum, Bonn. ◼️🎥

This statuette of the Virgin grieving over her son's distorted dead body in her lap reflects the increased interest in the 13th and 14th centuries in Jesus's suffering and his mother's grief.

subtly revealed the shape of Uta's right arm beneath her cloak and rendered the fall of drapery folds with an accuracy suggesting the sculptor used a living model. The two statues are arresting images of real people, even if they bear the names of aristocrats the artist never met. By the mid-13th century, in the Holy Roman Empire life-size images of secular personages had found their way into churches.

Röttgen Pietà The confident Naumburg portraits stand in marked contrast to a haunting 14th-century German painted wood statuette (FIG. **7-26**) of the Virgin Mary holding the dead Christ in her lap. This *Pietà* (Italian, "pity" or "compassion") reflects the increased interest during the 13th and 14th centuries in humanizing biblical figures and in the suffering of Jesus and grief of his mother and followers. This expressed emotionalism accompanied the shift toward representation of the human body in motion. As the figures of the church portals began to twist on their columns, then move within their niches, and then stand independently, their details became more outwardly related to the human audience as indicators of recognizable human emotions.

The sculptor of the *Röttgen Pietà* (named after a collector) portrayed Christ as a stunted, distorted human wreck, stiffened in death and covered with streams of blood gushing from a huge wound. The Virgin, who cradles him as if he were a child in her lap, is the very image of maternal anguish, her oversized face twisted in an expression of unbearable grief. This statue expresses nothing of the serenity of earlier Gothic depictions of Mary (FIG. 7-5, right tympanum). Nor does it have anything in common with the aloof, iconic images of the Theotokos with the infant Jesus in her lap common in Byzantine art (FIG. 4-19). Here the artist forcibly confronts the devout with an appalling icon of agony, death, and sorrow. The work calls out to the horrified believer, "What is your suffering compared to this?"

ITALY

Nowhere is the regional diversity of late medieval art and architecture more evident than in Italy. In fact, art historians debate whether the art of Italy between 1200 and 1400 is the last phase of medieval art or the beginning of the rebirth, or *Renaissance,* of Greco-Roman naturalism, the dawn of a new artistic age when artists broke away from medieval conventions and consciously revived the classical style. Both of these characterizations have merit.

A revived interest in classical cultures—indeed, the veneration of classical antiquity as a model—was central to the notion of a renaissance in Italy. Indeed, the belief the Renaissance represented the restoration of the glorious past of Greece and Rome gave rise to the concept of the "Middle Ages" as the era falling between antiquity and the Renaissance. This notion of artistic rebirth is the root of Vasari's condescending labeling of medieval art as "Gothic."

A significant development in 14th-century Italy was the blossoming of a vernacular (commonly spoken) literature,

which dramatically affected Italy's intellectual and cultural life. Latin remained the official language of Church liturgy and state documents. However, the creation of an Italian vernacular literature was one important sign that the essentially religious view of the world dominating medieval Europe was about to change dramatically. Although religion continued to occupy a primary position in the lives of Europeans, a growing concern with the natural world, the individual, and humanity's worldly existence characterized the Renaissance period—the 14th through the 16th centuries (see Chapters 8 and 9).

Humanism Fundamental to the development of the Italian Renaissance was *humanism.* Humanism was more a code of civil conduct, a theory of education, and a scholarly discipline than a philosophical system. As their name suggests, the Italian humanists were concerned chiefly with human values and interests as distinct from—but not opposed to—religion's otherworldly values. Humanists pointed to classical cultures as particularly praiseworthy. This enthusiasm for antiquity involved study of Latin literature and a conscious emulation of what proponents believed were the Roman civic virtues. These included self-sacrificing service to the state, participation in government, defense of state institutions (especially the administration of justice), and stoic indifference to personal misfortune in the performance of duty. Classical cultures provided humanists with a model for living in this world, a model primarily of human focus derived not from an authoritative and traditional religious dogma but from reason.

Sculpture and Painting

The Renaissance humanists quickly developed a keen interest in classical art as well as literature. Although the *Visitation* statues of Reims Cathedral (FIG. 7-14) show a familiarity with Roman statuary in 13th-century France, the emulation of Greco-Roman art was, not surprisingly, far more common in Italy, where Holy Roman Emperor Frederick II (r. 1220–1250) had been king of Sicily since 1197. Frederick's nostalgia for Rome's past grandeur fostered a revival of Roman sculpture in Sicily and southern Italy not unlike the neoclassical renewal Charlemagne encouraged in Germany and France four centuries earlier (see Chapter 6).

Nicola Pisano The sculptor known as NICOLA PISANO (Nicola of Pisa, active ca. 1258–1278) received his early training in southern Italy. After Frederick's death in 1250, Nicola traveled northward and eventually settled in Pisa. Then at the height of its political and economic power, the maritime city was a magnet for artists seeking lucrative commissions. Nicola specialized in carving marble reliefs and ornamentation for large *pulpits* (raised platforms from which priests lead church services), completing the first in 1260 for Pisa's baptistery (FIG. 6-27, *left*). Some elements of the pulpit's design carried on medieval traditions, but Nicola also incorporated classical elements. The large, bushy capitals are a Gothic

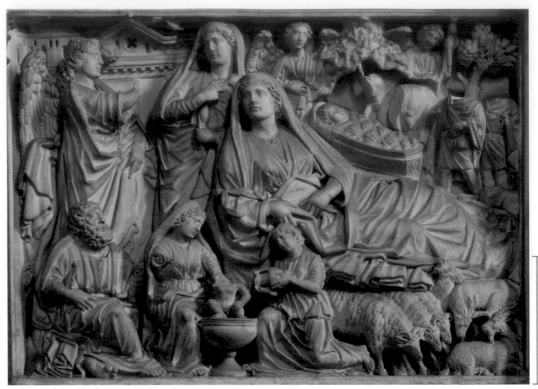

7-27 NICOLA PISANO, *Annunciation, Nativity,* and *Adoration of the Shepherds,* relief panel on the baptistery pulpit, Pisa, Italy, 1259–1260. Marble, 2′ 10″ × 3′ 9″. ■◀

Classical sculpture inspired the faces, beards, coiffures, and draperies, as well as the bulk and weight of Nicola's figures. The *Nativity* Madonna resembles lid figures on Roman sarcophagi.

1 ft.

variation of the Corinthian capital. The arches are round, as in Roman architecture, rather than pointed, as in Gothic buildings north of the Alps. Also, each of the large rectangular relief panels resembles the sculptured front of a Roman sarcophagus (FIG. 3-48).

One of these panels (FIG. **7-27**) depicts scenes from the infancy cycle of Christ (see "The Life of Jesus in Art," Chapter 4, pages 130–131), including *Annunciation* (*top left*), *Nativity* (*center* and *lower half*), and *Adoration of the Shepherds* (*top right*). The Virgin reclines in the manner of lid figures on Etruscan (FIG. 3-4) and Roman sarcophagi, and the face types, beards, coiffures, and draperies, as well as the bulk and weight of the figures, reveal the influence of classical relief sculpture. Art historians have even been able to pinpoint the models for some of the pulpit figures on Roman sarcophagi in Pisa.

Cimabue Late-13th-century Italian painting also differs sharply from the elegant court style popular north of the Alps. Byzantine style dominated Italian painting throughout the Middle Ages. The Italo-Byzantine style, or *maniera greca* (Greek style), still characterizes the art of Cenni di Pepo, called CIMABUE ("Bull's Head"; ca. 1240–1302). *Madonna Enthroned with Angels and Prophets* (FIG. **7-28**) is perhaps Cimabue's finest work. In this enormous (nearly 13 feet tall) panel painted for the church of the Holy Trinity in Florence, the heritage of Byzantine icon painting (FIGS. 4-19 and 4-26) is apparent in the careful structure and symmetry, the poses of the figures, the gold lines of Mary's garments, and the gold background. However, Cimabue constructed a deeper space for the Madonna and the surrounding figures to inhabit than was common in Byzantine painting, and he convincingly depicted the throne as receding into space. The overlapping

bodies of the angels reinforce the sense of depth, as do the half-length prophets who look outward or upward from beneath the massive throne.

Giotto Critics from Giorgio Vasari to the present day have regarded GIOTTO DI BONDONE (ca. 1266–1337) as the first Renaissance painter. A pioneer in pursuing a naturalistic approach to representation based on observation, he made a much more radical break with the maniera greca than did Cimabue, whom Vasari identified as Giotto's teacher. Scholars still debate the sources of Giotto's style, although one formative influence must have been Cimabue. Late medieval mural painting in Rome, French Gothic sculpture, and ancient Roman sculpture and painting must also have impressed the young Giotto. Yet no mere synthesis of these varied sources could have produced the significant shift in artistic approach that has led some scholars to describe Giotto as the father of Western pictorial art. Renowned in his own day, his reputation has never faltered. Regardless of the other influences on his artistic style, his true teacher was nature— the world of visible things.

Giotto's revolution in painting did not consist only of displacing the Byzantine style, establishing painting as a major art form for the next seven centuries, and restoring the naturalistic approach the ancients developed and medieval artists largely abandoned. He also inaugurated a method of pictorial expression based on observation and initiated an age that might be called "early scientific." By stressing the preeminence of sight for gaining knowledge of the world, Giotto and his successors contributed to the foundation of empirical science. They recognized the visual world must be observed before it can be analyzed and understood. Praised

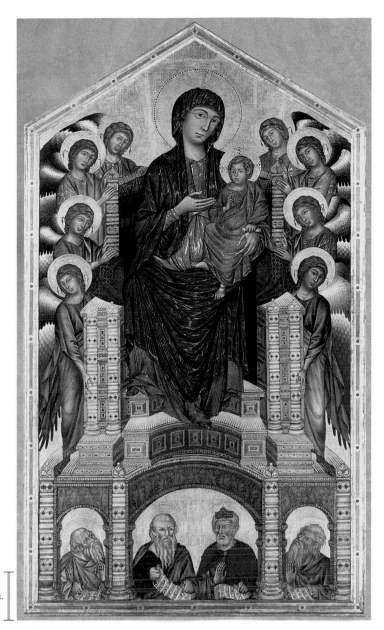

7-28 CIMABUE, *Madonna Enthroned with Angels and Prophets,* from Santa Trinità, Florence, Italy, ca. 1280–1290. Tempera and gold leaf on wood, 12' 7" × 7' 4". Galleria degli Uffizi, Florence. ■◀

Cimabue was a master of the Italo-Byzantine style. Here, the heritage of Byzantine icon painting is apparent, but Cimabue rendered the Madonna's massive throne as receding into space.

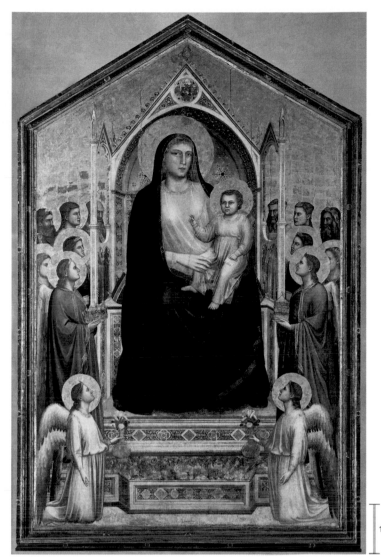

7-29 GIOTTO DI BONDONE, *Madonna Enthroned,* from the Church of the Ognissanti, Florence, Italy, ca. 1310. Tempera and gold leaf on wood, 10' 8" × 6' 8". Galleria degli Uffizi, Florence. ■◀

Giotto displaced the Byzantine style in Italian painting and revived classical naturalism. His figures have substance, dimensionality, and bulk, and give the illusion they could throw shadows.

in his own and later times for his fidelity to nature, Giotto was more than a mere imitator of it. He revealed nature while observing it and divining its visible order. In fact, he showed his generation a new way of seeing. With Giotto, Western artists turned resolutely toward the visible world as their source of knowledge of nature.

Madonna Enthroned On nearly the same great scale as Cimabue's enthroned Madonna (FIG. 7-28) is Giotto's *altarpiece* (FIG. 7-29) depicting the same subject. Giotto's Madonna rests within her Gothic throne with the unshakable stability of an ancient marble goddess. Giotto replaced Cimabue's slender Virgin, fragile beneath the thin ripplings of her

drapery, with a weighty, queenly mother. He even showed Mary's breasts pressing through the thin fabric of her white undergarment. Gold highlights have disappeared from her heavy robe. Giotto aimed instead to construct a figure with substance, dimensionality, and bulk—qualities suppressed in favor of a spiritual immateriality in Byzantine and Italo-Byzantine art. Works painted in the new style portray statuesque figures projecting into the light and giving the illusion they could throw shadows. Giotto's *Madonna Enthroned* marks the end of medieval painting in Italy and the beginning of a new naturalistic approach to art.

Arena Chapel Projecting onto a flat surface the illusion of solid bodies moving through space presents a double challenge. Constructing the illusion of a weighty, three-dimensional body also requires constructing the illusion of a space sufficiently ample to contain that body. In his fresco cycles (see "Fresco Painting," page 213), Giotto constantly strove to reconcile these two aspects of illusionistic painting. His murals in the Arena Chapel (Cappella Scrovegni; FIG. **7-30**) at Padua show his art at its finest. A banker, Enrico Scrovegni, built the chapel on a site adjacent to his palace in the hope it would expiate the moneylender's sin of usury. Consecrated in 1305, the chapel takes its name from an ancient Roman arena (amphitheater) nearby. Some scholars have suggested that Giotto himself may have been the architect because its design so perfectly suits its interior decoration.

The rectangular barrel-vaulted hall has only six windows, all in the south wall (FIG. 7-30, *left*), leaving the other walls as almost unbroken and well-illuminated surfaces for painting. In 38 framed scenes, Giotto presented one of the most impressive and complete Christian pictorial cycles ever rendered. The narrative unfolds on the north and south walls in three zones, reading from top to bottom: at the top, incidents from the lives of the Virgin and her parents, Joachim and Anna; in the middle, the life and mission of Christ; and in the lowest zone, his passion, crucifixion, and resurrection. Below, imitation marble veneer—reminiscent of ancient Roman wall decoration (FIG. 3-40)—alternates with personified Virtues and Vices painted in *grisaille* (monochrome grays, often used for modeling in paintings) to resemble sculpture. The climactic event of the cycle of human salvation, the *Last Judgment,* covers most of the west wall above the chapel's entrance.

Subtly scaled to the chapel's space (only about half life-size), Giotto's stately and slow-moving actors present their dramas convincingly and with great restraint. *Lamentation* (FIG. **7-31**) illustrates particularly well the revolutionary nature of Giotto's art. In the presence of boldly foreshortened angels darting about in hysterical grief, a congregation mourns over the dead savior just before his entombment. Mary cradles her son's body, while Mary Magdalene looks solemnly at the wounds in Christ's feet and John the Evangelist throws his arms back dramatically. Giotto arranged a shallow stage for the figures, bounded by a thick diagonal rock incline defining a horizontal ledge in the foreground. Though narrow, the ledge provides firm visual support for the figures, and the steep slope leads the viewer's eye toward the picture's dramatic focal point at the lower left. The figures are sculpturesque, and their postures and gestures convey a broad spectrum of grief, ranging from Mary's almost fierce despair to the passionate outbursts of Mary Magdalene

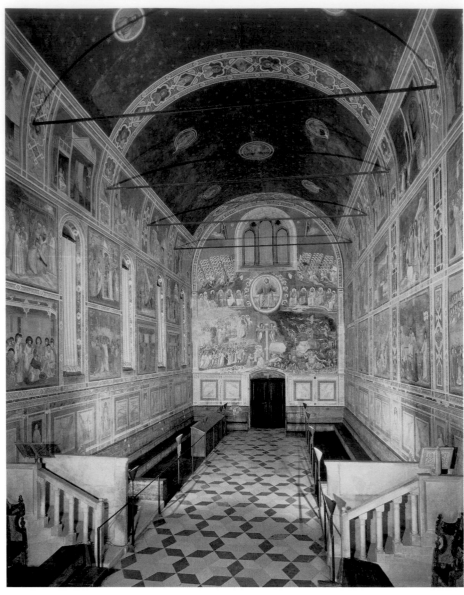

7-30 GIOTTO DI BONDONE, interior of the Arena Chapel (Cappella Scrovegni; looking west), Padua, Italy, 1305–1306.

The frescoes Giotto painted in the Arena Chapel show his art at its finest. In 38 framed panels, he presented the complete cycle of the life of Jesus, culminating in the *Last Judgment* on the entrance wall.

and John to the philosophical resignation of the two disciples at the right and the mute sorrow of the two hooded mourners in the foreground. Painters before Giotto rarely attempted, let alone achieved, this combination of naturalistic representation, compositional complexity, and emotional resonance.

The formal design of the *Lamentation* fresco—the way Giotto grouped the figures within the constructed space—is worth close study. Each group has its own definition, and each contributes to the rhythmic order of the composition. The strong diagonal of the rocky ledge, with its single dead tree (the tree of knowledge of good and evil, which withered after Adam and Eve's original sin), concentrates the viewer's attention on the heads of Christ and his mother, which Giotto positioned dynamically off center. The massive bulk of the seated mourner in the painting's left corner

Fresco Painting

Fresco painting has a long history, particularly in the Mediterranean region, where the Minoans (FIGS. 2-5 and 2-6) used it as early as the 17th century BCE. *Fresco* (Italian for "fresh") is a mural-painting technique involving the application of permanent lime-proof pigments, diluted in water, on freshly laid lime plaster. Because the surface of the wall absorbs the pigments as the plaster dries, fresco is one of the most durable painting techniques. The stable condition of frescoes such as those in the Arena Chapel (FIGS. 7-30 and 7-31) and the houses of Roman Pompeii (FIGS. 3-17 to 3-23) testify to the longevity of this painting method. The colors have remained vivid because of the chemically inert pigments the artists used. In addition to this *buon fresco* (good, that is, true fresco) technique, artists used *fresco secco* (dry fresco). Fresco secco involves painting on dried lime plaster. Although the finished product visually approximates buon fresco, the plaster wall does not absorb the pigments, which simply adhere to the surface, so fresco secco is not as permanent as buon fresco.

The buon fresco process is time-consuming and demanding and requires several layers of plaster. Although buon fresco methods vary, generally the artist prepares the wall with a rough layer of lime plaster called the *arriccio* (brown coat). The artist then transfers the composition to the wall, usually by drawing directly on the arriccio with a burnt orange pigment called *sinopia* (most popular during the 14th century) or by transferring a *cartoon* (a full-sized preparatory drawing). Cartoons increased in usage in the 15th and 16th centuries, largely replacing sinopia underdrawings. Finally, the painter lays the *intonaco* (painting

7-31 GIOTTO DI BONDONE, *Lamentation*, Arena Chapel (Cappella Scrovegni), Padua, Italy, ca. 1305. Fresco, 6' 6¾" × 6' ¾". ◼️

Giotto painted *Lamentation* in several sections, each corresponding to one painting session. Artists employing the buon fresco technique must complete each section before the plaster dries.

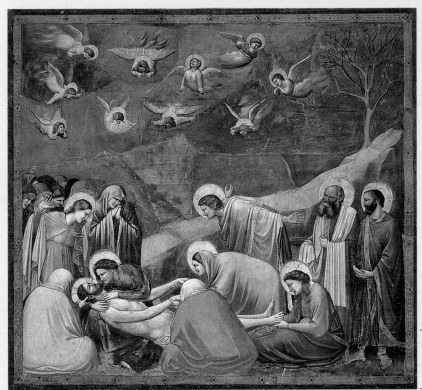

1 ft.

coat) smoothly over the drawing in sections (called *giornate,* Italian for "days") only as large as the artist expects to complete in that session. (In Giotto's *Lamentation* [FIG. 7-31], the giornate are easy to distinguish.) The buon fresco painter must apply the colors fairly quickly, because once the plaster is dry, it will no longer absorb the pigment. Any unpainted areas of the intonaco after a session must be cut away so that fresh plaster can be applied for the next giornata.

---

arrests and contains all movement. The seated mourner to the right establishes a relation with the central figures, who, by gazes and gestures, draw the viewer's attention back to Christ's head. Figures seen from the back, which are frequent in Giotto's compositions, represent an innovation in the development away from the maniera greca. These figures emphasize the foreground, aiding the visual placement of the intermediate figures farther back in space. This device, the very contradiction of Byzantine frontality, in effect puts the viewer behind the "observer figures," who, facing the action as spectators, reinforce the sense of stagecraft as a model for painting.

Giotto's new devices for depicting spatial depth and body mass could not, of course, have been possible without his management of light and shade. He shaded his figures to indicate both the direction of the light illuminating their bodies and the shadows (the diminished light), thereby giving the figures volume. In *Lamentation,* light falls upon the upper surfaces of the figures (especially the two central bending

figures) and passes down to dark in their garments, separating the volumes one from the other and pushing one to the fore, the other to the rear. The graded continuum of light and shade, directed by an even, neutral light from a single steady source—not shown in the picture—was the first step toward the development of *chiaroscuro* (the use of contrasts of dark and light to produce modeling) in Renaissance painting.

Giotto's stagelike settings are pictorial counterparts to contemporaneous *mystery plays,* in which actors extended the drama of the Mass into one- and two-act performances at church portals and in city squares. The great increase in popular sermons to huge city audiences prompted a public taste for narrative, recited as dramatically as possible. The arts of illusionistic painting, of drama, and of sermon rhetoric with all their theatrical flourishes developed simultaneously and were mutually influential. Giotto's art masterfully synthesized dramatic narrative, holy lesson, and truth to human experience in a visual idiom of his own invention, accessible to all.

Duccio The Republics of Siena and Florence were the two most powerful city-states in 14th-century Italy, home to wealthy bankers and merchants. The Sienese were particularly proud of their defeat of the Florentines at the battle of Monteperti in 1260 and believed the Virgin Mary had brought them victory. To honor the Virgin, in 1308 the Sienese commissioned DUCCIO DI BUONINSEGNA (active ca. 1278–1318) to paint an immense altarpiece for Siena Cathedral—the *Maestà* (*Virgin Enthroned in Majesty*). He and his assistants completed the ambitious work in 1311. As originally executed, the altarpiece consisted of a seven-foot-high center panel (FIG. **7-32**), surmounted by seven pinnacles above,

and a *predella,* or raised shelf, of panels at the base, altogether some 13 feet high.

The main panel on the front side of the altarpiece represents the Virgin enthroned in majesty as queen of Heaven amid choruses of angels and saints. Duccio derived the composition's formality and symmetry, along with the figures and facial types of the principal angels and saints, from Byzantine tradition. But the artist relaxed the strict frontality and rigidity of the figures. They turn to one another in quiet conversation. Further, Duccio individualized the faces of the four saints kneeling in the foreground, who perform their ceremonial gestures without stiffness. Similarly, Duccio

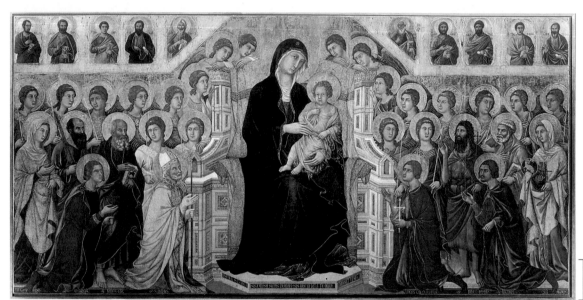

7-32 DUCCIO DI BUONINSEGNA, *Virgin and Child Enthroned with Saints,* principal panel of the *Maestà* altarpiece, from Siena Cathedral, Siena, Italy, 1308–1311. Tempera and gold leaf on wood, 7′ × 13′. Museo dell'Opera del Duomo, Siena. ◼️

Duccio derived the formality and symmetry of his composition from Byzantine painting, but relaxed the rigidity and frontality of the figures, softened the drapery, and individualized the faces.

1 ft.

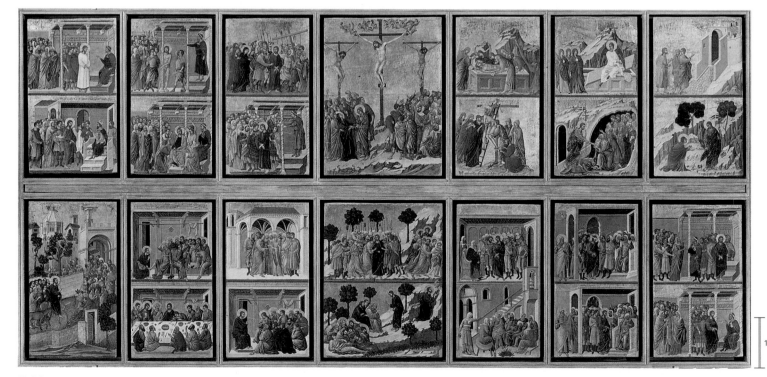

1 ft.

7-33 DUCCIO DI BUONINSEGNA, *Life of Jesus,* 14 panels from the back of the *Maestà* altarpiece, from Siena Cathedral, Siena, Italy, 1308–1311. Tempera and gold leaf on wood, 7′ × 13′. Museo dell'Opera del Duomo, Siena.

On the back of the *Maestà* altarpiece, Duccio presented Christ's passion in 24 scenes on 14 panels, beginning with *Entry into Jerusalem,* at the lower left, through *Noli me tangere,* at the top right.

softened the usual Byzantine hard body outlines and drapery patterning. The folds of the garments, particularly those of the female saints at both ends of the panel, fall and curve loosely. This is a feature familiar in French Gothic works (FIG. 7-19) and is a mark of the artistic dialogue between Italy and northern Europe in the 14th century.

Despite these changes revealing Duccio's interest in the new naturalism, he respected the age-old requirement that as an altarpiece the *Maestà* would be the focus of worship in Siena's largest and most important church. As such, Duccio knew the *Maestà* should be an object holy in itself—a work of splendor to the eyes, precious in its message and its materials. Duccio thus recognized how the function of the altarpiece limited experimentation in depicting narrative action and producing illusionistic effects (such as Giotto's) by modeling forms and adjusting their placement in pictorial space. Instead, the queen of Heaven panel is a miracle of color composition and texture manipulation, unfortunately not fully revealed in photographs. Close inspection of the original reveals what the Sienese artist learned from other sources. In the 13th and 14th centuries, Italy was the distribution center for the great silk trade from China and the Middle East. After processing in city-states such as Lucca and Florence, the Italians exported the precious fabric throughout Europe to satisfy an immense market for sumptuous dress. People throughout Europe prized fabrics from China, Byzantium, and the Islamic world. In the *Maestà,* Duccio created the glistening and shimmering effects of textiles, adapting the motifs and design patterns of exotic materials. Complementing the luxurious fabrics and the (lost) gilded wood frame are the halos of the holy figures, which feature tooled decorative designs in gold leaf (*punchwork*).

In contrast to the main panel, the back (FIG. **7-33**) of the altarpiece presents an extensive series of narrative panels of different sizes and shapes, beginning with *Annunciation* and culminating with Christ's *Resurrection*. The section reproduced here, consisting of 24 scenes in 14 panels, relates Christ's passion. In these scenes, Duccio allowed himself greater latitude for experimentation than in the *Maestà* panel. The bodies are not the flat frontal shapes of Italo-Byzantine art. Duccio imbued them with mass, modeled them with a range of tonalities from light to dark, and arranged their draperies around them convincingly. Even more novel and striking is the way the figures seem to react to events. Through posture, gesture, and even facial expression, they display a variety of emotions. Duccio's protagonists are actors in a religious drama the artist interpreted in terms of thoroughly human actions and reactions. In this passion cycle, Duccio took a decisive step toward the humanization of religious subject matter.

Simone Martini Duccio's successors in Siena included his pupil SIMONE MARTINI (ca. 1285–1344), who may have assisted in painting the *Maestà*. Martini was a close friend of the poet and scholar Francesco Petrarch (1304–1374), who praised the Sienese painter highly for his portrait of "Laura" (the woman to whom Petrarch dedicated his sonnets). Martini worked for the French kings in Naples and Sicily and, in his last years, produced paintings for the papal court, which in the 14th century was at Avignon, where he came in contact with French painters. By adapting the insubstantial but luxuriant patterns of the Gothic style to Sienese art and, in turn, by acquainting French painters with the Sienese style, Martini was instrumental in creating the so-called *International style*. This new style swept Europe during the late 14th and early 15th centuries because it appealed to the aristocratic taste for brilliant colors, lavish costumes, intricate ornamentation, and themes involving splendid processions.

Martini's *Annunciation* altarpiece (FIG. **7-34**) features elegant shapes and radiant color, flowing, fluttering line,

7-34 SIMONE MARTINI and LIPPO MEMMI (?), *Annunciation* altarpiece, from Siena Cathedral, Siena, Italy, 1333 (frame reconstructed in the 19th century). Tempera and gold leaf on wood; center panel, 10′ 1″ × 8′ 8¾″. Galleria degli Uffizi, Florence.

A pupil of Duccio, Martini was instrumental in the creation of the International style. Its hallmarks are elegant shapes, radiant color, flowing line, and weightless figures in golden, spaceless settings.

1 ft.

and weightless figures in a spaceless setting—all hallmarks of the artist's style. The complex etiquette of the European chivalric courts probably dictated the presentation. Gabriel has just alighted, the breeze of his passage lifting his mantle, his iridescent wings still beating. The gold of his sumptuous gown signals he has descended from Heaven. The Virgin, putting down her book of devotions, shrinks demurely from the angel's reverent genuflection—an appropriate act in the presence of royalty. Mary draws about her the deep blue, golden-hemmed mantle, colors befitting the queen of Heaven. Despite Mary's modesty and diffidence and the tremendous import of Gabriel's message, the scene subordinates drama to court ritual, and structural experimentation to surface splendor. The intricate tracery of the richly tooled French Gothic-inspired frame and the elaborate punchwork haloes enhance the tactile magnificence of the painting.

Simone Martini and his student and assistant, LIPPO MEMMI (active ca. 1317–1350), signed the altarpiece and dated it (1333). The latter's contribution to *Annunciation* is still a matter of debate, but most art historians believe he painted the two lateral saints. These figures, which are reminiscent of the jamb statues of Gothic church portals, have greater solidity and lack the linear elegance of Martini's central pair. Given the nature of medieval and Renaissance workshop practices, it is often difficult to distinguish the master's hand from those of his assistants, especially if the master corrected or redid part of the pupil's work.

Ambrogio Lorenzetti Another of Duccio's students, AMBROGIO LORENZETTI (active 1319–1348), contributed significantly to the general experiments in pictorial realism taking place in 14th-century Italy. In a vast fresco program he executed for the Sala della Pace (Hall of Peace; FIG. **7-35**) of Siena's Palazzo Pubblico ("public palace," or city hall), Lorenzetti both elaborated in spectacular fashion the advances in illusionistic representation made by other Italian painters and gave visual form to Sienese civic concerns. The subjects of Lorenzetti's murals are *Allegory of Good Government, Bad Government and the Effects of Bad Government in the City,* and *Effects of Good Government in the City and in the Country.* The turbulent politics of the Italian cities—the violent party struggles, the overthrow and reinstatement of governments—called for solemn reminders of fair and just administration, and the city hall was the perfect place to display these allegorical paintings. Indeed, the leaders of the Sienese government who commissioned this fresco series had undertaken the "ordering and reformation of the whole city and countryside of Siena."

In *Effects of Good Government in the City and in the Country* (FIG. 7-35, *right*), Lorenzetti depicted the urban and rural

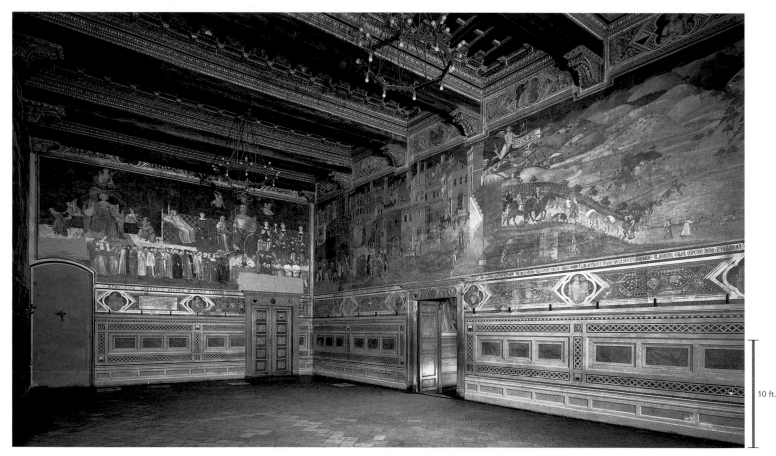

7-35 AMBROGIO LORENZETTI, *Effects of Good Government in the City and in the Country,* north (*left*) and east (*right*) walls of the Sala della Pace, Palazzo Pubblico, Siena, Italy, 1338–1339. Fresco, north wall 25′ 3″ wide, east wall 46′ wide.

In the Hall of Peace of Siena's city hall, Ambrogio Lorenzetti painted an illusionistic panorama of the bustling city. The fresco served as an allegory of good government in the Sienese republic.

10 ft.

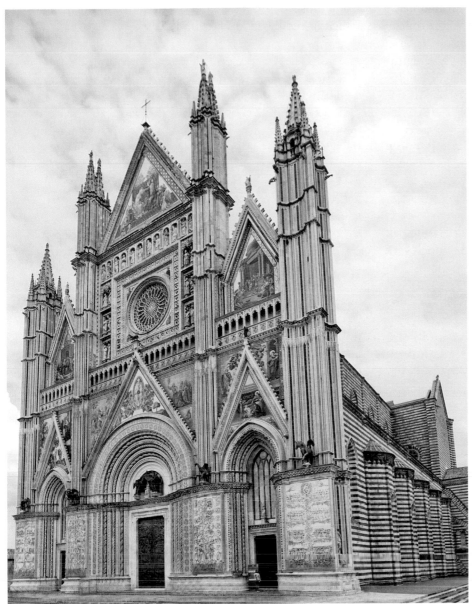

7-36 Lorenzo Maitani, Orvieto Cathedral (looking northeast), Orvieto, Italy, begun 1310. ◼◀

The pointed gables over the doorways, the rose window, and the large pinnacles derive from French Gothic architecture, but the facade of Orvieto Cathedral masks a traditional timber-roofed basilica.

first appearances of landscape in Western art since antiquity.

Architecture

The picture of Siena in the Sala della Pace frescoes could not be confused with a view of a French, German, or English city of the 14th century. Italian architects stood apart from developments north of the Alps.

Orvieto Cathedral The west facade of Orvieto Cathedral (FIG. **7-36**) is typical of late medieval architecture in Italy. Designed in the early 14th century by the Sienese architect Lorenzo Maitani, the Orvieto facade demonstrates the appeal of the French Gothic architectural vocabulary in Italy. Characteristically French are the pointed gables over the three doorways, the rose window and statues in niches in the upper zone, and in the four large pinnacles dividing the facade into three bays. The outer pinnacles serve as miniature substitutes for the tall northern European west-front towers. Maitani's facade, however, is a Gothic overlay masking a marble-revetted basilican structure in the Tuscan Romanesque tradition, as the three-quarter view of the cathedral in FIG. 7-36 reveals. The Orvieto facade resembles a great altar screen, its single plane covered with carefully placed carved and painted decoration. In principle, Orvieto belongs with Pisa Cathedral (FIG. 6-27) and other Italian buildings, rather than with Reims Cathedral (FIG. 7-13). Inside, Orvieto Cathedral has a timber-roofed nave with a two-story elevation (columnar arcade with round arches and a clerestory) in the Early Christian manner.

Florence Cathedral In the 14th century, the historian Giovanni Villani (ca. 1270–1348) described Florence as "the daughter and the creature of Rome," suggesting a preeminence inherited from the Roman Empire. Florentines were fiercely proud of what they perceived as their economic and cultural superiority. Florence controlled the textile industry in Italy, and the republic's gold *florin* was the standard coin of exchange everywhere in Europe.

Florentines translated their pride in their predominance into landmark buildings, such as the cathedral of Santa

effects of good government. One section of the fresco is a panoramic view of Siena, with its palaces, markets, towers, churches, streets, and walls. The city's traffic moves peacefully, guild members ply their trades and crafts, and radiant maidens, clustered hand in hand, perform a graceful circling dance. Dancers were regular features of festive springtime rituals. Here, their presence also serves as a metaphor for a peaceful commonwealth. The artist fondly observed the life of his city, and its architecture gave him an opportunity to apply Sienese painters' rapidly growing knowledge of perspective.

In the *Peaceful Country* section of the fresco, Lorenzetti presented a bird's-eye view of the undulating Tuscan countryside, with its villas, castles, plowed farmlands, and peasants going about their seasonal occupations. An allegorical figure of Security hovers above the landscape, unfurling a scroll promising safety to all who live under the rule of law. Although the mural is an allegory, Lorenzetti's particularized view of the Sienese countryside represents one of the

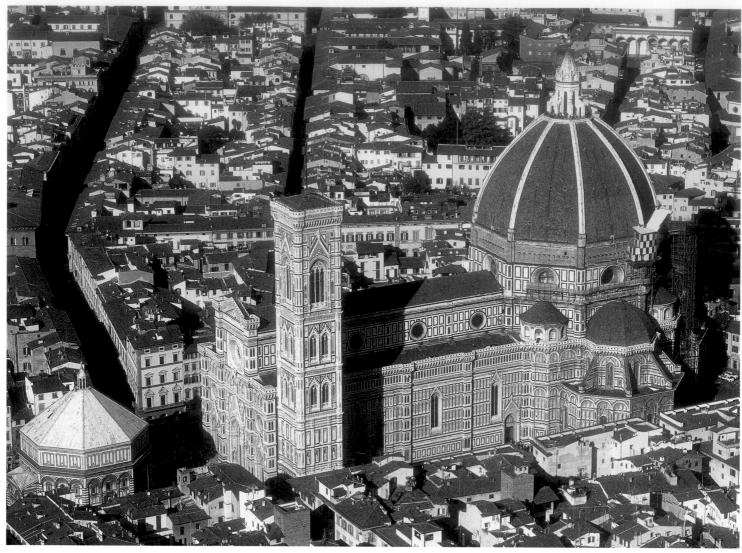

7-37 Arnolfo di Cambio and others, aerial view of Santa Maria del Fiore (and the Baptistery of San Giovanni; looking northeast), Florence, Italy, begun 1296. Campanile designed by Giotto di Bondone, 1334. ◼◀

The Florentine Duomo's marble revetment carries on the Tuscan Romanesque architectural tradition, linking this basilican church more closely to Early Christian Italy than to Gothic France.

Maria del Fiore (FIG. **7-37**). ARNOLFO DI CAMBIO (ca. 1245–1302) began work on the cathedral (*Duomo* in Italian) in 1296. Intended as the "most beautiful and honorable church in Tuscany," the Duomo reveals the competitiveness Florentines felt with such cities as Siena and Pisa (FIG. 6-27). Church authorities planned for the cathedral to hold the city's entire population, and although its capacity is only about 30,000 (Florence's population at the time was slightly less than 100,000), the building seemed so large even the noted architect Leon Battista Alberti (see Chapter 8) commented that it seemed to cover "all of Tuscany with its shade." The vast gulf separating this low, longitudinal basilican church with its Tuscan-style marble-revetted walls from its towering trans-alpine counterparts is strikingly evident in a comparison between the Italian church and Reims Cathedral (FIG. 7-13), completed several years before work began in Florence.

Giotto di Bondone designed the Duomo's campanile in 1334. In keeping with Italian tradition (FIG. 6-27), the bell tower stands apart from the church. In fact, it is essentially self-sufficient and could stand anywhere else in the city without looking out of place. The same cannot be said of Gothic towers. They are essential elements of the structures behind them, and it would be unthinkable to detach one of them and place it somewhere else. In contrast, not only could Giotto's tower be removed from the building without adverse effects, but also each of the parts—cleanly separated from one another by continuous moldings—seems capable of existing independently as an object of considerable aesthetic appeal. This compartmentalization is reminiscent of the Romanesque style, but it also forecasts the ideals of Renaissance architecture, discussed in Chapter 8.

Gothic and Late Medieval Europe

France

▌ The birthplace of Gothic art and architecture was Saint-Denis, where Abbot Suger rebuilt the Carolingian royal church using rib vaults with pointed arches and stained-glass windows. The Early Gothic (1140–1194) west facade of Suger's church also introduced sculpted figures on the portal jambs, a feature that appeared shortly later on the Royal Portal of Chartres Cathedral.

▌ After a fire in 1194, Chartres Cathedral was rebuilt with flying buttresses, four-part nave vaults, and a three-story elevation of nave arcade, triforium, and clerestory, setting the pattern for High Gothic (1194–1300) cathedrals, including Amiens with its 144-foot-high vaults.

▌ Flying buttresses made possible huge stained-glass windows, which converted natural light into divine colored light (*lux nova*), dramatically transforming the character of church interiors.

▌ High Gothic jamb statues broke out of the architectural straitjacket of their Early Gothic predecessors. In the west portals of Reims Cathedral, the sculpted figures move freely and use gestures to converse with their neighbors.

▌ In the 13th century, professional lay artists in Parisian workshops were renowned for producing illuminated manuscripts, usurping the role of monastic scriptoria.

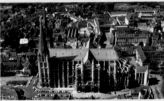
Chartres Cathedral, begun 1134; rebuilt after 1194

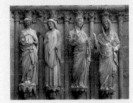
Annunciation and *Visitation*, Reims Cathedral, ca. 1230–1255

England and the Holy Roman Empire

▌ English Gothic churches, such as Salisbury Cathedral, differ from their French counterparts in their wider and shorter facades, and sparing use of flying buttresses. Especially characteristic of English Gothic architecture is the elaboration of architectural patterns. A prime example is the chapel of Henry VII in Westminster Abbey in London, which features Perpendicular-style fan vaults.

▌ In the Holy Roman Empire, architects eagerly embraced the French Gothic architectural style at Cologne Cathedral and elsewhere. German originality manifested itself most clearly in sculptures depicting emotionally charged figures in dramatic poses. The statues of secular historical figures in Naumburg Cathedral signal a revival of interest in portraiture.

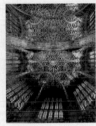
Chapel of Henry VII, London, 1503–1519

Italy

▌ Nicola Pisano was a master sculptor from southern Italy who carved pulpits incorporating marble panels that, both stylistically and in individual motifs, derive from ancient Roman sarcophagi.

▌ The leading Italian painter of the late 13th century was Cimabue, who worked in the Italo-Byzantine style, or maniera greca.

▌ Considered the first Renaissance painter, Giotto di Bondone forged a new path in the early 14th century. A pupil of Cimabue, he was a pioneer in pursuing a naturalistic approach to representation based on observation, which was at the core of the classical tradition in art.

▌ The greatest 14th-century Sienese painter was Duccio di Buoninsegna, whose *Maestà* still incorporates many Byzantine elements, but he relaxed the frontality and rigidity of his figures, and in narrative scenes took a decisive step toward humanizing religious subject matter.

▌ Secular themes also came to the fore in 14th-century Italy, most notably in Ambrogio Lorenzetti's frescoes for Siena's Palazzo Pubblico. His depictions of the city and its surrounding countryside are among the first landscapes in Western art since antiquity.

▌ Italian 14th-century architecture underscores the regional character of late medieval art. Orvieto Cathedral's facade incorporates elements of the French Gothic vocabulary, but it is a screen masking a traditional timber-roofed basilica with round arches in the nave arcade.

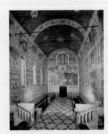
Giotto, Arena Chapel, Padua, ca. 1305

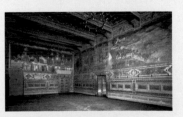
Lorenzetti, Sala della Pace, Siena, 1338–1339

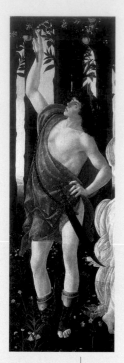

Mercury is the most enigmatic figure in Botticelli's lyrical painting celebrating love in springtime, probably a commemoration of the May 1482 wedding of Lorenzo di Pierfrancesco de' Medici.

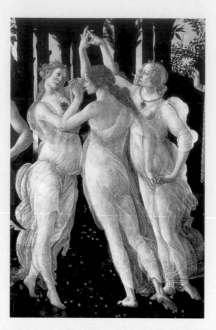

The dancing Three Graces closely resemble ancient prototypes Botticelli must have studied, but in 15th-century Florence, the Graces are clothed, albeit in thin, transparent garments.

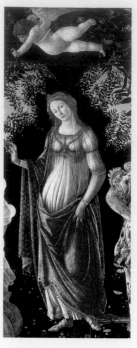

Cupid hovers over Venus, the central figure in this mythological allegory. The sky seen through the opening in the landscape behind Venus forms a kind of halo around the goddess of love's head.

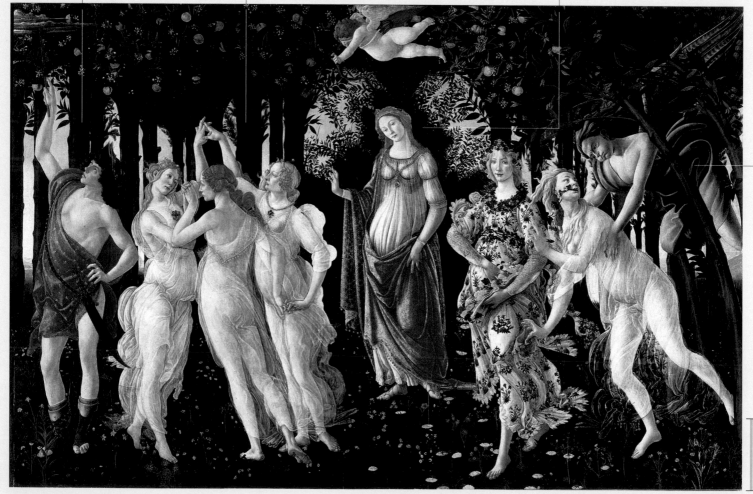

8-1 SANDRO BOTTICELLI, *Primavera,* ca. 1482. Tempera on wood, 6′ 8″ × 10′ 4″. Galleria degli Uffizi, Florence. ◼️

1 ft.

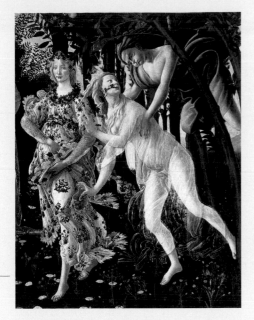

The blue ice-cold Zephyrus, the west wind, carries off and marries the nymph Chloris, whom he transforms into Flora, goddess of spring, appropriately shown wearing a rich floral gown.

The Early Renaissance in Europe

MEDICI PATRONAGE AND CLASSICAL LEARNING

The Medici family of Florence has become synonymous with the extraordinary cultural phenomenon called the Italian Renaissance. By the early 15th century (the '400s, or *Quattrocento* in Italian), the banker Giovanni di Bicci de' Medici (ca. 1360–1429) had established the family fortune. His son Cosimo (1389–1464) became a great patron of art and of learning in the broadest sense. For example, he founded the first public library since antiquity. Cosimo's grandson Lorenzo (1449–1492), called "the Magnificent," a member of the Platonic Academy of Philosophy, gathered about him artists and gifted men in all fields. He spent lavishly on buildings, paintings, and sculptures. Indeed, every great Quattrocento architect, painter, sculptor, philosopher, or humanist scholar enjoyed Medici patronage.

Of all the Florentine masters the Medici employed, perhaps the most famous today is SANDRO BOTTICELLI (1444–1510). His work is a testament to the intense interest the Medici and Quattrocento humanist scholars and artists had in the art, literature, and mythology of the Greco-Roman world—often interpreted by writers, painters, and sculptors alike in terms of Christianity according to the philosophical tenets of Neo-Platonism.

Botticelli painted *Primavera* (*Spring;* FIG. **8-1**) for Lorenzo di Pierfrancesco de' Medici (1463–1503), one of Lorenzo the Magnificent's cousins. Venus stands just to the right of center with her son Cupid hovering above her head. Botticelli drew attention to Venus by opening the landscape behind her to reveal a portion of sky that forms a kind of halo around the goddess of love's head. To her right, seemingly the target of Cupid's arrow, are the dancing Three Graces, based closely on ancient prototypes but clothed, albeit in thin, transparent garments. At the right, the blue ice-cold Zephyrus, the west wind, is about to carry off and marry the nymph Chloris, whom he transforms into Flora, goddess of spring, appropriately shown wearing a rich floral gown. At the far left, the enigmatic figure of Mercury turns away from all the others and reaches up with his distinctive staff, the *caduceus,* perhaps to dispel storm clouds. The sensuality of the representation, the appearance of Venus in springtime, and the abduction and marriage of Chloris all suggest the occasion for the painting was young Lorenzo's wedding in May 1482. But the painting also sums up the Neo-Platonists' view that earthly love is compatible with Christian theology. In their reinterpretation of classical mythology, Venus as the source of love provokes desire through Cupid. Desire can lead either to lust and violence (Zephyr) or through reason and faith (Mercury) to the love of God. *Primavera,* read from right to left, served to urge the newlyweds to seek God through love.

THE EARLY RENAISSANCE IN EUROPE

In the 14th and 15th centuries, Europe experienced the calamities of plague, war, and social upheaval. The Black Death that ravaged Italy in 1348, killing 50 to 60 percent of the population in the largest cities, also spread to much of the rest of Europe. Equally destabilizing—and far longer lasting—was the Hundred Years' War (1337–1453). Primarily a protracted series of conflicts between France and England, the war also involved Flanders, a region corresponding to parts of present-day northern France, Belgium, Holland, and Luxembourg (MAP 8-1). Crisis in the religious realm exacerbated the period's political instability. In 1305, the College of Cardinals elected a French pope, Clement V (r. 1305–1314). He and the French popes who succeeded him chose to reside in Avignon. Understandably, the Italians, who saw Rome as the rightful capital of the universal Church, resented the Avignon papacy. The conflict between the French and Italians resulted in the election in 1378 of two popes—Clement VII, who resided in Avignon, and Urban VI (r. 1378–1389), who remained in Rome. Thus began what became known as the Great Schism, which lasted until the election in 1417 of a new Roman pope, Martin V (r. 1417–1431), who was acceptable to all.

Despite the troubles of the age, a new economic system evolved—the early stage of European capitalism. In response to the financial requirements of trade, new credit and exchange systems created an economic network of enterprising European cities. Trade in money accompanied trade in commodities, and the former financed industry. Both were in the hands of international trading companies, such as the Medici bank of Florence. North of the Alps, in 1460 Flemish entrepreneurs established the first international commercial stock exchange in Antwerp, which became pivotal for Europe's integrated economic activity. Thriving commerce, industry, and finance contributed to the evolution of cities, as did the migration of a significant portion of the rural population to urban centers. With successful merchants and bankers joining kings, dukes, and popes as the leading patrons of painting, sculpture, and architecture, the arts also flourished.

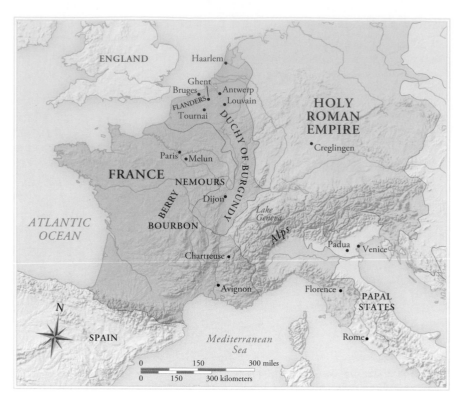

MAP 8-1 France, the duchy of Burgundy, and the Holy Roman Empire in 1477.

BURGUNDY AND FLANDERS

In the early 15th century, Philip the Good (r. 1419–1467) ruled a region known as the duchy of Burgundy (MAP 8-1), the fertile east-central region of France still famous for its wines. In 1369, one of Philip the Good's predecessors, Philip

---

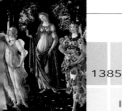

The Early Renaissance in Europe

1385	1425	1450	1475	1500
▮ Claus Sluter carves life-size statues of biblical figures with portraitlike features for Philip the Bold, duke of Burgundy	▮ Robert Campin, Jan van Eyck, and Rogier van der Weyden popularize the use of oil paints in Flanders	▮ In Germany, Johannes Gutenberg invents moveable type and prints the first Bibles on a letterpress	▮ The Late Gothic style lingers in Germany in the large wood retables of Tilman Riemenschneider	
▮ The Limbourg brothers expand the illusionistic capabilities of manuscript illumination for Jean, duke of Berry	▮ German graphic artists pioneer woodcut printing, making art affordable to the masses	▮ Federico da Montefeltro brings Piero della Francesca to the Urbino court	▮ Martin Schongauer becomes the first northern European master of engraving	
▮ Ghiberti wins the competition to design new doors for Florence's baptistery	▮ Ghiberti installs the *Gates of Paradise* facing Florence Cathedral	▮ Alberti rebuilds Sant'Andrea and Mantegna creates illusionistic paintings for Duke Ludovico Gonzaga of Mantua	▮ Botticelli paints Neo-Platonic mythological allegories for the Medici	
▮ Masaccio carries Giotto's naturalism further in frescoes	▮ Donatello revives freestanding nude male statuary		▮ Alberti publishes his treatise on architecture	
▮ Brunelleschi develops linear perspective and designs the Ospedale degli Innocenti	▮ Michelozzo builds the new Medici palace in Florence		▮ Savonarola condemns humanism and the Medici flee Florence	
	▮ Alberti publishes his treatise on painting			

the Bold (r. 1364–1404), married the daughter of the count of Flanders, and acquired territory in the Netherlands. Thereafter, the major source of Burgundian wealth and power was Bruges, the city that made Burgundy a dangerous rival of royal France. Bruges initially derived its wealth from the wool trade but soon expanded into banking, becoming the financial clearinghouse for all of northern Europe. Indeed, Bruges so dominated Flanders that the duke of Burgundy eventually chose to make the city his capital and moved his court there from Dijon. Due to the expanded territory and the prosperity of the duchy of Burgundy, Philip the Bold and his successors were probably the most powerful northern European rulers during the first three-quarters of the 15th century. Although cousins of the French kings, they usually supported England (on which they relied for the raw materials used in their wool industry) during the Hundred Years' War and, at times, controlled much of northern France, including Paris, the seat of the French monarchy. At the height of Burgundian power, the reigning duke's lands stretched from the Rhône River to the North Sea.

Chartreuse de Champmol

Philip the Bold was among the greatest art patrons in northern Europe. His largest artistic enterprise was the building of the Chartreuse de Champmol, near Dijon. A *chartreuse* ("charter house" in English) is a Carthusian monastery. The Carthusian order, founded in the late 11th century by Saint Bruno at Chartreuse in southeastern France, consisted of monks who devoted their lives to solitary living and prayer. Inspired by Saint-Denis, the burial site of the kings of France (see Chapter 7), Philip intended the Dijon chartreuse to become a ducal mausoleum and serve both as a means of securing salvation in perpetuity for the Burgundian dukes and as a dynastic symbol of Burgundian power.

For the Champmol cloister, Philip the Bold's head sculptor, CLAUS SLUTER (active ca. 1380–1406) of Haarlem (Netherlands), designed a large sculptural fountain located in a well that provided water for the monastery, but water probably did not spout from the fountain because the Carthusian commitment to silence and prayer would have precluded anything that produced sound. Sluter's *Well of Moses* (FIG. **8-2**) features statues of Moses and five other prophets (David, Daniel, Isaiah, Jeremiah, and Zachariah) surrounding a base that once supported a *Crucifixion* group. The Carthusians called the *Well of Moses* a *fons vitae*, a fountain of everlasting life. The blood of the crucified Christ symbolically flowed down over the grieving angels and Old Testament prophets, spilling into the well below, washing over Christ's prophetic predecessors and redeeming anyone who would drink water from the well.

Although the six prophets recall the jamb statues (FIG. 7-14) of Gothic portals, they are much more realistically rendered. Sluter's intense observation of natural appearance enabled him to sculpt the figures with portraitlike features and to differentiate textures from coarse drapery to smooth flesh and silky hair. Originally, paint, much of which has flaked off, further augmented the naturalism of the figures.

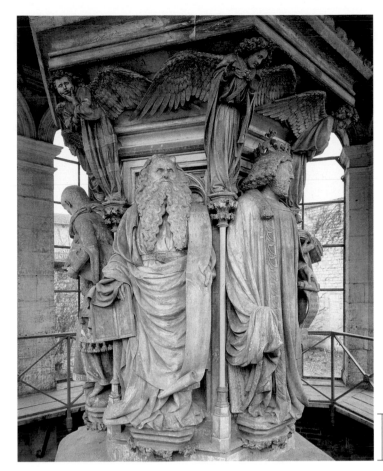

8-2 CLAUS SLUTER, *Well of Moses*, Chartreuse de Champmol, Dijon, France, 1395–1406. Limestone, painted and gilded by JEAN MALOUEL, Moses 6' high. ◼◀

The *Well of Moses*, a symbolic fountain of life made for the duke of Burgundy, originally supported a *Crucifixion* group. Sluter's figures recall French Gothic jamb statues but are far more realistic.

(The painter was JEAN MALOUEL [ca. 1365–1415], another Netherlandish master.) This fascination with the specific and tangible in the visible world became one of the chief characteristics of 15th-century Flemish art.

Robert Campin

One of the earliest Flemish masters—and one of the first to use the new medium of *oil painting* (see "Tempera and Oil Painting," page 224)—was the MASTER OF FLÉMALLE, whom many scholars identify as ROBERT CAMPIN (ca. 1378–1444) of Tournai. Although traditional scholarship credited Jan van Eyck (discussed next) with the invention of oil painting, another Flemish painter, Melchior Broederlam (active ca. 1387–1409), used oil-based pigments in the 1390s. Flemish painters built up their pictures by superimposing translucent paint layers over a carefully planned drawing made on a panel prepared with a white ground. With the oil medium, Flemish painters could create richer colors than previously possible, giving their paintings an intense tonality, the illusion of glowing light, and enamel-like surfaces. These traits differed significantly from the high-keyed color, sharp light, and rather *matte* (dull) surfaces of *tempera*. The brilliant and versatile oil medium suited perfectly the formal intentions of 15th-century Flemish painters, who aimed for

Tempera and Oil Painting

The generic words *paint* and *pigment* encompass a wide range of substances artists have used through the ages. Fresco aside (see "Fresco Painting," Chapter 7, page 213), during the 14th century, egg *tempera* was the material of choice for most painters, both in Italy and northern Europe. Tempera consists of egg combined with a wet paste of ground pigment. In his influential treatise *Il libro dell'arte* (*The Artist's Handbook*), Cennino Cennini (ca. 1370–1440), an Italian painter, noted that artists mixed only the egg yolk with the ground pigment, but analyses of paintings from this period have revealed some artists chose to use the entire egg. Images painted with tempera have a velvety sheen. Artists usually applied tempera to the surface with a light touch because thick application of the pigment mixture results in premature cracking and flaking.

Some artists used oil paints as far back as the eighth century, but not until the early 1400s did oil painting become widespread. Flemish artists were among the first to employ oils extensively (often mixing them with tempera), and Italian painters quickly followed suit. The discovery of better drying components in the early 15th century enhanced the setting capabilities of oils. Rather than apply these oils in the light, flecked brushstrokes that tempera encouraged, artists laid the oils down in transparent *glazes* over opaque or semiopaque underlayers. In this manner, painters could build up deep tones through repeated glazing. Unlike works in tempera, whose surface dries quickly due to water evaporation, oils dry more slowly, giving the artist time to rework areas. This flexibility must have been particularly appealing to artists who worked very deliberately, such as the Flemish masters Robert Campin (FIG. 8-3) and Jan van Eyck (FIGS. 8-4 to 8-6) and the Italian Leonardo da Vinci (see Chapter 9). Leonardo also preferred oil paint because its gradual drying process and consistency permitted him to blend the pigments, thereby creating the impressive *sfumato* (smoky) effect that contributed to his fame.

Both tempera and oils can be applied to various surfaces. Through the early 16th century, wood panels served as the foundation for most paintings. Italians painted on poplar. Northern European artists used oak, lime, beech, chestnut, cherry, pine, and silver fir. Availability of these timbers determined the choice of wood. Linen canvas became increasingly popular in the late 16th century. Although evidence suggests artists did not intend permanency for their early images on canvas, the material proved particularly useful in areas such as Venice where high humidity warped wood panels and made fresco unfeasible. Further, until artists began to use wooden bars to stretch the canvas to form a taut surface, canvas paintings were more portable than wood panels.

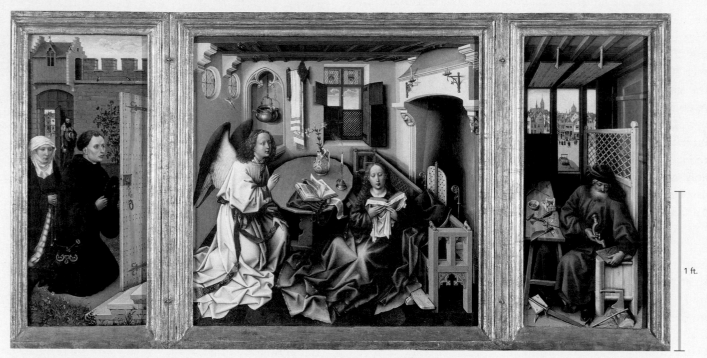

8-3 Robert Campin (Master of Flémalle), *Mérode Altarpiece* (open), ca. 1425–1428. Oil on wood, center panel 2′ 1⅜″ × 2′ ⅞″, each wing 2′ 1⅜″ × 10⅞″. Metropolitan Museum of Art, New York (The Cloisters Collection, 1956). ◼◀

Campin set *Annunciation* in a Flemish merchant's home in which the everyday objects have symbolic significance. Oil paints enabled Campin to depict all the details with loving fidelity.

sharply focused clarity of detail in their representation of objects ranging in scale from large to almost invisible.

Campin's most famous work is the *Mérode Altarpiece* (FIG. 8-3), a private commission for household prayer. It was not unusual in that respect. In 15th-century Flanders, lay patrons far outnumbered the clergy in commissioning religious artworks. At the time, various reform movements advocated personal devotion, and in the years leading up to the Protestant Reformation in the early 16th century, private devotional exercises and prayer grew in popularity. Perhaps the most striking feature of these private altarpieces is the integration of religious and secular concerns. For example, artists often presented biblical scenes as taking place in a Flemish house. Religion was such an integral part of Flemish life that separating the sacred from the secular became virtually impossible and undesirable. Moreover, the presentation in religious art of familiar settings and objects no doubt strengthened the direct bond the patron or viewer felt with biblical figures.

The *Mérode Altarpiece* is a small *triptych* (three-paneled painting) in which the center panel represents the popular *Annunciation* theme (as prophesied in Isaiah 7:14). The archangel Gabriel approaches Mary, who sits reading in a well-kept Flemish home. The view through the window in the right wing and the depicted accessories, furniture, and utensils confirm the locale as Flanders. However, the objects represented are not merely decorative. They also function as religious symbols. The book, extinguished candle, and lilies on the table, the copper basin in the corner niche, the towels, fire screen, and bench all symbolize the Virgin's purity and her divine mission.

In the right panel, Joseph, apparently unaware of Gabriel's arrival, has constructed a mousetrap, symbolic of the theological concept that Christ is bait set in the trap of the world to catch the Devil. The ax, saw, and rod Campin painted in the foreground of Joseph's workshop not only are tools of the carpenter's trade but also are mentioned in Isaiah 10:15. In the left panel, the closed garden is symbolic of Mary's purity, and the flowers Campin included relate to Mary's virtues, especially humility.

The altarpiece's donor, Peter Inghelbrecht, a wealthy merchant, and his wife, Margarete Scrynmakers, kneel in the garden and witness the momentous event through an open door. *Donor portraits*—portraits of the individual(s) who commissioned (or "donated") the work—became very popular in the 15th century. In this instance, in addition to asking to be represented in their altarpiece, the Inghelbrechts probably specified the subject. *Inghelbrecht* means "angel bringer," a reference to the *Annunciation* theme of the central panel. *Scrynmakers* means "cabinet- or shrine-makers," referring to the workshop scene in the right panel.

Jan van Eyck The first Netherlandish painter to achieve international fame was JAN VAN EYCK (ca. 1390–1441), who in 1425 became Philip the Good's court painter. In 1432, he moved his studio to Bruges, where the duke maintained his official residence. That same year he completed the *Ghent Altarpiece* (FIGS. 8-4 and 8-5)—which his older brother HUBERT VAN EYCK (ca. 1366–1426) had begun—for the church originally dedicated to John the Baptist (since 1540, Saint Bavo Cathedral) in Ghent. One of the most characteristic art forms in 15th-century Flanders was the monumental freestanding altarpiece, and the *Ghent Altarpiece* is one of the largest. Placed behind the altar, these imposing works served as backdrops for the Mass. Given their function, it is not surprising that many altarpieces depict scenes directly related to Christ's sacrifice. Flemish altarpieces most often took the form of *polyptychs*—hinged multipaneled paintings or relief panels. The hinges enabled the clergy to close the polyptych's side wings over the center panel(s). Artists decorated both the exterior and interior of the altarpieces. This multi-image format provided the opportunity to construct

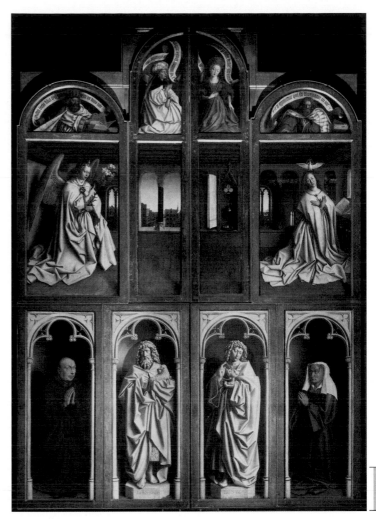

8-4 HUBERT and JAN VAN EYCK, *Ghent Altarpiece* (closed), Saint Bavo Cathedral, Ghent, Belgium, completed 1432. Oil on wood, 11′ 5″ × 7′ 6″. ◼◀

Monumental painted altarpieces were popular in Flemish churches. Artists decorated both the interiors and exteriors of these polyptychs, which often, as here, included donor portraits.

narratives through a sequence of images, somewhat as in manuscript illustration. Although concrete information is lacking about when the clergy opened and closed these altarpieces, the wings probably remained closed on regular days and open on Sundays and feast days. On this schedule, viewers could have seen both the interior and exterior—diverse imagery at various times according to the liturgical calendar.

Jodocus Vyd, diplomat-retainer of Philip the Good, and his wife, Isabel Borluut, commissioned the *Ghent Altarpiece*. Vyd's largesse contributed to his appointment as burgomeister (chief magistrate) of Ghent shortly after the unveiling of the work. Two of the exterior panels (FIG. 8-4) depict the donors. The husband and wife, painted in illusionistically rendered niches, kneel with their hands clasped in prayer. They gaze piously at illusionistic stone sculptures of Ghent's patron saints, John the Baptist and John the Evangelist. The *Annunciation* appears on the upper register, with a careful representation of a Flemish town outside the painted window of the center panel. In the uppermost arched panels, van

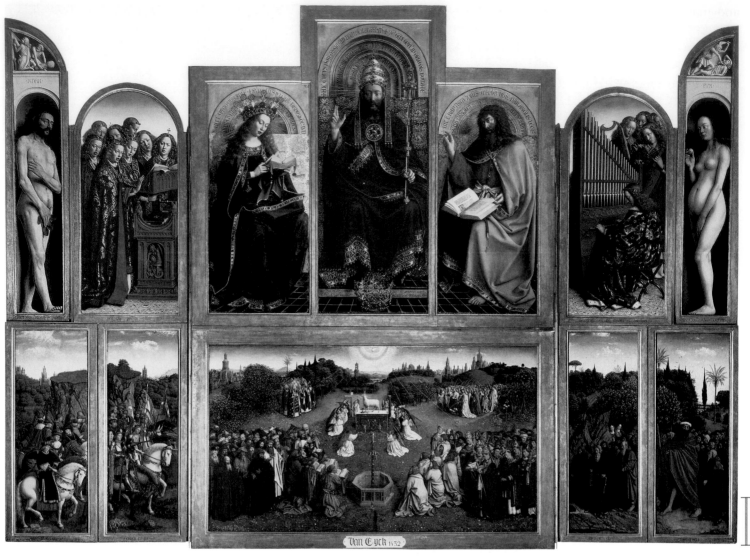

8-5 HUBERT and JAN VAN EYCK, *Ghent Altarpiece* (open), Saint Bavo Cathedral, Ghent, Belgium, completed 1432. Oil on wood, 11' 5" × 15' 1". ◼◀

In this sumptuous painting of salvation from the original sin of Adam and Eve (shown on the wings), God the Father presides in majesty between the Virgin Mary and John the Baptist.

1 ft.

Eyck depicted the Old Testament prophets Zachariah and Micah, along with *sibyls,* Greco-Roman mythological female prophets whose writings the Church interpreted as prophesies of Christ.

When open (FIG. 8-5), the altarpiece reveals a sumptuous, superbly colored painting of humanity's redemption through Christ. In the upper register, God the Father—wearing the pope's triple tiara, with a worldly crown at his feet, and resplendent in a deep-scarlet mantle—presides in majesty. To God's right is the Virgin, represented as the queen of Heaven, with a crown of 12 stars upon her head. John the Baptist sits to God's left. To either side is a choir of angels, with an angel playing an organ on the right. Adam and Eve appear in the far panels. The inscriptions in the arches above Mary and John the Baptist extol the Virgin's virtue and purity and John the Baptist's greatness as the forerunner of Christ. The inscription above the Lord's head translates as "This is God, all-powerful in his divine majesty; of all the best, by the gentleness of his goodness; the most liberal giver, because of his infinite generosity." The step behind the crown at the Lord's

feet bears the inscription "On his head, life without death. On his brow, youth without age. On his right, joy without sadness. On his left, security without fear." The entire altarpiece amplifies the central theme of salvation. Even though humans, symbolized by Adam and Eve, are sinful, they will be saved because God, in his infinite love, will sacrifice his own son for this purpose.

The panels of the lower register extend the symbolism of the upper. In the center panel, the community of saints comes from the four corners of the earth through an opulent, flower-spangled landscape. They proceed toward the altar of the lamb and the octagonal fountain of life. The lamb symbolizes the sacrificed Son of God, whose heart bleeds into a chalice, while into the fountain spills the "pure river of water of life, clear as crystal, proceeding out of the throne of God and of the Lamb" (Rev. 22:1). On the right, the 12 apostles and a group of martyrs in red robes advance. On the left appear prophets. In the right background come the virgin martyrs, and in the left background the holy confessors approach. On the lower wings, hermits, pilgrims, knights, and judges approach from left and right. They symbolize the four cardinal virtues: Temperance, Prudence, Fortitude, and Justice, respectively. The altarpiece celebrates the whole Christian cycle from the fall to the redemption, presenting the Church triumphant in heavenly Jerusalem.

Van Eyck used oil paints to render the entire altarpiece in a shimmering splendor of color that defies reproduction. No small detail escaped the painter. With pristine specificity, he revealed the beauty of the most insignificant object as if it were a work of piety as much as a work of art. He depicted the soft texture of hair, the glitter of gold in the heavy brocades, the luster of pearls, and the flashing of gems, all with loving fidelity to appearance.

Giovanni Arnolfini Both the *Mérode Altarpiece* and the *Ghent Altarpiece* include painted portraits of their donors. These paintings marked a significant revival of portraiture, a genre that had languished since antiquity. A purely secular portrait, but one with religious overtones, is Jan van Eyck's oil painting *Giovanni Arnolfini and His Wife* (FIG. **8-6**). Van Eyck depicted the Lucca financier (who had established himself in Bruges as an agent of the Medici family) and his second wife, whose name is not known, in their home, a setting that is simultaneously mundane and charged with the spiritual. As in the *Mérode Altarpiece,* almost every object carries meaning. The cast-aside clogs indicate this event takes place on holy ground. The little dog symbolizes fidelity. Behind the couple, the curtains of the marriage bed have been opened. The bedpost's *finial* (crowning ornament) is a tiny statue of Saint Margaret, patron saint of childbirth. (The bride is not yet pregnant, although the fashionable costume she wears makes her appear so.) From the finial hangs a whisk broom, symbolic of domestic care. The oranges on the chest below the window may refer to fertility. The single candle burning in the left rear holder of the ornate chandelier and the mirror, in which the viewer sees the entire room reflected, symbolize the all-seeing eye of God. The small medallions set into the mirror frame show tiny scenes from the passion of Christ and represent God's promise of salvation for the figures reflected on the mirror's convex surface. Viewers of the period would have been familiar with many of the objects included in the painting because of traditional Flemish customs. Husbands presented brides with clogs, and the solitary lit candle in the chandelier was part of Flemish marriage practices. Van Eyck's placement of the two figures suggests conventional gender roles—the woman stands near the bed and well into the room, whereas the man stands near the open window, symbolic of the outside world.

Van Eyck enhanced the documentary nature of this scene by exquisitely painting each object. He carefully distinguished textures and depicted the light from the window on the left reflecting off various surfaces. He also augmented the scene's credibility by including the convex mirror (complete with its spatial distortion, brilliantly recorded), because viewers can see not only the principals, Arnolfini and his wife, but also two persons who look into the room through the door. One of these must be the artist himself, as the

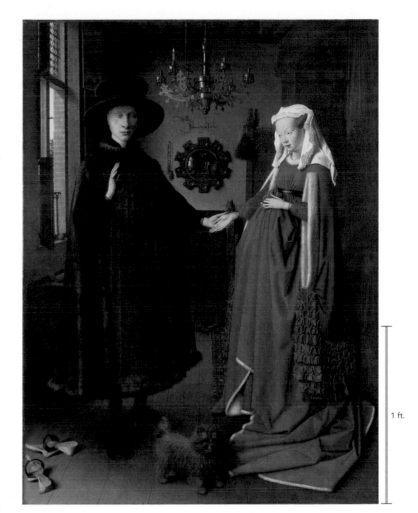

8-6 JAN VAN EYCK, *Giovanni Arnolfini and His Wife*, 1434. Oil on wood, 2′ 9″ × 1′ 10½″. National Gallery, London. ◼◀

Van Eyck played a major role in establishing portraiture as an important Flemish art form. In this portrait of an Italian financier and his wife, he also portrayed himself in the mirror.

florid inscription above the mirror—*Johannes de Eyck fuit hic* ("Jan van Eyck was here")—announces he was present. The picture's purpose, then, would have been to record and sanctify this marriage. Most scholars now reject this traditional reading, however, and it has been suggested that Arnolfini is conferring legal privileges on his wife to conduct business in his absence. In either case, the artist functions as a witness. The self-portrait of van Eyck in the mirror also underscores the painter's self-consciousness as a professional artist whose role deserves to be recorded and remembered.

Van Eyck and his contemporaries established portraiture as a major art form. Great patrons embraced the opportunity to have their likenesses painted. They wanted to memorialize themselves in their dynastic lines and to establish their identities, ranks, and stations with images far more concrete than heraldic coats of arms. Portraits also served to represent state officials at events they could not attend. Sometimes, royalty, nobility, and the very rich would send artists to paint the likeness of a prospective bride or groom. When young King Charles VI (r. 1380–1422) of France sought a bride, he dispatched a painter to three different royal courts to make portraits of the candidates.

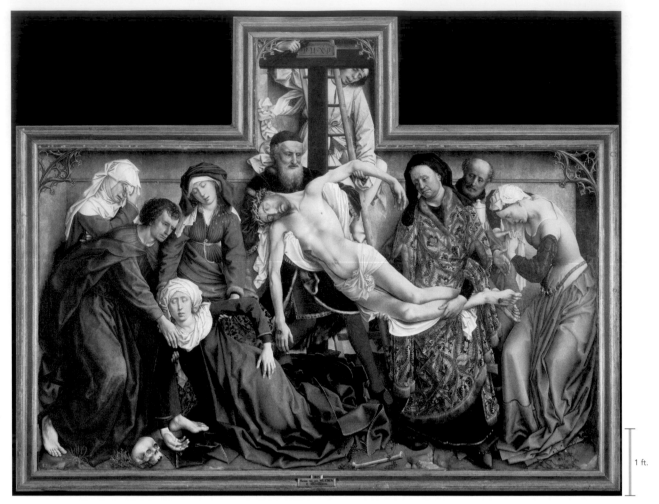

1 ft.

8-7 ROGIER VAN DER WEYDEN, *Deposition,* center panel of a triptych from Notre-Dame hors-les-murs, Louvain, Belgium, ca. 1435. Oil on wood, 7′ 2⅝″ × 8′ 7⅛″. Museo del Prado, Madrid. ◼◂

Deposition resembles a relief carving in which the biblical figures act out a drama of passionate sorrow as if on a shallow theatrical stage. The painting makes an unforgettable emotional impact.

Rogier van der Weyden A painter whose fame rivaled that of Jan van Eyck was ROGIER VAN DER WEYDEN (ca. 1400–1464), who was an assistant in the workshop of Robert Campin when van Eyck received the commission for the *Ghent Altarpiece.* Rogier quickly became renowned for his dynamic compositions stressing human action and drama. He concentrated on Christian themes such as *Deposition* (FIG. **8-7**) and other passion episodes that elicited powerful emotions, moving observers deeply by vividly portraying the suffering of Christ.

Deposition is the center panel of a triptych commissioned by the archers' guild of Louvain. Rogier acknowledged his patrons by incorporating the crossbow (the guild's symbol) into the decorative tracery in the corners. Instead of creating a deep landscape setting, as van Eyck might have, Rogier compressed the figures and action onto a shallow stage with a golden back wall. The painting, with the artist's crisp drawing and precise modeling of forms, resembles a stratified relief carving. A series of lateral undulating movements gives the group a compositional unity, a formal cohesion Rogier strengthened by depicting the desolating anguish many of the figures share. The similar poses of Christ and his mother

reflect the belief that Mary suffered the same pain at the crucifixion as her son. Few painters have equaled Rogier in the rendering of passionate sorrow as it vibrates through a figure or distorts a tear-stained face. His depiction of the agony of loss in *Deposition* is among the most authentic in religious art and creates an immediate and unforgettable emotional effect on the viewer.

Saint Luke Slightly later in date is Rogier's *Saint Luke Drawing the Virgin* (FIG. **8-8**), probably painted for the Guild of Saint Luke, the artists' guild in Brussels. The panel depicts the patron saint of painters drawing the Virgin Mary using a *silverpoint* (a sharp *stylus* that creates a fine line). The theme paid tribute to the profession of painting in Flanders by drawing attention to the venerable history of the painter's craft. Many scholars believe Rogier's Saint Luke is a self-portrait, identifying the Flemish painter with the first Christian artist and underscoring the holy nature of painting. Rogier shared with Campin and van Eyck the aim of recording every detail of the scene with loving fidelity to optical appearance, seen here in the rich fabrics, floor pattern, and the landscape visible through the window. Also, as his older

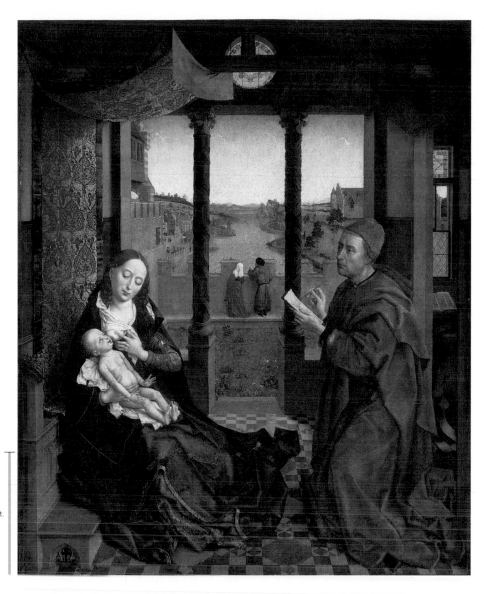

1 ft.

Probably commissioned by the painters' guild in Brussels, this panel honors the first Christian artist and the profession of painting. Saint Luke may be a self-portrait of Rogier van der Weyden.

colleagues did, Rogier imbued much of the representation with symbolic significance. At the right, the ox identifies the figure recording the Virgin's features as Saint Luke. The carved armrest of the Virgin's bench depicts Adam, Eve, and the serpent, reminding the viewer that Mary is the new Eve and Christ the new Adam who will redeem humanity from original sin.

Hugo van der Goes By the mid-15th century, Flemish art had achieved renown throughout Europe. The *Portinari Altarpiece* (FIG. **8-9**) is a large-scale Flemish triptych in a family chapel in Florence, Italy. The artist who received the commission was HUGO VAN DER GOES (ca. 1440–1482) of Ghent. Hugo painted the altarpiece for Tommaso Portinari, an Italian shipowner and agent for the Medici family. Portinari appears on the wings of the triptych with his family and their patron saints. In the central panel, *Adoration of the Shepherds*, the

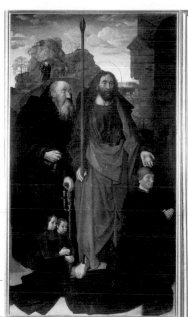
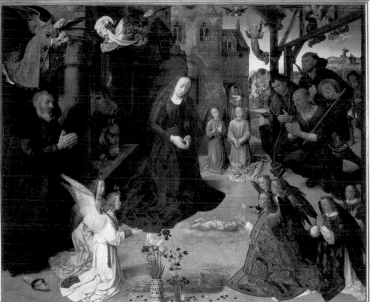
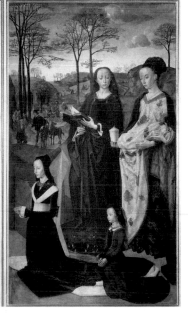

1 ft.

8-9 HUGO VAN DER GOES, *Portinari Altarpiece* (open), from Sant'Egidio, Florence, Italy, ca. 1476. Tempera and oil on wood, center panel 8′ 3½″ × 10′, each wing 8′ 3½″ × 4′ 7½″. Galleria degli Uffizi, Florence.

This altarpiece is a rare instance of the awarding of a major commission in Italy to a Flemish painter. The Florentines admired Hugo's realistic details and brilliant portrayal of human character.

Virgin, Joseph, and the angels seem to brood on the suffering to come rather than to meditate on the miracle of Jesus's birth. Mary kneels, somber and monumental, on a tilted ground—a compositional device that may derive from the tilted stage floors of mystery plays. Three shepherds enter from the right rear. Hugo represented them in attitudes of wonder, piety, and gaping curiosity. Their lined faces, work-worn hands, and uncouth dress and manner seem immediately familiar.

After Portinari placed his altarpiece in his family's chapel in the Florentine church of Sant'Egidio, it created a considerable stir among Italian artists. Although the painting may have seemed unstructured to them and the varying scale of the figures according to their importance perpetuated medieval conventions, Hugo's masterful technique and incredible realism in representing drapery, flowers, animals, and, above all, human character and emotion made a deep impression on them.

devotional prayers, litanies to the saints, and an illustrated calendar containing local religious feast days. Books of Hours became favorite possessions of the northern European aristocracy during the 14th and 15th centuries. These sumptuous books eventually became available to affluent merchants and contributed to the decentralization of religious practice that was one factor in the Protestant Reformation in the early 16th century (see Chapter 9).

The calendar pictures of *Les Très Riches Heures* represent the 12 months in terms of the associated seasonal tasks, alternating scenes of nobility and peasantry. Above each picture is a lunette depicting the zodiac signs and the chariot of the sun as it makes its yearly cycle through the heavens. Beyond its function as a religious book, *Les Très Riches Heures* also visually captures the power of the duke and his relationship to the peasants. The illustration for October (FIG. **8-10**) focuses on

FRANCE

In France, the anarchy of the Hundred Years' War and the weakness of the kings gave rise to a group of powerful duchies. The strongest and wealthiest—the duchy of Burgundy, which controlled Flanders—has already been examined. But the dukes of Berry, Bourbon, and Nemours as well as members of the French royal court were also important art patrons.

Limbourg Brothers During the 15th century, French artists built on the achievements of Gothic manuscript painters (see Chapter 7). Among the most significant developments was a new conception and presentation of space. The LIMBOURG BROTHERS—POL, HERMAN, and JEAN, three nephews of Jean Malouel (FIG. 8-2), the court artist of Philip the Bold—were pioneers in expanding the illusionistic capabilities of manuscript illumination. The Limbourgs produced a gorgeously illustrated Book of Hours for Jean, the duke of Berry (r. 1360–1416) and brother of King Charles V (r. 1364–1380) of France and Philip the Bold. The duke was an avid art patron and focused on collecting manuscripts, jewels, and rare artifacts. The three brothers worked on *Les Très Riches Heures du Duc de Berry* (*The Very Sumptuous Hours of the Duke of Berry*) until their deaths in 1416. A *Book of Hours*, like a *breviary,* was used for reading prayers. As prayer books, they replaced the traditional *psalters* (books of psalms), which had been the only liturgical books in private hands until the mid-13th century. A Book of Hours contained liturgical passages to be read privately at set times during the day, as well as penitential psalms,

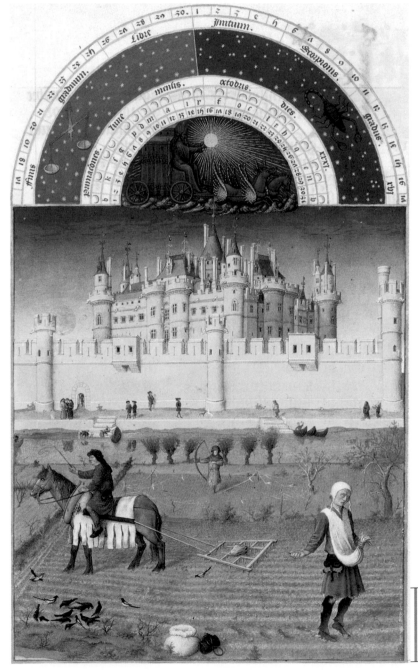

8-10 LIMBOURG BROTHERS (POL, HERMAN, JEAN), *October,* from *Les Très Riches Heures du Duc de Berry,* 1413–1416. Colors and ink on vellum, 8⅞″ × 5⅜″. Musée Condé, Chantilly. ◼

The Limbourg brothers expanded the illusionistic capabilities of manuscript painting with their sumptuous pictures in *Les Très Riches Heures* depicting characteristic activities of each month.

1 in.

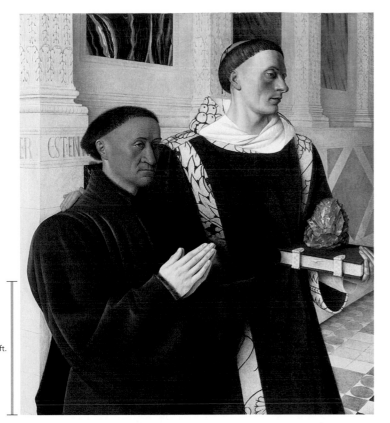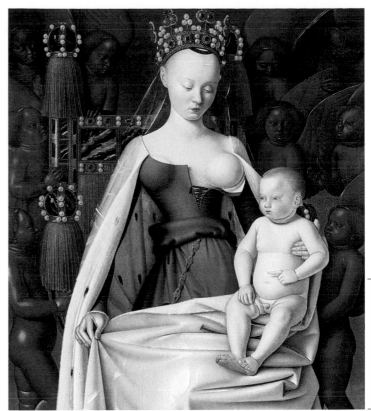

8-11 JEAN FOUQUET, *Melun Diptych.* Left wing: *Étienne Chevalier and Saint Stephen,* ca. 1450. Oil on wood, 3′ ½″ × 2′ 9½″. Gemäldegalerie, Staatliche Museen zu Berlin, Berlin. Right wing: *Virgin and Child,* ca. 1451. Oil on wood, 3′ 1¼″ × 2′ 9½″. Koninklijk Museum voor Schone Kunsten, Antwerp.

Fouquet's meticulous representation of a pious kneeling donor with a standing patron saint recalls Flemish painting, as do the three-quarter stances and the realism of the portraits.

the peasantry. The Limbourgs depicted a sower, a harrower on horseback, and washerwomen, along with city dwellers, who promenade in front of the Louvre (the French king's residence at the time). The peasants do not appear discontented as they go about their tasks. Surely, this imagery flattered the duke's sense of himself as a compassionate master. The growing artistic interest in naturalism is evident in the careful way the painter recorded the architectural details of the Louvre and in the convincing shadows of the people, animals, and objects (such as the archer scarecrow and the horse) in the scene.

As a whole, *Les Très Riches Heures* reinforced the image of the duke of Berry as a devout man, cultured bibliophile, sophisticated art patron, and powerful and magnanimous leader. Further, the expanded range of subject matter, especially the prominence of genre subjects in a religious book, reflected the increasing integration of religious and secular concerns in both art and life at the time. Although all three Limbourg brothers worked on *Les Très Riches Heures,* art historians have never been able to ascertain which brother painted which images. Given the common practice of collaboration on artistic projects at this time, however, the determination of specific authorship is not very important.

Jean Fouquet Images for private devotional use were popular in France, as in Flanders. Among the French artists whose paintings were in demand was JEAN FOUQUET (ca. 1420–1481), who worked for King Charles VII (r. 1422–1461)

and for the duke of Nemours. Fouquet painted a *diptych* (two-paneled painting; FIG. **8-11**) for Étienne Chevalier, the royal treasurer of France. In the left panel, Chevalier appears with his patron saint, Saint Stephen (Étienne in French). Appropriately, Fouquet depicted Chevalier as devout—kneeling, with hands clasped in prayer. The representation of the pious donor with his standing saint recalls Flemish art, as do the three-quarter stances, the realism of Chevalier's portrait, and the painting medium (oil on wood). The artist portrayed Saint Stephen holding the stone of his martyrdom (death by stoning) atop a Bible. Fouquet rendered the entire image in meticulous detail and included a highly ornamented architectural setting.

In its original diptych form in Melun Cathedral (the two panels are now in different museums), the viewer would follow the gaze of Chevalier and Saint Stephen over to the right panel, which depicts the Virgin Mary and Christ Child. The juxtaposition of these two images enabled the patron to bear witness to the sacred. However, the integration of sacred and secular (especially the political or personal) prevalent in other northern European artworks complicates the reading of this diptych. Agnès Sorel (1421–1450), the mistress of Charles VII, was Fouquet's model for the Virgin Mary. Chevalier commissioned this painting after Sorel's death, probably by poisoning while pregnant with the king's child. Thus, in addition to the religious interpretation of this diptych, there is surely a personal and political narrative here as well.

HOLY ROMAN EMPIRE

Because the Holy Roman Empire (whose core was Germany) did not participate in the drawn-out saga of the Hundred Years' War, its economy remained stable and prosperous. Without a dominant court to commission artworks, wealthy merchants and clergy became the primary German patrons during the 15th century.

Tilman Riemenschneider Carved wooden *retables* (altarpieces) were popular commissions for German churches. One prominent sculptor who specialized in producing retables was Tilman Riemenschneider (ca. 1460–1531), who created the *Creglingen Altarpiece* for a parish church in Creglingen, incorporating intricate Gothic forms, especially in the retable's elaborate canopy. The subject of the center panel (FIG. **8-12**) is *Assumption of the Virgin*. By employing an endless and restless line running through the garments of the figures, Riemenschneider succeeded in setting the whole design into fluid motion, and no individual element functions without the rest. The draperies float and flow around bodies lost within them, serving not as descriptions but as design elements that tie the figures to one another and to the framework. A look of psychic strain, a facial expression common in Riemenschneider's work, heightens the spirituality of the figures, immaterial and weightless as they appear.

Martin Schongauer A new age blossomed with the invention by Johannes Gutenberg (ca. 1400–1468) of moveable type around 1450 and the development of the printing press. Printing had been known in China centuries before but had never fostered, as it did in 15th-century Europe, a revolution in written communication and in the generation and management of information. Printing provided new and challenging media for artists, and the earliest form was the *woodcut* (see "Woodcuts, Engravings, and Etchings," page 233). Artists produced inexpensive woodblock prints before the development of moveable-type printing. But when a rise in literacy and the improved economy necessitated production of illustrated books on a grand scale, artists met the challenge of bringing the woodcut picture onto the same page as the letterpress. The woodcut medium hardly had matured when the technique of *engraving,* begun in the 1430s and well developed by 1450, proved much more flexible. Predictably, in the second half of the century,

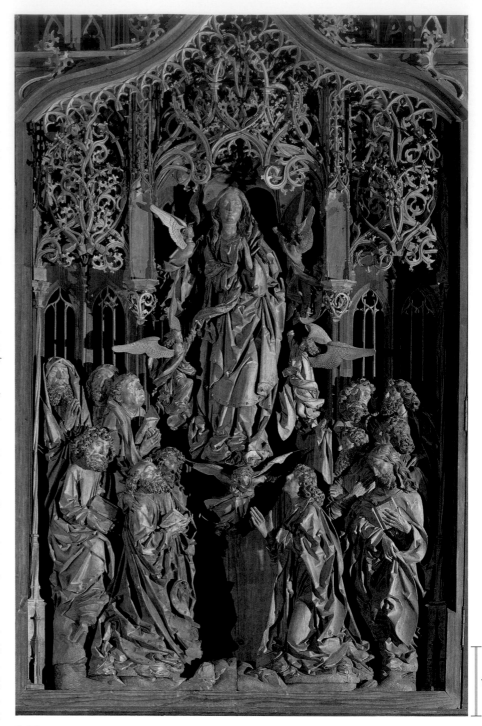

8-12 Tilman Riemenschneider, *Assumption of the Virgin,* center panel of *Creglingen Altarpiece,* parish church, Creglingen, Germany, ca. 1495–1499. Lindenwood, 6' 1" wide.

Riemenschneider specialized in carving large wood retables. His works feature intricate Gothic tracery and religious figures whose bodies are almost lost within their swirling garments.

engraving began to replace the woodcut process, for making both book illustrations and widely popular single prints.

Martin Schongauer (ca. 1430–1491) was the most skilled and subtle early master of metal engraving in northern Europe. His *Saint Anthony Tormented by Demons* (FIG. **8-13**) shows both the versatility of the medium and the artist's mastery of it. The stoic saint is caught in a revolving thornbush of spiky demons, who claw and tear at him furiously. With

Woodcuts, Engravings, and Etchings

With the invention of moveable type in the 15th century and the new widespread availability of paper from commercial mills, the art of printmaking developed rapidly in Europe. A *print* is an artwork on paper, usually produced in multiple impressions. The set of prints an artist creates from a single print surface is called an *edition*. The printmaking process involves the transfer of ink from a printing surface to paper. This can be accomplished in several ways. During the 15th and 16th centuries, artists most commonly used the *relief* and *intaglio* methods of printmaking.

Artists produce relief prints, the oldest and simplest printing method, by carving into a surface, usually wood. Relief printing requires artists to conceptualize their images negatively—that is, they remove the surface areas around the images using a gouging instrument. Thus, when the printmaker inks the ridges, the hollow areas remain dry, and a positive image results when the artist presses the printing block against paper. Because artists produce *woodcuts* through a subtractive process (removing parts of the material), it is difficult to create very thin, fluid, and closely spaced lines. As a result, woodcut prints tend to exhibit stark contrasts and sharp edges (for example, FIG. I-7).

In contrast to the production of relief prints, the intaglio method involves a positive process. The artist *incises* (cuts) an image into a metal plate, often copper. The image can be created on the plate manually (*engraving* or *drypoint*; for example, FIGS. 8-13 and 8-30) using a tool (*burin* or *stylus*) or chemically (*etching*; for example FIG. 10-24). In the etching process, an acid bath eats into the exposed parts of the plate where the artist has drawn through an acid-resistant coating. When the artist inks the surface of the intaglio plate and wipes it clean, the ink is forced into the incisions. Then the printmaker runs the plate and paper through a roller press, and the paper absorbs the remaining ink, creating the print. Because the engraver "draws" the image onto the plate, intaglio prints differ in character from relief prints. Engravings, drypoints, and etchings generally present a wider variety of linear effects. They also often reveal to a greater extent evidence of the artist's touch, the result of the hand's changing pressure and shifting directions.

The paper and inks artists use also affect the finished look of the printed image. During the 15th and 16th centuries, European printmakers used papers produced from cotton and linen rags that papermakers mashed with water into a pulp. The papermakers then applied a thin layer of this pulp to a wire screen and allowed it to dry to create the paper. As contact with Asia increased, printmakers made greater use of what was called Japan paper (of mulberry fibers) and China paper. Artists, then as now, could select from a wide variety of inks. The type and proportion of the ink ingredients affect the consistency, color, and oiliness of inks, which various papers absorb differently.

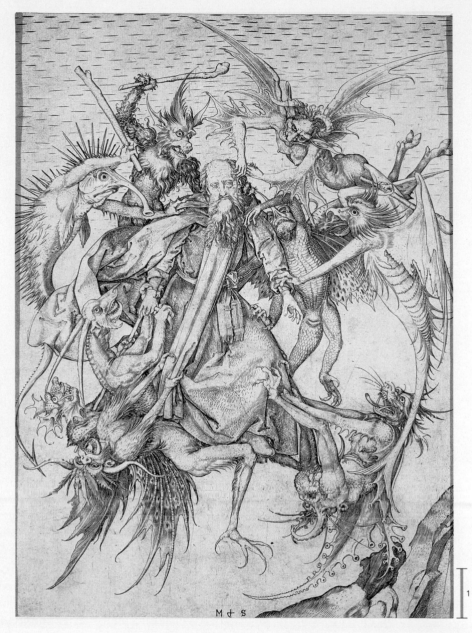

8-13 MARTIN SCHONGAUER, *Saint Anthony Tormented by Demons,* ca. 1480–1490. Engraving, 1' ¼″ × 9″. Fondazione Magnani Rocca, Corte di Mamiano.

Schongauer was the most skilled of the early masters of metal engraving. By using a burin to incise lines in a copper plate, he was able to create a marvelous variety of tonal values and textures.

M↑S

1 in.

unsurpassed skill and subtlety, Schongauer created marvelous distinctions of tonal values and textures—from smooth skin to rough cloth, from the furry and feathery to the hairy and scaly. The use of *cross-hatching* (sets of engraved lines at right angles) to describe forms, which Schongauer probably developed, became standard among German graphic artists. The Italians preferred *parallel hatching* (FIG. 8-30) and rarely adopted the other method, which, in keeping with the general northern European approach to art, tends to describe the surfaces of things rather than their underlying structures.

ITALY

During the 15th century, Italy witnessed constant fluctuations in its political and economic spheres, including shifting power relations among the numerous city-states and republics and the rise of princely courts (MAP 8-2). *Condottieri* (military leaders) with large numbers of mercenary troops at their disposal played a major role in the ongoing struggle for power. Papal Rome and the courts of Urbino, Mantua, and other cities emerged as cultural and artistic centers alongside the great art centers of the 14th century, especially the Republic of Florence. The association of humanism with education and culture appealed to accomplished individuals of high status, and humanism had its greatest impact among the elite and powerful, whether in the republics or the princely courts. These individuals were in the best position to commission art. As a result, humanist ideas permeate Italian Renaissance art. The intersection of art with humanist doctrines during the Quattrocento is evident in the popularity of subjects selected from classical history and mythology; in the increased concern with developing perspective systems and depicting anatomy accurately; in the revival of portraiture and other self-aggrandizing forms of patronage; and in citizens' extensive participation in civic and religious art commissions.

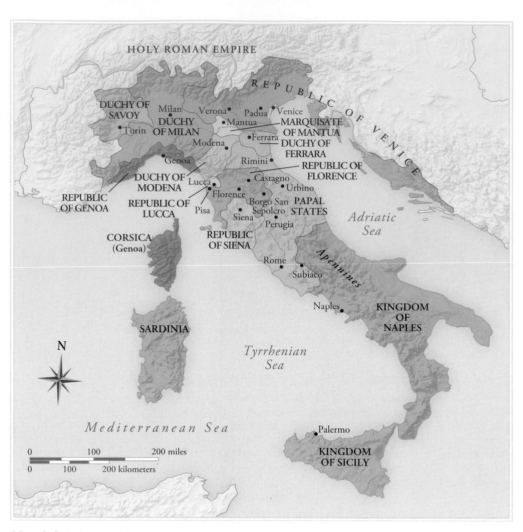

MAP 8-2 Italy around 1400.

Florence

Because high-level patronage required significant accumulated wealth, those individuals who had managed to prosper came to the fore in artistic circles. The best-known Italian Renaissance art patrons were the Medici of Florence (see "Medici Patronage," page 221), yet the first important artistic commission in Quattrocento Florence was not a Medici project but rather a competition held by the Cathedral of Santa Maria del Fiore and sponsored by the city's guild of wool merchants.

Baptistery Competition In 1401, Florence Cathedral's art directors held a competition to make bronze doors for the east portal of the Baptistery of San Giovanni. The commission was prestigious because the baptistery's east entrance faced the cathedral (FIG. 7-37). The jurors required each entrant to submit a relief panel depicting the *Sacrifice of Isaac,* a venerable biblical subject (FIG. 4-1, *top left*) that may have been chosen in part because of contemporary events. In the late 1390s, Giangaleazzo Visconti, the duke of Milan, began a military campaign to take over the Italian peninsula. By 1401, Visconti's troops had surrounded Florence, and its independence was in serious jeopardy. Despite dwindling water and food supplies, Florentine officials exhorted the public to defend the city's freedom. For example, the humanist chancellor Coluccio Salutati (1331–1406) urged his fellow citizens to adopt the republican ideal of civil and political liberty associated with ancient Rome and to identify themselves with its spirit. To be a Florentine citizen was to be Roman. Freedom was the distinguishing virtue of both societies. The story of Abraham and Isaac, with its theme of sacrifice, paralleled the message Florentine officials had conveyed to rally the public's support. The Florentines' reward for their faith and sacrifice came in 1402 when Visconti died suddenly, ending the invasion threat.

Only the panels of the two finalists, FILIPPO BRUNELLESCHI (1377–1446) and LORENZO GHIBERTI (1378–1455), have survived. As instructed, both artists used the same French Gothic *quatrefoil* frames employed earlier for the panels on

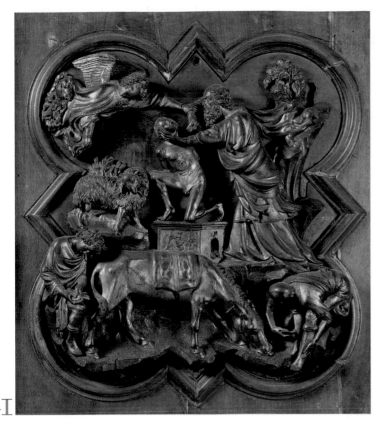

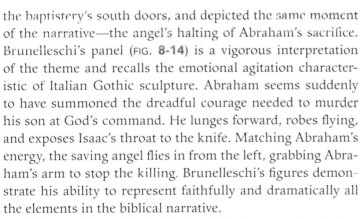

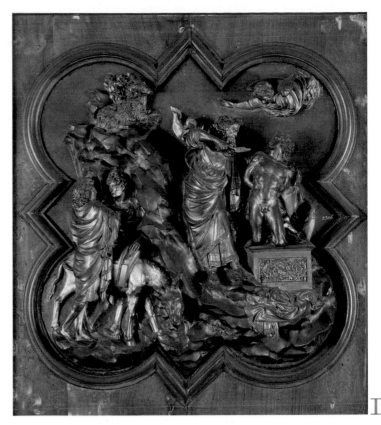

8-14 FILIPPO BRUNELLESCHI, *Sacrifice of Isaac,* competition panel for the east doors of the Baptistery of San Giovanni, Florence, Italy, 1401–1402. Gilded bronze, 1' 9" × 1' 5½". Museo Nazionale del Bargello, Florence.

Brunelleschi's entry in the competition to create new bronze doors for the Florentine baptistery shows a frantic angel about to halt an emotional, lunging Abraham clothed in swirling Gothic robes.

8-15 LORENZO GHIBERTI, *Sacrifice of Isaac,* competition panel for the east doors of the Baptistery of San Giovanni, Florence, Italy, 1401–1402. Gilded bronze, 1' 9" × 1' 5½". Museo Nazionale del Bargello, Florence.

In contrast to Brunelleschi's panel (FIG. 8-14), Ghiberti's entry in the baptistery competition features gracefully posed figures that recall classical statuary. Even Isaac's altar has a Roman acanthus frieze.

the baptistery's south doors, and depicted the same moment of the narrative—the angel's halting of Abraham's sacrifice. Brunelleschi's panel (FIG. **8-14**) is a vigorous interpretation of the theme and recalls the emotional agitation characteristic of Italian Gothic sculpture. Abraham seems suddenly to have summoned the dreadful courage needed to murder his son at God's command. He lunges forward, robes flying, and exposes Isaac's throat to the knife. Matching Abraham's energy, the saving angel flies in from the left, grabbing Abraham's arm to stop the killing. Brunelleschi's figures demonstrate his ability to represent faithfully and dramatically all the elements in the biblical narrative.

Whereas Brunelleschi imbued his image with violent movement and high emotion, Ghiberti, the youngest artist in the competition, emphasized grace and smoothness. In Ghiberti's panel (FIG. **8-15**), Abraham appears in a typically Gothic pose with outthrust hip (compare FIG. 7-19) and seems to contemplate the act he is about to perform, even as he draws his arm back to strike. The figure of Isaac, beautifully posed and rendered, recalls Greco-Roman statuary. Unlike his medieval predecessors, Ghiberti revealed a genuine appreciation of the nude male form and a deep interest in how

the muscular system and skeletal structure move the human body. Even the altar on which Isaac kneels displays Ghiberti's emulation of antique models. Decorating it are acanthus scrolls of a type that commonly adorned Roman buildings. These classical references reflect the increasing influence of humanism. Ghiberti's *Sacrifice of Isaac* is also noteworthy for the artist's interest in spatial illusion. The rocky landscape seems to emerge from the blank panel toward the viewer, as does the strongly foreshortened angel. Brunelleschi's image, in contrast, emphasizes the planar orientation of the surface.

Ghiberti's training included both painting and metalwork. His careful treatment of the gilded bronze surfaces, with their sharply and accurately incised detail, proves his skill as a goldsmith. That Ghiberti cast his panel in only two pieces (thereby reducing the amount of bronze needed) no doubt also impressed the selection committee. Brunelleschi's panel consists of several cast pieces. Thus, not only would Ghiberti's doors, as proposed, be lighter and more impervious to the elements, but they also represented a significant cost savings. The younger artist's submission clearly had much to recommend it, both stylistically and technically, and the judges awarded the commission to him.

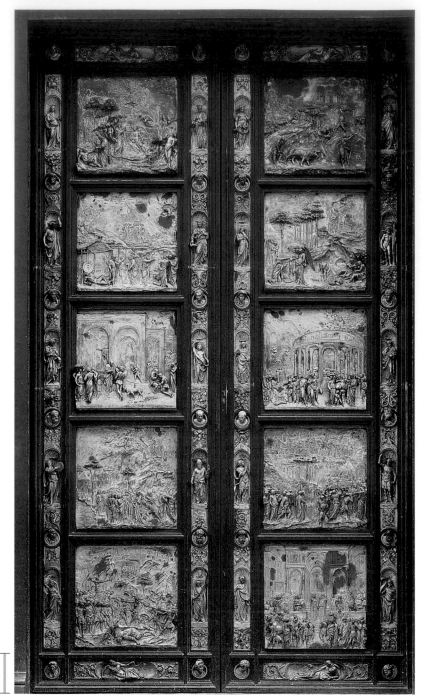

8-16 LORENZO GHIBERTI, east doors (*Gates of Paradise*), Baptistery of San Giovanni, Florence, Italy, 1425–1452. Gilded bronze, 17′ high. Modern copy, 1990. Original panels in Museo dell'Opera del Duomo, Florence. ◼◀

In Ghiberti's later doors for the Florentine baptistery, the sculptor abandoned the Gothic quatrefoil frames for the biblical scenes (compare FIG. 8-15) and employed painterly illusionistic devices.

1 ft.

Gates of Paradise Ghiberti completed the baptistery's east doors in 1424, but church officials moved them to the north entrance so he could execute another pair of doors for the eastern entrance. This second project (1425–1452) produced the famous east doors (FIG. **8-16**) that Michelangelo later declared were "so beautiful that they would do well for the gates of Paradise."[1] In the *Gates of Paradise,* Ghiberti abandoned the quatrefoil frames of his earlier doors and reduced the number of panels from 28 to 10. Each panel contains a

relief set in a plain molding and depicts an episode from the Old Testament. The complete gilding of the reliefs creates an effect of great splendor and elegance.

The individual panels, such as *Isaac and His Sons* (FIG. **8-17**), clearly recall painting techniques in their depiction of space as well as in their treatment of the narrative. Some exemplify more fully than painting many of the principles the architect and theorist Leon Battista Alberti formulated in his 1435 treatise, *On Painting*. In his relief, Ghiberti created the illusion of space partly through the use of linear perspective (see "Linear and Atmospheric Perspective," page 237, and FIG. **8-18**) and partly by sculptural means. He represented the pavement on which the figures stand according to a painter's *vanishing-point* perspective construction, but the figures themselves appear almost fully in the round. In fact, some of their heads stand completely free. As the eye progresses upward, the relief increasingly flattens, concluding with the architecture in the background, which Ghiberti depicted using barely raised lines. In this manner, the artist created a sort of sculptor's *atmospheric perspective,* with forms appearing less distinct the deeper they are in space.

In these panels, Ghiberti achieved a greater sense of depth than had previously seemed possible in a relief, but his principal figures do not occupy the architectural space he created for them. Rather, the artist arranged them along a parallel plane in front of the grandiose architecture. (According to Alberti in *On the Art of Building,* the grandeur of the architecture reflects the dignity of the events shown in the foreground.) Ghiberti's figure style mixes a Gothic patterning of rhythmic line, classical poses and motifs, and a new realism in characterization, movement, and surface detail. Ghiberti retained the medieval narrative method of presenting several episodes within a single frame. In *Isaac and His Sons,* the women in the left foreground attend the birth of Esau and Jacob in the left background. In the central foreground, Isaac sends Esau and his dogs to hunt game. In the right foreground, Isaac blesses the kneeling Jacob as Rebecca looks on. Yet viewers experience little confusion because of Ghiberti's careful and subtle placement of each scene. The figures, in varying degrees of projection, gracefully twist and turn, appearing to occupy and move through a convincing stage space, which Ghiberti deepened by showing some figures from behind. The classicism derives from the artist's close study of ancient art. Ghiberti admired and collected classical sculpture, bronzes, and coins. Their influence appears throughout the panel, particularly in the figure of Rebecca, which Ghiberti based on a popular Greco-Roman statuary type. The emerging practice of collecting classical art in the 15th century had much to do with the incorporation of classical motifs and the emulation of classical style in Renaissance art.

Linear and Atmospheric Perspective

Scholars long have noted the Renaissance fascination with perspective. In essence, portraying perspective involves constructing a convincing illusion of space in two-dimensional imagery while unifying all objects within a single spatial system. Renaissance artists were not the first to focus on depicting illusionistic space. Both the Greeks and the Romans were well versed in perspective rendering (FIG. 3-19, *right*). However, the Renaissance rediscovery of and interest in perspective contrasted sharply with the portrayal of space during the Middle Ages, when spiritual concerns superseded the desire to depict objects illusionistically.

Renaissance knowledge of perspective included both *linear perspective* and *atmospheric perspective*.

▌ **Linear perspective** Developed by Filippo Brunelleschi, linear perspective enables artists to determine mathematically the relative size of rendered objects to correlate them with the visual recession into space. The artist first must identify a horizontal line that marks, in the image, the horizon in the distance (hence the term *horizon line*). The artist then selects a *vanishing point* on that horizon line (often located at the exact center of the line). By drawing *orthogonals* (diagonal lines) from the edges of the picture to the vanishing point, the artist creates a structural grid that organizes the image and determines the size of objects within the image's illusionistic space. Among the works that provide clear examples of linear perspective are Ghiberti's *Isaac and His Sons* (FIGS. 8-17 and 8-18), Masaccio's *Holy Trinity* (FIG. 8-24), and Perugino's *Christ Delivering the Keys of the Kingdom to Saint Peter* (FIG. 8-36).

▌ **Atmospheric perspective** Unlike linear perspective, which relies on a structured mathematical system, atmospheric perspective involves optical phenomena. Artists using atmospheric perspective (sometimes called *aerial perspective*) exploit the principle that the farther back the object is in space, the blurrier and less detailed it appears. Leonardo da Vinci used atmospheric perspective to great effect, as seen in such works as *Madonna of the Rocks* (FIG. 9-2) and *Mona Lisa* (FIG. 9-4).

Earlier Italian artists, such as Giotto, Duccio, and Lorenzetti, had used several devices to indicate distance, but with the development of linear perspective, Quattrocento artists acquired a way to make the illusion of distance certain and consistent. In effect, they conceived the picture plane as a transparent window through which the observer looks to see the constructed pictorial world. This discovery was enormously important, for it made possible what has been called the "rationalization of sight." It brought all random and infinitely various visual sensations under a simple rule that could be expressed mathematically. Indeed, Renaissance artists' interest in linear perspective reflects the emergence at this time of modern science itself. Of course, 15th-century artists were not primarily scientists. They simply found perspective an effective way to order and clarify their compositions. Nonetheless, linear perspective, with its new mathematical certitude, conferred a kind of aesthetic legitimacy on painting and relief sculpture by making the picture measurable and exact. The projection of measurable objects on flat surfaces influenced the character of Renaissance paintings but also made possible scale drawings, maps, charts, graphs, and diagrams—means of exact representation that laid the foundation for modern science and technology.

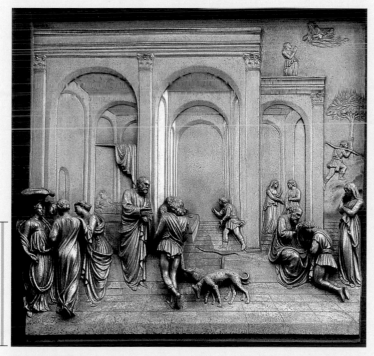

1 ft.

8-17 LORENZO GHIBERTI, *Isaac and His Sons* (detail of FIG. 8-16), east doors (*Gates of Paradise*), Baptistery of San Giovanni, Florence, Italy, 1425–1452. Gilded bronze, 2' 7½" × 2' 7½". Museo dell'Opera del Duomo, Florence. ■◀

In this relief, Ghiberti employed linear perspective to create the illusion of distance, but he also used sculptural atmospheric perspective, with forms appearing less distinct the deeper they are in space.

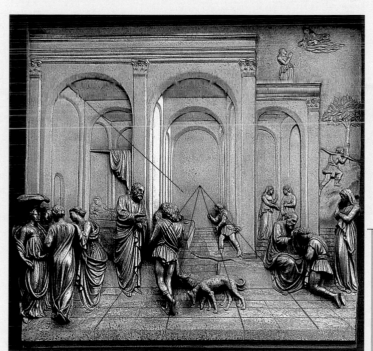

1 ft.

8-18 Perspective diagram of FIG. 8-17. ■◀

All of the orthogonals of the floor tiles in this early example of linear perspective converge on a vanishing point on the central axis of the composition, but the orthogonals of the architecture do not.

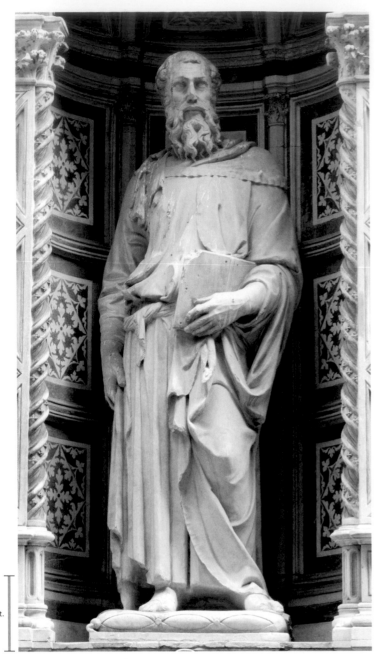

8-19 DONATELLO, *Saint Mark,* south facade of Or San Michele, Florence, Italy, ca. 1411–1413. Marble, figure 7′ 9″ high. Modern copy. Original sculpture in museum on second floor of Or San Michele, Florence. ◼◀

In this statue carved for the guild of linen makers and tailors, Donatello introduced classical contrapposto into Renaissance sculpture. The drapery falls naturally and moves with the body.

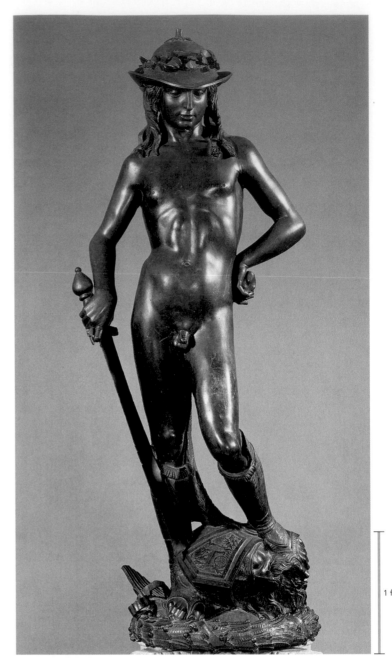

8-20 DONATELLO, *David,* ca. 1440–1460. Bronze, 5′ 2¼″ high. Museo Nazionale del Bargello, Florence. ◼◀

Donatello's *David* possesses both the relaxed contrapposto and the sensuous beauty of nude Greek gods (FIG. 2-48). The revival of classical statuary style appealed to the sculptor's patrons, the Medici.

Donatello A younger contemporary of Ghiberti was Donato di Niccolo Bardi, called DONATELLO (ca. 1386–1466). He participated along with other esteemed sculptors, including Ghiberti, in another major Florentine art program of the early 1400s, the decoration of Or San Michele. At various times, the building housed a church, a granary, and the headquarters of Florence's guilds. City officials had assigned each of the niches on the building's four sides to a specific guild to fill with a statue of its patron saint. Donatello carved *Saint Mark* (FIG. 8-19) for the guild of linen makers and tailors

in 1413. In this sculpture, Donatello introduced the classical principle of weight shift, or *contrapposto* (see Chapter 2), into Renaissance statuary. As the saint's body moves, his garment moves with it, hanging and folding naturally from and around different body parts so the viewer senses the figure as a nude human wearing clothing, not a stone statue with arbitrarily incised drapery. Donatello's *Saint Mark* is the first Renaissance statue whose voluminous robe (the pride of the Florentine guild that paid for the statue) does not conceal but accentuates the movement of the arms, legs, shoulders, and clergy regarded nude statues as both indecent and idolatrous, and nudity in general appeared only rarely in art—and then only in biblical or moralizing contexts, such as the story of Adam and Eve or depictions of sinners in Hell. With *David*, Donatello reinvented the classical nude. His subject, however, was not a Greco-Roman god, hero, or athlete but the youthful biblical slayer of Goliath who had become the symbol of the Florentine republic. *David* possesses both the relaxed classical contrapposto stance and the proportions and sensuous beauty of Greek images of gods (FIG. 2-48), qualities absent from medieval figures. The invoking of classical poses and formats appealed to the humanist Medici, who were aware of Donatello's earlier *David* in Florence's town hall, the Palazzo della Signoria, which the artist had produced during the threat of invasion by King Ladislaus (r. 1399–1414) of Naples. David had become a symbol of Florentine strength and independence, and the Medici's selection of the same subject for their private residence suggests the family identified themselves with Florence or, at the very least, saw themselves as responsible for the city's prosperity and freedom.

Gattamelata Given the increased emphasis on individual achievement and recognition that humanism fostered, it is not surprising that portraiture enjoyed a revival in 15th-century Italy. The grandest portrait of the era was a 12-foot-tall bronze equestrian statue (FIG. **8-21**) Donatello produced for the Republic of Venice. His assignment was to create a commemorative monument in honor of the recently deceased Venetian condottiere Erasmo da Narni, nicknamed Gattamelata ("honeyed cat," a wordplay on his mother's name, Melania Gattelli). Equestrian statues occasionally had been set up in Italy in the late Middle Ages, but Donatello's *Gattamelata* was the first to rival the grandeur of Roman imperial mounted portraits, such as that of Marcus Aurelius (FIG. 3-41), which the artist must have seen in Rome. Donatello's contemporaries, one of whom described Gattamelata as sitting on his horse "with great magnificence like a triumphant Caesar,"[2] recognized this reference to antiquity. The statue stands high on a lofty elliptical base in the square in front of the church of Sant'Antonio in Padua, the condottiere's birthplace. Massive and majestic, the great horse bears the armored general easily, for, unlike the sculptor of Marcus Aurelius, Donatello did not represent the Venetian commander as superhuman and disproportionately larger than his horse. Gattamelata dominates his mighty steed by force of character rather than sheer size. The condottiere, his face set in a mask of dauntless resolution and unshakable will, is the very portrait of the male Renaissance individualist. Such a man—intelligent, courageous, ambitious, and frequently of humble origin—could, by his own resourcefulness and on his own merits, rise to a commanding position in the world. Together, man and horse convey an overwhelming image of irresistible strength and unlimited power—an impression Donatello reinforced visually by placing the left forefoot of the horse on an orb, reviving a venerable ancient symbol for hegemony over the earth—a remarkable conceit because Erasmo da Narni was not a head of state.

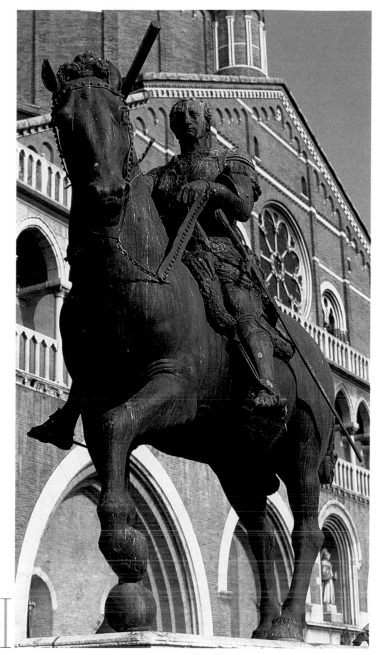

1 ft.

8-21 DONATELLO, *Gattamelata* (equestrian statue of Erasmo da Narni), Piazza del Santo, Padua, Italy, ca. 1445–1453. Bronze, 12′ 2″ high.

Donatello based his gigantic portrait of a Venetian general on equestrian statues of ancient Roman emperors (FIG. 3-41). Together, man and horse convey an overwhelming image of irresistible strength.

hips. This development further contributed to the sculpted figure's independence from its architectural setting. Saint Mark's stirring limbs, shifting weight, and mobile drapery suggest impending movement out of the niche.

David Donatello also enjoyed the patronage of the Medici. He cast the bronze statue *David* (FIG. **8-20**) sometime between 1440 and 1460 for display in the courtyard (FIG. 8-34) of the Medici palace in Florence. The sculpture was the first nude statue since ancient times. During the Middle Ages, the

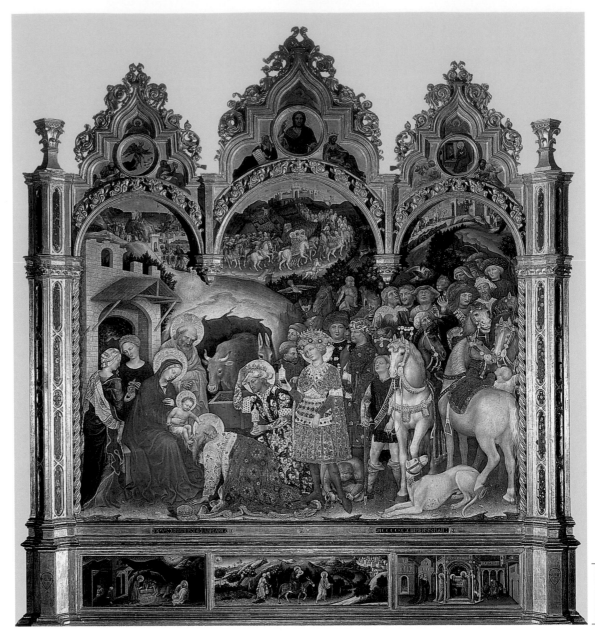

8-22 Gentile da Fabriano, *Adoration of the Magi,* altarpiece from the Strozzi chapel, Santa Trinità, Florence, Italy, 1423. Tempera on wood, 9′ 11″ × 9′ 3″. Galleria degli Uffizi, Florence.

Gentile was the leading Florentine painter working in the International style, but he successfully blended naturalistic details with Late Gothic splendor in color, costume, and framing ornamentation.

1 ft.

Gentile da Fabriano In Quattrocento Italy, humanism and the celebration of classical artistic values also largely determined the character of panel and mural painting. The new Renaissance style did not, however, immediately displace all vestiges of the Late Gothic style. In particular, the International style, the dominant mode in painting around 1400 (see Chapter 7), persisted well into the 15th century. The leading Quattrocento master of the International style was GENTILE DA FABRIANO (ca. 1370–1427), who in 1423 painted *Adoration of the Magi* (FIG. **8-22**) as the altarpiece for the family chapel of Palla Strozzi (1372–1462) in the church of Santa Trinità in Florence. At the beginning of the 15th century, the Strozzi family was the wealthiest in the city. The altarpiece, with its elaborate gilded Gothic frame, is testimony to the patron's lavish tastes. So too is the painting itself, with its gorgeous surface and sumptuously costumed kings, courtiers, captains, and retainers accompanied by a menagerie of exotic animals. Gentile portrayed all these elements in a rainbow of color with extensive use of gold. The painting presents all the pomp and ceremony of chivalric etiquette in a religious scene centered on the Madonna and Child. Although the style is fundamentally International Gothic, Gentile inserted striking naturalistic details. For example, the artist depicted animals from a variety of angles and foreshortened the forms convincingly, most notably the horse at the far right seen in a three-quarter rear view. Gentile did the same with human figures, such as the kneeling man removing the spurs from the standing *magus* (wise man) in the center foreground. In the left panel of the predella, Gentile painted what may have been the first nighttime *Nativity* scene with the central light source—the radiant Christ Child—introduced into the picture itself. Although predominantly conservative, Gentile demonstrated he was not oblivious to Quattrocento experimental trends and could blend naturalistic and inventive elements skillfully and subtly into a traditional composition without sacrificing Late Gothic splendor in color, costume, and framing ornamentation.

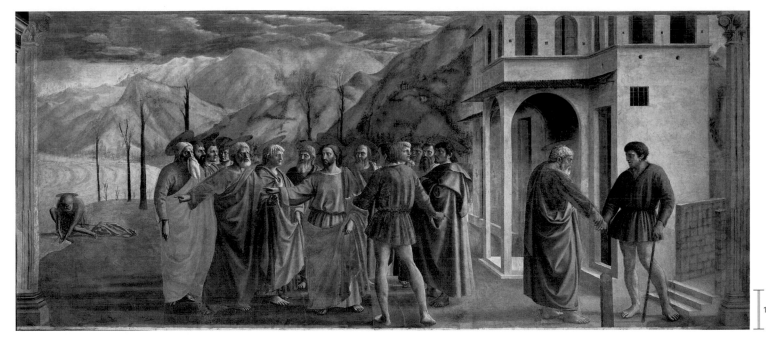

1 ft.

8-23 MASACCIO, *Tribute Money*, Brancacci chapel, Santa Maria del Carmine, Florence, Italy, ca. 1424–1427. Fresco, 8′ 4⅛″ × 19′ 7⅛″. ◼◀

Masaccio's figures recall Giotto's in their simple grandeur, but they convey a greater psychological and physical credibility. He modeled his figures with light coming from a source outside the picture.

Masaccio The artist who epitomizes the innovative spirit of early-15th-century Florentine painting was Tommaso di ser Giovanni di Mone Cassai, known as MASACCIO (1401–1428). Most art historians recognize no other painter in history who contributed so much to the development of a new style in so short a time as Masaccio, whose untimely death at age 27 cut short his brilliant career. Masaccio was the artistic descendant of Giotto (see Chapter 7), whose calm, monumental style he carried further by introducing a new repertoire of representational devices that generations of Renaissance painters later studied and developed.

Tribute Money (FIG. **8-23**), in the family chapel of Felice Brancacci (1382–1447) in Santa Maria del Carmine in Florence, displays Masaccio's innovations. The fresco depicts an episode from the Gospel of Matthew (17:24–27). As the tax collector confronts Jesus at the entrance to the Roman town of Capernaum, Jesus directs Saint Peter to the shore of Lake Galilee. There, as Jesus foresaw, Peter finds the tribute coin in the mouth of a fish and returns to pay the tax. Masaccio divided the story into three parts within the fresco. In the center, Jesus, surrounded by his disciples, tells Saint Peter to retrieve the coin from the fish, while the tax collector stands in the foreground, his back to spectators and hand extended, awaiting payment. At the left, in the middle distance, Peter extracts the coin from the fish's mouth, and, at the right, he thrusts the coin into the tax collector's hand. Masaccio's figures recall Giotto's in their simple grandeur, but they convey a greater psychological and physical credibility. Masaccio created the figures' bulk through modeling not with a flat, neutral light lacking an identifiable source but with a light coming from a specific source outside the picture. The light comes from the right and strikes the figures at

an angle, illuminating the parts of the solids that obstruct its path and leaving the rest in shadow, producing the illusion of deep sculptural relief. Between the extremes of light and dark, the light appears as a constantly active but fluctuating force highlighting the scene in varying degrees. In his frescoes, Giotto used light only to model the masses. In Masaccio's works, light has its own nature, and the masses are visible only because of its direction and intensity. The viewer can imagine the light as playing over forms—revealing some and concealing others, as the artist directs it. The individual figures in *Tribute Money* are solemn and weighty, but they also move freely and reveal body structure, as do Donatello's statues. Masaccio's representations adeptly suggest bones, muscles, and the pressures and tensions of joints. Each figure conveys a maximum of contained energy. *Tribute Money* helps the viewer understand Giorgio Vasari's comment: "[T]he works made before his [Masaccio's] day can be said to be painted, while his are living, real, and natural."[3]

Masaccio's arrangement of the figures is equally inventive. They do not stand in a line in the foreground. Instead, the artist grouped them in circular depth around Jesus, and he placed the whole group in a spacious landscape rather than in the confined stage space of earlier frescoes. The group itself generates the foreground space, and the architecture on the right amplifies it. Masaccio depicted the building in perspective, locating the vanishing point, where all the orthogonals converge, at Jesus's head. He also diminished the brightness of the colors as the distance increases, an aspect of atmospheric perspective (see "Linear and Atmospheric Perspective," page 237). Although ancient Roman painters used aerial perspective (FIG. 3-20), medieval artists had abandoned it. Thus, it virtually disappeared from art until Masaccio and

Masaccio's pioneering *Holy Trinity* is the premier early-15th-century example of the application of mathematics to the depiction of space according to Brunelleschi's system of perspective.

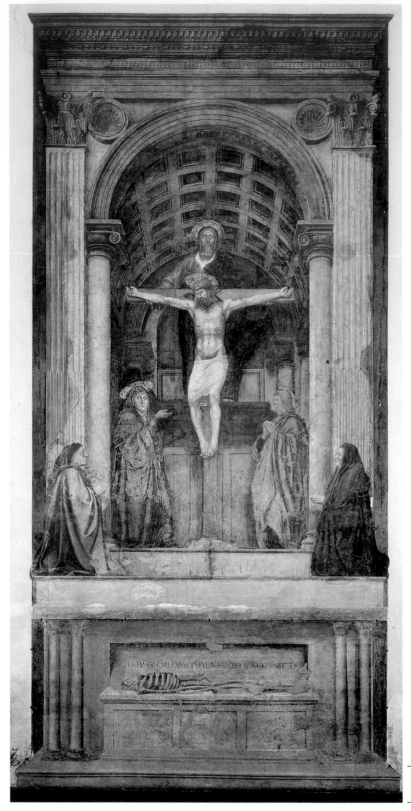

1 ft.

his contemporaries rediscovered it. They came to realize that the light and air interposed between viewers and what they see are two parts of the visual experience called "distance."

Holy Trinity Masaccio's *Holy Trinity* fresco (FIG. **8-24**) in Santa Maria Novella is another of the young artist's masterworks and the premier early-15th-century example of the application of mathematics to the depiction of space. Masaccio painted the composition on two levels of unequal height. Above, in a coffered barrel-vaulted chapel reminiscent of a Roman triumphal arch (FIG. 3-32), the Virgin Mary and Saint John appear on either side of the crucified Christ. God the Father emerges from behind Christ, supporting the arms of the cross and presenting his son to the worshiper as a devotional object. The dove of the Holy Spirit hovers between God's head and Christ's head. Masaccio also included portraits of the donors of the painting, Lorenzo Lenzi and his wife, who kneel just in front of the pilasters framing the chapel's entrance. Below, the artist painted a tomb containing a skeleton. An inscription in Italian above the skeleton reminds spectators, "I was once what you are, and what I am you will become."

The illusionism of *Holy Trinity* is breathtaking. In this fresco, Masaccio brilliantly demonstrated the principles and potential of Brunelleschi's new science of perspective. Indeed, some art historians have suggested Brunelleschi may have collaborated with Masaccio. The vanishing point of the composition is at the foot of the cross. With this point at eye level, spectators look up at the Trinity and down at the tomb. About five feet above the floor level, the vanishing point pulls the two views together, creating the illusion of a real structure transecting the wall's vertical plane. Whereas the tomb appears to project forward into the church, the chapel recedes visually behind the wall and appears as an extension of the spectators' space. This adjustment of the picture's space to the viewer's position was an important innovation in illusionistic painting that other artists of the Renaissance and the later Baroque period would develop further. Masaccio was so exact in his proportions that it is possible to calculate the dimensions of the chapel (for example, the span of the painted vault is seven feet and the depth of the chapel is nine feet). Thus, he achieved not only a successful illusion but also a rational measured coherence that is responsible for the unity and harmony of the fresco. *Holy Trinity* is, however, much more than a demonstration of Brunelleschi's perspective or of the painter's ability to represent fully modeled figures bathed in light. In this painting, Masaccio also powerfully conveyed one of the central tenets of Christian faith. The ascending pyramid of figures leads viewers from the despair of death to the hope of resurrection and eternal life through Christ's crucifixion.

Fra Angelico As Masaccio's *Holy Trinity* clearly demonstrates, humanism and religion were not mutually exclusive. In fact, for many Quattrocento artists, humanist concerns were not a primary consideration. The art of FRA ANGELICO (ca. 1400–1455) focused on serving the Roman Catholic

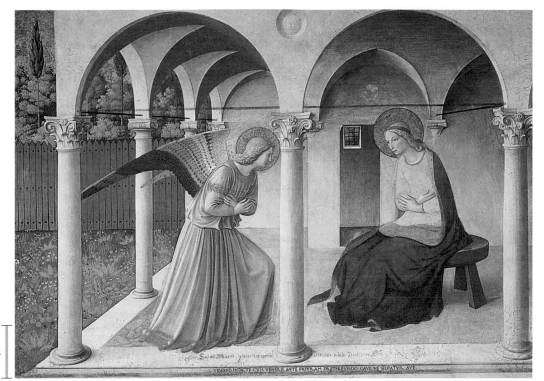

8-25 Fra Angelico, *Annunciation*, San Marco, Florence, Italy, ca. 1438–1447. Fresco, 7′ 1″ × 10′ 6″.

Painted for the Dominican monks of San Marco, Fra Angelico's fresco is simple and direct. Its figures and architecture have a pristine clarity befitting the fresco's function as a devotional image.

loggia (open arcade) resembling San Marco's cloister, and the artist painted all the fresco elements with a pristine clarity. As an admonition to heed the devotional function of the images, Fra Angelico included a small inscription at the base of the image: "As you venerate, while passing before it, this figure of the intact Virgin, beware lest you omit to say a Hail Mary." Like most of Fra Angelico's paintings, *Annunciation*, with its simplicity and direct-

Church. In the late 1430s, the abbot of the Dominican monastery of San Marco (Saint Mark) in Florence asked Fra Angelico to produce a series of frescoes for the monastery. The Dominicans had dedicated themselves to lives of prayer and work, and their religious compound was mostly spare and austere to encourage the monks to immerse themselves in their devotional lives. *Annunciation* (FIG. **8-25**) appears at the top of the stairs leading to the friars' cells. Appropriately, Fra Angelico presented the scene of the Virgin Mary and the Archangel Gabriel with simplicity and serenity. The two figures appear in a plain

ness, still has an almost universal appeal and fully reflects the artist's simple and humble character.

Andrea del Castagno Fra Angelico's younger contemporary ANDREA DEL CASTAGNO (ca. 1421–1457) also accepted a commission to produce a series of frescoes for a religious establishment. Castagno's *Last Supper* (FIG. **8-26**), painted in the refectory of Sant'Apollonia in Florence, a convent for Benedictine nuns, manifests both a commitment to the biblical narrative and an interest in perspective. The lavishly painted

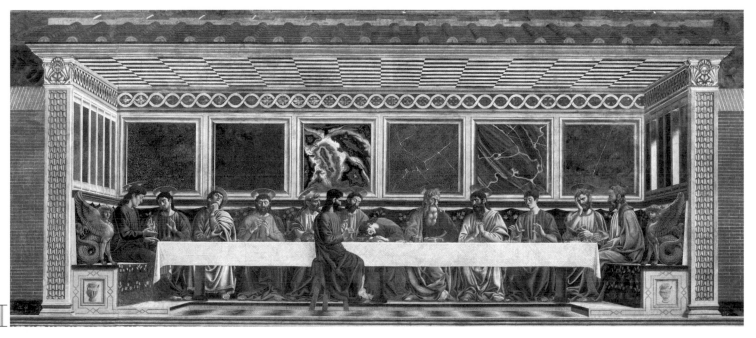

8-26 ANDREA DEL CASTAGNO, *Last Supper*, refectory of the convent of Sant'Apollonia, Florence, Italy, 1447. Fresco, 15′ 5″ × 32′. ◼▸

Judas sits isolated in this *Last Supper* based on the Gospel of Saint John. The figures are small compared with the setting, reflecting Castagno's preoccupation with the new science of perspective.

room Jesus and his 12 disciples occupy suggests the artist's absorption with creating the illusion of three-dimensional space. However, closer scrutiny reveals inconsistencies, such as how the Renaissance perspective system makes it impossible to see both the ceiling from inside and the roof from outside, as Castagno depicted. The two side walls also do not appear parallel. Castagno chose a conventional compositional format, with the figures seated at a horizontally placed table. He derived the apparent self-absorption of most of the disciples and the malevolent features of Judas (who sits alone on the outside of the table) from the Gospel of Saint John, rather than the more familiar version of the last supper recounted in the Gospel of Saint Luke. Castagno's dramatic and spatially convincing depiction of the event no doubt was a powerful presence for the nuns during their daily meals.

Fra Filippo Lippi Another younger contemporary of Fra Angelico, FRA FILIPPO LIPPI (ca. 1406–1469), was also a friar—but there all resemblance ends. Fra Filippo was unsuited for monastic life and indulged in misdemeanors ranging from forgery and embezzlement to the abduction of a pretty nun, Lucretia, who became his mistress and the mother of his son. Only the intervention of the Medici on his behalf at the papal court preserved Fra Filippo from severe punishment and total disgrace.

A painting from Fra Filippo's later years, *Madonna and Child with Angels* (FIG. **8-27**), shows his skill in employing a wonderfully fluid line, which unifies the composition and contributes to the precise and smooth delineation of forms. Fra Filippo interpreted his subject in a surprisingly worldly manner. The Madonna is a beautiful young mother, albeit with a transparent halo, seated in an elegantly furnished Florentine home. One of the angels holding up the Christ Child sports the mischievous, puckish grin of a boy refusing to behave for the pious occasion. Significantly, all figures reflect the use of live models (perhaps even Lucretia for the Madonna). Fra Filippo plainly relished the charm of youth and beauty as he found it in this world. He preferred the real in landscape also. The background, seen through the window, incorporates recognizable features of the Arno River valley. Compared with the earlier Madonnas by Giotto (FIG. 7-29) and Duccio (FIG. 7-32), this work shows how far artists had carried the humanization of the religious theme. Whatever the ideals of spiritual perfection may have meant to artists in past centuries, Renaissance artists realized those ideals in terms of the sensuous beauty of this world.

Piero della Francesca One of the most renowned painters in 15th-century Italy was PIERO DELLA FRANCESCA (ca. 1420–1492), of San Sepolcro in southeastern Tuscany, who painted a fresco of Christ's *Resurrection* (FIG. **8-28**) for the town hall of his birthplace. The viewer witnesses the miracle of the risen Christ through the Corinthian columns of a classical portico (preserved only in part because the painting was trimmed during its installation in a new location). Piero chose a viewpoint corresponding to the viewer's position and

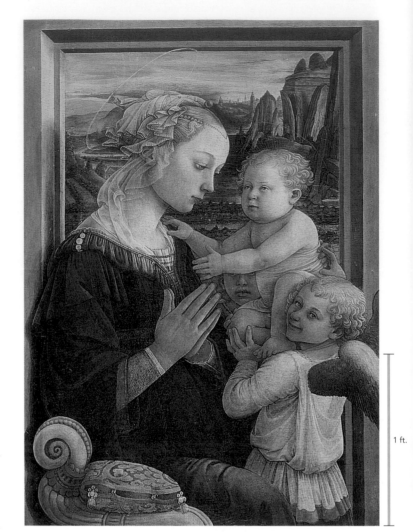

8-27 FRA FILIPPO LIPPI, *Madonna and Child with Angels,* ca. 1460–1465. Tempera on wood, 2′ 11½″ × 2′ 1″. Galleria degli Uffizi, Florence.

Fra Filippo, a monk guilty of many misdemeanors, represented the Virgin and Child in a distinctly worldly manner, carrying the humanization of the holy family further than any artist before him.

depicted the architectural frame at a sharp angle from below. The Roman soldiers who have fallen asleep when they should be guarding the tomb are also seen from below in a variety of foreshortened poses. The soldiers form the base of a compositional triangle culminating in Christ's head. For Christ, Piero violated the perspective of the rest of the fresco and used a head-on view of the resurrected savior, imbuing the figure with an iconic quality. Christ's muscular body has the proportions of Greco-Roman nude statues. His pastel cloak stands out prominently from the darker colors of the soldiers' costumes. Christ holds the banner of his victory over death and displays his wounds. His face has portraitlike features. The tired eyes and somber expression are the only indications of his suffering on the cross.

Sandro Botticelli About 20 years younger than Piero, Sandro Botticelli painted his most famous works for the Medici, including *Primavera* (FIG. 8-1) and *Birth of Venus* (FIG. **8-29**). The theme of the latter painting was the subject

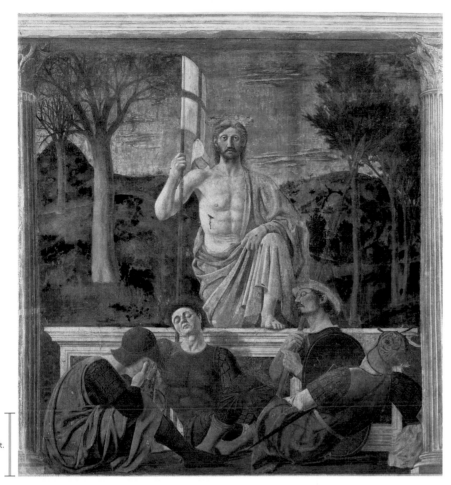

8-28 PIERO DELLA FRANCESCA, *Resurrection,* Palazzo Comunale, Borgo San Sepolcro, Italy, ca. 1463–1465. Fresco, 7' 4⅜" × 6' 6¼".

Christ miraculously rises from his tomb while the Roman guards sleep. The viewer sees the framing portico and the soldiers from below, but has a head-on view of the seminude muscular figure of Christ.

of a poem by Angelo Poliziano (1454–1494), a leading humanist of the day. In Botticelli's lyrical painting of Poliziano's retelling of the Greek myth, Zephyrus, carrying Chloris, blows Venus, born of the sea foam and carried on a cockle shell, to her sacred island, Cyprus. There, the nymph Pomona runs to meet her with a brocaded mantle. The lightness and bodilessness of the winds move all the figures without effort. Draperies undulate easily in the gentle gusts, perfumed by rose petals that fall on the whitecaps. In this painting, unlike in *Primavera,* Venus is nude. As noted earlier, the nude, especially the female nude, was exceedingly rare during the Middle Ages. The artist's use (especially on such a large scale—roughly life-size) of an ancient Venus statue—a Hellenistic variant of Praxiteles's famous *Aphrodite of Knidos* (FIG. 2-47)— as a model could have drawn harsh criticism. But in the more accommodating Renaissance culture and under the protection of the powerful Medici, the depiction went unchallenged, in part because *Birth of Venus* is susceptible to a Neo-Platonic reading, namely that those who embrace the contemplative life of reason will immediately contemplate spiritual and divine beauty whenever they behold physical beauty.

Botticelli's style is clearly distinct from the earnest search many other artists pursued to comprehend humanity and the natural world through a rational, empirical order. Indeed, Botticelli's elegant and beautiful linear style (he was a pupil of Fra Filippo Lippi, FIG. 8-27) seems removed from

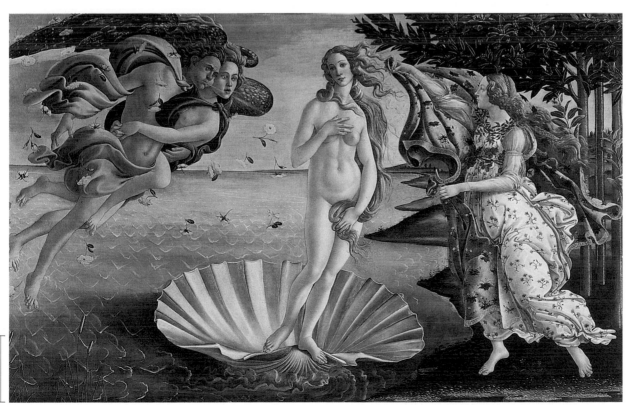

8-29 SANDRO BOTTICELLI, *Birth of Venus,* ca. 1484–1486. Tempera on canvas, 5' 9" × 9' 2". Galleria degli Uffizi, Florence.

Inspired by an Angelo Poliziano poem and classical Aphrodite statues (FIG. 2-47), Botticelli revived the theme of the female nude in this elegant and romantic representation of Venus born of sea foam.

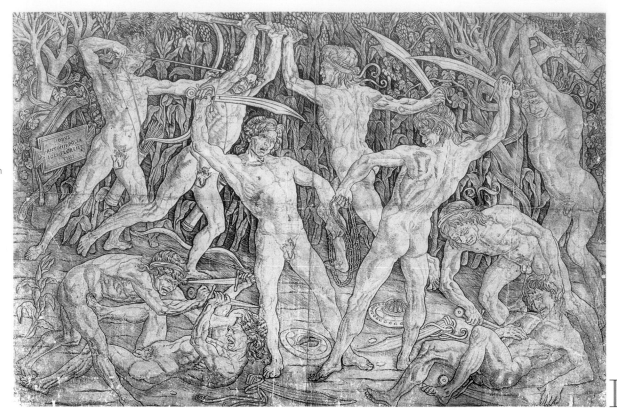

8-30 ANTONIO DEL POLLAIUOLO, *Battle of Ten Nudes,* ca. 1465. Engraving, 1' 3⅛" × 1' 11¼". Metropolitan Museum of Art, New York (bequest of Joseph Pulitzer, 1917).

Pollaiuolo was fascinated by how muscles and sinews activate the human skeleton. He delighted in showing nude figures in violent action and from numerous foreshortened viewpoints.

1 in.

all the scientific knowledge 15th-century artists had gained in the areas of perspective and anatomy. For example, the seascape in *Birth of Venus* is a flat backdrop devoid of atmospheric perspective. Botticelli's style paralleled the Florentine allegorical pageants that were chivalric tournaments structured around allusions to classical mythology. The same trend is evident in the poetry of the 1470s and 1480s. Artists and poets at this time did not directly imitate classical antiquity but used the myths, with delicate perception of their charm, in a way still tinged with medieval romance. Ultimately, Botticelli created a style of visual poetry parallel to the love poetry of Lorenzo de' Medici.

Antonio del Pollaiuolo Another of the many artists who produced sculptures and paintings for the Medici was ANTONIO DEL POLLAIUOLO (ca. 1431–1498), who took delight in showing human figures in violent action. Masaccio and his contemporaries had dealt effectively with the problem of rendering human anatomy, but they usually depicted their figures at rest or in restrained motion. Pollaiuolo conceived the body as a powerful machine and liked to display its mechanisms, such as knotted muscles and taut sinews that activate the skeleton as ropes pull levers. To show this to best effect, Pollaiuolo developed a figure so lean and muscular that it appears *écorché* (as if without skin), with strongly accentuated delineations at the wrists, elbows, shoulders, and knees. His *Battle of the Ten Nudes* (FIG. **8-30**), an early Italian example of the new engraving medium that northern European artists (FIG. **8-13**) had pioneered, shows this figure type in a variety of poses and from numerous viewpoints, enabling Pollaiuolo

to demonstrate his prowess in rendering the nude male figure. In this, he was a kindred spirit of late-sixth-century BCE Greek vase painters, such as Euthymides (FIG. **2-26**), who had experimented with foreshortening for the first time in history. Even though the figures in *Ten Nudes* hack and slash at one another without mercy, they nevertheless seem somewhat stiff and frozen because Pollaiuolo depicted *all* the muscle groups at maximum tension. Not until several decades later did an even greater anatomist, Leonardo da Vinci, observe that only some of the body's muscle groups are involved in any one action, while the others remain relaxed.

Ospedale degli Innocenti Filippo Brunelleschi's ability to codify a system of linear perspective derived in part from his skill as an architect. Although according to his biographer, Antonio Manetti (1423–1497), Brunelleschi turned to architecture out of disappointment over the loss of the commission for the baptistery doors, he continued to work as a sculptor for several years and received commissions for sculpture as late as 1416. It is true, however, that as the 15th century progressed, Brunelleschi's interest turned increasingly toward architecture. Several trips to Rome (the first in 1402, probably with his friend Donatello), where the ruins of ancient Rome captivated him, heightened his fascination with architecture. His close study of Roman monuments and his effort to make an accurate record of what he saw may have been the catalyst that led Brunelleschi to develop his revolutionary system of linear perspective.

Brunelleschi's most important early architectural commission was to design the Ospedale degli Innocenti (Hospital

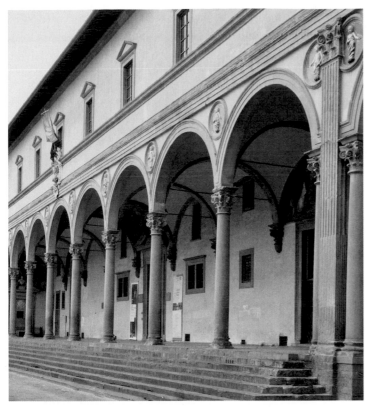

8-31 FILIPPO BRUNELLESCHI, loggia of the Ospedale degli Innocenti (looking northeast), Florence, Italy, begun 1419. ◼◀

Often called the first Renaissance building, the loggia of the orphanage sponsored by Florence's silk and goldsmith guild features a classically austere design based on a module of 10 braccia.

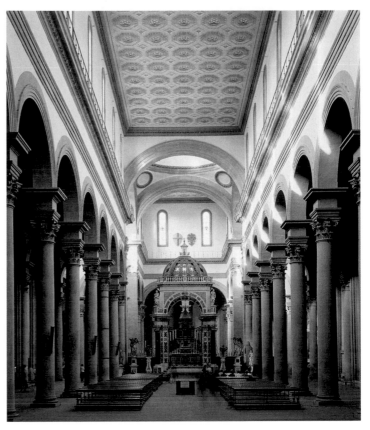

8-32 FILIPPO BRUNELLESCHI, interior of Santo Spirito (looking northeast), Florence, Italy, designed 1434–1436; begun 1446. ◼◀

Santo Spirito displays the classically inspired rationality of Brunelleschi's mature style in its all-encompassing modular scheme based on the dimensions of the dome-covered crossing square.

of the Innocents, FIG. **8-31**), a home for Florentine orphans and foundlings. Most scholars regard Brunelleschi's orphanage as the first building to embody the new Renaissance architectural style. As in earlier similar buildings, the facade is a loggia opening onto the street, a sheltered portico where, in this case, parents could anonymously deliver unwanted children to the care of the foundling hospital. Brunelleschi's arcade consists of a series of round arches on slender Corinthian columns. Each bay is a domed compartment with a pediment-capped window above. Both plan and elevation conform to a module that embodies the rationality of classical architecture. Each column is 10 *braccia* (approximately 20 feet; 1 braccia, or arm, equals 23 inches) tall. The distance between the columns of the facade and the distance between the columns and the wall are also 10 braccia. Thus, each of the bays is a cubical unit 10 braccia wide, deep, and high. The height of the columns also equals the diameter of the arches (except in the two outermost bays, which are slightly wider and serve as framing elements in the overall design).

Santo Spirito Designed around 1434, Santo Spirito (FIG. **8-32**) showcases the clarity and classically inspired rationality that characterize Brunelleschi's mature designs. Brunelleschi laid out this cruciform basilica in either multiples or segments of the dome-covered crossing square, creating a rhythmic harmony throughout the interior. For example, the nave is twice as high as it is wide, and the arcade and clerestory are of equal height, which means the height of the arcade equals the nave's width. The austerity of the decor enhances the restful and tranquil atmosphere. The calculated logic of the design—in essence, a series of mathematical equations—echoes that of classical buildings. The rationality of Santo Spirito contrasts sharply with the soaring drama and spirituality of the nave arcades and vaults of Gothic churches (FIGS. 7-9 and 7-12). Santo Spirito, like Brunelleschi's Ospedale, fully expresses the new Renaissance spirit that placed its faith in reason rather than in emotion.

Palazzo Medici The Medici family's consolidation of power in a city that prided itself on its republicanism did not go unchallenged. In the early 1430s, a power struggle with other wealthy families led to the expulsion of the Medici from Florence. In 1434, the family returned, but Cosimo, aware of the importance of public perception, attempted to maintain a lower profile and to wield his power from behind the scenes. He rejected an ostentatious design that Brunelleschi had proposed for a new Medici residence a short distance from the cathedral and awarded the commission instead to a younger architect, MICHELOZZO DI BARTOLOMMEO (1396–1472). Although Cosimo passed over Brunelleschi, his architectural style nevertheless deeply influenced Michelozzo. To a limited extent, the Palazzo Medici (FIG. **8-33**) reflects Brunelleschian principles.

Later bought by the Riccardi family (hence the name Palazzo Medici-Riccardi), who almost doubled the facade's length in the 18th century, the palace, both in its original and extended form, is a simple, massive structure. Heavy *rustication* (rough, unfinished masonry) on the ground floor accentuates its strength. Michelozzo divided the building block into stories of decreasing height by using long, unbroken *stringcourses* (horizontal bands), which give it coherence. *Dressed* (smooth, finished) *masonry* on the upper levels produces a smoother surface with each successive story and modifies the severity of the ground floor. The building thus appears progressively lighter as the eye moves upward. The extremely heavy cornice, which Michelozzo related not to the top story but to the building as a whole, dramatically reverses this effect. Like the ancient Roman cornices that served as Michelozzo's models, the Palazzo Medici-Riccardi cornice is a very effective lid for the structure, clearly and emphatically defining its proportions. Michelozzo perhaps also was inspired by the many extant examples of Roman rusticated masonry. However, nothing in the ancient world precisely compares with Michelozzo's design. The Palazzo Medici exemplifies the simultaneous respect for and independence from the antique—features that characterize the Early Renaissance in Italy.

The heart of the Palazzo Medici is an open colonnaded court (FIG. **8-34**) that clearly shows Michelozzo's debt to Brunelleschi. The round-arched colonnade, although more massive in its proportions, closely resembles Brunelleschi's foundling-hospital loggia (FIG. 8-31). The palace court surrounded by an arcade was the first of its kind and influenced a long line of descendants in Renaissance domestic architecture.

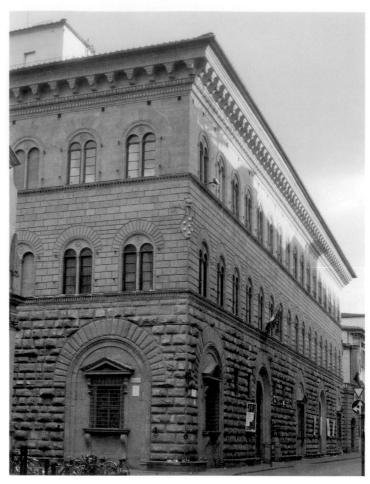

8-33 MICHELOZZO DI BARTOLOMMEO, Palazzo Medici-Riccardi (looking northwest), Florence, Italy, begun 1445. ◼◀

The Medici palace, with its combination of dressed and rusticated masonry and classical moldings, draws heavily on ancient Roman architecture, but Michelozzo creatively reinterpreted his models.

8-34 MICHELOZZO DI BARTOLOMMEO, interior court (looking west) of the Palazzo Medici-Riccardi, Florence, Italy, begun 1445. ◼◀

The Medici palace's interior court surrounded by a round-arched colonnade was the first of its kind, but the austere design clearly reveals Michelozzo's debt to Brunelleschi (FIG. 8-31).

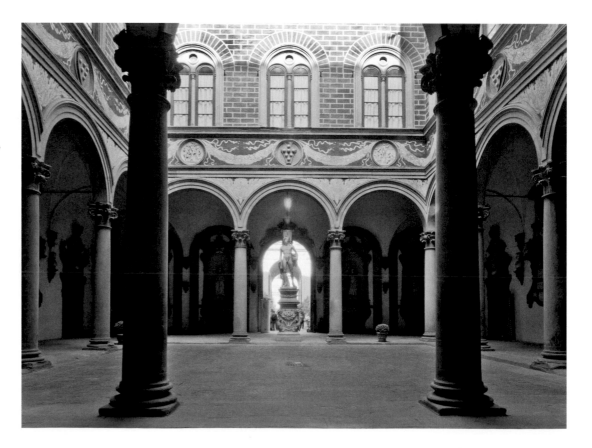

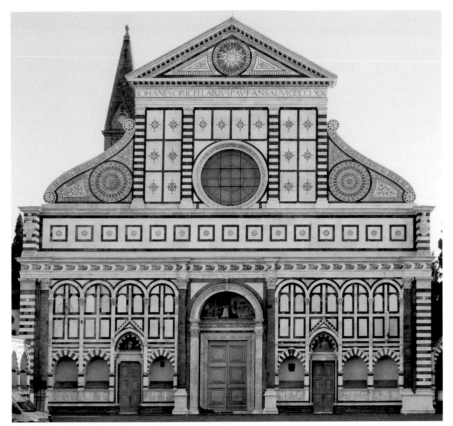

8-35 Leon Battista Alberti, west facade of Santa Maria Novella, Florence, Italy, 1456–1470. ◼◀

Alberti's design for the facade of this Gothic church features a pediment-capped temple front and pilaster-framed arcades. Numerical ratios are the basis of the proportions of all parts of the facade.

his treatise, Alberti wrote at length about the necessity of employing harmonic proportions to achieve beautiful buildings. Alberti shared this conviction with Brunelleschi, and this fundamental dependence on classically derived mathematics distinguished their architectural work from that of their medieval predecessors. They believed in the eternal and universal validity of numerical ratios as the source of beauty. In this respect, Alberti and Brunelleschi revived the true spirit of the High Classical age of ancient Greece, as epitomized by the architect Iktinos and the sculptor Polykleitos, who produced canons of proportions for the perfect temple and the perfect statue (see Chapter 2). Still, it was not only a desire to emulate Vitruvius and the Greek masters that motivated Alberti to turn to mathematics in his quest for beauty. His contemporary, the Florentine humanist Giannozzo Manetti (1396–1459), had argued that Christianity itself possessed the order and logic of mathematics. In his 1452 treatise, *On the Dignity and Excellence of Man*, Manetti insisted Christian religious truths were as self-evident as mathematical axioms.

The Santa Maria Novella facade was an ingenious solution to a difficult design problem. Alberti succeeded in subjecting preexisting and quintessentially medieval features, such as the large round window on the second level, to a rigid geometrical order that instilled a quality of classical calm and reason. This facade also introduced a feature of great historical consequence—the scrolls that simultaneously unite the broad lower and narrow upper levels and screen the sloping roofs over the aisles. With variations, similar spirals appeared in literally hundreds of church facades throughout the Renaissance and Baroque periods.

Leon Battista Alberti Although he entered the profession of architecture rather late in life, Leon Battista Alberti (1404–1472) made a remarkable contribution to architectural design. He was the first to study seriously the ancient Roman architectural treatise of Vitruvius (see page 89), and his knowledge of it, combined with his own archaeological investigations, made him the first Renaissance architect to understand Roman architecture in depth. Alberti's most influential theoretical work, *On the Art of Building* (written about 1450, published in 1486), although inspired by Vitruvius, contains much original material. Alberti advocated a system of ideal proportions and believed the central plan to be the ideal form for churches. He also considered incongruous the combination of column and arch, which had persisted since Roman times and throughout the Middle Ages. For Alberti, the arch was a wall opening that should be supported only by a section of wall (a pier), not by an independent sculptural element (a column), as in Brunelleschi's and Michelozzo's buildings.

Alberti's architectural style represents a scholarly application of classical elements to Quattrocento buildings. For the new facade (FIG. **8-35**) he designed for the 13th-century Gothic church of Santa Maria Novella in Florence, Alberti chose a small, pseudoclassical, pediment-capped temple front supported by a broad base of pilaster-framed arcades. Throughout the facade, Alberti defined areas and related them to one another in terms of proportions that can be expressed in simple numerical ratios. For example, the upper structure can be encased in a square one-fourth the size of the main square. The cornice separating the two levels divides the major square in half so that the lower portion of the building is a rectangle twice as wide as it is high. In

Girolamo Savonarola In the 1490s, Florence underwent a political, cultural, and religious upheaval. Florentine artists and their fellow citizens responded then not only to humanist ideas but also to the incursion of French armies and especially to the preaching of the Dominican monk Girolamo Savonarola (1452–1498), the reforming priest-dictator who denounced the humanistic secularism of the Medici and their artists, philosophers, and poets. Savonarola exhorted the people of Florence to repent their sins, and when Lorenzo de' Medici died in 1492, the priest prophesied the downfall of the city and of Italy and assumed absolute control of the state. As did a large number of citizens, Savonarola believed the Medici family's political, social, and religious power had corrupted Florence and invited the scourge of foreign invasion. Savonarola encouraged citizens to burn their classical texts, scientific treatises, and philosophical publications. Scholars still debate the significance of Savonarola's brief span of power. Apologists for the undoubtedly sincere monk deny his actions played a role in the decline of Florentine culture at the end of the 15th century. But the puritanical spirit that moved Savonarola must have dampened considerably the enthusiasm for classical antiquity of the Florentine Early Renaissance. Certainly, Savonarola's condemnation of humanism as heretical nonsense, and his banishing of the Medici and other wealthy families from Florence, deprived local artists of some of their major patrons, at least in the short term. There were, however, commissions aplenty for artists elsewhere in Italy.

The Princely Courts

Although Florentine artists led the way in creating the Renaissance in art and architecture, the arts flourished throughout Italy in the 15th century. The papacy in Rome and the princely courts in Urbino, Mantua, and elsewhere also deserve credit for nurturing Renaissance art.

Perugino Between 1481 and 1483, Pope Sixtus IV (r. 1414–1484) summoned a group of artists to Rome, including Sandro Botticelli and Pietro Vannucci of Perugia, known as PERUGINO (ca.1450–1523), to adorn the walls of the newly completed Sistine Chapel. Perugino's contribution to the fresco cycle was *Christ Delivering the Keys of the Kingdom to Saint Peter* (FIG. **8-36**). The papacy had, from the beginning, based its claim to infallible and total authority over the Roman Catholic Church on this biblical event. In Perugino's version, Christ hands the keys to Saint Peter, who stands amid an imaginary gathering of the 12 apostles and Renaissance contemporaries. These figures occupy the apron of a great stage space that extends into the distance to a point of convergence in the doorway of a central-plan temple. (Perugino used parallel and converging lines in the pavement to mark off the intervening space; compare FIG. 8-18.) Figures in the middle distance complement the near group, emphasizing its density and order by their scattered arrangement. At the corners of the great *piazza,* duplicate triumphal arches serve as the base angles of a distant compositional triangle whose apex is in the central building. Perugino modeled the arches very closely on the Arch of Constantine (FIG. 3-52) in Rome. Although an anachronism in a painting depicting a scene from Christ's life, the arches served to underscore the close ties between Saint Peter and Constantine, the first Christian emperor of Rome and builder of the great basilica (FIG. 4-3) over Saint Peter's tomb. Christ and Peter flank the triangle's central axis, which runs through the temple's doorway, the

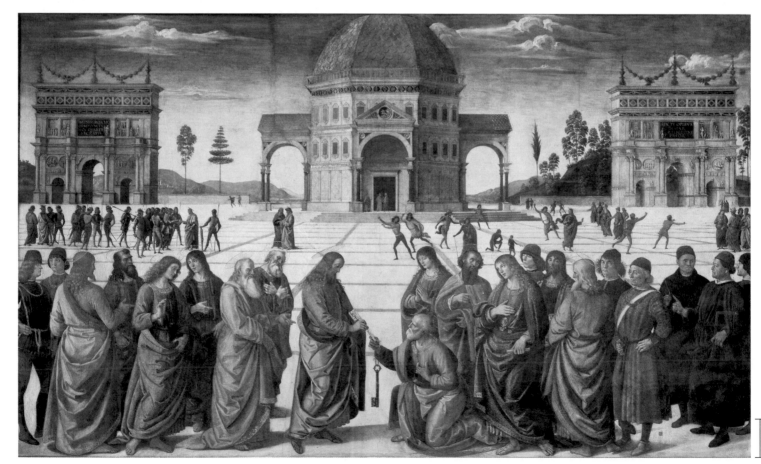

8-36 PERUGINO, *Christ Delivering the Keys of the Kingdom to Saint Peter,* Sistine Chapel, Vatican City, Rome, Italy, 1481–1483. Fresco, 11′ 5½″ × 18′ 8½″.

Painted for the Vatican, this fresco depicts the event on which the papacy bases its authority. The converging lines of the pavement connect the action in the foreground with the background.

vanishing point of Perugino's perspective scheme. Thus, the composition interlocks both two-dimensional and three-dimensional space, and the placement of the central actors emphasizes the axial center.

Urbino Under the patronage of Federico da Montefeltro (1422–1482), Urbino, southeast of Florence across the Apennines (MAP 8-2), became an important center of Renaissance art and culture. In fact, the humanist writer Paolo Cortese (1465–1540) described Federico as one of the two greatest artistic patrons of the 15th century (the other was Cosimo de' Medici). Federico was a condottiere so renowned for his military expertise that he was in demand by popes and kings, and soldiers came from across Europe to study under his direction.

One of the artists who received several commissions from Federico was Piero della Francesca (FIG. 8-28), who had already established a major reputation in his native Tuscany. At the Urbino court, Piero produced both official portraits and religious works for Federico, among them a double portrait (FIG. **8-37**) of the count and his second wife, Battista Sforza (1446–1472), whom Federico married in 1460 when she was 14 years old. The daughter of Alessandro Sforza (1409–1473), lord of Pesaro and brother of the duke of Milan, Battista was a well-educated humanist who proved to be an excellent administrator of Federico's territories during his frequent military campaigns. She gave birth to eight daughters in 11 years and finally, on January 25, 1472, to the male heir for which the couple had prayed. When the countess died of pneumonia five months later at age 26, Federico went into mourning for virtually the rest of his life. He never remarried.

Federico commissioned Piero della Francesca to paint their double portrait shortly after Battista's death to pay tribute to her and to have a memento of their marriage. The present frame is a 19th-century addition. Originally, the two portraits formed a hinged diptych. Piero depicted the Urbino count and countess in profile, in part to emulate the profile portraits of Roman rulers on coins that Renaissance humanists avidly collected, and in part to conceal the disfigured right side of Federico's face. (He lost his right eye and part of the bridge of his nose in a tournament in 1450.) Piero probably based Battista's portrait on her death mask, and the pallor of her skin may be a reference to her death. The backs of the panels also bear paintings. They represent Federico and Battista in triumphal chariots accompanied by personifications of their respective virtues, including Justice, Prudence, and Fortitude (Federico) and Faith, Charity, and Chastity (Battista). The placement of scenes of triumph on the reverse of profile portraits also emulates ancient Roman coinage.

Mantua Marquis Ludovico Gonzaga (1412–1478) ruled Mantua in northeastern Italy (MAP 8-2) during the mid-15th century. A famed condottiere like Federico da Montefeltro, Gonzaga established his reputation as a fierce military leader while general of the Milanese armies. The visit by Pope Pius II

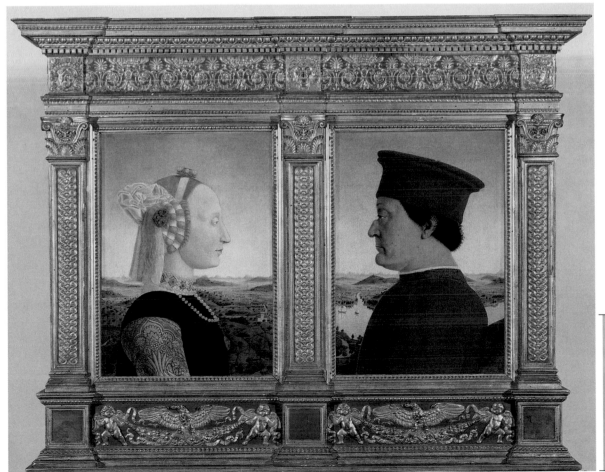

8-37 PIERO DELLA FRANCESCA, *Battista Sforza and Federico da Montefeltro*, ca. 1472–1474. Oil and tempera on wood in modern frame, each panel 1′ 6½″ × 1′ 1″. Galleria degli Uffizi, Florence. ▶

Piero's portraits of Federico da Montefeltro and his recently deceased wife, Battista Sforza, combine the profile views on Roman coins with the landscape backgrounds of Flemish portraiture.

1 ft.

(r. 1458–1464) in 1459 to Mantua stimulated the marquis's determination to transform his city into one all Italy would envy.

One of the major projects Gonzaga instituted was the rebuilding of Sant'Andrea, an 11th-century church. Gonzaga turned to Leon Battista Alberti for this important commission. The facade (FIG. **8-38**) Alberti designed incorporated two major ancient Roman architectural motifs—the temple front and the triumphal arch. The combination was already a feature of Roman buildings still standing in Italy. For example, many Roman triumphal arches incorporated a pediment over the arcuated passageway and engaged columns, but there is no close parallel in antiquity for Alberti's eclectic and ingenious design. The Renaissance architect's concern for proportion led him to equalize the vertical and horizontal dimensions of the facade, which left it considerably shorter than the church behind it. Because of the primary importance of visual appeal, many Renaissance architects made this concession not only to the demands of a purely visual proportionality in the facade but also to the facade's relation to the small square in front of it, even at the expense of continuity with the body of the building. Yet structural correspondences to the building do exist in Sant'Andrea's facade. The pilasters are the same height as those on the nave's in-

terior walls, and the large barrel vault over the central portal, with smaller barrel vaults branching off at right angles, introduces on a smaller scale the arrangement of the church's nave and aisles. The facade pilasters, as part of the wall, run uninterrupted through three stories in an early application of the *colossal* or *giant order* that became a favorite motif of Michelangelo (FIG. 9-15).

Inside (FIG. **8-39**), Alberti abandoned the medieval columned arcade Brunelleschi still used in Santo Spirito (FIG. 8-32). Thick walls alternating with vaulted chapels, interrupted by a massive dome over the crossing, support the huge barrel vault. The vaulted interior calls to mind the vast spaces and dense enclosing masses of Roman architecture, especially Constantine's Basilica Nova (FIG. 3-51), which may have served as a prototype for Alberti's design. In his architectural treatise, Alberti criticized the traditional basilican plan (with continuous aisles flanking the central nave) as impractical because the colonnades conceal the ceremonies from the faithful in the aisles. For this reason, he designed a single huge hall with independent chapels branching off at right angles. This break with a Christian building tradition that had endured for a thousand years was extremely influential in later Renaissance and Baroque church planning.

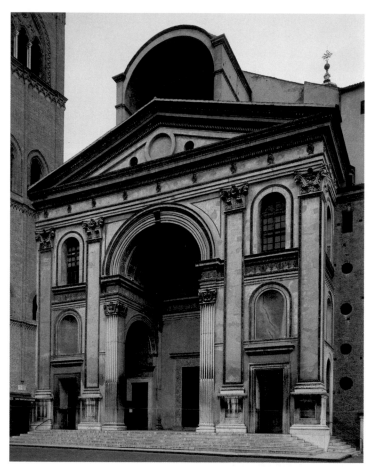

8-38 LEON BATTISTA ALBERTI, west facade of Sant'Andrea, Mantua, Italy, designed 1470, begun 1472.

Alberti's design for Sant'Andrea reflects his study of ancient Roman architecture. Employing a colossal order, the architect locked together a triumphal arch and a Roman temple front with pediment.

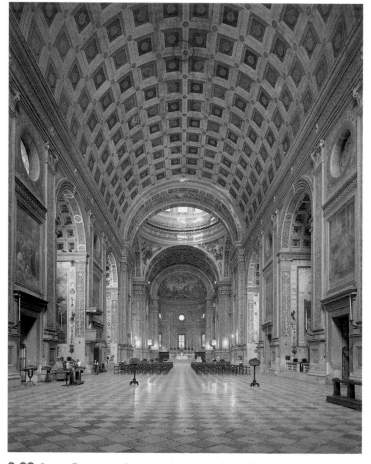

8-39 LEON BATTISTA ALBERTI, interior of Sant'Andrea (looking east), Mantua, Italy, designed 1470, begun 1472.

For the nave of Sant'Andrea, Alberti abandoned the medieval columnar arcade. The tremendous vaults suggest that Constantine's Basilica Nova (FIG. 3-51) in Rome may have served as a prototype.

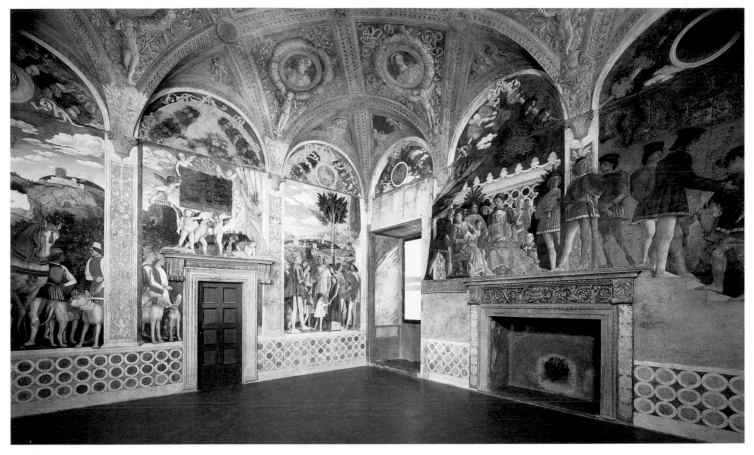

8-40 ANDREA MANTEGNA, interior of the Camera Picta, Palazzo Ducale, Mantua, Italy, 1465–1474. Fresco.

Working for Ludovico Gonzaga, who established Mantua as a great art city, Mantegna produced for the duke's palace the first completely consistent illusionistic fresco decoration of an entire room.

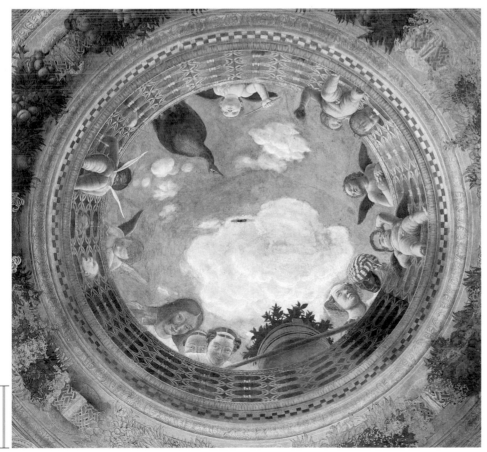

1 ft.

Andrea Mantegna As did other princes, Ludovico Gonzaga believed an impressive palace was an important visual expression of his authority. One of the most spectacular rooms in the Palazzo Ducale (Ducal Palace) in Mantua is the so-called Camera degli Sposi (Room of the Newlyweds), originally the Camera Picta (Painted Chamber; FIGS. **8-40** and **8-41**). ANDREA MANTEGNA (ca. 1431–1506) of Padua took almost nine years to complete the extensive fresco program, in which he sought to aggrandize Ludovico Gonzaga and his family. Any viewer standing in the Camera Picta, surrounded by the spectacle and majesty of courtly life cannot help

8-41 ANDREA MANTEGNA, ceiling of the Camera Picta, Palazzo Ducale, Mantua, Italy, 1465–1474. Fresco, 8' 9" in diameter. ◼

Inside the Camera Picta, the viewer becomes the viewed as figures gaze into the room from a painted oculus opening onto a blue sky. This is the first perspective view of a ceiling from below.

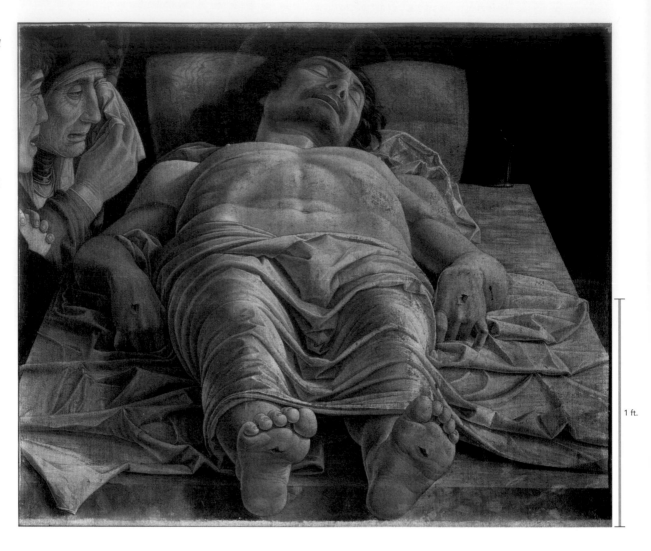

1 ft.

but be thoroughly impressed by both the commanding presence and elevated status of the patron and the dazzling artistic skills of Mantegna.

In the Camera Picta, Mantegna performed a triumphant feat by producing the first completely consistent illusionistic decoration of an entire room. By integrating real and painted architectural elements, Mantegna illusionistically dissolved the room's walls in a manner foretelling 17th-century Baroque decoration (see Chapter 10). The Camera Picta recalls the efforts of Italian painters more than 15 centuries earlier at Pompeii and elsewhere to integrate mural painting and architecture in frescoes of the so-called Second Style of Roman painting (FIG. 3-19). Mantegna's *trompe l'oeil* (French, "deceives the eye") design, however, went far beyond anything preserved from ancient Italy. The Renaissance painter's daring experimentalism led him to complete the room's decoration with the first perspective of a ceiling (FIG. 8-41) seen from below (called, in Italian, *di sotto in sù,* "from below upward"). Baroque ceiling decorators later broadly developed this technique. Inside the Camera Picta, the viewer becomes the viewed as figures look down into the room from the painted oculus. Seen against the convincing illusion of a cloud-filled blue sky, several *putti*

(cupids), strongly foreshortened, set the amorous mood of the Room of the Newlyweds, as the painted spectators smile down into the room. The prominent peacock is an attribute of Juno, Jupiter's bride, who oversees lawful marriages. This brilliant feat of illusionism is the climax of decades of experimentation with perspective.

Foreshortened Christ One of Mantegna's later paintings, *Foreshortened Christ* (FIG. **8-42**), is a work of overwhelming power as well as a demonstration of the artist's mastery of perspective. At first glance, this painting seems to be a strikingly realistic study in foreshortening. However, Manegna reduced the size of Christ's feet, which, as the painter clearly knew, would cover much of the Savior's body if properly represented according to Renaissance perspective rules. Thus, tempering naturalism with artistic license, Mantegna presented both a harrowing study of a strongly foreshortened cadaver and an intensely poignant depiction of a biblical tragedy. The painter's harsh, sharp line seems to cut the surface as if it were metal and conveys, by its grinding edge, the theme's corrosive emotion. Remarkably, in the supremely gifted hands of Mantegna, all of Quattrocento Italian science here serves the purpose of devotion.

The Early Renaissance in Europe

Burgundy and Flanders

▌ The most powerful rulers north of the Alps during the first three-quarters of the 15th century were the dukes of Burgundy, who controlled Flanders and were great art patrons.

▌ Flemish painters popularized the use of oil paints on wood panels. By superimposing translucent glazes, they created richer colors than possible using tempera or fresco. Robert Campin's *Mérode Altarpiece* is an early example. In the *Annunciation* triptych, the everyday objects depicted have symbolic significance.

▌ Jan van Eyck was largely responsible for establishing portraiture as an important art form in 15th-century Flanders.

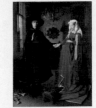

Van Eyck, *Giovanni Arnolfini and His Wife*, 1434

France and the Holy Roman Empire

▌ The Limbourg brothers expanded the illusionistic capabilities of manuscript illumination with full-page calendar pictures depicting naturalistic settings in a book of hours for Jean, duke of Berry.

▌ The major German innovation of the 15th century was the development of the printing press, which printers soon used to produce books with woodcut illustrations. Woodcuts are relief prints in which the artist carves out the areas around the lines to be printed. German artists such as Martin Schongauer were also the earliest masters of engraving. This intaglio technique allows for a wider variety of linear effects because the artist incises the image directly onto a metal plate.

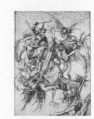

Schongauer, *Saint Anthony Tormented by Demons*, ca. 1480–1490

Italy

▌ The fortunate congruence of artistic genius, the spread of humanism, and economic prosperity nourished the flowering of the artistic culture historians call the Renaissance—the rebirth of classical values. The greatest center of Quattrocento Renaissance art was Florence, home of the Medici family, perhaps the most ambitious art patrons in history.

▌ Some of the earliest examples of the new Renaissance style in sculpture are Donatello's *Saint Mark*, which introduced the classical concept of contrapposto into Renaissance statuary, and his later *David*, the first nude male statue since antiquity.

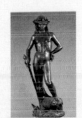

Donatello, *David*, ca. 1440–1460

▌ Masaccio's figures recall Giotto's but have a greater psychological and physical credibility, and the light shining on them comes from a source outside the picture. Masaccio's *Holy Trinity* in Santa Maria Novella in Florence epitomizes Early Renaissance painting in its convincing illusionism, achieved through Filippo Brunelleschi's new science of linear perspective, yet it remains effective as a devotional painting in a church setting.

▌ Italian architects also revived the classical style. Brunelleschi's Santo Spirito, a basilican church with a dome-covered crossing square, showcases the clarity and Roman-inspired rationality of Quattrocento Florentine architecture.

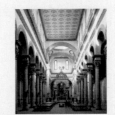

Brunelleschi, Santo Spirito, Florence, begun 1446

▌ Although Florentine artists led the way in creating the Renaissance in art and architecture, the papacy in Rome and the princely courts in Urbino and Mantua also were major art patrons. Among the important papal commissions of the 15th century was the decoration of the walls of the Sistine Chapel with frescoes, including Perugino's *Christ Delivering the Keys of the Kingdom to Saint Peter*, a prime example of linear perspective.

▌ Mantua became an important art center under Marquis Ludovico Gonzaga, who brought leading artists, such as Andrea Mantegna, to his court. Gonzaga also commissioned Leon Battista Alberti to rebuild the 11th-century church of Sant'Andrea. Alberti applied the principles he developed in his influential 1450 treatise *On the Art of Building* to the project and freely adapted forms from ancient Roman religious, triumphal, and civic architecture.

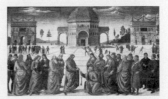

Perugino, *Christ Delivering the Keys to Saint Peter*, 1481–1483

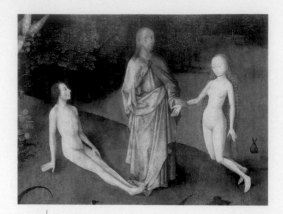

Garden of Earthly Delights is Bosch's most enigmatic painting, but scholars agree it depicts Paradise in the left and central panels and Hell in the right wing. At the left, God as Christ presents Eve to Adam.

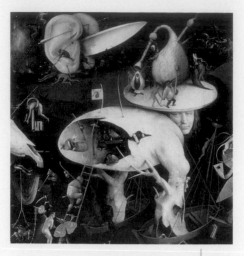

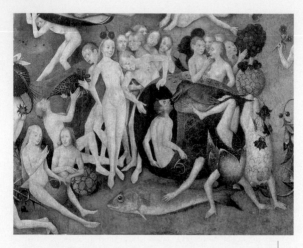

In the inky darkness of Bosch's Hell are unidentifiable objects that are imaginative variations on chemical apparatus of the day. Alchemy is a prominent theme of the work.

In the fantastic sunlit landscape that is Bosch's Paradise, scores of nude people in the prime of life blithely cavort. The oversized fruits are fertility symbols, and the scene celebrates procreation.

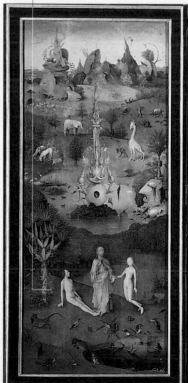
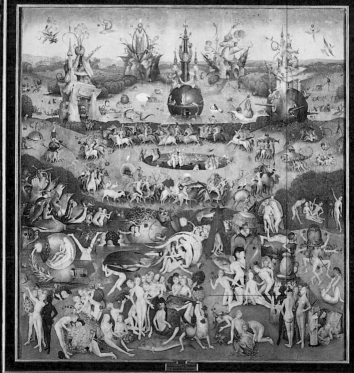
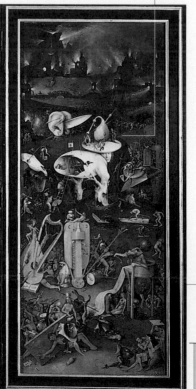

1 ft.

9-1 HIERONYMUS BOSCH, *Garden of Earthly Delights,* 1505–1510. Oil on wood, center panel 7′ 2⅝″ × 6′ 4¾″, each wing 7′ 2⅝″ × 3′ 2¼″. Museo del Prado, Madrid. ◼◀

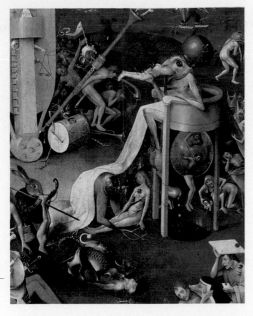

The horrors of Hell include beastly creatures devouring people and sinners enduring tortures tailored to their conduct while alive. A glutton vomits eternally. A miser defecates gold coins.

High Renaissance and Mannerism in Europe

EARTHLY DELIGHTS IN THE NETHERLANDS

HIERONYMUS BOSCH (ca. 1450–1516) was one of the most fascinating and puzzling artists in history—a unique artistic personality who nonetheless typifies the Renaissance era in the emergence of distinctive personal styles. Bosch's most famous painting, *Garden of Earthly Delights* (FIG. **9-1**), is also his most enigmatic, and no interpretation has ever won universal acceptance. Although the work is a monumental triptych, which would suggest a religious function as an altarpiece, the painting was on display in the palace of Henry III of Nassau, regent of the Netherlands, no later than seven years after its completion. This suggests the triptych was a secular commission, and given the work's central themes of sex and procreation, the painting may commemorate a wedding. Marriage was a familiar theme in Netherlandish painting. Any similarity to earlier paintings ends there, however, because *Garden of Earthly Delights* is unlike any other work. Bosch's triptych presents a visionary world of fantasy and intrigue—a painted world without close parallel until the advent of Surrealism more than 400 years later (see Chapter 14).

In the left panel, God (in the form of Christ) presents Eve to Adam in a landscape, presumably the Garden of Eden. Bosch's wildly imaginative setting includes an odd pink fountainlike structure in a body of water and an array of fanciful and unusual animals, including a giraffe, elephant, and winged fish.

The central panel is a continuation of Paradise, a sunlit landscape filled with nude people, all in the prime of youth, blithely cavorting amid bizarre creatures and unidentifiable objects. The youths play with abandon. Some stand on their hands or turn somersaults. The numerous fruits and birds (fertility symbols) in the scene suggest procreation, and, indeed, many of the figures pair off as couples.

In contrast to the orgiastic overtones of the central panel is the terrifying image of Hell in the right wing, where viewers must search through the inky darkness to find all of the fascinating though repulsive details Bosch recorded. Beastly creatures devour people, while other condemned souls endure tortures tailored to their conduct while alive. A glutton must vomit eternally. A miser defecates gold coins. A spidery monster fondles a promiscuous woman. Scholars have traditionally interpreted Bosch's triptych as a warning to viewers of the fate awaiting the sinful, decadent, and immoral, but as a secular work, *Garden of Earthly Delights* may have been intended for a learned audience fascinated by *alchemy*—the study of seemingly magical chemical changes. Details throughout the triptych seem to be based on chemical apparatus of the day, which Bosch knew well because his in-laws were pharmacists.

ITALY

The art and architecture of 16th-century (*Cinquecento*) Italy (MAP 9-1) built on the foundation of the Early Renaissance of the 15th century, but no single artistic style characterized Italian 16th-century art and regional differences abounded, especially between central Italy (Florence and Rome) and Venice.

The period opened with the brief era art historians call the High Renaissance—the quarter century between 1495 and the deaths of Leonardo da Vinci in 1519 and Raphael in 1520. The Renaissance style and the interest in classical culture, perspective, proportion, and human anatomy dominated the remainder of the 16th century (the Late Renaissance), but a new style, called Mannerism, challenged Renaissance naturalism almost as soon as Raphael had been laid to rest (in the ancient Roman Pantheon, FIG. 3-40). The one constant in Cinquecento Italy is the astounding quality, both technical and aesthetic, of the art and architecture produced. Indeed, the modern notion of the "fine arts" and the exaltation of the artist-genius originated in Renaissance Italy. During the High Renaissance, artists first became international celebrities, none more so than Leonardo da Vinci, Raphael, and Michelangelo.

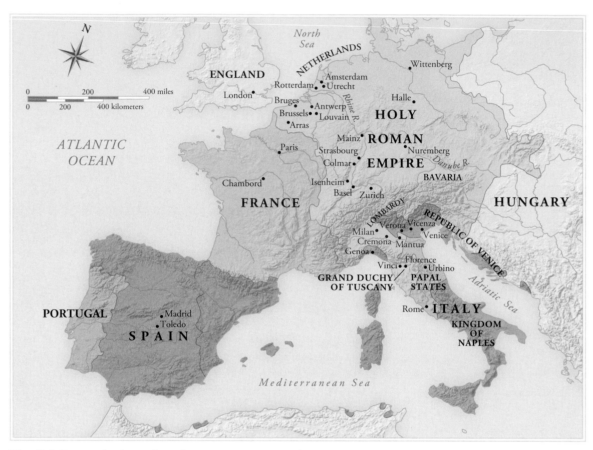

MAP 9-1 Europe in the early 16th century.

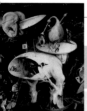

High Renaissance and Mannerism in Europe

1495	1520	1550	1575	1600

- The leading artists of the High Renaissance in Florence and Rome are Leonardo da Vinci, Raphael, and Michelangelo
- In Rome, Bramante champions the classical style in architecture
- In northern Europe, consistent with Protestant values, art patrons prefer secular to religious themes
- Albrecht Dürer, master print maker, becomes the first international art celebrity outside Italy

- Paul III launches the Counter-Reformation
- In Venice, Titian uses rich colors and establishes oil on canvas as the standard medium of Western painting
- Mannerism emerges as an alternative to High Renaissance style in the work of Pontormo, Parmigianino, Bronzino, and Giulio Romano
- Netherlandish painters inject moralizing religious messages into paintings of everyday life

- The Council of Trent defends religious art
- Andrea Palladio becomes chief architect of the Venetian Republic
- Giorgio Vasari publishes *Lives of the Most Eminent Painters, Sculptors, and Architects*
- Pieter Bruegel the Elder produces masterful landscapes that nonetheless focus on human activities

- Tintoretto is the leading Venetian Mannerist painter
- Giovanni da Bologna uses spiral compositions for Mannerist statuary groups
- Greek-born El Greco settles in Toledo and creates paintings that are a uniquely personal mix of Byzantine and Italian Mannerist elements. His hybrid style captures the fervor of Spanish Catholicism

Leonardo da Vinci on Painting

Leonardo da Vinci left copious notes stating his views on the purpose and technique of painting. He believed modeling with light and shadow and expressing emotional states were the heart of painting:

> A good painter has two chief objects to paint—man and the intention of his soul. The former is easy, the latter hard, for it must be expressed by gestures and the movement of the limbs. . . . A painting will only be wonderful for the beholder by making that which is not so appear raised and detached from the wall.*

The four figures in Leonardo's early masterpiece, *Madonna of the Rocks* (FIG. 9-2), certainly appear "detached from the wall." In this work, the Florentine painter achieved a groundbreaking feat—the unified representation of objects in an atmospheric setting. This innovation was a manifestation of Leonardo's scientific curiosity about the invisible substance surrounding things. The holy figures emerge through nuances of light and shade from the half-light of the cavernous visionary landscape. Light simultaneously veils and reveals the forms, immersing them in a layer of atmosphere. Leonardo's effective use of atmospheric perspective (see "Linear and Atmospheric Perspective," Chapter 8, page 237) was the result in large part of his mastery of the relatively new medium of oil painting, which had previously been used mostly by northern European painters (see "Tempera and Oil Painting," Chapter 8, page 224).

Leonardo wrote about the importance of atmospheric perspective in his so-called *Treatise on Painting,* where he set forth the reasons he believed painting was a greater art than sculpture:

> The painter will show you things at different distances with variation of color due to the air lying between the objects and the eye; he shows you mists through which visual images penetrate with difficulty; he shows you rain which discloses within it clouds with mountains and valleys; he shows the dust which discloses within it and beyond it the combatants who stirred it up; he shows streams of greater or lesser density; he shows fish playing between the surface of the water and its bottom; he shows the polished pebbles of various colors lying on the washed sand at the bottom of rivers, surrounded by green plants; he shows the stars at various heights above us, and thus he achieves innumerable effects which sculpture cannot attain.†

9-2 LEONARDO DA VINCI, *Madonna of the Rocks,* from San Francesco Grande, Milan, Italy, begun 1483. Oil on wood (transferred to canvas), 6' 6½" × 4'. Musée du Louvre, Paris. 🎥

Leonardo used gestures and a pyramidal composition to unite the Virgin, John the Baptist, the Christ Child, and an angel. The figures share the same light-infused environment.

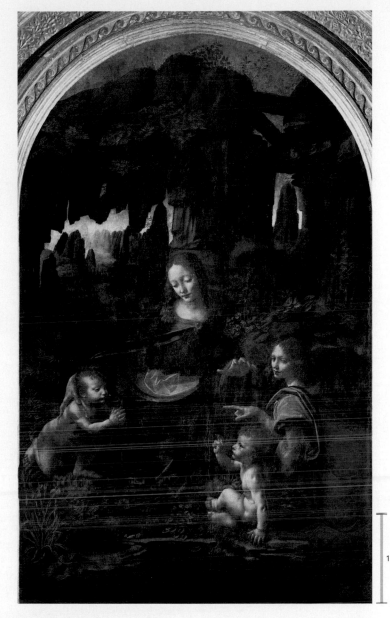

1 ft.

*Quoted in Anthony Blunt, *Artistic Theory in Italy, 1450–1600* (London: Oxford University Press, 1964), 34.
†Leonardo da Vinci, *Treatise on Painting,* 51, in Robert Klein and Henri Zerner, *Italian Art 1500–1600: Sources and Documents* (Evanston, Ill.: Northwestern University Press, 1966), 7–8.

Leonardo da Vinci

Born in the small town of Vinci, near Florence, LEONARDO DA VINCI (1452–1519) was the quintessential "Renaissance man." Art was but one of Leonardo's innumerable interests. His unquenchable curiosity is evident in the voluminous notes he interspersed with sketches in his notebooks dealing with botany, geology, geography, cartography, zoology, military engineering, animal lore, anatomy, and aspects of physical science, including hydraulics and mechanics. These studies informed his art. For example, Leonardo's in-depth explora-

tion of optics provided him with an understanding of perspective, light, and color. His scientific drawings (FIG. 9-5) are themselves artworks.

Leonardo's great ambition in his painting (see "Leonardo da Vinci on Painting," above, and FIG. 9-2), as well as in his scientific endeavors, was to discover the laws underlying the processes and flux of nature. With this end in mind, he also studied the human body and contributed immeasurably to knowledge of physiology and psychology. Leonardo believed reality in an absolute sense is inaccessible and humans could

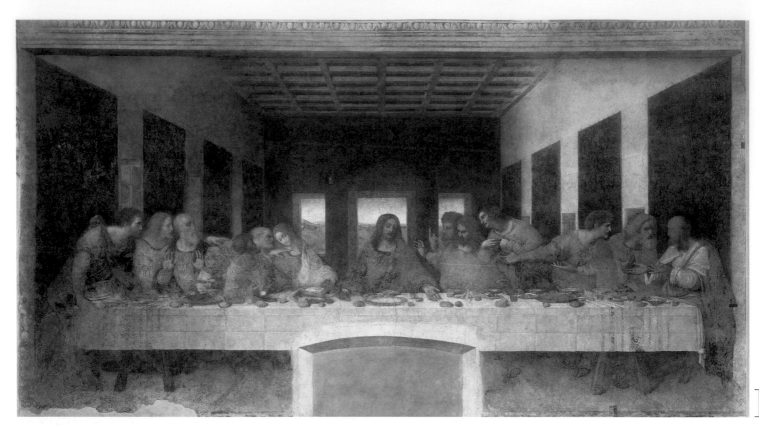

9-3 LEONARDO DA VINCI, *Last Supper,* ca. 1495–1498. Oil and tempera on plaster, 13′ 9″ × 29′ 10″. Refectory, Santa Maria delle Grazie, Milan. ◼◀

Christ has just announced that one of his disciples will betray him, and each one reacts. Christ is both the psychological focus of Leonardo's fresco and the focal point of all the converging perspective lines.

know it only through its changing images. He considered the eyes the most vital organs and sight the most essential function.

Around 1481, Leonardo left Florence after offering his services to Ludovico Sforza (1451–1508), the son and heir apparent of the ruler of Milan. The political situation in Florence was uncertain, and Leonardo may have felt his particular skills would be in greater demand in Milan, providing him with the opportunity for increased financial security. He devoted most of a letter to Ludovico to advertising his competence and his qualifications as a military engineer, mentioning only at the end his abilities as a painter and sculptor:

> And in short, according to the variety of cases, I can contrive various and endless means of offence and defence. . . . In time of peace I believe I can give perfect satisfaction and to the equal of any other in architecture and the composition of buildings, public and private; and in guiding water from one place to another. . . . I can carry out sculpture in marble, bronze, or clay, and also I can do in painting whatever may be done, as well as any other, be he whom he may."[1]

Madonna of the Rocks Ludovico accepted Leonardo's offer. Shortly after settling in Milan, the Florentine artist painted *Madonna of the Rocks* (FIG. **9-2**) as the center panel of an altarpiece in San Francesco Grande. The painting builds on Masaccio's understanding and usage of chiaroscuro, the

subtle play of light and dark. Leonardo presented the four figures in *Madonna of the Rocks* in a pyramidal grouping. The Madonna, Christ Child, infant John the Baptist, and angel pray, point, and bless, and these acts and gestures, although their meanings are uncertain, visually unite the individuals portrayed. The angel points to John and, through his outward glance, involves the viewer in the tableau. John prays to the Christ Child, who blesses him in return. The Virgin herself completes the series of interlocking gestures, her left hand reaching toward her son and her right hand resting protectively on John's shoulder. A melting mood of tenderness suffuses the entire composition. Nonetheless, the most remarkable aspect of *Madonna of the Rocks* is that the holy figures share the same light-infused environment, one of Leonardo's primary goals as a painter.

Last Supper For the refectory of Santa Maria delle Grazie in Milan, Leonardo painted *Last Supper* (FIG. **9-3**). The mural is unfortunately in a poor state, in part because, in a bold experiment, Leonardo mixed oil and tempera, and he applied the colors *a secco* (to dried, rather than wet, plaster). Because the wall did not absorb the pigment as in the *buon fresco* technique (see "Fresco Painting, Chapter 7, page 213), the paint quickly began to flake. The humidity of Milan further accelerated the deterioration. Nonetheless, the painting is both formally and emotionally Leonardo's most impressive work. Jesus and his 12 disciples sit at a long table placed parallel to the picture plane in a simple, spacious room. The austere setting amplifies the painting's highly dramatic action. Jesus, with outstretched hands, has just said, "One of you is about to betray me" (Matt. 26:21). A wave of intense excitement passes through the group as each disciple asks himself and, in some cases, his neighbor, "Is it I?" (Matt. 26:22). Leonardo linked Jesus's dramatic statement about betrayal with the initiation of the ancient liturgical ceremony of the Eucharist, when Jesus, blessing bread and wine, said, "This is my body, which is given for you. Do this for a commemoration of me. . . . This is the chalice, the new testament in my blood, which shall be shed for you" (Luke 22:19–20).

In the center, Jesus appears isolated from the disciples and in perfect repose, the calm eye of the emotional storm swirling around him. The central window at the back, whose curved pediment arches above his head, frames his figure. The pediment is the only curve in the architectural framework, and it serves here, along with the diffused light, as a halo. Jesus's head is the focal point of all converging perspective lines in the composition. Thus, the still, psychological focus and cause of the action is also the perspective focus, as well as the center of the two-dimensional surface. The two-dimensional, the three-dimensional, and the psychodimensional focuses are the same.

Leonardo presented the agitated disciples in four groups of three, united among and within themselves by the figures' gestures and postures. The artist sacrificed traditional iconography to pictorial and dramatic consistency by placing Judas on the same side of the table as Jesus and the other disciples (compare FIG. 8-26). The light source in the painting corresponds to the windows in the refectory. Judas's face is in shadow, and he clutches a money bag in his right hand as he reaches his left forward to fulfill Jesus's declaration: "But yet behold, the hand of him that betrayeth me is with me on the table" (Luke 22:21). The two disciples at the table ends are quieter than the others, as if to bracket the energy of the composition, which is more intense closer to Jesus, whose serenity both halts and intensifies it. The disciples register a broad range of emotional responses, including fear, doubt, protestation, rage, and love. Leonardo's numerous preparatory studies suggest he thought of each figure as carrying a particular charge and type of emotion. Like a stage director, he read the Gospel story carefully, and scrupulously cast his actors as the Bible described their roles. In this work, as in his other religious paintings, Leonardo revealed his extraordinary ability to apply his voluminous knowledge about the observable world to the pictorial representation of a religious scene, resulting in a psychologically complex and compelling painting.

Mona Lisa Leonardo's *Mona Lisa* (FIG. **9-4**) is probably the world's most famous portrait. The sitter's identity is still the subject of debate, but in his biography of Leonardo, Giorgio Vasari asserted she was Lisa di Antonio Maria Gherardini, the wife of Francesco del Giocondo, a wealthy Florentine—hence, "Mona (a contraction of *ma donna*, "my lady" in

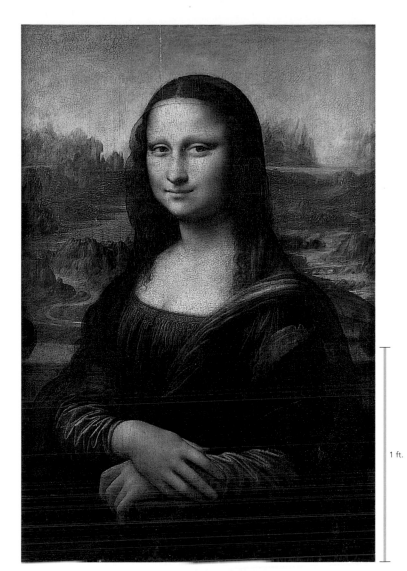

9-4 Leonardo da Vinci, *Mona Lisa,* ca. 1503–1505. Oil on wood, 2′ 6¼″ × 1′ 9″. Musée du Louvre, Paris.

Leonardo's skill with chiaroscuro and atmospheric perspective is on display in this new kind of portrait depicting the sitter as an individual personality who engages the viewer psychologically.

Italian) Lisa." Despite the uncertainty of this identification, Leonardo's portrait is a convincing representation of an individual. Unlike earlier portraits, it does not serve solely as an icon of status. Indeed, Mona Lisa wears no jewelry nor holds any attribute associated with wealth. She sits quietly, her hands folded, her mouth forming a gentle smile, and her gaze directed at the viewer. Renaissance etiquette dictated a woman should not look directly into a man's eyes. Leonardo's portrayal of this self-assured young woman without the trappings of power but engaging the audience psychologically is thus quite remarkable.

The enduring appeal of *Mona Lisa* derives in large part from Leonardo's decision to set his subject against the backdrop of a mysterious uninhabited landscape. This setting, with roads and bridges seemingly leading nowhere, recalls that of his *Madonna of the Rocks* (FIG. 9-2). The composition also resembles Fra Filippo Lippi's *Madonna and Child with*

Renaissance Drawings

In Cinquecento Italy, drawing (or *disegno*) assumed a position of greater artistic prominence than ever before. Until the late 15th century, the expense of drawing surfaces and their lack of availability limited the production of preparatory sketches. Most artists drew on *parchment* (prepared from the skins of calves, sheep, and goats) or on *vellum* (made from the skins of young animals). Because of the high cost of these materials, drawings in the 14th and 15th centuries tended to be extremely detailed and meticulously executed. Artists often drew using a silverpoint stylus (FIG. 8-8) because of the fine line it produced and the sharp point it maintained. The introduction in the late 15th century of less expensive paper made of fibrous pulp, from the developing printing industry (see "Woodcuts," Chapter 8, page 233), enabled artists to experiment more and to draw with greater freedom. As a result, sketches abounded. Artists executed these drawings in pen and ink, chalk, charcoal, brush, and graphite or lead. Leonardo da Vinci was especially prolific. His drawings are not only small-scale artworks of the highest quality but invaluable records of his wide range of interests, both artistic and scientific (FIG. 9-5).

During the Renaissance, the importance of drawing transcended the mechanical or technical possibilities it afforded artists, however. The term *disegno* referred also to design, an integral component of good art. Design was the foundation of art, and drawing was the fundamental element of design. Federico Zuccaro (1542–1609) summed up this philosophy when he stated that drawing is the external physical manifestation (*disegno esterno*) of an internal intellectual idea or design (*disegno interno*).

The design dimension of art production became increasingly important as artists cultivated their own styles. The early stages of an apprentice's training largely focused on the study and copying of exemplary artworks. But to achieve widespread recognition, artists had to develop their own styles. Although the artistic community and public at large acknowledged technical skill, the conceptualization of the artwork—its theoretical and formal development—was paramount. Disegno, design

9-5 LEONARDO DA VINCI, *The Fetus and Lining of the Uterus,* 1510–1513. Pen and ink with wash, over red chalk and traces of black chalk on paper, 1′ 8⅝″. Royal Library, Windsor Castle, Windsor. ◼️

The introduction of less expensive paper in the late 15th century enabled artists to draw more frequently. Leonardo's analytical anatomical studies epitomize the scientific spirit of the Renaissance.

1 in.

in this case, represented an artist's conceptualization and intention. In the literature of the period, the terms often invoked to praise esteemed artists included *invenzione* (invention), *ingegno* (innate talent), *fantasia* (imagination), and *capriccio* (originality).

Angels (FIG. 8-27) with figures seated in front of a window through which the viewer glimpses a distant landscape. Originally, the artist represented Mona Lisa in a loggia. A later owner trimmed the painting, eliminating the columns, but partial column bases remain to the left and right of Mona Lisa's shoulders. The painting is darker today than it was 500 years ago, and the colors are less vivid, but *Mona Lisa* still reveals Leonardo's fascination and skill with chiaroscuro and atmospheric perspective. The portrait is a prime example of Leonardo's famous smoky *sfumato* (misty haziness)—his subtle adjustment of light and blurring of precise planes.

Anatomical Studies Leonardo completed very few paintings. His perfectionism, relentless experimentation, and far-ranging curiosity diffused his efforts. However, the drawings in his notebooks preserve an extensive record of his ideas (see "Renaissance Drawings," above). His interests focused increasingly on science in his later years, and he embraced knowledge of all facets of the natural world. His investigations in anatomy yielded drawings of great precision and beauty of execution. *The Fetus and Lining of the Uterus* (FIG. 9-5), although it does not meet 21st-century standards for accuracy (for example, Leonardo regularized the uterus's shape to a sphere, and his characterization of the lining is incorrect), was an astounding achievement in its day. Leonardo's analytical anatomical studies epitomize the scientific spirit of the Renaissance, establishing that era as a prelude to the modern world and setting it in sharp contrast to the preceding Middle Ages. Although Leonardo may not have been the first scientist of the modern world (at least not in today's sense of the term), he certainly originated the modern method of scientific illustration incorporating *cutaway* views. Scholars have long recognized the importance of his drawings for the development of anatomy as a science, especially in an age predating photographic methods such as X-rays.

Leonardo also won renown in his time as both architect and sculptor, although no surviving buildings or sculptures can be definitively attributed to him. From his many drawings of central-plan structures, it is evident he shared the interest of other Renaissance architects in this building type. As for Leonardo's sculptures, numerous drawings of monumental equestrian statues survive, and he made a full-scale model for a monument to Francesco Sforza (1401–1466), Ludovico's father. The French used the statue as a target and shot it to pieces when they occupied Milan in 1499. Leonardo left Milan at that time and served for a while as a military engineer for Cesare Borgia (1476–1507), who, with the support of his father, Pope Alexander VI (r. 1492–1503), tried to conquer the cities of the Romagna region in north-central Italy and create a Borgia duchy. Leonardo eventually returned to Milan in the service of the French. At the invitation of King Francis I (see page 284), he then went to France, where he died at the château of Cloux in 1519.

Raphael

Raffaello Santi (or Sanzio), known as RAPHAEL (1483–1520) in English, was born in a small town in Umbria near Urbino. He probably learned the rudiments of his art from his father, Giovanni Santi (d. 1494), a painter connected with the ducal court of Federico da Montefeltro (FIG. 8-37), before entering the studio of Perugino (FIG. 8-36) in Perugia. Although strongly influenced by Perugino and Leonardo, Raphael developed an individual style exemplifying the ideals of High Renaissance art.

Madonna in the Meadow Raphael worked in Florence from 1504 to 1508, where he painted *Madonna in the Meadow* (FIG. 9-6) and adopted Leonardo's pyramidal composition and modeling of faces and figures in subtle chiaroscuro. But Raphael retained Perugino's lighter tonalities and blue skies, preferring clarity to obscurity, not fascinated, as Leonardo was, with mystery. Raphael's portrayals of the Madonna, of which this is an early example, unify Christian devotion and classical beauty. No artist ever has rivaled Raphael in his definitive rendering of this sublime theme of grace and dignity, of sweetness and lofty idealism.

School of Athens In 1508, Pope Julius II (r. 1503–1513) called Raphael to Rome. An immensely ambitious man, Julius sought to extend his spiritual authority to the temporal realm and selected his papal name to associate himself with Julius Caesar and the Roman Empire. His enthusiasm for engaging in battle earned Julius the designation "warrior-pope," but his 10-year papacy was most notable for his patronage of the arts. He understood well the propagandistic value of visual imagery, and upon his election immediately

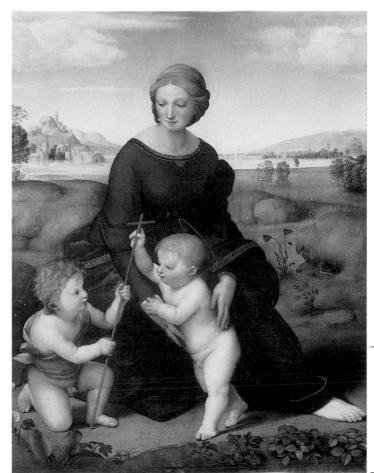

9-6 RAPHAEL, *Madonna in the Meadow*, 1505–1506. Oil on wood, 3′ 8½″ × 2′ 10¼″. Kunsthistorisches Museum, Vienna.

Emulating Leonardo's pyramidal composition (FIG. 9-2) but rejecting his dusky modeling and mystery, Raphael set his Madonna in a well-lit landscape and imbued her with grace, dignity, and beauty.

commissioned artworks that would present an authoritative image of his rule and reinforce the primacy of the Catholic Church. Among the many projects Julius commissioned were a new design for Saint Peter's basilica (FIG. 9-14), the painting of the Sistine Chapel ceiling (FIG. 9-10), and the decoration of the papal apartments (FIG. 9-7).

Although the commissions for Saint Peter's and the Sistine Chapel went to others, Julius awarded Raphael the responsibility of decorating the papal apartments. Of the suite's several rooms (*stanze*), Raphael painted two, including the Stanza della Segnatura ("Room of the Signature"—the papal library, where Julius signed official documents). Pupils completed the others, following Raphael's sketches. On the four walls of the library, Raphael presented images symbolizing the four branches of human knowledge and wisdom under the headings *Theology, Law, Poetry,* and *Philosophy*—the learning appropriate to a Renaissance pope. Given Julius II's desire for recognition as both a spiritual and temporal leader, it is appropriate the *Theology* and *Philosophy* frescoes face each other. The two images present a balanced picture of the pope—as a cultured, knowledgeable individual and as a wise, divinely ordained religious authority.

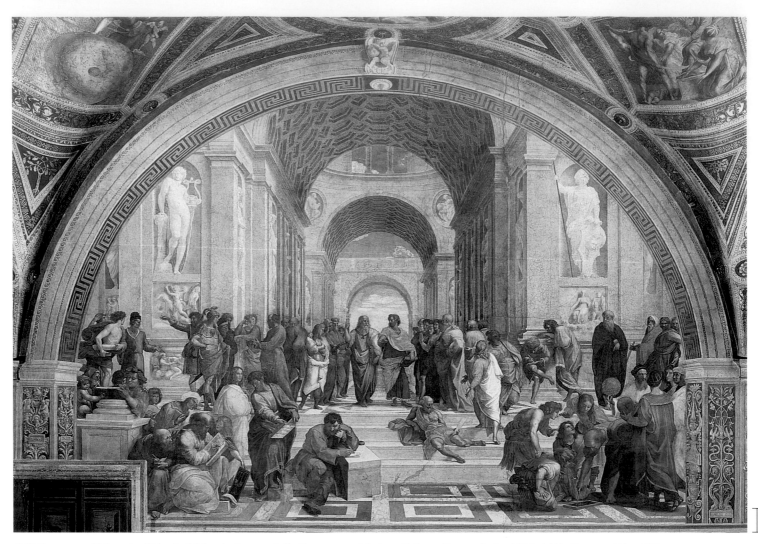

9-7 RAPHAEL, *Philosophy* (*School of Athens*), Stanza della Segnatura, Vatican Palace, Rome, Italy, 1509–1511. Fresco, 19′ × 27′. ◼◀

Raphael included himself in this gathering of great philosophers and scientists whose self-assurance conveys calm reason. The setting recalls the massive vaults of the Basilica Nova (FIG. 3-51).

In Raphael's *Philosophy* mural (commonly called *School of Athens,* FIG. **9-7**), the setting is not a "school" but a congregation of the great philosophers and scientists of the ancient world. Raphael depicted these luminaries, revered by Renaissance humanists, conversing and explaining their various theories and ideas. The setting is a vast hall covered by massive vaults recalling ancient Roman architecture, especially the coffered barrel vaults of Constantine's Basilica Nova (FIG. 3-51). Colossal statues of Apollo and Athena, patron deities of the arts and of wisdom, oversee the interactions. Plato and Aristotle are the central figures around whom Raphael carefully arranged the others. Plato holds his book *Timaeus* and points to Heaven, the source of his inspiration, whereas Aristotle carries his book *Nichomachean Ethics* and gestures toward the earth, from which his observations of reality sprang. Appropriately, ancient philosophers, men concerned with the ultimate mysteries that transcend this world, stand on Plato's side. On Aristotle's side are the philosophers and scientists concerned with nature and human affairs. At the lower left, Pythagoras writes as a servant holds up the harmonic scale. In the foreground, Heraclitus (probably a portrait of Michelangelo) broods alone. Diogenes sprawls on the steps. At the right, students surround Euclid, who demonstrates a theorem. Euclid may be a portrait of the architect Bramante (FIG. **9-13**). At the extreme right, just to the right of the astronomers Zoroaster and Ptolemy, both holding globes, Raphael included his self-portrait.

The groups appear to move easily and clearly, with eloquent poses and gestures that symbolize their doctrines and present an engaging variety of figural positions. The self-assurance and natural dignity of the figures convey calm reason, balance, and measure—those qualities Renaissance thinkers so admired as the heart of philosophy. Significantly, Raphael placed himself among the mathematicians and scientists in *School of Athens*. Certainly, the evolution of pictorial science approached perfection in this fresco in which Raphael convincingly depicted a vast space on a two-dimensional surface.

The artist's psychological insight matured along with his mastery of the problems of physical representation. All the characters in *School of Athens*, like those in Leonardo's *Last Supper* (FIG. **9-3**), communicate moods that reflect their beliefs, and the artist's placement of each figure tied these moods together. From the center, where Plato and Aristotle stand, Raphael arranged the groups of figures in an ellipse with a wide opening in the foreground. Moving along the floor's perspective pattern, the viewer's eye penetrates the assembly of philosophers and continues, by way of the reclining Diogenes, up to the here-reconciled leaders of the two great opposing camps of Renaissance philosophy. The vanishing point falls on Plato's left hand, drawing attention to *Timaeus*. In the Stanza della Segnatura, Raphael reconciled and harmonized not only the Platonists and Aristotelians but also classical humanism and Christianity, surely a major factor in the fresco's appeal to Julius II.

Michelangelo

The artist who received the most coveted commissions from Julius II was MICHELANGELO BUONARROTI (1475–1564). Although Michelangelo was an architect, sculptor, painter, poet, and engineer, he thought of himself first as a sculptor. He considered sculpture superior to painting because the sculptor shares in the divine power to "make man." Drawing a conceptual parallel to Plato's ideas, Michelangelo believed the image the artist's hand produces must come from the idea in the artist's mind. The idea, then, is the reality the artist's genius has to bring forth. But artists are not the creators of the ideas they conceive. Rather, they find their ideas in the natural world, reflecting the absolute idea, which, for the artist, is beauty. One of Michelangelo's best-known observations about sculpture is that the artist must proceed by finding the idea—the image locked in the stone. By removing the excess stone, the sculptor extricates the idea from the block (FIG. I-14). The artist, Michelangelo felt, works many years at this unceasing process of revelation and "arrives late at novel and lofty things."[2]

Michelangelo did indeed arrive at "novel and lofty things," for he broke sharply from the lessons of his predecessors and contemporaries in one important respect. He mistrusted the application of mathematical methods as guarantees of beauty in proportion. Measure and proportion, he believed, should be "kept in the eyes." Vasari quoted Michelangelo as declaring "it was necessary to have the compasses in the eyes and not in the hand, because the hands work and the eye judges."[3] Thus, Michelangelo set aside Vitruvius, Alberti, Leonardo, and others who tirelessly sought the perfect measure, and insisted the artist's inspired judgment could identify pleasing proportions. In addition, Michelangelo argued the artist must not be bound, except by the demands made by realizing the idea. This assertion of the artist's authority was typical of Michelangelo and anticipated the modern concept of the right to a self-expression of talent limited only by the artist's own judgment. The artistic license to aspire far beyond the "rules" was, in part, a manifestation of the pursuit of fame and success that humanism fostered. In this context, Michelangelo created works in architecture, sculpture, and painting that departed from High Renaissance regularity. He put in its stead a style of vast, expressive strength conveyed through complex, eccentric, and often titanic forms that loom before the viewer in tragic grandeur. Michelangelo's self-imposed isolation, creative furies, proud independence, and daring innovations led Italians of his era to speak of the charismatic personality of the man and the expressive character of his works in one word—*terribilità,* the sublime shadowed by the awesome and the fearful.

Pietà Michelangelo began his career in Florence, but when the Medici fell in 1494 (see pages 249–250), he fled to Bologna and then moved to Rome. There, still in his early 20s, he produced his first masterpiece—a *Pietà* (FIG. **9-8**)—for the French cardinal Jean de Bilhères Lagraulas (1439–1499). The cardinal

1 ft.

9-8 MICHELANGELO BUONARROTI, *Pietà,* ca. 1498–1500. Marble, 5′ 8½″ high. Saint Peter's, Vatican City, Rome.

Michelangelo's representation of Mary cradling Christ's corpse captures the sadness and beauty of the young Virgin but was controversial because the Madonna seems younger than her son.

commissioned the statue to be placed in the rotunda attached to the south transept of Old Saint Peter's (FIG. 4-3) in which he was to be buried. (The work is now on view in the new church [FIG. 10-3] that replaced the fourth-century basilica.) The theme—Mary cradling the dead body of Christ in her lap—was a staple in the repertoire of French and German artists (FIG. 7-26), and Michelangelo's French patron doubtless chose the subject. The Italian, however, rendered the northern European theme in an unforgettable manner. Michelangelo transformed marble into flesh, hair, and fabric with a sensitivity for texture almost without parallel. The polish and luminosity of the exquisite marble surface can be fully appreciated only in the presence of the original. Breathtaking, too, is the tender sadness of the beautiful and youthful Mary as she mourns the death of her son. In fact, her age—seemingly less than that of Christ—was a subject of controversy from the moment the statue was unveiled. Michelangelo explained Mary's ageless beauty as an integral part of her purity and virginity. The son whom she holds is also beautiful. Christ seems less to have died a martyr's crucifixion than to have drifted off into peaceful sleep in Mary's maternal arms. His wounds are barely visible.

David Michelangelo returned to Florence in 1501, when the Florence Cathedral building committee invited him to fashion a statue of *David* (FIG. **9-9**) from a great block of marble left over from an earlier aborted commission. In 1495, the Florentine Republic had ordered the transfer of Donatello's *David* (FIG. 8-20) from the Medici residence to the Palazzo della Signoria, the seat of the Florentine government. Michelangelo's *David,* like Donatello's, served as a symbol of Florentine liberty. The colossal statue—Florentines referred to it as "the Giant"—forever assured Michelangelo's reputation as an extraordinary talent. Vasari, for example, extolled the work, claiming "without any doubt the figure has put in the shade every other statue, ancient or modern, Greek or Roman."[4]

Despite the traditional association of David with heroic triumph, Michelangelo chose to represent the young biblical warrior not after his victory, with Goliath's head at his feet, but before the encounter, with David sternly watching his approaching foe. *David* exhibits the characteristic representation of energy in reserve that imbues Michelangelo's figures with the tension of a coiled spring. The anatomy of David's body plays an important part in this prelude to action. His rugged torso, sturdy limbs, and large hands and feet alert viewers to the triumph to come. Each swelling vein and tightening sinew amplifies the psychological energy of David's pose.

Michelangelo doubtless had the classical nude in mind. As did many of his colleagues, he greatly admired Greco-Roman statues, in particular the skillful and precise rendering of heroic physique. Without strictly imitating the antique style, the Renaissance sculptor captured in his *David* the tension of Lysippan athletes (FIG. 2-49) and the psychological insight and emotionalism of Hellenistic statuary (FIG. 2-54). His

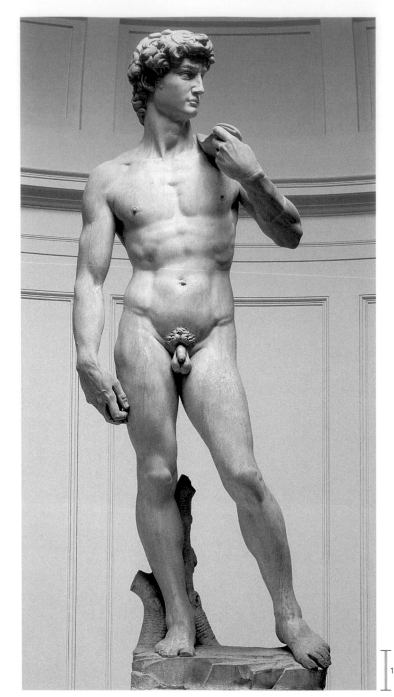

1 ft.

9-9 MICHELANGELO BUONARROTI, *David,* from Piazza della Signoria, Florence, Italy, 1501–1504. Marble, 17' high. Galleria dell'Accademia, Florence. ◼◀

In this colossal statue, Michelangelo represented David in heroic classical nudity, capturing the tension of Lysippan athletes (FIG. 2-49) and the emotionalism of Hellenistic statuary (FIG. 2-54).

David differs from Donatello's in much the same way Hellenistic statues departed from their Classical predecessors (see Chapter 2). Michelangelo abandoned the self-contained composition of the Quattrocento statue by abruptly turning the hero's head toward his gigantic adversary. This *David* is compositionally and emotionally connected to an unseen presence beyond the statue, a feature also of Hellenistic sculpture. As early as 1501 then, Michelangelo invested his efforts in presenting towering, pent-up emotion rather than calm, ideal beauty.

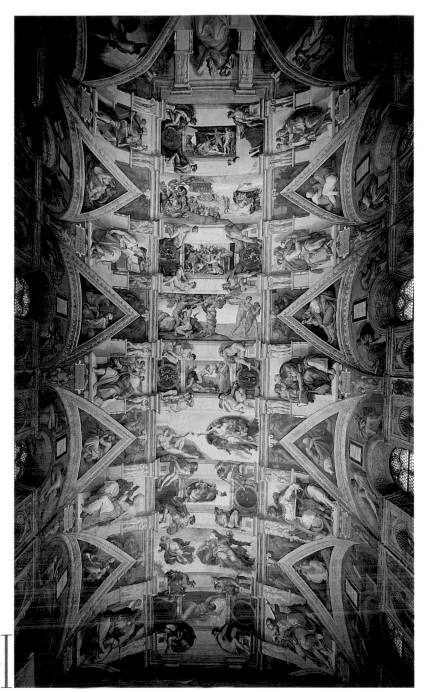

10 ft.

9-10 Michelangelo Buonarroti, ceiling of the Sistine Chapel, Vatican City, Rome, Italy, 1508–1512. Fresco, 128' × 45'. ◼◂

Michelangelo labored almost four years for Pope Julius II on the frescoes for the ceiling of the Sistine Chapel. He painted more than 300 figures illustrating the creation and fall of humankind.

Michelangelo succeeded in weaving together more than 300 figures in a grand drama of the human race.

A long sequence of narrative panels describing the creation, as recorded in Genesis, runs along the crown of the vault, from God's *Separation of Light and Darkness* (above the altar) to *Drunkenness of Noah* (nearest the entrance to the chapel). Thus, as viewers enter the chapel, look up, and walk toward the altar, they review, in reverse order, the history of the fall of humankind. The Hebrew prophets and ancient sibyls who foretold the coming of Christ appear seated in large thrones on both sides of the central row of scenes from Genesis, where the vault curves down. In the four corner pendentives, Michelangelo placed four Old Testament scenes with David, Judith, Haman, and Moses and the Brazen Serpent. Scores of lesser figures also appear. The ancestors of Christ fill the triangular compartments above the windows, nude youths punctuate the corners of the central panels, and small pairs of putti, painted in grisaille to imitate sculpture, support the painted cornice surrounding the entire central corridor. The overall conceptualization of the ceiling's design and narrative structure not only presents a sweeping chronology of Christianity but also is in keeping with Renaissance ideas about Christian history. These ideas included interest in the conflict between good and evil and between the energy of youth and the wisdom of age. The conception of the entire ceiling was astounding in itself, and the articulation of it in its thousands of details was a superhuman achievement.

Unlike Andrea Mantegna's decoration of the Camera Picta (FIGS. 8-40 and 8-41) in Mantua, the strongly marked unifying architectural framework in the Sistine Chapel does not produce "picture windows." Rather, the viewer focuses on figure after figure, each sharply outlined against the neutral tone of the architectural setting or the plain background of the panels. Here, as in his sculpture, Michelangelo relentlessly concentrated his expressive purpose on the human figure. To him, the body was beautiful not only in its natural form but also in its spiritual and philosophical significance. The body was the manifestation of the character of the soul. Michelangelo represented the body in its most elemental aspect—in the nude or simply draped, with no background and no ornamental embellishment. He always painted with a sculptor's eye for how light and shadow reveal volume and surface. It is no coincidence that many of the figures seem to be painted statues.

Sistine Chapel In 1508, the same year Julius II asked Raphael to decorate the papal *stanze*, the pope convinced a reluctant Michelangelo to paint the ceiling (FIG. 9-10) of the Sistine Chapel. The artist insisted painting was not his profession (a protest that rings hollow after the fact, but Michelangelo's major works until then had been in sculpture), but he accepted the commission. Michelangelo faced enormous difficulties in painting the Sistine ceiling: its dimensions (some 5,800 square feet), its height above the pavement (almost 70 feet), and the complicated perspective problems the vault's height and curve presented, as well as his inexperience as a fresco painter. Yet, in less than four years, Michelangelo produced an extraordinary series of monumental frescoes incorporating his patron's agenda, Church doctrine, and his own interests. Depicting the most august and solemn themes of all—the creation, fall, and redemption of humanity—

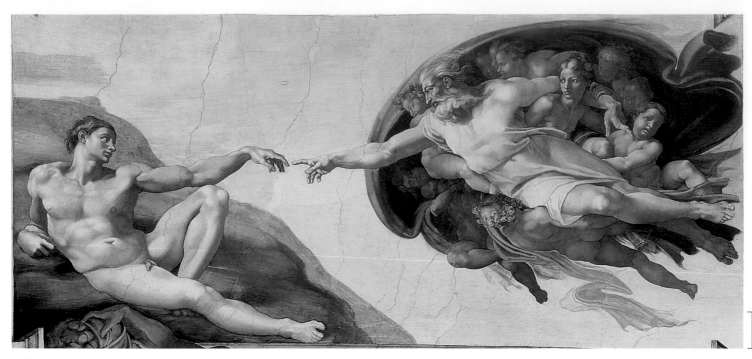

9-11 MICHELANGELO BUONARROTI, *Creation of Adam,* detail of the ceiling of the Sistine Chapel (FIG. 9-10), Vatican City, Rome, Italy, 1511–1512. Fresco, 9′ 2″ × 18′ 8″. ◼◀

Life leaps to Adam like a spark from the extended hand of God in this fresco, which recalls the communication between gods and heroes in the classical myths Renaissance humanists admired so much.

Creation of Adam One of the ceiling's central panels is *Creation of Adam* (FIG. **9-11**), in which Michelangelo rejected traditional iconography in favor of a bold new interpretation of the momentous event. God and Adam confront each other in a primordial unformed landscape of which Adam is still a material part, heavy as earth. The Lord transcends the earth, wrapped in a billowing cloud of drapery and borne up by his powers. Life leaps to Adam like a spark from the extended mighty hand of God. The communication between gods and heroes, so familiar in classical myth, is here concrete. This blunt depiction of the Lord as ruler of Heaven in the Olympian sense indicates how easily High Renaissance thought joined classical and Christian traditions. Yet the classical trappings do not obscure the essential Christian message.

Beneath the Lord's sheltering left arm is a female figure, apprehensively curious but as yet uncreated. Scholars traditionally believed she represented Eve, but many now think she is the Virgin Mary (with the Christ Child at her knee). If the second identification is correct, it suggests Michelangelo incorporated into his fresco one of the essential tenets of Christian faith—the belief that Adam's original sin eventually led to the sacrifice of Christ, which in turn made possible the redemption of all humankind. As God reaches out to Adam, the viewer's eye follows the motion from right to left, but Adam's extended left arm leads the eye back to the right, along the Lord's right arm, shoulders, and left arm to his left forefinger, which points to the Christ Child's face. The focal point of this right-to-left-to-right movement—the fingertips of Adam and the Lord—is dramatically off-center. Michelangelo replaced the straight architectural axes found in Leonardo's compositions with curves and diagonals. For

example, the bodies of the two great figures are complementary—the concave body of Adam fitting the convex body and billowing cloak of God. Thus, motion directs not only the figures but also the whole composition. The reclining positions of the figures, the heavy musculature, and the twisting poses are all intrinsic parts of Michelangelo's style.

The Counter-Reformation Paul III (r. 1534–1549) became pope at a time of widespread dissatisfaction with the leadership and policies of the Roman Catholic Church. Disgruntled Catholics voiced concerns about the sale of pardons for sins, favoritism in church appointments, and high Church officials pursuing personal wealth. This Reformation movement, based in the Holy Roman Empire (see page 280), resulted in the establishment of Protestantism, discussed in detail later. The Catholic Church, in response, mounted a full-fledged campaign—the Counter-Reformation—to counteract the defection of its members to Protestantism. The religious schism also had important consequences for artistic patronage (see "Religious Art in Counter-Reformation Italy," page 269).

Last Judgment Among Paul III's first papal commissions was *Last Judgment* (FIG. **9-12**), an enormous (48 feet tall) fresco for the Sistine Chapel. Here, Michelangelo depicted Christ as the stern judge of the world—a giant who raises his mighty right arm in a gesture of damnation so broad and universal as to suggest he will destroy all creation. The choirs of Heaven surrounding him pulse with anxiety and awe. Crowded into the spaces below are trumpeting angels, the ascending figures of the just, and the downward-hurtling figures of the damned. On the left, the dead awake and assume flesh. On

Religious Art in Counter-Reformation Italy

Led by Pope Paul III, who commissioned Michelangelo to paint *Last Judgment* (FIG. 9-12) in the Sistine Chapel, the Counter-Reformation consisted of numerous initiatives. The Council of Trent, which met intermittently from 1545 through 1563, was a major component of this effort. Composed of cardinals, archbishops, bishops, abbots, and theologians, the council dealt with issues of Church doctrine, including many the Protestants contested.

Catholics and Protestants had very different views of the role of devotional imagery in religious life. Catholics deemed art valuable for cultivating piety. They understood the power of visual imagery to construct and reinforce ideological claims, and Paul III, like his predecessors, especially Julius II, exploited this capability. Protestants rejected religious imagery and their churches were relatively bare. The Council of Trent validated the Catholic view and issued the following edict at the conclusion of its deliberations in 1563:

> The holy council commands all bishops and others who hold the office of teaching and have charge of the *cura animarum* [literally, "cure of souls"—the responsibility of laboring for the salvation of souls], that . . . they above all instruct the faithful diligently in matters relating to intercession and invocation of the saints, the veneration of relics, and the legitimate use of images. . . . [T]he images of Christ, of the Virgin Mother of God, and of the other saints are to be placed and retained especially in the churches, and due honor and veneration is to be given them; . . . because the honor which is shown them is referred to the prototypes which they represent, so that by means of the images which we kiss and before which we uncover the head and prostrate ourselves, we adore Christ and venerate the saints whose likeness they bear. . . . Moreover, let the bishops diligently teach that by means of the stories of the mysteries of our redemption portrayed in paintings and other representations the people are instructed and confirmed in the articles of faith, which ought to be borne in mind and constantly reflected upon; also that great profit is derived from all holy images, not only because the people are thereby reminded of the benefits and gifts bestowed on them by Christ, but also because through the saints the miracles of God and salutary examples are set before the eyes of the faithful, so that they may give God thanks for those things, may fashion their own life and conduct in imitation of the saints and be moved to adore and love God and cultivate piety. . . . That these things may be the more faithfully observed, the holy council decrees that no one is permitted to erect or cause to be erected in any place or church, howsoever exempt, any unusual image unless it has been approved by the bishop.*

*Canons and Decrees of the Council of Trent, December 3–4, 1563. Robert Klein and Henri Zerner, *Italian Art 1500–1600: Sources and Documents* (Evanston, Ill.: Northwestern University Press, 1966), 120–121.

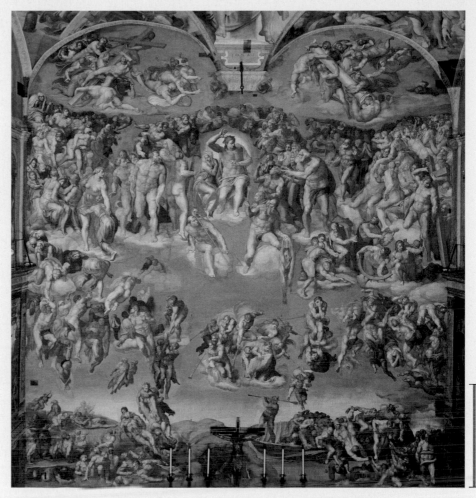

10 ft.

9-12 MICHELANGELO BUONARROTI, *Last Judgment,* altar wall of the Sistine Chapel, Vatican City, Rome, Italy, 1534–1541. Fresco, 48′ × 44′. ▪◀

For Pope Paul III, who launched the Catholic Counter-Reformation, Michelangelo completed the fresco cycle in the Sistine Chapel with this terrifying vision of the fate awaiting sinners on judgment day.

the right, demons, whose gargoyle masks and burning eyes revive the demons of Romanesque tympana (FIG. 6-21), torment the damned.

Michelangelo's terrifying vision of the fate awaiting sinners goes far beyond any previous rendition. Martyrs who suffered especially agonizing deaths crouch below the judge. One of them, Saint Bartholomew, who was skinned alive, holds the flaying knife and the skin, its face a grotesque self-portrait of Michelangelo. The figures are huge and violently twisted, with small heads and contorted features. Yet while this immense fresco impresses on viewers Christ's wrath on judgment day, it also holds out hope. A group of saved souls—the elect—crowd around Christ, and on the far right appears a figure with a cross, most likely the Good Thief (crucified with Christ) or a saint martyred by crucifixion, such as Saint Andrew.

Architecture

During the High Renaissance, consistent with the humanist interest in classical antiquity, architects and patrons alike turned to the buildings of ancient Rome for inspiration. There, they discovered the perfect prototypes for the domed architecture that became the hallmark of the 16th century.

Bramante The leading early Cinquecento proponent of this classical-revival style was DONATO D'ANGELO BRAMANTE (1444–1514). Born in Urbino and trained as a painter (perhaps by Piero della Francesca), Bramante went to Milan in 1481 and, as Leonardo did, stayed there until the French arrived in 1499. In Milan, he abandoned painting for architecture. Under the influence of Brunelleschi, Alberti, and perhaps Leonardo, Bramante developed the High Renaissance form of the central-plan church.

Bramante's first major project was the architectural gem known as the Tempietto (FIG. **9-13**), so named because, to contemporaries, it had the look of a small ancient temple. In fact, the round temples of Roman Italy provided the direct models for the lower story of Bramante's "little temple." Standing inside the cloister of San Pietro in Montorio on the Janiculum hill overlooking the Vatican, the Tempietto marked the presumed location of Saint Peter's crucifixion. Bramante planned, although never built, a circular colonnaded courtyard to frame the "temple." His intent was to coordinate the Tempietto and its surrounding portico by aligning the columns of the two structures.

The Tempietto design is severely rational with its sober circular *stylobate* (stepped temple platform) and the austere Tuscan style of the colonnade. Bramante achieved a wonderful balance and harmony in the relationship of the parts (dome, drum, and base) to one another and to the whole. Conceived as a tall domed cylinder projecting from the lower, wider cylinder of its colonnade, this small building incorporates all the qualities of a sculptured monument. Light and shadow play around the columns and balustrade and across the deep-set rectangular windows, which alternate with shallow shell-capped niches in the walls and drum. Although the Tempietto, superficially at least, may resemble a Greco-Roman *tholos* (a circular shrine), and although antique models provided the inspiration for all its details, the combination of parts and details was new and original. (Classical tholoi, for instance, had neither drum nor balustrade.)

One of the main differences between the Early and High Renaissance styles of architecture is the former's emphasis on detailing flat wall surfaces versus the latter's sculptural handling of architectural masses. Bramante's Tempietto initiated the High Renaissance era in architecture. Andrea Palladio, a brilliant theorist as well as a major later Cinquecento architect (FIG. **9-16**), included the Tempietto in his survey of ancient temples because Bramante was "the first to bring back to light the good and beautiful architecture that from antiquity to that time had been hidden."[5] Round in plan and elevated on a base that isolates it from its surroundings, the Tempietto conforms to Alberti's and Palladio's strictest demands for an ideal church.

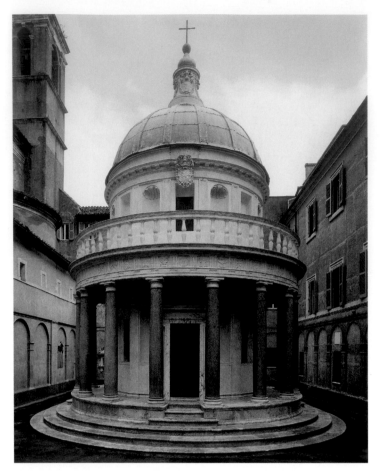

9-13 DONATO D'ANGELO BRAMANTE, Tempietto, San Pietro in Montorio, Rome, Italy, 1502(?).

Contemporaries celebrated Bramante as the first to revive the classical style in architecture. Roman round temples inspired his "little temple," but Bramante combined the classical parts in new ways.

New Saint Peter's One of the most important artistic projects Pope Julius II initiated was the replacement of the Constantinian basilican church of Old Saint Peter's (FIG. 4-3). The earlier building had fallen into considerable disrepair and, in any event, did not suit this ambitious pope's taste for the colossal. Julius wanted to gain control over all Italy and to make the Rome of the popes reminiscent of (if not more splendid than) the Rome of the caesars. He intended the new building to serve as a *martyrium* to mark Saint Peter's grave and also hoped to install his own tomb (designed by Michelangelo) in it. The choice of an architect for the new church was therefore of the highest importance. Julius chose Bramante.

Bramante's ambitious design consisted of a cross with arms of equal length, each terminating in an apse. A large dome would have covered the crossing, and smaller domes over subsidiary chapels would have covered the diagonal axes of the roughly square plan. Bramante's plan also called for a boldly sculptural treatment of the walls and piers under the dome. The organization of the interior space was complex in the extreme: nine interlocking crosses, five of them supporting domes. The scale was titanic. The architect boasted he would place the dome of the Pantheon (FIGS. 3-38 to 3-40) over the Basilica Nova (FIG. 3-51).

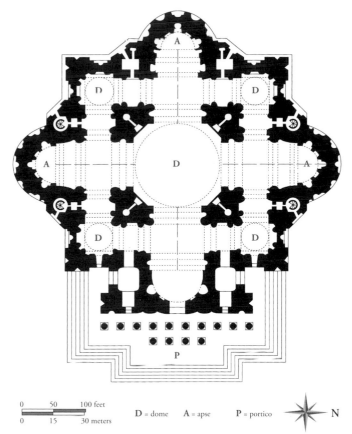

0   50   100 feet
0   15   30 meters   **D** = dome   **A** = apse   **P** = portico   N

9-14 MICHELANGELO BUONARROTI, plan for Saint Peter's, Vatican City, Rome, Italy, 1546.

Michelangelo's plan for the new Saint Peter's was radically different than that of the original basilica (FIG. 4-3). His central plan called for a domed Greek cross inscribed in a square and fronted by columns.

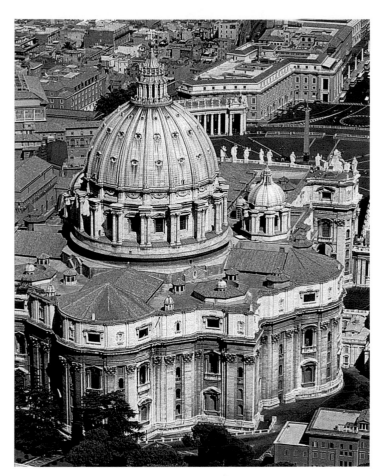

9-15 MICHELANGELO BUONARROTI, Saint Peter's (looking northeast), Vatican City, Rome, Italy, 1546–1564. Dome completed by GIACOMO DELLA PORTA, 1590.

The west end of Saint Peter's offers the best view of Michelangelo's intentions. The giant pilasters of his colossal order march around the undulating wall surfaces of the domed central-plan church.

During Bramante's lifetime, the Saint Peter's project did not advance beyond the construction of the crossing piers and the lower choir walls. After his death, the work passed from one architect to another and, in 1546, to Michelangelo, whose work on Saint Peter's became a long-term show of dedication, thankless and without pay. Among Michelangelo's difficulties was his struggle to preserve Bramante's central-plan design, which he praised. Michelangelo carried his obsession with human form over to architecture and reasoned that buildings should follow the form of the human body. This meant organizing their units symmetrically around a central axis, as the arms relate to the body or the eyes to the nose. "For it is an established fact," he once wrote, "that the members of architecture resemble the members of man. Whoever neither has been nor is a master at figures, and especially at anatomy, cannot really understand architecture."[6]

In his modification of Bramante's plan, Michelangelo reduced the central component from a number of interlocking crosses to a compact domed Greek cross inscribed in a square and fronted with a double-columned portico (FIG. **9-14**). Without destroying the centralizing features of Bramante's plan, Michelangelo, with a few strokes of the pen, converted its crystalline complexity into massive, cohesive unity. His treatment of the building's exterior further reveals his interest in creating a unified and cohesive design. Because of later changes to the front of the church (FIG. 10-2),

the west (apse) end (FIG. **9-15**) offers the best view of Michelangelo's style and intention. His design incorporated the colossal order, the two-story pilasters first used by Alberti at Sant'Andrea (FIG. 8-38) in Mantua. The giant pilasters seem to march around the undulating wall surfaces, confining the movement without interrupting it. The architectural sculpturing here extends up from the ground through the attic stories and into the drum and the dome, unifying the whole building from base to summit.

The domed west end—as majestic as it is today and as influential as it has been on architecture throughout the centuries—is not quite as Michelangelo intended it. Originally, he had planned a dome with an ogival section. But in his final version, he decided on a hemispherical dome to temper the verticality of the design of the lower stories and to establish a balance between dynamic and static elements. However, when GIACOMO DELLA PORTA (ca. 1533–1602) executed the dome after Michelangelo's death, he restored the earlier high design, ignoring Michelangelo's later version. Giacomo probably believed an ogival dome would provide greater stability and be easier to construct. Consequently, the dome seems to rise from its base, rather than rest firmly on it—an effect Michelangelo might not have approved.

Andrea Palladio The classical-revival style of High Renaissance architecture in Rome spread far and wide. One of its most accomplished practitioners was ANDREA PALLADIO (1508–1580), the chief architect of the Venetian Republic. In order to study the ancient buildings firsthand, Palladio made several trips to Rome. In 1556, he illustrated Daniel Barbaro's edition of Vitruvius's *De architectura* and later wrote his own treatise on architecture, *I quattro libri dell'architettura* (*The Four Books of Architecture*). Originally published in 1570, Palladio's treatise had a wide-ranging influence on succeeding generations of architects throughout Europe, most significantly in England and in colonial America.

Palladio accrued his significant reputation from his many designs for villas, built on the Venetian mainland. The same spirit that prompted the ancient Romans to build villas in the countryside motivated a similar villa-building boom in 16th-century Venice, which, with its very limited space, was highly congested. But a longing for the countryside was not the only motive. Declining fortunes prompted the Venetians to develop their mainland possessions with new land investment and reclamation projects. Citizens who could afford to do so set themselves up as aristocratic farmers and developed swamps into productive agricultural land. The villas were thus aristocratic farms (like the much later American plantations, which frequently emulated Palladio's architectural style). Palladio generally arranged the outbuildings in long, low wings branching out from the main building and enclosing a large rectangular court area.

Palladio's most famous villa, Villa Rotonda (FIG. **9-16**), near Vicenza, is exceptional because the architect did not build it for an aspiring gentleman farmer but for a retired monsignor who wanted a villa for social events. Palladio planned and designed Villa Rotonda, located on a hilltop, as a kind of *belvedere* (literally, "beautiful view"; in architecture, a structure with a view of the countryside or the sea), without the usual wings of secondary buildings. It has a central plan featuring four identical facades with projecting porches, each of which resembles a Roman Ionic temple and serves as a platform for enjoying a different view of the surrounding landscape. In placing a traditional temple porch in front of a dome-covered interior, Palladio doubtless had the Pantheon (FIG. 3-38) in his mind as a model.

Venetian Painting

In addition to Palladio, Cinquecento Venice boasted some of the most renowned painters of the era. Artists in the maritime republic showed a special interest in recording the effect of Venice's soft-colored light on figures and landscapes. The Venetian Renaissance style, noted for its *colorito* as opposed to *disegno*, is distinct from that of Florence and Rome.

Giorgione Art historians frequently describe Venetian painting as "poetic"—a characterization particularly appropriate given the development of *poesia*, or painting meant to operate in a manner similar to poetry. Both classical and Renaissance poetry inspired Venetian artists, and their paintings focused on the lyrical and sensual. Thus, in many Venetian artworks, discerning concrete narratives or subjects is virtually impossible. That is certainly the case with *The Tempest* (FIG. **9-17**), a painting that continues to defy interpretation. It is the greatest work attributed to the short-lived GIORGIONE DA CASTELFRANCO (ca. 1477–1510), the Venetian artist who deserves much of the credit for developing the poetic manner of painting. A lush landscape fills most of Giorgione's *Tempest,* but stormy skies and lightning in the middle background threaten the tranquility of the pastoral setting. Pushed off to both sides are the few human figures depicted—a young woman nursing a baby in the right foreground and a man carrying a *halberd* (a combination spear and battle-ax—but he is not a soldier) on the left. Much scholarly debate has centered on the painting's subject, fueled by X-rays of the canvas that revealed Giorgione altered many of the details as work progressed. Most notably, a seated nude woman originally occupied the position where Giorgione subsequently placed the standing man. The changes the painter made have led many art historians to believe Giorgione did not intend the painting to have a definitive narrative, which is appropriate for a Venetian poetic rendering. Other scholars have suggested various mythological and biblical narratives. The uncertainty about the subject contributes to the painting's intriguing air.

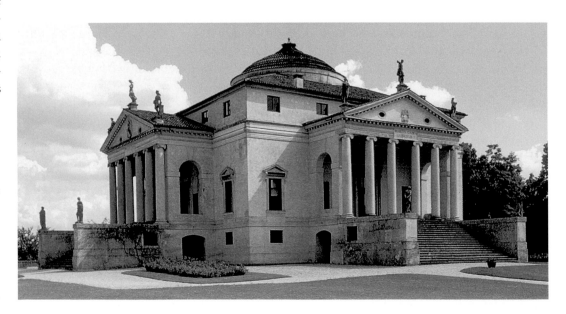

9-16 ANDREA PALLADIO, Villa Rotonda (formerly Villa Capra; looking south), near Vicenza, Italy, ca. 1550–1570.

Palladio's Villa Rotonda has four identical facades, each one resembling a Roman temple with a columnar porch. In the center is a great dome-covered rotunda modeled on the Pantheon (FIG. 3-38).

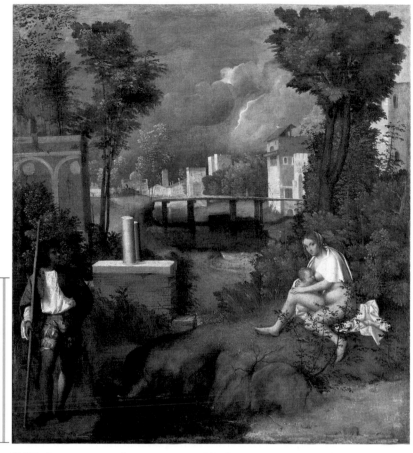

9-17 GIORGIONE DA CASTELFRANCO, *The Tempest*, ca. 1510. Oil on canvas, 2′ 8¼″ × 2′ 4¾″. Galleria dell'Accademia, Venice.

The subject of this painting set in a lush landscape beneath a stormy sky is uncertain, contributing, perhaps intentionally, to the painting's enigmatic quality and intriguing air.

Titian Giorgione's masterful handling of light and color and his interest in landscape, poetry, and music—Vasari reported he was an accomplished lutenist and singer—influenced his younger contemporary Tiziano Vecelli, called TITIAN (ca. 1490–1576) in English. Indeed, a masterpiece long attributed to Giorgione—*Pastoral Symphony* (FIG. **9-18**)—is now widely believed to be an early work of Titian. Out of dense shadow emerge the soft forms of figures and landscape. Titian, a supreme colorist and master of the oil medium, cast a mood of tranquil reverie and dreaminess over the entire scene, evoking the landscape of a lost but never forgotten paradise. As in Giorgione's *Tempest*, the theme is as enigmatic as the lighting. Two nude women, accompanied by two clothed young men, occupy the bountiful landscape through which a shepherd passes. In the distance, a villa crowns a hill. The artist so eloquently evoked the pastoral mood that the viewer does not find the uncertainty about the picture's precise meaning distressing. The mood is enough. The shepherd symbolizes the poet. The pipes and lute symbolize his poetry. The two women accompanying the young men may be thought of as their invisible inspiration, their muses. One turns to lift water from the sacred well of poetic inspiration. The voluptuous bodies of the women, softly modulated by the smoky shadow, became the standard in Venetian art. The fullness of their figures contributes to their effect as poetic personifications of nature's abundance.

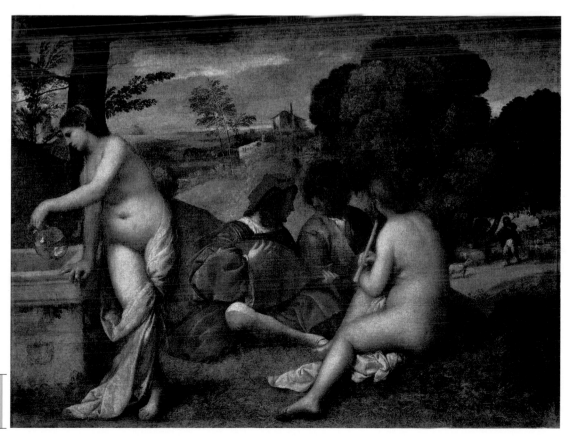

9-18 TITIAN, *Pastoral Symphony*, ca. 1508–1511. Oil on canvas, 3′ 7¼″ × 4′ 6¼″. Musée du Louvre, Paris.

Venetian art conjures poetry. In this painting, Titian so eloquently evoked the pastoral mood that the uncertainty about the picture's meaning is not distressing. The mood and rich color are enough.

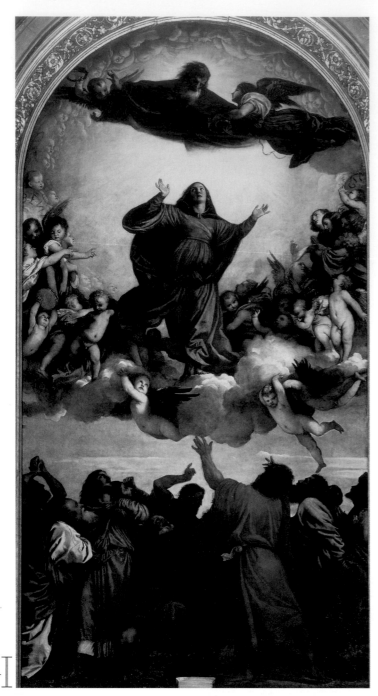

9-19 TITIAN, *Assumption of the Virgin*, 1515–1518. Oil on wood, 22′ 7½″ × 11′ 10″. Santa Maria Gloriosa dei Frari, Venice.

Titian won renown for his ability to convey light through color. In this dramatic depiction of the Virgin Mary's ascent to Heaven, the golden clouds seem to glow and radiate light into the church.

the glorious event. Through vibrant color, Titian infused the image with an intensity that amplifies the drama.

Venus of Urbino In 1538, at the height of his powers, Titian painted the so-called *Venus of Urbino* (FIG. **9-20**) for Guidobaldo II, who became the duke of Urbino (r. 1539–1574) the following year. The title (given to the painting later) elevates to the status of classical mythology what is probably a representation of a sensual Italian woman in her bedchamber. Whether the subject is divine or mortal, Titian based his version on an earlier (and pioneering) painting of Venus (not illustrated) by Giorgione. Here, Titian established the compositional elements and the standard for paintings of the reclining female nude, regardless of the many ensuing variations. This "Venus" reclines on the gentle slope of her luxurious pillowed couch. Her softly rounded body contrasts with the sharp vertical edge of the curtain behind her, which serves to direct the viewer's attention to her left hand and pelvis as well as to divide the foreground from the background. At the woman's feet is a slumbering lapdog—where Cupid would be if this were Venus. In the right background, two servants bend over a chest, apparently searching for garments to clothe their nude mistress. Beyond them, a window opens onto a landscape. Titian masterfully constructed the view backward into the room and the division of the space into progressively smaller units.

As in other Venetian paintings, color plays a prominent role in *Venus of Urbino*. The red tones of the matron's skirt and the muted reds of the tapestries against the neutral whites of the matron's sleeves and of the kneeling girl's gown echo the deep Venetian reds set off against the pale neutral whites of the linen and the warm ivory gold of the flesh. The viewer must study the picture carefully to realize the subtlety of color planning. For instance, the two deep reds (in the foreground cushions and in the background skirt) play a critical role in the composition as a gauge of distance and as indicators of an implied diagonal opposed to the real one of the reclining figure. Here, Titian used color not simply to record surface appearance but also to organize his placement of forms.

Mannerism

Mannerism emerged in the 1520s in Italy as a distinctive artistic style in reaction to the High Renaissance style of Florence, Rome, and Venice. The term derives from the Italian word *maniera,* meaning "style" or "manner." Art historians usually define *style* as a characteristic or representative mode, especially of an artist or period (see Introduction), but the term can also refer to an absolute quality of fashion (someone has "style"). Mannerism's style (or representative mode) is characterized by style (being stylish, cultured, elegant).

Among the features most closely associated with Mannerism is artifice. Of course, all art involves artifice, in the sense that art is not "natural"—it is something humans fashion. But many artists, including High Renaissance painters such as Leonardo and Raphael, chose to conceal that artifice by using such devices as perspective and shading to make their representations of the world look natural. In contrast, Mannerist

Assumption of the Virgin In 1516, Titian became the official painter of the Republic of Venice. Shortly thereafter, he received the commission to paint *Assumption of the Virgin* (FIG. **9-19**) for the main altar of Santa Maria Gloriosa dei Frari. The monumental altarpiece (nearly 23 feet tall) depicts the ascent of the Virgin to Heaven on a great white cloud borne aloft by putti. Above, golden clouds, so luminous they seem to glow and radiate light into the church interior, envelop the Virgin. God the Father appears above, awaiting Mary with open arms. Below, apostles gesticulate wildly as they witness

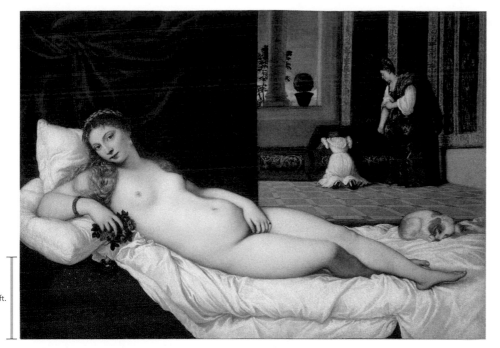

9-20 TITIAN, *Venus of Urbino*, 1536–1538. Oil on canvas, 3′ 11″ × 5′ 5″. Galleria degli Uffizi, Florence. ◼◀

Titian established oil color on canvas as the preferred painting medium in Western art. Here, he also set the standard for representations of the reclining female nude, whether divine or mortal.

painters consciously revealed the constructed nature of their art. In other words, Renaissance artists generally strove to create art that appeared natural, whereas Mannerist artists were less inclined to disguise the contrived nature of art production. This is why artifice is a central feature of discussions about Mannerism, and why Mannerist works can seem, appropriately, "mannered." The conscious display of artifice in Mannerism often reveals itself in imbalanced compositions and unusual complexities, both visual and conceptual. Ambiguous space, departures from expected conventions, and unique presentations of traditional themes also surface frequently in Mannerist art.

Pontormo *Entombment of Christ* (FIG. **9-21**) by the Florentine painter JACOPO DA PONTORMO (1494–1557) exhibits almost all the stylistic features characteristic of Mannerism's early phase. Painters had frequently depicted this subject, and Pontormo exploited the familiarity 16th-century viewers would have had by playing off their expectations. For example, he omitted from the painting both the cross and Christ's tomb, and instead of presenting the action as taking place across the perpendicular picture plane, as artists such as Rogier van der Weyden (FIG. 8-7) had done, Pontormo rotated the conventional figural groups along a vertical axis. As a result, the Virgin Mary falls back (away from the viewer) as she releases her dead son's hand. Unlike High Renaissance artists, who had concentrated the masses in the center of their paintings, Pontormo left a void. This emptiness accentuates the grouping of hands filling that hole, calling attention to the void—symbolic of loss and grief. In another departure from the norm, the Mannerist artist depicted the figures with curiously anxious glances cast in all directions. (The bearded young man at the upper right is probably a self-portrait). Athletic bending and distorted twisting characterize many of the figures, which have elastically elongated limbs and small oval heads. The contrasting colors, primarily light blues and pinks, add to the dynamism and complexity of the work. The painting breaks sharply from the balanced, harmoniously structured compositions of the High Renaissance.

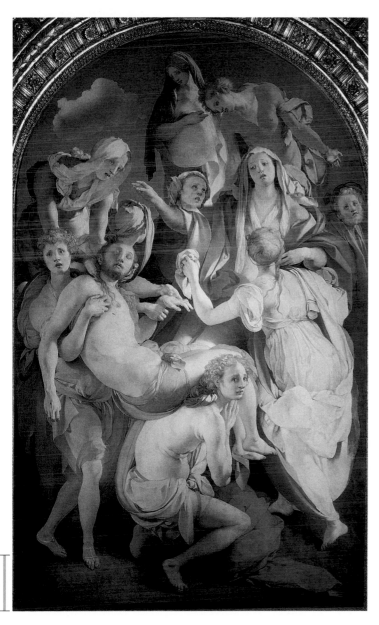

9-21 JACOPO DA PONTORMO, *Entombment of Christ*, Capponi chapel, Santa Felicità, Florence, Italy, 1525–1528. Oil on wood, 10′ 3″ × 6′ 4″.
◼◀

Mannerist paintings such as this one represent a departure from the compositions of the earlier Renaissance. Instead of concentrating masses in the center of the painting, Pontormo left a void.

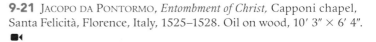

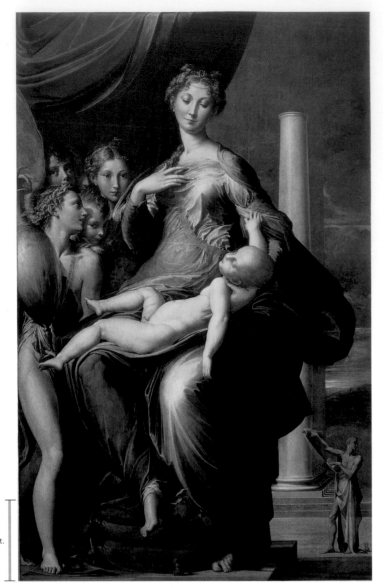

1 ft.

9-22 PARMIGIANINO, *Madonna with the Long Neck,* from the Baiardi chapel, Santa Maria dei Servi, Parma, Italy, 1534–1540. Oil on wood, 7' 1" × 4' 4". Galleria degli Uffizi, Florence. ■◀

Parmigianino's Madonna displays the stylish elegance that was a principal aim of Mannerism. Mary has a small oval head, a long slender neck, attenuated hands, and a sinuous body.

Parmigianino Girolamo Francesco Maria Mazzola, known as PARMIGIANINO (1503–1540), achieved in his best-known work, *Madonna with the Long Neck* (FIG. **9-22**), the elegant stylishness that was a principal aim of Mannerism. Parmigianino's rendition of this traditionally sedate subject is a picture of exquisite grace and precious sweetness. The Madonna's small oval head, her long and slender neck, the otherworldly attenuation and delicacy of her hand, and the sinuous, swaying elongation of her frame—all are marks of the aristocratic, sumptuously courtly taste of Mannerist artists and patrons alike. Parmigianino amplified this elegance by expanding the Madonna's form as viewed from head to toe. On the left stands a bevy of angelic creatures, melting with emotions as soft and smooth as their limbs. On the right,

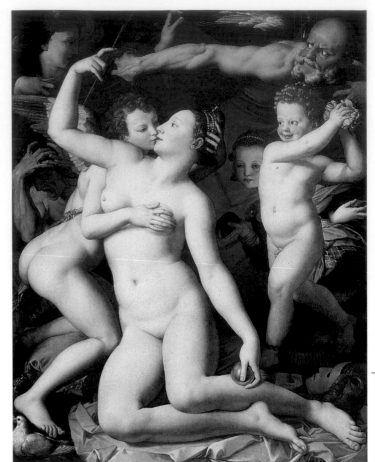

1 ft.

9-23 BRONZINO, *Venus, Cupid, Folly, and Time,* ca. 1546. Oil on wood, 5' 1" × 4' 8¼". National Gallery, London.

In this painting of Cupid fondling his mother, Venus, Bronzino demonstrated a fondness for learned allegories with lascivious undertones. As in many Mannerist paintings, the meaning is ambiguous.

the artist included a line of columns without capitals and an enigmatic figure with a scroll, whose distance from the foreground is immeasurable and ambiguous—the antithesis of rational Renaissance perspective diminution of size with distance.

Although the elegance and sophisticated beauty of the painting are due in large part to the Madonna's attenuated limbs, that exaggeration is not solely decorative in purpose. *Madonna with the Long Neck* takes its subject from a medieval simile that compared the Virgin's neck to a great ivory tower or column, such as the one Parmigianino inserted to the right of the Madonna.

Bronzino Pontormo's pupil, Agnolo di Cosimo, called BRONZINO (1503–1572), painted *Venus, Cupid, Folly, and Time* (FIG. **9-23**) for the first grand duke of Tuscany, Cosimo I de' Medici (r. 1537–1534), as a gift for King Francis I of France (see page 284). In this painting, Bronzino demonstrated the Mannerists' fondness for learned allegories that often had lascivious undertones, a shift from the simple and monumental statements and forms of the High Renaissance. Bronzino depicted Cupid—here an adolescent who has

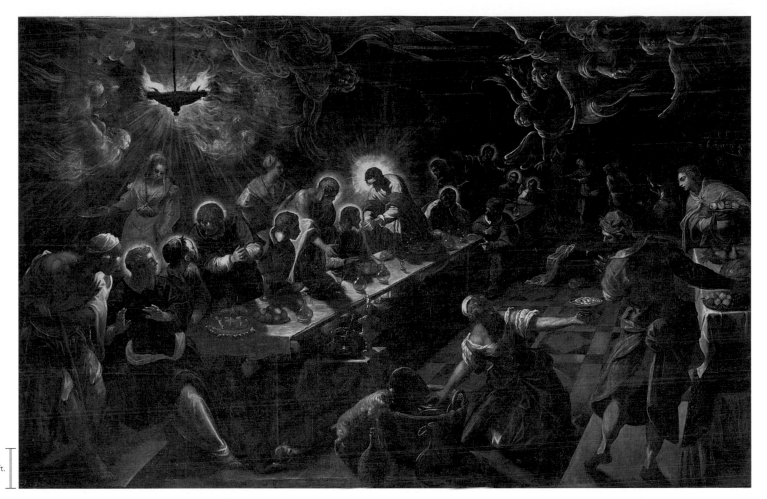

9-24 TINTORETTO, *Last Supper*, 1594. Oil on canvas, 12' × 18' 8". San Giorgio Maggiore, Venice. ◼◀

Tintoretto adopted many Mannerist pictorial devices to produce oil paintings imbued with emotional power, depth of spiritual vision, glowing Venetian color schemes, and dramatic lighting.

reached puberty, not an infant—fondling his mother, Venus, while Folly prepares to shower them with rose petals. Time, who appears in the upper right corner, draws back the curtain to reveal the playful incest in progress. Other figures in the painting represent other human qualities and emotions, including Envy. The masks, a favorite device of the Mannerists, symbolize deceit. The picture seems to suggest that love—accompanied by envy and plagued by inconstancy—is foolish and that lovers will discover its folly in time. But, as in many Mannerist paintings, the meaning is ambiguous, and interpretations of the painting vary. Compositionally, Bronzino placed the figures around the front plane, and they almost entirely block the space. The contours are strong and sculptural, the surfaces of enamel smoothness. The heads, hands, and feet are especially elegant. The Mannerists considered the extremities the carriers of grace, and the clever depiction of them as evidence of artistic skill.

Tintoretto Jacopo Robusti, known as TINTORETTO (1518–1594), claimed to be a student of Titian and aspired to combine Titian's color with Michelangelo's drawing, but he also adopted many Mannerist pictorial devices, which he employed to produce works imbued with dramatic power, depth

of spiritual vision, and glowing Venetian color schemes. Toward the end of Tintoretto's life, his art became spiritual, even visionary, as solid forms melted away into swirling clouds of dark shot through with fitful light. In *Last Supper* (FIG. **9-24**), the figures —many with shimmering halos—appear in a dark interior illuminated by a single light in the upper left of the image. The huge canvas incorporates many Mannerist devices, including an imbalanced composition and visual complexity. In terms of design, the contrast with Leonardo's *Last Supper* (FIG. 9-3) is both extreme and instructive. Leonardo's composition, balanced and symmetrical, parallels the picture plane in a geometrically organized and closed space. The figure of Christ is the tranquil center of the drama and the perspective focus. In Tintoretto's painting, Christ is above and beyond the converging perspective lines racing diagonally away from the picture surface, creating disturbing effects of limitless depth and motion. The viewer locates Tintoretto's Christ via the light flaring, beaconlike, out of darkness. The contrast of the two works reflects the direction Renaissance painting took in the 16th century, as it moved away from architectonic clarity of space and neutral lighting toward the dynamic perspectives and dramatic chiaroscuro of the coming Baroque.

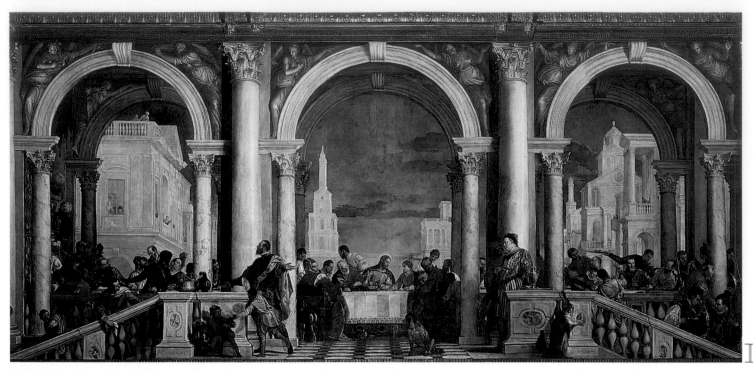

1 ft.

9-25 Paolo Veronese, *Christ in the House of Levi,* from the refectory of Santi Giovanni e Paolo, Venice, Italy, 1573. Oil on canvas, 18′ 3″ × 42′. Galleria dell'Accademia, Venice.

Veronese's paintings feature superb color and majestic classical settings. The Catholic Church accused him of impiety for including dogs and dwarfs near Christ in this work originally titled *Last Supper.*

Veronese Among the great Venetian masters was Paolo Cagliari of Verona, called Paolo Veronese (1528–1588). Whereas Tintoretto gloried in monumental drama and deep perspectives, Veronese specialized in splendid pageantry painted in superb color and set within majestic classical architecture. Like Tintoretto, Veronese painted on a huge scale, with canvases often as large as 20 by 30 feet or more. His usual subjects, painted for the refectories of wealthy monasteries, afforded him an opportunity to display magnificent companies at table. *Christ in the House of Levi* (FIG. **9-25**), originally called *Last Supper,* is an example. In a great open loggia framed by three monumental arches, Christ sits at the center of the splendidly garbed elite of Venice. In the foreground, with a courtly gesture, the very image of gracious grandeur, the chief steward welcomes guests. Robed lords, their colorful retainers, clowns, dogs, and dwarfs crowd into the spacious loggia. Painted during the Counter-Reformation, this depiction prompted criticism from the Catholic Church. The Holy Office of the Inquisition accused Veronese of impiety for painting such creatures so close to the Lord, and it ordered him to make changes at his own expense. Reluctant to do so, he simply changed the painting's title, converting the subject to a less solemn one. As Andrea Palladio looked to the example of classically inspired High Renaissance architecture, so Veronese returned to High Renaissance composition, its symmetrical balance, and its ordered architectonics. His shimmering colors span the whole spectrum, although he avoided solid colors for half shades (light blues, sea greens, lemon yellows, roses, and violets), creating veritable flowerbeds of tone.

Giovanni da Bologna Mannerism extended beyond painting. Artists translated its principles into sculpture and architecture as well. The lure of Italy drew a brilliant young Flemish sculptor, Jean de Boulogne, to Florence, where he practiced his art under the equivalent Italian name of Giovanni da Bologna (1529–1608). Giovanni's *Abduction of the Sabine Women* (FIG. **9-26**) exemplifies Mannerist principles of figure composition in sculpture. Drawn from the legendary history of Rome, the group received its present title—relating how the early Romans abducted wives for themselves from the neighboring Sabines—only after its exhibition. In fact, Giovanni did not intend to depict any particular subject. His goal was to achieve a dynamic spiral figural composition involving an old man, a young man, and a woman, all nude in the tradition of ancient statues portraying mythological figures. *Abduction of the Sabine Women* includes references to *Laocoön* (FIG. **2-59**) in the crouching old man and in the woman's up-flung arm. The three bodies interlock on a vertical axis, creating an ascending spiral movement.

To appreciate the sculpture fully, the viewer must walk around it because the work changes radically according to the vantage point. One factor contributing to the shifting imagery is the prominence of open spaces passing through the masses (for example, the space between an arm and a body), which have as great an effect as the solids. This sculpture was the first large-scale group since classical antiquity

9-26 GIOVANNI DA BOLOGNA, *Abduction of the Sabine Women*, Loggia dei Lanzi, Piazza della Signoria, Florence, Italy, 1579–1583. Marble, 13' 5½" high. ◼◂

This sculpture was the first large-scale group since classical antiquity designed to be seen from multiple viewpoints. The three bodies interlock to create a vertical spiral movement.

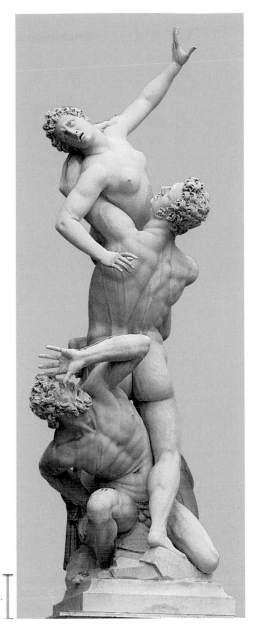

1 ft.

designed to be seen from multiple viewpoints. Giovanni's figures, however, do not break out of the spiral vortex of the composition but remain as if contained within a cylinder.

Giulio Romano Mannerist architects used classical architectural elements in a highly personal and unorthodox manner, rejecting the balance, order, and stability that were the hallmarks of the High Renaissance style, and aiming instead to reveal the contrived nature of architectural design. Applying that anticlassical principle was the goal of GIULIO ROMANO (ca. 1499–1546) when he designed the Palazzo del Tè (FIG. **9-27**) in Mantua for Duke Federigo Gonzaga (r. 1530–1540). In the facades facing the palace's courtyard, the divergences from architectural convention are especially pronounced. Indeed, the Palazzo del Tè constitutes an enormous parody of Bramante's classical style, a veritable Mannerist manifesto announcing the artifice of architectural design. In a building laden with structural surprises and contradictions, the courtyard is the most unconventional of all. The *keystones* (central voussoirs), for example, either have not fully settled or seem to be slipping from the arches—and, more eccentric still, Giulio even placed voussoirs in the pediments over the rectangular niches, where no arches exist. The massive Tuscan columns flanking these niches carry incongruously narrow architraves. That these architraves break midway between the columns stresses their apparent structural insufficiency, and they seem unable to support the weight of the triglyphs of the Doric frieze above, which threaten to crash down on the head of anyone foolish enough to stand below them. To be sure, only a highly sophisticated observer can appreciate Giulio's witticism. Recognizing some quite subtle departures from the norm presupposes a thorough familiarity with the established rules of classical architecture. That the duke delighted in Giulio's mannered architectural inventiveness speaks to his cultivated taste.

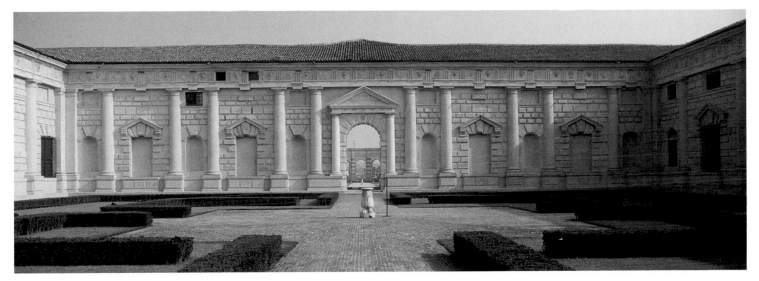

9-27 GIULIO ROMANO, courtyard of the Palazzo del Tè (looking southeast), Mantua, Italy, 1525–1535.

The Mannerist divergences from architectural convention, for example, the slipping triglyphs, are so pronounced in the Palazzo del Tè that they constitute a parody of Bramante's classical style.

HOLY ROMAN EMPIRE

The extraordinary flowering of art and architecture in Cinquecento Italy unfolded against the tumultuous backdrop of the split in Christendom between Catholicism and Protestantism. Prominent theologians, most notably Martin Luther (1483–1546) and John Calvin (1509–1564) in the Holy Roman Empire, directly challenged papal authority. Their major concerns were the sale of *indulgences* (pardons for sins, reducing the time a soul spent in Purgatory—equated with buying one's way into Heaven) and *nepotism* (the appointment of relatives to important positions). Particularly damaging was the perception that the Roman popes concerned themselves more with temporal power and material wealth than with the salvation of the faithful. The fact that many 15th-century popes and cardinals came from wealthy families, such as the Medici, intensified this perception.

Protestantism The northern European reform movement resulted in the establishment of Protestantism, with sects such as Lutheranism and Calvinism. Central to Protestantism was a belief in personal faith rather than adherence to decreed Church practices and doctrines. Because Protestants believed the only true religious relationship was the personal relationship between individuals and God, they were, in essence, eliminating the need for Church intercession, which is central to Catholicism.

In 1517, in Wittenberg, Luther posted for discussion his *Ninety-Five Theses,* in which he enumerated his objections to Church practices. Luther's goal was significant reform and clarification of major spiritual issues, but his ideas ultimately led to the splitting of Christendom. According to Luther, the Catholic Church's extensive ecclesiastical structure needed to be dismantled, for it had no basis in the Bible, which alone could serve as the foundation for Christianity. Luther declared the pope the Antichrist (for which the pope excommunicated him), called the Church the "whore of Babylon," and denounced ordained priests. He also rejected most of Catholicism's sacraments other than baptism and the Eucharist, decrying them as obstacles to salvation. He maintained that for Christianity to be restored to its original purity, the Church needed cleansing of all the doctrinal impurities that had collected through the ages.

A central concern of the Protestant reformers was the question of how Christians achieve salvation. Rather than perceive salvation as something for which weak and sinful humans must constantly strive through good deeds performed under a punitive God's watchful eye, Luther argued that faithful individuals attained redemption solely by God's bestowal of grace. Therefore, people cannot earn salvation. Further, no ecclesiastical machinery with all its miraculous rites and indulgent pardons could save sinners from God's judgment. Only absolute faith in Christ could ensure salvation. Redemption by faith alone, with the guidance of holy scripture, was the fundamental doctrine of Protestantism. The Bible was the word of God, the sole source of all religious truth, and the Church's councils, laws, and rituals carried no weight. Luther facilitated the lay public's access to biblical truths by producing the first translation of the Bible in a vernacular language (German).

Art and the Reformation In addition to doctrinal differences, Catholics and Protestants took divergent stances on the role of visual imagery in religion. Protestants believed representations of Christ, the Virgin, and saints could lead to idolatry and distracted viewers from focusing on the real reason for their presence in church—to communicate directly with God. Because of this belief, Protestant churches were relatively bare. The Protestant concern over the role of religious imagery at times progressed to outright *iconoclasm*—the destruction of religious artworks. Violent waves of iconoclastic fervor swept Basel, Zurich, Strasbourg, and Wittenberg in the 1520s. In an episode known as the Great Iconoclasm, bands of Calvinists visited Catholic churches in the Netherlands in 1566, shattering stained-glass windows, smashing statues, and destroying paintings and other artworks they perceived as idolatrous. The Roman Catholic Church's response to Protestantism—and to Protestant attitudes about the role of art in churches—was the Counter-Reformation (see "Religious Art in Counter-Reformation Italy," page 269).

Matthias Grünewald At the opening of the 16th century, however, Luther had not yet posted his *Ninety-Five Theses,* and the Catholic Church was still an important art patron in the Holy Roman Empire. Around 1510, Matthias Neithardt, known conventionally as MATTHIAS GRÜNEWALD (ca. 1480–1528), began work on the *Isenheim Altarpiece* (FIG. **9-28**), a complex and fascinating polyptych reflecting Catholic beliefs and incorporating several references to Catholic doctrines, such as the lamb (symbol of the son of God), whose wound spurts blood into a chalice in the *Crucifixion* scene. Created for the monastic hospital order Saint Anthony of Isenheim, the altarpiece takes the form of a wooden shrine (not illustrated) carved around 1505 by Nikolaus Hagenauer (active 1493–1538) featuring large gilded and polychrome statues of Saints Anthony Abbot, Augustine, and Jerome. To Hagenauer's centerpiece, Grünewald added two pairs of painted moveable wings that open at the center. Hinged at the sides, one pair stands directly behind the other. Grünewald's exterior panels (visible when the altarpiece is closed, as in FIG. 9-28) present four subjects: *Crucifixion* in the center, *Saint Sebastian* on the left, *Saint Anthony Abbot* on the right, and *Lamentation* in the predella. When these exterior wings are open, four additional scenes—*Annunciation, Angelic Concert, Madonna and Child,* and *Resurrection*—appear. Opening this second pair of wings exposes Hagenauer's interior shrine, flanked by Grünewald's *Meeting of Saints Anthony and Paul* and *Temptation of Saint Anthony* (not illustrated).

The placement of this shrine in the choir of a church adjacent to the monastery's hospital dictated much of the imagery. Saints associated with the plague and other diseases and with miraculous cures, such as Saints Anthony

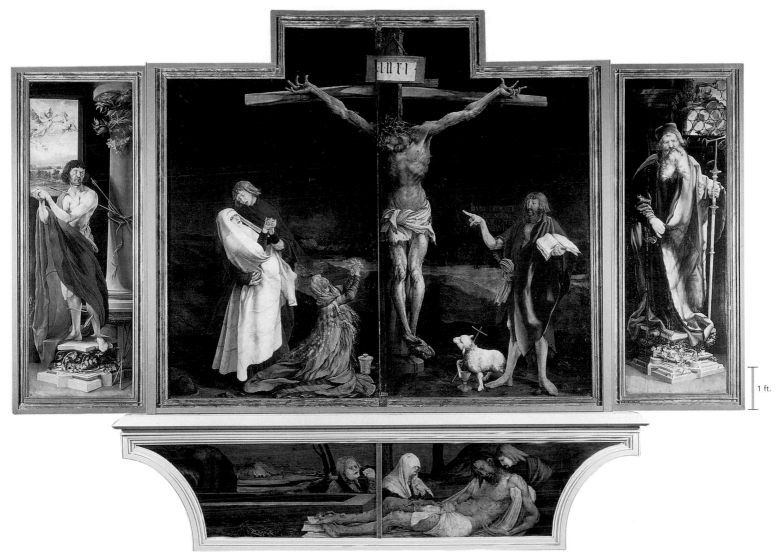

9-28 MATTHIAS GRÜNEWALD, *Isenheim Altarpiece* (closed), from the chapel of the Hospital of Saint Anthony, Isenheim, Germany, ca. 1510–1515. Oil on wood, center panel 9′ 9½″ × 10′ 9″, each wing 8′ 2½″ × 3′ ½″, predella 2′ 5½″ × 11′ 2″. Musée d'Unterlinden, Colmar.

Befitting its setting in a monastic hospital, Matthias Grünewald's *Isenheim Altarpiece* includes painted panels depicting suffering and disease but also miraculous healing, hope, and salvation.

and Sebastian, appear prominently in the *Isenheim Altarpiece*. Grünewald's panels specifically address the themes of dire illness and miraculous healing and accordingly feature the suffering of the order's patron saint, Anthony. The painted images served as warnings, encouraging increased devotion from monks and hospital patients. They also functioned therapeutically by offering some hope to the afflicted. Indeed, Saint Anthony's legend emphasized his dual role as vengeful dispenser of justice (by inflicting disease) and benevolent healer.

In the panel representing *Temptation of Saint Anthony*, Grünewald painted a grotesque image of a man, whose oozing boils, withered arm, and distended stomach all suggest a horrible disease. Medical experts have connected these symptoms with ergotism (a disease caused by ergot, a fungus that grows especially on rye). Although doctors did not discover the cause of ergotism until about 1600, people lived in fear of its recognizable symptoms (convulsions and gan-

grene). The public referred to this illness as "Saint Anthony's Fire," and it was one of the major diseases treated at the Isenheim hospital. The gangrene often compelled amputation, and scholars have noted that the two moveable halves of the altarpiece's predella, if slid apart, make it appear as if Christ's legs have been amputated. The same observation applies to the two main exterior panels. Due to the off-center placement of the cross, opening the left panel "severs" one arm from the crucified figure.

Thus, Grünewald carefully selected and presented his altarpiece's iconography to be particularly meaningful for viewers at this hospital. In the interior shrine, the artist balanced the horrors of the disease and the punishments that awaited those who did not repent with scenes such as the *Meeting of Saints Anthony and Paul*, depicting the two saints, healthy and aged, conversing peacefully. Even the exterior panels (the closed altarpiece; FIG. 9-28) convey these same concerns. *Crucifixion* emphasizes Christ's pain and suffering, but the knowledge that this act redeemed humanity tempers the misery. In addition, Saint Anthony appears in the right wing as a devout follower of Christ who, like Christ and for Christ, endured intense suffering for his faith. Saint Anthony's presence on the exterior thus reinforces the themes Grünewald intertwined throughout this entire altarpiece— themes of pain, illness, and death, as well as those of hope, comfort, and salvation. Grünewald also brilliantly used color to enhance the impact of the altarpiece. He intensified the contrast of horror and hope by playing subtle tones and soft harmonies against shocking dissonances of color.

Albrecht Dürer The dominant artist of the early 16th century in the Holy Roman Empire was ALBRECHT DÜRER (1471–1528) of Nuremberg. Like Leonardo da Vinci, he wrote theoretical treatises on a variety of subjects, such as perspective, fortification, and the ideal in human proportions. Dürer was the first artist outside Italy to become an international celebrity. He traveled extensively, visiting and studying in Colmar, Basel, Strasbourg, Venice, Antwerp, and Brussels, among other locales, and became personally acquainted with many of the leading humanists and artists of his time. His lofty reputation in his day—and ever since—rested primarily on his engravings and woodcuts. Indeed, few artists have ever rivaled the body of graphic work he produced. Dürer became a wealthy man from the sale of his prints. The lawsuit he brought in 1506 against an Italian artist for copying his prints reveals his business acumen. Scholars generally regard this lawsuit as the first in history over artistic copyright.

Fascinated with the classical ideas of Italian Renaissance artists, Dürer was among the first Northern Renaissance artists to travel to Italy expressly to study Italian art and its underlying theories at their source. After his first journey in 1494–1495 (the second was in 1505–1506), he incorporated many Italian Renaissance developments into his art. Art historians have acclaimed Dürer as the first artist north of the Alps to understand fully the basic aims of the Renaissance in Italy.

Fall of Man One of Dürer's early masterpieces, *Fall of Man* (*Adam and Eve*; FIG. **9-29**), represents the first distillation of his studies of the Vitruvian theory of human proportions, a theory based on arithmetic ratios. Clearly outlined against the dark background of a northern European forest, the two idealized figures of Adam and Eve stand in poses reminiscent of specific classical statues probably known to Dürer through graphic representations. Preceded by numerous geometric drawings in which the artist attempted to systematize sets of ideal human proportions in balanced contrapposto poses, the final engraving presents Dürer's concept of the "perfect" male and female figures. Yet he tempered this idealization with naturalism. The gnarled bark of the trees and the feathery leaves authenticate the scene, as do the various creatures skulking underfoot. The animals populating the print are symbolic. The choleric cat, the melancholic elk, the

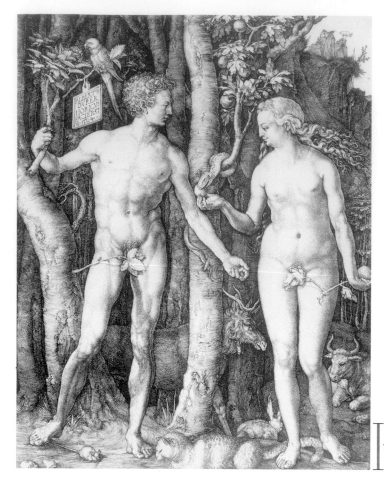

9-29 ALBRECHT DÜRER, *Fall of Man* (*Adam and Eve*), 1504. Engraving, $9\frac{7}{8}'' \times 7\frac{5}{8}''$. Museum of Fine Arts, Boston (centennial gift of Landon T. Clay).

Dürer was the first Northern Renaissance artist to achieve international celebrity. *Fall of Man*, with two figures based on ancient statues, reflects his studies of the Vitruvian theory of human proportions.

sanguine rabbit, and the phlegmatic ox represent humanity's temperaments based on the "four humors," fluids that were the basis of theories of the body's function developed by the ancient Greek physician Hippocrates and practiced in medieval physiology. The tension between cat and mouse in the foreground symbolizes the relation between Adam and Eve at the crucial moment in *Fall of Man*.

Melencolia I Dürer took up the theme of the four humors, specifically melancholy, in one of his most famous engravings, *Melencolia I* (FIG. **9-30**), which many scholars regard as a kind of self-portrait of Dürer's artistic psyche as well as a masterful example of the artist's ability to produce a wide range of tonal values and textures. (The renowned humanist Erasmus of Rotterdam [1466–1536] praised Dürer as "the Apelles [the most renowned ancient Greek painter] of black lines."[7])

The Italian humanist Marsilio Ficino (1433–1499) had written an influential treatise (*De vita triplici,* 1482–1489) in which he asserted that artists were distinct from the population at large because they were born under the sign of the

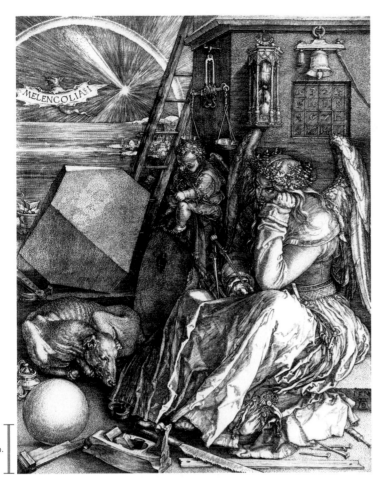

1 in.

9-30 ALBRECHT DÜRER, *Melencolia I*, 1514. Engraving, $9\frac{3}{8}$" × $7\frac{1}{2}$". Victoria & Albert Museum, London.

In this "self-portrait" of his artistic personality, Dürer portrayed Melancholy as a brooding winged woman surrounded by the tools of the artist and builder but incapable of using them.

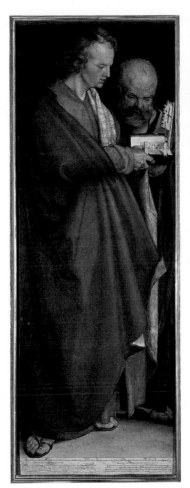
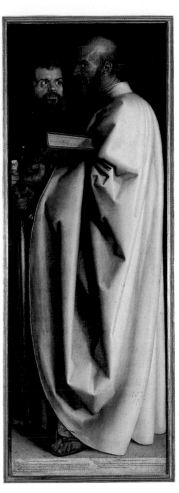

1 ft.

9-31 ALBRECHT DÜRER, *Four Apostles*, 1526. Oil on wood, each panel 7' 1" × 2' 6". Alte Pinakothek, Munich. ◼◀

Dürer's support for Lutheranism surfaces in these portraitlike depictions of four saints on two painted panels. Peter, representative of the pope in Rome, plays a secondary role behind John the Evangelist.

planet Saturn. They shared that Roman god's melancholic temperament because they had an excess of black bile, one of the four body humors, in their systems. Artists therefore were "saturnine"—eccentric and capable both of inspired artistic frenzy and melancholic depression. Raphael had depicted Michelangelo in the guise of the brooding Heraclitus in his *School of Athens* (FIG. 9-7), and Dürer used a similarly posed female figure for his winged personification of Melancholy in *Melencolia I*. (In 1510, in *De occulta philosophia*, Heinrich Cornelius Agrippa of Nettesheim [1486–1535] identified three levels of melancholy. The first was artistic melancholy, which explains the Roman numeral on the banner carried by the bat—a creature of the dark—in Dürer's engraving.) All around the brooding figure of Melancholy are the tools of the artist and builder (compare FIG. 7-17)—compass, hammer, nails, and saw among them—but they are useless to the frustrated artist while he is suffering from melancholy. Melancholy's face is obscured by shadow, underscoring her state of mind, but Dürer also included a burst of light on the far horizon behind the bat, an optimistic note suggesting artists can overcome their depression and produce works of genius—such as this engraving.

Four Apostles Dürer's impressive technical facility with different media extended also to painting. *Four Apostles* (FIG. 9-31) is a two-panel oil painting he produced without commission and presented to the city fathers of Nuremberg in 1526 to be hung in the city hall. Saints John and Peter appear on the left panel, Mark and Paul on the right. In addition to showcasing Dürer's mastery of the oil technique, of his brilliant use of color and light and shade, and of his ability to imbue the four saints with individual personalities and portraitlike features, *Four Apostles* documents the artist's support for Martin Luther by his positioning of the figures. Dürer relegated Saint Peter (as representative of the pope in Rome) to a secondary role by placing him behind John the Evangelist. John assumed particular prominence for Luther because of the evangelist's focus on Christ's person in his Gospel. In addition, Peter and John both read from the Bible, the single authoritative source of religious truth, according to Luther. At the bottom of the panels, Dürer included quotations from each of the apostles' books, using Luther's German translation of the New Testament. The excerpts warn against the coming of perilous times and the preaching of false prophets who will distort God's word.

Hans Holbein The leading artist of the Holy Roman Empire in the generation after Dürer was HANS HOLBEIN THE YOUNGER (ca. 1497–1543). The surfaces of Holbein's paintings are as lustrous as enamel, and the details are exact and exquisitely drawn. Holbein produced portraits in the northern European tradition of close realism that had emerged in 15th-century Flemish art (see Chapter 8). Yet he also incorporated Italian ideas about monumental composition and sculptural form.

Holbein began his artistic career in Basel, but due to the immediate threat of a religious civil war, he left for England, where he became painter to the court of King Henry VIII and produced a double portrait of the French ambassadors to England, Jean de Dinteville and Georges de Selve. *The French Ambassadors* (FIG. **9-32**) exhibits Holbein's considerable talents—his strong sense of composition, his subtle linear patterning, his gift for portraiture, his marvelous sensitivity to color, and his faultless technique. The two men, both ardent humanists, stand at opposite ends of a side table covered with an oriental rug and a collection of objects reflective of their worldliness and their interest in learning and the arts. These include mathematical and astronomical models and implements, a lute with a broken string, compasses, a sundial, flutes, globes, and an open hymn-book with Luther's translation of *Veni, Creator Spiritus* and of the Ten Commandments.

Of particular interest is the long gray shape that slashes diagonally across the picture plane and interrupts the stable, balanced, and serene composition. This form is an *anamorphic* image, a distorted image recognizable only when viewed with a special device, such as a cylindrical mirror, or by looking at the painting at an acute angle. In this case, if the viewer stands off to the right, the gray slash becomes a skull. Although scholars disagree on the skull's precise meaning, it certainly refers to death. Artists commonly incorporated skulls into paintings as reminders of mortality. Indeed, Holbein depicted a skull on the metal medallion on Jean de Dinteville's hat. Holbein may have intended the skulls, in conjunction with the crucifix that appears half hidden behind the curtain in the upper left corner, to encourage viewers to ponder death and resurrection.

The French Ambassadors may also allude to the growing tension between secular and religious authorities. Jean de

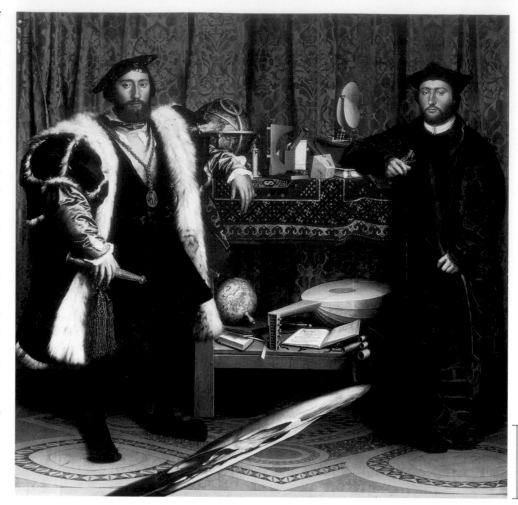

9-32 HANS HOLBEIN THE YOUNGER, *The French Ambassadors*, 1533. Oil and tempera on wood, 6′ 8″ × 6′ 9½″. National Gallery, London. ◼◣

In this double portrait, Holbein depicted two humanists with a collection of objects reflective of their worldliness and learning, but he also included an anamorphic skull, a reminder of death.

Dinteville was a titled landowner, Georges de Selve a bishop. The inclusion of Luther's translations next to the lute with the broken string (a symbol of discord) may also subtly refer to the religious strife. In any case, the painting is a supreme artistic achievement. Holbein rendered the still-life objects with the same meticulous care as the men themselves, the woven design of the deep emerald curtain behind them, and the floor tiles, drawn in faultless perspective.

FRANCE

As *The French Ambassadors* illustrates, France in the early 16th century continued its efforts to secure widespread recognition as a political power and cultural force. Under Francis I (r. 1515–1547), the French established a firm foothold in Milan and its environs. Francis waged a campaign (known as the Habsburg-Valois Wars) against Charles V (the Spanish king and Holy Roman Emperor; r. 1516–1558), which occupied him from 1521 to 1544. These wars involved disputed territories—southern France, the Netherlands, the Rhine-

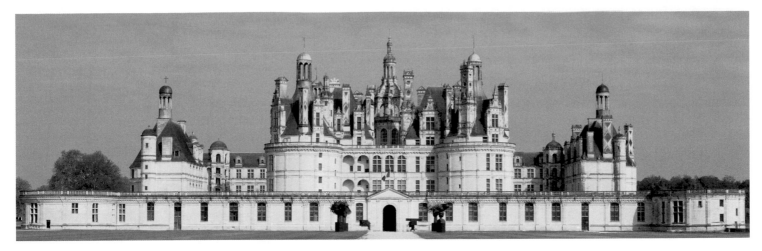

9-33 Château de Chambord (looking northwest), Chambord, France, begun 1519. ◼◢

French Renaissance châteaux, which developed from medieval castles, served as country houses for royalty. King Francis I's Château de Chambord reflects Italian palazzo design, but it has a Gothic roof.

land, northern Spain, and Italy—and reflected France's central role in the shifting geopolitical landscape. Despite these military preoccupations, Francis I also endeavored to elevate his country's cultural profile. To that end, he invited several esteemed Italian artists to his court, Leonardo da Vinci among them. Under Francis, the Church, the primary patron of art and architecture in medieval France, yielded that position to the French monarchy.

Château de Chambord Francis I indulged his passion for building by commissioning several large *châteaux*, among them the Château de Chambord (FIG. **9-33**). These châteaux, developed from medieval fortified castles, served as country houses for royalty, who usually built them near forests for use as hunting lodges. Construction of the Chambord château began in 1519, but Francis never saw its completion. The plan includes a central square block with four corridors, in the shape of a cross, and a broad, central staircase that gives access to groups of rooms—ancestors of the modern suite of rooms or apartments. At each of the four corners, a round tower punctuates the square plan, and a moat surrounds the whole. From the exterior, Chambord presents a carefully contrived horizontal accent on three levels, with continuous moldings separating its floors. Windows align precisely, one exactly over another. The Italian Renaissance palazzo (FIG. 8-33) served as the model for this matching of horizontal and vertical features, but above the third level the structure's lines break chaotically into a jumble of high dormers, chimneys, and lanterns that recall soaring ragged Gothic silhouettes on the skyline.

THE NETHERLANDS

With the demise of the duchy of Burgundy in 1477 and the division of that territory between France and the Holy Roman Empire, the Netherlands at the beginning of the 16th

century consisted of 17 provinces (corresponding to modern Holland, Belgium, and Luxembourg; see MAP 9-1). The Netherlands was among the most commercially advanced and prosperous European countries. Its extensive network of rivers and easy access to the Atlantic Ocean provided a setting conducive to overseas trade, and shipbuilding was one of the most profitable enterprises. The region's commercial center shifted toward the end of the 15th century, partly because of buildup of silt in the Bruges estuary. Traffic relocated to Antwerp, which became the hub of economic activity in the Netherlands after 1510. As many as 500 ships a day passed through Antwerp's harbor, and large trading companies from England, the Holy Roman Empire, Italy, Portugal, and Spain established themselves in the city.

During the second half of the 16th century, Philip II of Spain controlled the Netherlands, which he inherited from his father, Charles V (see page 289). Philip sought to force the entire population to become Catholic. His heavy-handed tactics and repressive measures led in 1579 to revolt and the formation of two federations: the Union of Arras, a Catholic union of southern Netherlandish provinces, which remained under Spanish dominion, and the Union of Utrecht, a Protestant union of northern provinces, which became the Dutch Republic.

Large-scale altarpieces and other religious works continued to be commissioned for Catholic churches, but with the rise of Protestantism in the Netherlands, artists and patrons increasingly favored secular subjects. Netherlandish art of this period provides a wonderful glimpse into the lives of various strata of society, from nobility to peasantry, capturing their activities, environment, and values.

Quinten Massys Antwerp's growth and prosperity, along with its wealthy merchants' propensity for collecting and purchasing art, attracted artists to the city. Among them was QUINTEN MASSYS (ca. 1466–1530) of Louvain, who became

Antwerp's leading master after 1510. In *Money-Changer and His Wife* (FIG. **9-34**), Massys presented a professional man transacting business. He holds scales, checking the weight of coins on the table. The artist's detailed rendering of the figures, setting, and objects suggests a fidelity to observable fact. But the painting is also a commentary on Netherlandish values and mores. *Money-Changer* highlights the financial transactions that in the 16th-century played an increasingly prominent role in secular life in the Netherlands, distracting Christians from their religious duties. The banker's wife, for example, shows more interest in watching her husband weigh money than in reading her prayer book. Massys incorporated into his painting numerous references to the importance of a moral, righteous, and spiritual life, including a carafe with water and a candlestick, traditional religious symbols. The couple ignores them, focusing solely on money. On the right, seen through a window, an old man talks with another man, a reference to idleness and gossip. The reflected image in the convex mirror on the counter offsets this

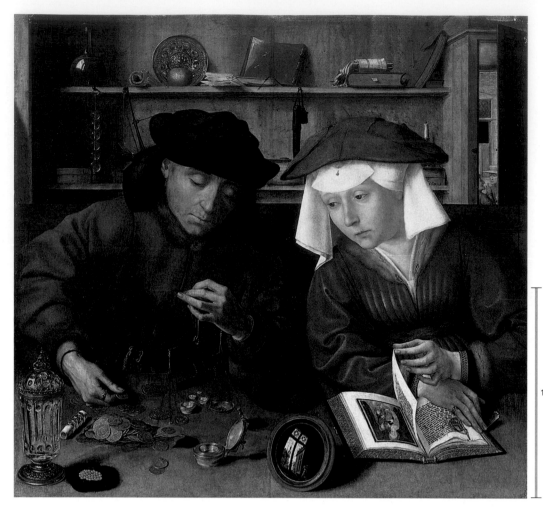

9-34 QUINTEN MASSYS, *Money-Changer and His Wife,* 1514. Oil on wood, 2′ 3¾″ × 2′ 2⅜″. Musée du Louvre, Paris.

Massys's depiction of a secular financial transaction is also a commentary on Netherlandish values. The banker's wife shows more interest in the money-weighing than in her prayer book.

image of sloth and foolish chatter. There, a man reads what is most likely a Bible or prayer book. Behind him is a church steeple. An inscription on the original frame (now lost) read, "Let the balance be just and the weights equal" (Lev. 19:36), an admonition that applies both to the money-changer's professional conduct and the eventual last judgment. Nonetheless, the couple in this painting has tipped the balance in favor of the pursuit of wealth.

Pieter Aertsen This tendency to inject reminders about spiritual well-being into paintings of everyday life emerges again in *Butcher's Stall* (FIG. **9-35**) by PIETER AERTSEN (ca. 1507–1575), who worked in Antwerp for more than three decades. At first glance, this painting appears to be a descriptive *genre* scene (one from everyday life). On display is an array of meat products—a side of a hog, chickens, sausages, a stuffed intestine, pig's feet, meat pies, a cow's head, a hog's head, and hanging entrails. Also visible are fish, pretzels, cheese, and butter. As did Massys, Aertsen embedded strategically placed religious images in his painting. In the background, Joseph leads a donkey carrying Mary and the Christ Child. The holy family stops to offer alms to a beggar and his son, while

the people behind the holy family wend their way toward a church. Furthermore, the crossed fishes on the platter and the pretzels and wine in the rafters on the upper left all refer to "spiritual food" (pretzels often served as bread during Lent). Aertsen accentuated these allusions to salvation through Christ by contrasting them to their opposite—a life of gluttony, lust, and sloth. He represented this degeneracy with the oyster and mussel shells (which Netherlanders believed possessed aphrodisiacal properties) scattered on the ground on the painting's right side, along with the people seen eating and carousing nearby under the roof. Underscoring the general theme is the placard at the right advertising land for sale—Aertsen's moralistic reference to a recent scandal involving the transfer of land from an Antwerp charitable institution to a land speculator. The sign appears directly above the vignette of the Virgin giving alms to the beggar.

Caterina van Hemessen With the accumulation of wealth in the Netherlands, portraits increased in popularity. *Self-Portrait* (FIG. **9-36**) by CATERINA VAN HEMESSEN (1528–1587) is the first known northern European self-portrait by a woman. Here, she

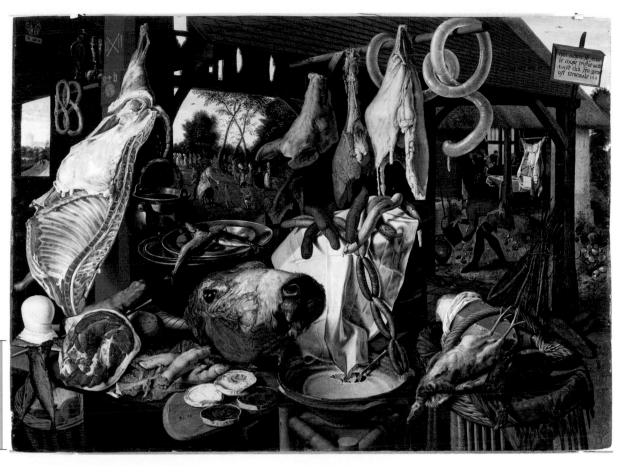

9-35 PIETER AERTSEN, *Butcher's Stall*, 1551. Oil on wood, 4' ⅜" × 6' 5¾". Uppsala University Art Collection, Uppsala.

Butcher's Stall appears to be a genre painting, but in the background, Joseph leads a donkey carrying Mary and the Christ Child. Aertsen balanced images of gluttony with allusions to salvation.

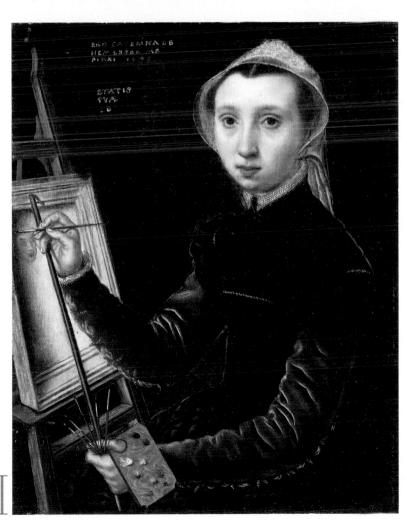

confidently presented herself as an artist who interrupts her work to look toward the viewer. She holds brushes, a palette, and a *maulstick* (a stick used to steady the hand while painting) in her left hand, and delicately applies pigment to the canvas with her right hand. The artist ensured proper identification (and credit) through the inscription in the painting: "Caterina van Hemessen painted me / 1548 / her age 20." Professional women artists remained unusual in the 16th century in large part because of the difficulty in obtaining formal training in a male master's workshop. Caterina was typical in having been trained by her father, the painter Jan Sanders van Hemessen (ca. 1500–1556).

Pieter Bruegel the Elder The greatest Netherlandish painter of the mid-16th century was PIETER BRUEGEL THE ELDER (ca. 1528–1569). Like many of his contemporaries, Bruegel traveled to Italy, where he probably spent almost two years, journeying as far south as Sicily. However, unlike other artists who visited the ruins of ancient Rome, Bruegel chose not to incorporate classical elements into his paintings. Landscapes were among his favorite subjects, but no matter how huge a slice of

9-36 CATERINA VAN HEMESSEN, *Self-Portrait*, 1548. Oil on wood, 1' ¾" × 9⅞". Kunstmuseum, Öffentliche Kunstsammlung Basel, Basel. ◼◀

In this first known northern European self-portrait by a woman, Caterina van Hemessen represented herself as a confident artist momentarily interrupting her work to look out at the viewer.

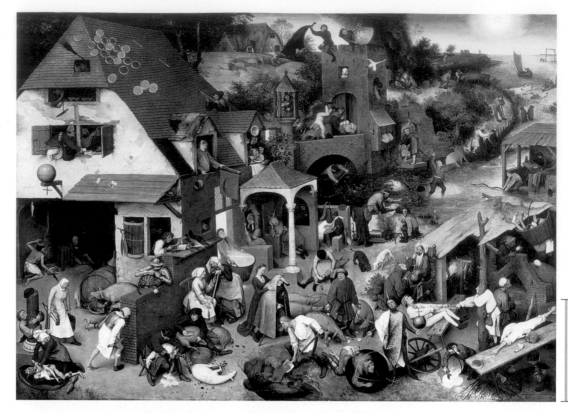

9-37 PIETER BRUEGEL THE ELDER, *Netherlandish Proverbs,* 1559. Oil on wood, 3′ 10″ × 5′ 4⅛″. Gemäldegalerie, Staatliche Museen zu Berlin, Berlin. ◼◣

In this painting of a Netherlandish village, Bruegel indulged his audience's obsession with proverbs and passion for clever imagery, and demonstrated his deep understanding of human nature.

1 ft.

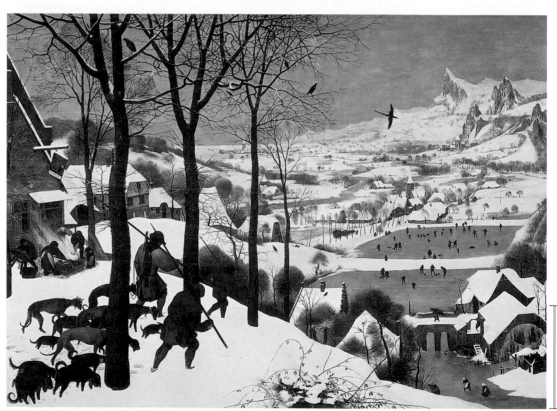

9-38 PIETER BRUEGEL THE ELDER, *Hunters in the Snow,* 1565. Oil on wood, 3′ 10″ × 5′ 3¾″. Kunsthistorisches Museum, Vienna.

In *Hunters in the Snow,* one of a series of paintings illustrating different seasons, Bruegel draws the viewer diagonally deep into the landscape by his mastery of line, shape, and composition.

1 ft.

the world he depicted, human activities remain the dominant theme. Bruegel's *Netherlandish Proverbs* (FIG. **9-37**) depicts a village populated by a wide range of people (nobility, peasants, and clerics). From a bird's-eye view, the spectator encounters a mesmerizing array of activities reminiscent of the topsy-turvy scenes of Hieronymus Bosch (FIG. 9-1), but the purpose and meaning of Bruegel's anecdotal details are

clear. By illustrating more than a hundred proverbs in this one painting, the artist indulged his Netherlandish audience's obsession with proverbs and passion for detailed and clever imagery. As the viewer scrutinizes the myriad vignettes within the painting, Bruegel's close observation and deep understanding of human nature become apparent. The proverbs depicted include, on the far left, a man in blue gnawing on a pillar ("He bites the column"—an image of hypocrisy). To his right, a man "beats his head against a wall" (an ambitious idiot). On the roof a man "shoots one arrow after the other, but hits nothing" (a shortsighted fool). In the far distance, the "blind lead the blind."

Hunters in the Snow (FIG. 9-38), one of six paintings illustrating seasonal changes, is very different in character and illustrates the dynamic variety of Bruegel's work. The series grew out of the tradition of depicting seasons and peasants in Books of Hours (FIG. 8-10). The painting shows human figures and landscape locked in winter cold. The weary hunters return with their hounds, women build fires, skaters skim the frozen pond, the town and its church huddle in their mantle of snow. Bruegel rendered the landscape in an optically accurate manner. It develops smoothly from foreground to background and draws the viewer diagonally into its depths. The painter's consummate skill in using line and shape and his subtlety in tonal harmony make this one of the great landscape paintings in Western art.

SPAIN

Spain emerged as the dominant European power at the end of the 16th century. Under Charles V of Habsburg (r. 1516–1556) and his son, Philip II (r. 1556–1598), the Spanish Empire encompassed a territory greater in extent than any ever known—a large part of Europe, the western Mediterranean, a strip of North Africa, and vast expanses in the New World. Spain acquired many of its New World colonies through aggressive overseas exploration. Among the most notable conquistadors sailing under the Spanish flag were Christopher Columbus (1451–1506), Vasco Nuñez de Balboa (ca. 1475–1517), Ferdinand Magellan (1480–1521), Hernán

Cortés (1485–1547), and Francisco Pizarro (ca. 1470–1541). The Habsburg Empire, enriched by New World plunder, supported the most powerful military force in Europe. Spain defended and then promoted the interests of the Catholic Church in its battle against the inroads of the Protestant Reformation. In fact, Philip II earned the title "Most Catholic King." Spain's crusading spirit, nourished by centuries of war with Islam, engaged body and soul in forming the most Catholic civilization of Europe and the Americas. In the 16th century, for good or for ill, Spain left the mark of its power, religion, language, and culture on two hemispheres.

El Escorial Philip II's major building project was El Escorial (FIG. 9-39), designed by JUAN DE HERRERA (ca. 1530–1597) and JUAN BAUTISTA DE TOLEDO (d. 1567), principally the former. In his will, Charles V stipulated that a "dynastic pantheon" be built to house the remains of past and future Spanish monarchs. Philip II chose a site some 30 miles northwest of Madrid for the enormous (625 feet wide and 520 feet deep) complex, which is not only a royal mausoleum but also a church, a monastery, and a palace. Legend has it that El Escorial's gridlike plan symbolized the gridiron on which Saint Lawrence suffered his martyrdom. The vast structure is in keeping with Philip's austere character, his passionate Catholic religiosity, his proud reverence for his dynasty, and his stern determination to impose his will worldwide. He insisted that in designing El Escorial, the architects focus on simplicity of form, severity in the whole, nobility without arrogance, and majesty without ostentation. The result is a classicism of Doric severity, ultimately derived from Italian architecture, but without close parallel elsewhere in Europe.

Only the three entrances, with the dominant central portal framed by superimposed orders and topped by a pedi-

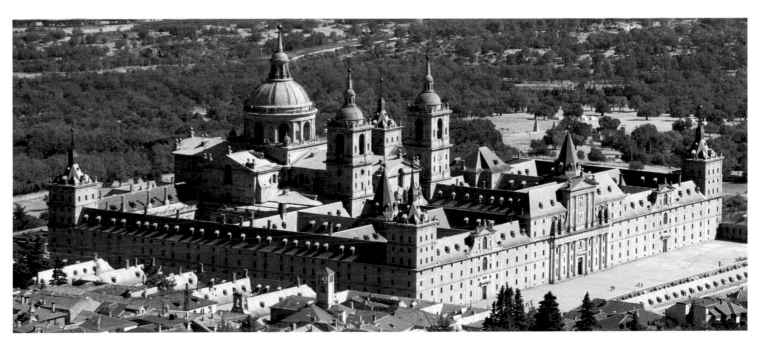

9-39 JUAN DE HERRERA and JUAN BAUTISTA DE TOLEDO, aerial view (looking southeast) of El Escorial, near Madrid, Spain, 1563–1584.

Conceived by Charles V and built by Philip II, El Escorial is a royal mausoleum, church, monastery, and palace in one. The complex is classical in style with severely plain walls and massive towers.

ment in the Italian fashion, break the long sweep of the structure's severely plain walls. Massive square towers punctuate the four corners. Within, the church's imposing granite facade produces an effect of overwhelming strength and weight. El Escorial stands as the overpowering architectural expression of Spain's spirit in its heroic epoch and of the character of Philip II, the extraordinary ruler who directed it.

El Greco Reflecting the increasingly international character of European art as well as the mobility of artists, the greatest Spanish painter of the era was not a Spaniard. Born in Crete, Doménikos Theotokópoulos, called EL GRECO (ca. 1547–1614), emigrated to Italy as a young man. In his youth, he absorbed the traditions of Late Byzantine frescoes and mosaics. While still young, El Greco went to Venice, where he worked in Titian's studio, although Tintoretto's paintings (FIG. 9-24) seem to have made a stronger impression on him. A brief trip to Rome explains the influences of Roman and Florentine Mannerism on his work. By 1577, he had left for Spain to spend the rest of his life in Toledo. El Greco's art is a strong personal blending of Byzantine and Mannerist elements. The intense emotionalism of his paintings, which naturally appealed to Spanish piety, and a great reliance on and mastery of color bound him to 16th-century Venetian art and to Mannerism. El Greco's art was not strictly Spanish (although it appealed to certain sectors of that society), for it had no Spanish antecedents and little effect on later Spanish painters. Nevertheless, El Greco's hybrid style captured the fervor of Spanish Catholicism.

Burial of Count Orgaz (FIG. **9-40**), painted in 1586 for Santo Tomé in Toledo, vividly expresses that fervor. El Greco based the painting on the legend that the count of Orgaz, who had died some three centuries before and who had been a great benefactor of Santo Tomé, was buried in the church by Saints Stephen and Augustine, who miraculously descended from Heaven to lower the count's body into its sepulcher. The brilliant Heaven that opens above irradiates the earthly scene. The painter represented the terrestrial realm with a firm realism, whereas he depicted the celestial, in his quite personal manner, with elongated undulating figures, fluttering draperies, and a visionary swirling cloud. Below, the two saints lovingly lower the count's armor-clad body, the armor and heavy robes painted with all the rich sensuousness of the Venetian school. A solemn chorus of personages dressed in black fills the background. In the carefully individualized features of these figures, El Greco demonstrated that he was also a great portraitist.

The upward glances of some of the figures below and the flight of an angel above link the painting's lower and upper sections. The action of the angel, who carries the count's

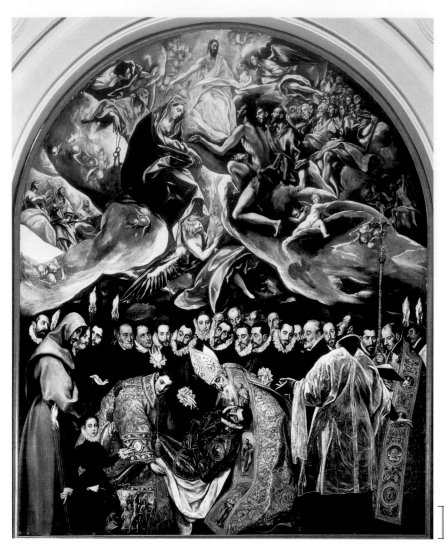

9-40 EL GRECO, *Burial of Count Orgaz*, Santo Tomé, Toledo, Spain, 1586. Oil on canvas, 16′ × 12′.

El Greco's art is a blend of Byzantine and Italian Mannerist elements. His intense emotional content captured the fervor of Spanish Catholicism, and his dramatic use of light foreshadowed the Baroque style.

1 ft.

soul in his arms as Saint John and the Virgin intercede for it before the throne of Christ, reinforces this connection. El Greco's deliberate change in style to distinguish between the two levels of reality gives the viewer an opportunity to see the artist's early and late manners in the same work, one below the other. His relatively sumptuous and realistic presentation of the earthly sphere is still strongly rooted in Venetian art, but the abstractions and distortions El Greco used to show the immaterial nature of the heavenly realm characterize his later style. His elongated figures existing in undefined spaces, bathed in a cool light of uncertain origin, explain El Greco's usual classification as a Mannerist, but it is difficult to apply that label to him without reservation. Although he used Mannerist formal devices, El Greco's primary concerns were emotion and conveying his religious passion or arousing that of observers. The forcefulness of his paintings is the result of his unique, highly developed expressive style. His strong sense of movement and use of light prefigured the Baroque style of the 17th century, examined next in Chapter 10.

High Renaissance and Mannerism in Europe

Italy

▮ During the High (1495–1520) and Late (1520–1600) Renaissance, the major Italian artistic centers were Florence, Rome, and Venice. Whereas most Florentine and Roman artists emphasized careful design preparation based on preliminary drawing (*disegno*), Venetian artists focused on color and the process of paint application (*colorito*).

▮ Leonardo da Vinci was a master of chiaroscuro and atmospheric perspective. He was famous for his *sfumato* (misty haziness) and for his psychological insight in depicting biblical narrative.

▮ Raphael favored lighter tonalities than Leonardo and clarity over obscurity. His sculpturesque figures appear in landscapes under blue skies or in grandiose architectural settings rendered in perfect perspective.

▮ In both sculpture and painting, Michelangelo won renown for his emotionally charged figures with heroic physiques. He preferred pent-up energy to Raphael's calm, ideal beauty.

▮ The leading early Cinquecento Italian architect was Bramante, who championed the classical style of the ancients, but combined classical elements in original ways. He favored the central plan for ecclesiastical buildings.

▮ The two greatest masters of the Venetian painting school were Giorgione, who developed the concept of *poesia*, poetical painting, and Titian, famed for his rich surface textures and dazzling display of color in all its nuances. Titian established oil color on canvas as the standard medium of the Western pictorial tradition.

▮ Mannerism (1520–1600) was a reaction to the High Renaissance style. A prime feature of Mannerist art is artifice. Renaissance artists generally strove to create art that appeared natural, whereas Mannerist artists such as Pontormo and Parmigianino were less inclined to disguise the contrived nature of art production. Ambiguous space, departures from expected conventions, and unique presentations of traditional themes are hallmarks of Mannerist art.

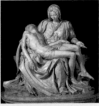

Michelangelo, *Pietà*, ca. 1498–1500

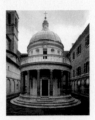

Bramante, Tempietto, Rome, 1502(?)

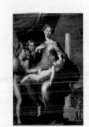

Parmigianino, *Madonna with the Long Neck*, 1534–1540

Northern Europe and Spain

▮ Dissatisfaction with the Church in Rome led to the Protestant Reformation, which began in the Holy Roman Empire. Protestants objected to the sale of indulgences and rejected most of the sacraments of Catholicism. They also condemned ostentatious church decoration as a form of idolatry. Art, however, especially prints, still played a role in Protestantism. Albrecht Dürer, the first artist outside Italy to achieve international celebrity, became a wealthy man through the sale of his woodcuts and engravings.

▮ The Netherlands was one of the most prosperous countries in 16th-century Europe. Netherlandish art provides a picture of contemporary life and values. Pieter Aertsen's *Butcher's Stall*, for example, seems to be a straightforward genre scene but includes the holy family offering alms to a beggar, providing a stark contrast between gluttony and religious piety.

▮ Landscapes were the specialty of Pieter Bruegel, the Elder. His *Hunters in the Snow* is one of a series of paintings depicting seasonal changes and the activities associated with them.

▮ The leading painter of 16th-century Spain was the Greek-born El Greco, whose art combined Byzantine style, Italian Mannerism, and the religious fervor of Catholic Spain.

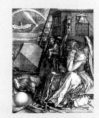

Dürer, *Melencolia I*, 1514

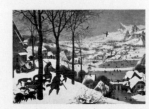

Bruegel, *Hunters in the Snow*, 1565

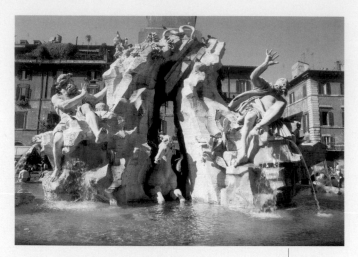

As water flows from a travertine grotto supporting an ancient Egyptian obelisk, Bernini's marble personifications of major rivers of four continents twist and gesticulate emphatically.

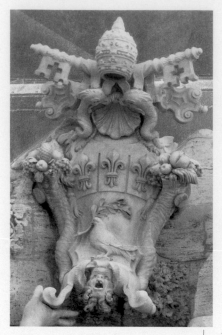

Crowning the grotto is Pope Innocent X's coat of arms and atop the obelisk is the Pamphili family's dove, symbolizing the Holy Spirit and Christianity's triumph in all parts of the then-known world.

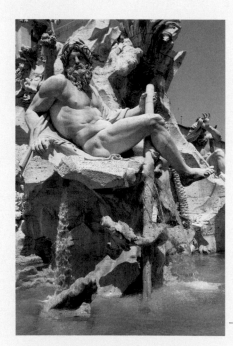

Each of the four rivers has an identifying attribute. The Ganges (Asia), easily navigable, holds an oar. The Plata (Americas) has a hoard of coins, signifying the wealth of the New World.

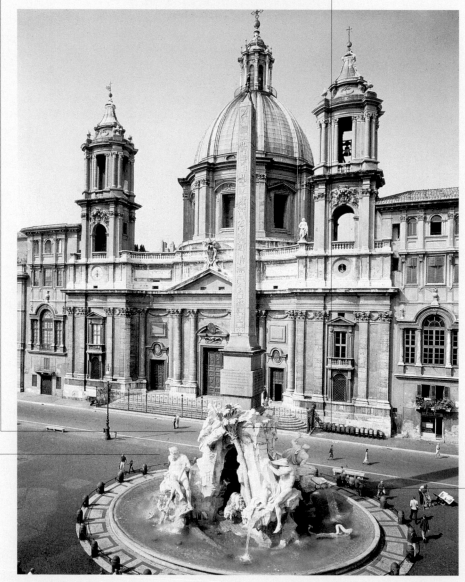

10-1 GIANLORENZO BERNINI, Fountain of the Four Rivers (looking southwest with Sant'Agnese in Agone in the background), Piazza Navona, Rome, Italy, 1648–1651.

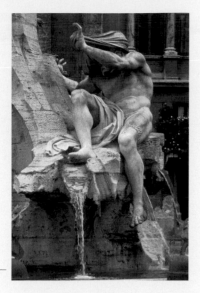

The Danube (Europe) gazes awestruck at the papal arms and the Nile (Africa) covers his face— Bernini's acknowledgment that the Nile's source was unknown to Europeans at the time.

Baroque Europe

BAROQUE ART AND SPECTACLE

One of the most popular tourist attractions in Rome is the Fountain of the Four Rivers (FIG. **10-1**) in Piazza Navona by GIANLORENZO BERNINI (1598–1680). Architect, painter, sculptor, playwright, and stage designer, Bernini was one of the most important and imaginative artists of the Baroque era in Italy and its most characteristic and sustaining spirit. Nonetheless, the fountain's patron, Pope Innocent X (r. 1644–1655), never wanted Bernini to win this commission. Bernini had been the favorite sculptor of the Pamphili pope's predecessor, Urban VIII (r. 1623–1644), who spent so extravagantly on art and on himself and his family that he nearly bankrupted the Vatican treasury. Innocent emphatically opposed the excesses of the Barberini pope and shunned Bernini, awarding new papal commissions to other sculptors and architects. Bernini was also in disgrace at the time because of his failed attempt to erect bell towers for the new facade (FIG. **10-2**) of Saint Peter's. When Innocent announced a competition for a fountain in Piazza Navona, site of the Pamphili family's palace and parish church, Sant'Agnese in Agone (FIG. **10-1**, *rear*), he pointedly did not invite Bernini to submit a design. However, the renowned sculptor succeeded in having a model of his proposed fountain placed where the pope would see it. When Innocent examined it, he was so captivated he declared the only way anyone could avoid employing Bernini was not to look at his work.

Bernini's bold design, executed in large part by his assistants, called for a sculptured travertine grotto supporting an ancient obelisk Innocent had transferred to Piazza Navona from the circus of the Roman emperor Maxentius (r. 305–312) on the Via Appia. The plaza was once the site of the stadium of Domitian (r. 81–96), a long and narrow arena for athletic contests, which explains the piazza's unusual shape and the church's name (*agone* means foot race in Italian). Water rushes from the artificial grotto into a basin filled with marble statues personifying major rivers of four continents—the Danube (Europe), Nile (Africa), Ganges (Asia), and Plata (Americas). The reclining figures twist and gesticulate, consistent with contemporary taste for movement and drama. The Nile covers his face—Bernini's way of acknowledging the source of that river was unknown at the time. The Rio de la Plata has a hoard of coins, signifying the wealth of the New World. The Ganges, easily navigable, holds an oar. The Danube, awestruck, reaches up to the papal coat of arms. A second reference to Innocent X is the Pamphili dove at the apex of the obelisk, which also symbolizes the Holy Spirit and the triumph of Christianity in all parts of the then-known world. The scenic effect of the cascading water would have been heightened whenever Piazza Navona was flooded for festival pageants. Bernini's fountain epitomizes the Baroque era's love for uniting art and spectacle.

EUROPE IN THE 17TH CENTURY

During the 17th century, numerous geopolitical shifts occurred in Europe as the fortunes of individual countries waxed and waned. Pronounced political and religious friction resulted in widespread unrest and warfare. Indeed, between 1562 and 1721, all of Europe was at peace for a mere four years. The major conflict of this period was the Thirty Years' War (1618–1648), which ensnared Spain, France, Sweden, Denmark, the Netherlands, Germany, Austria, Poland, the Ottoman Empire, and the Holy Roman Empire. Although the outbreak of this war had its roots in the conflict between militant Catholics and militant Protestants, the driving force quickly shifted to secular, dynastic, and nationalistic concerns. Among the major political entities vying for expanded power and authority in Europe were the Bourbon dynasty of France and the Habsburg dynasties of Spain and the Holy Roman Empire. The war, which concluded with the Treaty of Westphalia in 1648, was largely responsible for the political restructuring of Europe (MAP 10-1). As a result, the United Provinces of the Netherlands (the Dutch Republic), Sweden, and France expanded their authority. Spanish and Danish power diminished. In addition to reconfiguring territorial boundaries, the Treaty of Westphalia in essence granted freedom of religious choice throughout

MAP 10-1 Europe in 1648 after the Treaty of Westphalia.

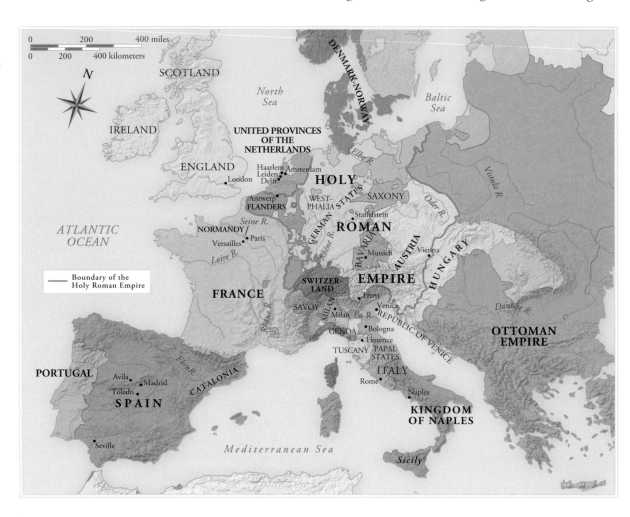

Baroque Europe

1600	1625	1650	1675	1700
▎ Paul V commissions Maderno to complete Saint Peter's ▎ Carracci introduces quadro riportato fresco painting ▎ Caravaggio pioneers tenebrism in oil painting ▎ Bernini incorporates drama and movement in marble statuary ▎ Rubens is the leading painter in Catholic Flanders ▎ In the northern Netherlands, Calvinist patrons favor genre scenes, portraits, and still lifes	▎ Borromini designs San Carlo alle Quattro Fontane ▎ Gentileschi is the leading woman artist in Europe ▎ Zurbarán paints scenes of martyrdom in Catholic Spain ▎ Hals achieves renown for his group portraits ▎ Rembrandt is the foremost Dutch Baroque painter and print maker	▎ Bernini designs the colonnaded oval piazza in front of Saint Peter's ▎ Velázquez paints *Las Meninas* ▎ Vermeer uses a camera obscura as an aid in painting domestic interiors ▎ Poussin champions "grand manner" painting	▎ Pozzo paints illusionistic ceiling frescoes in Sant'Ignazio ▎ Louis XIV, the "Sun King," builds the palace at Versailles ▎ Christopher Wren designs Saint Paul's Cathedral in London	

Europe. This treaty thus marked the abandonment of the idea of a united Christian Europe, and accepted the practical realities of secular political systems. The building of today's nation-states was emphatically under way.

The 17th century also brought heightened economic competition to Europe. Much of the foundation for worldwide mercantilism—extensive voyaging and geographic exploration, improved cartography, and advances in shipbuilding—had been laid in the previous century. In the 17th century, however, changes in financial systems, lifestyles, and trading patterns, along with expanding colonialism, fueled the creation of a worldwide marketplace. The Dutch founded the Bank of Amsterdam in 1609, which eventually became the center of European transfer banking. By establishing a system in which merchant firms held money on account, the bank relieved traders of having to transport precious metals as payment. Trading practices became more complex. Rather than reciprocal trading, triangular trade (trade among three parties) allowed for a larger pool of desirable goods. Exposure to an ever-growing array of goods affected European diets and lifestyles. Coffee (from island colonies) and tea (from China) became popular beverages during the early 17th century. Equally explosive was the growth of sugar use. Sugar, tobacco, and rice were slave crops, and the slave trade expanded to meet the demand for these goods. The resulting worldwide mercantile system permanently changed the face of Europe. The prosperity international trade generated affected social and political relationships, necessitating new rules of etiquette and careful diplomacy. With increased disposable income, more of the newly wealthy spent money on art, significantly expanding the market for artworks, especially small-scale paintings for private homes.

Baroque Art and Architecture Art historians traditionally describe 17th-century European art as *Baroque,* but the term is problematic because the period encompasses a broad range of styles and genres. Although its origin is unclear, Baroque may have come from the Portuguese word *barroco,* meaning an irregularly shaped pearl. Use of the term can be traced to the late 18th century, when critics disparaged the Baroque period's artistic production, in large part because of perceived deficiencies in comparison with the art of the Italian Renaissance. Over time, this negative connotation faded, but the term stuck. Baroque remains useful to describe the distinctive new style that emerged during the early 1600s—a style of complexity and drama seen especially in Italian art of this period. Whereas Renaissance artists reveled in the precise, orderly rationality of classical models, Baroque artists embraced dynamism, theatricality, and elaborate ornamentation, often on a grandiose scale, as in Bernini's Four Rivers Fountain (FIG. 10-1).

ITALY

Although the Protestant Reformation brought with it fundamental changes in artistic patronage in many northern European countries, in Italy the Catholic Church remained the leading source of artistic commissions. The aim of much of Italian Baroque art was to restore Roman Catholicism's predominance and centrality.

Architecture and Sculpture

Italian 17th-century art and architecture, especially in Rome, embodied the renewed energy of the Counter-Reformation (see "Religious Art in Counter-Reformation Italy," Chapter 9, page 269). At the end of the 16th century, Pope Sixtus V (r. 1585–1590) had augmented the papal treasury and intended to rebuild Rome as an even more magnificent showcase of Church power. Between 1606 and 1667, several strong and ambitious popes—Paul V, Urban VIII, Innocent X, and Alexander VII—made many of Sixtus V's dreams a reality. Rome still bears the marks of their patronage everywhere.

Saint Peter's In 1606, Pope Paul V (r. 1605–1621) commissioned CARLO MADERNO (1556–1629) to complete the centurylong project to rebuild Saint Peter's, the symbolic seat of the papacy and the emblem of Roman Catholicism. Because Maderno had to match the new facade (FIG. **10-2**) to the preexisting core of an incomplete building, he did not have the luxury of formulating a totally new concept for Saint Peter's. Maderno's facade nonetheless embodies the design principles of early Italian Baroque architecture. The rhythm of vigorously projecting

10-2 CARLO MADERNO, facade of Saint Peter's (looking west), Vatican City, Rome, Italy, 1606–1612.

Maderno's facade embodies the design principles of early Baroque architecture. The rhythm of columns and pilasters mounts dramatically toward the emphatically stressed central section.

columns and pilasters mounts dramatically toward the emphatically stressed pediment-capped central section. The recessed niches, which contain statues and create pockets of shadow, heighten the sculptural effect. The two outer bays with bell towers were not part of Maderno's original design, however. Had the facade been constructed according to the architect's concept, it would have exhibited greater verticality and visual coherence.

Behind the facade, Maderno's Saint Peter's also departed from the 16th-century plans of Bramante and Michelangelo (FIG. 9-14). Paul V asked Maderno to add three nave bays to the earlier nucleus because the central plan was too closely associated with ancient temples, such as the Pantheon (FIG. 3-38). Further, the traditional longitudinal basilica plan reinforced the symbolic distinction between clergy and laity and also was much better suited for large congregations and processional ceremonies. Lengthening the nave, however, pushed the dome farther back from the facade, and all but destroyed the effect Michelangelo had planned—a structure pulled together and dominated by its dome (FIG. 9-15). When viewed at close range, the dome hardly emerges above the facade's soaring frontal plane. Seen from farther back (FIG. 10-2), it appears to have no drum. Visitors must move back quite a distance from the front (or fly over the church, FIG. 10-3) to see the dome and drum together.

Bernini's Piazza Old Saint Peter's had a large forecourt, or atrium (FIG. 4-3), in front of the church proper, and in the mid-17th century Gianlorenzo Bernini received the prestigious commission to construct a monumental colonnade-framed piazza (FIG. **10-3**) in front of Maderno's facade. Bernini designed a vast paved oval embraced by two colonnades joined to the new facade. Four rows of huge Tuscan columns make up the two colonnades, which terminate in classical temple fronts. The colonnades extend a dramatic gesture of embrace to all who enter the piazza, symbolizing the welcome the Roman Catholic Church gave its members during the Counter-Reformation. Bernini himself referred to his colonnades as the welcoming arms of the church. Beyond their symbolic resonance, the colonnades served visually to counteract the natural perspective and bring the facade closer to the viewer. Emphasizing the facade's height in this manner, Bernini subtly and effectively compensated for its extensive width. Thus, a Baroque transformation expanded the compact central designs of Bramante and Michelangelo into a dynamic complex of axially ordered elements that reach out and enclose spaces of vast dimension. By its sheer scale and theatricality, the complete Saint Peter's fulfilled the desire of the Counter-Reformation Church to present an awe-inspiring and authoritative vision of itself.

Baldacchino Prior to being invited to design Saint Peter's piazza, Bernini had won the commission to erect a gigantic bronze *baldacchino* (FIG. **10-4**) under Giacomo della Porta's dome. Completed between 1624 and 1633, the canopy-like structure (*baldacco* is Italian for "silk from Baghdad," such as

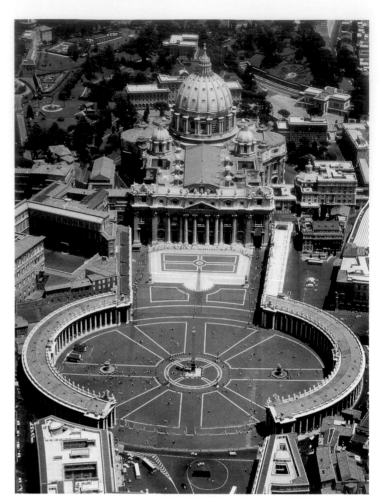

10-3 Aerial view of Saint Peter's (looking west), Vatican City, Rome, Italy. Piazza designed by GIANLORENZO BERNINI, 1656–1667.

The dramatic gesture of embrace Bernini's colonnade makes as worshipers enter Saint Peter's piazza symbolizes the welcome the Catholic Church wished to extend during the Counter-Reformation.

for a cloth canopy) stands about 100 feet high (the height of an eight-story building) and serves both functional and symbolic purposes. It marks the high altar and the tomb of Saint Peter, and it visually bridges human scale to the lofty vaults and dome above. Further, for worshipers entering the nave of the huge church, it provides a dramatic presence at the crossing. Its columns also create a visual frame for the elaborate sculpture representing the throne of Saint Peter (the Cathedra Petri) at the far end of Saint Peter's (FIG. 10-4, *rear*). On a symbolic level, the structure's decorative elements speak to the power of the Catholic Church and of Pope Urban VIII (r. 1623–1644). Partially fluted and wreathed with vines, the baldacchino's four spiral columns are Baroque versions of those of the ancient baldacchino over the same spot in Old Saint Peter's, thereby invoking the past to reinforce the primacy of the Roman Catholic Church in the 17th century. At the top of the columns, four colossal angels stand guard at the upper corners of the canopy. Forming the canopy's apex are four serpentine brackets that elevate the orb and the cross. Since the time of the emperor Constantine, builder of the original Saint Peter's basilica, the orb and the cross had served as symbols of the Church's triumph. The baldacchino also features

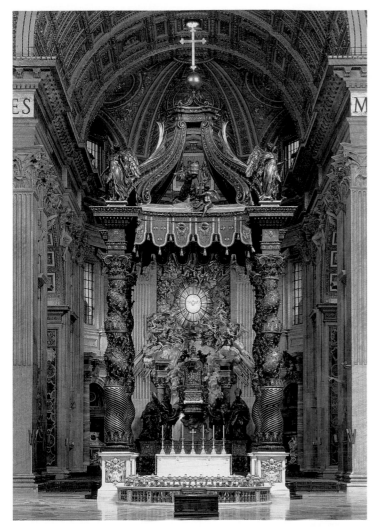

10-4 GIANLORENZO BERNINI, baldacchino (looking west), Saint Peter's, Vatican City, Rome, Italy, 1624–1633.

Bernini's baldacchino serves both functional and symbolic purposes. It marks Saint Peter's tomb and the high altar, and it visually bridges human scale to the lofty vaults and dome above.

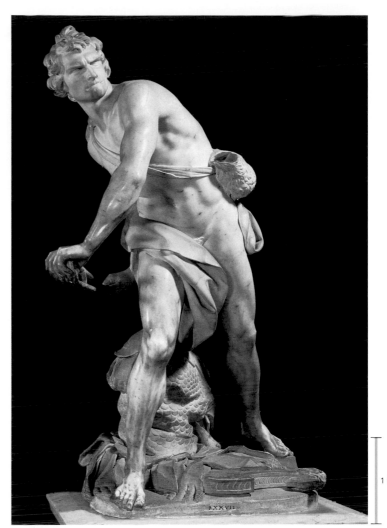

1 ft.

10-5 GIANLORENZO BERNINI, *David*, 1623. Marble, 5′ 7″ high. Galleria Borghese, Rome ◼

Bernini's sculptures are expansive and theatrical, and the element of time plays an important role in them. His emotion-packed *David* seems to be moving through both time and space.

numerous bees, symbols of Urban VIII's family, the Barberini. The structure effectively gives visual form to the triumph of Christianity and the papal claim to doctrinal supremacy.

David Although Bernini won fame as an architect, his international reputation rested primarily on his sculpture. The biographer Filippo Baldinucci (1625–1696) observed: "[No sculptor] manipulated marble with more facility and boldness. He gave his works a marvelous softness . . . making the marble, so to say, flexible."[1] Bernini's sculpture is expansive and theatrical, and the element of time usually plays an important role in it, as in the pronounced movement of the personified rivers—and the cascading water—in his Piazza Navona fountain (FIG. 10-1). An earlier masterwork is Bernini's *David* (FIG. **10-5**), which fundamentally differs from the Renaissance portrayals of the same subject by Donatello (FIG. 8-20) and Michelangelo (FIG. 9-9). Michelangelo portrayed David before his encounter with Goliath. Donatello depicted David after his triumph over the giant. Bernini chose to represent the combat itself and aimed to catch the

split second of maximum action. Bernini's David, his muscular legs widely and firmly planted, begins the violent, pivoting motion that will launch the stone from his sling. Unlike Myron, the fifth-century BCE Greek sculptor who froze his *Discus Thrower* (FIG. 2-34) at a fleeting moment of inaction, Bernini selected the most dramatic of an implied sequence of poses, requiring the viewer to think simultaneously of the continuum and of this tiny fraction of it. The suggested continuum imparts a dynamic burst of energy. *David* seems to be moving through time and through space, and the statue cannot be inscribed in a cylinder or confined in a niche. The action demands space around the statue, which is not self-sufficient in the Renaissance sense, as its pose and attitude direct attention beyond it to the unseen Goliath. Bernini's marble figure moves out into the space surrounding it. Further, the expression of intense concentration on David's face contrasts vividly with the classically placid visage of Donatello's biblical hero and is more emotionally charged even than Michelangelo's. The tension in David's face augments the dramatic impact of Bernini's sculpture.

Ecstasy of Saint Teresa Another work displaying the motion and emotion that are hallmarks of Italian Baroque art is Bernini's *Ecstasy of Saint Teresa* in the Cornaro chapel (FIG. **10-6**) of Santa Maria della Vittoria. The work exemplifies Bernini's refusal to limit his statues to firmly defined spatial settings. For this commission, Bernini marshaled the full capabilities of architecture, sculpture, and painting to charge the entire chapel with palpable tension. In Santa Maria della Vittoria, Bernini drew on the considerable knowledge of the theater he derived from writing plays and producing stage designs. The marble sculpture that serves as the chapel's focus depicts Saint Teresa of Avila (1515–1582), one of the great mystical saints of the Spanish Counter-Reformation. Her conversion occurred after the death of her father, when she fell into a series of trances, saw visions, and heard voices. Feeling a persistent pain, she attributed it to the fire-tipped arrow of divine love an angel had thrust repeatedly into her heart. In her writings, Saint Teresa described this experience as making her swoon in delightful anguish. In Bernini's hands, the entire Cornaro chapel became a theater for the production of this mystical drama. The niche in which it takes place appears as a shallow *proscenium* (the part of the stage in front of the curtain) crowned with a broken pediment and ornamented with polychrome marble. On either side of the chapel, sculpted relief portraits of the family of Cardinal Federico Cornaro (1579–1673) watch the heavenly drama unfold from choice balcony seats. Bernini depicted the saint in ecstasy, unmistakably a mingling of spiritual and physical passion, swooning back on a cloud, while the smiling angel aims his arrow. The sculptor's supreme technical virtuosity is evident in the visual differentiation in texture among the clouds, rough monk's cloth, gauzy material, smooth flesh, and feathery wings—all carved from the same white marble. Light from a hidden window of yellow glass pours down on golden rays suggesting the radiance of Heaven, whose painted representation covers the vault.

The passionate drama of Bernini's *Ecstasy of Saint Teresa* correlated with the ideas disseminated earlier by Ignatius Loyola (1491–1556), who founded the Jesuit order in 1534 and whom the Church canonized as Saint Ignatius in 1622. In his book *Spiritual Exercises,* Ignatius argued that the recreation of spiritual experiences in artworks would do much to increase devotion and piety. Thus, theatricality and

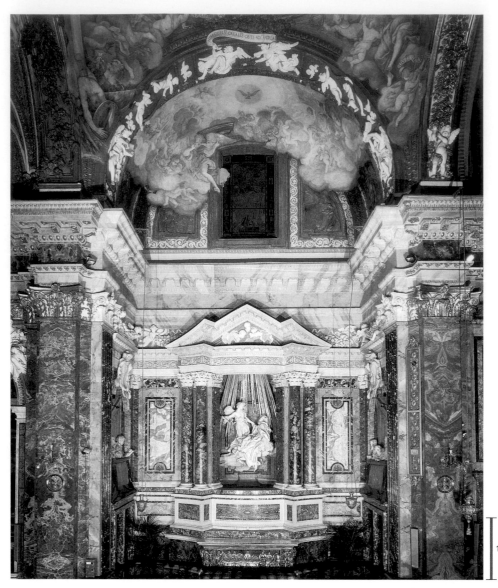

10 ft.

10-6 GIANLORENZO BERNINI, interior of the Cornaro chapel, Santa Maria della Vittoria, Rome, Italy, 1645–1652. *Ecstasy of Saint Teresa,* marble, 11′ 6″ high.

In the Cornaro chapel, Bernini, the quintessential Baroque artist, marshaled the full capabilities of architecture, sculpture, and painting to create an intensely emotional experience for worshipers.

sensory impact were useful vehicles for achieving Counter-Reformation goals (see "Religious Art in Counter-Reformation Italy," Chapter 9, page 269). Bernini was a devout Catholic, which undoubtedly contributed to his understanding of those goals. His inventiveness, technical skill, sensitivity to his patrons' needs, and energy made him the quintessential Italian Baroque artist.

Francesco Borromini As gifted as Bernini was as an architect, FRANCESCO BORROMINI (1599–1667) took Italian Baroque architecture to even greater dramatic heights. In San Carlo alle Quattro Fontane (Saint Charles at the Four Fountains; FIG. **10-7**), Borromini went much further than any of his predecessors or contemporaries in emphasizing a building's sculptural qualities. Although Maderno injected movement

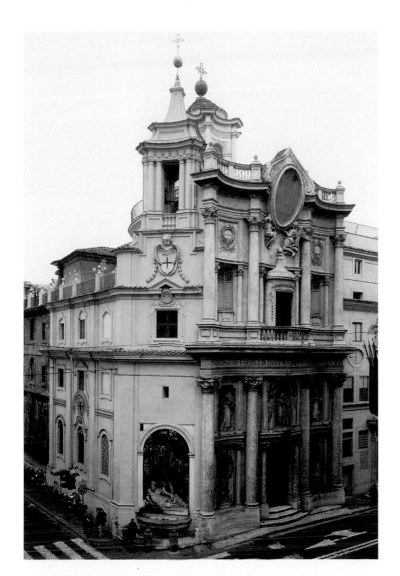

10-7 Francesco Borromini, San Carlo alle Quattro Fontane (looking south), Rome, Italy, 1638–1641.

Borromini rejected the notion that a church should have a flat frontis-piece. He set San Carlo's façade in undulating motion, creating a dynamic counterpoint of concave and convex elements.

into Saint Peter's facade (FIG. 10-2), Borromini set San Carlo's facade in undulating motion, creating a dynamic counterpoint of concave and convex elements. He enhanced the three-dimensional effect with deeply recessed niches. This facade is not the traditional flat frontispiece that defines a building's outer limits. It is a pulsating, engaging screen inserted between interior and exterior space, designed not to separate but to provide a fluid transition between the two. In fact, San Carlo has not one but two facades. The second, a narrow bay crowned with its own small tower, turns away from the main facade and, following the curve of the street, faces an intersection.

Inside, San Carlo is a hybrid of a Greek cross and an oval, with a long axis between entrance and apse. The side walls move in an undulating flow that reverses the facade's motion. Vigorously projecting columns define the space into which they protrude just as much as they accent the walls to which they are attached. Capping this molded interior space is a deeply coffered oval dome (FIG. **10-8**) that seems to float on the light entering through windows hidden in its base. Rich variations on the basic theme of the oval—dynamic relative to the static circle—create an interior that flows from entrance to altar, unimpeded by the segmentation so characteristic of Renaissance buildings.

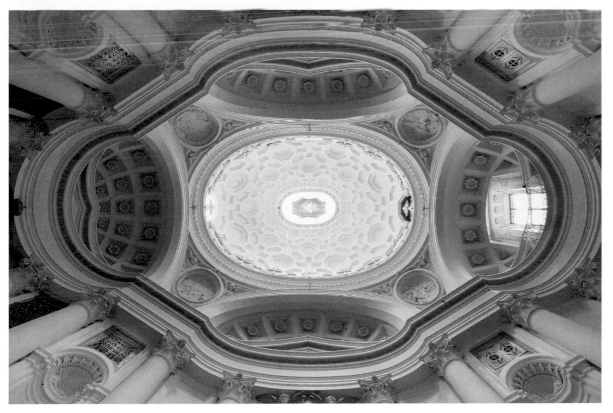

10-8 Francesco Borromini, view into the dome of San Carlo alle Quattro Fontane, Rome, Italy, 1638–1641.

In place of a traditional round dome, Borromini capped the interior of San Carlo with a deeply coffered oval dome that seems to float on the light entering through windows hidden in its base.

Painting

Although architecture and sculpture provided the most obvious vehicles for manipulating space and creating theatrical effects, painting continued to be an important art form in Baroque Italy.

Annibale Carracci One of the most renowned 17th-century Italian painters was ANNIBALE CARRACCI (1560–1609), who received much of his training at an art academy in his native Bologna founded by family members, among them his cousin Ludovico Carracci (1555–1619) and brother Agostino Carracci (1557–1602). The Bolognese academy was the first significant institution of its kind in the history of Western art. The Carracci established it on the premises that art can be taught—the basis of any academic philosophy of art—and that art instruction must include the classical and Renaissance traditions in addition to the study of anatomy and life drawing.

Annibale Carracci's most notable works are his frescoes (FIG. **10-9**) in the Palazzo Farnese in Rome. Cardinal Odoardo Farnese (1573–1626), a wealthy descendant of Pope Paul III, who built the palace, commissioned Carracci to decorate the ceiling of the palace's gallery to celebrate the wedding of the cardinal's brother. Appropriately, the title of its iconographic program is *Loves of the Gods*—interpretations of the varieties of earthly and divine love in classical mythology.

Carracci arranged the scenes in a format resembling framed easel paintings on a wall, but in the Farnese gallery the frescoes cover a shallow curved vault. The term for this type of simulation of easel painting for ceiling design is *quadro riportato* (transferred framed painting). Carracci made the quadro riportato format fashionable in Italy for more than a century. Flanking the framed pictures are polychrome seated nude youths, who turn their heads to gaze at the scenes around them, and standing Atlas figures painted to resemble marble statues. Carracci derived these motifs from the Sistine Chapel ceiling (FIG. 9-10), but he did not copy Michelangelo's figures. Notably, the chiaroscuro of the Farnese frescoes differs for the pictures and the figures surrounding them. Carracci modeled the figures inside the panels in an even light. In contrast, light from beneath illuminates the outside figures, as if they were tangible three-dimensional beings or statues illuminated by torches in the gallery below. In the crown of the vault, the long panel, *Triumph of Bacchus,* is an ingenious mixture of Raphael's drawing

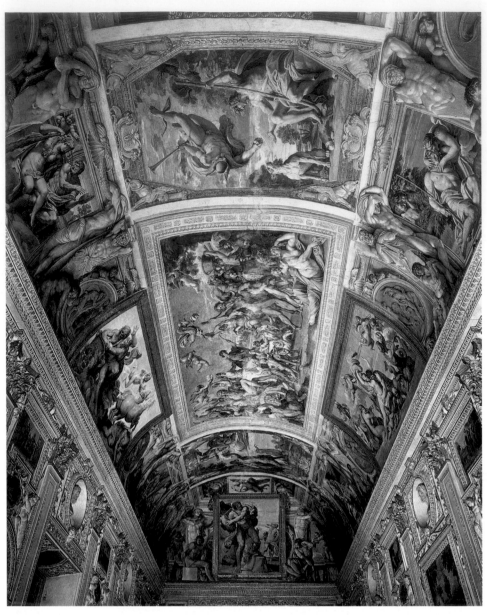

10-9 ANNIBALE CARRACCI, *Loves of the Gods,* ceiling frescoes in the gallery, Palazzo Farnese, Rome, Italy, 1597–1601. ◼◀

On the shallow curved vault of this large gallery in the Palazzo Farnese, Carracci arranged the mythological scenes in a quadro riportato format resembling easel paintings on a wall.

style and lighting and Titian's more sensuous and animated figures. Carracci succeeded in adjusting their authoritative styles to create something of his own—no easy achievement.

Caravaggio Michelangelo Merisi, known as CARAVAGGIO (1573–1610) after his northern Italian birthplace, developed a unique style that had tremendous influence throughout Europe. His outspoken disdain for the classical masters (probably more vocal than real) drew bitter criticism from many painters, one of whom denounced him as the "anti-Christ of painting." Giovanni Pietro Bellori, the most influential critic of the age and an admirer of Annibale Carracci, believed Caravaggio's refusal to emulate the models of his distinguished predecessors threatened the whole classical tradition of Italian painting that had reached its zenith in Raphael's work (see "Giovanni Pietro Bellori on Caravaggio," page 301). Yet despite this criticism and the problems in

Giovanni Pietro Bellori on Caravaggio

Giovanni Pietro Bellori (1613–1696), the leading biographer of Baroque artists, was an outspoken admirer of Renaissance classicism, especially the art of Raphael, and an ardent critic of Mannerism and of Caravaggio. In his *Vita* (*Life*) of Annibale Carracci, for example, Bellori praised "the divine Raphael . . . [whose art] raised its beauty to the summit, restoring it to the ancient majesty of . . . the Greeks and the Romans" and lamented that soon after, "artists, abandoning the study of nature, corrupted art with the *maniera*, that is to say, with the fantastic idea based on practice and not on imitation."*

Bellori characterized Caravaggio (FIGS. 10-10 and 10-11) as talented and widely imitated but condemned him for his rejection of classicism in favor of realism.

[Caravaggio] began to paint according to his own inclinations; not only ignoring but even despising the superb statuary of antiquity and the famous paintings of Raphael, he considered nature to be the only subject fit for his brush. As a result, when he was shown the most famous [ancient Greek] statues in order that he might use them as models, his only answer was to point toward a crowd of people, saying that nature had given him an abundance of masters. . . . [W]hen he came upon someone in town who pleased him he made no attempt to improve on the creations of nature †

[Caravaggio] claimed that he imitated his models so closely that he never made a single brushstroke that he called his own, but said rather that it was nature's. Repudiating all other rules, he considered the highest achievement not to be bound to art. For this innovation he was greatly acclaimed, and many talented and educated artists seemed compelled to follow him . . . Nevertheless he lacked *invenzione*, decorum, *disegno*, or any knowledge of the science of painting. The moment the model was taken from him, his hand and his mind became empty.‡

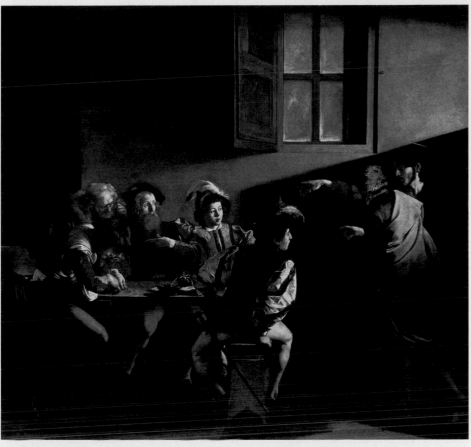

10-10 CARAVAGGIO, *Calling of Saint Matthew*, Contarelli chapel, San Luigi dei Francesi, Rome, ca. 1597–1601. Oil on canvas, 11' 1" × 11' 5". ◼

The stark contrast of light and dark was a key feature of Caravaggio's style. Here, Christ, cloaked in mysterious shadow, summons Levi the tax collector (Saint Matthew) to a higher calling.

1 ft.

*Giovanni Pietro Bellori, *Le vite de' pittori, scultori e architetti moderni* (Rome, 1672). Translated by Catherine Enggass, *The Lives of Annibale and Agostino Carracci by Giovanni Pietro Bellori* (University Park: Pennsylvania University Press, 1968), 5–6.
†Translated by Howard Hibbard, *Caravaggio* (New York: Harper & Row, 1983), 362.
‡*Ibid.*, 371–372.

Caravaggio's troubled life (police records are an important source of information about the artist), Caravaggio received many commissions, both public and private, and numerous painters paid him the supreme compliment of borrowing from his innovations. His influence on later artists, as much outside Italy as within, was immense. In his art, Caravaggio injected naturalism into both religion and the classics, reducing them to human dramas played out in the harsh and dingy settings of his time and place by unidealized figures he selected from the fields and the streets.

Calling of Saint Matthew The setting of Caravaggio's early masterpiece, *Calling of Saint Matthew* (FIG. **10-10**), is a modest tavern with unadorned walls. Into this mundane environment, cloaked in mysterious shadow and almost unseen, Jesus, identifiable initially only by his indistinct halo, enters from the right. With a commanding gesture, he summons Levi, the Roman tax collector, to a higher calling. The astonished Levi—his face illuminated by the beam of light emanating from an unspecified source above Jesus's head and outside the picture—points to himself in disbelief. Although Jesus's extended arm is reminiscent of the Lord's in *Creation of Adam* (FIG. 9-11), the position of his hand and wrist is similar to that of Adam's. This reference was highly appropriate because the Church considered Jesus the second Adam. Whereas Adam was responsible for the fall of humankind, Jesus is the vehicle of its redemption. The conversion of Levi (who became Matthew) brought his salvation.

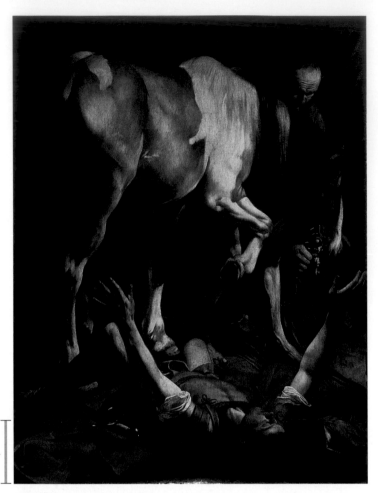

10-11 CARAVAGGIO, *Conversion of Saint Paul,* Cerasi chapel, Santa Maria del Popolo, Rome, ca. 1601. Oil on canvas, 7′ 6″ × 5′ 9″.

Caravaggio used perspective, chiaroscuro, and dramatic lighting to bring viewers into this painting's space and action, almost as if they were participants in Saint Paul's conversion to Christianity.

Conversion of Saint Paul A piercing ray of light illuminating a world of darkness and bearing a spiritual message is also a central feature of Caravaggio's *Conversion of Saint Paul* (FIG. **10-11**), which depicts the saint-to-be at the moment of his conversion, flat on his back with his arms thrown up. In the background, an old groom seems preoccupied with caring for the horse. At first inspection, little here suggests the momentous significance of the unfolding spiritual event. The viewer could be witnessing a mere stable accident, not a man overcome by a great miracle. To compel interest and involvement in Paul's conversion, Caravaggio used a perspective and a chiaroscuro intended to bring the viewer as close as possible to the scene's space and action, almost as if a participant. The low horizon line augments the sense of inclusion. Caravaggio designed *Conversion of Saint Paul* for its specific location in the church, positioned at the line of sight of a person standing at the chapel entrance. The sharply lit figures emerge from the dark of the background as if illuminated by the light from the chapel's windows. The lighting resembles that of a stage production analogous to the rays in Bernini's *Ecstasy of Saint Teresa* (FIG. **10-6**). The stark contrast of light and dark was a feature of Caravaggio's style that first shocked and then fascinated his contemporaries. Art historians call Caravaggio's use of dark settings enveloping their occupants *tenebrism,* from the Italian word *tenebroso,* or "shadowy" manner. In Caravaggio's work, tenebrism contributed greatly to the essential meaning of his pictures. In *Conversion of Saint Paul,* the dramatic spotlight shining down upon the fallen Paul is the light of divine revelation converting him to Christianity.

Artemisia Gentileschi Caravaggio's combination of naturalism and drama appealed both to patrons and artists, and he had many followers. Among them was the most celebrated woman artist of her era, ARTEMISIA GENTILESCHI (ca. 1593–1653), whose father Orazio (1563–1639), her teacher, was himself strongly influenced by Caravaggio. The daughter's successful career, pursued in Florence, Venice, Naples, and Rome, helped disseminate Caravaggio's manner throughout Italy. Gentileschi often painted narratives involving a heroic woman, for example, the biblical Judith slaying the Assyrian general Holofernes, enemy of the Israelites. Her most unusual work, but one of her best, is an allegory of *Painting* (*La Pittura;* FIG. **10-12**). Most art historians believe the painting, which was in the collection of the English king Charles I (r. 1625–1649) at the time of his execution in 1649, is a self-portrait.

Gentileschi's personified image of *Painting* as a woman closely follows the prescription for representing *La Pittura* in a widely circulated handbook by Cesare Ripa (d. 1622) called *Iconologia,* published in 1593. He describes *La Pittura* as a beautiful woman with disheveled hair painting with her brush in one hand and holding her palette in the other. She wears a gold chain with a pendant in the form of a mask, because masks imitate faces and painting is the art of imitation. The chain symbolizes the continuous linkage of master to pupil from generation to generation. Gentileschi represented *La Pittura* actively engaged in her craft, seen from her left side. The viewer's eye follows the line of her left arm through the curve of her shoulders and right arm to her right hand, the instrument of artistic genius. It is noteworthy that the canvas in this painting is blank. This is not a self-portrait of the artist at work on a specific painting but a portrait of Gentileschi as *Painting* herself.

In almost all Renaissance and Baroque self-portraits (for example, FIG. 9-36), the artist gazes at the viewer. The frontal view not only provides the fullest view of the artist's features, but it is also the easiest to paint because the artist needs only to look in a mirror in order to record his or her features. To create this self-portrait, however, Gentileschi had to set up two mirrors in order to paint her likeness from an angle, a highly original break from tradition and an assertion of her supreme skill in a field dominated by men (see "The Letters of Artemisia Gentileschi," page 303).

Fra Andrea Pozzo Inspired by the Sistine Chapel (FIG. 9-10), many Italian painters created ceiling decorations for churches and palaces. A master of this genre was FRA ANDREA POZZO (1642–1709), a lay brother of the Jesuit order and an expert on perspective, about which he wrote an influential treatise. Pozzo designed and executed the vast ceiling fresco *Glorification of Saint Ignatius* (FIG. **10-13**) for Sant'Ignazio, a prominent Counter-Reformation church because of its dedication to the

The Letters of Artemisia Gentileschi

Artemisia Gentileschi (FIG. 10-12) was the most renowned woman painter in Europe during the first half of the 17th century and the first woman ever admitted to membership in Florence's Accademia del Disegno. In addition to scores of paintings created for wealthy patrons, among them the king of England and the grand duke of Tuscany, Gentileschi left behind 28 letters, some of which reveal that she believed patrons treated her differently because of her gender. Two 1649 letters written in Naples to Don Antonio Ruffo (1610–1678) in Messina make her feelings explicit.

I fear that before you saw the painting you must have thought me arrogant and presumptuous. . . . [I]f it were not for Your Most Illustrious Lordship . . . I would not have been induced to give it for one hundred and sixty, because everywhere else I have been I was paid one hundred *scudi* per figure. . . . You think me pitiful, because a woman's name raises doubts until her work is seen.*

As for my doing a drawing and sending it, [tell the gentleman who wishes to know the price for a painting that] I have made a solemn vow never to send my drawings because people have cheated me. In particular, just today I found myself [in the situation] that, having done a drawing of souls in Purgatory for the Bishop of St. Gata, he, in order to spend less, commissioned another painter to do the painting using my work. If I were a man, I can't imagine it would have turned out this way, because when the concept has been realized and defined with lights and darks, and established by means of planes, the rest is a trifle.†

10-12 ARTEMISIA GENTILESCHI, *Self-Portrait as the Allegory of Painting*, ca. 1638–1639. Oil on canvas, 3' 2⅞" × 2' 5⅝". Royal Collection, Kensington Palace, London. ◼◀

Gentileschi here portrayed herself in the guise of *La Pittura* (*Painting*) with brush and palette. To paint a self-portrait from the side, Gentileschi had to set up a pair of mirrors to record her features.

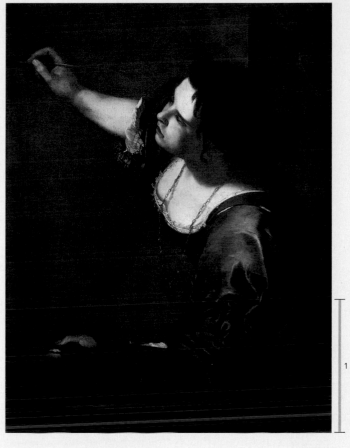

1 ft.

*Letter dated January 30, 1649. Translated by Mary D. Garrard, *Artemisia Gentileschi: The Image of the Female Hero in Italian Baroque Art* (Princeton, N.J.: Princeton University Press, 1989), 390.
†Letter dated November 13, 1649, ibid., 397–398.

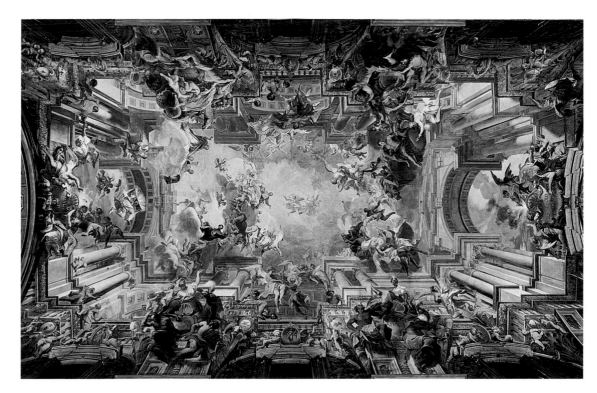

10-13 FRA ANDREA POZZO, *Glorification of Saint Ignatius*, ceiling fresco in the nave of Sant'Ignazio, Rome, Italy, 1691–1694.

By merging real and painted architecture, Pozzo created the illusion that the vaulted ceiling of Sant'Ignazio has been lifted off and the nave opens to Heaven above the worshipers' heads.

founder of the Jesuit order. The Jesuits played a major role in Catholic education and sent legions of missionaries to the New World and Asia. In *Glorification of Saint Ignatius,* Pozzo created the illusion of Heaven opening up above the congregation. To accomplish this, the artist painted an extension of the church's architecture into the vault so the roof seems to be lifted off. As Heaven and Earth commingle, Christ receives Saint Ignatius in the presence of figures personifying the four corners of the world. A disk in the nave floor marks the spot the viewer should stand to gain the whole perspective illusion. For worshipers looking up from this point, the vision is complete. They find themselves in the presence of the heavenly and spiritual.

The effectiveness of Italian Baroque religious art depended on the drama and theatricality of individual images, as well as on the interaction and fusion of architecture, sculpture, and painting. Sound enhanced this experience. Architects designed churches with acoustical effect in mind, and, in an Italian Baroque church filled with music, the power of both image and sound must have been immensely moving. Through simultaneous stimulation of both the senses of sight and hearing, the faithful might well have been transported into a trancelike state that would, indeed, as the great English poet John Milton (1608–1674) eloquently stated in *Il Penseroso* (1631), "bring all Heaven before [their] eyes."[2]

SPAIN

During the 16th century, Spain had established itself as an international power. The Habsburg kings had built a dynastic state encompassing Portugal, part of Italy, the Netherlands, and extensive areas of the New World. By the beginning of the 17th century, however, the Habsburg Empire was struggling, and although Spain mounted an aggressive effort during the Thirty Years' War, by 1660 the imperial age of the Spanish Habsburgs was over. In part, the demise of the Habsburg Empire was due to economic woes. The military campaigns of Philip III (r. 1598–1621) and his son Philip IV (r. 1621–1665) waged during the Thirty Years' War were costly and led to higher taxes. The increasing tax burden placed on Spanish subjects in turn incited revolts and civil war in Catalonia and Portugal in the 1640s, further straining an already fragile economy. Nevertheless, both Philip III and Philip IV continued to spend lavishly on art.

In a country passionately committed to Catholic orthodoxy, Spanish Baroque artists, like their counterparts in Counter-Reformation Italy, sought ways to move viewers and to encourage greater devotion and piety. Particularly appealing in this regard were scenes of death and martyrdom, which provided artists with opportunities both to depict extreme emotion and to elicit passionate feelings in viewers. Spain prided itself on its saints—Saint Teresa of Avila (FIG. 10-6) and Saint Ignatius Loyola (FIG. 10-13) were both Spanish-born—and martyrdom scenes surfaced frequently in Spanish Baroque art.

Francisco de Zurbarán One prominent Spanish Baroque painter of religious works was FRANCISCO DE ZURBARÁN (1598–1664), whose primary patrons were rich monastic

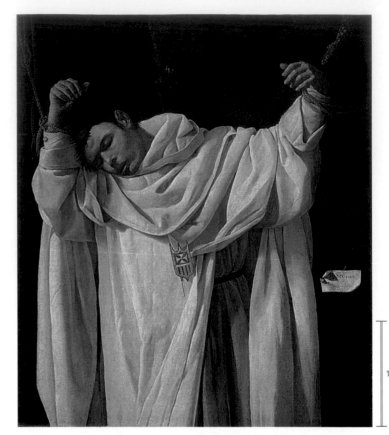

10-14 FRANCISCO DE ZURBARÁN, *Saint Serapion,* 1628. Oil on canvas, 3′ 11½″ × 3′ 4¾″. Wadsworth Atheneum, Hartford (Ella Gallup Sumner and Mary Catlin Sumner Collection Fund).

The light shining on Serapion calls attention to his tragic death and increases the painting's dramatic impact. The monk's coarse features label him as common, evoking empathy from a wide audience.

orders. Many of his paintings are quiet and contemplative, appropriate for prayer. Zurbarán painted *Saint Serapion* (FIG. 10-14) as a devotional image for the funerary chapel of the monastic Order of Mercy in Seville. The saint, who participated in the Third Crusade of 1196, suffered martyrdom while preaching the Gospel to Muslims. According to one account, the monk's captors tied him to a tree, and then tortured and decapitated him. The Order of Mercy dedicated itself to self-sacrifice, and Serapion's membership in this order amplified the resonance of Zurbarán's painting. In *Saint Serapion* the monk emerges from a dark background and fills the foreground. The bright light shining on him calls attention to the saint's tragic death and increases the dramatic impact of the image. In the background are two barely visible tree branches. A small note next to the saint identifies him. The coarse features of the Spanish monk label him as common, no doubt evoking empathy from a wide audience.

Diego Velázquez The foremost Spanish painter of the Baroque age—and the greatest beneficiary of royal patronage—was DIEGO VELÁZQUEZ (1599–1660). Trained in Seville, Velázquez was quite young when he came to the attention of Philip IV, who, struck by the artist's immense talent, named him chief court painter and palace chamberlain. With the exception of two extended trips to Italy and a few excursions, Velázquez remained in Madrid for the rest of his life. His

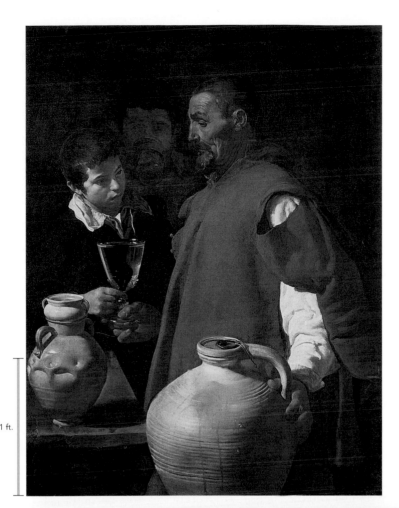

1 ft.

10-15 DIEGO VELÁZQUEZ, *Water Carrier of Seville*, ca. 1619. Oil on canvas, 3' 5½" × 2' 7½". Victoria & Albert Museum, London.

In this early work—a genre scene that seems to convey a deeper significance—the contrast of darks and lights and the plebeian nature of the figures reveal Velázquez's indebtedness to Caravaggio.

close relationship with Philip IV and his high office as chamberlain gave him prestige and a rare opportunity to fulfill the promise of his genius.

An early work, *Water Carrier of Seville* (FIG. **10-15**), painted when Velázquez was only about 20 years old, already reveals his impressive command of the painter's craft. In this genre scene that seems to carry a deeper significance, Velázquez rendered the figures with clarity and dignity, and his careful depiction of the water jugs in the foreground, complete with droplets of water, adds to the scene's credibility. As in Zurbarán's *Saint Serapion* (FIG. **10-14**), the plebeian nature of the figures and the contrast of darks and lights reveal the influence of Caravaggio, whose work Velázquez had studied.

Las Meninas After an extended visit to Rome from 1648 to 1651, Velázquez returned to Spain and, in 1656, painted his greatest work, *Las Meninas* (*The Maids of Honor*; FIG. **10-16**). The painter represented himself in his studio in the Alcázar, the royal residence in Madrid. The young Infanta (Princess) Margarita appears in the foreground with her two maids-in-waiting, her favorite dwarfs, and a large dog. In the middle ground are a woman in widow's attire and a male escort. In the background, a chamberlain stands in a brightly lit open doorway. Scholars have been able to identify everyone in the room, including the two meninas and the dwarfs.

Las Meninas is noteworthy for its visual and narrative complexity. Indeed, art historians have yet to agree on any particular reading or interpretation. A central issue has been what, exactly, is taking place in *Las Meninas*. What is Velázquez depicting on the huge canvas in front of him? He may be painting this very picture—an informal image of the infanta and her entourage. Alternately, Velázquez may be painting a portrait of King Philip IV and Queen Mariana, whose reflections appear in the mirror on the far wall. If so, that would suggest the presence of the king and queen in the viewer's space, outside the confines of the picture. Other scholars have proposed that the mirror image is not a reflection of the royal couple standing in Velázquez's studio but a reflection of the portrait the artist is in the process of painting on the canvas before him.

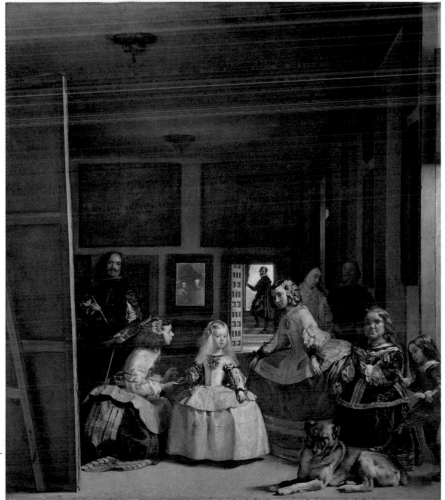

1 ft.

10-16 DIEGO VELÁZQUEZ, *Las Meninas* (*The Maids of Honor*), 1656. Oil on canvas, 10' 5" × 9'. Museo del Prado, Madrid. ◼◀

Velázquez intended this huge and complex work, with its cunning contrasts of real, mirrored, and picture spaces, to elevate both himself and the profession of painting in the eyes of Philip IV.

More generally, *Las Meninas* is Velázquez's attempt to elevate both himself and his profession. Throughout his career, Velázquez hoped to be ennobled by royal appointment to membership in the ancient and illustrious Order of Santiago (Saint James). Because he lacked a sufficiently noble lineage, he gained entrance only with difficulty at the very end of his life, and then only through the pope's dispensation. In the painting, Velázquez wears the order's red cross on his doublet, painted there, legend says, by Philip IV. In all likelihood, Velázquez painted it. In the artist's mind, *Las Meninas* might have embodied the idea of the great king visiting his studio, as Alexander the Great visited the studio of the painter Apelles. The figures in the painting all appear to acknowledge the royal presence. Placed among them in equal dignity is Velázquez, face-to-face with his sovereign.

The location of the completed painting reinforced this act of looking—of seeing and being seen. *Las Meninas* hung in Philip IV's personal office. Thus, although occasional visitors admitted to the king's private quarters may have seen this painting, Philip was the primary audience. Each time he stood before the canvas, he again participated in the work as the probable subject of Velázquez's painting within the painting and as the object of the figures' gazes. In *Las Meninas,* Velázquez elevated the art of painting, in the person of the painter, to the highest status. The king's presence enhanced this status—either in person as the viewer of *Las Meninas* or as a reflected image in the painting itself. The paintings that appear in *Las Meninas* further reinforced this celebration of the painter's craft. On the wall above the doorway and mirror, two faintly recognizable pictures are copies of paintings by Peter Paul Rubens (discussed next). The paintings depict the immortal gods as the source of art. Ultimately, Velázquez sought ennoblement not for himself alone but for his art as well.

Las Meninas is extraordinarily complex visually. Velázquez's optical report of the event, authentic in every detail, pictorially summarizes the various kinds of images in their different levels and degrees of reality. He portrayed the realities of image on canvas, of mirror image, of optical image, and of the two painted images. This work—with its cunning contrasts of real spaces, mirrored spaces, picture spaces, and pictures within pictures—itself appears to have been taken from a large mirror reflecting the entire scene. This would mean the artist did not paint the princess and her suite as the main subjects of *Las Meninas* but himself in the process of painting them. *Las Meninas* is a pictorial summary and a commentary on the essential mystery of the visual world, as well as on the ambiguity that results when different states or levels interact or are juxtaposed.

Velázquez employed several devices to achieve these results. The extension of the composition's pictorial depth in both directions is noteworthy. The open doorway and its ascending staircase lead the eye beyond the artist's studio, and the mirror and the outward glances of several of the figures incorporate the viewer's space into the picture as well. (Compare how the mirror in Jan van Eyck's *Giovanni Arnolfini and His Wife* [FIG. 8-6] similarly incorporates the area in front of the canvas into the picture, although less obviously and without a comparable extension of space beyond the rear wall of the room.) Velázquez also masterfully observed and represented form and shadow. Instead of putting lights abruptly beside darks, following Caravaggio, Velázquez allowed a great number of intermediate values of gray to come between the two extremes. His matching of tonal gradations approached effects that were later discovered in the photography age.

FLANDERS

In the 16th century, the Netherlands had come under the crown of Habsburg Spain when Emperor Charles V retired, leaving the Spanish kingdoms, their Italian and American possessions, and the Netherlandish provinces to his only legitimate son, Philip II (r. 1556–1598). (Charles bestowed his imperial title and German lands to his brother.) Philip's repressive measures against Protestants led the northern provinces to break from Spain and to set up the Dutch Republic. The southern provinces remained under Spanish control, and they retained Catholicism as their official religion. The political distinction between modern Holland and Belgium more or less reflects this original separation, which in the 17th century signaled not only religious but also artistic differences. The Baroque art of Flanders (the Spanish Netherlands) retained close connections to the Baroque art of Catholic Europe, whereas the Dutch schools of painting developed their own subjects and styles.

Peter Paul Rubens The greatest 17th-century Flemish painter was PETER PAUL RUBENS (1577–1640), who built on the innovations of the Italian Renaissance and Baroque masters to formulate the first truly pan-European painting style. Rubens's art is an original and powerful synthesis of the manners of many painters, especially Michelangelo, Titian, Carracci, and Caravaggio. His style had wide appeal, and his influence was international. Among the most learned individuals of his time, Rubens possessed an aristocratic education and a courtier's manner, diplomacy, and tact, which, with his facility for language, made him the associate of princes and scholars. He became court painter to the dukes of Mantua, friend of King Philip IV (r. 1621–1665) of Spain and his adviser on collecting art, painter to Charles I (r. 1625–1649) of England and Marie de' Medici (1573–1642) of France, and permanent court painter to the Spanish governors of Flanders. Rubens also won the confidence of his royal patrons in matters of state, and they often entrusted him with diplomatic missions of the highest importance. Rubens employed scores of associates and apprentices to produce a steady stream of paintings for an international clientele. In addition, he functioned as an art dealer, buying and selling contemporary artworks and classical antiquities. His many enterprises made him a rich man, able to afford a magnificent townhouse in Antwerp and a castle in the countryside.

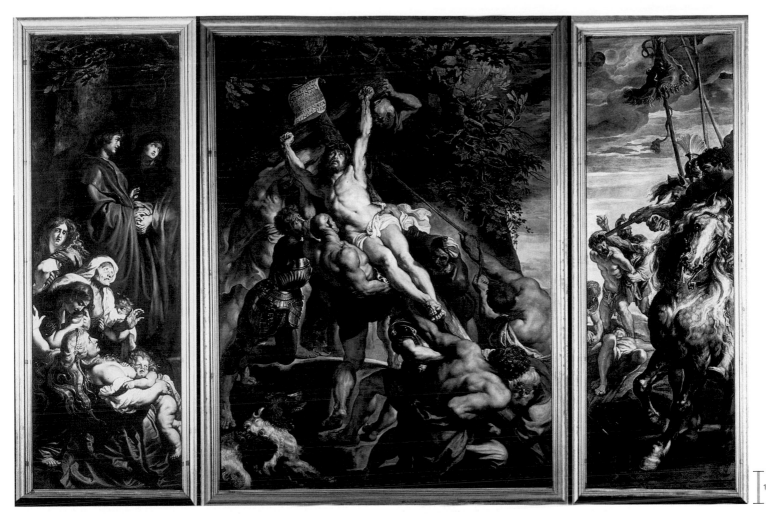

1 ft.

10-17 PETER PAUL RUBENS, *Elevation of the Cross*, from Saint Walburga, Antwerp, 1610. Oil on wood, center panel 15′ 1⅞″ × 11′ 1½″, each wing 15′ 1⅞″ × 4′ 11″. Antwerp Cathedral, Antwerp.

In this triptych, Rubens explored foreshortened anatomy and violent action. The whole composition seethes with a power that comes from heroic exertion. The tension is emotional as well as physical.

Elevation of the Cross Rubens departed Flanders for Italy in 1600 and remained there until 1608. During these years, he laid the foundations of his style. Shortly after returning home, he painted *Elevation of the Cross* (FIG. **10-17**) for Saint Walburga in Antwerp. The triptych reveals his careful study of the works of Michelangelo and Caravaggio, as well as ancient statuary. In a treatise he wrote in Latin—*De imitatione statuarum* (*On the Imitation of Statues*)—Rubens stated: "I am convinced that in order to achieve the highest perfection one needs a full understanding of the [ancient] statues, indeed a complete absorption in them; but one must make judicious use of them and before all avoid the effect of stone."[3] *Elevation of the Cross* provided Rubens with the opportunity to depict heavily muscled men in unusual poses straining to lift the heavy cross with Christ's body nailed to it. Here, as in his *Lion Hunt* (FIG. I-12), Rubens, deeply impressed by Michelangelo's twisting sculptured and painted figures, showed his prowess in representing foreshortened anatomy and the contortions of violent action. Rubens placed the body of Christ on the cross as a diagonal that cuts dynamically across the picture while inclining back into it. The whole composition

seethes with a power that comes from strenuous exertion, from elastic human sinew taut with effort. The tension is emotional as well as physical, as reflected not only in Christ's face but also in the features of his followers. Bright highlights and areas of deep shadow inspired by Caravaggio's tenebrism, hallmarks of Rubens's work at this stage of his career, enhance the drama. He later developed a much subtler coloristic style.

Marie de' Medici Rubens's interaction with royalty and aristocrats provided him with an understanding of the ostentation and spectacle of Baroque (particularly Italian) art that appealed to the wealthy and privileged. Rubens, the born courtier, reveled in the pomp and majesty of royalty. Likewise, those in power embraced the lavish spectacle that served the Catholic Church so well in Italy. The magnificence and splendor of Baroque imagery reinforced the authority and right to rule of the highborn. Among Rubens's royal patrons was Marie de' Medici, a member of the famous Florentine house and widow of Henry IV (r. 1589–1610), the first Bourbon king of France. She commissioned Rubens to

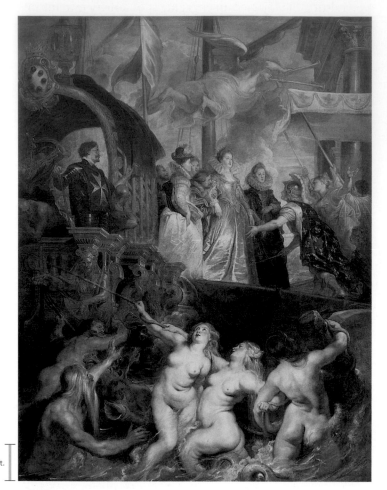

10-18 PETER PAUL RUBENS, *Arrival of Marie de' Medici at Marseilles,* 1622–1625. Oil on canvas, 12' 11½" × 9' 7". Musée du Louvre, Paris.

Rubens painted 21 large canvases glorifying Marie de' Medici's career. In this historical-allegorical picture of robust figures in an opulent setting, the sea and sky rejoice at the queen's arrival in France.

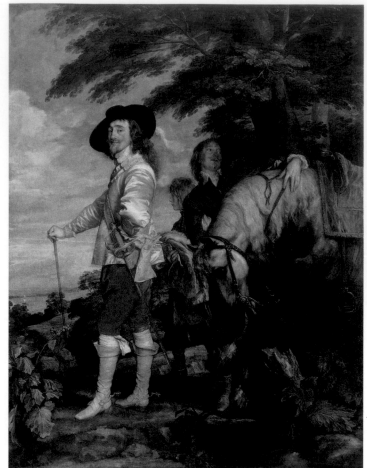

10-19 ANTHONY VAN DYCK, *Charles I Dismounted,* ca. 1635. Oil on canvas, 8' 11" × 6' 11½". Musée du Louvre, Paris.

Van Dyck specialized in court portraiture. In this painting, he depicted the absolutist monarch Charles I at a sharp angle so that the king, a short man, appears to be looking down at the viewer.

paint a series of huge canvases memorializing and glorifying her career. Between 1622 and 1626, Rubens, working with amazing creative energy, produced 21 huge historical-allegorical pictures designed to hang in the queen's new palace, the Luxembourg, in Paris.

In *Arrival of Marie de' Medici at Marseilles* (FIG. **10-18**), Marie disembarks after the sea voyage from Italy. A personification of France, draped in a cloak decorated with the royal fleur-de-lis (compare FIG. 10-31) welcomes her. The sea and sky rejoice at the queen's safe arrival. Neptune and the Nereids (daughters of the sea god Nereus) salute her, and the winged and trumpeting personified Fame swoops overhead. Conspicuous in the galley's opulently carved stern-castle, under the Medici coat of arms, stands the imperious commander of the vessel, the only immobile figure in the composition. In black and silver, this figure makes a sharp accent amid the swirling tonality of ivory, gold, and red. Rubens enriched the surfaces with a decorative splendor that pulls the whole composition together. The audacious vigor that customarily enlivens the artist's figures, beginning with the monumental, twisting sea creatures, vibrates through the entire design.

Anthony Van Dyck The most famous of Rubens's Flemish successors was ANTHONY VAN DYCK (1599–1641), who was an assistant in the master's studio. Early on, the younger man, unwilling to be overshadowed by Rubens's undisputed stature, left his native Antwerp for Genoa and then London, where he became court portraitist to Charles I. Although Van Dyck created dramatic compositions of high quality, his specialty became the portrait. In one of his finest works, *Charles I Dismounted* (FIG. **10-19**), the ill-fated English king stands with two attendants in a landscape with the Thames River in the background. The portrait is a stylish image of relaxed authority, as if the king is out for a casual ride in the park, but no one can mistake the regal poise and the air of absolute authority that Charles's Parliament resented and was soon to rise against. Van Dyck's placement of the monarch is exceedingly artful. He stands off center but balances the composition with a single keen glance at the viewer. Van Dyck even managed to portray Charles I, who was of short stature, in a position to look down on the observer. Van Dyck's elegant style resounded in English portrait painting well into the 19th century.

DUTCH REPUBLIC

With the founding of the Bank of Amsterdam in 1609, Amsterdam emerged as the financial center of the Continent. The Dutch economy also benefited enormously from the country's expertise on the open seas, which facilitated establishing far-flung colonies. By 1650, Dutch trade routes extended to the Americas, the west coast of Africa, China, Japan, Southeast Asia, and much of the Pacific. Due to this prosperity and in the absence of an absolute ruler, political power increasingly passed into the hands of an urban patrician class of merchants and manufacturers, especially in cities such as Amsterdam, Haarlem, and Delft. They in turn emerged as the most important sources of art commissions. As a result of this shift in patronage, and consistent with the Calvinist rejection of most religious art, 17th-century Dutch art centered on genre scenes, landscapes, portraits of middle-class men and women, and still lifes.

Frans Hals The leading painter in Haarlem was FRANS HALS (ca. 1581–1666), who made portraits his specialty. Portrait artists traditionally relied heavily on convention—for example, specific poses, settings, attire, and furnishings—to convey a sense of the sitter. Because the subject was usually someone of status or note, such as a pope, king, duchess, or wealthy banker, the artist's goal was to produce an image appropriate to the subject's station in life. With the increasing numbers of Dutch middle-class patrons, portrait painting became more challenging. The Calvinists shunned ostentation, instead wearing subdued and dark clothing with little variation or decoration, and the traditional conventions became inappropriate and thus unusable. Despite these difficulties, or perhaps because of them, Hals produced lively portraits that seem far more relaxed than traditional formulaic portraiture. He injected an engaging spontaneity into his images and conveyed the individuality of his sitters as well. His manner of execution intensified the casualness, immediacy, and intimacy in his paintings. Because the touch of Hals's brush was as light and fleeting as the moment he captured the pose, the figure, the highlights on clothing, and the facial expression all seem instantaneously created.

Hals's most ambitious paintings were group portraits, which multiplied the challenges of depicting a single sitter. *Archers of Saint Hadrian* (FIG. **10-20**) depicts the members of one of the many Dutch civic militia groups that claimed credit for liberating the Dutch Republic from Spain. As other companies did, the Archers met on their saint's feast day in dress uniform for a grand banquet. These events often included sitting for a group portrait, giving Hals the opportunity to attack the problem of how to represent each militia member satisfactorily yet retain action and variety in the composition. Whereas earlier group portraits in the Netherlands were rather ordered and regimented images, Hals sought to enliven his depictions. In *Archers of Saint Hadrian,* each man is both part of the troop and an individual with a distinct physiognomy. Further, the sitters' movements and moods vary markedly. Some engage the viewer directly. Others look away or at a companion. Some are stern, others animated. Each archer is equally visible and clearly recognizable. The uniformity of attire—black military dress, white ruffs, and sashes—did not deter Hals from injecting spontaneity into the work. Indeed, he used those elements to create a lively rhythm extending throughout the composition and energizing the portrait. The impromptu effect—the preservation of every detail and fleeting facial expression—is, of course, the result of careful planning. Yet Hals's vivacious brush appears to have moved instinctively, directed by a plan in his mind but not traceable in any preparatory scheme on the canvas.

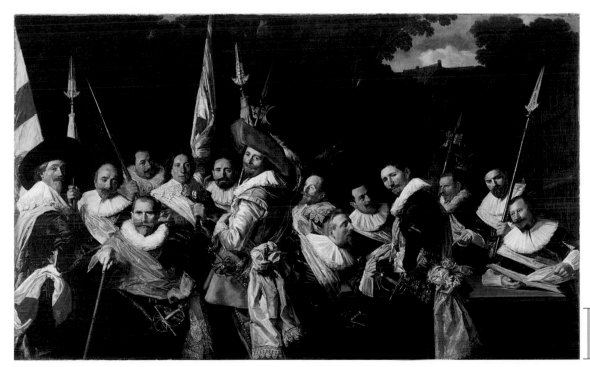

10-20 FRANS HALS, *Archers of Saint Hadrian,* ca. 1633. Oil on canvas, 6′ 9″ × 11′. Frans Halsmuseum, Haarlem.

In this brilliant composition, Hals succeeded in solving the problem of portraying each individual in a group portrait while retaining action and variety in the painting as a whole.

1 ft.

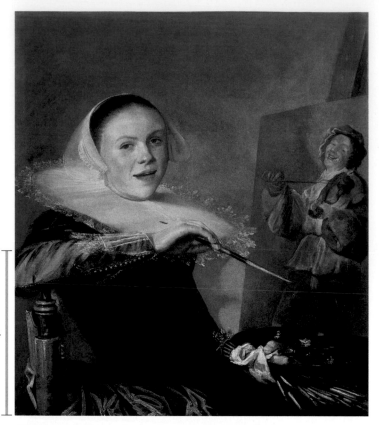

10-21 JUDITH LEYSTER, *Self-Portrait,* ca. 1630. Oil on canvas, 2′ 5¾″ × 2′ 1⅝″. National Gallery of Art, Washington, D.C. (gift of Mr. and Mrs. Robert Woods Bliss). ■❮

Although presenting herself as an artist specializing in genre scenes, Leyster wears elegant attire instead of a painter's smock, placing her socially as a member of a well-to-do family.

Judith Leyster Some of Hals's students developed thriving careers of their own as portraitists. One was JUDITH LEYSTER (1609–1660), whose *Self-Portrait* (FIG. **10-21**) is detailed, precise, and accurate, but also imbued with the spontaneity found in her master's works. In her portrait, Leyster succeeded at communicating a great deal about herself. She depicted herself as an artist, seated in front of a painting resting on an easel. The palette in her left hand and brush in her right announce the painting as her creation. She thus invites the viewer to evaluate her skill, which both the fiddler on the canvas and the image of herself demonstrate as considerable. Although she produced a wide range of paintings, including still lifes and floral pieces, her specialty was genre scenes such as the comic image seen on the easel. Leyster's quick smile and relaxed pose as she stops her work to meet the viewer's gaze reveal her self-assurance. Although presenting herself as an artist, Leyster did not depict herself wearing the traditional artist's smock (compare FIG. 10-23). Her elegant attire distinguishes her socially as a member of a well-to-do family, another important aspect of Leyster's identity.

Rembrandt van Rijn The foremost Dutch artist of the 17th century was REMBRANDT VAN RIJN (1606–1669), an undisputed genius and one of the greatest painters and print makers who ever lived. Born in Leiden, Rembrandt moved

around 1631 to Amsterdam, where he could attract a more extensive clientele. He quickly gained renown for his portraits, which delve deeply into the psyche and personality of his sitters. Like Hals, Rembrandt also produced memorable group portraits. The most famous is *The Company of Captain Frans Banning Cocq* (FIG. **10-22**), better known as *Night Watch*. This more commonly used title is a misnomer, however. The painting is not a nocturnal scene. The dark tonality today is the result of the varnish the artist used, which has darkened considerably over time. From the limited information available about the commission, it appears that Captain Frans Banning Cocq and his lieutenant, Willem van Ruytenburch, along with 16 members of their militia, contributed to Rembrandt's fee. *Night Watch* was one of six paintings by different artists commissioned by various groups around 1640 for the assembly and banquet hall of Amsterdam's new Musketeers' Hall. Unfortunately, in 1715, when city officials moved Rembrandt's painting to the town hall, they trimmed it on all sides. Even in its truncated form, *Night Watch* succeeds in capturing the excitement and frenetic activity of men preparing for a parade. Comparing this militia group portrait with Hals's *Archers of Saint Hadrian* (FIG. 10-20) reveals Rembrandt's inventiveness in enlivening what was, by then, becoming a conventional format for Dutch group portraits. Rather than present assembled men posed in orderly fashion, the younger artist chose to portray the company rushing about in the act of organizing themselves, thereby animating the image considerably. At the same time, Rembrandt managed to record the three most important stages of using a musket—loading, firing, and readying the weapon for reloading—details that must have pleased his patrons.

Rembrandt's use of light is among the hallmarks of his style. His pictorial method involved refining light and shade into finer and finer nuances until they blended with one another. Earlier painters' use of abrupt lights and darks gave way, in the work of artists such as Rembrandt and Velázquez (FIGS. 10-15 and 10-16), to gradation. Although these later artists sacrificed some of the dramatic effects of sharp chiaroscuro, a greater fidelity to actual appearances more than offset those sacrifices. This technique is closer to reality because the eye perceives light and dark not as static but as always subtly changing. In general, Renaissance artists represented forms and faces in a flat, neutral modeling light (even Leonardo's shading is of a standard kind). They represented the *idea* of light, rather than showed how humans perceive light. Artists such as Rembrandt discovered gradations of light and dark as well as degrees of differences in pose, in the movements of facial features, and in psychic states. They arrived at these differences optically, not conceptually or in terms of some ideal. Rembrandt found that by manipulating the direction, intensity, and distance of light and shadow, and by varying the surface texture with tactile brushstrokes, he could render subtle nuances of character and mood, both in individuals and whole scenes. He discovered for the modern world that variation of light and shade, subtly modulated, can be read as emotional differences. In the visible world,

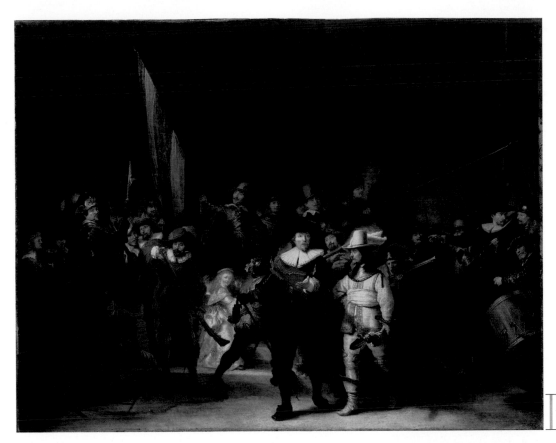

1 ft.

light, dark, and the wide spectrum of values between the two are charged with meanings and feelings that sometimes are independent of the shapes and figures they modify. The theater and the photographic arts have used these discoveries to great dramatic effect.

Self-Portrait Rembrandt's portraits reveal his complete understanding of what could be called the "psychology of light." Light and dark are not in conflict in his paintings. They are reconciled, merging softly and subtly to produce the visual equivalent of quietness. The prevailing mood of his portraits is one of tranquil meditation, of philosophical resignation, of musing recollection—indeed, a whole cluster of emotional tones heard only in silence. In the late *Self-Portrait* reproduced here (FIG. **10-23**), the light source outside the upper left of the painting bathes the artist's face in soft highlights, leaving the lower part of his body in shadow. Rembrandt depicted himself here as possessing dignity and strength, and the portrait serves as a summary of the many stylistic and professional concerns that occupied him throughout his career. Rembrandt's distinctive use of light is evident, as is the assertive brushwork suggesting his self-assurance. He presented himself as a working artist holding his brushes, palette, and maulstick and wearing his studio garb—a smock and painter's turban. The circles on the wall behind him may allude to a legendary sign of artistic virtuosity—the ability to draw a perfect circle freehand. Rembrandt's abiding interest in revealing the human soul emerges here in his careful focus on his expressive visage. His controlled use of light and the nonspecific setting contribute to this focus. Further, X-rays of the painting have revealed that Rembrandt

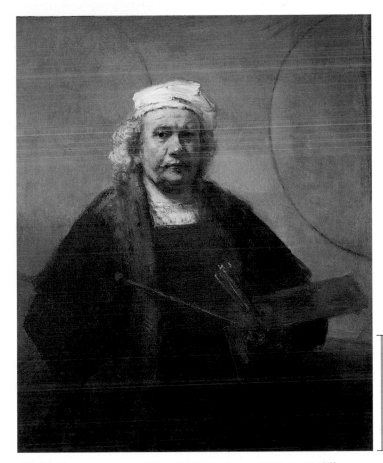

1 ft.

originally depicted himself in the act of painting. His final resolution, with the viewer's attention drawn to his face, produced a portrait not just of the artist but of the man as well.

Hundred-Guilder Print Many print makers adopted etching after its perfection early in the 17th century because the technique afforded greater freedom than engraving in drawing the design (see "Woodcuts, Engravings, and Etchings," Chapter 8, page 233). The etcher covers a copper plate with a layer of wax or varnish, and then incises the design into this surface with a pointed tool, exposing the metal below but not cutting into its surface. Next, the artist immerses the plate in acid, which etches, or eats away, the exposed parts of the metal, acting in the same way the burin does in engraving. The medium's softness gives etchers greater carving freedom than woodcutters and engravers have working directly in more resistant wood and metal. If Rembrandt had never painted, he still would be renowned, as he principally was in his lifetime, for his prints. Prints were a major source of income for Rembrandt, as they were for Albrecht Dürer (see Chapter 9), and he

often reworked the plates so they could be used to produce a new edition. This constant reworking was unusual within the context of 17th-century print-making practices.

Christ with the Sick around Him, Receiving the Children (FIG. **10-24**) is one of Rembrandt's most celebrated prints. Indeed, the title by which this work has been known since the early 18th century, *Hundred-Guilder Print*, refers to the high sale price it brought during Rembrandt's lifetime. Rembrandt produced the print using etching and engraving techniques. He suffused *Christ with the Sick* with a deep and abiding piety, presenting the viewer not the celestial triumph of the Catholic Church but the humanity and humility of Jesus. Christ appears in the center preaching compassionately to, and simultaneously blessing, the blind, the lame, and the young, who are spread throughout the composition in a dazzling array of standing, kneeling, and lying positions. Also present is a young man in elegant garments with his head in his hand, lamenting Christ's insistence that the wealthy need to give their possessions to the poor in order to gain entrance to Heaven. The tonal range of the print is remarkable. At the

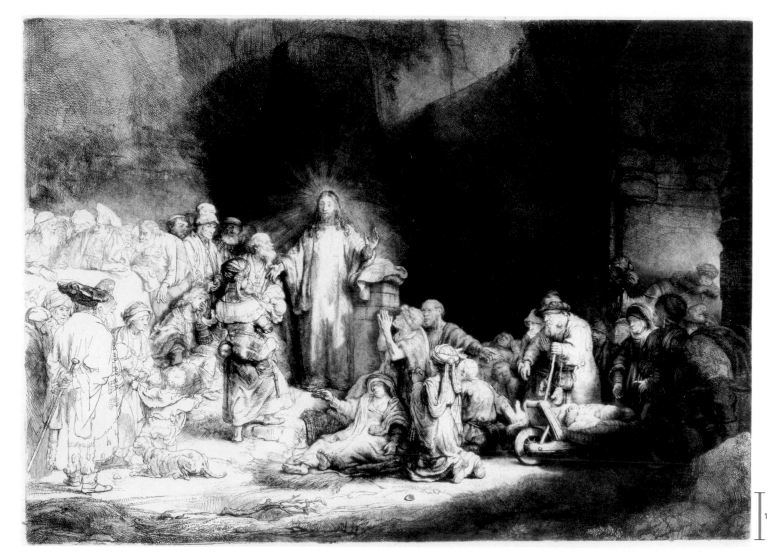

10-24 REMBRANDT VAN RIJN, *Christ with the Sick around Him, Receiving the Children* (*Hundred-Guilder Print*), ca. 1649. Etching, 11″ × 1′ 3¼″. Pierpont Morgan Library, New York.

Rembrandt's mastery of the newly perfected medium of etching is evident in his expert use of light and dark to draw attention to Christ as he preaches compassionately to the blind and lame.

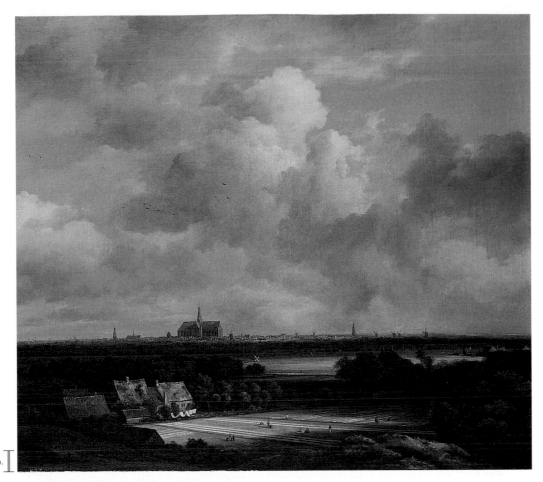

10-25 Jacob van Ruisdael, *View of Haarlem from the Dunes at Overveen*, ca. 1670. Oil on canvas, 1' 10" × 2' 1". Mauritshuis, The Hague.

In this painting, Ruisdael succeeded in capturing a realistic view of Haarlem, its windmills, and Saint Bavo church, but he also imbued the landscape with a quiet serenity approaching the spiritual.

right, the figures near the city gate are in deep shadow. At the left, the figures, some rendered almost exclusively in outline, are in bright light—not the light of day but the illumination radiating from Christ himself. A second, unseen source of light comes from the right and casts the shadow of the praying man's arms and head onto Christ's tunic. Technically and in terms of its humanity, the *Hundred-Guilder Print* is Rembrandt's supreme achievement as a print maker.

Jacob van Ruisdael In addition to portraiture, the Dutch avidly collected landscapes, interior scenes, and still lifes. Each of these painting genres dealt directly with the daily lives of the urban mercantile public, accounting for their appeal. Landscape scenes abound in 17th-century Dutch art. Due to topography and politics, the Dutch had a unique relationship to the land, one that differed from attitudes of people living in other European countries. After gaining independence from Spain, the Dutch undertook an extensive reclamation project lasting almost a century. Dikes and drainage systems cropped up across the countryside, and most Dutch families owned and worked their own farms, cultivating a feeling of closeness to the land.

   Jacob van Ruisdael (ca. 1628–1682) became famous for his precise and sensitive depictions of the Dutch landscape. In *View of Haarlem from the Dunes at Overveen* (FIG. **10-25**), Ruisdael provided an overarching view of this major Dutch city. The specificity of the artist's image—the Saint Bavo church in the background, the numerous windmills that were part of the land reclamation efforts, and the

figures in the foreground stretching linen to be bleached (a major industry in Haarlem)—reflects the pride Dutch painters took in recording their homeland and the activities of their fellow citizens. Nonetheless, in this painting the inhabitants and dwellings are so minuscule they blend into the land itself. Moreover, the horizon line is low, so the sky fills almost three-quarters of the picture space, and the sun illuminates the landscape only in patches, where it has broken through the clouds above. In *View of Haarlem*, Ruisdael not only captured the appearance of a specific locale but also succeeded in imbuing the work with a quiet serenity that becomes almost spiritual.

Jan Vermeer The sense of peace, familiarity, and comfort Dutch landscape paintings exude also emerges in interior scenes, another popular subject among middle-class patrons. These paintings offer the viewer glimpses into the lives of prosperous, responsible, and cultured citizens of the United Provinces. The foremost Dutch painter of interior scenes was Jan Vermeer (1632–1675) of Delft. Vermeer derived most of his income from his work as an innkeeper and art dealer, and he completed no more than 35 paintings that can be definitively attributed to him. Flemish artists had frequently painted domestic interiors, but sacred personages often occupied those scenes (for example, FIG. 8-3). In contrast, Vermeer and his contemporaries composed neat, quietly opulent interiors of Dutch middle-class homes with men, women, and children engaging in household tasks or at leisure. Women are the primary protagonists of Vermeer's paintings, which are highly idealized depictions of the social values of Dutch burghers.

   Vermeer, like Rembrandt, was a master of pictorial light and used it with immense virtuosity. He could render space so convincingly through his depiction of light that in his works, the picture surface functions as an invisible glass pane through which the viewer looks into the constructed illusion. Art historians believe Vermeer used as tools both mirrors and the *camera obscura* (literally, "dark room"), an ancestor of the modern camera based on passing light through a tiny pinhole or

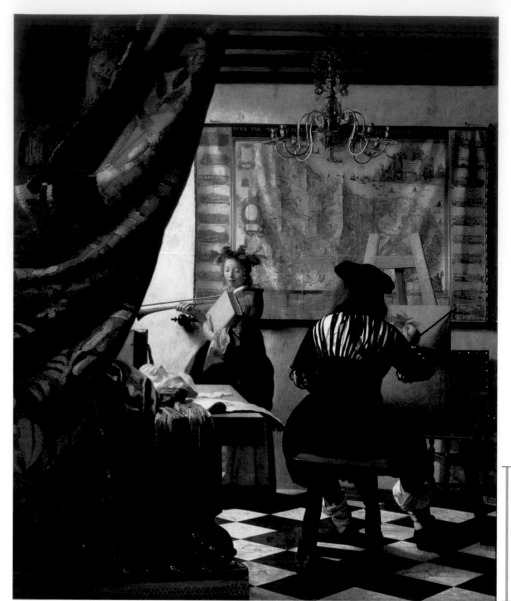

10-26 JAN VERMEER, *Allegory of the Art of Painting*, 1670–1675. Oil on canvas, 4′ 4″ × 3′ 8″. Kunsthistorisches Museum, Vienna.

Dutch painters often specialized in domestic scenes, but Vermeer's mother-in-law described this work as the "Art of Painting." Vermeer's tribute to his craft includes a model holding Clio's attributes.

1 ft.

lens to project an image on a screen or the wall of a room. (In later versions, artists projected the image on a ground-glass wall of a box whose opposite wall contained the pinhole or lens.) Vermeer did not simply copy the camera's image, however. Instead, the camera obscura and mirrors helped him obtain results he reworked compositionally, placing his figures and the furniture of a room in a beautiful stability of quadrilateral shapes. Vermeer's compositions evoke a classical serenity. Enhancing this quality are colors so true to the optical facts and so subtly modulated they suggest Vermeer was far ahead of his time in color science. For example, Vermeer realized shadows are not colorless and dark, adjoining colors affect each other, and light is composed of colors. Thus, he painted reflections off of surfaces in colors modified by others nearby. Some scholars have suggested Vermeer also perceived the phenomenon modern photographers call "circles of confusion," which appear on out-of-focus negatives. Vermeer could have seen them in images projected by the camera obscura's primitive lenses. He approximated these effects with light dabs that, in close view, give the impression of an image slightly "out of focus." When the observer draws back a step, however, as if adjusting the lens, the color spots cohere, giving an astonishingly accurate illusion of the third dimension.

The Art of Painting Vermeer's stylistic precision and commitment to his profession are evident in *Allegory of the Art of Painting* (FIG. **10-26**). The artist himself appears in the painting, with his back to the viewer and dressed in "historical" clothing. He is hard at work on a painting of the model standing before him wearing a laurel wreath and holding a trumpet and book, traditional attributes of Clio, the muse of history. The map of the provinces (an increasingly common wall adornment in Dutch homes) on the back wall serves as yet another reference to history. As in other Vermeer domestic scenes, the viewer is outside the space of the action, looking through the drawn curtain, which also separates the artist in his studio from the rest of the house.

Some art historians have suggested the light radiating from an unseen window on the left, illuminating both the model and the canvas being painted, alludes to the light of artistic inspiration. Accordingly, many scholars have interpreted this painting as an allegory—a reference to painting inspired by history. Vermeer's mother-in-law confirmed this allegorical reading in 1677 while seeking to retain the painting after the artist's death, when 26 of his works were scheduled to be sold to pay his widow's debts. She listed the painting in her written claim as "the piece . . . wherein the Art of Painting is portrayed."[4]

Pieter Claesz The prosperous Dutch were justifiably proud of their accomplishments, and the popularity of still-life paintings—particularly images of accumulated material goods—reflected this pride. These paintings, like Vermeer's interior scenes, are meticulously crafted images both scientific in their optical accuracy and poetic in their beauty and lyricism. Paintings such as *Vanitas Still Life* (FIG. **10-27**) by PIETER CLAESZ (1597–1660) celebrate material possessions,

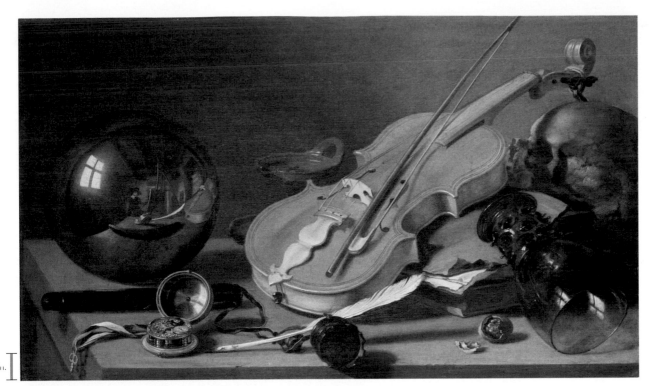

10-27 Pieter Claesz, *Vanitas Still Life*, 1630s. Oil on panel, 1' 2" × 1' 11½". Germanisches Nationalmuseum, Nuremberg.

Calvinist morality tempered Dutch citizens' delight in worldly possessions and accumulated wealth. In this *vanitas* still life, the skull and timepiece are *mementi mori*, reminders of life's transience.

1 in.

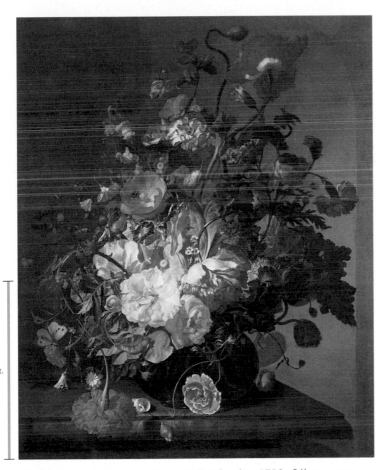

10-28 Rachel Ruysch, *Flower Still Life,* after 1700. Oil on canvas, 2' 5¾" × 1' 11⅞". Toledo Museum of Art, Toledo (purchased with funds from the Libbey Endowment, gift of Edward Drummond Libbey). ◼◖

Flower paintings were very popular in the Dutch Republic. Ruysch achieved international renown for her lush paintings of floral arrangements, noted also for their careful compositions.

1 ft.

here presented as if strewn across a tabletop or dresser. The ever-present morality and humility central to the Calvinist faith tempered Dutch pride in worldly goods, however. Thus, although Claesz fostered the appreciation and enjoyment of the beauty and value of the objects he depicted, he also reminded the viewer of life's transience by incorporating references to death. Art historians call works of this type *vanitas* (vanity) paintings, and each feature a *memento mori* (reminder of death). In *Vanitas Still Life,* references to mortality include the skull, timepiece, tipped glass, and cracked walnut. All suggest the passage of time or someone who was here but has departed. Claesz emphasized this element of time (and demonstrated his technical virtuosity) by including a self-portrait, reflected in the glass ball on the left side of the table. He appears to be painting this still life. But in an apparent challenge to the message of inevitable mortality that vanitas paintings convey, the portrait serves to immortalize the artist.

Rachel Ruysch As living objects that soon die, flowers, particularly cut blossoms, appeared frequently in vanitas paintings. However, floral painting as a distinct genre also flourished in the Dutch Republic. One of the leading practitioners of this art was Rachel Ruysch (1663–1750). Ruysch's father was a professor of botany and anatomy, which may account for her interest in and knowledge of plants and insects. She acquired an international reputation for lush paintings, such as *Flower Still Life* (FIG. **10-28**). In this image, the lavish floral arrangement is so full many of the blossoms seem to be spilling out of the vase. Ruysch's careful arrangement of the painting's elements is evident in her composing the flowers to create a diagonal running from the lower left to the upper right corner of the canvas, offsetting the opposing diagonal of the table edge.

Poussin's Notes for a Treatise on Painting

As the leading proponent of classical painting in 17th-century Rome, Nicolas Poussin outlined the principles of classicism in notes for an intended treatise on painting, left incomplete at his death. In those notes, Poussin described the essential ingredients necessary to produce a beautiful painting in "the grand manner":

> The grand manner consists of four things: subject-matter or theme, thought, structure, and style. The first thing that, as the foundation of all others, is required, is that the subject-matter shall be grand, as are battles, heroic actions, and divine things. But assuming that the subject on which the painter is laboring is grand, his next consideration is to keep away from minutiae . . . [and paint only] things magnificent and grand . . . Those who elect mean subjects take refuge in them because of the weakness of their talents.*

> The idea of beauty does not descend into matter unless this is prepared as carefully as possible. This preparation consists of three

things: arrangement, measure, and aspect or form. Arrangement means the relative position of the parts; measure refers to their size; and form consists of lines and colors. Arrangement and relative position of the parts and making every limb of the body hold its natural place are not sufficient unless measure is added, which gives to each limb its correct size, proportionate to that of the whole body [compare Polykleitos's *Canon*, discussed in Chapter 2], and unless form joins in, so that the lines will be drawn with grace and with a harmonious juxtaposition of light and shadow.†

Poussin applied these principles in paintings such as *Et in Arcadia Ego* (FIG. 10-29), a work peopled with perfectly proportioned statuesque figures attired in antique garb.

*Translated by Robert Goldwater and Marco Treves, eds., *Artists on Art*, 3d ed. (New York: Pantheon Books, 1958), 155.
†Ibid., 156.

10-29 NICOLAS POUSSIN, *Et in Arcadia Ego,* ca. 1655. Oil on canvas, 2′ 10″ × 4′. Musée du Louvre, Paris.

Poussin was the leading proponent of classicism in 17th-century Rome. His "grand manner" paintings are models of "arrangement and measure" and incorporate figures inspired by ancient statuary.

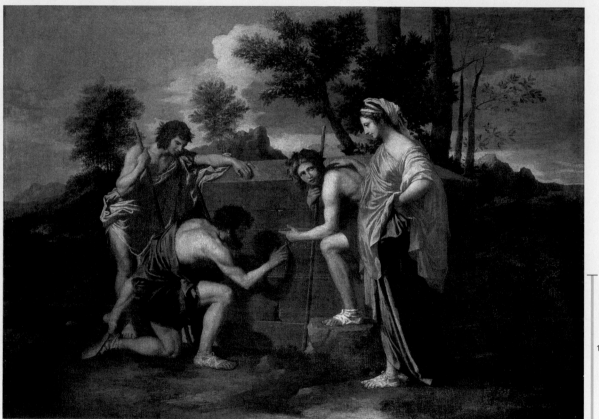

1 ft.

FRANCE

In France, monarchical authority had been increasing for centuries, culminating in the reign of Louis XIV (r. 1661–1715), who sought to determine the direction of French society and culture. Although its economy was not as expansive as the Dutch Republic's, France became Europe's largest and most powerful nation in the 17th century. Against this backdrop, the arts flourished.

Nicolas Poussin Rome's ancient and Renaissance monuments enticed many French artists to study there. For example, NICOLAS POUSSIN (1594–1665) of Normandy spent most of his life in Rome, where he produced grandly severe paintings modeled on those of Titian and Raphael. He also carefully formulated a theoretical explanation of his method and was ultimately responsible for establishing classical painting as an important ingredient of 17th-century French art (see "Poussin's Notes for a Treatise on Painting," above). Poussin's classical style presents a striking contrast to the contemporaneous Baroque style of his Italian counterparts in Rome, underscoring the multifaceted character of the art of 17th-century Europe.

Poussin's *Et in Arcadia Ego (Even in Arcadia, I* [am present]; FIG. **10-29**) exemplifies the "grand manner" of painting the artist advocated. It features a lofty subject rooted in the classical world and figures based on antique statuary. In contrast to contemporaneous painting in Italy, Poussin's canvas emulates the rational order and stability of Raphael's paintings. Dominating the foreground are three shepherds living in the idyllic land of Arcadia. They study an inscription on a tomb as a statuesque female figure quietly places her hand on the shoulder of one of them. She may be the spirit of death, reminding these mortals, as does the inscription, that death is found even in Arcadia, supposedly a spot of paradisiacal bliss. The countless draped female statues surviving in Italy from Roman times supplied the models for this figure, and the posture of the youth with one foot resting on a boulder derives from Greco-Roman statues of Neptune, the sea god, leaning on his trident. The classically compact, balanced grouping of the figures, the even light, and the thoughtful and reserved mood complement Poussin's classical figure types.

Claude Lorrain Claude Gellée, called CLAUDE LORRAIN (1600–1682) after his birthplace in the duchy of Lorraine, rivaled Poussin in fame. Claude modulated in a softer style Poussin's disciplined rational art, with its sophisticated revelation of the geometry of landscape. Unlike the figures in Poussin's pictures, those in Claude's landscapes tell no dramatic story, point out no moral, and praise no hero. Indeed,

they often appear to be added as mere excuses for the radiant landscape itself. For Claude, painting involved essentially one theme—the beauty of a broad sky suffused with the golden light of dawn or sunset glowing through a hazy atmosphere and reflecting brilliantly off rippling water.

In *Landscape with Cattle and Peasants* (FIG. **10-30**), the figures in the right foreground chat in animated fashion. In the left foreground, cattle relax contentedly. In the middle ground, cattle amble slowly away. The well-defined foreground, distinct middle ground, and dim background recede in serene orderliness, until all form dissolves in a luminous mist. Atmospheric and linear perspective reinforce each other to turn a vista into a typical Claudian vision, an ideal classical world bathed in sunlight in infinite space (compare FIG. I-10). Claude's formalizing of nature with balanced groups of architectural masses, screens of trees, and sheets of water followed the great tradition of classical landscape. It began with the backgrounds of Venetian painting (FIGS. 9-17 and 9-18) and continued in the art of Poussin (FIG. 10-29). Yet Claude, like the Dutch painters, studied the light and the atmospheric nuances of nature, making a unique contribution. He recorded carefully in hundreds of sketches the look of the Roman countryside, its gentle terrain accented by stone-pines, cypresses, and poplars and by ever-present ruins of ancient aqueducts, tombs, and towers. He made these the fundamental elements of his compositions.

Claude achieved his marvelous effects of light by painstakingly placing tiny value gradations, which imitated, though on a very small scale, the range of values of outdoor light and shade. Avoiding the problem of high-noon sunlight overhead, Claude preferred, and convincingly represented, the sun's rays as they gradually illuminated the morning sky or, with their dying glow, set the pensive mood of evening. Thus, he matched the moods of nature with those of human subjects. Claude's infusion of nature with human feeling and his recomposition of nature in a calm equilibrium greatly appealed to many landscape painters of the 18th and early 19th centuries.

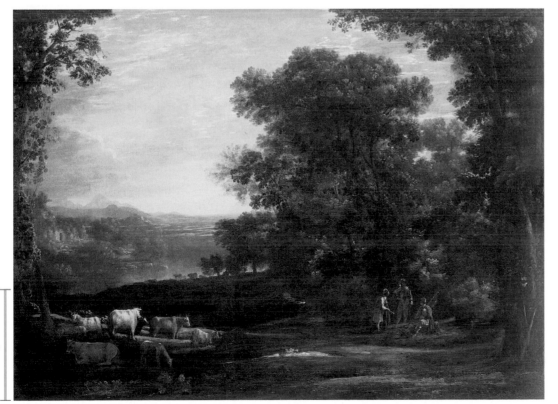

1 ft.

10-30 CLAUDE LORRAIN, *Landscape with Cattle and Peasants,* 1629. Oil on canvas, 3′ 6″ × 4′ 10½″. Philadelphia Museum of Art, Philadelphia (George W. Elkins Collection).

Claude used atmospheric and linear perspective to transform the rustic Roman countryside filled with peasants and animals into an ideal classical landscape bathed in sunlight in infinite space.

Louis XIV The preeminent French art patron of the 17th century was King Louis XIV. Determined to consolidate and expand his power, Louis was a master of political strategy and propaganda. He established a carefully crafted and nuanced relationship with the nobility, granting them sufficient benefits to keep them pacified but simultaneously maintaining rigorous control to avoid insurrection. He also ensured subservience by anchoring his rule in *divine right* (belief in a king's absolute power as God's will). So convinced was Louis of his indispensability that he eagerly adopted the title "the Sun King." Like the sun, Louis was the center of the universe.

The Sun King's desire for control extended to all realms of French life, including art. Louis and his principal adviser, Jean-Baptiste Colbert (1619–1683), strove to organize art and architecture in the service of the state. They understood well the power of art as propaganda and the value of visual imagery for cultivating a public persona, and they spared no pains to raise monuments to the king's absolute power. Louis and Colbert sought to regularize taste and establish the classical style as the preferred French manner. The founding of the Royal Academy of Painting and Sculpture in 1648 served to advance this goal.

Louis XIV (FIG. **10-31**) by HYACINTHE RIGAUD (1659–1743) successfully conveys the image of an absolute monarch. The king, age 63 when Rigaud painted this work, stands with his left hand on his hip and gazes directly at the viewer. His elegant ermine-lined fleur-de-lis coronation robes (compare FIG. 10-18) hang loosely from his shoulder, suggesting an air of haughtiness. Louis also draws his garment back to expose his legs. (The king was a ballet dancer in his youth and was proud of his well-toned legs.) The portrait's majesty derives in large part from the composition. The Sun King is the unmistakable focal point, and Rigaud placed him so that he seems to look down on the viewer. (Louis XIV was only 5′ 4″ tall—a fact that drove him to invent the high-heeled shoes he wears in the portrait.) The carefully detailed environment in which the king stands also contributes to the painting's stateliness and grandiosity. Indeed, when the king was not present, Rigaud's portrait, which hung over the throne, served in his place, and courtiers were not permitted to turn their backs on the painting.

Versailles Louis XIV was also a builder on a grand scale. One of his projects was to convert a royal hunting lodge at Versailles, south of Paris, into a great palace. He assembled a veritable army of architects, decorators, sculptors, painters, and landscape architects under the general management of CHARLES LE BRUN (1619–1690). In their hands, the conversion of a simple lodge into the palace of Versailles (FIG. **10-32**) became the greatest architectural project of the age—a defining statement of French Baroque style and an undeniable symbol of Louis XIV's power and ambition. Planned on a gigantic scale, the project called not only for a large palace flanking a vast park but also for the construction of a satellite city to house court and government officials, military and guard detachments, courtiers, and servants (undoubtedly to keep

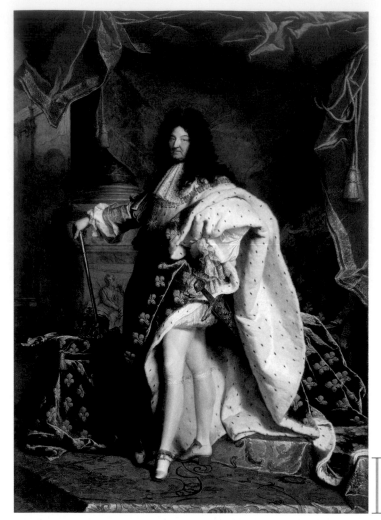

10-31 HYACINTHE RIGAUD, *Louis XIV,* 1701. Oil on canvas, 9′ 2″ × 6′ 3″. Musée du Louvre, Paris. ◼◀

In this portrait set against a stately backdrop, Rigaud portrayed the 5′ 4″ Sun King wearing red high-heeled shoes and with his ermine-lined coronation robes thrown over his left shoulder.

them all under the king's close supervision). Le Brun laid out this town to the east of the palace along three radial avenues that converge on the palace. Their axes, in a symbolic assertion of the ruler's absolute power over his domains, intersected in the king's spacious bedroom, which also served as an official audience chamber. The palace itself, more than a quarter mile long, is perpendicular to the dominant east-west axis running through the associated city and park.

Every detail of the extremely rich decoration of the palace's interior received careful attention. The architects and decorators designed everything from wall paintings to doorknobs in order to reinforce the splendor of Versailles and to exhibit the very finest sense of artisanship. Of the literally hundreds of rooms within the palace, the most famous is the Galerie des Glaces, or Hall of Mirrors (FIG. **10-33**), designed by JULES HARDOUIN-MANSART (1646–1708) and Le Brun. This hall overlooks the park from the second floor and extends along most of the width of the central block. Although deprived of its original sumptuous furniture, which included gold and silver chairs and bejeweled trees, the Galerie des Glaces retains much of its splendor today. Hundreds of

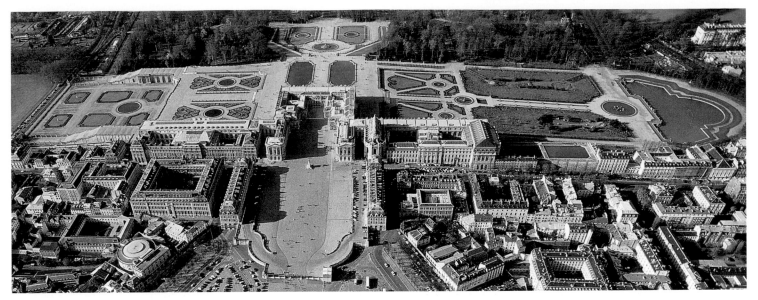

10-32 JULES HARDOUIN-MANSART, CHARLES LE BRUN, and ANDRÉ LE NÔTRE, aerial view of palace and gardens (looking northwest), Versailles, France, begun 1669.

Louis XIV ordered his architects to convert a royal hunting lodge at Versailles into a gigantic palace and park with a satellite city whose three radial avenues intersect in the king's bedroom.

mirrors, set into the wall opposite the windows, alleviate the hall's tunnel-like quality and illusionistically extend the width of the gallery. The mirror, that ultimate source of illusion, was a favorite element of Baroque interior design. Here, it also enhanced the dazzling extravagance of the great festivals Louis XIV was so fond of hosting.

The enormous palace might appear unbearably ostentatious were it not for its extraordinary setting in a vast park, which makes the palace seem almost an adjunct. From the

Galerie des Glaces, the king and his guests could enjoy a sweeping vista down the park's tree-lined central axis and across terraces, lawns, pools, and lakes toward the horizon. The park of Versailles, designed by ANDRÉ LE NÔTRE (1613–1700), must rank among the world's greatest artworks in both size and concept. Here, the French architect transformed an entire forest into a park. Although its geometric plan may appear stiff and formal, the park in fact offers an almost unlimited assortment of vistas, as Le Nôtre used not only the multiplicity of natural forms but also the terrain's slightly rolling contours with stunning effectiveness.

The formal gardens near the palace provide a rational transition from the frozen architectural forms to the natural living ones. Here, the elegant forms of trimmed shrubs and hedges define the tightly designed geometric units. Each unit differs from its neighbor and has a focal point

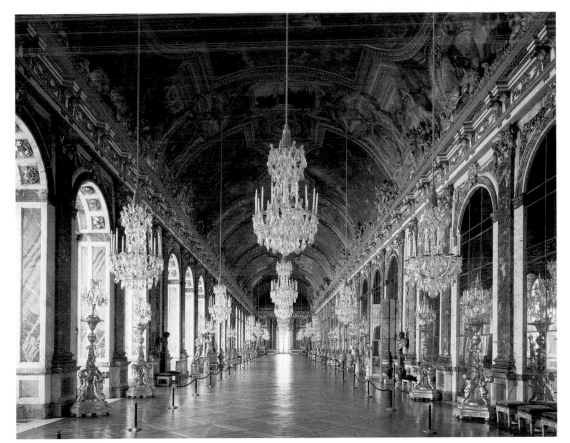

10-33 JULES HARDOUIN-MANSART and CHARLES LE BRUN, Galerie des Glaces (Hall of Mirrors), palace of Versailles, Versailles, France, ca. 1680.

This hall overlooks the Versailles park from the second floor of Louis XIV's palace. Hundreds of mirrors illusionistically extend the room's width and once reflected gilded and jeweled furnishings.

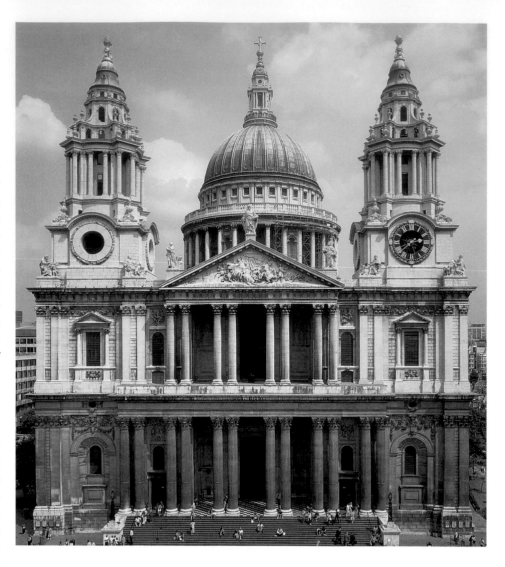

10-34 SIR CHRISTOPHER WREN, west facade of Saint Paul's Cathedral, London, England, 1675–1710.

Wren's cathedral replaced an old Gothic church. The facade design owes much to the Italian architects Andrea Palladio and Francesco Borromini. The great dome recalls Saint Peter's in Rome.

in the form of a sculptured group, a pavilion, a reflecting pool, or a fountain. Farther away from the palace, the design loosens as trees, in shadowy masses, screen or frame views of open countryside. Le Nôtre carefully composed all vistas for maximum effect. Light and shadow, formal and informal, dense growth and open meadows—all play against one another in unending combinations and variations. No photograph or series of photographs can reveal the design's full richness. The park unfolds itself only to those walking through it.

ENGLAND

In England, the common law and the Parliament kept royal power in check. England also differed from France (and Europe in general) in other significant ways. Although an important part of English life, religion was not the contentious issue it was on the Continent. The religious affiliations of the English included Catholicism, Anglicanism, Protestantism, and Puritanism (the English version of Calvinism). In the economic realm, England was the one country (other than the Dutch Republic) to take advantage of the opportunities overseas trade offered. England, like the Dutch Republic, possessed a large and powerful navy, as well as excellent maritime capabilities.

In the realm of art, the most important English contributions were in the field of architecture, much of it, as in France, incorporating classical elements.

Christopher Wren London's majestic Saint Paul's Cathedral (FIG. **10-34**) is the work of England's most renowned architect, CHRISTOPHER WREN (1632–1723). A mathematical genius and skilled engineer whose work won Isaac Newton's praise, Wren became professor of astronomy in London at age 25. Mathematics led to architecture, and Charles II (r. 1660–1685) asked Wren to prepare a plan for restoring the old Gothic church of Saint Paul. Wren proposed to remodel the building based on Roman structures. Within a few months, the Great Fire of London, which destroyed the old structure and many churches in the city in 1666, gave Wren his opportunity. Wren had traveled in France, where the splendid palaces and state buildings being created in and around Paris must have impressed him. Wren also closely studied prints illustrating Baroque architecture in Italy. In Saint Paul's, he harmonized Palladian, French, and Italian Baroque features.

In view of its size, the cathedral was built with remarkable speed—in little more than 30 years—and Wren lived to see it completed. The building's form underwent constant refinement during construction, and Wren did not determine the final appearance of the towers until after 1700. In the splendid skyline composition, two foreground towers act effectively as foils to the great dome. Wren must have known similar schemes that Italian architects devised for Saint Peter's (FIGS. 10-2 and 10-3) in Rome to solve the problem of the relationship between the facade and dome. The influence of Borromini (FIG. 10-7) is evident in the upper levels and lanterns of the towers. The lower levels owe a debt to Palladio, and the superposed paired columnar porticos have parallels in contemporaneous French architecture. Wren's skillful eclecticism brought all these foreign features into a monumental unity.

Wren designed many other churches after the Great Fire. Even today, Wren's towers and domes punctuate the London skyline. Saint Paul's dome is the tallest of all. Wren's legacy was significant and long-lasting, both in England and in colonial America (see Chapter 11).

Baroque Europe

Italy and Spain

▌ In contrast to Renaissance classicism, Italian Baroque architecture is dynamic, theatrical, and highly ornate. The facades of Francesco Borromini's churches—for example, San Carlo alle Quattro Fontane—are not flat frontispieces but undulating surfaces that provide a fluid transition from exterior to interior space. The interiors of his buildings pulsate with energy and feature complex domes that grow organically from curving walls.

▌ The greatest Italian Baroque sculptor was Gianlorenzo Bernini, who was also an important architect. In *Ecstasy of Saint Teresa*, he marshaled the full capabilities of architecture, sculpture, and painting to create an intensely emotional experience for worshipers, consistent with the Counter-Reformation principle of using artworks to inspire devotion and piety.

▌ In painting, Caravaggio broke new ground by employing stark and dramatic contrasts of light and dark (tenebrism) and by setting religious scenes, such as *Calling of Saint Matthew*, in everyday locales filled with rough-looking common people.

▌ The greatest Spanish Baroque painter was Diego Velázquez, court painter to Philip IV (r. 1621–1665). His masterwork, *Las Meninas*, is extraordinarily complex and mixes real spaces, mirrored spaces, picture spaces, and pictures within pictures. It is a celebration of the art of painting itself.

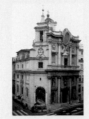

Borromini, San Carlo alle Quattro Fontane, Rome, 1638–1641

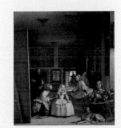

Velázquez, *Las Meninas*, 1656

Flanders and the Dutch Republic

▌ In the 17th century, Flanders remained Catholic and under Spanish control. Flemish Baroque art is more closely tied to the Baroque art of Italy than is the art of much of the rest of northern Europe. The leading Flemish painter of this era was Peter Paul Rubens, whose works feature robust and foreshortened figures in swirling motion.

▌ The Dutch Republic received official recognition of its independence from Spain in the Treaty of Westphalia of 1648. Worldwide trade and banking brought prosperity to its predominantly Protestant citizenry, which largely rejected church art in favor of private commissions of portraits, genre scenes, landscapes, and still lifes.

▌ Frans Hals produced innovative portraits of middle-class patrons in which a lively informality replaced the formulaic patterns of traditional portraiture. Jacob van Ruisdael specialized in landscapes depicting specific places, not idealized Renaissance settings. Pieter Claesz painted vanitas still lifes featuring meticulous depictions of worldly goods and reminders of death. Jan Vermeer specialized in painting Dutch families in serenely opulent homes. Vermeer's convincing representation of interior spaces depended in part on his use of the camera obscura.

▌ Rembrandt van Rijn was the greatest Dutch artist of the age. His oil paintings are notable for their dramatic impact and subtle gradations of light and shade as well as the artist's ability to convey human emotions. Rembrandt was also a master print maker renowned for his etchings, such as *Christ with the Sick*, known as the *Hundred-Guilder Print*.

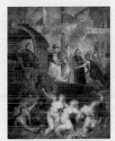

Rubens, *Arrival of Marie de'Medici at Marsailles*, 1622–1625

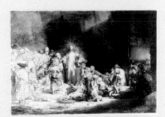

Rembrandt, *Hundred-Guilder Print*, ca. 1649

France and England

▌ The major art patron in 17th-century France was Louis XIV, the "Sun King," who built a gigantic palace-and-garden complex at Versailles featuring sumptuous furnishings and sweeping vistas. Among the architects Louis employed were Charles Le Brun and Jules Hardouin-Mansart, who succeeded in marrying Italian Baroque and French classical styles. The leading French proponent of classical painting was Nicolas Poussin, who spent most of his life in Rome and championed the "grand manner" of painting. This style called for heroic or divine subjects and classical compositions with figures often modeled on ancient statues, as in *Et in Arcadia Ego*.

▌ In England, architecture was the most important art form. Christopher Wren harmonized the architectural principles of Palladio with the Italian Baroque and French classical styles.

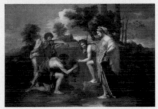

Poussin, *Et in Arcadia Ego*, ca. 1655

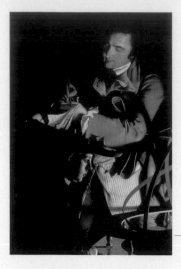

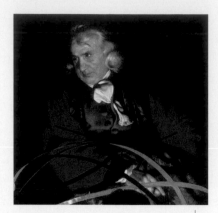

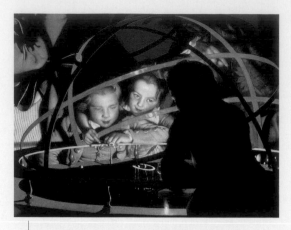

Joseph Wright of Derby specialized in dramatically lit paintings celebrating the scientific advances of the Enlightenment era. Here, a man listening to a learned lecture takes careful notes.

At the center of Wright's canvas, a scholar demonstrates an orrery, a mechanical model of the solar system in which each planet revolves around the sun at the correct relative velocity.

Awestruck children crowd close to the orbs representing the planets within the arcing bands symbolizing their orbits. Light from a lamp creates shadows, heightening the drama of the scene.

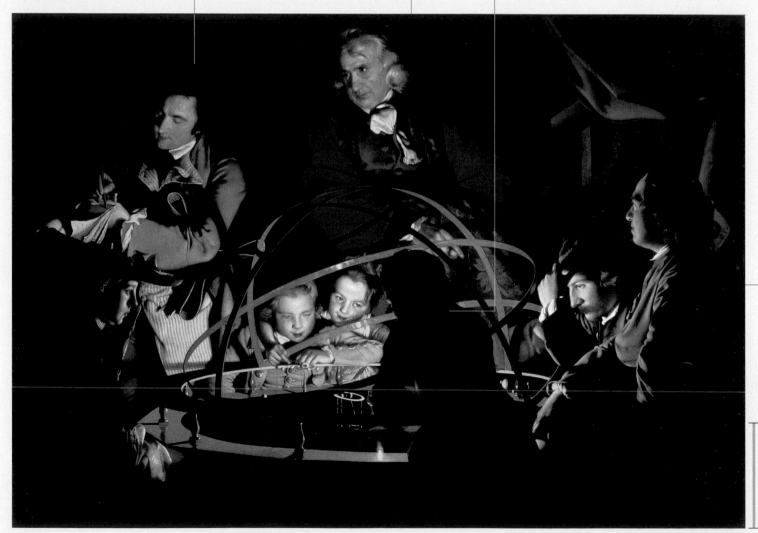

1 ft.

11-1 JOSEPH WRIGHT OF DERBY, *A Philosopher Giving a Lecture at the Orrery*, ca. 1763–1765. Oil on canvas, 4′ 10″ × 6′ 8″. Derby Museums and Art Gallery, Derby.

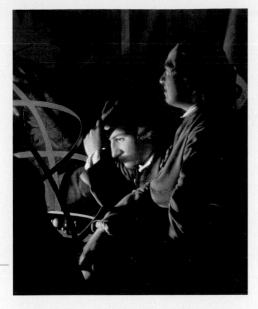

The wonders of scientific knowledge mesmerize everyone in Wright's painting, adults as well as children. At the right, two gentlemen look on with rapt attention to the demonstration.

Rococo to Neoclassicism in Europe and America

ART AND SCIENCE IN THE ERA OF ENLIGHTENMENT

The dawn of the *Enlightenment* in the 18th century brought a new way of thinking critically about the world and about humankind, independently of religion, myth, or tradition. Enlightenment thinkers rejected unfounded beliefs in favor of empirical evidence and promoted the questioning of all assertions. Thus, the Enlightenment encouraged and stimulated the habit and application of mind known as the "scientific method" and fostered technological invention. The scientific advances of the Enlightenment era affected the lives of everyone, and most people enthusiastically responded to wonders of the Industrial Revolution such as the steam engine, which gave birth to the modern manufacturing economy and the prospect of a seemingly limitless supply of goods and services.

The fascination science had for ordinary people as well as for the learned is the subject of *A Philosopher Giving a Lecture at the Orrery* (FIG. **11-1**) by the English painter JOSEPH WRIGHT OF DERBY (1734–1797). Wright studied painting near Birmingham, the center of the Industrial Revolution and specialized in dramatically lit scenes showcasing modern scientific instruments and experiments. In this painting, a scholar demonstrates a mechanical model of the solar system called an *orrery,* in which each planet (represented by a metal orb) revolves around the sun (a lamp) at the correct relative velocity. Light from the lamp pours forth from in front of the boy silhouetted in the foreground to create shadows that heighten the drama of the scene. Awestruck children crowd close to the tiny orbs representing the planets within the arcing bands symbolizing their orbits. An earnest listener makes notes, while the lone woman seated at the left and the two gentlemen at the right pay rapt attention. Science mesmerizes everyone in Wright's painting. The artist visually reinforced the fascination with the orrery by composing his image in a circular fashion, echoing the device's orbital design. The postures and gazes of all the participants and observers focus attention on the cosmic model. Wright scrupulously and accurately rendered every detail of the figures, the mechanisms of the orrery, and even the books and curtain in the shadowy background.

Wright's choice of subjects and realism in depicting them appealed to the great industrialists of his day, including Josiah Wedgwood (1730–1795), who pioneered many techniques of mass-produced pottery, and Sir Richard Arkwright (1732–1792), whose spinning frame revolutionized the textile industry. Both men often purchased paintings by Wright featuring scientific advances. To them, the Derby artist's elevation of the theories and inventions of the Industrial Revolution to the plane of history painting was exciting and appropriately in tune with the new era of Enlightenment.

THE 18TH CENTURY

In 1700, Louis XIV still ruled France as the Sun King, presiding over his realm and French culture from his palatial residence at Versailles (FIG. 10-32). By 1800, revolutions had overthrown the monarchy in France and achieved independence for the British colonies in America. The 18th century also gave birth to a revolution of a different kind—the Industrial Revolution, which began in England and soon transformed the economies of continental Europe and North America. Against this backdrop of revolutionary change, social as well as political, economic, and technological, came major transformations in the arts.

ROCOCO

The death of Louis XIV in 1715 had important repercussions in French high society. The grandiose palace-based culture of Baroque France gave way to a much more intimate and decentralized culture based in the elegant *hôtels* (townhouses) of Paris. These private homes became the centers of a new style called *Rococo,* which was primarily a style of interior design. The term derived from the French word *rocaille* (pebble), but it referred especially to the small stones and shells used to decorate grotto interiors. Shells or shell forms were the principal motifs in Rococo ornamentation.

In the early 1700s, Paris was the social capital of Europe, and the Rococo salon was the center of Parisian society. Wealthy, ambitious, and clever society hostesses competed to attract the most famous and the most accomplished people to their salons. The medium of social intercourse was conversation spiced with wit, repartee as quick and deft as a fencing match. Artifice reigned supreme, and participants considered enthusiasm or sincerity in bad taste. French Rococo salons were lively total works of art. Exquisitely wrought furniture, enchanting small sculptures, ornamented mirror frames, delightful ceramics and silver, small paintings, and decorative tapestries complemented the architecture, relief sculptures, and mural paintings.

Salon de la Princesse A typical French Rococo room is the Salon de la Princesse (FIG. **11-2**) in the Hôtel de Soubise in Paris, designed by GERMAIN BOFFRAND (1667–1754) in collaboration with the painter CHARLES-JOSEPH NATOIRE (1700–1777) and the sculptor JEAN-BAPTISTE LEMOYNE (1704–1778). A comparison between the Salon de la Princesse and the Galerie des Glaces (FIG. 10-33) at Versailles reveals how Boffrand softened the strong architectural lines and panels of the earlier style into flexible, sinuous curves luxuriantly multiplied in mirror reflections. The walls melt into the vault. Irregular painted shapes, surmounted by sculpture and separated by the ubiquitous rocaille shells, replace the hall's cornices. Painting, architecture, and sculpture combine to form a single ensemble. The profusion of curving tendrils and sprays of foliage blend with the shell forms to give an effect of freely growing nature, suggesting the designer permanently decked the Rococo room for a festival.

Antoine Watteau The painter most closely associated with French Rococo is ANTOINE WATTEAU (1684–1721). He was largely responsible for creating a specific type of Rococo painting, called a *fête galante* (amorous festival) painting. These paintings depicted the outdoor amusements of French high society. The premier example of a fête galante painting is Watteau's masterpiece, *Pilgrimage to Cythera* (FIG. **11-3**). The painting was the artist's entry for admission to the French Royal Academy of Painting and Sculpture. In 1717 the fête galante was not an acceptable category for submission, but rather than reject Watteau's candidacy, the academy created a new category to accommodate his entry. At the turn of the 18th century, two competing doctrines sharply divided the membership of the French academy. Many members followed Nicolas Poussin (FIG. 10-29) in teaching that form was the most important element in painting, whereas "colors in painting are as allurements for persuading the eyes."[1] Colors were additions for effect and not really essential. The other group took Peter Paul Rubens (FIGS. 10-17 and 10-18) as its model and proclaimed the supremacy of color. Depending on which doctrine they supported, academy members were either *Poussinistes* or *Rubénistes*. Watteau was Flemish, and Rubens's coloristic style heavily influenced his work. With Watteau in their ranks, the Rubénistes carried the day, establishing Rococo painting as the preferred style of the early 18th century.

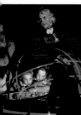

Rococo to Neoclassicism in Europe and America

1700	1725	1750	1775	1800
▮ The Rococo style becomes the rage in the opulent townhouses of Paris ▮ Watteau creates a new painting genre—the *fête galante*	▮ Chardin rejects the frivolity of Rococo painting in favor of "natural" art ▮ Canaletto paints views of Venice as souvenirs of the Grand Tour of Italy	▮ The Enlightenment admiration for Greece and Rome prompts a Neoclassical revival in architecture ▮ During the Industrial Revolution, Wright celebrates scientific advances in dramatic paintings	▮ Reynolds achieves renown for Grand Manner portraits ▮ David becomes the painter-ideologist of the French Revolution ▮ Jefferson promotes Neoclassicism as the official architectural style of the new American republic	

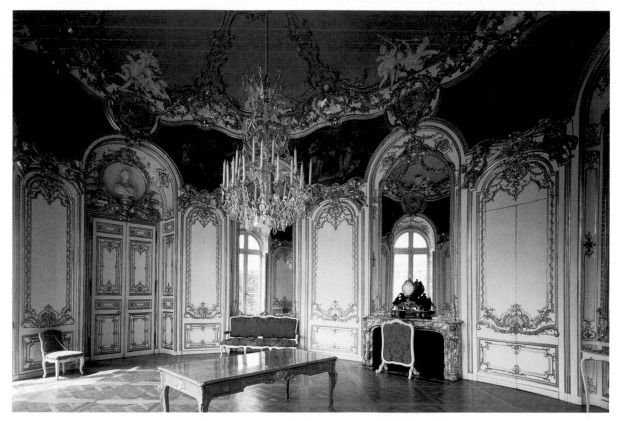

11-2 GERMAIN BOFFRAND, Salon de la Princesse, with painting by CHARLES-JOSEPH NATOIRE and sculpture by JEAN-BAPTISTE LEMOYNE, Hôtel de Soubise, Paris, France, 1737–1740.

Rococo rooms such as this one, featuring sinuous curves, gilded moldings and mirrors, small sculptures and paintings, and floral ornamentation, were the center of Parisian social and intellectual life.

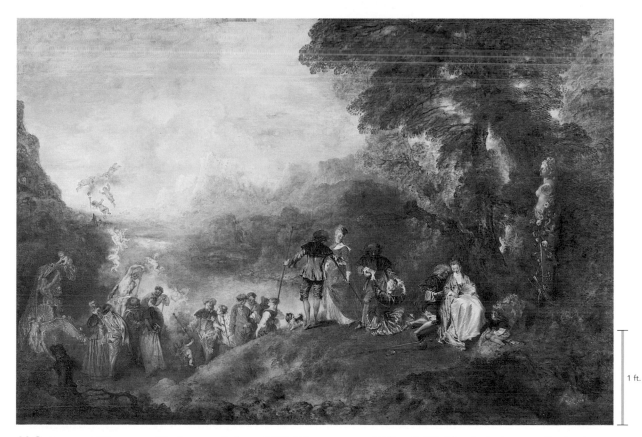

1 ft.

11-3 ANTOINE WATTEAU, *Pilgrimage to Cythera,* 1717. Oil on canvas, 4′ 3″ × 6′ 4½″. Musée du Louvre, Paris. ◼◀

Watteau's *fête galante* paintings depict the outdoor amusements of French high society and feature the Rococo taste for hazy color, subtly modeled shapes, gliding motion, and an air of suave gentility.

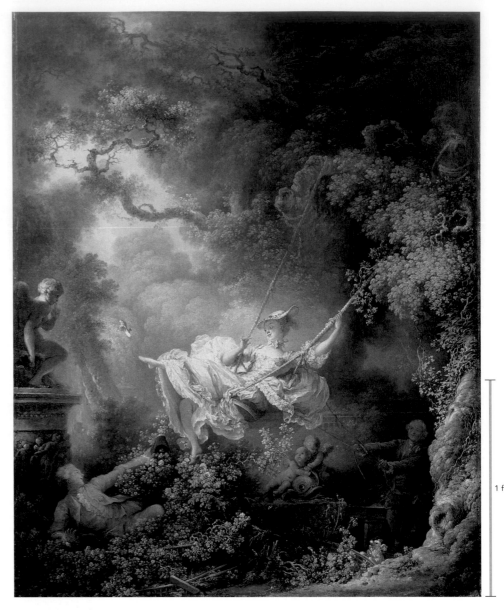

11-4 Jean-Honoré Fragonard, *The Swing*, 1766. Oil on canvas, 2′ 8⅝″ × 2′ 2″. Wallace Collection, London. ◼️

Fragonard's *Swing* epitomizes Rococo style. Pastel colors and soft light complement a scene in which a young lady flirtatiously kicks off her shoe at a statue of Cupid while her lover watches.

1 ft.

Pilgrimage to Cythera presents luxuriously costumed lovers who have made a "pilgrimage" to Cythera, the island of eternal youth and love, sacred to Aphrodite. The elegant figures move gracefully from the protective shade of a woodland park filled with amorous cupids and voluptuous statuary. Watteau's figural poses blend elegance and sweetness. He composed his generally quite small paintings from albums of drawings in which he sought to capture slow movement from difficult and unusual angles, searching for the smoothest, most poised, and most refined attitudes. Watteau also strove for the most exquisite shades of color difference, defining in a single stroke the shimmer of silk at a bent knee or the iridescence that touches a glossy surface as it emerges from shadow. The haze of color, the subtly modeled shapes, the gliding motion, and the air of suave gentility appealed greatly to Watteau's wealthy patrons.

Jean-Honoré Fragonard Watteau died of tuberculosis when he was only 37 years old, but his pupil Jean-Honoré Fragonard (1732–1806) and others carried on the Rococo painting manner Watteau pioneered. In *The Swing* (FIG. **11-4**), a young gentleman has convinced an unsuspecting old bishop to swing the young man's pretty sweetheart higher and higher, while her lover (and the work's patron), in the lower left-hand corner, stretches out to admire her ardently from a strategic position on the ground. The young lady flirtatiously and boldly kicks off her shoe toward the little statue of Cupid. The infant love god holds his finger to his lips. The landscape emulates Watteau's—a luxuriant perfumed bower in a park that very much resembles a stage scene for comic opera. The glowing pastel colors and soft light convey, almost by themselves, the theme's sensuality.

Clodion *The Swing* is a small painting. Indeed, Rococo was a style best suited for small-scale works projecting a mood of sensual intimacy. Claude Michel, called Clodion (1738–1814), specialized in small, lively sculptures representing sensuous Rococo fantasies. Clodion lived and worked in Rome for several years after winning a cherished Prix de Rome (Rome Prize) from the French royal academy to study art and paint or sculpt in the eternal city. Clodion's work incorporates echoes of Italian Mannerist sculpture. His small group, *Nymph and Satyr Carousing* (FIG. **11-5**), depicts two followers of Bacchus, the Roman god of wine. The sensuous nymph who rushes to pour wine from a cup into the open mouth of a semihuman goat-legged satyr is reminiscent of the nude female figures of Giovanni da Bologna (FIG. 9-26). The erotic playfulness of Fragonard is also evident in Clodion's two-foot-tall terracotta group destined for display on a marble tabletop in an elegant Rococo salon.

THE ENLIGHTENMENT

In the course of the 18th century, the feudal system that served as the foundation of social and economic life in Europe dissolved, and the rigid social hierarchies that provided the basis for Rococo art and patronage relaxed. A major factor in these societal changes was the Enlightenment. Enlightenment thinkers championed an approach to the acquisition of

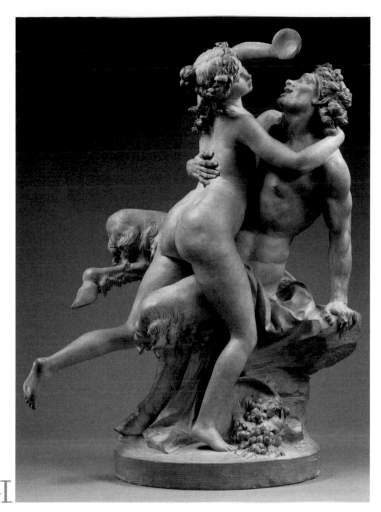

11-5 CLODION, *Nymph and Satyr Carousing*, ca. 1780–1790. Terracotta, 1' 11¼" high. Metropolitan Museum of Art, New York (bequest of Benjamin Altman, 1913).

The erotic playfulness of Fragonard's paintings is evident in Clodion's tabletop terracotta sculptures representing sensuous fantasies often involving satyrs and nymphs, the followers of Bacchus.

knowledge based on empirical observation and scientific experimentation (see "Art and Science in the Era of Enlightenment," page 323). Enlightenment-era science had its roots in the work of René Descartes, Blaise Pascal, Isaac Newton, and Gottfried Wilhelm von Leibniz in the 17th century. England and France were the principal centers of the Enlightenment, though its dictums influenced the thinking of intellectuals throughout Europe and in the American colonies. Benjamin Franklin, Thomas Jefferson, and other American notables embraced its principles.

Newton and Locke Of particular importance for Enlightenment thought was the work of Isaac Newton (1642–1727) and John Locke (1632–1704) in England. In his scientific studies, Newton insisted on empirical proof of his theories and encouraged others to avoid metaphysics and the supernatural—realms that extended beyond the natural physical world. This emphasis on both tangible data and concrete experience became a cornerstone of Enlightenment thought. Locke, whose works acquired the status of Enlightenment

gospel, developed these ideas further. According to Locke's "doctrine of empiricism," knowledge comes through sensory perception of the material world. From these perceptions alone people form ideas. Locke asserted human beings are born good, not cursed by original sin. The laws of nature grant them the natural rights of life, liberty, and property, as well as the right to freedom of conscience. Government is by contract, and its purpose is to protect these rights. If and when government abuses these rights, the citizenry has the further natural right of revolution.

Philosophes The work of Newton and Locke also inspired many French intellectuals, or *philosophes*. These thinkers conceived of individuals and societies at large as parts of physical nature. They shared the conviction the ills of humanity could be remedied by applying reason and common sense to human problems. They criticized the powers of church and state as irrational limits placed on political and intellectual freedom. They believed by accumulating and propagating knowledge, humanity could advance by degrees to a happier state than it had ever known. This conviction matured into the "doctrine of progress" and its corollary doctrine, the "perfectibility of humankind."

Animated by their belief in human progress and perfectibility, the philosophes took on the task of gathering knowledge and making it accessible to all who could read. Their program was, in effect, the democratization of knowledge. Denis Diderot (1713–1784) became editor of the groundbreaking 35-volume *Encyclopédie,* a compilation of articles written by more than a hundred contributors, including all the leading philosophes. The *Encyclopédie* was truly comprehensive (its formal title was *Systematic Dictionary of the Sciences, Arts, and Crafts*) and included all available knowledge—historical, scientific, and technical, as well as religious and moral—and political theory.

François Marie Arouet, better known as Voltaire (1694–1778), was the most representative figure—almost the personification—of the Enlightenment spirit. Voltaire was instrumental in introducing Newton and Locke to the French intelligentsia. He hated, and attacked through his writings, the arbitrary despotic rule of kings, the selfish privileges of the nobility and the church, religious intolerance, and, above all, the injustice of the *ancien regime* (the "old order"). Voltaire persuaded a whole generation that fundamental changes were necessary, paving the way for revolution in France and America at the end of the century.

Industrial Revolution The Enlightenment emphasis on scientific investigation and technological invention opened up new possibilities for human understanding of the world and for control of its material forces. Research into the phenomena of electricity and combustion, along with the discovery of oxygen and the power of steam, had enormous consequences. Steam power as an adjunct to, or replacement for, human labor initiated a new era in world history, beginning with the Industrial Revolution in England. These and

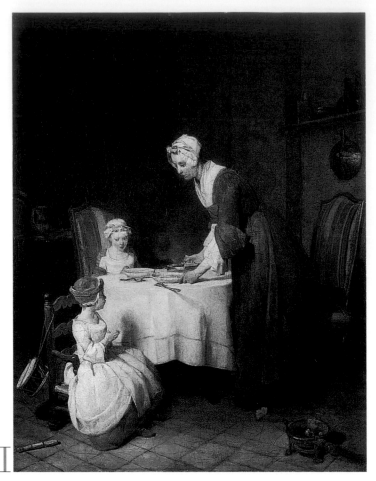

1 in.

11-6 JEAN-BAPTISTE-SIMÉON CHARDIN, *Saying Grace,* 1740. Oil on canvas, 1′ 7″ × 1′ 3″. Musée du Louvre, Paris.

Consistent with the ideas of Rousseau, Chardin celebrated the simple goodness of ordinary people, especially mothers and children, who lived in a world far from the frivolous Rococo salons of Paris.

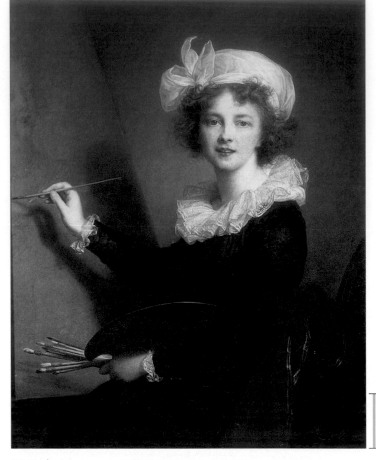

1 ft.

11-7 ÉLISABETH LOUISE VIGÉE-LEBRUN, *Self-Portrait,* 1790. Oil on canvas, 8′ 4″ × 6′ 9″. Galleria degli Uffizi, Florence.

Vigée-Lebrun was one of the few women admitted to France's Royal Academy of Painting and Sculpture. In this self-portrait, she depicted herself confidently painting the likeness of Queen Marie Antoinette.

other technological advances—admiringly recorded in the paintings of Joseph Wright of Derby (FIG. 11-1)—epitomized the Enlightenment notion of progress and gave birth to the Industrial Revolution. Most scholars mark the dawn of that technological revolution in the 1740s with the invention of steam engines in England for industrial production.

Rousseau The second key figure of the French Enlightenment, who was also instrumental in preparing the way ideologically for the French Revolution, was Jean-Jacques Rousseau (1712–1778). Voltaire believed the salvation of humanity lay in the advancement of science and in the rational improvement of society. In contrast, Rousseau argued the arts, sciences, society, and civilization in general had corrupted "natural man." According to Rousseau, "Man by nature is good . . . he is depraved and perverted by society." He rejected the idea of progress, insisting "Our minds have been corrupted in proportion as the arts and sciences have improved."[2] Rousseau's elevation of feelings above reason as the most "natural" human expression led him to exalt as the ideal the peasant's simple life, with its honest and unsullied emotions.

Chardin Rousseau's influential views were largely responsible for the turning away from the Rococo sensibility in the arts and the formation of a taste for the "natural," as opposed to the artificial and frivolous. Reflecting Rousseau's views, JEAN-BAPTISTE-SIMÉON CHARDIN (1699–1779) painted quiet scenes of domestic life, which offered the opportunity to praise the simple goodness of ordinary people, especially mothers and young children, who in spirit, occupation, and environment lived far from corrupt society. In *Saying Grace* (FIG. **11-6**), Chardin ushers the viewer into a modest room where a mother and her small daughters are about to dine. The mood of quiet attention is at one with the hushed lighting and mellow color and with the closely studied still-life accessories whose worn surfaces tell their own humble domestic history. The viewer witnesses a moment of social instruction, when mother and older sister supervise the younger sister in the simple, pious ritual of giving thanks to God before a meal. The simplicity of the composition reinforces the subdued charm of this scene, with the three figures highlighted against the dark background. Chardin was the poet of the commonplace and the master of its nuances. A gentle sentiment prevails in all his pictures, an emotion not contrived and artificial but born of

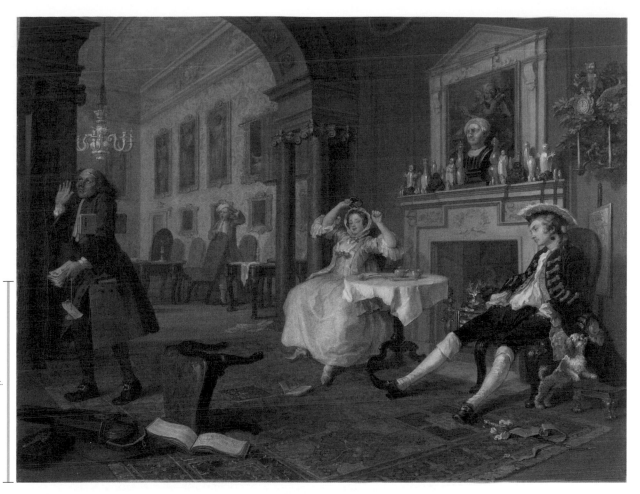

1 ft.

11-8 WILLIAM HOGARTH, *Breakfast Scene*, from *Marriage à la Mode*, ca. 1745. Oil on canvas, 2' 4" × 3'. National Gallery, London.

Hogarth won fame for his paintings and prints satirizing English life with comic zest. This is one of a series of six paintings in which he chronicled the marital immoralities of the moneyed class.

the painter's honesty, insight, and sympathy. Chardin's paintings had wide appeal, even in unexpected places. Louis XV, the royal personification of the Rococo in his life and tastes, once owned *Saying Grace*.

Vigée-Lebrun Another manifestation of the "naturalistic" impulse in 18th-century French art was the emergence of a new mode of portraiture exemplified by *Self-Portrait* (FIG. **11-7**) by ÉLISABETH LOUISE VIGÉE-LEBRUN (1755–1842). The painter looks directly at viewers and pauses in her work to return their gaze. Although her mood is lighthearted and her costume's details echo the serpentine curve Rococo artists and wealthy patrons loved, nothing about Vigée-Lebrun's pose or her mood speaks of Rococo frivolity. Hers is the self-confident stance of a woman whose art has won her an independent role in society. She portrayed herself in a close-up, intimate view at work on one of the many portraits she painted of her most important patron, Queen Marie Antoinette (1755–1793). Like many of her contemporaries, Vigée-Lebrun lived a life of extraordinary personal and economic independence, working for the nobility throughout Europe. She was famous for the force and grace of her portraits, especially those of highborn ladies and royalty. She was successful during the age of the late monarchy in France and was one of the few women admitted to the Royal Academy of Painting and Sculpture. After the French Revolution, however, the academy rescinded her membership because women were no longer welcome, but she enjoyed continued success owing to her talent, wit, and ability to forge connections with those in power in the postrevolutionary period.

William Hogarth Across the Channel, a truly English style of painting emerged with WILLIAM HOGARTH (1697–1764), who satirized the lifestyle of the newly prosperous middle class with comic zest. Traditionally, the British imported painters from the Continent—Holbein, Rubens, and Van Dyck among them. Hogarth waged a lively campaign throughout his career against the English feeling of dependence on, and inferiority to, these artists. Although Hogarth would have been the last to admit it, his own painting owed much to the work of his contemporaries in France, the Rococo artists. Yet his subject matter, frequently moral in tone, was distinctively English. This was the great age of English satirical writing, and Hogarth saw himself as translating satire into the visual arts.

Hogarth's favorite device was to make a series of narrative paintings and prints, in a sequence similar to chapters in a book or scenes in a play, following a character or group of characters in their encounters with some social evil. *Breakfast Scene* (FIG. **11-8**), from *Marriage à la Mode*, is one of six paintings satirizing the marital immoralities of the

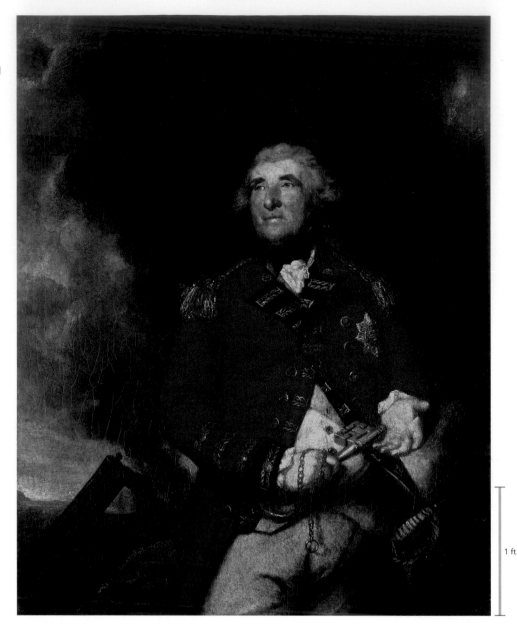

11-9 SIR JOSHUA REYNOLDS, *Lord Heathfield,* 1787. Oil on canvas, 4' 8" × 3' 9". National Gallery, London.

In this Grand Manner portrait, Reynolds depicted the English commander who defended Gibraltar. Heathfield stands in a dramatic pose, and his figure takes up most of the canvas.

1 ft.

moneyed classes in England. In it, a marriage is just beginning to founder. The husband and wife are tired after a long night spent in separate pursuits. While the wife stayed at home for an evening of cards and music-making, her young husband had been away from the house for a night of suspicious business. He thrusts his hands deep into the empty money-pockets of his breeches, while his wife's small dog sniffs inquiringly at a woman's lacy cap protruding from his coat pocket. A steward, his hands full of unpaid bills, raises his eyes in despair at the actions of his noble master and mistress. The house is palatial, but Hogarth filled it with witty clues to the dubious taste of its occupants. For example, the row of pious religious paintings on the upper wall of the distant room concludes with a curtained canvas undoubtedly depicting an erotic subject. According to the custom of the day, ladies could not view this discretely hidden painting, but at the pull of a cord, the master and his male guests could enjoy a tableau of cavorting figures. In *Breakfast Scene,* as in all his work, Hogarth proceeded as a novelist might, elaborating

on his subject with carefully chosen detail, the discovery of which heightens the comedy.

Sir Joshua Reynolds The Enlightenment concept of "nobility," especially in the view of Rousseau, referred to character, not to aristocratic birth, and in a century marked by revolutions, the virtues of courage and resolution, patriotism, and self-sacrifice assumed great importance. SIR JOSHUA REYNOLDS (1723–1792) specialized in what became known as *Grand Manner portraiture.* Although likenesses of specific individuals, Grand Manner portraits elevated the sitters by conveying refinement and elegance. Painters communicated a person's grace and class through certain standardized conventions, such as the large scale of the figure relative to the canvas, the controlled pose, the landscape setting, and the low horizon line.

Reynolds painted *Lord Heathfield* (FIG. **11-9**) in 1787. The sitter was a perfect subject for a Grand Manner portrait—a burly, ruddy English officer, the commandant of the fortress at Gibraltar. Heathfield had doggedly defended the British

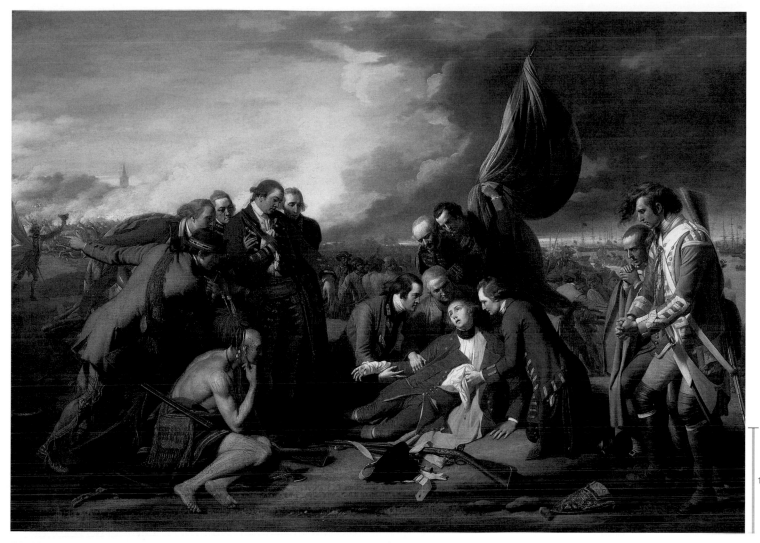

11-10 Benjamin West, *Death of General Wolfe*, 1771. Oil on canvas. 4' 11½" × 7'. National Gallery of Canada, Ottawa (gift of the Duke of Westminster, 1918).

West's great innovation was to blend contemporary subject matter and costumes with the grand tradition of history painting. Here, the painter likened General Wolfe's death to that of a martyred saint.

fortress against the Spanish and French, and later received the honorary title Baron Heathfield of Gibraltar. Here, he holds the huge key to the fortress, the symbol of his victory. He stands in front of a curtain of dark smoke rising from the battleground, flanked by one cannon pointing ineffectively downward and another whose tilted barrel indicates it lies uselessly on its back. Reynolds portrayed the features of the general's heavy, honest face and his uniform with unidealized realism. But Lord Heathfield's posture and the setting dramatically suggest the heroic themes of battle, courage, and patriotism.

Benjamin West Some American artists also became well known in England. Benjamin West (1738–1820), born in Pennsylvania on what was then the colonial frontier, traveled to Europe early in life to study art and then went to England, where he met with almost immediate success. A cofounder of the Royal Academy of Arts, West became official painter to King George III (r. 1760–1801) and retained that position

during the strained period of the American Revolution. In *Death of General Wolfe* (FIG. **11-10**), West depicted the mortally wounded young English commander just after his defeat of the French in the decisive battle of Quebec in 1759, which gave Canada to Great Britain. Because his subject was a recent event, West clothed his characters in contemporary costumes (although the military uniforms are not completely accurate). However, West blended this realism of detail with the grand tradition of history painting by arranging his figures in a complex, theatrically ordered composition. His modern hero dies among grieving officers on the field of victorious battle in a way that suggests the death of a saint. (The composition, in fact, derives from paintings of the lamentation over the dead Christ.) West wanted to present this hero's death in the service of the state as a martyrdom charged with religious emotions. His innovative combination of the conventions of traditional heroic painting with a look of modern realism influenced history painting well into the 19th century.

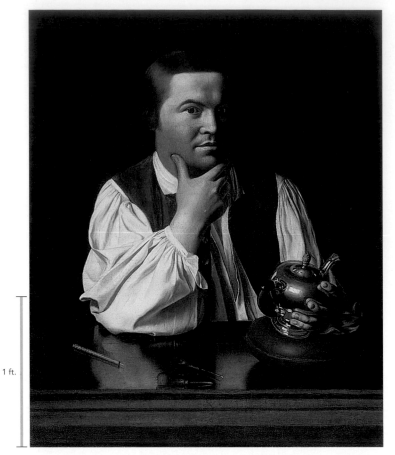

1 ft.

11-11 JOHN SINGLETON COPLEY, *Portrait of Paul Revere,* ca. 1768–1770. Oil on canvas, 2′ 11⅛″ × 2′ 4″. Museum of Fine Arts, Boston (gift of Joseph W., William B., and Edward H. R. Revere).

In contrast to Grand Manner portraiture, Copley's *Paul Revere* emphasizes his subject's down-to-earth character, differentiating this American work from its European counterparts.

John Singleton Copley American artist JOHN SINGLETON COPLEY (1738–1815) matured as a painter in the Massachusetts Bay Colony. Like West, Copley later emigrated to England, where he absorbed the fashionable English portrait style. But unlike Grand Manner portraiture, Copley's *Portrait of Paul Revere* (FIG. **11-11**), painted before the artist left Boston, conveys a sense of directness and faithfulness to visual fact that marked the taste for honesty and plainness noted by many late-18th- and early-19th-century visitors to America. When Copley painted his portrait, Revere was not yet the familiar hero of the American Revolution. In the picture, he is working at his profession of silversmithing. The setting is plain, the lighting clear and revealing. Revere sits in his shirtsleeves, bent over a teapot in progress. He pauses and turns his head to look the observer straight in the eye. The painter treated the reflections in the polished wood of the tabletop with as much care as he did Revere's figure, his tools, and the teapot resting on its leather graver's pillow. Copley gave special prominence to Revere's eyes by reflecting intense reddish light onto the darkened side of his face and hands. The informality and the sense of the moment link this painting to contemporaneous English and Continental

portraits. But the spare style and the emphasis on the sitter's down-to-earth character differentiate this American work from its European counterparts.

The Grand Tour The 18th-century public also sought "naturalness" in artists' depictions of landscapes. Documentation of specific places became popular, in part due to growing travel opportunities and expanding colonialism. These depictions of geographic settings also served the needs of the many scientific expeditions mounted during the century and satisfied the desires of genteel tourists for mementos of their journeys. By this time, a Grand Tour of the major sites of Europe was an essential part of every well-bred person's education (see "The Grand Tour and Veduta Painting," page 333). Those who embarked on a tour of the Continent wished to return with souvenirs to help them remember their experiences and impress those at home with the wonders they had seen. The English were especially eager collectors of travel pictures. Venetian artists in particular found it profitable to produce paintings of the most characteristic *vedute* (scenic views) of their city to sell to British visitors. Chief among those artists was ANTONIO CANALETTO (1697–1768), whose works, for example *Riva degli Schiavoni, Venice* (FIG. **11-12**), English tourists avidly acquired as evidence of their visit to Italy's magical city of water.

NEOCLASSICISM

One of the defining characteristics of the late 18th century was a renewed interest in classical antiquity, which the Grand Tour was instrumental in fueling. This interest gave rise to the artistic movement known as *Neoclassicism*. The geometric harmony and rationality of classical art and architecture embodied Enlightenment ideals. In addition, classical cultures represented the pinnacle of civilized society, and Greece and Rome served as models of enlightened political organization. With their traditions of liberty, civic virtue, morality, and sacrifice, these cultures were ideal models during a period of great political upheaval. Given these traditional associations, it is not coincidental that Neoclassicism was particularly appealing during the French and American Revolutions.

Winckelmann In the late 18th century, the ancient world also increasingly became the focus of academic research. In 1755, Johann Joachim Winckelmann (1717–1768), widely recognized as the first modern art historian, published *Reflections on the Imitation of Greek Works in Painting and Sculpture,* in which the German scholar unequivocally designated Greek art as the most perfect to come from human hands. For Winckelmann, classical art was far superior to the "natural" art of his day.

> [An enlightened person] will find beauties hitherto seldom revealed when he compares the total structure of Greek figures with most modern ones, especially those modelled more on nature than on Greek taste.[3]

The Grand Tour and Veduta Painting

Although travel throughout Europe was commonplace in the 18th century, Italy became an especially popular destination. This "pilgrimage" of the wealthy from France, England, Germany, the United States, and elsewhere came to be known as the Grand Tour. The Grand Tour was not simply leisure travel. The education available in Italy to the inquisitive mind made the trip an indispensable experience for anyone who wished to make a mark in society. The Enlightenment had made knowledge of ancient Rome imperative, and a steady stream of Europeans and Americans traveled to Italy in the late 18th and early 19th centuries. These tourists aimed to increase their knowledge of literature, the visual arts, architecture, theater, music, history, customs, and folklore. Given this extensive agenda, it is not surprising a Grand Tour could take a number of years to complete.

The British were the most avid travelers, and they conceived the initial "tour code," including required itineraries and important destinations. Although they designated Rome early on as the primary destination in Italy, visitors traveled as far north as Venice and as far south as Naples and even Sicily. Many returned home from their Grand Tour with a painting by Antonio Canaletto, the leading painter of scenic views (*vedute*) of Venice. It must have been very cheering on a gray winter afternoon in England to look up and see a sunny, panoramic view such as that in Canaletto's *Riva degli Schiavoni, Venice* (FIG. 11-12), with its cloud-studded sky, picturesque water traffic, and well-known Venetian landmarks painted in scrupulous perspective and minute detail. Canaletto usually made drawings "on location" to take back to his studio and use as sources for paintings. To help make the on-site drawings true to life, he often used a camera obscura, as Vermeer (FIG. 10-26) did before him, enabling Canaletto to create convincing representations incorporating the variable focus of objects at different distances. Canaletto's paintings give the impression of capturing every detail, with no "editing." In fact, he presented each site within Renaissance perspective conventions and exercised great selectivity about which details to include and which to omit to make a coherent and engagingly attractive veduta.

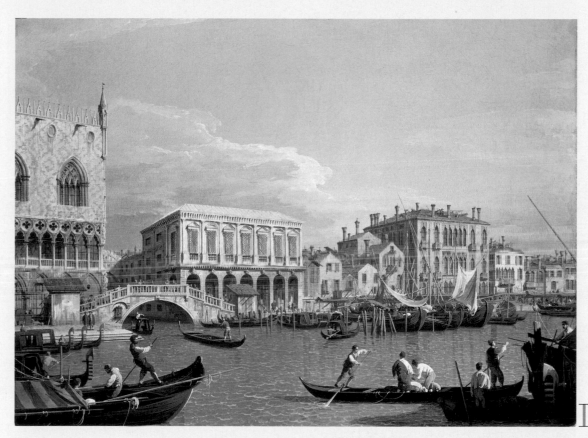

1 in.

11-12 ANTONIO CANALETTO, *Riva degli Schiavoni, Venice*, ca. 1735–1740. Oil on canvas, 1′ 6½″ × 2′ ⅞″. Toledo Museum of Art, Toledo.

Canaletto was the leading painter of Venetian *vedute*, which were treasured souvenirs for 18th-century travelers visiting Italy on a Grand Tour. He used a camera obscura for his on-site drawings.

In his later *History of Ancient Art* (1764), Winckelmann carefully described major works of classical art and positioned each one within a huge inventory organized by subject matter, style, and period. Before Winckelmann, art historians had focused on biography, as did Giorgio Vasari and Giovanni Pietro Bellori in the 16th and 17th centuries. Winckelmann thus initiated one modern art historical method thoroughly in accord with Enlightenment ideas of ordering knowledge—a system of description and classification that provided a pioneering model for the understanding of stylistic evolution.

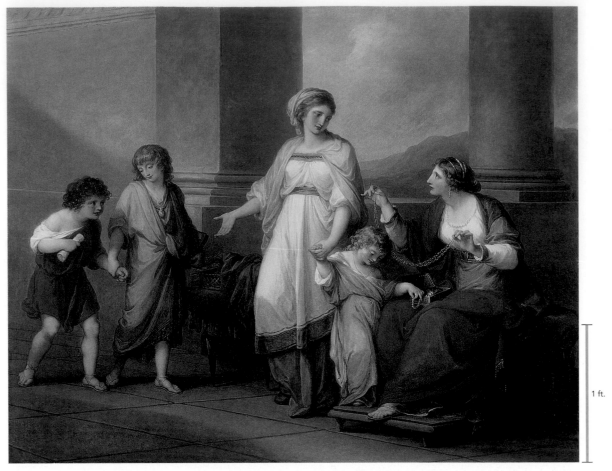

11-13 ANGELICA KAUFFMANN, *Cornelia Presenting Her Children as Her Treasures,* or *Mother of the Gracchi,* ca. 1785. Oil on canvas, 3′ 4″ × 4′ 2″. Virginia Museum of Fine Arts, Richmond (Adolph D. and Wilkins C. Williams Fund).

Kauffmann's painting of a virtuous Roman mother who presented her children to a visitor as her jewels exemplifies the Enlightenment fascination with classical antiquity and with classical art.

Angelica Kauffmann One of the pioneers of Neoclassical painting was ANGELICA KAUFFMANN (1741–1807). Born in Switzerland and trained in Italy, Kauffmann spent many of her productive years in England. A student of Reynolds, she was a founding member of the British Royal Academy of Arts and enjoyed an enviable reputation. Her *Cornelia Presenting Her Children as Her Treasures,* or *Mother of the Gracchi* (FIG. **11-13**), is an *exemplum virtutis* (example, or model, of virtue) drawn from Greek and Roman history and literature. The moralizing pictures of Hogarth (FIG. 11-8) already had marked a change in taste, but Kauffmann replaced the modern setting and characters of his works. She clothed her actors in ancient Roman garb and posed them in statuesque attitudes within Roman interiors. The theme of *Mother of the Gracchi* is the virtue of Cornelia, mother of the future political leaders Tiberius and Gaius Gracchus, who, in the second century BCE, attempted to reform the Roman Republic. Cornelia reveals her character in this scene, which takes place after a visitor had shown off her fine jewelry and then haughtily insisted Cornelia show hers. Instead of taking out her own precious adornments, Cornelia brought her sons forward, presenting them as her jewels. The architectural

setting is severely Roman, with no Rococo motif in evidence, and the composition and drawing have the simplicity and firmness of low-relief carving.

Jacques-Louis David Although his early paintings were in the Rococo manner, a period of study in Rome converted JACQUES-LOUIS DAVID (1748–1825) to Neoclassicism. David's preferred models were the works of the ancient and Renaissance masters. He rebelled against the Rococo style as an "artificial taste" and exalted the "perfect form" of Greek art (see "David on Greek Style and Public Art," page 335). David, who became the Neoclassical painter-ideologist of the French Revolution, concurred with the Enlightenment idea that the subject of an artwork should have a moral. He believed paintings representing noble deeds in the past could inspire virtue in the present.

A milestone painting in David's career, *Oath of the Horatii* (FIG. **11-14**), depicts a story from pre-Republican Rome, the heroic phase of Roman history. The topic was not too obscure for David's audience. Pierre Corneille (1606–1684) had retold this story of conflict between love and patriotism, first recounted by the ancient Roman historian Livy,

David on Greek Style and Public Art

Jacques-Louis David was the leading Neoclassical painter in France at the end of the 18th century. He championed a return to Greek style and the painting of inspiring heroic and patriotic subjects. In 1796 he made the following statement to his pupils:

> I want to work in a pure Greek style. I feed my eyes on antique statues, I even have the intention of imitating some of them. The Greeks had no scruples about copying a composition, a gesture, a type that had already been accepted and used. They put all their attention and all their art on perfecting an idea that had been already conceived. They thought, and they were right, that in the arts the way in which an idea is rendered, and the manner in which it is expressed, is much more important than the idea itself. To give a body and a perfect form to one's thought, this—and only this—is to be an artist.*

David also strongly believed paintings depicting noble events in ancient history, such as his *Oath of the Horatii* (FIG. 11-14), would serve to instill patriotism and civic virtue in the public at large in postrevolutionary France. In November 1793 he wrote:

> [The arts] should help to spread the progress of the human spirit, and to propagate and transmit to posterity the striking examples of the efforts of a tremendous people who, guided by reason and philosophy, are bringing back to earth the reign of liberty, equality, and law. The arts must therefore contribute forcefully to the education of the public. . . . The arts are the imitation of nature in her most beautiful and perfect form. . . . [T]hose marks of heroism and civic virtue offered the eyes of the people [will] electrify the soul, and plant the seeds of glory and devotion to the fatherland.†

*Translated by Robert Goldwater and Marco Treves, eds., *Artists on Art*, 3d ed. (New York: Pantheon Books, 1958), 206.
†Ibid., 205.

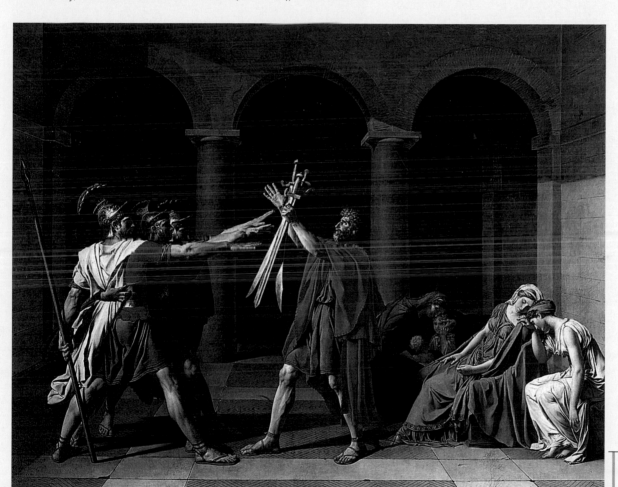

11-14 JACQUES-LOUIS DAVID, *Oath of the Horatii,* 1784. Oil on canvas, 10′ 10″ × 13′ 11″. Musée du Louvre, Paris. ◼◀

David was the Neoclassical painter-ideologist of the French Revolution. This huge canvas celebrating ancient Roman patriotism and sacrifice features statuesque figures and classical architecture.

1 ft.

in a play performed in Paris several years earlier. The leaders of the warring cities of Rome and Alba decided to resolve their conflicts in a series of encounters waged by three representatives from each side. The Romans chose as their champions the three Horatius brothers, who had to face the three sons of the Curatius family from Alba. A sister of the Horatii, Camilla, was the bride-to-be of one of the Curatius sons, and the wife of the youngest Horatius was the sister of the Curatii. David's painting shows the Horatii as they swear on their swords, held high by their father, to win or die for Rome, oblivious to the anguish and sorrow of their female relatives.

Oath of the Horatii is a paragon of the Neoclassical style. Not only was the subject a narrative of patriotism and sacrifice excerpted from Roman history, but the painter presented it with force and clarity. The action unfolds in a shallow space much like a stage setting, defined by a severely simple architectural framework. David deployed his statuesque and carefully modeled figures across the space, close to the foreground, in a manner reminiscent of ancient relief sculpture. The rigid, angular, and virile forms of the men on the left effectively contrast with the soft curvilinear shapes of the distraught women on the right. This juxtaposition visually pits virtues Enlightenment thinkers ascribed to men (such as courage, patriotism, and unwavering loyalty to a cause) against the emotions of love, sorrow, and despair the women in the painting express. The French viewing audience perceived such emotionalism as characteristic of the female nature. The message was clear and of a type readily identifiable to the prerevolutionary French public. The picture created a sensation at its first exhibition in Paris in 1785. Although David had painted it under royal patronage and did not intend the painting as a revolutionary statement, the Neoclassical style of *Oath of the Horatii* soon became the semiofficial voice of the revolution.

Death of Marat When the French Revolution broke out in 1789, David threw in his lot with the Jacobins, the radical and militant revolutionary faction. He accepted the role of de facto minister of propaganda, organizing political pageants and ceremonies requiring floats, costumes, and sculptural props. David believed art could play an important role in educating the public and that dramatic paintings emphasizing patriotism and civic virtue would prove effective as rallying calls. However, rather than continuing to create artworks focused on scenes from antiquity, David began to portray scenes from the French Revolution itself. He intended *Death of Marat* (FIG. **11-15**) not only to serve as a record of an important event in the struggle to overthrow the monarchy but also to provide inspiration and encouragement to the revolutionary forces. The painting commemorates the assassination of Jean-Paul Marat (1743–1793), an influential writer and David's friend. The artist depicted the martyred revolutionary in his medicinal bath after Charlotte Corday (1768–1793), a member of a rival political faction, stabbed him to death. (Marat suffered from a painful skin disease.) The cold neutral space above Marat's figure slumped in the tub produces a chilling oppressiveness. David vividly placed all narrative details in the foreground—the knife, the wound, the blood, the letter with which Corday gained entrance— to sharpen the sense of pain and outrage. David masterfully composed the painting to present Marat as a tragic martyr who died in the service of the revolution. David based Marat's figure on Christ in Michelangelo's *Pietà* (FIG. 9-8). The reference to Christ's martyrdom made the painting a kind of "altarpiece" for the new civic "religion," inspiring the French people with the saintly dedication of their slain leader.

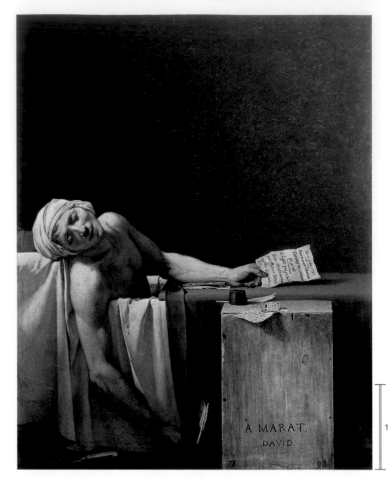

1 ft.

11-15 JACQUES-LOUIS DAVID, *Death of Marat*, 1793. Oil on canvas, 5′ 5″ × 4′ 2½″. Musées Royaux des Beaux-Arts de Belgique, Brussels. ◼◀

David depicted the revolutionary Marat as a tragic martyr, stabbed to death in his bath. Although the painting displays severe Neoclassical spareness, its convincing realism conveys pain and outrage.

Panthéon, Paris Architecture in the Enlightenment era also exhibits a dependence on classical models. Early in the 18th century, architects began to turn away from the theatricality and ostentation of Baroque and Rococo design and embraced a more streamlined antique look. Sainte-Geneviève, now called the Panthéon (FIG. **11-16**), by JACQUES-GERMAIN SOUFFLOT (1713–1780) stands as testament to the revived interest in classical architecture. The columns, based on those of a Roman temple in Lebanon (reproduced with studied archaeological precision), stand out from walls that are severely blank, except for a repeated garland motif near the top. The colonnaded dome, a Neoclassical version of the domes of Saint Peter's (FIGS. 9-15 and 10-3) in Rome and Saint Paul's (FIG. 10-34) in London, rises above a Greek-cross plan. Both the dome and the vaults rest on an interior grid of splendid freestanding Corinthian columns, as if the portico's colonnade continued within. Although the whole effect, inside and out, is Roman, the structural principles employed were essentially Gothic. Soufflot was one of the first 18th-century builders to apply the logical engineering of Gothic cathedrals (see "The Gothic Cathedral," Chapter 7, page 197) to modern buildings.

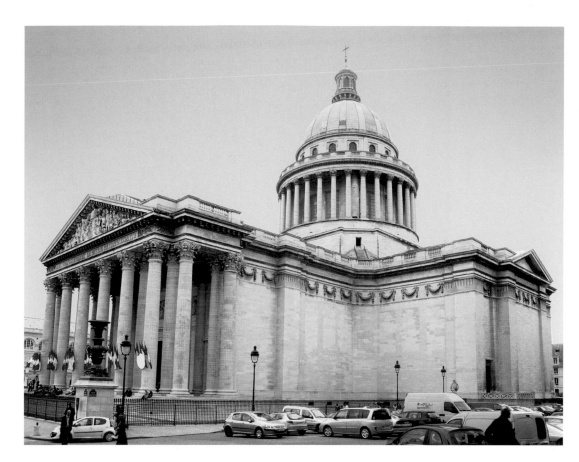

11-16 JACQUES-GERMAIN SOUFFLOT, Panthéon (Sainte-Geneviève; looking northeast), Paris, France, 1755–1792. ■◀

Soufflot's Panthéon is a testament to the Enlightenment admiration for Greece and Rome. It combines a portico based on an ancient Roman temple with a colonnaded dome and a Greek-cross plan.

Thomas Jefferson Because the appeal of Neoclassicism was due in part to the values with which it was associated—morality, idealism, patriotism, and civic virtue—it is not surprising that in the new American republic, THOMAS JEFFERSON (1743–1826)—scholar, economist, educational theorist, statesman, and gifted amateur architect—spearheaded a movement to adopt Neoclassicism as the national architectural style.

Jefferson admired Palladio immensely and read carefully the Italian architect's *Four Books of Architecture*. Later, while minister to France, he studied French 18th-century classi-

cal architecture and visited Roman ruins in Provence. When Jefferson became president, he selected Benjamin Latrobe (1764–1820) to build the US Capitol in Washington, D.C., specifying that Latrobe use a Roman style.

Jefferson's choice in part reflected his admiration for the beauty of the Roman buildings he had seen in Europe and in part his association of those buildings with an idealized Roman republican government and, through that, with the democracy of ancient Greece. For the University of Virginia (FIG. **11-17**), which he founded, Jefferson selected the Pan-

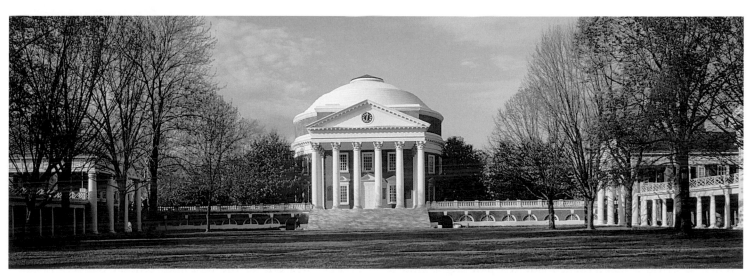

11-17 THOMAS JEFFERSON, Rotunda and Lawn (looking north), University of Virginia, Charlottesville, Virginia, 1819–1826. ■◀

Modeled on the Pantheon (FIG. 3-38), Jefferson's Rotunda sits like a temple in a Roman forum on an elevated platform overlooking the colonnaded Lawn of the University of Virginia.

11-18 JEAN-ANTOINE HOUDON, *George Washington*, 1788–1792. Marble, 6′ 2″ high. State Capitol, Richmond.

Houdon portrayed Washington in contemporary garb, but he incorporated the Roman *fasces* and Cincinnatus's plow in the statue because Washington similarly had returned to his farm after his war service.

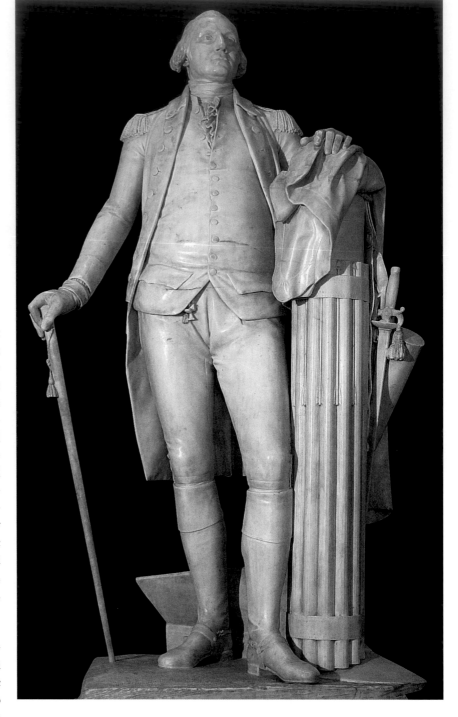

theon (FIG. 3-38) as his model for the Rotunda, the centerpiece of the "academical village" he built in Charlottesville. The domed building sits on an elevated platform at one end of a grassy quadrangle ("the Lawn"), framed by Neoclassical pavilions and colonnades—just as temples in Roman forums (FIGS. 3-12 and 3-35) stood at one short end of a colonnaded square. Each of the ten pavilions (five on each side) resembles a small classical temple. No two are exactly alike. Jefferson experimented with variations of all the different classical orders in his pavilions. He had thoroughly absorbed the principles of classical architecture and clearly delighted in borrowing motifs from major buildings. Jefferson was no mere copyist, however. His designs were highly original—and, in turn, frequently emulated.

Jean-Antoine Houdon Neoclassicism also became the preferred style for public sculpture in the newly independent United States. When the members of the Virginia legislature wanted to erect a life-size marble statue of Virginia-born George Washington (1732–1799), they awarded the commission to the leading French Neoclassical sculptor of the late 18th century, JEAN-ANTOINE HOUDON (1741–1828). Houdon had already carved a bust portrait of Benjamin Franklin (1706–1790) when he was America's ambassador to France. Houdon's portrait of Washington (FIG. **11-18**) is the sculptural equivalent of a Grand Manner portrait (FIG. 11-9). But although the first American president wears contemporary garb, the statue makes an overt reference to the Roman Republic. The "column" on which Washington leans is a bundle of rods with an ax attached—the ancient Roman *fasces,* an emblem of authority. The 13 rods symbolize the 13 original states. The plow behind Washington and the fasces allude to Cincinnatus, a patrician of the early Roman Republic

who was elected dictator during a time of war and resigned his position as soon as victory had been achieved in order to return to his farm. Washington wears the badge of the Society of the Cincinnati (visible beneath the bottom of his waistcoat), an association founded in 1783 for officers in the revolutionary army who had resumed their peacetime roles. Tellingly, Washington no longer holds his sword in Houdon's statue.

The Neoclassical style, so closely associated with revolution and democracy in the late 18th century, ironically also became the ideal vehicle for promoting the empire of Napoleon Bonaparte in the opening decade of the 19th century. Napoleonic art and the revolutionary new styles that eventually displaced Neoclassicism are the subjects of Chapter 12.

Rococo to Neoclassicism in Europe and America

Rococo

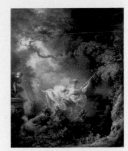

Fragonard, *The Swing*, 1766

I In the early 18th century, the centralized and grandiose palace-based culture of Baroque France gave way to the much more intimate Rococo culture based in the townhouses of Paris. There, aristocrats and intellectuals gathered for witty conversation in salons featuring delicate colors, sinuous lines, gilded mirrors, elegant furniture, and small paintings and sculptures.

I The leading Rococo painter was Antoine Watteau, whose usually small canvases feature light colors and elegant figures in ornate costumes moving gracefully through lush landscapes. Jean-Honoré Fragonard carried on the Rococo style late into the 18th century.

The Enlightenment

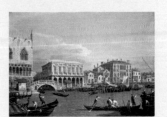

Wright, *A Lecture at the Orrery*, ca. 1763–1765

I By the end of the 18th century, revolutions had overthrown the monarchy in France and achieved independence for the British colonies in America. A major factor was the Enlightenment, a new way of thinking critically about the world independently of religion and tradition that also helped foster the Industrial Revolution, which began in England in the 1740s. The paintings of Joseph Wright of Derby celebrated the scientific inventions of the Enlightenment era.

I The Enlightenment also made knowledge of ancient Rome imperative for the cultured elite, and Europeans and Americans in large numbers undertook a Grand Tour of Italy. Among the most popular souvenirs of the Grand Tour were Antonio Canaletto's *vedute* of Venice rendered in precise Renaissance perspective with the aid of a camera obscura.

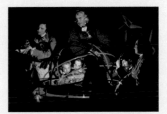

Canaletto, *Riva degli Schiavoni, Venice*, ca. 1735–1740

I Rejecting the idea of progress, Jean-Jacques Rousseau, one of the leading French *philosophes*, argued for a return to natural values and exalted the simple, honest life of peasants. His ideas influenced artists such as Jean-Baptiste-Siméon Chardin, who painted sentimental narratives about rural families.

I The taste for naturalism also led to a reawakening of an interest in realism. Benjamin West represented the protagonists in his history paintings wearing contemporary costumes.

Neoclassicism

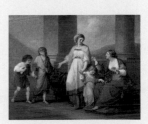

Kauffmann, *Mother of the Gracchi*, ca. 1785

I The Enlightenment revival of interest in Greece and Rome also gave rise in the late 18th century to the artistic movement known as Neoclassicism, which incorporated the subjects and styles of ancient art.

I One pioneer of the new style was Angelica Kauffmann, who often chose subjects drawn from Roman history for her paintings. Jacques-Louis David, who exalted classical art as "the imitation of nature in her most beautiful and perfect form," also favored ancient Roman themes. Painted on the eve of the French Revolution, *Oath of the Horatii*, set in a severe classical hall, is an example of patriotism and sacrifice.

I Neoclassicism also became the dominant style in 18th-century architecture. Ancient Roman and Italian Renaissance structures inspired Jacques-Germain Soufflot's Panthéon in Paris. In the United States, Thomas Jefferson championed Neoclassicism as the official architectural style of the new American republic. It represented for him idealism, patriotism, and civic virtue. He used the Pantheon in Rome as the model for the Rotunda of the University of Virginia.

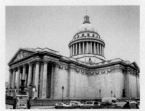

Soufflot, Panthéon, Paris, 1755–1792

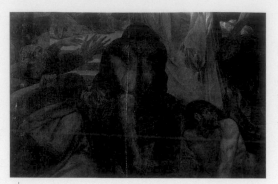

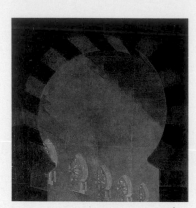

In the shadows of the left side of the huge canvas are dying and dead Arabs, including a seated man in despair. Gros based the figure on one of the damned in Michelangelo's *Last Judgment* (FIG. 9-12).

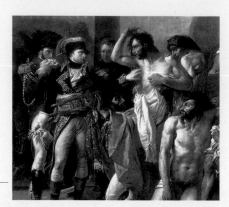

Napoleon, fearless among the plague-stricken, reaches out to touch one man's sores. Gros portrayed the French general as Christlike, implying he possessed miraculous power to heal the sick.

Foreshadowing Romanticism, Gros carefully recorded the exotic people, costumes, and architecture of Jaffa, including the distinctive Islamic striped horseshoe arches of the mosque-hospital.

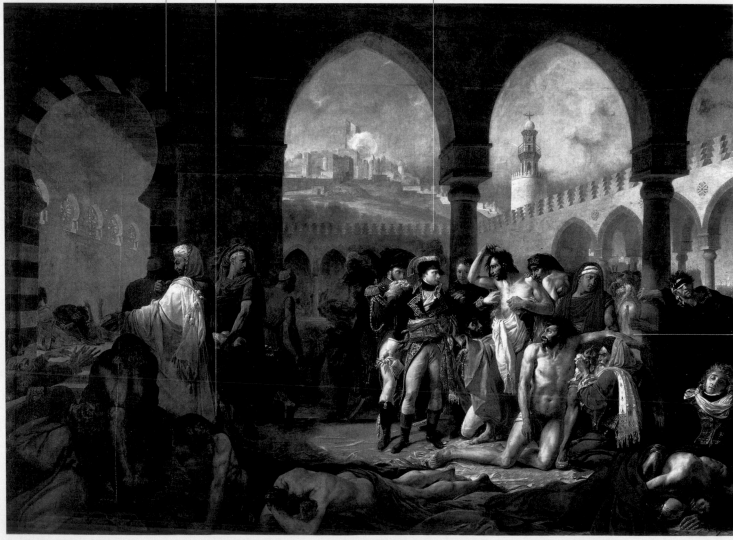

1 ft.

12-1 Antoine-Jean Gros, *Napoleon at the Plague House at Jaffa,* 1804. Oil on canvas, 17′ 5″ × 23′ 7″. Musée du Louvre, Paris.

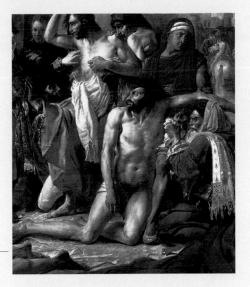

Among the dying Napoleon has come to comfort is a kneeling nude man with left arm extended. His posture recalls that of the dead Christ in a *Pietà* Michelangelo carved near the end of his life.

Romanticism, Realism, and Photography, 1800 to 1870

NAPOLEON AT JAFFA

In the opening decade of the 19th century, many of the leading French artists produced major artworks glorifying the most powerful man in Europe at the time—Napoleon Bonaparte (1769–1821), since 1799 First Consul of the French Republic and from 1804 to 1815, Emperor of the French. One of those artists was ANTOINE-JEAN GROS (1771–1835), a pupil of Jacques-Louis David (FIGS. 11-14 and 11-15), Napoleon's favorite painter. Gros, like David, produced several paintings that contributed to Napoleon's growing mythic status. In *Napoleon at the Plague House at Jaffa* (FIG. 12-1), the artist, at Napoleon's request, recorded an incident during an outbreak of the bubonic plague in the course of the general's Syrian campaign of 1799. This fearsome disease struck Muslim and French forces alike, and to quell the growing panic and hysteria, on March 11, 1799, Napoleon himself visited the mosque at Jaffa that had been converted into a hospital for those who had contracted the dreaded disease. Gros depicted Napoleon's staff officers covering their noses against the stench of the place, whereas Napoleon, amid the dead and dying, is fearless and in control. He comforts those still alive, who are clearly awed by his presence and authority. Indeed, by depicting the French leader having removed his glove to touch the sores of a plague victim, Gros implied Napoleon possessed the miraculous power to heal. The composition recalls scenes of the doubting Thomas touching Christ's wound. Here, however, Napoleon is not Saint Thomas but a Christlike figure tending to the sick, as in Rembrandt's *Hundred-Guilder Print* (FIG. 10-24), which Gros certainly knew. The French painter also based the despairing seated figure at the lower left on the comparable figure (one of the damned) in Michelangelo's *Last Judgment* (FIG. 9-12). The kneeling nude man with extended arm at the right recalls the dead Christ in a late *Pietà* by Michelangelo.

The action in *Napoleon at the Plague House in Jaffa* unfolds against the exotic backdrop of the horseshoe arches and Moorish arcades of the mosque-hospital's courtyard (compare FIG. 5-6). On the left are Muslim doctors distributing bread and ministering to plague-stricken Arabs in the shadows. On the right, in radiant light, are Napoleon and his soldiers in their splendid tailored uniforms. David had used this polarized compositional scheme and an arcaded backdrop to great effect in his *Oath of the Horatii* (FIG. 11-14), and Gros emulated these features in this painting. However, the younger artist's fascination with the exoticism of the Muslim world, as is evident in his attention to the details of architecture and costume, represented a departure from Neoclassicism. This, along with Gros's emphasis on death, suffering, and an emotional rendering of the scene, presaged core elements of the artistic movement that would soon displace Neoclassicism—Romanticism.

ART UNDER NAPOLEON

The revolution of 1789 initiated a new era in France, but the overthrow of the monarchy also opened the door for Corsican-born Napoleon Bonaparte to exploit the resulting disarray and establish a different kind of monarchy with himself at its head. In 1799, after serving in various French army commands, Napoleon became First Consul of the French Republic, a title with clear and intentional links to the ancient Roman Republic (see Chapter 3). During the next 15 years, the ambitious general gained control of almost all of continental Europe in name or through alliances, and in 1804 the pope journeyed to Paris for Napoleon's coronation as Emperor of the French. In 1812, however, Napoleon launched a disastrous invasion of Russia that ended in retreat, and in 1815 he suffered a devastating defeat at the hands of the British at Waterloo in present-day Belgium. Forced to abdicate the imperial throne, Napoleon went into exile on the island of Saint Helena in the South Atlantic, where he died six years later.

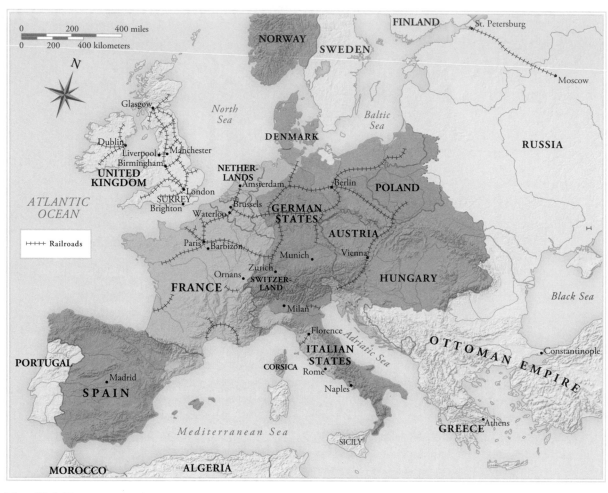

MAP 12-1 Europe around 1850.

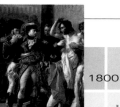

Romanticism, Realism, and Photography, 1800 to 1870

1800	1815	1840	1870
▌ Napoleon appoints David as First Painter of the Empire and brings Canova from Rome to Paris ▌ Gros and Ingres form a bridge between Neoclassicism and Romanticism	▌ Romanticism is the leading art movement in Europe. Delacroix and other painters favor exotic and fantastic subjects featuring unleashed emotion, vibrant color, and bold brushstrokes ▌ Friedrich, Turner, Cole, and other Romantic artists specialize in painting transcendental landscapes ▌ Gothic style enjoys a revival in architecture ▌ Daguerre and Talbot invent photography	▌ Courbet and other Realist painters in Europe and America insist people and events of their own time are the only valid subjects for art ▌ Manet's paintings get a hostile reception because of their shocking subject matter and nonillusionistic style ▌ Paxton pioneers prefabricated glass-and-iron construction in the Crystal Palace ▌ O'Sullivan makes on-the-spot photographs of the Civil War	

After Napoleon's death, the political geography of Europe changed dramatically (MAP 12-1), but in many ways the more significant changes during the first half of the 19th century were technological and economic. The Industrial Revolution caused a population boom in European cities, and railroads spread to many parts of the Continent, facilitating the transportation of both goods and people. Transformation also occurred in the art world. The century opened with Neoclassicism still supreme, but by 1870 Romanticism and Realism in turn had captured the imagination of artists and public alike. New construction techniques had a major impact on architectural design, and the invention of photography revolutionized picture making of all kinds.

Antonio Canova Napoleon embraced all links with the classical past as sources of symbolic authority for his short-lived imperial state, and it is not surprising that the artistic style that most appealed to him was Neoclassicism. He appointed Jacques-Louis David First Painter of the Empire and commissioned various architects to design buildings and monuments based on ancient Roman models. Napoleon's favorite sculptor was ANTONIO CANOVA (1757–1822), who somewhat reluctantly left a successful career in Italy to settle in Paris and serve the emperor. Once in France, Canova became Napoleon's admirer and made numerous portraits, all in the Neoclassical style, of the emperor and his family. The most remarkable is the marble portrait (FIG. 12-2) of Napoleon's

sister, Pauline Borghese (1780–1825), as Venus. Initially, Canova had suggested depicting Borghese as Diana, goddess of the hunt. Pauline, however, demanded she be portrayed as Venus, the goddess of love. Thus, she appears, seminude and reclining on a divan, gracefully holding a golden apple—the symbol of the goddess's triumph in the judgment of Paris. Canova clearly based his work on Greek statuary and on the reclining figures on Roman sarcophagus lids. The French public never got to admire Canova's portrait, however. Napoleon had arranged the marriage of his sister to an heir of the noble Roman Borghese family. Once Pauline was in Rome, her behavior was less than dignified, and the public gossiped extensively about her affairs. Pauline's insistence on being represented as the goddess of love reflected her self-perception. Because of his wife's questionable reputation, Prince Camillo Borghese (1775–1832), the work's official patron, kept the sculpture sequestered in the Villa Borghese and allowed relatively few people to see the portrait.

Ingres In the late 1790s, JEAN-AUGUSTE-DOMINIQUE INGRES (1780–1867) arrived at David's studio, but his study there was to be short-lived. Ingres soon broke with his master on matters of style and adopted what he believed to be a truer and purer Greek style than David's Neoclassical manner. The younger artist employed flat, linear forms approximating those found in Greek vase painting (see Chapter 2), and often placed the main figures in the foreground of his

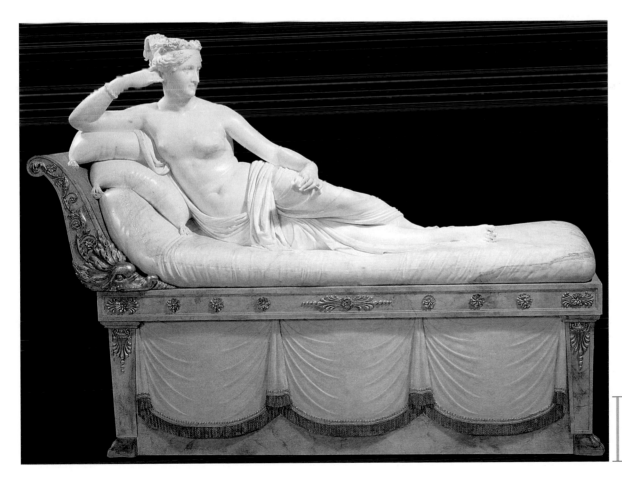

12-2 ANTONIO CANOVA, *Pauline Borghese as Venus*, 1808. Marble, 6' 7" long. Galleria Borghese, Rome.

Canova was Napoleon Bonaparte's favorite sculptor. Here, the artist depicted the emperor's sister—at her request—as the nude Roman goddess of love in a marble statue inspired by classical models.

1 ft.

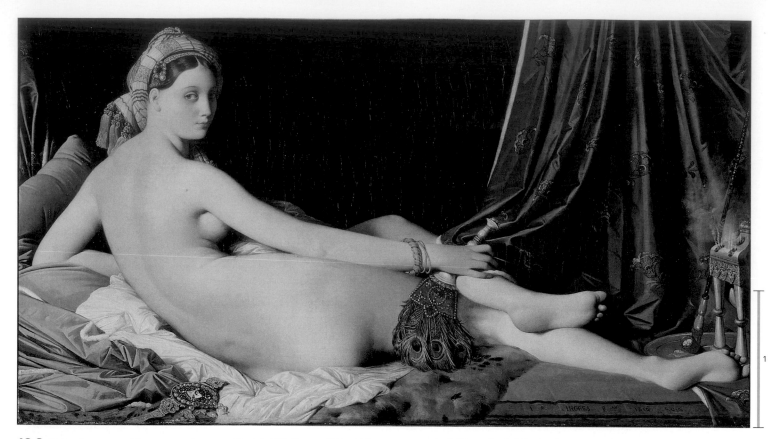

12-3 JEAN-AUGUSTE-DOMINIQUE INGRES, *Grande Odalisque*, 1814. Oil on canvas, 2′ 11⅞″ × 5′ 4″. Musée du Louvre, Paris. ◼◀

The reclining female nude was a Greco-Roman subject, but Ingres converted his Neoclassical figure into an odalisque in a Turkish harem, consistent with the new Romantic taste for the exotic.

composition, emulating low-relief sculpture. In *Grande Odalisque* (FIG. **12-3**), Ingres's subject, the reclining nude female figure, followed the grand tradition of classical antiquity and the Renaissance (FIG. 9-20). The work also shows Ingres's admiration for Raphael in his borrowing of that master's type of female head (FIG. 9-6). However, by converting the figure to an *odalisque* (woman in a Turkish harem), Ingres, unlike Canova (FIG. 12-2), made a strong concession to the burgeoning Romantic taste for the exotic.

ROMANTICISM

Whereas Neoclassicism's rationality reinforced Enlightenment thought (see Chapter 11), particularly Voltaire's views, Rousseau's ideas contributed to the rise of *Romanticism*. Rousseau's exclamation, "Man is born free, but is everywhere in chains!"—the opening line of his *Social Contract* (1762)—summarizes a fundamental Romantic premise. Romanticism emerged from a desire for freedom—not only political freedom but also freedom of thought, of feeling, of action, of worship, of speech, and of taste. Romantics asserted freedom was the right and property of all. They believed the path to freedom was through imagination rather than reason. Romanticism as a phenomenon began around 1750 and ended about 1850, but most art historians use the term more narrowly to denote a movement that flourished from about 1800 to 1840, between Neoclassicism and Realism.

The transition from Neoclassicism to Romanticism represented a shift in emphasis from reason to feeling, from calculation to intuition, and from objective nature to subjective emotion. Among Romanticism's manifestations were the interests in the medieval period and in the sublime. For people living in the 18th century, the Middle Ages were the "dark ages," a time of barbarism, superstition, dark mystery, and miracle. The Romantic imagination stretched its perception of the Middle Ages into all the worlds of fantasy open to it, including the ghoulish, the infernal, the terrible, the nightmarish, the grotesque, the sadistic, and all the imagery that comes from the chamber of horrors when reason sleeps (FIG. 12-4).

Related to the imaginative sensibility was the period's notion of the sublime. Among the individuals most involved in studying the sublime was the British politician and philosopher Edmund Burke (1729–1797). In *A Philosophical Enquiry into the Origins of Our Ideas of the Sublime and Beautiful* (1757), Burke articulated his definition of the sublime—feelings of awe mixed with terror. Burke observed that pain or fear evoked the most intense human emotions and that these emotions can also be thrilling. Thus, raging rivers and great storms at sea could be sublime to their viewers. Accompanying this taste for the sublime was the taste for the fantastic, the occult, and the macabre—for the adventures of the soul voyaging into the dangerous reaches of the imagination.

The Romantic Spirit in Art, Music, and Literature

The appeal of Romanticism, with its emphasis on freedom and emotions unrestrained by rational thought (FIG. 12-4), extended well beyond the realm of the visual arts. In European music, literature, and poetry, the Romantic spirit dominated the late 18th and early 19th centuries. Composers and authors as well as painters rejected classicism's structured order in favor of the emotive and expressive. In music, the compositions of Franz Schubert (1797–1828), Franz Liszt (1811–1886), Frédéric Chopin (1810–1849), and Johannes Brahms (1833–1897) all emphasized the melodic or lyrical. For these composers, music had the power to express the unspeakable and to communicate the subtlest and most powerful human emotions.

In literature, Romantic poets such as John Keats (1795–1821), William Wordsworth (1770–1850), and Samuel Taylor Coleridge (1772–1834) published volumes of poetry manifesting the Romantic interest in lyrical drama. *Ozymandias*, by Percy Bysshe Shelley (1792–1822), transported readers to faraway, exotic locales. The setting of *Sardanapalus* (1821) by Lord Byron (1788–1824) is the ancient Assyrian Empire (see pages 28–30). Byron's poem conjures images of eroticism and fury unleashed—images Eugène Delacroix made concrete in his painting *Death of Sardanapalus* (FIG. 12-7). One of the best examples of the Romantic spirit is the engrossing novel *Frankenstein*, written in 1818 by Shelley's wife, Mary Wollstonecraft Shelley (1797–1851). This fantastic tale of a monstrous creature run amok not only embraced emotionalism but also rejected the rationalism underlying Enlightenment thought. Dr. Frankenstein's monster was a product of science, and the novel is an indictment of the tenacious belief in science that Voltaire and other Enlightenment thinkers promoted. *Frankenstein* served as a cautionary tale of the havoc that could result from unrestrained scientific experimentation and from the arrogance of scientists.

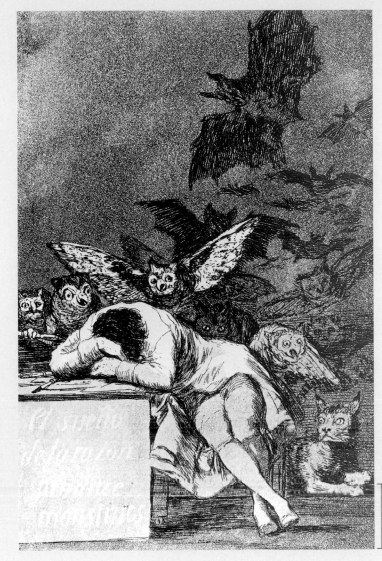

12-4 FRANCISCO GOYA, *The Sleep of Reason Produces Monsters*, from *Los Caprichos*, ca. 1798. Etching and aquatint, $8\frac{7}{16}'' \times 5\frac{7}{8}''$. Metropolitan Museum of Art, New York (gift of M. Knoedler & Co., 1918).

In this print, Goya depicted himself asleep while threatening creatures converge on him, revealing his commitment to the Romantic spirit— the unleashing of imagination, emotions, and nightmares.

1 in.

Francisco Goya Although Spaniard FRANCISCO JOSE DE GOYA LUCIENTES (1746–1828) was Jacques-Louis David's contemporary, their work has little in common. Both, however, rose to prominence as official court artists. In 1786, Goya entered the employ of Charles IV (r. 1788–1808) of Spain, and in 1799, the king promoted him to First Court Painter. At about that time, Goya produced perhaps his most famous print, *The Sleep of Reason Produces Monsters* (FIG. **12-4**), from the series titled *Los Caprichos* (*The Caprices*). *Sleep of Reason* exemplifies Romantic artists' rejection of the Neoclassical penchant for rationality and order. Goya depicted himself asleep, slumped onto a desk, while threatening creatures converge on him. Seemingly poised to attack the artist are owls (symbols of folly) and bats (symbols of ignorance). The viewer might read this as a portrayal of what emerges when reason is suppressed and, therefore, as advocating Enlightenment ideals. However, the print should be interpreted as

Goya's commitment to the creative process and the Romantic spirit—the unleashing of imagination, emotions, and even nightmares (see "The Romantic Spirit in Art, Music, and Literature," above).

Third of May, 1808 Much of Goya's multifaceted work deals not with Romantic fantasies but with contemporary events. Dissatisfaction with the rule of Charles IV increased dramatically during Goya's tenure at the court, and the Spanish people eventually threw their support behind the king's son, Ferdinand VII, in the hope he would initiate reform. To overthrow his father, Ferdinand enlisted the aid of Napoleon Bonaparte, who had designs on the Spanish throne and thus readily agreed to send French troops to Spain. Not surprisingly, as soon as he ousted Charles IV, Napoleon revealed his plan to rule Spain himself by installing his brother Joseph Bonaparte (r. 1808–1813) on the Spanish throne. The

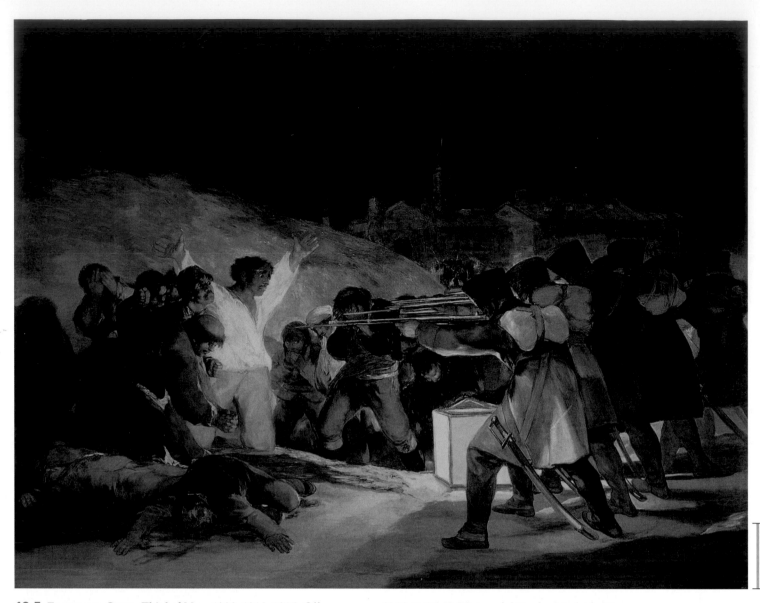

12-5 FRANCISCO GOYA, *Third of May, 1808*, 1814–1815. Oil on canvas, 8′ 9″ × 13′ 4″. Museo del Prado, Madrid. ◼◂

Goya encouraged viewer empathy for the massacred Spanish peasants by portraying horrified expressions on their faces, endowing them with a humanity lacking in the French firing squad.

Spanish people, finally recognizing the French as invaders, sought a way to expel the foreign troops. On May 2, 1808, Spaniards attacked Napoleon's soldiers in a chaotic and violent clash. In retaliation and as a show of force, the French responded the next day by rounding up and executing Spanish citizens.

This tragic event is the subject of Goya's most famous painting, *Third of May, 1808* (FIG. **12-5**). In emotional fashion, Goya depicted the anonymous murderous wall of Napoleonic soldiers ruthlessly executing the unarmed and terrified Spanish peasants. The artist encouraged empathy for the Spaniards by portraying horrified expressions and anguish on their faces, endowing them with a humanity lacking in the French firing squad. Moreover, the peasant about to be shot throws his arms out in a cruciform gesture reminiscent of Christ's position on the cross. Goya enhanced the emotional drama of the massacre by using stark darks and lights and by extending the time frame depicted. Although Goya

captured the specific moment when one man is about to be executed, he also recorded the bloody bodies of others lying dead on the ground. Still others have been herded together and will be shot in a few moments.

Théodore Géricault In France, one of the two greatest Romantic painters was THÉODORE GÉRICAULT (1791–1824). Although Géricault retained an interest in the heroic and the epic and completed rigorous training in classical drawing, he chafed at the rigidity of the Neoclassical style, instead producing works that captivate viewers with their drama, visual complexity, and emotional force. His most ambitious project was a gigantic (16 by 23 feet) canvas titled *Raft of the Medusa* (FIG. **12-6**). In this work, Géricault abandoned the idealism of Neoclassicism and embraced the theatricality of Romanticism. The subject is the 1816 shipwreck off the African coast of the French frigate *Medusa*, which ran aground on a reef due to the incompetence of the captain, a political appointee.

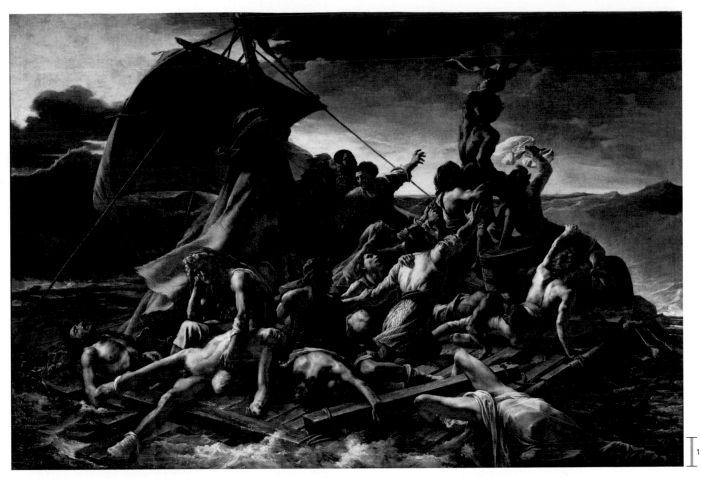

12-6 THÉODORE GÉRICAULT, *Raft of the Medusa,* 1818–1819. Oil on canvas, 16′ 1″ × 23′ 6″. Musée du Louvre, Paris. ◼◀

In this gigantic history painting, Géricault rejected Neoclassical compositional principles and, in the Romantic spirit, presented a jumble of writhing bodies in every attitude of suffering, despair, and death.

In an attempt to survive, 150 passengers built a makeshift raft from pieces of the disintegrating ship. The raft drifted for 12 days, and the number of survivors dwindled to 15. Finally, a ship spotted the raft and rescued the emaciated survivors. This horrendous event was political dynamite once it became public knowledge.

In *Raft of the Medusa,* Géricault sought to capture the horror, chaos, and emotion of the tragedy yet invoke the grandeur and impact of Neoclassical history painting. *Medusa* took eight months to complete, not only because of its size, but because Géricault went to great lengths to ensure the accuracy of his representation. He visited hospitals and morgues to examine corpses, interviewed the survivors, and had a model of the raft constructed in his studio. In the painting, the few despairing survivors summon what little strength they have left to flag down the passing ship far on the horizon. The subdued palette and prominent shadows lend an ominous pall to the scene. Géricault departed from the straightforward organization of Neoclassical compositions and instead presented a jumble of writhing bodies. He arranged the survivors and several corpses in a powerful X-shaped composition, and piled one body on another in every attitude of suffering, despair, and death (compare FIG. 12-1). One light-filled diagonal axis stretches from bodies at the

lower left up to the black man raised on his comrades' shoulders and waving a piece of cloth toward the horizon. The cross axis descends from the storm clouds and the dark, billowing sail at the upper left to the shadowed upper torso of the body trailing in the open sea. Géricault's decision to place the raft at a diagonal so that a corner juts outward further draws viewers into the tragic scene. Indeed, it seems as though some of the corpses are sliding off the raft into the viewing space.

Raft of the Medusa is also Géricault's commentary on the practice of slavery. The artist was a member of an abolitionist group that sought ways to end the slave trade in the colonies. Given Géricault's antipathy to slavery, it is appropriate he placed Jean Charles, a black soldier and one of the few survivors, at the top of the pyramidal heap of bodies.

Eugène Delacroix Art historians often present the history of painting during the first half of the 19th century as a contest between two major artists—Ingres, the Neoclassical draftsman, and EUGÈNE DELACROIX (1798–1863), the Romantic colorist. Their dialogue recalls the quarrel at the end of the 17th century and the beginning of the 18th between the Poussinistes and the Rubénistes (see page 324). No other painter of the time explored the domain of Romantic subject

Delacroix on David and Neoclassicism

Eugène Delacroix, the leading French Romantic painter of the 19th century, expressed his contempt for the Neoclassical style of Jacques-Louis David (FIGS. 11-14 and 11-15) and others in a series of letters he wrote in 1832 from Morocco. Romantic artists often depicted exotic faraway places they had never seen, but Delacroix journeyed to northern Africa in search of fresh inspiration for his paintings. He discovered in the sun-drenched Moroccan landscape—and in the hardy and colorful Moroccans dressed in robes reminiscent of the Roman toga—new insights into a culture he believed was more classical than anything European Neoclassicism could conceive. In a letter to his friend Fréderic Villot dated February 29, 1832, he wrote:

> This place is made for painters. . . . [B]eauty abounds here; not the over-praised beauty of fashionable paintings. The heroes of David and Co. with their rose-pink limbs would cut a sorry figure beside

these children of the sun, who moreover wear the dress of classical antiquity with a nobler air, I dare assert.*

In a second letter, written June 4, 1832, he reported to Auguste Jal:

> I have Romans and Greeks on my doorstep: it makes me laugh heartily at David's Greeks, . . . I know now what they were really like; . . . If painting schools persist in [depicting classical subjects], I am convinced, and you will agree with me, that they would gain far more from being shipped off as cabin boys on the first boat bound for the Barbary coast than from spending any more time wearing out the classical soil of Rome. Rome is no longer to be found in Rome.†

*Translated by Jean Stewart, in Charles Harrison, Paul Wood, and Jason Gaiger, eds., *Art in Theory 1815–1900: An Anthology of Changing Ideas* (Oxford: Blackwell, 1998), 87.
†Ibid., 88.

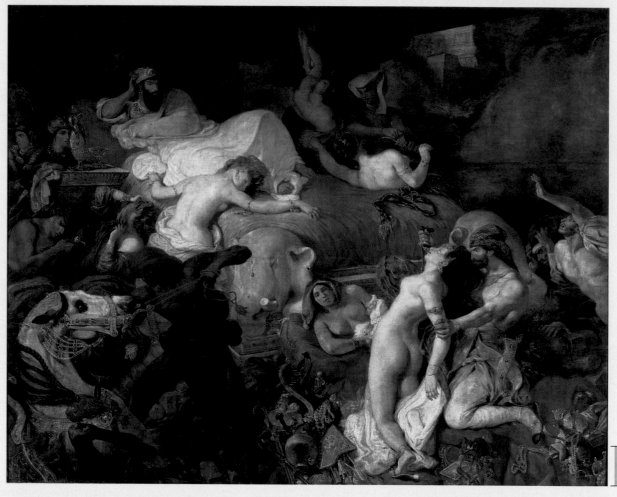

12-7 EUGÈNE DELACROIX, *Death of Sardanapalus*, 1827. Oil on canvas, 12′ 1½″ × 16′ 2⅞″. Musée du Louvre, Paris. ◼◀

Inspired by Lord Byron's 1821 poem, Delacroix painted the Romantic spectacle of an Assyrian king on his funeral pyre. The richly colored and emotionally charged canvas is filled with exotic figures.

1 ft.

and mood as thoroughly and definitively as Delacroix. His technique was impetuous, improvisational, and instinctive, rather than the deliberate, studious, and cold method of the Neoclassicists (see "Delacroix on David and Neoclassicism," above). His work epitomized Romantic colorist painting, catching the impression quickly and developing it in the execution process. His contemporaries commented on how furiously Delacroix worked once he had an idea, keeping the

whole painting progressing at once. The fury of his attack matched the fury of his imagination and his subjects.

Death of Sardanapalus Delacroix's richly colored and emotionally charged *Death of Sardanapalus* (FIG. **12-7**) is perhaps the grandest Romantic pictorial drama ever painted. Although inspired by Lord Byron's poem *Sardanapalus* (see "The Romantic Spirit," page 345), the painting does not illustrate

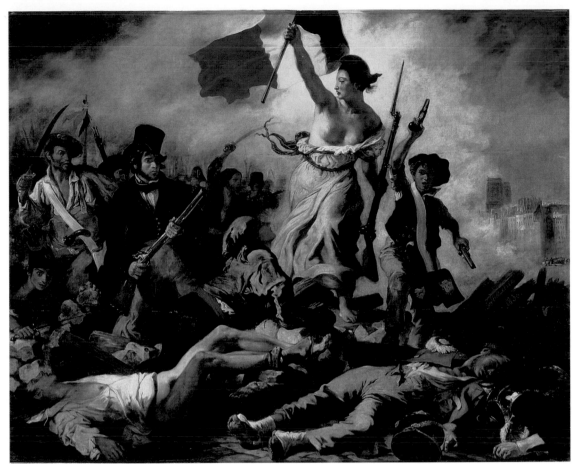

12-8 Eugène Delacroix, *Liberty Leading the People,* 1830. Oil on canvas, 8′ 6″ × 10′ 8″. Musée du Louvre, Paris. ◼◀

In a balanced mix of history and poetic allegory, Delacroix captured the passion and energy of the 1830 revolution in this painting of Liberty leading the Parisian uprising against Charles X.

1 ft.

that text faithfully. Delacroix depicted the last hour of the Assyrian king Ashurbanipal (r. 668–627 BCE), whom the Greeks called Sardanapalus. The king has just received news of his army's defeat and the enemy's entry into his city. The setting is much more tempestuous and crowded than Byron described, and orgiastic destruction has replaced the sacrificial suicide of the poem. Sardanapalus reclines on his funeral pyre, soon to be set alight, and gloomily watches the destruction of all of his most precious possessions—his women, slaves, horses, and treasure. Sardanapalus's favorite concubine throws herself on the bed, determined to go up in flames with her master. The Assyrian king presides like a genius of evil over the tragic scene. Most conspicuous are the tortured and dying bodies of the harem women. In the foreground, a muscular slave plunges his knife into the neck of one woman. Delacroix filled this awful spectacle of suffering and death with the most daringly difficult and tortuous poses, and chose the richest intensities of hue. With its exotic and erotic overtones, *Death of Sardanapalus* tapped into the Romantic fantasies of 19th-century viewers.

Liberty Leading the People Although *Death of Sardanapalus* is a seventh-century BCE drama, Delacroix, as Géricault, also turned to current events, particularly tragic or sensational ones, for his subject matter. In *Liberty Leading the People* (FIG. **12-8**), Delacroix captured the passion and the energy of the 1830 revolution in France. Based on the Parisian uprising against Charles X (r. 1824–1830) at the end of July 1830,

it depicts the allegorical personification of Liberty, defiantly thrusting forth the French Republic's tricolor banner as she urges the masses to fight on. The scarlet Phrygian cap (the symbol of a freed slave in antiquity) she wears reinforces the urgency of this struggle. Arrayed around Liberty are bold Parisian types—the street boy brandishing his pistols, the menacing worker with a cutlass, and the intellectual dandy in top hat with sawed-off musket. As in Géricault's *Raft of the Medusa* (FIG. 12-6), dead bodies lie all around. In the background, the Gothic towers of Notre-Dame (FIG. 7-7) rise through the smoke and haze. The painter's inclusion of this recognizable Parisian landmark specifies the locale and event, balancing contemporary historical fact with poetic allegory.

Caspar David Friedrich Landscape painting came into its own in the 19th century as a fully independent and respected genre. Briefly eclipsed at the century's beginning by the taste for ideal form, which favored figural composition and history, landscape painting expressed the Romantic view (first extolled by Rousseau) of nature as a "being" that included the totality of existence in organic unity and harmony. In nature—"the living garment of God," as German poet and dramatist Johann Wolfgang von Goethe (1749–1832) called it—artists found an ideal subject to express the Romantic theme of the soul unified with the natural world. As all nature was mysteriously permeated by "being," landscape artists had the task of interpreting the signs, symbols, and emblems of universal spirit disguised within visible material things. Artists

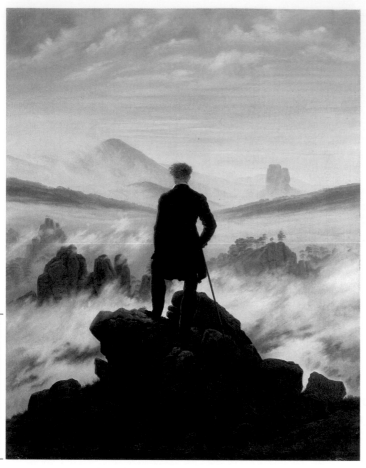

12-9 CASPAR DAVID FRIEDRICH, *Wanderer above a Sea of Mist*, 1817–1818. Oil on canvas, 3′ 1¾″ × 2′ 5⅜″. Hamburger Kunsthalle, Hamburg.

Friedrich's painting of a solitary man on a rocky promontory gazing at a vast panorama of clouds, mountains, and thick mist perfectly expresses the Romantic notion of the sublime in nature.

no longer merely beheld a landscape but rather participated in its spirit, becoming translators of nature's transcendent meanings.

Among the artists best known for their Romantic transcendental landscape paintings is CASPAR DAVID FRIEDRICH (1774–1840). For Friedrich, landscapes were temples and his paintings were altarpieces. The reverential mood of his works demands from the viewer the silence appropriate to sacred places filled with a divine presence. Friedrich's work balances inner and outer experience. "The artist," he wrote, "should not only paint what he sees before him, but also what he sees within him."[1] In many of Friedrich's landscapes, the human figure plays an insignificant role. Indeed, the human actors are often difficult even to discern. But in other paintings, one or more figures seen from behind gazing at the natural vista dominate the canvas. In *Wanderer above a Sea of Mist* (FIG. **12-9**), a solitary man, dressed in attire suggestive of a bygone era in Germany, stands on a rocky promontory and leans on his cane. He surveys a vast panorama of clouds, mountains, and thick mist. Because Friedrich chose a point of view on the level of the man's head, the viewer has the sensation of hovering in space behind him—an impossible position that

enhances the aura of mystery the scene conveys. Scholars dispute whether Friedrich intended the viewer to identify with the man seen from behind or if he wanted the viewer to contemplate the man gazing at the misty landscape. In either case, the painter communicated an almost religious awe at the beauty and vastness of the natural world. *Wanderer above a Sea of Mist* perfectly expresses the Romantic notion of the sublime in nature.

John Constable In England, one of the most momentous developments in Western history—the Industrial Revolution—had a profound impact on the evolution of Romantic landscape painting. Although discussion of the Industrial Revolution invariably focuses on technological advances, factory development, and growth of urban centers, industrialization had no less pronounced an effect on the countryside and the land itself. The detrimental economic effect the Industrial Revolution had on prices for agrarian products produced significant unrest in the English countryside. In particular, increasing numbers of displaced farmers could no longer afford to farm their small land plots. JOHN CONSTABLE (1776–1837) addressed this agrarian situation in his landscape paintings. He made countless sketches from nature for each of his canvases, studying nature as a meteorologist (which he was by avocation). His special gift was for capturing the texture that climate and weather give to landscape. Constable's use of tiny dabs of local color, stippled with white, created a sparkling shimmer of light and hue across the canvas surface—the vibration itself suggestive of movement and process.

The Haywain (FIG. **12-10**) is a placid, picturesque scene of the countryside. A small cottage is on the left, and in the center foreground a man leads a horse and wagon across the stream. Billowy clouds float lazily across the sky. The muted greens and golds and the delicacy of Constable's brushstrokes complement the scene's tranquility. The artist portrayed the oneness with nature the Romantic poets sought. The relaxed figures are not observers but participants in the landscape's "being." *The Haywain* is also significant for precisely what it does not show—the civil unrest of the agrarian working class and the resulting outbreaks of violence and arson. The figures populating Constable's landscapes blend into the scenes and are one with nature. Rarely does the viewer see workers engaged in tedious labor. Indeed, this painting has a nostalgic, wistful air to it. It is Constable's lament for a disappearing rural pastoralism. This nostalgia, presented in such naturalistic terms, renders Constable's works Romantic in tone. That the painter felt a kindred spirit with the Romantic artists is revealed by his comment, "Painting is but another word for feeling."[2]

J.M.W. Turner Constable's contemporary in the English school of landscape painting, JOSEPH MALLORD WILLIAM TURNER (1775–1851), produced work that also responded to encroaching industrialization. However, whereas Constable's paintings are serene and precisely painted, Turner's feature

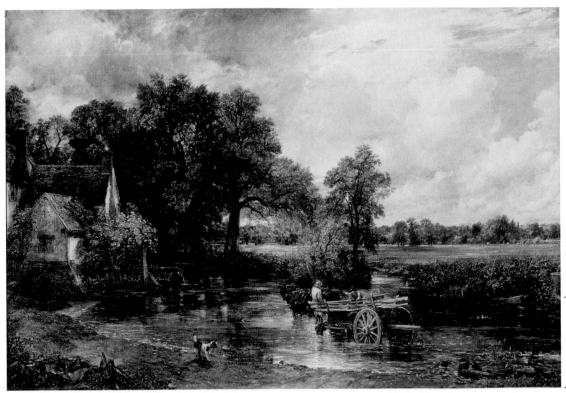

12-10 JOHN CONSTABLE, *The Haywain,* 1821. Oil on canvas, 4′ 3¼″ × 6′ 1″. National Gallery, London.

The Haywain is a nostalgic view of the disappearing English countryside during the Industrial Revolution. Constable had a special gift for capturing the texture that climate and weather give to landscape.

1 ft.

turbulent swirls of frothy pigment. The passion and energy of Turner's works reveal the Romantic sensibility that was the foundation for his art and also clearly illustrate Edmund Burke's concept of the sublime—awe mixed with terror.

Among Turner's most notable works is *The Slave Ship* (FIG. **12-11**). Its subject is a 1783 incident reported in a widely read book titled *The History of the Abolition of the Slave Trade,* by Thomas Clarkson. Because the book had just been reprinted in 1839, Clarkson's account probably prompted Turner's choice of subject for this 1840 painting. The incident involved the captain of a slave ship who, on realizing his insurance company would reimburse him only for slaves lost at sea but not for those who died en route, ordered the sick and dying slaves thrown overboard. Turner's frenzied

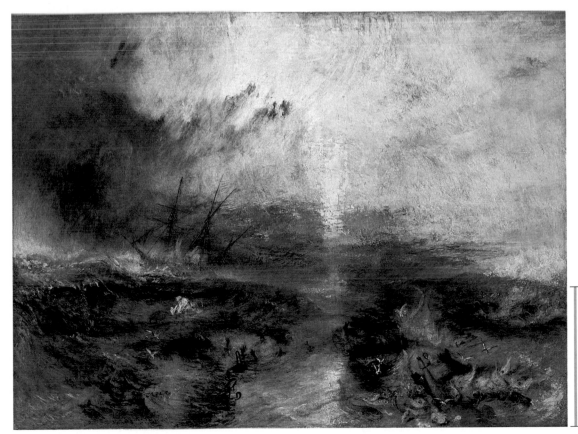

12-11 JOSEPH MALLORD WILLIAM TURNER, *The Slave Ship* (*Slavers Throwing Overboard the Dead and Dying, Typhoon Coming On*), 1840. Oil on canvas, 2′ 11¼″ × 4′. Museum of Fine Arts, Boston (Henry Lillie Pierce Fund).

The essence of Turner's innovative style is the emotive power of color. He released color from any defining outlines to express both the forces of nature and the painter's emotional response to them.

1 ft.

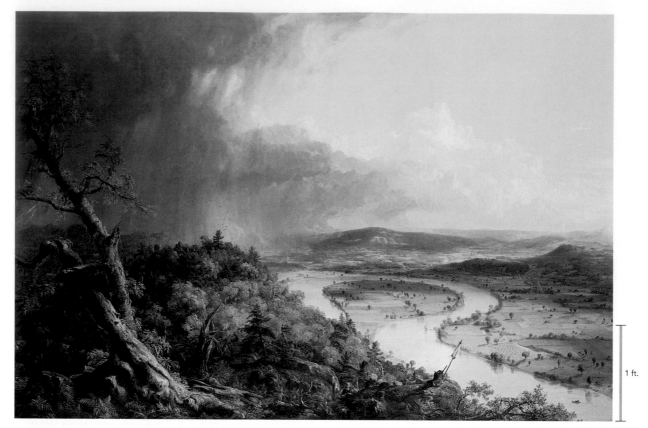

12-12 THOMAS COLE, *The Oxbow* (*View from Mount Holyoke, Northampton, Massachusetts, after a Thunderstorm*), 1836. Oil on canvas, 4′ 3½″ × 6′ 4″. Metropolitan Museum of Art, New York (gift of Mrs. Russell Sage, 1908). ◼️◄

Cole divided his canvas into dark wilderness on the left and sunlit civilization on the right. The minuscule painter at the bottom center seems to be asking for advice about America's future course.

1 ft.

emotional depiction of this act matches its barbaric nature. The artist transformed the sun into an incandescent comet amid flying scarlet clouds. The slave ship moves into the distance, leaving in its wake a turbulent sea choked with the bodies of slaves sinking to their deaths. The scale of the minuscule human forms compared with the vast sea and overarching sky reinforces the sense of the sublime, especially the immense power of nature over humans. Almost lost in the boiling colors are the event's particulars, but on close inspection, the viewer can discern the iron shackles and manacles around the wrists and ankles of the drowning slaves, denying them any chance of saving themselves.

A key ingredient of Turner's highly personal style is the emotive power of pure color. The haziness of the painter's forms and the indistinctness of his compositions intensify the colors and energetic brushstrokes. Turner's innovation was to release color from any defining outlines so as to express both the forces of nature and the painter's emotional response to them. In his paintings, the reality of color is at one with the reality of feeling. Turner's methods had an incalculable effect on the later development of painting. His discovery of the aesthetic and emotive power of pure color and his pushing of the medium's fluidity to a point where the paint itself is almost the subject were important steps toward 20th-century abstract art, which dispensed with shape and form altogether (see Chapter 15).

Thomas Cole In America, landscape painting was the specialty of a group of artists known as the Hudson River School, so named because its members drew their subjects primarily from the uncultivated regions of New York's Hudson River Valley, although many of these painters depicted scenes from across the country. As did the early-19th-century landscape painters in Germany and England, the artists of the Hudson River School not only presented Romantic panoramic landscape views but also participated in the ongoing exploration of the individual's and the country's relationship to the land. American landscape painters frequently focused on identifying qualities that made America unique. One American painter of English birth, THOMAS COLE (1801–1848), often considered the leader of the Hudson River School, articulated this idea:

> Whether he [an American] beholds the Hudson mingling waters with the Atlantic—explores the central wilds of this vast continent, or stands on the margin of the distant Oregon, he is still in the midst of American scenery—it is his own land; its beauty, its magnificence, its sublimity—all are his; and how undeserving of such a birthright, if he can turn towards it an unobserving eye, an unaffected heart![3]

Another issue that surfaced frequently in Hudson River School paintings was the moral question of America's direction as a civilization. Cole addressed this question in *The*

Oxbow (FIG. **12-12**). A splendid scene opens before the viewer, dominated by the lazy oxbow-shaped curve of the Connecticut River near Northampton, Massachusetts. Cole divided the composition in two, with the dark, stormy wilderness on the left and the more developed civilization on the right. The minuscule artist in the bottom center of the painting (wearing a top hat), dwarfed by the landscape's scale, turns to the viewer as if to ask for input in deciding the country's future course. Cole's depiction of expansive wilderness incorporated reflections and moods romantically appealing to the public.

REALISM

Advances in industrial technology during the early 19th century reinforced Enlightenment faith in the connection between science and progress. Both intellectuals and the general public increasingly embraced *empiricism* and *positivism*. To empiricists, the basis of knowledge is observation and direct experience. Positivists ascribe to the philosophical model developed by Auguste Comte (1798–1857), who believed scientific laws governed the environment and human activity and could be revealed through careful recording and analysis of observable data. Comte's followers promoted science as the mind's highest achievement and advocated a purely empirical approach to nature and society.

Realism was a movement that developed in France around mid-century against this backdrop of an increasing emphasis on science. Consistent with the philosophical tenets of the empiricists and positivists, Realist artists argued that only the contemporary world—what people could see—was "real." Accordingly, Realists focused their attention on the people and events of their own time and disapproved of historical and fictional subjects on the grounds they were neither visible nor present and therefore were not real.

Gustave Courbet The leading figure of the Realist movement was GUSTAVE COURBET (1819–1877). In fact, even though he shunned labels, Courbet used the term *Realism* when exhibiting his works (see "Courbet on Realism," page 354). The Realists' sincerity about scrutinizing their environment led them to paint subjects artists had traditionally deemed unworthy of depiction—the mundane and trivial, working-class laborers and peasants, and so forth. Moreover, the Realists depicted these scenes on a scale and with an earnestness and seriousness previously reserved for historical, mythological, and religious painting.

The Stone Breakers In *The Stone Breakers* (FIG. **12-13**), Courbet captured on canvas in a straightforward manner two men—one about 70, the other quite young—in the act of breaking stones, traditionally the lot of the lowest members of French society. By juxtaposing youth and age, Courbet suggested those born to poverty remain poor their entire lives. The artist neither romanticized nor idealized the men's menial labor but depicted their thankless toil with directness and accuracy. Courbet's palette of dirty browns and grays further conveys the dreary and dismal nature of the task, and the angular positioning of the older stone breaker's limbs suggests a mechanical monotony.

Courbet's portrayal of the working poor had a special resonance for his mid-19th-century French audience. In 1848, laborers rebelled against the bourgeois leaders of the newly formed Second Republic and against the rest of the nation, demanding better working conditions and a redistribution of property. The army quelled the uprising in three days, but not without long-lasting trauma and significant loss of life. The 1848 revolution raised the issue of labor as a national concern. Courbet's depiction of stone breakers in 1849 was thus both timely and populist.

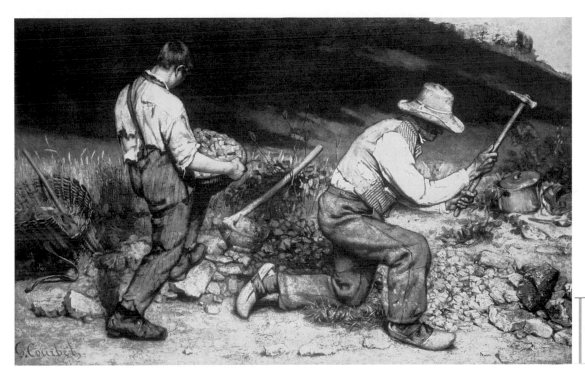

12-13 GUSTAVE COURBET, *The Stone Breakers*, 1849. Oil on canvas, 5′ 3″ × 8′ 6″. Formerly Gemäldegalerie, Dresden (destroyed in 1945).

Courbet was the leading figure in the Realist movement. Using a palette of dirty browns and grays, he conveyed the dreary and dismal nature of menial labor in mid-19th-century France.

1 ft.

Courbet on Realism

The academic jury selecting work for the 1855 Salon (part of the Exposition Universelle in Paris that year) rejected two of Courbet's paintings, declaring the subjects and figures of his canvases (FIGS. 12-13 and 12-14) were too coarse and too large. In response, Courbet withdrew all of his works and set up his own exhibition outside the grounds, calling it the Pavilion of Realism. Courbet was the first artist ever known to have staged a private exhibition of his own work. His pavilion and the statement he issued to explain the paintings shown there amounted to the Realist movement's manifestos.

> The title of "realist" has been imposed upon me . . . . Titles have never given a just idea of things; were it otherwise, the work would be superfluous. . . . I have studied the art of the moderns, avoiding any preconceived system and without prejudice. I have no more wanted to imitate the former than to copy the latter; nor have I thought of achieving the idle aim of "art for art's sake." No! I have simply wanted to draw from a thorough knowledge of tradition the reasoned and free sense of my own individuality. . . . To be able to translate the customs, ideas, and appearances of my time as I see them—in a word, to create a living art—this has been my aim.*

Six years later, on Christmas Day, 1861, Courbet wrote an open letter, published a few days later in the *Courier du dimanche*, addressed to prospective students.

> [An artist must apply] his personal faculties to the ideas and the events of the times in which he lives. . . . [A]rt in painting should consist only of the representation of things that are visible and tangible to the artist. Every age should be represented only by its own artists, that is to say, by the artists who have lived in it. I also maintain that painting is an essentially concrete art form and can consist only of the representation of both real and existing things. . . . An abstract object, not visible, nonexistent, is not within the domain of painting.†

Courbet's most famous statement, however, is his blunt dismissal of academic painting, in which he concisely summed up the core principle of Realist painting:

> I have never seen an angel. Show me an angel, and I'll paint one.‡

*Translated by Robert Goldwater and Marco Treves, eds., *Artists on Art from the XIV to the XX Century* (New York: Pantheon, 1958), 295.
†Translated by Petra ten-Doesschate Chu, *Letters of Gustave Courbet* (Chicago: University of Chicago Press, 1992), 203–204.
‡Quoted by Vincent van Gogh in a July 1885 letter to his brother Theo. Ronald de Leeuw, *The Letters of Vincent van Gogh* (New York: Penguin, 1996), 302.

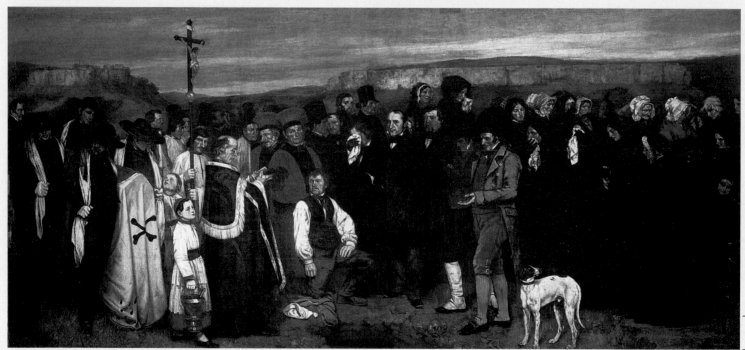

1 ft.

12-14 GUSTAVE COURBET, *Burial at Ornans,* 1849. Oil on canvas, 10′ 3½″ × 21′ 9½″. Musée d'Orsay, Paris.

Although as monumental in scale as a traditional history painting, *Burial at Ornans* horrified critics because of the ordinary nature of the subject and Courbet's starkly antiheroic composition.

Burial at Ornans Many art historians regard Courbet's *Burial at Ornans* (FIG. **12-14**) as his masterpiece. The huge (10 by 22 feet) canvas depicts a funeral set in a bleak provincial landscape outside the artist's hometown. Attending the funeral are the types of ordinary people Honoré de Balzac (1799–1850) and Gustave Flaubert (1821–1880) presented in their novels. The mourners' faces register all degrees of response to the ceremony. Although the painting has the monumental scale of a traditional history painting, the subject's ordinariness and the starkly antiheroic composition horrified critics. Arranged in a wavering line extending across the breadth of the canvas are three groups—the somberly clad women at the back right, a semicircle of similarly clad men by the open grave, and assorted churchmen at the left. This wall of figures blocks any view into deep space. Behind and above the figures are bands of overcast sky and barren cliffs. The dark pit of the grave opens into the viewer's space in the center foreground. Despite the unposed look of the figures, Courbet controlled the composition in a masterful way by his sparing use of bright color. In place of the heroic, the sublime, and the dramatic, Courbet aggressively presented the viewer with the mundane realities of daily life and death. Unlike the theatricality of Romanticism, Realism captured the ordinary rhythms of daily life.

Of great importance for the later history of art, Realism also involved a reconsideration of the painter's primary goals and departed from the established priority on illusionism. Accordingly, Realists called attention to painting as a pictorial construction by the ways they applied pigment or manipulated composition. Courbet's intentionally simple and direct methods of expression in composition and technique seemed unbearably crude to many of his more traditional contemporaries, who called him a primitive. Although his bold, somber palette was essentially traditional, Courbet often used the *palette knife* for quickly placing and unifying large daubs of paint, producing a roughly wrought surface. The public accused him of carelessness and critics wrote of his "brutalities."

Jean-Francois Millet As did Courbet, JEAN-FRANCOIS MILLET (1814–1878) found his subjects in the people and occupations of the everyday world. Millet was the most prominent member of the group of French painters of country life who, to be close to their rural subjects, settled near the village of Barbizon. This Barbizon School specialized in detailed pictures of forest and countryside. In *The Gleaners* (FIG. **12-15**), Millet depicted three impoverished women—members of the lowest level of peasant society—performing the backbreaking task of gleaning. Landowning nobles traditionally permitted peasants to glean, or collect, the wheat scraps left in the field after the harvest. Millet characteristically placed his monumental figures in the foreground, against a broad sky. Although the field stretches back to a rim of haystacks, cottages, trees, and distant workers and a flat horizon, the gleaners quietly doing their tedious and time-consuming work dominate the canvas.

Although Millet's paintings evoke a sentimentality absent from Courbet's, the French public still reacted to his work with disdain and suspicion. In the aftermath of the 1848 revolution, Millet's investiture of the poor with solemn grandeur did not meet with approval from the prosperous classes. Further, the middle class linked the poor with the dangerous, newly defined working class, which was finding outspoken champions in men such as Karl Marx (1818–1883), Friedrich Engels (1820–1895), and the novelists Émile Zola (1840–1902) and Charles Dickens (1812–1870). Socialism was a growing movement, and both its views on property and

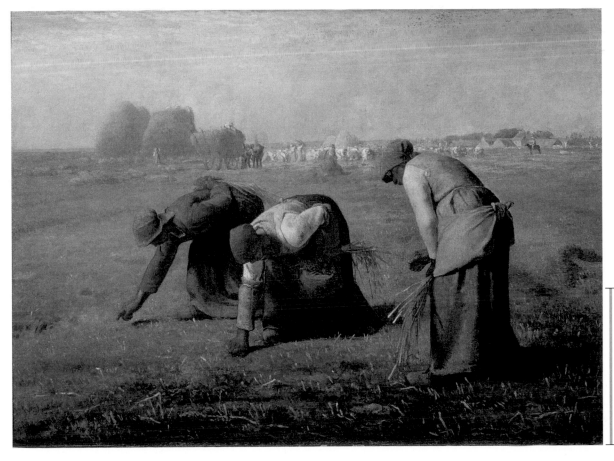

12-15 JEAN-FRANCOIS MILLET, *The Gleaners*, 1857. Oil on canvas, 2' 9" × 3' 8". Musée d'Orsay, Paris.

Millet and the Barbizon School painters specialized in depictions of French country life. Here, Millet portrayed three impoverished women gathering the remainders left in the field after a harvest.

1 ft.

Lithography

In 1798, the German print maker Alois Senefelder (1771–1834) created the first prints using stone instead of metal plates or wood blocks. In contrast to earlier printing techniques (see "Woodcuts, Engravings, and Etchings," Chapter 8, page 233), in which the artist applied ink either to a raised or incised surface, in *lithography* (Greek, "stone writing") the printing and nonprinting areas of the plate are on the same plane.

The chemical phenomenon fundamental to lithography is the repellence of oil and water. The lithographer uses a greasy, oil-based crayon to draw directly on a stone plate, and then wipes water onto the stone, which clings only to the areas the drawing does not cover. Next, the artist rolls oil-based ink onto the stone, which adheres to the drawing but is repelled by the water. When the artist presses the stone against paper, only the inked areas—the drawing—transfer to the paper. Color lithography requires multiple plates, one for each color, and the print maker must take special care to make sure that each impression lines up perfectly with the previous one so that each color prints in its proper place.

One of the earliest masters of this new printmaking process was Honoré Daumier, whose politically biting lithographs (FIG. 12-16) published in a widely read French journal reached an audience of unprecedented size.

12-16 HONORÉ DAUMIER, *Rue Transnonain, le 15 avril, 1834*, 1834. Lithograph, 1' × 1' 5½". Philadelphia Museum of Art, Philadelphia (bequest of Fiske and Marie Kimball).

Daumier used the recent invention of lithography to reach a wide audience for his social criticism and political protest. This print records the horrific 1834 massacre in a workers' housing block in Paris.

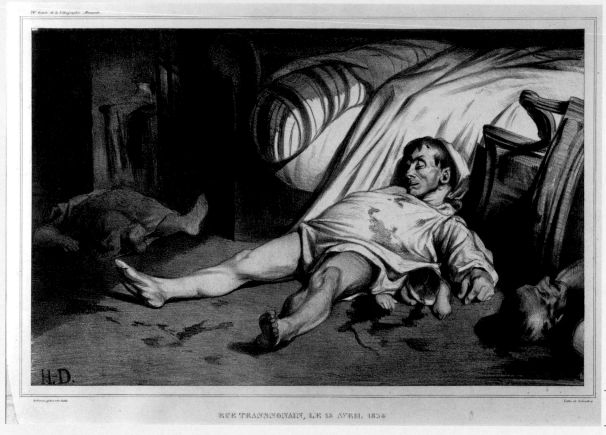

RUE TRANSNONAIN, LE 15 AVRIL 1834

1 in.

its call for social justice, even economic equality, threatened the bourgeoisie. Much of the public saw Millet's sympathetic portrayal of the poor as a political manifesto.

Honoré Daumier Because people widely recognized the power of art to serve political ends, the political and social agitation accompanying the violent revolutions in France and the rest of Europe in the later 18th and early 19th centuries prompted the French people to suspect artists of subversive intention. Realist artist HONORÉ DAUMIER (1808–1879) was a defender of the urban working classes, and in his art, he boldly confronted authority with social criticism and political protest. In response, the authorities imprisoned the artist. A painter, sculptor, and one of history's great print makers, Daumier produced *lithographs* (see "Lithography," above) that enabled him to create an unprecedented number of prints, thereby reaching a broader audience. Daumier also contributed satirical lithographs to the widely read, liberal French Republican journal *Caricature*. In these prints, he mercilessly lampooned the foibles and misbehavior of politicians, lawyers, doctors, and the rich bourgeoisie in general.

Daumier's lithograph *Rue Transnonain* (FIG. **12-16**) depicts an atrocity that unfolded in the street in Paris in which an unknown sniper killed a civil guard, part of a government force trying to repress a worker demonstration in April 1834. Because the fatal shot had come from a workers' housing block, the remaining guards immediately stormed the building and massacred all of its inhabitants. With the power Goya

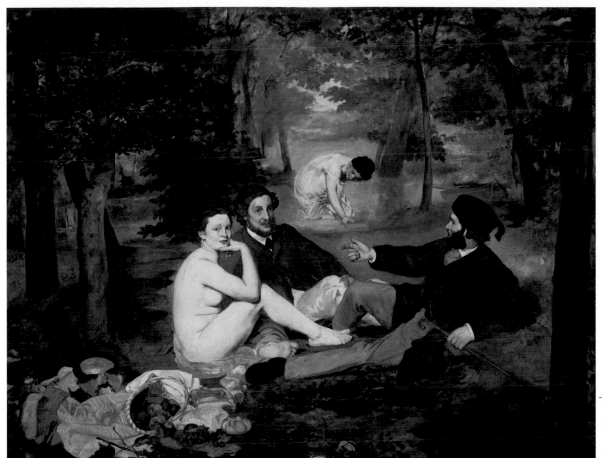

12-17 ÉDOUARD MANET, *Le Déjeuner sur l'Herbe* (*Luncheon on the Grass*), 1863. Oil on canvas, 7′ × 8′ 8″. Musée d'Orsay, Paris.

Manet shocked his contemporaries with both his subject matter and manner of painting. Moving away from illusionism, he used colors to flatten form and to draw attention to the painting surface.

1 ft.

displayed in *Third of May, 1808* (FIG. 12-5), Daumier created a view of the slaughter from a sharp angle of vision. But unlike Goya, he depicted not the dramatic moment of execution but the terrible, quiet aftermath. The limp bodies of the workers lie amid violent disorder. Daumier's pictorial manner is rough and spontaneous, and that approach to representation, which is a central characteristic of Realist art, accounts in large measure for its remarkable force.

Édouard Manet Like Gustave Courbet, ÉDOUARD MANET (1832–1883) was a pivotal figure in 19th-century European art. Not only was his work influential in articulating Realist principles, but the younger artist also played an important role in the development of Impressionism in the 1870s (see Chapter 13). Manet's *Le Déjeuner sur l'Herbe* (*Luncheon on the Grass;* FIG. **12-17**), widely recognized as a seminal work in the history of art, depicts two clothed men and one nude and one clothed woman at a picnic. Consistent with Realist principles, Manet based all four figures on real people. The seated nude is Manet's favorite model at the time, and the gentlemen are his brother (with cane) and the sculptor Ferdinand Leenhof. The two men wear fashionable Parisian attire of the 1860s. The nude woman is a distressingly unidealized figure who also seems disturbingly unabashed and at ease, gazing directly at the viewer without shame or flirtatiousness.

This audacious painting outraged the French public. Rather than depicting a traditional pastoral scene (compare FIG. 9-18), *Le Déjeuner* features ordinary men and promiscuous women in a Parisian park. Manet surely anticipated criticism of his painting, but shocking the public was not his primary aim. His goal was more complex and far more ambitious. He sought to reassess the nature of painting. The work contains sophisticated references and allusions to many painting genres—history painting, portraiture, pastoral scenes, nudes, and even religious scenes. *Le Déjeuner sur l'Herbe* is Manet's synthesis and critique of the history of painting.

The negative response to Manet's painting on the part of public and critics alike extended beyond the artist's subject matter. He rendered the men and women in soft focus and broadly painted the landscape, including the pool in which the second woman bathes. The loose manner of painting contrasts with the clear forms of the harshly lit foreground trio as well as the pile of discarded female clothes and picnic foods at the lower left. The lighting creates strong contrasts between dark and highlighted areas. In the main figures, many values are summed up in one or two lights or darks. The effect is both to flatten the forms and set them off sharply from the setting. Form, rather than being a matter of line, is only a function of paint and light. Manet aimed to move away from illusionism toward an open acknowledgment of painting's properties, such as the flatness of the painting surface, which would become a core principle of many later 19th- and 20th-century painters.

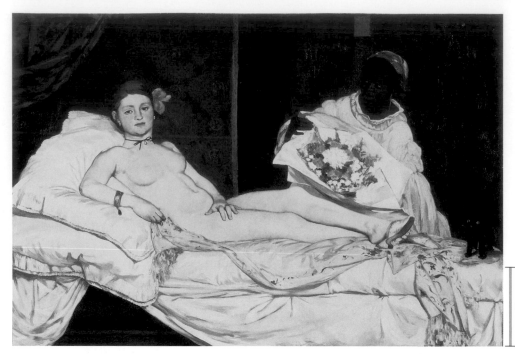

12-18 ÉDOUARD MANET, *Olympia*, 1863. Oil on canvas, 4′ 3″ × 6′ 2¼″. Musée d'Orsay, Paris. ◼◣

Manet's painting of a nude prostitute and her black maid carrying a bouquet from a client scandalized the public. Critics also faulted his rough brushstrokes and abruptly shifting tonalities.

1 ft.

Olympia Even more scandalous to the French viewing public was Manet's *Olympia* (FIG. **12-18**). This work depicts a young white prostitute (Olympia was a common "professional" name for prostitutes) reclining on a bed. Nude except for a thin black ribbon tied around her neck, a bracelet on her arm, an orchid in her hair, and fashionable slippers on her feet, Olympia meets the viewer's eye with a look of cool indifference. The only other figure in the painting is a black maid, who presents Olympia with a bouquet of flowers from a client.

Olympia horrified public and critics alike. Although images of prostitutes were not unheard of during this period, the shamelessness of Olympia and her look verging on defiance shocked viewers. The depiction of a black woman was also not new to painting, but the French public perceived Manet's inclusion of both a black maid and a nude prostitute as evoking moral depravity, inferiority, and animalistic sexuality. The contrast of the black servant with the fair-skinned courtesan also conjured racial divisions. One critic described Olympia as "a courtesan with dirty hands and wrinkled feet . . . her body has the livid tint of a cadaver displayed in the morgue; her outlines are drawn in charcoal and her greenish, bloodshot eyes appear to be provoking the public, protected all the while by a hideous Negress."[4] From this statement, it is clear that viewers were responding not only to the subject matter but to Manet's artistic style as well. The painter's brushstrokes are rougher and the shifts in tonality more abrupt than those found in traditional painting. This departure from accepted practice exacerbated the audacity of the subject matter.

Winslow Homer Although French artists took the lead in promoting the depiction of the realities of modern life, the Realist movement was neither exclusively French nor confined to Europe. One of the leading American Realist painters was WINSLOW HOMER (1836–1910) of Boston. During the Civil War, Homer joined the Union campaign as an artist-reporter for *Harper's Weekly*. At the end of the war, he painted *Veteran in a New Field* (FIG. **12-19**). Although it is relatively simple and direct, Homer's painting is a significant commentary on the effects and aftermath of America's catastrophic national conflict. At the center of the canvas is a man with his back to the viewer, harvesting wheat. Homer identified him as a veteran by including his uniform and canteen carelessly thrown

12-19 WINSLOW HOMER, *Veteran in a New Field*, 1865. Oil on canvas, 2′ ⅛″ × 3′ 2⅛″. Metropolitan Museum of Art, New York (bequest of Miss Adelaide Milton de Groot, 1967).

This veteran's productive work implies a smooth transition to peace after the Civil War, but Homer placed a single-bladed scythe—the Grim Reaper's tool—in his hands, symbolizing the deaths of soldiers.

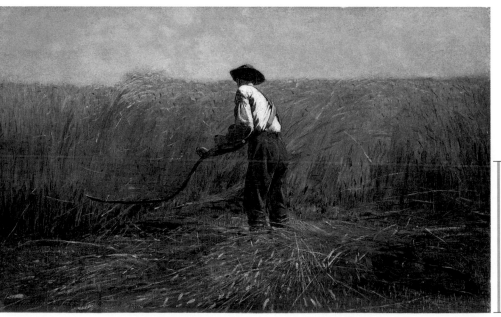

1 ft.

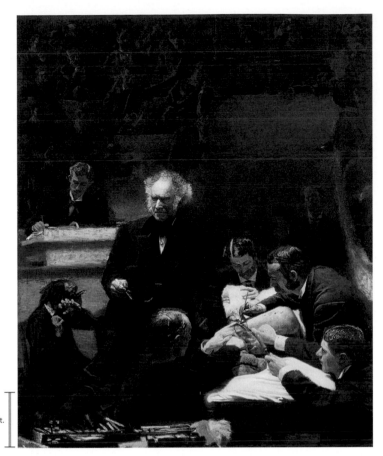

12-20 THOMAS EAKINS, *The Gross Clinic*, 1875. Oil on canvas, 8′ × 6′ 6″. Philadelphia Museum of Art, Philadelphia. ◼◀

The too-brutal realism of Eakins's depiction of a medical college operating amphitheater caused this painting's rejection from the Philadelphia exhibition celebrating America's centennial.

on the ground. The veteran's involvement in meaningful and productive work as a farmer implies a smooth transition from war to peace, which contemporaries considered evidence of America's strength. "The peaceful and harmonious disbanding of the armies in the summer of 1865," poet Walt Whitman (1819–1892) wrote, was one of the "immortal proofs of democracy, unequall'd in all the history of the past."[5]

Veteran in a New Field also comments symbolically about death. By the 1860s, farmers used cradled scythes to harvest wheat. For this detail, however, Homer rejected realism in favor of symbolism. The former soldier's tool is a single-bladed scythe. The artist thus transformed the veteran into a symbol of Death—the Grim Reaper himself—and the painting into an elegy to the thousands of soldiers who did not return from the war.

Thomas Eakins Even more resolutely a Realist than Homer was Philadelphia-born THOMAS EAKINS (1844–1916). The too-brutal Realism of Eakins's early masterpiece, *The Gross Clinic* (FIG. **12-20**), prompted the art jury to reject it for the Philadelphia exhibition celebrating the American independence centennial in 1876. The painting portrays the renowned surgeon Samuel Gross in the operating amphitheater of the Jefferson Medical College in Philadelphia. Dr. Gross, with bloody

fingers and scalpel, lectures about his surgery on a young man's leg. Watching the surgeon are several colleagues, all of whom historians have identified, and the patient's mother, who covers her face. The painting is an unsparing description of an unfolding event, with a good deal more reality than many viewers could endure. "It is a picture," one critic said, "that even strong men find difficult to look at long, if they can look at it at all."[6]

Edmonia Lewis Realism also appealed to some American sculptors. EDMONIA LEWIS (ca. 1845–after 1909), the daughter of a Chippewa mother and African American father, produced work stylistically indebted to Neoclassicism but depicting contemporary Realist themes. *Forever Free* (FIG. **12-21**) is a marble sculpture Lewis carved while living in Rome, surrounded by examples of both classical and Renaissance art. It represents two freed African American slaves. The man stands heroically in a contrapposto stance reminiscent of classical statues. His right hand rests on the shoulder of the kneeling woman, and his left hand holds aloft a broken manacle and chain as literal and symbolic references to his former servitude. Produced four years after President Abraham Lincoln (1809–1865) issued the Emancipation Proclamation, *Forever Free* was widely perceived as an abolitionist

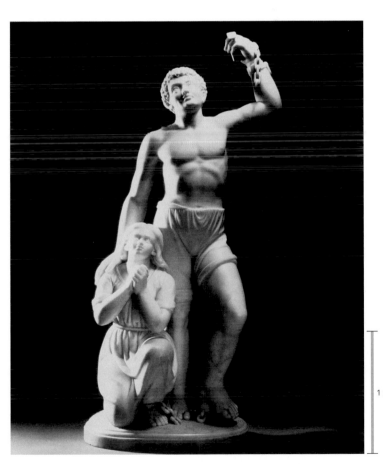

12-21 EDMONIA LEWIS, *Forever Free*, 1867. Marble, 3′ 5¼″ high. James A. Porter Gallery of Afro-American Art, Howard University, Washington, D.C.

Lewis was a sculptor whose work owes a stylistic debt to Neoclassicism but depicts contemporary Realist themes. She carved *Forever Free* four years after Lincoln's Emancipation Proclamation.

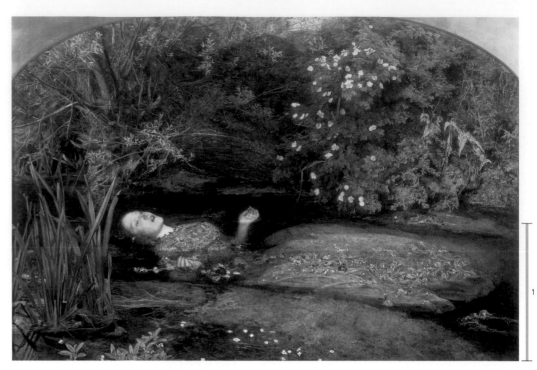

12-22 John Everett Millais, *Ophelia*, 1852. Oil on canvas, 2′ 6″ × 3′ 8″. Tate Gallery, London. ◼◢

Millet was a founder of the Pre-Raphaelite Brotherhood, whose members refused to be limited to the contemporary scenes strict Realists portrayed. The drowning of Ophelia is a Shakespearean subject.

1 ft.

statement. However, other factors caution against a simplistic reading. For example, scholars have debated the degree to which Lewis attempted to inject a statement about gender relationships into this statue and whether the kneeling position of the woman is a reference to female subordination in the African American community.

Lewis's accomplishments as a sculptor speak to the increasing access to training available to women in the 19th century. Educated at Oberlin College (the first American college to grant degrees to women), Lewis financed her trip to Rome with the sale of medallions and marble busts. Her success in a field dominated by white male artists is a testament to both her skill and her determination.

John Everett Millais Realism did not appeal to all artists, of course. In England, a group of painters who called themselves the *Pre-Raphaelite Brotherhood* refused to be limited to the contemporary scenes strict Realists portrayed. These artists chose instead to represent fictional and historical subjects, albeit with a significant degree of convincing illusion. Organized in 1848, the Pre-Raphaelites wished to create fresh and sincere art, free from what they considered the tired and artificial manner propagated in the academies by the successors of Raphael. Influenced by the well-known critic, artist, and writer John Ruskin (1819–1900), the Brotherhood shared his distaste for the materialism and ugliness of the contemporary industrializing world. The Pre-Raphaelites also appreciated the spirituality and idealism (as well as the art and artisanship) of past times, especially the Middle Ages and the Early Renaissance.

One of the founders of the Pre-Raphaelite Brotherhood was John Everett Millais (1829–1896). Millais's painstaking observation of nature is evident in *Ophelia* (FIG. **12-22**), which he exhibited in the Universal Exposition in Paris in 1855—the exhibition at which Courbet set up his Pavilion of Realism. The subject, from Shakespeare's *Hamlet* (4.7.176–179) is the drowning of Ophelia. To make the pathos of the scene visible, Millais became a faithful and feeling witness of its every detail, reconstructing it with a lyricism worthy of the original poetry. Although the scene is fictitious, Millais worked diligently to present it with unswerving fidelity to visual fact. He painted the background at a spot along the Hogsmill River in Surrey. For the figure of Ophelia, Millais had a friend lie in a heated bathtub full of water for hours at a time.

ARCHITECTURE

The buildings constructed during the 19th century are among the most stylistically diverse in history, ranging from the Neoclassical architecture of the Napoleonic Empire to the Neo-Gothic. At the same time, architects were exploring the expressive possibilities that new construction technologies had made possible.

Houses of Parliament The revival of historical styles often was a reflection of nationalistic pride. England, for example, celebrated its medieval heritage with *Neo-Gothic* buildings. In London, when the old Houses of Parliament burned in 1834, Charles Barry (1795–1860), with the assistance of Augustus Welby Northmore Pugin (1812–1852), submitted the winning design (FIG. **12-23**) for the new government complex. Barry had traveled widely in Europe, Greece, Turkey, Egypt, and Palestine, studying the architecture of each place. He preferred the classical Renaissance styles, but he had designed some earlier Neo-Gothic buildings, and Pugin successfully influenced him in the direction of English Late Gothic. Pugin was one of a group of English artists and critics who saw moral purity and spiritual authenticity in the religious architecture of the Middle Ages and revered the careful medieval artisans who built the great cathedrals. The Industrial Revolution was flooding the market with cheaply made and ill-designed commodities. Machine work was replacing handicraft. Many, Pugin included, believed in the necessity of restoring the old artisanship, which they felt embodied honesty as well as quality. The design of the Houses of Parliament, however, is not genuinely Gothic, despite its picturesque tower groupings (the Clock Tower, containing Big Ben, at one end, and the Victoria Tower at the other). The building has a formal axial plan and a kind of Palladian regularity beneath its Neo-Gothic detail.

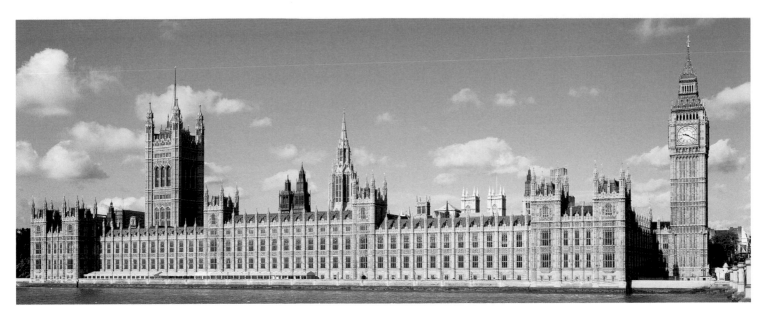

12-23 CHARLES BARRY and AUGUSTUS WELBY NORTHMORE PUGIN, Houses of Parliament (looking west), London, England, designed 1835. ◼◀

During the 19th century, architects revived many historical styles, often reflecting nationalistic pride. The Houses of Parliament have an exterior veneer and towers that recall English Late Gothic style.

Royal Pavilion Although the Neoclassical and Neo-Gothic styles dominated early-19th-century architecture, exotic new approaches of all manner soon began to appear, due in part to European imperialism and in part to the Romantic spirit permeating all the arts. Great Britain's forays throughout the world, particularly India, had exposed English culture to a broad range of non-Western artistic styles. The Royal Pavilion (FIG. 12-24), designed by JOHN NASH (1752–1835), exhibits a wide variety of these styles. Nash was an established architect, known for Neoclassical buildings in London, when the prince regent (later King George IV) asked him to design a royal pleasure palace in the seaside resort of Brighton. The architecture of Greece, Egypt, and China influenced the interior décor of the Royal Pavilion, but the fantastic exterior

is a conglomeration of Islamic domes, minarets, and screens architectural historians describe as "Indian Gothic." Underlying the exotic facade is a cast-iron skeleton, an early (if hidden) use of this material in noncommercial construction. Nash also put this metal to fanciful use, creating life-size palm-tree columns in cast iron to support the Royal Pavilion's kitchen ceiling.

Crystal Palace Other architects abandoned sentimental and Romantic designs from the past. Most utilitarian structures—factories, warehouses, dockyard structures, mills, bridges, and the like—long had been built simply and without historical ornamentation, often, as in the Royal Pavilion, using cast iron because of its tensile strength and resistance

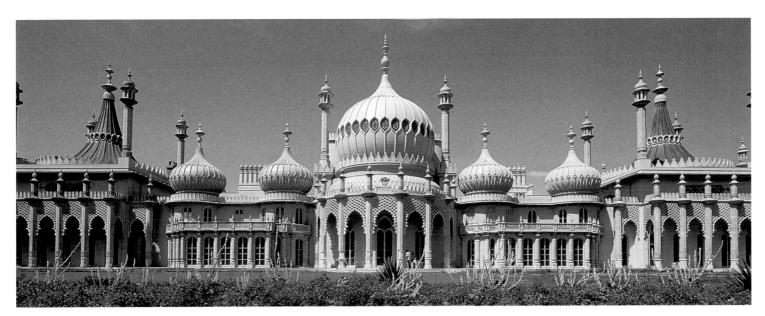

12-24 JOHN NASH, Royal Pavilion (looking northwest), Brighton, England, 1815–1818.

British territorial expansion brought a familiarity with many exotic styles. This palatial "Indian Gothic" seaside pavilion is a conglomeration of Islamic domes, minarets, and screens.

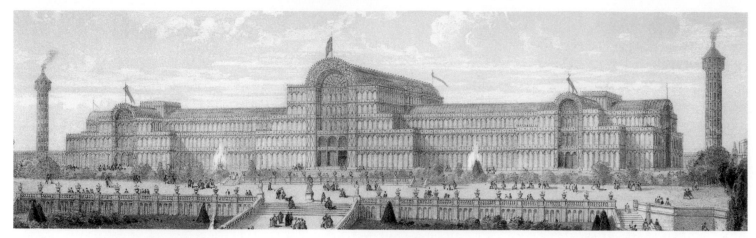

12-25 Joseph Paxton, Crystal Palace, London, England, 1850–1851; enlarged and relocated at Sydenham, England, 1852–1854. Detail of a color lithograph by Achille-Louis Martinet, ca. 1862. Private collection.

The tensile strength of iron enabled Paxton to experiment with a new system of glass-and-metal roof construction. Assembled using prefabricated parts, the vast Crystal Palace required only six months to build.

to fire. After 1860, steel became available, enabling architects to create new designs involving vast enclosed spaces, as in the great train sheds of railroad stations and in exposition halls.

Joseph Paxton (1801–1865) had built several conservatories (greenhouses) in the English countryside. In the largest—300 feet long—he used an experimental system of glass-and-metal roof construction. Encouraged by the success of this system, Paxton submitted a glass-and-iron building design for the hall to house the Great Exhibition of 1851 and won the competition for the commission. The London exhibition was organized to present "works of industry of all nations." Paxton constructed the exhibition building, the Crystal Palace (FIG. **12-25**), with prefabricated parts. This enabled workers to build the vast structure in the then-unheard-of time of six months and to dismantle it quickly at the exhibition's closing to avoid permanent obstruction of the park. The plan borrowed much from ancient Roman and Christian basilicas, with a central flat-roofed "nave" and a barrel-vaulted crossing "transept." The design provided ample interior space to contain displays of huge machines as well as to accommodate decorative touches in the form of large working fountains and giant trees. The public admired the Crystal Palace so much that the workers who dismantled it put up an enlarged version of the glass-and-steel exhibition hall at a new location on the outskirts of London at Sydenham, where it remained until fire destroyed it in 1936.

PHOTOGRAPHY

A technological device of immense consequence for the modern experience was invented shortly before the mid-19th century: the camera, with its attendant art of photography. From the time Frenchman Louis-Jacques-Mandé Daguerre (1789–1851) and Briton William Henry Fox Talbot (1800–1877) announced the first practical photographic processes in 1839, people have celebrated photography's ability to make convincing pictures of people, places, and things.

The relative ease of the process, even in its earliest and most primitive form, seemed a dream come true for 19th-century scientists and artists, who for centuries had grappled with less satisfying methods for capturing accurate images of their subjects. Photography also perfectly suited an age that saw the emergence of Realism as an art movement and a pronounced shift of artistic patronage away from the elite few toward a broader base of support. The growing and increasingly powerful middle class embraced both the comprehensible images of the new medium and their lower cost.

For the traditional artist, photography suggested new answers to the great debate about what is real and how to represent the real in art. Because photography easily and accurately enabled the representation of three-dimensional objects on a two-dimensional surface, the new medium also challenged the place of traditional modes of pictorial representation originating in the Renaissance. Artists as diverse as Ingres, Delacroix, and Courbet welcomed photography as a helpful auxiliary to painting. Other artists, however, feared the camera was a mechanism that would displace the painstaking work of skilled painters. From the moment of its invention, photography threatened to expropriate the realistic image, until then the exclusive property of painting.

Artists themselves were instrumental in the development of the new photographic technology. The camera obscura was familiar to 17th- and 18th-century artists (see pages 313–314). In 1807, the invention of the *camera lucida* (lighted room) replaced the enclosed chamber of the camera obscura. Now the photographer aimed a small prism lens, hung on a stand, downward at an object. The lens projected the image of the object onto a sheet of paper. Artists using either of these devices found this process long and arduous, no matter how accurate the resulting work. All yearned for a more direct way to capture a subject's image. Two very different scientific inventions that accomplished this—the *daguerreotype* and the *calotype* (see "Daguerreotype, Calotype, and Wet-Plate Photography," page 363)—appeared almost simultaneously in France and England in 1839.

Daguerreotype, Calotype, and Wet-Plate Photography

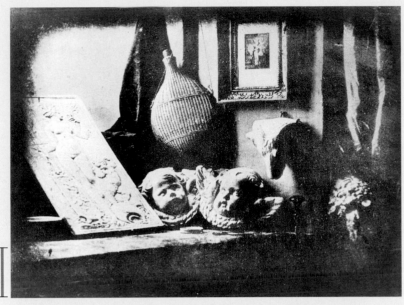

12-26 LOUIS-JACQUES-MANDÉ DAGUERRE, *Still Life in Studio,* 1837. Daguerreotype, 6¼" × 8¼". Collection Société Française de Photographie, Paris. ◼

One of the first plates Daguerre produced after perfecting his new photographic process was this still life, in which he was able to capture amazing detail and finely graduated tones of light and shadow.

The earliest photographic processes were the *daguerreotype* (FIG. 12-26), named after L.J.M. Daguerre, and the *calotype*. Daguerre was an architect and theatrical set painter and designer who used a camera obscura in his work. Through a mutual acquaintance, he met Joseph Nicéphore Niépce (1765–1833), who in 1826 had successfully made a permanent picture of the cityscape outside his upper-story window by exposing, in a camera obscura, a metal plate covered with a light-sensitive coating. Niépce's process, however, had the significant drawback that it required an eight-hour exposure time. After Niépce died in 1833, Daguerre continued his work, making two important discoveries. Latent development—that is, bringing out the image through treatment in chemical solutions—considerably shortened the length of time needed for exposure. Daguerre also discovered a better way to "fix" the image by chemically stopping the action of light on the photographic plate, which otherwise would continue to darken until the image turned solid black.

The daguerreotype reigned supreme in photography until the 1850s, but the second major photographic invention, the ancestor of the modern negative-print system, eventually replaced it. On January 31, 1839, less than three weeks after Daguerre unveiled his method in Paris, William Henry Fox Talbot presented a paper on his "photogenic drawings" to the Royal Institution in London. As early as 1835, Talbot made "negative" images by placing objects on sensitized paper and exposing the arrangement to light. This created a design of light-colored silhouettes recording the places where opaque or translucent objects had blocked light from darkening the paper's emulsion. In his experiments, Talbot next exposed sensitized papers inside simple cameras and, with a second sheet, created "positive" images. He further improved the process with more light-sensitive chemicals and a chemical development of the negative image. This technique enabled multiple prints. However, in Talbot's process, which he named the *calotype* (from the Greek word *kalos*, "beautiful"), the photographic images incorporated the texture of the paper. This produced a slightly blurred, grainy effect very different from the crisp detail and wide tonal range available with the daguerreotype. Also discouraging widespread adoption of the calotype were the stiff licensing and equipment fees charged for many years after Talbot patented his new process in 1841.

One of the earliest masters of an improved kind of calotype photography was the multitalented Frenchman known as Nadar (FIG. 12-27). He used glass negatives and albumen (prepared with egg white) printing paper, which could record finer detail and a wider range of light and shadow than Talbot's calotype process. The new *wet-plate* technology (so named because the photographic plate was exposed, developed, and fixed while wet) almost at once became the universal way of making negatives until 1880. However, wet-plate photography (FIG. 12-28) had drawbacks. The plates had to be prepared and processed on the spot. Working outdoors meant taking along a portable darkroom—a wagon, tent, or box with light-tight sleeves for the photographer's arms.

Daguerreotypes The French government presented the new daguerreotype process at the Academy of Science in Paris on January 7, 1839, with the understanding that its details would be made available to all interested parties without charge (although the inventor received a large annuity in appreciation). Soon, people worldwide began making daguerreotype pictures in a process almost immediately christened "photography," from the Greek *photos* (light) and *graphos* (writing). Each daguerreotype was a unique work. *Still Life in Studio* (FIG. 12-26) is one of the first successful plates Daguerre produced after perfecting his method. The process captured every detail—the subtle forms, the varied textures, the finely graduated tones of light and shadow—in Daguerre's carefully constructed tableau. The three-dimensional forms of the sculptures, the basket, and the bits of cloth spring into high relief. The inspiration for the composition came from 17th-century Dutch still lifes, such as those of Pieter Claesz

(FIG. 10-27). As did Claesz, Daguerre arranged his objects to reveal their textures and shapes clearly. Unlike a painter, Daguerre could not alter anything within his arrangement to create a stronger image. However, he could suggest a symbolic meaning through his choice of objects. Like the skull and timepiece in Claesz's painting, Daguerre's sculptural and architectural fragments and the framed print of an embrace suggest even art is vanitas and will not endure forever.

Nadar Making portraits was an important economic opportunity for most photographers, and portraiture quickly became one of the most popular early photographic genres. The greatest of the early portrait photographers was French novelist, journalist, and caricaturist Gaspar-Félix Tournachon, known simply as NADAR (1828–1910). Photographic studies for his caricatures led Nadar to open a portrait studio. The new calotype photographic process enabled Nadar

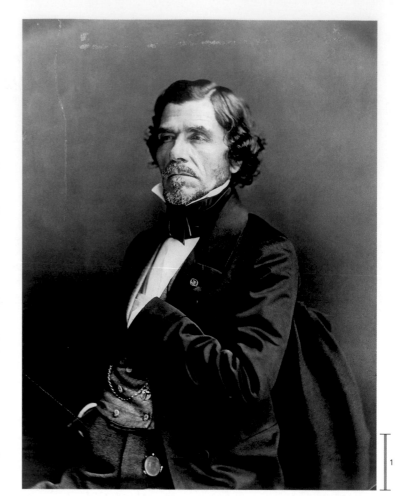

12-27 NADAR, *Eugène Delacroix,* ca. 1855. Modern print, 8½″ × 6⅔″, from the original negative. Bibliothèque Nationale, Paris.

Nadar was one of the earliest portrait photographers. His prints of the leading artists of the day, such as this one of Eugène Delacroix, reveal the sitters' personalities as well as record their features.

to produce portraits with a rich range of tones. So talented was he at capturing the essence of his subjects that the most important people in France, including Delacroix, Daumier, Courbet, and Manet, flocked to his studio to have their portraits made. Nadar said he sought in his work "that instant of understanding that puts you in touch with the model—helps you sum him up, guides you to his habits, his ideas, and character and enables you to produce . . . a really convincing and sympathetic likeness, an intimate portrait."[7] Nadar's *Eugène Delacroix* (FIG. **12-27**) shows the painter at the height of his career. Even in half-length, the painter's gesture and expression create a mood that seems to reveal much about him. Perhaps Delacroix responded to Nadar's famous gift for putting his clients at ease by assuming the pose that best expressed his personality.

Timothy O'Sullivan Photographers were quick to realize the documentary power of their new medium. Thus began the story of photography's influence on modern life and of the immense changes it brought to communication and information management. Historical events could be recorded in permanent form on the spot for the first time. The photographs taken of the American Civil War by Mathew B. Brady (1823–1896), ALEXANDER GARDNER (1821–1882), and TIMOTHY O'SULLIVAN (1840–1882) remain unsurpassed as incisive accounts of military life, unsparing in their truthful detail and poignant as expressions of human experience. The most moving are the inhumanly objective records of combat deaths. Perhaps the most reproduced of these is Gardner's print of O'Sullivan's *A Harvest of Death, Gettysburg, Pennsylvania* (FIG. **12-28**). Although viewers could regard this image as simple news reportage, it also functions to impress on people the high price of war. Corpses litter the battlefield as far as the eye can see. As the photograph modulates from the precise clarity of the bodies of Union soldiers in the foreground, boots stolen and pockets picked, to the indistinct corpses in the distance, the suggestion of innumerable other dead soldiers is unavoidable. This "harvest" is far more sobering and depressing than that in Winslow Homer's Civil War painting, *Veteran in a New Field* (FIG. 12-19). Though it was years before photolithography could reproduce photographs such as this in newspapers, photographers exhibited them publicly. They made an impression that newsprint engravings never could.

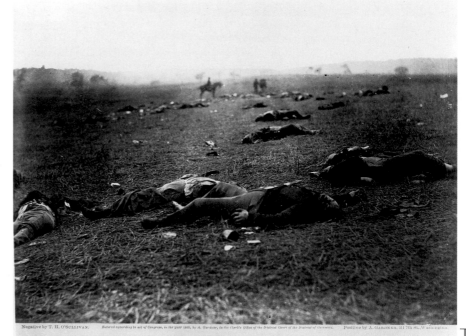

A HARVEST OF DEATH, GETTYSBURG, PENNSYLVANIA.

12-28 TIMOTHY O'SULLIVAN, *A Harvest of Death, Gettysburg, Pennsylvania.* Negative by Timothy O'Sullivan. Original print by ALEXANDER GARDNER, 6¾″ × 8¾″. New York Public Library (Astor, Lenox, and Tilden Foundations, Rare Books and Manuscript Division), New York. ◼◀

Wet-plate technology enabled photographers to record historical events on the spot—and to comment on the high price of war, as in this photograph of dead Union soldiers at Gettysburg in July 1863.

Romanticism, Realism, and Photography, 1800 to 1870

Art under Napoleon

❙ As Emperor of the French from 1804 to 1815, Napoleon embraced the Neoclassical style in order to associate his regime with the empire of ancient Rome. Napoleon chose Jacques-Louis David as First Painter of the Empire. Napoleon's favorite sculptor was Antonio Canova, who carved marble Neoclassical portraits of the imperial family, including a reclining image of Napoleon's sister, Pauline Borghese, in the guise of Venus.

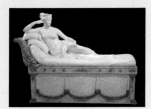

Canova, *Pauline Borghese as Venus*, 1808

Romanticism

❙ The term *Romanticism* denotes the artistic movement that flourished from 1800 to 1840. Romantic artists gave precedence to feeling and imagination over Enlightenment reason, and explored the exotic, erotic, and fantastic. The leading Romantic artist in Spain was Francisco Goya, whose *Sleep of Reason* celebrates the unleashing of imagination, emotions, and even nightmares. In France, Eugène Delacroix led the way in depicting Romantic narratives set in faraway places and distant times, for example, *Death of Sardanapalus*. Romantic painters often chose landscapes as an ideal subject to express the theme of the soul unified with the natural world. Masters of the transcendental landscape include Friedrich in Germany, Constable and Turner in England, and Cole in the United States.

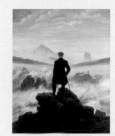

Friedrich, *Wanderer above a Sea of Mist*, 1817–1818

Realism

❙ Realism developed as an artistic movement in mid-19th-century France. Its leading proponent was Gustave Courbet, whose paintings of menial labor and ordinary people exemplify his belief that painters should depict only their own time and place. Honoré Daumier boldly confronted authority with his satirical lithographs commenting on the plight of the urban working classes. Édouard Manet shocked the public with his paintings featuring promiscuous women, and his rough brushstrokes, which emphasized the flatness of the painting surface, paving the way for modern abstract art. Among the leading American Realists were Winslow Homer and Thomas Eakins.

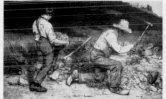

Courbet, *The Stone Breakers*, 1849

Architecture

❙ Territorial expansion, the Romantic interest in exotic locales and earlier eras, and nationalistic pride led to the revival in the 19th century of older architectural styles, especially the Gothic, exemplified by London's Houses of Parliament. By the middle of the century, many architects had already abandoned sentimental and Romantic designs from the past in favor of exploring the possibilities of cast-iron construction, as in Joseph Paxton's Crystal Palace in London.

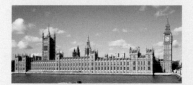

Barry and Pugin, Houses of Parliament, London, 1835

Photography

❙ In 1839, Daguerre in Paris and Talbot in London invented the first practical photographic processes. Many of the earliest photographers, chief among them Nadar in France, specialized in portrait photography, but others, including O'Sullivan in the United States, quickly realized the documentary power of the new medium.

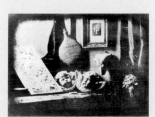

Daguerre, *Still Life in Studio*, 1837

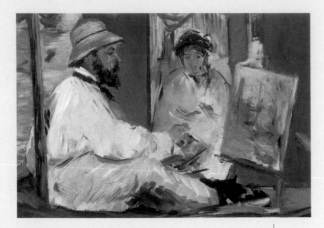

In summer 1874, Manet recorded Monet painting—*en plein air* directly on canvas without any preliminary sketch—in his floating studio on the Seine at Argenteuil, 22 minutes from Paris by train.

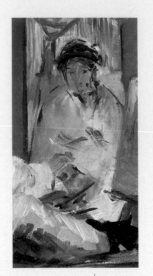

With Monet is his wife, Camille Doncieux. Monet, underappreciated as an artist, had recently sold some paintings, enabling the couple to purchase the small boat he equipped with a cabin and easel.

In this painting, Manet adopted not only Monet's Impressionist subject matter but also the younger artist's short brushstrokes and fascination with the reflection of sunlight on water.

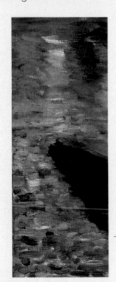

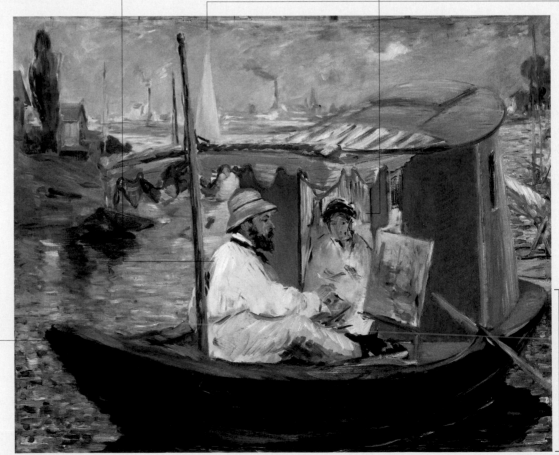

13-1 ÉDOUARD MANET, *Claude Monet in His Studio Boat*, 1874. Oil on canvas, 2′ 8″ × 3′ 3¼″. Neue Pinakothek, Munich. ◼◂

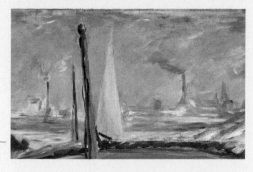

In the distance are the factories and smokestacks of Argenteuil. Manet thus recorded the two poles of modern life—the leisure activities of the bourgeoisie and the industrialization along the Seine.

Impressionism, Post-Impressionism, and Symbolism, 1870 to 1900

FRAMING THE ERA

IMPRESSIONS OF MODERN LIFE

Impressionism was an art movement born in industrialized, urbanized Paris as a reaction to the sometimes brutal and chaotic transformation of late-19th-century French life, which made the world seem unstable and insubstantial. As the poet and critic Charles Baudelaire (1821–1867) observed in his 1860 essay *The Painter of Modern Life:* "[M]odernity is the transitory, the fugitive, the contingent,"[1] Accordingly, Impressionist painters built upon the innovations of the Realists in turning away from traditional mythological and religious themes in favor of daily life, but they sought to convey the elusiveness and impermanence of the subjects they portrayed.

In 1872, the painter CLAUDE MONET (1840–1926), a leading Impressionist, moved to Argenteuil, a prosperous industrial town on the Seine that was also a favorite leisure destination of Parisians—only 22 minutes away by train from the city. Situated at a point where the river widened into a deep basin, Argenteuil was an ideal spot for boating of all kinds, from casual rowing to formal regattas. In 1873, after accumulating enough money from recent sales of his paintings, the underappreciated and financially strapped Monet was able to purchase a small boat, which he equipped with a tiny wooden cabin and a striped awning and used as his floating studio.

During the summer of 1874, ÉDOUARD MANET (FIGS. 12-17 and 12-18) joined Monet at Argenteuil and painted side-by-side with the younger artist. One day, Manet recorded Monet in his studio boat (FIG. **13-1**) at work on *Sailboats on the Seine, Argenteuil,* a painting now in the Fine Arts Museum of San Francisco. Monet, wearing a straw hat, sits at the front of the boat with his easel before him. Camille Doncieux (1847–1879), Monet's wife, is at once the painter's admirer and his muse. In the distance are the factories and smokestacks that represent the opposite pole of life at Argenteuil. In capturing both the leisure activities of the bourgeoisie and the industrialization along the Seine in the 1870s on the same canvas, Manet, like Monet, was fulfilling Baudelaire's definition of "the painter of modern life."

Claude Monet in His Studio Boat is noteworthy as a document of Monet's preference for painting outdoors (*en plein air*)—a radical practice at the time—in order to record his "impression" of the Seine by placing colors directly on a white canvas without any preliminary sketch—also a sharp break from traditional studio techniques. The painting further attests to Monet's influence on his older friend Manet, who here adopted the younger painter's subject matter, short brushstrokes, and fascination with the reflection of light on water.

MARXISM, DARWINISM, MODERNISM

The Industrial Revolution, born in England, spread so rapidly to France (MAP 13-1) and throughout the Continent and the United States that historians often refer to the third quarter of the 19th century as the second Industrial Revolution. Whereas the first Industrial Revolution centered on textiles, steam, and iron, the second focused on steel, electricity, chemicals, and oil. The discoveries in these fields provided the foundation for developments in plastics, machinery, building construction, and automobile manufacturing and paved the way for the invention of the radio, electric light, telephone, and electric streetcar.

A significant consequence of industrialization was urbanization. The number and size of Western cities grew dramatically during the latter part of the 19th century, largely due to migration from the countryside. Farmers in large numbers relocated to urban centers because expanded agricultural enterprises squeezed smaller property owners from their land. The widely available work opportunities in the cities, especially in the factories, were also a major factor in this population shift. Improving health and living conditions in the cities further contributed to their explosive growth.

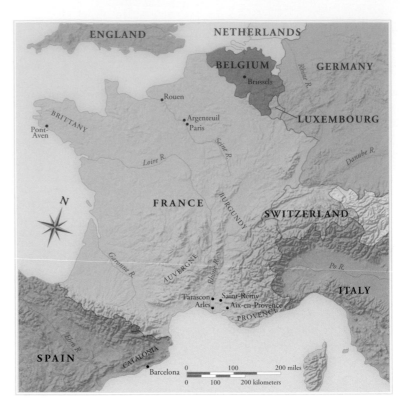

MAP 13-1 France around 1870.

Marxism and Darwinism The rise of the urban working class was fundamental to the ideas of German political and social theorist Karl Marx (1818–1883), whose *Communist Manifesto* (1848), written with Friedrich Engels (1820–1895), called for workers to overthrow the capitalist system. As did other 19th-century empiricists, Marx believed scientific, rational law governed nature and, indeed, all human history. For Marx, economic forces based on class struggle induced historical change. Throughout history, insisted Marx, those who controlled the means of production conflicted with those whose labor they exploited for their own enrichment. Marx advocated the creation of a socialist state in which the working class seized power. Marxism held great appeal for many intellectuals as well as for oppressed laborers.

Equally influential was the English naturalist Charles Darwin (1809–1882), whose theory of natural selection did much to increase interest in science. Darwin's concept of evolution, based on a competitive system in which only the fittest survived, as presented in *On the Origin of Species by Means of Natural Selection* (1859), contradicted the biblical narrative of creation. By challenging traditional religious beliefs, Darwinism contributed to growing secularism. Other theorists and social thinkers, notably British philosopher Herbert Spencer (1820–1903), applied Darwin's principles to the rapidly changing socioeconomic realm. As in the biological world, they asserted, intense competition led to the survival of the most economically fit companies, enterprises, and countries. The social Darwinists provided Western nations with justification for the colonization of peoples and cultures they deemed less advanced (see "Primitivism and Colonialism," Chapter 14, page 394).

Modernism The combination of extensive technological changes and increased exposure to other cultures, coupled with the rapidity of these changes, led to an acute sense in Western cultures of the world's impermanence. These societal changes in turn fostered a new and multifaceted artistic approach that art historians call *modernism*. Modernist artists seek to capture the images and sensibilities of their age, but

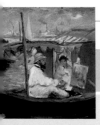

Impressionism, Post-Impressionism, and Symbolism, 1870 to 1900

Academic Salons and Independent Art Exhibitions

For both artists and art historians, modernist art stands in marked contrast—indeed in forceful opposition—to academic art, that is to the art promoted by established art schools such as the Royal Academy of Painting and Sculpture in France (founded in 1648) and the Royal Academy of Arts in Britain (founded in 1768). These government-subsidized academies, which supported a limited range of artistic expression focusing on traditional subjects and highly polished technique, held annual exhibitions, called "Salons" in France. Because of the challenges modernist art presented to established artistic conventions, the juries for the Salons and other exhibitions often rejected the works more adventurous artists wished to display. When, however, the 1855 jury rejected some of Gustave Courbet's paintings, the artist reacted by setting up his own Pavilion of Realism (see "Courbet on Realism," Chapter 12, page 354).

Growing dissatisfaction with the decisions of the French Academy's jurors prompted Napoleon III (r. 1852–1870) in 1863 to establish the Salon des Refusés (Salon of the Rejected) to show all of the works not accepted for exhibition in the regular Salon. Manet's *Le Déjeuner sur l'Herbe* (FIG. 12-17) was among them. The public greeted it and the entire exhibition with derision. In 1867, after further rejections, Manet, following Courbet, mounted a private exhibition of 50 of his paintings outside the Paris World's Fair. Six years later, Claude Monet (FIGS. 13-1 and 13-2) and the other Impressionists formed their own society and began mounting shows of their works in Paris. This action allowed the Impressionists much freedom, for they did not have to contend with the Royal Academy's authoritative and confining viewpoint. The Impressionist exhibitions took place at one- or two-year intervals from 1874 until 1886.

Another group of artists unhappy with the official Salon's conservative nature adopted the same renegade idea. In 1884, these artists formed the Société des Artistes Indépendants (Society of Independent Artists) and held annual Salons des Indépendants. Georges Seurat's *A Sunday on La Grande Jatte* (FIG. 13-8) was one of the paintings in the Independents' 1886 Salon.

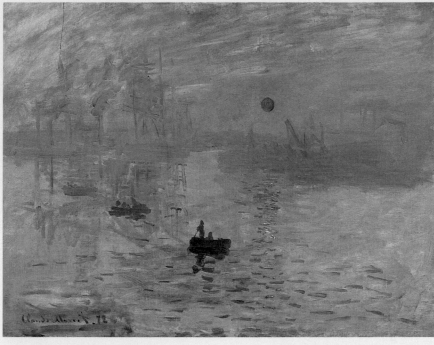

13-2 Claude Monet, *Impression: Sunrise*, 1872. Oil on canvas, 1' 7½" × 2' 1½". Musée Marmottan, Paris.

A hostile critic applied the derogatory term *Impressionism* to this painting because of its sketchy quality and undisguised brushstrokes. Monet and his circle embraced the label for their movement.

As the art market expanded, venues for the exhibition of art increased. Art circles and societies sponsored private shows in which both amateurs and professionals participated. Dealers became more aggressive in promoting the artists they represented by mounting exhibitions in a variety of spaces, some fairly intimate and small, others large and grandiose. All of these proliferating opportunities for exhibition gave French artists alternatives to the traditional constraints of the Salon and provided fertile breeding ground for the development of radically new art forms and styles.

---

modernism transcends the simple depiction of the contemporary world—the goal of Realism (see Chapter 12). Modernist artists also critically examine the premises of art itself, as Manet did in his seminal 1863 painting *Le Déjeuner sur l'Herbe* (FIG. 12-17). Modernism thus implies certain concerns about art and aesthetics that are internal to art production, regardless of whether the artist is portraying modern life.

Clement Greenberg (1909–1994), an influential American art critic, explained:

> The essence of Modernism lies . . . in the use of the characteristic methods of a discipline to criticize the discipline itself. . . . Realistic, illusionist art had dissembled the medium, using art to conceal art. Modernism used art to call attention to art. The limitations that constitute the medium of painting—the flat surface, the shape of the support, the properties of pigment—were treated by the Old Masters as negative factors that could be acknowledged only implicitly or indirectly.

Modernist painting has come to regard these same limitations as positive factors that are to be acknowledged openly.[2]

Although the work of Gustave Courbet and the Realists already expressed this modernist viewpoint, modernism emerged even more forcefully in the late-19th-century movements that art historians call Impressionism, Post-Impressionism, and Symbolism.

IMPRESSIONISM

A hostile critic applied the label *Impressionism* in response to Claude Monet's *Impression: Sunrise* (FIG. 13-2), exhibited in the first Impressionist show in 1874 (see "Academic Salons and Independent Art Exhibitions," above). Although the critic intended the label to be derogatory, by the third Impressionist show in 1878, the artists had embraced it and were calling themselves Impressionists.

Claude Monet Artists and critics had used the term *Impressionism* before, but only in relation to sketches. Impressionist paintings do incorporate the qualities of sketches—abbreviation, speed, and spontaneity. This is apparent in *Impression: Sunrise,* in which Monet made no attempt to disguise the brushstrokes or blend the pigment to create smooth tonal gradations and an optically accurate scene. This concern with acknowledging the paint and the canvas surface continued the modernist exploration the Realists began. Beyond this connection to the sketch, Impressionism operated at the intersection of what the artists saw and what they felt. In other words, the "impressions" these artists recorded in their paintings were neither purely objective descriptions of the exterior world nor solely subjective responses but the interaction between the two. They were sensations—the artists' subjective and personal responses to nature.

In sharp contrast to traditional studio artists, Monet worked outdoors. Painting *en plein air* sharpened Monet's focus on the roles light and color play in capturing an instantaneous representation of atmosphere and climate. Scientific studies of light and the invention of chemically synthesized pigments increased artists' sensitivity to the multiplicity of colors in nature and gave them new colors for their work. After scrutinizing the effects of light and color on forms, the Impressionists concluded that *local color*—an object's true color in white light—becomes modified by the quality of the light shining on it, by reflections from other objects, and by the effects juxtaposed colors produce. Shadows do not appear gray or black, as many earlier painters thought, but seem to be composed of colors modified by reflections or other conditions. Using various colors and short, choppy brushstrokes, Monet was able to catch accurately the vibrating quality of light. The fact that Impressionist canvas surfaces look unintelligible at close range and their forms and objects appear only when the eye fuses the strokes at a certain distance accounts for much of the early adverse criticism leveled at Monet and his fellow Impressionists.

Pierre-Auguste Renoir Modern industrialized Paris provided ample time for leisure activities, and scenes of dining, dancing, café-concerts, opera, and ballet became mainstays of Impressionism. *Le Moulin de la Galette* (FIG. **13-3**) by PIERRE-AUGUSTE RENOIR (1841–1919) depicts a popular Parisian dance hall. Some people crowd the tables and chatter, while others dance energetically. So lively is the atmosphere the viewer can virtually hear the sounds of music, laughter, and tinkling glasses. The painter dappled the whole scene with sunlight and shade, artfully blurred into the figures to produce precisely the effect of floating and fleeting light the

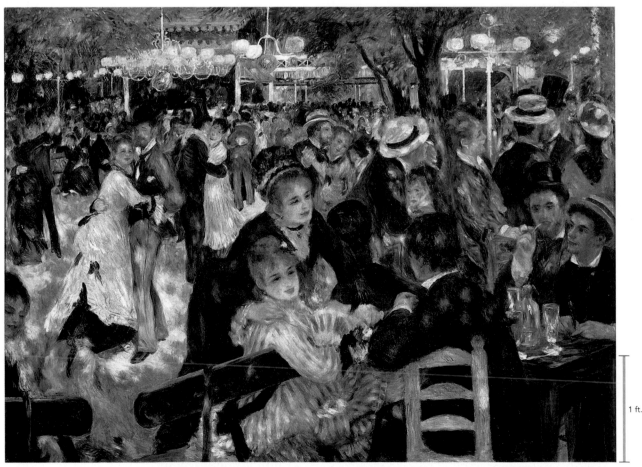

1 ft.

13-3 PIERRE-AUGUSTE RENOIR, *Le Moulin de la Galette,* 1876. Oil on canvas, 4′ 3″ × 5′ 8″. Musée d'Orsay, Paris. ◼◂

Renoir's painting of this popular Parisian dance hall is dappled by sunlight and shade, artfully blurred into the figures to produce just the effect of floating and fleeting light the Impressionists cultivated.

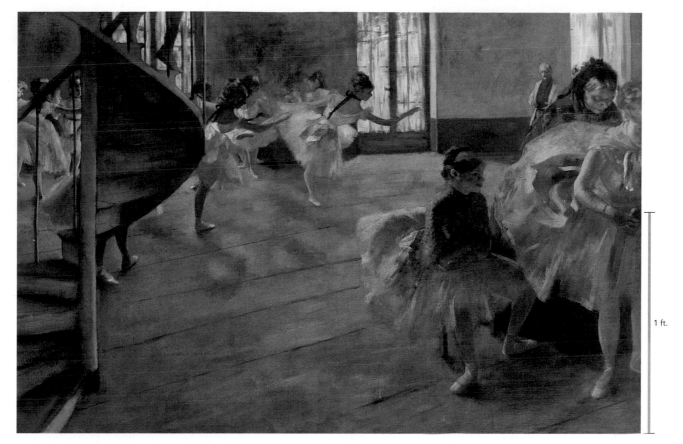

13-4 EDGAR DEGAS, *The Rehearsal,* 1874. Oil on canvas, 1′ 11″ × 2′ 9″. Glasgow Art Galleries and Museum, Glasgow (Burrell Collection). ◼◀

The arbitrarily cut-off figures of dancers, the patterns of light splotches, and the blurry images reveal Degas's interest in reproducing fleeting moments, as well as his fascination with photography.

Impressionists cultivated. Renoir's casual unposed placement of the figures and the suggested continuity of space, spreading in all directions and only accidentally limited by the frame, position the viewer as a participant rather than as an outsider. Whereas classical artists sought to express universal and timeless qualities, the Impressionists attempted to depict just the opposite—the incidental and the momentary.

Edgar Degas Impressionists also depicted more formal leisure activities. The fascination EDGAR DEGAS (1834–1917) had with patterns of motion brought him to the Paris Opéra and its ballet school. There, his keen observational power took in the formalized movements of classical ballet, one of his favorite subjects. In *The Rehearsal* (FIG. **13-4**), Degas used several devices to bring the observer into the pictorial space. The frame cuts off the spiral stair, the windows in the background, and the group of figures in the right foreground. The figures are not at the center of a classically balanced composition. Instead, Degas arranged them in a seemingly random manner. The prominent diagonals of the wall bases and floorboards lead the viewer's eye into and along the directional lines of the dancers. Finally, as is customary in Degas's ballet pictures, a large, off-center, empty space creates the illusion of a continuous floor connecting the observer with the pictured figures.

The often arbitrarily cut-off figures, the patterns of light splotches, and the blurriness of the images in this and other Degas works indicate the artist's interest in reproducing single moments. They also reveal his fascination with photography. Degas not only studied the photographs of others but also used a camera to make preliminary studies for his works, particularly photographing figures in interiors. Japanese art was another inspirational source for Degas's paintings. The cunning spatial projections in works such as *The Rehearsal* probably derived in part from Japanese prints (see "Japanese Woodblock Prints," Chapter 19, page 528). Japanese artists used diverging lines not only to organize the flat shapes of figures but also to direct the viewer's attention into the picture space (compare FIG. 19-18). The Impressionists, acquainted with these prints as early as the 1860s, greatly admired their spatial organization, familiar and intimate themes, and flat, unmodeled color areas.

Mary Cassatt In the Salon of 1874, Degas admired a painting by a young American artist, MARY CASSATT (1844–1926), who had moved from Philadelphia to Europe to study masterworks in France and Italy. Degas befriended Cassatt, who exhibited regularly with the Impressionists, but as a woman, she could not easily frequent the cafés with her male artist friends. She also had the responsibility of caring for her aging parents, who had joined her in Paris. Because of these restrictions, Cassatt's subjects were principally women and children, whom she presented with a combination of objectivity

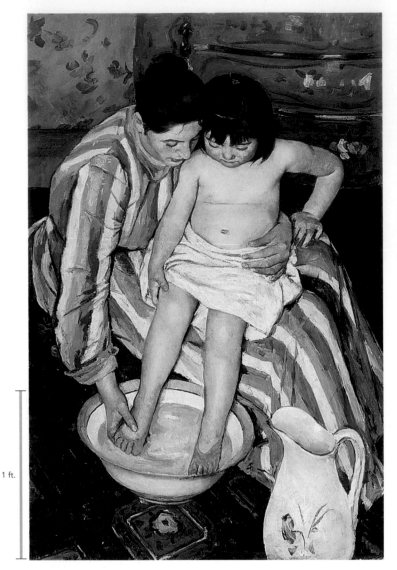

1 ft.

13-5 Mary Cassatt, *The Bath,* ca. 1892. Oil on canvas, 3′ 3″ × 2′ 2″. Art Institute of Chicago, Chicago (Robert A. Walker Fund). ◼◀

Cassatt's compositions owed much to Degas and Japanese prints, but her subjects differ from those of most Impressionist painters, in part because, as a woman, she could not frequent cafés.

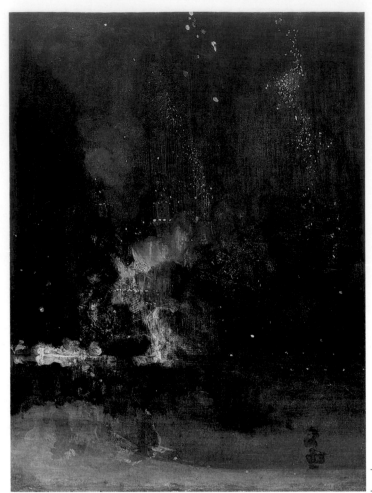

1 in

13-6 James Abbott McNeill Whistler, *Nocturne in Black and Gold* (*The Falling Rocket*), ca. 1875. Oil on panel, 1′ 11⅝″ × 1′ 6⅓″. Detroit Institute of the Arts, Detroit (gift of Dexter M. Ferry Jr.).

In this painting, Whistler displayed an Impressionist's interest in conveying atmospheric effects of fireworks at night, but he also emphasized the abstract arrangement of shapes and colors.

and genuine sentiment. Works such as *The Bath* (FIG. **13-5**) show the tender relationship between a mother and child. The visual solidity of the mother and child contrasts with the flattened patterning of the wallpaper and rug. Cassatt's style in this work owed much to the compositional devices of Degas and of Japanese prints, but the painting's design has an originality and strength all its own.

James Whistler Another American expatriate artist in Europe was James Abbott McNeill Whistler (1834–1903), who spent time in Paris before settling finally in London. He met many of the French Impressionists, and his art is a unique combination of some of their concerns and his own. Whistler shared the Impressionists' interest in the subjects of contemporary life and the sensations color produces on the eye. To these influences he added his own desire to create harmonies

paralleling those achieved in music. To underscore his artistic intentions, Whistler began calling his paintings "arrangements" or "nocturnes." *Nocturne in Black and Gold,* or *The Falling Rocket* (FIG. **13-6**), is a daring painting with gold flecks and splatters representing an exploded firework punctuating the darkness of the night sky. More interested in conveying the atmospheric effects than in providing details of the scene, Whistler emphasized creating a harmonious arrangement of shapes and colors on the rectangle of his canvas, an approach many 20th-century painters adopted. Whistler's works angered many 19th-century viewers, however. The British critic John Ruskin (1819–1900) responded to this painting with a scathing review accusing Whistler of "flinging a pot of paint in the public's face."[3] In reply, Whistler sued Ruskin for libel. Although Whistler won the case, his victory had sadly ironic consequences for him. The judge, showing where his—and the public's—sympathies lay, awarded the artist only one farthing (less than a penny) in damages and required Whistler to pay all of the court costs, which ruined him financially.

POST-IMPRESSIONISM

By 1886 most critics and a large segment of the public accepted the Impressionists as serious artists. Just when their images of contemporary life no longer seemed crude and unfinished, however, a group of younger artists came to feel the Impressionists were neglecting too many of the traditional elements of picturemaking in their attempts to capture momentary sensations of light and color on canvas. These artists were much more interested in systematically examining the properties and expressive qualities of line, pattern, form, and color. Because their art had its roots in Impressionism, but was not stylistically homogeneous, these artists became known as the *Post-Impressionists*.

Henri de Toulouse-Lautrec Closest to the Impressionists in many ways was the French artist HENRI DE TOULOUSE-LAUTREC (1864–1901), who deeply admired Degas and shared the Impressionists' interest in capturing the sensibility of modern life. His work, however, has an added satirical edge to it and often borders on caricature. Genetic defects stunted his growth and partially crippled him, leading to his self-exile from the high society his ancient aristocratic name entitled him to enter. He became a denizen of the night world of Paris, consorting with a tawdry population of entertainers, prostitutes, and other social outcasts. He reveled in the energy of the city's music halls, cafés, and bordellos. *At the Moulin Rouge* (FIG. **13-7**) reveals the influences of De-

gas, of Japanese prints, and of photography in the oblique and asymmetrical composition, the spatial diagonals, and the strong line patterns with added dissonant colors. But Toulouse-Lautrec so emphasized or exaggerated each element that the tone is new. Compare, for example, the mood of *Moulin Rouge* with the relaxed and casual atmosphere of Renoir's *Le Moulin de la Galette* (FIG. 13-3). Toulouse-Lautrec's scene is nightlife, with its glaring artificial light, brassy music, and assortment of corrupt, cruel, and masklike faces. (He included himself in the background—the diminutive man wearing a derby hat accompanying the very tall man, his cousin.) Such distortions by simplification of the figures and faces anticipated Expressionism (see Chapter 14), when artists' use of formal elements—for example, brighter colors and bolder lines than ever before—increased the effect of their images on observers.

Georges Seurat The themes GEORGES SEURAT (1859–1891) addressed in his paintings were also Impressionist subjects, but he depicted them in a resolutely intellectual way. He devised a disciplined and painstaking system of painting focused on color analysis. Seurat was less concerned with the recording of immediate color sensations than he was with their careful and systematic organization into a new kind of pictorial order. He disciplined the free and fluent play of color characterizing Impressionism into a calculated arrangement based on scientific color theory. Seurat's system, known as *pointillism* or *divisionism*, involved carefully observing color and separating it into its component parts (see "Pointillism and 19th-Century Color Theory," page 374). The artist then applies these pure component colors to the canvas in tiny dots (points) or daubs. Thus, the shapes, figures, and spaces in the image become comprehensible only from a distance, when the viewer's eye blends the many pigment dots.

Seurat introduced pointillism to the French public at the eighth and last Impressionist exhibition in 1886, where he displayed

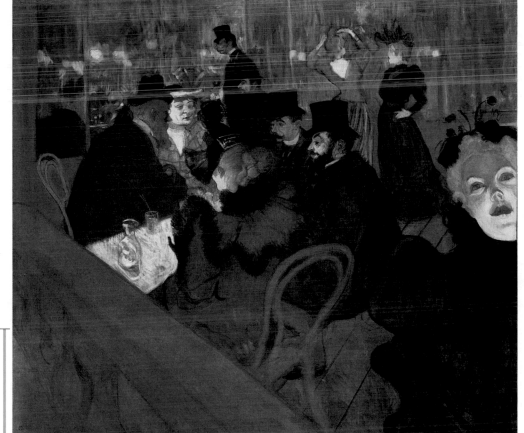

13-7 HENRI DE TOULOUSE-LAUTREC, *At the Moulin Rouge,* 1892–1895. Oil on canvas, 4' × 4' 7". Art Institute of Chicago, Chicago (Helen Birch Bartlett Memorial Collection).

Degas, Japanese prints, and photography influenced this painting's oblique composition, but the glaring lighting, masklike faces, and dissonant colors are distinctly Toulouse-Lautrec's.

1 ft.

Pointillism and 19th-Century Color Theory

n the 19th century, advances in the sciences contributed to changing theories about color and how people perceive it. Many physicists and chemists studied optical reception and the behavior of the human eye in response to light of differing wavelengths. They also investigated the psychological dimension of color. Their discoveries provided a framework within which artists such as Georges Seurat (FIG. 13-8), the inventor of pointillism, worked.

Discussions of color often focus on *hue* (for example, red, yellow, and blue), but it is important to consider the other facets of color— *saturation* (the hue's brightness or dullness) and *value* (the hue's lightness or darkness). Most artists during the 19th century understood the concepts of *primary, secondary,* and *complementary colors* (see Introduction, page 7). Chemist Michel-Eugène Chevreul (1786–1889) extended artists' understanding of color dynamics by formulating the law of *simultaneous contrasts* of colors. Chevreul asserted juxtaposed colors affect the eye's reception of each, making the two colors as dissimilar as possible, both in hue and value. For example, placing light green next to dark green has the effect of making the light green look even lighter and the dark green darker. Chevreul further provided an explanation of *successive contrasts*—the phenomenon of colored afterimages. When a person looks intently at a color (green, for example) and then shifts to a white area, the eye momentarily perceives the complementary color (red).

Charles Blanc (1813–1882), who coined the term *optical mixture* to describe the visual effect of juxtaposed complementary colors, asserted the smaller the areas of adjoining complementary colors, the greater the tendency for the eye to "mix" the colors, so that the viewer perceives a grayish or neutral tint. Seurat used this principle frequently in his paintings. Also influential for Seurat was the work of physicist Ogden Rood (1831–1902), who constructed an accurate and understandable diagram of contrasting colors. Further (and particularly significant to Seurat), Rood suggested artists could achieve color gradation by placing small dots or lines of color side by side, which blended in the eye when viewed from a distance.

The color experiments of Seurat and other late-19th-century artists were also part of a larger discourse about human vision and how people see and understand the world. The theories of physicist Ernst Mach (1838–1916) focused on the psychological experience of sensation. He believed humans perceive their environments in isolated units of sensation the brain then recomposes into a comprehensible world. Another scientist, Charles Henry (1859–1926), also pursued research into the psychological dimension of color—how colors affect people, and under what conditions. He went even further to explore the physiological effects of perception.

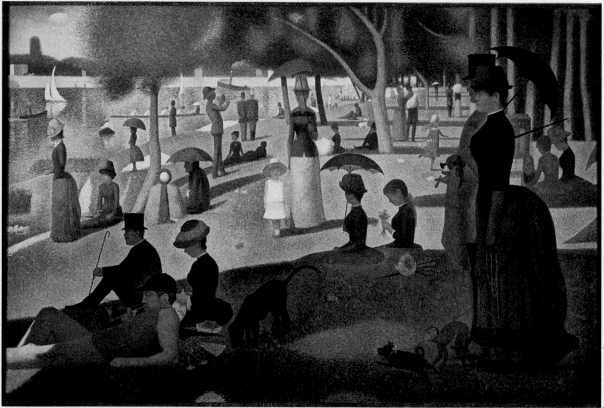

13-8 GEORGES SEURAT, *A Sunday on La Grande Jatte,* 1884–1886. Oil on canvas, 6′ 9″ × 10′. Art Institute of Chicago, Chicago (Helen Birch Bartlett Memorial Collection). ◼◀

Seurat's color system— pointillism—involved dividing colors into their component parts and applying those colors to the canvas in tiny dots. The forms become comprehensible only from a distance.

1 ft.

A Sunday on La Grande Jatte (FIG. **13-8**). The subject of the painting is consistent with Impressionist recreational themes, but Seurat's rendition of Parisians at leisure is strangely rigid and remote, unlike the spontaneous representations of Impressionism. By using meticulously calculated values, Seurat carved out a deep rectangular space. He played on repeated motifs both to create flat patterns and to suggest spatial depth. Reiterating the profile of the female form, the parasol, and the cylindrical forms of the figures, Seurat placed each in space to set up a rhythmic movement in depth as well as from side to side. Sunshine fills the picture, but the painter did not break the light into transient patches of color. Light,

The Letters of Vincent van Gogh

Throughout his life, Vincent van Gogh wrote letters to his brother, Theo van Gogh (1857–1891), a Parisian art dealer, on matters both mundane and philosophical. The letters are precious documents of the vicissitudes of the painter's life and reveal his emotional anguish. In many of the letters, van Gogh also forcefully stated his views about art, including his admiration for Japanese prints, which he collected and in some cases copied.

In one letter, Vincent told Theo: "In both my life and in my painting, I can very well do without God but I cannot, ill as I am, do without something which is greater than I, . . . the power to create."* For van Gogh, the power to create involved the expressive use of color. "Instead of trying to reproduce exactly what I have before my eyes, I use color more arbitrarily so as to express myself forcibly."† Color in painting, he argued, is "not locally true from the point of view of the delusive realist, but color suggesting some emotion of an ardent temperament."‡

Some of van Gogh's letters contain vivid descriptions of his paintings. For example, about *Night Café* (FIG. 13-9), a place in which the artist believed one could "go mad," he wrote:

I have tried to express the terrible passions of humanity by means of red and green. The room is blood red and dark yellow with a green billiard table in the middle; there are four citron-yellow lamps with a glow of orange and green. Everywhere there is a clash and contrast of the most disparate reds and greens in the figures of little sleeping hooligans, in the empty, dreary room, in violet and blue. The blood-red and the yellow-green of the billiard table, for instance, contrast with the soft, tender Louis XV green of the counter, on which there is a pink nosegay. The white coat of the landlord,

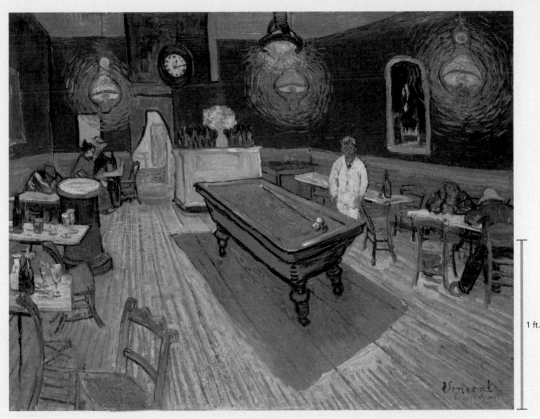

13-9 VINCENT VAN GOGH, *Night Café*, 1888. Oil on canvas, 2' 4½" × 3'. Yale University Art Gallery, New Haven (bequest of Stephen Carlton Clark).

In *Night Café*, van Gogh explored ways colors and distorted forms can express emotions. The thickness, shape, and direction of his brushstrokes create a tactile counterpart to the intense colors.

awake in a corner of that furnace, turns citron-yellow, or pale luminous green.§

*Vincent van Gogh to Theo van Gogh, September 3, 1888, in W. H. Auden, ed., *Van Gogh: A Self-Portrait. Letters Revealing His Life as a Painter* (New York: Dutton, 1963), 319.
†August 11, 1888. Ibid., 313.
‡September 8, 1888. Ibid., 321.
§September 8, 1888. Ibid., 320.

---

air, people, and landscape are formal elements in an abstract design in which line, color, value, and shape cohere in a precise and tightly controlled organization.

Vincent van Gogh In marked contrast to Seurat, VINCENT VAN GOGH (1853–1890) explored the capabilities of colors and distorted forms to express his emotions. The son of a Dutch Protestant pastor, van Gogh believed he had a religious calling and did missionary work in the coal-mining area of Belgium. Repeated professional and personal failures brought him close to despair. Only after he turned to painting did he find a way to communicate his experiences. When van Gogh died of a self-inflicted gunshot wound at age 37, he considered himself a failure as an artist. He sold only one painting during his lifetime, but after his death his work profoundly influenced later artists, especially the Fauves and German Expressionists (see Chapter 14), who built on van Gogh's use of color and the expressiveness of his art.

Van Gogh moved to Paris in 1886, and then, in 1888, to Arles in southern France, where he painted *Night Café* (FIG. 13-9). Although the subject is apparently benign, van Gogh invested it with a charged energy. As he stated in a letter to his brother, Theo (see "The Letters of Vincent van Gogh," above), he wanted the painting to convey an oppressive atmosphere—"a place where one can ruin oneself, go mad, or commit a crime."[4] The proprietor rises like a specter

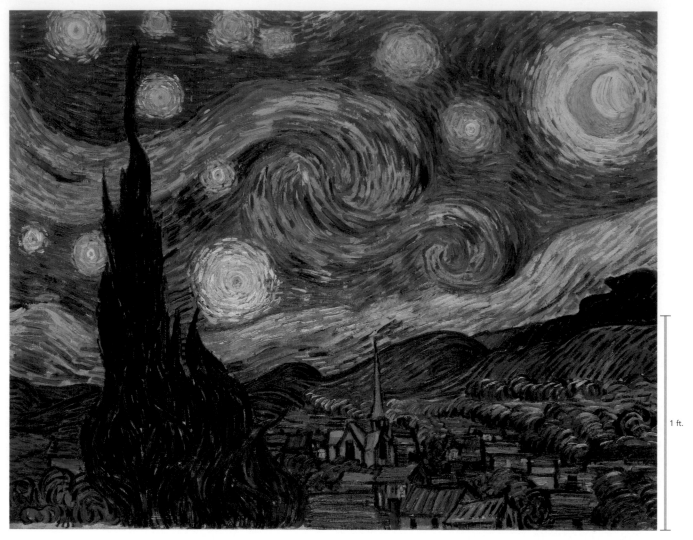

1 ft.

13-10 VINCENT VAN GOGH, *Starry Night,* 1889. Oil on canvas, 2′ 5″ × 3′ ¼″. Museum of Modern Art, New York (acquired through the Lillie P. Bliss Bequest). ◼◀

In this late work, van Gogh painted the vast night sky filled with whirling and exploding stars, the earth huddled beneath it. The painting is an almost abstract pattern of expressive line, shape, and color.

from the edge of the billiard table, which the painter depicted in such a steeply tilted perspective that it threatens to slide out of the painting into the viewer's space. Van Gogh communicated the "madness" of the place by selecting vivid hues whose juxtaposition augmented their intensity. His insistence on the expressive values of color led him to develop a corresponding expressiveness in his paint application. The thickness, shape, and direction of his brushstrokes created a tactile counterpart to his intense color schemes. He often moved the brush vehemently back and forth or at right angles, giving a textilelike effect, or squeezed dots or streaks directly onto his canvas from his paint tube. This bold, almost slapdash attack enhanced the intensity of his colors.

Starry Night Similarly illustrative of van Gogh's "expressionist" method is *Starry Night* (FIG. **13-10**), which the artist painted in 1889, the year before his death. At this time, van Gogh was living in an asylum in Saint-Rémy, near Arles, where he had committed himself. In *Starry Night,* the artist did not represent the sky's appearance. Rather, he communi-

cated his feelings about the electrifying vastness of the universe, filled with whirling and exploding stars, with the earth and humanity huddling beneath it. Given van Gogh's determination to "use color . . . to express [him]self forcibly," the dark, deep blue suffusing the entire painting cannot be overlooked. Together with the turbulent brushstrokes, the color suggests a quiet but pervasive depression. A letter Vincent wrote to his brother reveals his state of mind at this time:

> [L]ooking at the stars always makes me dream, . . . Why, I ask myself, shouldn't the shining dots of the sky be as accessible as the black dots on the map of France? Just as we take the train to get to Tarascon or Rouen, we take death to reach a star.[5]

Paul Gauguin As van Gogh did, PAUL GAUGUIN (1848–1903) rejected objective representation in favor of subjective expression. He also broke with the Impressionists' studies of minutely contrasted hues because he believed color above all must be expressive. For Gauguin, the artist's power to

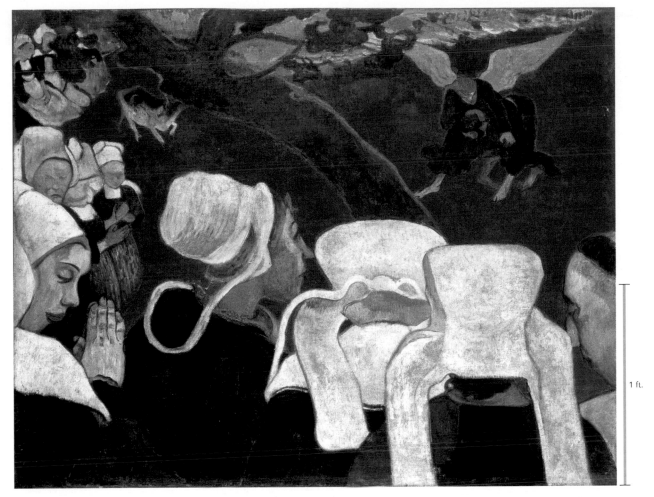

1 ft.

13-11 PAUL GAUGUIN, *Vision after the Sermon* (*Jacob Wrestling with the Angel*), 1888. Oil on canvas, 2′ 4¾″ × 3′ ½″. National Gallery of Scotland, Edinburgh. ■◀

Gauguin admired Japanese prints, stained glass, and cloisonné enamels. Their influences are evident in this painting of Breton women, in which firm outlines enclose large areas of unmodulated color.

determine the colors in a painting was a central element of creativity. However, whereas van Gogh's heavy, thick brushstrokes were an important component of his expressive style, Gauguin's color areas appear flatter, often visually dissolving into abstract patches or patterns.

In 1883, Gauguin gave up his prosperous brokerage business in Paris to devote his time entirely to painting. Three years later, attracted by Brittany's unspoiled culture, Gauguin moved from Paris to Pont-Aven. Although in the 1870s and 1880s, Brittany had been transformed into a profitable market economy, Gauguin still viewed the Bretons as "natural" men and women at ease in their environment. At Pont-Aven, he painted *Vision after the Sermon,* or *Jacob Wrestling with the Angel* (FIG. **13-11**), a work in which he decisively rejected both Realism and Impressionism. The painting shows Breton women, wearing their starched white Sunday caps and black dresses, visualizing the sermon they have just heard at church on Jacob's encounter with the Holy Spirit (Gen. 32:24–30). The women pray devoutly before the apparition. Gauguin departed from optical realism and composed the picture elements to focus the viewer's attention on the idea and intensify its message. The images are not what the

Impressionist eye would have seen and replicated but what memory would have recalled and imagination would have modified. Thus, the artist twisted the perspective and allotted the space to emphasize the innocent faith of the unquestioning women, and he shrank Jacob and the angel, wrestling in a ring enclosed by a Breton stone fence, to the size of fighting cocks. Wrestling matches were regular features at the entertainment held after high mass, so Gauguin's women are spectators at a contest that was, for them, a familiar part of their culture.

Gauguin did not unify the picture with a horizon perspective, light and shade, or naturalistic use of color. Instead, he abstracted the scene into a pattern. Pure unmodulated color fills flat planes and shapes bounded by firm lines: white caps, black dresses, and the red field of combat. The shapes are angular, even harsh. The caps, sharp profiles, and hard contours suggest the austerity of peasant life and ritual. Gauguin admired Japanese prints, stained glass (FIG. 7-10), and cloisonné metalwork (FIG. 6-2). These art forms contributed to his own daring experiment to transform traditional painting and Impressionism into abstract, expressive patterns of line, shape, and pure color.

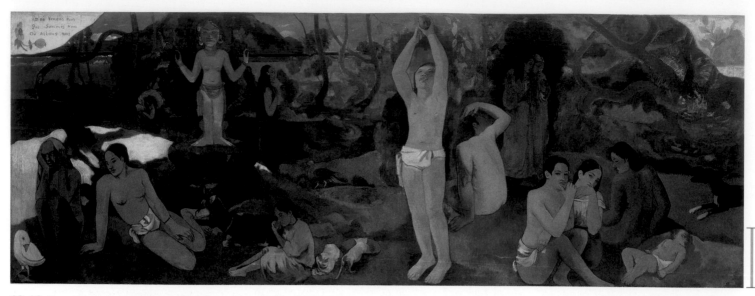

13-12 PAUL GAUGUIN, *Where Do We Come From? What Are We? Where Are We Going?* 1897. Oil on canvas, 4′ 6 13/16″ × 12′ 3″. Museum of Fine Arts, Boston (Tompkins Collection).

In search of a place far removed from European materialism, Gauguin moved to Tahiti, where he used native women and tropical colors to present a pessimistic view of the inevitability of the life cycle.

Where Do We Come From? After a brief period of association with van Gogh in Arles in 1888, Gauguin settled in Tahiti because he believed it offered him a life far removed from materialistic Europe and an opportunity to reconnect with nature. Upon his arrival, he discovered that the South Pacific island, under French control since 1842, had been extensively colonized. Disappointed, Gauguin tried to maintain his vision of an untamed paradise by moving to the Tahitian countryside, where he expressed his fascination with primitive life in a series of canvases in which he often based the design on native motifs. The tropical flora of the island inspired the harmonies of lilac, pink, and lemon in his paintings.

In 1897, worn down by failing health and the hostile reception of his work, Gauguin tried unsuccessfully to take his own life, but not before painting *Where Do We Come From? What Are We? Where Are We Going?* (FIG. **13-12**). Gauguin judged this to be his most important painting. It can be read as a summary of his art and his views on life. The scene is a tropical landscape, populated with native women and children. Gauguin described the monumental canvas in a letter to a friend:

> Where are we going? Near to death an old woman. . . . What are we? Day to day existence. . . . Where do we come from? Source. Child. Life begins. . . . Behind a tree two sinister figures, cloaked in garments of sombre colour, introduce, near the tree of knowledge, their note of anguish caused by that very knowledge in contrast to some simple beings in a virgin nature, which might be paradise as conceived by humanity, who give themselves up to the happiness of living.[6]

Where Do We Come From? is, therefore, a sobering, pessimistic image of the life cycle's inevitability. Gauguin died a few years later in the Marquesas Islands, his artistic genius still unrecognized.

Paul Cézanne Although at first he accepted the Impressionists' color theories and their faith in subjects chosen from everyday life, studying Renaissance and Baroque paintings in the Louvre persuaded PAUL CÉZANNE (1839–1906) that Impressionism lacked form and structure. Cézanne decided he wanted to "make of Impressionism something solid and durable like the art of the museums."[7] *Mont Sainte-Victoire* (FIG. **13-13**) is one of many views Cézanne painted of this mountain near his home in Aix-en-Provence. His aim in all of his mature works was not truth in appearance, especially not photographic truth, nor was it the "truth" of Impressionism. Rather, he sought a lasting structure behind the formless and fleeting visual information the eye absorbs. Instead of employing the Impressionists' random approach when he was face-to-face with nature, Cézanne, like Seurat, developed a more analytical style. His goal was to order the lines, planes, and colors comprising nature. He constantly and painstakingly checked his painting against the part of the scene—he called it the "motif"—he was studying at the moment. Cézanne sought "[to do] Poussin over entirely from nature . . . in the open air, with color and light, instead of . . . in a studio."[8] He wished to achieve Poussin's effects of distance, depth, structure, and solidity not by using traditional perspective and chiaroscuro but by recording the color patterns he deduced from an optical analysis of nature.

With special care, Cézanne explored the properties of line, plane, and color and their interrelationships. He studied the effect of every kind of linear direction, the capacity of planes to create the sensation of depth, the intrinsic qualities of color, and the power of colors to modify the direction and depth of lines and planes. To create the illusion of three-dimensional form and space, Cézanne focused on carefully selecting colors. He understood that the visual properties—hue, saturation, and value—of different colors vary (see "Color Theory," page 374).

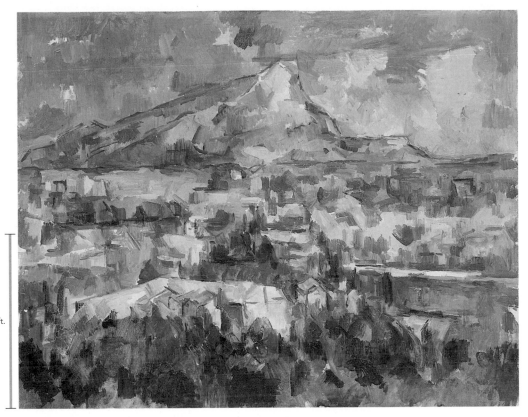

13-13 PAUL CÉZANNE, *Mont Sainte-Victoire,* 1902–1904. Oil on canvas, 2′ 3½″ × 2′ 11¼″. Philadelphia Museum of Art, Philadelphia (George W. Elkins Collection). ■◀

In his landscapes, Cézanne replaced the transitory visual effects of changing atmospheric conditions—the Impressionists' focus—with careful analysis of the lines, planes, and colors of nature.

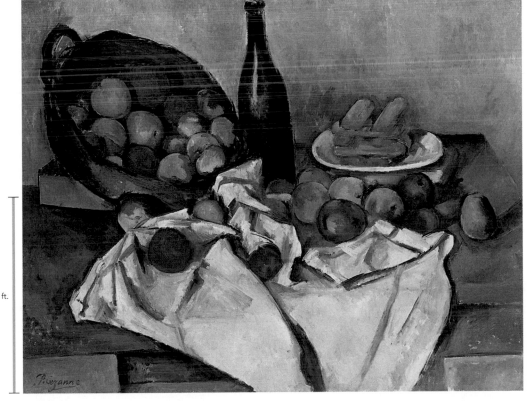

13-14 PAUL CÉZANNE, *Basket of Apples,* ca. 1895. Oil on canvas, 2′ ⅜″ × 2′ 7″. Art Institute of Chicago, Chicago (Helen Birch Bartlett Memorial Collection, 1926). ■◀

Cézanne's still lifes reveal his analytical approach to painting. He captured the solidity of bottles and fruit by juxtaposing color patches, but the resulting abstract shapes are not optically realistic.

Cool colors tend to recede, whereas warm ones advance. By applying to the canvas small patches of juxtaposed colors, some advancing and some receding, Cézanne created volume and spatial depth in his works. On occasion, the artist depicted objects chiefly in one hue and achieved convincing solidity by modulating the intensity (or saturation). At other times, he juxtaposed contrasting colors of similar saturation to compose specific objects, such as fruit or bowls.

In *Mont Sainte-Victoire,* Cézanne replaced the transitory visual effects of changing atmospheric conditions—effects that preoccupied Monet—with a more concentrated, lengthier analysis of the colors in large lighted spaces. The main space stretches out behind and beyond the canvas plane and includes numerous small elements, such as roads, fields, houses, and the viaduct at the far right, each seen from a slightly different viewpoint. Above this shifting, receding perspective rises the largest mass of all, the mountain, with an effect—achieved by equally stressing background and foreground contours—of being simultaneously near and far away. This portrayal approximates the real experience a person has when viewing a landscape's forms piecemeal. The relative proportions of objects vary rather than being fixed by strict perspective, such as that normally found in a photograph. Cézanne immobilized the shifting colors of Impressionism into an array of clearly defined planes composing the objects and spaces in his scene.

Basket of Apples Still life was another good vehicle for Cézanne's experiments, as he could arrange a limited number of selected objects to provide a well-ordered point of departure. So analytical was Cézanne in preparing, observing, and painting still lifes (in contrast to the Impressionist emphasis on spontaneity) that he had to abandon using real fruit and flowers because they tended to rot. In *Basket of Apples* (FIG. **13-14**), the objects have lost something of their individual character. The bottle and fruit have almost become a cylinder and spheres. Cézanne captured the solidity of each object by juxtaposing color patches. His interest in the study of volume and solidity is evident from the disjunctures in the painting—the table edges are discontinuous, and various objects seem to be depicted from different vantage points. In his zeal to understand three-dimensionality and to convey the placement of forms relative to the space around them, Cézanne explored his still-life arrangements from different viewpoints. This resulted in paintings that, although conceptually coherent, do not appear optically realistic. In keeping with the modernist concern with the integrity of the painting surface, Cézanne's methods never allow the viewer to disregard the two-dimensionality of the picture plane. In this manner, Cézanne achieved a remarkable feat—presenting the viewer with two-dimensional and three-dimensional images simultaneously.

SYMBOLISM

The Impressionists and Post-Impressionists believed their emotions and sensations were important elements for interpreting the world, but the depiction of reality remained the primary focus of their efforts. By the end of the 19th century, the representation of nature became completely subjective. Artists rejected the optical world as observed in favor of a fantasy world, of forms they conjured in their free imagination, with or without reference to things conventionally seen. Color, line, and shape, divorced from conformity to the optical image, became symbols of personal emotions in response to the world. Many of the artists following this path adopted an approach to subject and form that associated them with a general European movement called *Symbolism*. Symbolists, whether painters or writers, disdained Realism as trivial. The task of Symbolist artists was not to see things but to see through them to a significance and reality far deeper than what superficial appearance revealed. Symbolists cultivated all the resources of imagination, and their subjects became increasingly esoteric as well as exotic, mysterious, visionary, dreamlike, and fantastic. Perhaps not coincidentally, at about this time Sigmund Freud (1856–1939), the founder of psychoanalysis, published his classic work *Interpretations of Dreams*

(1900), an introduction to the concept and the world of unconscious experience.

Henri Rousseau Paul Gauguin had journeyed to the South Seas in search of primitive innocence. HENRI ROUSSEAU (1844–1910) was a "primitive" without leaving Paris—a self-taught amateur painter. Derided by the critics, Rousseau compensated for his apparent visual, conceptual, and technical naïveté with a natural talent for design and an imagination teeming with exotic images of mysterious tropical landscapes. In *Sleeping Gypsy* (FIG. **13-15**), the recumbent figure occupies a desert world, silent and secret, and dreams beneath a pale, perfectly round moon. In the foreground, a lion resembling a stuffed, but somehow menacing, animal doll sniffs at the gypsy. A critical encounter impends—an encounter of the type that recalls the uneasiness of a person's vulnerable subconscious self during sleep. Rousseau's art of drama and fantasy has its own sophistication and, after the artist's death, influenced the development of Surrealism (see Chapter 14).

Edvard Munch Linked in spirit to the Symbolists was the Norwegian painter and graphic artist EDVARD MUNCH (1863–1944). Munch felt deeply the pain of human life and believed humans were powerless before the great natural forces of death and love. The emotions associated with them—jealousy, loneliness, fear, desire, despair—became the theme of most of his art. Because Munch's goal was to describe the conditions of "modern psychic life," as he put it, Realist and Impressionist techniques were inappropriate, focusing as they did on the tangible world. In the spirit of Symbolism, Munch used color, line, and figural distortion to expressive ends.

The Scream (FIG. **13-16**) exemplifies Munch's style. The image—a man standing on a bridge or jetty in a landscape—comes from the real world, but Munch's treatment of the image departs significantly from visual reality. *The Scream* evokes

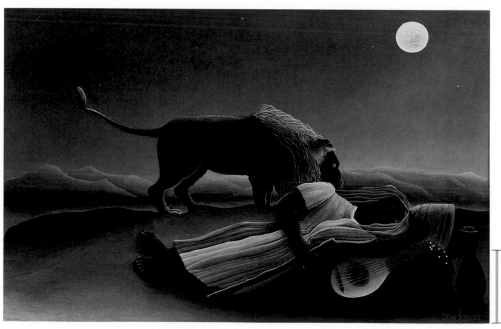

13-15 HENRI ROUSSEAU, *Sleeping Gypsy*, 1897. Oil on canvas, 4' 3" × 6' 7". Museum of Modern Art, New York (gift of Mrs. Simon Guggenheim).

In *Sleeping Gypsy*, Henri Rousseau depicted a doll-like but menacing lion sniffing at a recumbent dreaming figure in a mysterious landscape. The painting conjures the vulnerable subconscious during sleep.

1 ft.

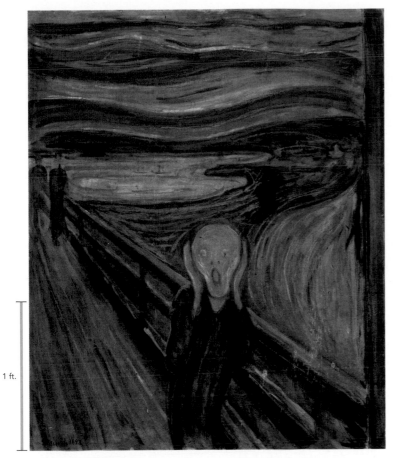

13-16 EDVARD MUNCH, *The Scream,* 1893. Tempera and pastels on cardboard, 2′ 11¾″ × 2′ 5″. National Gallery, Oslo.

Although grounded in the real world, *The Scream* departs significantly from visual reality. Munch used color, line, and figural distortion to evoke a strong emotional response from the viewer.

a visceral, emotional response from the viewer because of the painter's dramatic presentation. The man in the foreground, simplified to almost skeletal form, emits a primal scream. The landscape's sweeping curvilinear lines reiterate the shapes of the man's mouth and head, almost like an echo, as the cry seems to reverberate through the setting. The fiery red and yellow stripes that give the sky an eerie glow also contribute to this work's resonance. Munch wrote a revealing epigraph to accompany the painting: "I stopped and leaned against the balustrade, almost dead with fatigue. Above the blue-black fjord hung the clouds, red as blood and tongues of fire. My friends had left me, and alone, trembling with anguish, I became aware of the vast, infinite cry of nature."[9] Appropriately, the original title of this work was *Despair.*

Fin-de-Siècle Historians have adopted the term *fin-de-siècle* (French, "end of the century") to describe the culture of the late 1800s. This designation is not merely chronological but also refers to a certain sensibility. The increasingly large and prosperous middle classes aspired to the advantages the aristocracy traditionally enjoyed. They too strove to live "the good life," which evolved into a culture of decadence and indulgence. Characteristic of the fin-de-siècle period was an intense preoccupation with sexual drives, powers, and perversions. People at the end of the century also immersed themselves in an exploration of the unconscious. This culture was unrestrained and freewheeling, but the determination to enjoy life masked an anxiety prompted by significant political upheaval and an uncertain future. The country most closely associated with fin-de-siècle culture was Austria.

Gustav Klimt The Viennese artist GUSTAV KLIMT (1863–1918) captured this period's flamboyance in his work but tempered it with unsettling undertones. In *The Kiss* (FIG. **13-17**), Klimt depicted a couple locked in an embrace. The setting is ambiguous and all the viewer sees is a small segment of each body—and virtually nothing of the man's face. The rest of the canvas dissolves into shimmering, extravagant flat patterning, evoking the conflict between two- and three-dimensionality intrinsic to the work of many other modernists. In *The Kiss,* however, those patterns also signify gender contrasts—rectangles for the man's garment, circles for the woman's. Yet the patterning also unites the two lovers into a single formal entity, underscoring their erotic union.

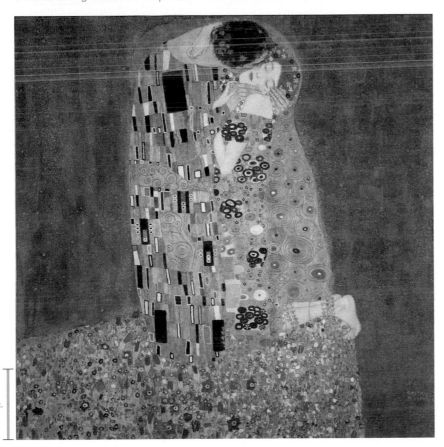

13-17 GUSTAV KLIMT, *The Kiss,* 1907–1908. Oil on canvas, 5′ 10¾″ × 5′ 10¾″. Österreichische Galerie Belvedere, Vienna. ◼◀

In this opulent Viennese fin-de-siècle painting, Gustav Klimt revealed only a small segment of each lover's body. The rest of the painting dissolves into shimmering, extravagant flat patterning.

SCULPTURE

The three-dimensional art of sculpture could not capture the optical sensations many painters favored in the later 19th century. Its very nature—its tangibility and solidity—suggests permanence. Consequently, the sculptors of this period pursued artistic goals markedly different from those of contemporaneous painters.

Auguste Rodin The leading French sculptor of the era was AUGUSTE RODIN (1840–1917), who conceived and executed his sculptures with a Realist sensibility. Rodin was also well aware of the Impressionists' innovations. Although color was not a significant factor in his work, the influence of Impressionism is evident in Rodin's abiding concern for the effect of light on sculpted surfaces. When focusing on the human form, he joined his profound knowledge of anatomy and movement with special attention to the body's exterior, saying, "The sculptor must learn to reproduce the surface, which means all that vibrates on the surface, soul, love, passion, life. . . . Sculpture is thus the art of hollows and mounds, not of smoothness, or even polished planes."[10] Primarily a modeler of pliable material rather than a carver of hard wood or stone, Rodin worked his sculptures with fingers sensitive to the subtlest variations of surface, catching the fugitive play of constantly shifting light on the body. In his studio, he often would have a model move around in front of him while he created preliminary versions of his sculptures with coils of clay. Rodin was able to capture the quality of the transitory through his highly textured surfaces while revealing larger themes and deeper, lasting sensibilities.

The Gates of Hell Rodin's most ambitious work, the nearly 21-feet-tall *Gates of Hell* (FIG. **13-18**), occupied him for two decades. On August 16, 1880, Rodin received the commission to design a pair of doors for a planned Museum of Decorative Arts in Paris. The museum was never built, however, and it was not until after the sculptor's death that others cast his still-unfinished doors in bronze. Rodin derived the theme of his doors from Dante's *Inferno* and Baudelaire's *Flowers of Evil*. Originally inspired by Lorenzo Ghiberti's *Gates of Paradise* (FIG. **8-16**), Rodin quickly abandoned the idea of a series of framed narrative panels and decided instead to cover each of the doors with a continuous writhing mass of tormented men and women, sinners condemned to Dante's second circle of Hell for their lust. Because of the varying height of the relief and the variegated surfaces, the figures seem to be in flux, moving in and out of an undefined space in a reflection of their psychic turmoil. The dreamlike (or rather, the nightmarish) vision connects Rodin with the Symbolists, and the pessimistic mood exemplifies the fin-de-siècle spirit. The swirling composition and emotionalism

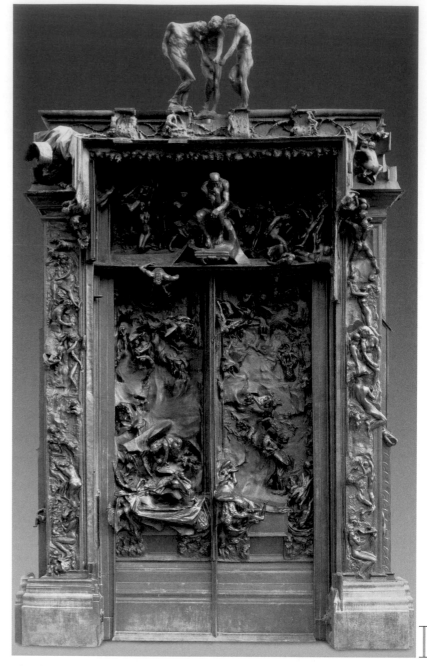

13-18 AUGUSTE RODIN, *The Gates of Hell,* 1880–1900 (cast in 1917). Bronze, 20′ 10″ × 13′ 1″. Musée Rodin, Paris.

Rodin's most ambitious work, inspired by Dante's *Inferno* and Ghiberti's *Gates of Paradise* (FIG. 8-16), presents nearly 200 tormented sinners in relief below *The Three Shades* and *The Thinker*.

recall Delacroix's *Death of Sardanapalus* (FIG. **12-7**) and Michelangelo's *Last Judgment* (FIG. **9-12**). But Rodin's work defies easy stylistic classification.

The nearly 200 figures of *The Gates of Hell* spill over onto the jambs and the lintel. Rodin also included freestanding figures, which, cast separately in multiple versions, are among his most famous works. Above the doors, *The Three Shades* is a trio of twisted nude male figures, essentially the same figure with elongated arms in three different positions. *The Thinker,* Rodin's famous seated nude man with a powerful body who rests his chin on his clenched right hand, ponders the fate of the tormented souls on the doors below.

ARCHITECTURE

In the later 19th century, new technologies, the availability of steel, and the changing needs of urbanized, industrialized society affected architecture throughout the Western world. The Realist impulse also encouraged architectural designs that honestly expressed a building's purpose rather than elaborately disguised a building's function. But the taste for elaborate ornamentation also remained strong in an era characterized by stylistic diversity.

Art Nouveau One important international architectural and design movement that developed in the closing decades of the 19th century was *Art Nouveau* (New Art), which took its name from a shop in Paris called L'Art Nouveau. Proponents of this movement tried to synthesize all the arts in a determined attempt to create art based on natural forms that could be mass-produced for a large audience. The Art Nouveau style adapted the twining-plant form to the needs of architecture, painting, sculpture, and the decorative arts.

The mature Art Nouveau style is on display in the staircase (FIG. **13-19**) of the Van Eetvelde House in Brussels, which the Belgian architect VICTOR HORTA (1861–1947) designed. Every detail of the Van Eetvelde interior functions as part of a living whole. Furniture, drapery folds, veining in the lavish stone paneling, and the patterning of the door moldings join with real plants to provide graceful counterpoints for the twining-plant theme. Metallic tendrils curl around the railings and posts, delicate metal tracery fills the glass dome, and floral and leaf motifs spread across the fabric panels of the screen.

Alexandre-Gustave Eiffel The French engineer-architect whose work epitomizes the exploitation of new technologies to create larger, stronger, and more fire-resistant structures free of superfluous ornamentation was ALEXANDRE-GUSTAVE EIFFEL (1832–1923). Eiffel created the interior armature for France's anniversary gift to the United States—the *Statue of Liberty*—but he designed his best-known work, the Eiffel Tower (FIG. **13-20**), for an exhibition in Paris in 1889. Still re-

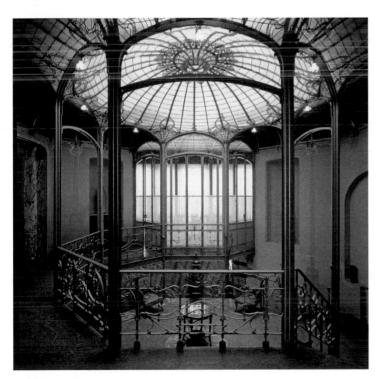

13-19 VICTOR HORTA, staircase in the Van Eetvelde House, Brussels, 1895.

The Art Nouveau movement was an attempt to create art and architecture based on natural forms. Here, every detail conforms to the theme of the twining plant and functions as part of a living whole.

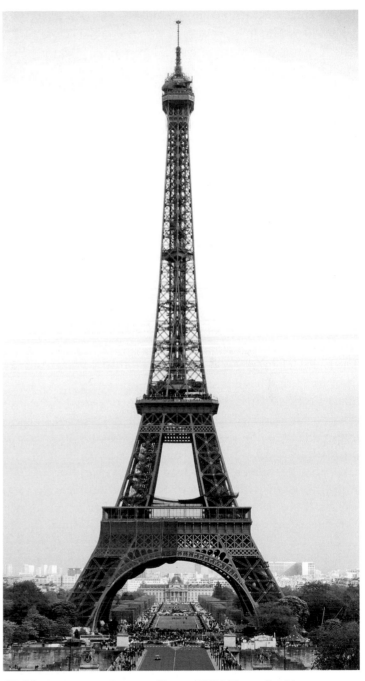

13-20 ALEXANDRE-GUSTAVE EIFFEL, Eiffel Tower (looking northwest), Paris, France, 1889. ◼◀

New materials and technologies and the modernist aesthetic fueled radically new architectural designs in the late 19th century. Eiffel jolted the world with the exposed iron skeleton of his tower.

garded as the symbol of modern Paris, the elegant iron tower thrusts its needle shaft 984 feet above the city, making it at the time of its construction the world's tallest structure. The tower rests on four giant supports connected by gracefully arching open-frame skirts that provide a pleasing mask for the heavy horizontal girders needed to strengthen the legs. The transparency of the structure blurs the distinction between interior and exterior to an extent never before achieved or even attempted. Eiffel jolted the architectural profession into a realization that modern materials and processes could germinate a radically innovative approach to architectural design.

Louis Henry Sullivan The desire for greater speed and economy in building, as well as for a reduction in fire hazards, prompted the use of cast and wrought iron for many building programs, especially commercial ones. Architects in the United States enthusiastically developed cast-iron architecture until a series of disastrous fires in the early 1870s in New York, Boston, and Chicago demonstrated that cast iron by itself was far from impervious to fire. This discovery led to encasing the metal in masonry, combining the first material's strength with the second's fire resistance. In cities, convenience required closely grouped buildings, and increased property values forced architects literally to raise the roof. The new construction materials, which could support structures of unprecedented height, gave birth to the American skyscraper.

As skyscrapers proliferated, in large part because of the introduction of elevators beginning in 1868, architects refined the visual vocabulary of these buildings. LOUIS HENRY SULLIVAN (1856–1924) arrived at a synthesis of industrial structure and ornamentation that perfectly expressed the spirit of late-19th-century commerce. To achieve this, he used the latest technological developments to create light-filled, well-ventilated office buildings and adorned both exteriors and interiors with ornate embellishments. Such decoration served to connect commerce and culture, and imbued these white-collar workspaces with a sense of refinement and taste. These characteristics are evident in Sullivan's Guaranty (Prudential) Building (FIG. **13-21**) in Buffalo. The skyscraper is steel, sheathed with terracotta. The imposing size of the building and the regularity of the window placements served as an expression of the large-scale, refined, and orderly office work taking place within. Sullivan tempered the severity of the structure with lively ornamentation, both on the piers and cornice on the exterior of the building and on the stairway balustrades, elevator cages, and ceiling in the

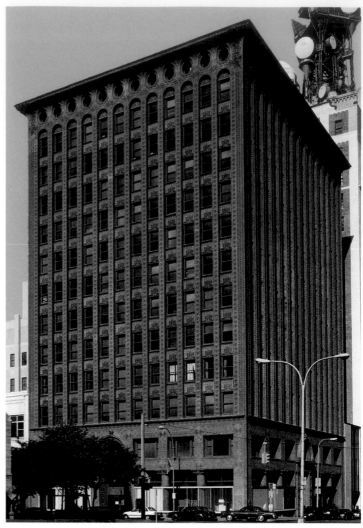

13-21 LOUIS HENRY SULLIVAN, Guaranty (Prudential) Building (looking southwest), Buffalo, 1894–1896.

Sullivan drew on the latest technologies to create this light-filled, well-ventilated, early steel-and-glass skyscraper. He added ornate surface embellishments to impart a sense of refinement and taste.

interior. The Guaranty Building illustrates Sullivan's famous dictum that "form follows function," which became the slogan of many early-20th-century architects.

Thus, in architecture as well as in the pictorial arts, the late 19th century was a period during which artists challenged traditional modes of expression, often emphatically rejecting the past. Architects and painters as different as Sullivan, Monet, van Gogh, and Cézanne, each in his own way, contributed significantly to the entrenchment of modernism as the new cultural orthodoxy of the early 20th century (see Chapter 14).

Impressionism, Post-Impressionism, and Symbolism, 1870 to 1900

Impressionism

- A hostile critic applied the term *Impressionism* to the paintings of Claude Monet because of their sketchy quality. The Impressionists—Monet, Pierre-Auguste Renoir, Edgar Degas, and others—strove to capture fleeting moments and transient effects of light and climate on canvas. They also focused on recording the contemporary urban scene in Paris, frequently painting in bars and dance halls, such as the Moulin de la Galette.

- Complementing the Impressionists' sketchy, seemingly spontaneous brushstrokes are the compositions of their paintings. Reflecting the influence of Japanese prints and photography, Impressionist works often have arbitrarily cut-off figures and settings seen at sharply oblique angles.

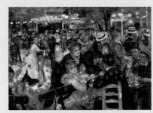

Renoir, *Le Moulin de la Galette*, 1876

Post-Impressionism

- Post-Impressionism is not a unified style. The term refers to the group of late-19th-century artists who followed the Impressionists and took painting in new directions.

- Georges Seurat refined the Impressionist approach to color and light into pointillism—the disciplined application of pure color in tiny daubs. Vincent van Gogh explored the capabilities of colors and distorted forms to express emotions, as in his dramatic depiction of the sky in *Starry Night*. Paul Gauguin, an admirer of Japanese prints, moved away from Impressionism in favor of large areas of flat color bounded by firm lines. Paul Cézanne replaced the transitory visual effects of the Impressionists with a rigorous analysis of the lines, planes, and colors that make up landscapes and still lifes.

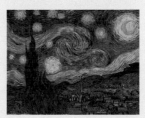

Van Gogh, *Starry Night*, 1889

Symbolism

- The Symbolists disdained Realism as trivial and sought to depict a reality beyond that of the everyday world, rejecting materialism and celebrating fantasy and imagination. Their subjects were often mysterious, exotic, and sensuous. Henri Rousseau's *Sleeping Gypsy*, which alludes to the world of the subconscious during sleep, is a characteristic example.

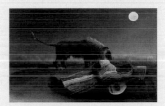

Rousseau, *Sleeping Gypsy*, 1897

Sculpture

- Sculpture cannot capture transitory optical effects or explore the properties of color and line, and late-19th-century sculptors pursued goals different from those of the Impressionists and Post-Impressionists.

- The leading sculptor of the era was Auguste Rodin, who explored Realist themes and the representation of movement. His vision of tormented, writhing figures in Hell connects his work with the Symbolists.

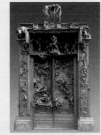

Rodin, *Gates of Hell*, 1880–1900

Architecture

- New technologies and the changing needs of urbanized, industrialized society transformed Western architecture in the late 19th century. The exposed iron skeleton of the Eiffel Tower, which blurs the distinction between interior and exterior, jolted architects into a realization that modern materials and processes could revolutionize architectural design.

- In the United States, Louis Sullivan was a pioneer in designing the first metal, stone, and glass skyscrapers.

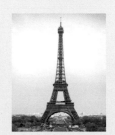

Eiffel, Eiffel Tower, Paris, 1889

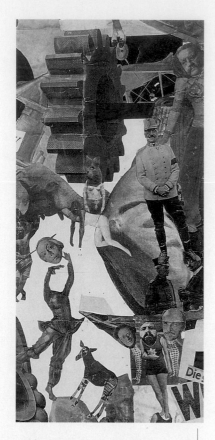

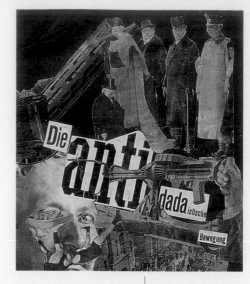

The cut-out photos in Höch's photomontage appear to be randomly selected, but they are carefully arranged. The leading figures of the Weimar Republic (the "anti-Dadaists") are at the top right.

The many photos pasted together in *Cut with a Kitchen Knife* include mass-produced machine parts. In the lower left of this detail, the artist Käthe Kollwitz's head floats above a dancer's body.

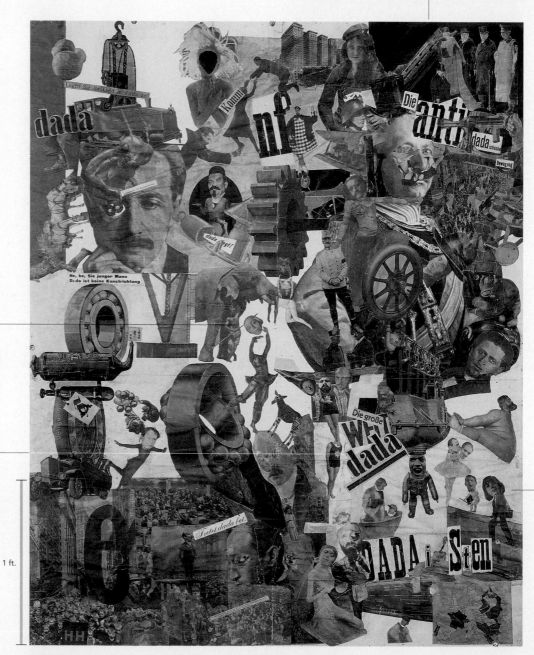

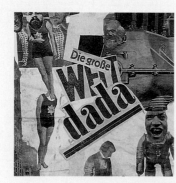

The letters cut from various publications are of different typefaces and font sizes, contributing to the sense of dislocation throughout. Near the center are the words *The great Dada world.*

1 ft.

14-1 HANNAH HÖCH, *Cut with the Kitchen Knife Dada through the Last Weimar Beer Belly Cultural Epoch of Germany,* 1919–1920. Photomontage, 3′ 9″ × 2′ 11½″. Neue Nationalgalerie, Staatliche Museen zu Berlin, Berlin. ◼

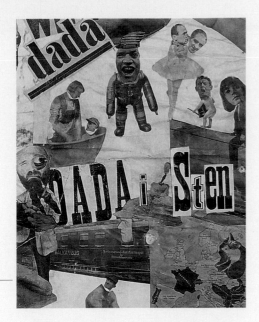

At the lower right, in the section labeled *Dadaists*, Höch juxtaposed a photo of her own face with a map of Europe showing those countries that had granted women the right to vote.

Modernism in Europe and America, 1900 to 1945

GLOBAL WAR, ANARCHY, AND DADA

World War I—the "Great War"—broke out in 1914, unleashing slaughter and devastation on a scale unprecedented in history. More than nine million soldiers died in four years. Britain alone lost 60,000 men on the opening day of the battle of the Somme. The negotiated formal end of hostilities in 1919 redrew the political map of Europe (MAP **14-1**). Peace, however, could not erase the scars of a global conflict that had altered the worldview of millions. One major consequence of the Great War was the emergence of an artistic movement known as *Dada*. The Dadaists believed reason and logic had been responsible for the insane spectacle of collective homicide that was World War I, and they concluded the only route to salvation was through political anarchy, the irrational, and the intuitive.

In Berlin, Dada took on an activist political edge. The Berlin Dadaists pioneered a variation of the technique called *collage* in French—creating artistic compositions from cut pieces of paper. The Berliners christened their version *photomontage* because their assemblages consisted almost entirely of pieces of magazine photographs, usually combined into deliberately antilogical compositions. Collage lent itself well to the Dada desire to exploit chance in the creation of art—and anti-art.

One of the Berlin Dadaists who perfected the photomontage technique was HANNAH HÖCH (1889–1978). Höch's photomontages advanced the absurd illogic of Dada by presenting viewers with chaotic, contradictory, and satiric compositions. They also provided scathing and insightful commentary on two of the most dramatic developments during the Weimar Republic (1918–1933) in Germany—the redefinition of women's social roles and the explosive growth of mass print media. Höch incorporated both themes in *Cut with the Kitchen Knife Dada through the Last Weimar Beer Belly Cultural Epoch of Germany* (FIG. **14-1**), in which she arranged in seemingly haphazard fashion—often with a touch of typically wicked Dada humor—an eclectic mixture of cutout photos. Closer inspection, however, reveals the artist's careful selection and placement of the photographs. For example, the key figures in the Weimar Republic are together at the upper right (identified as the "anti-Dada movement"). Some of Höch's fellow Dadaists appear among images of Karl Marx and Vladimir Lenin, aligning Dada with other revolutionary forces in what she prominently labeled with cutout lettering "Die grosse Welt dada" (the great Dada world). Höch also positioned herself in the topsy-turvy Dada world she created. A photograph of her head appears in the lower right corner, juxtaposed with a map of Europe showing which countries had granted women the right to vote—a commentary on the power both women and Dada had to destabilize society.

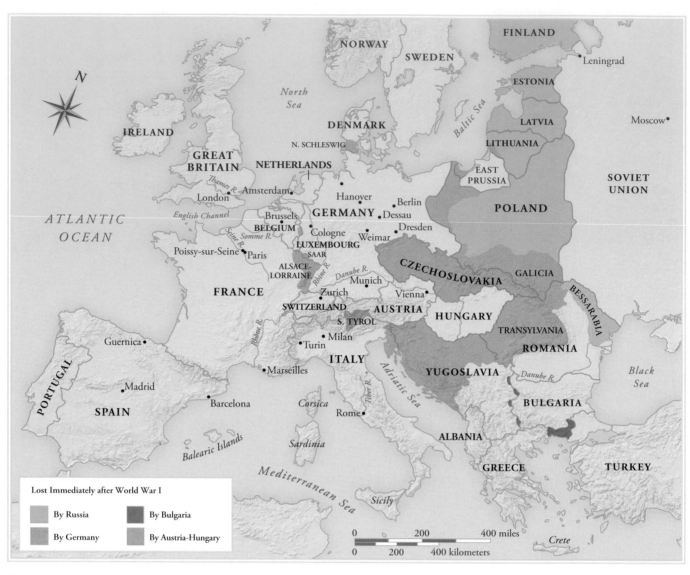

MAP 14-1 Europe at the end of World War I.

Lost Immediately after World War I
- By Russia
- By Germany
- By Bulgaria
- By Austria-Hungary

0   200   400 miles
0 200 400 kilometers

(Map labels)
FINLAND, NORWAY, SWEDEN, Leningrad, ESTONIA, Moscow, DENMARK, LATVIA, N. SCHLESWIG, LITHUANIA, IRELAND, GREAT BRITAIN, NETHERLANDS, EAST PRUSSIA, SOVIET UNION, POLAND, Amsterdam, Hanover, Berlin, London, GERMANY, Dessau, Thames R., Brussels, Cologne, Dresden, BELGIUM, Weimar, ATLANTIC OCEAN, English Channel, Seine R., Somme R., LUXEMBOURG, SAAR, CZECHOSLOVAKIA, GALICIA, Poissy-sur-Seine, Paris, ALSACE-LORRAINE, Rhine R., Danube R., Munich, BESSARABIA, Vienna, FRANCE, Zurich, AUSTRIA, HUNGARY, SWITZERLAND, S. TYROL, TRANSYLVANIA, Rhone R., Milan, ROMANIA, Guernica, Turin, YUGOSLAVIA, Danube R., Black Sea, PORTUGAL, ITALY, Marseilles, Adriatic Sea, Tiber R., BULGARIA, Madrid, Corsica, Rome, ALBANIA, SPAIN, Barcelona, TURKEY, GREECE, Balearic Islands, Sardinia, Mediterranean Sea, Sicily, Crete, North Sea, Baltic Sea

Modernism in Europe and America, 1900 to 1945

1900 — 1910 — 1920 — 1930 — 1945

1900
- European artists build on the innovations of the Impressionists and Post-Impressionists and explore new avenues of artistic expression
- Henri Matisse and the Fauves free color from its descriptive function
- German Expressionist groups— Die Brücke and Der Blaue Reiter—produce paintings featuring bold colors and distorted forms

1910
- Pablo Picasso and Georges Braque radically challenge tradition with their Cubist dissection of forms
- Futurist artists celebrate dynamic motion and modern technology
- Vassily Kandinsky produces completely abstract paintings
- The Dadaists explore the role of chance in irreverent artworks
- The Armory Show introduces America to avant-garde developments in Europe

1920
- Neue Sachlichkeit painters depict the horrors of global conflict
- The Surrealists seek ways to visualize the world of the unconscious
- De Stijl artists create "pure plastic art" using geometric forms and primary colors
- Constantine Brancusi and Barbara Hepworth promote abstraction in sculpture
- The Bauhaus advocates the integration of all the arts

1930
- Aaron Douglas and Jacob Lawrence explore African American history
- Alexander Calder creates abstract sculptures with moving parts
- The Regionalists reject European abstraction and celebrate life in rural America
- Diego Rivera paints vast mural cycles recording Mexican history
- Dorothea Lange and Margaret Bourke-White achieve renown for their documentary photography

GLOBAL UPHEAVAL AND ARTISTIC REVOLUTION

The first half of the 20th century was a period of significant upheaval worldwide. Between 1900 and 1945, the major industrial powers fought two global wars, witnessed the rise of Communism, Fascism, and Nazism, and suffered the Great Depression. These decades were also a time of radical change in the arts when painters and sculptors challenged some of the most basic assumptions about the purpose of art and what form an artwork should take. Throughout history, artistic revolution has often accompanied political, social, and economic upheaval, but never before had the new directions artists explored been as pronounced or as long-lasting as those born during the first half of the last century.

Avant-Garde As did other members of society, artists deeply felt the effects of the political and economic disruptions of the early 20th century. As the old social orders collapsed and new ones, from communism to corporate capitalism, took their places, artists searched for new definitions of and uses for art in a radically changed world. Already in the 19th century, each successive modernist movement had challenged artistic conventions with ever-greater intensity. This relentless questioning of the status quo gave rise to the notion of an artistic *avant-garde*. The term, which means "front guard," derives from French military usage. Avant-garde artists were the vanguard, or trailblazers. They rejected the classical, academic, and traditional, and zealously explored the premises and formal qualities of painting and sculpture.

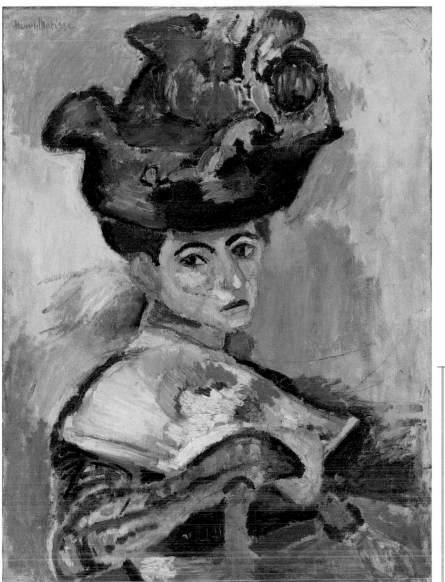

14-2 HENRI MATISSE, *Woman with the Hat*, 1905. Oil on canvas, 2′ 7¾″ × 1′ 11½″. San Francisco Museum of Modern Art, San Francisco (bequest of Elise S. Haas).

Matisse's portrayal of his wife, Amélie, features patches and splotches of seemingly arbitrary colors. He and the other Fauve painters used color not to imitate nature but to produce a reaction in the viewer.

EUROPE, 1900 TO 1920

Avant-garde artists in all their diversity became a major force during the opening decades of the 20th century, beginning with the artistic movement known as *Fauvism*.

Fauvism

In 1905 a group of young painters exhibited canvases so simplified in design and so shockingly bright in color that a startled critic, Louis Vauxcelles (1870–1943), described the artists as *fauves* (wild beasts). Driving the Fauve movement was a desire to develop an art having the directness of Impressionism but employing intense color juxtapositions for expressive ends. Building on the legacy of artists such as Vincent van Gogh and Paul Gauguin (see Chapter 13), the Fauves went even further in liberating color from its descriptive function and exploring the effects different colors have on emotions.

Henri Matisse The dominant figure of the Fauve group was HENRI MATISSE (1869–1954), who believed color could play a primary role in conveying meaning and focused his efforts on developing this notion (see "Matisse on Color," page 390). In an early painting, *Woman with the Hat* (FIG. **14-2**), Matisse depicted his wife, Amélie, in a rather conventional manner compositionally, but the seemingly arbitrary colors startle the viewer. The entire image—the woman's face, clothes, hat, and background—consists of patches and splotches of color juxtaposed in ways that sometimes produce jarring contrasts. Matisse explained his approach: "What characterized fauvism was that we rejected imitative colors, and that with pure colors we obtained stronger reactions."[1]

Matisse's exploration of the expressive power of color reached maturity in *Red Room* (*Harmony in Red;* FIG. **14-3**). The

Matisse on Color

In an essay entitled "Notes of a Painter," published in the Parisian journal *La Grande Revue* on Christmas Day 1908, Henri Matisse responded to his critics and set forth his principles and goals as a painter. The following excerpts help explain what Matisse was trying to achieve in paintings such as *Harmony in Red* (FIG. 14-3) .

What I am after, above all, is expression. . . . Expression, for me, does not reside in passions glowing in a human face or manifested by violent movement. The entire arrangement of my picture is expressive: the place occupied by the figures, the empty spaces around them, the proportions, everything has its share. Composition is the art of arranging in a decorative manner the diverse elements at the painter's command to express his feelings. . . .

Both harmonies and dissonances of colour can produce agreeable effects. . . . Suppose I have to paint an interior: I have before me a cupboard; it gives me a sensation of vivid red, and I put down a red which satisfies me. A relation is established between this red and the white of the canvas. Let me put a green near the red, and make the floor yellow; and again there will be relationships between the green or yellow and the white of the canvas which will satisfy me. . . . A new combination of colours will succeed the first. . . . From the relationship I have found in all the tones there must result a living harmony of colours, a harmony analogous to that of a musical composition. . . .

The chief function of colour should be to serve expression as well as possible. . . . My choice of colours does not rest on any scientific theory; it is based on observation, on sensitivity, on felt experiences. . . . I simply try to put down colours which render my sensation. There is an impelling proportion of tones that may lead me to change the shape of a figure or to transform my composition. Until I have achieved this proportion in all parts of the composition I strive towards it and keep on working. Then a moment comes when all the parts have found their definite relationships, and from then on it would be impossible for me to add a stroke to my picture without having to repaint it entirely.*

*Translated by Jack D. Flam, *Matisse on Art* (London: Phaidon, 1973), 32–40.

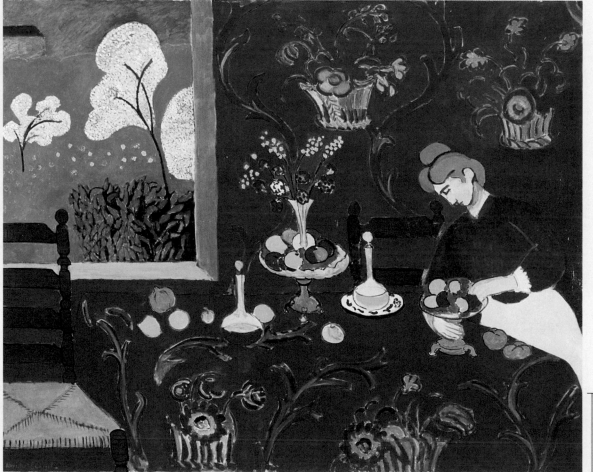

14-3 HENRI MATISSE, *Red Room* (*Harmony in Red*), 1908–1909. Oil on canvas, 5′ 11″ × 8′ 1″. State Hermitage Museum, Saint Petersburg. ◼◀

Matisse believed painters should choose compositions and colors that express their feelings. Here, the table and the wall seem to merge because they are the same color and have identical patterning.

1 ft.

subject is the interior of a comfortable, prosperous household with a maid placing fruit and wine on the table, but Matisse's canvas is radically different from traditional paintings of domestic interiors (FIG. 10-26). The Fauve painter depicted objects in simplified and schematized fashion and flattened out the forms. For example, Matisse eliminated the front edge of the table, rendering the table, with its identical patterning, as flat as the wall behind it. The window at the upper left could also be a painting on the wall, further flattening the space. Everywhere, the colors contrast richly and intensely. Initially, this work was predominantly green, and then Matisse repainted it blue. Neither color seemed appropriate. Not until he repainted the canvas red did he feel he had found the right color for the "harmony" he wished to compose.

German Expressionism

The immediacy and boldness of the Fauve images appealed to many artists, including the German *Expressionists*. However, although color plays a prominent role in German painting of the early 20th century, the "expressiveness" of the German images is due as much to wrenching distortions of form, ragged outline, and agitated brushstrokes.

Ernst Ludwig Kirchner The first group of German Expressionists—*Die Brücke* (The Bridge)—gathered in Dresden in 1905 under the leadership of ERNST LUDWIG KIRCHNER (1880–1938). The group members thought of themselves as paving the way for a more perfect age by bridging the old age and the new, hence their name. The Bridge artists protested the hypocrisy and materialistic decadence of those in power. Kirchner, in particular, focused much of his attention on the detrimental effects of industrialization, such as the alienation of individuals in cities, which he felt fostered a mechanized and impersonal society. His *Street, Dresden* (FIG. **14-4**) provides a glimpse into the frenzied urban activity of a bustling German city before World War I. Rather than offering the distant, panoramic urban view of the Impressionists, Kirchner's street scene is jarring and dissonant in both composition and color. The women in the foreground loom large, approaching somewhat menacingly. The steep perspective of the street, which threatens to push the women into the viewer's space, increases their confrontational nature. Harshly rendered, the women's features make them appear ghoulish, and the garish, clashing colors—juxtapositions of bright orange, emerald green, chartreuse, and pink—add to the expressive impact of the image. Kirchner's perspective distortions, disquieting figures, and color choices reflect the influence of the work of Edvard Munch, who made similar expressive use of formal elements in *The Scream* (FIG. 13-16).

Vassily Kandinsky A second major German Expressionist group, *Der Blaue Reiter* (The Blue Rider), formed in Munich in 1911. The two founding members, Vassily Kandinsky and Franz Marc, whimsically selected this name because of their mutual interest in the color blue and in horses. As did Die Brücke, this group produced paintings that captured the artists' feelings in visual form while also eliciting intense visceral responses from viewers.

Born in Russia, VASSILY KANDINSKY (1866–1944) moved to Munich in 1896 and soon developed a spontaneous and aggressively avant-garde expressive style. Indeed, Kandinsky was one of the first artists to explore complete abstraction,

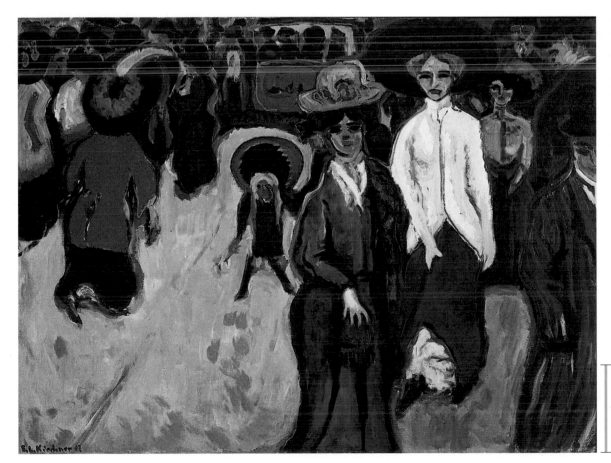

14-4 ERNST LUDWIG KIRCHNER, *Street, Dresden*, 1908 (dated 1907). Oil on canvas, 4′ 11¼″ × 6′ 6⅞″. Museum of Modern Art, New York. ▮◀

Kirchner's perspective distortions, disquieting figures, and color choices reflect the influence of the Fauves and of Edvard Munch (FIG. 13-16), who made similar expressive use of formal elements.

1 ft.

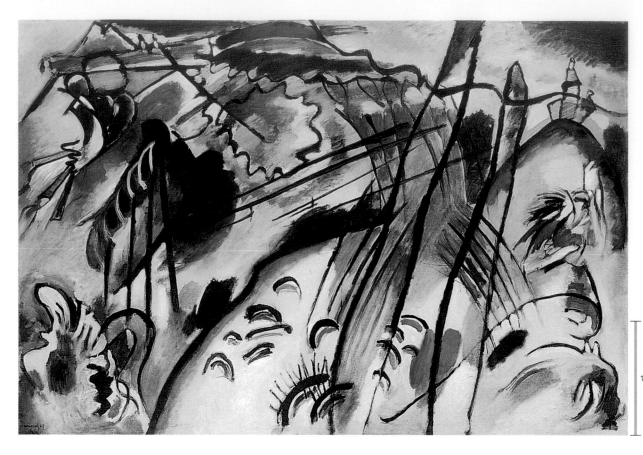

14-5 VASSILY KANDINSKY, *Improvisation 28* (second version), 1912. Oil on canvas, 3' 7⅞" × 5' 3⅞". Solomon R. Guggenheim Museum, New York (gift of Solomon R. Guggenheim, 1937).

Kandinsky believed artists must express their innermost feelings by orchestrating color, form, line, and space. He was one of the first artists to explore complete abstraction in paintings he called *Improvisations*.

1 ft.

as in *Improvisation 28* (FIG. **14-5**). A true intellectual, Kandinsky was one of the few artists to read with some comprehension the new scientific theories of the era formulated by Max Planck (1858–1947), Ernest Rutherford (1871–1937), Albert Einstein (1879–1955), and Niels Bohr (1885–1962). Fundamental to Enlightenment thought was faith in science, but the discoveries of these scientists shattered people's confidence in the objective reality of matter. Rutherford's and Bohr's exploration of atomic structure, for example, convinced Kandinsky material objects had no real substance. The painter articulated his ideas in an influential 1912 treatise, *Concerning the Spiritual in Art,* which contributed to the growing interest in abstraction. Artists, Kandinsky believed, must express their innermost feelings by orchestrating color, form, line, and space. *Improvisation 28* is one of numerous works Kandinsky produced that convey feelings with color juxtapositions, intersecting linear elements, and implied spatial relationships. Ultimately, Kandinsky saw these abstractions as evolving blueprints for a more enlightened and liberated society emphasizing spirituality.

Franz Marc As did many of the other German Expressionists, FRANZ MARC (1880–1916) grew increasingly pessimistic about the state of humanity, especially as World War I loomed on the horizon. His perception of human beings as deeply flawed led him to turn to the natural world for his subjects. Animals, he believed, were more pure than humanity and thus more appropriate vehicles to express an inner truth. In his quest to imbue his paintings with greater emotional intensity, Marc focused on color and developed a

system of correspondences between specific colors and feelings or ideas. According to Marc, "Blue is the *male* principle, severe and spiritual. Yellow is the *female* principle, gentle, happy and sensual. Red is *matter,* brutal and heavy."[2]

Fate of the Animals (FIG. **14-6**) represents the culmination of Marc's efforts to create, in a sense, an iconography of color. Painted in 1913, when the tension of impending cataclysm had pervaded society, the animals appear trapped in a forest amid falling trees, some apocalyptic event destroying both the forest and the animals inhabiting it. The painter distorted the entire scene and shattered it into fragments. Significantly, the lighter and brighter colors—the passive, gentle, and cheerful ones—are absent, and the colors of severity and brutality dominate the work. Marc discovered just how well his painting portended war's anguish and tragedy when he ended up at the front the following year. His experiences in battle prompted him to write to tell his wife in a letter: "[*Fate of the Animals*] is like a premonition of this war—horrible and shattering. I can hardly conceive that I painted it."[3] Marc's contempt for people's inhumanity and his attempt to express that through his art ended, with tragic irony, in his death in action in World War I in 1916.

Käthe Kollwitz The emotional power of postwar German Expressionism is evident in the graphic work of KÄTHE KOLLWITZ (1867–1945), although she had no formal association with any Expressionist group. Kollwitz explored a range of issues from the overtly political to the deeply personal. One subject she treated repeatedly was a mother with her dead child. Although she initially derived the theme from the

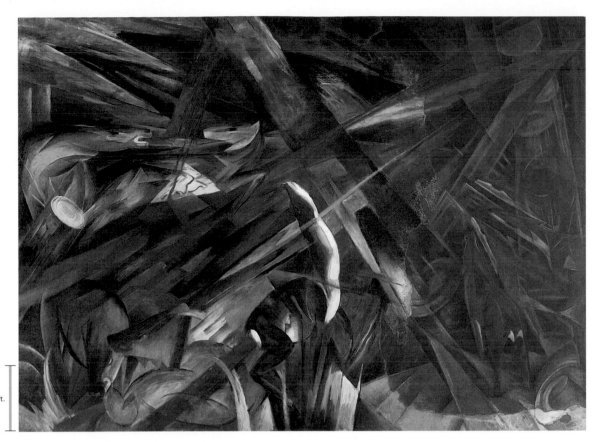

14-6 FRANZ MARC, *Fate of the Animals,* 1913. Oil on canvas, 6′ 4¼″ × 8′ 9½″. Kunstmuseum Basel, Basel.

Marc developed a system of correspondences between specific colors and feelings or ideas. In this apocalyptic scene of animals trapped in a forest, the colors of severity and brutality dominate.

1 ft.

Christian *Pietà,* Kollwitz transformed it into a universal statement of maternal loss and grief. In *Woman with Dead Child* (FIG. **14-7**), she replaced the reverence and grace pervading most depictions of Mary holding the dead Christ (FIG. 9-8) with an animalistic passion. The grieving mother ferociously grips the body of her dead child. The primal nature of the undeniably powerful image is in keeping with the aims of the Expressionists. Because Kollwitz used her son Peter as the model for the dead child, the image was no doubt all the more personal to her. The print proved to be a poignant premonition. Peter died fighting in World War I at age 21.

Primitivism and Cubism

The Expressionist departure from any strict adherence to illusionism in art was a path other artists followed. Among those who most radically challenged prevailing artistic conventions and moved most aggressively into the realm of abstraction was Pablo Picasso.

Pablo Picasso An artist whose importance in the history of art is uncontested, PABLO PICASSO (1881–1973) made staggering contributions to new ways of representing the surrounding world. Perhaps the most prolific artist in history, he explored virtually every artistic medium during his lengthy career and experimented with a wide range of visual expression, first in his native Spain and then in Paris, where he settled in 1904. Picasso remained a traditional artist in making careful preparatory studies for each major work, but he epitomized modernism in his enduring quest for innovation, which resulted in sudden shifts from one style to another.

Les Demoiselles d'Avignon By 1906, Picasso was searching restlessly for new ways to depict form. He found clues in the ancient sculpture of his homeland and the art

1 in.

14-7 KÄTHE KOLLWITZ, *Woman with Dead Child,* 1903. Etching overprinted lithographically with a gold tone plate, 1′ 4⅝″ × 1′ 7⅛″. British Museum, London.

The theme of the mother mourning over her dead child derives from images of the *Pietà* in Christian art, but Kollwitz transformed it into a powerful universal statement of maternal loss and grief.

Primitivism and Colonialism

Many early-20th-century artists incorporated in their work stylistic elements from the artifacts of Africa, Oceania, and the native peoples of the Americas—a phenomenon art historians call *primitivism*. Some of them, for example Henri Matisse and Pablo Picasso, were enthusiastic collectors of "primitive art," but all artists could study the "non-Western" objects displayed in the many European and American anthropological and ethnographic museums that had begun to proliferate during the second half of the 19th century. The formation of these collections was a by-product of the frenzied imperial expansion central to the geopolitical dynamics of the 19th century and much of the 20th century. Most of the Western powers maintained colonies in Africa or the Pacific. Westerners often perceived these colonial cultures as "primitive" and referred to many of the non-Western artifacts exhibited in museums as "artificial curiosities" or "fetish objects." These objects, which often depicted strange gods or creatures, reinforced the perception these peoples were "barbarians" who needed to be "civilized" or "saved," thereby justifying colonialism and missionary work worldwide.

Whether avant-garde artists were aware of the imperialistic implications of their appropriation of non-Western cultures is unclear. Certainly, however, many artists reveled in the energy and freshness of non-Western images and forms. These different cultural products provided Western artists with new ways of looking at their own art. Picasso, for example, believed

African masks "were magic things . . . mediators" between humans and the forces of evil, and he sought to capture their power as well as their forms in his paintings. "I understood why I was a painter. . . . All alone in that awful museum [the Trocadéro in Paris, now the Musée du quai Branly], with masks, dolls . . . *Les Demoiselles d'Avignon* [FIG. 14-8] must have come to me that day."*

*Jean-Louis Paudrat, "From Africa," in William Rubin, ed., *"Primitivism" in 20th Century Art: Affinity of the Tribal and the Modern* (New York: Museum of Modern Art, 1984), 1:141.

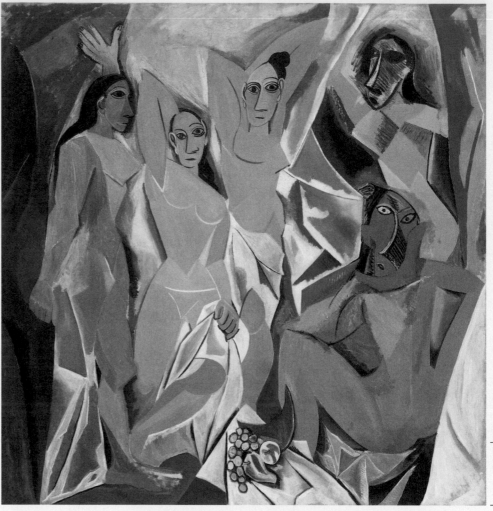

14-8 PABLO PICASSO, *Les Demoiselles d'Avignon,* 1907. Oil on canvas, 8′ × 7′ 8″. Museum of Modern Art, New York (acquired through the Lillie P. Bliss Bequest). ■◀

African and ancient Iberian sculpture and Cézanne's late paintings influenced this pivotal work, with which Picasso opened the door to a radically new method of representing forms in space.

1 ft.

of other "primitive" cultures (see "Primitivism and Colonialism," above). These diverse sources lie behind *Les Demoiselles d'Avignon* (*The Young Ladies of Avignon*; FIG. **14-8**), which opened the door to a radically new method of representing form in space. Picasso began the work as a symbolic picture to be titled *Philosophical Bordello,* portraying male clients intermingling with women in the reception room of a brothel on Avignon Street in Barcelona. By the time the artist finished, he had eliminated the men and simplified the room's details to a suggestion of drapery and a schematic foreground still life. Picasso had become wholly absorbed in the problem of

finding a new way to represent the five women in their interior space. Instead of depicting the figures as continuous volumes, he fractured their shapes and interwove them with the equally jagged planes representing drapery and empty space. Indeed, the space, so entwined with the bodies, is virtually illegible. Here Picasso pushed Cézanne's treatment of form and space (FIGS. 13-13 and 13-14) to a new level. The tension between Picasso's representation of three-dimensional space and his conviction that a painting is a two-dimensional design lying flat on the surface of a stretched canvas is a tension between representation and abstraction.

The artist extended the radical nature of *Les Demoiselles d'Avignon* even further by depicting the figures inconsistently. Ancient Iberian sculptures inspired the calm, ideal features of the three young women at the left. The energetic, violently striated features of the two heads to the right emerged late in Picasso's production of the work and grew directly from his increasing fascination with the power of African sculpture, which he collected and kept in his Paris studio. Perhaps responding to the energy of these two new heads, Picasso also revised their bodies. He broke them into more ambiguous planes suggesting a combination of views, as if the observer sees the figures from more than one place in space at once. The woman seated at the lower right shows these multiple angles most clearly, seeming to present the viewer simultaneously with a three-quarter back view from the left, another from the right, and a front view of the head that suggests seeing the figure frontally as well. Gone is the traditional concept of an orderly, constructed, and unified pictorial space mirroring the world. In its place are the rudimentary beginnings of a new representation of the world as a dynamic interplay of time and space. Clearly, *Les Demoiselles d'Avignon* represents a dramatic departure from the careful presentation of a visual reality. Explained Picasso: "I paint forms as I think them, not as I see them."[4]

Analytic Cubism For many years, Picasso showed *Les Demoiselles* only to other painters. One of the first to see it was GEORGES BRAQUE (1882–1963), a Fauve painter who found it so challenging that he began to rethink his own painting style. Using the painting's revolutionary elements as a point of departure, together Braque and Picasso formulated *Cubism* around 1908 in the belief the art of painting had to move far beyond the description of visual reality. Cubism represented a radical turning point in the history of art, nothing less than a dismissal of the pictorial illusionism that had dominated Western art since the Renaissance. The Cubists rejected naturalistic depictions, preferring compositions of shapes and forms abstracted from the conventionally perceived world. These artists pursued the analysis of form central to Cézanne's artistic explorations, and by dissecting everything around them into their many constituent features, which they then recomposed, by a new logic of design, into a coherent, independent aesthetic picture. The Cubists' rejection of accepted artistic practice illustrates both the period's aggressive avant-garde critique of pictorial convention and the public's dwindling faith, in light of modern physics, in a safe, concrete Enlightenment world.

The new style received its name after Matisse described some of Braque's work to the critic Louis Vauxcelles as having been painted "with little cubes." In his review, Vauxcelles described the new paintings as "cubic oddities."[5] The French writer and theorist Guillaume Apollinaire (1880–1918) summarized well the central concepts of Cubism in 1913:

> Authentic cubism [is] the art of depicting new wholes with formal elements borrowed not from the reality of vision, but from that of conception. This tendency leads to a poetic

kind of painting which stands outside the world of observation; for, even in a simple cubism, the geometrical surfaces of an object must be opened out in order to give a complete representation of it. . . . Everyone must agree that a chair, from whichever side it is viewed, never ceases to have four legs, a seat and back, and that if it is robbed of one of these elements, it is robbed of an important part.[6]

Most art historians refer to the first phase of Cubism, developed jointly by Picasso and Braque, as *Analytic Cubism*. Because Cubists could not achieve the kind of total view Apollinaire described by the traditional method of drawing or painting models from one position, they began to dissect the forms of their subjects and to present their analysis of form across the canvas surface.

Georges Braque's painting *The Portuguese* (FIG. **14-9**) exemplifies Analytic Cubism. The subject is a Portuguese musician the artist recalled seeing years earlier in a bar in Marseilles. Braque dissected the man and his instrument in dynamic interaction with the space around them. Unlike

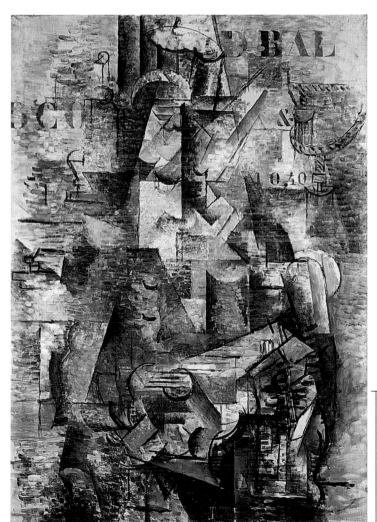

1 ft.

14-9 GEORGES BRAQUE, *The Portuguese*, 1911. Oil on canvas, 3′ 10⅛″ × 2′ 8″. Kunstmuseum Basel, Basel (gift of Raoul La Roche, 1952). ◼◀

The Cubists rejected the pictorial illusionism that had dominated Western art for centuries. Here, Braque concentrated on dissecting form and placing it in dynamic interaction with space.

the Fauves and German Expressionists, who used vibrant colors, the Cubists chose subdued hues—here solely brown tones—in order to focus attention on form. In *The Portuguese,* Braque carried his analysis so far the viewer must work diligently to discover clues to the subject. The construction of large intersecting planes suggests the forms of a man and a guitar. Smaller shapes interpenetrate and hover in the large planes. The way Braque treated light and shadow reveals his departure from conventional artistic practice. Light and dark passages suggest both chiaroscuro modeling and transparent planes that enable the viewer to see through one level to another. Solid forms emerge only to be canceled almost immediately by a different reading of the subject.

The stenciled letters and numbers add to the painting's complexity. Letters and numbers are flat shapes, but as elements of a Cubist painting such as *The Portuguese,* they allow the painter to play with the viewer's perception of two- and three-dimensional space. The letters and numbers lie flat on the painted canvas surface, yet the shading and shapes of other forms flow behind and underneath them, pushing the letters and numbers forward into the viewing space. Occasionally, they seem attached to the surface of some object within the painting. Ultimately, the constantly shifting imagery makes it impossible to arrive at any definitive reading of the image. Analytical Cubist paintings radically disrupt expectations about the representation of space and time.

Synthetic Cubism In 1912, Cubism entered a new phase called *Synthetic Cubism,* in which, instead of dissecting forms, artists constructed paintings and drawings from objects and shapes cut from paper or other materials. The point of departure for this new style was Picasso's *Still Life with Chair-Caning* (FIG. **14-10**), a mixed-media work in which the artist imprinted a photolithographed pattern of a cane chair seat on the canvas, and then pasted a piece of oilcloth on it. Framed with rope, this work challenges the viewer's understanding of reality. The photographically replicated chair caning seems so "real" one expects the holes to break any brushstrokes laid upon it. But the chair caning, although optically suggestive of the real, is only an illusion or representation of an object. In contrast, the painted abstract areas do not refer to tangible objects in the real world. Yet the fact they do not imitate anything makes them more "real" than the chair caning. No pretense exists. Picasso extended the visual play by making the letter *U* escape from the space of the accompanying *J* and *O* and partially covering it with a cylindrical shape that pushes across its left side. The letters *JOU,* which appear in many Cubist paintings, formed part of the masthead of the daily French newspapers (*journaux*) often found among the objects represented. Picasso and Braque

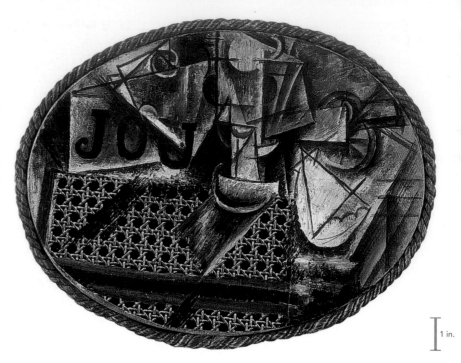

14-10 PABLO PICASSO, *Still Life with Chair-Caning,* 1912. Oil, oilcloth, and rope on canvas, $10\frac{5}{8}''$ × 1' $1\frac{3}{4}''$. Musée Picasso, Paris. ◼◀

This painting includes a piece of oilcloth imprinted with the photolithographed pattern of a cane chair seat. Framed with a piece of rope, the still life challenges the viewer's understanding of reality.

especially delighted in the punning references to *jouer* and *jouir*—the French verbs meaning "to play" and "to enjoy."

After *Still Life with Chair-Caning,* both Picasso and Braque continued to explore the medium of *collage* introduced into the realm of "high art" (as opposed to unselfconscious "folk art") in that work. From the French *coller* (to stick), a collage is a composition of bits of objects, such as newspaper or cloth, glued to a surface. Although most discussions of Cubism and collage focus on the innovations in artistic form they represented, it is important to note that the public also viewed the revolutionary nature of Cubism in sociopolitical terms. Many people considered Cubism's challenge to artistic convention and tradition a subversive attack on 20th-century society. In fact, many modernist artists and writers of the period allied themselves with various anarchist groups whose social critiques and utopian visions appealed to progressive thinkers. Many critics in the French press consistently equated Cubism's disdain for tradition with anarchism and revolution.

Guernica Picasso continued to experiment with different artistic styles and media right up until his death in 1973. Celebrated primarily for his brilliant formal innovations, he was nonetheless acutely aware of politics throughout his life. As Picasso watched his homeland descend into civil war in the late 1930s, his involvement in political issues grew even stronger. He declared: "[P]ainting is not made to decorate apartments. It is an instrument for offensive and defensive

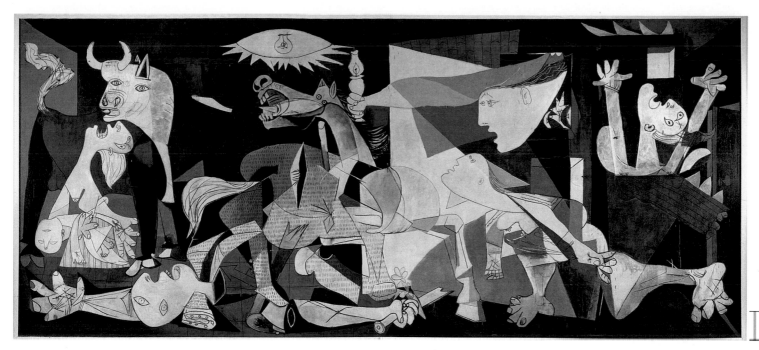

14-11 PABLO PICASSO, *Guernica,* 1937. Oil on canvas, 11' 5½" × 25' 5¾". Museo Nacional Centro de Arte Reina Sofia, Madrid. ◼◗

Picasso used Cubist techniques, especially the fragmentation of objects and dislocation of anatomical features, to expressive effect in this condemnation of the Nazi bombing of the Basque capital.

war against the enemy."[7] In January 1937, the Spanish Republican government-in-exile in Paris asked Picasso to produce a monumental work for the Spanish Pavilion at the Paris International Exposition that summer. He did not formally accept the invitation, however, until he received word that Guernica, capital of the Basque region in southern France and northern Spain, had been almost totally destroyed in an air raid on April 26. Nazi pilots acting on behalf of the rebel general Francisco Franco (1892–1975) bombed the city at the busiest hour of a market day, killing or wounding many of Guernica's 7,000 citizens. The event jolted Picasso into action. By the end of June, he had completed *Guernica* (FIG. **14-11**), a mural-sized canvas of immense power.

Despite the painting's title, Picasso made no specific reference to the event in *Guernica.* The imagery includes no bombs and no German planes. It is a universal visceral outcry of human grief. In the center, along the lower edge of the painting, lies a slain warrior clutching a broken and useless sword. A gored horse tramples him and rears back in fright as it dies. On the left, a shrieking, anguished woman cradles her dead child. On the far right, a woman on fire runs screaming from a burning building, while another woman flees mindlessly. In the upper right corner, a woman, represented only by a head, emerges from the burning building, thrusting forth a light to illuminate the horror. Overlooking the destruction is a bull, which, according to the artist, represents "brutality and darkness."[8]

In *Guernica,* Picasso brilliantly used aspects of his earlier Cubist discoveries to expressive effect, particularly the fragmentation of objects and the dislocation of anatomical features. The dissections and contortions of the human form paralleled what happened to the Basque people in real life. To emphasize the scene's severity and starkness, Picasso reduced his palette to black, white, and shades of gray, suppressing color once again, as he had in his Analytic Cubist works.

Futurism

A contemporaneous modernist art movement, *Futurism,* did indeed have a well-defined sociopolitical agenda. Inaugurated and named by the charismatic Italian poet and playwright Filippo Tommaso Marinetti (1876–1944) in 1909, Futurism began as a literary movement but soon encompassed the visual arts, cinema, theater, music, and architecture. Indignant over the political and cultural decline of Italy, the Futurists published numerous manifestos in which they aggressively advocated revolution, both in society and in art. In their quest to launch Italian society toward a glorious future, the Futurists championed war as a means of washing away the stagnant past and agitated for the destruction of museums, libraries, and similar repositories of accumulated culture, which they described as mausoleums. They also called for radical innovation in the arts. Of particular interest to the Futurists were the speed and dynamism of modern technology. Marinetti insisted a racing "automobile adorned with great pipes like serpents with explosive breath . . . is more beautiful than the *Victory of Samothrace"* (FIG. 2-55), which in the early 20th century exemplified classicism and the glories of past civilizations.[9] Appropriately, Futurist art often focused on motion in time and space, incorporating the Cubist discoveries derived from the analysis of form.

Futurist Manifestos

On April 11, 1910, a group of young Italian artists published *Futurist Painting: Technical Manifesto* in Milan in an attempt to apply the writer Filippo Tommaso Marinetti's views on literature to the visual arts. Signed jointly by Giacomo Balla, Umberto Boccioni, and three other artists, the manifesto states in part:

> On account of the persistency of an image on the retina, moving objects constantly multiply themselves [and] their form changes . . . . Thus a running horse has not four legs, but twenty. . . .

> What was true for the painters of yesterday is but a falsehood today. . . . To paint a human figure you must not paint it; you must render the whole of its surrounding atmosphere. . . . The shadows which we shall paint shall be more luminous than the highlights of our predecessors, and our pictures, next to those of the museums, will shine like blinding daylight compared with deepest night. . . .

> We declare . . . that all forms of imitation must be despised, all forms of originality glorified . . . that all subjects previously used must be swept aside in order to express our whirling life of steel, of pride, of fever and of speed . . . that movement and light destroy the materiality of bodies.*

Two years later, Boccioni published *Technical Manifesto of Futurist Sculpture,* in which he argued that traditional sculpture was "a monstrous anachronism" and that modern sculpture should be

> a translation, in plaster, bronze, glass, wood or any other material, of those atmospheric planes which bind and intersect things. . . . Let's . . . proclaim the absolute and complete abolition of finite lines and the contained statue. Let's split open our figures and place the environment inside them. We declare that the environment must form part of the plastic whole.†

The sculptures of Boccioni (FIG. 14-13) and the paintings of Balla (FIG. 14-12) are the perfect expressions of these Futurist principles and goals.

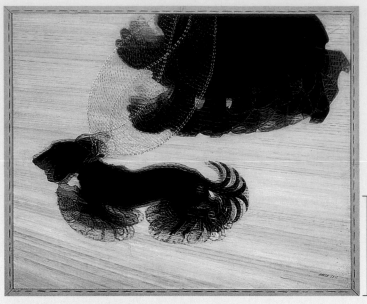

14-12 GIACOMO BALLA, *Dynamism of a Dog on a Leash,* 1912. Oil on canvas, 2′ 11¾″ × 3′ 7¼″. Albright-Knox Art Gallery, Buffalo (bequest of A. Conger Goodyear, gift of George F. Goodyear, 1964). ◼◀

The Futurists' interest in motion and in the Cubist dissection of form is evident in Balla's painting of a passing dog and its owner. Simultaneity of views was central to the Futurist program.

Futurist Painting: Technical Manifesto (*Poesia,* April 11, 1910). Translated by Filippo Tommaso Marinetti, in Umbro Apollonio, ed., *Futurist Manifestos* (Boston: Museum of Fine Arts, 1970), 27–31.
†Translated by Robert Brain, in ibid., 51–65.

Giacomo Balla The Futurists' interest in motion and in the Cubist dissection of form is evident in *Dynamism of a Dog on a Leash* (FIG. **14-12**), in which GIACOMO BALLA (1871–1958) represented a passing dog and its owner, whose skirts are just within visual range. Balla achieved the effect of motion by repeating shapes, for example, the dog's legs and tail and in the swinging line of the leash. Simultaneity of views was central to the Futurist program (see "Futurist Manifestos," above), as it was to Cubism.

Umberto Boccioni One of the cosigners of the Futurist manifesto was UMBERTO BOCCIONI (1882–1916), who produced what is perhaps the definitive work of Futurist sculpture, *Unique Forms of Continuity in Space* (FIG. **14-13**). This piece highlights the formal and spatial effects of motion rather than their source, the striding human figure. The figure is so expanded, interrupted, and broken in plane and contour that

it almost disappears behind the blur of its movement—just as people, buildings, and stationary objects become blurred when seen from an automobile traveling at great speed on a highway. Although Boccioni's figure bears a curious resemblance to the ancient *Nike of Samothrace* (FIG. 2-55), the ancient sculptor suggested motion only through posture and agitated drapery, not through distortion and fragmentation of the human body.

This Futurist representation of motion in sculpture has its limitations, however. The eventual development of the motion picture, based on the rapid sequential projection of fixed images, produced more convincing illusions of movement. And several decades later in sculpture, Alexander Calder (FIG. 14-30) pioneered the development of kinetic sculpture—with parts that really move. But in the early 20th century, Boccioni was unsurpassed for his ability to capture the sensation of motion in statuary.

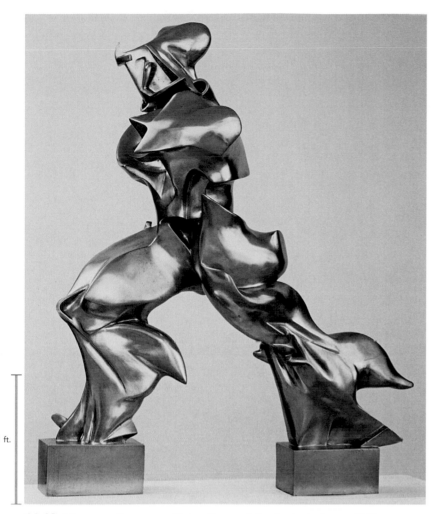

14-13 UMBERTO BOCCIONI, *Unique Forms of Continuity in Space,* 1913 (cast 1931). Bronze, 3′ 7⅞″ × 2′ 10⅞″ × 1′ 3¾″. Museum of Modern Art, New York (acquired through the Lillie P. Bliss Bequest). ■◀

Boccioni's Futurist manifesto for sculpture advocated abolishing the enclosed statue. This running figure's body is so expanded it almost disappears behind the blur of its movement.

DADA

Although the Futurists celebrated World War I and the changes they hoped it would effect, the mass destruction and chaos that conflict unleashed horrified other artists. Humanity had never before witnessed such wholesale slaughter on so grand a scale over such an extended period. The new technology of armaments, bred of the age of steel, changed the nature of combat. In the face of massed artillery hurling millions of tons of high explosives and gas shells and in the sheets of fire from thousands of machine guns, attack was suicidal, and battle movement congealed into the stalemate of trench warfare. The mud, filth, and blood of the trenches, the pounding and shattering of incessant shell fire, and the terrible deaths and mutilations were a devastating psychological, as well as physical, experience for a generation brought up with the doctrine of progress and a belief in the fundamental values of civilization.

With the war as a backdrop, many artists contributed to an artistic and literary movement that became known as *Dada*

(see "Global War, Anarchy, and Dada," page 387). This movement emerged, in large part, in reaction to what many of these artists saw as nothing more than an insane spectacle of collective homicide. Although Dada began independently in New York and Zurich, it also emerged in Paris, Berlin, and Cologne, among other cities. Dada was more a mind-set or attitude than a single identifiable style. The Dadaists believed Enlightenment reasoning had produced global devastation, and consequently they turned away from logic in favor of the irrational. Thus, an element of absurdity is a cornerstone of Dada—reflected even in the movement's name. According to an oft-repeated anecdote, the Dadaists chose *Dada* at random by sticking a knife into a French-German dictionary (hence the title of FIG. 14-1). *Dada* is French for "child's hobby horse." The word satisfied the Dadaists' desire for something irrational and nonsensical.

Art historians often describe Dada as a nihilistic enterprise because of its goal of undermining cherished notions about art. However, by attacking convention and logic, the Dada artists unlocked new avenues for creative invention, thereby fostering a more serious examination of the basic premises of art. But the Dadaists could also be lighthearted in subversion. Although horror and disgust about the war initially prompted Dada, an undercurrent of humor and whimsy runs through much of the art. In its emphasis on the spontaneous and intuitive, Dada paralleled the views of Sigmund Freud (1856–1939) and Carl Jung (1875–1961). Freud was a Viennese doctor who formulated the fundamental principles of psychoanalysis. In *The Interpretation of Dreams* (1900), Freud argued that unconscious and inner drives control human behavior. Jung, a Swiss psychiatrist who developed Freud's theories further, believed the unconscious is composed of two facets, one personal and one collective. The collective unconscious comprises memories and associations all humans share. According to Jung, the collective unconscious accounts for the development of myths, religions, and philosophies. The Dadaists were particularly interested in exploring the unconscious. They believed art was a powerfully practical means of self-revelation and catharsis, and the images arising out of the subconscious mind had a truth of their own, independent of conventional vision.

Jean Arp The Zurich-based Dada artist JEAN (HANS) ARP (1887–1966) pioneered the use of chance in composing his images. Tiring of the look of some Cubist-related collages he was making, he tore some sheets of paper into roughly shaped squares, haphazardly dropped them onto a sheet of paper on the floor, and glued them into the resulting arrangement. The rectilinearity of the shapes guaranteed a somewhat regular design, but chance had introduced an imbalance that seemed to Arp to restore to his work a special mysterious vitality he wanted to preserve. *Collage Arranged*

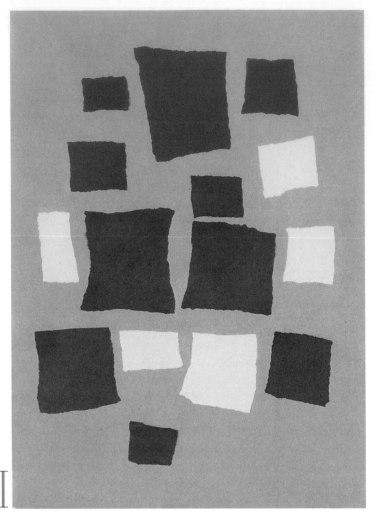

1 in.

14-14 JEAN (HANS) ARP, *Collage Arranged According to the Laws of Chance,* 1916–1917. Torn and pasted paper, 1' 1⅞" × 1' 1⅝". Museum of Modern Art, New York. ◼◀

In this collage, Arp dropped torn paper squares onto a sheet of paper, and then glued them into the resulting arrangement. His reliance on chance in composing images reinforced the anarchy inherent in Dada.

According to the Laws of Chance (FIG. **14-14**) is one of the works he created by this method. As the Dada filmmaker Hans Richter (1888–1976) stated, "For us chance was the 'unconscious mind' that Freud had discovered in 1900. . . . Adoption of chance had another purpose, a secret one. This was to restore to the work of art its primeval magic power and to find a way back to the immediacy it had lost through contact with . . . classicism."[10] Arp's renunciation of artistic control and reliance on chance in creating his compositions reinforced the anarchy and subversiveness inherent in Dada.

Marcel Duchamp Perhaps the most influential Dadaist was MARCEL DUCHAMP (1887–1968), a Frenchman who became the central artist of New York Dada. In 1913, he exhibited his first "readymade" sculptures, which were mass-produced common objects the artist selected and sometimes "rectified" by modifying their substance or combining them with another object. The creation of readymades, he insisted, was free from any consideration of either good or bad taste, qualities shaped by a society he and other Dada artists found

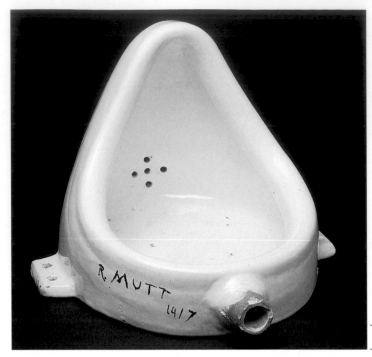

1 in.

14-15 MARCEL DUCHAMP, *Fountain* (second version), 1950 (original version produced 1917). Glazed sanitary china with black paint, 1' high. Philadelphia Museum of Art, Philadelphia.

Duchamp's "readymade" sculptures were mass-produced objects the Dada artist modified. In *Fountain,* he conferred the status of art on a urinal and forced people to see the object in a new light.

aesthetically bankrupt. Perhaps his most outrageous readymade was *Fountain* (FIG. **14-15**), a porcelain urinal presented on its back, signed "R. Mutt," and dated (1917). The "artist's signature" was, in fact, a witty pseudonym derived from the Mott plumbing company's name and that of the shorter man of the then-popular Mutt and Jeff comic-strip duo. The "art" of this "artwork" lay in the artist's choice of object, which had the effect of conferring the status of art on it and forcing the viewer to see the object in a new light.

Suprematism

Dada was a movement born of pessimism and cynicism. Not all early-20th-century artists, however, reacted to the profound turmoil of the times by retreating from society. Some artists promoted utopian ideals, believing staunchly in art's ability to contribute to improving society. These efforts often surfaced in the face of significant political upheaval, as was the case with Suprematism in Russia.

Kazimir Malevich Russian artist KAZIMIR MALEVICH (1878–1935) developed an abstract style to convey his belief that the supreme reality in the world is "pure feeling," which attaches to no object. Thus, this belief called for new, nonobjective forms in art—shapes not related to objects in the visible world. Malevich christened his new artistic approach *Suprematism,* explaining:

> Under Suprematism I understand the supremacy of pure feeling in creative art. To the Suprematist, the visual

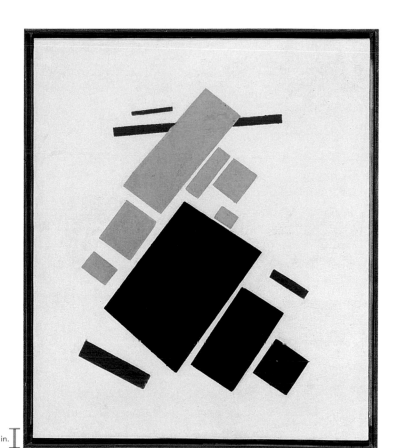

14-16 KAZIMIR MALEVICH, *Suprematist Composition: Airplane Flying*, 1915 (dated 1914). Oil on canvas, 1' 10⅞" × 1' 7". Museum of Modern Art, New York. ◼◀

Malevich developed an abstract style he called Suprematism to convey that the supreme reality in the world is pure feeling. Here, the brightly colored rectilinear shapes float against white space.

phenomena of the objective world are, in themselves, meaningless; the significant thing is feeling, as such, quite apart from the environment in which it is called forth.[11]

The basic form of Malevich's new Suprematist nonobjective art was the square. Combined with its relatives, the straight line and the rectangle, the square soon filled his paintings, such as *Suprematist Composition: Airplane Flying* (FIG. **14-16**). In this work, the brightly colored shapes float against and within a white space, and the artist placed them in dynamic relationship to one another. Malevich believed everyone would easily understand his new art because of the universality of its symbols. It used the pure language of shape and color to which all people could respond intuitively.

UNITED STATES, 1900 TO 1930

Avant-garde experiments in the arts were not limited to Europe. Increasingly common transatlantic travel resulted in a lively exchange of artistic ideas. American artists wishing to pursue modernist ideas at home received encouragement from a number of wealthy and visionary patrons, mostly women (see "Art 'Matronage' in America," at right).

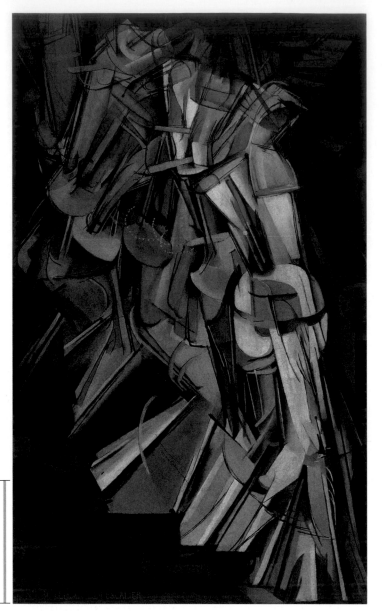

14-17 MARCEL DUCHAMP, *Nude Descending a Staircase, No. 2,* 1912. Oil on canvas, 4′ 10″ × 2′ 11″. Philadelphia Museum of Art, Philadelphia (Louise and Walter Arensberg Collection).

The Armory Show of 1913 introduced European avant-garde art to America. Duchamp's figure moving down a staircase in a time continuum reveals the artist's debt to Cubism and Futurism.

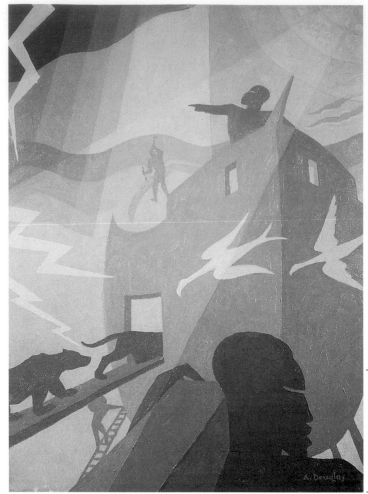

14-18 AARON DOUGLAS, *Noah's Ark,* ca. 1927. Oil on Masonite, 4′ × 3′. Fisk University Galleries, University of Tennessee, Nashville.

In *Noah's Ark* and other paintings of the cultural history of African Americans, Douglas incorporated motifs from African sculpture and the transparent angular planes characteristic of Synthetic Cubism.

Armory Show Artists did not have to travel to Europe to become exposed to modernist art. On February 17, 1913, an exhibition of more than 1,600 works by American and European artists, including Matisse, Kandinsky, Picasso, Braque, and Duchamp, opened at the armory of the National Guard's 69th Regiment in New York City. In addition to exposing American artists and the public to the latest in European artistic developments, the Armory Show also provided American artists with a prime showcase for their work. The provocative exhibition, which traveled to Chicago and Boston after New York, served as a lightning rod for commentary, immediately attracting heated controversy. Some critics even demanded the exhibition be closed as a menace to public morality. The work the press most maligned was Marcel Duchamp's *Nude Descending a Staircase, No. 2* (FIG. **14-17**). The painting represents a single figure in motion down a staircase in a time continuum and suggests the effect of a sequence of overlaid film stills. Unlike Duchamp's Dadaist work (FIG. **14-15**), *Nude Descending a Staircase* shares many characteristics with the work of the Cubists and the Futurists. The monochromatic palette is reminiscent of Analytic Cubism, as is Duchamp's faceted presentation of the human form. The artist's interest in depicting the figure in motion reveals an affinity to the Futurists' ideas. One critic described this work as "an explosion in a shingle factory,"[12] and newspaper cartoonists delighted in lampooning the painting.

Aaron Douglas The influence of Synthetic Cubism is evident in the work of African American artist AARON DOUGLAS (1898–1979), who used the style to represent symbolically the historical and cultural memories of African Americans. Born in Kansas, Douglas settled in New York City in 1924 and became a key figure in the Harlem Renaissance. The artists and writers who spearheaded this movement aimed to cultivate pride among fellow African Americans and to foster racial tolerance across the United States. Encouraged to create art that would express the cultural history of his race, Douglas incorporated motifs from African sculpture into compositions painted in a version of Synthetic Cubism stressing transparent angular planes. *Noah's Ark* (FIG. **14-18**) was one of seven paintings based on a book of poems by James Weldon Johnson (1871–1938) called *God's Trombones: Seven Negro Sermons in Verse*. Douglas used flat planes to evoke a sense of mystical space and miraculous happenings. In *Noah's Ark,* lightning strikes and rays of light crisscross the pairs of animals entering the ark, while men load supplies in preparation for departure. The artist suggested deep space by differentiating the size of the large human head and shoulders of the worker at the bottom and the small person at work on the far deck of the ship. Yet the composition's unmodulated color shapes create a surface pattern that cancels any illusion of three-dimensional depth. Here, Douglas used Cubism's formal language to express a powerful religious vision.

Georgia O'Keeffe In 1918, Wisconsin-born GEORGIA O'KEEFFE (1887–1986) moved from the tiny town of Canyon, Texas, to New York City, where she met Alfred Stieglitz (FIG. 14-19), who played a major role in promoting the avant-garde in the United States through "291," his gallery at 291 Fifth Avenue. Stieglitz had seen and exhibited some of O'Keeffe's work, and he drew her into his circle of avant-garde painters and photographers. He became one of O'Keeffe's staunchest supporters and, eventually, her husband. O'Keeffe is best known for her paintings of cow skulls and of flowers, for example, *Jack-in-the-Pulpit No. 4* (FIG. I-5), which reveals her interest in stripping subjects to their purest forms and colors to heighten their expressive power. In this work, O'Keeffe reduced the incredible details of a flower to a symphony of basic colors, shapes, textures, and vital rhythms, simplifying the flower's curved planes and contours almost to the point of complete abstraction. The fluid planes unfold like undulant petals from a subtly placed axis—the white jetlike streak—in a vision of the slow, controlled motion of growing life. O'Keeffe's painting, in its graceful, quiet poetry, reveals the organic reality of the object by strengthening its characteristic features.

Alfred Stieglitz As an artist, ALFRED STIEGLITZ (1864–1946) is best known for his photographs. Taking his camera everywhere he went, he photographed whatever he saw around him, from the bustling streets of New York City to cloudscapes in upstate New York to the faces of friends and relatives. He believed in making only "straight, unmanipulated" photographs. Thus, he exposed and printed them using basic photographic processes, without resorting to techniques such as double-exposure or double-printing that would add information absent in the subject when he released the shutter. Stieglitz said he wanted the photographs he made with this direct technique "to hold a moment, to record some-

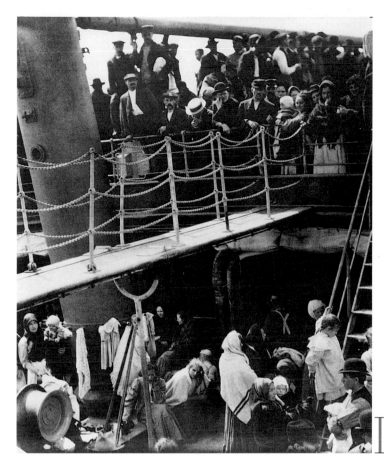

14-19 ALFRED STIEGLITZ, *The Steerage,* 1907 (print 1915). Photogravure (on tissue), 1′ ⅞″ × 10⅛″. Amon Carter Museum, Fort Worth. ◼◀

Stieglitz waged a lifelong campaign to win a place for photography among the fine arts. This 1907 image is a haunting mixture of found patterns of forms and human activity. It stirs deep emotions.

thing so completely that those who see it would relive an equivalent of what has been expressed."[13]

Stieglitz conducted a lifelong campaign to win a place for photography among the fine arts. He founded the Photo-Secession group, which mounted traveling exhibitions in the United States and sent loan collections abroad, and he also published an influential journal titled *Camera Work*. Stieglitz's own specialty was photographing subjects in terms of arrangements of forms and of the "colors" of his black-and-white materials. His aesthetic approach crystallized in *The Steerage* (FIG. **14-19**), taken during a voyage to Europe with his first wife and daughter in 1907. Traveling first class, Stieglitz rapidly grew bored with the company of prosperous passengers. From his section of the ship he could see the lower deck reserved for steerage passengers the government sent back to Europe after refusing them entrance into the United States. Stieglitz described what he saw:

> The scene fascinated me: A round hat; the funnel leaning left, the stairway leaning right; the white drawbridge, its railing made of chain; white suspenders crossed on the back of a man below; circular iron machinery; a mast that cut into the sky, completing a triangle. I stood spellbound.

I saw shapes related to one another—a picture of shapes, and underlying it, a new vision that held me: simple people; the feeling of ship, ocean, sky; a sense of release that I was away from the mob called rich. . . . I had only one plate holder with one unexposed plate. Could I catch what I saw and felt? I released the shutter. If I had captured what I wanted, the photograph would go far beyond any of my previous prints. It would be a picture based on related shapes and deepest human feeling—a step in my own evolution, a spontaneous discovery.[14]

This description reveals Stieglitz's abiding interest in the formal elements of the photograph—an insistently modernist focus. The finished print fulfilled Stieglitz's vision so well it shaped his future photographic work, and its haunting mixture of found patterns and human activity continues to stir viewers' emotions to this day.

Edward Weston Like Alfred Stieglitz, in whose 291 Gallery he exhibited his work, EDWARD WESTON (1886–1958) played a major role in establishing photography as an important artistic medium. But unlike Stieglitz, who worked outdoors and sought to capture transitory moments in his photographs, Weston meticulously composed and carefully lit his subjects in a controlled studio setting, whether he was doing still lifes of peppers, shells, and other natural forms of irregular shape or figure studies. In the 1930 photograph of a pepper illustrated here (FIG. **14-20**), the artificial lighting accentuates the undulating surfaces and crevices of the vegetable. Weston left nothing to chance, choosing the exact angle and play of light over the object, "previsualizing" the final photographic print before snapping the camera's shutter. Weston frequently chose peppers whose shapes reminded him of human bodies. *Pepper No. 30* looks like a seated nude figure seen from behind with raised arms emerging from broad shoulders. Viewers can read the vertical crease down the center of the vegetable as the spinal column leading to the buttocks. Although highly successful as a purely abstract composition of shapes and of light and dark, Weston's still life also conveys mystery and sensuality through its dramatic lighting and rich texture.

EUROPE, 1920 TO 1945

Because World War I was fought entirely in Europe, European artists experienced its devastating effects to a much greater degree than did their American counterparts. The war had a profound impact on Europe's geopolitical terrain, on individual and national psyches, and on the art of the 1920s and 1930s.

Neue Sachlichkeit

In Germany, World War I gave rise to an artistic movement called *Neue Sachlichkeit* (New Objectivity). All of the artists associated with Neue Sachlichkeit served, at some point, in the German army. Their military experiences deeply influenced their worldviews and informed their art, which aimed to present an objective image of the war and its effects.

Max Beckmann Initially a supporter of the Great War, MAX BECKMANN (1884–1950) enlisted in the German army because he believed the chaos would lead to a better society, but over time the massive loss of life and widespread destruction increasingly disillusioned him. Soon his work began to emphasize the horrors of war and of a society he saw descending into madness. His disturbing view of society is evident in *Night* (FIG. **14-21**), which depicts a cramped room three intruders have invaded. A bound woman, apparently raped, is splayed across the foreground of the painting. At the left, one of the intruders hangs her husband, while another one twists his left arm out of its socket. An unidentified woman cowers in the background. On the far right, the third intruder prepares to flee with the child.

Although this image does not depict a war scene, the wrenching brutality pervading the home is a searing and horrifying comment on society's condition. Beckmann also injected a personal reference by using himself, his wife, and his son as the models for the three family members. The stilted angularity of the figures and the roughness of the paint

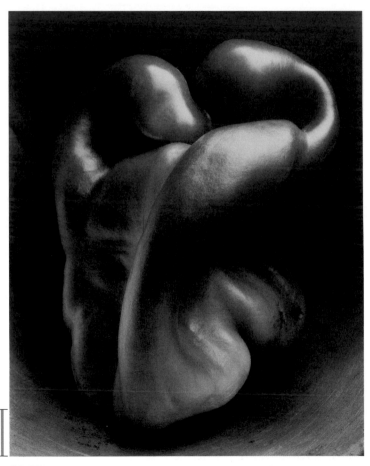

1 in.

14-20 EDWARD WESTON, *Pepper No. 30,* 1930. Gelatin silver print, $9\frac{1}{2}'' \times 7\frac{1}{2}''$. Center for Creative Photography, University of Arizona, Tucson.

Weston "previsualized" his still lifes, choosing the exact angle, lighting, and framing he desired. His vegetables often resemble human bodies, in this case a seated nude seen from behind.

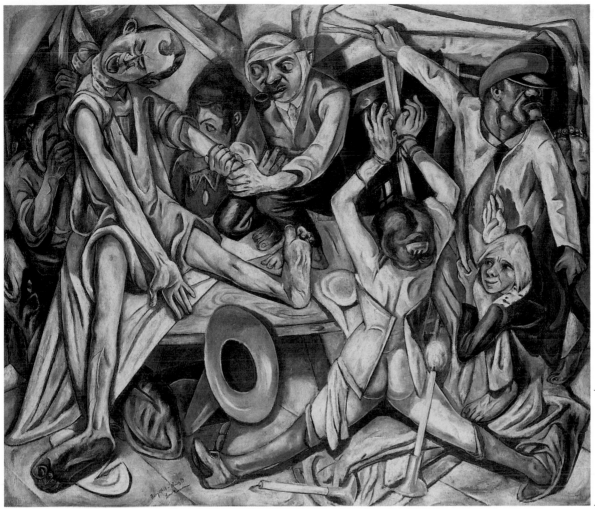

14-21 MAX BECKMANN, *Night*, 1918–1919. Oil on canvas, 4′ 4⅜″ × 5′ ¼″. Kunstsammlung Nordrhein-Westfalen, Düsseldorf.

Beckmann's treatment of forms and space in *Night* matched his view of the brutality of early-20th-century society. Objects are dislocated and contorted, and the space is buckled and illogical.

1 ft.

surface contribute to the image's savageness. In addition, the artist's treatment of forms and space reflects the world's violence. Objects are dislocated and contorted, and the space is buckled and illogical. For example, the woman's hands are bound to the window that opens from the room's back wall, but her body appears to hang vertically, rather than lying across the plane of the intervening table.

Surrealism

In 1924, the *First Surrealist Manifesto* appeared in France, and most of the artists associated with Dada joined that new movement. Not surprisingly, *Surrealism* incorporated many of the Dadaists' improvisational techniques. The Surrealists believed those methods important for engaging the elements of fantasy and activating the unconscious forces deep within every human being. Inspired in part by the ideas of Freud and Jung, the Surrealists sought to explore the inner world of the psyche, the realm of fantasy and the unconscious, and had a special interest in the nature of dreams. According to André Breton (1896–1966), one of the leading Surrealist thinkers:

> Surrealism is based on the belief in the superior reality of certain forms of association heretofore neglected, in the omnipotence of dreams, in the undirected play of

thought. . . . I believe in the future resolution of the states of dream and reality, in appearance so contradictory, in a sort of absolute reality, or surreality."[15]

Thus, the Surrealists' dominant motivation was to bring the aspects of outer and inner "reality" together into a single position, in much the same way life's seemingly unrelated fragments combine in the vivid world of dreams. Surrealism developed along two lines. In *Naturalistic Surrealism,* artists present recognizable scenes that seem to have metamorphosed into a dream or nightmare image. In *Biomorphic Surrealism,* artists produce largely abstract compositions, although the imagery sometimes suggests organisms or natural forms.

Giorgio de Chirico The widely recognized precursor of Surrealism was the Italian painter GIORGIO DE CHIRICO (1888–1978). De Chirico's emphatically ambiguous paintings are the most famous examples of a movement called *Pittura Metafisica,* or Metaphysical Painting. Returning to Italy after study in Munich, de Chirico found hidden reality revealed through strange juxtapositions, such as those seen on late autumn afternoons in the city of Turin, when the long shadows of the setting sun transformed vast open squares and silent public monuments into what the painter called "metaphysical towns." De Chirico translated this vision into paint in works such as *The Song of Love* (FIG. **14-22**), a dreamlike scene set in the deserted piazza of an Italian town. A huge Greco-Roman marble head is suspended in midair above a green ball. To the right is a gigantic red glove nailed to a wall. The buildings and the three over-life-size objects cast shadows that direct the viewer's eye to the left and to a locomotive puffing smoke—a favorite Futurist motif and here shown in slow motion and incongruously placed near the central square. The choice of the term *metaphysical* to describe de Chirico's paintings suggests that these images transcend their physical appearances. *The Song of Love,* for all its clarity and simplicity, takes on a rather sinister air. The sense of strangeness de Chirico could conjure with familiar objects and scenes recalls the observation of philosopher Friedrich Nietzsche (1844–1900) that "underneath this reality in which we live and have our being, another and altogether different reality lies concealed."[16]

Salvador Dalí Spaniard SALVADOR DALÍ (1904–1989) was the most famous Naturalistic Surrealist painter. As he described it, in his painting he aimed "to materialize the images of concrete irrationality with the most imperialistic fury of precision . . . in order that the world of imagination and of concrete irrationality may be as objectively evident . . . as that of the exterior world of phenomenal reality."[17] In *The Persistence of Memory* (FIG. **14-23**), Dalí created a haunting allegory of empty space where time has ended. An eerie, never-setting sun illuminates the barren landscape. An amorphous creature draped with a limp pocket watch sleeps in the foreground. Another watch hangs from the branch of a dead tree springing unexpectedly from a blocky

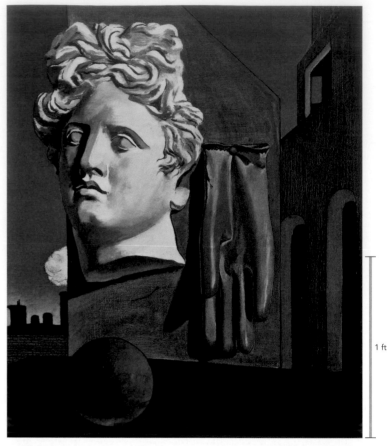

1 ft.

14-22 GIORGIO DE CHIRICO, *The Song of Love,* 1914. Oil on canvas, 2′ 4¾″ × 1′ 11⅜″. Museum of Modern Art, New York (Nelson A. Rockefeller bequest).

De Chirico's Metaphysical Painting movement was a precursor of Surrealism. Here, a Greco-Roman head floats mysteriously next to a gigantic red glove in a deserted shadow-filled Italian city square.

14-23 SALVADOR DALÍ, *The Persistence of Memory,* 1931. Oil on canvas, 9½″ × 1′ 1″. Museum of Modern Art, New York. ◼◀

Dalí aimed to paint "images of concrete irrationality." In this realistically rendered landscape featuring three "decaying" watches, he created a haunting allegory of empty space where time has ended.

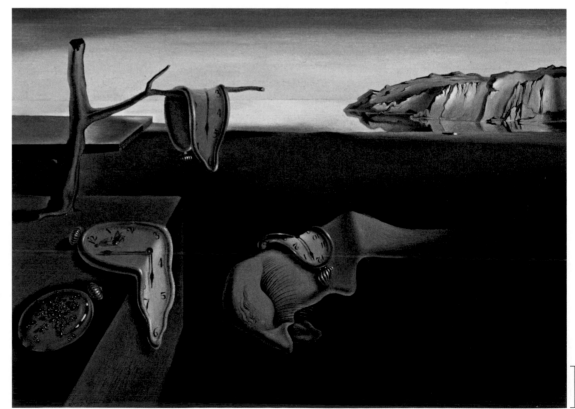

1 in.

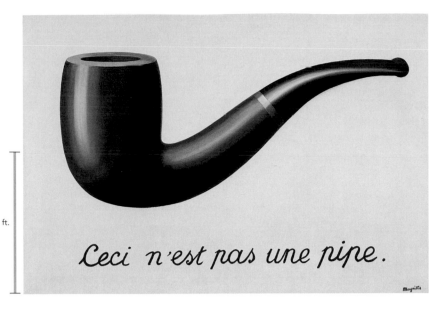

14-24 RENÉ MAGRITTE, *The Treachery (or Perfidy) of Images,* 1928–1929. Oil on canvas, 1′ 11⅝″ × 3′ 1″. Los Angeles County Museum of Art, Los Angeles (purchased with funds provided by the Mr. and Mrs. William Preston Harrison Collection). ■◀

The discrepancy between Magritte's meticulously painted briar pipe and his caption, "This is not a pipe," challenges the viewer's reliance on the conscious and the rational in the reading of visual art.

architectural form. A third watch hangs half over the edge of the rectangular form, beside a small timepiece resting dial-down on the block's surface. Ants swarm mysteriously over the small watch, while a fly walks along the face of its large neighbor, almost as if this assembly of watches were decaying organic life—soft and sticky. Dalí rendered every detail of this dreamscape with precise control, striving to make the world of his paintings convincingly real—in his words, to make the irrational concrete.

René Magritte The Belgian painter RENÉ MAGRITTE (1898–1967) moved to Paris in 1927 and joined the intellectual circle of André Breton. In 1929, Magritte published an important essay in the Surrealist journal *La revolution surréaliste* in which he discussed the disjunction between objects, pictures of objects, and names of objects and pictures. The essay explains the intellectual basis for *The Treachery (or Perfidy) of Images* (FIG. **14-24**), in which Magritte presented a meticulously rendered depiction of a briar pipe. The caption beneath the image, however, contradicts what seems obvious: "Ceci n'est pas une pipe" ("This is not a pipe"). The discrepancy between image and caption clearly challenges the assumptions

underlying the reading of visual art. As is true of other Surrealists' work, this painting wreaks havoc on the viewer's reliance on the conscious and the rational.

Meret Oppenheim Sculpture especially appealed to the Surrealists because its concrete tangibility made their art all the more disquieting. *Object* (FIG. **14-25**), also called *Le Déjeuner en Fourrure (Luncheon in Fur)*, by Swiss artist MERET OPPENHEIM (1913–1985) captures the incongruity, humor, visual appeal, and, often, eroticism characterizing Surrealism. The artist presented a fur-lined teacup inspired by a conversation she had with Picasso. After admiring a bracelet Oppenheim had made from a piece of brass covered with fur, Picasso noted that anything might be covered with fur. When her tea grew cold, Oppenheim responded to Picasso's comment by ordering "un peu plus de fourrure" (a little more fur), and the sculpture had its genesis. *Object* takes on an anthropomorphic quality, animated by the quirky combination of the fur with a functional object. Further, the sculpture captures the Surrealist flair for alchemical, seemingly magical or mystical, transformation. It incorporates a sensuality and eroticism (seen here in the seductively soft, tactile fur lining the concave form) that are also components of much of Surrealist art.

Joan Miró Like the Dadaists, the Surrealists used many methods to free the creative process from reliance on the kind of conscious control they believed society had shaped too much. The Spanish artist JOAN MIRÓ (1893–1983) used *automatism*—the creation of art without conscious control—and various types of planned "accidents" to provoke reactions closely related to subconscious experience. Although Miró resisted formal association with any movement or group, including the Surrealists, Breton identified him as "the most Surrealist of us all."[18] From the beginning, Miró's work contained an element of fantasy and hallucination. After Surrealist poets in Paris introduced him to the use of chance

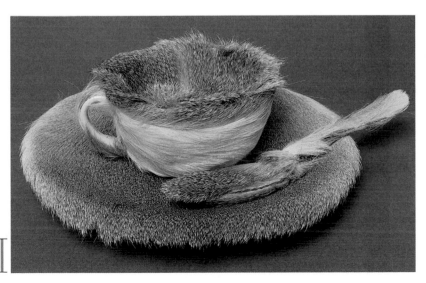

14-25 MERET OPPENHEIM, *Object (Le Déjeuner en Fourrure)*, 1936. Fur-covered cup, 4⅜″ diameter; saucer, 9⅜″ diameter; spoon, 8″ long. Museum of Modern Art, New York.

The Surrealists loved the concrete tangibility of sculpture, which made their art even more disquieting. Oppenheim's functional fur-covered object captures the Surrealist flair for magical transformation.

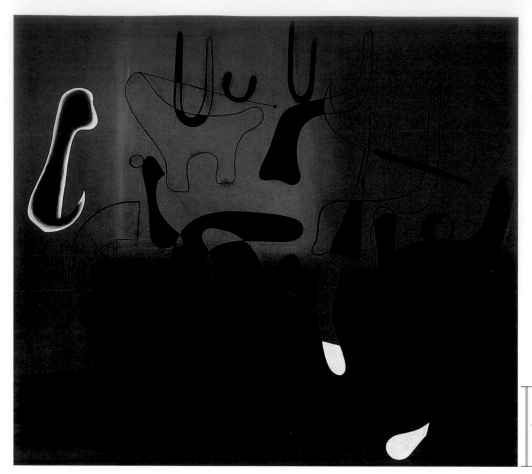

1 ft.

in the creation of art, the young Spaniard devised a new painting method that enabled him to create works such as *Painting* (FIG. **14-26**). Miró began this piece by making a scattered collage composition with assembled fragments cut from a catalog for machinery. The shapes in the collage became motifs the artist freely reshaped on the canvas to create black silhouettes—solid or in outline, with dramatic accents of white and vermilion. They suggest a host of amoebic organisms or constellations in outer space floating in an immaterial background space filled with soft reds, blues, and greens.

Miró described his creative process as a switching back and forth between unconscious and conscious image-making: "Rather than setting out to paint something, I begin painting and as I paint the picture begins to assert itself, or suggest itself under my brush. The form becomes a sign for a woman or a bird as I work. . . . The first stage is free, unconscious. . . . The second stage is carefully calculated."[19] Even the artist could not always explain the meanings of pictures such as *Painting*. They are, in the truest sense, spontaneous and intuitive expressions of the little-understood, submerged unconscious part of life.

De Stijl

The utopian spirit and ideals of the Suprematists (FIG. 14-16) in Russia were shared by a group of young Dutch artists. They formed a new movement in 1917 called *De Stijl* (The Style). The name reflected confidence that De Stijl revealed the underlying eternal structure of existence. Accordingly, De Stijl artists reduced their formal vocabulary to simple geometric elements.

Piet Mondrian The cofounders of De Stijl were the painters PIET MONDRIAN (FIG. 14-27) and Theo van Doesburg (1883–1931). Their goal, according to van Doesburg and

architect Cor van Eesteren (1897–1988), was a total integration of art and life:

> We must realize that life and art are no longer separate domains. That is why the "idea" of "art" as an illusion separate from real life must disappear. The word "Art" no longer means anything to us. In its place we demand the construction of our environment in accordance with creative laws based upon a fixed principle. These laws, following those of economics, mathematics, technique, sanitation, etc., are leading to a new, plastic unity.[20]

Time spent in Paris before World War I introduced Mondrian to Cubism. However, as his attraction to contemporary theological writings grew, Mondrian sought to purge his art of every overt reference to individual objects in the external world. He formulated a conception of nonobjective design—"pure plastic art"—that he believed expressed universal reality:

> Art is higher than reality and has no direct relation to reality. . . . To approach the spiritual in art, one will make as little use as possible of reality, because reality is opposed to the spiritual. . . . [W]e find ourselves in the presence of an abstract art. Art should be above reality, otherwise it would have no value for man."[21]

Mondrian soon moved beyond Cubism because he felt "Cubism did not accept the logical consequences of its own discoveries; it was not developing towards its own goal, the expression of pure plastics."[22] To achieve "pure plastic art,"

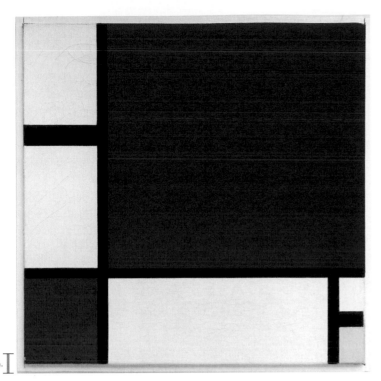

1 in.

14-27 PIET MONDRIAN, *Composition with Red, Blue, and Yellow,* 1930. Oil on canvas, 1' 6⅛" × 1' 6⅛". Kunsthaus, Zurich. © Mondrian/ Holtzman Trust c/o HCR International, Warrenton, VA, USA. ◼◀

Mondrian's "pure plastic" paintings consist of primary colors locked into a grid of intersecting vertical and horizontal lines. By altering the grid patterns, he created a dynamic tension.

or *Neoplasticism,* as Mondrian called it, he eventually limited his formal vocabulary to the three primary colors (red, blue, and yellow), the three primary values (black, white, and gray), and the two primary directions (horizontal and vertical). He believed primary colors and values were the purest colors and therefore the perfect tools to help an artist construct a harmonious composition. Mondrian created numerous paintings locking color planes into a grid of intersecting vertical and horizontal lines, as in *Composition with Red, Blue, and Yellow* (FIG. **14-27**). In each of these paintings, he altered the grid patterns and the size and placement of the color planes to create an internal cohesion and harmony. This did not mean inertia. Rather, Mondrian worked to maintain a dynamic tension in his paintings through the size and position of lines, shapes, and colors.

Sculpture

During the second quarter of the 20th century, European sculptors also explored avant-garde ideas in their work, especially abstraction.

Constantin Brancusi In his sculptures, Romanian artist CONSTANTIN BRANCUSI (1876–1957) sought to move beyond surface appearances to capture the essence or spirit of the object depicted. He asserted: "What is real is not the external form but the essence of things. Starting from this truth

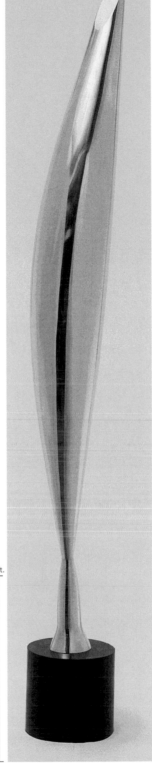

14-28 CONSTANTIN BRANCUSI, *Bird in Space,* 1924. Bronze, 4' 2⁵⁄₁₆" high. Philadelphia Museum of Art, Philadelphia (Louise and Walter Arensberg Collection, 1950). ◼◀

Although not a literal depiction of a bird, Brancusi's softly curving, light-reflecting abstract sculpture in polished bronze suggests a bird about to soar in free flight through the heavens.

1 ft.

it is impossible for anyone to express anything essentially real by imitating its exterior surface."[23] Brancusi's ability to design rhythmic, elegant sculptures conveying the essence of his subjects is evident in *Bird in Space* (FIG. **14-28**). Clearly not a literal depiction of a bird, the abstract form of the work is the final result of a long process. Brancusi started with the image of a bird at rest with its wings folded at its sides and ended with a gently curving columnar form sharply tapered at each end. Despite the abstraction, the sculpture retains the suggestion of a bird about to soar in free flight through the heavens. The highly reflective surface of the polished bronze does not allow the viewer's eye to linger on the sculpture itself. Instead, the eye follows the gleaming reflection along the delicate curves right off the tip of the work, thereby inducing a feeling of flight.

The British sculptor Henry Moore (1898–1986) summed up Brancusi's contribution to the history of sculpture as follows: "Since the Gothic, European sculpture had become overgrown with moss, weeds—all sorts of surface excrescences which completely concealed shape. It has been Brancusi's special mission to get rid of this overgrowth, and to make us once more shape-conscious. To do this he has had to concentrate on very simple direct shapes. . . . Abstract qualities of design are essential to the value of a work."[24]

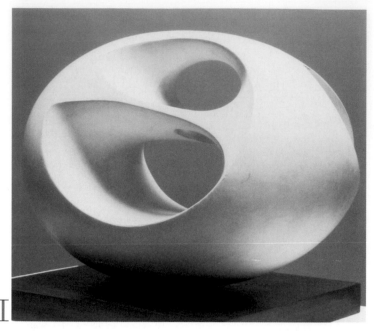

1 in.

14-29 BARBARA HEPWORTH, *Oval Sculpture* (*No. 2*), 1943. Plaster cast, 11¼″ × 1′ 4¼″ × 10″. Tate, London.

Hepworth's major contribution to the history of sculpture was the introduction of the hole, or negative space, as an abstract element that is as integral and important to the sculpture as its mass.

Barbara Hepworth Another leading British artist of this era was BARBARA HEPWORTH (1903–1975), who developed her personal kind of essential sculptural form, combining pristine shape with a sense of organic vitality. She sought a sculptural idiom that would express her sense both of nature and the landscape and of the person who is in and observes nature. By 1929, Hepworth arrived at a breakthrough that evolved into an enduring and commanding element in her work from that point on. It represents her major contribution to the history of sculpture: the hole, or negative space. In Hepworth's sculptures, holes are not abstract elements. They do not represent anything specific, but they are as integral and important to the sculpture as the masses. *Oval Sculpture* (*No. 2*) is a plaster cast (FIG. **14-29**) of an earlier wood sculpture Hepworth carved in 1943. Pierced in four places, the work is as much defined by the smooth, curving holes as by the volume of white plaster. Like the forms in all of Hepworth's mature works, those in *Oval Sculpture* are basic and universal, expressing a sense of eternity's timelessness.

UNITED STATES AND MEXICO, 1930 TO 1945

In the years leading up to and during World War II, many European artists emigrated to the United States. Their collective presence in the United States was critical for the development of American art in the decades following the 1913 Armory Show. Yet few of the leading American artists of this period pursued abstraction, either in painting or sculpture.

Alexander Calder One exception was ALEXANDER CALDER (1898–1976), who rose to international prominence because of his contributions to the development of abstract art. The son and grandson of sculptors, Calder initially studied mechanical engineering. Fascinated all his life by motion, he

14-30 ALEXANDER CALDER, *Lobster Trap and Fish Tail,* 1939. Painted sheet aluminum and steel wire, 8′ 6″ × 9′ 6″. Museum of Modern Art, New York.

Using his thorough knowledge of engineering to combine nonobjective organic forms and motion, Calder created a new kind of sculpture—the mobile—that expressed reality's innate dynamism.

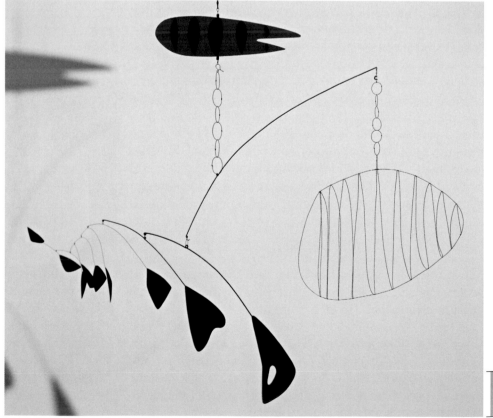

1 ft.

explored movement in relationship to three-dimensional form in much of his work. As a young artist in Paris in the late 1920s, Calder invented a circus full of wire-based miniature performers he activated into analogues of the motion of their real-life counterparts. After a visit to Piet Mondrian's studio in the early 1930s, Calder set out to put the Dutch painter's brightly colored rectangular shapes (FIG. 14-27) into motion. (Marcel Duchamp, intrigued by Calder's early motorized and hand-cranked examples of moving abstract pieces, named them *mobiles*.) Calder's engineering skills soon helped him to fashion a series of balanced structures hanging from rods, wires, and colored, organically shaped plates. This new kind of sculpture, which combined nonobjective organic forms and motion, succeeded in expressing the innate dynamism of the natural world.

An early Calder mobile is *Lobster Trap and Fish Tail* (FIG. **14-30**). The artist carefully planned each nonmechanized mobile so any air current would set the parts moving to create a constantly shifting dance in space. Mondrian's work may have provided the initial inspiration for the mobiles, but their organic shapes resemble those in Joan Miró's Surrealist paintings (FIG. 14-26). Indeed, viewers can read Calder's forms as either geometric or organic. Geometrically, the lines suggest circuitry and rigging, and the shapes derive from circles and ovoid forms. Organically, the lines suggest nerve axons, and the shapes resemble cells, leaves, fins, wings, and other bioforms.

Great Depression The catastrophic US stock market crash of October 1929 marked the onset of the Great Depression, which dramatically changed the nation, and artists were among the millions of economic victims. The limited art market virtually disappeared, and museums curtailed both their purchases and exhibition schedules. Many artists sought financial support from the federal government, which established numerous programs to provide relief, assist recovery, and promote reform. Among the programs supporting artists were the Treasury Relief Art Project, founded in 1934 to commission art for federal buildings, and the Works Progress Administration (WPA), founded in 1935 to relieve widespread unemployment. Under the WPA, the government paid artists, writers, and theater people a regular wage in exchange for work in their professions. Another important program was the Resettlement Administration (RA), better known by its later name, the Farm Security Administration (FSA), which oversaw emergency aid programs for farm families.

Dorothea Lange The RA hired American photographer DOROTHEA LANGE (1895–1965) in 1936 and dispatched her to document the deplorable living conditions of the rural poor. At the end of an assignment photographing migratory pea pickers in California, Lange stopped at a camp in Nipomo and found the workers there starving because the crops had frozen in the fields. Among the pictures Lange made on this occasion was *Migrant Mother, Nipomo Valley* (FIG. **14-31**), in which she captured the mixture of strength and worry in the

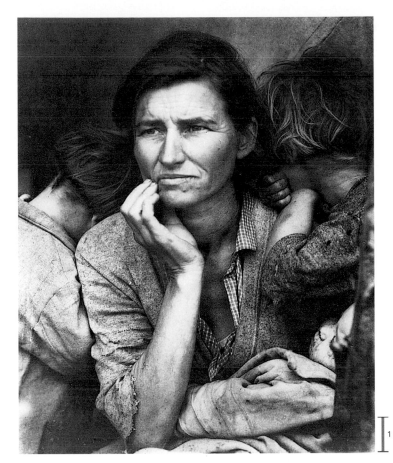

14-31 DOROTHEA LANGE, *Migrant Mother, Nipomo Valley*, 1935. Gelatin silver print, 1' 1" × 9". Oakland Museum of California, Oakland (gift of Paul S. Taylor). ◼◀

While documenting the lives of migratory farm workers during the Depression, Lange made this unforgettable photograph of a mother in which she captured the woman's strength and worry.

raised hand and careworn face of a mother, who holds a baby on her lap. Two older children cling to their mother trustingly while turning their faces away from the camera. Within days after Lange's powerful photograph appeared in a San Francisco newspaper, people rushed food to Nipomo to feed the hungry workers.

Margaret Bourke-White Almost 10 years younger than Dorothea Lange, MARGARET BOURKE-WHITE (1904–1971) also made her reputation as a photojournalist in Depression-era America. She was the first staff photographer Henry Luce (1898–1967) hired to furnish illustrations for the magazines in his publishing empire. Beginning in 1929, Bourke-White worked for *Fortune*, then for *Life* when Luce launched the renowned newsweekly in 1936. Her most famous photographs for Luce were not of people or events but of the triumphs of 20th-century engineering, and they served to instill pride in an American public severely lacking in confidence during the Depression. For example, Bourke-White photographed the Chrysler Building (FIG. 14-41) while it was under construction in New York, attracting media attention for her daring balancing act on steel girders high above the pavement. Her

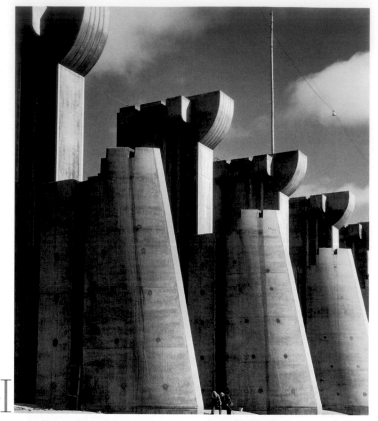

1 in.

14-32 MARGARET BOURKE-WHITE, *Fort Peck Dam, Montana,* 1936. Gelatin silver print, 1' 1" × 10½". Metropolitan Museum of Art, New York (gift of Ford Motor Company and John C. Waddell, 1987).

Bourke-White's dramatic photograph of Fort Peck Dam graced the cover of the first issue of *Life* magazine and celebrated the achievements of modern industry at the height of the Great Depression.

angle from below to communicate the dam's soaring height, underscoring the immense scale by including two dwarfed figures of men in the foreground. The tight framing, which shuts out all of the landscape and much of the sky, transforms the dam into an almost-abstract composition, a kind of still life, like Edward Weston's peppers (FIG. 14-20).

Edward Hopper Trained as a commercial artist, EDWARD HOPPER (1882–1967) studied painting and printmaking in New York and then in Paris. When he returned to the United States, he concentrated on scenes of contemporary American city and country life. His paintings depict buildings, streets, and landscapes that are curiously muted, still, and filled with empty spaces, evoking the national mind-set during the Depression era. Hopper did not paint historically specific scenes. He took as his subject the more generalized theme of the overwhelming loneliness and echoing isolation of modern life in the United States. In his paintings, motion is stopped and time suspended. From the darkened streets outside a restaurant in Hopper's *Nighthawks* (FIG. **14-33**), the viewer glimpses the lighted interior through huge windows, which lend the inner space the paradoxical sense of being both a safe refuge and a vulnerable place for the three customers and the man behind the counter. The seeming indifference of Hopper's characters to one another as well as the echoing spaces surrounding them evoke the pervasive loneliness of modern humans. *Nighthawks* recalls the work of 19th-century Realist painters (see Chapter 12), but in keeping with more recent trends in painting, Hopper simplified the shapes in a move toward abstraction.

Jacob Lawrence African American artist JACOB LAWRENCE (1917–2000) moved to Harlem, New York, in 1927 while still a boy. There, he came under the spell of the African art and the African American history he found in lectures and exhibitions and in the special programs sponsored by the 135th Street branch of the New York Public Library. The everyday life of Harlem and African American history became the

photograph of *Fort Peck Dam, Montana* (FIG. **14-32**) appeared on the cover of the first issue of *Life* (November 23, 1936). Fort Peck Dam was at the time the largest earth-filled dam in the world. Bourke-White photographed its towers (designed to conjure a crenellated medieval fortress) at a sharp

14-33 EDWARD HOPPER, *Nighthawks,* 1942. Oil on canvas, 2' 6" × 4' 8¾". Art Institute of Chicago, Chicago (Friends of American Art Collection).

The seeming indifference of Hopper's characters to one another, and the echoing spaces that surround them, evoke the overwhelming loneliness and isolation of Depression-era life in the United States.

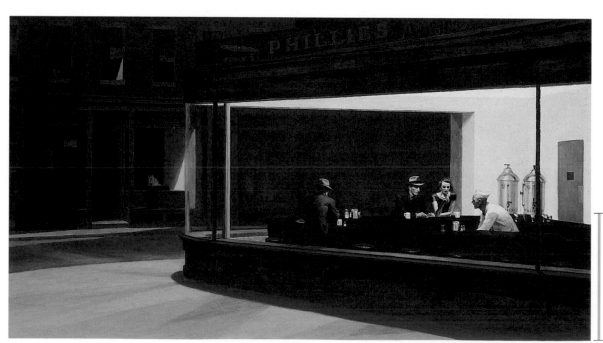

1 ft.

subjects of Lawrence's paintings. In 1941, he began a series titled *The Migration of the Negro,* in which he defined his own vision of the continuing African American struggle against discrimination. The series of 60 paintings chronicles the ongoing exodus of black labor from the southern United States. Disillusioned with their lives in the South, hundreds of thousands of African Americans migrated north in the years following World War I, seeking improved economic opportunities and a more hospitable political and social environment. But the conditions African Americans encountered in the North were often as difficult and discriminatory as those they had left behind in the South.

Lawrence's *Migration* paintings provide numerous vignettes capturing the African Americans who had moved to the North. Often, a sense of the bleakness and of the degradation of their new life dominates the images. *No. 49* (FIG. **14-34**) bears the caption "They also found discrimination in the North although it was much different from that which they had known in the South." Lawrence depicted a blatantly segregated dining room with a barrier running down the room's center separating the whites on the left from the African Americans on the right. To ensure a continuity and visual integrity among all 60 paintings, Lawrence interpreted his themes systematically in rhythmic arrangements of bold, flat, and strongly colored shapes. His style drew equally from his interest in the push-pull effects of Cubist space and his memories of the patterns made by the colored scatter rugs brightening the floors of his childhood homes. He unified the narrative with a consistent palette of bluish green, orange, yellow, and grayish brown throughout the entire series.

Grant Wood At a 1931 conference, GRANT WOOD (1891–1942) announced a new movement developing in the Midwest, known as *Regionalism,* which he described as focused on American subjects and as standing in reaction to the modernist abstraction of Europe and New York. Wood and the Regionalists turned their attention instead to rural life as America's cultural backbone. Wood's paintings focus on rural Iowa, where he was born and raised. The work that catapulted Wood to national prominence was *American Gothic* (FIG. **14-35**), which became an American icon. The artist depicted a farmer and his spinster daughter standing in front of a neat house with a small Gothic lancet window, a motif

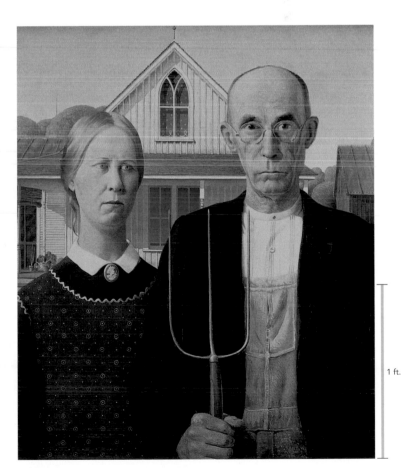

14-34 JACOB LAWRENCE, *No. 49* from *The Migration of the Negro,* 1940–1941. Tempera on Masonite, 1′ 6″ × 1′. Phillips Collection, Washington, D.C.

The 49th in a series of 60 paintings documenting African American life in the North, Lawrence's depiction of a segregated dining room underscored that the migrants had not left discrimination behind.

14-35 GRANT WOOD, *American Gothic,* 1930. Oil on beaverboard, 2′ 5⅞″ × 2′ ⅞″. Art Institute of Chicago, Chicago (Friends of American Art Collection). ◼◀

In reaction to modernist abstract painting, the Midwestern Regionalism movement focused on American subjects. Wood's painting of an Iowa farmer and his daughter became an American icon.

Rivera on Art for the People

Diego Rivera was an avid proponent of a social and political role for art in the lives of common people, and he wrote passionately about the proper goals for an artist—goals that he fully met in his own murals depicting Mexican history (FIG. 14-36). Rivera's views stand in sharp contrast to the growing interest in abstraction on the part of many early-20th-century painters and sculptors.

Art has always been employed by the different social classes who hold the balance of power as one instrument of domination—hence, as a political instrument. One can analyze epoch after epoch—from the stone age to our own day—and see that there is no form of art which does not also play an essential political role. . . . What is it then that we really need? . . . An art with revolution as its subject: because the principal interest in the worker's life has to be touched first. It is necessary that he find aesthetic satisfaction and the highest pleasure appareled in the essential interest of his life. . . . The subject is to the painter what the rails are to a locomotive. He cannot do without it. In fact, when he refuses to seek or accept a subject, his own plastic methods and his own aesthetic theories become his subject instead. . . . [H]e himself becomes the subject of his work. He becomes nothing but an illustrator of his own state of mind. . . . That is the deception practiced under the name of "Pure Art."*

*Quoted in Robert Goldwater and Marco Treves, eds., *Artists on Art from the XIV to the XX Century* (New York: Pantheon, 1945), 475–477.

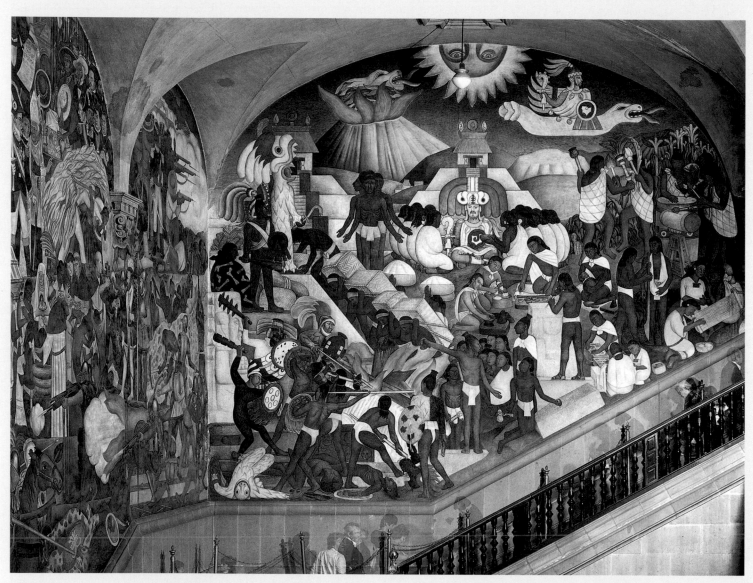

14-36 DIEGO RIVERA, *Ancient Mexico,* detail of *History of Mexico,* fresco in the Palacio Nacional, Mexico City, 1929–1935.

A staunch Marxist, Rivera painted vast mural cycles in public buildings to dramatize the history of his native land. This fresco depicts the conflicts between indigenous Mexicans and Spanish colonizers.

associated with churches and religious piety. The man and woman wear traditional attire. He appears in worn overalls and she in an apron trimmed with rickrack. The dour expression on both faces gives the painting a severe quality, which Wood enhanced with his meticulous brushwork. The public immediately embraced *American Gothic* as embodying qualities that represented the true spirit of America.

Wood's Regionalist vision involved more than his subjects. It extended to a rejection of avant-garde styles in favor of a clearly readable, Realist style. Surely, this approach appealed to many people alienated by the increasing presence of abstraction in art. However, despite the accolades this painting received, it also attracted criticism. Not everyone saw the painting as a sympathetic portrayal of Midwestern life. Indeed, some Iowans considered the depiction of life in their state insulting. In addition, despite the seemingly reportorial nature of *American Gothic,* some viewed it as a political statement—one of staunch nationalism. In light of the problematic nationalism in Germany at the time, many observers found Wood's nationalistic attitude disturbing. Nonetheless, during the Great Depression, Regionalist paintings had a popular appeal because they often projected a reassuring image of America's heartland.

Diego Rivera During the period between the two world wars, several Mexican painters achieved international renown for their work. DIEGO RIVERA (1886–1957) was one of a group of Mexican artists determined to base their art on the culture of their homeland. The movement these artists formed was part of the idealistic rethinking of society that occurred in conjunction with the Mexican Revolution (1910–1920) and the lingering political turmoil of the 1920s. Among the projects these politically motivated artists undertook were vast mural cycles placed in public buildings to dramatize and validate the history of Mexico's native peoples. A staunch Marxist, Rivera strove to develop an art that served his people's needs (see "Rivera on Art for the People," page 414). Toward that end, he sought to create a national Mexican style incorporating a popular, generally accessible aesthetic in keeping with the socialist spirit of the Mexican Revolution.

Perhaps Rivera's finest mural cycle is the one lining the staircase of the National Palace in Mexico City. In these images, painted between 1929 and 1935, he depicted scenes from Mexico's history, of which *Ancient Mexico* (FIG. **14-36**) is one. This section of the mural represents the conflicts between the indigenous people and the Spanish colonizers. Rivera included portraits of important figures in Mexican history, especially those involved in the struggle for Mexican independence. Although the composition is complex, the simple monumental shapes and areas of bold color make the story easy to read.

Frida Kahlo Born to a Mexican mother and German father, the painter FRIDA KAHLO (1907–1954), who married Diego Rivera, used the details of her life as powerful symbols for the psychological pain of human existence. Art historians often consider Kahlo a Surrealist due to the psychic and autobiographical issues she dealt with in her art. Indeed, André Breton described her as a Naturalistic Surrealist. Kahlo herself, however, rejected any association with the Surrealists. She began painting seriously as a young student, during convalescence from an accident that tragically left her in constant pain. Her life became a heroic and tumultuous battle for survival against illness and stormy personal relationships.

Typical of her long series of unflinching self-portraits is *The Two Fridas* (FIG. **14-37**). The twin figures sit side by

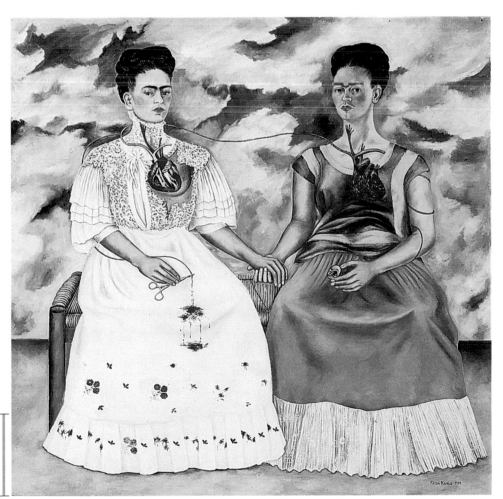

14-37 FRIDA KAHLO, *The Two Fridas,* 1939. Oil on canvas, 5′ 7″ × 5′ 7″. Museo de Arte Moderno, Mexico City.

Kahlo's deeply personal paintings touch sensual and psychological memories in her audience. Here, twin self-portraits linked by clasped hands and a common artery suggest two sides of her personality.

1 ft.

side on a low bench in a barren landscape under a stormy sky. The figures suggest different sides of the artist's personality, inextricably linked by the clasped hands and by the thin artery stretching between them, joining their exposed hearts. The artery ends on one side in surgical forceps and on the other in a miniature portrait of her husband as a child. Kahlo's deeply personal paintings touch sensual and psychological memories in her audience.

However, to read these paintings solely as autobiographical overlooks the powerful political dimension of Kahlo's art. She was deeply nationalistic and committed to her Mexican heritage. Politically active, she joined the Communist Party in 1920 and participated in public political protests. *The Two Fridas* incorporates Kahlo's commentary on the struggle facing Mexicans in the early 20th century in defining their national cultural identity. The Frida on the right (representing indigenous culture) appears in a Tehuana dress, the traditional costume of Zapotec women from the Isthmus of Tehuantepec, whereas the Frida on the left (representing imperialist forces) wears a European-style white lace dress. The heart, depicted here in such dramatic fashion, was an important symbol in the art of the Aztecs (see Chapter 20), whom Mexican nationalists idealized as the last independent rulers of their land. Thus, *The Two Fridas* represents both Kahlo's personal struggles and the struggles of her homeland.

ARCHITECTURE

The first half of the 20th century was a time of great innovation in architecture too. As in painting, sculpture, and photography, new ideas came from both sides of the Atlantic.

Walter Gropius The De Stijl group not only developed an appealing simplified geometric style but also promoted the notion that art should be thoroughly incorporated into living environments. As Mondrian had insisted, "[A]rt and life are *one;* art and life are both expressions of truth."[25] In Germany, WALTER GROPIUS (1883–1969) developed the concept of "total architecture" at a school called the *Bauhaus.* In 1919, Gropius became the director of the Weimar School of Arts and Crafts, founded in 1906. Under Gropius, the school assumed a new name—Das Staatliche Bauhaus (State School of Building). Gropius's goal was to train artists, architects, and designers to accept and anticipate 20th-century needs. He developed an extensive curriculum based on certain principles. Gropius staunchly advocated the importance of

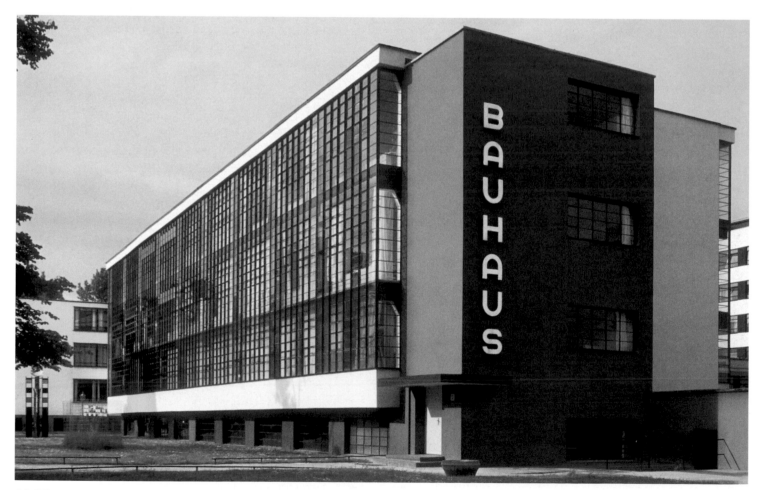

14-38 WALTER GROPIUS, Shop Block (looking northeast), the Bauhaus, Dessau, Germany, 1925–1926.

Gropius constructed this Bauhaus building by sheathing a reinforced concrete skeleton in glass. The design followed his dictum that architecture should avoid "all romantic embellishment and whimsy."

strong basic design and craftsmanship as fundamental to good art and architecture, and he promoted the unity of art, architecture, and design. Further, Gropius emphasized the need for thorough knowledge of machine-age technologies and materials. "Architects, painters, and sculptors," he insisted, "must recognize anew the composite character of a building as an entity."[26] To encourage the elimination of the boundaries that traditionally separated art from architecture and art from craft, the Bauhaus offered courses in a wide range of artistic disciplines. These included weaving, pottery, bookbinding, carpentry, metalwork, stained glass, mural painting, stage design, advertising, and typography, in addition to architecture, painting, and sculpture. Ultimately, Gropius hoped to achieve a marriage between art and industry—a synthesis of design and production. As did the De Stijl movement, the Bauhaus philosophy had its roots in utopian principles. Gropius declared: "Let us collectively desire, conceive, and create the new building of the future, which will be everything in one structure: architecture and sculpture and painting, which, from the million hands of draftsmen, will one day rise towards heaven as the crystalline symbol of a new and coming faith."[27] In its reference to a unity of workers, this statement also reveals the undercurrent of socialism in Germany at the time.

Bauhaus in Dessau After encountering increasing hostility from a new government elected in 1924, the Bauhaus moved north to Dessau (FIG. 14-38) in early 1925. By this time, the Bauhaus program had matured. In a statement, Gropius listed the school's goals:

- A decidedly positive attitude to the living environment of vehicles and machines.
- The organic shaping of things in accordance with their own current laws, avoiding all romantic embellishment and whimsy.
- Restriction of basic forms and colours to what is typical and universally intelligible.
- Simplicity in complexity, economy in the use of space, materials, time, and money.[28]

The building Gropius designed for the Dessau Bauhaus was the school's architectural manifesto. The Dessau complex consisted of workshop and class areas, a dining room, a theater, a gymnasium, a wing with studio apartments, and an enclosed two-story bridge housing administrative offices. Of the major wings, the most dramatic was the Shop Block (FIG. 14-38). Three stories tall, the Shop Block housed a printing shop and dye works facility, in addition to other work areas. The builders constructed the skeleton of reinforced concrete but set these supports well back, sheathing the entire structure in glass, creating a streamlined and light effect. This design's simplicity followed Gropius's dictum that architecture should avoid "all romantic embellishment and whimsy." Further, he realized his principle of "economy in the use of space" in his interior layout of the Shop Block, which consisted of large areas of free-flowing undivided space. Gropius believed this kind of spatial organization encouraged interaction and the sharing of ideas.

Ludwig Mies van der Rohe In 1928, Gropius left the Bauhaus, and LUDWIG MIES VAN DER ROHE (1886–1969) eventually took over the directorship, moving the school to Berlin. Taking as his motto "less is more" and calling his architecture "skin and bones," the new Bauhaus director had already fully formed his aesthetic when he conceived the model (FIG. 14-39) for a glass skyscraper building in 1921. Three irregularly shaped towers flow outward from a central court

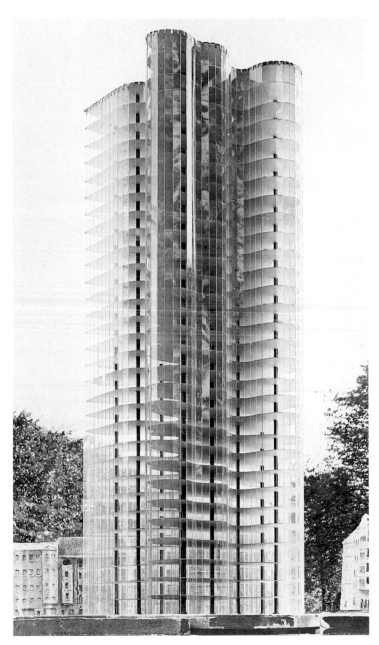

14-39 LUDWIG MIES VAN DER ROHE, model for a glass skyscraper, Berlin, Germany, 1922 (no longer extant).

In this technically and aesthetically adventurous design, the architect whose motto was "less is more" proposed a transparent building that revealed its cantilevered floor planes and thin supports.

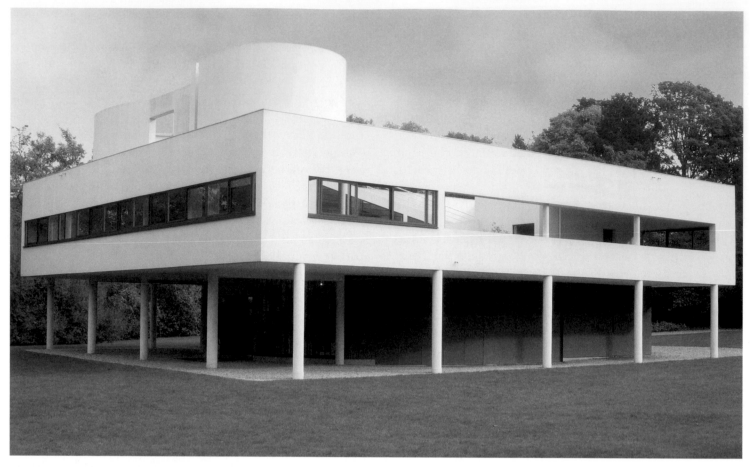

14-40 Le Corbusier, Villa Savoye (looking southeast), Poissy-sur-Seine, France, 1929. ◼◀

Steel and ferroconcrete made it possible for Le Corbusier to invert the traditional practice of placing light architectural elements above heavy ones and to eliminate weight-bearing walls on the ground story.

designed to hold a lobby, a porter's room, and a community center. Two cylindrical entrance shafts rise at the ends of the court, each containing elevators, stairways, and toilets. Wholly transparent, the perimeter walls reveal the regular horizontal patterning of the cantilevered floor planes and their thin vertical supporting elements. The bold use of glass sheathing and inset supports was, at the time, technically and aesthetically adventurous. The weblike delicacy of the lines of the model, as well as the illusion of movement created by reflection and by light changes seen through the glass, prefigured the design of many of the glass-and-steel skyscrapers found in major cities throughout the world today.

End of the Bauhaus One of Adolf Hitler's first acts after coming to power was to close the Bauhaus in 1933. During its 14-year existence, the school graduated fewer than 500 students, yet it achieved legendary status. Its phenomenal influence extended beyond architecture, painting, and sculpture to interior design, graphic design, and advertising. Moreover, art schools everywhere began to structure their curricula in line with the program the Bauhaus pioneered. The numerous Bauhaus instructors who fled Nazi Germany disseminated the school's philosophy and aesthetic widely.

Many, including Gropius and Mies van der Rohe, settled in the United States.

Le Corbusier The simple geometric aesthetic developed by Gropius and Mies van der Rohe became known as the *International style* because of its widespread popularity. The first and purest proponent of this style was the Swiss architect Charles-Edouard Jeanneret, who took the name Le Corbusier (1887–1965). An influential theorist as well as practitioner, Le Corbusier sought to design a functional living space, which he described as a "machine for living."[29]

Le Corbusier's Villa Savoye (FIG. **14-40**) at Poissy-sur-Seine near Paris is a cube of lightly enclosed and deeply penetrated space with only a partially confined ground floor (containing a three-car garage, bedrooms, a bathroom, and utility rooms). Much of the house's interior is open space, with thin columns supporting the main living floor and roof garden area. The major living rooms in the Villa Savoye are on the second floor, wrapping around an open central court. Strip windows running along the membranelike exterior walls provide illumination to the rooms as well as views out to nature. From the second-floor court, a ramp leads up to a flat roof-terrace and an interior garden protected by a curving

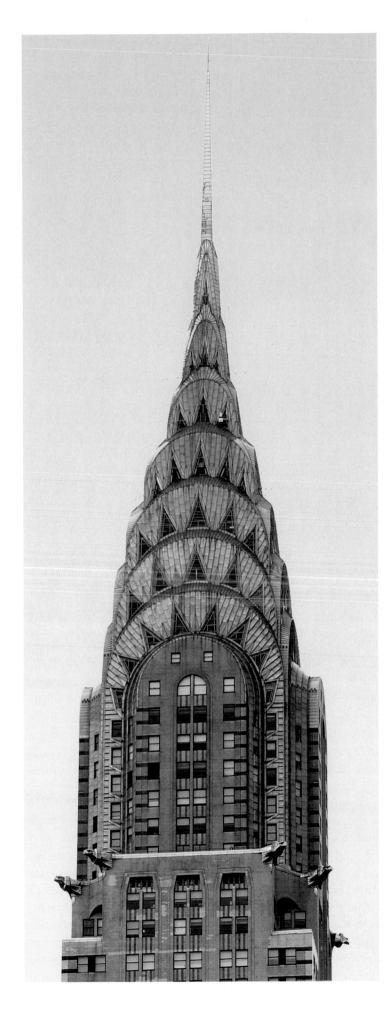

windbreak along the north side. The Villa Savoye has no traditional facade. The ostensible approach to the house does not define an entrance. Visitors must walk around and through the house to comprehend its layout, which incorporates several changes of direction and spiral staircases. Spaces and masses interpenetrate so fluidly that inside and outside space intermingle. In the Villa Savoye, Le Corbusier inverted traditional design practice by placing heavy elements above and light ones below, and by refusing to enclose the ground story of the Villa Savoye with masonry walls. This openness, made possible by the use of steel and ferroconcrete, makes the "load" of the Villa Savoye's upper stories appear to hover lightly on the slender column supports.

Art Deco Although the Bauhaus condemned ornamentation in the design of buildings, popular taste still favored decoration as an important element in architecture. *Art Deco* was a movement in the 1920s and 1930s that acquired its name at the Exposition des Arts Décoratifs et Industriels Modernes (Exposition of Modern Decorative and Industrial Arts) held in Paris in 1925. Art Deco had universal application—to buildings, interiors, furniture, utensils, jewelry, fashions, illustration, and commercial products of every sort. Art Deco products have a "streamlined," elongated symmetrical aspect. Simple flat shapes alternate with shallow volumes in hard patterns. The exemplary Art Deco masterpiece is the stainless-steel spire of the Chrysler Building (FIG. **14-41**) in New York City, designed by WILLIAM VAN ALEN (1882–1954). The building and spire are monuments to the fabulous 1920s, when American millionaires and corporations competed with one another to raise the tallest skyscrapers in the biggest cities. Built up of diminishing fan shapes, the spire glitters triumphantly in the sky, a resplendent crown honoring the business achievements of the great auto manufacturer. As a temple of commerce, the Chrysler Building celebrated the principles and success of American business before the onset of the Great Depression.

Frank Lloyd Wright Perhaps America's greatest architect, FRANK LLOYD WRIGHT (1867–1959) was born in Wisconsin and moved to Chicago, where he eventually joined the firm headed by Louis Sullivan (FIG. 13-21). Wright believed in "natural" or "organic" architecture serving free individuals who have the right to move within a "free" space, which he envisioned as a nonsymmetrical design interacting spatially with its natural surroundings. He sought to develop an organic unity of planning, structure, materials, and site.

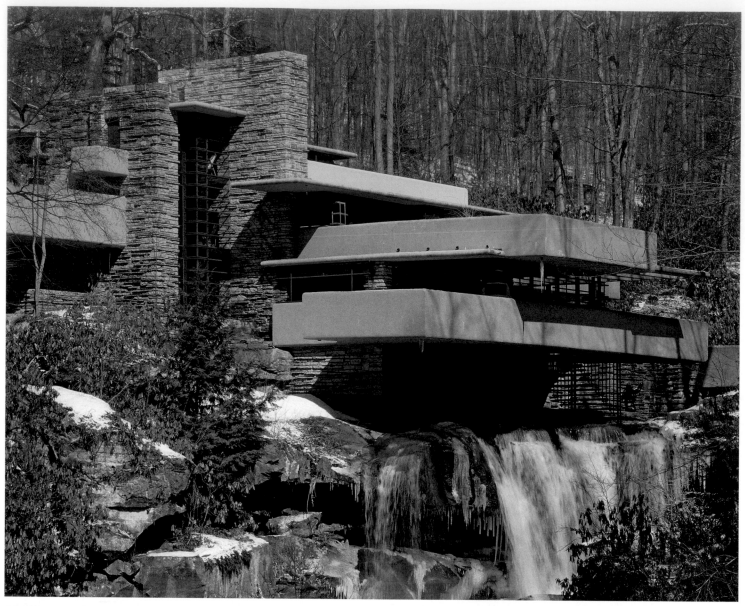

14-42 FRANK LLOYD WRIGHT, Kaufmann House (Fallingwater; looking northeast), Bear Run, Pennsylvania, 1936–1939.

Perched on a rocky hillside over a waterfall, Wright's Fallingwater has long sweeping lines, unconfined by abrupt wall limits, reaching out and capturing the expansiveness of the natural environment.

Wright's universally acclaimed masterpiece is the house nicknamed "Fallingwater" (FIG. **14-42**), which the architect designed as a weekend retreat at Bear Run, Pennsylvania, for the Pittsburgh department store magnate Edgar Kaufmann Sr. The Kaufmann House exemplifies Wright's "naturalistic" approach to architecture. Perched on a rocky hillside over a small waterfall, the house has long sweeping lines, unconfined by abrupt wall limits, reaching out toward and capturing the expansiveness of the natural environment. Rather than build the house overlooking or next to the waterfall, Wright decided to build it over the waterfall because he believed the inhabitants would become desensitized to the waterfall's presence and power if they merely overlooked it. To take advantage of the location, Wright designed a series of terraces that extend on three levels from a central core structure. Abandoning all symmetry, he eliminated a facade, extended the roofs far beyond the walls, and all but concealed the entrance. The contrast in texture among concrete, painted metal, and natural stones in the house's walls enliven its shapes, as does Wright's use of full-length strip windows to create a stunning interweaving of interior and exterior space. The implied message of Wright's new architecture was space, not mass—a space designed to fit the patron's life and enclosed and divided as required.

Frank Lloyd Wright achieved international fame. As early as 1940, Mies van der Rohe wrote that the "dynamic impulse from [Wright's] work invigorated a whole generation."[30] Wright's influence in Europe was exceptional, however, for any American artist before World War II. But in the decades following that global conflict, American painters, sculptors, and architects often took the lead in establishing new styles artists elsewhere quickly emulated. This new preeminence of the United States in the arts is the subject of Chapter 15.

Modernism in Europe and America, 1900 to 1945

Europe, 1900 to 1920

- In the early 1900s, avant-garde artists searched for new definitions of art in a changed world. The Fauves used bold colors as the primary means of conveying feeling. German Expressionist paintings featured clashing colors, disquieting figures, and perspective distortions.

- Picasso and Braque radically challenged prevailing artistic conventions with Cubism, in which artists dissect forms and place them in interaction with the space around them.

- The Futurists focused on motion in time and space to create paintings and sculptures capturing the dynamic quality of modern life. The Dadaists celebrated the spontaneous and intuitive, often incorporating found objects in their artworks.

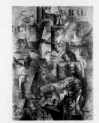

Braque, *The Portuguese*, 1911

United States, 1900 to 1930

- The Armory Show of 1913 introduced European avant-garde art to American artists. The most notorious work in the exhibition was Duchamp's *Nude Descending a Staircase*.

- Photography emerged as an important American art form in the work of Stieglitz and Weston, who emphasized the careful arrangement of forms and patterns of light and dark.

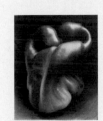

Weston, *Pepper No. 30*, 1930

Europe, 1920 to 1945

- World War I gave rise to the Neue Sachlichkeit movement in Germany. "New Objectivity" artists focused on depicting the horrors of war.

- The Surrealists investigated ways to express in art the world of dreams and the unconscious. Naturalistic Surrealists aimed for "concrete irrationality" in their naturalistic paintings of dreamlike scenes. Biomorphic Surrealists experimented with automatism and employed abstract imagery.

- Many European modernists pursued utopian ideals. The Suprematists developed an abstract style to express pure feeling. De Stijl artists employed simple geometric forms in their "pure plastic art." Brancusi and Hepworth also turned to abstraction and emphasized voids as well as masses in their sculptures.

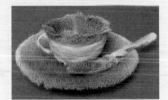

Oppenheim, *Object (Le Déjeuner en fourrure)*, 1936

United States and Mexico, 1930 to 1945

- Although Calder created abstract works between the wars, other American artists favored figural art. Hopper explored the loneliness of life in the Depression era. Lawrence recorded the struggle of African Americans. Wood depicted life in rural Iowa.

- Mexican artists achieved international renown. Rivera painted epic mural cycles of the history of Mexico. Kahlo's powerful paintings explored the human psyche.

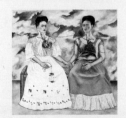

Kahlo, *The Two Fridas*, 1939

Architecture

- The Bauhaus in Germany promoted the vision of "total architecture," which called for the integration of all the arts in constructing modern living environments. In France, Le Corbusier used modern construction materials in his "machines for living"—simple houses with open plans and unadorned surfaces.

- The leading American architect of the first half of the 20th century was Wright. Fallingwater is a bold asymmetrical design integrating a private home with nature.

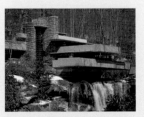

Wright, Fallingwater, 1936–1939

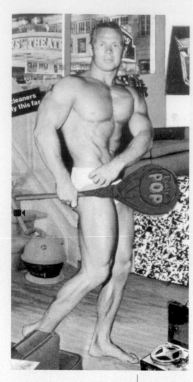

Toying with mass-media imagery typifies British Pop Art. The central motif in Hamilton's modern home is the body builder Charles Atlas, who holds a Tootsie Pop in place of a weightlifter's barbell.

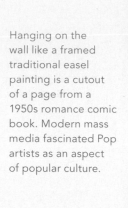

Hanging on the wall like a framed traditional easel painting is a cutout of a page from a 1950s romance comic book. Modern mass media fascinated Pop artists as an aspect of popular culture.

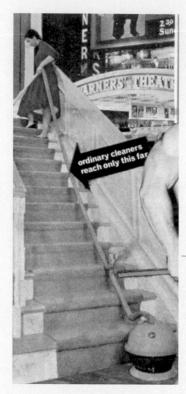

The fantasy interior in Hamilton's collage reflects the values of modern consumer culture. The figures and objects cut from glossy magazines include an advertisement for Hoover vacuum cleaners.

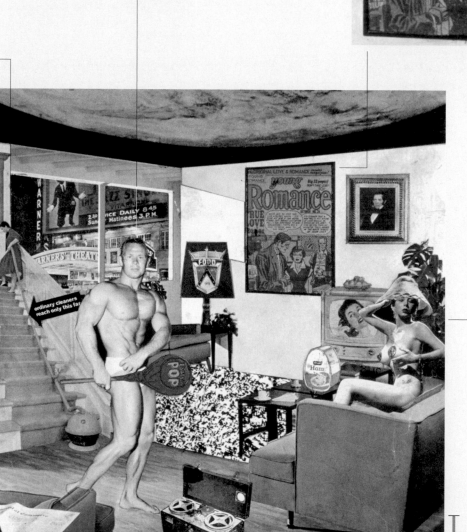

1 in.

15-1 RICHARD HAMILTON, *Just What Is It That Makes Today's Homes So Different, So Appealing?* 1956. Collage, $10\frac{1}{4}'' \times 9\frac{3}{4}''$. Kunsthalle Tübingen, Tübingen.

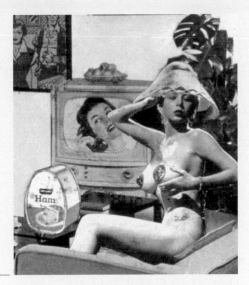

Modernism and Postmodernism in Europe and America, 1945 to 1980

Also included in Hamilton's "appealing" modern home are a television, a can of Armour ham, and a photograph taken from a "girlie magazine" to stimulate speculation about society's values.

ART AND CONSUMER CULTURE

The interest in abstraction that emerged so forcefully in avant-garde artistic circles during the first half of the 20th century gained even greater momentum in the decades after the end of World War II. However, a reaction to pure formalism in painting and sculpture also set in. The artists of the *Pop Art* movement reintroduced all of the devices the postwar abstractionists had purged from their artworks. Pop artists revived the tools traditionally used to convey meaning in art, such as signs, symbols, metaphors, allusions, illusions, and figural imagery. They not only embraced representation but also firmly grounded their art in the consumer culture and mass media of the postwar period, thereby making it much more accessible and understandable to the average person. Indeed, the name "Pop Art"—credited to the British art critic Lawrence Alloway (1926–1990)—is short for "popular art" and referred to the popular mass culture and familiar imagery of the contemporary urban environment.

Art historians trace the roots of Pop Art to the young British artists, architects, and writers who formed the Independent Group at the Institute of Contemporary Art in London in the early 1950s. They sought to initiate fresh thinking in art, in part by sharing their fascination with the aesthetics and content of such facets of popular culture as advertising, comic books, and movies. In 1956, an Independent Group member, RICHARD HAMILTON (b. 1922), made a small collage, *Just What Is It That Makes Today's Homes So Different, So Appealing?* (FIG. **15-1**), which exemplifies British Pop Art. Trained as an engineering draftsman, exhibition designer, and painter, Hamilton studied the way advertising shapes public attitudes. Long intrigued by Marcel Duchamp's ideas (see page 400), Hamilton consistently combined elements of popular art and fine art, seeing both as belonging to the whole world of visual communication. He created *Just What Is It?* for the poster and catalog of one section of an exhibition titled *This Is Tomorrow,* which included images from Hollywood cinema, science fiction, and the mass media.

The fantasy interior in Hamilton's collage reflects the values of mid-20th-century consumer culture through figures and objects cut from glossy magazines. *Just What Is It?* includes references to mass media (the television, the theater marquee outside the window, the newspaper), to advertising (Hoover vacuum cleaners, Ford cars, Armour hams, Tootsie Pops), and to popular culture (the "girlie magazine," the body builder Charles Atlas, romance comic books). Artworks of this sort stimulated viewers' wide-ranging speculation about society's values. This kind of intellectual toying with mass-media meaning and imagery typified Pop Art both in Europe and America.

THE AFTERMATH OF WORLD WAR II

World War II, with the global devastation it unleashed, set the stage for further conflict and upheaval during the second half of the 20th century. In 1947, the British left India, dividing the subcontinent into two hostile nations, India and Pakistan. After a bloody civil war, Communists came to power in China in 1949. North Korea invaded South Korea in 1950 and fought a grim war with the United States and its allies. The Soviets brutally suppressed uprisings in East Germany, Poland, Hungary, and Czechoslovakia. The United States intervened in disputes in Central and South America. Almost as soon as many African nations—Kenya, Uganda, Nigeria, Angola, Mozambique, the Sudan, Rwanda, and the Congo—won their independence from colonial powers, civil wars devastated them. In Indonesia, civil war left more than 100,000 dead. Algeria expelled France in 1962 after the French waged a prolonged war with Algeria's Muslim natives. After 15 years of bitter fighting in Southeast Asia, the United States suffered defeat in Vietnam.

The period from 1945 to 1980 also brought upheaval in the cultural sphere. In the United States, for example, the struggle for civil rights for African Americans, for free speech on university campuses, and for disengagement from the Vietnam War led to a rebellion of the young. A new system of values emerged—a "youth culture," expressed in the radical rejection not only of national policies but often also of the society generating them. Young Americans derided their elders' lifestyles and adopted unconventional dress, manners, habits, and morals deliberately subversive of mainstream social standards. The youth era witnessed the sexual revolution, the widespread use and abuse of drugs, and the development of rock music. Young people "dropped out" of regulated society, embraced alternative belief systems, and rejected Western university curricula as irrelevant.

The civil rights movement of the 1960s and the women's liberation movement of the 1970s reflected this spirit of rebellion, coupled with the rejection of racism and sexism. African Americans fought discrimination and sought equal rights. Women systematically began to challenge the male-dominated culture, which they perceived as having limited their political and economic opportunities for centuries. Gays and lesbians and various ethnic groups also mounted challenges to discriminatory policies and attitudes. Painters, sculptors, and photographers fully participated in these challenges to the established institutions of Western society, producing compelling artworks addressing the pressing social and political issues of the day.

PAINTING, SCULPTURE, AND PHOTOGRAPHY

The end of World War II in 1945 left devastated cities, ruptured economies, and governments in chaos throughout Europe. These factors, coupled with the massive loss of life and the indelible horrors of the bombing of Hiroshima and Nagasaki and of the Holocaust, resulted in a pervasive sense of despair, disillusionment, and skepticism. Although many people (for example, the Futurists in Italy; see Chapter 14) had tried to find redemptive value in World War I, it was nearly impossible to do the same with World War II, coming as it did so soon after the "war to end all wars." Additionally, World War I was largely a European conflict that left roughly 10 million people dead, whereas World War II was a truly global catastrophe, claiming 35 million lives.

Postwar Expressionism in Europe

The cynicism pervading Europe in the 1940s found voice in existentialism, a philosophy asserting the absurdity of human existence and the impossibility of achieving certitude. Many existentialists also promoted atheism. The writings

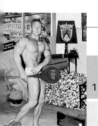

Modernism and Postmodernism in Europe and America, 1945 to 1980

1945	1960	1970	1980
▌ European Expressionists capture in paintings and sculptures the revulsion and cynicism that emerged in the wake of World War II ▌ New York School painters develop Abstract Expressionism, emphasizing form and raw energy over subject matter ▌ Sleek, geometrically rigid modernist skyscrapers become familiar sights in cities throughout the world	▌ Post-Painterly Abstractionists reject the passion and texture of action painting and celebrate the flatness of pigment on canvas ▌ Op artists produce the illusion of motion and depth using only geometric forms ▌ Minimalists reduce sculpture to basic shapes and emphasize their works' "objecthood" ▌ Pop artists find inspiration in popular culture and represent commonplace commercial products ▌ Superrealists create paintings and sculptures characterized by scrupulous reproduction of the appearance of people and objects ▌ Performance artists replace traditional stationary artworks with temporal action-artworks	▌ Artists play a leading role in the feminist movement by promoting women's themes and employing materials traditionally associated with women, such as china and fabric ▌ Postmodern architects erect complex and eclectic buildings that often incorporate references to historical styles ▌ Environmental artists redefine what constitutes "art" by manipulating natural materials in monumental earthworks ▌ Artists increasingly embrace new media—video recorders, computers—as tools for creating artworks	

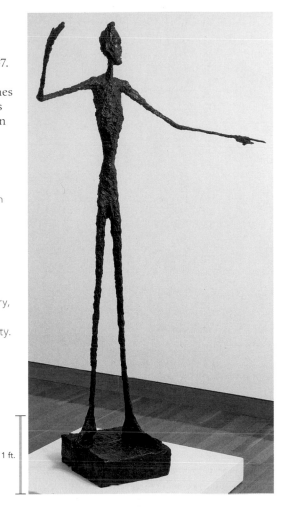

15-2 Alberto Giacometti, *Man Pointing* (no. 5 of 6), 1947. Bronze, 5′ 10″ high. Des Moines Art Center, Des Moines (Nathan Emory Coffin Collection).

The writer Jean-Paul Sartre saw Giacometti's thin and virtually featureless sculpted figures as the epitome of existentialist humanity—alienated, solitary, and lost in the world's immensity.

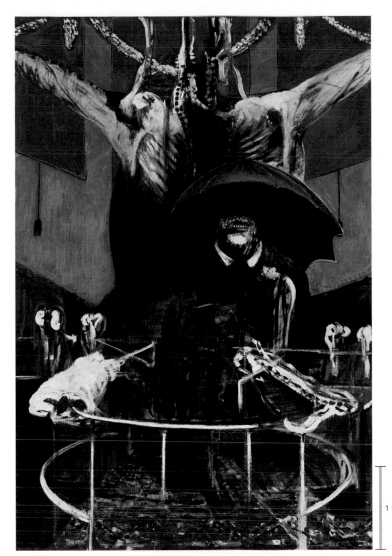

15-3 Francis Bacon, *Painting*, 1946. Oil and pastel on linen, 6′ 5⅞″ × 4′ 4″. Museum of Modern Art, New York.

Painted in the aftermath of World War II, this intentionally revolting image of a powerful figure presiding over a slaughter is Bacon's indictment of humanity and a reflection of war's butchery.

of French author Jean-Paul Sartre (1905–1980) most clearly captured the existentialist spirit. According to Sartre, if God does not exist, then individuals must constantly struggle in isolation with the anguish of making decisions in a world without absolutes or traditional values. This spirit of pessimism and despair emerged frequently in European art of the immediate postwar period. A brutality or roughness appropriately expressing both the artist's state of mind and the larger cultural sensibility characterized the work of many European sculptors and painters.

Alberto Giacometti The sculpture of Swiss artist Alberto Giacometti (1901–1966) perhaps best expresses the spirit of existentialism. Although Giacometti never claimed he pursued existentialist ideas in his art, his works capture the spirit of that philosophy. Indeed, Sartre, Giacometti's friend, saw the artist's figural sculptures as the epitome of existentialist humanity—alienated, solitary, and lost in the world's immensity. Giacometti's sculptures of the 1940s, such as *Man Pointing* (FIG. **15-2**), are thin, nearly featureless figures with rough, agitated surfaces. Rather than conveying the solidity and mass of conventional bronze sculpture, these severely attenuated figures seem swallowed up by the space surrounding them, imparting a sense of isolation and fragility. Giacometti's evocative sculptures spoke to the pervasive despair that emerged in the aftermath of world war.

Francis Bacon Created in the year after World War II ended, *Painting* (FIG. **15-3**) by British artist Francis Bacon (1910–1992) is an indictment of humanity and a reflection of war's butchery. Bacon presented a compelling and revolting image of a powerful, stocky man with a gaping mouth and a vivid red stain on his upper lip, as if he were a carnivore devouring the raw meat sitting on the railing surrounding him. Bacon may have based his depiction of this central figure on news photos of similarly dressed European and American officials. The umbrella in particular recalls images of Neville Chamberlain (1869–1940), the wartime British prime minister who frequently appeared in photographs with an umbrella. The artist added to the visceral impact of the painting by depicting the flayed carcass hanging behind the central figure as if it were a crucified human form. *Painting* is unmistakably "an attempt to remake the violence of reality itself," as Bacon often described his art based on what he referred to as "the brutality of fact."[1]

Abstract Expressionism

In the 1960s, the center of the Western art world shifted from Paris to New York because of the devastation World War II had inflicted across Europe and the resulting influx of émigré artists escaping to the United States. It was in New York that the first major American avant-garde art movement—Abstract Expressionism—emerged. The most important forerunner of the Abstract Expressionists, however, was an Armenian.

Arshile Gorky Born a Christian in Islamic Turkish Armenia, ARSHILE GORKY (1904–1948) was four years old when his father escaped being drafted into the Turkish army by fleeing the country. His mother died of starvation in her 15-year-old son's arms in a refugee camp for victims of the Turkish campaign of genocide against the Christian minority. Penniless, Gorky managed in 1920 to make his way to America, settling in New York City four years later. In a career lasting only two decades, Gorky contributed significantly to the artistic revolution born in New York. His work is the bridge between the Biomorphic Surrealism of Joan Miró (FIG. 14-26) and the totally abstract canvases of Jackson Pollock (FIG. 15-5).

Garden in Sochi (FIG. **15-4**), painted in 1943, is the third in a series of canvases with identical titles named after a Black Sea resort but inspired by Gorky's childhood memories of the Garden of Wish Fulfillment in his birthplace. The women of the Armenian village of Khorkom believed their wishes would be granted if they rubbed their bare breasts against a rock in that garden beneath a tree to which they tied torn strips of their clothing. The brightly colored and thinly outlined forms in *Garden in Sochi,* which initially appear to be purely abstract biomorphic shapes, are loose sketches representing, at the left, a bare-breasted woman, and, at the center, a tree trunk with fluttering fabric. At the bottom are two oversized shoes—the Armenian slippers Gorky's father gave his son shortly before abandoning the family.

Clement Greenberg The few traces of representational art in Gorky's work disappeared in *Abstract Expressionism.* As the name suggests, the artists associated with the New York School of Abstract Expressionism produced paintings that are, for the most part, abstract but express the artist's state of mind, with the goal also of striking emotional chords in the viewer. The most important champion of this strict *formalism*—an emphasis on an artwork's visual elements rather than its subject—was the American art critic Clement Greenberg (1909–1994), who wielded considerable influence

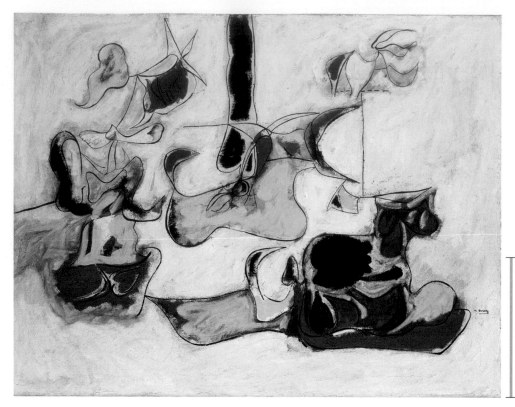

15-4 ARSHILE GORKY, *Garden in Sochi,* ca. 1943. Oil on canvas, 2′ 7″ × 3′ 3″. Museum of Modern Art, New York (acquired through the Lillie P. Bliss Bequest).

Gorky's paintings of the 1940s, which still incorporate recognizable forms, are the bridge between the Biomorphic Surrealist canvases of Miró and the Abstract Expressionist paintings of Pollock.

from the 1940s through the 1970s. Greenberg helped redefine the parameters of modernism by advocating the rejection of illusionism and the exploration of the properties of each artistic medium. So dominant was Greenberg that scholars often refer to the general modernist tenets during this period as Greenbergian formalism. Greenberg promoted the idea of artistic purity. He believed artists should strive for a more explicit focus on the properties exclusive to each medium—for example, flatness in painting and three-dimensionality in sculpture. Greenberg argued that

> a modernist work of art must try, in principle, to avoid communication with any order of experience not inherent in the most literally and essentially construed nature of its medium. Among other things, this means renouncing illusion and explicit subject matter. The arts are to achieve concreteness, "purity," by dealing solely with their respective selves—that is, by becoming "abstract" or nonfigurative.[2]

The Abstract Expressionist movement developed along two lines—*gestural abstraction* and *chromatic abstraction*. The gestural abstractionists relied on the expressiveness of energetically applied pigment. In contrast, the chromatic abstractionists focused on color's emotional resonance.

Jackson Pollock The artist whose work best exemplifies gestural abstraction is JACKSON POLLOCK (1912–1956), who developed his signature style in the mid-1940s. By 1950, Pollock had refined his technique and was producing large-scale

Jackson Pollock on Action Painting

The kind of physical interaction between the painter and the canvas that Jackson Pollock championed led the critic Harold Rosenberg (1896–1989) to label Pollock's work (FIG. 15-5) *action painting*. In an influential 1952 article, Rosenberg described the attempts of Pollock and other Abstract Expressionists to get "in the painting":

> At a certain moment the canvas began to appear to one American painter after another as an arena in which to act—rather than as a space in which to reproduce, redesign, analyze or "express" an object, actual or imagined. What was to go on the canvas was not a picture but an event. The painter no longer approached his easel with an image in his mind; he went up to it with material in his hand to do something to that other piece of material in front of him. The image would be the result of this encounter.*

In an essay he published in 1947, Pollock explained the motivations for his action painting and described the manner in which he applied pigment to canvas.

> My painting does not come from the easel. I hardly ever stretch my canvas before painting. I prefer to tack the unstretched canvas to the hard wall or the floor. I need the resistance of a hard surface. On the floor I am more at ease. I feel nearer, more a part of the painting, since this way I can walk around it, work from the four sides and literally be *in* the painting. . . . I continue to get further away from the usual painter's tools such as easel, palette, brushes, etc. I prefer sticks, trowels, knives and dripping fluid paint or a heavy impasto with sand, broken glass and other foreign matter added. When I am *in* my painting, I'm not aware of what I'm doing. . . . [T]he painting has a life of its own. I try to let it come through. . . . The source of my painting is the unconscious.†

*Harold Rosenberg, "The American Action Painters," reprinted in *The Tradition of the New* (New York: Horizon Press, 1959), 25.
†Quoted in Francis V. O'Connor, *Jackson Pollock* (New York: Museum of Modern Art, 1967), 39–40.

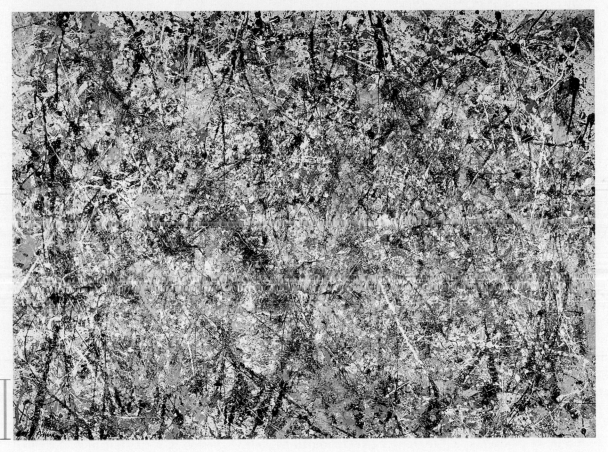

1 ft.

15-5 JACKSON POLLOCK, *Number 1, 1950 (Lavender Mist)*, 1950. Oil, enamel, and aluminum paint on canvas, 7′ 3″ × 9′ 10″. National Gallery of Art, Washington, D.C. (Ailsa Mellon Bruce Fund).

Pollock's "action paintings" emphasize the creative process. His mural-size canvases consist of rhythmic drips, splatters, and dribbles of paint that envelop viewers, drawing them into a lacy spider web.

abstract paintings such as *Number 1, 1950* (*Lavender Mist;* FIG. **15-5**). These works consist of rhythmic drips, splatters, and dribbles of paint. The mural-sized fields of energetic skeins of pigment envelop viewers, drawing them into a lacy spider web. Using sticks or brushes, Pollock flung, poured, and dripped paint (not only traditional oil paints but aluminum paints and household enamels as well) onto a section of canvas he simply unrolled across his studio floor. This working method earned Pollock the derisive nickname "Jack the Dripper." Responding to the image as it developed, he created art that was spontaneous yet choreographed. Pollock's painting technique highlights the most significant aspect of gestural abstraction—its emphasis on the creative process. Indeed, Pollock literally immersed himself in the painting during its creation (see "Jackson Pollock on Action Painting," above). Art historians have linked his ideas about improvisation in the creative process to his interest in what psychiatrist Carl Jung called the collective unconscious. Pollock's reliance on improvisation and the subconscious has parallels in Surrealism and the work of Vassily Kandinsky (FIG. 14-5), whom critics described as an Abstract Expressionist as early as 1919.

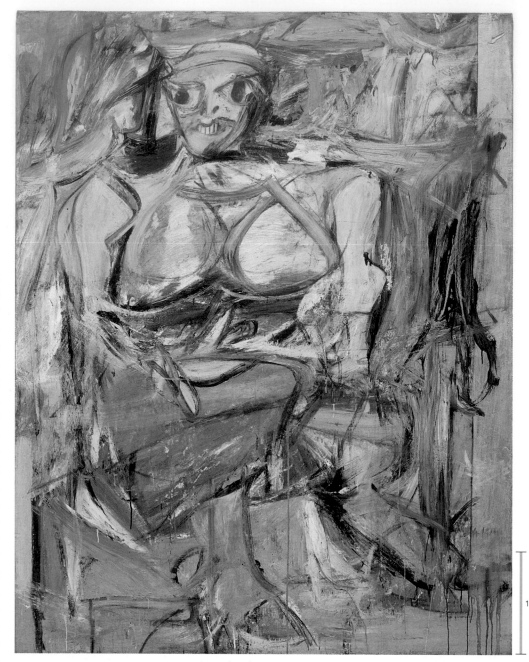

15-6 WILLEM DE KOONING, *Woman I,* 1950–1952. Oil on canvas, 6′ 3⅞″ × 4′ 10″. Museum of Modern Art, New York. ▪️

Although rooted in figuration, including pictures of female models on advertising billboards, de Kooning's *Woman I* displays the energetic application of pigment typical of gestural abstraction.

1 ft.

Willem de Kooning Despite the public's skepticism about Pollock's art, other artists enthusiastically pursued similar avenues of expression. Dutch-born WILLEM DE KOONING (1904–1997) also developed a gestural abstractionist style. Even images such as *Woman I* (FIG. **15-6**), although rooted in figuration, display the sweeping gestural brushstrokes and energetic application of pigment typical of gestural abstraction. Out of the jumbled array of slashing lines and agitated patches of color appears a ferocious-looking woman with staring eyes and ponderous breasts. Her toothy smile, derived from an ad for Camel cigarettes, seems to devolve into a grimace. Female models on advertising billboards partly inspired *Woman I,* one of a series of female images, but de Kooning's female forms also suggest fertility figures and a satiric inversion of the traditional image of Venus, goddess of love. Process was important to de Kooning, as it was for Pollock. Continually working on *Woman I* for almost two years, de Kooning painted an image and then scraped it away the next day and began anew. His wife Elaine, also an accomplished painter, estimated he painted approximately 200 scraped-away images of women on this canvas before settling on the final one.

Mark Rothko In contrast to the aggressively energetic images of the gestural abstractionists, the work of the chromatic abstractionists exudes a quieter aesthetic, exemplified by the work of Russian-born MARK ROTHKO (1903–1970). Rothko believed that references to anything specific in the physical world conflicted with the sublime idea of the universal, supernatural "spirit of myth," which he saw as the core of meaning in art. Rothko's mature paintings are compositionally simple, with color serving as the primary conveyor of meaning. In works such as *No. 14* (FIG. **15-7**), Rothko created compelling visual experiences consisting of two or three large rectangles of pure color with hazy edges that seem to float on the canvas surface, hovering in front of a colored background. His compositions present shimmering veils of intensely luminous colors that appear to be suspended in front of the canvases. Although the color juxtapositions are visually captivating, Rothko intended them as more than decorative. He saw color as a doorway to another reality and insisted color could express "basic human emotions—tragedy, ecstasy, doom. . . . The people who weep before my pictures are having the same religious experience I had when I painted them."[3] As did the other Abstract Expressionists, Rothko produced highly evocative paintings reliant on formal elements rather than on specific representational content to elicit emotional responses in viewers.

Post-Painterly Abstraction

Post-Painterly Abstraction, another postwar American art movement, developed out of Abstract Expressionism. Yet *Post-Painterly Abstraction,* a term Clement Greenberg coined, manifests a radically different sensibility from Abstract Expressionism. Whereas Abstract Expressionism conveys a feeling of passion and visceral intensity, a cool, detached rationality emphasizing tighter pictorial control characterizes Post-Painterly Abstraction. Greenberg saw this art as contrasting with "painterly" art, characterized by loose, visible pigment application. Evidence of the artist's hand, so prominent in gestural abstraction, is conspicuously absent in Post-Painterly Abstraction. Greenberg championed this art form because it embodied his idea of purity in art.

Frank Stella Attempting to arrive at pure painting, the Post-Painterly Abstractionists distilled painting down to its essential elements, producing spare, elemental images. One of the primary practitioners of *hard-edge painting,* one variant of Post-Painterly Abstraction, was Massachusetts-born FRANK STELLA (b. 1936), who moved to New York City in 1958, but did not favor the expressive brushwork of the Abstract Expressionists. In works such as *Mas o Menos* (*More or Less*; FIG. **15-8**), Stella eliminated many of the variables associated with painting. His canvases are composed of thin, evenly spaced pinstripes on colored grounds. They have no central focus, no painterly or expressive elements, only limited surface modulation, and no tactile quality. Stella's systematic method of painting illustrates Greenberg's insistence on purity in art. The artist's famous comment on his work, "What you see is what you see," reinforces the notions that painters interested in producing advanced art must reduce their work to its essential elements and that the viewer must acknowledge that a painting is simply pigment on a flat surface.

15-7 MARK ROTHKO, *No. 14,* 1960. Oil on canvas, 9′ 6″ × 8′ 9″. San Francisco Museum of Modern Art, San Francisco (Helen Crocker Russell Fund Purchase).

Rothko's chromatic abstractionist paintings—consisting of hazy rectangles of pure color hovering in front of a colored background—are compositionally simple but compelling visual experiences.

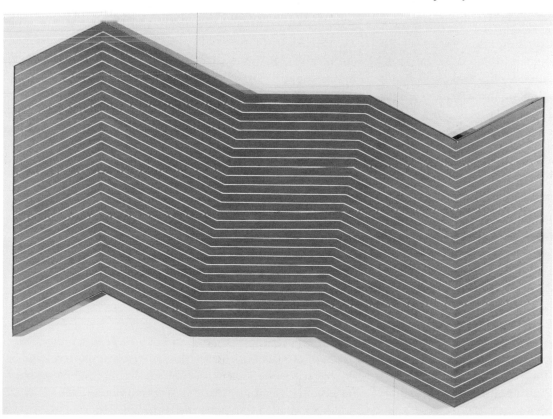

15-8 FRANK STELLA, *Mas o Menos* (*More or Less*), 1964. Metallic powder in acrylic emulsion on canvas, 9′ 10″ × 13′ 8½″. Musée National d'Art Moderne, Centre Georges Pompidou, Paris (purchase 1983 with participation of Scaler Foundation).

Stella tried to achieve purity in painting using evenly spaced pinstripes on colored grounds. His canvases have no central focus, no painterly or expressive elements, and no tactile quality.

Helen Frankenthaler on Color-Field Painting

In 1965 the art critic Henry Geldzahler (1935–1994) interviewed Helen Frankenthaler about her work as an abstract painter. In the following excerpt, Frankenthaler described her approach to placing color on canvas in works such as *The Bay* (FIG. 15-9) and compared her method with the way earlier modernist artists used color in their paintings.

> I will sometimes start a picture feeling "What will happen if I work with three blues and another color, and maybe more or less of the other color than the combined blues?" And very often midway through the picture I have to change the basis of the experience. . . .
>
> When you first saw a Cubist or Impressionist picture there was a whole way of instructing the eye or the subconscious. Dabs of color had to stand for real things; it was an abstraction of a guitar or a hillside. The opposite is going on now. If you have bands of blue, green, and pink, the mind doesn't think sky, grass, and flesh. These are colors and the question is what are they doing with themselves and with each other. Sentiment and nuance are being squeezed out.*

*Henry Geldzahler, "Interview with Helen Frankenthaler," *Artforum* 4, no. 2 (October 1965), 37–38.

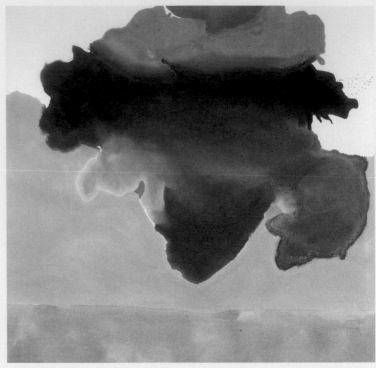

15-9 HELEN FRANKENTHALER, *The Bay*, 1963. Acrylic on canvas, 6′ 8⅞″ × 6′ 9⅞″. Detroit Institute of Arts, Detroit.

Frankenthaler and other color-field painters poured paint onto unprimed canvas, allowing the pigments to soak into the fabric. Her works underscore that a painting is simply pigment on a flat surface.

1 ft.

Helen Frankenthaler *Color-field painting,* another variant of Post-Painterly Abstraction, also emphasized painting's basic properties. However, rather than produce sharp, unmodulated shapes as the hard-edge artists had done, the color-field painters poured diluted paint onto unprimed canvas and allowed the pigments to soak in. No other painting method results in such literal flatness. The images created, such as *The Bay* (FIG. 15-9) by lifelong New Yorker HELEN FRANKENTHALER (b. 1928), appear spontaneous and almost accidental (see "Helen Frankenthaler on Color-Field Painting," above).

Op Art

A major artistic movement of the 1960s was *Op Art* (short for Optical Art), in which painters sought to produce optical illusions of motion and depth using only geometric forms on flat surfaces.

Bridget Riley The artist whose name is synonymous with Op Art is the British artist BRIDGET RILEY (b. 1931), who developed her signature black-and-white Op Art style in the early 1960s. Her paintings, for example, *Fission* (FIG. 15-10), came to the public's attention after being featured in the December 1964 issue of *Life* magazine. The publicity unleashed a craze for Op Art designs in clothing. In 1965, the exhibition *The Responsive Eye* at the Museum of Modern Art be-

stowed an official stamp of approval on the movement. In *Fission,* Riley filled the canvas with black dots of varied sizes and shapes, creating the illusion of a pulsating surface that caves in at the center (hence the painting's title). The effect on the viewer of Op Art paintings such as this one is disorienting and sometimes disturbing, and some works can even induce motion sickness. Thoroughly modernist in the insistence a painting is a two-dimensional surface covered with pigment and not a representation of any person, object, or place, the Op Art movement nonetheless embraced the Renaissance notion that the painter can create the illusion of depth through perspective.

Abstraction in Sculpture

Painters were not the only artists interested in Greenberg's formalist ideas. American sculptors also strove for purity in their medium. Whereas painters worked to emphasize flatness, sculptors, understandably, chose to focus on three-dimensionality as the unique characteristic and inherent limitation of the sculptural idiom.

David Smith Indiana-born and Ohio-raised sculptor DAVID SMITH (1906–1965) produced metal sculptures that have affinities with the Abstract Expressionist movement in painting. Smith learned to weld in an automobile plant in 1925 and later applied to his art the technical expertise he gained

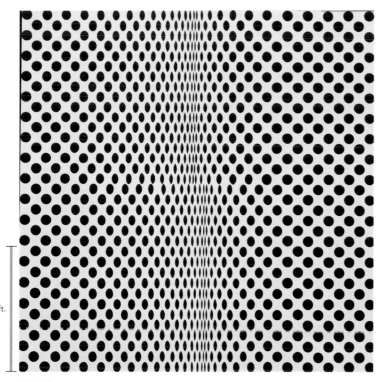

15-10 BRIDGET RILEY, *Fission,* 1963. Tempera on composition board, 2′ 11″ × 2′ 10″. Museum of Modern Art, New York (gift of Philip Johnson).

Op Art paintings create the illusion of motion and depth using only geometric forms. The effect can be disorienting. The pattern of black dots in Riley's *Fission* appears to cave in at the center.

from that experience. After experimenting with a variety of sculptural styles and materials, Smith created his *Cubi* series in the early 1960s. These works, for example *Cubi XII* (FIG. **15-11**), consist of simple geometric forms—cubes and rectangular bars. Made of stainless steel sections piled on top of one another, often at unstable angles, and then welded together, these large-scale sculptures make a striking visual statement. Smith added gestural elements reminiscent of Abstract Expressionism by burnishing the metal with steel wool, producing swirling random-looking patterns that draw attention to the two-dimensionality of the sculptural surface. This treatment, which captures the light hitting the sculpture, activates the surface and imparts a texture to his pieces. Smith created the *Cubi* series for display in the open air. The metal sculptures lose much of their character in the sterile lighting of a museum.

Donald Judd A predominantly sculptural movement that emerged in the 1960s among artists seeking Greenbergian purity was *Minimalism*. Minimalist artworks generally lack identifiable subjects, colors, surface textures, and narrative elements. By rejecting illusionism and reducing sculpture to basic geometric forms, Minimalists emphasized their art's "objecthood" and concrete tangibility. In so doing, they reduced experience to its most fundamental level. One leading Minimalist was Missouri native DONALD JUDD (1928–1994),

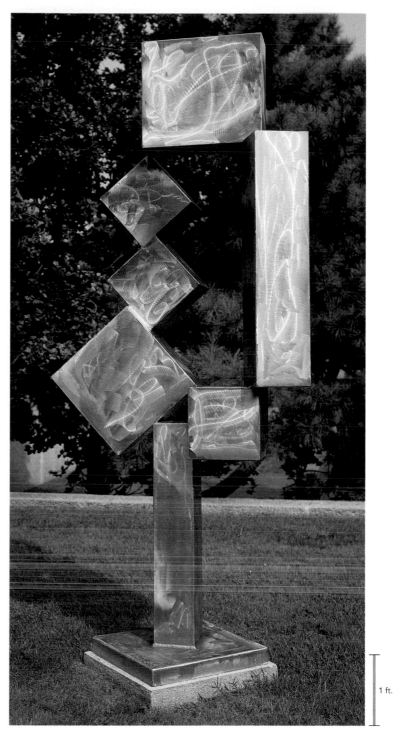

15-11 DAVID SMITH, *Cubi XII,* 1963. Stainless steel, 9′ 1⅝″ high. Hirshhorn Museum and Sculpture Garden, Smithsonian Institution, Washington, D.C. (gift of the Joseph H. Hirshhorn Foundation, 1972).

David Smith's metal sculptures have affinities with Abstract Expressionism. They consist of simple geometric forms—cubes, cylinders, and rectangular bars—piled up and then welded together.

who produced most of his major works in New York City. Judd's determination to arrive at a visual vocabulary devoid of deception or ambiguity propelled him away from representation and toward precise and simple sculpture. For Judd, a work's power derived from its character as a whole

Painting, Sculpture, and Photography **431**

and from the specificity of its materials. *Untitled* (FIG. **15-12**) presents basic geometric boxes constructed of brass and red Plexiglas, undisguised by paint or other materials. The artist did not intend the work to be metaphorical or symbolic but a straightforward declaration of sculpture's objecthood. Judd used Plexiglas because its translucency enables the viewer access to the interior, thereby rendering the sculpture both open and enclosed. This aspect of the design reflects Judd's desire to banish ambiguity or falseness from his works.

Louise Nevelson Although Minimalism was a dominant sculptural trend in the 1960s, many sculptors pursued other styles. Russian-born LOUISE NEVELSON (1899–1988) created sculpture combining a sense of the architectural fragment with the power of Dada and Surrealist found objects to express her personal sense of life's underlying significance. Beginning in the late 1950s, Nevelson assembled sculptures of found wooden objects and forms, enclosing small sculptural compositions in boxes of varied sizes, and joined the boxes to one another to form "walls," which she then painted in a single hue—usually black, white, or gold. This monochromatic color scheme unifies the diverse parts of pieces such as *Tropical Garden II* (FIG. **15-13**) and creates a mysterious field of shapes and shadows. The structures suggest magical environments resembling the treasured secret hideaways dimly remembered from childhood. Yet the boxy frames and the precision of the manufactured found objects create a rough geometric structure the eye roams over freely, lingering on some details. The effect is rather like viewing the side of an apartment building from a moving elevated train.

Louise Bourgeois In contrast to the architectural nature of Nevelson's work, a sensuous organic quality recalling the evocative Biomorphic Surrealist forms of Joan Miró (FIG. 14-26) pervades the work of the French-American artist LOUISE BOURGEOIS (1911–2010). *Cumul I* (FIG. **15-14**) is a collection of round-headed units huddled, with their heads protruding, within a collective cloak dotted with holes. The units differ in size, and their position within the group lends a distinctive personality to each. Although the shapes remain abstract, they refer strongly to human figures. Bourgeois used a wide variety of materials in her

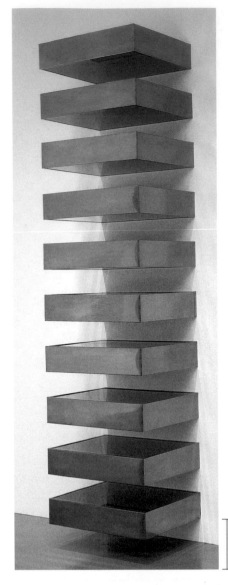

15-12 DONALD JUDD, *Untitled,* 1969. Brass and colored fluorescent Plexiglas on steel brackets, 10 units, $6\frac{1}{8}$" $\times$ 2' $\times$ 2' 3" each, with 6" intervals. Hirshhorn Museum and Sculpture Garden, Smithsonian Institution, Washington, D.C. (gift of Joseph H. Hirshhorn, 1972). © Donald Judd Estate/Licensed by VAGA, New York.

By rejecting illusionism and symbolism and reducing sculpture to basic geometric forms, Donald Judd and other Minimalist artists emphasized their works' "objecthood" and concrete tangibility.

1 ft.

15-13 LOUISE NEVELSON, *Tropical Garden II,* 1957–1959. Wood painted black, 5' $11\frac{1}{2}$" $\times$ 10' $11\frac{3}{4}$" $\times$ 1'. Musée National d'Art Moderne, Centre Georges Pompidou, Paris.

The monochromatic color scheme unifies the diverse sculpted forms and found objects in Nevelson's "walls" and creates a mysterious field of shapes and shadows suggesting magical environments.

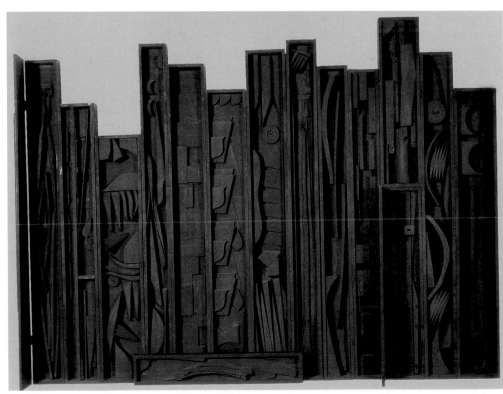

1 ft.

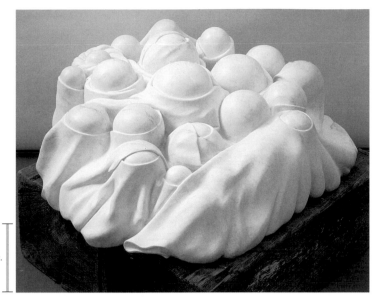

15-14 LOUISE BOURGEOIS, *Cumul I,* 1969. Marble, 1' 10¾" × 4' 2" × 4'. Musée National d'Art Moderne, Centre Georges Pompidou, Paris. © Louise Bourgeois/Licensed by VAGA, New York. ◼

Bourgeois's sculptures consist of sensuous organic forms that recall the Biomorphic Surrealist forms of Miró (FIG. 14-26). Although the shapes remain abstract, they refer strongly to human figures.

works, including wood, plaster, latex, and plastics, in addition to alabaster, marble, and bronze. She exploited each material's qualities to suit the expressiveness of the piece. In *Cumul I,* the alternating high gloss and matte finish of the marble increases the sensuous distinction between the group of swelling forms and the soft folds swaddling them. Bourgeois connected her sculpture with the body's multiple relationships to landscape: "[My pieces] are anthropomorphic and they are landscape also, since our body could be considered from a topographical point of view, as a land with mounds and valleys and caves and holes." Sculptures such as *Cumul I*

are openly sexual: "There has always been sexual suggestiveness in my work. Sometimes I am totally concerned with female shapes—characters of breasts like clouds—but often I merge the activity—phallic breasts, male and female, active and passive."[4]

Pop Art

Despite their differences, the Abstract Expressionists, Post-Painterly Abstractionists, Op Art painters, and Minimalist sculptors all adopted an artistic vocabulary of resolute abstraction. The artists of the Pop Art movement, however, observing that the insular and introspective attitude of the avant-garde had alienated the public, reintroduced traditional imagery in their artworks and embraced popular culture (see "Art and Consumer Culture," page 423). Although Pop Art originated in England, the movement found its greatest success in the United States, in large part because the more fully matured American consumer culture provided a fertile environment for the movement. Indeed, Independent Group members claimed their inspiration came from Hollywood, Detroit, and New York's Madison Avenue, paying homage to America's predominance in the realms of mass media, mass production, and advertising.

Jasper Johns One of the artists pivotal to the early development of American Pop Art was JASPER JOHNS (b. 1930), who moved to New York City from South Carolina in 1952. Johns sought to draw attention to common objects in the world—what he called things "seen but not looked at."[5] To this end, he did several series of paintings of numbers, letters, flags, and maps of the United States. For example, *Three Flags* (FIG. 15-15) depicts an object people view frequently but rarely scrutinize. Johns painted the flags on three overlapping canvases using *encaustic*—an ancient method of painting with liquid wax and dissolved pigment (FIG. 3-42)—mixed with newsprint. The flags thus have a pronounced surface texture, emphasizing that the viewer is looking at a handmade painting, not a machine-made fabric. Moreover, the flags increase in size from front to back, reversing traditional perspective. By reducing the American flag to a repetitive pattern, Johns drained meaning from the patriotic emblem. This is not the flag itself but three pictures of a flag in one.

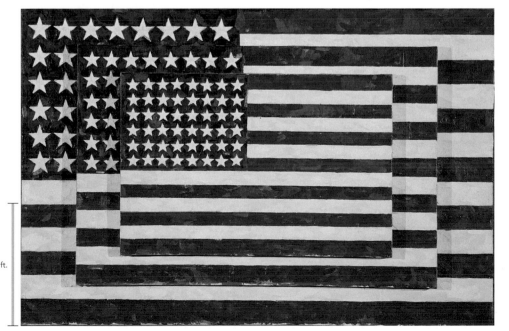

15-15 JASPER JOHNS, *Three Flags,* 1958. Encaustic on canvas, 2' 6⅞" × 3' 9½". Whitney Museum of American Art, New York (50th Anniversary Gift of the Gilman Foundation, the Lauder Foundation, and A. Alfred Taubman).

American Pop artist Jasper Johns wanted to draw attention to common objects people view frequently but rarely scrutinize. He made many paintings of flags, maps, numbers, and letters.

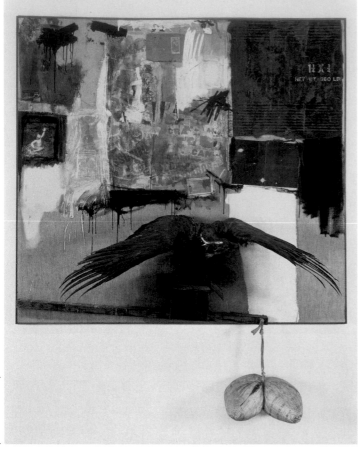

1 ft.

15-16 ROBERT RAUSCHENBERG, *Canyon*, 1959. Oil, pencil, paper, fabric, metal, cardboard box, printed paper, printed reproductions, photograph, wood, paint tube, and mirror on canvas, with oil on eagle, string, and pillow, 6′ 9¾″ × 5′ 10″ × 2′. Sonnabend Collection, New York. © Robert Rauschenberg/Licensed by VAGA, New York.

Rauschenberg's "combines" intersperse painted passages with sculptural elements. *Canyon* incorporates pigment on canvas with pieces of printed paper, photographs, a pillow, and a stuffed eagle.

Robert Rauschenberg A close friend of Johns's, ROBERT RAUSCHENBERG (1925–2008), also began using mass-media images in his work in the 1950s. Rauschenberg set out to create works that would be open and indeterminate, and he began making *combines*, combinations of paintings and sculptures. Some Rauschenberg combines seem to be sculptures with painting incorporated into certain sections. Others are paintings with three-dimensional objects attached to the surface. In the early 1960s, Rauschenberg adopted the commercial medium of *silk-screen printing*, first in black and white and then in color, and began filling entire canvases with appropriated news images and anonymous photographs of city scenes.

Canyon (FIG. **15-16**) is typical of his combines. Pieces of printed paper and photographs cover parts of the canvas. Much of the unevenly painted surface consists of pigment roughly applied in a manner reminiscent of de Kooning's work (FIG. 15-6). A stuffed bald eagle attached to the lower part of the combine spreads its wings as if lifting off in flight toward the viewer. Completing the combine, a pillow dangles from a string attached to a wood stick below the eagle.

Rauschenberg tilted or turned some of the images sideways, and each overlays part of another image. The compositional confusion may resemble that of a Dada collage, but the combine's parts maintain their individuality. The various recognizable images and objects seem unrelated and defy a consistent reading, although Rauschenberg chose all the elements of his combines with specific meanings in mind. For example, he based *Canyon* on a Rembrandt painting of Jupiter in the form of an eagle carrying the boy Ganymede heavenward. The photo in the combine is a reference to the Greek boy, and the hanging pillow is a visual pun on his buttocks.

Roy Lichtenstein As the Pop Art movement matured, the images became more concrete and tightly controlled. Manhattanite ROY LICHTENSTEIN (1923–1997) turned his attention to the comic book as a mainstay of popular culture. In paintings such as *Hopeless* (FIG. **15-17**), Lichtenstein excerpted an image from a comic book, a form of entertainment meant to be read and discarded, and immortalized the image on a large canvas. Aside from that modification, Lichtenstein remained remarkably faithful to the original comic-strip image. His subjects were typically the melodramatic scenes that were hallmarks of the popular romance comic books at the time and included "balloons" with the words the characters speak. Lichtenstein also used the visual vocabulary of the comic strip, with its dark black outlines and unmodulated color areas, and retained the familiar square dimensions. Moreover, his printing technique, *benday dots,* called attention

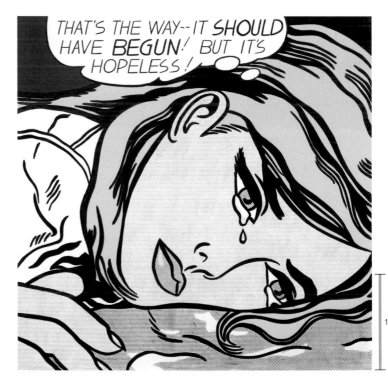

1 ft.

15-17 ROY LICHTENSTEIN, *Hopeless*, 1963. Oil and synthetic polymer paint on canvas, 3′ 8″ × 3′ 8″. Kunstmuseum Basel, Basel. © Estate of Roy Lichtenstein.

Comic books appealed to Pop artist Lichtenstein because they were a mainstay of popular culture, meant to be read and discarded. He immortalized their images on large canvases.

to the mass-produced derivation of the image. Named after its inventor, the newspaper printer Benjamin Day (1810–1889), the benday-dot system involves the modulation of colors through the placement and size of colored dots.

Andy Warhol The quintessential American Pop artist was ANDY WARHOL (1928–1987). An early successful career as a commercial artist and illustrator grounded Warhol in the sensibility and visual rhetoric of advertising and the mass media. This knowledge proved useful for his Pop artworks, which often depicted icons of mass-produced consumer culture, such as *Green Coca-Cola Bottles* (FIG. **15-18**). Warhol favored reassuringly familiar objects and people. He explained his attraction to the ubiquitous curved Coke bottle:

> What's great about this country is that America started the tradition where the richest consumers buy essentially the same things as the poorest. You can be watching TV and see Coca-Cola, and you can know that the President drinks Coke, Liz Taylor drinks Coke, and just think, you can drink Coke, too. A Coke is a Coke and no amount of money can get you a better Coke.[6]

As did other Pop artists, Warhol used a visual vocabulary and a printing method that reinforced the image's connections to consumer culture. The silk-screen technique enabled Warhol to print the image endlessly (although he varied each bottle slightly). The repetition and redundancy of the Coke bottle reflect the saturation of this product in American society.

Claes Oldenburg In the 1960s, CLAES OLDENBURG (b. 1929) also produced Pop artworks that incisively commented on American consumer culture, but his medium was sculpture. Born in Sweden, Oldenburg graduated from Yale University in 1950. He is best known for his mammoth outdoor sculptures, for example, *Lipstick* (*Ascending*) *on Caterpillar Tracks* (FIG. **15-19**), which, at the request of a group of graduate students at the Yale School of Architecture, he created (in secret and without a fee) as a gift to his alma mater. He installed the 21-foot-tall sculpture on Ascension Day, May 15, 1969, on Beineke Plaza across from the office of the university's president, the site of many raucous protests against the Vietnam War. Oldenburg's characteristic humor emerges

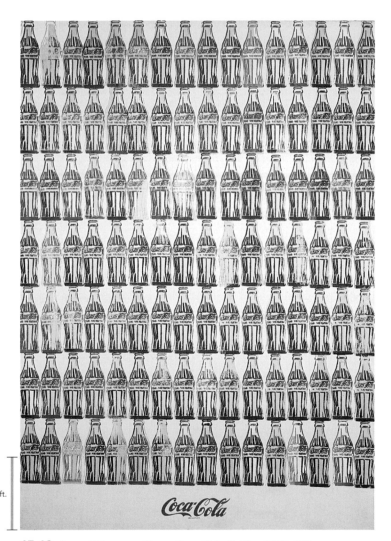

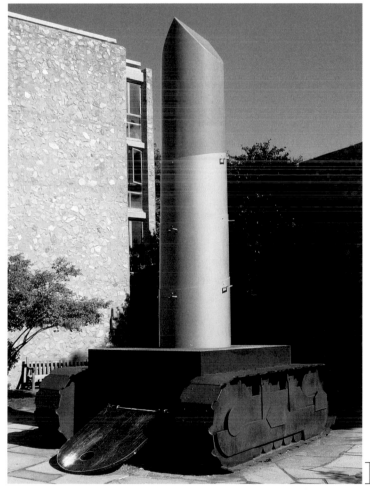

15-18 ANDY WARHOL, *Green Coca-Cola Bottles,* 1962. Oil on canvas, 6' 10½" × 4' 9". Whitney Museum of American Art, New York.

Warhol was the quintessential American Pop artist. Here, he selected an icon of mass-produced, consumer culture, and then multiplied it, reflecting Coke's omnipresence in American society.

15-19 CLAES OLDENBURG, *Lipstick* (*Ascending*) *on Caterpillar Tracks,* 1969; reworked, 1974. Painted steel, aluminum, and fiberglass, 21' high. Morse College, Yale University, New Haven (gift of Colossal Keepsake Corporation).

Designed as a speaker's platform for antiwar protesters, *Lipstick* humorously combines phallic and militaristic imagery. Originally, the lipstick tip was soft red vinyl and had to be inflated.

unmistakably in the combination of phallic and militaristic imagery, especially in the double irony of the "phallus" being a woman's cosmetic item, and the Caterpillar-type endless-loop metal tracks suggesting not a tractor-earthmover for construction work but a military tank designed for destruction in warfare. *Lipstick* was to be a speaker's platform for protesters, and originally the lipstick tip was a drooping red vinyl balloon the speaker had to inflate, underscoring the sexual innuendo. Vandalism and exposure to the elements (the original tractor was plywood) caused so much damage to *Lipstick* that it had to be removed. Oldenburg reconstructed it in metal and fiberglass.

Superrealism and Photography

Like the Pop artists, the artists associated with *Superrealism* sought a form of artistic communication that was more accessible to the public than the remote, unfamiliar visual language of the postwar abstractionists. The Superrealists expanded Pop's iconography in both painting and sculpture by making images in the late 1960s and 1970s involving scrupulous fidelity to optical fact. Because many Superrealists used photographs as sources for their imagery, art historians also refer to this movement as *Photorealism*.

Audrey Flack One of Superrealism's pioneers was lifelong New Yorker AUDREY FLACK (b. 1931), who was intrigued by both the formal and technical qualities of photography. For paintings such as *Marilyn* (FIG. **15-20**), Flack first projected an image

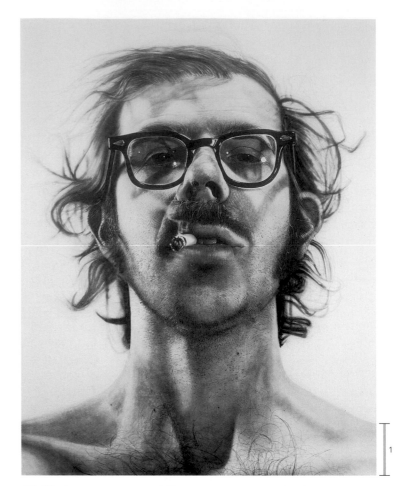

15-21 CHUCK CLOSE, *Big Self-Portrait,* 1967–1968. Acrylic on canvas, 8′ 11″ × 6′ 11″. Walker Art Center, Minneapolis (Art Center Acquisition Fund, 1969). ◼◀

Close's goal was to translate photographic information into painted information. In his portraits, he deliberately avoided creative compositions, flattering lighting effects, and revealing facial expressions.

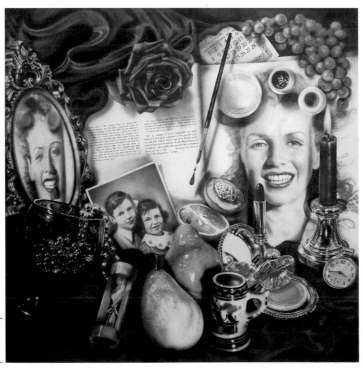

1 ft.

15-20 AUDREY FLACK, *Marilyn,* 1977. Oil over acrylic on canvas, 8′ × 8′. University of Arizona Museum, Tucson (museum purchase with funds provided by the Edward J. Gallagher Jr. Memorial Fund).

Flack's pioneering Photorealist still lifes record objects with great optical fidelity. *Marilyn* alludes to Dutch vanitas paintings and incorporates multiple references to the transience of life.

in slide form onto the canvas. By next using an *airbrush* (a device originally designed as a photo-retouching tool that sprays paint with compressed air), she could duplicate the smooth gradations of tone and color found in photographs. Most of her paintings are still lifes that present the viewer with a collection of familiar objects painted with great optical fidelity. *Marilyn* is a still life incorporating photographs of the face of Hollywood actress Marilyn Monroe (1926–1962). Rather than being a celebration of Monroe's fame, Flack's still life is a poignant commentary on her tragic life and includes multiple references to death and alludes to Dutch vanitas paintings (FIG. 10-27). The fresh fruit, hourglass, burning candle, watch, and calendar all refer to the passage of time and the transience of life.

Chuck Close Also usually considered a Superrealist is Seattle-born CHUCK CLOSE (b. 1940), best known for his large-scale portraits. Close, developed an intellectually rigorous, systematic approach to painting using airbrushes and razor blades in order to purge his paintings of visible brushstrokes. He based his paintings of the late 1960s and early 1970s, such as *Big Self-Portrait* (FIG. **15-21**), on photographs, and his main goal was to translate photographic information

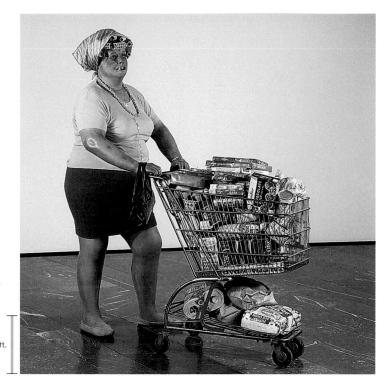

15-22 DUANE HANSON, *Supermarket Shopper,* 1970. Polyester resin and fiberglass polychromed in oil, with clothing, steel cart, and groceries, life-size. Nachfolgeinstitut, Neue Galerie, Sammlung Ludwig, Aachen. © Estate of Duane Hanson/Licensed by VAGA, New York.

Hanson used molds from live models to create his Superrealistic life-size painted plaster sculptures. His aim was to capture the emptiness and loneliness of average Americans in familiar settings.

into painted information. Because he aimed simply to record visual information about his subject's appearance, he deliberately avoided creative compositions, flattering lighting effects, and revealing facial expressions. Not interested in providing insight into the personalities of those portrayed, Close painted anonymous and generic people, mostly friends. By reducing the variables in his paintings (even their canvas size is a constant 9 by 7 feet), Close could focus on employing his methodical presentations of faces, thereby encouraging the viewer to deal with the formal aspects of his works. Indeed, because of the large scale of the artist's paintings, close scrutiny causes the images to dissolve into abstract patterns.

Duane Hanson Not surprisingly, many sculptors also were Superrealists, including Minnesota-born DUANE HANSON (1925–1996), who spent much of his career in southern Florida. Hanson perfected a casting technique that enabled him to create life-size sculptures many viewers mistake at first for real people. Hanson began by making plaster molds from live models and then filled the molds with polyester resin. After the resin hardened, he removed the outer molds and cleaned and painted the sculptures with an airbrush, and added wigs, clothes, and other accessories. These works, such as *Supermarket Shopper* (FIG. **15-22**), depict stereotypical average Americans, striking chords with the public precisely because of their familiarity.

The subject matter that I like best deals with the familiar lower and middle-class American types of today. To me, the resignation, emptiness and loneliness of their existence captures the true reality of life for these people. . . . I want to achieve a certain tough realism which speaks of the fascinating idiosyncrasies of our time.[7]

Diane Arbus In the postwar period, many photographers explored abstraction, but others embraced the medium's ability to reproduce faithfully the appearance of people, objects, and places. During the 1960s, the most famous photographer of people—with all their blemishes, both physical and psychological—was DIANE ARBUS (1923–1971). New York–born and –educated, Diane Nemerov married Allan Arbus when she was 18 and worked as a fashion photographer in the 1940s and 1950s. In the 1960s, however, she began photographing ordinary people living ordinary lives, people with physical deformities, and people at the margins of society, for example, transvestites—in short, people who rarely were the chosen subjects of professional photographers.

One of Arbus's most memorable photographs (FIG. **15-23**) is of a boy she encountered in New York City's Central Park in 1962 carrying a toy hand grenade. She asked him to stand still and pose for her, and as she moved around him searching

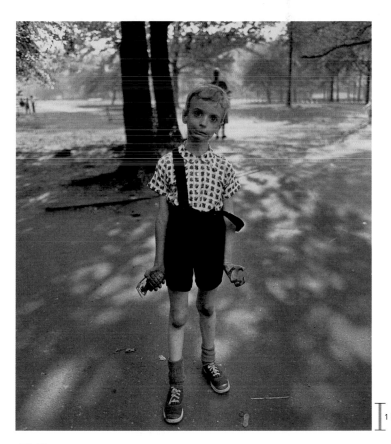

15-23 DIANE ARBUS, *Child with Toy Hand Grenade in Central Park, N.Y.C.,* 1962. Gelatin silver print, 1' 3½" × 1' 3". Metropolitan Museum of Art, New York (gift of Jennifer and Joseph Duke, 2001).

Arbus specialized in photographs of people on the margins of society. Her photograph of a boy holding a toy hand grenade in New York's Central Park presents him as a menacing, isolated personality.

Painting, Sculpture, and Photography   **437**

Judy Chicago on The Dinner Party

One of the acknowledged masterpieces of feminist art is Judy Chicago's *The Dinner Party* (FIG. 15-24), which required a team of nearly 400 to create and assemble. In 1979, Chicago published a book explaining the genesis and symbolism of the work.

[By 1974] I had discarded [my original] idea of painting a hundred abstract portraits on plates, each paying tribute to a different historic female figure. . . . In my research I realized over and over again that women's achievements had been left out of history . . . . My new idea was to try to symbolize this. . . . [I thought] about putting the plates on a table with silver, glasses, napkins, and tablecloths, and over the next year and a half the concept of *The Dinner Party* slowly evolved. I began to think about the piece as a reinterpreta-

tion of the Last Supper from the point of view of women, who, throughout history, had prepared the meals and set the table. In my "Last Supper," however, the women would be the honored guests. Their representation in the form of plates set on the table would express the way women had been confined, and the piece would thus reflect both women's achievements and their oppression. . . . My goal with *The Dinner Party* was . . . to forge a new kind of art expressing women's experience . . . . [It] seemed appropriate to relate our history through art, particularly through techniques traditionally associated with women—china-painting and needlework.*

*Judy Chicago, "The Dinner Party": A Symbol of Our Heritage (Garden City, N.Y.: Anchor Press, 1979), 11–12.

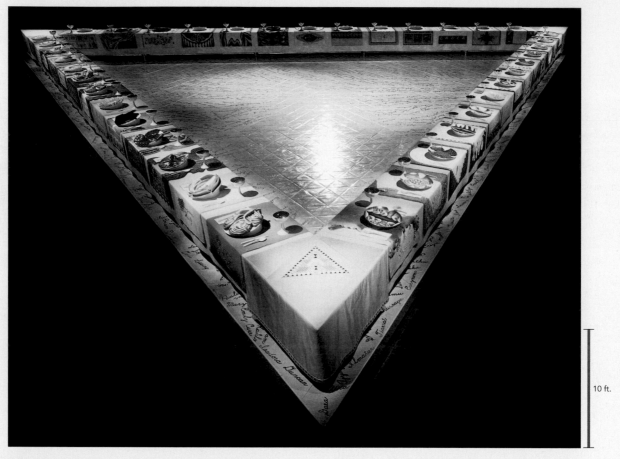

10 ft.

15-24 JUDY CHICAGO, *The Dinner Party,* 1979. Multimedia, including ceramics and stitchery, 48′ × 48′ × 48′. Brooklyn Museum, Brooklyn.

Chicago's *Dinner Party* honors 39 women from antiquity to the 20th century. The triangular form and the materials—painted china and fabric—are traditionally associated with women.

for the perfect angle, he became impatient, his body tensed, and his face formed a menacing expression. She snapped the shutter and recorded his peculiar grimace and eerie clawlike left hand. The empty space all around the boy contributes to the sense he is a disturbed personality isolated from society, in contrast to the "normal" family at the top right of the photograph.

Feminist Art

With the renewed interest in representation the Pop artists and Superrealists introduced in the 1960s and 1970s, painters and sculptors once again began to embrace the persuasive powers of art to communicate with a wide audience. In the 1970s, many artists began to investigate the social dynamics of power and privilege, especially in relation to gender, although racial, ethnic, and sexual orientation issues have also figured prominently in the art of recent decades (see Chapter 16).

Judy Chicago Women artists played a significant role in the feminist movement, which sought equal rights for women and focused attention on the subservient place of women in societies throughout history. Chicago native JUDY CHICAGO (Judy Cohen, b. 1939), a cofounder of the Feminist Art Program in California, was a leader of that movement. In the early 1970s, she began planning an ambitious piece, *The Dinner Party* (FIG. **15-24**), using craft techniques (such as china painting and needlework) traditionally practiced by women, to celebrate the achievements and contributions women made throughout history (see "Judy Chicago on *The Dinner Party*," page 438). She originally conceived the work as a feminist *Last Supper* for 13 "honored guests," as in the biblical account of Christ's passion, but at Chicago's table the guests are women instead of men. A witches' coven also comprises 13 women, and Chicago's *Dinner Party* additionally refers to witchcraft and the worship of the Mother Goddess. But because Chicago had uncovered so many worthy women in the course of her research, she tripled the number of guests and placed table settings for 39 women around a triangular table 48 feet long on each side. The triangular form refers to the ancient symbol for both woman and the Goddess. The notion of a dinner party also alludes to women's traditional role as homemakers.

The Dinner Party rests on a triangular white tile floor inscribed with the names of 999 additional women of achievement to signify that the accomplishments of the 39 honored guests rest on a foundation other women laid. Among those with place settings are American painter Georgia O'Keeffe (FIG. I-5), Egyptian pharaoh Hatshepsut (FIG. 1-30), British writer Virginia Woolf, Native American guide Sacajawea, and American suffragist Susan B. Anthony. Each woman's place has identical eating utensils and a goblet but features a unique oversized porcelain plate and a long placemat covered with imagery reflecting that woman's life and culture. The plates range from simple concave shapes with china-painted imagery to dishes whose sculptured three-dimensional designs almost seem to struggle to free themselves. The designs on each plate incorporate both butterfly and vulval motifs—the butterfly as the ancient symbol of liberation and the vulva as the symbol of female sexuality. Each placemat combines traditional needlework techniques, including needlepoint, embroidery, crochet, beading, patchwork, and appliqué.

Cindy Sherman After studying painting in Buffalo, CINDY SHERMAN (b. 1954) switched to photography as her primary means of expression. She addresses in her work how traditionally Western artists have presented female beauty for the enjoyment of the "male gaze," a primary focus of contemporary feminist theory, which explores gender as a socially constructed concept. Since 1977, Sherman has produced more than 80 black-and-white photographs called *Untitled Film*

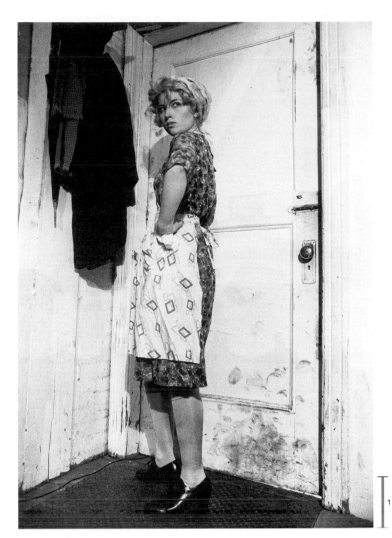

1 in.

15-25 CINDY SHERMAN, *Untitled Film Still #35*, 1979. Gelatin silver-print, 10" × 8". Private collection. 🎥

Sherman here assumed a role for one of a series of 80 photographs resembling film stills in which she addressed the way women have been presented in Western art for the enjoyment of the "male gaze."

Stills. She got the idea for the series after examining soft-core pornography magazines and noting the stereotypical ways they depicted women. She decided to produce photographs showing herself designing, acting in, directing, and photographing the works. In so doing, Sherman took control of her own image and constructed her own identity, a primary feminist concern. In *Untitled Film Still #35* (FIG. **15-25**), for example, Sherman appears in costume and wig in a photograph that seems to be a film still. Most of the images in this series recall popular film genres but are sufficiently generic that the viewer cannot relate them to specific movies. Sherman often reveals the constructed nature of these images with the shutter release cable she holds in her hand to take the pictures. (The cord runs across the floor in *#35*.) Although the artist is still the object of the viewer's gaze in these photographs, the identity is one she alone chose to assume.

Magdalena Abakanowicz Not strictly feminist in subject, but created using materials traditionally associated with women, are the sculptures of Polish fiber artist MAGDALENA

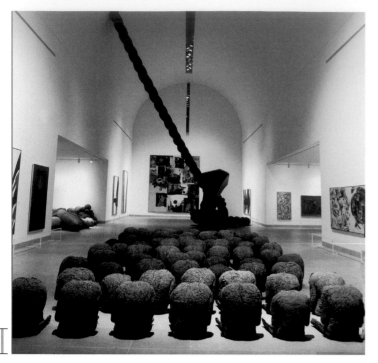

15-26 Magdalena Abakanowicz, *80 Backs,* 1976–1980. Burlap and resin, each 2′ 3″ high. Museum of Modern Art, Dallas. © Magdalena Abakanowicz/Licensed by VAGA, New York.

Polish fiber artist Abakanowicz explored the stoic, everyday toughness of the human spirit in this group of nearly identical sculptures that serve as symbols of distinctive individuals lost in the crowd.

ABAKANOWICZ (b. 1930). A leader in the exploration of the expressive powers of weaving techniques in large-scale artworks, Abakanowicz gained fame with experimental freestanding figural works expressing the stoic, everyday toughness of the human spirit. For Abakanowicz, fiber materials are deeply symbolic:

> I see fiber as the basic element constructing the organic world on our planet, as the greatest mystery of our environment. It is from fiber that all living organisms are built—the tissues of plants and ourselves. . . . Fabric is our covering and our attire. Made with our hands, it is a record of our souls.[8]

Abakanowicz's sculptures are to a great degree reflections of her early life experiences as a member of an aristocratic family disturbed by the dislocations of World War II and its aftermath. Best known for her works based on human forms, she multiplies each form for exhibition in groups as symbols for the individual in society, lost in the crowd yet retaining some distinctiveness. This impression is especially powerful in *80 Backs* (FIG. **15-26**). Abakanowicz made each piece by pressing layers of natural organic fibers into a plaster mold. Every sculpture depicts the slumping shoulders, back, and arms of a figure of indeterminate sex and rests legless directly on the floor. The repeated pose of the figures in *80 Backs* suggests meditation, submission, and anticipation. Although made from a single mold, the figures achieve a touching sense of individuality because each assumed a slightly different posture as the material dried and because the artist imprinted a different pattern of fiber texture on each.

ARCHITECTURE AND SITE-SPECIFIC ART

Some of the most innovative architects of the first half of the 20th century, most notably Frank Lloyd Wright (FIG. 14-42), Le Corbusier (FIG. 14-40), and Ludwig Mies van der Rohe (FIG. 14-39), concluded their long and productive careers in the postwar period. At the same time, younger architects rose to international prominence, some working in the modernist idiom but others taking architectural design in new "postmodern" directions.

Modernism

In parallel with the progressive postwar movement toward formal abstraction in painting and sculpture, modernist architects stressed formalist simplicity in buildings adhering to a rigid geometry as well as buildings featuring organic sculptural qualities.

Frank Lloyd Wright The last great building Frank Lloyd Wright designed was the Solomon R. Guggenheim Museum (FIG. **15-27**) in New York City. Using reinforced concrete almost as a sculptor might use resilient clay, Wright, who often described his architecture as "organic," designed a structure inspired by the spiral of a snail's shell. The shape of the shell expands toward the top, and a winding interior ramp (FIG. 16-22) spirals to connect the gallery bays. A skylight strip embedded in the museum's outer wall provides illumination to the ramp, which visitors can stroll up or down, viewing the artworks displayed along the gently sloping pathway. Thick walls and the solid organic shape give the building, outside and inside, the sense of turning in on itself, and the long interior viewing area opening onto a 90-foot central well of space creates a sheltered environment, secure from the bustling city outside.

Le Corbusier Completed in 1955 at Ronchamp, France, Le Corbusier's Notre-Dame-du-Haut (FIG. **15-28**) is an organic fusion of architecture and sculpture, and a testament to the boundless creativity of this great architect. The monumental impression of this small pilgrimage chapel seen from afar is deceptive. Although one massive exterior wall contains a pulpit facing a spacious outdoor area for large-scale open-air services on holy days, the interior holds at most 200 people. The intimate scale, stark and heavy walls, and mysterious illumination (jewel tones cast from deeply recessed stained-glass windows) give this space an aura reminiscent of a sacred cave.

Notre-Dame-du-Haut's structure may look free-form at first, but Le Corbusier based it, as did the designers of late medieval cathedrals, on an underlying mathematical system. The church has a frame of steel and metal mesh, which the builders sprayed with concrete and painted white, except for two interior private chapel niches with colored walls and the roof, which Le Corbusier wished to have darken naturally

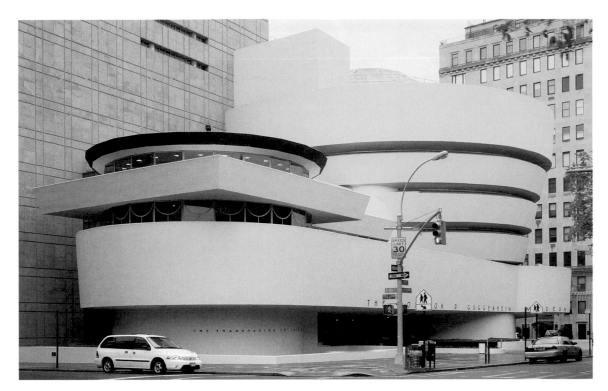

15-27 FRANK LLOYD WRIGHT, Solomon R. Guggenheim Museum (looking southeast), New York, 1943–1959. ■◀

Using reinforced concrete almost as a sculptor might use resilient clay, Wright designed a snail shell–shaped museum with a winding, gently inclined interior ramp for the display of artworks.

with the passage of time. The preliminary sketches for the building indicate Le Corbusier linked the design with the shape of praying hands, with the wings of a dove (representing both peace and the Holy Spirit), and with the prow of a ship (a reminder the term for the central aisle in a basilican church is *nave*—Latin for "ship"). The architect hoped that in the mystical interior he created and in the rolling hills around the chapel, worshipers would reflect on the sacred and the natural. No one who has visited Notre-Dame-du-Haut, whether on a bright sunlit day or in a thundering storm, has come away unmoved.

Mies van der Rohe In contrast to the sculpturesque postwar idiom of Wright and Le Corbusier, other modernist architects created massive, sleek, and geometrically rigid buildings, following Bauhaus architect Ludwig Mies van der Rohe's contention that "less is more" (see page 417). Many of these more Minimalist designs are heroic presences in the

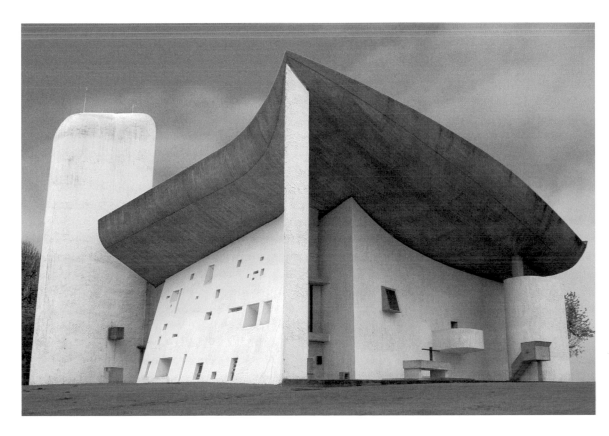

15-28 LE CORBUSIER, Notre-Dame-du-Haut (looking northwest), Ronchamp, France, 1950–1955. ■◀

The organic forms of Le Corbusier's mountaintop chapel present a fusion of architecture and sculpture. The architect based the shapes on praying hands, a dove's wings, and a ship's prow.

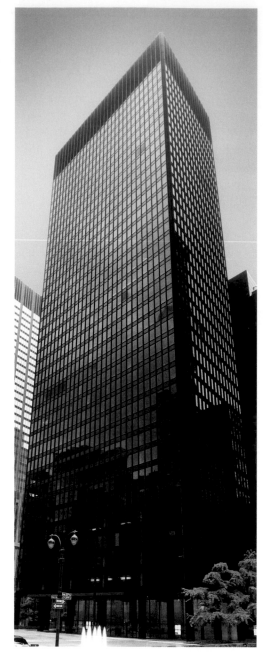

15-29 Ludwig Mies van der Rohe and Philip Johnson, Seagram Building (looking northeast), New York, 1956–1958. ◼◀

Massive, sleek, and geometrically rigid, this modernist skyscraper has a bronze-and-glass skin that masks its concrete-and-steel frame. The giant corporate tower appears to rise from the pavement on stilts.

it appear to have a glass skin, interrupted only by the thin strips of bronze anchoring the windows. The bronze strips and the amber glass windows give the tower a richness found in few of its neighbors.

Postmodernism

The impersonality and sterility of many modernist structures eventually led to a rejection of modernism's authority in architecture, ushering in *postmodernism,* one of the most dramatic developments in later-20th-century architecture as well as in contemporary painting and sculpture (see Chapter 16). Postmodernism in architecture is not a unified style. In contrast to the simplicity of modernist architecture, postmodern architecture is complex, pluralistic, and eclectic. Whereas the modernist program was reductive, the postmodern vocabulary of the 1970s and 1980s was expansive and inclusive. Among the first to explore this new direction in architecture were Jane Jacobs (1916–2006) and Robert Venturi (b. 1925). In their influential books *The Death and Life of Great American Cities* (Jacobs, 1961) and *Complexity and Contradiction in Architecture* (Venturi, 1966), Jacobs and Venturi argued that the uniformity and anonymity of modernist architecture (in particular, the corporate skyscrapers dominating many urban skylines) were unsuited to human social interaction and that diversity is the great advantage of urban life. Postmodern architects accepted, indeed embraced, the messy and chaotic nature of big-city life. When designing these varied buildings, many postmodern architects consciously selected past architectural elements or references and juxtaposed them with contemporary elements or fashioned them of high-tech materials, thereby creating a dialogue between past and present. Postmodern architecture incorporates not only traditional architectural references but references to mass culture and popular imagery as well.

Michael Graves The Portland Building (FIG. **15-30**) by Indianapolis-born architect MICHAEL GRAVES (b. 1934) reasserts the wall's horizontality against the verticality of modernist skyscrapers. Graves favored the square's solidity and stability, making it the main body of his composition (echoed in the windows), which rests on a wider base and carries a set-back penthouse crown. Narrow vertical windows tying together seven stories open two paired facades. These support capital-like large hoods on one pair of opposite facades and a frieze of stylized Baroque roundels tied by bands on the other pair. A huge painted keystone motif joins five upper levels on one facade pair, and painted surfaces further define the building's base, body, and penthouse levels. The modernist purist surely would not welcome the ornamental wall, color painting, or symbolic references. These features, taken together, raised a storm of criticism. Various critics denounced Graves's Portland Building as "an enlarged jukebox" and an "oversized Christmas package," but others approvingly noted its classical references as constituting a "symbolic temple" and praised the building as a courageous architectural adventure. Whatever history's verdict will be, the Portland Building

urban landscape that effectively symbolize the giant corporations they often house. The purest example of these corporate skyscrapers is the rectilinear glass-and-bronze Seagram Building (FIG. **15-29**) in Manhattan, designed by Mies van der Rohe and American architect PHILIP JOHNSON (1906–2005). By the mid-1950s, the steel-and-glass towers pioneered by Louis Sullivan (FIG. 13-21) and carried further by Mies van der Rohe himself (FIG. 14-39) had become a familiar sight in cities throughout the world. Appealing in its structural logic and clarity, the style, easily imitated, quickly became the norm for postwar commercial high-rise buildings. The architects of the Seagram Building deliberately designed it as a thin shaft, leaving the front quarter of its midtown site as an open pedestrian plaza. The tower appears to rise from the pavement on stilts. Glass walls even surround the recessed lobby. The building's recessed structural elements make tect RENZO PIANO (b. 1937) used motifs and techniques from ordinary industrial buildings in their design for the Georges Pompidou National Center of Art and Culture (FIG. **15-31**) in Paris. The architects fully exposed the anatomy of this six-level building, which is a kind of updated version of the Crystal Palace (FIG. 12-25), and made its "metabolism" visible. They color-coded pipes, ducts, tubes, and corridors according to function (red for the movement of people, green for water, blue for air-conditioning, and yellow for electricity), much as in a sophisticated factory. Critics who deplore the building's vernacular qualities disparagingly refer to the complex as a "cultural supermarket" and point out that its exposed entrails require excessive maintenance to protect them from the elements. Nevertheless, the Pompidou Center has been popular with visitors since it opened. The flexible interior spaces and the colorful structural body provide a festive environment for the crowds flowing through the building enjoying its art galleries, industrial design center, library, science and music centers, conference rooms, research and archival facilities, movie theaters, rest areas, and restaurant (which looks down and through the building), as well as dramatic panoramas of Paris from its terrace.

Environmental and Site-Specific Art

One of the most exciting developments in postwar art and architecture has been *Environmental Art,* which stands at the intersection of architecture and sculpture. Environmental Art, sometimes called *earthworks,* emerged in the 1960s and includes a wide range of artworks, most of which are *site-specific* (created for a unique location). Many artists associated with the movement also use natural or organic materials, including the land itself. It is no coincidence that this art form developed during a period of increased concern for the environment. The ecology movement of the 1960s and

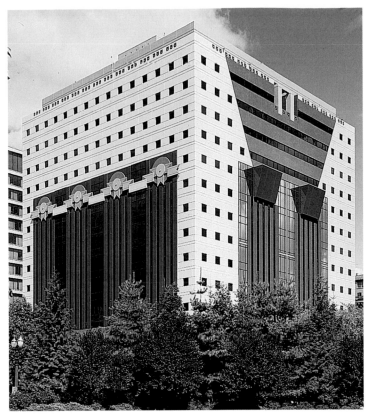

15-30 MICHAEL GRAVES, Portland Building (looking northwest), Portland, Oregon, 1980.

In this early example of postmodern architecture, Graves reasserted the horizontality and solidity of the wall. He drew attention to the mural surfaces through polychromy and ornamental motifs.

is an early marker of postmodernist innovation that borrowed from the lively, garish language of pop culture.

Rogers and Piano During their short-lived partnership, British architect RICHARD ROGERS (b. 1933) and Italian archi-

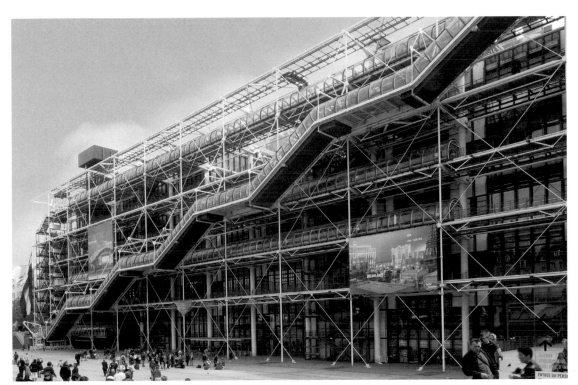

15-31 RICHARD ROGERS and RENZO PIANO, Georges Pompidou National Center of Art and Culture (looking northeast), Paris, France, 1977. ◼◀

Rogers and Piano fully exposed the anatomy of this six-level building, as in the century-earlier Crystal Palace (FIG. 12-25), and color-coded the internal parts according to function, as in a factory.

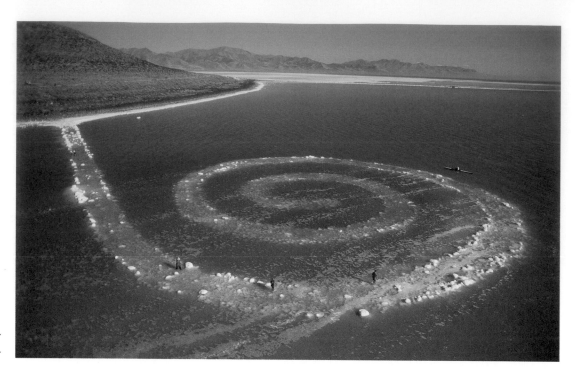

15-32 ROBERT SMITHSON, *Spiral Jetty* (looking northeast), Great Salt Lake, Utah, 1970. © Estate of Robert Smithson/Licensed by VAGA, New York. ◼◣

Smithson used industrial equipment to create Environmental artworks by manipulating earth and rock. *Spiral Jetty* is a mammoth spiral of black basalt, limestone, and earth extending into Great Salt Lake.

1970s aimed to publicize and combat escalating pollution, depletion of natural resources, and the dangers of toxic waste. The problems of public aesthetics (for example, litter, urban sprawl, and compromised scenic areas) were also at issue. Widespread concern about the environment led to the passage of the National Environmental Policy Act in 1969 and the creation of the federal Environmental Protection Agency. Environmental artists use their art to call attention to the landscape and, in so doing, are an important part of this national dialogue.

As an innovative art form challenging traditional assumptions about art making, Environmental Art clearly had an avant-garde, progressive dimension. But as Pop artists did, Environmental artists insist on moving art out of the rarefied atmosphere of museums and galleries and into the public sphere. Most encourage spectator interaction with their works. Ironically, the remote locations of many earthworks have limited public access.

Robert Smithson One of the pioneering Environmental artists was New Jersey–born ROBERT SMITHSON (1938–1973), who used industrial construction equipment to manipulate vast quantities of earth and rock on isolated sites. Smithson's best-known project is *Spiral Jetty* (FIG. **15-32**), a mammoth coil of black basalt, limestone rocks, and earth extending out into Great Salt Lake in Utah. As he was driving by the lake one day, Smithson came across some abandoned mining equipment, left there by a company that had tried and failed to extract oil from the site. Smithson saw this as a testament to the enduring power of nature and to the inability of humans to conquer it. He decided to create an artwork in the lake that ultimately became a monumental spiral curving out from the shoreline and running 1,500 linear feet into the water. Smithson insisted on designing his work in response to the location itself. He wanted to avoid the arrogance of an artist merely imposing an unrelated concept on the site. The spiral idea grew from Smithson's first impression of the location. Then, while researching Great Salt Lake, Smithson discovered that the molecular structure of the salt crystals coating the rocks at the water's edge is spiral in form.

> As I looked at the site, it reverberated out to the horizons only to suggest an immobile cyclone while flickering light made the entire landscape appear to quake. A dormant earthquake spread into the fluttering stillness, into a spinning sensation without movement. The site was a rotary that enclosed itself in an immense roundness. From that gyrating space emerged the possibility of the Spiral Jetty.[9]

PERFORMANCE AND CONCEPTUAL ART AND NEW MEDIA

Environmental art, although a singular artistic phenomenon, typifies postwar developments in the art world in redefining the nature of an "artwork" and expanding the range of works artists and the public at large consider "art." Some of the new types of artworks are the result of the invention of new media, such as computers and video cameras. But the new art forms also reflect avant-garde artists' continued questioning of the status quo.

Performance Art

One of the new artistic genres is *Performance Art*. Performance artists replace traditional stationary artworks with movements, gestures, and sounds performed before an audience, whose members sometimes participate in the performance. The informal and spontaneous events Performance artists staged anticipated the rebellion and youthful exuberance of the 1960s and at first pushed art outside the confines of mainstream art institutions (museums and galleries). Performance Art also served as an antidote to the pretentiousness of most traditional art objects and challenged art's function as a commodity. In the later 1960s, however, museums commissioned performances with increasing frequency, thereby neutralizing much of the subversiveness characteristic of this new art form.

Carolee Schneemann Born in Pennsylvania, CAROLEE SCHNEEMANN (b. 1939) settled in New York City in 1962, where she became one of the pioneering Performance artists of the 1960s. In notes she wrote in 1962–1963, Schneemann reflected on the nature of art production and contrasted her kinetic works with more traditional art forms.

> Environments, happenings—concretions—are an extension of my painting-constructions which often have moving (motorized) sections. . . . [But, the] steady exploration and repeated viewing which the eye is required to make with my painting-constructions is reversed in the performance situation where the spectator is overwhelmed with changing recognitions, carried emotionally by a flux of evocative actions and led or held by the specified time sequence which marks the duration of a performance. In this way the audience is actually *visually* more *passive* than when confronting a . . . "still" work . . . With paintings, constructions and sculptures the viewers are able to carry out repeated examinations of the work, to select and vary viewing positions (to walk with the eye), to touch surfaces and to freely indulge responses to areas of color and texture at their chosen speed.[10]

Schneemann's self-described "kinetic theater" radically transformed the nature of Performance art by introducing a feminist dimension through the use of her body (often nude) to challenge gender stereotypes. In her 1964 performance, *Meat Joy* (FIG. **15-33**), Schneemann reveled in the taste, smell, and feel of raw sausages, chickens, and fish.

Conceptual Art

The relentless challenges to artistic convention fundamental to the historical avant-garde reached a logical conclusion with *Conceptual Art* in the late 1960s. Conceptual artists maintained that the "artfulness" of art lay in the artist's idea, rather than in its final expression. These artists regarded the idea, or concept, as the defining component of the artwork. Indeed, some Conceptual artists eliminated the object altogether.

Joseph Kosuth Toledo, Ohio, native JOSEPH KOSUTH (b. 1945) was one of the early proponents of Conceptual Art. His work operates at the intersection of language and vision, dealing with the relationship between the abstract and the concrete. For example, in *One and Three Chairs* (FIG. **15-34**) Kosuth juxtaposed a real chair, a full-scale photograph of the same chair, and an enlarged reproduction of a dictionary definition of the word *chair*. By so doing, the Conceptual

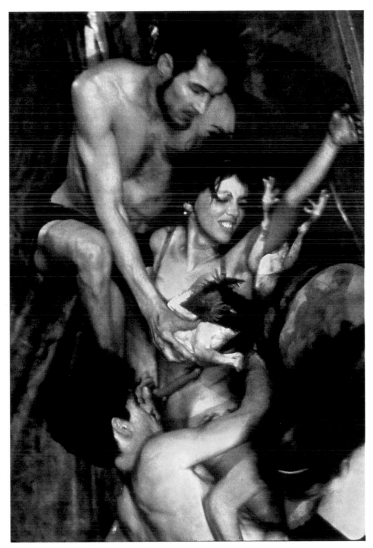

15-33 CAROLEE SCHNEEMANN, *Meat Joy* (performance at Judson Church, New York City), 1964.

In her performances, Schneemann transformed the nature of Performance Art by introducing a feminist dimension through the use of her body (often nude) to challenge traditional gender roles.

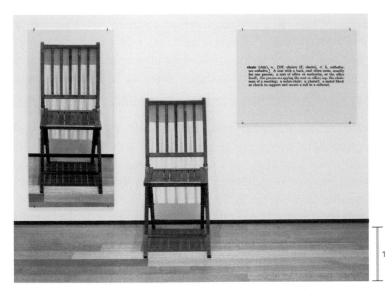

1 ft.

15-34 JOSEPH KOSUTH, *One and Three Chairs*, 1965. Wooden folding chair, photographic copy of a chair, and photographic enlargement of a dictionary definition of *chair*; chair, 2′ 8⅜″ × 1′ 2⅞″ × 1′ 8⅞″; photo panel, 3′ × 2′ ⅛″; text panel, 2′ × 2′ ⅛″. Museum of Modern Art, New York (Larry Aldrich Foundation Fund).

Conceptual artists regard the concept as an artwork's defining component. To portray "chairness," Kosuth juxtaposed a chair, a photograph of the chair, and a dictionary definition of *chair*.

artist asked viewers to ponder the notion of what constitutes "chairness." He explained:

> Like everyone else I inherited the idea of art as a set of *formal* problems. . . . [T]he radical shift was in changing the idea of art itself. . . . It meant you could have an art work which was that *idea* of an art work, and its formal components weren't important. I felt I had found a way to make art without formal components being confused for an expressionist composition. The expression was in the idea, not the form—the forms were only a device in the service of the idea.[11]

Conceptual artists such as Kosuth challenge the very premises of artistic production, pushing art's boundaries to a point where no concrete definition of *art* is possible.

New Media

During the 1960s and 1970s, many avant-garde artists eagerly embraced technologies previously unavailable in their attempt to find new avenues of artistic expression. Among the most popular new media were video recording and computer graphics. Initially, only commercial television studios possessed video equipment, but in the 1960s, with the development of relatively inexpensive portable video recorders and of electronic devices allowing manipulation of recorded video material, artists began to explore in earnest the expressive possibilities of this new technology. In its basic form, video recording involves a special motion-picture camera that captures visible images and translates them into electronic data for display on a video monitor or television screen. Video pictures resemble photographs in the amount of detail they contain, but a video image consists of a series of points of light on a grid. Viewers looking at television or video art are not aware of the monitor's surface. Instead, fulfilling the ideal of Renaissance artists, they concentrate on the image and look through the glass surface, as through a window, into the "space" beyond. Video images combine the optical realism of photography with the sense that the subjects move in real time in a deep space "inside" the monitor.

Nam June Paik When video introduced the possibility of manipulating subjects in real time, artists such as Korean-born NAM JUNE PAIK (1932–2006) were eager to work with the medium. After studying music performance, art history, and Eastern philosophy in Korea and Japan, Paik worked with electronic music in Germany in the late 1950s. In 1965, after relocating to New York City, Paik acquired the first inexpensive video recorder sold in Manhattan (the Sony Porta-Pak) and immediately recorded everything he saw out the window of his taxi on the return trip to his studio downtown. Experience acquired as artist-in-residence at television stations WGBH in Boston and WNET in New York enabled him to experiment with the most advanced broadcast video technology.

Paik collaborated with the gifted Japanese engineer-inventor Shuya Abe (b. 1932) in developing a video synthe-

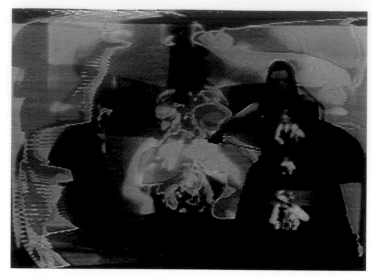

15-35 NAM JUNE PAIK, video still from *Global Groove,* 1973. Color videotape, sound, 30 minutes. Collection of the artist. ◼◀

Korean-born video artist Paik's best-known work is a cascade of fragmented sequences of performances and commercials intended as a sample of the rich worldwide television menu of the future.

sizer. This instrument enables artists to manipulate and change electronic video information in various ways, causing images or parts of images to stretch, shrink, change color, or break up. With the synthesizer, artists can also layer images, inset one image into another, or merge images from various cameras with those from video recorders to make a single visual kaleidoscopic "time-collage." This kind of compositional freedom enabled Paik to combine his interests in painting, music, Eastern philosophy, global politics for survival, humanized technology, and cybernetics. Paik called his video works "physical music" and said his musical background enabled him to understand time better than could video artists trained only in painting or sculpture.

Paik's best-known video work, *Global Groove* (FIG. **15-35**), combines in quick succession fragmented sequences of female tap dancers, poet Allen Ginsberg (1926–1997) reading his work, a performance by cellist Charlotte Moorman (1933–1991) using a man's back as her instrument, Pepsi-Cola commercials from Japanese television, Korean drummers, and a shot of the Living Theatre group performing a controversial piece called *Paradise Now.* Commissioned originally for broadcast over the United Nations satellite, the cascade of imagery in *Global Groove* gives viewers a glimpse of the rich worldwide television menu Paik predicted would be available in the future—a prediction that has been fulfilled with the advent of affordable cable and satellite television service.

After 1980 The decades following the conclusion of World War II were unparalleled in the history of art through the ages for innovation in form and content and for the development of new media. Those exciting trends have continued unabated since 1980—and with an increasingly international dimension that will be explored in Chapter 16.

Modernism and Postmodernism in Europe and America, 1945 to 1980

Painting, Sculpture, and Photography

▌ The art of the decades following World War II reflects cultural upheaval—the rejection of traditional values, the civil rights and feminist movements, and the new consumer society.

▌ The first major postwar avant-garde art movement was Abstract Expressionism, which championed an artwork's formal elements rather than its subject. Gestural abstractionists, such as Pollock and de Kooning, sought expressiveness through energetically applied pigment. Chromatic abstractionists, such as Rothko, struck emotional chords through large areas of pure color.

▌ Post-Painterly Abstraction promoted a cool rationality in contrast to Abstract Expressionism's passion. Both hard-edge painters, such as Stella, and color-field painters, such as Frankenthaler, pursued purity in art by emphasizing the flatness of pigment on canvas.

▌ Pop artists, such as Johns, Lichtenstein, and Warhol, turned away from abstraction to the representation of subjects grounded in popular culture—flags, comic strips, Coca-Cola bottles—sometimes employing commercial printing techniques.

▌ Riley and other Op artists sought to produce optical illusions of motion and depth using only geometric forms on two-dimensional surfaces.

▌ Superrealists, such as Flack, Close, and Hanson—kindred spirits to Pop artists in many ways—created paintings and sculptures featuring scrupulous fidelity to optical fact.

▌ The leading sculptural movement of this period was Minimalism. Judd created artworks consisting of simple and unadorned geometric shapes to underscore the "objecthood" of his sculptures.

▌ Many artists pursued social agendas in their work. Postwar feminist artists include Chicago, whose *Dinner Party* honors important women throughout history and features crafts traditionally associated with women, and Sherman, who explored the "male gaze" in her photographs resembling film stills.

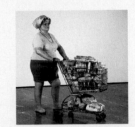

Pollock, *Lavender Mist*, 1950

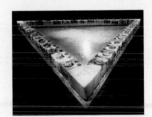

Hanson, *Supermarket Shopper*, 1970

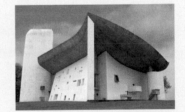

Chicago, *Dinner Party*, 1979

Architecture and Site-Specific Art

▌ Some of the leading early-20th-century modernist architects remained active after 1945. Wright built the snail-shell Guggenheim Museum, Le Corbusier the sculpturesque Notre-Dame-du-Haut, and Mies van der Rohe the Minimalist Seagram skyscraper.

▌ In contrast to modernist architecture, postmodern architecture is complex and eclectic and often incorporates references to historical styles. A pioneering postmodern project was Graves's Portland Building, which incorporates classical and Baroque motifs.

▌ Site-specific art stands at the intersection of architecture and sculpture. Smithson's *Spiral Jetty* is a mammoth coil of natural materials in Utah's Great Salt Lake.

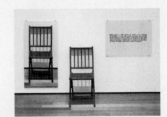

Le Corbusier, Notre-Dame-du-Haut, Ronchamp, 1950–1955

Performance and Conceptual Art and New Media

▌ Among the most significant developments in the art world after World War II has been the expansion of the range of works considered "art."

▌ Performance artists, such as Schneemann, replace traditional stationary artworks with movements and sounds performed before an audience. Performance Art often addresses the same social and political issues that contemporaneous painters and sculptors explore.

▌ Kosuth and other Conceptual artists believe the "artfulness" of art is in the artist's idea, not the work resulting from the idea.

▌ Paik and others have embraced video recording technology to produce artworks combining images and sounds.

Kosuth, *One and Three Chairs*, 1965

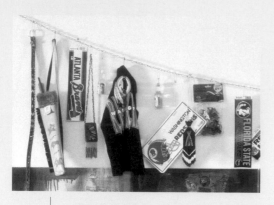

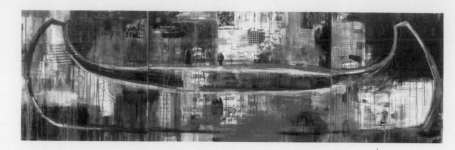

Smith's mixed-media canvases celebrate her Native American identity. Above the painting, as if hung from a clothesline, are cheap trinkets she proposes to trade for the return of confiscated land.

Overlapping the collage and the central motif of the canoe in Smith's anti-Columbus Quincentenary Celebration is dripping red paint, symbolic of the shedding of Native American blood.

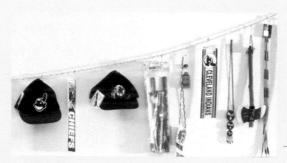

The sports teams represented in *Trade* all have American Indian-derived names, reminding viewers of the vocal opposition to these names and to practices such as the Atlanta Braves' "tomahawk chop."

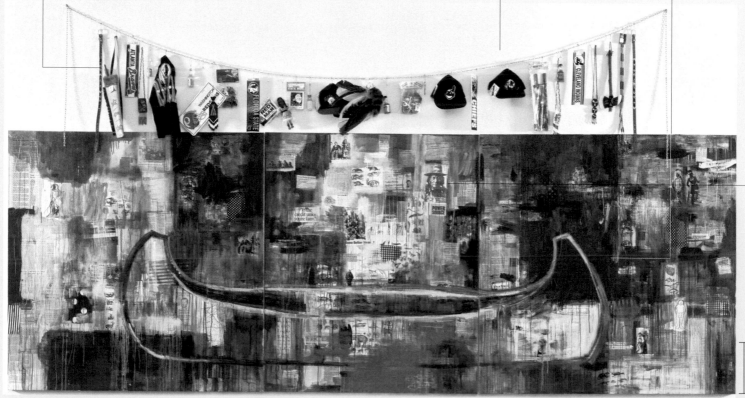

1 ft.

16-1 JAUNE QUICK-TO-SEE SMITH, *Trade* (*Gifts for Trading Land with White People*), 1992. Oil and mixed media on canvas, 5′ × 14′ 2″. Chrysler Museum of Art, Norfolk.

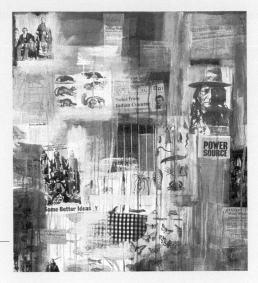

Newspaper clippings chronicle the conquest of Native America by Europeans and include references to the problems facing those living on reservations today—poverty, alcoholism, disease.

Contemporary Art Worldwide

ART AS SOCIOPOLITICAL MESSAGE

Although televisions, cell phones, and the Internet have brought people all over the world closer together than ever before in history, national, ethnic, religious, and racial conflicts are unfortunate and unavoidable facts of contemporary life. Some of the most eloquent voices raised in protest about the major political and social issues of the day have been those of painters and sculptors, who can harness the power of art to amplify the power of the written and spoken word.

JAUNE QUICK-TO-SEE SMITH (b. 1940) is a Native American artist descended from the Shoshone, Salish, and Cree peoples. Raised on the Flatrock Reservation in Montana, she is steeped in the traditional culture of her ancestors, but she trained as an artist in the European American tradition at Framingham State College in Massachusetts and at the University of New Mexico. Smith's ethnic heritage has always informed her art, however, and her concern about the invisibility of Native American artists has led her to organize exhibitions of their art. Her self-identity has also been the central theme of her mature work as an artist.

In 1992, Smith created what many critics consider her masterpiece: *Trade* (FIG. **16-1**), subtitled *Gifts for Trading Land with White People*. A complex multimedia work of monumental size, *Trade* is Smith's response to what she called "the Quincentenary Non-Celebration," that is, White America's celebration of the 500th anniversary of Christopher Columbus's arrival in what Europeans called the New World. *Trade* combines collage elements and attached objects, reminiscent of a Rauschenberg combine (FIG. 15-16), with energetic brushwork recalling de Kooning's Abstract Expressionist canvases (FIG. 15-6) and clippings from Native American newspapers. The clippings include images chronicling the conquest of Native America by Europeans and references to the problems facing those living on reservations today—poverty, alcoholism, disease. The dripping red paint overlaying the collage with the central motif of the canoe is symbolic of the shedding of Native American blood.

Above the painting, as if hung from a clothesline, is an array of objects. These include Native American artifacts, such as beaded belts and feather headdresses, plastic tomahawks and "Indian princess" dolls, and contemporary sports memorabilia from teams with American Indian-derived names—the Cleveland Indians, Atlanta Braves, and Washington Redskins. The inclusion of these objects reminds viewers of the vocal opposition to the use of these and similar names for high school and college as well as professional sports teams. All the cheap artifacts together also have a deeper significance. As the title indicates and Smith explained:

> Why won't you consider trading the land we handed over to you for these silly trinkets that so honor us? Sound like a bad deal? Well, that's the deal you gave us.[1]

SOCIAL AND POLITICAL ART

Jaune Quick-to-See Smith's *Trade* (FIG. 16-1) is the unique product of the artist's heritage as a Native American who has sought to bridge native and European artistic traditions, but her work parallels that of many other innovative artists of the decades since 1980 in addressing contemporary social and political issues. This focus on the content and meaning of art represents, as did the earlier work of the Pop artists and Superrealists (see Chapter 15), a rejection of modernist formalist doctrine and a desire on the part of artists once again to embrace the persuasive powers of art to communicate with a wide audience.

Postmodernism The rejection of the principles underlying modernism is a central element in the diverse phenomenon in art, as in architecture, known as postmodernism (see page 422). No simple definition of *postmodernism* is possible, but it represents the erosion of the boundaries between high culture and popular culture—a separation Clement Greenberg and the modernists had staunchly defended.

For many contemporary artists, postmodernism involves examining the process by which meaning is generated and the negotiation or dialogue that transpires between viewers and artworks. This kind of examination of the nature of art parallels the literary field of study known as critical theory. Critical theorists view art and architecture, as well as literature and the other humanities, as a culture's intellectual products or "constructs." These constructs unconsciously suppress or conceal the real premises informing the culture, primarily the values of those politically in control. Thus, cultural products function in an ideological capacity, obscuring, for example, racist or sexist attitudes. When revealed by analysis, the facts behind these constructs, according to critical theorists, contribute to a more substantial understanding of artworks, buildings, books, and the overall culture.

Many critical theorists use an analytical strategy called *deconstruction,* after a method developed by French intellectuals in the 1960s and 1970s. In deconstruction theory, all cultural contexts are "texts." Critical theorists who employ this approach seek to uncover—to deconstruct—the facts of power, privilege, and prejudice underlying the practices and institutions of any given culture. In so doing, scholars can reveal the precariousness of structures and systems, such as language and cultural practices, along with the assumptions underlying them. Critical theorists do not agree upon any single philosophy or analytical method because in principle they oppose firm definitions. They do share a healthy suspicion of all traditional truth claims and value standards, all hierarchical authority and institutions. For them, deconstruction means destabilizing established meanings, definitions, and interpretations while encouraging subjectivity and individual differences.

Indeed, if there is any common denominator in the art of the decades since 1980, it is precisely the absence of any common denominator. Diversity of style and content and the celebration of individual personalities, backgrounds, and approaches to art are central to the notion of postmodern art. The art of the 1980s and 1990s and of the opening decades of the 21st century is worldwide in scope, encompasses both abstraction and realism, and addresses a wide range of contemporary social and political issues.

Social Art: Gender and Sexuality

Many artists who have embraced the postmodern interest in investigating the dynamics of power and privilege have focused on issues of gender and sexuality in the contemporary world.

Barbara Kruger In the 1970s, some feminist artists, chief among them Cindy Sherman (FIG. 15-25), explored the "male gaze" and the culturally constructed notion of gender in their art. BARBARA KRUGER (b. 1945), who studied in New York under Diane Arbus (FIG. 15-23), examines similar issues in her photographs. The strategies and techniques of contemporary mass media fascinate Kruger, who was the art director of *Mademoiselle* magazine in the late 1960s. In *Untitled*

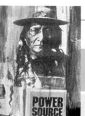

Contemporary Art Worldwide

1980	1990	2000
Social and political issues—gender and sexuality, ethnic, religious, and national identity—figure prominently in the art of Kruger, Mapplethorpe, Ringgold, Basquiat, and many others	Artworks addressing pressing political and social issues continue to be produced in great numbers by, among others, Quick-to-See Smith, Sikander, Bester, and Neshat	Modern, postmodern, and traditional art forms coexist today in the increasingly interconnected worldwide art scene as artists on all continents work with age-old materials and also experiment with the new media of digital photography, computer graphics, and video
Foster and Rogers are the leading proponents of High-Tech architecture, which incorporates advanced engineering and technology	Saville, Kiki Smith, and others revive realistic figure painting and sculpture as vital components of the contemporary art scene	
Lin's Vietnam Veterans Memorial and exhibitions of the work of Mapplethorpe and Ofili become lightning rods for debate over public financing of art	Deconstructivism (Gehry) and green architecture (Piano) emerge as major architectural movements	

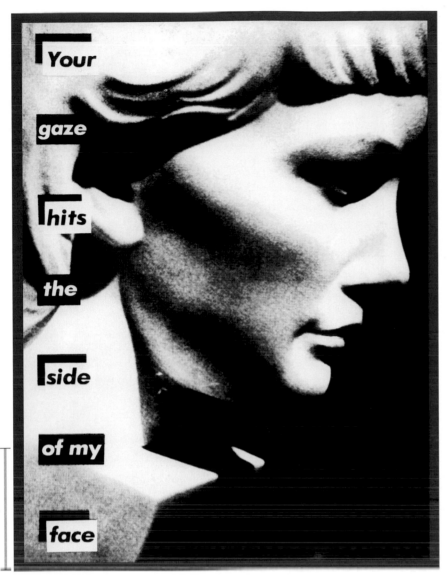

1 ft.

16-2 BARBARA KRUGER, *Untitled* (*Your Gaze Hits the Side of My Face*), 1981. Photograph, red painted frame, 4′ 7″ × 3′ 5″. Courtesy Mary Boone Gallery, New York. ◼◂

Kruger has explored the "male gaze" in her art. Using the layout techniques of mass media, she constructed this word-and-photograph collage to challenge culturally constructed notions of gender.

Robert Mapplethorpe For many artists, their homosexuality is as important—or even more important—an element of their personal identity as their gender, ethnicity, or race. One brilliant gay artist who became the central figure in a heated debate in the halls of the US Congress as well as among the public at large was lifelong New Yorker ROBERT MAPPLETHORPE (1946–1989). Mapplethorpe's *The Perfect Moment* traveling exhibition, funded in part by the National Endowment for the Arts, featured his photographs of flowers and people, many nude, some depicting children, some homoerotic and sadomasochistic in nature. The show led to a landmark court case in Cincinnati on freedom of expression for artists and prompted new legislation establishing restrictions on government funding of the arts (see "Public Funding of Controversial Art," page 452).

Never at issue was Mapplethorpe's technical mastery of the photographic medium. His gelatin silver prints have glowing textures with rich tonal gradations of black, gray, and white. In many ways, Mapplethorpe was the heir of Edward Weston, whose innovative compositions of still lifes (FIG. 14-20) and nudes helped establish photography as an art form on a par with painting and sculpture. What shocked the public was not nudity per se—a traditional subject with roots in antiquity—but the openly gay character of many of Mapplethorpe's images. *The Perfect Moment* photographs included, in addition to some very graphic images of homosexual men, a series of self-portraits documenting Mapplethorpe's changing appearance almost up until he died from AIDS only months after the show opened in Philadelphia in December 1988. The self-portrait reproduced here (FIG. 16-3) presents Mapplethorpe as an androgynous young man with long hair and makeup, confronting the viewer with a steady gaze. Mapplethorpe's photographs, like the work of other gay and lesbian artists of the time, are inextricably bound up with the social upheavals in American society and the struggle for equal rights for women, homosexuals, minorities, and the disabled during the second half of the 20th century.

(*Your Gaze Hits the Side of My Face*; FIG. **16-2**), Kruger incorporated the layout techniques magazines and billboards use to sell consumer goods. Although she favored the reassuringly familiar format and look of advertising, Kruger's goal was to subvert the typical use of advertising imagery. She aimed to expose the deceptiveness of the media messages the viewer complacently absorbs. Kruger wanted to undermine the myths—particularly those about women—the media constantly reinforce. Her word-and-photograph collages challenge the cultural attitudes embedded in commercial advertising. In *Your Gaze*, Kruger overlaid a photograph of a classically beautiful sculpted head of a woman with a vertical row of text composed of eight words. The words cannot be taken in with a single glance. Reading them is a staccato exercise, with an overlaid cumulative quality that delays understanding and intensifies the meaning (rather like reading a series of roadside billboards from a speeding car). Kruger's use of text in her work is significant. Many cultural theorists have asserted language is one of the most powerful vehicles for internalizing stereotypes and conditioned roles.

Public Funding of Controversial Art

Although art can be beautiful and uplifting, throughout history art has also challenged and offended. Since the early 1980s, a number of heated controversies about art have surfaced in the United States. There have been many calls to remove "offensive" works from public view and, in reaction, accusations of censorship. The central questions in all cases have been whether there are limits to what art can appropriately be exhibited and whether governmental authorities have the right to monitor and pass judgment on creative endeavors. A related question is whether the acceptability of a work should be a criterion in determining the public funding of art.

Two exhibits in 1989 placed the National Endowment for the Arts (NEA), a US government agency charged with distributing federal funds to support the arts, squarely in the middle of this debate. One of the exhibitions, devoted to recipients of the Awards for the Visual Arts (AVA), took place at the Southeastern Center for Contemporary Art in North Carolina. Among the award winners was Andres Serrano (b. 1950), whose *Piss Christ,* a photograph of a crucifix submerged in urine, sparked an uproar. Responding to this artwork, Reverend Donald Wildmon, an evangelical minister from Mississippi and head of the American Family Association, expressed outrage that this kind of work was in an exhibition funded by the NEA and the Equitable Life Assurance Society (a sponsor of the AVA). He demanded *Piss Christ* be removed and launched a letter-writing campaign that caused Equitable Life to cancel its sponsorship of the awards. To staunch conservatives, this exhibition, along with *Robert Mapplethorpe: The Perfect Moment,* which included erotic and openly homosexual images of the artist (FIG. 16-3) and others, served as evidence of cultural depravity and immorality. These critics insisted that art of an offensive character should not receive public funding. As a result of media furor over *The Perfect Moment,* the director of the Corcoran Museum of Art canceled the scheduled exhibition of this traveling show. But the director of the Contemporary Arts Center in Cincinnati did mount the show, resulting in his indictment on charges of obscenity, but a jury acquitted him six months later.

These controversies intensified public criticism of the NEA and its funding practices. The next year, the head of the NEA, John Frohnmayer, vetoed grants for four lesbian, gay, or feminist performance artists, who became known as the "NEA Four." Infuriated by what they perceived as overt censorship, the artists filed suit, eventually settling the case and winning reinstatement of their grants. Congress responded by dramatically reducing the NEA's budget, and the agency no longer awards grants or fellowships to individual artists.

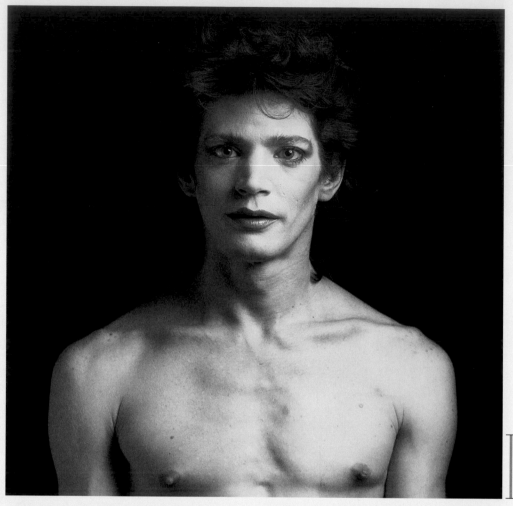

1 in.

16-3 ROBERT MAPPLETHORPE, *Self-Portrait,* 1980. Gelatin silver print, 7¾″ × 7¾″. Robert Mapplethorpe Foundation, New York.

Mapplethorpe's *Perfect Moment* show led to a landmark court case on freedom of expression for artists. In this self-portrait, an androgynous Mapplethorpe confronts the viewer with a steady gaze.

Controversies have also erupted on the municipal level. In 1999, Rudolph Giuliani, then mayor of New York, joined the protest over the inclusion of several artworks in the exhibition *Sensation: Young British Artists from the Saatchi Collection* at the Brooklyn Museum. Chris Ofili's *The Holy Virgin Mary* (FIG. 16-7) became the flashpoint for public furor. Denouncing the show as "sick stuff," the mayor threatened to cut off all city subsidies to the museum.

Artworks that seek to unsettle and challenge are critical to the cultural, political, and psychological life of a society. The regularity with which unconventional kinds of art raise controversy suggests they operate at the intersection of two competing principles: free speech and artistic expression on the one hand and a reluctance to impose images upon an audience that finds them repugnant or offensive on the other. What these controversies do demonstrate, beyond doubt, is the enduring power of art—and artists.

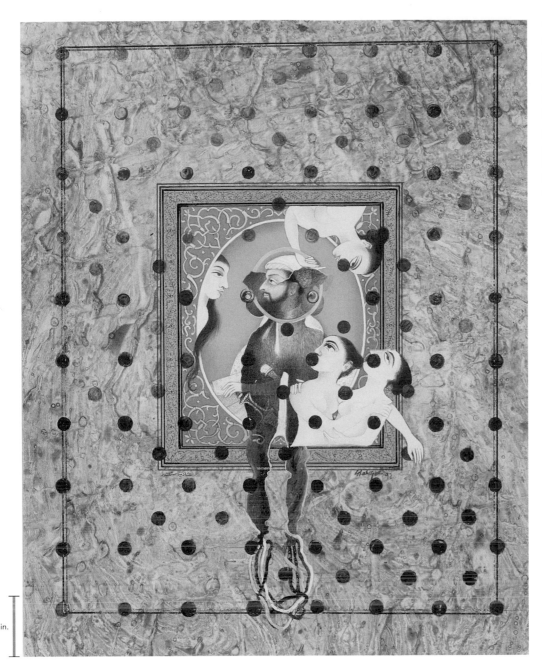

1 in.

16-4 SHAHZIA SIKANDER, *Perilous Order*, 1994–1997. Vegetable color, dry pigment, watercolor, and tea on Wasli paper, $10\frac{1}{2}$″ × 8″. Whitney Museum of American Art, New York (purchase, with funds from the Drawing Committee).

Imbuing miniature painting with a contemporary message about hypocrisy and intolerance, Sikander portrayed a gay friend as a homosexual Mughal emperor who enforced Muslim orthodoxy.

Shahzia Sikander The struggle for recognition and equal rights has never been confined to the United States. In the Muslim world, women and homosexuals face especially difficult challenges, which Pakistani artist SHAHZIA SIKANDER (b. 1969) brilliantly addresses in her work. Sikander, who now lives in New York City, has revived the demanding South Asian/Persian art of miniature painting (see Chapter 17), but imbued this traditional art form with contemporary meaning. In *Perilous Order* (FIG. **16-4**), she addresses homosexuality, intolerance, and hypocrisy by portraying a gay friend in the guise of the Mughal emperor Aurangzeb (r. 1658–1707), who was a strict enforcer of Islamic orthodoxy although reputed to be a homosexual. Sikander depicted him framed against a magnificent marbleized background ringed by voluptuous nude Hindu nymphs and behind the shadow of a veiled Hindu goddess. *Perilous Order* thus also incorporates a reference to the tensions between the Muslim and Hindu populations of Pakistan and India today.

Social Art: Race, Ethnicity, and National Identity

Gender and sexual-orientation issues are by no means the only societal concerns contemporary artists have addressed in their work. Race, ethnicity, and national identity are among the other pressing issues that have given rise to important artworks during the past few decades.

Faith Ringgold One of the leading artists addressing issues associated with African American women is Harlem native FAITH RINGGOLD (b. 1930). In the 1960s, Ringgold produced

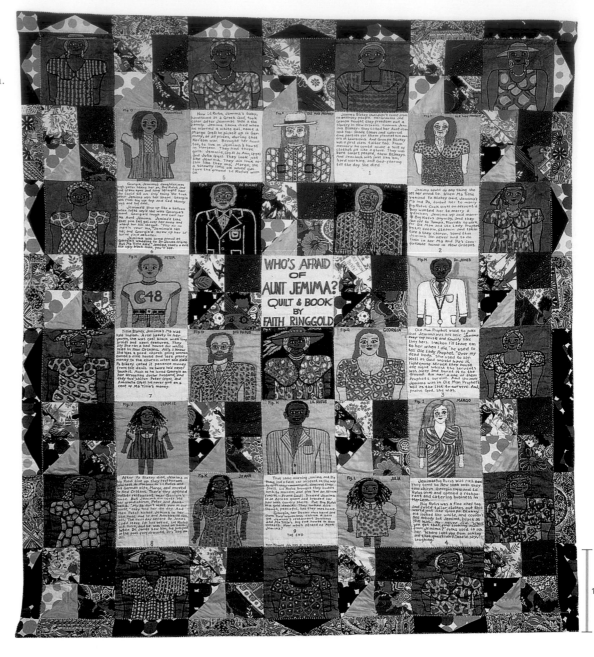

16-5 FAITH RINGGOLD, *Who's Afraid of Aunt Jemima?* 1983. Acrylic on canvas with fabric borders, quilted, 7′ 6″ × 6′ 8″. Private collection.

In this quilt, a medium associated with women, Ringgold presented a tribute to her mother that also addresses African American culture and the struggles of women to overcome oppression.

1 ft.

numerous works that provided pointed and incisive commentary on the realities of racial prejudice. She increasingly incorporated references to gender as well and, in the 1970s, turned to fabric as the predominant material in her art. Using fabric enabled Ringgold to make more pointed reference to the domestic sphere, traditionally associated with women, and to collaborate with her mother, Willi Posey, a fashion designer. After her mother's death in 1981, Ringgold created *Who's Afraid of Aunt Jemima?* (FIG. **16-5**), a quilt composed of dyed, painted, and pieced fabric. A moving tribute to her mother, this "story quilt"—Ringgold's signature art form—merges the personal and the political. The quilt tells the witty story of the family of Aunt Jemima, the stereotypical black "mammy" in the mind of the public, but here Jemima is a successful African American businesswoman. Ringgold narrates the story using black dialect interspersed with embroidered portraits and traditional patterned squares. *Aunt Jemima,* while resonating with autobiographical references, also speaks to the larger issues of

the history of African American culture and the struggles of women to overcome oppression.

Jean-Michel Basquiat The work of JEAN-MICHEL BASQUIAT (1960–1988) focuses on still another facet of the minority cultural experience in America. Born in Brooklyn, the son of an accountant from Haiti and a black Puerto Rican mother, Basquiat rebelled against middle-class values, dropped out of school at 17, and took to the streets. He first drew attention as an artist in 1980 when he participated in a group show—the "Times Square Show"—in an abandoned 42nd Street building. Eight years later, after a meteoric rise to fame, he died of a heroin overdose at age 27. Basquiat was self-taught, both as an artist and about the history of art, but he was not a "primitive." His sophisticated style owes a debt to diverse sources, including the late paintings of Pablo Picasso, Abstract Expressionism, and urban graffiti. Many of Basquiat's paintings celebrate black heroes, for example, the legendary jazz

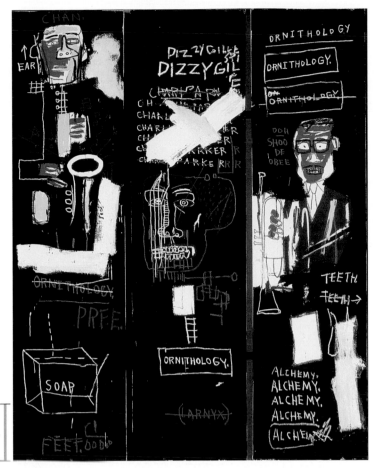

16-6 JEAN-MICHEL BASQUIAT, *Horn Players*, 1983. Acrylic and oil paintstick on three canvas panels, 8′ × 6′ 3″. Broad Art Foundation, Santa Monica.

In this tribute to two legendary African American musicians, Basquiat combined bold colors, fractured figures, and graffiti to capture the dynamic rhythms of jazz and the excitement of New York.

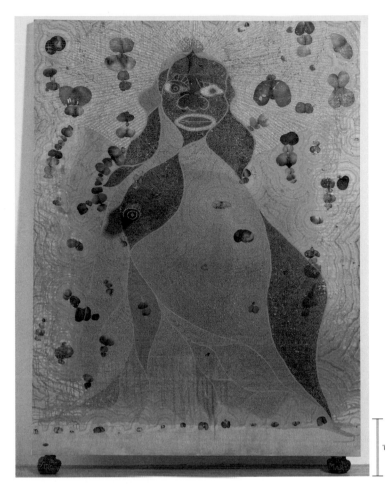

16-7 CHRIS OFILI, *The Holy Virgin Mary*, 1996. Acrylic, oil, polyester resin, paper collage, glitter, map pins, elephant dung on linen, 8′ × 6′. Victoria Miro Gallery, London.

Ofili, a British-born Catholic of Nigerian descent, represented the Virgin Mary with African elephant dung on one breast and surrounded by genitalia and buttocks. The painting produced a public outcry.

musicians Charlie "Bird" Parker and Dizzy Gillespie, whom he memorialized in *Horn Players* (FIG. **16-6**). The fractured figures, the bold colors against a black background, and the deliberately scrawled, crossed-out, and misspelled graffiti (*ornithology*, "the study of birds," is a pun on Parker's nickname) create a dynamic composition suggesting the rhythms of jazz music and the excitement of the streets of New York.

Chris Ofili In the global artistic community of the contemporary world, the exploration of personal social, ethnic, and national identity is a universal theme. CHRIS OFILI (b. 1968) is a British-born Catholic of Nigerian descent. Ofili's *The Holy Virgin Mary* (FIG. **16-7**) depicts Mary in a manner that departs radically from traditional representations. Ofili's work presents the Virgin in simplified form, and she appears to float in an indeterminate space. Surrounding the Virgin are tiny images of genitalia and buttocks cut out from pornographic magazines. The artist employed brightly colored pigments, applied to the canvas in multiple layers of beadlike dots (inspired by images from ancient caves in Zimbabwe). Another reference to Ofili's African heritage surfaces in the clumps of

elephant dung—one attached to the Virgin's breast, and two more on which the canvas rests, serving as supports. The dung enabled Ofili to incorporate Africa into his work in a literal way. Still, he wants the viewer to move beyond the cultural associations of the materials and see them in new ways. Not surprisingly, *The Holy Virgin Mary* elicited strong reactions from the public (see "Public Funding of Controversial Art," page 452).

Political Art

Although almost all of the works discussed thus far are commentaries on contemporary society—seen through the lens of these artists' personal experiences—they do not incorporate references to specific events. Other artists, however, have addressed contemporary political issues in their work.

Willie Bester Political oppression in South Africa figures prominently in the paintings of WILLIE BESTER (b. 1956), one of many South African artists who were vocal critics of apartheid (government-sponsored racial separation). Bester's 1992

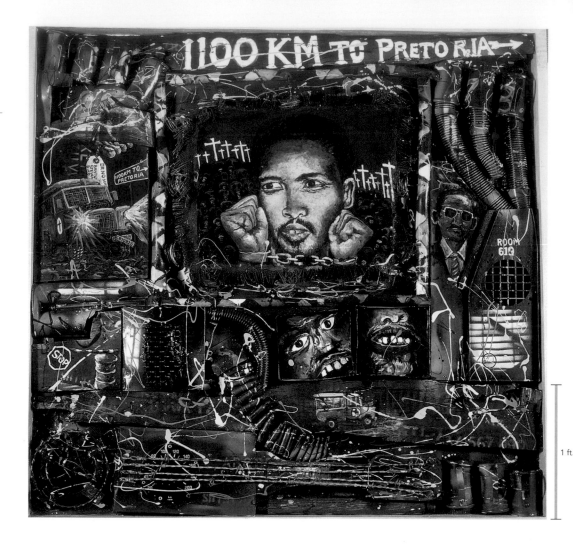

1 ft.

Homage to Steve Biko (FIG. 16-8) is a tribute to the gentle and heroic leader of the South African Black Liberation Movement whom the authorities killed while in detention. The exoneration of the two white doctors in charge of him sparked protests around the world. Bester packed his picture with references to death and injustice. Biko's portrait, at the center, is near another of the police minister, James Kruger, who had Biko transported 1,100 miles to Pretoria in the yellow Land Rover ambulance seen left of center and again beneath Biko's portrait. Bester portrayed Biko with his chained fists raised in the classic worldwide protest gesture. This portrait memorializes both Biko and the many other antiapartheid activists, as indicated by the white graveyard crosses above a blue sea of skulls beside Biko's head. The crosses stand out against a red background, recalling the inferno of burned townships. The stop sign (lower left) seems to mean "stop Kruger," or perhaps "stop apartheid." The tagged foot, as if in a morgue, above the ambulance (to the left) also refers to Biko's death. The red crosses on this vehicle's door and on Kruger's reflective dark glasses repeat, with sad irony, the graveyard crosses.

Blood-red and ambulance-yellow are in fact unifying colors dripped or painted on many parts of the canvas. Writing and numbers, found fragments and signs, both stenciled and painted—favorite Cubist motifs (FIGS. 14-9 and 14-10)—also appear throughout the composition. Numbers refer to

dehumanized life under apartheid. Found objects—wire, sticks, cardboard, sheet metal, cans, and other discards—from which the poor construct fragile, impermanent township dwellings, remind viewers of the degraded lives of most South African people of color. The oilcan guitar (bottom center), another recurrent Bester symbol, refers both to the social harmony and joy provided by music and to the control imposed by apartheid policies. The whole composition is rich in texture and dense in its collage combinations of objects, photographs, signs, symbols, and pigment. *Homage to Steve Biko* is a powerful critique of an oppressive sociopolitical system, and it exemplifies the extent to which art can be invoked in the political process.

Shirin Neshat Political and social oppression also play a significant role in the art of SHIRIN NESHAT (b. 1957), who grew up in a Westernized Iranian home and attended a Catholic boarding school in Tehran before leaving her homeland for the United States. Neshat produces films, video, and photographs critical of the fundamentalist Islamic regime in Iran, especially in its treatment of women. She often poses for her photographs wearing a veil—the symbol for Neshat of the repression of Muslim women—and with her face and exposed parts of her body covered with Farsi (Persian) messages. A rifle often figures prominently in the photographs

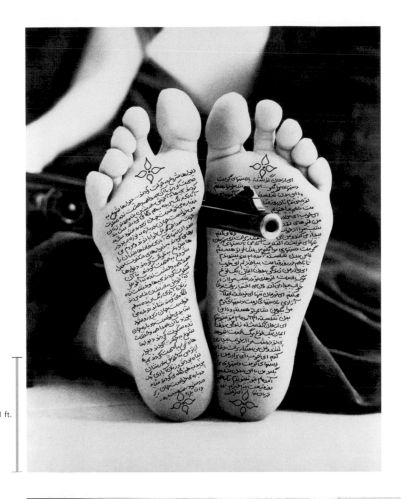

as an emblem of militant feminism, a notion foreign to the Muslim faith. In *Allegiance and Wakefulness* (FIG. **16-9**) from her *Women of Allah* series, the viewer sees only the barrel of a rifle and Neshat's feet covered with verses of militant Farsi poetry handwritten in ink.

Xu Bing A different kind of political/cultural commentary has been the hallmark of XU BING (b. 1955), a Chongqing, China, native who was forced to work in the countryside with peasants during the Cultural Revolution of 1966 to 1976 under Mao Tse-tung (1893–1976). Xu moved to the United States in 1990 at the invitation of the University of Wisconsin, where two years earlier he had exhibited his most famous work, a large *installation* (artwork creating an artistic environment in a gallery) called *A Book from the Sky* (FIG. **16-10**). The work presents an enormous number of woodblock-printed texts in characters evocative of Chinese writing but

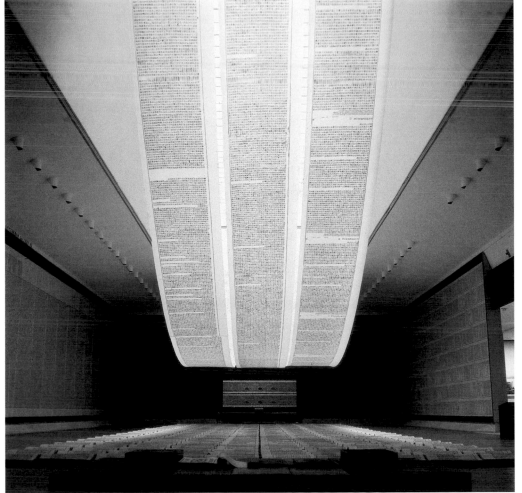

invented by the artist. Producing them required both an intimate knowledge of genuine Chinese characters and extensive training in block carving. *A Book from the Sky,* however, is no hymn to tradition. Critics have interpreted it both as a stinging critique of the meaninglessness of contemporary political language and as a commentary on the illegibility of the past. Like many works of art, past and present, Eastern and Western, Xu's postmodern masterpiece can be read on many levels.

OTHER MOVEMENTS AND THEMES

Despite the high visibility of contemporary artists whose work deals with the pressing social and political issues of the world, some critically acclaimed living artists have produced innovative modernist art during the postmodern era. Abstraction remains a valid and compelling approach to painting and sculpture in the 21st century, as does more traditional figural art.

Figural Painting and Sculpture

The work of three artists—Jenny Saville, Kiki Smith, and Jeff Koons—underscores the diversity and vitality of figure painting and sculpture today.

Jenny Saville Briton JENNY SAVILLE (b. 1970), who now lives and paints in an old palace in Palermo, Italy, is best known for her over-life-size self-portraits in which she exaggerates the girth of her body and delights in depicting heavy folds of flesh with visible veins in minute detail and from a sharply foreshortened angle, which further distorts the body's proportions. Saville's nude self-portraits are a commentary on the contemporary obsession with the lithe bodies of fashion models. In *Branded* (FIG. **16-11**), she highlights the dichotomy between the popular notion of a beautiful body and the imperfect bodies of most people by "branding" her body with words inscribed in her flesh—*delicate, decorative, petite.*

Kiki Smith A distinctly unflattering approach to the representation of the human body is also the hallmark of New York–based KIKI SMITH (b. 1954). In her work, Smith has explored the question of who controls the human body, an interest that grew out of her training as an emergency medical service technician. Smith, however, also wants to reveal the socially constructed nature of the body, and she encourages the viewer to consider how external forces shape people's perceptions of their bodies. In works such as *Untitled* (FIG. **16-12**), the artist dramatically departed from conventional

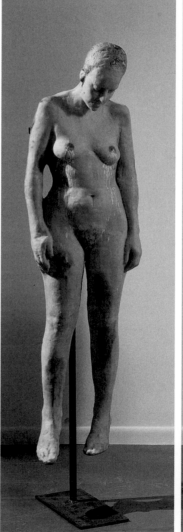
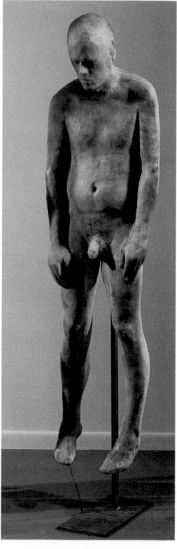

16-12 KIKI SMITH, *Untitled,* 1990. Beeswax and microcrystalline wax figures on metal stands, female figure installed height 6′ 1½″ and male figure installed height 6′ 4$\frac{15}{16}$″. Whitney Museum of American Art, New York (purchased with funds from the Painting and Sculpture Committee).

Asking "Who controls the body?" Kiki Smith sculpted two life-size wax figures of a nude man and woman with body fluids running from the woman's breasts and down the man's leg.

16-11 JENNY SAVILLE, *Branded,* 1992. Oil on canvas, 7′ × 6′. Charles Saatchi Collection, London.

Saville's unflattering foreshortened self-portrait "branded" with words such as *delicate* and *petite* underscores the dichotomy between the perfect bodies of fashion models and those of most people.

representations of the body, both in art and in the media. She suspended two life-size wax figures, one male and one female, both nude, from metal stands. Smith marked each of the sculptures with long white drips—body fluids running from the woman's breasts and down the man's leg. She commented:

> Most of the functions of the body are hidden . . . from society. . . . [W]e separate our bodies from our lives. But, when people are dying, they are losing control of their bodies. That loss of function can seem humiliating and frightening. But, on the other hand, you can look at it as a kind of liberation of the body. It seems like a nice metaphor—a way

16-13 Jeff Koons, *Pink Panther*, 1988. Porcelain, 3′ 5″ high. Museum of Contemporary Art, Chicago (Gerald S. Elliot Collection). ◼️◀

Koons creates sculptures highlighting everything he considers wrong with contemporary American consumer culture. In this work, he intertwined a centerfold nude and a cartoon character.

1 ft.

to think about the social   that people lose control despite the many agendas of different ideologies in society, which are trying to control the body(ies) . . . medicine, religion, law, etc. Just thinking about control—who has control of the body? . . . Does the mind have control of the body? Does the social? [2]

Jeff Koons The sculptures of Jeff Koons (b. 1955) form a striking counterpoint to the figural art of Kiki Smith. Koons first became prominent in the art world for a series of works in the early 1980s involving the exhibition of everyday commercial products such as vacuum cleaners. Clearly following in the footsteps of Marcel Duchamp (FIG. 14-15), Koons made no attempt to manipulate or alter the machine-made objects. More recently, he turned to ceramic sculpture. In *Pink Panther* (FIG. **16-13**), Koons intertwined a magazine centerfold nude with a famous cartoon character. He reinforced the trite and kitschy nature of this imagery by including the work in an exhibition he titled *The Banality Show*. Some art critics have argued Koons and his work instruct viewers because both artist and artwork serve as the most visible symbols of everything wrong with contemporary American society. Regardless of whether this is true, Koons's prominence in the art world indicates he, like Andy Warhol (FIG. 15-18) before him, has developed an acute understanding of the dynamics of consumer culture.

ARCHITECTURE AND SITE-SPECIFIC ART

The work of architects and Environmental artists today is as varied as that of contemporary painters and sculptors, but the common denominator in the diversity of contemporary architectural design and site-specific projects is the breaking down of national boundaries.

Architecture

In the late 20th and early 21st century, one of the byproducts of the globalization of the world's economy has been that leading architects have received commissions to design buildings far from their home bases. In the rapidly developing emerging markets of Asia, the Middle East, Africa, Latin America, and elsewhere, virtually every architect with an international reputation can list a recent building in Beijing or another urban center on his or her résumé.

Norman Foster British architect Norman Foster (b. 1935) met Richard Rogers (FIG. 15-31) at the Yale School of Architecture, and they opened a joint architectural firm when they returned to London in 1962, although they established separate practices several years later. Foster and Rogers are the leading proponents of what critics call *High-Tech architecture,* the roots of which can be traced to Joseph Paxton's mid-19th-century Crystal Palace (FIG. 12-25) in London. High-Tech architects design buildings incorporating the latest innovations in engineering and technology and exposing the base of the building is a plaza opening onto the neighboring streets. Visitors ascend on escalators from the plaza to a spectacular 10-story, 170-feet-tall atrium bordered by balconies with additional workspaces. What Foster calls "sun scoops"—computerized mirrors on the south side of the building—track the movement of the sun across the Hong Kong sky and reflect the sunlight into the atrium and plaza, flooding the dramatic spaces with light at all hours of the day. Not surprisingly, the roof of this High-Tech skyscraper serves as a landing pad for corporate helicopters.

Green Architecture The harnessing of solar energy as a power source is one of the key features of what critics commonly refer to as *green architecture*—ecologically friendly buildings that use "clean energy" and sustain the natural environment. Green architecture is the most important trend in architectural design in the early 21st century. A pioneer in this field is Renzo Piano, the codesigner with Richard Rogers of the Pompidou Center (FIG. 15-31) in Paris. Piano won an international competition to design the Tjibaou Cultural Centre (FIG. **16-15**) in Noumea. Rooted in the village architecture of the Kanak people of New Caledonia, the center consists of 10 beehive-shaped bamboo "huts" nestled in pine trees on a narrow island peninsula in the Pacific Ocean. Each unit of Piano's postmodern complex has an adjustable skylight as a roof to provide natural—sustainable—climate control. The curved profile of the Tjibaou pavilions also helps the structures withstand the pressure of the hurricane-force winds common in the South Pacific.

Deconstructivism In architecture, as in painting and sculpture, deconstruction as an analytical and design strategy emerged in the 1970s. *Deconstructivist* architects attempt to disrupt the conventional categories of architecture and to rupture the viewer's expectations based on them. Disorder, dissonance, imbalance, asymmetry, irregularity, and unconformity replace their opposites—order, harmony, balance, symmetry, regularity, and clarity. The seemingly haphazardly presented volumes, masses, planes, borders, lighting, locations, directions, spatial relations, as well as the disguised structural facts of Deconstructivist design, challenge the viewer's assumptions about architectural form as it relates to function. According to Deconstructivist principles, the very absence of the stability of traditional categories of architecture in a structure announces a "deconstructed" building.

Frank Gehry The architect most closely identified with Deconstructivist architecture is Canadian FRANK GEHRY (b. 1929). Gehry works up his designs by constructing models and then cutting them up and arranging the parts until he has a satisfying composition. Among Gehry's most notable projects is the Guggenheim Museum (FIG. **16-16**) in Bilbao, Spain, which appears to be a collapsed or collapsing aggregate of units. Visitors approaching the building see a mass of irregular asymmetrical and imbalanced forms whose

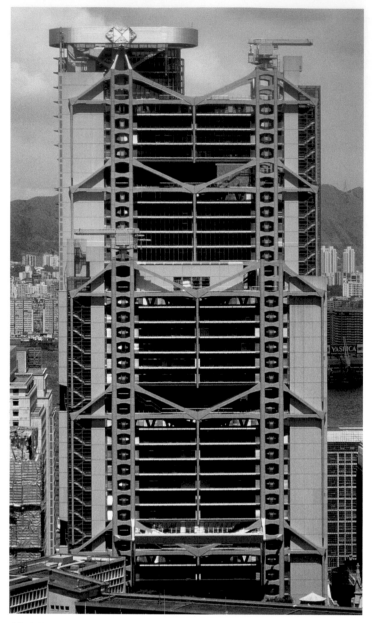

16-14 NORMAN FOSTER, Hong Kong and Shanghai Bank (looking southwest), Hong Kong, China, 1979–1986.

Foster's High-Tech tower has an exposed steel skeleton featuring floors with uninterrupted working spaces. At the base is a 10-story atrium illuminated by computerized mirrors that reflect sunlight.

the structures' component parts. High-Tech architecture is distinct from other postmodern architectural movements in dispensing with all historical references.

Foster's design for the headquarters (FIG. **16-14**) of the Hong Kong and Shanghai Bank Corporation (HSBC), which cost $1 billion to build, exemplifies the High-Tech approach to architecture. The 47-story skyscraper has an exposed steel skeleton with the elevators and other service elements located in giant piers at the short ends of the building, a design that provides uninterrupted communal working spaces on each cantilevered floor. Foster divided the tower into five horizontal units of six to nine floors each that he calls "villages," suspended from steel girders resembling bridges. At

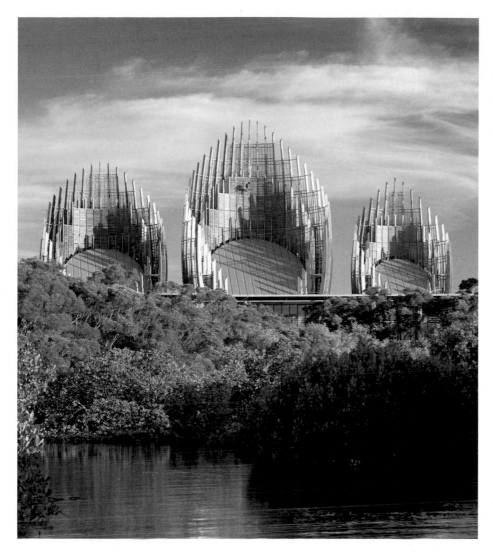

16-15 RENZO PIANO, Tjibaou Cultural Centre (looking southeast), Noumea, New Caledonia, 1998.

A pioneering example of "green architecture," Piano's complex of 10 bamboo units, based on traditional New Caledonian village huts, has adjustable skylights in the roofs for natural climate control.

museum. In the center of the building, an enormous glass-walled atrium soars 165 feet above the ground, serving as the focal point for the three levels of galleries radiating from it. The seemingly weightless screens, vaults, and volumes of the interior float and flow into one another, guided only by light and dark cues. The Guggenheim Museum in Bilbao is a profoundly compelling structure. Its disorder, its deceptive randomness of design, and the disequilibrium it prompts in viewers epitomize Deconstructivist principles.

Environmental and Site-Specific Art

When Robert Smithson created *Spiral Jetty* (FIG. 15-32) in Utah's Great Salt Lake in 1970, he was a trailblazer in the new genre of Environmental Art, or earthworks. In recent decades, earthworks and other site-specific artworks that bridge the gap between architecture and sculpture have become an established mode of artistic expression. As is true of all other media in the postmodern era, these artworks take a dazzling variety of forms.

profiles change dramatically with every shift of the viewer's position. The limestone- and titanium-clad exterior lends a space-age character to the structure and highlights further the unique cluster effect of the many forms. A group of organic forms Gehry refers to as a "metallic flower" tops the

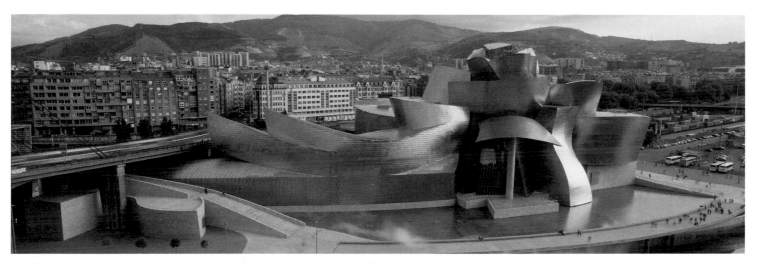

16-16 FRANK GEHRY, Guggenheim Bilbao Museo (looking south), Bilbao, Spain, 1997.

Gehry's limestone-and-titanium Bilbao museum is an immensely dramatic building. Its disorder and seeming randomness of design epitomize Deconstructivist architectural principles.

Maya Lin's Vietnam Veterans Memorial

Maya Lin's Vietnam Veterans Memorial (FIG. 16-17) is, like Minimalist sculptures (FIG. 15-12), an unadorned geometric form. Yet the monument, despite its serene simplicity, actively engages viewers in a psychological dialogue, giving visitors the opportunity to explore their feelings about the Vietnam War. The history of the memorial provides dramatic testimony to this monument's power. In 1981, a jury of architects, sculptors, and landscape architects selected Lin's design from among 1,400 entries in a blind competition. Conceivably, the jurors not only found her design compelling but also thought its simplicity would be the least likely to provoke controversy. But when the jury made its selection public, heated debate ensued. Even the wall's color came under attack. One veteran charged that black is "the universal color of shame, sorrow and degradation in all races, all societies worldwide."* But the sharpest protests concerned the form and siting of the monument. Because of the stark contrast between the massive white memorials (the Washington Monument and the Lincoln Memorial) bracketing Lin's sunken wall, some people interpreted her Minimalist design as minimizing the Vietnam War and, by extension, Vietnam veterans. Lin herself, however, described the wall as follows:

> The Vietnam Veterans Memorial is not an object inserted into the earth but a work formed from the act of cutting open the earth and polishing the earth's surface—dematerializing the stone to pare surface, creating an interface between the world of the light and the quieter world beyond the names.†

Due to the vocal opposition, a compromise was necessary to ensure the memorial's completion. In 1983, the Commission of Fine Arts, the federal group overseeing the project, commissioned a larger-than-life-size realistic bronze sculpture by artist Frederick Hart (1943–1999) of three soldiers, armed and uniformed, which stands approximately 120 feet from Lin's wall. Several years later, a group of nurses won approval for a sculpture honoring women's service in the Vietnam War. The 7-foot-tall bronze statue by Glenna Goodacre (b. 1939) depicts three female figures, one cradling a wounded soldier in her arms. Unveiled in 1993, the work occupies a site about 300 feet south of the Lin memorial.

Commonly, visitors react very emotionally to Lin's Vietnam Veterans Memorial, even those who know none of the soldiers named on the monument. The polished granite surface prompts individual soul-searching—viewers see themselves reflected among the names. Many leave mementos at the foot of the wall in memory of loved ones they lost in the Vietnam War or make rubbings from the incised names. It can be argued that much of this memorial's power derives from its Minimalist simplicity. It does not dictate response and therefore successfully encourages personal exploration.

*Elizabeth Hess, "A Tale of Two Memorials," *Art in America* 71, no. 4 (April 1983): 122.
†Excerpt from an unpublished 1995 lecture, quoted in Kristine Stiles and Peter Selz, *Theories and Documents of Contemporary Art: A Sourcebook of Artists' Writings* (Berkeley and Los Angeles: University of California Press, 1996), 525.

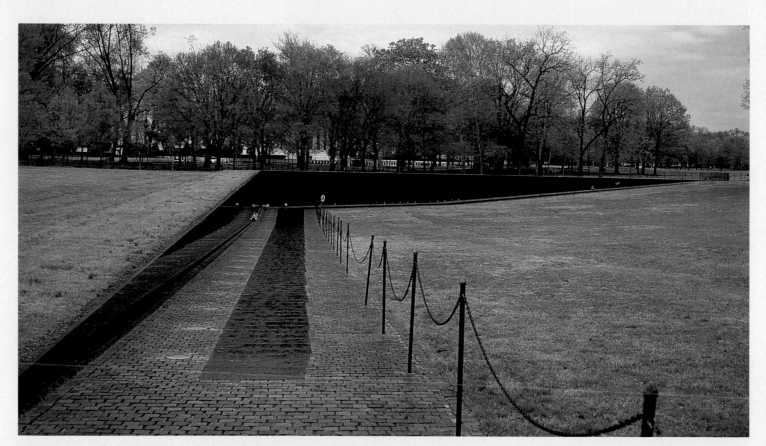

16-17 MAYA YING LIN, Vietnam Veterans Memorial (looking north), Washington, D.C., 1981–1983.

Like Minimalist sculpture, Lin's memorial to veterans of the Vietnam War is a simple geometric form. Its inscribed polished walls actively engage viewers in a psychological dialogue about the war.

Maya Ying Lin Variously classified as a work either of Minimalist sculpture or architecture is the Vietnam Veterans Memorial (FIG. **16-17**) in Washington, D.C., designed in 1981 by MAYA YING LIN (b. 1960) when she was a 21-year-old student at the Yale School of Architecture. The austere, simple memorial, a V-shaped wall constructed of polished black granite panels, begins at ground level at each end and gradually ascends to a height of 10 feet at the center of the V. Each wing is 246 feet long. Lin set the wall into the landscape, enhancing visitors' awareness of descent as they walk along the wall toward the center. The names of the Vietnam War's 57,939 American casualties (and those missing in action) incised on the memorial's walls, in the order of their deaths, contribute to the monument's dramatic effect.

When Lin designed this pristinely simple monument, she gave a great deal of thought to the purpose of war memorials. Her conclusion was a memorial

> should be honest about the reality of war and be for the people who gave their lives. . . . [I] didn't want a static object that people would just look at, but something they could relate to as on a journey, or passage, that would bring each to his own conclusions. . . . I wanted to work with the land and not dominate it. I had an impulse to cut open the earth . . . an initial violence that in time would heal. The grass would grow back, but the cut would remain.[3]

In light of the tragedy of the war, this unpretentious memorial's allusion to a wound and long-lasting scar contributes to its communicative ability (see "Maya Lin's Vietnam Veterans Memorial," page 462).

Rachel Whiteread Another controversial memorial commissioned for a specific historical setting is the Viennese Holocaust Memorial (FIG. **16-18**) by British sculptor RACHEL WHITEREAD (b. 1963). In 1996, the city of Vienna chose Whiteread as the winner of the competition for a monument commemorating the 65,000 Austrian Jews who perished at the hands of the Nazis during World War II. The decision to focus attention on a past most Austrians wished to forget unleashed a controversy that delayed construction of the monument until 2000. Whiteread modulated the surface of the Holocaust memorial only slightly by depicting in low relief the shapes of two doors and hundreds of identical books on shelves, with the edges of the covers and the pages rather than the spines facing outward. The book motif was a reference both to Jews as the "People of the Book" and to the book burnings that accompanied Jewish persecutions throughout the centuries and under the Nazis. Around the base, Whiteread inscribed the names of Nazi concentration camps in German, Hebrew, and English. The setting for the memorial is Judenplatz (Jewish Square), the site of a synagogue destroyed in 1421. The brutality of the tomblike monument—it cannot be entered, and its shape suggests a prison block—was a visual as well as psychological shock in the Baroque Viennese square. Whiteread's purpose, however, was not to please but to create a memorial that met the jury's charge to "combine dignity with reserve and spark an aesthetic dialogue with the past in a place that is replete with history."

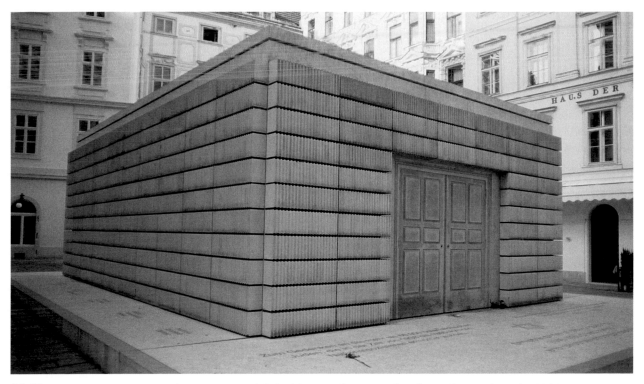

16-18 RACHEL WHITEREAD, Holocaust Memorial (looking northwest), Judenplatz, Vienna, Austria, 2000.

Whiteread's monument to the 65,000 Austrian Jews who perished in the Holocaust is a tomblike concrete block with doors that cannot be opened and library books seen from behind.

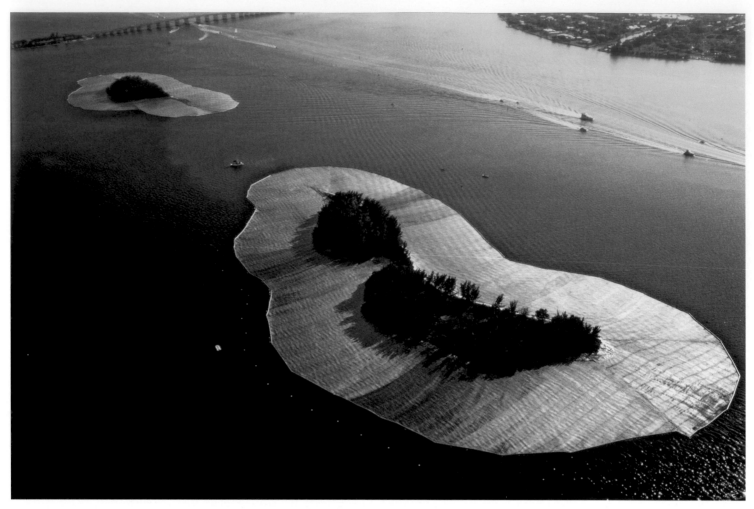

16-19 CHRISTO and JEANNE-CLAUDE, *Surrounded Islands, Biscayne Bay, Miami, Florida, 1980–1983.* ■◀

Christo and Jeanne-Claude created this Environmental artwork by surrounding 11 small islands with 6.5 million square feet of pink fabric. Characteristically, the work existed for only two weeks.

Christo and Jeanne-Claude The most famous Environmental artists of the past few decades are CHRISTO (b. 1935) and his deceased spouse JEANNE-CLAUDE (1935–2009). In their works they sought to intensify the viewer's awareness of the space and features of rural and urban sites. However, rather than physically alter the land itself, as Robert Smithson (FIG. 15-32) often did, Christo and Jeanne-Claude prompted this awareness by temporarily modifying the landscape with cloth. Their projects require years of preparation and research, and scores of meetings with local authorities and interested groups of local citizens. These temporary artworks are usually on view for only a few weeks.

Surrounded Islands (FIG. **16-19**), created in Biscayne Bay in Miami, Florida, for two weeks in May 1983, typifies Christo and Jeanne-Claude's work. For this project, they surrounded 11 small artificial islands in the bay (created from a dredging project) with 6.5 million square feet of specially fabricated pink polypropylene floating fabric. This Environmental artwork required three years of preparation to obtain the required permits and to assemble the labor force and obtain the $3.2 million needed to complete the project. The artists

raised the money by selling Christo's original preparatory drawings, collages, and models of works they created in the 1950s and 1960s. Huge crowds watched as crews removed accumulated trash from the 11 islands (to assure maximum contrast between their dark colors, the pink of the cloth, and the blue of the bay) and then unfurled the fabric "cocoons" to form magical floating "skirts" around each tiny bit of land.

NEW MEDIA

In addition to taking the ancient arts of painting and sculpture in new directions, contemporary artists have continued to explore the expressive possibilities of the various new media developed in the postwar period, especially digital photography, computer graphics, and video.

Andreas Gursky Since the mid-1990s, German photographer ANDREAS GURSKY (b. 1955) has used computer and digital technology to produce gigantic color prints in which he combines and manipulates photographs taken with a wide-angle lens, usually from a high vantage point. The size

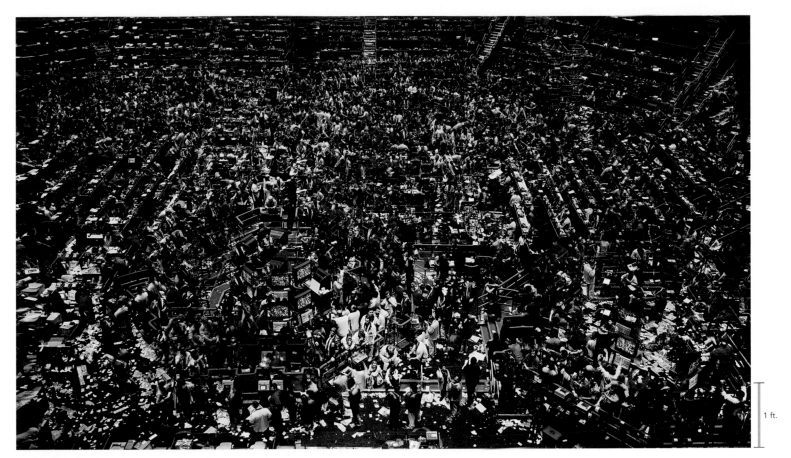

16-20 ANDREAS GURSKY, *Chicago Board of Trade II,* 1999. C-print, 6′ 9½″ × 11′ 5⅝″. Matthew Marks Gallery, New York.

Gursky manipulates digital photographs to produce vast tableaus depicting characteristic places of the modern global economy. The size of his prints rivals 19th-century history paintings.

of his photographs, sometimes almost a dozen feet wide, intentionally rivals 19th-century history paintings. But as was true of Gustave Courbet (FIGS. 12-13 and 12-14) in his day, Gursky's subjects come from everyday life. He records the mundane world of the modern global economy—vast industrial plants, major department stores, hotel lobbies, and stock and commodity exchanges—and transforms the commonplace into striking, almost abstract, compositions.

Gursky's enormous 1999 print (FIG. **16-20**) documenting the frenzied activity on the main floor of the Chicago Board of Trade is a characteristic example of his work. He took a series of photographs from a gallery, creating a panoramic view of the traders in their brightly colored jackets. He then combined several digital images using commercial photo-editing software to produce a blurred tableau of bodies, desks, computer terminals, and strewn paper in which both mass and color are so evenly distributed as to negate the traditional Renaissance notion of perspective. In using the computer to modify the "objective truth" and spatial recession of "straight photography," Gursky blurs the distinction between painting and photography.

Bill Viola For much of his artistic career, BILL VIOLA (b. 1951) has also explored the capabilities of digitized imagery, producing many video installations and single-channel works. Often focusing on sensory perception, the pieces not only heighten viewer awareness of the senses but also suggest an exploration into the spiritual realm. Viola spent years seriously studying Buddhist, Christian, Sufi, and Zen mysticism. Because he fervently believes in art's transformative power and in a spiritual view of human nature, Viola designs works encouraging spectator introspection. His video projects have involved using techniques such as extreme slow motion, contrasts in scale, shifts in focus, mirrored reflections, staccato editing, and multiple or layered screens to achieve dramatic effects.

The power of Viola's work is evident in *The Crossing* (FIG. **16-21**), an installation piece involving two color video channels projected on 16-foot-high screens. The artist either shows the two projections on the front and back of the same screen or on two separate screens in the same installation. In these two companion videos, shown simultaneously on the two screens, a man surrounded in darkness appears, moving closer until he fills the screen. On one screen, drops of water fall from above onto the man's head, while on the other screen, a small fire breaks out at the man's feet. Over the next few minutes, the water and fire increase in intensity until the man disappears in a torrent of water on one screen (FIG. 16-21) and flames consume the man on the other screen. The

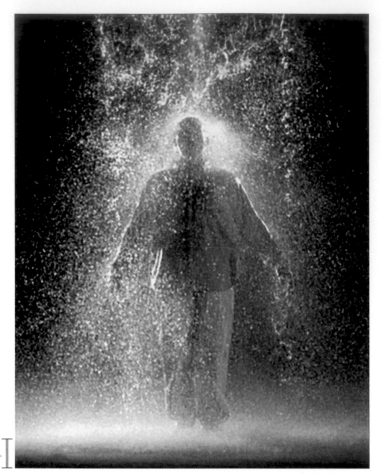

16-21 Bill Viola, *The Crossing*, 1996. Video/sound installation with two channels of color video projection onto screens 16' high. ■◀

Viola's video projects use extreme slow motion, contrasts in scale, shifts in focus, mirrored reflections, and staccato editing to create dramatic sensory experiences rooted in tangible reality.

1 ft.

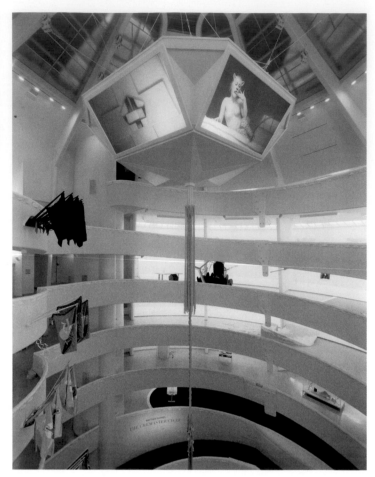

16-22 Matthew Barney, *Cremaster* cycle, installation at the Solomon R. Guggenheim Museum, New York, 2003.

Barney's vast multimedia installations of drawings, photographs, sculptures, and videos typify the relaxation at the opening of the 21st century of the traditional boundaries among artistic media.

deafening roar of a raging fire and a torrential downpour accompany these visual images. Eventually, everything subsides and fades into darkness. This installation's elemental nature and its presentation in a dark space immerse viewers in a pure sensory experience very much rooted in tangible reality.

Matthew Barney A major trend in the art world today is the relaxation of the traditional boundaries between artistic media. In fact, many contemporary artists are creating vast and complex multimedia installations combining new and traditional media. One of these artists is Matthew Barney (b. 1967), whose 2003 installation (FIG. **16-22**) of his epic *Cremaster* cycle (1994–2002) at the Guggenheim Museum in New York typifies the expansive scale of many contemporary works. A multimedia extravaganza involving drawings, photographs, sculptures, videos, films, and performances (presented in videos), the *Cremaster* cycle is a lengthy narrative set in a self-enclosed universe Barney created. The title of the work refers to the cremaster muscle, which controls testicular contractions in response to external stimuli. Barney uses the development of this muscle in the embryonic process of sexual differentiation as the conceptual springboard for the entire *Cremaster* project, in which he explores the notion of creation in expansive and complicated ways. The cycle's narrative, revealed in

the five feature-length films and the artworks, makes reference to, among other things, a musical revue in Boise, Idaho (where Barney grew up), the life cycle of bees, the execution of convicted murderer Gary Gilmore, the construction of the Chrysler Building (FIG. 14-41), Celtic mythology, Masonic rituals, a motorcycle race, and a lyric opera set in late-19th-century Budapest. In the installation, Barney tied the artworks together conceptually by a five-channel video piece projected on screens hanging in the Guggenheim's rotunda. Immersion in Barney's constructed world is disorienting and overwhelming and has a force that competes with the immense scale and often frenzied pace of contemporary life.

What Next? No one knows what the next years and decades will bring, but given the expansive scope of postmodernism, it is certain no single approach to or style of art will dominate. New technologies will undoubtedly continue to redefine what constitutes a "work of art." The universally expanding presence of computers, digital technology, and the Internet may well erode what few conceptual and geographical boundaries remain, and make art and information about art available to virtually everyone, thereby creating a truly global artistic community. As this chapter has revealed, substantial progress has already been made in that direction.

Contemporary Art Worldwide

Painting, Sculpture, and Photography

I Many contemporary artists use art to address pressing social and political issues and to define their personal identities.

I Gender and sexuality are central themes in the work of Barbara Kruger, Robert Mapplethorpe, and Shahzia Sikander.

I Faith Ringgold and Jean-Michel Basquiat address issues of concern to African Americans.

I Jaune Quick-to-See Smith focuses on Native American heritage and Chris Ofili on his African roots.

I Other artists have treated political and economic issues: Willie Bester, apartheid in South Africa, and Shirin Neshat, the challenges facing Muslim women.

I Abstraction continues to be a major mode of artistic expression, but the past few decades have also witnessed a revival of realistic figural art. Among today's best-known figural painters and sculptors are Kiki Smith and Jeff Koons in the United States and expatriate Englishwoman Jenny Saville in Italy.

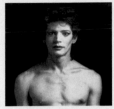

Mapplethorpe,
Self-Portrait, 1980

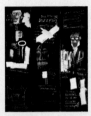

Basquiat,
Horn Players, 1983

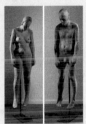

Smith,
Untitled, 1990

Architecture, Site-Specific Art, and New Media

I Postmodern architecture is as diverse as contemporary painting and sculpture. Leading Hi-Tech architects include Norman Foster and Renzo Piano.

I Frank Gehry is the major champion of Deconstructivism.

I The monuments designed by Maya Lin and Rachel Whiteread bridge the gap between architecture and sculpture, as do the Environmental artworks of Christo and Jeanne-Claude.

I Many contemporary artists have harnessed new technologies in their artistic production: in Germany, Andreas Gursky, digital photography; in the United States, Bill Viola, video; and Matthew Barney, complex multimedia installations.

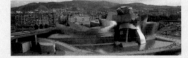

Gehry, Guggenheim Bilbao Museo,
1997

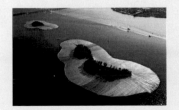

Christo and Jeanne-Claude,
Surrounded Islands, 1980–1983

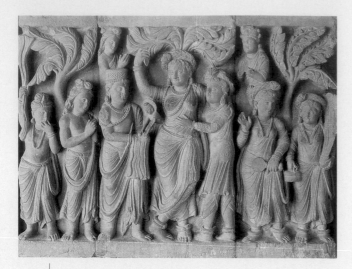

This frieze is one of the earliest pictorial narratives of the Buddha's life. At the left, Queen Maya gives birth to Prince Siddhartha, the future Buddha, who emerges from her right hip.

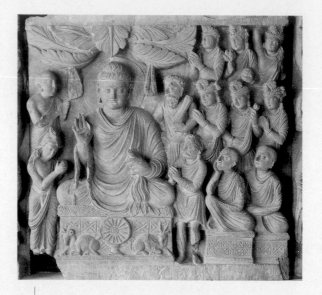

Here, the Buddha, seated in the Deer Park at Sarnath with his right hand raised in a gesture of blessing, preaches his first sermon in which he reveals the Eightfold Path to nirvana.

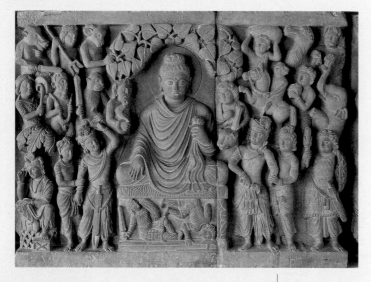

In the next scene, the Buddha sits beneath the Bodhi tree while the soldiers and demons of the evil Mara attempt to distract him from his quest for knowledge, but they are not successful.

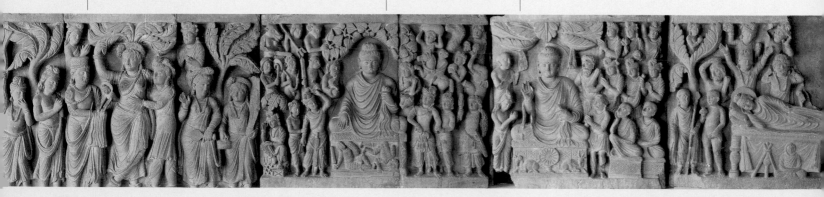

17-1 The life and death of the Buddha, frieze from Gandhara, Pakistan, second century CE. Schist, 2′ 2⅜″ × 9′ 6⅛″. Freer Gallery of Art, Washington, D.C.

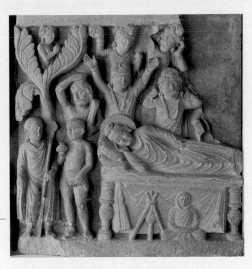

South and Southeast Asia

In the final scene, the Buddha lies dying among his devotees, who wail in grief, save for one meditating monk who realizes the Buddha has achieved nirvana and release from suffering.

THE LIFE OF THE BUDDHA

The Buddha (Enlightened One) was born around 563 BCE as Prince Siddhartha Gautama, the eldest son of the king of the Shakya clan. A prophecy foretold he would grow up to be either a world conqueror or a great religious leader. His father preferred the secular role for young Siddhartha and groomed him for kingship by shielding the boy from the hardships of the world. When he was 29, however, the prince rode out of the palace, abandoned his wife and family, and encountered for himself the pain of old age, sickness, and death. Siddhartha responded to the suffering he witnessed by renouncing his opulent life and becoming a wandering ascetic searching for knowledge through meditation. Six years later, he achieved complete enlightenment, or buddhahood, while meditating beneath a pipal tree (the Bodhi tree) at Bodh Gaya (place of enlightenment) in eastern India. Known from that day on as Shakyamuni (wise man of the Shakya clan), the Buddha preached his first sermon in the Deer Park at Sarnath. There he set in motion the Wheel (*chakra*) of the Law (*dharma*) and expounded the Four Noble Truths, the core insights of Buddhism: (1) life is suffering; (2) the cause of suffering is desire; (3) one can overcome and extinguish desire; (4) the way to conquer desire and end suffering is to follow the Buddha's Eightfold Path of right understanding, right thought, right speech, right action, right livelihood, right effort, right mindfulness, and right concentration. The Buddha's path leads to *nirvana,* the cessation of the endless cycle of painful life, death, and rebirth. The Buddha continued to preach until his death at age 80.

One of the earliest pictorial narrative cycles of the Buddha's life is a stone frieze (FIG. **17-1**) from Gandhara, a region largely in Pakistan today, close to the Afghanistan border. Depicted, in chronological order from left to right, are the Buddha's birth at Lumbini, the enlightenment at Bodh Gaya, the first sermon at Sarnath, and the Buddha's death at Kushinagara. At the left, Queen Maya gives birth to Prince Siddhartha, who emerges from her right hip. Receiving him is the god Indra. Elegantly dressed ladies, one with a fan of peacock feathers, suggest the opulent court life the Buddha left behind. In the next scene, the Buddha sits beneath the Bodhi tree while the soldiers and demons of the evil Mara attempt to distract him from his quest for knowledge. They are unsuccessful, and the Buddha then preaches the Eightfold Path to nirvana in the Deer Park at Sarnath. The sculptor set the scene by placing two deer and the Wheel of the Law beneath the figure of the Buddha. In the final section of the frieze, the parinirvana, the Buddha lies dying among his devotees, some of whom wail in grief, while one monk, who realizes the Buddha has been permanently released from suffering, remains tranquil in meditation.

SOUTH ASIA

In the third millennium BCE, a great civilization arose over a wide geographical area along the Indus River in Pakistan and extended into India as far south as Gujarat and east beyond Delhi (MAP **17-1**). Thus, when Alexander the Great and his army reached India in 326 BCE, they encountered a civilization already more than 2,000 years old. Archaeologists have dubbed this early South Asian culture the Indus Civilization.

Indus Civilization

The Indus Civilization flourished from about 2600 to 1500 BCE. The most important excavated Indus sites are Harappa and Mohenjo-daro. Both were fully developed cities featuring streets oriented to compass points and multistoried houses built of carefully formed and precisely laid kiln-baked bricks. The Indus cities also boasted one of the world's first sophisticated systems of water supply and sewage. In Mohenjo-daro, hundreds of wells throughout the city provided fresh water to homes incorporating some of the oldest recorded private bathing areas and toilet facilities, with drainage into public sewers. The inhabitants of the Indus cities engaged in trade with cities as far away as modern Iraq, but in sharp contrast to the contemporaneous civilizations of Mesopotamia and Egypt, no excavated Indus building has yet been identified as a temple or palace.

Indus Seals Surprisingly, archaeologists have discovered little art from the long-lived Indus Civilization, and all of the objects found are small. The most common are steatite seals with incised designs. They are similar in many ways to the seals found at contemporaneous sites in Mesopotamia. Most of the Indus examples have an animal or tiny narrative carved on the face, along with an as-yet-untranslated script. On the back, a *boss* (circular knob) with a hole enabled insertion of a string so the owner could wear the seal or hang it on a wall. As in Mesopotamia, the Indus peoples sometimes used the seals to make impressions on clay, apparently for securing trade goods wrapped in textiles. The animals most frequently represented include the humped bull, elephant, rhinoceros, and tiger—always shown in strict profile. Some of the narrative seals indicate the Indus peoples considered trees sacred, as both Buddhists and Hindus later did. Many scholars have suggested religious and ritual continuities between the Indus Civilization and later Indian culture.

One of the most elaborate seals (FIG. **17-2**) depicts a male figure with a horned headdress and, perhaps, three faces, seated (with erect penis) among the profile animals that regularly appear alone on other seals. The figure's position—folded legs with heels pressed together and arms resting on the knees—suggests a *yogic* posture. *Yoga* is a method for controlling the body and relaxing the mind used in later Indian religions to yoke, or unite, the practitioner to the divine. Although most scholars reject the identification of this figure as a prototype of the multiheaded Hindu god Shiva (FIG. 17-9) as Lord of Beasts, the yogic posture proves this important Indian meditative practice began as early as the Indus Civilization.

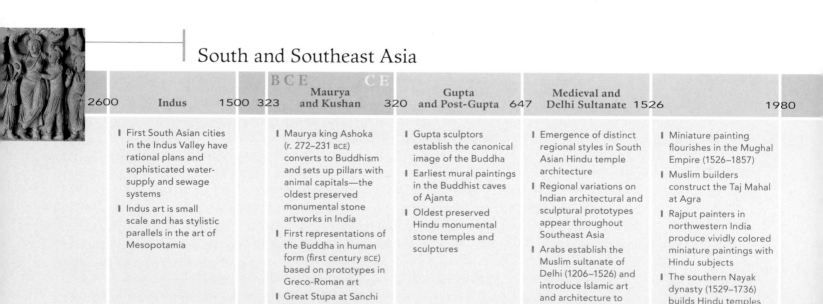

South and Southeast Asia

			BCE	CE					
2600	**Indus**	1500	323	**Maurya and Kushan**	320	**Gupta and Post-Gupta**	647	**Medieval and Delhi Sultanate** 1526	1980

▮ First South Asian cities in the Indus Valley have rational plans and sophisticated water-supply and sewage systems ▮ Indus art is small scale and has stylistic parallels in the art of Mesopotamia	▮ Maurya king Ashoka (r. 272–231 BCE) converts to Buddhism and sets up pillars with animal capitals—the oldest preserved monumental stone artworks in India ▮ First representations of the Buddha in human form (first century BCE) based on prototypes in Greco-Roman art ▮ Great Stupa at Sanchi assumes its present monumental form under the Kushan dynasty between 50 BCE and 50 CE	▮ Gupta sculptors establish the canonical image of the Buddha ▮ Earliest mural paintings in the Buddhist caves of Ajanta ▮ Oldest preserved Hindu monumental stone temples and sculptures	▮ Emergence of distinct regional styles in South Asian Hindu temple architecture ▮ Regional variations on Indian architectural and sculptural prototypes appear throughout Southeast Asia ▮ Arabs establish the Muslim sultanate of Delhi (1206–1526) and introduce Islamic art and architecture to northern India	▮ Miniature painting flourishes in the Mughal Empire (1526–1857) ▮ Muslim builders construct the Taj Mahal at Agra ▮ Rajput painters in northwestern India produce vividly colored miniature paintings with Hindu subjects ▮ The southern Nayak dynasty (1529–1736) builds Hindu temples featuring gateways decorated with painted sculptures ▮ Buddhism and Buddhist art and architecture dominate Southeast Asia ▮ Modern art in South and Southeast Asia is a mix of traditional and Western styles

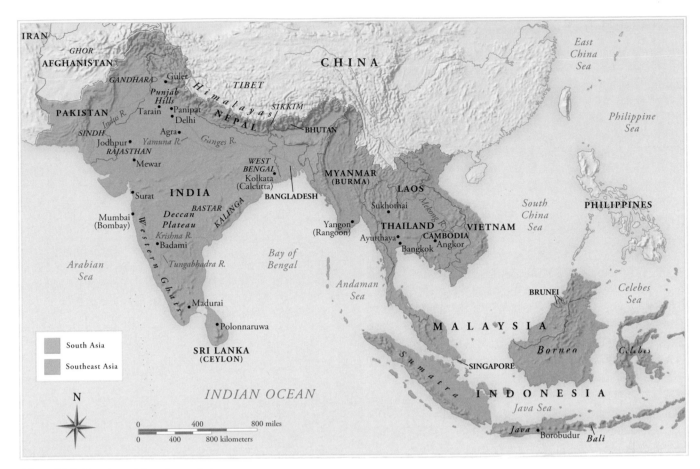

MAP 17-1 South and Southeast Asia.

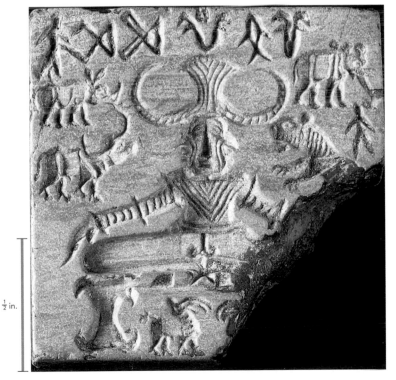

½ in.

17-2 Seal with seated figure in yogic posture, from Mohenjo-daro, Pakistan, ca. 2300–1750 BCE. Steatite coated with alkali and baked, $1\frac{3}{8}'' \times 1\frac{3}{8}''$. National Museum, New Delhi.

This seal depicting a (three-faced?) figure wearing a horned headdress and seated in a yogic posture indicates this important Indian meditative practice began as early as the Indus Civilization.

Vedic and Upanishadic Period

By 1700 BCE, the urban phase of the Indus Civilization had ended in most areas. Very little art survives from the next thousand years, but the religious foundations laid during this period helped define most later South Asian art.

Vedas The basis for the new religious ideas were the oral hymns of the Aryans, a mobile herding people from Central Asia who occupied northwestern India in the second millennium BCE. The Aryans (Noble Ones) spoke Sanskrit, the earliest language yet identified in South Asia. Around 1500 BCE, they composed the first of four Vedas. These Sanskrit compilations of religious learning (*Veda* means "knowledge") included hymns intended for priests (called Brahmins) to chant or sing. The Aryan religion centered on sacrifice, the ritual enactment of often highly intricate and lengthy ceremonies in which the priests placed materials, such as milk and soma (an intoxicating drink), into a fire that took the sacrifices to the gods in the heavens. If the Brahmins performed these rituals accurately, the gods would fulfill the prayers of those who sponsored the sacrifices. These gods, primarily male, included Indra, Varuna, Surya, and Agni, gods associated, respectively, with rain, the ocean, the sun, and fire. The Aryans did not make images of these deities.

Upanishads The next phase of South Asian urban civilization developed east of the Indus heartland, in the Ganges

River valley. Here, from 800 to 500 BCE, religious thinkers composed a variety of texts called the *Upanishads*. Among the innovative ideas of the Upanishads were samsara, karma, and moksha (or nirvana). *Samsara* is the belief that individuals are born again after death in an almost endless round of rebirths. The type of rebirth can vary. One can be reborn as a human being, an animal, or even a god. An individual's past actions (*karma*), either good or bad, determine the nature of future rebirths. The ultimate goal of a person's religious life is to escape—*moksha* (liberation in Hinduism) or *nirvana* (cessation in Buddhism)—from the cycle of birth and death by merging the individual self into the vital force of the universe.

Hinduism and Buddhism Hinduism and Buddhism, the two major modern religions originating in Asia, developed in the late centuries BCE and the early centuries CE. Hinduism, the dominant religion in India today, discussed in more detail later, has its origins in Aryan religion. The founder of Buddhism was the Buddha (see "The Life of the Buddha," page 469), who advocated the path of *asceticism,* or self-discipline and self-denial, as the means to free oneself from attachments to people and possessions, thus ending rebirth (see "Buddhism and Buddhist Iconography," page 473). Unlike their predecessors in South Asia, both Hindus and Buddhists use images of gods and holy persons in religious rituals. Buddhism has the older artistic tradition. The earliest Buddhist monuments date to the Maurya period.

Maurya Dynasty

When Alexander the Great reached the Indus River in 326 BCE, his troops refused to go forward. Reluctantly, Alexander abandoned his dream of conquering India and headed home. After Alexander's death, his generals divided his empire among themselves. One of them, Seleucus Nicator, reinvaded India, but Chandragupta Maurya (r. 323–298 BCE), founder of the Maurya dynasty (r. 323–185 BCE), defeated him in 305 BCE and eventually consolidated almost all of present-day India under his domain.

Ashoka The greatest Maurya ruler, Ashoka (r. 272–231 BCE), left his imprint on history by converting to Buddhism and spreading the Buddha's teaching throughout and beyond India. Ashoka formulated a legal code based on the Buddha's dharma and inscribed his laws on enormous monolithic stone columns set up throughout his kingdom. Ashoka's pillars reached 30 to 40 feet high and are the earliest known monumental stone artworks in India. The pillars penetrated deep into the ground, connecting earth and sky, forming an "axis of the universe," a pre-Buddhist concept that became an important motif in Buddhist architecture. The columns stood along pilgrimage routes to sites associated with the Buddha and on the roads leading to Pataliputra (modern Patna), the Maurya capital.

Capping Ashoka's pillars were elaborate capitals, also carved from a single block of stone. The finest (FIG. **17-3**) is 7 feet high and comes from Sarnath, where the Buddha gave his first sermon and set the Wheel of the Law into motion. Stylistically, the Sarnath capital owes much to ancient Mesopotamia and Persia, but its iconography is Buddhist. Two pairs of back-to-back lions (texts often refer to the Buddha as "the lion") stand on a round abacus decorated with four wheels and four animals symbolizing the four quarters of the world. The lions once carried a large stone wheel on their backs. The wheel (chakra) is a reference to the Wheel of the Law but also indicated Ashoka's stature as a *chakravartin* (holder of the wheel), a universal king imbued with divine authority. The open mouths of the four lions facing the four quarters of the world may signify the worldwide announcement of the Buddha's message.

Kushan Dynasty

The Maurya dynasty came to an abrupt end when its last ruler was assassinated by one of his generals, who founded a new dynasty in his own name. The Shungas (r. 185–72 BCE), however, ruled an empire confined to central India. Their successors were the Andhras (r. ca. 50–320 CE), who also controlled the Deccan plateau to the south. By the middle of the first century CE, an even greater empire, the Kushan (r. ca. 50–320 CE), rose in northern India. Its most celebrated king was Kanishka (r. 78–144 CE), whose capital was at Peshawar in Gandhara. The Kushans grew rich on trade between China and the west along one of the main caravan routes (the "Silk Road"—see Chapter 18) bringing the luxuries of the Orient to the Roman Empire.

Sanchi The unifying characteristic of this age of regional dynasties in South Asia was the patronage of Buddhism. One important Buddhist monastery, founded during Ashoka's reign and in use for more than a thousand years, is at Sanchi in central India. It consists of many buildings constructed over the centuries, including temples, *viharas* (celled structures where monks live), and large *stupas* (see "The Stupa," page 474). Sanchi's Great Stupa dates originally to Ashoka's reign, but in its present form (FIG. **17-4**), with its tall stone fence and four gates, dates from around 50 BCE to 50 CE. The solid earth-and-rubble dome stands 50 feet high. Worshipers enter through one of the gateways, walk on the lower circumambulation path, then climb the stairs on the south side to circumambulate at the second level. Veneration of the Buddha was open to all, not just the monks, and common laypeople, who hoped to accrue merit for future rebirths with their gifts, made most of the dedications.

The reliefs on the four toranas at Sanchi depict the story of the Buddha's life and those of his past lives (*jatakas*). In Buddhist belief, everyone has had innumerable past lives, including Siddhartha. During Siddhartha's former lives, he accumulated sufficient merit to achieve enlightenment and become the Buddha. In the life stories recounted in the Sanchi torana reliefs, however, the Buddha never appears in human form. Instead, the artists used symbols, for example, footprints, a parasol, or

Buddhism and Buddhist Iconography

Buddhism The earliest form of Buddhism is Theravada (Path of the Elders) Buddhism, practiced by the Buddha's disciples after his death. The new religion developed and changed over time as the Buddha's teachings spread from India throughout Asia. The second major school of Buddhist thought, Mahayana (Great Path) Buddhism, emerged around the beginning of the Common Era (CE). Mahayana Buddhists refer to Theravada Buddhism as Hinayana (Lesser Path) Buddhism and believe in a larger goal than nirvana for an individual—namely, buddhahood for all. Mahayana Buddhists also revere *bodhisattvas* (Buddhas-to-be), exemplars of compassion who restrain themselves at the threshold of nirvana to aid others in achieving buddhahood. Theravada Buddhism became the dominant sect in southern India, Sri Lanka, and mainland Southeast Asia, whereas Mahayana Buddhism took root in northern India and spread to China, Korea, Japan, and Nepal.

A third important Buddhist sect, especially popular in East Asia, venerates the Amitabha Buddha (Amida in Japanese), the Buddha of Infinite Light and Life. The devotees of this Buddha hope to be reborn in the Pure Land Paradise of the West, where the Amitabha resides and can grant them salvation. In Pure Land teachings, people have no possibility of attaining enlightenment on their own but can achieve paradise by faith alone.

Buddhist Iconography The earliest (first century CE) depictions of the Buddha in human form show him as a robed monk. Artists distinguished the Enlightened One from monks and bodhisattvas by *lakshanas*, body attributes indicating the Buddha's suprahuman nature. These distinguishing marks include an *urna*, or curl of hair between the eyebrows, shown as a dot (FIG. 17-1), and an *ushnisha*, a cranial bump shown as hair on the earliest images (FIG. 17-1) but later as part of the head (FIG. 17-6). Artists also often depicted the Buddha with elongated ears FIGS. 17-1 and 17-6), the result of wearing heavy royal jewelry in his youth, but the enlightened Shakyamuni is rarely bejeweled, though many bodhisattvas are (FIG. 17-7). Sometimes the Buddha appears with a halo, or sun disk, behind his head (FIG. 17-6).

Representations of the Buddha also feature a repertory of *mudras*, or hand gestures, conveying fixed meanings. These include the *dhyana* (meditation) mudra, with the right hand over the left hand, palms upward; the *bhumisparsha* (earth-touching) mudra, right hand down reaching to the ground, calling the earth to witness the Buddha's enlightenment (FIG. 17-1, *left center*); the *dharmachakra* (Wheel of the Law, or teaching) mudra, a two-handed gesture with right thumb and index finger forming a circle (FIG. 17-6); and the *abhaya* (do not fear) mudra, right hand up, palm outward, a gesture of protection or blessing (FIG. 17-1, *right*).

Episodes from the Buddha's life are among the most popular subjects in all Buddhist artistic traditions. No single text provides the complete or authoritative narrative of the Buddha's life and death. Thus, numerous versions and variations exist, allowing for a rich artistic repertory. Four of the most important events—all represented on the early frieze reproduced in FIG. 17-1—are his birth at Lumbini from the side of his mother, Queen Maya; the achievement of buddhahood while meditating beneath the Bodhi tree at Bodh Gaya; the Buddha's first sermon at Sarnath; and his attainment of nirvana (*parinirvana*) when he died at Kushinagara (compare FIG. 17-19).

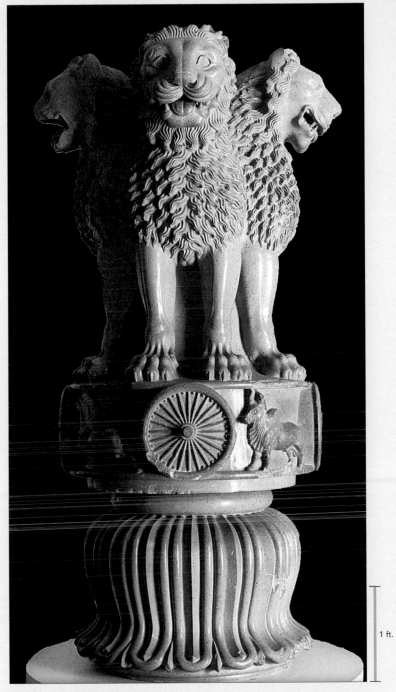

1 ft.

17-3 Lion capital of the column set up by Ashoka at Sarnath, India, ca. 250 BCE. Polished sandstone, 7' high. Archaeological Museum, Sarnath.

Ashoka formulated a legal code based on the Buddha's teachings and inscribed those laws on columns he set up throughout his kingdom. The lions on this capital once supported the Wheel of the Law.

The Stupa

An essential element of Buddhist sanctuaries is the *stupa*, a large circular mound modeled on earlier South Asian burial mounds of a type familiar in many other ancient cultures (for example, FIG. 2-11). The stupa was not a tomb, however, but a monument housing relics of the Buddha. When the Buddha died, his followers placed his cremated remains in eight reliquaries. Unlike their Western equivalents, which were put on display in churches (see "Pilgrimages and the Cult of Relics," Chapter 6, page 173), the Buddha's relics were buried in solid earthen mounds (stupas) that could not be entered. In the mid-third century BCE, Ashoka opened the original eight stupas and spread the Buddha's relics among thousands of stupas in all corners of his realm. Buddhists venerate the Buddha's remains by *circumambulation*, walking around the stupa in a clockwise direction. The circular movement, echoing the movement of the earth and the sun, brings the devotee into harmony with the cosmos.

Stupas come in many sizes. The largest, such as the Great Stupa at Sanchi (FIG. 17-4) erected originally by King Ashoka in the mid-third century BCE, are three-dimensional *mandalas*, or sacred diagrams of the universe. The domed stupa itself represents the world mountain, with the cardinal points marked by *toranas*, or gateways. The *harmika*, positioned atop the stupa dome, is a stone fence that encloses a square area symbolizing the sacred domain of the gods. At the harmika's center, a *yasti*, or pole, corresponds to the axis of the universe, a motif already present in Ashoka's pillars (FIG. 17-3). Three *chatras*, or stone disks, assigned various meanings, crown the yasti. The yasti rises from the mountain-dome and passes through the harmika, thus uniting this world with the heavenly paradise. A stone fence often encloses the entire structure, separating the sacred space containing the Buddha's relics from the profane world outside.

17-4 Diagram (*top*) and view looking north (*bottom*) of the Great Stupa, Sanchi, India, third century BCE to first century CE.

The Sanchi stupa is an earthen mound containing relics of the Buddha. Buddhists walk around stupas in a clockwise direction. They believe the circular motion brings devotees into harmony with the cosmos.

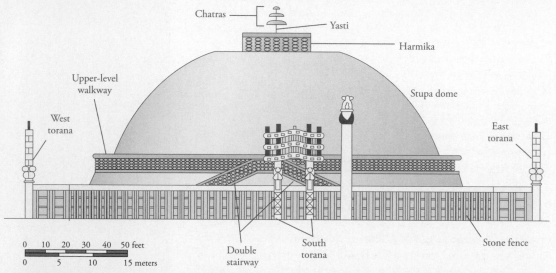

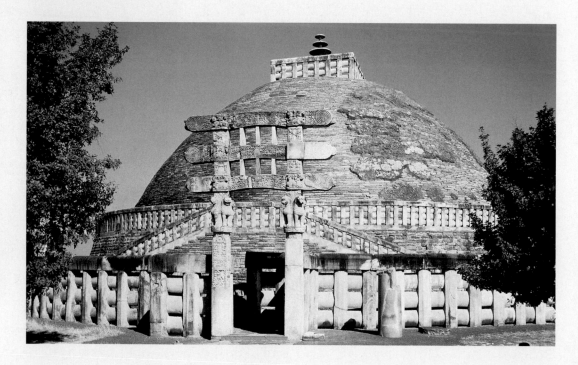

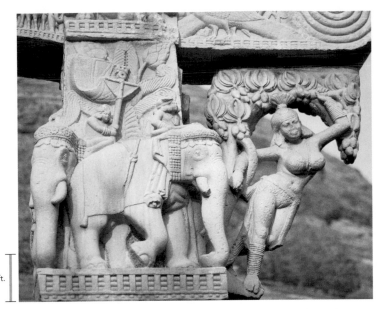

17-5 Elephants and yakshi, detail of the east torana, Great Stupa, Sanchi, India, mid-first century BCE to early first century CE. Sandstone, 5′ high.

Yakshis are scantily clad goddesses personifying fertility and vegetation. The Sanchi yakshis make mango trees flower. Buddhist artists later adapted the motif for Queen Maya giving birth to the Buddha.

an empty seat, to indicate the Buddha's presence. Some scholars regard these symbols as markers of where the Buddha once was so others can follow in his footsteps.

Also carved on the east torana is a scantily clad, sensuous woman called a *yakshi* (FIG. 17-5), a goddess personifying fertility and vegetation. She reaches up to hold a mango tree branch while pressing her left foot against the trunk, which causes the tree to flower. Buddhist artists later adopted this pose, with its rich associations of procreation and abundance, for representing the Buddha's mother, Maya, giving birth (FIG. 17-1, *top left*).

Gandhara The first anthropomorphic representations of the Buddha probably appeared in the first century CE. Scholars still debate what brought about this momentous shift in Buddhist iconography, but one factor may have been the changing perception of the Buddha himself. Originally revered as an enlightened mortal, the Buddha increasingly became regarded as a divinity. Consequently, the Buddha's followers desired images of him to worship.

One of the earliest pictorial narratives in which the Buddha appears in human form is the Gandharan frieze (FIG. 17-1) discussed in the introduction to this chapter. Although the iconography of the frieze is Buddhist, Roman sculptures must have served as stylistic models for the Gandharan artist. For example, the distribution of standing and equestrian figures over the relief ground, with those behind the first row seemingly suspended in the air, is familiar in Roman art of the second and third centuries CE (FIG. 3-48). The figure of the Buddha on his deathbed has parallels in the reclining figures on the lids of Etruscan (FIG. 3-4) and Roman

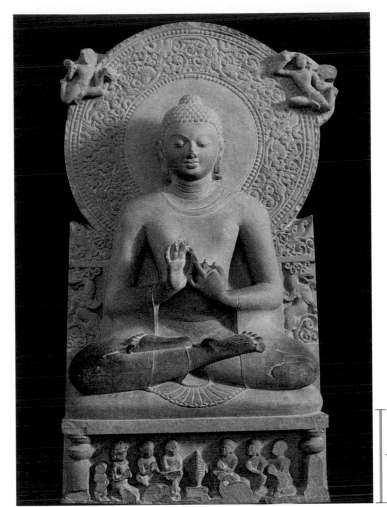

17-6 Seated Buddha preaching first sermon, from Sarnath, India, second half of fifth century. Tan sandstone, 5′ 3″ high. Archaeological Museum, Sarnath.

Gupta artists formulated the canonical image of the Buddha. The smooth unadorned surfaces conform to the Indian notion of perfect body form and emphasize the figure's spirituality.

sarcophagi. The type of hierarchical composition in which a large central figure sits between balanced tiers of smaller onlookers is also common in Roman imperial art (FIG. 3-53).

The Gupta and Post-Gupta Periods

Around 320* a new empire arose in north-central India. The Gupta emperors (r. ca. 320–450) chose Pataliputra as their capital, deliberately associating themselves with the prestige of the former Maurya Empire. The heyday of this dynasty was under Chandragupta II (r. 375–415), whose very name recalled the first Maurya emperor.

Sarnath Under the Guptas, artists formulated what became the canonical image of the Buddha. A fifth-century statue (FIG. 17-6) of the Buddha from Sarnath is a characteristic example. The Buddha wears a clinging monastic robe covering

*From this point on, all dates in this chapter are CE unless otherwise stated.

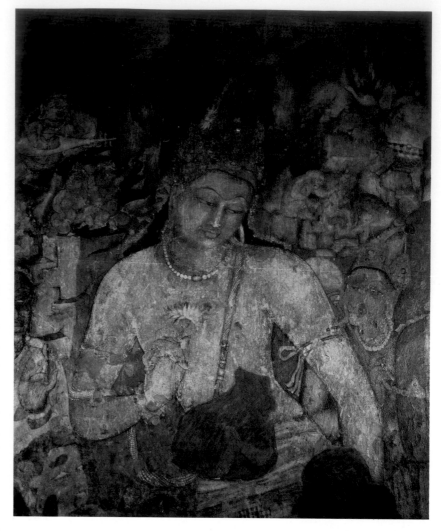

17-7 Bodhisattva Padmapani, detail of a wall painting in the antechamber of cave 1, Ajanta, India, second half of fifth century.

The Ajanta caves are renowned for their mural paintings. This artist rendered the sensuous form of the richly attired bodhisattva with gentle gradations of color and delicate highlights and shadows.

both shoulders. His eyes are downcast in meditation, and he holds his hands in front of his body in the Wheel-turning gesture, preaching his first sermon. Below the Buddha is a scene with the Wheel of the Law at the center between two deer symbolizing the Deer Park at Sarnath. The statue's smooth, unadorned surfaces conform to the Indian notion of perfect body form and emphasize the figure's spirituality. Buddha images such as this one became so popular that temples housing Buddha statues seem largely to have superseded the stupa as the norm in Buddhist sacred architecture.

Ajanta The new popularity of Buddha imagery may be seen at Ajanta, northeast of Bombay. Ajanta had been home to a small Buddhist monastery for centuries, but during the second half of the fifth century, royal patrons of the local Vakataka dynasty, allied to the Guptas by marriage, added more than 20 new caves to the site. Ajanta owes its fame today to the painted walls and ceilings in many of those caves. Illustrated here (FIG. **17-7**) is a detail of one of the restored painted walls in cave 1 depicting the bodhisattva Padmapani among a crowd of devotees, both princes and commoners. With long, dark hair hanging down below a jeweled crown, he stands holding his attribute, a blue lotus flower, in his right hand. The painter rendered with finesse the sensuous form of the richly attired bodhisattva, gently modeling the figure with gradations of color and delicate highlights and shadows, especially evident in the face and neck. The artist also carefully considered the placement of the painting in the cave. The bodhisattva gazes downward at worshipers entering the antechamber on their way to the rock-cut Buddha image in a cell at the back of the cave.

At Ajanta, as at many other sites in India, Buddhists and Hindus practiced their religions side by side. For example, the Hindu Vakataka king Harishena (r. 462–481) and members of his court were the sponsors of new Hindu caves at the Buddhist monastery. Buddhism and Hinduism are not monotheistic religions, such as Judaism, Christianity, and Islam. Instead, Buddhists and Hindus approach the spiritual through many gods and varying paths, which permits mutually tolerated differences. In fact, in Hinduism, the Buddha is one of the ten incarnations of Vishnu, one of the three principal Hindu deities (see "Hinduism and Hindu Iconography," page 477).

Badami More early Buddhist than Hindu art has survived in India because the Buddhists constructed their monasteries with durable materials such as stone and brick. But in the Gupta period, Hindu stone sculpture and architecture began to rival the great Buddhist monuments of South Asia. During the sixth century, the Huns brought down the Gupta Empire, and various regional dynasties rose to power. In the Deccan plateau of central India, the Chalukya kings ruled from their capital at Badami. There, Chalukya sculptors carved a series of reliefs in the walls of halls cut into the cliff above the city. One relief (FIG. **17-8**) shows Shiva dancing the cosmic dance, his 18 arms swinging rhythmically in an arc. Some of the hands hold objects, and others form prescribed mudras. At the lower right, the elephant-headed Ganesha tentatively mimics Shiva. Nandi, Shiva's bull mount, stands at the left. Artists often represented Hindu deities as part human and part animal or, as in the Badami relief, as figures with multiple body parts. Such composite and multilimbed forms indicate the subjects are not human but suprahuman gods with supernatural powers.

Elephanta Another portrayal of Shiva as a suprahuman being is in a cave temple on Elephanta, an island in Bombay's harbor that in the sixth century was under the control of the Kalachuri dynasty. Deep within the temple, in a niche once

Hinduism and Hindu Iconography

Unlike Buddhism (and Christianity, Islam, and other religions), Hinduism recognizes no founder or great prophet. Hinduism also has no simple definition but means "the religion of the Indians." Both *India* and *Hindu* have a common root in the name of the Indus River. The practices and beliefs of Hindus vary tremendously, but the literary origins of Hinduism date to the Vedic period, and some aspects of Hindu practice apparently were already present in the Indus Civilization of the third millennium BCE. Ritual sacrifice by Brahmin priests is central to Hinduism, as it was to the Aryans. The goal of sacrifice is to please a deity in order to achieve liberation (moksha) from the endless cycle of birth, death, and rebirth (samsara) and become one with the universal spirit.

Hinduism is a religion of many gods, who have various natures and take many forms. This multiplicity suggests the all-pervasive nature of the Hindu gods. The three most important deities are the gods Shiva and Vishnu and the goddess Devi.

▎ *Shiva* is the Destroyer, but, consistent with the multiplicity of Hindu belief, he is also a regenerative force. In the latter role, Shiva can be represented in the form of a *linga* (a phallus or cosmic pillar). When Shiva appears in human form in Hindu art, he frequently has multiple limbs and heads (FIGS. 17-8 and 17-9), signs of his suprahuman nature, and matted locks piled atop his head, crowned by a crescent moon. Sometimes he wears a serpent scarf and has a third eye on his forehead (the emblem of his all-seeing nature). Shiva rides the bull **Nandi** (FIG. 17-8) and often carries a *trident*, a three-pronged pitchfork.

▎ *Vishnu* is the Preserver of the Universe. Artists frequently portray him with four arms holding various attributes. He sometimes reclines on a serpent floating on the waters of the cosmic sea (FIG. 17-10). When the evil forces of the universe become too strong, he descends to earth to restore balance and assumes different forms (*avatars*, or incarnations), including a boar, fish, and tortoise, as well as **Krishna**, the divine lover (FIG. 17-17), and even the Buddha himself.

▎ *Devi* is the Great Goddess who takes many forms and has many names. Hindus worship her alone or as a consort of male gods (**Parvati** or **Uma**, wife of Shiva; **Lakshmi**, wife of Vishnu), as well as **Radha**, lover of Krishna (FIG. 17-17). She has both benign and horrific forms, and she creates as well as destroys. In one manifestation, she is **Durga**, a multi-armed goddess who often rides a lion. Her son is the elephant-headed **Ganesha** (FIG. 17-8).

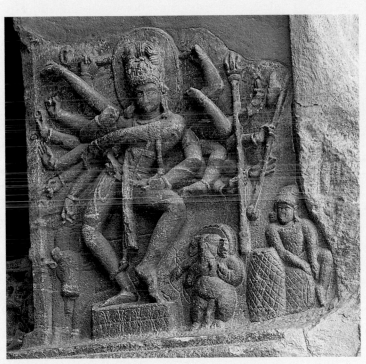

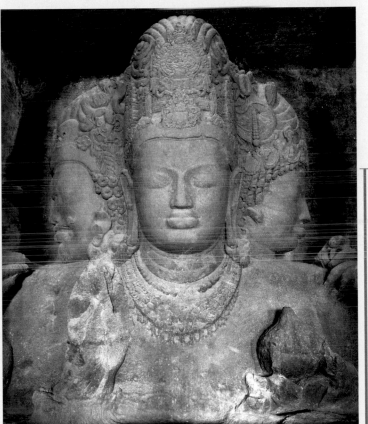

10 ft.

17-8 Dancing Shiva, rock-cut relief, cave 1, Badami, India, late sixth century.

Shiva dances the cosmic dance and has 18 arms, some holding objects, others forming mudras. Hindu gods often have multiple limbs to indicate their suprahuman nature and divine powers.

17-9 Shiva as Mahadeva, cave 1, Elephanta, India, ca. 550–575. Basalt, Shiva 17' 10" high.

This immense rock-cut image of Shiva as Mahadeva (Great God) emerges out of the depths of the Elephanta cave as worshipers' eyes adjust to the darkness. Shiva has both male and female faces.

closed off with wooden doors, is a nearly 18-foot-high rock-cut image (FIG. 17-9) of Shiva as Mahadeva, the "Great God" or Lord of Lords. Mahadeva appears to emerge out of the depths of the cave as worshipers' eyes become accustomed to the darkness. This image of Shiva has three faces, each showing a different aspect of the deity. (A fourth, unseen at the back, is implied—the god has not emerged fully from the rock.) The central face expresses Shiva's quiet, balanced

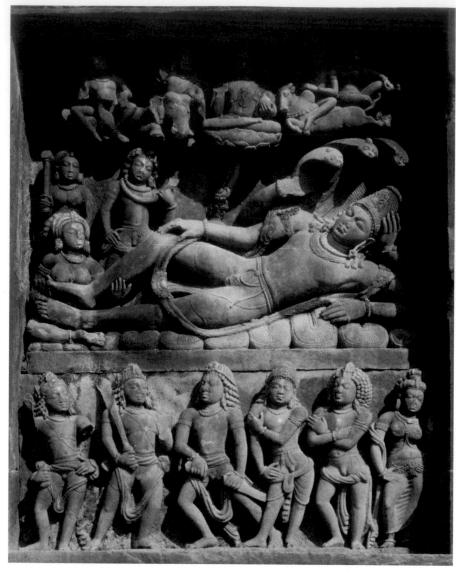

17-10 *Vishnu Asleep on the Serpent Ananta,* relief panel on the south facade of the Vishnu Temple, Deogarh, India, early sixth century.

The Deogarh temple is one of the first Hindu stone temples. Its reliefs celebrate Vishnu. Here, the god sleeps on the serpent Ananta and dreams the universe into reality.

among the first Hindu temples constructed with stone blocks. A simple square tower, it has an elaborately decorated doorway at the front and a relief in a niche on each of the other three sides. Sculpted guardians protect the doorway at Deogarh because it is the transition point between the dangerous outside and the sacred interior.

The reliefs in the three niches depict important episodes in the saga of Vishnu. On the south (FIG. **17-10**), Vishnu sleeps on the coils of the giant serpent Ananta, whose multiple heads form a kind of umbrella around the god's face. While Lakshmi massages her husband's legs (he has cramps as he gives birth), the four-armed Vishnu dreams the universe into reality. A lotus plant (said to have grown out of Vishnu's navel) supports the four-headed Hindu god of creation, Brahma. Flanking him are other important Hindu divinities, including Shiva on his bull. Below are six figures. The four at the right are personifications of Vishnu's various powers. They will defeat the two armed demons at the left. The sculptor carved all the figures in the classic Gupta style, with smooth bodies and clinging garments (compare FIG. 17-6).

Medieval Period

During the 7th through the 12th centuries, regional dynasties ruled parts of India. Whereas Buddhism spread rapidly throughout East Asia, in medieval India it gradually declined, and the various local kings vied with one another to build glorious shrines to the Hindu gods.

Thanjavur Under the Chola dynasty, whose territories extended into part of Sri Lanka and even Java, architects constructed temples of unprecedented size and grandeur in the southern Indian tradition (see "Hindu Temples," page 479). The Rajarajeshvara Temple (FIG. **17-11**) at Thanjavur, dedicated in 1010 to Shiva as the Lord of Rajaraja, was the largest and tallest temple (210 feet high) in India at the time. The temple stands inside a walled precinct. It consists of a stairway leading to two flat-roofed mandapas, the larger one having 36 pillars, and to the garbha griha in the base of the enormous pyramidal vimana, which is as much an emblem of the Cholas' secular power as of their devotion to Shiva. On the exterior walls of the lower stories are numerous reliefs in niches depicting the god in his various forms.

Khajuraho At the same time the Cholas were building the Rajarajeshvara Temple at Thanjavur in the south, the Chandella dynasty was constructing northern-style temples at Khajuraho. The Vishvanatha Temple (FIG. **17-12**) is one of

demeanor. The clean planes of the face contrast with the richness of the piled hair encrusted with jewels. The two side faces differ significantly. The one on the right is female, with framing hair curls. The left face is a grimacing male with a curling mustache who wears a cobra as an earring. The female (Uma) indicates the creative aspect of Shiva. The fierce male (Bhairava) represents Shiva's destructive side. Shiva holds these two opposing forces in check, and the central face expresses their balance. The cyclic destruction and creation of the universe, which the side faces also symbolize, are part of Indian notions of time, matched by the cyclic pattern of death and rebirth.

Deogarh The rock-cut Badami and Elephanta cave shrines are characteristic of early Hindu religious architecture, but temples constructed using quarried stone became more important as Hinduism evolved. The Vishnu Temple at Deogarh in north-central India, datable to the early sixth century, is

Hindu Temples

The Hindu temple is the home of the gods on earth and the place where they make themselves visible to humans. At the core of all Hindu temples is the *garbha griha* (womb chamber), which houses images or symbols of the deity—for example, Shiva's linga (see "Hinduism," page 477). Only Brahmin priests may enter this inner sanctuary to make offerings to the gods. Worshipers, however, may stand at the threshold and behold the deity as manifest by its image. In the elaborate multiroomed temples of later Hindu architecture, the worshipers and priests progress through a series of ever more sacred spaces, usually on an east-west axis. Hindu priests and architects attached great importance to each temple's plan and sought to make it conform to the sacred geometric diagram (*mandala*) of the universe.

Architectural historians, following ancient Indian texts, divide Hindu temples into two major typological groups tied to geography.

▌ **Northern temples** (FIG. 17-12). The most important distinguishing feature of the northern style of temple is its beehivelike tower or *shikhara* (mountain peak), capped by an *amalaka*, a ribbed cushionlike form, derived from the shape of the amala fruit (believed to have medicinal powers). Amalakas appear on the corners of the lower levels of the shikhara too. Northern temples also have smaller towerlike roofs over the halls (*mandapas*) leading to the garbha griha.

▌ **Southern temples** (FIG. 17-11). Hindu temples of the southern type have flat roofs over their pillared mandapas, and shorter towered shrines, called *vimanas*, which lack the curved profile of their northern counterparts and resemble multilevel pyramids.

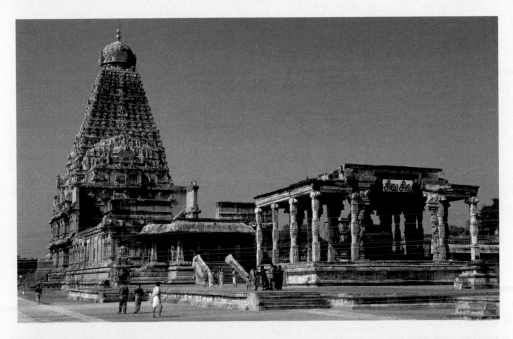

17-11 Rajarajeshvara Temple (looking southeast), Thanjavur, India, ca. 1010.

The Rajarajeshvara Temple at Thanjavur is an example of the southern type of Hindu temple. Two flat-roofed mandapas lead to the garbha griha in the base of its 210-foot-tall pyramidal vimana.

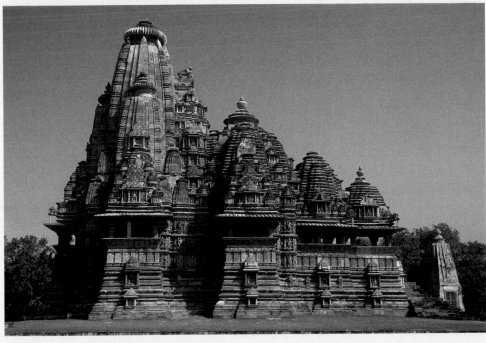

17-12 Vishvanatha Temple (looking north), Khajuraho, India, ca. 1000.

The Vishvanatha Temple is a northern Hindu temple type. It has four towers, each taller than the preceding one, symbolizing Shiva's mountain home. The largest tower is the beehive-shaped shikhara.

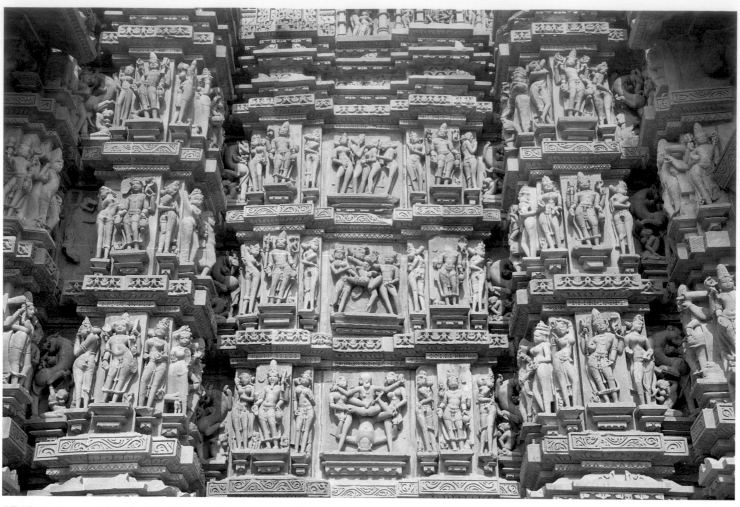

17-13 Mithuna reliefs, detail of the north side of the Vishvanatha Temple, Khajuraho, India, ca. 1000.

Northern Hindu temples usually feature reliefs depicting deities and amorous couples (mithunas). The erotic sculptures suggest the propagation of life and serve as protectors of the sacred precinct.

more than 20 large, elaborate temples at that site. Vishvanatha (Lord of the World) is another of the many names for Shiva. Dedicated in 1002, the structure has four towers over the mandapas, each rising higher than the preceding one, leading to the tallest tower at the rear, in much the same way the foothills of the Himalayas, Shiva's home, rise to meet their highest peak. The mountain symbolism applies to the interior of the Vishvanatha Temple as well. Under the tallest tower, the shikhara, is the garbha griha, the small and dark inner sanctuary chamber, like a cave, which houses the image of the deity. Thus, temples such as the Vishvanatha symbolize constructed mountains with caves, comparable to the cave temples at Elephanta and other Indian sites. In all cases, the deity manifests himself or herself within the cave and takes various forms in sculptures. The temple-mountains, however, are not intended to appear natural but rather are perfect mountains designed using ideal mathematical proportions.

The reliefs of Thanjavur's Rajarajeshvara Temple are typical of southern temple decoration, which is generally limited to images of deities. The exterior walls of Khajuraho's Vishvanatha Temple are equally typical of northern temples in the profusion of sculptures (FIG. **17-13**) depicting mortals as well as gods, especially pairs of men and women (*mithunas*) embracing or engaged in sexual intercourse in an extraordinary range of positions. The use of seminude yakshis and amorous couples as motifs on religious buildings in India has a very long history, going back to the earliest architectural traditions, both Hindu and Buddhist (FIG. **17-5**). As in the earlier examples, the erotic sculptures of Khajuraho suggest fertility and the propagation of life and serve as auspicious protectors of the sacred precinct.

Islam Arab armies first appeared in South Asia—at Sindh (Pakistan)—in 712. With them came Islam, the new religion that had already spread with astonishing speed from the Arabian peninsula to Syria, Iraq, Iran, Egypt, North Africa, and even southern Spain (see Chapter 5). At first, the Muslims established trading settlements in South Asia but did not press deeper into the subcontinent. At the Battle of Tarain in 1192, however, Muhammad of Ghor (Afghanistan) defeated the armies of a confederation of Indian states. His general, Qutb al-Din Aybak, established the sultanate of Delhi (1206–1526). On his death in 1211, he passed power on to his son Iltutmish (r. 1211–1236), who extended Ghorid rule across northern India.

Mughal Empire

In 1526, a Muslim prince named Babur defeated the last of the Ghorid sultans of northern India at the Battle of Panipat. Declaring himself the ruler of India, Babur established the Mughal Empire (1526–1857) at Delhi.

Akbar the Great The first great flowering of Mughal art and architecture occurred during the long reign of Babur's grandson, Akbar (r. 1556–1605), called the Great. Akbar enlarged the imperial painting workshop to about a hundred artists and kept them busy working on a series of ambitious projects. One of these was to illustrate the text of the biography he had commissioned Abul Fazl (1551–1602), a member of his court and a close friend, to write. The *Akbarnama* (*History of Akbar*) includes many full-page *miniatures,* so called because of their small size (about the size of a page in this book) compared with paintings on walls, wood panels, or canvas. Indian miniatures were watercolor paintings on paper. They served either as illustrations in books or as loose-leaf pages in albums. Owners did not place the miniatures in frames and only rarely hung them on walls.

One miniature (FIG. **17-14**) in the emperor's personal copy of the *Akbarnama* was a collaborative effort between the painter BASAWAN, who designed and drew the composition, and CHATAR MUNI, who colored it. The painting depicts the episode of Akbar and Hawai, a wild elephant the 19-year-old ruler mounted and pitted against another ferocious elephant. When the second animal fled in defeat, Hawai, still carrying Akbar, chased it to a pontoon bridge. The enormous weight of the elephants capsized the boats, but Akbar managed to bring Hawai under control and dismount safely. The young ruler viewed the episode as an allegory of his ability to govern—that is, to take charge of an unruly state.

For his pictorial record of that frightening day, Basawan chose the moment of maximum chaos and danger—when the elephants crossed the pontoon bridge, sending boatmen flying into the water. The composition is a bold one, with a very high horizon and two strong diagonal lines formed by the bridge and the shore. Together these devices tend to flatten out the vista, yet at the same time Basawan created a sense of depth by diminishing the size of the figures in the background. He was also a master of vivid gestures and anecdotal detail. Note especially the bare-chested figure in the foreground clinging to the end of a boat, the figure near the lower right corner with outstretched arms sliding into the water as the bridge sinks, and the oarsman just beyond the bridge who strains to steady his vessel while his three passengers stand up or lean overboard in reaction to the surrounding commotion.

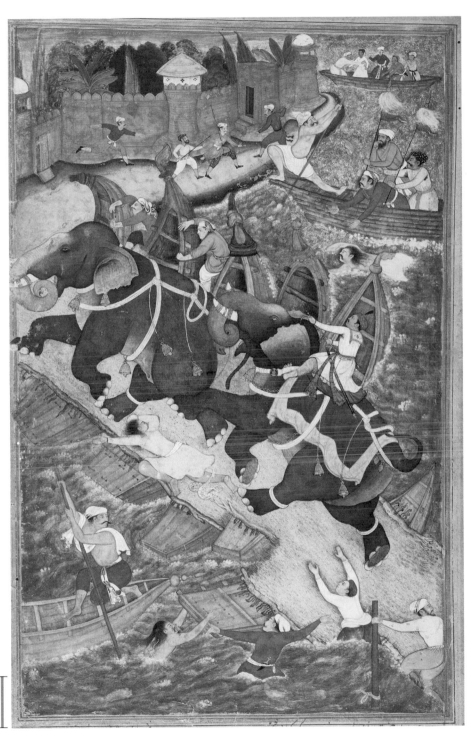

1 in.

17-14 BASAWAN and CHATAR MUNI, *Akbar and the Elephant Hawai,* folio 22 from the *Akbarnama* (*History of Akbar*) by Abul Fazl, ca. 1590. Opaque watercolor on paper, 1' 1⅞" × 8¾". Victoria & Albert Museum, London.

The Mughal rulers of India were great patrons of miniature painting. This example, showing the young emperor Akbar bringing an elephant under control, is an allegory of Akbar's ability to rule.

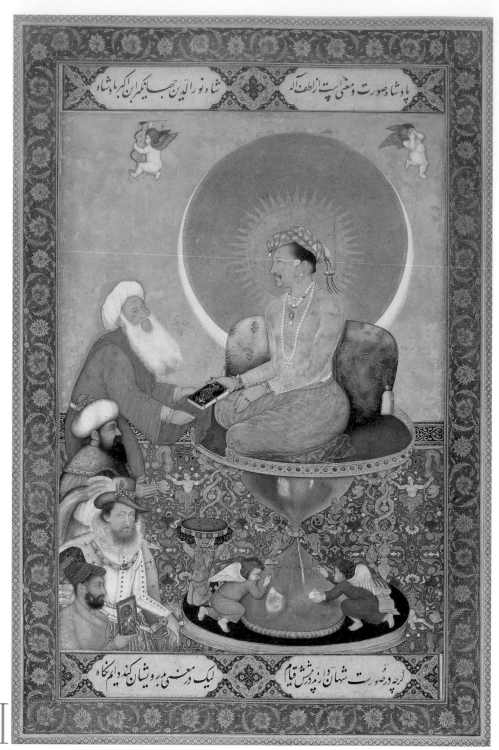

17-15 BICHITR, *Jahangir Preferring a Sufi Shaykh to Kings*, ca. 1615–1618. Opaque watercolor on paper, 1′ 6⅞″ × 1′ 1″. Freer Gallery of Art, Washington, D.C. ◼️

European influence on Mughal painting is evident in this allegorical portrait of the haloed emperor Jahangir on an hourglass throne, seated above time, favoring spiritual over worldly power.

British ambassadors and merchants were frequent visitors, and Jahangir, like his father, acquired many European luxury goods, including globes, hourglasses, prints, and portraits.

The influence of European art on Mughal miniature painting under Jahangir is evident in Bichitr's allegorical portrait (FIG. **17-15**) of Jahangir seated on an hourglass throne. As the sands of time run out, two cupids (clothed, unlike their European models more closely copied at the top of the painting) inscribe the throne with the wish that Jahangir would live a thousand years. Bichitr portrayed his patron as an emperor above time and placed behind Jahangir's head a radiant halo combining a golden sun and a white crescent moon, indicating Jahangir is the center of the universe and its light source. One of the inscriptions on the painting gives the emperor's title as "Light of the Faith."

At the left are four figures. The lowest, both spatially and in the social hierarchy, is the Hindu painter Bichitr himself, wearing a red turban. He holds a painting representing two horses and an elephant, costly gifts from Jahangir, and another self-portrait. In the painting-within-the-painting, Bichitr bows deeply before the emperor. In the larger painting, the artist signed his name across the top of the footstool Jahangir uses to step up to his hourglass throne. Thus, the ruler steps on Bichitr's name, further indicating the painter's inferior status.

Above Bichitr is a portrait in full European style of King James I of England (r. 1603–1625), copied from a painting by John de Critz (ca. 1552–1641) that the English ambassador to the Mughal court had given as a gift to Jahangir. Above the king is a Turkish sultan, a convincing study of physiognomy but probably not a specific portrait. The highest member of the foursome is an elderly Muslim Sufi *shaykh* (mystic saint). Jahangir's father, Akbar, had gone to the mystic to pray for an heir. The current emperor, the answer to Akbar's prayers, presents the holy man with a sumptuous book as a gift. An inscription explains that "although to all appearances kings stand before him, Jahangir looks inwardly toward the dervishes [Islamic holy men]" for guidance. Bichitr's allegorical painting portrays his emperor in both words and pictures as favoring spiritual over worldly power.

Jahangir That the names Basawan and Chatar Muni are known is significant in itself. In contrast to the anonymity of pre-Mughal artists in India, many of those whom the Mughal emperors employed signed their artworks. Another of these was BICHITR, an artist in the imperial workshop of Akbar's son and successor, Jahangir (r. 1605–1627). The Mughal dynasty presided over a cosmopolitan court with refined tastes.

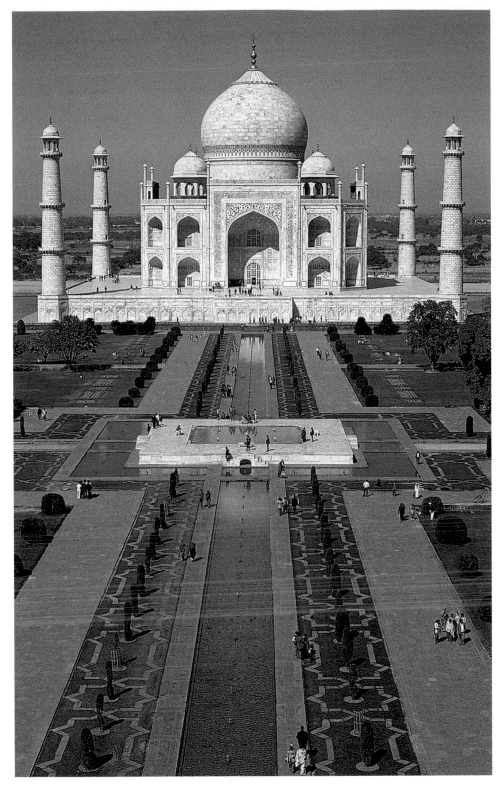

17-16 Taj Mahal (looking north), Agra, India, 1632–1647. ■◄

This Mughal mausoleum seems to float magically over reflecting pools in a vast garden. The tomb may have been conceived as the throne of God perched above the gardens of Paradise on judgment day.

Taj Mahal Monumental tombs were not part of either the Hindu or Buddhist traditions but had a long history in Islamic architecture. The Delhi sultans had erected tombs in India, but none could compare in grandeur to the fabled Taj Mahal (FIG. **17-16**) at Agra. Shah Jahan (r. 1628–1658), Jahangir's son, built the immense *mausoleum* as a memorial to his favorite wife, Mumtaz Mahal (1593–1631), although it eventually became the ruler's tomb as well. The dome-on-cube shape of the central block has antecedents in earlier Islamic mausoleums, but modifications and refinements in the design of the Agra tomb created an almost weightless vision of glistening white marble. The Agra mausoleum seems to float magically above the tree-lined reflecting pools punctuating the garden leading to it. Reinforcing the illusion of the marble tomb being suspended above water is the absence of any visible means of ascent to the upper platform. A stairway does exist, but the architect intentionally hid it from the view of anyone who approaches the memorial.

The Taj Mahal follows the plan of Iranian garden pavilions, except that the building stands at one end rather than in the center of the formal garden. The tomb is octagonal in plan and has typically Iranian arcuated niches (FIGS. 5-10 and 5-11) on each side. The interplay of shadowy voids with light-reflecting marble walls that seem paper-thin creates an impression of translucency. The pointed arches lead the eye in a sweeping upward movement toward the climactic dome, shaped like a crown (*taj*). Four carefully related minarets and two flanking pavilions (not visible in FIG. 17-16) enhance and stabilize this soaring form of the mausoleum. The architect achieved this delicate balance between verticality and horizontality by strictly applying an all-encompassing system of proportions. The Taj Mahal (excluding the minarets) is exactly as wide as it is tall, and the height of its dome is equal to the height of the facade.

Abd al-Hamid Lahori (d. 1654), a court historian who witnessed the construction of the Taj Mahal, compared its minarets to ladders reaching toward Heaven and its surrounding gardens to Paradise. In fact, inscribed on the gateway to the gardens and the walls of the mausoleum are selected excerpts from the Koran confirming the historian's interpretation of the tomb's symbolism. The designer of the Taj Mahal may have conceived the mausoleum as the throne of God perched above the gardens of Paradise on judgment day. The minarets hold up the canopy of that throne. In Islam, the most revered place of burial is beneath the throne of God.

Later Hindu Kingdoms

The Mughal emperors ruled vast territories, but much of northwestern India (present-day Rajasthan) remained under the control of Hindu Rajput (sons of kings) dynasties. These small kingdoms had stubbornly resisted Mughal expansion, but even the strongest of them, Mewar, eventually submitted to the Mughal emperors. When Jahangir defeated the Mewari forces in 1615, the Mewar maharana (great king), like the other Rajput rulers, maintained a degree of independence but had to pay tribute to the Mughal treasury.

Rajput painting resembles Mughal painting in format and material, but it differs sharply in other respects. Most Rajput artists, for example, worked in anonymity, never inserting self-portraits into their paintings as the Mughal painter Bichitr did in his miniature (FIG. 17-15) of Jahangir on an hourglass throne.

Krishna and Radha One of the most common subjects for Rajput paintings was the amorous adventures of Krishna, the "Blue God," the most popular avatar of Vishnu. Krishna was a herdsman who spent an idyllic existence tending his cows, playing the flute, and sporting with beautiful herdswomen. His favorite lover was Radha. The 12th-century poet Jayadeva related the story of Krishna and Radha in the *Gita Govinda* (*Song of the Cowherd*). Their love was a model of the devotion, or *bhakti,* paid to Vishnu. Jayadeva's poem was the source for hundreds of later paintings, including *Krishna and Radha in a Pavilion* (FIG. **17-17**), a miniature painted in the Punjab Hills by a member of the "Pahari School," probably for Raja Govardhan Chand (r. 1741–1773) of Guler. Although Pahari painting owed much to Mughal drawing style, its coloration, lyricism, and sensuality are distinctive. In *Krishna and Radha in a Pavilion,* the lovers sit naked on a bed beneath a jeweled pavilion in a lush garden of ripe mangoes and flowering shrubs. Krishna gently touches Radha's breast while looking directly into her face. Radha shyly averts her gaze. It is night, the time of illicit trysts, and the dark monsoon sky momentarily lights up with a lightning flash indicating the moment's electric passion. Lightning is one of the standard symbols used in Rajput and Pahari miniatures to represent sexual excitement.

Madurai Construction of some of the largest Hindu temple complexes in southern India occurred under the Nayak dynasty (r. 1529–1736). The most striking features of these huge complexes are their gateway towers called *gopuras* (FIG. **17-18**), decorated from top to bottom with painted sculptures. After erecting the gopuras, the builders constructed walls to connect them and then built more gopuras, always expanding outward from the center. Each set of gopuras was taller than those of the previous circuit. The outermost towers reached colossal size, dwarfing the temples at the heart of the complexes. The tallest gopuras of the Great Temple at Madurai, dedicated to Shiva under his local name, Sundareshvara (the Handsome One), and his consort Minakshi (the Fish-Eyed One), stand about 150 feet tall. Rising in a series of tiers of diminishing size, they culminate in a barrel-vaulted roof with finials. The ornamentation is extremely rich, consisting of row after row of brightly painted stucco sculptures representing the vast pantheon of Hindu deities and a host of attendant figures. Reconsecration of the temple occurs at 12-year intervals, at which time the gopura sculptures receive a new coat of paint, which accounts for the vibrancy of their colors today.

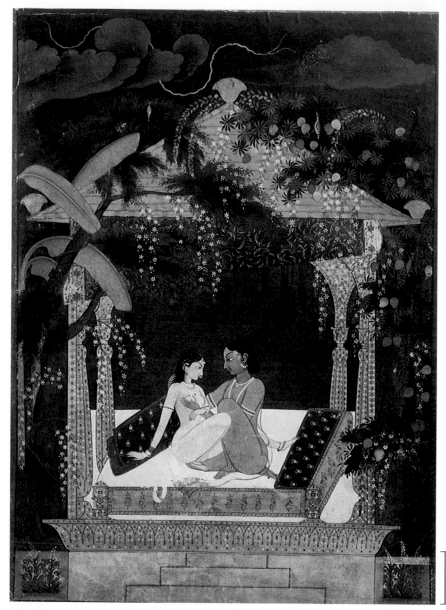

1 in.

17-17 *Krishna and Radha in a Pavilion,* ca. 1760. Opaque watercolor on paper, 11⅛″ × 7¾″. National Museum, New Delhi.

The love of Krishna, the "Blue God," for Radha is the subject of this colorful, lyrical, and sensual Pahari watercolor. Krishna's love was a model of the devotion paid to the Hindu god Vishnu.

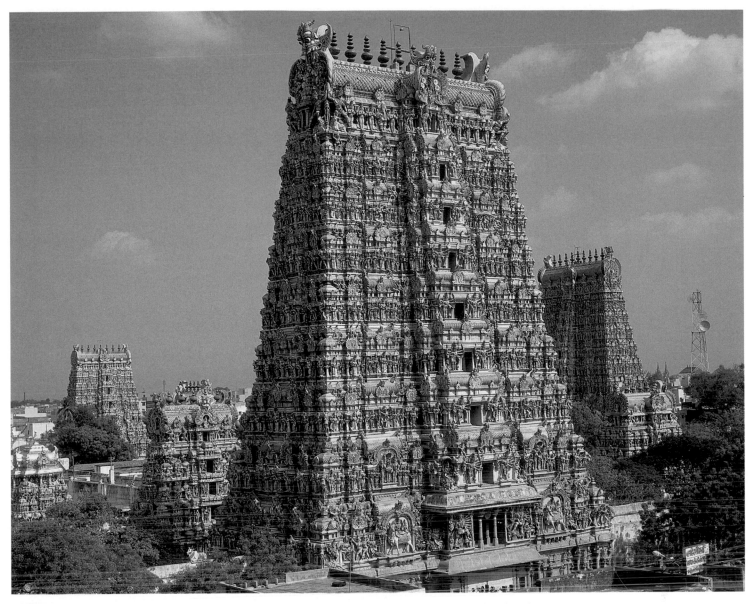

17-18 Outermost gopuras of the Great Temple (looking southeast), Madurai, India, completed 17th century.

The colossal gateway towers set up during the Nayak dynasty at the Great Temple at Madurai feature brightly painted stucco sculptures representing the vast pantheon of Hindu deities.

The Mughal Empire came to an end in 1857, and for nearly a century thereafter, the British ruled India. Under the leadership of Mahatma Gandhi (1869–1948), India and Pakistan attained independence in 1947. Throughout the period of British sovereignty, local traditions mixed with imported European styles in both art and architecture. The rich and varied contemporary art of South Asia continues to draw upon these diverse traditions.

SOUTHEAST ASIA

Art historians once considered the art of Southeast Asia an extension of Indian civilization. Because of the Indian character of many Southeast Asian monuments, scholars hypothesized that Indian artists had constructed and decorated them and that Indians had colonized Southeast Asia. Today, researchers have concluded that the expansion of Indian culture to Southeast Asia during the first millennium CE was peaceful and nonimperialistic, a by-product of trade. Accompanying the trade goods from India were Sanskrit, Buddhism, and Hinduism—and Buddhist and Hindu art. But the Southeast Asian peoples soon modified Indian art to make it their own. Art historians now recognize Southeast Asian art and architecture as a distinctive and multifaceted tradition.

Sri Lanka

Sri Lanka (formerly Ceylon) is an island located at the very tip of the Indian subcontinent. Theravada Buddhism, the oldest form of Buddhism, stressing worship of the historical Buddha, arrived in Sri Lanka as early as the third century BCE. From there it spread to other parts of Southeast Asia. With the demise of Buddhism in India in about the 13th century, Sri Lanka now has the longest-lived Buddhist tradition in the world.

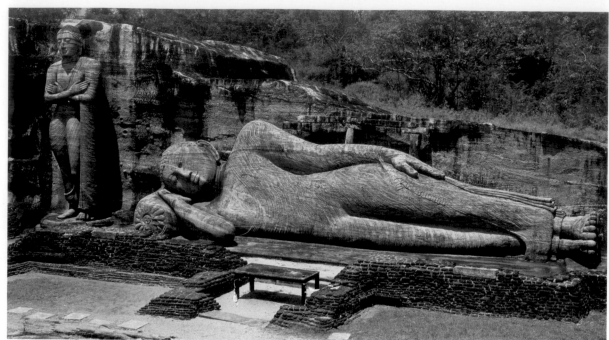

17-19 *Death of the Buddha (Parinirvana)*, Gal Vihara, near Polonnaruwa, Sri Lanka, 11th to 12th century. Granulite, Buddha 10′ × 46′.

The sculptor of this colossal recumbent Sri Lankan Buddha emulated the classic Gupta style of a half millennium earlier in the figure's clinging robe, rounded face, and coiffure.

Gal Vihara One of the largest sculptures in Southeast Asia is the 46-foot-long recumbent Buddha (FIG. **17-19**) carved out of a rocky outcropping at Gal Vihara. To the left of the Buddha, much smaller in scale, stands his cousin and chief disciple, Ananda, arms crossed, mourning Shakyamuni's death. Although more than a half millennium later in date, the Sri Lankan representation of the Buddha's parinirvana reveals its sculptor's debt to the classic Gupta sculptures of India, with their clinging garments, rounded faces, and distinctive renditions of hair (compare FIG. 17-6).

Java

In contrast to the Buddhist monuments of Sri Lanka, those on the island of Java, part of the modern nation of Indonesia, exhibit a marked independence from Indian models.

Borobudur Unique in both form and meaning, Borobudur (FIG. **17-20**) is a Buddhist monument of colossal size, measuring about 400 feet per side at the base and about 98 feet tall. Built over a small hill on nine terraces accessed by four stairways aligned with the cardinal points, the structure contains literally millions of blocks of volcanic stone. Visitors ascending the massive monument on their way to the summit encounter more than 500 life-size Buddha images, at least 1,000 relief panels, and some 1,500 stupas of various sizes.

Scholars debate the intended meaning of Borobudur. Most think it is a constructed cosmic mountain, a three-dimensional mandala where worshipers pass through various realms on their way to ultimate enlightenment. As they circumambulate the structure, pilgrims first see reliefs

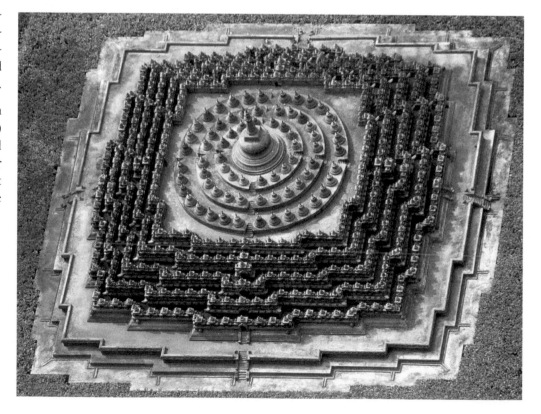

17-20 Aerial view of Borobudur, Java, Indonesia, ca. 800.

Borobudur is a gigantic, unique Buddhist monument. Built on nine terraces with more than 1,500 stupas and 1,500 statues and reliefs, it takes the form of a cosmic mountain, which worshipers circumambulate.

illustrating the karmic effects of different kinds of human behavior, then reliefs depicting jatakas of the Buddha's earlier lives, and, farther up, events from the life of Shakyamuni. On the circular terraces near the summit, each stupa is hollow and houses a statue of the seated Buddha, who has achieved spiritual enlightenment and preaches using the Wheel-turning mudra. At the very top is the largest, sealed stupa. It may once have contained another Buddha image, but it may also have been left empty to symbolize the formlessness of true enlightenment. Although scholars have interpreted the iconographic program in different ways, all agree on two essential points: that Borobudur is dependent on Indian art, literature, and religion, and that nothing comparable exists in India itself. Borobudur's sophistication, complexity, and originality underline how completely the Javanese, and Southeast Asians in general, had absorbed, rethought, and reformulated Indian religion and art by 800.

Cambodia

In 802, at about the same time the Javanese built Borobudur, the Khmer king Jayavarman II (r. 802–850) founded the Angkor dynasty, which ruled Cambodia for the next 400 years and sponsored the construction of hundreds of monuments, including gigantic Buddhist monasteries (*wats*).

Angkor Wat Founded by Indravarman (r. 877–889), Angkor is a vast complex of temples and palaces within a rectangular grid of canals and reservoirs fed by local rivers. Each of the Khmer kings who succeeded Indravarman built a temple mountain at Angkor and installed his personal god—Shiva, Vishnu, or the Buddha—on top and gave the god part of his own royal name, implying the king was a manifestation of the deity. When the king died, the Khmer believed the god reabsorbed him because he had been the earthly portion of the deity during his lifetime, so they worshiped the king's image as the god. This concept of kingship approaches deification of the ruler, familiar in many other societies, such as pharaonic Egypt (see Chapter 1).

Of the Khmer kings' monuments, Angkor Wat (FIG. **17-21**) is the most spectacular. Built by Suryavarman II (r. 1113–1150), it is the largest of the many Khmer temple complexes. Angkor Wat rises from a huge rectangle of land delineated by a moat measuring about 5,000 by 4,000 feet. Like the other Khmer temples, its purpose was to associate the king with his personal god, in this case Vishnu. The centerpiece of the complex is a tall stepped tower surrounded by four smaller towers connected by covered galleries. The five towers symbolize the five peaks of Mount Meru, the sacred mountain at the center of the universe. Two more circuit walls with galleries, towers, and gates enclose the central block. Thus, as Hindus progress inward through the complex, the towers rise ever higher, paralleling the towers of Khajuraho's Vishvanatha Temple (FIG. 17-12) but in a more complex sequence and on a much grander scale. Throughout Angkor Wat, stone reliefs glorify both Vishnu in his various avatars and Suryavarman II.

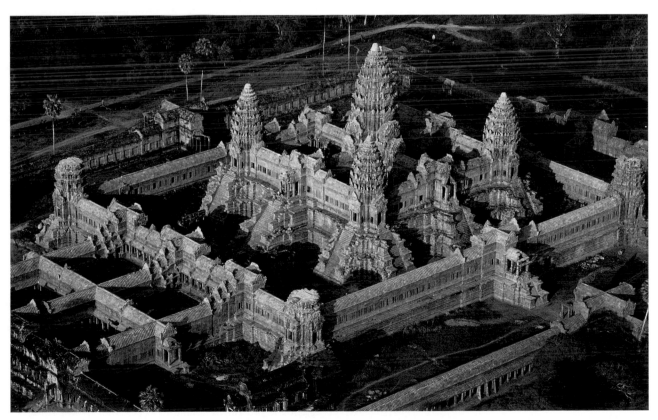

17-21 Aerial view of Angkor Wat (looking northeast), Angkor, Cambodia, first half of 12th century.

Angkor Wat, built by Suryavarman II to associate the Khmer king with the god Vishnu, has five towers symbolizing the five peaks of Mount Meru, the sacred mountain at the center of the universe.

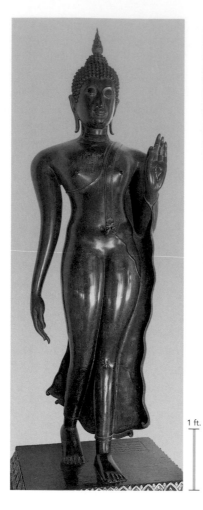

Walking-Buddha statues are unique to Thailand and display a distinctive human anatomy. The Buddha's body is soft and elastic, and the right arm hangs loosely, like an elephant trunk.

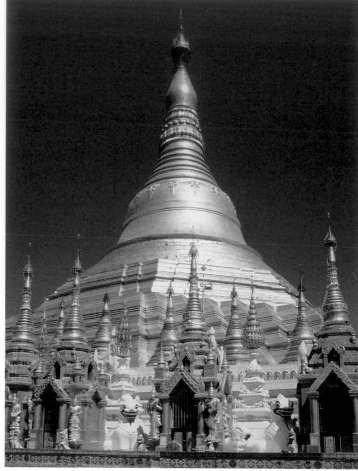

Thailand

Southeast Asians practiced both Buddhism and Hinduism, but by the 13th century, in contrast to developments in India, Hinduism was in decline and Buddhism dominated much of the mainland. Historians date the beginning of the Sukhothai kingdom in Thailand to 1292, the year King Ramkhamhaeng (r. 1279–1299) set up a four-sided stele bearing the first inscription written in the Thai language.

Walking Buddha Sukhothai's crowning artistic achievement was the development of a type of walking-Buddha statue (FIG. **17-22**) displaying a distinctively Thai approach to body form. The bronze Buddha has broad shoulders and a narrow waist and wears a clinging monk's robe. He strides forward, his right heel off the ground and his left arm raised with the hand held in the do-not-fear mudra to encourage worshipers to come forward in reverence. A flame leaps from the top of the Buddha's head, and a sharp nose projects from his rounded face. The right arm hangs loosely, seemingly without muscles or joints, and resembles an elephant's trunk. The Sukhothai artists intended the body type to suggest a supernatural being and to express the Buddha's beauty and perfection. Although images in stone exist, the Sukhothai artists handled bronze best, a material well suited to their conception of the Buddha's body as elastic. The Sukhothai walking-Buddha statuary type is unique in Buddhist art.

Myanmar

Myanmar, like Thailand, is overwhelmingly a Theravada Buddhist country today. Important Buddhist monasteries and monuments dot the countryside.

17-23 Schwedagon Pagoda (looking northeast), Rangoon (Yangon), Myanmar, 14th century or earlier (rebuilt several times).

The 344-foot-tall Schwedagon Pagoda houses two of the Buddha's hairs. Silver and jewels and 13,153 gold plates sheathe its exterior. The gold ball at the top is inlaid with 4,351 diamonds.

Schwedagon Pagoda In Rangoon, an enormous complex of buildings, including shrines filled with Buddha images, has as its centerpiece one of the largest stupas in the world, the Schwedagon Pagoda (FIG. **17-23**). (*Pagoda* derives from the Portuguese version of a word for *stupa*.) The Rangoon pagoda houses two of the Buddha's hairs, traditionally said to have been brought to Myanmar by merchants who received them from the Buddha himself. Rebuilt several times, this highly revered stupa is famous for the gold, silver, and jewels encrusting its surface. The Schwedagon Pagoda stands 344 feet high. Covering its upper part are 13,153 plates of gold, each about a foot square. At the very top is a seven-tiered umbrella crowned with a gold ball inlaid with 4,351 diamonds, one of which weighs 76 carats. This great wealth was a gift to the Buddha from the laypeople of Myanmar to produce merit.

Buddhism and Buddhist art gradually spread from India not only to Southeast Asia but also to China, Korea, and Japan, where architects, sculptors, and painters created some of the most impressive surviving Buddhist monuments as well as a distinguished tradition of secular art (see Chapters 18 and 19).

South and Southeast Asia

Indus Civilization and Maurya Dynasty

▌ The Indus Civilization (ca. 2600–1500 BCE) was one of the world's earliest civilizations. Indus cities had streets oriented to the compass points and sophisticated water-supply and sewage systems, but little Indus art survives, most of it seals with incised designs and small-scale sculptures.

▌ The greatest ruler of the Maurya dynasty (323–185 BCE) was Ashoka (r. 272–231 BCE), who converted to Buddhism and spread the Buddha's teaching throughout South Asia. Ashoka built the original Great Stupa at Sanchi. His pillars are the first monumental stone artworks in India.

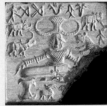

Seal, Mohenjo-daro,
ca. 2300–1750 BCE

Kushan, Gupta, and Post-Gupta Periods

▌ The first representations of the Buddha in human form date to the Kushan Empire (mid-first century to 320 CE). Gandharan Buddhist art owes a strong stylistic debt to Greco-Roman art. By the second century CE, the iconography of the life of the Buddha was well established.

▌ Gupta sculptors formulated the canonical Buddha image in the fifth century, combining Gandharan iconography with a soft, full-bodied figure in clinging garments. The Gupta-period Buddhist caves of Ajanta are the best surviving examples of early mural painting in India.

▌ The oldest Hindu monumental stone temples and sculptures—at Badami, Elephanta, Deogarh, and elsewhere—date to the fifth and sixth centuries.

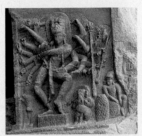

Dancing Shiva, Badami,
late sixth century CE

Medieval Period

▌ The Chola, Chandella, and other regional dynasties ruled South Asia from the 7th to the 12th century, and distinctive regional styles emerged in Hindu religious architecture. Northern temples, such as the Vishvanatha Temple at Khajuraho, have a series of small towers leading to a tall beehive-shaped tower, or shikhara, over the garbha griha. Southern temples have flat-roofed pillared halls (mandapas) leading to a pyramidal tower (vimana).

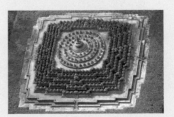

Vishvanatha Temple,
Khajuraho, ca. 1000

Mughal Empire

▌ The first great flowering of art and architecture in the Mughal Empire (1526–1857) occurred under Akbar the Great (r. 1556–1605), whose imperial painting workshop produced magnificent miniatures. Shah Jahan (r. 1628–1658) built the Taj Mahal as a memorial to his favorite wife.

▌ During the Mughal Empire, Hindu Rajput kings ruled much of northwestern India. The coloration and sensuality of Rajput painting distinguish it from the contemporaneous Mughal style.

▌ Between 1529 and 1736, the Hindu Nayak dynasty controlled southern India and built immense temple complexes with towers (gopuras) featuring painted stucco sculptures of Hindu deities.

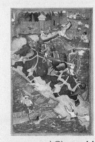

Basawan and Chatar Muni,
Akbar and the Elephant Hawai, ca. 1590

Southeast Asia

▌ Southeast Asian art and architecture reflect Indian prototypes, but many local styles developed.

▌ Borobudur in Indonesia has no parallel in India. The Khmer kings of Cambodia built vast Buddhist temple complexes at Angkor. In Thailand, the Sukhothai walking-Buddha statuary type displays a unique approach to body form. Myanmar's Schwedagon Pagoda in Rangoon, one of the world's largest stupas, is encrusted with gold, silver, and jewels.

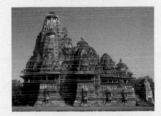

Borobudur, Java, ca. 800

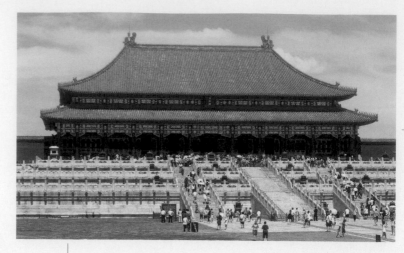

The Hall of Supreme Harmony, the largest wooden building in China, was the climax of the Forbidden City's long north-south axis. It housed the Ming emperor's throne room.

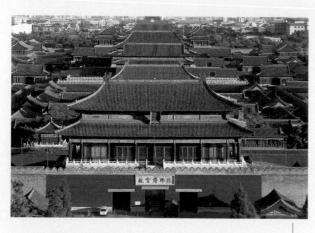

The Forbidden City provided the perfect setting for the rituals surrounding the Ming emperor. Successive gates, such as the Gate of Divine Prowess, regulated access to increasingly restricted areas.

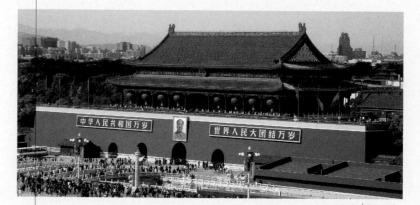

The southern entrance to the Beijing palace complex was the Noon Gate. Only the emperor could walk through the central portal. Those of decreasing rank used the lateral passageways.

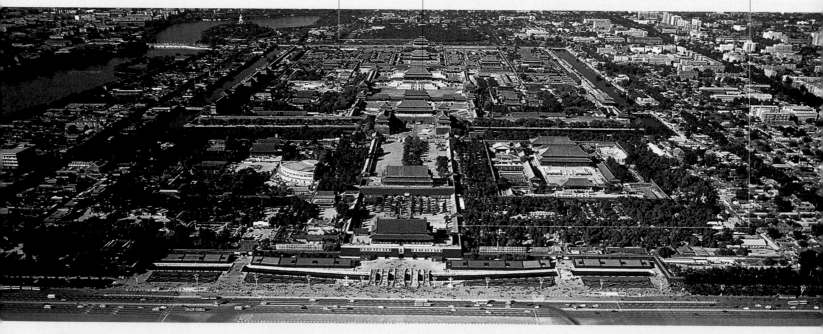

18-1 Aerial view (looking north) of the Forbidden City, Beijing, China, Ming dynasty, 15th century and later.

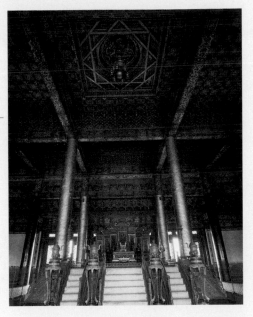

For the columns of the opulently appointed throne room of the Son of Heaven, the Chinese builders had to transport gigantic tree trunks from Sichuan Province down the Yangtze River.

18

China and Korea

THE FORBIDDEN CITY

Since ancient times, emperors and regional kings ruled the vast territory of present-day China. In 1368, Zhu Yuanzhong led a popular uprising that expelled the foreign Yuan dynasty from their capital at Beijing. Zhu then founded the native Chinese Ming dynasty, proclaiming himself its first emperor under the official name of Hongwu ("Abundantly Martial," r. 1368–1398). The new emperor built his capital at Nanjing (Southern Capital), but the third Ming emperor, Yongle ("Perpetual Happiness," r. 1403–1424), moved the imperial seat back to Beijing (Northern Capital).

The Ming architects laid out Beijing as three nested, walled cities. The outer perimeter wall was 15 miles long and enclosed the walled Imperial City, with a perimeter of 6 miles, and the vast imperial palace compound, the Forbidden City (FIG. **18-1**), surrounded by a 50-yard-wide moat. The name "Forbidden City" dates to 1576 and aptly describes the highly restricted access to the inner compound, where the Ming emperor, the Son of Heaven, resided. The layout of the Forbidden City provided the perfect setting for the elaborate ritual of the imperial court. For example, the entrance gateway to the complex, the Noon Gate, has five portals. Only the emperor could walk through the central doorway. The two entrances to its left and right were reserved for the imperial family and high officials. Others had to use the outermost passageways. Entrance to the Forbidden City proper was through the nearly 40-yard-tall triple-passageway Meridian Gate. Only the emperor and his retinue and foreign ambassadors who had been granted an official audience could pass through the Meridian Gate.

Within the Forbidden City, more gates and a series of courtyards, gardens, temples, and other buildings led eventually to the Hall of Supreme Harmony, in which the emperor, seated on his dragon throne on a high stepped platform, received important visitors. The hall is the largest wooden building in China. For its columns, the Ming builders had to transport gigantic tree trunks from Sichuan Province down the Yangtze River. Perched on an immense platform above marble staircases, the Hall of Supreme Harmony was the climax of a long north-south axis. The fill for the platform consists of the soil and rocks the Ming engineers collected from the excavation of the great moat around the imperial complex.

Beyond that grand reception hall is the even more restricted Inner Court and the Palace of Heavenly Purity—the private living quarters of the emperor and his extended family of wives, concubines, and children. At the northern end of the central axis of the Forbidden City is the Gate of Divine Prowess, through which the palace servants gained access to the complex.

FRAMING THE ERA

CHINA

Vast and varied both topographically and climatically, China (MAP 18-1) comprises sandy plains, mighty rivers, towering mountains, and fertile farmlands. Its political and cultural boundaries have varied over the millennia, and at times it has grown geographically to about twice the area of the United States. China boasts the world's largest population and is ethnically diverse. The spoken language varies so much that speakers of different dialects do not understand one another. The written language, however, which employs *characters* (signs recording meaning rather than sounds), has made possible a shared Chinese literary, philosophic, and religious tradition.

China traces its beginnings to long before the dawn of recorded history. Discoveries in recent years have provided

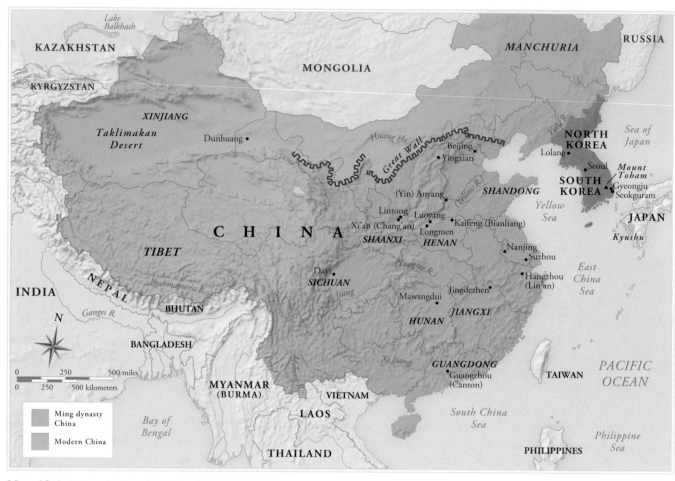

MAP 18-1 China during the Ming dynasty.

China and Korea

	BCE		CE				
1600	Shang to Qin	206	Han and Tang	907	Song to Yuan	1368	Ming to People's Republic	1980

Shang to Qin
- Shang (1600–1050 BCE) artists perfect the technique of bronze-casting
- Zhou (1050–256 BCE) artists excel in fashioning luxurious objects in bronze, lacquer, and jade
- The First Emperor of Qin (221–210 BCE) builds an immense burial mound guarded by 6,000 terracotta soldiers

Han and Tang
- Han (206 BCE–220 CE) buildings feature interlocking clusters of wooden brackets
- Tang dynasty (618–906) is the golden age of Chinese painting on silk scrolls
- Chang'an, the Tang capital, is the most magnificent city in the world

Song to Yuan
- Song (907–1279) China is the world's most technologically advanced society
- Apogee of landscape painting under the Song emperors
- Liao dynasty (907–1125) builds the world's tallest wooden building
- Mongols establish the Yuan dynasty (1279–1368)
- The Jingdezhen kilns produce porcelain pottery with cobalt-blue underglaze decoration

Ming to People's Republic
- Ming (1368–1644) emperors build the Forbidden City in Beijing
- Ming landscape architects design uncultivated scenic gardens at Suzhou
- Joseon dynasty (1392–1910) in Korea erects Namdaemun gate in Seoul
- Manchus rule China as the Qing dynasty (1644–1911)
- Marxist themes dominate the state-sponsored art of the People's Republic of China (1911–)

evidence of settled village life as far back as the seventh or early sixth millennium BCE. Mastery of the art of pottery soon followed. The potters of the Yangshao Culture, which arose along the Yellow River in northeastern China, produced fine decorated ceramic bowls even before the invention of the potter's wheel in the fourth millennium BCE. Archaeologists have begun to confirm the existence of China's earliest royal dynasty, the Xia (ca. 2000–1600 BCE), long thought to have been mythical.

Shang and Zhou Dynasties

The first great Chinese dynasty of the Bronze Age was the Shang (ca. 1600–1050 BCE), whose kings ruled from a series of royal capitals in the Yellow River valley. In 1928 excavations at Anyang (ancient Yin) brought to light the last Shang capital. There, archaeologists found a large number of objects inscribed in the earliest form of the Chinese language. These fragmentary records and the other finds at Anyang reveal a warlike, highly stratified society. The excavated tomb furnishings include weapons and a great wealth of objects in jade, ivory, lacquer (sap-coated wood), and bronze. Not only the kings received lavish burials. The tomb of Fu Hao, the wife of Wu Ding (r. ca. 1215–1190 BCE), for example, contained more than a thousand bronze and jade objects and an ivory beaker inlaid with turquoise.

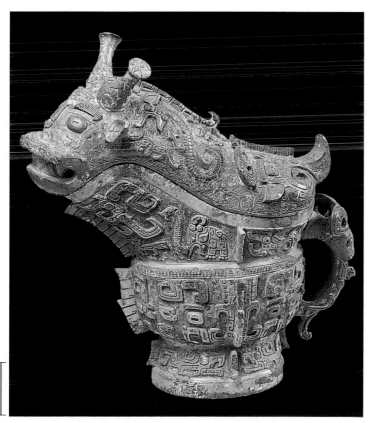

1 in.

18-2 Guang, probably from Anyang, China, Shang dynasty, 12th or 11th century BCE. Bronze, 6½" high. Asian Art Museum of San Francisco, San Francisco (Avery Brundage Collection).

Shang artists perfected casting elaborate bronze vessels covered with animal motifs. The animal forms, real and imaginary, on this libation guang are probably connected with the world of spirits.

Shang Bronzes Shang artists perfected the casting of elaborate bronze vessels. Used in sacrifices to ancestors and in funerary ceremonies, Shang bronzes held wine, water, grain, or meat for sacrificial rites. Each vessel's shape matched its intended purpose. The *guang* illustrated here (FIG. **18-2**) is a libation vessel shaped like a covered gravy boat, characteristically densely decorated with abstract and animal motifs. The multiple designs and their fields of background spirals integrate so closely with the form of the guang that they are not merely an external embellishment but an integral part of the sculptural whole. Some motifs on the guang's side may represent the eyes of a tiger and the horns of a ram. A horned animal forms the front of the lid, and at the rear is a horned head with a bird's beak. Another horned head appears on the handle. Fish, birds, elephants, rabbits, and more abstract composite creatures swarm over the surface against a background of spirals. The fabulous animal forms, real and imaginary, are unlikely to have been purely decorative. They probably inhabit the world of spirits addressed in the rituals.

Zhou Dynasty Around 1050 BCE, the Zhou, former vassals of the Shang, captured Anyang and overthrew their Shang overlords. The Zhou dynasty (ca. 1050–256 BCE) proved to be the longest lasting in China's history. The closing centuries of Zhou rule include a long period of warfare among competing states, the so-called Warring States Period (ca. 475–221 BCE). This period of political and social turmoil was also a time of intellectual upheaval, when conflicting schools of philosophy, including Legalism, Daoism, and Confucianism, emerged (see "Daoism and Confucianism," page 496).

Qin Dynasty

The ruler of the state of Qin (from which the modern name *China* derives) brought the Warring States Period to an end by conquering all rival states, including the Zhou. Known to history by his title, Qin Shi Huangdi (First Emperor of Qin), between 221 and 210 BCE he controlled an area equal to about half of modern China. During his reign, Shi Huangdi ordered the linkage of active fortifications along the northern border of his realm to form the famous Great Wall (MAP 18-1), which defended China against the fierce nomadic peoples of the north, especially the Huns. By sometimes brutal methods, the First Emperor consolidated rule through a centralized bureaucracy and adopted standardized written language, weights and measures, and coinage. He also repressed all schools of thought other than Legalism, which espoused absolute obedience to the state's authority and advocated strict laws and punishments. Chinese historians have harshly condemned the First Emperor, but the bureaucratic system he put in place long outlasted his reign. Its success was due in large part to Shi Huangdi's decision to replace the feudal lords with talented salaried administrators and to reward merit rather than favor high birth.

Lintong In 1974, excavations started at the site of the immense burial mound of Shi Huangdi at Lintong. For its

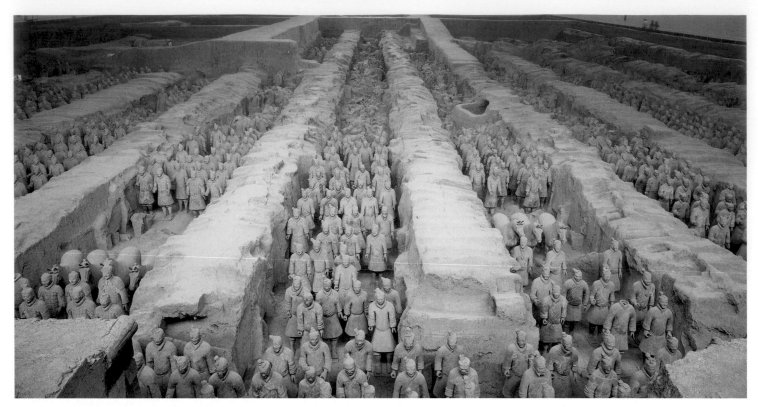

18-3 Army of the First Emperor of Qin in pits next to his burial mound, Lintong, China, Qin dynasty, ca. 210 BCE. Painted terracotta, average figure 5′ 10⅞″ high. ◼

The First Emperor was buried beneath an immense mound guarded by more than 6,000 life-size terracotta soldiers. Although produced from common molds, every figure has an individualized appearance.

construction, the First Emperor conscripted more than 700,000 laborers. The mound itself remains largely unexcavated, but researchers believe it contains a vast treasure-filled underground funerary palace designed to match the fabulous palace the emperor occupied in life. The historian Sima Qian (136–85 BCE) described both palaces, but scholars did not take his account seriously until the discovery of pits around the tomb containing more than 6,000 life-size painted terracotta figures of soldiers and horses, as well as bronze horses and chariots. The terracotta army (FIG. **18-3**) served as the First Emperor's bodyguard deployed in perpetuity outside his tomb.

The Lintong army, consisting of statues of cavalry, chariots, archers, lancers, and hand-to-hand fighters, was one of the 20th century's greatest archaeological discoveries. The huge assemblage testifies to a high degree of organization in the Qin imperial workshop. Manufacturing this army of statues required a veritable army of sculptors and painters as well as a large number of huge kilns. The First Emperor's artisans could have opted to use the same molds over and over again to produce thousands of identical soldiers standing in strict formation. In fact, they did employ the same molds repeatedly for different parts of the statues but assembled the parts in many different combinations. Consequently, the stances, arm positions, garment folds, equipment, coiffures, and facial features vary, sometimes slightly, sometimes markedly, from statue to statue. Additional hand modeling of the cast

body parts before firing enabled the sculptors to differentiate the figures even more. The Qin painters undoubtedly added further variations to the appearance of the terracotta army. The result of these efforts was a brilliant balance between uniformity and individuality.

Han Dynasty

Soon after the First Emperor's death, the people who had suffered under his reign revolted, assassinated his son, and founded the Han dynasty (206 BCE–220 CE). The Han extended China's southern and western boundaries, penetrating far into Central Asia (present-day Xinjiang) and even traded indirectly with distant Rome via the fabled Silk Road, a network of caravan routes linking China and the Mediterranean world. Very few traders traveled the entire distance. Along the way, goods usually passed through the hands of people from many lands, who often only dimly understood the origins and destinations of what they traded. The Roman passion for silk ultimately led to the modern name for the Central Asian routes, but gold, ivory, gems, glass, lacquer, incense, furs, spices, cotton, linens, exotic animals, and other merchandise precious enough to warrant the risks also passed along the Silk Road.

Marquise of Dai In 1972, archaeologists excavated the tomb of the marquise of Dai at Mawangdui. The tomb contained a rich array of goods for use during the burial

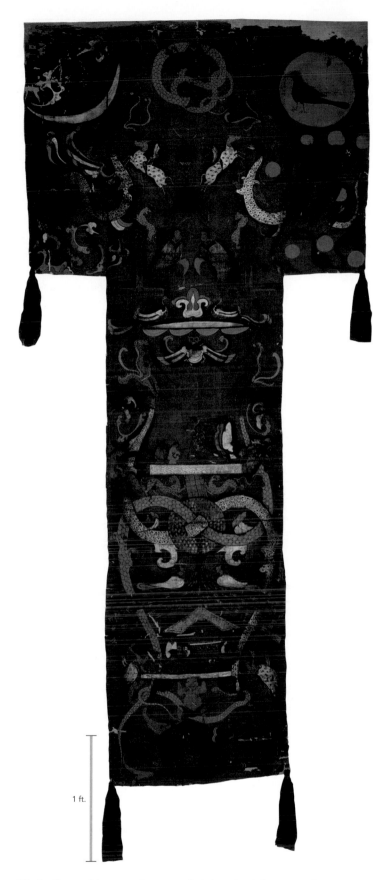

ceremonies and to accompany the noblewoman into the afterlife. Among the finds were decorated lacquer utensils, rich textiles, and an astonishingly well-preserved corpse in the innermost of four nested sarcophagi. Most remarkable, however, was the discovery of a painted T-shaped silk banner (FIG. 18-4) draped over the marquise's coffin. Scholars generally agree the area within the cross at the top of the T represents Heaven. Most of the vertical section below is the human realm. At the bottom is the Underworld. In the heavenly realm, dragons and immortal beings appear between and below two orbs—the red sun and its symbol, the raven, on the right, and the silvery moon and its symbol, the toad, on the left. Below, the standing figure on the first white platform near the center of the vertical section is probably the marquise of Dai herself—one of the first portraits in Chinese art. The woman awaits her ascent to Heaven, where she can attain immortality. Nearer the bottom, the artist depicted her funeral. Between these two sections are two intertwining dragons. Their tails reach down to the Underworld and their heads point to Heaven, unifying the entire composition.

Wuwei Flying Horse Another Han tomb of special interest is that of Governor-General Zhang, discovered in 1969 at Wuwei in Gansu Province. The tomb contained almost 100 cast-bronze sculptures of horses, chariots, and soldiers—a miniature version of the life-size army (FIG. 18-3) guarding the tomb of the First Emperor of Qin. The figurine illustrated here (FIG. 18-5) represents a distinctive breed of horse from Turkestan. It differs from all the others in Zhang's

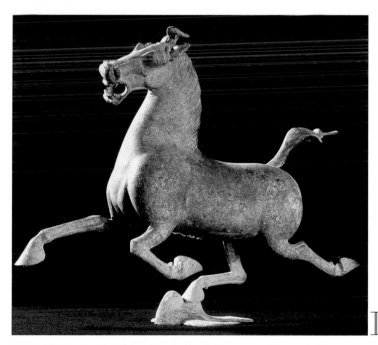

18-5 Flying horse, from the tomb of Governor-General Zhang, Wuwei, China, Han dynasty, late second century CE. Bronze, 1' 1½" high. Gansu Provincial Museum, Lanzhou.

Found in a late Han dynasty tomb, this cast-bronze galloping, flying horse has one hoof on a swallow with spread wings, suggesting the deceased's heavenward journey to the afterlife.

1 ft.

18-4 Funeral banner, from tomb 1 (tomb of the marquise of Dai), Mawangdui, China, Han dynasty, ca. 168 BCE. Painted silk, 6' 8¾" × 3' ¼". Hunan Provincial Museum, Changsha.

This T-shaped silk banner was draped over the coffin of the marquise of Dai, who is shown at the center awaiting her ascent to immortality in Heaven, the realm of the silvery moon and red sun.

China   495

Daoism and Confucianism

Daoism and Confucianism are both philosophies and religions native to China. Both schools of thought attracted wide followings during the fifth to third centuries BCE (Warring States Period), when political turbulence led to social unrest.

Daoism emerged out of the metaphysical teachings attributed to Laozi (604?–531? BCE) and Zhuangzi (370?–301? BCE). It takes its name from Laozi's treatise *Daodejing* (*The Way and Its Power*). Daoist philosophy stresses an intuitive awareness, nurtured by harmonious contact with nature, and shuns everything artificial. Daoists seek to follow the universal path, or principle, called the Dao, whose features cannot be described but only suggested through analogies. For example, the Dao is said to be like water, always yielding but eventually wearing away the hard stone that does not yield. For Daoists, strength comes from flexibility and inaction. Historically, Daoist principles encouraged retreat from society in favor of personal cultivation in nature.

Confucius (Kong Fuzi, or Master Kong, 551–479 BCE) was born in the state of Lu (roughly modern Shandong Province) to an aristocratic family that had fallen on hard times. From an early age, he showed a strong interest in the rites and ceremonies that helped unite people into an orderly society. As he grew older, he developed a deep concern for the suffering the civil conflict of his day caused. Thus, he adopted a philosophy he hoped would lead to order and stability. The *junzi* ("superior person" or "gentleman"), who possesses *ren* (human-heartedness), personified the ideal social order Confucius sought. Although originally a junzi had to be of noble birth, in Confucian thought anyone can become a junzi by cultivating

the virtues Confucius espoused, especially empathy for suffering, pursuit of morality and justice, respect for ancient ceremonies, and adherence to traditional social relationships, such as those between parent and child, elder and younger sibling, husband and wife, and ruler and subject.

Confucius's disciple Mencius (or Mengzi, 371?–289? BCE) developed his master's ideas further, stressing that the deference to age and rank at the heart of the Confucian social order brings a reciprocal responsibility. For example, a king's legitimacy depends on the goodwill of his people. A ruler should share his joys with his subjects and will know his laws are unjust if they bring suffering to the people.

Confucius spent much of his adult life trying to find rulers willing to apply his teachings, but he died in disappointment. However, he and Mencius profoundly influenced Chinese thought and social practice. Chinese traditions of venerating deceased ancestors and outstanding leaders encouraged the development of Confucianism as a religion as well as a philosophic tradition. Eventually, Emperor Wu (r. 140–87 BCE) of the Han dynasty established Confucianism as the state's official doctrine. Thereafter, it became the primary subject of the civil service exams required for admission into and advancement within government service.

Confucian and *Daoist* are broad, imprecise terms scholars often use to distinguish aspects of Chinese culture stressing social responsibility and order (Confucian, for example, FIGS. 18-6 and 18-9) from those emphasizing cultivation of individuals, often in reclusion (Daoist, for example, FIGS. 18-10 and 18-14). But both philosophies share the idea that anyone can cultivate wisdom or ability, regardless of birth.

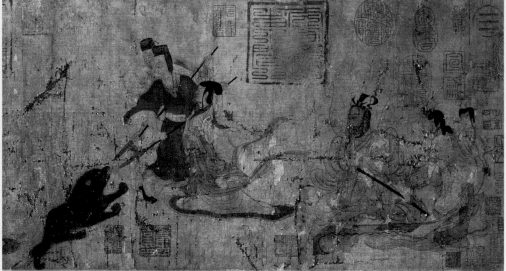

18-6 Attributed to GU KAIZHI, *Lady Feng and the Bear,* detail of *Admonitions of the Instructress to the Court Ladies,* Period of Disunity, late fourth century. Handscroll, ink and colors on silk, 9¾" high (scroll 11' 4½" long). British Museum, London.

Lady Feng's act of heroism to save the life of her emperor was a perfect model of Confucian behavior. In this early Chinese representation of the episode, the painter set the figures against a blank background.

1 in.

tomb because it is not prancing or standing still but galloping, or, more accurately, flying because one hoof rests on a swallow with spread wings. The sculptor posed the horse with its head tilted to one side but presented the animal's body in a pure profile. The Wuwei horse has an elegant silhouette, with its legs spread widely and its tail lifted behind it like a fifth leg, balancing the curved neck and the rear left leg. Zhang's airborne horse suggests the journey from his tomb will take him heavenward to an immortal afterlife.

Period of Disunity

For three and a half centuries, from 220 to 581,* civil strife divided China into competing states. The history of this so-called Period of Disunity is extremely complex, but one development deserves special mention—the occupation of northern China by peoples who were not ethnically Han

*From this point on, all dates in this chapter are CE unless otherwise stated.

Chinese and who spoke non-Chinese languages. It was in the northern states, connected to India by the Silk Road, that Buddhism first took root in China during the Han dynasty. Certain practices shared with Daoism (see "Daoism and Confucianism," page 496), such as withdrawal from ordinary society, helped Buddhism gain an initial foothold in the north. But Buddhism's promise of hope beyond the troubles of this world earned it an ever broader audience during the upheavals of the Period of Disunity. In addition, the fully developed Buddhist system of thought attracted intellectuals. Buddhism never fully displaced Daoism and Confucianism, but it did prosper throughout China for centuries and had a profound influence on the further development of the religious forms of those two native traditions.

Gu Kaizhi   Secular arts also flourished in the Period of Disunity, as rulers sought artists to lend prestige to their courts. The most famous early Chinese painter with whom extant works can be associated was GU KAIZHI (ca. 344–406). Gu was a friend of important members of the Eastern Jin dynasty (317–420) and won renown as a calligrapher, a painter of court portraits, and a pioneer of landscape painting. A *handscroll* (see "Chinese Painting Materials and Formats," page 499) attributed to Gu Kaizhi in the 11th century is not by his hand, but it exemplifies the key elements of his art. Called *Admonitions of the Instructress to the Court Ladies,* the horizontal scroll contains painted scenes and accompanying explanatory text. Like all Chinese handscrolls, this one was unrolled and read from right to left, with only a small section exposed for viewing at one time. The section illustrated here (FIG. **18-6**) records a well-known act of heroism—Lady Feng saving her emperor's life by placing herself between him and an attacking bear, a perfect model of Confucian behavior. As in many early Chinese paintings, the artist set the figures against a blank background with only a minimal setting for the scene, although in other works, Gu provided landscape settings for his narratives. The figures' poses and fluttering drapery ribbons, in concert with individualized facial expressions, convey a clear quality of animation.

Tang Dynasty

The emperors of the short-lived Sui dynasty (r. 581–618) succeeded in reuniting China and prepared the way for the brilliant Tang dynasty (r. 618–906). Under the Tang emperors, China entered a period of unequaled magnificence. Chinese armies marched across Central Asia, prompting an influx of foreign peoples, wealth, and ideas into China. Traders, missionaries, and other travelers journeyed to the cosmopolitan Tang capital at Chang'an (present-day Xi'an), and the Chinese, in turn, ventured westward. Chang'an, laid out on a grid scheme, occupied more than 30 square miles. It was the greatest city in the world during the seventh and eighth centuries.

Longmen Caves   The Tang emperors were lavish art patrons. One of the most spectacular Tang commissions was the group of sculptures (FIG. **18-7**) carved into the face of a cliff in the Longmen Caves complex near Luoyang. The central figure of the Buddha is 44 feet tall—seated. An inscription records that the project was completed in 676 when Gaozong (r. 649–683) was emperor and that in 672 the empress Wu Zetian underwrote a substantial portion of the considerable cost with her private funds. Wu Zetian was an exceptional woman by any standard, and when Gaozong died in 683, she declared herself emperor and ruled until 705, when she was forced to abdicate at age 82.

Wu Zetian's Buddha is the Vairocana Buddha, or the Mahayana Cosmic Buddha, the Buddha of Boundless Space and Time (see "Buddhism," Chapter 17, page 473). Flanking him are two of his monks, attendant bodhisattvas, and guardian figures—all smaller than the Buddha but still of colossal size. The sculptors represented the Buddha in serene

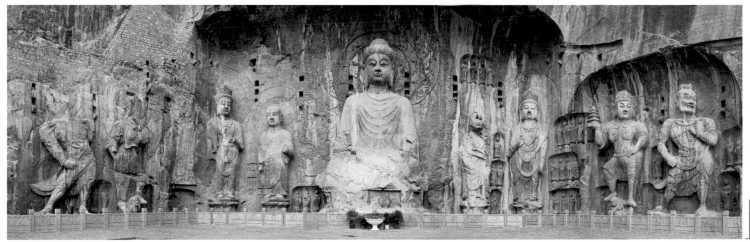

18-7 Vairocana Buddha, disciples, and bodhisattvas, Fengxian Temple, Longmen Caves, Luoyang, China, Tang dynasty, completed 676. Buddha 44′ high. ◼◀

Empress Wu Zetian sponsored these colossal rock-cut sculptures. The Tang artists represented the Mahayana Cosmic Buddha in serene majesty, suppressing surface detail in favor of monumental simplicity.

majesty. An almost geometric regularity of contour and smoothness of planes emphasize the volume of the massive figure. The folds of the Buddha's robes fall in a few concentric arcs. The artists suppressed surface detail in the interest of monumental simplicity and dignity.

Dunhuang Grottoes The westward expansion of the Tang Empire increased the importance of Dunhuang, the westernmost gateway to China on the Silk Road. Dunhuang long had been a wealthy, cosmopolitan trade center, a Buddhist pilgrimage destination, and home to thriving communities of Buddhist monks and nuns of varied ethnicity, as well as to adherents of other religions. In the course of several centuries beginning in the Period of Disunity—when work also began at the Longmen Caves—the Chinese cut hundreds of sanctuaries with painted murals into the soft rock of the cliffs near Dunhuang. Known today as the Mogao Grottoes and in antiquity as the Caves of a Thousand Buddhas, the Dunhuang cave temples are especially important because in 845 the emperor Wuzong instituted a major persecution, destroying 4,600 Buddhist temples and 40,000 shrines and forcing the return of 260,500 monks and nuns to lay life. Wuzong's policies did not affect Dunhuang, then under Tibetan rule, so the site preserves much of the type of art lost elsewhere.

Paradise of Amitabha (FIG. **18-8**) in Dunhuang cave 172 shows how the splendor of the Tang era and religious teachings could come together in a powerful image. Buddhist Pure Land sects, especially those centered on Amitabha, Buddha of the West, had captured the popular imagination in the Period of Disunity and continued to flourish during the Tang dynasty. Pure Land teachings asserted individuals had no hope of attaining enlightenment through their own power because of the waning of the Buddha's law. Instead, they could obtain rebirth in a realm free from spiritual corruption simply through faith in Amitabha's promise of salvation. Richly detailed, brilliantly colored pictures steeped in the opulence of the Tang dynasty, such as this one, greatly aided worshipers in gaining faith by visualizing the wonders of the Pure Land Paradise. Amitabha sits in the center of a raised platform against a backdrop of ornate buildings characteristic of the Tang era. The Buddha's principal bodhisattvas and lesser divine attendants surround him. Before them a celestial dance takes place. Bodhisattvas had strong appeal in East Asia as compassionate beings ready to achieve buddhahood but dedicated to humanity's salvation. Some received direct worship and became the main subjects of sculpture and painting.

Yan Liben The Tang emperors also fostered a brilliant tradition of scroll painting (see "Chinese Painting Materials and Formats," page 499). Although few examples exist today, many art historians regard the early Tang dynasty as the golden age of Chinese figure painting. *The Thirteen Emperors* (FIG. **18-9**) is a masterpiece of line drawing and colored washes long attributed to YAN LIBEN (d. 673). Born into an aristocratic family and the son of a famous artist, Yan was prime minister under the Tang emperor Gaozong as well as a celebrated painter. This handscroll depicts 13 Chinese rulers from the Han to the Sui dynasties. Its purpose was to portray

18-8 *Paradise of Amitabha,* cave 172, Dunhuang, China, Tang dynasty, mid-eighth century. Wall painting, 10′ high.

This richly detailed, brilliantly colored mural aided worshipers at Dunhuang to visualize the wonders of the Pure Land Paradise promised to those who had faith in Amitabha, the Buddha of the West.

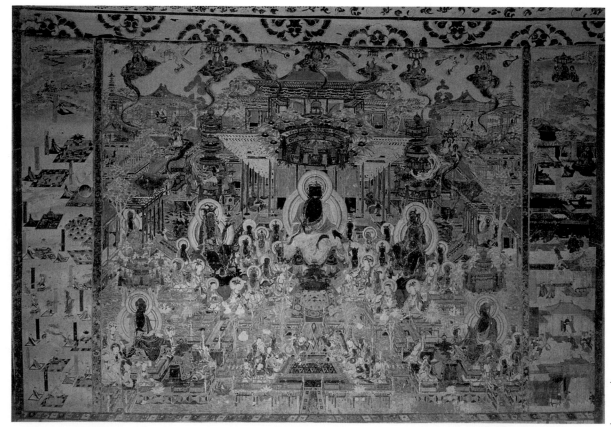

1 ft.

Chinese Painting Materials and Formats

Mural paintings in caves (FIG. 18-8) were popular in China, as they were in South Asia (FIG. 17-7), but Chinese artists also employed several other materials and formats for their paintings. The basic requirements for paintings not on walls were the same as for writing—a round tapered brush, soot-based ink, and either silk or paper. The Chinese were masters of the brush. Sometimes they used modulated lines for contours and interior details that elastically thicken and thin to convey depth and mass. In other works, they used *iron-wire lines* (thin, unmodulated lines with a suggestion of tensile strength) to define the figures. Chinese painters also used richly colored minerals as pigments, finely ground and suspended in a gluey medium, and watery washes of mineral and vegetable dyes. The formats of Chinese paintings on silk or paper tend to be personal

and intimate, and they are usually best viewed by only one or two people at a time. The most common types are listed here.

- *Hanging scrolls* (FIGS. 18-10, 18-15, and 18-18) Chinese painters often mounted pictures on, or painted directly on, unrolled vertical scrolls for display on walls.

- *Handscrolls* (FIGS. 18-6, 18-9, and 18-11) Artists also frequently attached paintings to, or painted on, long, narrow scrolls the viewer unrolled horizontally, section by section from right to left.

- *Album leaves* (FIGS. 18-14 and 18-19) Many Chinese artists painted small panels on paper leaves, which collectors placed in albums.

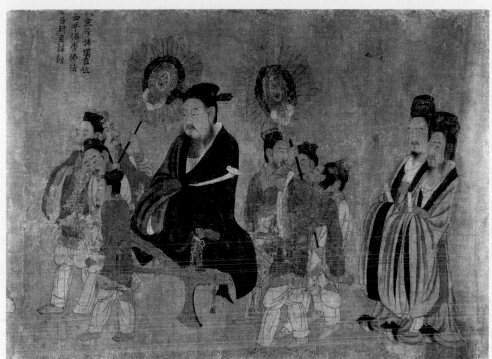

18-9 Attributed to YAN LIBEN, *Emperor Xuan and Attendants*, detail of *The Thirteen Emperors*, Tang dynasty, ca. 650. Handscroll, ink and colors on silk; detail 1' 8¼" high (scroll 17' 5" long). Museum of Fine Arts, Boston.

This handscroll portrays 13 Chinese rulers as Confucian exemplars of moral and political virtue. Yan Liben, a celebrated Tang painter, was a master of line drawing and colored washes.

1 in.

these historical figures as exemplars of moral and political virtue, in keeping with the Confucian ideal of learning from the past. Each emperor stands or sits in an undefined space. The emperor's great size relative to his attendants immediately establishes his superior stature. Simple shading in the faces and the robes gives the figures an added semblance of volume and presence. The detail in FIG. 18-9 represents Emperor Xuan of the Chen dynasty (557–589) seated among his attendants, two of whom carry the ceremonial fans that signify his rank. Xuan stands out from the others also because of his dark robes. His majestic serenity contrasts with his attendants' animated poses, which vary sharply from figure to figure, lending vitality to the composition.

Song Dynasty

The last century of Tang rule witnessed many popular uprisings and the empire's gradual disintegration. After an interim of internal strife known as the Five Dynasties period

(907–960), General Zhao Kuangyin succeeded in consolidating the country once again. He established himself as the first emperor (r. 960–976) of the Song dynasty (960–1279), which ruled China from a capital in the north at Bianliang (present-day Kaifeng) during the Northern Song period (960–1127). The Song emperors curtailed many of the hereditary privileges of the elite class. They also made political appointments on the basis of scores on civil service examinations, and education became a more important prerequisite for Song officials than high birth. The three centuries of Song rule, including the Southern Song period (1127–1279) when the capital was at Lin'an (present-day Hangzhou) in southern China, were also a time of extraordinary technological innovation. Under the Song emperors, the Chinese invented the magnetic compass for sea navigation, printing with moveable clay type, paper money, and gunpowder. Song China was the most technologically advanced society in the world in the early second millennium.

China   499

Fan Kuan For many art historians, the Song dynasty also marks the apogee of Chinese landscape painting, which first emerged as a major subject during the Period of Disunity. Although many of the great Northern Song masters worked for the imperial court, FAN KUAN (ca. 960–1030) was a Daoist recluse (see "Daoism and Confucianism," page 496) who shunned the cosmopolitan life of Bianliang. He believed nature was a better teacher than were other artists, and he spent long days in the mountains studying configurations of rocks and trees and the effect of sunlight and moonlight on natural forms. Song critics lauded Fan and other leading Chinese painters of the day as the first masters of the recording of light, shade, distance, and texture.

In *Travelers among Mountains and Streams* (FIG. **18-10**), Fan painted a vertical landscape of massive mountains rising from the distance. The overwhelming natural forms dwarf the few human and animal figures (for example, the mule train in the lower right corner), which the artist reduced to minute proportions. The nearly seven-foot-long silk hanging scroll cannot contain nature's grandeur, and the landscape continues in all directions beyond its borders. Fan showed some elements from level ground (for example, the great boulder in the foreground), and others obliquely from the top (the shrubbery on the highest cliff). The shifting perspectives lead the viewer on a journey through the mountains. To appreciate the painted landscape fully, the viewer must focus not only on the larger composition but also on intricate details and on the character of each brushstroke. Numerous "texture strokes" help model massive forms and convey a sense of tactile surfaces. For the face of the mountain, for example, Fan Kuan employed small, pale brush marks, the kind of texture strokes the Chinese call "raindrop strokes."

Huizong A century after Fan painted in the mountains of Shanxi, HUIZONG (1082–1135; r. 1101–1126) assumed the Song throne at Bianliang. Less interested in governing than in the arts, he brought the country to near bankruptcy and lost much of China's territory to the armies of the Tartar Jin dynasty (1115–1234), who captured the Song capital in 1126 and took Huizong as a prisoner. He died in their hands nine years later. An accomplished poet, calligrapher, and painter, Huizong reorganized the imperial painting academy and required the study of poetry and calligraphy as part of the official training of court painters. Prominent inscriptions are frequent elements of Chinese paintings (see "Calligraphy and Inscriptions on Chinese Paintings," page 501).

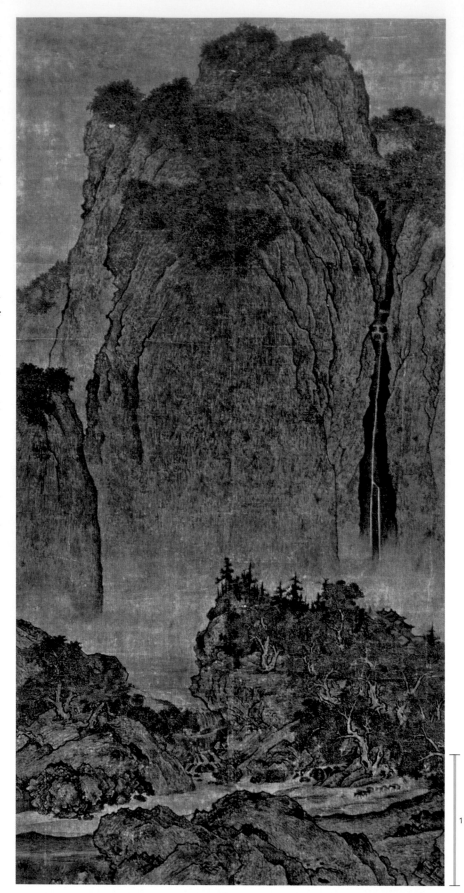

18-10 FAN KUAN, *Travelers among Mountains and Streams,* Northern Song period, early 11th century. Hanging scroll, ink and colors on silk, 6′ 7¼″ × 3′ 4¼″. National Palace Museum, Taibei.

Fan Kuan, a Daoist recluse, spent long days in the mountains studying the effects of light on rock formations and trees. He was one of the first masters of recording light, shade, distance, and texture.

1 ft

Calligraphy and Inscriptions on Chinese Paintings

Many Chinese paintings (FIGS. 18-6, 18-9, 18-11, 18-14, 18-15, and 18-18) bear inscriptions, texts written on the same surface as the picture, or *colophons*, texts written on attached pieces of paper or silk. Throughout Chinese history, calligraphy and painting have been closely connected. Even the primary implements and materials for writing and drawing are the same—a brush, ink, and paper or silk (see "Chinese Painting Materials," page 499). Calligraphy depends for its effects on the controlled vitality of individual brushstrokes and on the dynamic relationships of strokes within a character and among the characters themselves. Training in calligraphy was a fundamental part of the education and self-cultivation of Chinese scholars and officials. Many stylistic variations exist in Chinese calligraphy. At the most formal extreme, each character consists of distinct straight and angular strokes and is separate from the next character. At the other extreme, the characters flow together as cursive abbreviations with many rounded forms.

A long tradition in China links pictures and texts. Famous poems frequently provided subjects for paintings, and poets composed poems inspired by paintings. Either practice might prompt inscriptions on artworks.

Some inscriptions address the painting's subject. Others praise the painting's quality or the character of the painter. Some inscriptions explain the circumstances of the work. Later admirers and owners of paintings frequently inscribed their own appreciative words.

Painters, inscribers, and even owners usually also added *seal* impressions in red ink (FIGS. 18-14, 18-15, 18-18, and 18-19) to identify themselves. With all these textual additions, some paintings that have passed through many collections may seem cluttered to Western eyes. However, the historical importance given to these inscriptions and to the ownership history of paintings has been a critical aspect of art appreciation in China.

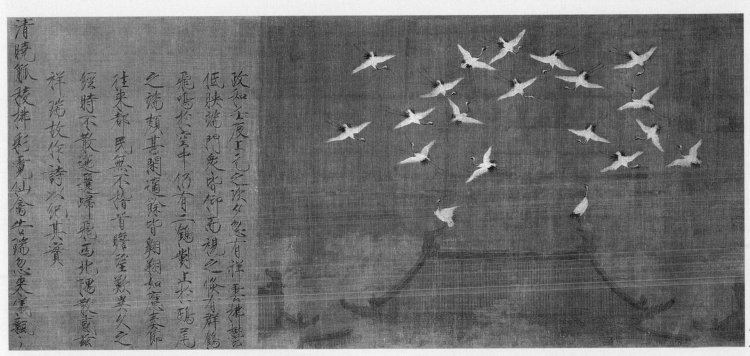

1 in.

18-11 Attributed to HUIZONG, *Auspicious Cranes*, Northern Song period, 1112. Section of a handscroll, ink and colors on silk, 1′ 8⅛″ × 4′ 6⅜″. Liaoning Provincial Museum, Shenyang.

The Chinese regarded the white cranes that appeared at Huizong's palace as an auspicious sign. This painting of that event is a masterful balance of pictorial and calligraphic elements.

A short handscroll (FIG. **18-11**) usually attributed to Huizong is more likely the work of court painters under his direction, but it displays the emperor's style as both calligrapher and painter. Huizong's characters represent one of many styles of Chinese calligraphy. They consist of thin strokes, and each character is meticulously aligned with its neighbors to form neat vertical rows. The painting depicts cranes flying over the roofs of Bianliang. It is a masterful combination of elegant composition and realistic observation. The painter carefully recorded the black and red feathers of the white cranes and depicted the birds from a variety of viewpoints to

suggest they were circling around the roof. Huizong did not, however, choose this subject because of his interest in the anatomy and flight patterns of birds. The painting was a propaganda piece commemorating the appearance of 20 white cranes at the palace gates during a festival in 1112. The Chinese regarded the cranes as an auspicious sign, proof Heaven had blessed Huizong's rule.

Foguang Si Pagoda For two centuries during the Northern Song period, the Liao dynasty (907–1125) ruled part of northern China. In 1056, the Liao rulers built the tallest

Chinese Wooden Construction

Although the basic unit of Chinese architecture, the rectangular hall with columns supporting a roof, was common in many ancient civilizations, Chinese buildings have two major distinguishing features: the curving silhouettes of their roofs and their method of construction. The Chinese, like other ancient peoples, used wood to construct their earliest buildings. Although those structures do not survive, scholars believe that many of the features giving East Asian architecture its specific character may date to the Zhou dynasty.

The typical Chinese hall has a pitched roof with projecting eaves. Wooden columns, lintels, and brackets provide the support. The walls have no weight-bearing function but serve only as screens. The colors of Chinese buildings, predominantly red, black, yellow, and white, are also distinctive. Chinese timber architecture is customarily multicolored throughout, save for certain parts left in natural color, such as railings made of white marble. The builders usually painted the screen walls and the columns red. Chinese designers often chose dazzling combinations of colors and elaborate patterns for the beams, brackets, eaves, rafters, and ceilings. Artists painted or lacquered the surfaces to protect the timber from rot and wood parasites, as well as to produce an arresting aesthetic effect.

The drawing reproduced here (FIG. 18-12) shows the basic construction method of Chinese architecture, with the major components of a Chinese building labeled. The builders laid *beams* between columns, decreasing the length of the beams as the structure rose. The beams supported vertical *struts*, which in turn supported higher beams and eventually the *purlins* running the length of the building and carrying the roof's sloping *rafters*. Unlike the rigid elements of the triangular trussed timber roof common in the West, which produce flat sloping rooflines, the varying lengths of the Chinese structures' cross beams and the variously placed purlins can create curved profiles, which eventually became the norm throughout East Asia. The interlocking clusters of brackets were capable of supporting roofs with broad overhanging *eaves*, another typical feature of Chinese architecture (FIGS. 18-1 and 18-13). Multiplication of the *bays* (spaces between the columns) could extend the building's length to any dimension desired, although each bay could be no wider or longer than the length of a single tree trunk. The proportions of the structural elements could be fixed into modules, allowing for standardization of parts and thus rapid construction. Remarkably, the highly skilled Chinese workers fit the parts together without using any adhesive substance, such as mortar or glue.

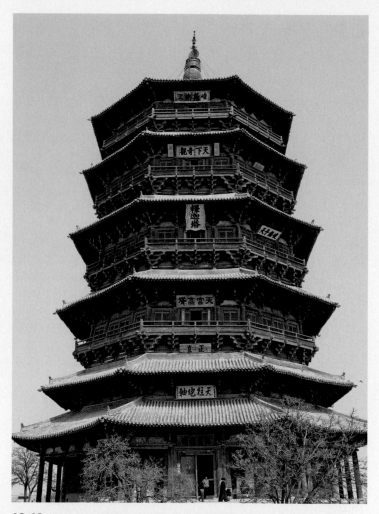

18-12 Chinese raised-beam construction (after L. Liu).

Chinese walls have no weight-bearing function. They serve only as screens separating inside from outside and room from room. Curved rafters and eaves are distinctive features of Chinese architecture.

18-13 Foguang Si Pagoda, Yingxian, China, Liao dynasty, 1056.

The tallest wooden building in the world is this Buddhist pagoda at Yingxian. The nine-story tower shows the Chinese wooden beam-and-bracket construction system at its most ingenious.

wooden building ever constructed (see "Chinese Wooden Construction," above, and FIG. 18-12)—the Foguang Si Pagoda (FIG. 18-13) at Yingxian. The *pagoda,* or tower—the building type most often associated with Buddhism in China and other parts of East Asia—is the most eye-catching feature of a Buddhist temple complex. It somewhat resembles the tall towers of Indian temples (see "Hindu Temples," Chapter 17, page 479) and their distant ancestor, the Buddhist stupa (see "The Stupa," Chapter 17, page 474). As did stupas, many early pagodas housed relics and provided a focus for devotion to the Buddha. Later pagodas served other functions, such as housing sacred images and texts.

The octagonal pagoda at Yingxian is 216 feet tall. Sixty giant, four-tiered bracket clusters carry the floor beams and projecting eaves of the five main stories. They rest on two concentric rings of columns at each level. Alternating main stories and windowless mezzanines with cantilevered balconies, set back farther on each story as the tower rises, form a combined elevation of nine stories. Along with the open veranda on the ground level and the soaring pinnacle, the balconies visually lighten the building's mass.

Ma Yuan Gaozong (r. 1127–1162), Huizong's sixth son, fled Bianling after his father's capture, established a new Southern Song capital at Lin'an, and resumed court sponsorship of the arts. During the reign of Ningzong (r. 1194–1224), both the emperor and empress, Yang, frequently added brief poems to the paintings created under their direction. Some of these painters belonged to families that had worked for the Song emperors for several generations. The most famous was the Ma family. MA YUAN (ca. 1160–1225) painted *On a Mountain Path in Spring* (FIG. **18-14**), a silk album leaf, for Ningzong in the early 13th century. In his composition, in striking contrast to Fan's much larger *Travelers among Mountains*

and Streams (FIG. 18-10), Ma reduced the landscape to a few elements and confined the natural setting to the foreground and left side of the page. A large, solitary figure gazes out into the infinite distance. Framing him are the carefully placed diagonals of willow branches. Near the upper right corner, a bird flies toward the couplet Ningzong added in ink:

> *Brushed by his sleeves, wild flowers dance in the wind;*
> *Fleeing from him, hidden birds cut short their songs.*

Some scholars have suggested the author of the two-line poem was Empress Yang, but the inscription is in Ningzong's hand. In any case, landscape paintings such as this one are perfect embodiments of the Chinese ideals of peace and unity with nature.

Yuan Dynasty

The 13th century was a time of profound political upheaval in Asia. During the opening decade, the Islamic armies of Muhammad of Ghor (1162–1206) wrested power from India's Hindu kings and established a Muslim sultanate at Delhi (see page 480). Then, in 1210, the Mongols, led by Genghis Khan (1167–1230), invaded China from Central Asia. By 1215 they had destroyed the Jin dynasty's capital at Beijing and taken control of northern China. Two decades later, they attacked

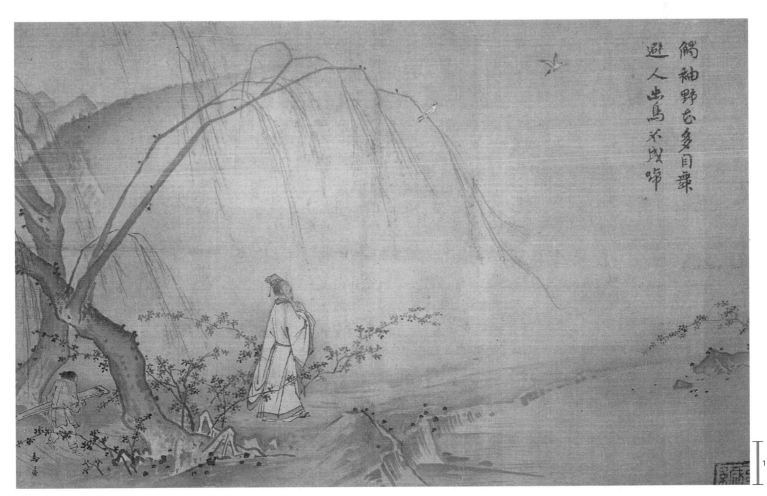

18-14 MA YUAN, *On a Mountain Path in Spring,* Southern Song period, early 13th century. Album leaf, ink and colors on silk, 10¾″ × 1′ 5″. National Palace Museum, Taibei.

In contrast to Fan (FIG. 18-10), Ma reduced the landscape on this silk album leaf to a few elements and confined them to one part of the page. A large, solitary figure gazes into the infinite distance.

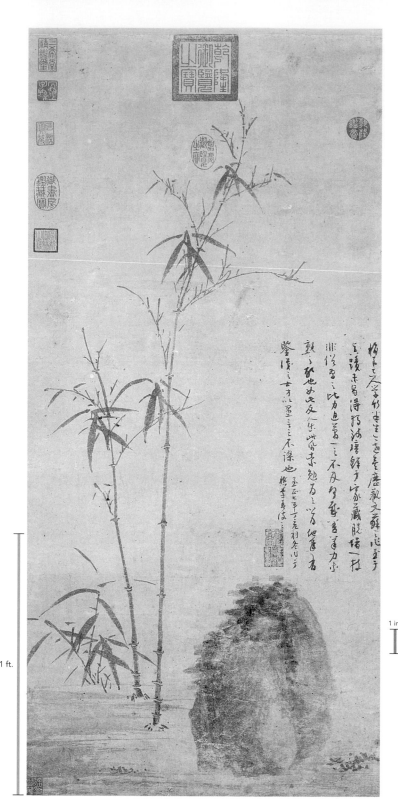

18-15 WU ZHEN, *Stalks of Bamboo by a Rock,* Yuan dynasty, 1347. Hanging scroll, ink on paper, 2′ 11½″ × 1′ 4⅝″. National Palace Museum, Taibei. 🎥

Wu Zhen was one of the leading Yuan literati (scholar-artists). The bamboo plants in this hanging scroll are perfect complements to the prominently featured black Chinese calligraphic characters.

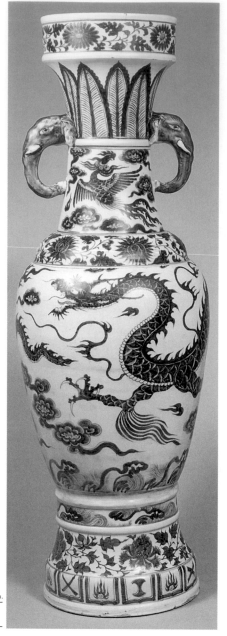

18-16 Temple vase, Yuan dynasty, 1351. White porcelain with cobalt-blue underglaze, 2′ 1″ × 8⅛″. Percival David Foundation of Chinese Art, London.

This vase is an early example of porcelain with cobalt-blue underglaze decoration. Dragons and phoenixes, auspicious symbols of male and female energy, respectively, are the major painted motifs.

During the relatively brief tenure of the Yuan, trade between Europe and Asia increased dramatically. It was no coincidence that Marco Polo (1254–1324), the most famous early European visitor to China, arrived during the reign of Kublai Khan. Part fact and part fable, Marco Polo's chronicle of his travels to and within China was the only eyewitness description of East Asia available in Europe for several centuries. The Venetian's account makes clear he profoundly admired Yuan China. He marveled not only at Kublai Khan's opulent lifestyle and palaces but also at the volume of commercial traffic on the Yangtze River; the splendors of Hangzhou; the use of paper currency, porcelain, and coal; the efficiency of the Chinese postal system; and the hygiene of the Chinese people. In the early second millennium, China was richer and technologically more advanced than late medieval Europe.

Wu Zhen The Mongols were great admirers of Chinese art and culture, but they were very selective in admitting former Southern Song subjects into their administration. In addition, many Chinese loyal to the former emperors refused to collaborate with their new foreign overlords, whom they considered barbarian usurpers. WU ZHEN (1280–1354), for example, chose to live as a hermit, far from the luxurious milieu of the Yuan emperors. He was among the *literati,* or scholar-artists, who emerged during the Song dynasty. The literati were men and women from prominent families who

the Song dynasty in southern China, but it was not until 1279 that the last Song emperor fell at the hands of Genghis Khan's grandson, Kublai Khan, who proclaimed himself emperor (r. 1279–1294) of the new Yuan dynasty (r. 1279–1368).

painted primarily for a small audience of their social peers. Highly educated and steeped in traditional Chinese culture, they cultivated poetry, calligraphy, painting, and other arts as a sign of social status and refined taste. Literati art is usually personal in nature and often shows nostalgia for the past.

Bamboo was a popular subject of literati painters because the plant was a symbol of the ideal Chinese gentleman, who bends in adversity but does not break, and because depicting bamboo branches and leaves approximated the cherished art of calligraphy. In *Stalks of Bamboo by a Rock* (FIG. **18-15**), Wu clearly differentiated the individual bamboo plants and reveled in the abstract patterns the stalks and leaves formed. The bamboo plants are perfect complements to the calligraphic beauty of the Chinese black characters and red seals so prominently featured on this hanging scroll (see "Calligraphy and Inscriptions," page 501). Both the bamboo and the inscriptions gave the artist the opportunity to display his proficiency with the brush.

Jingdezhen Porcelain Chinese potters had produced stunning ceramic wares since the Neolithic period. By the Yuan period, the Chinese had extended their mastery to fully developed porcelains, a very technically demanding medium. *Porcelain* is made from a fine white clay called kaolin mixed with ground petuntse (a type of feldspar), fired in a kiln at an extremely high temperature (well over 2,000 degrees F) until the clay fully fuses into a dense, hard substance resembling stone or glass. True porcelain is translucent and rings when struck. No other Chinese art form has achieved such worldwide admiration, inspired such imitation, or penetrated so deeply into everyday life as porcelain. Long imported by China's neighbors as luxury goods, Chinese porcelains later captured great attention in the West, where potters did not succeed in mastering the production process until the early 18th century.

A tall porcelain vase (FIG. **18-16**) from the Jingdezhen kilns is one of a nearly identical pair dated by inscription to 1351. The inscription also says the vases, together with an incense burner, composed an altar set donated to a Buddhist temple as a prayer for peace, protection, and prosperity for the donor's family. The vase is one of the earliest dated examples of fine porcelain with cobalt-blue *underglaze* decoration. The painter applied a cobalt compound to the clay surface before the main firing and then a clear *glaze* over the decoration. The underglaze decoration fully bonds to the piece in the kiln and emerges as an intense blue. The ornamentation on this example consists of bands of floral motifs between broader zones containing auspicious symbols, including phoenixes in the lower part of the neck and dragons on the main body of the vessel, both among clouds. These motifs may suggest the donor's high status or invoke prosperity blessings. Because of their vast power and associations with nobility and prosperity, the dragon and the phoenix also symbolize the emperor and empress, respectively, and often appear on objects made for the imperial household. The dragon also may represent *yang*, the Chinese principle of active masculine energy, and the phoenix may represent *yin*, the principle of passive feminine energy.

Ming Dynasty

The major building project of the Ming emperors who succeeded the Yuan rulers of China was the imperial palace complex in Beijing (see "The Forbidden City," page 491, and FIG. 18-1). Strictly organized along a north-south axis with traditional wooden buildings featuring curved rooflines alternating with courtyards, the Forbidden City culminated with the Hall of Supreme Harmony in which the Son of Heaven received official visitors.

Suzhou Gardens At the opposite architectural pole from the formality and rigid axiality of Ming palace architecture is the Chinese pleasure garden. Several Ming gardens at Suzhou have been meticulously restored, including the huge (almost 54,000 square feet) Wangshi Yuan (Garden of the Master of the Fishing Nets; FIG. **18-17**). Designing a Ming garden was not a

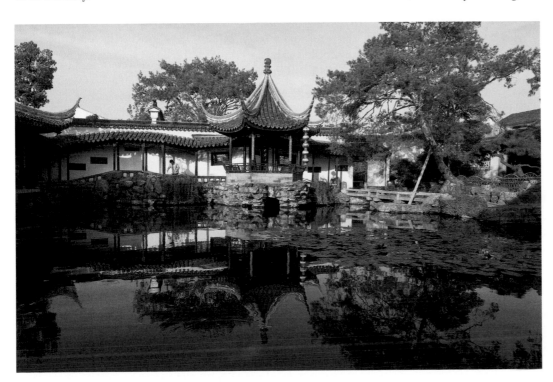

18-17 Wangshi Yuan (Garden of the Master of the Fishing Nets), Suzhou, China, Ming dynasty, 16th century and later.

Ming gardens are arrangements of natural and artificial elements mimicking the irregularities of nature. This approach to design is the opposite of the formality and axiality of the Ming palace (FIG. 18-1).

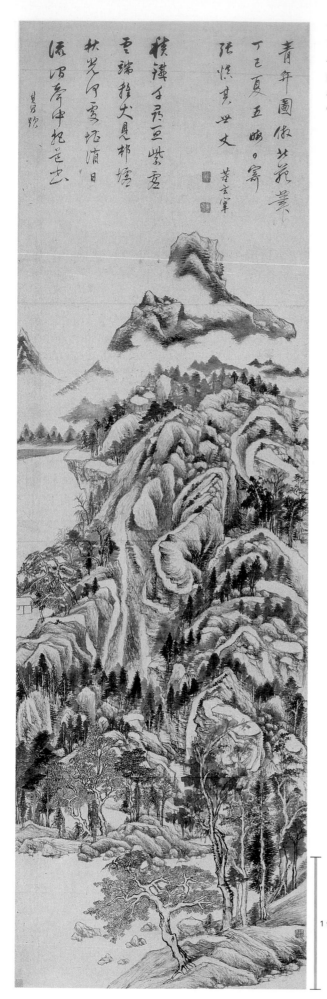

18-18 Dong Qichang, *Dwelling in the Qingbian Mountains*, Ming dynasty, 1617. Hanging scroll, ink on paper, 7' 3½" × 2' 2½". Cleveland Museum of Art, Cleveland (Leonard C. Hanna Jr. bequest). ■◀

Dong Qichang, the "first modernist painter," conceived his landscapes as shaded masses of rocks alternating with blank bands, flattening the composition and creating expressive, abstract patterns.

1 ft.

matter of cultivating plants in rows or of laying out terraces, flowerbeds, and avenues in geometric fashion, as was the case in many other cultures (compare, for example, the 17th-century French gardens at Versailles, FIG. 10-32). Instead, Ming gardens were often scenic arrangements of natural and artificial elements intended to reproduce the irregularities of uncultivated nature. Verandas and pavilions rise on pillars above the water, and stone bridges, paths, and causeways encourage wandering through ever-changing vistas of trees, flowers, rocks, and their reflections in the ponds. The typical design was a sequence of carefully contrived visual surprises.

Dong Qichang The Ming emperors maintained an official workshop of painters in the Forbidden City itself, but the venerable tradition of literati painting also flourished. One of the most intriguing and influential literati of the late Ming dynasty was DONG QICHANG (1555–1636), a wealthy landowner and high official who was a poet, calligrapher, and painter. He also amassed a vast collection of Chinese art and achieved great fame as an art critic. In Dong's view, most Chinese landscape painters could be classified as belonging to either the Northern School of precise, academic painting or the Southern School of more subjective, freer painting. "Northern" and "Southern" were not geographic but stylistic labels. Dong chose these names for the two schools because he determined their characteristic styles had parallels in the northern and southern schools of *Chan* Buddhism. Northern Chan Buddhists were "gradualists" and believed enlightenment could be achieved only after long training. The Southern Chan Buddhists believed enlightenment could come suddenly. Dong's Northern School therefore comprised professional, highly trained court painters, whose role was to promote Ming ideology. The leading painters of the Southern School were the literati, whose freer and more expressive style Dong judged to be far superior.

Dong's own work—for example, *Dwelling in the Qingbian Mountains* (FIG. **18-18**)—belongs to the Southern School he admired so much. Subject and style, as well as the incorporation of a long inscription at the top, immediately reveal the artist's debt to earlier literati painters. But Dong was also an innovator, especially in his treatment of the towering mountains, where shaded masses of rocks alternate with flat, blank bands, flattening the composition and creating highly expressive and abstract patterns. Some critics have called Dong Qichang the first *modernist* painter, foreshadowing developments in 19th-century European landscape painting (FIG. 13-13).

Qing Dynasty

The Ming bureaucracy's internal decay enabled another group of invaders, the Manchus of Manchuria, to overrun China in the 17th century. The Qing dynasty (r. 1644–1911) the Manchus established quickly restored effective imperial rule in the north. Southern China remained rebellious until the second Qing emperor, Kangxi ("Lasting Prosperity," r. 1662–1722), succeeded in pacifying all of China. The Manchus adapted themselves to Chinese life and cultivated knowledge of China's arts.

Shitao Traditional literati painting continued to be fashionable among conservative Qing artists, but other painters experimented with extreme effects of massed ink or individualized brushwork patterns. Bold and freely manipulated compositions with a new, expressive force began to appear. A prominent painter in this mode was SHITAO (DAOJI, 1642–1707), a descendant of the Ming imperial family who became a Chan Buddhist monk at age 20. His theoretical writings, most notably his *Sayings on Painting from Monk Bitter Gourd*, called for the use of the "single brushstroke" or "primordial line" as the root of all phenomena and representation. Although he carefully studied classical paintings, Shitao opposed mimicking earlier works and believed that he could not learn anything from the paintings of others unless he changed them. In *Man in a House beneath a Cliff* (FIG. **18-19**), Shitao surrounded the figure in a hut with vibrant, free-floating colored dots and multiple sinuous contour lines. Unlike traditional literati, Shitao did not so much depict the landscape's appearance as animate it, molding the forces running through it.

People's Republic

The overthrow of the Qing dynasty and establishment of the Republic of China under the Nationalist Party in 1912 did not bring an end to the traditional themes and modes of Chinese

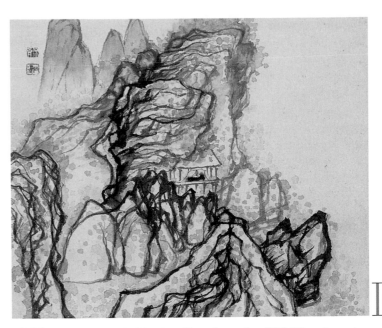

18-19 SHITAO (DAOJI), *Man in a House beneath a Cliff,* Qing dynasty, late 17th century. Album leaf, ink and colors on paper, $9\frac{1}{2}'' \times 11''$. C. C. Wang Collection, New York. ◼◀

Shitao experimented with extreme effects of massed ink and individualized brushwork patterns. In this album leaf, vibrant, free-floating colored dots and sinuous contour lines surround a hut.

art. But the triumph of Marxism in 1949, when the Communists took control of China and founded the People's Republic, inspired a social realism that broke drastically with the past. The intended purpose of Communist art was to serve the people in the struggle to liberate and elevate the masses.

Ye Yushan In *Rent Collection Courtyard* (FIG. **18-20**), a 1965 tableau 100 yards long and incorporating 114 life-size figures, YE YUSHAN (b. 1935) and a team of sculptors depicted the grim times before the People's Republic. Peasants, worn

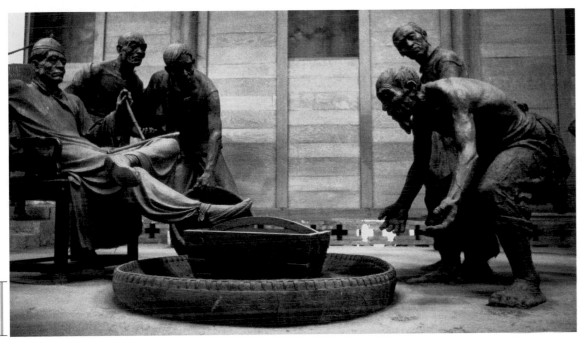

18-20 YE YUSHAN and others, *Rent Collection Courtyard* (detail of larger tableau), Dayi, China, 1965. Clay, 100 yards long with life-size figures. ◼◀

In this propagandistic tableau incorporating 114 figures, sculptors depicted the exploitation of peasants by their merciless landlords during the grim times before the Communist takeover of China.

and bent by toil, bring their taxes (in produce) to the courtyard of their merciless, plundering landlord. The message
is clear—this kind of exploitation must not happen again.
Initially, the authorities did not reveal the artists' names.
The anonymity of those who depicted the event was significant in itself. The secondary message was that only collective action could bring about the transformations the People's Republic sought.

KOREA

Korea is a peninsula that shares borders with China and
Russia and faces the islands of Japan (MAPS 18-1 and 19-1).
Korea's pivotal location is a key factor in understanding the
relationship of its art to that of China and the influence of
Korean art on Japanese art.

Three Kingdoms Period

About 100 BCE, during the Han dynasty, the Chinese established outposts in Korea. The most important was Lolang,
which became a prosperous commercial center. By the middle
of the century, however, three native kingdoms—Goguryeo,
Baekje, and Silla—controlled most of the Korean peninsula
and reigned for more than seven centuries until Silla completed its conquest of its neighbors in 668. During this era,
known as the Three Kingdoms period (ca. 57 BCE–688 CE),
Korea remained in continuous contact with both China and
Japan. Buddhism came to Korea from China in the fourth
century CE. The Koreans in turn transmitted it from the peninsula to Japan in the sixth century.

Silla Crown Tombs of the Silla kingdom have yielded spectacular artifacts representative of the wealth and power of
its rulers. Finds in the region of Gyeongju, the Silla capital, justify the city's ancient name—Kumsong (City of Gold).
The gold-and-jade crown (FIG. 18-21) from the Cheonmachong (Heavenly Horse) tomb at Hwangnam-dong, near
Gyeongju, dated to the fifth or sixth century, also attests
to the high quality of artisanship among Silla artists. The
crown's major elements, the band and the uprights, as well
as the myriad spangles adorning them, were cut from sheet
gold and embossed along the edges. Gold rivets and wires
secure the whole, as do the comma-shaped pieces of jade
further embellishing the crown. Archaeologists interpret the
uprights as stylized tree and antler forms believed to symbolize life and supernatural power. The Cheonmachong
crown has no Chinese counterpart, although the technique
of working sheet gold may have come to Korea from northeast China.

Unified Silla Kingdom

Aided by China's emperor, the Silla kingdom conquered
the Goguryeo and Baekje kingdoms and unified Korea
in 668. The era of the Unified Silla Kingdom (688–935) is

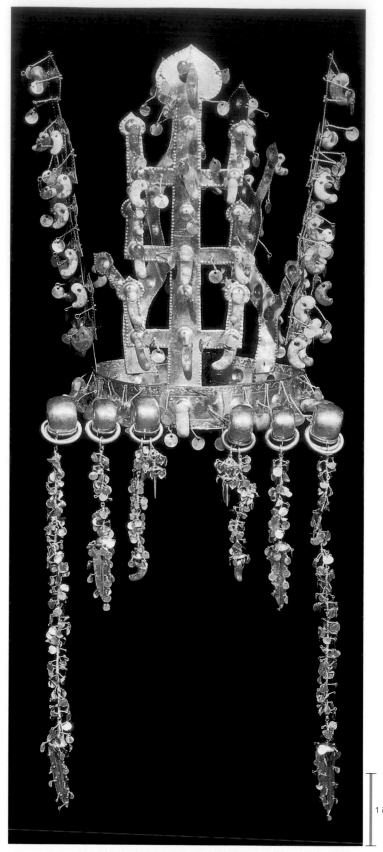

18-21 Crown, from the north mound of the Cheonmachong
tomb (tomb 98), Hwangnam-dong, near Gyeongju, Korea, Three
Kingdoms Period, fifth to sixth century. Gold and jade, 10¾″ high.
Gyeongju National Museum, Gyeongju.

This gold-and-jade crown from a Silla tomb attests to the wealth of that
kingdom and the skill of its artists. The uprights may be stylized tree
and antler forms symbolizing life and supernatural power.

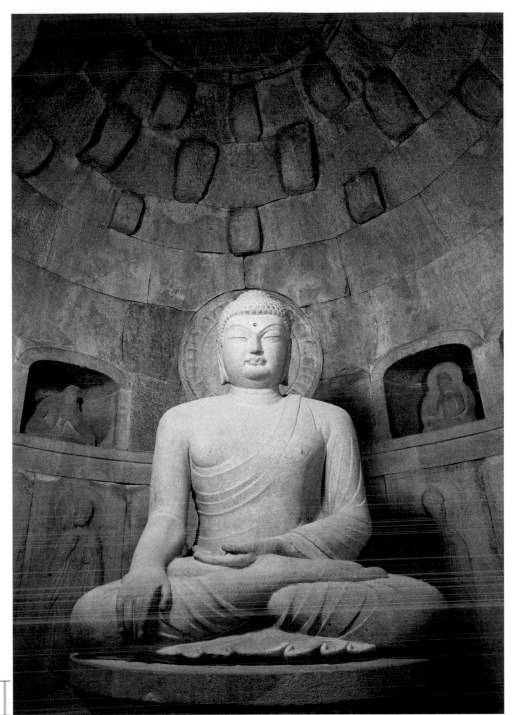

18-22 Shakyamuni Buddha, in the rotunda of the cave temple, Seokguram, Korea, Unified Silla Kingdom, 751–774. Granite, 11′ high.

Unlike rock-cut Chinese Buddhist shrines, this Korean cave temple was constructed using granite blocks. Dominating the rotunda is a huge statue depicting the Buddha at the moment of his enlightenment.

1 ft.

was built under the supervision of Kim Tae-song, a member of the royal family who served as prime minister. He initiated construction in 742 to honor his parents in his previous life. Certainly, the intimate scale of Seokguram and the quality of its reliefs and freestanding figures support the idea it was a private chapel for royalty.

The main *rotunda* (circular area under a dome; FIG. **18-22**) measures about 21 feet in diameter. Despite its modest size, the Seokguram project required substantial resources. Unlike the Chinese Buddhist caves at Longmen (FIG. 18-7) and Dunhuang (FIG. 18-8), the interior wall surfaces and sculpture were not cut from the rock in the process of excavation. Instead, workers assembled hundreds of granite pieces of various shapes and sizes, attaching them with stone rivets instead of mortar. Sculpted images of bodhisattvas, *lohans,* and guardians line the lower zone of the wall. Above, 10 niches contain miniature statues of seated bodhisattvas and believers. All these figures face inward toward the 11-foot-tall statue of Shakyamuni, the historical Buddha, which dominates the chamber and faces the entrance. Carved from a single block of granite, the image represents the Buddha as he touched the earth to call it to witness the realization of his enlightenment at Bodh Gaya (FIG. 17-1). Although remote in time and place from the Sarnath Buddha (FIG. 17-6) in India, this majestic image remains faithful to its iconographic prototype. However, no close precedents exist for the figure's distinctly broad-shouldered dignity combined with harmonious proportions. Art historians consider this Korean statue one of the finest images of the Buddha in East Asia.

roughly contemporaneous with the Tang dynasty's brilliant culture in China, and many consider the era to be Korea's golden age.

Seokguram The Silla rulers embraced Buddhism both as a source of religious enlightenment and as a protective force. They considered the magnificent Buddhist temples they constructed in and around their capital of Gyeongju to be supernatural defenses against external threats as well as places of worship. Unfortunately, none of these temples survived Korea's turbulent history. However, there remains at Seokguram, near the summit of Mount Toham, northeast of the city, a splendid granite Buddhist monument. Records suggest it

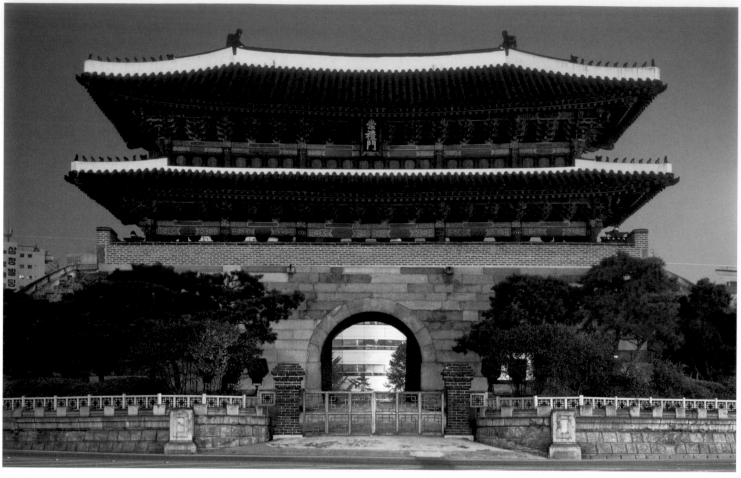

18-23 Namdaemun, Seoul, South Korea, Joseon dynasty, first built in 1398.

The new Joseon dynasty constructed the south gate to their new capital of Seoul as a symbol of their authority. Namdaemun combines stone foundations with Chinese-style bracketed wooden construction.

Joseon Dynasty

At the time the Yuan overthrew the Song dynasty in China, the Goryeo dynasty (r. 918–1392), which had ruled Korea since the downfall of China's Tang dynasty, was still in power. The Goryeo kings outlasted the Yuan as well. Toward the end of the Goryeo dynasty, however, the Ming emperors of China attempted to take control of northeastern Korea. General Yi Seonggye repelled them and founded the last Korean dynasty, the Joseon in 1392. The long rule of the Joseon kings ended only in 1910, when Japan annexed Korea.

Namdaemun, Seoul Public building projects helped give the new Joseon state an image of dignity and power. One impressive early monument, built for the new Joseon capital of Seoul, is the city's south gate, or Namdaemun (FIG. **18-23**). It combines the imposing strength of its impressive stone foundations with the sophistication of its intricately bracketed wooden superstructure. In East Asia, elaborate gateways, often in a processional series, are a standard element in city designs, as well as royal and sacred compounds, all usually surrounded by walls, as at Beijing's Forbidden City (FIG. 18-1). These gateways served as magnificent symbols of the ruler's authority, as did the triumphal arches of imperial Rome (see Chapter 3).

Modern Korea

After its annexation in 1910, Korea remained part of Japan until 1945, when the Western Allies and the Soviet Union took control of the peninsula nation at the end of World War II. Korea was divided into the Democratic People's Republic of Korea (North Korea) and the Republic of Korea (South Korea) in 1948. South Korea soon emerged as a fully industrialized nation, and its artists have had a wide exposure to art styles from around the globe. While some Korean and Chinese artists continue to work in a traditional East Asian manner, others have embraced developments in Europe and America. Contemporary East Asian art is examined in Chapter 16.

China and Korea

Shang to Qin Dynasties

▌ The Shang dynasty (ca. 1600–1050 BCE) was the first great Chinese dynasty of the Bronze Age. The Shang kings ruled from a series of capitals in the Yellow River valley. Shang bronze-workers were among the best in the ancient world. The Zhou dynasty (ca. 1050–256 BCE) was the longest in China's history. During the last centuries of Zhou rule, Daoism and Confucianism gained wide followings in China. Shi Huangdi founded the short-lived Qin dynasty (221–206 BCE) after defeating the Zhou and other rival states. A terracotta army of more than 6,000 soldiers guarded the First Emperor's burial mound at Lintong.

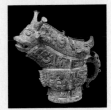

Shang guang,
12th or 11th century BCE

Han to Tang Dynasties

▌ The Han dynasty (206 BCE–220 CE) extended China's boundaries. Han tombs have yielded rich finds, including painted silks and bronze figurines. Civil strife divided China into competing states during the Period of Disunity (220–581 CE). China enjoyed unequaled prosperity and power under the Tang emperors (618–906), whose capital at Chang'an became the most cosmopolitan city in the world. The Tang dynasty was the golden age of Chinese figure painting. Yan Liben's *The Thirteen Emperors* handscroll illustrates historical figures as exemplars of Confucian ideals. The Dunhuang mural paintings provide evidence of the magnificence of Tang Buddhist art.

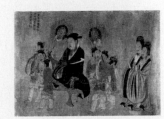

Yan Liben, *The Thirteen Emperors*, ca. 650

Song and Yuan Dynasties

▌ Song China (Northern Song, 960–1127, capital at Bianliang; Southern Song, 1127–1279, capital at Lin'an) was the most technologically advanced society in the world in the early second millennium. In art, the Song era marked the apogee of Chinese landscape painting. Fan Kuan, a Daoist recluse, was a pioneer in recording light, shade, distance, and texture in his hanging scrolls. The Mongols invaded northern China in 1210 and defeated the last Song emperor in 1279 to establish the Yuan dynasty (1279–1368). Yuan China was richer and technologically more advanced than Europe. The Jingdezhen kilns gained renown for porcelain pottery with cobalt-blue underglaze decoration.

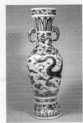

Temple vase,
Yuan dynasty, 1351

Ming Dynasty to 1980

▌ The Ming dynasty (1368–1644) constructed a vast new imperial palace compound, the Forbidden City, at its capital of Beijing. Surrounded by a moat and featuring an axial plan, it was the ideal setting for court ritual. At the opposite architectural pole are the gardens of Suzhou, which reproduce the irregularities of uncultivated nature.

▌ Under the Qing dynasty (1644–1911), traditional painting styles remained fashionable, but some Qing painters, such as Shitao, experimented with extreme effects of massed ink and free brushwork patterns. The overthrow of the Qing dynasty did not bring a dramatic change in Chinese art, but when the Communists gained control in 1949, state art focused on promoting Marxist ideals in vast propaganda pieces, such as *Rent Collection Courtyard*.

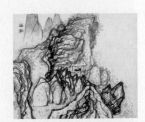

Shitao, *Man in a House beneath a Cliff*, late 17th century

Korea

▌ The art of Korea is closely related to both Chinese and Japanese art. The first golden age of Korean art and architecture was under the Unified Silla Kingdom (688–935), when a magnificent Buddhist complex was constructed at Seokguram.

▌ The last Korean dynasty was the Joseon (1392–1910), which established its capital at Seoul and erected impressive public monuments, such as the Namdaemun gate, to serve as symbols of imperial authority.

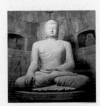

Shakyamuni Buddha,
Seokguram, 751–774

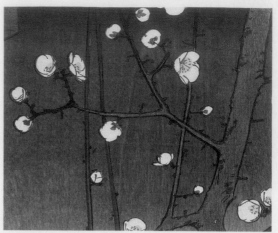

Ando Hiroshige's woodblock print shows only a partial view of the Sleeping Dragon Plum, whose branches spread out in abstract patterns resembling the beloved Japanese art of calligraphy.

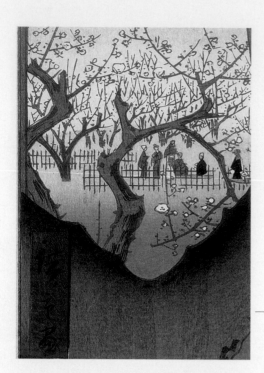

In the 19th century, residents of Edo (modern Tokyo) sought to escape from the noise and pressures of city life to visit places of natural beauty, such as the plum-tree estate at Kameido.

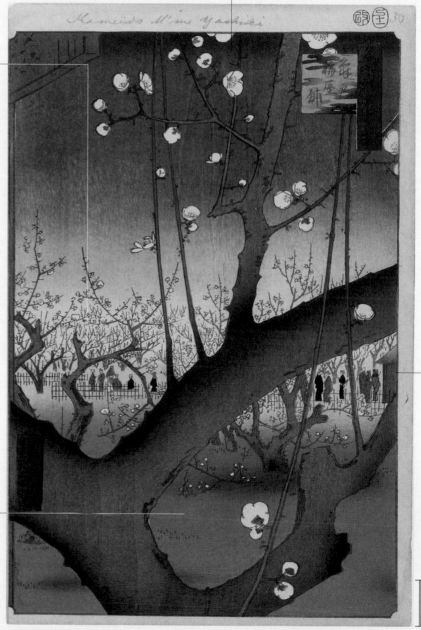

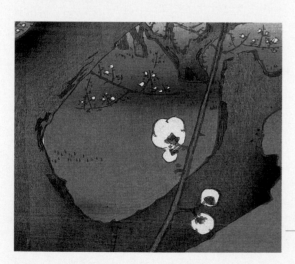

The main attraction of the Kameido estate was the venerable Sleeping Dragon Plum, the most famous tree in Edo, celebrated for its large white blossoms and aromatic fragrance.

19-1 ANDO HIROSHIGE, *Plum Estate, Kameido,* from *One Hundred Famous Views of Edo,* Edo period, 1857. Woodblock print, ink and color on paper, 1' 1¼" × 8⅝". Brooklyn Museum, Brooklyn (gift of Anna Ferris). ◼

Japan

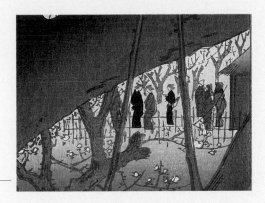

The bold patterns of the Kameido plum tree's limbs seen against the unnaturally colored red sky so dominate the print that the viewer hardly notices the crowd of onlookers behind a fence.

FAMOUS VIEWS OF EDO

Landscape painting—long revered as a major genre of Chinese and Korean painting (see Chapter 18)—emerged in the 18th century in Japan as an immensely popular subject with the proliferation of inexpensive multicolor woodblock prints (see "Japanese Woodblock Prints," page 528). Although inspired in part by Dutch landscape engravings imported into Japan at a time when the ruling Tokugawa government was pursuing an isolationist policy (see page 525), Japanese printmakers radically transformed the compositions and coloration of their Western models.

ANDO HIROSHIGE (1797–1858) and the older Katsushika Hokusai (FIG. 19-19) were the two most renowned Japanese printmakers specializing in landscapes. Hiroshige, born into a wealthy family, decided early on to pursue a career as an artist rather than to follow in his father's footsteps as chief of a fire brigade. In August 1832, he traveled on an official government mission to the emperor in Kyoto and the following year published a series of prints based on sketches he made on that journey—*Fifty-three Stations of the Tokaido Highway*. That collection of views of the countryside along the major roadway on Japan's east coast was an instant success. Many other editions followed, including views of Kyoto (1834) and his last and most ambitious series, published shortly before his death, *One Hundred Famous Views of Edo*.

Plum Estate, Kameido (FIG. **19-1**), dated "11th Month, 1857," comes from the *Edo* series. The "famous views" are not monuments and buildings but places of leisure and natural beauty where the Japanese sought to escape from the noise and pressures of city life. Many of the sites are religious shrines. Others, including the plum orchard of Kameido, were favorite spots to visit at particular times of the year, when their natural beauty was at its peak. The main attraction of the Kameido estate was the Sleeping Dragon Plum, the most famous tree in Edo (present-day Tokyo), celebrated for its large white blossoms and aromatic fragrance. Hiroshige's print shows only a partial view of the venerable tree, with its branches spreading out to touch all sides of the print and forming a bold abstract pattern resembling the beloved Japanese art of calligraphy. The pattern of the tree's limbs so dominates the print the viewer hardly notices the crowd of onlookers behind a fence in the background. The unnatural coloration of the red sky enhances the abstract effect, flattening the pictorial space in a manner completely foreign to the Western notion of perspective. It was precisely this quality that fascinated 19th-century European painters who were trying to break free of the Renaissance ideals perpetuated by the official painting academies (see Chapter 13). One such artist was Vincent van Gogh, who paid tribute to Hiroshige by painting his own version of the Kameido woodblock print.

JAPAN BEFORE BUDDHISM

The Japanese archipelago (MAP **19-1**) consists of four main islands—Hokkaido, Honshu, Shikoku, and Kyushu—and hundreds of smaller ones, a surprising number of them inhabited. The earliest Japanese art-producing culture antedates the birth of the Buddha by roughly 10,000 years.

Jomon and Yayoi

The Jomon period (ca. 10,500–300 BCE) takes its name from the Japanese word *jomon* (cord markings) and refers to the technique Japanese potters of this era used to decorate ceramic vessels. The Jomon people were hunter-gatherers, but unlike most such societies, which were nomadic, the Jomon inhabited villages. Their settled lives enabled them to develop a distinctive ceramic technology, even before their development of agriculture. In fact, archaeologists have dated some pottery fragments found in Japan to before 10,000 BCE— older than the ceramics in any other area of the world.

Jomon culture gradually gave way to Yayoi (ca. 300 BCE– 300 CE) in Kyushu, the southernmost of the main Japanese islands. Increased interaction with both China and Korea and immigration from Korea brought dramatic social and technological transformations. Japanese villages grew in size, and their inhabitants built fortifications around them, indicating a perceived need for defense. In the third century CE, Chinese visitors noted that Japan had walled towns, many small kingdoms, and a highly stratified social structure. Wet-rice agriculture provided the social and economic foundations for this development. During the Yayoi period, the Japanese also developed bronze-casting and loom weaving.

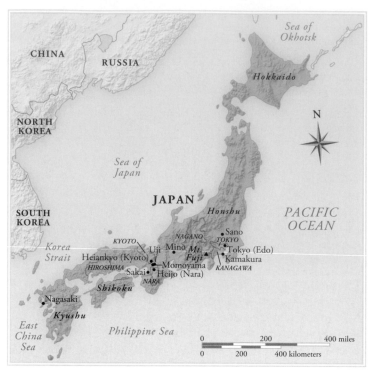

MAP 19-1 Japan.

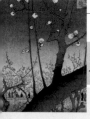

Japan

	Jomon, Yayoi, Kofun		Asuka, Nara, Heian		Kamakura and Muromachi		Momoyama		Edo		Meiji and Showa	
BCE	10,500	CE 552		1185		1573		1615		1868		1980

- Jomon (10,500–300 BCE) and Yayoi (300 BCE–300 CE) artisans produce fine pottery and bronzes
- Kofun (300–552) elite construct monumental keyhole-shaped burial mounds and place cylindrical clay figures (haniwa) around and on top of them

- Buddhism arrives in Japan from Korea in 552, initiating the Asuka period (552–645)
- The imperial government establishes its capital at Nara in 710 and builds Buddhist temple complexes following Chinese models during the Nara period (645–784)
- The imperial capital moves to Heiankyo (Kyoto) in 794, and Esoteric Buddhism takes hold in Japan during the Heian period (794–1185), during which narrative scroll painting becomes a major art form

- The Japanese emperor yields power to shoguns during the Kamakura period (1185–1332). Sculptors create realistic portraits in wood with rock-crystal eyes
- During the Muromachi period (1336–1573) Zen Buddhism rises to prominence. Kano Motonobu helps establish the Kano School as a virtual Japanese national painting academy

- Japanese shoguns decorate their palatial fortress-castles with painted folding screens featuring lavish use of gold leaf
- Sen no Rikyu becomes the most renowned master of the Japanese tea ceremony and designs teahouses that foster humility
- Shino ceramics exemplify the aesthetic principles of wabi and sabi

- The Katsura Imperial Villa at Kyoto sets the standard for Japanese domestic architecture
- The Rinpa School emerges as the major alternative style of painting to the Kano School
- Japanese woodblock prints depicting the sensual pleasures of Edo's "floating world" reach a wide audience

- Ceramic master Hamada Shoji receives official recognition as a Living National Treasure
- Kenzo Tange designs the modernist stadiums for the 1964 Olympics in Tokyo

Kofun

Historians named the succeeding Kofun period (ca. 300–552)* after the enormous earthen burial mounds, or *tumuli,* that had begun to appear in the third century. (*Ko* means "old"; *fun* means "tomb.") As in other ancient cultures, these gigantic tombs served to proclaim the power and wealth of those buried beneath them.

Tomb of Nintoku The largest tumulus (FIG. **19-2**) in Japan, at Sakai, is usually identified as the tomb of Emperor Nintoku, although some scholars think the tumulus postdates his death in 399. The central mound, which takes the standard Kofun "keyhole" form, is 1,574 feet long and rises to a height of 114 feet. Surrounded by three moats, the entire site covers 458 acres. Kofun tumuli usually had a stone-walled burial chamber near the summit of the mound. Inside were the deceased's coffin and numerous objects to take into the afterlife. The objects buried with exalted individuals such as Emperor Nintoku included imperial regalia, swords, and bronze mirrors. The mirrors were imports from China, but the form of the Kofun keyhole tombs and many of the other burial goods, for example, comma-shaped jewels, suggest even closer connections with Korea (compare FIG. 18-21).

* From this point on, all dates in this chapter are CE unless otherwise stated.

Haniwa The Japanese also placed unglazed ceramic sculptures called *haniwa* on and around the Kofun tumuli. These sculptures, usually several feet in height, as is the warrior shown here (FIG. **19-3**), are distinctly Japanese. Compared with the Chinese terracotta soldiers and horses (FIG. 18-3) buried with the First Emperor of Qin, these statues appear deceptively whimsical as variations on a cylindrical theme (*hani* means "clay"; *wa* means "circle"). Yet haniwa sculptors skillfully adapted the basic clay cylinder into a host of forms, from abstract shapes to objects, animals, and human figures. These artists altered the shapes of the cylinders, emblazoned them with applied ornaments, excised or built up forms, and then painted the haniwa. The variety of figure types suggests the haniwa did not function as military guards but perhaps represented the realm the deceased ruled during life. The Japanese set the statues both in curving rows around the tumulus and in groups around a haniwa house placed directly over the deceased's burial chamber. The arrangement may mimic a funeral procession in honor of the dead. Presumably, the number of sculptures reflected the stature of the dead person. Emperor Nintoku's tumulus had about 20,000 haniwa statues placed around the mound.

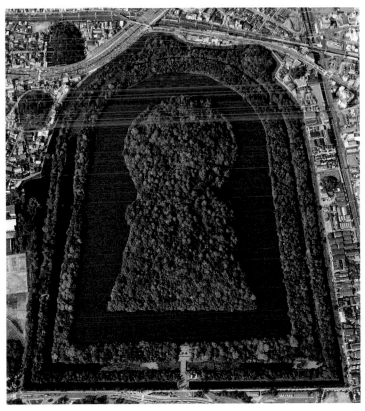

19-2 Tomb of Emperor Nintoku (looking northeast), Sakai, Osaka Prefecture, Japan, Kofun period, late fourth to early fifth century.

The largest Kofun tumulus, attributed to Emperor Nintoku, has a keyhole shape and three surrounding moats. About 20,000 clay haniwa originally stood on the gigantic earthen mound.

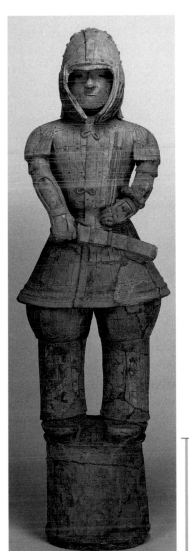

19-3 Haniwa warrior figure, from Gunma Prefecture, Japan, late Kofun period, fifth to mid-sixth century. Low-fired clay, 4′ 3¼″ high. Tokyo National Museum, Tokyo. ◼◀

During the Kofun period, the Japanese set up cylindrical clay statues (haniwa) of humans, animals, and objects on burial tumuli. They may represent the realm the deceased ruled during life.

1 ft.

BUDDHIST JAPAN

In 552, according to traditional interpretation, King Syong Myong of Baekje, one of Korea's Three Kingdoms (see page 508), sent Emperor Kimmei (r. 539–571) a gilded-bronze statue of the Buddha along with *sutras* (Buddhist scriptures) translated into Chinese, at the time the written language of eastern Asia. This event marked the beginning of the Asuka period (552–645), during which the ruling elite embraced major elements of continental culture that had been gradually filtering into Japan. These cultural components, which ultimately became firmly established in Japan, included Chinese writing, Confucianism, and Buddhism. Older beliefs and practices (those that came to be known as Shinto) continued to have significance (and still do), especially as agricultural rituals and imperial court rites. As time passed, Shinto deities even gained new identities as local manifestations of Buddhist deities.

In 645, a series of reforms led to the establishment of a centralized government in place of the individual clans that controlled Japan's different regions. This shift marked the beginning of the Nara period (645–784), when the Japanese court, ruling from a series of capitals south of Kyoto, increasingly adopted the forms and rites of the Chinese court. In 710, the Japanese finally established what they intended as a permanent capital at Heijo (present-day Nara). City planners laid out the new capital on a symmetrical grid closely modeled on the plan of the Chinese capital of Chang'an.

Asuka and Nara

In the arts associated with Buddhist practices, Japan followed Korean and Chinese prototypes very closely, especially during the Asuka and Nara periods. In fact, early Buddhist architecture in Japan adhered so closely to mainland standards (although generally with a considerable time lag) that surviving Japanese temples have helped greatly in the reconstruction of what was almost completely lost on the continent.

Tori Busshi Among the earliest extant examples of Japanese Buddhist sculpture is a bronze *Buddha triad* (Buddha flanked by two bodhisattvas; FIG. **19-4**) dated 623. Empress Suiko (r. 593–628) commissioned the work as a votive offering when her nephew, Prince Shotoku Taishi, fell ill in 621. When he died, the empress dedicated the triad to the prince's well-being in his next life and to his hoped-for rebirth in Paradise. The central figure in the triad is Shaka (the Japanese name for Shakyamuni, the historical Buddha), seated with his right hand raised in the abhaya mudra (fear-not gesture; see "Buddhism and Buddhist Iconography," Chapter 17, page 473). Behind Shaka is a flaming *mandorla* (a lotus-petal-shaped *nimbus*) incorporating small figures of other Buddhas. The sculptor, TORI BUSSHI (*busshi* means "maker of Buddhist images"), was a descendant of a Chinese immigrant. Tori's Buddha triad reflects the style of the early to mid-sixth century in China and Korea characterized by elongated heads

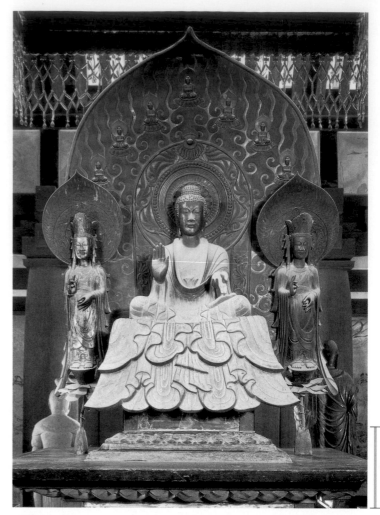

19-4 TORI BUSSHI, Shaka triad, kondo, Horyuji, Nara Prefecture, Japan, Asuka period, 623. Bronze, central figure 2′ 10″ high. ◾

Tori's Shaka triad (the historical Buddha and two bodhisattvas) is among the earliest Japanese Buddhist sculptures. The elongated heads and elegant swirling drapery reflect Chinese models.

and elegantly stylized drapery folds forming gravity-defying swirls. The vibrant patterns of the Buddha's garment contrast with the serenity of his pose and expression.

Horyuji Kondo Tori Busshi created his Shaka triad for an Asuka Buddhist temple complex at Horyuji, seven miles south of modern Nara. Fire destroyed the temple, but the priests rescued Tori's statue and reinstalled it around 680 in the *kondo,* or Golden Hall, of the successor Nara period complex (FIG. **19-5**). The kondo was the main hall for worship and housed statues of the Buddha and the bodhisattvas the temple honored. Although periodically repaired and somewhat altered, the Horyuji kondo retains its graceful but sturdy forms beneath the modifications. The main pillars (not visible in FIG. 19-5 due to the addition of a porch in the eighth century) decrease in diameter from bottom to top. The tapering provides an effective transition between the more delicate brackets above and the columns' stout forms. Also somewhat masked by the later porch is the harmonious

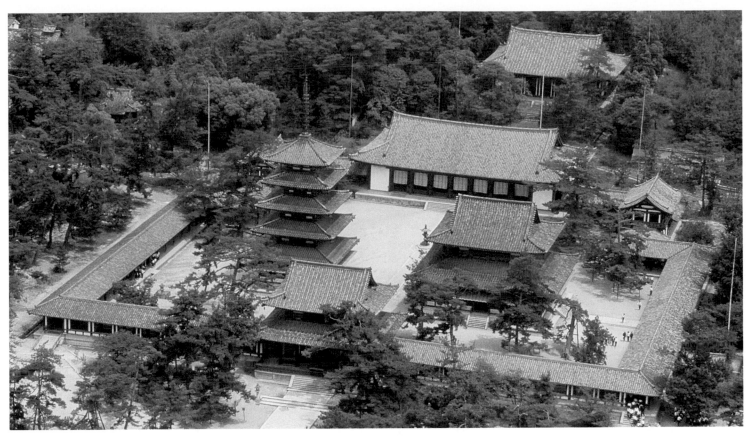

19-5 Aerial view of the Horyuji temple complex (looking northwest), Nara Prefecture, Japan, Nara period, ca. 680.

The main components of a Japanese Buddhist temple complex were the kondo (Golden Hall), which housed statues of the Buddha and bodhisattvas, and the pagoda, which contained relics of the Buddha.

reduction in scale from the first to the second story. Following Chinese models, the builders used ceramic tiles as roofing material and adopted the distinctive curved roofline of Chinese architecture (see "Chinese Wooden Construction," Chapter 18, page 502). Other buildings at the site include a five-story pagoda that serves as a reliquary.

Heian

In 784, possibly to escape the power of the Buddhist priests in Nara, the imperial house moved its capital north, eventually relocating in 794 to what became its home until modern times. Originally called Heiankyo (capital of peace and tranquility), its name today is Kyoto. The Heian period (794–1185) of Japanese art takes its name from the new capital. Early in the Heian period, Japan maintained fairly close ties with China, but from the middle of the ninth century on, relations between the two deteriorated so rapidly that by the end of that century, court-sponsored contacts had ceased. Japanese culture became much more self-directed than it had been in the preceding few centuries.

Esoteric Buddhism Among the major developments during the early Heian period was the introduction of Esoteric Buddhism to Japan from China. The name reflects the secret transmission of its teachings. Two Esoteric sects made their appearance: Tendai in 805 and Shingon in 806. The teachings of Tendai were based on the *Lotus Sutra,* one of the Buddhist scriptural narratives, and Shingon (True Word) teachings on two other sutras. Both Tendai and Shingon Buddhists believe all individuals possess buddha nature and can achieve enlightenment through meditation rituals and careful living. To aid focus during meditation, Shingon disciples use special hand gestures (mudras) and recite particular words or syllables. Shingon became the primary form of Buddhism in Japan through the mid-10th century.

Taizokai Mandara Because of the emphasis on ritual and meditation in Shingon, the arts flourished during the early Heian period. Both paintings and sculptures provided followers with visualizations of specific Buddhist deities and allowed them to contemplate the transcendental concepts central to the religion. Of particular importance in Shingon meditation was the *mandara* (*mandala* in Sanskrit), a diagram of the cosmic universe. The most famous Japanese mandaras are the Womb World (Taizokai) and the Diamond World (Kongokai). Together they formed a complementary pair on the wall of a Shingon kondo. The Womb World is composed of 12 zones, each representing one of the various dimensions of buddha nature (for example, universal knowledge, wisdom, achievement, and purity). The mandara illustrated

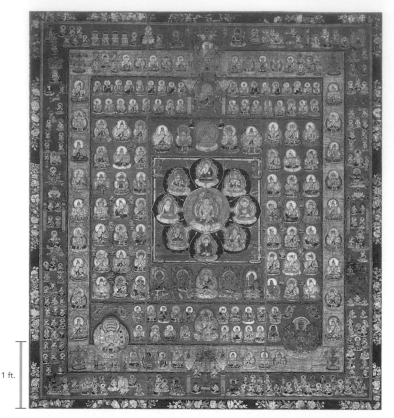

1 ft.

19-6 Taizokai (Womb World) mandara, Kyoogokokuji (Toji), Kyoto, Japan, Heian period, second half of ninth century. Hanging scroll, color on silk, 6′ × 5′ ⅝″.

The Womb World mandara is a diagram of the cosmic universe, composed of 12 zones representing the dimensions of Buddha nature. Mandaras played a central role in Esoteric Buddhist meditation.

here (FIG. **19-6**)—at Kyoogokokuji (Toji), the Shingon teaching center established at Kyoto in 823—is among the oldest and best preserved. Many of the figures hold lightning bolts, symbolizing the power of the mind to destroy human passion.

Phoenix Hall, Uji During the middle and later Heian period, belief in the vow of Amida, the Buddha of the Western Pure Land, to save believers through rebirth in his realm gained prominence among the Japanese aristocracy. Eventually, the simple message of Pure Land Buddhism—universal salvation—facilitated the spread of Buddhism to all classes of Japanese society. The most important surviving monument in Japan related to Pure Land beliefs is the Phoenix Hall (FIG. **19-7**) of the Byodoin at Uji. Fujiwara Yorimichi (990–1074), the powerful regent for three emperors between 1016 and 1068, built the temple in memory of his father on the grounds of his family's summer villa south of Kyoto. Dedicated in 1053, the Phoenix Hall's elaborate winged form evokes images of the Buddha's palace in his Pure Land, as depicted in East Asian paintings (FIG. 18-8) in which the architecture reflects the design of Chinese palaces. By placing only light pillars on the exterior, elevating the wings, and situating the whole on a pond, the Phoenix Hall builders suggested the floating weightlessness of celestial architecture. The building's name derives from its overall birdlike shape and from two bronze phoenixes decorating the ridgepole ends. In eastern Asia, people believed these birds alighted on lands properly ruled. Phoenixes are also associated with empresses. The authority of the Fujiwara family derived primarily from the marriage of daughters to the imperial line.

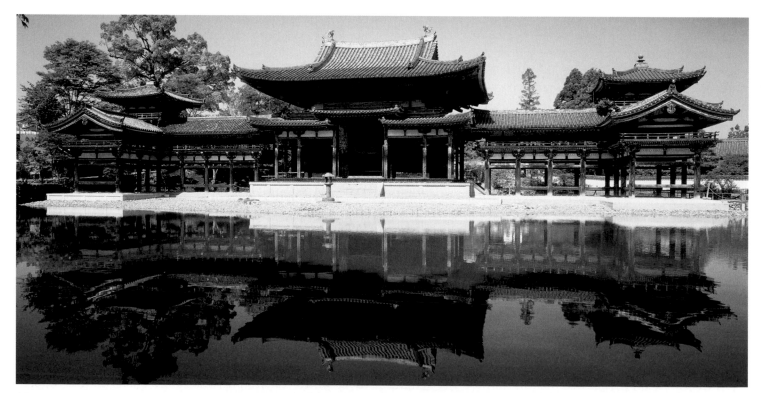

19-7 Phoenix Hall (looking west), Byodoin, Uji, Kyoto Prefecture, Japan, Heian period, 1053.

The Phoenix Hall's elaborate winged form evokes images of Amida's palace in the Western Pure Land. Situated on a pond, the temple suggests the floating weightlessness of celestial architecture.

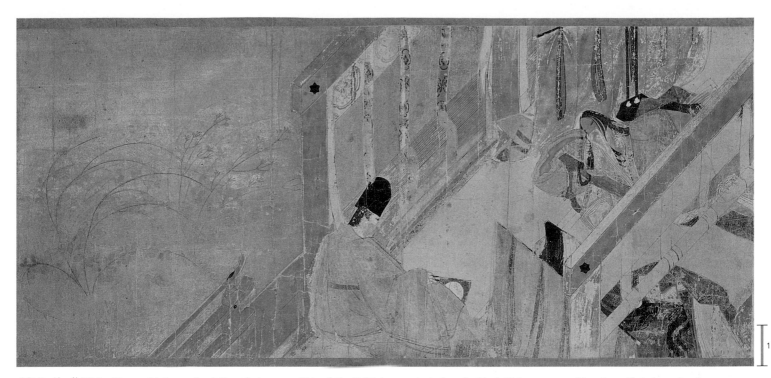

19-8 *Genji Visits Murasaki,* from the Minori chapter, *Tale of Genji,* Heian period, first half of 12th century. Handscroll, ink and color on paper, 8⅝″ high. Goto Art Museum, Tokyo. ◼◀

In this handscroll of Lady Murasaki's *Tale of Genji,* the upturned ground and diagonal lines suggest three-dimensional space. Flat color fields emphasize the painting's two-dimensionality.

Tale of Genji Japan's most admired literary classic is *Tale of Genji,* written around 1000 by Murasaki Shikubu (usually referred to as Lady Murasaki; ca. 978–ca. 1025), a lady-in-waiting at the court. Recounting the lives and loves of Prince Genji and his descendants, *Tale of Genji* provides readers with a view of Heian court culture. The oldest extant examples of illustrated copies are fragments from a deluxe set of early-12th-century handscrolls produced by five teams consisting of a nobleman talented in calligraphy, a chief painter who drew the compositions in ink, and assistants who added the color. The script is primarily *hiragana,* a sound-based writing system developed in Japan from Chinese characters. Hiragana originally served the needs of women (who were not taught Chinese) and became the primary script for Japanese court poetry. In these handscrolls, pictures alternate with text, as in Gu Kaizhi's *Admonitions* scrolls (FIG. 18-6). However, the Japanese work focuses on emotionally charged moments in personal relationships, rather than on lessons in exemplary behavior.

In the scene illustrated here (FIG. **19-8**), Genji meets with his greatest love near the time of her death. The bush-clover in the garden identifies the season as autumn, a time associated with the fading of life and love. A radically upturned ground plane and strong diagonal lines suggest three-dimensional space. The painter omitted roofs and ceilings to provide a view of the interior spaces where the action takes place. Flat fields of color emphasize the painting's two-dimensional character. Rich patterns in the textiles and architectural ornamentation give a feeling of sumptuousness.

The human figures appear constructed of stiff layers of contrasting fabrics, and the artist simplified and generalized the aristocratic faces, using a horizontal line for each eye and a hook for the nose. This lack of individualization may reflect societal restrictions on looking directly at exalted persons. Later Japanese critics considered several formal features of the *Genji* illustrations—native subjects, bright mineral pigments, lack of emphasis on strong brushwork, and general flatness—typical of *yamato-e,* or "native-style painting." *Yamato* means "Japan."

JAPAN UNDER THE SHOGUNS

A series of civil wars in the late 12th century brought an end to imperial power. In 1185, the Japanese emperor in Kyoto appointed Minamoto Yoritomo (1147–1199) the first *shogun* (military governor) at Kamakura in eastern Japan. Although the imperial family theoretically remained the source of political authority, real power was in the hands of the shogun and the *daimyo* (local lords), the leaders of powerful bands of *samurai* (warriors), who paid obeisance to the shogun.

Kamakura

During the Kamakura *shogunate* (1185–1332), more frequent and positive contact with China brought with it an appreciation for more recent cultural developments there, ranging from new architectural styles to Chan (in Japan, *Zen*) Buddhism.

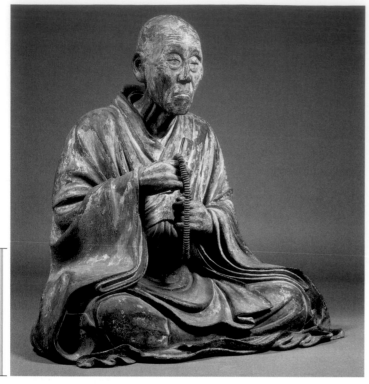

1 ft.

19-9 Portrait statue of the priest Shunjobo Chogen, Todaiji, Nara, Japan, Kamakura period, ca. 1206. Painted cypress wood, 2′ 8⅜″ high.

Kamakura artists' interest in naturalism is evident in this moving portrait of a seated priest. The statue is noteworthy for its finely painted details and powerful rendering of personality and old age.

Shunjobo Chogen Rebuilding in Nara after the destruction the civil wars inflicted presented an early opportunity for architectural experimentation. A leading figure in planning and directing the reconstruction efforts was the Shingon priest Shunjobo Chogen (1121–1206), who sources say made three trips to China between 1166 and 1176. After learning about contemporary Chinese architecture, he oversaw the rebuilding of the Todaiji Buddhist complex, among other projects. Chogen's portrait statue (FIG. **19-9**) is one of the most striking examples of the high level of naturalism prevalent in the early Kamakura period. It features finely painted details and a powerful rendering of the signs of aging, including sunken cheeks and eye sockets, lined face and neck, and slumping posture. Details such as the nervous handling of the prayer beads capture the personality as well as the appearance of the priest. The statue is the work of the Kei School of sculptors, known for their expert craftsmanship and use of inlaid rock crystal for the eyes, a technique unique to Japan.

The Kei School, which traced its lineage to Jocho, a master sculptor of the mid-11th century, typified traditional Japanese artistic practice. Indeed, until recently, hierarchically organized male workshops produced most Japanese art. Membership in these workshops was often based on familial relationships. Dominating each workshop was a master, and many of his main assistants and apprentices were relatives. Outsiders of considerable skill sometimes joined workshops, often through marriage or adoption. The eldest son usually inherited the master's position, after rigorous training in

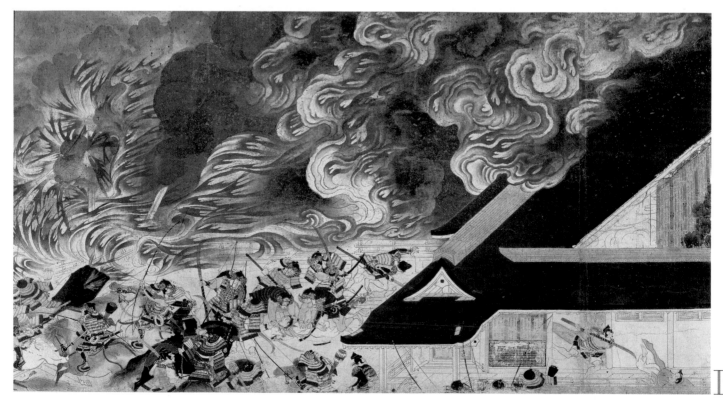

1 in.

19-10 *Night Attack on the Sanjo Palace,* from *Events of the Heiji Period,* Kamakura period, 13th century. Handscroll, ink and colors on paper, 1′ 4¼″ high (scroll 22′ 10″ long). Museum of Fine Arts, Boston (Fenollosa-Weld Collection).

The *Heiji* scroll is an example of Japanese historical narrative painting. Staccato brushwork and vivid flashes of color capture the drama of the night attack and burning of Emperor Goshirakawa's palace.

the necessary skills from a very young age. Therefore, one meaning of the term *art school* in Japan is a network of work shops tracing their origins back to the same master, a kind of artistic clan.

Attack on Sanjo Palace Handscroll painting also flourished in the Kamakura period. *Events of the Heiji Period* is a 13th-century masterpiece of historical narrative painting. The scroll depicts some of the civil-war battles at the end of the Heian period. The section reproduced here (FIG. **19-10**) represents the nighttime attack on the Sanjo palace during which the retired emperor Goshirakawa (r. 1155–1158) was taken prisoner and his palace burned. Swirling flames and billowing clouds of smoke dominate the composition. Below, soldiers on horseback and on foot do battle. As in other Heian and Kamakura scrolls, the artist depicted the buildings from above at a sharp angle. Noteworthy here are the painter's staccato brushwork and the vivid flashes of color that beautifully capture the drama of the event.

Muromachi

In 1336, after years of upheaval and conflict, Ashikaga Takauji (1305–1358) succeeded in establishing domination of his clan over all of Japan and became the new imperially recognized shogun. This marked the beginning of the Muromachi period (1336–1573), named after the district in Kyoto in which the Ashikaga shogunate maintained its headquarters.

During the Muromachi period, Zen Buddhism (see "Zen Buddhism," page 522) rose to prominence. Unlike Pure Land Buddhism, which stressed reliance on the saving power of Amida, the Buddha of the West, Zen emphasized rigorous discipline and personal responsibility. For this reason, Zen held a special attraction for the upper echelons of samurai, whose behavioral codes placed high values on loyalty, courage, and self-control. Further, familiarity with Chinese Chan culture carried implications of superior knowledge and refinement, thereby legitimizing the elevated status of the warrior elite. Zen, however, was not exclusively the religion of Zen monks and highly placed warriors. Aristocrats, merchants, and others studied at and supported Zen temples. Zen Buddhists generally accepted other Buddhist teachings, especially the ideas of the Pure Land sects. These sects gave much greater attention to the problems of death and salvation. Zen temples stood out not only as religious institutions but also as centers of secular culture, where people could study Chinese art, literature, and learning, which the Japanese imported along with Zen Buddhism.

Sesshu Toyo As was common in earlier eras of Japanese history, Muromachi painters usually closely followed Chinese precedents (often arriving by way of Korea), which artists throughout East Asia regarded as part of a shared cultural heritage. Among the most celebrated Muromachi artists was the Zen priest SESSHU TOYO (1420–1506), one of the few Japanese painters who traveled to China and studied contemporaneous Ming painting. His most dramatic works are in the *splashed-ink* (*haboku*) style, a technique with Chinese roots. The

19-11 SESSHU TOYO, splashed-ink (haboku) landscape, detail of the lower part of a hanging scroll, Muromachi period, 1495. Ink on paper, full scroll 4′ 10¼″ × 1′ ⅞″; detail 4½″ high. Tokyo National Museum, Tokyo.

In this haboku landscape, the artist applied primarily broad, rapid strokes, sometimes dripping the ink on the paper. The result hovers at the edge of legibility, without dissolving into abstraction.

painter of a haboku picture pauses to visualize the image, loads the brush with ink, and then applies primarily broad, rapid strokes, sometimes even dripping the ink onto the paper. The result often hovers at the edge of legibility, without dissolving into sheer abstraction. This balance between spontaneity and a thorough knowledge of the painting tradition gives the pictures their artistic strength. In the haboku landscape illustrated here (FIG. **19-11**), images of mountains, trees, and buildings

Zen Buddhism

Zen (*Chan* in Chinese), as a fully developed Buddhist tradition, began filtering into Japan in the 12th century and had its most pervasive impact on Japanese culture starting in the 14th century during the Muromachi period. As in other forms of Buddhism, Zen followers hoped to achieve enlightenment. Zen teachings assert everyone has the potential for enlightenment, but worldly knowledge and mundane thought patterns are barriers to achieving it. Thus, followers must succeed in breaking through the boundaries of everyday perception and logic. This is most often accomplished through meditation. Indeed, the word *zen* means "meditation." Some Zen schools stress meditation as a long-term practice eventually leading to enlightenment, whereas others stress the benefits of sudden shocks to the worldly mind. One of these shocks is the subject of Kano Motonobu's *Zen Patriarch Xiangyen Zhixian Sweeping with a Broom* (FIG. 19-12), in which the shattering of a fallen roof tile opens the monk's mind.

The guidance of an enlightened Zen teacher is essential to arriving at enlightenment. Years of strict training involving manual labor under the tutelage of this master, coupled with meditation, provide the foundation for a receptive mind. According to Zen beliefs, by cultivating discipline and intense concentration, Buddhists can transcend their ego and release themselves from the shackles of the mundane world. Although Zen is not primarily devotional, followers do pray to specific deities. In general, Zen teachings view mental calm, lack of fear, and spontaneity as signs of a person's advancement on the path to enlightenment.

Zen training for Muromachi monks took place at temples, some of which also served as centers of Chinese learning and handled funeral rites. These temples even embraced many traditional Buddhist observances, such as devotional rituals before images, which had little to do with meditation per se.

As the teachings spread, Zen ideals reverberated throughout Japanese culture. Lay followers as well as Zen monks painted pictures and

19-12 KANO MOTONOBU, *Zen Patriarch Xiangyen Zhixian Sweeping with a Broom,* from Daitokuji, Kyoto, Japan, Muromachi period, ca. 1513. Hanging scroll, ink and color on paper, 5′ 7¾″ × 2′ 10¾″. Tokyo National Museum, Tokyo.

The Kano School represents the opposite pole of Muromachi style from splashed-ink painting. In this scroll depicting a Zen patriarch experiencing enlightenment, bold outlines define the forms.

1 ft.

produced other artworks that appear to reach toward Zen ideals through their subjects and means of expression. Other cultural practices reflected the widespread appeal of Zen. For example, the tea ceremony (see page 523) offered a temporary respite from everyday concerns, a brief visit to a quiet retreat with a meditative atmosphere, such as the Taian teahouse (FIG. 19-14).

emerge from the ink-washed surface. Two figures appear in a boat (to the lower right), and the two swift strokes nearby represent the pole and banner of a wine shop.

Kano Motonobu Representing the opposite pole of Muromachi painting is the Kano School, which by the 17th century had become virtually a national painting academy. KANO MOTONOBU (1476–1559) was largely responsible for establishing the Kano style. His *Zen Patriarch Xiangyen Zhixian Sweeping with a Broom* (FIG. **19-12**) depicts Xiangyen (d. 898) at the moment he achieved enlightenment. As the patriarch sweeps the ground near his rustic retreat, a roof tile falls at his feet and shatters. Xiangyen's Zen training is so deep the resonant sound propels him into an awakening (see "Zen Buddhism," above). In contrast to Muromachi splashed-ink

painting, Motonobu's work displays exacting precision in applying ink in bold outlines. Thick clouds obscure the mountainous setting and focus the viewer's attention on the sharp, angular rocks, bamboo branches, and modest hut framing the patriarch. Lightly applied colors also draw attention to Xiangyen, whom Motonobu showed as having dropped his broom with his right hand as he recoils in astonishment.

Momoyama

In 1573, Oda Nobunaga (1534–1582) overthrew the Ashigara shogunate in Kyoto but was later killed by one of his generals. Toyotomi Hideyoshi (1536–1598) then took control of the government until his death in 1598. In the ensuing power struggle, Tokugawa Ieyasu (1542–1616) emerged victorious and assumed the title of shogun in 1603. Ieyasu continued to

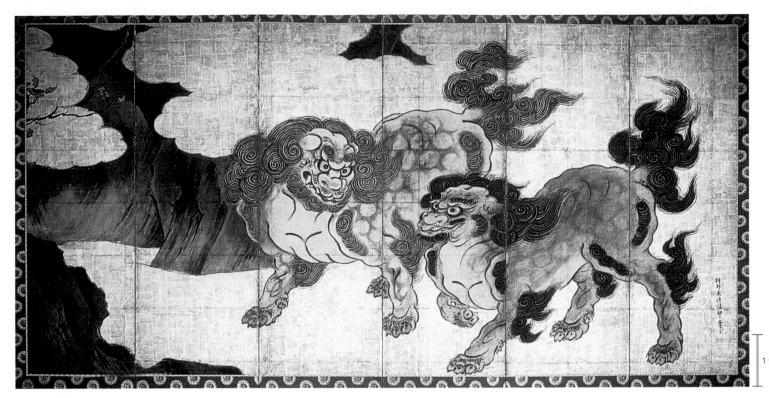

1 ft.

19-13 Kano Eitoku, *Chinese Lions*, Momoyama period, late 16th century. Six-panel screen, color, ink, and gold leaf on paper, 7′ 4″ × 14′ 10″. Museum of the Imperial Collections, Tokyo.

Chinese lions were fitting imagery for the castle of a Momoyama warlord because they exemplified power and bravery. Eitoku's huge screen features boldly outlined forms on a gold ground.

face challenges, but by 1615 he had eliminated his last rival, initiating a new era in Japan's long history, the Edo period (see page 525). During the brief intervening Momoyama period (1573–1615), the successive warlords constructed huge castles with palatial residences—partly as symbols of their authority and partly as fortresses. The era's designation, Momoyama (Peach Blossom Hill), derives from the scenic foliage at one of those castles. Each warlord commissioned lavish decorations for the interior of his castle, including paintings, sliding doors, and folding screens (*byobu*) in ink, color, and gold leaf.

Kano Eitoku The grandson of Kano Motonobu, Kano Eitoku (1543–1590), was the leading Momoyama painter of murals and screens and received numerous commissions to provide paintings for the warlords' castles. So extensive were these commissions that Eitoku adopted a painting system developed by his grandfather, which depended on a team of specialized painters to assist him. Unfortunately, little of Eitoku's elaborate work remains because of the subsequent destruction of the Momoyama shoguns' ostentatious castles. However, a painting of Chinese lions on a six-panel screen (FIG. **19-13**) offers a glimpse of his work's grandeur. Possibly created for Toyotomi Hideyoshi, this screen, originally one of a pair, appropriately speaks to the emphasis on militarism so prevalent at the time. The lions Eitoku depicted are ancient Chinese mythological beasts. Appearing in both religious and secular contexts, the lions came to be associated with power and bravery, and are thus fitting imagery for a shogun.

In Eitoku's painting, the colorful beasts' powerfully muscled bodies, defined and flattened by broad contour lines, stride forward within a gold field and minimal setting elements. The dramatic effect of this work derives in part from its scale—it is more than 7 feet tall and nearly 15 feet long.

Sen no Rikyu A favorite exercise of cultivation and refinement in the Momoyama period was the tea ceremony, which involved the ritual preparation, serving, and drinking of green tea. The host's responsibilities included serving the guests, selecting utensils, and determining the tearoom's decoration, which changed according to occasion and season. The tea ceremony eventually came to carry important political and ideological implications. It provided a means for those relatively new to political or economic power to assert authority in the cultural realm. For instance, upon returning from a major military campaign, Toyotomi Hideyoshi held an immense tea ceremony lasting 10 days and open to everyone in Kyoto. The tea ceremony's political implications became so important that warlords granted or refused their vassals the right to host tea rituals.

The most venerated tea master of the Momoyama period was Sen no Rikyu (1522–1591), who was instrumental in establishing the rituals and aesthetics of the tea ceremony, for example, the manner of entry into a teahouse (crawling on one's hands and knees). Rikyu believed crawling fostered humility and created the impression, however unrealistic, that there was no rank in a teahouse. Rikyu was the designer

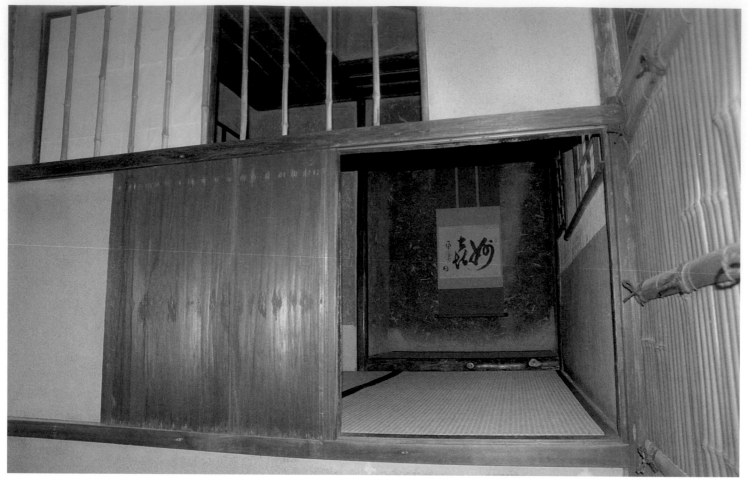

19-14 SEN NO RIKYU, view into the Taian teahouse, Myokian Temple, Kyoto, Japan, Momoyama period, ca. 1582.

The dimness and tiny size of the Taian tearoom and its alcove produce a cavelike feel and encourage intimacy among the host and guests, who must crawl through a small door to enter.

of the first Japanese teahouse built as an independent structure as opposed to being part of a house. The Taian teahouse (FIG. **19-14**) at the Myokian temple in Kyoto, also attributed to Rikyu, is the oldest in Japan. The interior displays two standard features of late Muromachi residential architecture—very thick, rigid straw mats called *tatami* (a Heian innovation) and an alcove called a *tokonoma*. The tatami accommodate the traditional Japanese customs of not wearing shoes indoors and of sitting on the floor. The tokonoma served as places to hang scrolls of painting or calligraphy and to display other prized objects.

The Taian tearoom has unusually dark walls, with earthen plaster covering even some of the square corner posts. The room's dimness and tiny size (about 6 feet square, the size of two tatami mats) produce a cavelike feel and encourage intimacy among the tea host and guests. The guests enter from the garden outside by crawling through a small sliding door. The means of entrance emphasizes a guest's passage into a ceremonial space set apart from the ordinary world.

Shino Ceramics Sen no Rikyu also was influential in determining the aesthetics of tea-ceremony utensils. In his view, value and refinement lay in character and ability and not in bloodline or rank, and he therefore encouraged the use of tea items whose value was their inherent beauty rather than their monetary worth. Even before Rikyu, in the late 15th century, admiration of the technical brilliance of Chinese objects had begun to give way to greater appreciation of the virtues of rustic wares. This new aesthetic of refined rusticity, or *wabi,* was consistent with Zen concepts. Wabi suggests austerity and simplicity. Related to wabi and also important as a philosophical and aesthetic principle was *sabi*—the value found in the old and weathered, suggesting the tranquility reached in old age.

Wabi and sabi aesthetics underlie the ceramic vessels produced for the tea ceremony, such as the Shino water jar named *Kogan* (FIG. **19-15**). The name, which means "ancient stream bank," comes from the painted design on the jar's surface as well as from its coarse texture and rough form. The term *Shino* generally refers to ceramic wares produced during the late 16th and early 17th centuries in kilns in Mino. Shino vessels typically have rough surfaces and feature heavy glazes containing feldspar. The Kogan illustrated here has a prominent crack in one side and sagging contours (both intentional) to suggest the accidental and natural, qualities essential to the values of wabi and sabi.

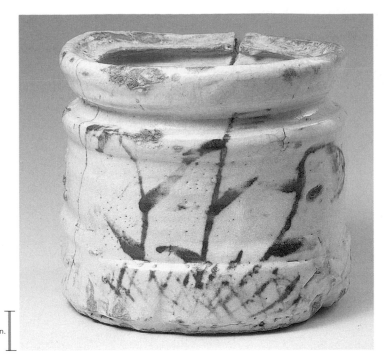

1 in.

19-15 Kogan (tea-ceremony water jar), Momoyama period, late 16th century. Shino ware with underglaze design, 7" high. Hatakeyama Memorial Museum, Tokyo.

The vessels used in the Japanese tea ceremony reflect the concepts of wabi, the aesthetic of refined rusticity, and sabi, the value found in weathered objects, suggesting the tranquility of old age.

Edo

When Tokugawa Ieyasu consolidated his power in 1615, he abandoned Kyoto, the official capital, and set up his headquarters in Edo (Tokyo), initiating the Edo period (1615–1868). The new regime instituted many policies designed to limit severely the pace of social and cultural change in Japan. Fearing destabilization of the social order, the Tokugawa rulers banned Christianity and expelled all Western foreigners except the Dutch. The Tokugawa also instituted Confucian ideas of social stratification and civic responsibility as public policy, and they tried to control the social influence of urban merchants, some of whose wealth far outstripped that of most warrior leaders. However, the population's great expansion in urban centers, the spread of literacy in the cities and beyond, and a growing thirst for knowledge and diversion made for a very lively popular culture not easily subject to tight control.

Katsura Imperial Villa In the Edo period, the imperial court's power remained as it had been for centuries, symbolic and ceremonial, but the court continued to wield influence in matters of taste and culture. For example, for a 50-year period in the 17th century, a princely family developed a modest country retreat into a villa that became the standard for domestic Japanese architecture. The Katsura Imperial Villa (FIG. **19-16**), built between 1620 and 1663 on the Katsura River

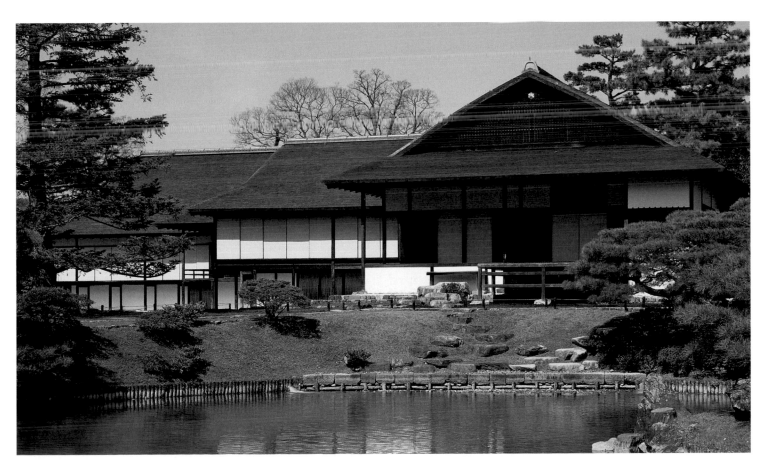

19-16 East facade of the Katsura Imperial Villa, Kyoto, Japan, Edo period, 1620–1663.

The Katsura Imperial Villa became the standard for Japanese residential architecture. The design relies on subtleties of proportion, color, and texture instead of ornamentation for its aesthetic appeal.

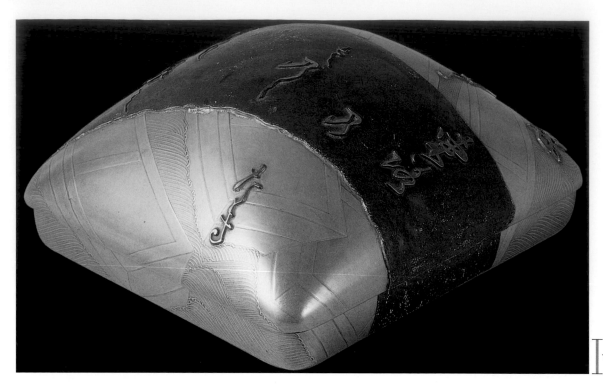

19-17 Honami Koetsu, *Boat Bridge,* writing box, Edo period, early 17th century. Lacquered wood with sprinkled gold and lead overlay, $9\frac{1}{2}'' \times 9'' \times 4\frac{3}{8}''$. Tokyo National Museum, Tokyo.

Koetsu's writing box is an early work of the Rinpa School, which drew on ancient traditions of painting and craft decoration to develop a style that collapsed boundaries between the two arts.

1 in.

southwest of Kyoto, has many features derived from earlier teahouses, such as Rikyu's Taian (FIG. **19-14**). However, the villa's designers incorporated elements of courtly gracefulness as well. Ornamentation that disguises structural forms has little place in the Katsura villa's appeal, which relies instead on subtleties of proportion, color, and texture. A variety of textures (stone, wood, tile, plaster) and subdued colors and tonal values enrich the villa's lines, planes, and volumes. Artisans painstakingly rubbed and burnished all surfaces to bring out the natural beauty of their grains and textures. The rooms are not large, but parting or removing the sliding doors between them can create broad rectangular spaces. Perhaps most important, the residents can open the doors to the outside to achieve a harmonious integration of building and garden—one of the primary ideals of Japanese residential architecture.

Rinpa In painting, the Kano School enjoyed official governmental sponsorship during the Edo period, and its workshops provided paintings to the Tokugawa shoguns and their major vassals. By the mid-18th century, Kano masters also served as the primary painting teachers for nearly everyone aspiring to a career in the field. Even so, individualist painters and other schools emerged and flourished, working in quite distinct styles.

The earliest major alternative school to emerge in the Edo period, Rinpa, was quite different in nature from the Kano School. It did not have a similar continuity of lineage and training through father and son, master and pupil. Instead, over time, Rinpa aesthetics and principles attracted a variety of individuals as practitioners and champions. Stylistically, Rinpa works feature vivid color and extensive use of gold and silver and often incorporate decorative patterns. Rinpa takes its first syllable from the last syllable in the name of OGATA

KORIN (1658–1716; FIG. I-11), the scion of a wealthy merchant family with close connections to the Japanese court. Many Rinpa works incorporate literary themes the nobility favored.

Honami Koetsu One of the earliest Rinpa masters was HONAMI KOETSU (1558–1637), the heir of an important family in the ancient capital of Kyoto and a greatly admired calligrapher. He also participated in and produced ceramics for the tea ceremony, as well as wooden objects with lacquer decoration, drawing on ancient traditions of painting and craft decoration to develop a style that collapsed boundaries between the two arts.

In typical Rinpa fashion, Koetsu's *Boat Bridge* writing box (FIG. **19-17**) exhibits motifs drawn from a 10th-century poem about the boat bridge at Sano, in the eastern provinces. The lid presents a subtle, gold-on-gold scene of small boats lined up side by side in the water to support the planks of a temporary bridge. The bridge itself, a lead overlay, forms a band across the lid's convex surface. The raised metallic lines on the water, boats, and bridge are a few Japanese characters from the poem, which describes the experience of crossing a bridge as evoking reflection on life's insecurities. The box also shows the dramatic contrasts of form, texture, and color typifying Rinpa aesthetics, especially the juxtaposition of the bridge's dark metal and the box's brilliant gold surface. The gold decoration comes from careful sprinkling of gold dust in wet lacquer.

Ukiyo-e The growing urbanization in cities such as Osaka, Kyoto, and Edo led to an increase in the pursuit of sensual pleasure and entertainment in the brash popular theaters and pleasure houses found in locales such as Edo's Yoshiwara brothel district. The Tokugawa tried to hold these

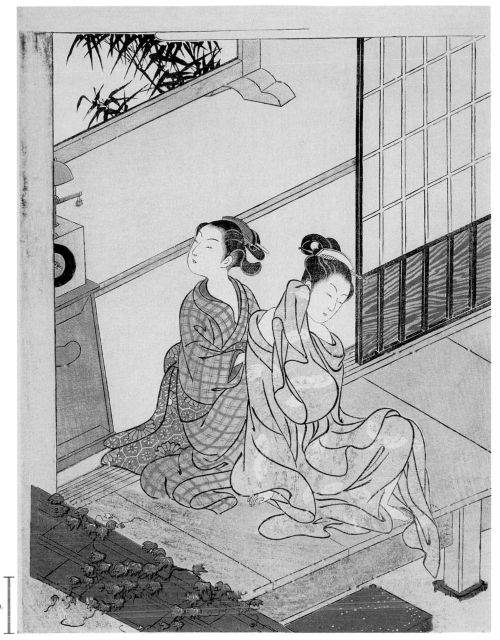

ukiyo-e—"pictures of the floating world," a term suggesting the transience of human life and the ephemerality of the material world. The main subjects of these paintings and especially prints come from the realms of pleasure, but Edo printmakers also frequently depicted beautiful young women in domestic settings (FIG. 19-18) and landscapes (FIGS. 19-1 and 19-19).

Suzuki Harunobu The urban appetite for ukiyo pleasures and for their depiction in woodblock prints provided fertile ground for many graphic designers to flourish. Consequently, competition among publishing houses led to ever greater refinement and experimentation in printmaking. One of the most admired and emulated 18th-century designers, SUZUKI HARUNOBU (ca 1725–1770), played a key role in developing multi-colored prints. Called *nishiki-e* (brocade pictures) because of their sumptuous and brilliant color, these prints employed the highest-quality paper and costly pigments. Harunobu gained a tremendous advantage over his competitors when he received commissions from members of a poetry club to design limited-edition nishiki-e prints. He transferred much of the knowledge he derived from nishiki-e to his design of more commercial prints. Harunobu even issued some of the private designs later under his own name for popular consumption.

The sophistication of Harunobu's work is evident in *Evening Bell at the Clock* (FIG. **19-18**), from *Eight Views of the Parlor.* This series draws upon Chinese series, usually titled *Eight Views of the Xiao and Xiang Rivers,* in which each image focuses on a particular time of day or year. In Harunobu's adaptation, beautiful young

19-18 SUZUKI HARUNOBU, *Evening Bell at the Clock,* from *Eight Views of the Parlor,* Edo period, ca. 1765. Woodblock print, 11¼″ × 8½″. Art Institute of Chicago, Chicago (Clarence Buckingham Collection). ◼◀

Harunobu's nishiki-e (brocade pictures) took their name from their costly pigments and paper. The rich color and flatness of the objects, women, and setting in this print exemplify the artist's style.

activities in check, but their efforts were largely in vain. Those of lesser means could partake in the Yoshiwara pleasures and amusements vicariously. Rapid developments in the printing industry led to the availability of numerous books and printed images (see "Japanese Woodblock Prints," page 528), and these could convey the city's delights for a fraction of the cost of direct participation. Taking part in the emerging urban culture involved more than simple physical satisfactions and rowdy entertainments. Many participants were also admirers of literature, music, and art. The best-known products of this sophisticated counterculture are the

women and the activities occupying their daily lives became subjects. In *Evening Bell at the Clock,* two young women seen from the typically Japanese elevated viewpoint (compare FIG. 19-8) sit on a veranda. One is drying herself after a bath (erotic themes are quite common in ukiyo-e), while the other—her maid—turns to face the chiming clock. Here, the artist has playfully transformed the great temple bell ringing over the waters in the Chinese series into a modern Japanese clock. This image incorporates the refined techniques characteristic of nishiki-e. Further, the flatness of the depicted objects and the rich color recall the traditions of court painting, a comparison many nishiki-e artists openly sought.

Japanese Woodblock Prints

During the Edo period, woodblock prints with ukiyo-e themes became enormously popular. Sold in small shops and on the street, an ordinary print went for the price of a bowl of noodles. People with modest incomes could therefore collect prints in albums or paste them on walls. Ukiyo-e artists were generally painters who did not themselves manufacture the prints that made them so famous. As the designers, they sold drawings to publishers, who in turn oversaw their printing. The publishers also played a role in creating ukiyo-e prints by commissioning specific designs or adapting them before printing. Certainly, the names of both designer and publisher appeared on the final prints. Unacknowledged in nearly all cases, however, were the individuals who made the prints, the block carvers and printers. Using skills honed since childhood, they worked with both speed and precision for relatively low wages and thus made ukiyo-e prints affordable.

Stylistically, Japanese prints during the Edo period tend to have black outlines separating distinct color areas (FIG. 19-18). This format is a result of the printing process. A master carver pasted painted designs facedown on a wooden block. Wetting and gently scraping the thin paper revealed the reversed image to guide the cutting of the block. After the carving, only the outlines of the forms and other elements that would be black in the final print remained raised in relief. The master printer then coated the block with black ink and printed several initial outline prints. These master prints became the guides for carving the other blocks, one for each color used. On each color block, the carver left in relief only the areas to be printed in that color. Even ordinary prints sometimes required up to 20 colors and thus 20 blocks. To print a color, a printer applied the appropriate pigment to a block's raised surface, laid a sheet of paper on it, and rubbed the back of the paper with a smooth flat object. Then another printer would print a different color on the same sheet of paper. Perfect alignment of the paper in each step was critical to prevent overlapping of colors, so the carvers included printing guides in their blocks—an L-shaped ridge in one corner and a straight ridge on one side. The printers could cover small alignment errors with a final printing of the black outlines from the last block.

The materials used in printing varied over time, but by the mid-18th century had reached a level of standardization. The blocks were planks of fine-grained hardwood, usually cherry. The best paper came from the white layer beneath the bark of mulberry trees because its long fibers helped the paper stand up to repeated rubbing on the blocks. The printers used a few mineral pigments but favored inexpensive dyes made from plants for most colors. As a result, the colors of ukiyo-e prints are highly susceptible to fading, especially when exposed to strong light. In the early 19th century, more permanent European synthetic dyes began to enter Japan. The first, Prussian blue, appears in Hokusai's *The Great Wave off Kanagawa* (FIG. 19-19).

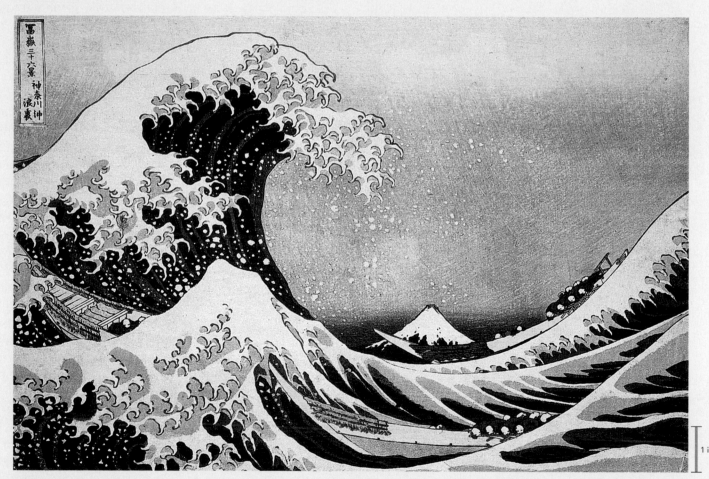

1 in.

19-19 KATSUSHIKA HOKUSAI, *The Great Wave off Kanagawa*, from *Thirty-six Views of Mount Fuji*, Edo period, ca. 1826–1833. Woodblock print, ink and colors on paper, $9\frac{7}{8}$″ × 1′ $2\frac{3}{4}$″. Museum of Fine Arts, Boston (Bigelow Collection). ◼️

Adopting the low horizon line of Western painting, Hokusai used the traditional flat and powerful graphic forms of Japanese art to depict the threatening wave in the foreground.

Katsushika Hokusai Woodblock prints afforded artists great opportunity for experimentation. For example, in producing landscapes, Japanese artists often incorporated Western perspective techniques, although others, Ando Hiroshige (FIG. 19-1) among them, did not. One of the foremost Japanese landscape artists was KATSUSHIKA HOKUSAI (1760–1849). In *The Great Wave off Kanagawa* (FIG. **19-19**), from *Thirty-six Views of Mount Fuji*, the huge foreground wave dwarfs the artist's representation of a distant Fuji. This contrast and the whitecaps' ominous fingers magnify the wave's threatening aspect. The men in the boats bend low to dig their oars against the rough sea and drive their long low vessels past the danger. Although Hokusai's print draws on Western techniques and incorporates the distinctive European color called Prussian blue, it also engages the Japanese pictorial tradition. Against a background with the low horizon typical of Western painting, Hokusai placed in the foreground the wave's more traditionally flat and powerful graphic forms.

MODERN JAPAN

The Edo period and the rule of the shoguns ended in 1868, when rebellious samurai from provinces far removed from Edo toppled the Tokugawa. Facilitating this revolution was the shogunate's inability to handle increasing pressure from Western nations for Japan to throw open its doors to the outside world. Although the rebellion restored direct sovereignty to the imperial throne, real power rested with the emperor's cabinet. As a symbol of imperial authority, however, the official name of this new period was Meiji ("Enlightened Rule"; 1868–1912), after the emperor's chosen regnal name.

During the Showa period (1926–1989), Japan became increasingly prominent on the world stage in economics, politics, and culture, and played a leading role in World War II. The most tragic consequences of that conflict for Japan were the widespread devastation and loss of life resulting from the atomic bombings of Hiroshima and Nagasaki in 1945. During the succeeding occupation period, the United States imposed new democratic institutions on Japan, with the emperor serving as a ceremonial head of state. Japan's economy rebounded with remarkable speed, and during the past several decades, Japanese artists have also made a mark in the international art world. As they did in earlier times with the art and culture of China and Korea, many Japanese artists and architects internalized Western styles and techniques and incorporated them as part of Japan's own vital culture.

Kenzo Tange In the postwar period, Japanese architecture, especially public and commercial building, underwent rapid transformation along Western lines. In fact, architecture may be the most influential Japanese art form on the world stage today. Japanese architects have made major contributions to both modern and postmodern developments (see Chapters 15 and 16). One of the most daringly experimental architects was KENZO TANGE (1913–2005). In his design of the stadiums (FIG. **19-20**) for the 1964 Olympics, he employed a cable suspension system that enabled him to shape steel and concrete into remarkably graceful structures. His attention to both the sculptural qualities of each building's raw concrete form and the fluidity of its spaces allied him with architects worldwide who carried on the legacy of the late style of Le Corbusier (FIG. 15-28) in France.

19-20 KENZO TANGE, aerial view of the national indoor Olympic stadiums, Tokyo, Japan, Showa period, 1961–1964.

Tange was one of the most daring architects of postwar Japan. His Olympic stadiums employ a cable suspension system that enabled him to shape steel and concrete into remarkably graceful structures.

A leading figure in the modern folk art movement in Japan, Hamada Shoji gained international fame. His unsigned ceramics feature casual slip designs and a coarser, darker texture than porcelain.

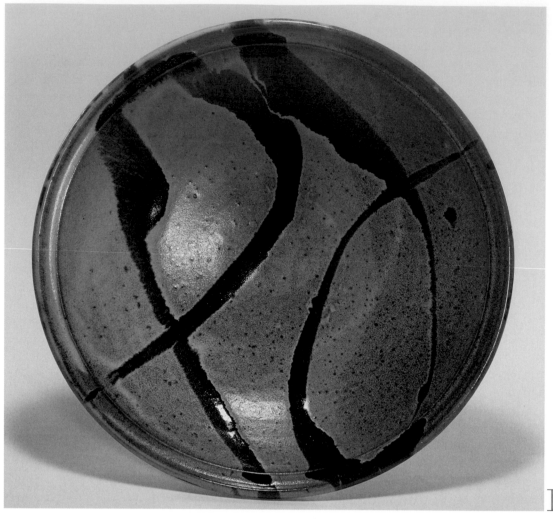

1 in.

Hamada Shoji Another modern Japanese art form that has attracted great attention worldwide is ceramics, which has ancient roots in Japan. A formative figure in Japan's folk art movement, the philosopher Yanagi Soetsu (1889–1961), promoted an ideal of beauty inspired by the tea ceremony. He argued that true beauty could only be achieved in functional objects made of natural materials by anonymous craftspeople, such as the Shino water jar (FIG. 19-15). Among the ceramists who produced this type of folk pottery, known as *mingei,* was HAMADA SHOJI (1894–1978). Although Hamada espoused Yanagi's selfless ideals, he still gained international fame and in 1955 received official recognition in Japan as a Living National Treasure. Works such as his dish (FIG. **19-21**) with casual slip designs are unsigned, but connoisseurs easily recognize them as his. This kind of pottery is coarser, darker, and heavier than porcelain and lacks the latter's fine decoration. To those who appreciate simpler, earthier beauty, however, this dish holds great attraction.

Hamada's artistic influence extended beyond the production of pots. He traveled to England in 1920 and, along with English potter Bernard Leach (1887–1978), established a community of ceramists committed to the mingei aesthetic. Together, Hamada and Leach expanded international knowledge of Japanese ceramics, and even now, the "Hamada-Leach aesthetic" is part of potters' education worldwide, underscoring the productive exchange of artistic ideas between Asia and the West today—discussed more fully in Chapter 16.

Japan

Japan before Buddhism

I The Jomon (ca. 10,500–300 BCE) is Japan's earliest distinct culture. It takes its name from the applied clay cordlike coil decoration of Jomon pottery.

I During the Kofun (Old Tomb) period (ca. 300–552 CE), the Japanese erected great earthen keyhole-shaped burial mounds and placed clay cylindrical figures (haniwa) on top of them. The largest tumulus in Japan, attributed to Emperor Nintoku, is at Sakai.

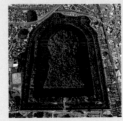

Tomb of Emperor Nintoku, Sakai, late fourth to early fifth century

Buddhist Japan

I Buddhism came to Japan from Korea in 552, and the first Japanese Buddhist artworks, such as Tori Busshi's Shaka triad, date to the Asuka period (552–645).

I During the Nara period (645–784), architecture, for example, the Horyuji Buddhist temple complex, followed Chinese models in construction technique and curved roofline.

I In 794, the imperial house moved its capital to Kyoto, initiating the Heian period (794–1185). A masterpiece of Heian Buddhist architecture is the Phoenix Hall at Uji, which evokes images of the celestial architecture of the Buddha's Pure Land of the West. Heian scroll paintings, for example, *Tale of Genji*, feature elevated viewpoints suggesting three-dimensional space and flat colors emphasizing the painting's two-dimensional character.

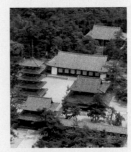

Horyuji, Nara, ca. 680

Japan under the Shoguns

I In 1185, power shifted from the Japanese emperor to the Kamakura shogunate (1185–1332). Kamakura painting is diverse in both subject and style and includes historical narratives and Buddhist hanging scrolls. Kamakura portraits—for example, the seated statue of Shunjobo Chogen—are noteworthy for their realism and the use of rock crystal for the eyes.

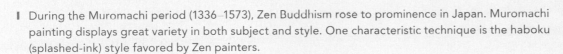

I During the Muromachi period (1336–1573), Zen Buddhism rose to prominence in Japan. Muromachi painting displays great variety in both subject and style. One characteristic technique is the haboku (splashed-ink) style favored by Zen painters.

Shunjobo Chogen, ca. 1206

I The Momoyama period (1573–1615) was a brief interlude between two long-lasting shogunates, but it was then that the tea ceremony became an important social ritual. Sen no Rikyu designed the first teahouse built as an independent structure. The favored tea utensils were rustic Shino wares.

I The Edo period (1615–1868) began when Tokugawa Ieyasu moved his headquarters from Kyoto to Edo (Tokyo). Ukiyo-e woodblock prints of Edo's "floating world" by Suzuki Harunobu and others depict scenes from brothels and the theater as well as beautiful women in domestic settings.

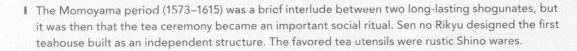

Harunobu, *Evening Bell at the Clock*, ca. 1765

Modern Japan

I The Tokugawa shogunate toppled in 1868, opening the modern era of Japanese history. In the post–World War II period, Japanese architects achieved international reputations. Kenzo Tange was a master of creating dramatic shapes using a cable suspension system for his concrete-and-steel buildings.

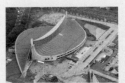

Tange, Olympic stadiums, Tokyo, 1961–1964

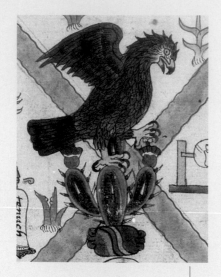

Produced for Charles V, the *Codex Mendoza* recounts the history of the Aztec Empire. The frontispiece represents the legendary landing of the eagle on a cactus and the founding of Tenochtitlán in 1325.

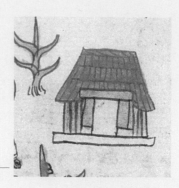

At the heart of Tenochtitlán was the Templo Mayor, a gigantic pyramid surmounted by temples to Huitzilopochtli and Tlaloc, represented in the *Codex Mendoza* in abbreviated form as a single shrine.

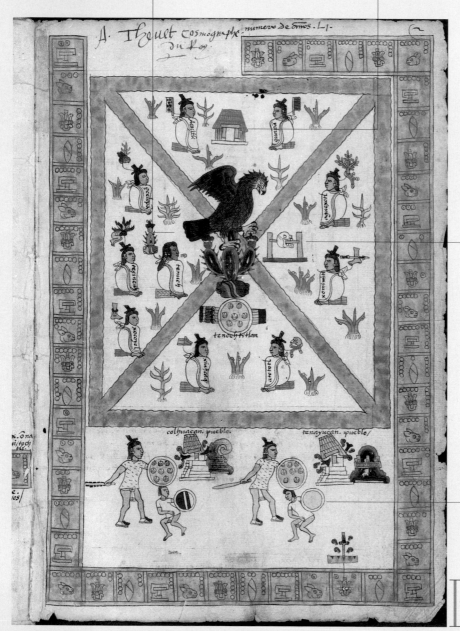

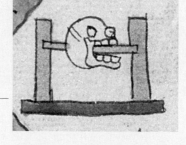

The representation of Tenochtitlán's sacred precinct also includes a rack of skulls of the sacrificial victims the Aztecs threw down the steps of the lofty pyramid after cutting out their hearts.

20-1 The founding of Tenochtitlán, folio 2 recto of the *Codex Mendoza*, Aztec, from Mexico City, Mexico, ca. 1540–1542. Ink and color on paper, $1' \frac{7}{8}'' \times 8\frac{5}{8}''$. Bodleian Library, Oxford University, Oxford.

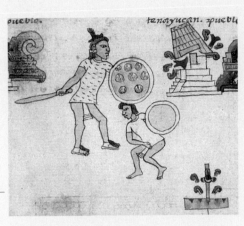

At the bottom of the page, the painter depicted two historical events. Aztec warriors with clubs and shields conquer the cities of Colhuacán and Tenayuca, shown as temple-pyramids set ablaze.

Native America

THE FOUNDING OF TENOCHTITLÁN

When their insatiable quest for gold brought the Spaniards, led by Hernán Cortés (1485–1547), into contact in 1519 with the Aztec Empire in what is today Mexico, they encountered the latest of a series of highly sophisticated indigenous Mesoamerican art-producing cultures. Two decades later, the first Spanish viceroy of New Spain, Antonio de Mendoza, commissioned native scribes and painters to produce a remarkable illustrated manuscript (on European paper). The *Codex Mendoza* recounted the history of the empire Cortés had vanquished and included a description of the customs of the people who called themselves Mexica. The book took the form of a *codex*—a bound volume resembling a modern book, in contrast to earlier books in the form of scrolls. The intended audience for the *Codex Mendoza* was Charles V of Spain, but the king never saw the manuscript because French pirates intercepted the Spanish ship at sea. Although produced for a Spanish patron, the *Codex Mendoza* closely reflects the format and style of contemporaneous Aztec illustrated manuscripts.

The opening 16 pages of the 71-page codex summarize the 196-year history of the Mexica through the Spanish conquest of 1521. The frontispiece (FIG. **20-1**), with explanatory labels in Aztec hieroglyphs and Spanish, represents the founding of the capital city of Tenochtitlán in 1325 on an island in Lake Texcoco (Lake of the Moon). There, according to legend, an eagle landed on a prickly pear cactus, marking the spot where the chief Aztec deity, Huitzilopochtli, instructed the nomadic warriors to settle. The artist depicted the eagle on the cactus (now the central motif on the Mexican flag) at the intersection of two canals, referring to the division of Tenochtitlán into four quarters. At the center of the city—considered the center of the universe—was the sacred precinct archaeologists call the Templo Mayor (Great Temple, FIG. 20-13), which featured two temples surmounting a great pyramid. (The painter represented the shrine in abbreviated form as a single temple.) To the right of the eagle and cactus is the rack of skulls of the sacrificial victims whose bodies the Aztec priests threw down the pyramid's steps after cutting out their hearts. The labeled figures seated on reed mats in Tenochtitlán's four quarters are the legendary founders of the city. Below, the painter represented two historical events in stereotypical form. Aztec warriors with clubs and shields conquer two cities, Colhuacán and Tenayuca, shown as temple-pyramids set ablaze. The border contains the hieroglyphs for 51 of the 52 years of one of the recurring cycles of the Aztec calendar system.

Today, Tenochtitlán lies at the heart of densely populated Mexico City. In the early 16th century, the Aztec capital was home to more than 100,000 people. The total population of the area of Mexico the Aztecs dominated was approximately 11 million.

THE ANCIENT AMERICAS

The origins of the indigenous peoples of the Americas are still uncertain. Sometime no later than 30,000 to 10,000 BCE, these first Americans probably crossed the now-submerged land bridge connecting Asia and North America at the Bering Strait. Some migrants may have reached the Western Hemisphere via boat. By 8000 to 2000 BCE, these Stone Age hunter-gatherer nomads had settled in villages and learned to fish and farm, and by the early centuries CE, several population groups had reached a high level of social complexity and technological achievement. Although most relied on stone tools, did not use the wheel (except for toys), and had no pack animals but the llama (in South America), ancient Americans excelled in the engineering arts associated with the planning and construction of cities, roads and bridges, and irrigation and drainage systems. They built towering temples, carved monumental stone statues and reliefs, painted extensive murals, and mastered the arts of weaving, pottery, and metalwork. This chapter examines in turn the greatest artistic achievements of the native peoples of Mesoamerica, South America, and North America.

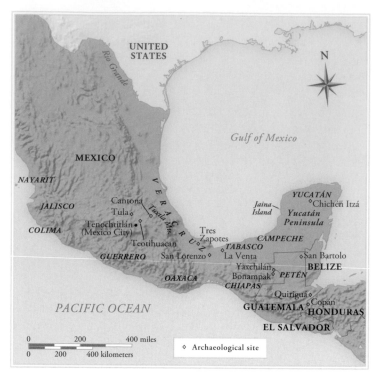

MAP 20-1 Mesoamerica.

MESOAMERICA

The term *Mesoamerica* describes the region comprising part of present-day Mexico, Guatemala, Belize, Honduras, and the Pacific coast of El Salvador (MAP 20-1). Mesoamerica was the homeland of several of the great civilizations that flourished before Cortés conquered the Aztec Empire in the 16th century. The Europeans destroyed most of the once-glorious American cities in their zeal to obliterate native religious beliefs and practices. The forces of nature—erosion and the encroachment of tropical forests—caused the abandonment of other sites. But despite the ruined state of the pre-Hispanic cities, archaeologists and art historians have been able to reconstruct much of the history of the art and architecture of ancient Mesoamerica. Historians have established a widely accepted chronology divided into three epochs: Preclassic, from 2000 BCE to about 300 CE; Classic, from about 300 to 900; and Postclassic, from 900 to the Spanish conquest of 1521.

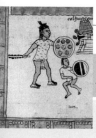

Native America

BCE	CE					
1200	300	900	1300	1532	1800	1980

- The Olmec (ca. 900–400 BCE), the "mother culture" of Mesoamerica, carve colossal ruler portraits
- Construction of the Avenue of the Dead and the pyramids of Teotihuacán in Preclassic (ca. 400 BCE–300 CE) Mesoamerica
- The Paracas (ca. 400 BCE–200 CE) culture in Peru produces extraordinary textiles
- Adena (ca. 500–1 BCE) build the first great mounds in North America

- The Maya construct vast complexes of temple-pyramids, palaces, plazas, and ball courts in Classic (ca. 300–900 CE) Mesoamerica
- The Nasca (ca. 200 BCE–600 CE) create 800 miles of earth drawings around 500 CE

- Construction of a huge pyramid-temple and the largest ball court in Mesoamerica at the Postclassic (ca. 900–1521) Maya site of Chichén Itzá
- Cahokia, Illinois, with 120 mounds is the largest city in North America during the Mississippian culture (ca. 800–1500 CE)
- In the American Southwest, the Ancestral Puebloans build Cliff Palace in Colorado between 1150 and 1300

- Aztecs build the Templo Mayor at Tenochtitlán and place monumental statues and reliefs in the sacred precinct
- Inka construct 14,000 miles of roads in the Andes and build the city of Machu Picchu and the Temple of the Sun in Cuzco

- Kwakiutl carve transformation masks
- Hopi produce katsina figurines
- Great Plains artists fashion elaborate robes and regalia for the elite
- Southwest ceramists develop black-on-black glazed pottery

Olmec

Archaeologists often refer to the Preclassic Olmec culture of the present-day states of Veracruz and Tabasco as the "mother culture" of Mesoamerica because many distinctive Mesoamerican religious, social, and artistic traditions can be traced to it. Settling in the tropical lowlands of the Gulf of Mexico, the Olmec peoples cultivated a terrain of rain forest and alluvial lowland. Here, between approximately 1500 and 400 BCE, social organization assumed the form later Mesoamerican cultures developed. The mass of the population—food-producing farmers scattered in hinterland villages—provided the sustenance and labor that maintained a hereditary caste of rulers, hierarchies of priests, functionaries, and artisans. At regular intervals, the whole community convened for ritual observances at religious-civic centers such as La Venta.

La Venta At La Venta, stone fences enclosed two great courtyards. At one end of the larger area was a pyramidal mound almost 100 feet high and adorned with colored clays. Its form may have mimicked a mountain, held sacred by Mesoamerican peoples as both a life-giving source of water and a feared destructive force. The La Venta layout is an early form of the temple-pyramid-plaza complex aligned on a north-south axis that characterized later Mesoamerican ceremonial center design.

Four colossal basalt heads (FIG. **20-2**), weighing about 10 tons each and standing between 6 and 10 feet high, face out from the plaza. Archaeologists have discovered more than a dozen similar heads at San Lorenzo and Tres Zapotes. Al-

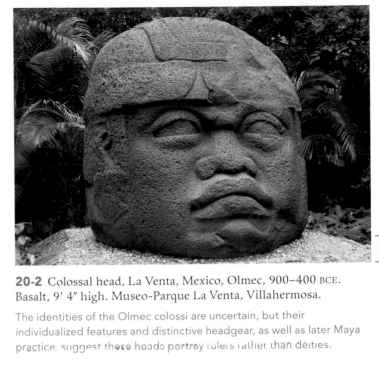

20-2 Colossal head, La Venta, Mexico, Olmec, 900–400 BCE. Basalt, 9′ 4″ high. Museo-Parque La Venta, Villahermosa.

The identities of the Olmec colossi are uncertain, but their individualized features and distinctive headgear, as well as later Maya practice, suggest these heads portray rulers rather than deities.

most as much of an achievement as the carving of these huge heads with stone tools was their transportation across the 60 miles of swampland from the nearest known basalt source, the Tuxtla Mountains. Although the identities of the colossi are uncertain, their individualized features and distinctive headgear and ear ornaments, as well as the later Maya practice of carving monumental ruler portraits, suggest that the Olmec heads portray rulers rather than gods.

The sheer size of the heads and their intensity of expression evoke great power, whether mortal or divine.

Teotihuacán

The late Preclassic site of Teotihuacán (FIG. **20-3**), northeast of Mexico City, was a large, densely populated metropolis that fulfilled a central civic, economic, and religious role for the region and indeed for much of Mesoamerica. The city covers 9 square miles, laid out in a grid pattern with the axes oriented by sophisticated surveying. Its major monuments date between 50 and 250 CE. At its

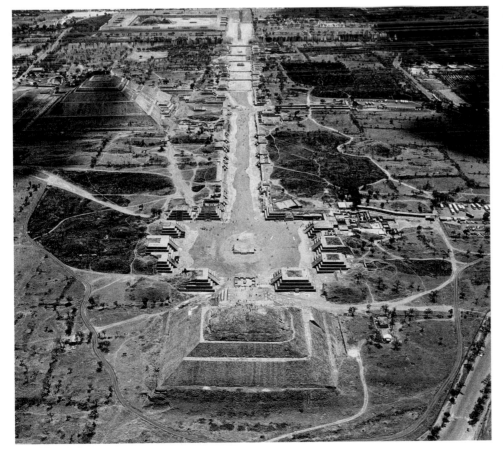

20-3 Aerial view of Teotihuacán (looking south), Mexico. Pyramid of the Moon (*foreground*), Pyramid of the Sun (*top left*), and the Citadel (*background*), all connected by the Avenue of the Dead; main structures ca. 50–250 CE. ◼◀

At its peak around 600 CE, Teotihuacán was the world's sixth-largest city. It featured a grid plan, a 2-mile-long main avenue, and monumental pyramids echoing the shapes of nearby mountains.

peak, around 600 CE, Teotihuacán may have had as many as 125,000 to 200,000 residents, making it the sixth-largest city in the world at that time. Hundreds of years later, the Aztecs gave Teotihuacán its current name, which means "the place of the gods." Because the city's inhabitants left only a handful of undeciphered hieroglyphs, the names of many major features of the site are unknown. The Avenue of the Dead and the Pyramids of the Sun and Moon are Aztec designations that do not necessarily relate to the original names.

North-south and east-west axes, each 4 miles in length, divide the grid plan into quarters. The main north-south axis (FIG. 20-3), the Avenue of the Dead, is 130 feet wide and connects the Pyramid of the Moon complex with the Citadel and its Temple of Quetzalcoatl, the "feathered serpent," a major god in the Mesoamerican pantheon associated with wind, rain clouds, and life. The 2-mile stretch of the Avenue of the Dead is not a continuously flat street but is broken by sets of stairs, giving pedestrians a constantly changing view of the surrounding buildings and landscape.

Pyramids The largest structures at Teotihuacán are the stepped temple platforms popularly called pyramids, as in Egypt (see Chapter 1), but there is no connection between these two ancient cultures. The Pyramid of the Sun (FIG. 20-3, *top left*), facing west on the east side of the Avenue of the Dead, dates to the first century CE. The city's centerpiece, it rises to a height of more than 200 feet. The Pyramid of the Moon (FIG. 20-3, *foreground*) dates to a century or more later, around 150 to 250 CE. The shapes of the pyramids echo the surrounding mountains. Their imposing mass and scale surpass those of all other Mesoamerican sites. Rubble-filled and faced with the local volcanic stone, the pyramids consist of stacked square platforms diminishing in perimeter from the base to the top. Ramped stairways once led to crowning

temples constructed of perishable materials such as wood and thatch.

The Teotihuacanos built the Pyramid of the Sun over a now-dry cave that once may have contained a sacred spring. Excavators found children buried at the four corners of each of the pyramid's tiers. The Aztec sacrificed children to bring rainfall, and Teotihuacán art abounds with references to water, so the Teotihuacanos may have shared the Aztec preoccupation with rain and agricultural fertility. The city's inhabitants rebuilt the Pyramid of the Moon at least five times in Teotihuacán's early history. The builders may have positioned it to mimic the shape of Cerro Gordo, the volcanic mountain behind it.

Mural Painting As in most ancient Mesoamerican cities, brightly painted stucco once covered Teotihuacán's buildings and streets. Elaborate murals also decorated the walls of the rooms of its elite residential compounds. The Teotihuacano artists applied pigments to a smooth lime-plaster surface coated with clay, and then polished the surface to a high sheen. Although some preserved murals have a restricted palette of varying tones of red, creating subtle contrasts between figure and ground, most employ vivid hues arranged in flat, carefully outlined patterns.

The mural illustrated here (FIG. **20-4**) depicts an earth or nature goddess. Some scholars think she was the city's principal deity. Always shown frontally with her face covered by a jade mask, she is dwarfed by her large feathered headdress and reduced to a bust placed upon a stylized pyramid. She stretches her hands out to provide liquid streams filled with bounty. The stylized human hearts flanking the frontal bird mask in the Teotihuacano goddess's headdress reflect the ancient Mesoamerican belief that human sacrifice is essential to agricultural renewal.

20-4 Goddess, wall painting from the Tetitla apartment complex at Teotihuacán, Mexico, 650–750 CE. Pigments over clay and plaster.

Elaborate mural paintings adorned Teotihuacán's elite residential compound. This example may depict the city's principal deity, a goddess wearing a jade mask and a large feathered headdress.

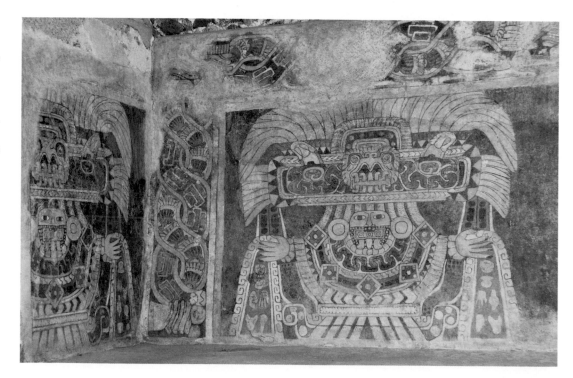

Maya

As was true of Teotihuacán, the foundations of Maya civilization date to the Preclassic period, perhaps 600 BCE or even earlier. At that time, the Maya, who occupied the moist lowland areas of Belize, southern Mexico, Guatemala, and Honduras, seem to have abandoned their early, somewhat egalitarian pattern of village life and adopted a hierarchical autocratic society. This system evolved into the typical Classic Maya city-state governed by hereditary rulers and ranked nobility. How and why this happened are still unknown, but the Classic Maya culture endured for 600 years.

Although the causes of the beginning and end of Classic Maya civilization are obscure, researchers are gradually revealing its history, religion, ceremonies, conventions, and patterns of daily life through scientific excavation and progress made in decoding Mayan script. Two important breakthroughs radically altered the understanding of both Mayan writing and the Maya worldview. The first was the realization the Maya depicted their rulers (rather than gods or anonymous priests) in their art and noted their rulers' achievements in their texts. The second was that Mayan writing is largely phonetic—that is, the hieroglyphs consist of signs representing sounds in the Mayan language. Fortunately, the Spaniards recorded the various Mayan languages in colonial texts and dictionaries. The Maya possessed a highly developed knowledge of mathematical calculation and the ability to observe and record the movements of the sun, the moon, and several planets. Their calendar, although radically different in form from the Western calendar used today, was just as precise and efficient. It enabled the Maya to establish the genealogical lines of their rulers and to create the only true written history in ancient America.

Architecture and Ritual Vast complexes of terraced temple-pyramids, palaces, plazas, and residences of the governing elite dotted the Classic Maya area. Unlike Teotihuacán, no single Maya site ever achieved dominance as the center of power. The new architecture, and the art embellishing it, advertised the power of the rulers, who appropriated cosmic symbolism and stressed their descent from gods to reinforce their claims to legitimate rule.

The Maya erected their most sacred and majestic buildings in enclosed, centrally located precincts within their cities. There, the Maya rulers staged dramatic rituals within spacious sculpture-filled plazas. In both life and art, the Maya elite wore extravagant, vividly colorful cotton textiles, feathers, jaguar skins, and jade, all emblematic of their rank and wealth. On the different levels of the painted and polished temple platforms, the ruling classes performed the rites in clouds of incense to the music of maracas, flutes, and drums. The Maya thus transformed the architectural complex at each city's center into a theater of religion and statecraft.

Copán Because Copán, on the western border of Honduras, has more hieroglyphic inscriptions and well-preserved carved monuments than any other site in the Americas, it was one of the first Maya sites excavated. It also has proved one of the richest in the trove of architecture, sculpture, and artifacts recovered. In Copán's Great Plaza, the Maya set up tall stone stelae featuring sculpted portraits of their rulers and inscriptions recording their names, dates of reign, and notable achievements. Stele D (FIG. 20-5), dated 736 CE, represents Waxaklajuun-Ub'aah-K'awiil (r. 695–738), the 13th in the Copán dynastic sequence of 16 rulers. During his long reign, the city may have reached its greatest physical extent and range of political influence. On Stele D, Ruler 13, as scholars call him, wears an elaborate headdress and ornamented kilt and sandals. He holds across his chest a double-headed serpent bar, symbol of his sacred authority. His features are distinctly Maya, although highly idealized. The Maya elite usually required sculptors and painters to portray them as eternally youthful. The dense, deeply carved

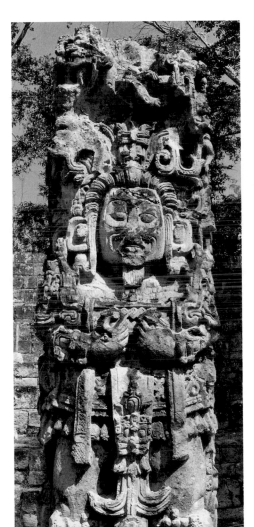

20-5 Stele D portraying Ruler 13 (Waxaklajuun-Ub'aah-K'awiil), Great Plaza, Copán, Honduras, Maya, 736 CE. Stone, 11′ 9″ high.

This 12-foot stele portrays one of Copán's most important rulers as an over-life-size figure wearing an elaborate headdress and holding a double-headed serpent bar, symbol of his sacred authority

1 ft.

The Mesoamerican Ball Game

After witnessing the native ball game of Mexico soon after their arrival, the 16th-century Spanish conquerors took Aztec ball players back to Europe to demonstrate the novel sport. Their chronicles remark on the athletes' great skill, the heavy wagering that accompanied the competition, and the ball itself, made of rubber, a substance the Spaniards had never seen before.

Native Americans played the game throughout Mesoamerica and into the southwestern United States, beginning at least 3,400 years ago, the date of the earliest known ball court. The Olmec were apparently avid players. Their very name—a modern invention in Nahuatl, the Aztec language—means "rubber people," after the latex-growing region they inhabited. Not only do ball players appear in Olmec art, but archaeologists have found remnants of sunken earthen ball courts and even rubber balls at Olmec sites.

The Olmec earthen playing field evolved in other Mesoamerican cultures into a plastered masonry surface, I- or T-shaped in plan, flanked by two parallel sloping or straight walls. Sometimes the walls were wide enough to support small structures on top, as at Copán (FIG. 20-6). At other sites, temples stood at either end of the ball court. These structures were common features of Mesoamerican cities. At Cantona, for example, archaeologists have uncovered 22 ball courts even though only a small portion of the site has been excavated. Teotihuacán (FIG. 20-3) is an exception. Excavators have not yet found a ball court there, but mural paintings at the site illustrate people playing the game with portable markers and sticks. Most ball courts were adjacent to the important civic structures of Mesoamerican cities, such as palaces and temple-pyramids, as at Copán.

Historians know surprisingly little about the rules of the ball game itself, not even how many players were on the field or how they scored goals. Unlike a modern soccer field with its standard dimensions, Mesoamerican ball courts vary widely in size. The largest known—at Chichén Itzá—is nearly 500 feet long. Copán's is about 93 feet long. Some have stone rings set high up on their walls at right angles to the ground, but many courts lack this feature, so it is uncertain whether the players aimed to get the ball through a ring in order to score a point. Alternatively, players may have scored goals by bouncing the ball against the walls and into the end zones. As in soccer, players could not touch the ball with their hands but used their heads, elbows, hips, and legs. They wore thick leather belts, and sometimes even helmets, and padded their knees and arms against the blows of the fast-moving solid rubber ball (FIG. 20-7).

Although widely enjoyed as a competitive spectator sport, the ball game did not serve solely for entertainment. The ball, for example, may have represented a celestial body such as the sun, its movements over the court imitating the sun's daily passage through the sky. Reliefs on the walls of some ball courts make clear the game sometimes culminated in human sacrifice, probably of captives taken in battle and then forced to participate in a game they were predestined to lose.

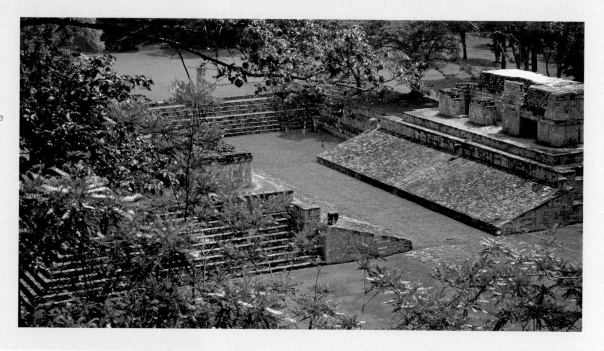

20-6 Ball court (looking northeast), Middle Plaza, Copán, Honduras, Maya, 738 CE.

Ball courts were common in Mesoamerican cities. Copán's is 93 feet long. The rules of the ball game itself are unknown, but games sometimes ended in the sacrifice of captives taken in battle.

ornamental details framing the face and figure in florid profusion stand almost clear of the block and wrap around the sides of the stele. The high relief, originally painted, gives the impression of an over-life-size freestanding statue, although an incised hieroglyphic text is on the flat back of the stele. Ruler 13 erected many stelae and buildings at Copán, including one of Mesoamerica's best-preserved (and carefully restored) ball courts (FIG. **20-6**; see "The Mesoamerican Ball Game," above), but suffered a humiliating death when the king of neighboring Quiriguá captured and beheaded him.

Jaina The Maya produced small-scale sculptures as well, especially in clay. Remarkably lifelike, the figurines represent a wider range of human types and activities than those depicted on Maya stelae. Ball players, women weaving, supernatural beings, and amorous couples, as well as elaborately attired rulers and warriors, are the most common subjects. Burials in the island cemetery of Jaina, off the western coast of Yucatán, have yielded hundreds of clay statuettes, including the ball player illustrated here (FIG. **20-7**). Traces of blue remain on the man's belt, remnants of the vivid pigments that

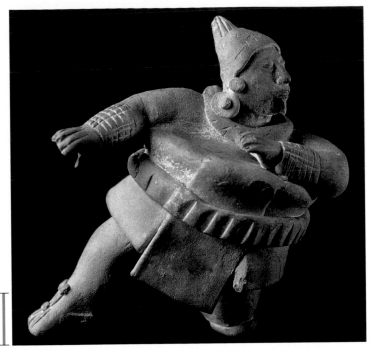

20-7 Ball player, from Jaina Island, Mexico, Maya, 700–900 CE. Painted clay, 6¼" high. Museo Nacional de Antropología, Mexico City.

Maya ceramic figurines represent a wide range of human types and activities. This kneeling ball player wears a thick leather belt and arm- and kneepads to protect him from the hard rubber ball.

once covered many of these figurines. The Maya used "Maya blue," a combination of a particular kind of clay and indigo, a vegetable dye, to paint both ceramics and murals. This pig-

ment has proved virtually indestructible, unlike other colors the Maya used. The Jaina figurines accompanied the dead on their inevitable voyage to the Underworld, but excavations have revealed nothing more that might clarify the meaning and function of the figures. Male figurines do not come exclusively from burials of male individuals, for example.

Bonampak Bonampak (Mayan, "painted walls") in southeastern Mexico is, as its name suggests, famous for its mural paintings. The example reproduced here (FIG. **20-8**) shows warriors and captives on a terraced platform. The figures have naturalistic proportions and overlap, twist, turn, and gesture. The artists used fluid lines to outline the forms, working with color to indicate both texture and volume. The Bonampak painters combined their pigments with a mixture of water, crushed limestone, and vegetable gums and applied them to their stucco walls in a technique best described as a cross between fresco and tempera.

Circumstantial details abound in the Bonampak murals. The information given is comprehensive, explicit, and presented with the fidelity of an eyewitness report. Royal personages are identifiable by both their physical features and their costumes, and accompanying inscriptions provide the precise day, month, and year for the events recorded. All the scenes at Bonampak relate the events and ceremonies welcoming a new royal heir (shown as a toddler in some scenes). They include presentations, preparations for a royal fete, dancing, battle, and the taking and sacrificing of prisoners. On all occasions of state, public bloodletting was an integral part of Maya ritual. The ruler, his consort, and certain

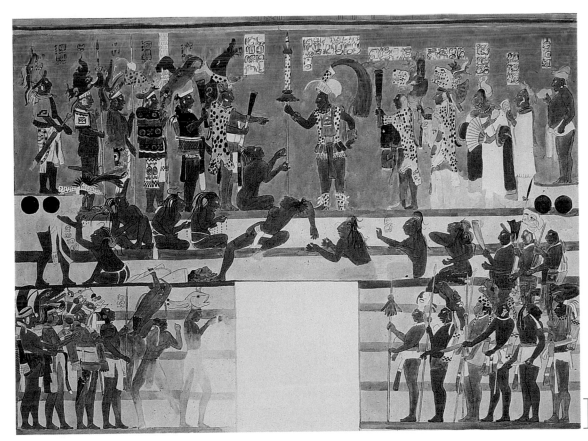

20-8 Presentation of captives to Lord Chan Muwan, room 2 of structure 1, Bonampak, Mexico, Maya, ca. 790 CE. Mural, 17' × 15'; watercolor copy by Antonio Tejeda. Peabody Museum of Archaeology and Ethnology, Harvard University, Cambridge.

The figures in this mural—a cross between fresco and tempera—may be standing on a pyramid's steps. At the top, the richly attired Chan Muwan reviews naked captives, with mutilated hands, awaiting death.

members of the nobility drew blood from their own bodies and sought union with the supernatural world. The slaughter of captives taken in war regularly accompanied this ceremony. Indeed, Mesoamerican cultures undertook warfare largely to provide victims for sacrifice. The torture and eventual execution of prisoners served both to nourish the gods and to strike fear into enemies and the general populace.

The illustrated scene (FIG. 20-8) depicts the presentation of captives to Lord Chan Muwan. The painter arranged the figures in registers that may represent a pyramid's steps. On the uppermost step, against a blue background, is a file of gorgeously appareled nobles wearing animal headgear. Conspicuous among them on the right are retainers clad in jaguar pelts and jaguar headdresses. Also present is Chan Muwan's wife (third from right). The ruler himself, in jaguar jerkin and high-backed sandals, stands at the center, facing a crouching victim who begs for mercy. Naked captives, anticipating death, crowd the middle level. One of them, already dead, sprawls at the ruler's feet. Others dumbly contemplate the blood dripping from their mutilated hands. The lower zone (cut through by a doorway) shows clusters of attendants who are doubtless of inferior rank to the lords of the upper zone. The stiff formality of the victors contrasts graphically with the supple imploring attitudes and gestures of the hapless victims. The Bonampak victory was short-lived, however. The artists never finished the murals, and soon after the dates written on the walls, the Maya abandoned the site.

The Bonampak murals are the most famous Maya wall paintings, but they are not unique. At San Bartolo in northeastern Guatemala, archaeologists from Boston University have discovered the earliest examples yet found. They date to about 100 BCE, almost a millennium before the Bonampak murals.

Yaxchilán Elite women played an important role in Maya society, and some surviving artworks, such as the painted reliefs on the lintels of temple 23 at Yaxchilán, document their high status. Lintel 24 (FIG. **20-9**) depicts Itzamna B'ahlam II (r. 681–742 CE), known as Shield Jaguar, and his principal wife, Lady Xoc, who is magnificently outfitted in an elaborate woven garment, headdress, and jewels. With a barbed cord she pierces her tongue in a bloodletting ceremony that, according to accompanying inscriptions, celebrated the birth of a son to one of the ruler's other wives as well as an alignment between the planets Saturn and Jupiter. The celebration must have taken place in a dark chamber or at night because Shield Jaguar provides illumination with a blazing torch. These ceremonies induced an altered state of consciousness in order to connect the bloodletter with the supernatural world. (Lintel 25 depicts Lady Xoc and her vision of an ancestor emerging from the mouth of a serpent.)

Chichén Itzá Throughout Mesoamerica, the Classic period ended at different times with the disintegration of the great civilizations. Teotihuacán's political and cultural empire, for example, began to wane around 600, when fire destroyed

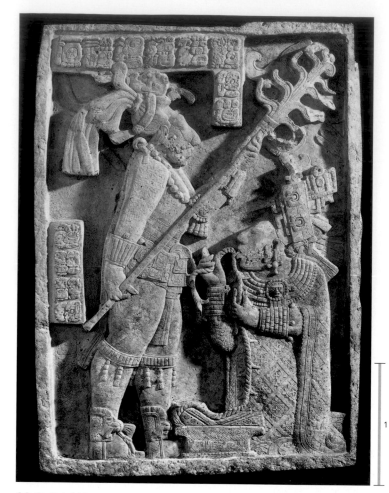

20-9 Shield Jaguar and Lady Xoc, lintel 24 of temple 23, Yaxchilán, Mexico, Maya, ca. 725 CE. Limestone, 3′ 7″ × 2′ 6½″. British Museum, London.

The carved lintels of this eighth-century temple document the central role elite women played in Maya society. Lady Xoc pierces her tongue in a bloodletting ritual intended to induce a visionary state.

the city center. Within a century Teotihuacán was deserted. Around 900, the Maya abandoned many of their sites to the jungle, leaving a few northern Maya cities to flourish for another century or two during the Postclassic period before they, too, became depopulated. The war and confusion that followed the collapse of the Classic civilizations fractured the great states into small, local political entities isolated in fortified sites. In central Mexico the Toltec and the later Aztec peoples, both ambitious migrants from the north, forged empires by force of arms, while the militant city-state of Chichén Itzá dominated Yucatán, a flat, low limestone peninsula covered with scrub vegetation. During the Classic period, Mayan-speaking peoples sparsely inhabited this northern region. For reasons scholars still debate, when the southern Maya abandoned their Classic sites after 900, the northern Maya continued to build many new temples in this area.

Dominating the main plaza of Chichén Itzá is the 98-foot-high pyramid (FIG. 20-10) the Spaniards nicknamed the Castillo (Castle). The pyramid has nine levels, probably a reference to the nine levels of the Underworld. The design of the Castillo is also tied to the solar year. The north side has

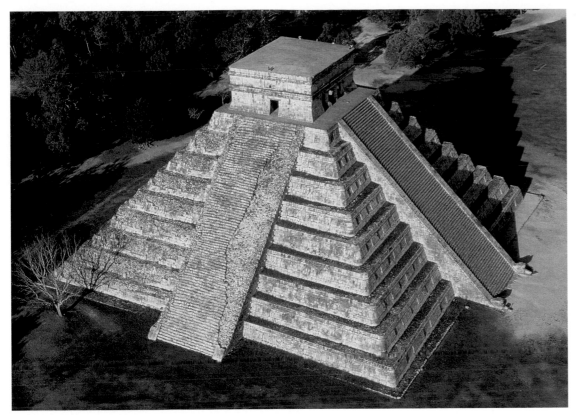

A temple to Kulkulcán sits atop this pyramid featuring 365 stairs on its four sides. At the winter and summer equinoxes, the sun casts a shadow in the shape of a serpent along the northern staircase.

92 steps and the other three sides 91 steps each for a total of 365. At the winter and summer equinoxes, the sun casts a shadow along the northern staircase of the pyramid. Because of the pyramid's silhouette and the angle of the sun, the shadow takes the shape of a serpent slithering along the pyramid's face as the sun moves across the sky. Atop the structure is a temple dedicated to Kulkulcán, the Maya equivalent of Quetzalcoatl.

Excavations inside the Castillo in 1937 revealed an earlier nine-level pyramid within the later and larger structure. Inside was a royal burial chamber with a throne in the form of a red jaguar and a stone figure of a type called a *chacmool* (red jaguar paw) depicting a fallen warrior. Chacmools (for example, FIG. **20-11**, found near the Castillo) recline on their backs and have receptacles on their chests to receive sacrificial offerings, probably of defeated enemies.

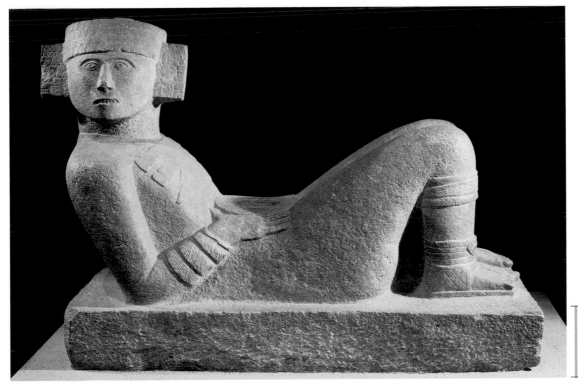

20-11 Chacmool, from the Platform of the Eagles, Chichén Itzá, Mexico, Maya, ca. 800–900 CE. Stone, 4′ 10½″ high. Museo Nacional de Antropología, Mexico City. ◼◀

Chacmools represent fallen warriors reclining on their backs with receptacles on their chests to receive sacrificial offerings. Excavators discovered one in the throne chamber inside the Castillo (FIG. 20-10).

1 ft.

Toltec

The name *Toltec* (makers of things) refers to a powerful northern Mesoamerican population group whose arrival in central Mexico coincided with the fall of the Classic civilizations, although they may have not been the cause. In any case, the Toltecs occupied Tula, north of Mexico City, from about 900 to 1200, the early part of the Postclassic period. Master artisans as well as feared warriors, the Toltecs constructed imposing temples and set up monumental statues.

Tula Most impressive are the four colossal *atlantids* (male statue-columns; FIG. **20-12**) built up of four stacked stone *drums* each that stand atop Pyramid B at Tula. Whether the atlantids portray rulers in military dress or anonymous armed warriors is uncertain, but their function is clear. These images of brutal authority stand eternally at attention, warding off all hostile forces. They wear feathered headdresses and, as breastplates, stylized butterflies, heraldic symbols of the Toltec. In one hand they clutch a bundle of darts and in the other an *atlatl* (spear-thrower), typical weapons of highland Mexico. The figures originally supported a temple roof, now missing.

By 1180 the last Toltec ruler abandoned Tula, and most of his people followed. Some years later, the city was catastrophically destroyed, its ceremonial buildings burned to their foundations, its walls torn down, and the straggling remainder of its population scattered. The exact reasons for the Toltecs' departure and for their city's destruction are unknown.

Aztec

The fall of the Toltecs brought a century of anarchy to the Valley of Mexico, the vast highland valley 7,000 feet above sea level now home to sprawling Mexico City. Waves of northern invaders established warring city-states and wrought destruction in the valley. The last and greatest of these conquerors were the Aztecs, who called themselves Mexica and claimed descent from the Toltecs. Fulfilling a legendary prophecy that they would build a city where they saw an eagle perched on a cactus with a serpent in its mouth, they settled on an island in Lake Texcoco (Lake of the Moon). Their settlement grew into the magnificent city of Tenochtitlán (see "The Founding of Tenochtitlán," page 533).

Recognized by those they subdued as fierce in war and cruel in peace, the Aztecs radically changed the social and political situation in Mexico. Subservient groups not only had to submit to Aztec military power but also had to provide victims to be sacrificed to Huitzilopochtli, the hummingbird god of war, and to other Aztec deities (see "Aztec Religion," page 543). As did other Mesoamerican peoples before them, the Mexica practiced bloodletting and human sacrifice to please the gods and sustain the great cycles of the universe. The Aztecs, however, engaged in human sacrifice on a greater scale than any of their predecessors, even waging wars expressly to obtain captives for future sacrifice.

Tenochtitlán The ruins of the Aztec capital, Tenochtitlán, lie directly beneath the center of Mexico City. The Mexica laid out Tenochtitlán on a grid plan dividing the city into quarters (FIG. 20-1) and wards, reminiscent of Teotihuacán (FIG. 20-3), which, long abandoned, had become a pilgrimage site for the Aztecs. Tenochtitlán's island location required conducting communication and transport via canals and other waterways. Many of the Spaniards thought of Venice in Italy when they saw the city rising from the waters like a radiant vision. Crowded with buildings, plazas, and courtyards, the city also boasted a vast and bustling marketplace. In the words of Bernal Díaz del Castillo (1492–1581), who accompanied Cortés, "Some of the soldiers among us who had been in many parts of the world, in Constantinople, and all over Italy, and in Rome, said that so large a marketplace and so full of people, and so well regulated and arranged, they had never beheld before."[1]

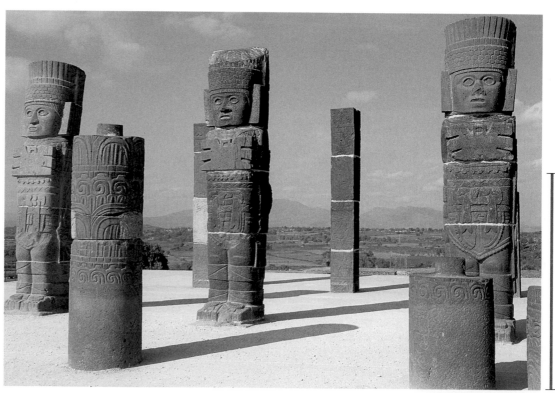

20-12 Colossal atlantids, pyramid B, Tula, Mexico, Toltec, ca. 900–1180 CE. Stone, each 16' high.

Little is known about the Toltecs, but they left behind these colossal stone statue-columns atop a pyramid-temple at Tula. The atlantids portray warriors or rulers armed with darts and spear-throwers.

10 ft.

Aztec Religion

The Aztecs saw their world as a flat disk resting on the back of a monstrous earth deity. Tenochtitlán, their capital, was at its center. Hueteocalli, the Great Temple (FIG. 20-13), at the heart of the city, represented the Hill of Coatepec, the Serpent Mountain, and formed the axis passing up to the heavens and down through the Underworld—a concept with parallels in other cultures (see, for example, "The Stupa," Chapter 17, page 474). Each of the four cardinal points had its own god, color, tree, and calendar symbol. The sky consisted of 13 layers, whereas the Underworld had nine.

Because the Aztecs often adopted the gods of conquered peoples, their pantheon was complex and varied. When the Aztecs arrived in the Valley of Mexico, their own chief god, Huitzilopochtli (Hummingbird of the South), a war and sun/fire deity, joined such well-established Mesoamerican gods as the rain and fertility god Tlaloc and the feathered serpent Quetzalcoatl, who was a benevolent god of life, wind, learning, and culture. Huitzilopochtli was the son of Coatlicue ("She of the Serpent Skirt"; FIG. 20-15). Coatlicue was also the mother of Coyolxauhqui ("She of the Golden Bells"; FIG. 20-14) and 400 sons, the Centzon Huitznahua (Four Hundred Southerners), who, jealous their mother was pregnant with Huitzilopochtli, banded together to murder her. At the moment of her death, she gave birth to Huitzilopochtli, who slaughtered Coyolxauhqui and most of her brothers, then cut his sister's body into pieces and threw it down Coatepec Mountain.

Most Aztec ceremonies involved colorfully attired dancers and actors, and musicians playing conch-shell trumpets, drums, rattles, rasps, bells, and whistles. Almost every Aztec festival also included human sacrifice. To Tlaloc, the priests offered small children because their tears brought the rains. Distinctive hairstyles, clothing, and black body paint identified the priests. Women served as priestesses, particularly in temples dedicated to various earth-mother cults. When Cortés and his men encountered a group of foul-smelling priests with uncut fingernails, long hair matted with blood, and ears covered in cuts, they recoiled in shock, not realizing they were performing rites in honor of the deities

20-13 Reconstruction drawing with cutaway view of various rebuildings of the Great Temple, Tenochtitlán, Mexico City, Mexico, Aztec, ca. 1400–1500. C = Coyolxauhqui disk (FIG. 20-14).

The Great Temple in the Aztec capital encases successive earlier structures. The latest temple honored the gods Huitzilopochtli and Tlaloc, whose sanctuaries were at the top of a stepped pyramid.

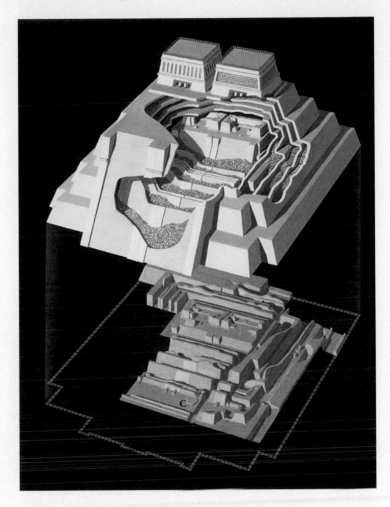

they served, including piercing their skin with cactus spines to draw blood. These priests were the opposite of the "barbarians" the European conquerors considered them to be. They were, in fact, the most highly educated Aztecs. The religious practices that horrified the Spaniards, however, were not unique to the Aztecs but were deeply rooted in earlier Mesoamerican society.

Hueteocalli In the 1970s, Mexican archaeologists identified the exact location of many of the most important structures within Tenochtitlán's sacred precinct. The principal building was Hueteocalli—the Templo Mayor, or Great Temple (FIG. 20-13), a temple-pyramid honoring the Aztec god Huitzilopochtli and the local rain god Tlaloc (see "Aztec Religion," above). Two great staircases originally swept upward from the plaza level to the two sanctuaries at the summit. Hueteocalli is a remarkable example of *superimposition,* a common trait in Mesoamerican architecture, already noted in the Castillo (FIG. 20-10) at Chichén Itzá. The excavated structure, composed of seven shells, indicates how earlier walls nested within the later ones. (Today, only two of the inner structures remain. The Spaniards destroyed the later ones in the 16th

century.) The sacred precinct also contained the temples of other deities, a ball court, a skull rack for the exhibition of the heads of victims killed in sacrificial rites (FIG. 20-1, *top right*), and a school for the children of the nobility.

Coyolxauhqui The Temple of Huitzilopochtli at Tenochtitlán commemorated the god's victory over his sister and 400 brothers, who had plotted to kill their mother, Coatlicue. The myth signifies the birth of the sun at dawn, a role Huitzilopochtli sometimes assumed, and the sun's battle with the forces of darkness, the stars and moon. Huitzilopochtli killed or chased away his brothers and dismembered the body of his sister, the moon goddess Coyolxauhqui, at Coatepec Mountain near Tula (represented by the pyramid

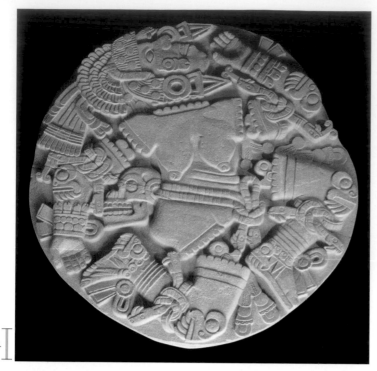

1 ft.

20-14 Coyolxauhqui, from the Great Temple of Tenochtitlán, Mexico City, Aztec, ca. 1469. Stone, diameter 10′ 10″. Museo del Templo Mayor, Mexico City.

The bodies of sacrificed foes the Aztecs hurled down the stairs of the Great Temple landed on this disk, which depicts the segmented body of the moon goddess Coyolxauhqui, Huitzilopochtli's sister.

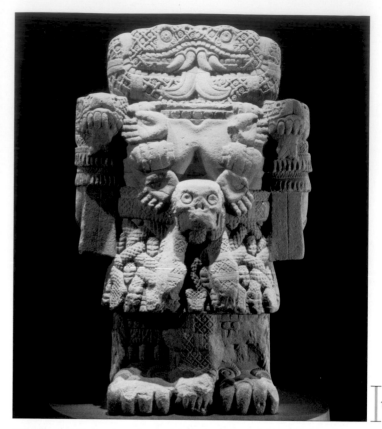

1 ft.

20-15 Coatlicue, from Tenochtitlán, Mexico City, Aztec, ca. 1487–1520. Andesite, 11′ 6″ high. Museo Nacional de Antropología, Mexico City.

This colossal statue may have stood near the Great Temple. The be-headed goddess wears a necklace of human hands and hearts. Entwined snakes form her skirt. All her attributes symbolize sacrificial death.

itself). The mythical event is the subject of a huge stone disk (FIG. **20-14**) the Aztecs placed at the foot of the staircase leading up to one of Huitzilopochtli's earlier temples on the site. (Cortés and his army never saw it because it lay within the outermost shell of the Great Temple.) The relief presents the image of the murdered and segmented body of Coyolxauhqui. The mythological theme also carried a contemporary political message. The Aztecs sacrificed their conquered enemies at the top of the Great Temple and then hurled their bodies down the temple stairs to land on this stone. The victors thus forced their foes to reenact the horrible fate of the dismembered goddess. The unforgettable image of the fragmented goddess proclaimed the power of the Mexica over their enemies and the inevitable fate that must befall their foes when defeated. Marvelously composed, the relief has a kind of dreadful yet formal beauty. Within the circular space, the design's carefully balanced and richly detailed components have a slow turning rhythm reminiscent of a revolving galaxy. The carving is in low relief, a smoothly even, flat surface raised from a flat ground.

Coatlicue The Aztecs also produced freestanding statues. Perhaps the most impressive is the colossal image (FIG. **20-15**) of the beheaded Coatlicue. The main forms are in high relief, the details executed either in low relief or by incising. The overall aspect is of an enormous blocky mass, its ponderous weight looming over awed viewers. From the beheaded goddess's neck writhe two serpents whose heads meet to form a

tusked mask. Coatlicue wears a necklace of severed human hands and excised human hearts. The pendant of the necklace is a skull. Entwined snakes form her skirt. From between her legs emerges another serpent, symbolic perhaps of both menses and the male member. Like most Aztec deities, Coatlicue has both masculine and feminine traits. Her hands and feet have great claws, which she used to tear the human flesh she consumes. All her attributes symbolize sacrificial death. Yet, in Aztec thought, this mother of the gods combined savagery and tenderness, for out of destruction arose new life.

Cortés and Moctezuma Unfortunately, most Aztec art did not survive the Spanish conquest and its aftermath. The conquerors took Aztec gold artifacts back to Spain and melted them down, and evangelical friars destroyed countless "idols" and illustrated books. The Europeans found it impossible to reconcile the beauty of the great city of Tenochtitlán with what they regarded as its hideous cults. They admired its splendid buildings ablaze with color, its luxuriant and spacious gardens, its sparkling waterways, its teeming markets, and its grandees resplendent in exotic bird feathers. But in 1519, when Emperor Moctezuma II (r. 1502–1521) brought Cortés and his entourage into Huitzilopochtli's temple, the Spaniards started back in horror, recoiling in disgust at the huge statues clotted with dried blood. Denouncing Huitzilopochtli as a devil, Cortés proposed to put a high cross above the pyramid and a statue of the Virgin in the sanctuary to exorcise its evil. The ensuing clash of cultures led to a century of turmoil and an enormous population decline throughout the Spanish king's new domains, due in part to a host of new diseases for which the Native Americans had no immunity.

SOUTH AMERICA

As in Mesoamerica, until their defeat at the hands of Spanish conquistadors, the indigenous civilizations of Andean South America (MAP 20-2) built impressive temples and other monuments and produced sophisticated paintings, sculptures, ceramics, and textiles. Although less well studied than the ancient Mesoamerican cultures, the South American civilizations are older, and in some ways they surpassed the accomplishments of their northern counterparts. Andean peoples, for example, mastered metalworking much earlier, and their monumental architecture predates the Olmec pyramids by more than a millennium.

The Central Andean region of South America lies between Ecuador and northern Chile, with its western border the Pacific Ocean. Andean civilizations flourished both in the highlands and on the coast. The most important are the Paracas, Nasca, and Moche cultures and the Inka Empire.

Paracas, Nasca, and Moche

Three major coastal traditions developed during the millennium from ca. 400 BCE to 700 CE: the Paracas (ca. 400 BCE–200 CE), Nasca (ca. 200 BCE–600 CE), and Moche (ca. 1–700 CE). Together they exemplify the great variations within ancient Peruvian art styles.

Paracas Outstanding among the Paracas arts are the mantles used to wrap the bodies of the dead in multiple layers. These textiles are among the enduring masterpieces of Andean art. Most are of woven cotton with designs embroidered onto the fabric in alpaca or vicuña wool imported from the highlands.

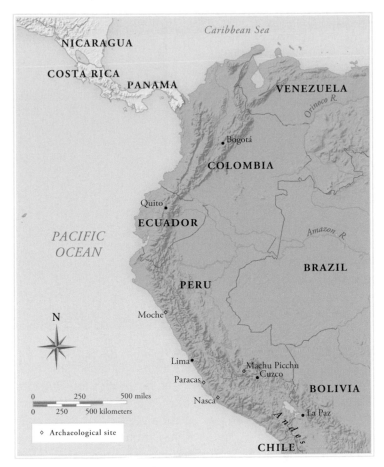

MAP 20-2 Andean South America.

The weavers, probably exclusively women, used more than 150 vivid colors, and sometimes sewed rare tropical bird feathers and small plaques of gold and silver onto cloth destined for the nobility. Feline, bird, and serpent motifs appear on many of the textiles, but the human figure, real or mythological, predominates. Humans dressed up as or transforming into animals are common motifs on the funerary mantles. On one well-preserved example (FIG. 20-16), a figure with prominent eyes

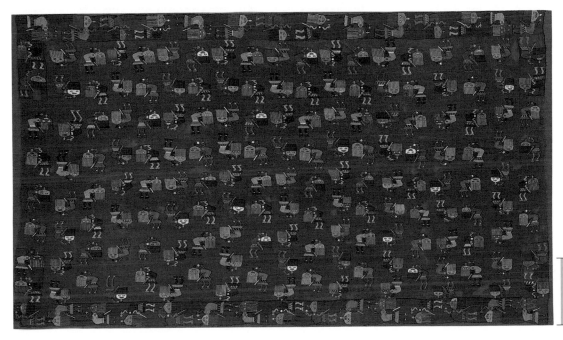

20-16 Embroidered funerary mantle, from the southern coast of Peru, Paracas, first century CE. Plain-weave camelid fiber with embroidery of camelid wool, 4′ 7⅞″ × 7′ 10⅞″. Museum of Fine Arts, Boston (William A. Paine Fund).

Paracas weavers created elaborate mantles to wrap around the bodies of the dead. The flying or floating figure repeated endlessly on this mantle is probably the deceased or a religious practitioner.

1 ft.

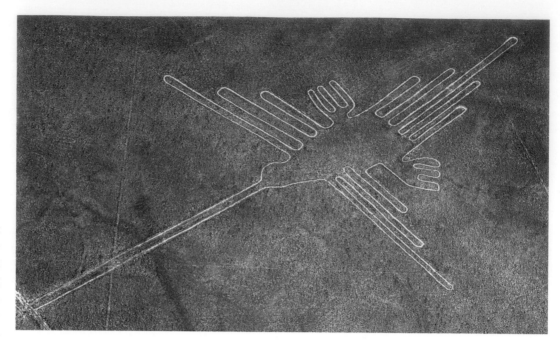

20-17 Hummingbird, Nasca Plain, Peru, Nasca, ca. 500 CE. Dark layer of pebbles scraped aside to reveal lighter clay and calcite beneath.

The earth drawings known as Nasca Lines represent birds, fish, plants, and geometric forms. They may have marked pilgrimage routes leading to religious shrines, but their function is uncertain.

appears scores of times. The flowing hair and the slow kicking motion of the legs suggest the figure is flying or floating while carrying batons and fans or, according to some scholars, knives and hallucinogenic mushrooms. On other mantles, the figures carry the skulls or severed heads of enemies. Art historians have interpreted the flying figures either as Paracas religious practitioners dancing or flying during an ecstatic trance or as images of the deceased. Despite endless repetitions, variations of detail occur throughout each textile, notably in the figures' positions and in subtle color changes.

Nasca The Nasca culture takes its name from the Nasca River valley south of Paracas. The Nasca are most famous for the figures they depicted on a gigantic scale. Some 800 miles of lines drawn in complex networks on the dry surface of the Nasca Plain have long attracted world attention because of their colossal size, which defies human perception from the ground. Preserved today are about three dozen images of plants, fish, and birds, including a hummingbird (FIG. **20-17**) several hundred feet long. The Nasca artists also drew geometric forms, such as trapezoids, spirals, and straight lines running for miles. Artists produced the Nasca Lines, as art historians call these immense earth drawings, by selectively removing the dark top layer of stones to expose the light clay and calcite below. The Nasca created the lines quite easily from available materials and using rudimentary geometry. Small groups of workers have made modern reproductions of them with relative ease. The lines seem to be paths laid out using simple stone-and-string methods. Some lead in traceable directions across the deserts of the Nasca River drainage. Others have many shrinelike nodes punctuating the lines, like the knots on a cord. Some lines converge at central places usually situated close to water sources and seem to be associated with water supply and irrigation. They may have marked routes for those journeying to local or regional shrines on foot. Altogether, the vast arrangement of the Nasca Lines is a system—not a meaningless maze but a traversable map that plotted the whole terrain of Nasca material and spiritual concerns.

Moche The Moche occupied a series of river valleys on the north coast of Peru around the same time the Nasca flourished to the south. The Moche have left behind an extraordinary variety of painted vessels illustrating architecture, metallurgy, weaving, the brewing of maize beer, human deformities and diseases, and even sexual acts. Predominantly flat-bottomed, stirrup-spouted jars, they are generally

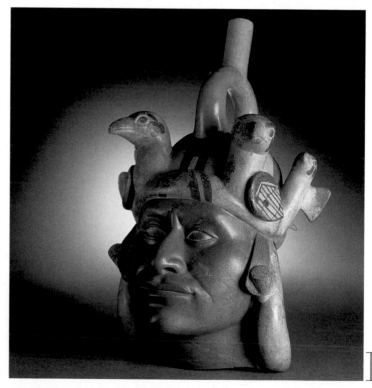

1 in.

20-18 Vessel in the shape of a portrait head, from north coast Peru, Moche, fifth to sixth century CE. Painted clay, 1' ½" high. Museo Arqueológico Rafael Larco Herrera, Lima.

The Moche culture produced an extraordinary variety of painted vessels. This one in the shape of a head may depict a warrior, ruler, or royal retainer. The realistic face is particularly striking.

decorated with a two-color slip. Although the Moche made early vessels by hand without the aid of a potter's wheel, they fashioned later ones in two-piece molds. Thus, numerous near-duplicates survive. The portrait vessel illustrated here (FIG. **20-18**) is an elaborate example of a common Moche type. It may depict the face of a warrior, a ruler, or even a royal retainer whose image may have been buried with many other pots to accompany his dead master. The realistic rendering of the physiognomy is particularly striking.

Inka

The Inka were a small highland group who established themselves in the Cuzco Valley around 1000.* In the 15th century, however, they rapidly extended their power until their empire stretched from modern Quito, Ecuador, to central Chile, a distance of more than 3,000 miles, and boasted a population of some 12 million. At the time of the Spanish conquest, the Inka Empire, although barely a century old, was the largest in the world. Expertise in mining and metalwork enabled the Inka to accumulate enormous wealth and to amass the fabled troves of gold and silver the Spaniards coveted. An empire as vast and rich as the Inka's required skillful organizational and administrative control. The Inka had rare talent for both. They divided their Andean empire, which they called Tawantinsuyu, the Land of the Four Quarters, into sections and subsections, provinces and communities, whose boundaries all converged on, or radiated from, the capital city of Cuzco.

The engineering prowess of the Inka matched their talent for governing. They mastered the difficult problems of agriculture in a mountainous region with expert terracing and irrigation, and knitted their extensive territories with a network of more than 14,000 miles of roads and bridges. Shunning wheeled vehicles and horses, they used their highway system to move goods by llama herds. They also established a highly efficient, swift communication system of relay runners who carried messages the length of the empire. Where the terrain was too steep for a paved flat surface, the Inka built stone steps, and their rope bridges crossed canyons high over impassable rivers. They placed small settlements along the roads no more than a day apart where travelers could rest and obtain supplies for the journey.

The Inka never developed a writing system, but they employed a remarkably sophisticated record-keeping system using a device known as the *khipu*, with which they recorded calendar and astronomical information, census and tribute totals, and inventories. For example, the Spaniards noted admiringly that Inka officials always knew exactly how much maize or cloth was in any storeroom in their empire. Not a book or a tablet, the khipu consisted of a main fiber cord and other knotted threads hanging perpendicularly off it. The color and position of each thread, as well as the kind of knot and its location, signified numbers and categories of things, whether people, llamas, or crops. Studies of khipus have demonstrated the Inka used the decimal system, were familiar with the concept of zero, and could record numbers up to five digits.

Machu Picchu The imperial Inka were gifted architects, and their masons were masters of shaping and fitting stone. As a militant people, they selected breathtaking, naturally fortified sites and further strengthened them by building various defensive structures. Inka city planning reveals an almost instinctive grasp of the harmonious relationship of architecture to site.

One of the world's most awe-inspiring sights is the Inka city of Machu Picchu (FIG. **20-19**), which perches on a ridge

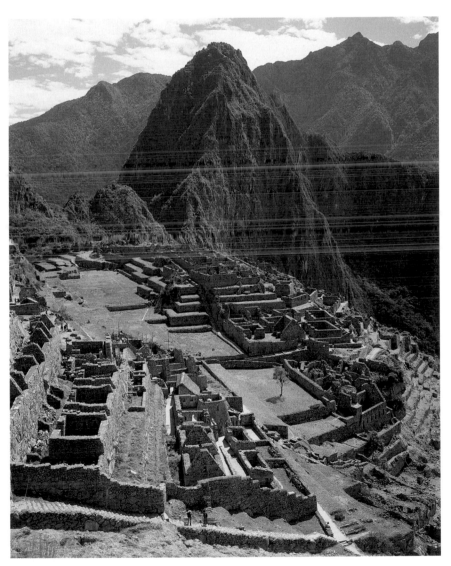

20-19 Machu Picchu (looking northwest), Peru, Inka, 15th century.

Machu Picchu was the estate of an Inka ruler. Large upright stones echo the contours of nearby sacred peaks. Precisely placed windows and doors facilitated astronomical observations.

*From this point on all dates in this chapter are CE unless otherwise stated.

between two jagged peaks 9,000 feet above sea level. Invisible from the Urubamba River valley some 1,600 feet below, the site remained unknown to the outside world until its rediscovery in 1911. In the very heart of the Andes, Machu Picchu is about 50 miles north of Cuzco and, like some of the region's other cities, was the estate of a powerful mid-15th-century Inka ruler. Though relatively small and insignificant among its neighbors (its resident population was a little more than a thousand), the city is of great archaeological importance as a rare site left undisturbed since Inka times. The accommodation of its architecture to the landscape is so complete that Machu Picchu seems a natural part of the mountain ranges surrounding it on all sides. The Inka even cut large stones to echo the shapes of the mountains beyond. Terraces spill down the mountainsides and extend even up to the very peak of Huayna Picchu, the great hill just beyond the city's main plaza. The Inka carefully sited buildings so that windows and doors framed spectacular views of sacred peaks and facilitated the recording of important astronomical events.

Cuzco In the 16th century, the Spanish conquistadors largely destroyed the Inka capital at Cuzco. However, some

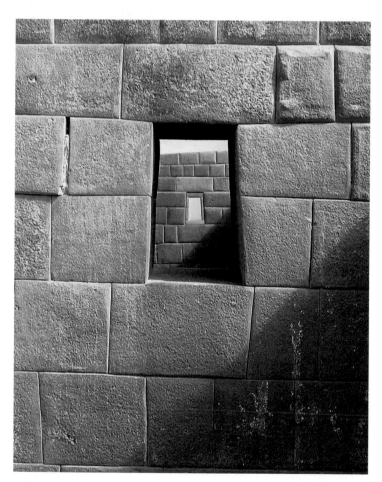

20-20 Detail of the ashlar masonry walls of the Temple of the Sun, Cuzco, Peru, Inka, 15th century.

Perfectly constructed ashlar masonry walls are all that remain of the Temple of the Sun, the most important shrine in the Inka capital. Gold, silver, and emeralds covered the temple's interior walls.

Spanish accounts describe Cuzco's plan as having the shape of a puma, with a great shrine-fortress on a hill above the city representing its head and the southeastern convergence of two rivers forming its tail. A great plaza, still the hub of the modern city, nestled below the animal's stomach. The puma was a symbol of Inka royal power.

One Inka building at Cuzco that survives in small part is the Temple of the Sun (FIG. **20-20**), built of stone blocks fit together without mortar. Cuzco masons laid the stones with perfectly joined faces. Remarkably, the Inka produced the close joints of their masonry by abrasion alone, grinding the surfaces to a perfect fit. Known to the Spanish as Coricancha (Golden Enclosure), the Temple of the Sun was the most magnificent of all Inka shrines. The 16th-century Spanish chroniclers wrote in awe of Coricancha's splendor, its interior veneered with sheets of gold, silver, and emeralds and housing life-size statues of silver and gold. Dedicated to the worship of several Inka deities, including the creator god Viracocha and the gods of the sun, moon, stars, and the elements, the temple was the center point of a network of radiating sight lines leading to some 350 shrines, which had both calendar and astronomical significance.

Pizarro and Atawalpa Smallpox spreading south from Spanish-occupied Mesoamerica killed the last Inka emperor and his heir and unleashed a civil war. In 1532, Francisco Pizarro (1471–1541) ambushed the would-be emperor Atawalpa on his way to be crowned at Cuzco after vanquishing his rival half-brother. Although Atawalpa paid a huge ransom of gold and silver, the Spaniards killed him and took control of his vast domain, only a decade after Cortés had defeated the Aztecs in Mexico. Following the murder of Atawalpa, the Spaniards erected the church of Santo Domingo, in an imported European style, on what remained of the Inka Temple of the Sun at Cuzco. A curved section of Inka wall serves to this day as the foundation for the church's apse. The two contrasting structures remain standing one atop the other. The juxtaposition is a symbol of the Spanish conquest of the Americas and serves as a composite monument to it.

NORTH AMERICA

In many parts of the United States and Canada, archaeologists have identified indigenous cultures dating back as far as 12,000 years ago. Most of the surviving art objects, however, come from the past 2,000 years. Scholars divide the vast and varied territory of North America (MAP **20-3**) into cultural regions based on the relative homogeneity of language and social and artistic patterns. Lifestyles varied widely over the continent, ranging from small bands of migratory hunters to settled—at times even urban—agriculturalists, and Native American art and architecture are more varied in the United States and Canada than in Mesoamerica and Andean South America. Four major regions are of special interest: the Eastern Woodlands, the American Southwest, the

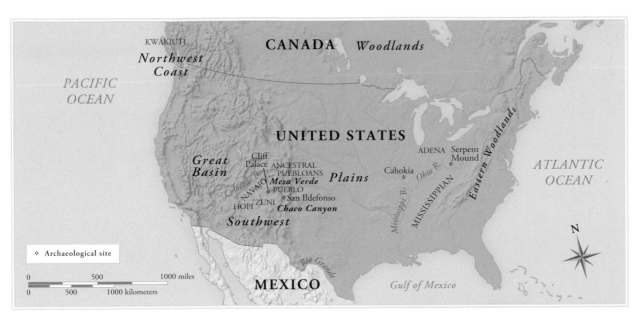

Northwest Coast (Washington and British Columbia), and the Great Plains.

Woodlands

The Adena and Mississippian cultures of the Woodlands east of the Mississippi River are noteworthy for their great urban centers.

Adena Archaeologists have found remains of the Adena culture of Ohio at about 500 sites. The Adena buried their elite in great earthen mounds and often placed ceremonial pipes in the graves. Smoking was an important social and religious ritual in many Native American cultures, and pipes were treasured status symbols men wanted to take with them into the afterlife. The Adena pipe shown here (FIG. 20-21), carved between 500 BCE and the end of the millennium, takes the shape of a standing man. The figure has naturalistic joint articulations and musculature, a lively flexed-leg pose, and an alert facial expression—all combining to suggest movement. In form and costume (note the prominent ear spools), the figure resembles some Mesoamerican sculptures.

Mississippian The Adena were the first great mound builders of North America, but the Mississippian culture, which emerged around 800 and eventually encompassed much of the eastern United States, surpassed all earlier Woodlands groups in the size and complexity of their communities. One Mississippian mound site, Cahokia in southern Illinois, was the largest city in North America in the early second millennium, with a population of at least 20,000 and an area of more than 6 square miles. There were approximately 120 mounds at Cahokia. The grandest, 100 feet tall and built in stages between about 900 and 1200, was Monk's Mound. Aligned with the position of the sun at the equinoxes, it may have served as an astronomical observatory as well as the site of agricultural ceremonies. Topping each stage were wooden structures the Mississippians eventually destroyed in preparation for the building of a new layer.

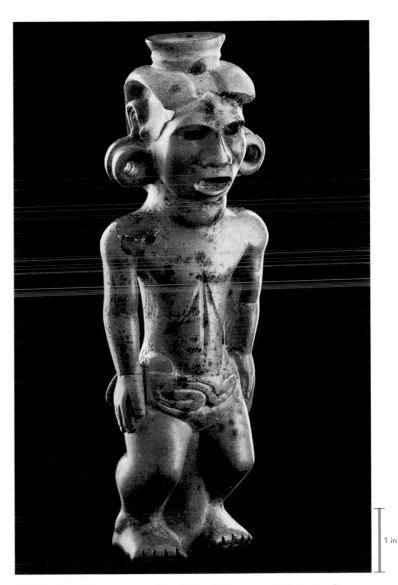

1 in.

20-21 Pipe, from a mound in Ohio, Adena, ca. 500–1 BCE. Stone, 8″ high. Ohio Historical Society, Columbus.

Smoking was an important ritual in ancient North America, and the Adena often buried pipes with men for use in the afterlife. This example resembles some Mesoamerican sculptures in form and costume.

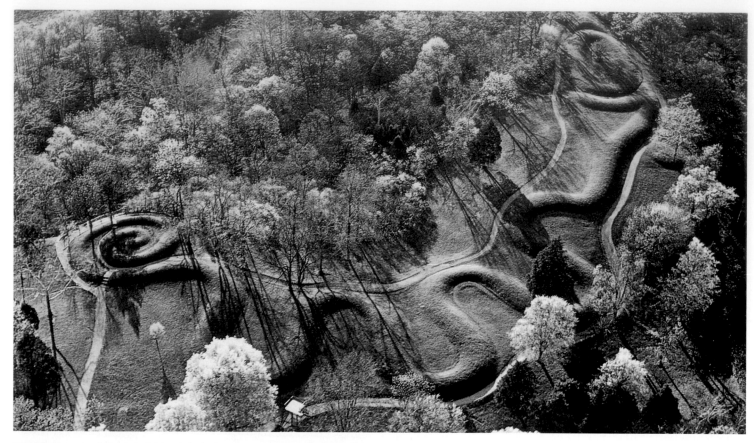

20-22 Serpent Mound, Ohio, Mississippian, ca. 1070. 1,200' long, 20' wide, 5' high.

The Mississippians constructed effigy mounds in the form of animals and birds. This mound seems to depict a serpent. Some scholars, however, think it replicates the path of Halley's Comet in 1066.

Serpent Mound The Mississippians also constructed *effigy mounds* (mounds built in the form of animals or birds). One of the largest and best preserved is Serpent Mound, a twisting earthwork on a bluff overlooking a creek in Ohio. It measures nearly a quarter mile from its open jaw (FIG. **20-22**, *top right*), which seems to clasp an oval-shaped mound in its mouth, to its tightly coiled tail (*far left*). Both its date and meaning are controversial.

For a long time after the first excavations in the 1880s, archaeologists attributed construction of Serpent Mound to the Adena culture. Radiocarbon dates taken from the mound, however, indicate the Mississippians built it much later. Unlike most other Woodlands mounds, Serpent Mound contained no evidence of burials or temples. The Mississippians, however, associated serpents with the earth and the fertility of crops, and the serpent is an important motif in Mississippian art. Nonetheless, some researchers have proposed another possible meaning for the shape of Serpent Mound. The date suggested for it is 1070, not long after the brightest appearance in recorded history of Halley's Comet in 1066. Could Serpent Mound have been built in response to this important astronomical event? The serpentine form of the mound may replicate the comet streaking across the night sky. Whatever its meaning, an earthwork as large and elaborate as Serpent Mound could only have been built by a large labor force under the firm direction of a powerful elite eager to leave their mark on the landscape forever.

Southwest

The dominant culture of the American Southwest during the centuries preceding the arrival of Europeans was the Ancestral Puebloan, formerly known as the Anasazi (Navajo, "enemy ancestors"), which emerged around 200 but did not reach its peak until about 1000. The many ruined *pueblos* (Spanish, "urban settlements") scattered throughout the Southwest reveal the Ancestral Puebloans' masterful construction skills. In Chaco Canyon, New Mexico, for example, they built a great semicircle of 800 rooms reaching to five stepped-back stories, the largest of several similar sites in and around the canyon. Chaco Canyon was the center of a wide trade network extending as far as Mexico.

Cliff Palace Sometime in the late 12th century, a drought occurred, and the Ancestral Puebloans largely abandoned their open canyon-floor dwelling sites to move farther north to the steep-sided canyons and lusher environment of Mesa Verde in southwestern Colorado. Cliff Palace (FIG. **20-23**) is wedged into a sheltered ledge above a valley floor. It contains about 200 rectangular rooms (mostly communal dwellings) of carefully laid stone and timber, once plastered inside and out with *adobe* (sun-dried mud brick). The location for Cliff Palace was not accidental. The Ancestral Puebloans designed it to take advantage of the sun to heat the pueblo in winter. The cliff shaded the pueblo during the hot summer months.

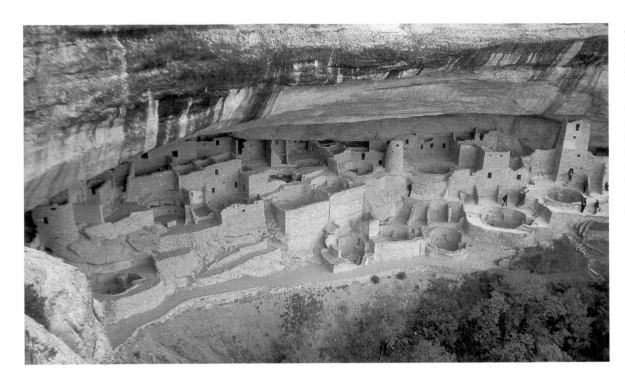

20-23 Cliff Palace, Mesa Verde National Park, Colorado, Ancestral Puebloan, ca. 1150–1300

Cliff Palace, wedged into a sheltered ledge to heat the pueblo in winter and shade it during the hot summer months, contains about 200 stone-and-timber rooms plastered inside and out with adobe.

Kuaua Pueblo Scattered in the foreground of FIG. 20-23 are two dozen large circular semisubterranean structures, called *kivas*. The Ancestral Puebloans entered the kivas using a ladder extending through a hole in the (now-lost) flat roof. These rooms were the spiritual centers of native Southwest life, male council houses where the elders stored ritual regalia and where private rituals and preparations for public ceremonies took place—and still do.

Between 1300 and 1500, the Ancestral Puebloans decorated their kivas with elaborate mural paintings representing deities associated with agricultural fertility. According to their descendants, the present-day Hopi and Zuni, the detail of the Kuaua Pueblo mural shown here (FIG. **20-24**) depicts a "lightning man" on the left side. Fish and eagle images (associated with rain) appear on the right side. Seeds, a lightning bolt, and a rainbow stream from the eagle's mouth. All these figures are associated with the fertility of the earth and the life-giving properties of the seasonal rains, a constant preoccupation of Southwest farmers.

The painter depicted the figures with great economy, using thick black lines, dots, and a restricted palette of black, brown, yellow, and white. The frontal figure of the lightning man seen against a neutral ground makes an immediate visual impact.

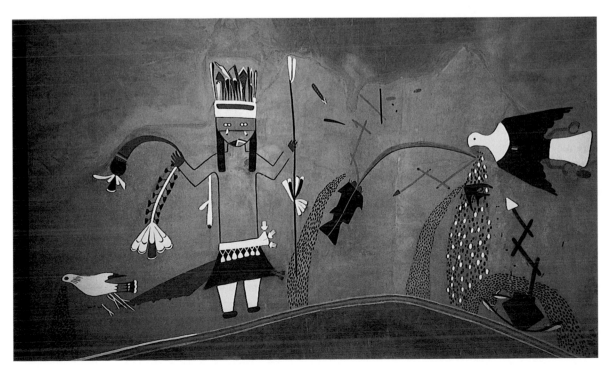

20-24 Detail of a kiva mural from Kuaua Pueblo (Coronado State Monument), New Mexico, Ancestral Puebloan, late 15th to early 16th century. Interior of the kiva, 18' × 18'. Museum of New Mexico, Santa Fe.

The kiva, or male council house, was the spiritual center of Puebloan life. Kivas were decorated with mural paintings associated with agricultural fertility. This one depicts a lightning man, fish, birds, and seeds.

20-25 OTTO PENTEWA, katsina figurine, New Oraibi, Arizona, Hopi, carved before 1959. Cottonwood root and feathers, 1′ high. Arizona State Museum, University of Arizona, Tucson.

Katsinas are benevolent spirits living in mountains and water sources. This Hopi katsina represents a rain-bringing deity wearing a decorated mask symbolic of water and agricultural fertility.

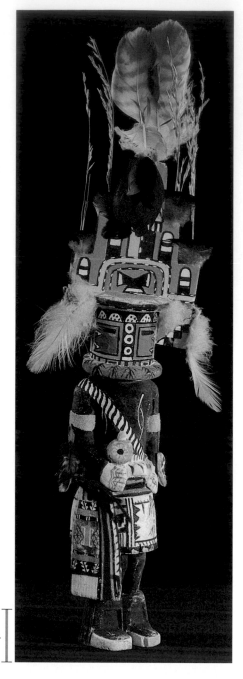

1 in.

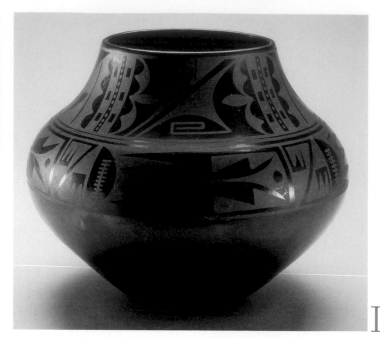

1 in.

20-26 MARÍA MONTOYA MARTÍNEZ, jar, San Ildefonso Pueblo, New Mexico, ca. 1939. Blackware, $11\frac{1}{8}″ \times 1′\ 1″$. National Museum of Women in the Arts, Washington, D.C. (gift of Wallace and Wilhelmina Hollachy).

María Montoya Martínez revived old techniques to produce pottery of striking shapes, proportions, and textures. Her black-on-black vessels feature matte designs on highly polished surfaces.

introduced during the colonial period). However, the cult is probably very ancient.

Pueblo Pottery The Southwest has also provided the finest examples of North American pottery. Originally producing utilitarian forms, Southwest potters worked without the potter's wheel and instead coiled shapes they then covered with slip, polished, and fired. Decorative motifs, often abstract and conventionalized, dealt largely with forces of nature—clouds, wind, and rain. In the early decades of the 20th century, San Ildefonso Pueblo potter MARÍA MONTOYA MARTÍNEZ (1887–1980) revived old techniques to produce forms of striking shape, proportion, and texture. Her black-on-black pieces (FIG. **20-26**) feature matte designs on high-gloss surfaces achieved by extensive polishing and special firing in an oxygen-poor atmosphere.

Northwest Coast

The Native Americans of the coasts and islands of northern Washington State, the province of British Columbia in Canada, and southern Alaska have long enjoyed a rich and reliable environment. They fished, hunted, gathered edible plants, and made their homes, utensils, and ritual objects from the region's great cedar forests.

Kwakiutl Among the numerous groups who settled the Northwest Coast are the Kwakiutl of southern British Columbia. Kwakiutl religious specialists used masks in their

Hopi Katsinas Another art form from the Southwest is the *katsina* figurine. Katsinas are benevolent supernatural spirits personifying ancestors and natural elements living in mountains and water sources. Humans join their world after death. Among contemporary Pueblo groups, masked dancers ritually impersonate katsinas during yearly festivals dedicated to rain, fertility, and good hunting. To educate young girls in ritual lore, the Hopi traditionally give them miniature representations of the masked dancers. The illustrated Hopi katsina (FIG. **20-25**), fashioned by OTTO PENTEWA (d. 1963), represents a rain-bringing deity who wears a mask painted in geometric patterns symbolic of water and agricultural fertility. Topping the mask is a stepped shape signifying thunderclouds and feathers to carry the Hopis' airborne prayers. The origins of the katsina figurines have been lost in time (they even may have developed from carved saints the Spaniards

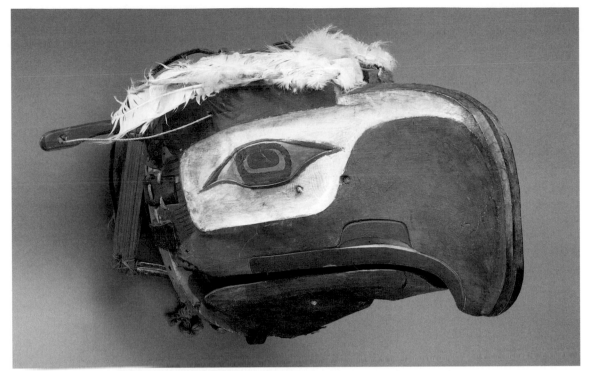

20-27 Eagle transformation mask, closed (*top*) and
open (*bottom*) views, Alert
Bay, Canada, Kwakiutl,
late 19th century. Wood,
feathers, and string,
1' 10" × 11". American
Museum of Natural
History, New York.

The wearer of this Kwakiutl
mask could open and close
it rapidly by manipulating
hidden strings, magically
transforming himself from
human to eagle and back
again as he danced.

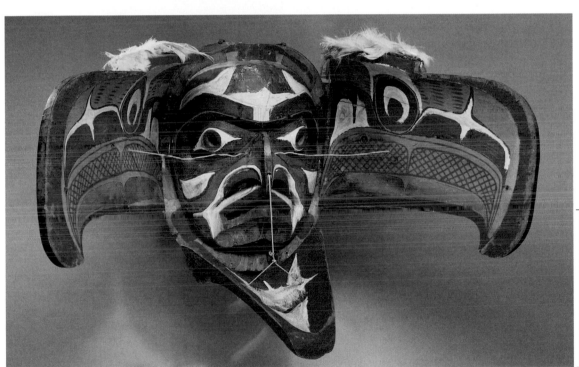

1 ft.

healing rituals. Men also wore masks in dramatic public performances during the winter ceremonial season. The animals
and mythological creatures represented in masks and a host
of other carvings derive from the Northwest Coast's rich oral
tradition and celebrate the mythological origins and inherited privileges of high-ranking families. The artist who made
the Kwakiutl mask illustrated here (FIG. **20-27**) meant it to be
seen in flickering firelight, and ingeniously constructed it to
open and close rapidly when the wearer manipulated hidden
strings. He could thus magically transform himself from human to eagle and back again as he danced. The transformation theme, in myriad forms, is a central aspect of the art and
religion of the Americas. The Kwakiutl mask's human aspect also owes its dramatic character to the exaggeration and
distortion of facial parts—such as the hooked beaklike nose
and flat flaring nostrils—and to the deeply undercut curvilinear depressions, which form strong shadows. In contrast
to the carved human face, but painted in the same colors, is
the two-dimensional abstract image of the eagle painted on
the inside of the outer mask.

20-28 Karl Bodmer, *Hidatsa Warrior Pehriska-Ruhpa (Two Ravens)*, 1833. Engraving by Paul Legrand after the original watercolor in the Joslyn Art Museum, Omaha, 1′ 3⅞″ × 11½″. Engraving: Buffalo Bill Historical Center, Cody. ◼◀

The personal regalia of a Hidatsa warrior included his pipe, painted buffalo-hide robe, bear-claw necklace, and feather decorations, all symbols of his affiliations and military accomplishments.

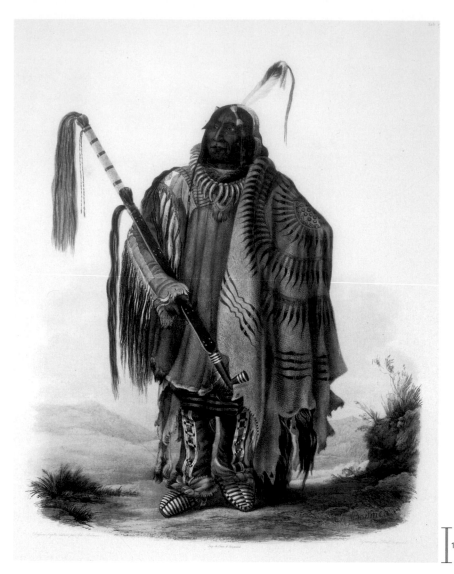

1 in.

Great Plains

After colonial governments disrupted settled indigenous communities on the East Coast and the Europeans introduced the horse to North America, a new mobile Native American culture flourished on the Great Plains for a short time. Great Plains artists worked in materials and styles quite different from those of the Northwest Coast and Eskimo/Inuit peoples. Much artistic energy went into the decoration of leather garments, pouches, horse trappings, tipis, and buffalo-skin robes.

Hidatsa Regalia Because most Plains peoples were nomadic, they focused their aesthetic attention largely on their clothing and bodies and on other portable objects, such as shields, clubs, pipes, tomahawks, and various containers. Transient but important Plains art forms can sometimes be found in the paintings and drawings of visiting American and European artists, who recorded Native American costumes as anthropological curiosities, relics of a soon-to-be-lost era as the descendants of Europeans pursued their Manifest Destiny to take over the continent (see Chapter 11). In 1833, for example, Karl Bodmer (1809–1893) of Switzerland, portrayed the personal decoration of Pehriska-Ruhpa (Two Ravens). The portrait (FIG. **20-28**) includes the Hidatsa warrior's pipe, painted buffalo-hide robe, bear-claw necklace, and feather decorations, all symbolic of his affiliations and military accomplishments. These items represent his life story—a composite artistic statement in several media immediately intelligible to other Native Americans. The concentric circle design over his left shoulder, for example, is an abstract rendering of an eagle-feather war bonnet.

Whether secular and decorative or spiritual and highly symbolic, the diverse styles and forms of Native American art in the United States and Canada have traditionally reflected the indigenous peoples' reliance on and reverence toward the environment they considered it their privilege to inhabit. Today, some Native American artists work in media and styles indistinguishable from those of other contemporary artists worldwide, but in the work of others, for example, Jaune Quick-to-See Smith (FIG. 16-1), the Native American experience remains central to their artistic identity.

Native America

Mesoamerica

▌ The Olmec (ca. 1200–400 BCE) is often called the "mother culture" of Mesoamerica. The Olmec built pyramids and ball courts and carved colossal basalt portraits of their rulers during the Preclassic period.

▌ In contrast to the embryonic civic centers of the Olmec, Teotihuacán in the Valley of Mexico was a huge metropolis laid out on a strict grid plan. Its major pyramids and plazas date to the late Preclassic period, ca. 50–250 CE.

▌ During the Classic period (ca. 300–900), the Maya built vast complexes of temple-pyramids, palaces, plazas, and ball courts and decorated them with monumental sculptures and mural paintings glorifying their rulers and gods.

▌ The Aztec Empire was the dominant power in Mesoamerica at the time of the Spanish conquest. Tenochtitlán, the capital, was a magnificent island city laid out on a grid plan. Statues and reliefs adorned the main religious complex centered on the pyramid-temple of Huitzilopochtli and Tlaloc.

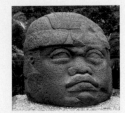

Colossal head, La Venta, Olmec,
ca. 900–400 BCE

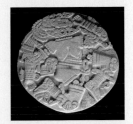

Coyolxauhqui, Tenochtitlán,
Aztec, ca. 1469

South America

▌ The ancient civilizations of South America are even older than those of Mesoamerica. The earliest Andean sites began to develop around 3000 BCE.

▌ The Paracas (ca. 400 BCE–200 CE) and Moche (ca. 1–700 CE) cultures of Peru produced extraordinary textiles and distinctive painted ceramics. The subjects range from composite human-animals to ruler portraits.

▌ The Nasca (ca. 200 BCE–600 CE) are famous for their immense earth drawings representing birds, fish, plants, and geometric forms. Known as Nasca Lines, they may have marked pilgrimage routes.

▌ In the 15th century, the Inka ruled a vast empire from their capital at Cuzco in Peru. The most impressive preserved Inka site is Machu Picchu, constructed on a terraced hillside with spectacular views of sacred peaks.

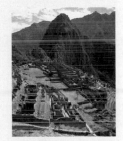

Machu Picchu, Inka,
15th century

North America

▌ The indigenous cultures of the United States and Canada date as far back as 10,000 BCE, but most of the surviving art objects date from the past 2,000 years.

▌ The peoples of the Mississippian culture (ca. 800–1500) were great mound builders. Cahokia in Illinois encompassed about 120 mounds and had a population of at least 20,000. It was the largest city in North America during the early second millennium.

▌ In the American Southwest, native peoples have been producing distinctive pottery for more than 2,000 years. The Ancestral Puebloans constructed urban settlements (pueblos) and decorated their council houses (kivas) with mural paintings.

▌ On the Northwest Coast, masks played an important role in religious rituals. Some examples enabled the wearer to transform himself from human to animal and back again.

▌ The people of the Great Plains produced magnificent painted robes and shields, bead necklaces, and feathered headdresses.

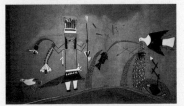

Kuaua Pueblo, Ancestral Puebloan,
late 15th to early 16th century

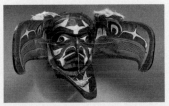

Eagle transformation mask, Kwakiutl,
late 19th century

The name for these screens is *nduen fobara* (foreheads of the deceased). The chief's headdress is in the form of a 19th-century European sailing ship, a reference to the deceased's trading business.

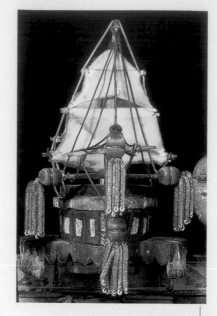

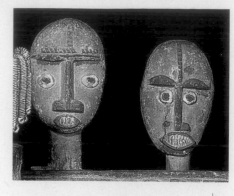

To either side of the chief are his attendants and, at the top of the shrine, the heads of his slaves. Both attendants and slaves are smaller in size than the chief, as is appropriate for their lower rank.

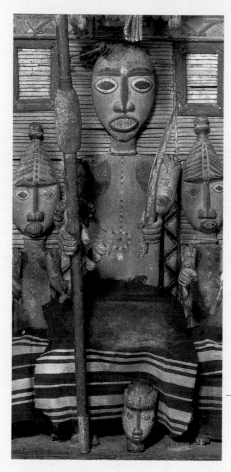

Kalabari Ijaw ancestral screens are memorials to the chiefs of trading companies called canoe houses. The deceased, the central figure holding a long staff and curved knife, is also the largest.

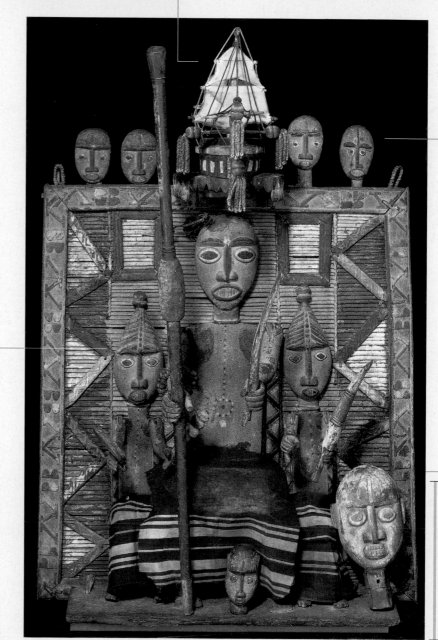

1 ft.

21-1 Ancestral screen (nduen fobara), Kalabari Ijaw, Nigeria, late 19th century. Wood, fiber, and cloth, 3' 9½" high. British Museum, London.

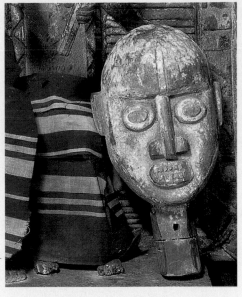

The chief is bare-chested with colorful drapery covering the lower part of his body. At his feet are the heads of conquered rivals, completing the exceptionally rich iconographical program.

Africa

KALABARI IJAW ANCESTRAL SCREENS

Throughout the continent, Africans have, since ancient times, venerated ancestors for the continuing aid they believe they provide the living, including help in maintaining the productivity of the earth for bountiful crop production and ensuring successful hunts. In some African societies, for example the Kota of Gabon, people place the bones of their ancestors in containers guarded by sculptured figures (FIG. 21-11) in order to protect these treasured relics from theft or harm. In highly stratified societies headed by a monarch, for example, the Benin kingdom, the royal family maintains altars (FIG. 21-17) at which the current king offers animal sacrifices to honor his ancestors and enlist their help in protecting the living and assuring prosperity.

The Kalabari Ijaw peoples have hunted and fished in the eastern delta of the Niger River in present-day Nigeria for several centuries. As in so many other African cultures, Kalabari artists and patrons have lavished attention on memorials to ancestors. Their shrines, however, take a unique form because a cornerstone of the Kalabari economy has long been trade, and trading organizations known locally as "canoe houses" play a central role in Kalabari society. Kalabari ancestor shrines are elaborate screens of wood, fiber, textiles, and other materials. An especially elaborate example (FIG. 21-1) is the almost four-foot-tall *nduen fobara* (foreheads of the deceased) honoring a former chief of a trading company. The chief's family usually commissioned these memorial screens on the one-year anniversary of his death. Displayed in the house in which the chief lived, the screen represents the deceased himself at the center, holding a long silver-tipped staff in his right hand and a curved knife in his left hand. His chest is bare and drapery covers the lower part of his body. His impressive headdress is in the form of a 19th-century European sailing ship, a reference to the chief's successful trading business. Flanking him are his attendants, smaller in size as is appropriate for their lower rank. The heads of his slaves are at the top of the screen and those of his conquered rivals are at the bottom. The hierarchical composition and the stylized rendition of human anatomy and facial features are common in African art, but the richness and complexity of this shrine are exceptional.

Unusual, too, is the way the sculptor created the shrine by assembling it from separately carved sections and then painting it. Most African sculptors fashioned their works from a single block of wood. The carpentry technique employed for the Kalabari screens may be the result of sustained contact with European traders and first-hand knowledge of European woodworking techniques.

AFRICAN PEOPLES AND ART FORMS

Africa (MAP 21-1) is a vast continent of more than 50 nations comprising more than one-fifth of the world's land mass and many distinct topographical and ecological zones. Parched deserts occupy northern and southern regions, high mountains rise in the east, and three great rivers—the Niger, the Congo, and the Nile—and their lush valleys support agriculture and large settled populations. More than 2,000 distinct ethnic, cultural, and linguistic groups long have inhabited this enormous continent. These population groups historically have ranged in size from a few hundred, in hunting and gathering bands, to 20 million or more. Councils of elders often governed smaller groups, whereas larger populations sometimes formed a centralized state under a king.

Despite this great variety, African peoples share many core beliefs and practices. These include honoring ancestors (FIG. 21-1), worshiping nature deities, and elevating rulers to sacred status. Most peoples also consult diviners or fortune tellers. These beliefs have given rise to many richly expressive art traditions, including rock engraving and painting, body decoration, masquerades and other lavish festivals, figural sculpture, and sacred and secular architecture. Given the size of the African continent and the diversity of ethnic groups, it is not surprising that African art varies enormously in subject, materials, and function. Nomadic and seminomadic peoples excel in the arts of personal adornment and also produce rock engravings and paintings depicting animals and rituals. Farmers, in contrast, often create figural sculpture in terracotta, wood, and metal for display in shrines to legendary ancestors or nature deities held responsible for the health of crops and the well-being of the people. The regalia, art, and architecture of kings and their courts, as elsewhere in the world, celebrate the wealth and power of the rulers themselves. Nearly all African peoples lavish artistic energy on the decoration of their own bodies to express their identity and status, and many communities mount richly layered festivals, including masquerades, to celebrate harvests and the New Year and to commemorate the deaths of leaders. In Africa, art helps define and create culture. Closely integrated within communal life and thought, African art was not created solely for display until the late 20th century.

PREHISTORY AND EARLY CULTURES

Thousands of rock engravings and paintings found at hundreds of sites across the continent constitute the earliest known African art. Some painted animals from the Apollo 11 Cave in Namibia date to perhaps as long ago as 23,000 BCE, earlier than all but the oldest Paleolithic art of Europe (see Chapter 1). Because humankind apparently originated in Africa, archaeologists may yet discover the world's earliest art there as well. The greatest concentrations of rock art are in the Sahara Desert to the north, the Horn of Africa in the east, and the Kalahari Desert to the south, as well as in caves and on rock outcroppings in southern Africa. Accurately naturalistic renderings as well as stylized images on rock surfaces show animals and humans in many different positions and activities, singly or in groups, stationary or in motion. Most of these works date to within the past 4,000 to 6,000 years, but some may have been created as early as 8000 BCE. They provide a rich record of the environment, human activities, and animal species in prehistoric times.

Although the precise dating and meaning of most African rock art remain uncertain, a considerable literature exists describing, analyzing, and interpreting the varied human and animal activities shown, as well as the evidently symbolic, more abstract patterns. The human and humanlike figures may include representations of supernatural beings as well as mortals. The general significance and function

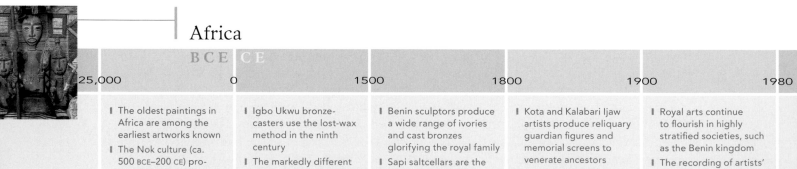

Africa

	BCE	CE				
25,000		0	1500	1800	1900	1980

- The oldest paintings in Africa are among the earliest artworks known
- The Nok culture (ca. 500 BCE–200 CE) produces the first African sculptures in the round

- Igbo Ukwu bronze-casters use the lost-wax method in the ninth century
- The markedly different styles of sculptures from Ile-Ife and from Djenne underscore the regional diversity of African art
- Djenne builds an adobe mosque in the 13th century
- Great Zimbabwe constructs fortification walls and towers in the 14th century

- Benin sculptors produce a wide range of ivories and cast bronzes glorifying the royal family
- Sapi saltcellars are the earliest evidence for interaction between African artists and European patrons

- Kota and Kalabari Ijaw artists produce reliquary guardian figures and memorial screens to venerate ancestors
- Royal arts include the throne of Bamum king Ngansu and Fon king Glele's bocio of the god Gu

- Royal arts continue to flourish in highly stratified societies, such as the Benin kingdom
- The recording of artists' names becomes more common. Osei Bonsu and Ilowe of Ise achieve wide renown as sculptors
- Throughout the continent, African peoples produce elaborate masks to be danced at masquerades

MAP 21-1 Africa.

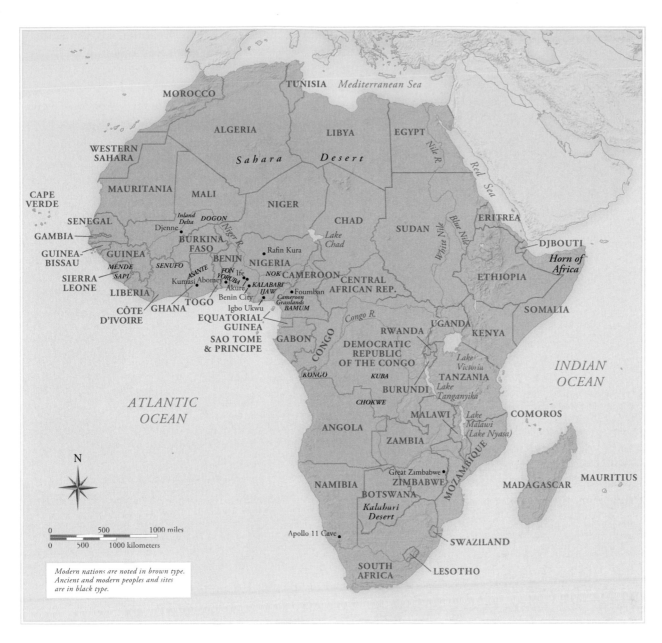

MAP 21-1 Africa.

of prehistoric art in Africa probably coincide with those of the later arts, which portray ideas and rituals about the origin, survival, health, and continuity of human populations.

Nok Outside Egypt and neighboring Nubia (see Chapter 1), the earliest African sculptures in the round have been found at several sites in central Nigeria archaeologists collectively call the Nok culture. Scholars disagree on whether the Nok sites were unified politically or socially. Named after the site where these sculptures were first discovered in 1928, Nok art dates between 500 BCE and 200 CE. Hundreds of Nok-style human and animal heads, body parts, and figures have been found accidentally during tin-mining operations, but not in their original context. A representative terracotta head (FIG. **21-2**), found at Rafin Kura, is a fragment of what was originally a full figure. Preserved fragments of other statues indicate the Nok sculptors fashioned standing, seated, and kneeling figures. The heads are disproportionately large compared with the bodies. The head shown here has an expressive face with large alert eyes, flaring nostrils, and

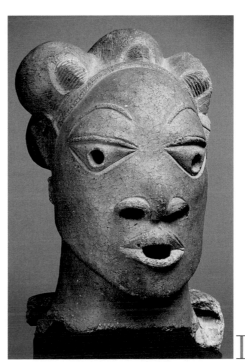

21-2 Nok head, from Rafin Kura, Nigeria, ca. 500 BCE–200 CE. Terracotta, 1' 2 3/16" high. National Museum, Lagos.

The earliest African sculptures in the round come from Nigeria. The Nok culture produced expressive terracotta heads with large eyes, mouths, and ears. Piercing equalized the heat during the firing process.

Prehistory and Early Cultures 559

Art and Leadership in Africa

The relationships between leaders and art forms are strong, complex, and universal in Africa. Political, spiritual, and social leaders—kings, chiefs, titled people, and religious specialists—have the power and wealth to obtain the services of the best artists and acquire the most sumptuous materials to adorn themselves, furnish their homes and palaces, and make visible the cultural and religious organizations they lead. Leaders also possess the power to dispense art or the prerogative to use it.

Several formal or structural principles characterize leaders' arts and thus set them off from the popular arts of ordinary Africans. Leaders' arts—for example, the lavish and layered regalia of chiefs and kings—tend to be durable and fashioned of costly materials, such as ivory, beads, copper alloys, and other luxurious metals. Some of the objects made specifically for African leaders, such as thrones and footstools (FIG. 21-12), ornate clothing (FIG. 21-22), and special weaponry, draw attention to their superior status. Handheld objects—for example, staffs (FIG. 21-9), spears, knives (FIG. 21-1), scepters, pipes, and fly whisks (FIG. 21-3)—extend a leader's reach and magnify his or her gestures. Other objects associated with leaders, such as fans (FIG. I-1), shields, and umbrellas, protect the leaders both physically and spiritually. Sometimes the regalia and implements of an important person are so heavy they render the leader virtually immobile (FIG. 21-22), suggesting that the temporary holder of an office is less significant than the eternal office itself.

Although leaders' arts are easy to recognize in centralized, hierarchical societies, such as the Benin (FIGS. I-1, 21-8, 21-9, and 21-17) and Bamum (FIG. 21-12) kingdoms, leaders among less centralized peoples have been no less conversant with the power of art to move people and effect change. For example, African leaders often oversee religious rituals in which they may be less visible than the forms used in those rituals: shrines, altars, festivals, and rites of passage such as funerals, the last being especially elaborate and festive in many parts of Africa. The arts that leaders control thus help create pageantry, mystery, and spectacle, enriching and changing the lives of the people.

21-3 Equestrian figure on fly-whisk hilt, from Igbo Ukwu, Nigeria, 9th to 10th century CE. Copper-alloy bronze, figure 6³⁄₁₆″ high. National Museum, Lagos. ◼◂

The oldest known African lost-wax cast bronze is this fly-whisk hilt, which a leader used to extend his reach and magnify his gestures. The artist exaggerated the size of the ruler compared with his steed.

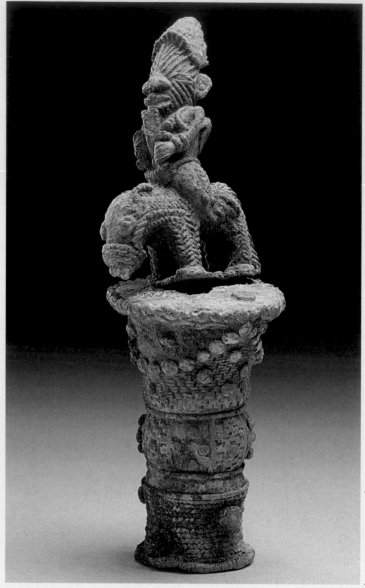

1 in.

---

parted lips. The pierced eyes, mouth, and ear holes are characteristic of Nok sculpture and probably helped to equalize the heating of the hollow clay head during the firing process. The coiffure with incised grooves, the raised eyebrows, the perforated triangular eyes, and the sharp jaw line suggest the sculptor carved some details of the head while modeling the rest. The function of the Nok terracottas is unclear, but the broken tube around the neck of the Rafin Kura figure may be a bead necklace, an indication the person portrayed held an elevated position in Nok society. The gender of the Nok artists is unknown, but because the primary ceramists and clay sculptors across the continent have traditionally been women, Nok women may have sculpted these heads as well.

Igbo Ukwu By the 9th or 10th century CE, a West African bronze-casting tradition of great sophistication had developed in the lower Niger area, just east of that great river. Dozens of objects in an intricate, refined style have been unearthed at Igbo Ukwu. The ceramic, copper, bronze, and iron artifacts include basins, bowls, altar stands, staffs, swords, scabbards, knives, and pendants. In one grave archaeologists discovered numerous prestige objects—copper anklets, armlets, spiral ornaments, a fan handle, and more than 100,000 beads, which may have been used as a form of currency. The tomb also contained three elephant tusks, a crown, and a bronze leopard's skull. These items, doubtless the regalia of a leader (see "Art and Leadership in Africa," page 560), whether secular or religious, are the earliest cast-metal objects known from regions south of the Sahara.

A lost-wax cast bronze sculpture (FIG. 21-3), the earliest yet found in Africa, came from the same grave at Igbo Ukwu. It depicts an equestrian figure on a fly-whisk hilt. The African artist made the handle using a casting method similar to that documented much earlier in Mesopotamia (FIG. 1-15) and the Mediterranean (see "Hollow-Casting," Chapter 2, page 67). The hilt's upper section consists of a figure seated on a horse, and the lower part is an elaborately embellished handle with beaded and threadlike patterns. The rider's head is of exaggerated size, a common trait in the art of many early cultures. The prominent facial stripes (scarification) probably represent marks of titled status, a practice still current among Igbo-speaking peoples today.

11TH TO 18TH CENTURIES

Although kings ruled some African population groups from an early date, the best evidence for royal arts in Africa comes from the several centuries between about 1000 and the beginning of European colonization in the 19th century.* During this period, Africans also constructed major houses of worship for the religions of Christianity and Islam, both of which originated in the Middle East but quickly gained adherents south of the Sahara.

Ile-Ife Africans have long considered Ile-Ife, about 200 miles west of Igbo Ukwu in southwestern Nigeria, the cradle of Yoruba civilization, the place where the gods Oduduwa and Obatala created the earth and its peoples. Tradition also names Oduduwa the first *oni* (ruler) of Ile-Ife and the ancestor of all Yoruba kings. Ife artists often portrayed their sacred kings in sculpture. One of the most impressive examples is a statuette (FIG. 21-4) of an Ife king cast in a zinc-brass alloy, datable to the 11th or 12th century. This and many similar representations of Ife rulers are exceptional in Africa because of the naturalistic recording of facial features and fleshy anatomy. The naturalism does not extend to body proportions, however. The heads of the rulers, for example, are disproportionately large compared with their bodies. For modern Yoruba, the head is the locus of wisdom, destiny, and the essence of being, and these ideas probably developed at least 800 years ago, accounting for the emphasis on the head in Ife statuary and African art in general. The artist also took great care to indicate the man's status as a sacred ruler by precisely reproducing the details of the heavily beaded costume, crown, and jewelry.

Djenne Terracottas The inland floodplain of the Niger River was for the African continent a kind of "fertile crescent" analogous to ancient Mesopotamia (see Chapter 1). By

*From this point on, all dates in this chapter are CE unless otherwise stated.

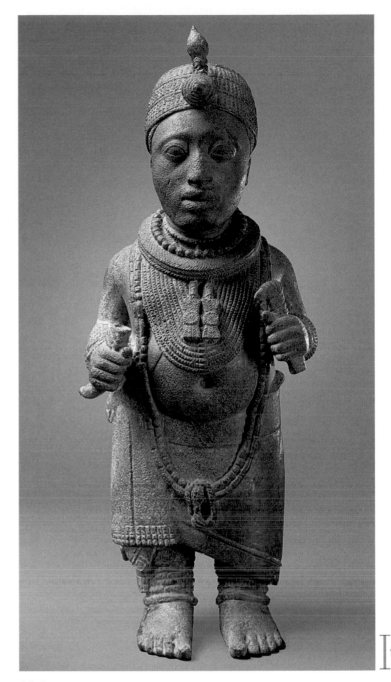

21-4 King, from Ita Yemoo (Ife), Nigeria, 11th to 12th century. Zinc-brass, 1' 6½" high. Museum of Ife Antiquities, Ife. ◼️

Unlike most African sculptures, this royal figure has a naturalistically modeled torso and facial features approaching portraiture. The head, however, the locus of wisdom, is disproportionately large.

about 800, a walled town, Djenne in present-day Mali, had been built on high ground left dry during the flooding season. Hundreds of sensitively modeled terracotta sculptures, most dating to between 1100 and 1500, have been found at numerous sites in the Djenne region. Production tapered off sharply, however, with the arrival of Islam, whose adherents shunned figural art in religious contexts (see Chapter 5). Unfortunately, as is true of the Nok terracottas, the vast majority of the surviving Djenne sculptures came from illegal excavations, and all contextual information about them has

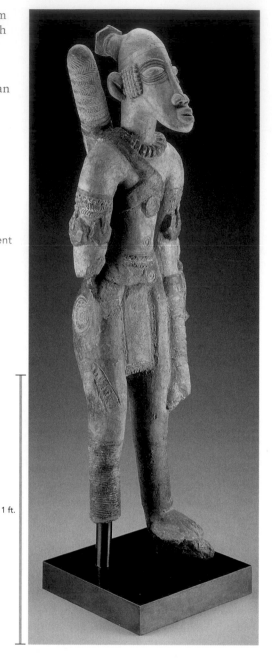

21-5 Archer, from Djenne, Mali, 13th to 15th centuries. Terracotta, 2' ⅜" high. National Museum of African Art, Washington, D.C.

Djenne terracottas present a striking contrast to statues from Ile-Ife. This archer is thin with tubular limbs and an elongated head featuring a prominent chin, bulging eyes, and large nose.

1 ft.

been destroyed. The artists depicted the human figures in a variety of postures—seated, reclining, kneeling, standing, and on horseback. Some are warriors. Others wear elaborate jewelry, but many are without adornment or attributes. The range of subjects and postures is extraordinary at this date. The terracotta figure illustrated here (FIG. **21-5**) dates to the 13th to 15th centuries and represents a Djenne warrior with a quiver of arrows on his back and knives strapped to his left arm. The proportions of the figure present a striking contrast to those from Ile-Ife (FIG. **21-4**)—thin and tall with tubular limbs and an elongated head with a prominent chin, bulging eyes, and large nose, characteristic features of the distinctive Djenne style.

Djenne Mosque Djenne boasts one of the most ambitious examples of adobe architecture in the world, the city's Great Mosque (FIG. **21-6**), first built in the 13th century and

reconstructed in 1906–1907 after a fire destroyed the earlier building in 1830. The mosque has a large courtyard and a roofed prayer hall, emulating the plan of many of the oldest mosques known (see "The Mosque," Chapter 5, page 151). The facade, however, is unlike any in the Middle East and features soaring adobe towers and vertical buttresses resembling engaged columns. The many rows of protruding wooden beams further enliven the walls but also serve a practical function as perches for workers undertaking the essential recoating of sacred clay on the exterior that occurs during an annual festival.

Great Zimbabwe The most famous southern African site of this period is a complex of stone ruins at the large southeastern political center called Great Zimbabwe. First occupied in the 11th century, the site features walled enclosures and towers dating from about the late 13th to the middle of the 15th centuries. At that time, Great Zimbabwe had a wide trade network. Finds of beads and pottery from Mesopotamia and China, along with copper and gold objects, underscore that Great Zimbabwe was a prosperous trade center well before Europeans began their coastal voyaging in the late 15th century.

Most scholars agree Great Zimbabwe was a royal residence with special areas for the ruler, his wives, and nobles, including an open court for ceremonial gatherings (the royal hill complex). At the city's zenith, as many as 18,000 people may have lived in the surrounding area, with most of the commoners living outside the enclosed complex reserved for royalty. Although the habitations themselves have not survived, the enclosures remain. They are unusual for their size and the excellence of their stonework. Some perimeter walls are 30 feet tall. One of these, known as the Great Enclosure (FIG. **21-7**), houses one large and several small conical, tower-like stone structures, which archaeologists have interpreted symbolically as masculine (large) and feminine (small) forms, but their precise significance is unknown. The form of the large tower suggests a granary. Grain bins were symbols of royal power and generosity, as the ruler received tribute in grain and dispensed it to the people in times of need.

Benin The founding of the Benin kingdom (not to be confused with the modern Republic of Benin; see MAP 21-1) most likely occurred in the 13th century. According to oral tradition, the first Benin king was the grandson of a Yoruba king of Ile-Ife. Benin reached its greatest power and geographical extent in the 16th century. The kingdom's vicissitudes and slow decline thereafter culminated in 1897, when the British burned and sacked the Benin palace and city. Benin City thrives today, however, and the palace, where the Benin king continues to live, has been partially rebuilt. Benin artists have produced many complex, finely cast copper-alloy sculptures as well as sophisticated artworks in ivory, wood, ceramic, and wrought iron. The hereditary *oba,* or sacred king, and his court still use and dispense art objects as royal favors to title holders and other chiefs (see "Art and Leadership," page 560).

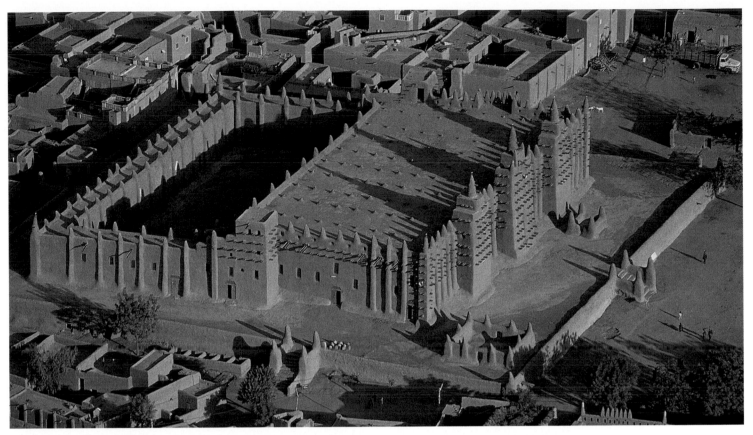

21-6 Aerial view of the Great Mosque (looking northwest), Djenne, Mali, begun 13th century, rebuilt 1906–1907.

The Great Mosque at Djenne resembles Middle Eastern mosques in plan (large courtyard in front of a roofed prayer hall), but the construction materials—adobe and wood—are distinctly African.

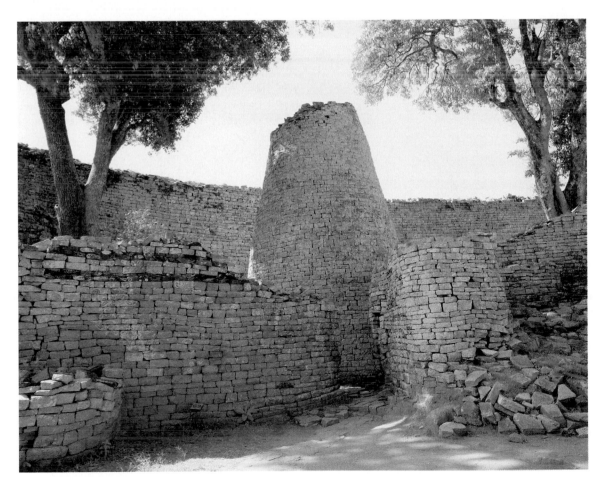

21-7 Walls and tower, Great Enclosure, Great Zimbabwe, Zimbabwe, 14th century.

The Great Zimbabwe Empire in southern Africa had a trade network that extended to Mesopotamia and China. Thirty-foot-high stone walls and conical towers surrounded the royal residence.

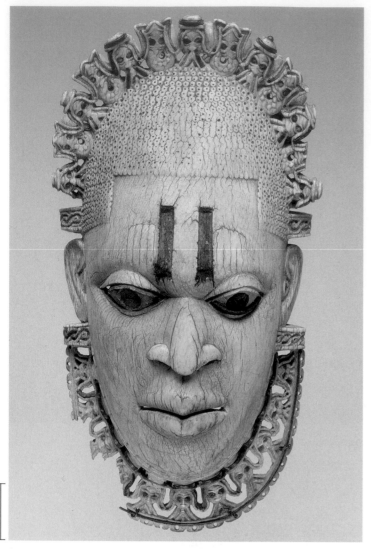

1 in.

21-8 Waist pendant of a queen mother, from Benin, Nigeria, ca. 1520. Ivory and iron, $9\frac{3}{8}$" high. Metropolitan Museum of Art, New York (Michael C. Rockefeller Memorial Collection, gift of Nelson A. Rockefeller, 1972).

This ivory head probably portrays Idia, mother of Oba Esigie, who wore it on his waist. Above Idia's head are Portuguese heads and mudfish, symbols of trade and of the sea god Olokun.

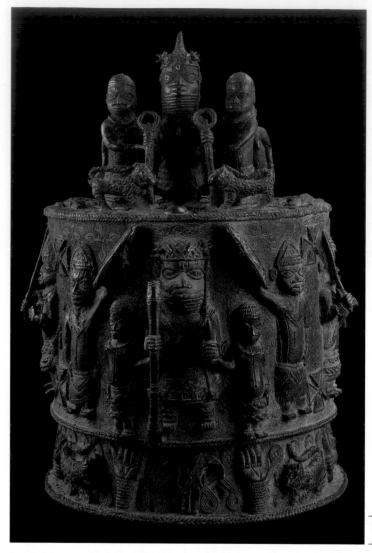

1 in.

21-9 Altar to the Hand (ikegobo), from Benin, Nigeria, ca. 1735–1750. Bronze, 1' $5\frac{1}{2}$" high. British Museum, London (gift of Sir William Ingram). ◼◀

An ikegobo is an altar to the hand, the symbol of personal achievement in Benin society. The band at the bottom of this altar features hands alternating with other emblems of royal power.

Queen Mother Idia One of the masterworks of Benin sculpture is an ivory head of a woman (FIG. **21-8**), which a Benin king almost certainly wore at his waist. Oba Esigie (r. ca. 1504–1550), under whom the Benin kingdom flourished and expanded with Portuguese aid, probably commissioned the head to honor his mother, Idia, for whom he created the title of Queen Mother (*iy'oba*), and built a separate palace. The head, remarkable for its sensitive naturalism, most likely represents Idia. On its crown are alternating Portuguese heads and mudfish, symbolic references respectively to Benin's trade and diplomatic relationships with the Portuguese and to Olokun, god of the sea, wealth, and creativity. Another series of Portuguese heads also adorns the lower part of the carving. In the late 15th and 16th centuries, the Benin people probably associated the Portuguese, with their large ships from across

the sea, their powerful weapons, and their wealth in metals, cloth, and other goods, with Olokun, the deity they deemed responsible for abundance and prosperity.

Ikegobo of Eresonyen A cast-brass royal shrine—an *ikegobo* or "altar to the hand" (FIG. **21-9**)—underscores the centrality of the sacred king in Benin culture. The altar features symmetrical hierarchical compositions centered on a Benin king, probably Eresonyen (r. ca. 1735–1750). At the top, flanking and supporting the oba, are smaller (and therefore lesser) members of his court, usually identified as priests. In front of them is a pair of leopards, animals the sacred king sacrificed and symbolic of his power over all creatures. Similar compositions are common in Benin arts, as exemplified by the royal plaque (FIG. I-1) discussed in the Introduction. Here, the artist also distorted the king's proportions to emphasize his head, the seat of his will and power. Benin men celebrate a festival of the head called Igue, and one of the king's praise names is "great head." King Eresonyen appears again as the largest figure on the cylindrical body of the altar. The oba and other high-ranking officials offered sacrifices at the ikegobo to ensure the king's continued strength and achievement.

Sapi Between 1490 and 1540, some peoples on the Atlantic coast of Africa in present-day Sierra Leone, whom the Portuguese collectively called the Sapi, created art not only for themselves but also for Portuguese explorers and traders, who took the objects back to Europe. The Portuguese commissions included delicate spoons, forks, and elaborate containers usually referred to as saltcellars, as well as boxes, hunting horns, and knife handles. Salt was a valuable commodity, used both as a flavoring and as a food preservative. Costly saltcellars were prestige items that graced the tables of the European elite. Sapi sculptors meticulously carved the saltcellars from elephant tusk ivory, which was plentiful in those early days and was one of the coveted exports in early West and Central African trade with Europe. The Sapi export ivories are a fascinating hybrid art form. Characterized by refined detail and careful finish, they are the earliest examples of African tourist art.

Art historians have attributed the saltcellar shown here (FIG. **21-10**), almost 17 inches high, to the MASTER OF THE SYMBOLIC EXECUTION, one of the three major Sapi ivory carvers during the period. The saltcellar, which depicts an execution scene, is the source of the artist's assigned name. A kneeling figure with a shield in one hand holds an ax (restored) in the other hand over another seated figure about to lose his head. On the ground before the executioner, severed heads grimly testify to the executioner's power. A double zigzag line separates the lid of the globular container from the rest of the vessel. This vessel rests in turn on a circular platform held up by slender rods adorned with crocodile images. Two male and two female figures sit between these rods, grasping them. The men wear European-style pants and have long, straight hair. The women wear skirts, and the elaborate raised patterns on their upper chests surely represent decorative scars. The European components of this saltcellar include the overall design of a spherical container on a pedestal and some of the geometric patterning on the base and the sphere, as well as certain elements of dress, such as the shirts and hats. Distinctly African are the style of the human heads and figures and their proportions, the latter skewed to emphasize the head. Identical large noses with flaring nostrils, as well as the conventions for rendering eyes and lips, characterize Sapi stone figures from the same region and period. Scholars do not know whether it was the African carver or the European patron who specified the subject matter and the configurations of various parts, but the Sapi works testify to a fruitful artistic interaction between Africans and Europeans during the early 16th century.

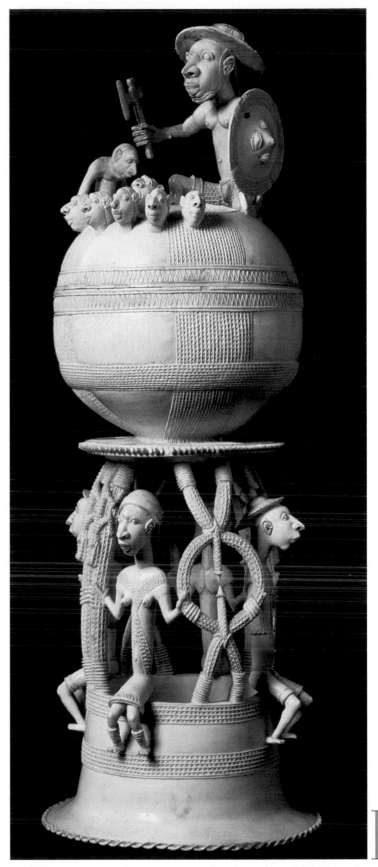

1 in.

21-10 MASTER OF THE SYMBOLIC EXECUTION, saltcellar, Sapi-Portuguese, from Sierra Leone, ca. 1490–1540. Ivory, 1' 4⅞" high. Museo Nazionale Preistorico e Etnografico Luigi Pigorini, Rome.

The Sapi exported saltcellars combining African and Portuguese traits. This one represents an execution scene with an African-featured man wearing European pants seated among severed heads.

19TH CENTURY

Archaeology and field research in Africa (mainly interviews with local people) have provided much more detail on the use, function, and meaning of African art objects produced during the past two centuries.

Kota Among the many African peoples who venerate their ancestors are the Kalabari Ijaw (FIG. 21-1) and the Kota, who collect the cranial and other bones (*relics*) of the deceased and place them in special containers (*reliquaries*) crowned by guardian figures called *mbulu ngulu* (FIG. **21-11**). These figures have severely stylized bodies in the form of an open diamond below a wood head. The Kota sculptors covered both the head and the abstract body with strips and sheets of polished copper and brass. The Kota believe the gleaming surfaces repel evil. The simplified heads have hairstyles flattened out laterally above and beside the face. Geometric ridges, borders,

and subdivisions add a textured elegance to the shiny forms. The copper alloy on most of these images is reworked sheet brass (or copper wire) taken from brass basins originating in Europe and traded into this area of equatorial Africa in the 18th and 19th centuries. The Kota inserted the lower portion of the image into the box of ancestral relics.

Bamum Art crafted to honor royalty was also a major genre of 19th-century African art production. In the kingdom of Bamum in present-day Cameroon, the ruler lived in a palace compound at the capital city of Foumban until its destruction in 1910. The royal arts of Bamum make extensive use of richly colored textiles and luminous materials, such as glass beads and cowrie shells. The ultimate status symbol was the king's throne. The throne illustrated here (FIG. **21-12**) belonged to King Nsangu (r. 1865–1872 and 1885–1887). Intertwining blue and black serpents decorate the cylindrical seat. Above are the figures of two of the king's retainers, perpetually at his service. One, a man, holds the royal drinking horn. The other is a woman carrying a serving bowl in her hands. Below

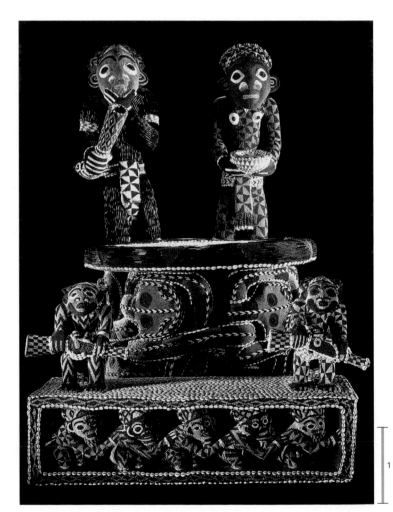

21-11 Reliquary guardian figure (mbulu ngulu), Kota, Gabon, 19th or early 20th century. Wood, copper, iron, and brass, 1' 9 1/16" high. Musée Barbier-Mueller, Geneva.

Kota guardian figures have large heads and bodies in the form of an open diamond. Polished copper and brass sheets cover the wood forms. The Kota believe gleaming surfaces repel evil.

21-12 Throne and footstool of King Nsangu, Bamum, Cameroon, ca. 1870. Wood, textile, glass beads, and cowrie shells, 5' 9" high. Museum für Völkerkunde, Staatliche Museen zu Berlin, Berlin.

King Nsangu's throne features luminous beads and shells and richly colored textiles. The decoration includes intertwining serpents, male and female retainers, and bodyguards with European rifles.

are two of the king's bodyguards wielding European rifles. Dancing figures decorate the rectangular footstool. When the king sat on this throne (compare FIG. 21-22), his rich garments complemented the bright colors of his seat, advertising his wealth and power to all who were admitted to his palace.

Fon The founding of the Fon kingdom in the present-day Republic of Benin dates to around 1600. Under King Guezo (r. 1818–1858), the Fon became a regional power with an economy based on trade in palm oil. After his first military victory, Guezo's son Glele (r. 1858–1889) commissioned a prisoner of war, AKATI AKPELE KENDO, to make a life-size iron statue (FIG. 21-13) of a warrior, probably Gu, the Fon god of war, for a battle shrine in Glele's palace at Ahomey. This *bocio,* or empowerment figure, was the centerpiece of a circle of iron swords and other weapons set vertically into the ground. The warrior strides forward with swords in both hands, ready to do battle. He wears a crown of miniature weapons and tools on his head. The form of the crown echoes the circle of swords around the statue. The Fon believed the bocio

protected their king, and they transported it to the battlefield whenever they set out to fight an enemy force. King Glele's iron warrior is remarkable for its size and for the fact that not only is the patron's name known but so, too, is the artist's name—a rare instance in Africa before the 20th century.

Kongo The Congo River formed the principal transportation route for the peoples of Central Africa during the 19th century. Some of the most distinctive African artworks of that period come from Kongo, for example, the large standing statue (FIG. 21-14) shown here. It represents a man bristling with nails and blades—a Kongo *nkisi n'kondi* (power figure). Consecrated by priests using precise ritual formulas, these images embodied spirits believed to heal and give life, or sometimes to inflict harm, disease, or even death. Each figure had its specific role, just as it wore particular medicines—here protruding from the abdomen and featuring a large cowrie shell. The Kongo also activated every image differently. Owners appealed to a figure's forces every time they inserted a nail or blade, as if to prod the spirit to do its work

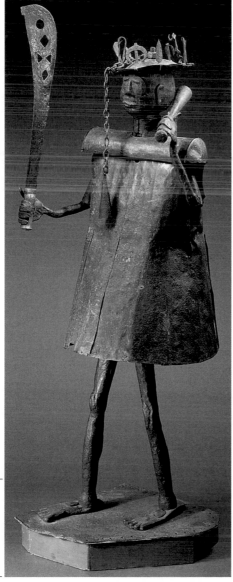

21-13 AKATI AKPELE KENDO, warrior figure (Gu?), from the palace of King Glele, Abomey, Fon, Republic of Benin, 1858–1859. Iron, 5' 5" high. Musée du quai Branly, Paris (on loan to the Musée du Louvre, Paris).

This bocio, or empowerment figure, probably representing the war god Gu, was the centerpiece of a circle of iron swords. The Fon believed it protected their king, and they set it up on the battlefield.

1 ft.

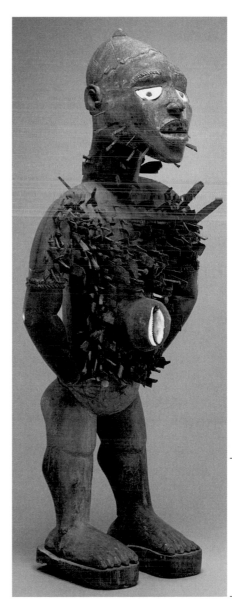

21-14 Nail figure (nkisi n'kondi), Kongo, from Shiloango River area, Democratic Republic of Congo, ca. 1875–1900. Wood, nails, blades, medicinal materials, and cowrie shell, 3' 10¾" high. Detroit Institute of Arts, Detroit.

Only priests using ritual formulas could consecrate Kongo power figures, which embody spirits that can heal or inflict harm. The statue has simplified anatomical forms and an oversized head.

1 ft.

People invoked other spirits by repeating certain chants, by rubbing the images, or by applying special powders. The roles of power figures varied enormously, from curing minor ailments to stimulating crop growth, from punishing thieves to weakening an enemy. Very large Kongo figures, such as this one, had exceptional ascribed powers and aided entire communities. Although benevolent for their owners, the figures stood at the boundary between life and death, and most villagers held them in awe. Compared with the sculptures of most other African peoples, this Kongo figure is relatively naturalistic, although the carver simplified the facial features and magnified the size of the head for emphasis.

Chokwe The Chokwe occupy the area of west-central Africa corresponding to parts of northeastern Angola and southwestern Democratic Republic of Congo. Local legend claims the Chokwe are the descendants of the widely traveled Chibinda Ilunga, who won fame as a hunter. He married a princess named Lueji, who was a hereditary ruler of one of the kingdoms of the Lunda Empire, an important regional power during the 16th through 19th centuries. Lueji gave Chibinda a sacred bracelet, the basis and symbol of her rule, and he taught the Lunda to be great hunters, enriched the kingdom, and extended its territory. The Chokwe, one of the population groups resulting from that territorial expansion,

became skilled elephant hunters and ivory traders. They eventually revolted against the Lunda kings and brought about the collapse of the Lunda Empire in the mid-19th century.

The Chokwe revere Chibinda Ilunga as founder, hunter, and civilizing hero, and he figures prominently in their royal arts. The statue illustrated here (FIG. **21-15**) is one of the finest examples. It shows the legendary hunter-king wearing a chief's barkcloth-and-rattan headdress and holding a staff in his right hand and, in his left hand, a medicine horn containing powerful substances to aid hunters. The sculptor portrayed Chibinda with a muscular body and oversized arms and feet to underscore the hunter's manual dexterity and ability to undertake long journeys. A rare feature of this and other Chokwe figures is the use of human hair for Chibinda's beard.

Dogon The Dogon live south of the inland delta region of the great Niger River in what is today Mali. One of the most common themes in Dogon art—and in African art in general—is the human couple. A characteristic Dogon example is the statue of a linked man and woman illustrated here (FIG. **21-16**). It dates to the early 19th century and is probably a shrine or altar, although contextual information is lacking. Interpretations vary, but the image vividly documents primary gender roles in traditional African

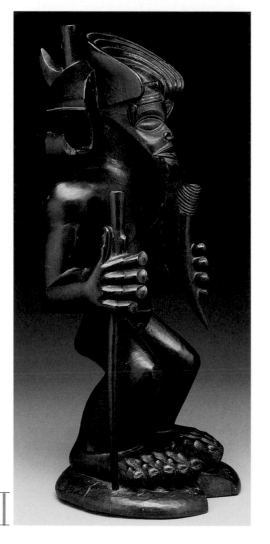

21-15 Chibinda Ilunga, Chokwe, from Angola or Democratic Republic of Congo, late 19th to 20th century. Wood and human hair, 1′ 4″ high. Kimbell Art Museum, Fort Worth.

The Chokwe claim descent from the legendary hunter Chibinda Ilunga, portrayed in art as a muscular man with a chief's headdress, oversized hands and feet, and a beard of human hair.

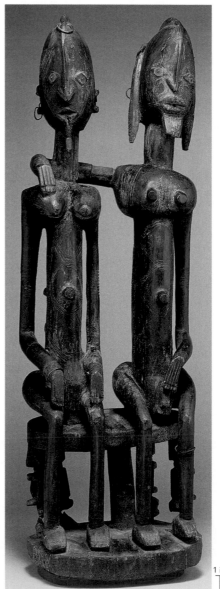

21-16 Seated couple, Dogon, Mali, ca. 1800–1850. Wood, 2′ 4″ high. Metropolitan Museum of Art, New York (gift of Lester Wunderman).

This Dogon carving of a linked man and woman documents gender roles in traditional African society. The protective man wears a quiver on his back. The nurturing woman carries a child on hers.

society. The man wears a quiver on his back. The woman carries a child on hers. Thus, the man assumes a protective role as hunter or warrior, the woman a nurturing role. The slightly larger man reaches behind his mate's neck and touches her breast, as if to protect her. His left hand points to his genitalia. Four stylized figures support the stool upon which they sit. They are probably either spirits or ancestors, but the identity of the larger figures is uncertain.

The strong stylization of Dogon sculptures contrasts sharply with the organic, relatively realistic treatment of the human body in Kongo and Chokwe art (FIGS. 21-14 and 21-15). The artist who carved the Dogon couple (FIG. 21-16) based the forms more on the idea or concept of the human body than on observation of individual heads, torsos, and limbs. The linked body parts are tubes and columns articulated inorganically. The carver reinforced the almost abstract geometry of the overall composition by incising rectilinear and diagonal patterns on the surfaces. The Dogon artist also understood the importance of space, and charged the voids, as well as the sculptural forms, with rhythm and tension.

20TH CENTURY

The art of Africa during the past 100 years ranges from traditional works depicting age-old African themes to modern works that are international in both content and style (for example, FIG. 16-8).

Benin In 1897, when the British sacked Benin City, there were still 17 shrines to ancestors in the Benin royal palace. Today, only one 20th-century altar (FIG. 21-17) remains. According to oral history, it is similar to centuries-earlier versions. With a base of sacred riverbank clay, it is an assemblage of varied materials, objects, and symbols: a central copper-alloy altarpiece depicting a sacred king flanked by members of his entourage, plus copper-alloy heads, each fitted on top with an ivory tusk carved in relief. Behind are wood staffs and metal bells. The heads represent both the kings themselves and, through the durability of their material, the enduring nature of kingship. Their glistening surfaces, seen as red and signaling danger, repel evil forces that might adversely affect the shrine and thus the king and kingdom. Elephant-tusk relief carvings atop the heads commemorate important events and personages in Benin history. Their bleached white color signifies purity and goodness (probably of royal ancestors), and the tusks themselves represent male physical power. The carved wood rattle-staffs standing at the back refer to generations of dynastic ancestors by their bamboolike, segmented forms. The rattle-staffs and the pyramidal copper-alloy bells serve the important function of calling royal ancestral spirits to rituals performed at the altar.

The Benin king's head stands for wisdom, good judgment, and divine guidance for the kingdom (compare FIG. 21-9). The several heads in the ancestral altar multiply these qualities. By means of animal sacrifices at this site, the living king annually purifies his own head (and being) by invoking the collective strength of his ancestors. Thus, the varied objects, symbols, colors, and materials composing this shrine contribute both visually and ritually to the imaging of royal power, as well as to its history, renewal, and perpetuation.

Osei Bonsu Traditionally, Africans have tended not to exalt artistic individuality as much as Westerners have. Many people, in fact, still consider African art as anonymous, but that is primarily because early researchers rarely asked for artists' names. Nonetheless, art historians can recognize many individual hands even when an artist's name has not been recorded. During the past century, art historians and anthropologists have been systematically noting the names and life histories of individual artists, many of whom have strong regional reputations. One of these was OSEI BONSU (1900–1976), a master carver based in the Asante capital, Kumasi, in present-day Ghana. A more naturalistic rendering of the face and cross-hatched eyebrows are distinctive features of Bonsu's personal style.

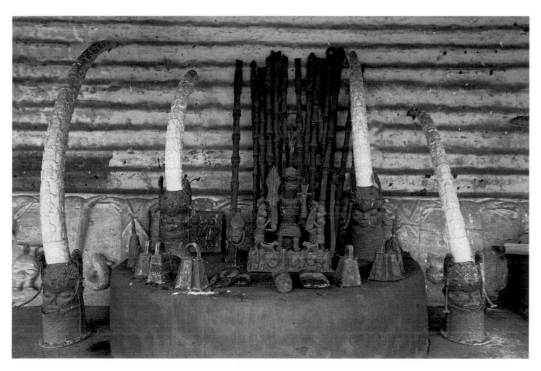

21-17 Royal ancestral altar of King Eweka II, in the palace in Benin City, Nigeria, photographed in 1970. Clay, copper alloy, wood, and ivory.

This shrine to the heads of royal ancestors is an assemblage of materials, objects, and symbols. By sacrificing animals at this altar, the Benin king annually invokes the collective strength of his ancestors.

The gold-covered wood sculpture illustrated here (FIG. 21-18) is a characteristic example of Bonsu's work. It depicts two men sitting at a table of food, and is a *linguist's staff*, so named because its carrier often speaks for a king or chief. The form of the staff reflects an Asante proverb: "Food is for its rightful owner, not for the one who happens to be hungry." Food is a metaphor for the office the king or chief rightfully holds. The "hungry" man lusts for the office. The linguist, who is an important counselor and adviser to the king, might carry this staff to a meeting at which a rival contests the king's title to the stool (his throne, the office). Many hundreds of Asante sculptures have proverbs or other sayings associated with them, resulting in a rich verbal tradition related to Asante visual arts.

Olowe of Ise The leading Yoruba sculptor of the early 20th century was OLOWE OF ISE (ca. 1873–1938). Kings throughout Yorubaland (southern Nigeria and southern Benin) commissioned Olowe to carve reliefs, masks, bowls, veranda posts, and other works. The king of Ikere, for example, employed Olowe for four years starting in 1910, during which he resided at Ikere and produced the magnificent carved and painted doors (FIG. 21-19) that marked the entrance to the shrine of

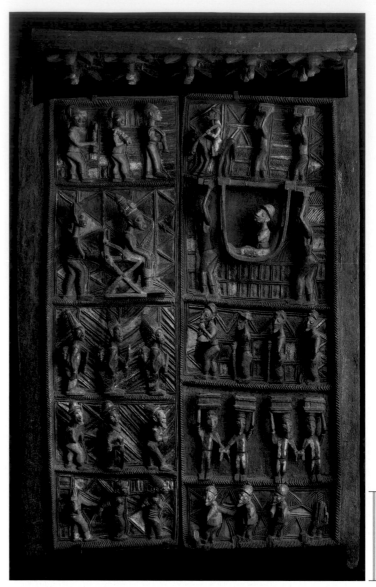

21-19 OLOWE OF ISE, doors from the shrine of the king's head in the royal palace, Ikere, Yoruba, Nigeria, 1910–1914. Painted wood, 6' high. British Museum, London.

Olowe's painted high-relief doors to the shrine of the king's head depict the 1897 visit of the British provincial commissioner to the Ikere palace. The enthroned Yoruba king is the largest figure.

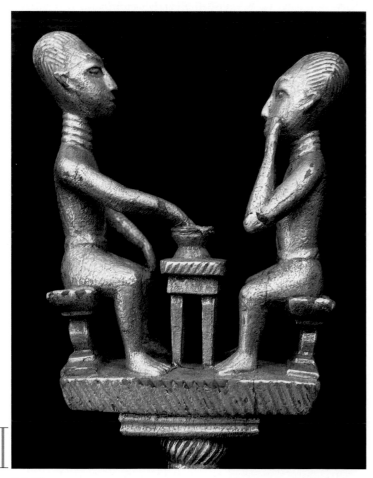

1 in.

21-18 OSEI BONSU, two men sitting at a table of food (linguist's staff), Asante, Ghana, mid-20th century. Wood and gold leaf, section shown 10" high. Collection of the Paramount Chief of Offinso, Asante.

Bonsu carved this gold-covered wood linguist's staff for someone who could speak for the Asante king. At the top are two men sitting at a table of food—a metaphor for the office of the king.

the king's head in his palace in northeastern Yorubaland. Departing from convention, Olowe made the two doors of unequal width to accommodate a rare historical narrative in 10 panels in five registers. The reliefs recount the 1897 visit of the representative of the British Empire, Captain Ambrose, commissioner of Ondo province. Litter-bearers carry Ambrose into the palace compound, where the enthroned king—far larger than the British emissary—and his principal wife receive him. The other panels on each door depict the entourage of the two protagonists including, at the left, the king's bodyguards and other wives, and, on the right door, shackled slaves carrying chests. Characteristically for Olowe, the relief is so high some of the figures project as much as 6 inches from the surface, which has a vividly colored patterned background. Olowe also carved the veranda posts of the courtyard in front of the shrine.

African Masquerades

The art of masquerade has long been a quintessential African expressive form, laden with meaning and cultural importance. This is so today but was even more critically true in colonial times and earlier, when African masking societies boasted extensive regulatory and judicial powers. In stateless societies, such as those of the Senufo (FIG. 21-20) and Mende (FIG. 21-21), masks sometimes became so influential they had their own priests and served as power sources or as oracles. Societies empowered maskers to levy fines and to apprehend witches (usually defined as socially destructive people) and criminals, and to judge and punish them. Normally, however—especially today—masks are less threatening and more secular and educational and serve as diversions from the humdrum of daily life. Masked dancers usually embody either ancestors, seen as briefly returning to the human realm, or various nature spirits called upon for their special powers.

The mask, a costume ensemble's focal point, combines with held objects, music, and dance gestures to invoke a specific named character, almost always considered a spirit. A few masked spirits appear by themselves, but more often several characters come out together or in turn. Maskers enact a broad range of human, animal, and fantastic otherworldly behavior that is usually both stimulating and didactic. Masquerades, in fact, vary in function or effect along a continuum from weak spirit power and strong entertainment value to those rarely seen but possessing vast executive powers backed by powerful shrines. Most operate between these extremes, crystallizing varieties of human and animal behavior—caricatured, ordinary, comic, bizarre, serious, or threatening. These actions inform and affect audience members because of their dramatic staging. It is the purpose of most masquerades to move people, to affect them, to effect change.

Thus, masks and masquerades are mediators—between men and women, youths and elders, initiated and uninitiated, powers of nature and those of human agency, and even life and death. For many groups in West and Central Africa, masking plays (or once played) an active role in the socialization process, especially for men, who control most masks. Maskers carry boys (and, more rarely, girls) away from their mothers to bush initiation camps, put them through ordeals and schooling, and welcome them back to society as men months or even years later. A second major role is in aiding the transformation of important deceased persons

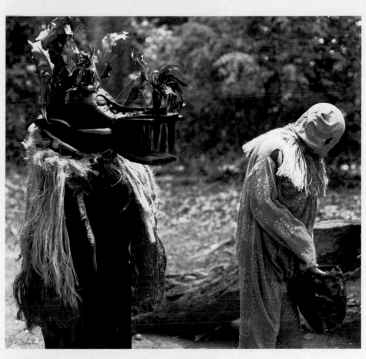

21-20 Senufo masqueraders, Côte d'Ivoire, photographed ca. 1980–1990. ■◀

Senufo masqueraders are always men. Their masks often represent composite creatures incarnating both ancestors and bush powers. They fight malevolent spirits with their aggressively powerful forms.

into productive ancestors who, in their new roles, can bring benefits to the living community. Because most masking cultures are agricultural, it is not surprising that Africans often invoke masquerades to increase the productivity of the fields, to stimulate the growth of crops, and later to celebrate the harvest.

Senufo The Senufo of the western Sudan region in what is now northern Côte d'Ivoire number more than a million today and produce many different art forms. Perhaps the most interesting are the masks used in the important communal rite of the masquerade (see "African Masquerades," above). Senufo men dance many masks, mostly in the context of Poro, the primary men's association for socialization and initiation, a protracted process taking nearly 20 years to complete. Maskers also perform at funerals and other public spectacles. Large Senufo masks (for example, FIG. **21-20**) are composite creatures, combining characteristics of antelope, crocodile, warthog, hyena, and human: sweeping horns, a head, and an open-jawed snout with sharp teeth. These masks incarnate both ancestors and bush powers that combat witchcraft and sorcery, malevolent spirits, and the wandering dead. They are protectors who fight evil with their aggressively powerful forms and their medicines. At funerals, Senufo maskers attend the corpse and help expel the deceased

from the village. This is the deceased individual's final transition, a rite of passage parallel to that undergone by all men during their years of Poro socialization. When an important person dies, the masquerades, music, dancing, costuming, and feasting together constitute a festive and complex work of art that transcends any one mask or character.

Mende The Mende are farmers who occupy the Atlantic coast of Africa in Sierra Leone. Although men own and perform most masks in Africa, in Mende society the women control and dance Sande society masks. Mende men perform the Poro society masks. The Sande society controls the initiation, education, and acculturation of Mende girls. The glistening black surface of Mende Sowie masks (FIG. **21-21**) evokes female ancestral spirits newly emergent from their underwater homes (also symbolized by the turtle on top). The mask and its parts refer to ideals of female beauty, morality, and behavior. A high, broad forehead signifies wisdom and

21-21 Female mask, Mende, Sierra Leone, mid- to late 20th century. Painted wood, 1' 2½" high. Fowler Museum of Cultural History, University of California, Los Angeles (gift of the Wellcome Trust). ◼

This Mende mask refers to ideals of female beauty, morality, and behavior. The large fore-head signifies wisdom, the neck design beauty and health, and the plaited hair the order of ideal households.

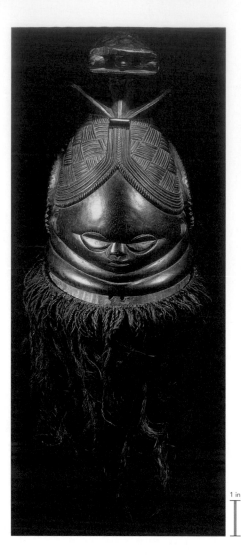

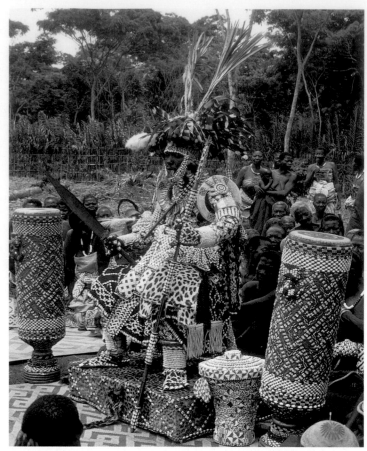

21-22 Kuba King Kot a-Mbweeky III during a display for photographer and filmmaker Eliot Elisofon in 1970, Mushenge, Democratic Republic of Congo.

Eagle feathers, leopard skin, cowrie shells, imported beads, raffia, and other materials combine to make the Kuba king larger than life. His costume underscores his wealth, dignity, and military might.

success. The neck ridges have multiple meanings. They are signs of beauty, good health, and prosperity and also refer to the ripples in the water from which the water spirits emerge. Intricately woven or plaited hair is the essence of harmony and order found in ideal households. A small closed mouth and downcast eyes indicate the silent, serious demeanor expected of recent initiates. Sande women wear these masks on top of their heads as headdresses, with black raffia and cloth costumes to hide the wearers' identity during public performances. Elaborate coiffures, shiny black color, dainty triangular-shaped faces with slit eyes, rolls around the neck, and actual and carved versions of amulets and various emblems on the top commonly characterize Sowie masks. These symbolize the adult women's roles as wives, mothers, providers for the family, and keepers of medicines for use within the Sande association and the society at large.

Kuba Throughout history, African costumes have been laden with meaning and have projected messages that all members of the society could read. A photograph (FIG. **21-22**) taken in 1970 shows the Kuba (Democratic Republic of Congo) king Kot a-Mbweeky III (r. 1969–) seated in state before his court, bedecked in a dazzling multimedia costume with many symbolic elements. The king commissioned the costume he wears and now has become art himself. Eagle feathers, leopard skin, cowrie shells, imported beads, raffia, and other materials combine to overload and expand the image of the man, making him larger than life and most certainly a multimedia work of art. He holds not one but two

weapons, symbolic of his military might and underscoring his wealth, dignity, and grandeur. The man, with his regalia, embodies the office of sacred kingship. He is a superior being, in fact and figuratively, raised upon a dais, flanked by ornate drums, with a treasure basket of sacred relics by his left foot. The geometric patterns on the king's costume and nearby objects, and the abundance and redundancy of rich materials, epitomize the opulent style of Kuba court arts.

African Art Today During the past two centuries and especially in recent decades, the encroachments of Christianity, Islam, Western education, and market economies have led to increasing secularization in all the arts of Africa. Many contemporary African artists have trained or worked abroad and have achieved international prominence (see Chapter 16). Also, in many areas of the continent, traditional figures and masks earlier commissioned for shrines or as incarnations of ancestors or spirits are now made mostly for sale as tourist arts. Nonetheless, despite the growing importance of urbanism, most African people still live in rural communities. Traditional values, although under pressure, hold considerable force in villages especially, and some people adhere to spiritual beliefs that uphold traditional art forms. African art remains as varied as the vast continent itself and continues to evolve.

Africa

Prehistory and Early Cultures

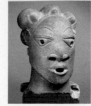

▌ Humankind apparently originated in Africa, and some of the oldest known artworks come from the Apollo 11 Cave in Namibia. They date around 23,000 BCE.

▌ The Nok culture of central Nigeria produced the oldest African sculptures in the round between 500 BCE and 200 CE. The earliest examples of African bronze-casting using the lost-wax method are the 9th- or 10th-century CE sculptures found at Igbo Ukwu (Nigeria).

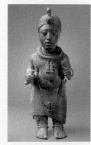

Nok terracotta head,
ca. 500 BCE–200 CE

11th to 18th Centuries

▌ The sculptors of Ile-Ife (Nigeria) fashioned images of their kings in an unusually naturalistic style during the 11th and 12th centuries, but the heads of the figures are disproportionately large, as in most African artworks.

▌ This period saw the construction of Islamic and Christian shrines emulating foreign models but employing African building methods, for example, the adobe Great Mosque at Djenne (Mali).

▌ In southern Africa, Great Zimbabwe conducted prosperous trade with Mesopotamia and China long before the first contact with Europeans. Impressive stone walls and towers enclosed the royal palace complex.

▌ The Benin kingdom in the Lower Niger region, probably founded in the 13th century, reached its zenith in the 16th century. Benin sculptors excelled in ivory carving and bronze-casting, producing artworks glorifying the royal family.

▌ An early example of the interaction between African artists and European patrons is the series of Sapi ivory saltcellars from Sierra Leone datable between 1490 and 1540.

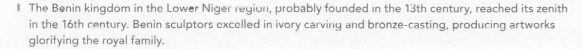

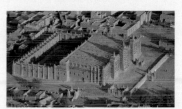

Ife king,
11th to 12th century

Great Mosque, Djenne, 13th century

19th Century

▌ Most of the traditional forms of African art continued into the 19th century. Among these are sculptures and shrines connected with the veneration of ancestors, such as the Kalabari Ijaw screen honoring a deceased chief. Especially impressive examples of African woodcarving are the Kongo power figures bristling with nails and blades and the Dogon sculptures of male and female couples. Although stylistically diverse, most African sculpture exhibits hierarchy of scale, both among figures and within the human body, where enlarged heads are common.

▌ The royal arts also flourished in the 19th century. One of the earliest African artists whose name survives is Akati Akpele Kendo, who worked for the Fon king Glele around 1858, but most African art remains anonymous.

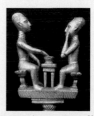

Kalabari Ijaw ancestral screen,
late 19th century

20th Century

▌ As in the 19th century, traditional arts flourished in 20th-century Africa, but the names of many more individual 20th-century artists are known. Two of the most famous are the Asante sculptor Osei Bonsu and the Yoruba sculptor Olowe of Ise.

▌ The fashioning of masks for festive performances remains important in many parts of Africa today. Senufo masqueraders are almost always men, even when the masks they dance are female, but in Mende society, women are maskers too.

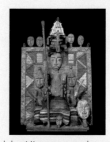

Bonsu, linguist's staff,
mid-20th century

Notes

INTRODUCTION

1. Quoted in George Heard Hamilton, *Painting and Sculpture in Europe, 1880–1940,* 6th ed. (New Haven, Conn.: Yale University Press, 1993), 345.

2. Quoted in *Josef Albers: Homage to the Square* (New York: Museum of Modern Art, 1964), n.p.

CHAPTER 1

1. The chronology adopted in this chapter is that of John Baines and Jaromír Malék, *Atlas of Ancient Egypt* (Oxford: Oxford University Press, 1980), 36–37, and the division of kingdoms is that of, among others, Mark Lehner, *The Complete Pyramids* (New York: Thames & Hudson, 1997), 8–9, and David P. Silverman, ed., *Ancient Egypt* (New York: Oxford University Press, 1997), 20–39.

CHAPTER 2

1. Galen, *De placitis Hippocratis et Platonis,* 5. Translated by J. J. Pollitt, *The Art of Ancient Greece: Sources and Documents* (New York: Cambridge University Press, 1990), 76.

2. Pliny the Elder, *Natural History,* 34.55. Translated by Pollitt, 75.

3. Pliny, *Natural History,* 36.20.

4. Lucian, *Amores,* 13–14; *Imagines,* 6.

5. Pliny, *Natural History,* 35.110.

CHAPTER 3

1. Livy, *History of Rome,* 25.40.1–3.

2. Pliny the Elder, *Natural History,* 35.133.

CHAPTER 4

1. Augustine, *City of God,* 16.26.

2. Procopius, *De aedificiis,* 1.1.23ff. Translated by Cyril Mango, *The Art of the Byzantine Empire, 312–1453: Sources and Documents* (reprint of 1972 ed., Toronto: University of Toronto Press, 1986), 74.

3. Paulus Silentarius, *Descriptio Sanctae Sophiae,* 489, 668. Translated by Mango, 83, 86.

4. Procopius, op. cit., 1.1.23ff. Translated by Mango, 75.

5. *Libri Carolini,* 4.2. Translated by Herbert L. Kessler, *Spiritual Seeing: Picturing God's Invisibility in Medieval Art* (Philadelphia: University of Pennsylvania Press, 2000), 119.

CHAPTER 6

1. Translated by Françoise Henry, *The Book of Kells* (New York: Alfred A. Knopf, 1974), 165.

2. *Beowulf,* 3162–3164, translated by Kevin Crossley-Holland (New York: Farrar, Straus & Giroux, 1968), 119.

3. Translated by Charles P. Parkhurst, Jr., in Elizabeth G. Holt, *A Documentary History of Art,* 2d ed. (Princeton, N.J.: Princeton University Press, 1981), 1: 18.

4. Bernard of Clairvaux, *Apologia,* 12.28–29. Translated by Conrad Rudolph, *The "Things of Greater Importance": Bernard of Clairvaux's* Apologia *and the Medieval Attitude toward Art* (Philadelphia: University of Pennsylvania Press, 1990), 279, 283.

5. Translated by Calvin B. Kendall, *The Allegory of the Church: Romanesque Portals and Their Verse Inscriptions* (Toronto: University of Toronto Press, 1998), 207.

CHAPTER 7

1. Giorgio Vasari, *Introduzione alle tre arti del disegno* (1550), ch. 3. Translated in Paul Frankl, *The Gothic: Literary Sources and Interpretation through Eight Centuries* (Princeton, N.J.: Princeton University Press, 1960), 290–291, 859–860.

2. Translated by Erwin Panofsky, *Abbot Suger on the Abbey Church of Saint-Denis and Its Art Treasures,* 2d ed. (Princeton, N.J.: Princeton University Press, 1979), 101.

3. Ibid., 65.

4. Dante, *Divine Comedy,* Purgatory, 11.81.

5. Translated by Roland Behrendt, *Johannes Trithemius, In Praise of Scribes: De laude scriptorum* (Lawrence, Kans.: Coronado Press, 1974), 71.

6. Frankl, 55.

CHAPTER 8

1. Giorgio Vasari, *Lives of the Painters, Sculptors and Architects,* translated by Gaston du C. de Vere (New York: Knopf, 1996), 1: 304.

2. Quoted in H. W. Janson, *The Sculpture of Donatello* (Princeton, N.J.: Princeton University Press, 1965), 154.

3. Vasari, *Lives,* 1: 318.

CHAPTER 9

1. Leonardo da Vinci to Ludovico Sforza, ca. 1480–1481. Elizabeth Gilmore Holt, ed., *A Documentary History of Art* (Princeton: Princeton University Press, 1981), 1: 274–275.

2. Quoted in James M. Saslow, *The Poetry of Michelangelo: An Annotated Translation* (New Haven, Conn.: Yale University Press, 1991), 407.

3. Giorgio Vasari, *Lives of the Painters, Sculptors and Architects,* translated by Gaston du C. de Vere (New York: Knopf, 1996), 2: 736.

4. Quoted in A. Richard Turner, *Renaissance Florence: The Invention of a New Art* (New York: Abrams, 1997), 163.

5. Quoted in Bruce Boucher, *Andrea Palladio: The Architect in His Time* (New York: Abbeville Press, 1998), 229.

6. Quoted in Robert J. Clements, *Michelangelo's Theory of Art* (New York: New York University Press, 1961), 320.

7. Translated by Erwin Panofsky, in Wolfgang Stechow, *Northern Renaissance Art 1400–1600: Sources and Documents* (Evanston, Ill.: Northwestern University Press, 1989), 123.

CHAPTER 10

1. Filippo Baldinucci, *Vita del Cavaliere Giovanni Lorenzo Bernini* (1681). Translated by Robert Enggass, in Robert Enggass and Jonathan Brown, *Italian and Spanish Art 1600–1750: Sources and Documents* (Evanston, Ill.: Northwestern University Press, 1992), 116.

2. John Milton, *Il Penseroso* (1631, published 1645), 166.

3. Translated by Kristin Lohse Belkin, *Rubens* (London: Phaidon, 1998), 47.

4. Albert Blankert, *Johannes Vermeer van Delft 1632–1675* (Utrecht: Spectrum, 1975), 133, no. 51. Translated by Bob Haak, *The Golden Age: Dutch Painters of the Seventeenth Century* (New York: Abrams, 1984), 450.

CHAPTER 11

1. Translated by Robert Goldwater and Marco Treves, eds., *Artists on Art,* 3d ed. (New York: Pantheon Books, 1958), 157.

2. Quoted in Thomas A. Bailey, *The American Pageant: A History of the Republic,* 2d ed. (Boston: Heath, 1961), 280.

3. Translated by Elfriede Heyer and Roger C. Norton in Charles Harrison, Paul Wood, and Jason Gaiger, eds., *Art in Theory 1648–1815: An Anthology of Changing Ideas* (Oxford: Blackwell, 2000), 453.

CHAPTER 12

1. Translated by Jason Gaiger, in Charles Harrison, Paul Wood, and Jason Gaiger, eds., *Art in Theory 1815–1900: An Anthology of Changing Ideas* (Oxford: Blackwell, 1998), 54.

2. Quoted by Brian Lukacher, in Stephen F. Eisenman, ed., *Nineteenth Century Art: A Critical History,* 4th ed. (New York: Thames & Hudson, 2011), 126.

3. Quoted in John W. McCoubrey, *American Art 1700–1960: Sources and Documents* (Englewood Cliffs, N.J.: Prentice Hall, 1965), 98.

4. Quoted in Eisenman, 336.

5. Quoted in Nikolai Cikovsky Jr. and Franklin Kelly, *Winslow Homer* (Washington, D.C.: National Gallery of Art, 1995), 26.

6. Quoted in Lloyd Goodrich, *Thomas Eakins, His Life and Work* (New York: Whitney Museum of American Art, 1933), 51–52.

7. Quoted in Naomi Rosenblum, *A World History of Photography,* 4th ed. (New York: Abbeville Press, 2007), 69.

CHAPTER 13

1. Quoted in Linda Nochlin, *Realism* (Harmondsworth: Penguin, 1971), 28.

2. Clement Greenberg, "Modernist Painting," *Art and Literature,* no. 4 (Spring 1965): 193–194.

3. Quoted in John W. McCoubrey, *American Art 1700–1960: Sources and Documents* (Englewood Cliffs, N.J.: Prentice Hall, 1965), 184.

4. Vincent van Gogh to Theo van Gogh, September 1888, in J. van Gogh–Bonger and V. W. van Gogh, eds., *The Complete Letters of Vincent van Gogh* (Greenwich, Conn.: 1979), 3: 534.

5. Vincent van Gogh to Theo van Gogh, July 16, 1888, in W. H. Auden, ed., *Van Gogh: A Self-Portrait. Letters Revealing His Life as a Painter* (New York: Dutton, 1963), 299.

6. Quoted in Belinda Thompson, ed., *Gauguin by Himself* (Boston: Little, Brown, 1993), 270–271.

7. Cézanne to Émile Bernard, March 1904. Quoted in Robert Goldwater and Marco Treves, eds., *Artists on Art,* 3d ed. (New York: Pantheon, 1945), 363.

8. Cézanne to Émile Bernard, April 15, 1904. Ibid., 363.

9. Quoted in George Heard Hamilton, *Painting and Sculpture in Europe, 1880–1940,* 6th ed. (New Haven, Conn.: Yale University Press, 1993), 124.

10. Quoted in Victor Frisch and Joseph T. Shipley, *Auguste Rodin* (New York: Stokes, 1939), 203.

CHAPTER 14

1. Quoted in John Elderfield, *The "Wild Beasts": Fauvism and Its Affinities* (New York: Museum of Modern Art, 1976), 29.

2. Quoted in Frederick S. Levine, *The Apocalyptic Vision: The Art of Franz Marc as German Expressionism* (New York: Harper & Row, 1979), 57.

3. Quoted in Sam Hunter, John Jacobus, and Daniel Wheeler, *Modern Art,* Rev. 3d. ed. (Upper Saddle River, N.J.: Prentice Hall, 2004), 121.

4. Quoted in George Heard Hamilton, *Painting and Sculpture in Europe, 1880–1940,* 6th ed. (New Haven, Conn.: Yale University Press, 1993), 246.

5. Ibid., 238.

6. Quoted in Edward Fry, ed., *Cubism* (London: Thames & Hudson, 1966), 112–113.

7. Pablo Picasso, "Statement to Simone Téry," in Charles Harrison and Paul Wood, eds., *Art in Theory 1900–2000: An Anthology of Changing Ideas* (Oxford: Blackwell, 2003), 649.

8. Quoted in Roland Penrose, *Picasso: His Life and Work,* Rev. ed. (New York: Harper & Row, 1971), 311.

9. Filippo Tommaso Marinetti, *The Foundation and Manifesto of Futurism* (*Le Figaro,* 20 February 1909). Translated by Joshua C. Taylor, in Herschel B. Chipp, *Theories of Modern Art: A Source Book by Artists and Critics* (Berkeley and Los Angeles: University of California Press, 1968), 286.

10. Hans Richter, *Dada: Art and Anti-Art* (London: Thames & Hudson, 1961), 57.

11. Translated by Howard Dearstyne, in Robert L. Herbert, *Modern Artists on Art,* 2d ed. (Mineola, N.Y.: Dover, 2000), 117.

12. Charles C. Eldredge, "The Arrival of European Modernism," *Art in America,* 61 (July–August 1973): 35.

13. Dorothy Norman, *Alfred Stieglitz: An American Seer* (Millerton, N.Y.: Aperture, 1973), 9–10.

14. Ibid., 161.

15. Quoted in William S. Rubin, *Dada, Surrealism, and Their Heritage* (New York: Museum of Modern Art, 1968), 64.

16. Quoted in Hamilton, *Painting and Sculpture,* 392.

17. Quoted in Rubin, *Dada, Surrealism,* 111.

18. Quoted in Hunter, Jacobus, and Wheeler, *Modern Art,* 179.

19. Quoted in William S. Rubin, *Miró in the Collection of the Museum of Modern Art* (New York: Museum of Modern Art, 1973), 32.

20. Quoted in Kenneth Frampton, *Modern Architecture: A Critical History,* 4th ed. (New York: Thames & Hudson, 2007), 147.

21. Quoted in Michel Seuphor, *Piet Mondrian: Life and Work* (New York: Abrams, 1956), 117.

22. Piet Mondrian, *Plastic Art and Pure Plastic Art* (1937), quoted in Hamilton, *Painting and Sculpture,* 319.

23. Quoted in Hamilton, *Painting and Sculpture,* 426.

24. Quoted in Robert L. Herbert, *Modern Artists on Art,* 2d ed. (Mineola, N.Y.: Dover, 2000), 173–179.

25. Piet Mondrian, *Dialogue on the New Plastic* (1919). Translated by Harry Holzman and Martin S. James, in Harrison and Wood, *Art in Theory 1900–1990,* 285.

26. Walter Gropius, from *The Manifesto of the Bauhaus,* April 1919.

27. Translated by Charles Haxthausen, in Barry Bergdoll, ed., *Bauhaus 1919–1933* (New York: Museum of Modern Art, 2009), 64.

28. Quoted in John Willett, *Art and Politics in the Weimar Period: The New Sobriety, 1917–1933* (New York: Da Capo Press, 1978), 119.

29. Quoted in Wayne Craven, *American Art: History and Culture* (Madison, Wis.: Brown & Benchmark, 2003), 403.

30. Quoted in Philip Johnson, *Mies van der Rohe,* Rev. ed. (New York: Museum of Modern Art, 1954), 200–201.

CHAPTER 15

1. Quoted in Dawn Ades and Andrew Forge, *Francis Bacon* (London: Thames & Hudson, 1985), 8; and David Sylvester, *The Brutality of Fact: Interviews with Francis Bacon,* 3d ed. (London: Thames & Hudson, 1987), 182.

2. Clement Greenberg, "Sculpture in Our Time," *Arts Magazine,* 32, no. 9 (June 1956): 22.

3. Quoted in Selden Rodman, *Conversations with Artists* (New York: Devin-Adair, 1957), 93–94.

4. Quoted in Deborah Wye, *Louise Bourgeois* (New York: Museum of Modern Art, 1982), 25.

5. Quoted in Richard Francis, *Jasper Johns* (New York: Abbeville, 1984), 21.

6. Andy Warhol, *The Philosophy of Andy Warhol* (New York: Harcourt Brace Jovanovich, 1975), 100.

7. Quoted in Christine Lindey, *Superrealist Painting and Sculpture* (London: Orbis, 1980), 130.

8. Quoted in Mary Jane Jacob, *Magdalena Abakanowicz* (New York: Abbeville, 1982), 94.

9. Quoted in Nancy Holt, ed., *The Writings of Robert Smithson* (New York: New York University Press, 1975), 111.

10. Quoted in Bruce McPherson, ed., *More Than "Meat Joy": Complete Performance Works and Selected Writings* (New Paltz, N.Y.: Documentext, 1979), 10–11.

11. Quoted in "Joseph Kosuth: Art as Idea as Idea," in Jeanne Siegel, ed., *Artwords: Discourse on the 60s and 70s* (Ann Arbor, Mich.: UMI Research Press, 1985), 221, 225.

CHAPTER 16

1. Quoted in Arlene Hirschfelder, *Artists and Craftspeople* (New York: Facts on File, 1994), 115.

2. Quoted in Donald Hall, *Corporal Politics* (Cambridge, Mass.: MIT List Visual Arts Center, 1993), 46.

3. Quoted in "Vietnam Memorial: America Remembers," *National Geographic,* 167, no. 5 (May 1985): 557.

CHAPTER 20

1. Bernal Díaz del Castillo, *The Discovery and Conquest of Mexico,* translated by A. P. Maudslay (New York: Farrar, Straus & Giroux, 1956), 218–219.

Glossary

A

a secco Italian, "dried." See *fresco*.

abacus The uppermost portion of the *capital* of a *column*, usually a thin slab.

abbess See *abbey*.

abbey A religious community under the direction of an abbot (for monks) or an abbess (for nuns).

abbot See *abbey*.

abhaya See *mudra*.

abrasion The rubbing or grinding of stone or another material to produce a smooth finish.

abstract Non-representational; *forms* and *colors* arranged without reference to the depiction of an object.

Abstract Expressionism The first major American avant-garde movement, Abstract Expressionism emerged in New York City in the 1940s. The artists produced *abstract* paintings that expressed their state of mind and that they hoped would strike emotional chords in viewers. The movement developed along two lines: *gestural abstraction* and *chromatic abstraction*.

acropolis Greek, "high city." In ancient Greece, usually the site of the city's most important temple(s).

action painting Also called *gestural abstraction*. The kind of *Abstract Expressionism* practiced by Jackson Pollock, in which the emphasis was on the creation process, the artist's gesture in making art. Pollock poured liquid paint in linear webs on his canvases, which he laid out on the floor, thereby physically surrounding himself in the painting during its creation.

additive light Natural light, or sunlight, the sum of all the wavelengths of the visible *spectrum*. See also *subtractive light*.

additive sculpture A kind of sculpture *technique* in which materials (for example, clay) are built up or "added" to create form.

adobe The clay used to make a kind of sun-dried mud brick of the same name; a building made of such brick.

aerial perspective See *perspective*.

agone Italian, "foot race."

airbrush A tool that uses compressed air to spray paint onto a surface.

aisle The portion of a *basilica* flanking the *nave* and separated from it by a row of *columns* or *piers*.

ala (pl. **alae**) One of a pair of rectangular recesses at the back of the *atrium* of a Roman *domus*.

album leaf A painting on a single sheet of paper for a collection stored in an album.

alchemy The study of seemingly magical changes, especially chemical changes.

altarpiece A panel, painted or sculpted, situated above and behind an altar. See also *retable*.

alternate-support system In church architecture, the use of alternating wall supports in the *nave*, usually *piers* and *columns* or *compound piers* of alternating form.

amalaka In Hindu temple design, the large flat disk with ribbed edges surmounting the beehive-shaped tower (*shikara*).

Amazonomachy In Greek mythology, the battle between the Greeks and Amazons.

ambulatory A covered walkway, outdoors (as in a church *cloister*) or indoors; especially the passageway around the *apse* and the *choir* of a church.

amphiprostyle A *classical* temple *plan* in which the *columns* are placed across both the front and back but not along the sides.

amphitheater Greek, "double theater." A Roman building type resembling two Greek theaters put together. The Roman amphitheater featured a continuous elliptical *cavea* around a central *arena*.

amphora An ancient Greek two-handled jar used for general storage purposes, usually to hold wine or oil.

amulet An object worn to ward off evil or to aid the wearer.

Analytic Cubism The first phase of *Cubism*, developed jointly by Pablo Picasso and Georges Braque, in which the artists analyzed form from every possible vantage point to combine the various views into one pictorial whole.

anamorphic image A distorted image that must be viewed by some special means (such as a mirror) to be recognized.

ancien régime French, "old order." The term used to describe the political, social, and religious order in France before the Revolution at the end of the 18th century.

antae The molded projecting ends of the walls forming the *pronaos* or *opisthodomos* of an ancient Greek temple.

apadana The great audience hall in ancient Persian palaces.

apostle Greek, "messenger." One of the 12 disciples of Jesus.

apoxyomenos Greek, "athlete scraping oil from his body."

apse A recess, usually semicircular, in the wall of a building, commonly found at the east end of a church.

apsidal Rounded; *apse*-shaped.

arcade A series of *arches* supported by *piers* or *columns*.

arch A curved structural member that spans an opening and is generally composed of wedge-shaped blocks (*voussoirs*) that transmit the downward pressure laterally. See also *thrust*.

Archaic The artistic style of 600–480 BCE in Greece, characterized in part by the use of the *composite view* for painted and *relief* figures and of Egyptian stances for statues.

Archaic smile The smile that appears on all *Archaic* Greek statues from about 570 to 480 BCE. The smile is the Archaic sculptor's way of indicating the person portrayed is alive.

architrave The *lintel* or lowest division of the *entablature*.

archivolt The continuous molding framing an *arch*. In *Romanesque* and *Gothic* architecture, one of the series of concentric bands framing the *tympanum*.

arcuated *Arch*-shaped.

arena In a Roman *amphitheater*, the central area where bloody *gladiatorial* combats and other boisterous events took place.

armature The crossed, or diagonal, *arches* that form the skeletal framework of a *Gothic rib vault*. In sculpture, the framework for a clay form.

arriccio In *fresco* painting, the first layer of rough lime plaster applied to the wall.

Art Deco Descended from *Art Nouveau*, this movement of the 1920s and 1930s sought to upgrade industrial design as a "fine art" and to work new materials into decorative patterns that could be either machined or handcrafted. Characterized by streamlined, elongated, and symmetrical design.

Art Nouveau French, "new art." A late-19th- and early-20th-century art movement whose proponents tried to synthesize all the arts in an effort to create art based on natural forms that could be mass produced by technologies of the industrial age.

asceticism Self-discipline and self-denial.

ashlar masonry Carefully cut and regularly shaped blocks of stone used in construction, fitted together without mortar.

assemblage An artwork constructed from already existing objects.

atlantid A male figure that functions as a supporting *column*. See also *caryatid*.

atlatl Spear-thrower, the typical weapon of the Toltecs of ancient Mexico.

atmospheric perspective See *perspective*.

atrium The central reception room of a Roman *domus* that is partly open to the sky. Also the open, *colonnaded* court in front of and attached to a Christian *basilica*.

attic The uppermost story of a building, *triumphal arch*, or city gate.

attribute (n.) The distinctive identifying aspect of a person, for example, an object held, an associated animal, or a mark on the body. (v.) To make an *attribution*.

attribution Assignment of a work to a maker or makers.

automatism In painting, the process of yielding oneself to instinctive motions of the hands after establishing a set of conditions (such as size of paper or *medium*) within which a work is to be created.

avant-garde French, "advance guard" (in a platoon). Late-19th- and 20th-century artists who emphasized innovation and challenged established convention in their work. Also used as an adjective.

avatar A manifestation of a deity incarnated in some visible form in which the deity performs a sacred function on earth. In Hinduism, an incarnation of a god.

axial plan See *plan*.

B

baldacchino A canopy on *columns*, frequently built over an altar. The term derives from *baldacco*.

baldacco Italian, "silk from Baghdad." See *baldacchino*.

baptism The Christian bathing ceremony in which an infant or a convert becomes a member of the Christian community.

baptistery In Christian architecture, the building used for *baptism*, usually situated next to a church. Also, the designated area or hall within a church for baptismal rites.

bar tracery See *tracery*.

Baroque The traditional blanket designation for European art from 1600 to 1750. The stylistic term *Baroque*, which describes art that features dramatic theatricality and elaborate ornamentation in contrast to the simplicity and orderly rationality of *Renaissance* art, is most appropriately applied to Italian art of this period. The term derives from *barroco*.

barrel vault See *vault*.

barroco Portuguese, "irregularly shaped pearl." See *Baroque*.

base In ancient Greek architecture, the molded projecting lowest part of *Ionic* and *Corinthian columns*. (*Doric* columns do not have bases.)

basilica (adj. **basilican**) In Roman architecture, a public building for legal and other civic proceedings, rectangular in plan with an entrance usually on a long side. In Christian architecture, a church somewhat resembling the Roman basilica, usually entered from one end and with an *apse* at the other.

bas-relief See *relief*.

Bauhaus A *school* of architecture in Germany in the 1920s under the aegis of Walter Gropius, who emphasized the unity of art, architecture, and design.

bay The space between two columns, or one unit in the *nave arcade* of a church; also, the passageway in an *arcuated* gate.

beam A horizontal structural member that carries the load of the superstructure of a building; a timber *lintel*.

belvedere Italian, "beautiful view." A building or other structure with a view of a *landscape* or seascape.

ben-ben A pyramidal stone; emblem of the Egyptian god Re.

benday dots Named after the newspaper printer Benjamin Day, the benday dot system involves the modulation of *colors* through the placement and size of colored dots.

bent-axis plan A *plan* that incorporates two or more angular changes of direction, characteristic of Sumerian architecture.

bestiary A collection of illustrations of real and imaginary animals.

bhumisparsha See *mudra*.

bilateral symmetry Having the same *forms* on either side of a central axis.

Biomorphic Surrealism See *Surrealism*.

black-figure painting In early Greek pottery, the silhouetting of dark figures against a light background of natural, reddish clay, with linear details *incised* through the silhouettes.

blind arcade An *arcade* having no true openings, applied as decoration to a wall surface.

bocio A Fon (Republic of Benin) empowerment figure.

bodhisattva In Buddhist thought, a potential Buddha who chooses not to achieve enlightenment in order to help save humanity.

Book of Hours A Christian religious book for private devotion containing prayers to be read at specified times of the day.

boss A circular knob.

braccia Italian, "arm." A unit of measurement; 1 braccia equals 23 inches.

breviary A Christian religious book of selected daily prayers and Psalms.

Buddha triad A three-figure group with a central Buddha flanked on each side by a *bodhisattva*.

buon fresco See *fresco*.

burin A pointed tool used for *engraving* or *incising*.

busshi Japanese, "maker of Buddhist images."

buttress An exterior masonry structure that opposes the lateral *thrust* of an *arch* or a *vault*. A pier buttress is a solid mass of masonry. A flying buttress consists typically of an inclined member carried on an arch or a series of arches and a solid buttress to which it transmits lateral thrust.

Byzantine The art, territory, history, and culture of the Eastern Christian Empire and its capital of Constantinople (ancient Byzantium).

C

caduceus In ancient Greek mythology, a magical rod entwined with serpents, the attribute of Hermes (Roman, Mercury), the messenger of the gods.

caldarium The hot-bath section of a Roman bathing establishment.

caliph(s) Islamic rulers, regarded as successors of Muhammad.

calligrapher One who practices *calligraphy*.

calligraphy Greek, "beautiful writing." Handwriting or penmanship, especially elegant writing as a decorative art.

calotype From the Greek *kalos*, "beautiful." A photographic process in which a positive image is made by shining light through a negative image onto a sheet of sensitized paper.

came A lead strip in a *stained-glass* window that joins separate pieces of colored glass.

camera lucida Latin, "lighted room." A device in which a small lens projects the image of an object downward onto a sheet of paper.

camera obscura Latin, "dark room." An ancestor of the modern camera in which a tiny pinhole, acting as a lens, projects an image on a screen, the wall of a room, or the ground-glass wall of a box; used by artists in the 17th, 18th, and early 19th centuries as an aid in drawing from nature.

campanile A bell tower of a church, usually, but not always, freestanding.

canon A rule, for example, of proportion. The ancient Greeks considered beauty to be a matter of "correct" proportion and sought a canon of proportion, for the human figure and for buildings. The fifth-century BCE sculptor Polykleitos wrote the *Canon*, a treatise incorporating his formula for the perfectly proportioned *statue*.

capital The uppermost member of a *column*, serving as a transition from the *shaft* to the *lintel*. In *classical* architecture, the form of the capital varies with the *order*.

Capitolium An ancient Roman temple dedicated to the gods Jupiter, Juno, and Minerva.

capriccio Italian, "originality." One of several terms used in Italian *Renaissance* literature to praise the originality and talent of artists.

caput mundi Latin, "head (capital) of the world."

Carolingian (adj.) Pertaining to the empire of Charlemagne (Latin, "Carolus Magnus") and his successors.

carpet page In early medieval manuscripts, a decorative page resembling a textile.

cartoon In painting, a full-size preliminary drawing from which a painting is made.

carving A *technique* of sculpture in which the artist cuts away material (for example, from a stone block) in order to create a *statue* or a *relief*.

caryatid A female figure that functions as a supporting *column*. See also *atlantid*.

casting A sculptural *technique* in which the artist pours liquid metal, plaster, clay, or another material into a *mold*. When the material dries, the sculptor removes the cast piece from the mold.

catacombs Subterranean networks of rock-cut galleries and chambers designed as cemeteries for the burial of the dead.

cathedral A bishop's church. The word derives from Latin *cathedra*, referring to the bishop's chair.

cavea Latin, "hollow place or cavity." The seating area in ancient Greek and Roman theaters and *amphitheaters*.

cella The chamber at the center of an ancient temple; in a classical temple, the room (Greek, *naos*) in which the *cult statue* usually stood.

centaur In ancient Greek mythology, a creature with the front or top half of a human and the back or bottom half of a horse.

centauromachy In ancient Greek mythology, the battle between the Greeks and *centaurs*.

central plan See *plan*.

chacmool A *Mesoamerican* statuary type depicting a fallen warrior on his back with a receptacle on his chest for sacrificial offerings.

chakra The Buddha's wheel, set in motion at Sarnath.

chakravartin In South Asia, the ideal king, the Universal Lord who ruled through goodness.

Chan See *Zen*.

chaplet A metal pin used in hollow-casting to connect the *investment* with the clay core.

characters In Chinese writing, signs that record spoken words.

chartreuse A Carthusian *monastery*.

château (pl. **châteaux**) French, "castle." A luxurious country residence for French royalty, developed from medieval castles.

chatra See *yasti*.

chiaroscuro In drawing or painting, the treatment and use of light and dark, especially the gradations of light that produce the effect of *modeling*.

chisel A tool with a straight blade at one end for cutting and shaping stone or wood.

chiton A Greek tunic, the essential (and often only) garment of both men and women, the other being the *himation*, or mantle.

choir The space reserved for the clergy and singers in the church, usually east of the *transept* but, in some instances, extending into the *nave*.

Christogram The three initial letters (chi-rho-iota) of Christ's name in Greek, which came to serve as a monogram for Christ.

chromatic abstraction A kind of *Abstract Expressionism* that focuses on the emotional resonance of color, as exemplified by the work of Mark Rothko.

chronology In art history, the dating of art objects and buildings.

chryselephantine Fashioned of gold and ivory.

Cinquecento Italian, "500," that is, the 1500s or 16th century.

circumambulation In Buddhist worship, walking around the *stupa* in a clockwise direction, a process intended to bring the worshiper into harmony with the cosmos.

cire perdue See *lost-wax process*.

city-state An independent, self-governing city.

Classical The art and culture of ancient Greece between 480 and 323 BCE. Lowercase *classical* refers more generally to Greco-Roman art and culture.

clerestory The *fenestrated* part of a building that rises above the roofs of the other parts. The oldest known clerestories are Egyptian. In Roman *basilicas* and medieval churches, clerestories are the windows that form the *nave*'s uppermost level below the timber ceiling or the *vaults*.

cloison French, "partition." A cell made of metal wire or a narrow metal strip soldered edge-up to a metal base to hold *enamel*, semiprecious stones, pieces of colored glass, or glass paste fired to resemble sparkling jewels.

cloisonné A decorative metalwork technique employing *cloisons*.

cloister A *monastery* courtyard, usually with covered walks or *ambulatories* along its sides.

cluster pier See *compound pier*.

codex (pl. **codices**) Separate pages of *vellum* or *parchment* bound together at one side; the predecessor of the modern book. The codex superseded the *rotulus*. In *Mesoamerica*, a painted and inscribed book on long sheets of bark paper or deerskin coated with fine white plaster and folded into accordion-like pleats.

coffer A sunken panel, often ornamental, in a *vault* or a ceiling.

collage A composition made by combining on a flat surface various materials, such as newspaper, wallpaper, printed text and illustrations, photographs, and cloth.

coller French, "to stick." See *collage*.

colonnade A series or row of *columns*, usually spanned by *lintels*.

colonnette A thin *column*.

colophon An inscription, usually on the last page, giving information about a book's manufacture. In Chinese painting, written texts on attached pieces of paper or silk.

color The value, or tonality, of a color is the degree of its lightness or darkness. The intensity, or saturation, of a color is its purity, its brightness or dullness. See also *primary colors, secondary colors*, and *complementary colors*.

color-field painting A variant of *Post-Painterly Abstraction* in which artists sought to reduce painting to its physical essence by pouring diluted paint onto unprimed canvas and letting these pigments soak into the fabric, as exemplified by the work of Helen Frankenthaler.

colorito Italian, "colored" or "painted." A term used to describe the application of paint. Characteristic of the work of 16th-century Venetian artists who emphasized the application of paint as an important element of the creative process. Central Italian artists, in contrast, largely emphasized *disegno*—the careful design preparation based on preliminary drawing.

colossal order An architectural design in which the *columns* or *pilasters* are two or more stories tall. Also called a giant order.

column A vertical, weight-carrying architectural member, circular in cross-*section* and consisting of a *base* (sometimes omitted), a *shaft*, and a *capital*.

combines The name American artist Robert Rauschenberg gave to his *assemblages* of painted passages and sculptural elements.

complementary colors Those pairs of *colors*, such as red and green, that together embrace the entire *spectrum*. The complement of one of the three *primary colors* is a mixture of the other two.

compose See *composition*.

composite view A convention of representation in which part of a figure is shown in profile and another part of the same figure is shown frontally; also called twisted perspective.

composition The way in which an artist organizes *forms* in an artwork, either by placing shapes on a flat surface or by arranging forms in space.

compound pier A *pier* with a group, or cluster, of attached *shafts*, or *responds*, especially characteristic of *Gothic* architecture.

Conceptual Art An American *avant-garde* art movement of the 1960s whose premise was that the "artfulness" of art lay in the artist's idea rather than its final expression.

concrete A building material invented by the Romans and consisting of various proportions of lime mortar, volcanic sand, water, and small stones.

condottiere (pl. **condottieri**) An Italian mercenary general.

congregational mosque A city's main *mosque*, designed to accommodate the entire *Muslim* population for the Friday noonday prayer. Also called the great mosque or Friday mosque.

connoisseur An expert in *attributing* artworks to one artist rather than another. More generally, an expert on artistic *style*.

consuls In the Roman Republic, the two chief magistrates.

contour line In art, a continuous *line* defining the outer shape of an object.

contrapposto The disposition of the human figure in which one part is turned in opposition to another part (usually hips and legs one way, shoulders and chest another), creating a counterpositioning of the body about its central axis. Sometimes called "weight shift" because the weight of the body tends to be thrown to one foot, creating tension on one side and relaxation on the other.

corbel A projecting wall member used as a support for some element in the superstructure. Also, *courses* of stone or brick in which each course projects beyond the one beneath it. Two such walls, meeting at the topmost course, create a corbeled *arch* or corbeled *vault*.

corbeled arch An *arch* formed by the piling of stone blocks in horizontal *courses*, cantilevered inward until the blocks meet at a *keystone*.

corbeled vault A *vault* formed by the piling of stone blocks in horizontal *courses*, cantilevered inward until the two walls meet in an *arch*.

Corinthian capital A more ornate form than *Doric* or *Ionic*, it consists of a double row of acanthus leaves from which tendrils and flowers grow, wrapped around a bell-shaped *echinus*. Although this *capital* form is often cited as the distinguishing feature of the Corinthian *order*, no such order exists, in strict terms, but only this type of capital used in the *Ionic* order.

cornice The projecting, crowning member of the *entablature* framing the *pediment*; also, any crowning projection.

corona civica Latin, "civic crown." A Roman honorary wreath worn on the head.

course In masonry construction, a horizontal row of stone blocks.

cross vault See *vault*.

cross-hatching See *hatching*.

crossing The space in a *cruciform* church formed by the intersection of the *nave* and the *transept*.

crossing square The area in a church formed by the intersection (*crossing*) of a *nave* and a *transept* of equal width, often used as a standard *module* of interior proportion.

crossing tower The tower over the *crossing* of a church.

cruciform Cross-shaped.

Crusades In medieval Europe, armed pilgrimages aimed at recapturing the Holy Land from the *Muslims*.

cubiculum (pl. **cubicula**) A small cubicle or bedroom that opened onto the *atrium* of a Roman *domus*. Also, a chamber in an Early Christian *catacomb* that served as a mortuary chapel.

Cubism An early-20th-century art movement that rejected *naturalistic* depictions, preferring *compositions* of shapes and *forms abstracted* from the conventionally perceived world. See also *Analytic Cubism* and *Synthetic Cubism*.

cult statue The *statue* of the deity that stood in the *cella* of an ancient temple.

cuneiform Latin, "wedge-shaped." A system of writing used in ancient Mesopotamia, in which wedge-shaped characters were produced by pressing a *stylus* into a soft clay tablet, which was then baked or otherwise allowed to harden.

cutaway An architectural drawing that combines an exterior view with an interior view of part of a building.

Cycladic The prehistoric art of the Aegean islands around Delos, excluding Crete.

Cyclopean masonry A method of stone construction, named after the mythical *Cyclopes*, using massive, irregular blocks without mortar, characteristic of the Bronze Age fortifications of Tiryns and other *Mycenaean* sites.

Cyclops (pl. **Cyclopes**) A mythical Greek one-eyed giant.

D

Dada An early-20th-century art movement prompted by a revulsion against the horror of World War I. Dada embraced political anarchy, the irrational, and the intuitive. A disdain for convention, often enlivened by humor or whimsy, is characteristic of the art the Dadaists produced.

Daedalic The Greek sculptural style of the seventh century BCE named after the legendary artist Daedalus.

daguerreotype A photograph made by an early method on a plate of chemically treated metal; developed by Louis J. M. Daguerre.

daimyo Local lords who controlled small regions and owed obeisance to the *shogun* in the Japanese *shogunate* system.

damnatio memoriae The Roman decree condemning those who ran afoul of the Senate. Those who suffered damnatio memoriae had their memorials demolished and their names erased from public inscriptions.

De Stijl Dutch, "the style." An early-20th-century art movement, founded by Piet Mondrian and Theo van Doesburg, whose members promoted utopian ideals and developed a simplified geometric style.

deconstruction An analytical strategy developed in the late 20th century according to which all cultural "constructs" (art, architecture, literature) are "texts." People can read these texts in a variety of ways, but they cannot arrive at fixed or uniform meanings. Any interpretation can be valid, and readings differ from time to time, place to place, and person to person. For those employing this approach, deconstruction means destabilizing established meanings and interpretations while encouraging subjectivity and individual differences.

Deconstructivism An architectural *style* using *deconstruction* as an analytical strategy. Deconstructivist architects attempt to disorient the observer by disrupting the conventional categories of architecture. The haphazard presentation of *volumes*, *masses*, *planes*, lighting, and so forth challenges the viewer's assumptions about *form* as it relates to function.

Deësis Greek, "supplication." An image of Christ flanked by the figures of the Virgin Mary and John the Baptist, who intercede on behalf of humankind.

Der Blaue Reiter German, "the blue rider." An early-20th-century *German Expressionist* art movement founded by Vassily Kandinsky and Franz Marc. The artists selected the whimsical name because of their mutual interest in the color blue and horses.

dharma In Buddhism, moral law based on the Buddha's teaching.

dharmachakra See *mudra*.

dhyana See *mudra*.

di sotto in sù Italian, "from below upward." A *perspective* view seen from below.

diagonal rib See *rib*.

dictator In the Roman Republic, the supreme magistrate with extraordinary powers, appointed during a crisis for a specified period.

Die Brücke German, "the bridge." An early-20th-century *German Expressionist* art movement under the leadership of Ernst Ludwig Kirchner. The group thought of itself as the bridge between the old age and the new.

diptych A two-paneled painting or *altarpiece;* also, an ancient Roman, Early Christian, or Byzantine hinged writing tablet, often of ivory and carved on the external sides.

disegno Italian, "drawing" and "design." *Renaissance* artists considered drawing to be the external physical manifestation (*disegno esterno*) of an internal intellectual idea of design (*disegno interno*).

disputatio Latin, "logical argument." The philosophical methodology used in *Scholasticism.*

divine right The belief in a king's absolute power as God's will.

divisionism See *pointillism.*

documentary evidence In art history, the examination of written sources in order to determine the date of an artwork, the circumstances of its creation, or the identity of the artist(s) who made it.

dome A hemispherical *vault;* theoretically, an *arch* rotated on its vertical axis. In *Mycenaean* architecture, domes are beehive-shaped.

domus A Roman private house.

donor portrait A portrait of the individual(s) who commissioned (donated) a religious work, for example, an *altarpiece,* as evidence of devotion.

Doric One of the two systems (or *orders*) invented in ancient Greece for articulating the three units of the *elevation* of a *classical* building—the platform, the *colonnade,* and the superstructure (*entablature*). The Doric order is characterized by, among other features, *capitals* with funnel-shaped *echinuses, columns* without *bases,* and a *frieze* of *triglyphs* and *metopes.* See also *Ionic.*

doryphoros Greek, "spear bearer."

dressed masonry Stone blocks shaped to the exact dimensions required, with smooth faces for a perfect fit.

drum One of the stacked cylindrical stones that form the *shaft* of a *column.* Also, the cylindrical wall that supports a *dome.*

dry secco See *fresco.*

drypoint An *engraving* in which the design, instead of being cut into the plate with a *burin,* is scratched into the surface with a hard steel "pencil." See also *etching, intaglio.*

duomo Italian, "cathedral."

E

earthworks See *Environmental Art.*

eaves The lower part of a roof that overhangs the wall.

echinus The convex element of a *capital* directly below the *abacus.*

écorché The representation of a nude body as if without skin.

edition A set of impressions taken from a single *print* surface.

effigy mounds Ceremonial mounds built in the shape of animals or birds by native North American peoples.

elevation In architecture, a head-on view of an external or internal wall, showing its features and often other elements that would be visible beyond or before the wall.

embroidery The technique of sewing threads onto a finished ground to form contrasting designs.

en plein air See *plein air.*

enamel A decorative coating, usually colored, fused onto the surface of metal, glass, or ceramics.

encaustic A painting *technique* in which pigment is mixed with melted wax and applied to the surface while the mixture is hot.

engaged column A half-round *column* attached to a wall. See also *pilaster.*

engraving The process of *incising* a design in hard material, often a metal plate (usually copper); also, the *print* or impression made from such a plate.

Enlightenment The Western philosophy based on empirical evidence that dominated the 18th century. The Enlightenment was a new way of thinking critically about the world and about humankind, independently of religion, myth, or tradition.

entablature The part of a building above the *columns* and below the roof. The entablature has three parts: *architrave, frieze,* and *pediment.*

entasis The convex profile (an apparent swelling) in the *shaft* of a *column.*

Environmental Art An American art form that emerged in the 1960s. Often using the land itself as their material, Environmental artists construct monuments of great scale and minimal form. Permanent or impermanent, these works transform some section of the environment, calling attention both to the land itself and to the hand of the artist. Sometimes referred to as earthworks.

etching A kind of *engraving* in which the design is *incised* in a layer of wax or varnish on a metal plate. The parts of the plate left exposed are then etched (slightly eaten away) by the acid in which the plate is immersed after incising. See also *drypoint, intaglio.*

Eucharist In Christianity, the partaking of the bread and wine, which believers hold to be either Christ himself or symbolic of him.

evangelist One of the four authors (Matthew, Mark, Luke, John) of the New Testament *Gospels.*

exedra Recessed area, usually semicircular.

exemplum virtutis Latin, "example or model of virtue."

Expressionism (adj. **Expressionist**) Twentieth-century art that is the result of the artist's unique inner or personal vision and that often has an emotional dimension. Expressionism contrasts with art focused on visually describing the empirical world.

F

facade Usually, the front of a building; also, the other sides when they are emphasized architecturally.

faience A low-fired opaque glasslike silicate.

fan vault See *vault.*

fantasia Italian, "imagination." One of several terms used in Italian *Renaissance* literature to praise the originality and talent of artists.

fauces Latin, "jaws." In a Roman *domus,* the narrow foyer leading to the *atrium.*

Fauves French, "wild beasts." See *Fauvism.*

Fauvism An early-20th-century art movement led by Henri Matisse. For the Fauves, *color* became the formal element most responsible for pictorial coherence and the primary conveyor of meaning.

fenestrated Having windows.

fenestration The arrangement of the windows of a building.

fête galante French, "amorous festival." A type of *Rococo* painting depicting the outdoor amusements of French upper-class society.

fin-de-siècle French, "end of the century." A period in Western cultural history from the end of the 19th century until just before World War I, when decadence and indulgence masked anxiety about an uncertain future.

findspot Place where an artifact was found; *provenance.*

finial A crowning ornament.

First Style mural The earliest style of Roman *mural* painting. The aim of the artist was to imitate, using painted *stucco relief,* the appearance of costly marble panels.

flashing In making *stained-glass* windows, fusing one layer of colored glass to another to produce a greater range of *colors.*

fleur-de-lis A three-petaled iris flower; the royal flower of France.

flute or **fluting** Vertical channeling, roughly semicircular in cross-*section* and used principally on *columns* and *pilasters.*

flying buttress See *buttress.*

folio A page of a manuscript or book.

fons vitae Latin, "fountain of life." A symbolic fountain of everlasting life.

foreshortening The use of *perspective* to represent in art the apparent visual contraction of an object that extends back in space at an angle to the perpendicular plane of sight.

form In art, an object's shape and structure, either in two dimensions (for example, a figure painted on a surface) or in three dimensions (such as a *statue*).

formal analysis The visual analysis of artistic *form*.

formalism Strict adherence to, or dependence on, stylized shapes and methods of *composition*. An emphasis on an artwork's visual elements rather than its subject.

forum The public square of an ancient Roman city.

Fourth Style mural In Roman *mural* painting, the Fourth Style marks a return to architectural *illusionism,* but the architectural vistas of the Fourth Style are irrational fantasies.

freestanding sculpture See *sculpture in the round.*

fresco Painting on lime plaster, either dry (dry fresco, or fresco secco) or wet (true, or buon, fresco). In the latter method, the pigments are mixed with water and become chemically bound to the freshly laid lime plaster. Also, a painting executed in either method.

fresco secco See *fresco.*

Friday mosque See *congregational mosque.*

frieze The part of the *entablature* between the *architrave* and the *cornice;* also, any sculptured or painted band in a building. See *register.*

frigidarium The cold-bath section of a Roman bathing establishment.

Futurism An early-20th-century Italian art movement that championed war as a cleansing agent and that celebrated the speed and dynamism of modern technology.

G

garbha griha Hindi, "womb chamber." In Hindu temples, the *cella,* the holy inner sanctum often housing the god's image or *symbol.*

genre A *style* or category of art; also, a kind of painting that realistically depicts scenes from everyday life.

Geometric The *style* of Greek art during the ninth and eighth centuries BCE, characterized by *abstract* geometric ornament and schematic figures.

German Expressionism An early-20th-century regional *Expressionist* movement.

gestural abstraction Also known as *action painting.* A kind of *abstract* painting in which the gesture, or act of painting, is seen as the subject of art. Its most renowned proponent was Jackson Pollock. See also *Abstract Expressionism.*

giant order See *colossal order.*

gigantomachy In ancient Greek mythology, the battle between gods and giants.

giornata (pl. **giornate**) Italian, "day." The section of plaster that a *fresco* painter expects to complete in one session.

gladiator An ancient Roman professional fighter, usually a slave, who competed in an *amphitheater.*

glaze A vitreous coating applied to pottery to seal and decorate the surface; it may be colored, transparent, or opaque, and glossy or *matte.* In *oil painting,* a thin, transparent, or semitransparent layer applied over a *color* to alter it slightly.

glazier A glassworker.

gold leaf Gold beaten into tissue-paper-thin sheets that then can be applied to surfaces.

gopuras The massive, ornamented entrance gateway towers of southern Indian temple compounds.

gorgon In ancient Greek mythology, a hideous female demon with snake hair. Medusa, the most famous gorgon, was capable of turning anyone who gazed at her into stone.

Gospels The four New Testament books that relate the life and teachings of Jesus.

Gothic Originally, a derogatory term named after the Goths, used to describe the history, culture, and art of western Europe in the 12th to 14th centuries. Typically divided into periods designated Early (1140–1194), High (1194–1300), and Late (1300–1500).

gouache A painting *medium* consisting of watercolor mixed with gum.

Grand Manner portraiture A type of 18th-century portrait painting designed to communicate a person's grace and class through certain standardized conventions, such as the large scale of the figure relative to the canvas, the controlled pose, the *landscape* setting, and the low *horizon line.*

graver An *engraving* tool. See also *burin.*

great mosque See *congregational mosque.*

Greek cross A cross with four arms of equal length.

green architecture Ecologically friendly architectural design using clean energy to sustain the natural environment.

griffin An eagle-headed winged lion.

grisaille A *monochrome* painting done mainly in neutral grays to simulate sculpture.

groin The edge formed by the intersection of two barrel *vaults.*

groin vault See *vault.*

ground line In paintings and *reliefs,* a painted or carved baseline on which figures appear to stand.

guang An ancient Chinese covered vessel, often in animal form, holding wine, water, grain, or meat for sacrificial rites.

guild An association of merchants, craftspersons, or scholars in medieval and *Renaissance* Europe.

H

haboku In Japanese art, a loose and rapidly executed painting *style* in which the ink seems to have been applied by flinging or splashing it onto the paper.

Hadith The words and exemplary deeds of the Prophet Muhammad.

halberd A combination spear and battle-ax.

handscroll In Asian art, a horizontal painted scroll that is unrolled right to left, section by section, and often used to present illustrated religious texts or *landscapes.*

hanging scroll In Asian art, a vertical scroll hung on a wall with pictures mounted or painted directly on it.

haniwa Sculpted fired pottery cylinders, modeled in human, animal, or other forms and placed on Japanese *tumuli* of the Kofun period.

hard-edge painting A variant of *Post-Painterly Abstraction* that rigidly excluded all reference to gesture and incorporated smooth knife-edge geometric forms to express the notion that painting should be reduced to its visual components.

harmika In Buddhist architecture, a stone fence or railing that encloses an area surmounting the *dome* of a *stupa* that represents one of the Buddhist heavens; from the center arises the *yasti.*

hatching A series of closely spaced drawn or *engraved* parallel *lines.* Cross-hatching employs sets of lines placed at right angles.

Hellas The ancient name of Greece.

Hellenes (adj. **Hellenic**) The name the ancient Greeks called themselves as the people of *Hellas.*

Hellenistic The term given to the art and culture of the roughly three centuries between the death of Alexander the Great in 323 BCE and the death of Queen Cleopatra in 30 BCE, when Egypt became a Roman province.

henge An arrangement of *megalithic* stones in a circle, often surrounded by a ditch.

Hiberno-Saxon An art *style* that flourished in the *monasteries* of the British Isles in the early Middle Ages.

hierarchy of scale An artistic convention in which greater size indicates greater importance.

hieroglyph A *symbol* or picture in the ancient Egyptian writing system.

hieroglyphic A system of writing using *symbols* or pictures.

high relief See *relief.*

High-Tech architecture A contemporary architectural *style* calling for buildings that incorporate the latest innovations in engineering and technology and expose the structures' component parts.

Hijra The flight of Muhammad from Mecca to Medina in 622, the year from which Islam dates its beginnings.

himation An ancient Greek mantle worn by men and women over the *chiton* and draped in various ways.

hiragana A phonetic cursive script developed in Japan from Chinese *characters;* it came to be the primary script for Japanese court poetry.

historiated Ornamented with representations, such as plants, animals, or human figures, that have a narrative—as distinct from a purely decorative—function.

horizon line See *perspective.*

hôtel French, "town house."

hue The name of a *color.* See also *primary colors, secondary colors,* and *complementary colors.*

humanism In the *Renaissance,* an emphasis on education and on expanding knowledge (especially of *classical* antiquity), the exploration of individual potential and a desire to excel, and a commitment to civic responsibility and moral duty.

hydria An ancient Greek three-handled water pitcher.

hypostyle hall A hall with a roof supported by *columns.*

I

icon A portrait or image; especially in *Byzantine* churches, a panel with a painting of sacred personages that are objects of veneration. In the visual arts, a painting, a piece of sculpture, or even a building regarded as an object of veneration.

iconoclasm The destruction of religious or sacred images. In Byzantium, the period from 726 to 843 when there was an imperial ban on such images. The destroyers of images were known as iconoclasts. Those who opposed such a ban were known as iconophiles.

iconoclast See *iconoclasm.*

iconography Greek, the "writing of images." The term refers both to the content, or subject, of an artwork and to the study of content in art. It also includes the study of the symbolic, often religious, meaning of objects, persons, or events depicted in works of art.

iconophile See *iconoclasm.*

ikegobo A Benin royal shrine.

illuminare Latin, "to adorn, ornament, or brighten."

illuminated manuscript A luxurious handmade book with painted illustrations and decorations.

illusionism (adj. **illusionistic**) The representation of the three-dimensional world on a two-dimensional surface in a manner that creates the illusion that the person, object, or place represented is three-dimensional. See also *perspective.*

imagines In ancient Rome, wax portraits of ancestors.

imam In Islam, the leader of collective worship.

impasto A layer of thickly applied pigment.

imperator Latin, "commander in chief," from which the word *emperor* derives.

impluvium In a Roman *domus,* the basin located in the *atrium* that collected rainwater.

Impressionism A late-19th-century art movement that sought to capture a fleeting moment, thereby conveying the elusiveness and impermanence of images and conditions.

in antis In ancient Greek architecture, the area between the *antae.*

incise To cut into a surface with a sharp instrument; also, a method of decoration, especially on metal and pottery.

indulgence A religious pardon for a sin committed.

ingegno Italian, "innate talent." One of several terms used in Italian *Renaissance* literature to praise the originality and talent of artists.

installation An artwork that creates an artistic environment in a room or gallery.

intaglio A graphic *technique* in which the design is *incised,* or scratched, on a metal plate, either manually (*engraving, drypoint*) or chemically (*etching*). The incised lines of the design take the ink, making this the reverse of the *woodcut* technique.

internal evidence In art history, the examination of what an artwork represents (people, clothing, hairstyles, and so on) in order to determine its date. Also, the examination of the *style* of an artwork to identify the artist who created it.

International style A *style* of 14th- and 15th-century painting begun by Simone Martini, who adapted the French *Gothic* manner to Sienese art fused with influences from northern Europe. This style appealed to the aristocracy because of its brilliant *color,* lavish costumes, intricate ornamentation, and themes involving splendid processions of knights and ladies. Also, a style of 20th-century architecture associated with Le Corbusier, whose elegance of design came to influence the look of modern office buildings and skyscrapers.

intonaco In *fresco* painting, the last layer of smooth lime plaster applied to the wall; the painting layer.

invenzione Italian, "invention." One of several terms used in Italian *Renaissance* literature to praise the originality and talent of artists.

investment In hollow-casting, the final clay *mold* applied to the exterior of the wax model.

Ionic One of the two systems (or *orders*) invented in ancient Greece for articulating the three units of the *elevation* of a *classical* building: the platform, the *colonnade,* and the superstructure (*entablature*). The Ionic order is characterized by, among other features, *volutes, capitals, columns* with *bases,* and an uninterrupted *frieze.*

iron-wire lines In ancient Chinese painting, thin brush *lines* suggesting tensile strength.

iwan In Islamic architecture, a *vaulted* rectangular recess opening onto a courtyard.

iy'oba In the Benin kingdom, the title of "queen mother."

J

jambs In architecture, the side posts of a doorway.

jataka Tales of the past lives of the Buddha. See also *sutra.*

jomon Japanese, "cord markings." A type of Japanese ceramic *technique* characterized by ropelike markings.

journaux French, "newspapers."

junzi Chinese, "superior person" or "gentleman." A person who is a model of Confucian behavior.

K

Kaaba Arabic, "cube." A small cubical building in Mecca, the Islamic world's symbolic center.

ka In ancient Egypt, the immortal human life force.

karma In Vedic religions (see *Veda*), the ethical consequences of a person's life, which determine his or her fate.

katsina An art form of Native Americans of the Southwest, the katsina doll represents benevolent supernatural spirits (katsinas) living in mountains and water sources.

keystone See *voussoir.*

khipu Andean record-keeping device consisting of numerous knotted strings hanging from a main cord; the strings signified, by position and *color,* numbers and categories of things.

kings' gallery The band of *statues* running the full width of the *facade* of a *Gothic cathedral* directly above the *rose window.*

kiva A square or circular underground structure that is the spiritual and ceremonial center of *Pueblo* Indian life.

Kogan The name of a distinctive type of *Shino* water jar.

kondo Japanese, "golden hall." The main hall for worship in a Japanese Buddhist temple complex. The kondo contained *statues* of the Buddha and the *bodhisattvas* to whom the temple was dedicated.

Koran Islam's sacred book, composed of *surahs* (chapters) divided into verses.

kore (pl. **korai**)   Greek, "young woman." An *Archaic* Greek *statue* of a young woman.

kouros (pl. **kouroi**)   Greek, "young man." An *Archaic* Greek *statue* of a young man.

krater   An ancient Greek wide-mouthed bowl for mixing wine and water.

Kufic   An early form of Arabic script, characterized by angularity, with the uprights forming almost right angles with the baseline.

kylix   An ancient Greek drinking cup with a wide bowl and two horizontal handles.

L

labyrinth   Maze. The English word derives from the mazelike plan of the *Minoan* palace at Knossos.

lacquer   A varnishlike substance made from the sap of the Asiatic sumac tree, used to decorate wood and other organic materials. Often colored with mineral pigments, lacquer cures to great hardness and has a lustrous surface.

lakshana   One of the distinguishing marks of the Buddha. The lakshanas include the *urna* and *ushnisha*.

lamassu   Assyrian guardian in the form of a man-headed winged bull.

lancet   In *Gothic* architecture, a tall narrow window ending in a *pointed arch*.

landscape   A picture showing natural scenery, without narrative content.

lateral section   See *section*.

leading   In the manufacture of *stained-glass* windows, the joining of colored glass pieces using lead *cames*.

lekythos (pl. **lekythoi**)   A flask containing perfumed oil; lekythoi were often placed in Greek graves as offerings to the deceased.

line   The extension of a point along a path, made concrete in art by drawing on or chiseling into a *plane*.

linear perspective   See *perspective*.

linga   In Hindu art, the depiction of Shiva as a phallus or cosmic *pillar*.

linguist's staff   In Africa, a staff carried by a person authorized to speak for a king or chief.

lintel   A horizontal *beam* used to span an opening.

literati   In China, talented amateur painters and scholars from the landed gentry.

lithograph   See *lithography*.

lithography   A printmaking technique in which the artist uses an oil-based crayon to draw directly on a stone plate and then wipes water onto the stone. When ink is rolled onto the plate, it adheres only to the drawing. The *print* produced by this method is a lithograph.

lithos   Greek, "stone."

liturgy (adj. **liturgical**)   The official ritual of public worship.

local color   An object's true *color* in white light.

loggia   A gallery with an open *arcade* or a *colonnade* on one or both sides.

lohan   A Buddhist holy person who has achieved enlightenment and *nirvana* by suppression of all desire for earthly things.

longitudinal plan   See *plan*.

longitudinal section   See *section*.

lost-wax (cire perdue) process   A bronze-*casting* method in which a figure is modeled in wax and covered with clay; the whole is fired, melting away the wax (French, cire perdue) and hardening the clay, which then becomes a *mold* for molten metal.

low relief   See *relief*.

lunette   A semicircular area (with the flat side down) in a wall over a door, niche, or window; also, a painting or *relief* with a semicircular frame.

lux nova   Latin, "new light." Abbot Suger's term for the light that enters a *Gothic* church through *stained-glass* windows.

M

madrasa   An Islamic theological college adjoining and often containing a *mosque*.

magus (pl. **magi**)   One of the three wise men from the East who presented gifts to the infant Jesus.

mandala   Sanskrit term for the sacred diagram of the universe; Japanese, mandara.

mandapa   *Pillared* hall of a Hindu temple.

mandara   See *mandala*.

mandorla   An almond-shaped *nimbus* surrounding the figure of Christ or other sacred figure. In Buddhist Japan, a lotus-petal-shaped nimbus.

maniera   Italian, "style" or "manner." See *Mannerism*.

maniera greca   Italian, "Greek manner." The Italo-*Byzantine* painting *style* of the 13th century.

Mannerism   A *style* of later *Renaissance* art that emphasized "artifice," often involving contrived imagery not derived directly from nature. Such artworks showed a self-conscious stylization involving complexity, caprice, fantasy, and polish. Mannerist architecture tended to flout the *classical* rules of order, stability, and symmetry, sometimes to the point of parody.

manu scriptus   Latin, "handwritten."

maqsura   In some *mosques*, a screened area in front of the *mihrab* reserved for a ruler.

martyr   A person who chooses to die rather than deny his or her religious belief. See also *saint*.

martyrium   A shrine to a Christian *martyr*.

mass   The bulk, density, and weight of matter in *space*.

Mass   The Catholic and Orthodox ritual in which believers understand that Christ's redeeming sacrifice on the cross is repeated when the priest consecrates the bread and wine in the *Eucharist*.

mastaba   Arabic, "bench." An ancient Egyptian rectangular brick or stone structure with sloping sides erected over a subterranean tomb chamber connected with the outside by a shaft.

matte   In painting, pottery, and photography, a dull finish.

maulstick   A stick used to steady the hand while painting.

mausoleum   A monumental tomb. The name derives from the mid-fourth-century BCE tomb of Mausolos at Halikarnassos, one of the Seven Wonders of the ancient world.

mbulu ngulu   The wood-and-metal *reliquary* guardian figures of the Kota of Gabon.

meander   An ornament, usually in bands but also covering broad surfaces, consisting of interlocking geometric motifs. An ornamental pattern of contiguous straight lines joined usually at right angles.

medium (pl. **media**)   The material (for example, marble, bronze, clay, *fresco*) in which an artist works; also, in painting, the vehicle (usually liquid) that carries the pigment.

megalith (adj. **megalithic**)   Greek, "great stone." A large, roughly hewn stone used in the construction of monumental prehistoric structures.

Mesoamerica   The region that comprises Mexico, Guatemala, Belize, Honduras, and the Pacific coast of El Salvador.

Mesolithic   The "middle" Stone Age, between the *Paleolithic* and the *Neolithic* ages.

Messiah   The savior of the Jews prophesied in Hebrew scripture. Christians believe that Jesus of Nazareth was the Messiah.

metope   The square panel between the *triglyphs* in a *Doric frieze*, often sculpted in *relief*.

mihrab   A semicircular niche set into the *qibla* wall of a *mosque*.

minaret   A distinctive feature of *mosque* architecture, a tower from which the faithful are called to worship.

minbar   In a *mosque*, the *pulpit* on which the *imam* stands.

mingei   A type of modern Japanese folk pottery.

miniatures   Small individual Indian paintings intended to be held in the hand and viewed by one or two individuals at one time.

Minimalism   A predominantly sculptural American trend of the 1960s characterized by works featuring a severe reduction of *form*, often to single, homogeneous units.

Minoan   The prehistoric art of Crete, named after the legendary King Minos of Knossos.

Minotaur   The mythical beast, half man and half bull, that inhabited the *labyrinth* of the *Minoan* palace at Knossos.

Miraj   The ascension of the Prophet Muhammad to Heaven.

mithuna   In South Asian art, a male-female couple embracing or engaged in sexual intercourse.

mobile   A kind of sculpture, invented by Alexander Calder, combining nonobjective organic forms and motion in balanced structures hanging from rods, wires, and colored, organically shaped plates.

modeling   The shaping or fashioning of three-dimensional forms in a soft material, such as clay; also, the gradations of light and shade reflected from the surfaces of matter in space, or the illusion of such gradations produced by alterations of value in a drawing, painting, or print.

modernism   A movement in Western art that developed in the second half of the 19th century and sought to capture the images and sensibilities of the age. Modernist art goes beyond simply dealing with the present and involves the artist's critical examination of the premises of art itself.

module (adj. **modular**)   A basic unit of which the dimensions of the major parts of a work are multiples. The principle is used in sculpture and other art forms, but it is most often employed in architecture, where the module may be the dimensions of an important part of a building, such as the diameter of a *column*.

moksha   See *nirvana*.

mold   A hollow form for *casting*.

molding   In architecture, a continuous, narrow surface (projecting or recessed, plain or ornamented) designed to break up a surface, to accent, or to decorate.

monastery   A group of buildings in which monks live together, set apart from the secular community of a town.

monastic   Relating to life in a *monastery*.

monastic order   An organization of monks living according to the same rules, for example, the Benedictine, Franciscan, and Dominican orders.

monasticism   A religious movement originating in the third century in which those seeking a spiritual way of life live in isolation in the wilderness or in communities of monks in *monasteries*.

monochrome (adj. **monochromatic**)   One *color*.

monolith (adj. **monolithic**)   A stone *column shaft* that is all in one piece (not composed of *drums*); a large, single block or piece of stone used in *megalithic* structures. Also, a colossal *statue* carved from a single piece of stone.

monotheism   The worship of one all-powerful god.

moralized Bible   A heavily illustrated Bible, each page pairing paintings of Old and New Testament episodes with explanations of their moral significance.

mortuary temple   In Egyptian architecture, a temple erected for the worship of a deceased *pharaoh*.

mosaic   Patterns or pictures made by embedding small pieces (*tesserae*) of stone or glass in cement on surfaces such as walls and floors; also, the *technique* of making such works.

mosaic tilework   An Islamic decorative *technique* in which large ceramic panels are fired, cut into smaller pieces, and set in plaster.

mosque   The Islamic building for collective worship. From the Arabic word *masjid*, meaning a "place for bowing down."

mudra   In Buddhist and Hindu iconography, a stylized and symbolic hand gesture. The dhyana (meditation) mudra consists of the right hand over the left, palms upward, in the lap. In the bhumisparsha

(earth-touching) mudra, the right hand reaches down to the ground, calling the earth to witness the Buddha's enlightenment. The dharmachakra (Wheel of the Law, or "teaching") mudra is a two-handed gesture with right thumb and index finger forming a circle. The abhaya (do not fear) mudra, with the right hand up, palm outward, is a gesture of protection or blessing.

Mughal   "Descended from the Mongols." The Muslim rulers of India, 1526–1857.

Muhaqqaq   A cursive *style* of Islamic *calligraphy*.

mullion   A vertical member that divides a window or that separates one window from another.

mummification   A *technique* used by ancient Egyptians to preserve human bodies so that they may serve as the eternal home of the immortal *ka*.

mummy   An embalmed corpse.

muqarnas   Stucco decorations of Islamic buildings in which stalactite-like forms break a structure's solidity.

mural   A wall painting.

Muslim   A believer in Islam.

Mycenaean   The prehistoric art of Greece, named after the citadel of Mycenae.

mystery play   A dramatic enactment of the holy mysteries of the Christian faith performed at church portals and in city squares.

N

naos   See *cella*.

narthex   A porch or vestibule of a church, generally *colonnaded* or *arcaded* and preceding the *nave*.

natatio   The swimming pool in a Roman bathing establishment.

naturalism   The style of painted or sculptured representation based on close observation of the natural world that was at the core of the *classical* tradition.

Naturalistic Surrealism   See *Surrealism*.

nave   The central area of an ancient Roman *basilica* or of a church, demarcated from *aisles* by *piers* or *columns*.

nave arcade   In *basilica* architecture, the series of *arches* supported by *piers* or *columns* separating the *nave* from the *aisles*.

nduen fobara   A Kalabari Ijaw (Nigeria) ancestral screen in honor of a deceased chief of a trading house.

necropolis   Greek, "city of the dead." A large burial area or cemetery.

nemes   In ancient Egypt, the linen headdress worn by the *pharaoh*, with the *uraeus* cobra of kingship on the front.

Neoclassicism   A *style* of art and architecture that emerged in the late 18th century as part of a general revival of interest in *classical* cultures. Neoclassical artists adopted themes and *styles* from ancient Greece and Rome.

Neo-Gothic   The revival of the *Gothic style* in architecture, especially in the 19th century.

Neolithic   The "new" Stone Age.

Neoplasticism   The Dutch artist Piet Mondrian's theory of "pure plastic art," an ideal balance between the universal and the individual using an *abstract* formal vocabulary.

nepotism   The appointment of relatives to important positions.

Neue Sachlichkeit   German, "new objectivity." An art movement that grew directly out of the World War I experiences of a group of German artists who sought to show the horrors of the war and its effects.

nimbus   A halo or aureole appearing around the head of a holy figure to signify divinity.

nirvana   In Buddhism and Hinduism, a blissful state brought about by absorption of the individual soul or consciousness into the supreme spirit. Also called moksha.

nishiki-e   Japanese, "brocade pictures." Japanese polychrome *woodcut prints* valued for their sumptuous *colors*.

nkisi n'kondi A power figure carved by the Kongo people of the Democratic Republic of Congo. Such images embodied spirits believed to heal and give life or to be capable of inflicting harm or death.

nymphs In *classical* mythology, female divinities of springs, caves, and woods.

O

oba An African sacred king.

oculus (pl. **oculi**) Latin, "eye." The round central opening of a *dome*. Also, a small round window in a *Gothic cathedral*.

odalisque A woman in a Turkish harem.

ogive (adj. **ogival**) The diagonal *rib* of a *Gothic vault*; a pointed, or Gothic, *arch*.

oil painting A painting *technique* using oil-based pigments that rose to prominence in northern Europe in the 15th century and is now the standard medium for painting on canvas.

oni An African ruler.

Op Art An artistic movement of the 1960s in which painters sought to produce optical illusions of motion and depth using only geometric forms on two-dimensional surfaces.

opere francigeno See *opus francigenum.*

opisthodomos In ancient Greek architecture, a porch at the rear of a temple, set against the blank back wall of the *cella*.

optical mixture The visual effect of juxtaposed *complementary colors.*

opus francigenum Latin, "French work." Architecture in the *style* of Gothic France; *opere francigeno* (adj.), "in the French manner."

opus modernum Latin, "modern work." The late medieval term for *Gothic* art and architecture. Also called *opus francigenum.*

orant In Early Christian art, a figure with both arms raised in the ancient gesture of prayer.

oratory The church of a Christian *monastery.*

orchestra Greek, "dancing place." In ancient Greek theaters, the circular piece of earth with a hard and level surface on which the performance took place.

order In *classical* architecture, a *style* represented by a characteristic design of the *columns* and *entablature*. See also *superimposed orders.*

orrery A mechanical model of the solar system demonstrating how the planets revolve around the sun.

orthogonal A line imagined to be behind and perpendicular to the picture *plane*; the orthogonals in a painting appear to recede toward a *vanishing point* on the horizon.

orthogonal plan The imposition of a strict grid *plan* on a site, regardless of the terrain, so that all streets meet at right angles.

Ottonian (adj.) Pertaining to the empire of Otto I and his successors.

P

pagoda An East Asian tower, usually associated with a Buddhist temple, having a multiplicity of winged *eaves*; thought to be derived from the Indian *stupa.*

palaestra An ancient Greek and Roman exercise area, usually framed by a *colonnade*. In Greece, the palaestra was an independent building; in Rome, palaestras were also frequently incorporated into a bathing complex.

paleo Greek, "old."

Paleolithic The "old" Stone Age, during which humankind produced the first sculptures and paintings.

palette A thin board with a thumb hole at one end on which an artist lays and mixes *colors*; any surface so used. Also, the colors or kinds of colors characteristically used by an artist. In ancient Egypt, a slate slab used for preparing makeup.

palette knife A flat tool used to scrape paint off the *palette*. Artists sometimes also use the palette knife in place of a brush to apply paint directly to the canvas.

Pantokrator Greek, "ruler of all." Christ as ruler and judge.

papyrus A plant native to Egypt and adjacent lands used to make paperlike writing material; also, the material or any writing on it.

parallel hatching See *hatching.*

parapet A low, protective wall along the edge of a balcony, roof, or bastion.

parchment Lambskin prepared as a surface for painting or writing.

parinirvana Image of the reclining Buddha, a position often interpreted as representing his death.

parthenos Greek, "virgin." The epithet of Athena, the virgin goddess.

passio Latin, "suffering."

Passover The annual feast celebrating the release of the Jews from bondage to the *pharaohs* of Egypt.

paten A large shallow bowl or plate for the bread used in the *Eucharist.*

patrician A Roman freeborn landowner.

patron The person or entity that pays an artist to produce individual artworks or employs an artist on a continuing basis.

Pax Augusta Latin, "Augustan peace."

Pax Romana Latin, "Roman peace."

pebble mosaic A *mosaic* made of irregularly shaped stones of various *colors.*

pediment In *classical* architecture, the triangular space (gable) at the end of a building, formed by the ends of the sloping roof above the *colonnade*; also, an ornamental feature having this shape.

pendant The large hanging terminal element of a *Gothic* fan *vault.*

pendentive A concave, triangular section of a hemisphere, four of which provide the transition from a square area to the circular base of a covering *dome*. Although pendentives appear to be hanging (pendant) from the dome, they in fact support it.

peplos (pl. **peploi**) A simple, long belted garment of wool worn by women in ancient Greece.

Performance Art An American *avant-garde* art trend of the 1960s that made time an integral element of art. It produced works in which movements, gestures, and sounds of persons communicating with an audience replace physical objects.

period style See *style.*

peripteral See *peristyle.*

peristyle In *classical* architecture, a *colonnade* all around the *cella* and its porch(es). A peripteral colonnade consists of a single row of *columns* on all sides.

Perpendicular A Late English *Gothic style* of architecture distinguished by the pronounced verticality of its decorative details.

personal style See *style.*

personification An *abstract* idea represented in bodily form.

perspective A method used to present an illusion of the three-dimensional world on a two-dimensional surface. In linear perspective, the most common type, all parallel lines or surface edges converge on one, two, or three vanishing points located with reference to the eye level of the viewer (the horizon line of the picture), and associated objects are rendered smaller the farther from the viewer they are intended to seem. Atmospheric, or aerial, perspective creates the illusion of distance by the greater diminution of *color* intensity, the shift in color toward an almost neutral blue, and the blurring of contours as the intended distance between eye and object increases.

pharaoh (adj. **pharaonic**) An ancient Egyptian king.

philosophe French, "thinker, philosopher." The term applied to French intellectuals of the *Enlightenment.*

Phoibos Greek, "radiant." The epithet of the Greek god Apollo.

photomontage A *composition* made by pasting together pictures or parts of pictures, especially photographs. See also *collage.*

Photorealism See *Superrealism.*

physical evidence In art history, the examination of the materials used to produce an artwork in order to determine its date.

piazza Italian, "plaza."

pier A vertical, freestanding masonry support.

Pietà A painted or sculpted representation of the Virgin Mary mourning over the body of the dead Christ.

pilaster A flat, rectangular, vertical member projecting from a wall of which it forms a part. It usually has a *base* and a *capital* and is often *fluted*.

pillar Usually a weight-carrying member, such as a *pier* or a *column*; sometimes an isolated, freestanding structure used for commemorative purposes.

pinnacle In *Gothic* churches, a sharply pointed ornament capping the *piers* or flying *buttresses*; also used on church *facades*.

Pittura Metafisica Italian, "metaphysical painting." An early-20th-century Italian art movement led by Giorgio de Chirico, whose work conveys an eerie mood and visionary quality.

plan The horizontal arrangement of the parts of a building or of the buildings and streets of a city or town, or a drawing or diagram showing such an arrangement. In an axial plan, the parts of a building are organized longitudinally, or along a given axis; in a central plan, the parts of the structure are of equal or almost equal dimensions around the center.

plane A flat surface.

plate tracery See *tracery*.

plein air An approach to painting popular among the *Impressionists*, in which an artist sketches outdoors to achieve a quick impression of light, air, and *color*. The artist then takes the sketches to the studio for reworking into more finished works of art.

poesia A term describing "poetic" art, notably Venetian *Renaissance* painting, which emphasizes the lyrical and sensual.

pointed arch A narrow *arch* of pointed profile, in contrast to a semicircular arch.

pointillism A system of painting devised by the 19th-century French painter Georges Seurat. The artist separates *color* into its component parts and then applies the component colors to the canvas in tiny dots (points). The image becomes comprehensible only from a distance, when the viewer's eyes optically blend the pigment dots. Sometimes referred to as divisionism.

polyptych An *altarpiece* composed of more than three sections.

polytheism The belief in multiple gods.

pontifex maximus Latin, "chief priest." The high priest of the Roman state religion, often the emperor himself.

Pop Art A term coined by British art critic Lawrence Alloway to refer to art, first appearing in the 1950s, that incorporated elements from consumer culture, the mass media, and popular culture, such as images from motion pictures and advertising.

porcelain Extremely fine, hard, white ceramic made from a fine white clay called kaolin mixed with ground petuntse, a type of feldspar. True porcelain is translucent and rings when struck.

portico A roofed *colonnade*; also an entrance porch.

post-and-lintel system A system of construction in which two posts support a *lintel*.

Post-Impressionism The term used to describe the stylistically heterogeneous work of the group of late-19th-century painters in France, including van Gogh, Gauguin, Seurat, and Cézanne, who more systematically examined the properties and expressive qualities of *line*, pattern, *form*, and *color* than the *Impressionists* did.

postmodernism A reaction against *modernist formalism*, seen as elitist. Far more encompassing and accepting than the more rigid confines of modernist practice, postmodernism offers something for everyone by accommodating a wide range of *styles*, subjects, and formats, from traditional easel painting to *installation* and from *abstraction* to *illusionistic* scenes. Postmodern art often includes irony or reveals a self-conscious awareness on the part of the artist of art-making processes or the workings of the art world.

Post-Painterly Abstraction An American art movement that emerged in the 1960s and was characterized by a cool, detached rationality emphasizing tighter pictorial control. See also *color-field painting* and *hard-edge painting*.

Poussiniste A member of the French Royal Academy of Painting and Sculpture during the early 18th century who followed Nicolas Poussin in insisting that *form* was the most important element of painting. See also *Rubéniste*.

predella The narrow ledge on which an *altarpiece* rests on an altar.

prefiguration In Early Christian art, the depiction of Old Testament persons and events as prophetic forerunners of Christ and New Testament events.

primary colors Red, yellow, and blue—the *colors* from which all other colors may be derived.

primitivism The incorporation in early-20th-century Western art of stylistic elements from the artifacts of Africa, Oceania, and the native peoples of the Americas.

princeps Latin, "first citizen." The title Augustus and his successors as Roman emperor used to distinguish themselves from Hellenistic monarchs.

print An artwork on paper, usually produced in multiple impressions.

pronaos The space, or porch, in front of the *cella*, or naos, of an ancient Greek temple.

proportion The relationship in size of the parts of persons, buildings, or objects, often based on a *module*.

prostyle A *classical* temple *plan* in which the *columns* are only in front of the *cella* and not on the sides or back.

provenance Origin or source; *findspot*.

psalter A book containing the Psalms.

pseudoperipteral In Roman architecture, a pseudoperipteral temple has a series of *engaged columns* all around the sides and back of the *cella* to give the appearance of a *peripteral colonnade*.

pueblo A communal multistoried dwelling made of stone or *adobe* brick by the Native Americans of the Southwest. Uppercase *Pueblo* refers to various groups that occupied such dwellings.

pulpit A raised platform in a church or *mosque* on which a priest or *imam* stands while leading the religious service.

punchwork Tooled decorative work in *gold leaf*.

purlins Horizontal *beams* in a roof structure, parallel to the *ridgepoles*, resting on the main *rafters* and giving support to the secondary rafters.

putto (pl. **putti**) A cherubic young boy.

pylon The wide entrance gateway of an Egyptian temple, characterized by its sloping walls.

Q

qibla The direction (toward Mecca) Muslims face when praying.

quadrant arch An *arch* whose curve extends for one-quarter of a circle's circumference.

quadro riportato A ceiling design in which painted scenes are arranged in panels that resemble framed pictures transferred to the surface of a shallow, curved *vault*.

quatrefoil A shape or *plan* in which the parts assume the form of a cloverleaf.

Quattrocento Italian, "400," that is, the 1400s or 15th century.

R

radiating chapels In medieval churches, chapels for the display of *relics* that opened directly onto the *ambulatory* and the *transept*.

rafters The sloping supporting timber planks that run from the *ridgepole* of a roof to its edge.

raking cornice The *cornice* on the sloping sides of a *pediment*.

Rayonnant The "radiant" style of *Gothic* architecture, dominant in the second half of the 13th century and associated with the French royal court of Louis IX at Paris.

Realism A movement that emerged in mid-19th-century France. Realist artists represented the subject matter of everyday life (especially subjects that previously had been considered inappropriate for depiction) in a relatively *naturalistic* mode.

red-figure painting In later Greek pottery, the silhouetting of red figures against a black background, with painted linear details; the reverse of *black-figure painting*.

refectory The dining hall of a Christian *monastery*.

regional style See *style*.

Regionalism A 20th-century American art movement that portrayed American rural life in a clearly readable, *Realist* style. Major Regionalists include Grant Wood and Thomas Hart Benton.

register One of a series of superimposed bands or *friezes* in a pictorial narrative, or the particular levels on which motifs are placed.

relics The body parts, clothing, or objects associated with a holy figure, such as the Buddha or Christ or a Christian *saint*.

relief In sculpture, figures projecting from a background of which they are part. The degree of relief is designated high or low (bas). See also *repoussé*.

relief sculpture See *relief*.

relieving triangle In *Mycenaean* architecture, the triangular opening above the *lintel* that serves to lighten the weight to be carried by the lintel itself.

reliquary A container for holding *relics*.

ren Chinese, "human-heartedness." The quality that the ideal Confucian *junzi* possesses.

Renaissance French, "rebirth." The term used to describe the history, culture, and art of 14th- through 16th-century western Europe during which artists consciously revived the *classical* style.

renovatio Latin, "renewal." During the *Carolingian* period, Charlemagne sought to revive the culture of ancient Rome (*renovatio imperi Romani*).

repoussé Formed in *relief* by beating a metal plate from the back, leaving the impression on the face. The metal sheet is hammered into a hollow *mold* of wood or some other pliable material and finished with a *graver*. See also *relief*.

respond An engaged *column, pilaster,* or similar element that either projects from a *compound pier* or some other supporting device or is bonded to a wall and carries one end of an *arch*.

retable An architectural screen or wall above and behind an altar, usually containing painting, sculpture, or other decorations. See also *altarpiece*.

revetment In architecture, a wall covering or facing.

rib A relatively slender, molded masonry *arch* that projects from a surface. In *Gothic* architecture, the ribs form the framework of the *vaulting*. A diagonal rib is one of the ribs that form the X of a *groin vault*. A transverse rib crosses the *nave* or *aisle* at a 90-degree angle.

rib vault A *vault* in which the diagonal and transverse *ribs* compose a structural skeleton that partially supports the masonry *web* between them.

ridgepole The *beam* running the length of a building below the peak of the gabled roof.

rocaille See *Rococo*.

Rococo A style, primarily of interior design, that appeared in France around 1700. Rococo interiors featured lavish decoration, including small sculptures, ornamental mirrors, easel paintings, *tapestries, reliefs,* wall paintings, and elegant furniture. The term *Rococo* derived from the French word *rocaille* (pebble) and referred to the small stones and shells used to decorate grotto interiors.

Romanesque "Roman-like." A term used to describe the history, culture, and art of medieval western Europe from ca. 1050 to ca. 1200.

Romanticism A Western cultural phenomenon, beginning around 1750 and ending about 1850, that gave precedence to feeling and imagination over reason and thought. More narrowly, the art movement that flourished from about 1800 to 1840.

rose window A circular *stained-glass* window.

rotulus The manuscript scroll used by Egyptians, Greeks, Etruscans, and Romans; predecessor of the *codex*.

rotunda The circular area under a *dome;* also a domed round building.

roundel See *tondo*.

Rubéniste A member of the French Royal Academy of Painting and Sculpture during the early 18th century who followed Peter Paul Rubens in insisting that *color* was the most important element of painting. See also *Poussiniste*.

rusticate (n. **rustication**) To give a rustic appearance by roughening the surfaces and beveling the edges of stone blocks to emphasize the joints between them. Rustication is a *technique* employed in ancient Roman architecture and was also popular during the *Renaissance,* especially for stone *courses* at the ground-floor level.

S

sabi Japanese; the value found in the old and weathered, suggesting the tranquility reached in old age.

saint From the Latin word *sanctus,* meaning "made holy by God." Applied to persons who suffered and died for their Christian faith or who merited reverence for their Christian devotion while alive. In the Roman Catholic Church, a worthy deceased Catholic who is canonized by the pope.

samsara In Hindu belief, the rebirth of the soul into a succession of lives.

samurai Medieval Japanese warriors.

sarcophagus (pl. **sarcophagi**) Greek, "consumer of flesh." A coffin, usually of stone.

saturation See *color*.

satyr A Greek mythological follower of Dionysos having a man's upper body, a goat's hindquarters and horns, and a horse's ears and tail.

scarification Decorative markings on the human body made by cutting or piercing the flesh to create scars.

Scholasticism The *Gothic* school of philosophy in which scholars applied Aristotle's system of rational inquiry to the interpretation of religious belief.

school A chronological and stylistic classification of works of art with a stipulation of place.

scriptorium (pl. **scriptoria**) The writing studio of a *monastery*.

sculpture in the round Freestanding figures, *carved* or *modeled* in three dimensions.

seal In Asian painting, a stamp affixed to a painting to identify the artist, the *calligrapher,* or the owner.

secco Italian, "dry." See also *fresco*.

Second Style mural The style of Roman *mural* painting in which the aim was to dissolve the confining walls of a room and replace them with the illusion of a three-dimensional world constructed in the artist's imagination.

secondary colors Orange, green, and purple, obtained by mixing pairs of *primary colors* (red, yellow, blue).

section In architecture, a diagram or representation of a part of a structure or building along an imaginary *plane* that passes through it vertically. Drawings showing a theoretical slice across a structure's width are lateral sections. Those cutting through a building's length are longitudinal sections. See also *elevation* and *cutaway*.

senate Latin senatus, "council of elders." The Senate was the main legislative body in Roman constitutional government.

serdab A small concealed chamber in an Egyptian *mastaba* for the *statue* of the deceased.

Severe Style The Early *Classical* style of Greek sculpture, ca. 480–450 BCE.

sexpartite vault See *vault*.

sfumato Italian, "smoky." A smokelike haziness that subtly softens outlines in painting; particularly applied to the paintings of Leonardo da Vinci.

shaft The tall, cylindrical part of a *column* between the *capital* and the *base*.

shaykh An Islamic mystic *saint*.

shikara The beehive-shaped tower of a northern-style Hindu temple.

Shino Japanese ceramic wares produced during the late 16th and early 17th centuries in kilns in Mino.

shogun In 12th- through 19th-century Japan, a military governor who managed the country on behalf of a figurehead emperor.

shogunate The Japanese military government of the 12th through 19th centuries.

sibyl A Greco-Roman mythological prophetess.

silentiary An usher responsible for maintaining silence in the *Byzantine* imperial palace in Constantinople.

silk-screen printing An industrial printing *technique* that creates a sharp-edged image by pressing ink through a design on silk or a similar tightly woven porous fabric stretched tight on a frame.

silverpoint A *stylus* made of silver, used in drawing in the 14th and 15th centuries because of the fine *line* it produced and the sharp point it maintained.

simultaneous contrasts The phenomenon of juxtaposed *colors* affecting the eye's reception of each, as when a painter places dark green next to light green, making the former appear even darker and the latter even lighter. See also *successive contrasts*.

sinopia A burnt-orange pigment used in *fresco* painting to transfer a *cartoon* to the *arriccio* before the artist paints the plaster.

site-specific art Art created for a specific location. See also *Environmental Art*.

skene Greek, "stage." The stage of a *classical* theater.

skenographia Greek, "scene painting"; the Greek term for *perspective* painting.

slip A mixture of fine clay and water used in ceramic decoration.

solidus (pl. **solidi**) A *Byzantine* gold coin.

space In art history, both the actual area an object occupies or a building encloses and the *illusionistic* representation of space in painting and sculpture.

spandrel The roughly triangular space enclosed by the curves of adjacent *arches* and a horizontal member connecting their vertexes; also, the space enclosed by the curve of an *arch* and an enclosing right angle. The area between the arch proper and the framing *columns* and *entablature*.

spectrum The range or band of visible colors in natural light.

sphinx A mythical Egyptian beast with the body of a lion and the head of a human.

splashed-ink painting See *haboku*.

springing The lowest stone of an *arch*, resting on the *impost block*. In *Gothic vaulting*, the lowest stone of a diagonal or transverse *rib*.

stained glass In *Gothic* architecture, the colored glass used for windows.

stanza (pl. **stanze**) Italian, "room."

statue A three-dimensional sculpture.

stele (pl. **stelae**) A *carved* stone slab used to mark graves or to commemorate historical events.

still life A picture depicting an arrangement of inanimate objects.

strigil A tool ancient Greek athletes used to scrape oil from their bodies after exercising.

stringcourse A raised horizontal *molding*, or band, in masonry. Its principal use is ornamental but it usually reflects interior structure.

strut A timber plank or other structural member used as a support in a building. Also a short section of marble used to support an arm or leg in a *statue*.

stucco A type of plaster used as a coating on exterior and interior walls. Also used as a sculptural *medium*.

stupa A large, mound-shaped Buddhist shrine.

style A distinctive artistic manner. Period style is the characteristic style of a specific time. Regional style is the style of a particular geographical area. Personal style is an individual artist's unique manner.

stylistic evidence In art history, the examination of the *style* of an artwork in order to determine its date or the identity of the artist.

stylobate The uppermost course of the platform of a *classical* Greek temple, which supports the *columns*.

stylus A needlelike tool used in *engraving* and *incising*; also, an ancient writing instrument used to inscribe clay or wax tablets.

subtractive light The painter's light in art; the light reflected from pigments and objects. See also *additive light*.

subtractive sculpture A kind of sculpture *technique* in which materials are taken away from the original mass; *carving*.

successive contrasts The phenomenon of colored afterimages. When a person looks intently at a *color* (green, for example) and then shifts to a white area, the fatigued eye momentarily perceives the *complementary color* (red). See also *simultaneous contrasts*.

sultan A *Muslim* ruler.

Sunnah The collection of the Prophet Muhammad's moral sayings and descriptions of his deeds.

superimposition In *Mesoamerican* architecture, the erection of a new structure on top of, and incorporating, an earlier structure; the nesting of a series of buildings inside one another.

Superrealism A *school* of painting and sculpture of the 1960s and 1970s that emphasized producing artworks based on scrupulous fidelity to optical fact. The Superrealist painters were also called Photorealists because many used photographs as sources for their imagery.

Suprematism A type of art formulated by Kazimir Malevich to convey his belief that the supreme reality in the world is pure feeling, which attaches to no object and thus calls for new, nonobjective forms in art—shapes not related to objects in the visible world.

surah A chapter of the *Koran*, divided into verses.

Surrealism A successor to *Dada*, Surrealism incorporated the improvisational nature of its predecessor into its exploration of the ways to express in art the world of dreams and the unconscious. Biomorphic Surrealists, such as Joan Miró, produced largely *abstract compositions*. *Naturalistic* Surrealists, notably Salvador Dalí, presented recognizable scenes transformed into a dream or nightmare image.

sutra In Buddhism, an account of a sermon by or a dialogue involving the Buddha. A scriptural account of the Buddha. See also *jataka*.

symbol An image that stands for another image or encapsulates an idea.

Symbolism A late-19th-century movement based on the idea that the artist was not an imitator of nature but a creator who transformed the facts of nature into a *symbol* of the inner experience of that fact.

symmetria Greek, "commensurability of parts." Polykleitos's treatise on his *canon* of proportions incorporated the principle of symmetria.

Synthetic Cubism A later phase of *Cubism*, in which paintings and drawings were constructed from objects and shapes cut from paper or other materials to represent parts of a subject, in order to engage the viewer with pictorial issues, such as figuration, realism, and abstraction.

T

taberna In Roman architecture, a single-room shop usually covered by a barrel *vault*.

tablinum The study or office in a Roman *domus*.

taj Arabic and Persian, "crown."

tapestry A weaving *technique* in which the *weft* threads are packed densely over the *warp* threads so that the designs are woven directly into the fabric.

tatami The traditional woven straw mat used for floor covering in Japanese architecture.

tattoo A permanent design on the skin produced using indelible dyes.

technique The processes artists employ to create *form*, as well as the distinctive, personal ways in which they handle their materials and tools.

tempera A *technique* of painting using pigment mixed with egg yolk, glue, or casein; also, the *medium* itself.

templon The columnar screen separating the sanctuary from the main body of a *Byzantine* church.

tenebrism Painting in the "shadowy manner," using violent contrasts of light and dark, as in the work of Caravaggio. The term derives from *tenebroso*.

tenebroso Italian, "shadowy." See *tenebrism*.

tepidarium The warm-bath section of a Roman bathing establishment.

terracotta Hard-baked clay, used for sculpture and as a building material. It may be *glazed* or painted.

terribilità Italian, "the sublime shadowed by the awesome and the fearful."

tessera (pl. **tesserae**) Greek, "cube." A tiny stone or piece of glass cut to the desired shape and size for use in forming a *mosaic*.

tetrarch One of four corulers.

tetrarchy Greek, "rule by four." A type of Roman government established in the late third century CE by Diocletian in an attempt to foster order by sharing power with potential rivals.

texture The quality of a surface (rough, smooth, hard, soft, shiny, dull) as revealed by light. In represented texture, a painter depicts an object as having a certain texture even though the pigment is the real texture.

theatron Greek, "place for seeing." In ancient Greek theaters, the slope overlooking the *orchestra* on which the spectators sat.

Theotokos Greek, "she who bore God." The Virgin Mary, the mother of Jesus.

Third Style mural In Roman *mural* painting, the *style* in which delicate linear fantasies were sketched on predominantly *monochromatic* backgrounds.

tholos (pl. **tholoi**) A temple with a circular plan. Also, the burial chamber of a *tholos tomb*.

tholos tomb In *Mycenaean* architecture, a beehive-shaped tomb with a circular plan.

thrust The outward force exerted by an *arch* or a *vault* that must be counterbalanced by a *buttress*.

toga The garment worn by an ancient Roman male citizen.

tokonoma A shallow alcove in a Japanese room, which is used for decoration, such as a painting or stylized flower arrangement.

tonality See *color*.

tondo (pl. **tondi**) A circular painting or *relief* sculpture.

torana Gateway in the stone fence around a *stupa,* located at the cardinal points of the compass.

torque The distinctive necklace worn by the Gauls.

tracery Ornamental stonework for holding *stained glass* in place, characteristic of *Gothic cathedrals*. In plate tracery, the glass fills only the "punched holes" in the heavy ornamental stonework. In bar tracery, the stained-glass windows fill almost the entire opening, and the stonework is unobtrusive.

transept The part of a church with an axis that crosses the *nave* at a right angle.

transverse arch An *arch* separating one *vaulted bay* from the next.

transverse rib See *rib*.

tribune In church architecture, a gallery over the inner *aisle* flanking the *nave*.

triclinium The dining room of a Roman *domus*.

trident The three-pronged pitchfork associated with the ancient Greek sea god Poseidon (Roman, Neptune).

triforium In a *Gothic cathedral*, the *blind arcaded* gallery below the *clerestory;* occasionally, the *arcades* are filled with *stained glass*.

triglyph A triple projecting, grooved member of a *Doric frieze* that alternates with *metopes*.

trilithon A pair of *monoliths* topped with a *lintel;* found in *megalithic* structures.

Trinity In Christianity, God the Father, his son Jesus Christ, and the Holy Spirit.

triptych A three-paneled painting, ivory plaque, or *altarpiece*. Also, a small, portable shrine with hinged wings used for private devotion.

triumphal arch In Roman architecture, a freestanding *arch* commemorating an important event, such as a military victory or the opening of a new road.

trompe l'oeil French, "fools the eye." A form of *illusionistic* painting that aims to deceive viewers into believing they are seeing real objects rather than a representation of those objects.

true fresco See *fresco*.

trumeau In church architecture, the *pillar* or center post supporting the *lintel* in the middle of the doorway.

tubicen Latin, "trumpet player."

tumulus (pl. **tumuli**) Latin, "burial mound." In Etruscan architecture, tumuli cover one or more subterranean multichambered tombs cut out of the local tufa (limestone). Also characteristic of the Japanese Kofun period of the third and fourth centuries CE.

tunnel vault See *vault*.

Tuscan column The standard type of Etruscan *column*. It resembles ancient Greek *Doric* columns but is made of wood, is unfluted, and has a *base*. Also a popular motif in *Renaissance* and *Baroque* architecture.

twisted perspective See *composite view*.

tympanum (pl. **tympana**) The space enclosed by a *lintel* and an *arch* over a doorway.

U

ukiyo-e Japanese, "pictures of the floating world." During the Edo period, *woodcut prints* depicting brothels, popular entertainment, and beautiful women.

underglaze In *porcelain* decoration, the *technique* of applying mineral colors to the surface before the main firing, followed by an application of clear *glaze*.

Upanishads South Asian religious texts of ca. 800–300 BCE that introduced the concepts of *samsara, karma,* and *moksha*.

uraeus An Egyptian cobra; one of the emblems of *pharaonic* kingship.

urna A whorl of hair, represented as a dot, between the brows; one of the *lakshanas* of the Buddha.

ushabti In ancient Egypt, a figurine placed in a tomb to act as a servant to the deceased in the afterlife.

ushnisha A knot of hair on the top of the head; one of the *lakshanas* of the Buddha.

V

valley temple The temple closest to the Nile River associated with each of the Great Pyramids at Gizeh in ancient Egypt.

value See *color*.

vanishing point See *perspective*.

vanitas Latin, "vanity." A term describing paintings (particularly 17th-century Dutch *still lifes*) that include references to death.

vault (adj. **vaulted**) A masonry roof or ceiling constructed on the *arch* principle, or a concrete roof of the same shape. A barrel (or tunnel) vault, semicylindrical in cross-*section,* is in effect a deep arch or an uninterrupted series of arches, one behind the other, over an oblong space. A quadrant vault is a half-barrel vault. A groin (or cross) vault is formed at the point at which two barrel vaults intersect at right angles. In a ribbed vault, there is a framework of *ribs* or arches under the intersections of the vaulting sections. A sexpartite vault is one whose ribs divide the vault into six compartments. A fan vault is a vault characteristic of English *Perpendicular Gothic* architecture, in which radiating ribs form a fanlike pattern.

vaulting web   See *web.*

Veda   Sanskrit, "knowledge." One of four second-millennium BCE South Asian compilations of religious learning.

veduta (pl. **vedute**)   Italian, "scenic view."

velarium   In a Roman *amphitheater,* the cloth awning that could be rolled down from the top of the *cavea* to shield spectators from sun or rain.

vellum   Calfskin prepared as a surface for writing or painting.

veristic   True to natural appearance; superrealistic.

vihara   A Buddhist *monastery,* often cut into a hill.

vimana   A pyramidal tower over the *garbha griha* of a Hindu temple of the southern style.

vita contemplativa   Latin, "contemplative life." The secluded spiritual life of monks and nuns.

volume   The *space* that *mass* organizes, divides, or encloses.

volute   A spiral, scroll-like form characteristic of the ancient Greek *Ionic capital.*

votive offering   A gift of gratitude to a deity.

voussoir   A wedge-shaped stone block used in the construction of a true *arch.* The central voussoir, which sets the arch, is called the keystone.

W

wabi   A 16th-century Japanese art style characterized by refined rusticity and an appreciation of simplicity and austerity.

wat   A Buddhist *monastery* in Cambodia.

web   The masonry blocks that fill the area between the *ribs* of a *groin vault.* Also called vaulting web.

weld   To join metal parts by heating, as in assembling the separate parts of a *statue* made by *casting.*

westwork   German, "western entrance structure." The *facade* and towers at the western end of a medieval church, principally in Germany.

wet-plate photography   An early photographic process in which the photographic plate is exposed, developed, and fixed while wet.

wet secco   See *fresco.*

white-ground painting   An ancient Greek vase-painting *technique* in which the pot was first covered with a *slip* of very fine white clay, over which black *glaze* was used to outline figures, and diluted brown, purple, red, and white were used to color them.

woodcut   A wooden block on the surface of which those parts not intended to *print* are cut away to a slight depth, leaving the design raised; also, the printed impression made with such a block.

Y

yakshi   Lesser local female Buddhist and Hindu goddesses associated with fertility and vegetation.

yamato-e   Also known as native-style painting, a purely Japanese style that often involves colorful, decorative representations of Japanese narratives or *landscapes.*

yang   In Chinese cosmology, the principle of active masculine energy, which permeates the universe in varying proportions with yin, the principle of passive feminine energy.

yasti   In Buddhist architecture, the mast or pole that arises from the dome of the *stupa* and its *harmika* and symbolizes the axis of the universe; it is adorned with a series of chatras (stone disks).

yin   See *yang.*

yoga   A method for controlling the body and relaxing the mind used in later Indian religions to yoke, or unite, the practitioner to the divine.

Z

Zen   A Japanese Buddhist sect and its doctrine, emphasizing enlightenment through intuition and introspection rather than the study of scripture. In Chinese, Chan.

ziggurat   In ancient Mesopotamian architecture, a monumental platform for a temple.

Bibliography

This list of books is very selective, but comprehensive enough to satisfy the reading interests of the beginning art history student and general reader. The resources listed range from works that are valuable primarily for their reproductions to those that are scholarly surveys of schools and periods or monographs on individual artists. The emphasis is on recent in-print books and on books likely to be found in college and municipal libraries. No entries for periodical articles appear, but the bibliography begins with a list of some the major journals that publish art historical scholarship in English.

SELECTED PERIODICALS

African Arts
American Art
American Indian Art
American Journal of Archaeology
Antiquity
Archaeology
Archives of American Art
Archives of Asian Art
Ars Orientalis
Art Bulletin
Art History
Art in America
Art Journal
Artforum International
Artnews
Burlington Magazine
Gesta
History of Photography
Journal of Egyptian Archaeology
Journal of Roman Archaeology
Journal of the Society of Architectural Historians
Journal of the Warburg and Courtauld Institutes
Latin American Antiquity
October
Oxford Art Journal
Women's Art Journal

GENERAL STUDIES

Baxandall, Michael. *Patterns of Intention: On the Historical Explanation of Pictures.* New Haven, Conn.: Yale University Press, 1985.

Boström, Antonia. *The Encyclopedia of Sculpture.* 3 vols. London: Routledge, 2003.

Broude, Norma, and Mary D. Garrard, eds. *The Expanding Discourse: Feminism and Art History.* New York: HarperCollins, 1992.

Bryson, Norman, Michael Ann Holly, and Keith Moxey. *Visual Theory: Painting and Interpretation.* New York: Cambridge University Press, 1991.

Burden, Ernst. *Illustrated Dictionary of Architecture.* 2d ed. New York: McGraw-Hill, 2002.

Büttner, Nils. *Landscape Painting: A History.* New York: Abbeville, 2006.

Carrier, David. *A World Art History and Its Objects.* University Park: Pennsylvania State University Press, 2009.

Chadwick, Whitney. *Women, Art, and Society.* 4th ed. New York: Thames & Hudson, 2007.

Cheetham, Mark A., Michael Ann Holly, and Keith Moxey, eds. *The Subjects of Art History: Historical Objects in Contemporary Perspective.* New York: Cambridge University Press, 1998.

Chilvers, Ian, and Harold Osborne, eds. *The Oxford Dictionary of Art.* 3d ed. New York: Oxford University Press, 2004.

Corbin, George A. *Native Arts of North America, Africa, and the South Pacific: An Introduction.* New York: HarperCollins, 1988.

Crouch, Dora P., and June G. Johnson. *Traditions in Architecture: Africa, America, Asia, and Oceania.* New York: Oxford University Press, 2000.

Curl, James Stevens. *Oxford Dictionary of Architecture and Landscape Architecture.* 2d ed. New York: Oxford University Press, 2006.

Duby, Georges, ed. *Sculpture: From Antiquity to the Present.* 2 vols. Cologne: Taschen, 1999.

Encyclopedia of World Art. 17 vols. New York: McGraw-Hill, 1959–1987.

Fine, Sylvia Honig. *Women and Art: A History of Women Painters and Sculptors from the Renaissance to the 20th Century.* Montclair: Alanheld & Schram, 1978.

Fleming, John, Hugh Honour, and Nikolaus Pevsner. *The Penguin Dictionary of Architecture and Landscape Architecture.* 5th ed. New York: Penguin, 2000.

Frazier, Nancy. *The Penguin Concise Dictionary of Art History.* New York: Penguin, 2000.

Freedberg, David. *The Power of Images: Studies in the History and Theory of Response.* Chicago: University of Chicago Press, 1989.

Gaze, Delia, ed. *Dictionary of Women Artists.* 2 vols. London: Routledge, 1997.

Hall, James. *Illustrated Dictionary of Subjects and Symbols in Eastern and Western Art.* 2d ed. Boulder, Colo.: Westview, 2008.

Harris, Anne Sutherland, and Linda Nochlin. *Women Artists: 1550–1950.* Los Angeles: Los Angeles County Museum of Art, 1977.

Hults, Linda C. *The Print in the Western World: An Introductory History.* Madison: University of Wisconsin Press, 1996.

Kemp, Martin. *The Science of Art: Optical Themes in Western Art from Brunelleschi to Seurat.* New Haven, Conn.: Yale University Press, 1990.

Kostof, Spiro, and Gregory Castillo. *A History of Architecture: Settings and Rituals.* 2d ed. Oxford: Oxford University Press, 1995.

Kultermann, Udo. *The History of Art History.* New York: Abaris, 1993.

Lucie Smith, Edward. *The Thames & Hudson Dictionary of Art Terms.* 2d ed. New York: Thames & Hudson, 2004.

Moffett, Marian, Michael Fazio, and Lawrence Wadehouse. *A World History of Architecture.* Boston: McGraw-Hill, 2004.

Murray, Peter, and Linda Murray. *The Penguin Dictionary of Art and Artists.* 7th ed. New York: Penguin, 1998.

Nelson, Robert S., and Richard Shiff, eds. *Critical Terms for Art History.* Chicago: University of Chicago Press, 1996.

Pazanelli, Roberta, ed. *The Color of Life: Polychromy in Sculpture from Antiquity to the Present.* Los Angeles: J. Paul Getty Museum, 2008.

Penny, Nicholas. *The Materials of Sculpture.* New Haven, Conn.: Yale University Press, 1993.

Pevsner, Nikolaus. *A History of Building Types.* London: Thames & Hudson, 1987. Reprint of 1979 ed.

———. *An Outline of European Architecture.* 8th ed. Baltimore: Penguin, 1974.

Pierce, James Smith. *From Abacus to Zeus: A Handbook of Art History.* 7th ed. Upper Saddle River, N.J.: Pearson Prentice Hall, 2003.

Placzek, Adolf K., ed. *Macmillan Encyclopedia of Architects.* 4 vols. New York: Macmillan, 1982.

Podro, Michael. *The Critical Historians of Art*. New Haven, Conn.: Yale University Press, 1982.

Pollock, Griselda. *Vision and Difference: Femininity, Feminism and Histories of Art*. London: Routledge, 1988.

Preziosi, Donald, ed. *The Art of Art History: A Critical Anthology*. New York: Oxford University Press, 1998.

Read, Herbert. *The Thames & Hudson Dictionary of Art and Artists*. Rev. ed. New York: Thames & Hudson, 1994.

Reid, Jane D. *The Oxford Guide to Classical Mythology in the Arts 1300–1990s*. 2 vols. New York: Oxford University Press, 1993.

Roth, Leland M. *Understanding Architecture: Its Elements, History, and Meaning*. 2d ed. Boulder, Colo.: Westview, 2006.

Schama, Simon. *The Power of Art*. New York: Ecco, 2006.

Slatkin, Wendy. *Women Artists in History: From Antiquity to the 20th Century*. 4th ed. Upper Saddle River, N.J.: Prentice Hall, 2000.

Steer, John, and Antony White. *Atlas of Western Art History: Artists, Sites and Monuments from Ancient Greece to the Modern Age*. New York: Facts on File, 1994.

Stratton, Arthur. *The Orders of Architecture: Greek, Roman and Renaissance*. London: Studio, 1986.

Summers, David. *Real Spaces: World Art History and the Rise of Western Modernism*. London: Phaidon, 2003.

Sutton, Ian. *Western Architecture: From Ancient Greece to the Present*. New York: Thames & Hudson, 1999.

Trachtenberg, Marvin, and Isabelle Hyman. *Architecture: From Prehistory to Post-Modernism*. 2d ed. Upper Saddle River, N.J.: Prentice Hall, 2003.

Turner, Jane, ed. *The Dictionary of Art*. 34 vols. New ed. New York: Oxford University Press, 2003.

Watkin, David. *A History of Western Architecture*. 5th ed. London: Laurence King, 2011.

West, Shearer. *Portraiture*. New York: Oxford University Press, 2004.

Wittkower, Rudolf. *Sculpture Processes and Principles*. New York: Harper & Row, 1977.

Zijlmans, Kitty, and Wilfried van Damme, eds. *World Art Studies: Exploring Concepts and Approaches*. Amsterdam: Valiz, 2008.

ANCIENT ART, GENERAL

Boardman, John. *The World of Ancient Art*. London: Thames & Hudson, 2006.

———, ed. *The Oxford History of Classical Art*. New York: Oxford University Press, 1997.

Chitham, Robert. *The Classical Orders of Architecture*. 2d ed. Boston: Architectural Press, 2005.

Dunbabin, Katherine. *Mosaics of the Greek and Roman World*. New York: Cambridge University Press, 1999.

Gates, Charles. *Ancient Cities: The Archaeology of Urban Life in the Ancient Near East and Egypt, Greece, and Rome*. 2d ed. London: Routledge, 2011.

Grossman, Janet Burnett. *Looking at Greek and Roman Sculpture in Stone: A Guide to Terms, Styles, and Techniques*. Los Angeles: J. Paul Getty Museum, 2003.

Ling, Roger. *Ancient Mosaics*. Princeton, N.J.: Princeton University Press, 1998.

Renfrew, Colin, and Paul G. Bahn. *Archaeology: Theories, Methods, and Practices*. London: Thames & Hudson, 1991.

Trigger, Bruce. *Understanding Early Civilizations: A Comparative Study*. New York: Cambridge University Press, 2003.

CHAPTER 1: Prehistory and the First Civilizations

Prehistory

Aujoulat, Norbert. *Lascaux: Movement, Space, and Time*. New York: Abrams, 2005.

Bahn, Paul G. *The Cambridge Illustrated History of Prehistoric Art*. New York: Cambridge University Press, 1998.

———. *Cave Art: A Guide to the Decorated Ice Age Caves of Europe*. London: Frances Lincoln, 2007.

Bahn, Paul G., and Jean Vertut. *Journey through the Ice Age*. Berkeley: University of California Press, 1997.

Clottes, Jean. *Cave Art*. London: Phaidon, 2008.

Cunliffe, Barry, ed. *The Oxford Illustrated Prehistory of Europe*. New York: Oxford University Press, 1994.

Guthrie, R. Dale. *The Nature of Paleolithic Art*. Chicago: University of Chicago Press, 2005.

Hodder, Ian. *The Leopard's Tale: Revealing the Mysteries of Çatalhöyük*. London: Thames & Hudson, 2006.

Scarre, Chris. *Exploring Prehistoric Europe*. New York: Oxford University Press, 1998.

White, Randall. *Prehistoric Art: The Symbolic Journey of Humankind*. New York: Abrams, 2003.

Ancient Near East

Allen, Lindsay. *The Persian Empire*. Chicago: University of Chicago Press, 2005.

Amiet, Pierre. *Art of the Ancient Near East*. New York: Abrams, 1980.

Ascalone, Enrico. *Mesopotamia: Assyrians, Sumerians, Babylonians*. Berkeley and Los Angeles: University of California Press, 2007.

Bahrani, Zainab. *The Graven Image: Representation in Babylonia and Assyria*. Philadelphia: University of Pennsylvania Press, 2003.

Collins, Paul. *Assyrian Palace Sculptures*. Austin: University of Texas Press, 2008.

Collon, Dominique. *Ancient Near Eastern Art*. Berkeley: University of California Press, 1995.

Crawford, Harriet. *Sumer and the Sumerians*. 2d ed. New York: Cambridge University Press, 2004.

Curatola, Giovanni, ed. *The Art and Architecture of Mesopotamia*. New York: Abbeville, 2007.

Curtis, John E., and Nigel Tallis. *Forgotten Empire: The World of Ancient Persia*. Berkeley: University of California Press, 2005.

Finkel, Irving L., and Michael J. Seymour, eds. *Babylon*. New York: Oxford University Press, 2008.

Foster, Benjamin R., and Karen Polinger Foster. *Civilizations of Ancient Iraq*. Princeton, N.J.: Princeton University Press, 2009.

Frankfort, Henri. *The Art and Architecture of the Ancient Orient*. 5th ed. New Haven, Conn.: Yale University Press, 1996.

Meyers, Eric M., ed. *The Oxford Encyclopedia of Archaeology in the Near East*. 5 vols. New York: Oxford University Press, 1997.

Moortgat, Anton. *The Art of Ancient Mesopotamia*. New York: Phaidon, 1969.

Parrot, André. *The Arts of Assyria*. New York: Golden Press, 1961.

———. *Sumer: The Dawn of Art*. New York: Golden Press, 1961.

Reade, Julian E. *Assyrian Sculpture*. Cambridge, Mass.: Harvard University Press, 1999.

———. *Mesopotamia*. Cambridge, Mass.: Harvard University Press, 1991.

Roaf, Michael. *Cultural Atlas of Mesopotamia and the Ancient Near East*. New York: Facts on File, 1990.

Sasson, Jack M., ed. *Civilizations of the Ancient Near East*. 4 vols. New York: Scribner, 1995.

Snell, Daniel C. *Life in the Ancient Near East: 3100–332 B.C.* New Haven, Conn.: Yale University Press, 1997.

Strommenger, Eva, and Max Hirmer. *5,000 Years of the Art of Mesopotamia*. New York: Abrams, 1964.

Egypt

Arnold, Dieter. *Building in Egypt: Pharaonic Stone Masonry*. New York: Oxford University Press, 1991.

Arnold, Dorothea. *When the Pyramids Were Built: Egyptian Art of the Old Kingdom*. New York: Rizzoli, 1999.

Baines, John, and Jaromír Málek. *Atlas of Ancient Egypt*. New York: Facts on File, 1980.

Bard, Kathryn A. *An Introduction to the Archaeology of Ancient Egypt*. Oxford: Blackwell, 2007.

———, ed. *Encyclopedia of the Archaeology of Ancient Egypt*. London: Routledge, 1999.

Davis, Whitney. *The Canonical Tradition in Ancient Egyptian Art*. New York: Cambridge University Press, 1989.

Dodson, Aidam, and Salima Ikram. *The Tomb in Ancient Egypt*. New York: Thames & Hudson, 2008.

Ikram, Salima, and Aidan Dodson. *The Mummy in Ancient Egypt: Equipping the Dead for Eternity*. New York: Thames & Hudson, 1998.

Kemp, Barry J. *Ancient Egypt: Anatomy of a Civilization*. 2d ed. New York: Routledge, 2006.

Lehner, Mark. *The Complete Pyramids: Solving the Ancient Mysteries*. New York: Thames & Hudson, 1997.

Málek, Jaromír. *Egypt: 4,000 Years of Art*. New York: Phaidon, 2003.
——. *Egyptian Art*. London: Phaidon, 1999.
O'Neill, John P. *Egyptian Art in the Age of the Pyramids*. New York: Abrams, 1999.
Redford, Donald B., ed. *The Oxford Encyclopedia of Ancient Egypt*. 3 vols. New York: Oxford University Press, 2001.
Robins, Gay. *The Art of Ancient Egypt*. Rev. ed. Cambridge, Mass.: Harvard University Press, 2008.
Schulz, Regina, and Matthias Seidel, eds. *Egypt: The World of the Pharaohs*. Cologne: Könemann, 1999.
Shafer, Byron E., ed. *Temples of Ancient Egypt*. Ithaca, N.Y.: Cornell University Press, 1997.
Shaw, Ian, and Paul Nicholson. *The Dictionary of Ancient Egypt*. London: British Museum, 1995.
Silverman, David P., ed. *Ancient Egypt*. New York: Oxford University Press, 1997.
Smith, William Stevenson, and William Kelly Simpson. *The Art and Architecture of Ancient Egypt*. Rev. ed. New Haven, Conn.: Yale University Press, 1998.
Weeks, Kent R., ed. *Valley of the Kings*. Vercelli: White Star, 2001.
Wildung, Dietrich. *Egypt: From Prehistory to the Romans*. Cologne: Taschen, 1997.

CHAPTER 2: Ancient Greece

Prehistoric Aegean

Betancourt, Philip P. *Introduction to Aegean Art*. New York: Institute for Aegean Prehistory, 2007.
Castleden, Rodney. *Mycenaeans*. London: Routledge, 2005.
Cullen, Tracey, ed. *Aegean Prehistory: A Review*. Boston: Archaeological Institute of America, 2001.
Dickinson, Oliver P.T.K. *The Aegean Bronze Age*. New York: Cambridge University Press, 1994.
Doumas, Christos. *The Wall-Paintings of Thera*. Athens: Thera Foundation, 1992.
Fitton, J. Lesley. *Cycladic Art*. 2d ed. Cambridge, Mass.: Harvard University Press, 1999.
——. *The Discovery of the Greek Bronze Age*. London: British Museum, 1995.
Forsyth, Phyllis Young. *Thera in the Bronze Age*. New York: Peter Lang, 1997.
Getz-Preziosi, Patricia. *Sculptors of the Cyclades: Individual and Tradition in the Third Millennium B.C.* Ann Arbor. University of Michigan Press, 1987.
Graham, James W. *The Palaces of Crete*. Princeton, N.J.: Princeton University Press, 1987.
Hood, Sinclair. *The Arts in Prehistoric Greece*. New Haven, Conn.: Yale University Press, 1992.
Immerwahr, Sarah A. *Aegean Painting in the Bronze Age*. University Park: Pennsylvania State University Press, 1990.
Marinatos, Spyridon, and Max Hirmer. *Crete and Mycenae*. London: Thames & Hudson, 1960.
Preziosi, Donald, and Louise A. Hitchcock. *Aegean Art and Architecture*. New York: Oxford University Press, 1999.
Schofield, Louise. *The Mycenaeans*. London: British Museum, 2007.
Shelmerdine, Cynthia W., ed. *The Cambridge Companion to the Aegean Bronze Age*. New York: Cambridge University Press, 2008.
Warren, Peter. *The Aegean Civilizations: The Making of the Past*. New York: Peter Bedrick, 1989.

Greece

Biers, William. *The Archaeology of Greece: An Introduction*. 2d ed. Ithaca, N.Y.: Cornell University Press, 1996.
Boardman, John. *Athenian Black Figure Vases*. Rev. ed. New York: Thames & Hudson, 1985.
——. *Athenian Red Figure Vases: The Archaic Period*. New York: Thames & Hudson, 1988.
——. *Athenian Red Figure Vases: The Classical Period*. New York: Thames & Hudson, 1989.
——. *Greek Sculpture: The Archaic Period*. Rev. ed. New York: Thames & Hudson, 1985.
——. *Greek Sculpture: The Classical Period*. New York: Thames & Hudson, 1987.
——. *Greek Sculpture: The Late Classical Period and Sculpture in Colonies and Overseas*. New York: Thames & Hudson, 1995.
Camp, John M. *The Archaeology of Athens*. New Haven, Conn.: Yale University Press, 2001.
Clark, Andrew J., Maya Elston, and Mary Louise Hart. *Understanding Greek Vases: A Guide to Terms, Styles, and Techniques*. Los Angeles: J. Paul Getty Museum, 2002.
Fullerton, Mark D. *Greek Art*. New York: Cambridge University Press, 2000.
Haynes, Denys E. L. *The Technique of Greek Bronze Statuary*. Mainz: von Zabern, 1992.
Hurwit, Jeffrey M. *The Art and Culture of Early Greece, 1100–480 B.C.* Ithaca, N.Y.: Cornell University Press, 1985.
——. *The Athenian Acropolis: History, Mythology, and Archaeology from the Neolithic Era to the Present*. New York: Cambridge University Press, 1999.
Jenkins, Ian. *Greek Architecture and Its Sculpture*. Cambridge, Mass.: Harvard University Press, 2006.
Lawrence, Arnold W., and R. A. Tomlinson. *Greek Architecture*. Rev. ed. New Haven, Conn.: Yale University Press, 1996.
Mattusch, Carol C. *Classical Bronzes: The Art and Craft of Greek and Roman Statuary*. Ithaca, N.Y.: Cornell University Press, 1996.
Mee, Christopher. *Greek Archaeology*. Hoboken, N.J.: Wiley-Blackwell, 2011.
Mee, Christopher, and Tony Spawforth. *Greece: An Oxford Archaeological Guide*. New York: Oxford University Press, 2001.
Morris, Sarah P. *Daidalos and the Origins of Greek Art*. Princeton, N.J.: Princeton University Press, 1992.
Neer, Richard T. *The Emergence of the Classical Style in Greek Sculpture*. Chicago: University of Chicago Press, 2010.
——. *Greek Art and Archaeology: A New History, c. 2500–c. 150 BCE*. New York: Thames & Hudson, 2011.
Osborne, Robin. *Archaic and Classical Greek Art*. New York: Oxford University Press, 1998.
Palagia, Olga, ed. *Greek Sculpture. Functions, Materials, and Techniques in the Archaic and Classical Periods*. New York: Cambridge University Press, 2006.
Pedley, John Griffiths. *Greek Art and Archaeology*. 4th ed. Upper Saddle River, N.J.: Prentice Hall, 2007.
Pollitt, Jerome J. *Art in the Hellenistic Age*. New York: Cambridge University Press, 1986.
——. *The Art of Ancient Greece: Sources and Documents*. 2d ed. New York: Cambridge University Press, 1990.
Rhodes, Robin F. *Architecture and Meaning on the Athenian Acropolis*. New York: Cambridge University Press, 1995.
Ridgway, Brunilde S. *The Archaic Style in Greek Sculpture*. 2d ed. Chicago: Ares, 1993.
——. *Fifth Century Styles in Greek Sculpture*. Princeton, N.J.: Princeton University Press, 1981.
——. *Fourth-Century Styles in Greek Sculpture*. Madison: University of Wisconsin Press, 1997.
——. *Hellenistic Sculpture I: The Styles of ca. 331–200 B.C.* Madison: University of Wisconsin Press, 1990.
——. *Hellenistic Sculpture II: The Styles of ca. 200–100 B.C.* Madison: University of Wisconsin Press, 2000.
——. *Prayers in Stone: Greek Architectural Sculpture*. Berkeley: University of California Press, 1999.
Robertson, Martin. *A History of Greek Art*. Rev. ed. 2 vols. New York: Cambridge University Press, 1986.
Smith, R.R.R. *Hellenistic Sculpture*. New York: Thames & Hudson, 1991.
Spawforth, Tony. *The Complete Greek Temples*. London: Thames & Hudson, 2006.
Spivey, Nigel. *Greek Art*. London: Phaidon, 1997.
Stansbury-O'Donnell, Mark D. *Looking at Greek Art*. New York: Cambridge University Press, 2010.
——. *Pictorial Narrative in Ancient Greek Art*. New York: Cambridge University Press, 1999.
Stewart, Andrew. *Classical Greece and the Birth of Western Art*. New York: Cambridge University Press, 2008.
——. *Greek Sculpture: An Exploration*. 2 vols. New Haven, Conn.: Yale University Press, 1990.

CHAPTER 3: The Roman Empire

Etruria

Barker, Graeme, and Tom Rasmussen. *The Etruscans*. Oxford: Blackwell, 1998.

Bonfante, Larissa, ed. *Etruscan Life and Afterlife: A Handbook of Etruscan Studies*. Detroit: Wayne State University Press, 1986.

Brendel, Otto J. *Etruscan Art*. 2d ed. New Haven, Conn.: Yale University Press, 1995.

Haynes, Sybille. *Etruscan Civilization: A Cultural History*. Los Angeles: J. Paul Getty Museum, 2000.

Spivey, Nigel. *Etruscan Art*. New York: Thames & Hudson, 1997.

Sprenger, Maja, Gilda Bartoloni, and Max Hirmer. *The Etruscans: Their History, Art, and Architecture*. New York: Abrams, 1983.

Steingräber, Stephan. *Abundance of Life: Etruscan Wall Painting*. Los Angeles: J. Paul Getty Museum, 2006.

Torelli, Mario, ed. *The Etruscans*. New York: Rizzoli, 2001.

Rome

Anderson, James C., Jr. *Roman Architecture and Society*. Baltimore: Johns Hopkins University Press, 1997.

Barton, Ian M., ed. *Roman Domestic Buildings*. Exeter: University of Exeter Press, 1996.

———. *Roman Public Buildings*. 2d ed. Exeter: University of Exeter Press, 1995.

Claridge, Amanda. *Rome: An Oxford Archaeological Guide*. 2d ed. New York: Oxford University Press, 2010.

Clarke, John R. *The Houses of Roman Italy, 100 B.C.–A.D. 250*. Berkeley and Los Angeles: University of California Press, 1991.

Coarelli, Filippo. *Rome and Environs: An Archaeological Guide*. Berkeley and Los Angeles: University of California Press, 2007.

D'Ambra, Eve. *Roman Art*. New York: Cambridge University Press, 1998.

Dobbins, John J., and Pedar W. Foss, eds. *The World of Pompeii*. London: Routledge, 2007.

Dyson, Stephen L. *Rome: A Living Portrait of an Ancient City*. Baltimore: Johns Hopkins University Press, 2010.

Hannestad, Niels. *Roman Art and Imperial Policy*. Aarhus: Aarhus University Press, 1986.

Kleiner, Diana E. E. *Roman Sculpture*. New Haven, Conn.: Yale University Press, 1992.

Kleiner, Fred S. *A History of Roman Art*. Enhanced ed. Belmont, Calif.: Wadsworth, 2010.

Kraus, Theodor. *Pompeii and Herculaneum: The Living Cities of the Dead*. New York: Abrams, 1975.

Lancaster, Lynne. *Concrete Vaulted Construction in Imperial Rome*. New York: Cambridge University Press, 2006.

Ling, Roger. *Roman Painting*. New York: Cambridge University Press, 1991.

MacDonald, William L. *The Architecture of the Roman Empire I: An Introductory Study*. Rev. ed. New Haven, Conn.: Yale University Press, 1982.

Mattusch, Carol C., ed. *Pompeii and the Roman Villa: Art and Culture around the Bay of Naples*. New York: Thames & Hudson, 2008.

Mazzoleni, Donatella. *Domus: Wall Painting in the Roman House*. Los Angeles: J. Paul Getty Museum, 2004.

Pollitt, Jerome J. *The Art of Rome, 753 B.C.–A.D. 337: Sources and Documents*. Rev. ed. New York: Cambridge University Press, 1983.

Richardson, Lawrence, Jr. *A New Topographical Dictionary of Ancient Rome*. Baltimore: Johns Hopkins University Press, 1992.

———. *Pompeii: An Architectural History*. Baltimore: Johns Hopkins University Press, 1988.

Stewart, Peter. *The Social History of Roman Art*. New York: Cambridge University Press, 2008.

Taylor, Rabun. *Roman Builders*. New York: Cambridge University Press, 2003.

Toynbee, Jocelyn M. C. *Death and Burial in the Roman World*. London: Thames & Hudson, 1971.

Wallace-Hadrill, Andrew. *Houses and Society in Pompeii and Herculaneum*. Princeton, N.J.: Princeton University Press, 1994.

Ward-Perkins, John B. *Roman Imperial Architecture*. 2d ed. New Haven, Conn.: Yale University Press, 1981.

Wilson-Jones, Mark. *Principles of Roman Architecture*. New Haven, Conn.: Yale University Press, 2000.

Zanker, Paul. *The Power of Images in the Age of Augustus*. Ann Arbor: University of Michigan Press, 1988.

———. *Roman Art*. Los Angeles: J. Paul Getty Museum, 2010.

MEDIEVAL ART, GENERAL

Alexander, Jonathan J. G. *Medieval Illuminators and Their Methods of Work*. New Haven, Conn.: Yale University Press, 1992.

Andrews, Francis B. *The Mediaeval Builders and Their Methods*. New York: Barnes & Noble, 1993.

Calkins, Robert G. *Medieval Architecture in Western Europe: From A.D. 300 to 1500*. New York: Oxford University Press, 1998.

Coldstream, Nicola. *Medieval Architecture*. New York: Oxford University Press, 2002.

Cross, Frank L., and Elizabeth A. Livingstone, eds. *The Oxford Dictionary of the Christian Church*. 3d ed. New York: Oxford University Press, 1997.

De Hamel, Christopher. *A History of Illuminated Manuscripts*. Oxford: Phaidon, 1986.

Kessler, Herbert L. *Seeing Medieval Art*. Toronto: Broadview Press, 2004.

Murray, Peter, and Linda Murray. *The Oxford Companion to Christian Art and Architecture*. New York: Oxford University Press, 1996.

Ross, Leslie. *Medieval Art: A Topical Dictionary*. Westport, Conn.: Greenwood, 1996.

Sekules, Veronica. *Medieval Art*. New York: Oxford University Press, 2001.

Snyder, James, Henry Luttikhuizen, and Dorothy Verkerk. *Art of the Middle Ages*. 2d ed. Upper Saddle River, N.J.: Prentice Hall, 2006.

Stokstad, Marilyn. *Medieval Art*. 2d ed. Boulder, Colo.: Westview, 2004.

CHAPTER 4: Early Christianity and Byzantium

Bowersock, G. W., Peter Brown, and Oleg Grabar, eds. *Late Antiquity: A Guide to the Postclassical World*. Cambridge, Mass.: Harvard University Press, 1998.

Cioffarelli, Ada. *Guide to the Catacombs of Rome and Its Surroundings*. Rome: Bonsignori, 2000.

Cormack, Robin. *Byzantine Art*. New York: Oxford University Press, 2000.

———. *Icons*. Cambridge, Mass.: Harvard University Press, 2007.

Cormack, Robin, and Maria Vassiliki. *Byzantium, 330–1453*. London: Royal Academy of Arts, 2008.

Deliyannis, Deborah Mauskopf. *Ravenna in Late Antiquity*. New York: Cambridge University Press, 2010.

Elsner, Jás. *Art and the Roman Viewer: The Transformation of Art from the Pagan World to Christianity*. New York: Cambridge University Press, 1995.

———. *Imperial Rome and Christian Triumph*. New York: Oxford University Press, 1998.

Freely, John. *Byzantine Monuments of Istanbul*. New York: Cambridge University Press, 2004.

Grabar, André. *The Beginnings of Christian Art, 200–395*. London: Thames & Hudson, 1967.

———. *Christian Iconography*. Princeton, N.J.: Princeton University Press, 1980.

———. *The Golden Age of Justinian: From the Death of Theodosius to the Rise of Islam*. New York: Odyssey Press, 1967.

Jensen, Robin Margaret. *Understanding Early Christian Art*. New York: Routledge, 2000.

Kleinbauer, W. Eugene. *Hagia Sophia*. London: Scala, 2004.

Koch, Guntram. *Early Christian Art and Architecture*. London: SCM Press, 1996.

Krautheimer, Richard, and Slobodan Ćurčić. *Early Christian and Byzantine Architecture*. 4th ed. New Haven, Conn.: Yale University Press, 1986.

Lowden, John. *Early Christian and Byzantine Art*. London: Phaidon, 1997.

Mango, Cyril. *Art of the Byzantine Empire, 312–1453: Sources and Documents*. Toronto: University of Toronto Press, 1986. Reprint of 1972 ed.

———. *Byzantine Architecture*. New York: Electa/Rizzoli, 1985.

Mathews, Thomas F. *Byzantium: From Antiquity to the Renaissance*. New York: Abrams, 1998.

———. *The Clash of Gods: A Reinterpretation of Early Christian Art*. Rev. ed. Princeton, N.J.: Princeton University Press, 1999.

Ousterhout, Robert. *Master Builders of Byzantium*. Princeton, N.J.: Princeton University Press, 2000.

Pelikan, Jaroslav. *Imago Dei: The Byzantine Apologia for Icons*. Princeton, N.J.: Princeton University Press, 1990.

Poeschke, Joachim. *Italian Mosaics, 300–1300*. New York: Abbeville, 2010.

Rodley, Lyn. *Byzantine Art and Architecture: An Introduction*. New York: Cambridge University Press, 1994.

Spier, Jeffrey, ed. *Picturing the Bible: The Earliest Christian Art*. New Haven, Conn.: Yale University Press, 2007.

Webster, Leslie, and Michelle Brown, eds. *The Transformation of the Roman World, A.D. 400–900*. Berkeley: University of California Press, 1997.

CHAPTER 5: The Islamic World

Baker, Patricia L. *Islam and the Religious Arts*. London: Continuum, 2004.

Blair, Sheila S., and Jonathan Bloom. *The Art and Architecture of Islam 1250–1800*. New Haven, Conn.: Yale University Press, 1994.

Bloom, Jonathan, and Sheila S. Blair. *The Grove Encyclopedia of Islamic Art and Architecture*. New York: Oxford University Press, 2009.

———. *Islamic Arts*. London: Phaidon, 1997.

Brend, Barbara. *Islamic Art*. Cambridge, Mass.: Harvard University Press, 1991.

Ettinghausen, Richard, Oleg Grabar, and Marilyn Jenkins-Madina. *The Art and Architecture of Islam, 650–1250*. Rev. ed. New Haven, Conn.: Yale University Press, 2001.

Frishman, Martin, and Hasan-Uddin Khan. *The Mosque: History, Architectural Development and Regional Diversity*. New York: Thames & Hudson, 1994.

Grabar, Oleg. *The Formation of Islamic Art*. Rev. ed. New Haven, Conn.: Yale University Press, 1987.

———. *Islamic Visual Culture, 1100–1800*. New York: Ashgate, 2006.

Grube, Ernst J. *Architecture of the Islamic World: Its History and Social Meaning*. 2d ed. New York: Thames & Hudson, 1984.

Hattstein, Markus, and Peter Delius, eds. *Islam: Art and Architecture*. Cologne: Könemann, 2000.

Hillenbrand, Robert. *Islamic Architecture: Form, Function, Meaning*. Edinburgh: Edinburgh University Press, 1994.

———. *Islamic Art and Architecture*. New York: Thames & Hudson, 1999.

Irwin, Robert. *The Alhambra*. Cambridge, Mass.: Harvard University Press, 2004.

———. *Islamic Art in Context: Art, Architecture, and the Literary World*. New York: Abrams, 1997.

Schimmel, Annemarie. *Calligraphy and Islamic Culture*. New York: New York University Press, 1984.

Tadgell, Christopher. *Four Caliphates: The Formation and Development of the Islamic Tradition*. London: Ellipsis, 1998.

CHAPTER 6: Early Medieval and Romanesque Europe

Ashley, Kathleen, and Marilyn Deegan. *Being a Pilgrim: Art and Ritual on the Medieval Routes to Santiago*. Burlington, Vt.: Lund Humphries, 2009.

Bagnoli, Martina, Holger A. Kleiner, C. Griffith Mann, and James Robinson, eds. *Treasures of Heaven: Saints, Relics, and Devotion in Medieval Europe*. New Haven, Conn.: Yale University Press, 2010.

Cahn, Walter. *Romanesque Manuscripts: The Twelfth Century*. 2 vols. London: Miller, 1998.

Collins, Roger. *Early Medieval Europe, 200–1000*. New York: St. Martin's, 1991.

Conant, Kenneth J. *Carolingian and Romanesque Architecture, 800–1200*. 4th ed. New Haven, Conn.: Yale University Press, 1992.

Davis-Weyer, Caecilia. *Early Medieval Art, 300–1150: Sources and Documents*. Toronto: University of Toronto Press, 1986. Reprint of 1971 ed.

Diebold, William J. *Word and Image: An Introduction to Early Medieval Art*. Boulder, Colo.: Westview Press, 2000.

Dodwell, Charles R. *The Pictorial Arts of the West, 800–1200*. New Haven, Conn.: Yale University Press, 1993.

Harbison, Peter. *The Golden Age of Irish Art: The Medieval Achievement 600–1200*. New York: Thames & Hudson, 1999.

Hearn, Millard F. *Romanesque Sculpture: The Revival of Monumental Stone Sculpture in the Eleventh and Twelfth Centuries*. Ithaca, N.Y.: Cornell University Press, 1981.

Henderson, George. *From Durrow to Kells: The Insular Gospel-Books, 650–800*. London: Thames & Hudson, 1987.

Hubert, Jean, Jean Porcher, and Wolfgang Fritz Volbach. *The Carolingian Renaissance*. New York: Braziller, 1970.

Lasko, Peter. *Ars Sacra, 800–1200*. 2d ed. New Haven, Conn.: Yale University Press, 1994.

McClendon, Charles. *The Origins of Medieval Architecture: Building in Europe, A.D. 600–900*. New Haven, Conn.: Yale University Press, 2005.

Minne-Sève, Viviane, and Hervé Kergall. *Romanesque and Gothic France: Architecture and Sculpture*. New York: Abrams, 2000.

Nees, Lawrence J. *Early Medieval Art*. New York: Oxford University Press, 2002.

Petzold, Andreas. *Romanesque Art*. New York: Abrams, 1995.

Stalley, Roger. *Early Medieval Architecture*. New York: Oxford University Press, 1999.

Toman, Rolf, ed. *Romanesque: Architecture, Sculpture, Painting*. Cologne: Könemann, 1997.

CHAPTER 7: Gothic and Late Medieval Europe

Bony, Jean. *French Gothic Architecture of the Twelfth and Thirteenth Centuries*. Berkeley: University of California Press, 1983.

Branner, Robert. *Manuscript Painting in Paris during the Reign of St. Louis*. Berkeley: University of California Press, 1977.

———. *St. Louis and the Court Style in Gothic Architecture*. London: Zwemmer, 1965.

Camille, Michael. *Gothic Art: Glorious Visions*. New York: Abrams, 1996.

Cole, Bruce. *Sienese Painting: From Its Origins to the Fifteenth Century*. New York: HarperCollins, 1987.

Courtenay, Lynn T., ed. *The Engineering of Medieval Cathedrals*. Aldershot: Scolar, 1997.

Derbes, Anne, and Mark Sandona, eds. *The Cambridge Companion to Giotto*. New York: Cambridge University Press, 2004.

Erlande-Brandenburg, Alain. *The Cathedral: The Social and Architectural Dynamics of Construction*. New York: Cambridge University Press, 1994.

Frankl, Paul, and Paul Crossley. *Gothic Architecture*. New Haven, Conn.: Yale University Press, 2000.

Frisch, Teresa G. *Gothic Art 1140–c. 1450: Sources and Documents*. Toronto: University of Toronto Press, 1987. Reprint of 1971 ed.

Grodecki, Louis. *Gothic Architecture*. New York: Electa/Rizzoli, 1985.

Grodecki, Louis, and Catherine Brisac. *Gothic Stained Glass, 1200–1300*. Ithaca, N.Y.: Cornell University Press, 1985.

Maginnis, Hayden B. J. *Painting in the Age of Giotto: A Historical Reevaluation*. University Park: Pennsylvania State University Press, 1997.

———. *The World of the Early Sienese Painter*. University Park: Pennsylvania State University Press, 2001.

Minne-Sève, Viviane, and Hervé Kergall. *Romanesque and Gothic France: Architecture and Sculpture*. New York: Abrams, 2000.

Moskowitz, Anita Fiderer. *Italian Gothic Sculpture: c. 1250–c. 1400*. New York: Cambridge University Press, 2001.

Norman, Diana, ed. *Siena, Florence, and Padua: Art, Society, and Religion 1280–1400*. New Haven, Conn.: Yale University Press, 1995.

Poeschke, Joachim. *Italian Frescoes: The Age of Giotto, 1280–1400*. New York: Abbeville, 2005.

Radding, Charles M., and William W. Clark. *Medieval Architecture, Medieval Learning*. New Haven, Conn.: Yale University Press, 1992.

Raguin, Virginia Chieffo. *Stained Glass from its Origins to the Present*. New York: Abrams, 2003.

Rudolph, Conrad. *Artistic Change at St-Denis: Abbot Suger's Program and the Early Twelfth-Century Controversy over Art*. Princeton, N.J.: Princeton University Press, 1990.

Sauerländer, Willibald, and Max Hirmer. *Gothic Sculpture in France, 1140–1270*. New York: Abrams, 1973.

Stubblebine, James H. *Duccio di Buoninsegna and His School*. Princeton, N.J.: Princeton University Press, 1979.

Toman, Rolf, ed. *The Art of Gothic: Architecture, Sculpture, Painting*. Cologne: Könemann, 1999.

White, John. *Art and Architecture in Italy: 1250–1400*. 3d ed. New Haven, Conn.: Yale University Press, 1993.

Williamson, Paul. *Gothic Sculpture, 1140–1300*. New Haven, Conn.: Yale University Press, 1995.

Wilson, Christopher. *The Gothic Cathedral: The Architecture of the Great Church, 1130–1530*. London: Thames & Hudson, 1990.

RENAISSANCE ART, GENERAL

Andrés, Glenn M., John M. Hunisak, and Richard Turner. *The Art of Florence*. 2 vols. New York: Abbeville Press, 1988.

Campbell, Gordon, ed. *The Grove Encyclopedia of Northern Renaissance Art*. New York: Oxford University Press, 2009.

Christian, Kathleen, and David J. Drogin, eds. *Patronage and Italian Renaissance Sculpture*. Burlington, Vt.: Ashgate, 2010.

Cole, Bruce. *Italian Art, 1250–1550: The Relation of Renaissance Art to Life and Society*. New York: Harper & Row, 1987.

———. *The Renaissance Artist at Work: From Pisano to Titian*. New York: HarperCollins, 1983.

Frommel, Christoph Luitpold. *The Architecture of the Italian Renaissance*. London: Thames & Hudson, 2007.

Hartt, Frederick, and David G. Wilkins. *History of Italian Renaissance Art*. 7th ed. Upper Saddle River, N.J.: Prentice Hall, 2010.

Levey, Michael. *Florence: A Portrait*. Cambridge, Mass.: Harvard University Press, 1998.

Paoletti, John T., and Gary M. Radke. *Art, Power, and Patronage in Renaissance Italy*. Upper Saddle River, N.J.: Prentice Hall, 2005.

Partridge, Loren. *Art of Renaissance Florence, 1400–1600*. Berkeley and Los Angeles: University of California Press, 2009.

Richardson, Carol M., Kim W. Woods, and Michael W. Franklin. *Renaissance Art Reconsidered: An Anthology of Primary Sources*. Oxford: Blackwell, 2007.

Smith, Jeffrey Chipps. *The Northern Renaissance*. New York: Phaidon, 2004.

Snyder, James, Larry Silver, and Henry Luttikhuizen. *Northern Renaissance Art: Painting, Sculpture, the Graphic Arts from 1350 to 1575*. 2d ed. Upper Saddle River, N.J.: Prentice Hall, 2005.

Thomson, David. *Renaissance Architecture: Critics, Patrons, and Luxury*. Manchester: Manchester University Press, 1993.

Tingali, Paola. *Women in Italian Renaissance Art: Gender, Representation, Identity*. Manchester: Manchester University Press, 1997.

Woods, Kim W. *Making Renaissance Art*. New Haven, Conn.: Yale University Press, 2007.

———. *Viewing Renaissance Art*. New Haven, Conn.: Yale University Press, 2007.

CHAPTER 8: The Early Renaissance in Europe

Ahl, Diane Cole. *Fra Angelico*. New York: Phaidon, 2008.

Baxandall, Michael. *Painting and Experience in Fifteenth Century Italy: A Primer in the Social History of Pictorial Style*. 2d ed. New York: Oxford University Press, 1988.

Campbell, Lorne. *The Fifteenth Century Netherlandish Schools*. London: National Gallery Publications, 1998.

Cole, Alison. *Virtue and Magnificence: Art of the Italian Renaissance Courts*. New York: Abrams, 1995.

Cole, Bruce. *Masaccio and the Art of Early Renaissance Florence*. Bloomington: Indiana University Press, 1980.

Edgerton, Samuel Y., Jr. *The Heritage of Giotto's Geometry: Art and Science on the Eve of the Scientific Revolution*. Ithaca, N.Y.: Cornell University Press, 1991.

Gilbert, Creighton, ed. *Italian Art 1400–1500: Sources and Documents*. Evanston, Ill.: Northwestern University Press, 1992.

Harbison, Craig. *The Mirror of the Artist: Northern Renaissance Art in Its Historical Context*. New York: Abrams, 1995.

Heydenreich, Ludwig H. *Architecture in Italy, 1400–1500*. 2d ed. New Haven, Conn.: Yale University Press, 1996.

Hollingsworth, Mary. *Patronage in Renaissance Italy: From 1400 to the Early Sixteenth Century*. Baltimore: Johns Hopkins University Press, 1994.

Kemperdick, Stephan, and Jochen Sander, eds. *The Master of Flémalle and Rogier van der Weyden*. Ostfildern: Hatje Cantz, 2009.

Kempers, Bram. *Painting, Power, and Patronage: The Rise of the Professional Artist in the Italian Renaissance*. London: Penguin, 1992.

Kent, Dale. *Cosimo de' Medici and the Florentine Renaissance: The Patron's Oeuvre*. New Haven, Conn.: Yale University Press, 2000.

Lane, Barbara G. *The Altar and the Altarpiece: Sacramental Themes in Early Netherlandish Painting*. New York: Harper & Row, 1984.

Manca, Joseph. *Andrea Mantegna and the Italian Renaissance*. New York: Parkstone, 2006.

Michels, Alfred. *Hans Memling*. London: Parkstone, 2008.

Müller, Theodor. *Sculpture in the Netherlands, Germany, France and Spain: 1400–1500*. New Haven, Conn.: Yale University Press, 1986.

Nash, Susie. *Northern Renaissance Art*. New York: Oxford University Press, 2008.

Olson, Roberta J. M. *Italian Renaissance Sculpture*. London: Thames & Hudson, 1992.

Pächt, Otto. *Early Netherlandish Painting from Rogier van der Weyden to Gerard David*. New York: Harvey Miller, 1997.

Parshall, Peter, and Rainer Schoch. *Origins of European Printmaking: Fifteenth-Century Woodcuts and Their Public*. New Haven, Conn.: Yale University Press, 2005.

Poeschke, Joachim. *Donatello and His World: Sculpture of the Italian Renaissance*. New York: Abrams, 1993.

Seymour, Charles. *Sculpture in Italy: 1400–1500*. New Haven, Conn.: Yale University Press, 1992.

Smith, Jeffrey Chipps. *The Northern Renaissance*. New York: Phaidon, 2004.

Tomlinson, Amanda. *Van Eyck*. London: Chaucer, 2007.

Turner, A. Richard. *Renaissance Florence: The Invention of a New Art*. New York: Abrams, 1997.

Welch, Evelyn. *Art and Society in Italy 1350–1500*. Oxford: Oxford University Press, 1997.

White, John. *The Birth and Rebirth of Pictorial Space*. 3d ed. Boston: Faber & Faber, 1987.

CHAPTER 9: High Renaissance and Mannerism in Europe

Bartrum, Giulia, ed. *Albrecht Dürer and His Legacy: The Graphic Work of a Renaissance Artist*. Princeton, N.J.: Princeton University Press, 2003.

Blunt, Anthony. *Art and Architecture in France, 1500–1700*. Rev. ed. New Haven, Conn.: Yale University Press, 1999.

Brock, Maurice. *Bronzino*. Paris: Flammarion, 2002.

Brown, David Alan, and Sylvia Ferino-Pagden. *Bellini, Giorgione, Titian and the Renaissance of Venetian Painting*. New Haven, Conn.: Yale University Press, 2006.

Brown, Patricia Fortini. *Art and Life in Renaissance Venice*. New York: Abrams, 1997.

Cole, Bruce. *Titian and Venetian Painting, 1450–1590*. Boulder, Colo.: Westview, 2000.

Dal Pozzolo, Enrico. *Giorgione*. Milan: Motta, 2010.

Ekserdjian, David. *Parmigianino*. New Haven, Conn.: Yale University Press, 2006.

Franklin, David. *Painting in Renaissance Florence, 1500–1550*. New Haven, Conn.: Yale University Press, 2001.

Freedberg, Sydney J. *Painting in Italy: 1500–1600*. 3d ed. New Haven, Conn.: Yale University Press, 1993.

Goffen, Rona. *Renaissance Rivals. Michelangelo, Leonardo, Raphael, Titian*. New Haven, Conn.: Yale University Press, 2002.

Hall, Marcia B. *After Raphael: Painting in Central Italy in the Sixteenth Century*. New York: Cambridge University Press, 1999.

Hall, Marcia B., ed. *Rome (Artistic Centers of the Italian Renaissance)*. New York: Cambridge University Press, 2005.

Humfry, Peter. *Painting in Renaissance Venice*. New Haven, Conn.: Yale University Press, 1995.

———. *Titian*. London: Phaidon, 2007.

Huse, Norbert, and Wolfgang Wolters. *The Art of Renaissance Venice: Architecture, Sculpture, and Painting*. Chicago: University of Chicago Press, 1990.

Kliemann, Julian-Matthias, and Michael Rohlmann. *Italian Frescoes: High Renaissance and Mannerism, 1510–1600*. New York: Abbeville, 2004.

Koerner, Joseph Leo. *The Reformation of the Image*. Chicago: University of Chicago Press, 2004.

Landau, David, and Peter Parshall. *The Renaissance Print: 1470–1550*. New Haven, Conn.: Yale University Press, 1994.

Lotz, Wolfgang. *Architecture in Italy, 1500–1600*. 2d ed. New Haven, Conn.: Yale University Press, 1995.

Partridge, Loren. *The Art of Renaissance Rome*. New York: Abrams, 1996.

Rowe, Colin, and Leon Satkowski. *Italian Architecture of the 16th Century*. New York: Princeton Architectural Press, 2002.

Shearman, John K. G. *Mannerism*. Baltimore: Penguin, 1978.

———. *Only Connect . . . Art and the Spectator in the Italian Renaissance*. Princeton, N.J.: Princeton University Press, 1990.

Silver, Larry. *Hieronymous Bosch*. New York: Abbeville, 2006.

———. *Pieter Bruegel*. New York: Abbeville, 2011.

Smith, Jeffrey C. *German Sculpture of the Later Renaissance, c. 1520–1580: Art in an Age of Uncertainty*. Princeton, N.J.: Princeton University Press, 1993.

Stechow, Wolfgang. *Northern Renaissance Art, 1400–1600: Sources and Documents.* Upper Saddle River, N.J.: Prentice Hall, 1966.

Summers, David. *Michelangelo and the Language of Art.* Princeton, N.J.: Princeton University Press, 1981.

Talvacchia, Bette. *Raphael.* London: Phaidon, 2007.

Tronzo, William, ed. *St. Peter's in the Vatican.* New York: Cambridge University Press, 2005.

Wolf, Norbert. *Albrecht Dürer.* New York: Prestel, 2010.

Zerner, Henri. *Renaissance Art in France: The Invention of Classicism.* Paris: Flammarion, 2003.

Zöllner, Frank. *Leonardo da Vinci: The Complete Paintings and Drawings.* Cologne: Taschen, 2007.

CHAPTER 10: Baroque Europe

Alpers, Svetlana. *The Art of Describing: Dutch Art in the Seventeenth Century.* Chicago: University of Chicago Press, 1984.

Belkin, Kristin Lohse. *Rubens.* London: Phaidon, 1998.

Bissel, R. Ward. *Artemisia Gentileschi and the Authority of Art.* University Park: Pennsylvania State University Press, 1999.

Blunt, Anthony. *Art and Architecture in France, 1500–1700.* Rev. ed. New Haven, Conn.: Yale University Press, 1999.

Brown, Jonathan. *The Golden Age of Painting in Spain.* New Haven, Conn.: Yale University Press, 1991.

Carr, Dawson W., ed. *Velázquez.* London: National Gallery, 2006.

Enggass, Robert, and Jonathan Brown. *Italy and Spain, 1600–1750: Sources and Documents.* Upper Saddle River, N.J.: Prentice Hall, 1970.

Franits, Wayne. *Dutch Seventeenth-Century Genre Painting: Its Stylistic and Thematic Evolution.* New Haven, Conn.: Yale University Press, 2008.

Haak, Bob. *The Golden Age: Dutch Painters of the Seventeenth Century.* New York: Abrams, 1984.

Harris, Ann Sutherland. *Seventeenth-Century Art & Architecture.* Upper Saddle River, N.J.: Prentice Hall, 2005.

Harrison, Charles, Paul Wood, and Jason Gaiger, eds. *Art in Theory 1648–1815: An Anthology of Changing Ideas.* Oxford: Blackwell, 2000.

Held, Julius, and Donald Posner. *17th and 18th Century Art: Baroque Painting, Sculpture, Architecture.* New York: Abrams, 1971.

Keazor, Henry. *Nicholas Poussin, 1594–1665.* Cologne: Taschen, 2007.

Lagerlöf, Margaretha R. *Ideal Landscape: Annibale Carracci, Nicolas Poussin and Claude Lorrain.* New Haven, Conn.: Yale University Press, 1990.

Lawrence, Cynthia, ed. *Women and Art in Early Modern Europe: Patrons, Collectors, and Connoisseurs.* University Park: Pennsylvania State University Press, 1997.

Lemerle, Frédérique, and Yves Pauwels. *Baroque Architecture, 1600–1750.* Paris: Flammarion, 2008.

Liedtke, Walter. *Vermeer: The Complete Paintings.* Antwerp: Ludion, 2008.

Mérot, Alain. *French Painting in the Seventeenth Century.* New Haven, Conn.: Yale University Press, 1995.

Montagu, Jennifer. *Roman Baroque Sculpture: The Industry of Art.* New Haven, Conn.: Yale University Press, 1989.

Norberg-Schulz, Christian. *Baroque Architecture.* New York: Rizzoli, 1986.

North, Michael. *Art and Commerce in the Dutch Golden Age.* New Haven, Conn.: Yale University Press, 1997.

Puglisi, Catherine. *Caravaggio.* London: Phaidon, 2000.

Rosenberg, Jakob, Seymour Slive, and E. H. ter Kuile. *Dutch Art and Architecture, 1600–1800.* New Haven, Conn.: Yale University Press, 1979.

Schama, Simon. *The Embarrassment of Riches: An Interpretation of Dutch Culture in the Golden Age.* Berkeley: University of California Press, 1988.

Strinati, Claudio, and Jordana Pomeroy. *Italian Women Artists from Renaissance to Baroque.* Milan: Skira, 2007.

Toman, Rolf. *Baroque: Architecture, Sculpture, Painting.* Cologne: Könemann, 1998.

Varriano, John. *Italian Baroque and Rococo Architecture.* New York: Oxford University Press, 1986.

Vlieghe, Hans. *Flemish Art and Architecture, 1585–1700.* New Haven, Conn.: Yale University Press, 1998.

Westermann, Mariët. *Rembrandt.* London: Phaidon, 2000.

———. *A Worldly Art: The Dutch Republic 1585–1718.* New Haven, Conn.: Yale University Press, 1996.

Wittkower, Rudolf. *Art and Architecture in Italy 1600–1750.* 3 vols. 6th ed., revised by Joseph Connors and Jennifer Montagu. New Haven, Conn.: Yale University Press, 1999.

CHAPTER 11: Rococo to Neoclassicism in Europe and America

Bermingham, Ann. *Landscape and Ideology: The English Rustic Tradition, 1740–1850.* Berkeley: University of California Press, 1986.

Boime, Albert. *Art in the Age of Revolution, 1750–1800.* Chicago: University of Chicago Press, 1987.

Craske, Matthew. *Art in Europe, 1700–1830: A History of the Visual Arts in an Era of Unprecedented Urban Economic Growth.* New York: Oxford University Press, 1997.

Gaunt, W. *The Great Century of British Painting: Hogarth to Turner.* New York: Phaidon, 1971.

Goodman, Elise, ed. *Art and Culture in the Eighteenth Century: New Dimensions and Multiple Perspectives.* Newark: University of Delaware Press, 2001.

Herrmann, Luke. *British Landscape Painting of the Eighteenth Century.* New York: Oxford University Press, 1974.

Irwin, David. *Neoclassicism.* London: Phaidon, 1997.

Jarrassé, Dominique. *18th-Century French Painting.* Paris: Terrail, 1999.

Lee, Simon. *David.* London: Phaidon, 1999.

Stillman, Damie. *English Neo-Classical Architecture.* 2 vols. London: Zwemmer, 1988.

Waterhouse, Ellis Kirkham. *Painting in Britain: 1530–1790.* 4th ed. New Haven, Conn.: Yale University Press, 1979.

19TH AND 20TH CENTURIES, GENERAL

Arnason, H. H., and Elizabeth C. Mansfield. *History of Modern Art: Painting, Sculpture, Architecture, Photography.* 6th ed. Upper Saddle River, N.J.: Prentice Hall, 2009.

Ashton, Dore. *Twentieth-Century Artists on Art.* New York: Pantheon Books, 1985.

Butler, Cornelia, and Alexandra Schwartz, eds. *Modern Women: Women Artists at the Museum of Modern Art.* New York: Museum of Modern Art, 2010.

Chipp, Herschel B. *Theories of Modern Art.* Berkeley: University of California Press, 1968.

Chu, Petra ten-Doesschate. *Nineteenth-Century European Art.* 2d ed. Upper Saddle River, N.J.: Prentice Hall, 2006.

Coke, Van Deren. *The Painter and the Photograph from Delacroix to Warhol.* Rev. and enl. ed. Albuquerque: University of New Mexico Press, 1972.

Colquhoun, Alan. *Modern Architecture.* New York: Oxford University Press, 2002.

Craven, Wayne. *American Art: History and Culture.* Rev. ed. New York: McGraw Hill, 2002.

Doss, Erika. *Twentieth-Century American Art.* New York: Oxford University Press, 2002.

Eisenman, Stephen F., ed. *Nineteenth Century Art: A Critical History.* 4th ed. New York: Thames & Hudson, 2011.

Facos, Michelle. *An Introduction to Nineteenth-Century Art.* New York: Routledge, 2011.

Foster, Hal, Rosalind Krauss, Yve-Alain Bois, and Benjamin H. D. Buchloh. *Art since 1900: Modernism, Antimodernism, Postmodernism.* 2d ed. New York: Thames & Hudson, 2011.

Frampton, Kenneth. *Modern Architecture: A Critical History.* 4th ed. New York: Thames & Hudson, 2007.

Hamilton, George H. *Painting and Sculpture in Europe, 1880–1940.* 6th ed. New Haven, Conn.: Yale University Press, 1993.

Harrison, Charles, and Paul Wood. *Art in Theory 1900–2000: An Anthology of Changing Ideas.* Oxford: Blackwell, 2003.

Herbert, Robert L., ed. *Modern Artists on Art.* Upper Saddle River, N.J.: Prentice Hall, 1971.

Hertz, Richard, and Norman M. Klein, eds. *Twentieth-Century Art Theory: Urbanism, Politics, and Mass Culture.* Englewood Cliffs: Prentice-Hall, 1990.

Heyer, Paul. *Architects on Architecture: New Directions in America.* New York: Van Nostrand Reinhold, 1993.

Hills, Patricia. *Modern Art in the USA: Issues and Controversies of the 20th Century.* Upper Saddle River, N.J.: Prentice Hall, 2000.

Hunter, Sam, John Jacobus, and Daniel Wheeler. *Modern Art: Painting, Sculpture, Architecture, Photography.* Rev. 3d ed. Upper Saddle River, N.J.: Prentice Hall, 2004.

Lewis, Samella S. *African American Art and Artists.* Rev. ed. Berkeley and Los Angeles: University of California Press, 1994.

Marien, Mary Warner. *Photography: A Cultural History.* 3d ed. Upper Saddle River, N.J.: Prentice Hall, 2011.

Pohl, Frances K. *Framing America: A Social History of American Art*. 2d ed. New York: Thames & Hudson, 2008.

Rosenblum, Naomi. *A World History of Photography*. 4th ed. New York: Abbeville, 2007.

Rosenblum, Robert, and Horst W. Janson. *19th-Century Art*. Rev. ed. Upper Saddle River, N.J.: Prentice Hall, 2005.

Upton, Dell. *Architecture in the United States*. Oxford: Oxford University Press, 1998.

CHAPTER 12: Romanticism, Realism, and Photography, 1800 to 1870

Amic, Sylvain, et al. *Gustave Courbet*. Ostfildern: Hatje Cantz, 2008.

Bergdoll, Barry. *European Architecture 1750–1890*. New York: Oxford University Press, 2000.

Boime, Albert. *The Academy and French Painting in the 19th Century*. London: Phaidon, 1971.

———. *Art in the Age of Bonapartism, 1800–1815*. Chicago: University of Chicago Press, 1990.

Bordes, Philippe. *Jacques-Louis David: Empire to Exile*. New Haven, Conn.: Yale University Press, 2007.

Brown, David Blayney. *Romanticism*. London: Phaidon, 2001.

Bryson, Norman. *Tradition and Desire: From David to Delacroix*. New York: Cambridge University Press, 1984.

Clark, T. J. *The Painting of Modern Life: Paris in the Art of Manet and His Followers*. Princeton, N.J.: Princeton University Press, 1984.

Eitner, Lorenz. *Neoclassicism and Romanticism, 1750–1850: An Anthology of Sources and Documents*. New York: Harper & Row, 1989.

Fried, Michael. *Manet's Modernism, or, The Face of Painting in the 1860s*. Chicago: University of Chicago Press, 1996.

Hofmann, Werner. *Goya*. New York: Thames & Hudson, 2003.

Holt, Elizabeth Gilmore, ed. *From the Classicists to the Impressionists: A Documentary History of Art and Architecture in the Nineteenth Century*. Garden City, N.J.: Anchor Books/Doubleday, 1966.

Koerner, Joseph Leo. *Caspar David Friedrich and the Subject of Landscape*. 2d ed. London: Reaktion, 2009.

Krell, Alain. *Manet and the Painters of Contemporary Life*. London: Thames & Hudson, 1996.

Kroeber, Karl. *British Romantic Art*. Berkeley: University of California Press, 1986.

Le Men, Ségolène. *Courbet*. New York: Abbeville, 2008.

Licht, Fred. *Goya*. New York: Abbeville, 2001.

Middleton, Robin. *Architecture of the Nineteenth Century*. London: Phaidon, 2003.

Nochlin, Linda. *Realism and Tradition in Art, 1848–1900: Sources and Documents*. Upper Saddle River, N.J.: Prentice Hall, 1966.

Novotny, Fritz. *Painting and Sculpture in Europe, 1780–1880*. 3d ed. New Haven, Conn.: Yale University Press, 1988.

Porterfield, Todd. *The Allure of Empire: Art in the Service of French Imperialism 1798–1836*. Princeton, N.J.: Princeton University Press, 1998.

Rubin, James Henry. *Manet: Initial M, Hand and Eye*. Paris: Flammarion, 2010.

Shelton, Andrew Carrington. *Ingres*. London: Phaidon, 2008.

Toman, Rolf, ed. *Neoclassicism and Romanticism: Architecture, Sculpture, Painting, Drawings, 1750–1848*. Cologne: Könemann, 2006.

Vaughn, William. *German Romantic Painting*. New Haven, Conn.: Yale University Press, 1980.

CHAPTER 13: Impressionism, Post-Impressionism, and Symbolism, 1870 to 1900

Broude, Norma. *Impressionism: A Feminist Reading*. New York: Rizzoli, 1991.

Clark, T. J. *The Painting of Modern Life: Paris in the Art of Manet and His Followers*. Princeton, N.J.: Princeton University Press, 1984.

Cogeval, Guy, ed. *Claude Monet, 1840–1926*. Paris: Réunion des Musées Nationaux, 2010.

Distel, Anne. *Renoir*. New York: Abbeville, 2010.

Escritt, Stephen. *Art Nouveau*. London: Phaidon, 2000.

Facos, Michelle. *Symbolism in Context*. Berkeley and Los Angeles: University of California Press, 2009.

Herbert, Robert L. *Impressionism: Art, Leisure, and Parisian Society*. New Haven, Conn.: Yale University Press, 1988.

Lewis, Mary Tompkins. *Cézanne*. London: Phaidon, 2000.

Loyette, Henri, Sebastien Allard, and Laurence Des Cars. *Nineteenth Century French Art: From Romanticism to Impressionism, Post-Impressionism, and Art Nouveau*. Paris: Flammarion, 2007.

Masson, Raphaël, and Véronique Mattiussi. *Rodin*. Paris: Flammarion, 2004.

Nochlin, Linda. *Impressionism and Post-Impressionism, 1874–1904: Sources and Documents*. Upper Saddle River, N.J.: Prentice Hall, 1966.

Pfeiffer, Ingrid, et al. *Women Impressionists*. Ostfildern: Hatje Cantz, 2008.

Rachman, Carla. *Monet*. London: Phaidon, 1997.

Rubin, James H. *Impressionism*. London: Phaidon, 1999.

Shiff, Richard. *Cézanne and the End of Impressionism: A Study of the Theory, Technique, and Critical Evaluation of Modern Art*. Chicago: University of Chicago Press, 1984.

Smith, Paul. *Impressionism: Beneath the Surface*. New York: Abrams, 1995.

Sund, Judy. *Van Gogh*. London: Phaidon, 2002.

Thomson, Belinda, ed. *Gauguin: Maker of Myth*. London: Tate, 2010.

CHAPTER 14: Modernism in Europe and America, 1900 to 1945

Antliff, Mark. *Cultural Politics and the Parisian Avant-Garde*. Princeton, N.J.: Princeton University Press, 1993.

Antliff, Mark, and Patricia Leighten. *Cubism and Culture*. New York: Thames & Hudson, 2001.

Bearden, Romare, and Harry Henderson. *A History of African-American Artists from 1792 to the Present*. New York: Pantheon Books, 1993.

Bergdoll, Barry. *Bauhaus 1919–1933*. New York: Museum of Modern Art, 2009.

Bouvet, Vincent, and Gérard Durozoi. *Paris between the Wars 1919–1939: Art, Life & Culture*. New York: Vendome, 2010.

Breton, André. *Surrealism and Painting*. New York: Harper & Row, 1972.

Brown, Milton. *Story of the Armory Show: The 1913 Exhibition That Changed American Art*. 2d ed. New York: Abbeville, 1988.

Cowling, Elizabeth, ed. *Picasso: Challenging the Past*. London: National Gallery, 2011.

Cox, Neil. *Cubism*. London: Phaidon: 2000.

Curtis, Penelope. *Sculpture 1900–1945*. New York: Oxford University Press, 1999.

Curtis, William J. R. *Modern Architecture since 1900*. Upper Saddle River, N.J.: Prentice Hall, 1996.

Davidson, Abraham A. *Early American Modernist Painting, 1910–1935*. New York: Harper & Row, 1981.

Dietrich, Dorothea, ed. *Dada: Zurich, Berlin, Hannover, Cologne, New York, Paris*. Washington, D.C.: National Gallery, 2008.

Eberle, Matthias. *World War I and the Weimar Artists: Dix, Grosz, Beckmann, Schlemmer*. New Haven, Conn.: Yale University Press, 1985.

Edwards, Steve, and Paul Wood, eds. *Art of the Avant-Gardes*. New Haven, Conn.: Yale University Press, 2004.

Gale, Matthew. *Dada and Surrealism*. London: Phaidon, 1997.

Gordon, Donald E. *Expressionism: Art and Idea*. New Haven, Conn.: Yale University Press, 1987.

Harrison, Charles, Francis Frascina, and Gil Perry. *Primitivism, Cubism, Abstraction: The Early Twentieth Century*. New Haven, Conn.: Yale University Press, 1993.

Herbert, James D. *Fauve Painting: The Making of Cultural Politics*. New Haven, Conn.: Yale University Press, 1992.

Hurlburt, Laurance P. *The Mexican Muralists in the United States*. Albuquerque: University of New Mexico Press, 1989.

Krauss, Rosalind. *The Originality of the Avant-Garde and Other Modernist Myths*. Cambridge: MIT Press, 1986.

Lloyd, Jill. *German Expressionism: Primitivism and Modernity*. New Haven, Conn.: Yale University Press, 1991.

Motherwell, Robert, ed. *The Dada Painters and Poets: An Anthology*. 2d ed. Boston: Hall, 1981.

Orvell, Miles. *American Photography*. New York: Oxford University Press, 2003.

Rhodes, Colin. *Primitivism and Modern Art*. New York: Thames & Hudson, 1994.

Rubin, William S. *Dada and Surrealist Art*. New York: Abrams, 1968.

———, ed. *Pablo Picasso: A Retrospective*. New York: Museum of Modern Art; Boston: New York Graphic Society, 1980.

———, ed. *"Primitivism" in 20th-Century Art: Affinity of the Tribal and the Modern*. 2 vols. New York: Museum of Modern Art, 1984.

Stott, William. *Documentary Expression and Thirties America*. New York: Oxford University Press, 1973.

Taylor, Michael R., ed. *Arshile Gorky: A Retrospective*. New Haven, Conn.: Yale University Press, 2009.

Terraroli, Valerio, ed. *Art of the Twentieth Century, 1900–1919: The Avant-Garde Movements*. Milan: Skira, 2006.

———. *Art of the Twentieth Century, 1920–1945: The Artistic Culture between the Wars*. Milan: Skira, 2006.

Tisdall, Caroline, and Angelo Bozzolla. *Futurism*. New York: Oxford University Press, 1978.

Vogt, Paul. *Expressionism: German Painting, 1905–1920*. New York: Abrams, 1980.

CHAPTER 15: **Modernism and Postmodernism in Europe and America, 1945 to 1980**

Anfam, David. *Abstract Expressionism*. New York: Thames & Hudson, 1990.

Archer, Michael. *Art since 1960*. New ed. New York: Thames & Hudson, 2002.

Ashton, Dore. *American Art since 1945*. New York: Oxford University Press, 1983.

Battcock, Gregory, and Robert Nickas, eds. *The Art of Performance: A Critical Anthology*. New York: Dutton, 1984.

Beardsley, Richard. *Earthworks and Beyond: Contemporary Art in the Landscape*. New York: Abbeville Press, 1984.

Broude, Norma, and Mary D. Garrard. *The Power of Feminist Art: The American Movement of the 1970s, History and Impact*. New York: Abrams, 1994.

Butler, Cornelia H., ed. *WACK! Art and the Feminist Revolution*. Cambridge, Mass.: MIT Press, 2007.

Causey, Andrew. *Sculpture since 1945*. New York: Oxford University Press, 1998.

Crow, Thomas. *The Rise of the Sixties: American and European Art in the Era of Dissent*. New Haven, Conn.: Yale University Press, 2005.

Frascina, Francis, ed. *Pollock and After: The Critical Debate*. New York: Harper & Row, 1985.

Godfrey, Tony. *Conceptual Art*. London: Phaidon, 1998.

Goldberg, Rose Lee. *Performance Art: From Futurism to the Present*. Rev. ed. New York: Abrams, 1988.

Goldhagen, Sarah Williams, and Réjean Legault, *Anxious Modernisms: Experimentation in Postwar Architectural Culture*. Cambridge, Mass.: MIT Press, 2002.

Goodman, Cynthia. *Digital Visions: Computers and Art*. New York: Abrams, 1987.

Green, Jonathan. *American Photography: A Critical History since 1945 to the Present*. New York: Abrams, 1984.

Greenberg, Clement. *Clement Greenberg: The Collected Essays and Criticism*. Edited by J. O'Brien. 4 vols. Chicago: University of Chicago Press, 1986–1993.

Grundberg, Andy. *Photography and Art: Interactions since 1945*. New York: Abbeville, 1987.

Hopkins, David. *After Modern Art, 1945–2000*. New York: Oxford University Press, 2000.

Jacobus, John. *Twentieth-Century Architecture: The Middle Years, 1940–1964*. New York: Praeger, 1966.

Jencks, Charles. *The Language of Post-Modern Architecture*. 6th ed. New York: Rizzoli, 1991.

———. *What Is Post-Modernism?* 3d rev. ed. London: Academy Editions, 1989.

Joselit, David. *American Art since 1945*. New York: Thames & Hudson, 2003.

Leja, Michael. *Reframing Abstract Expressionism: Subjectivity and Painting in the 1940s*. New Haven, Conn.: Yale University Press, 1993.

Lippard, Lucy R. *Pop Art*. New York: Praeger, 1966.

Lovejoy, Margot. *Postmodern Currents: Art and Artists in the Age of the Electronic Media*. Ann Arbor, Mich.: UMI Research Press, 1989.

Lucie-Smith, Edward. *Movements in Art since 1945*. New ed. New York: Thames & Hudson, 2001.

Mamiya, Christin J. *Pop Art and Consumer Culture: American Super Market*. Austin: University of Texas Press, 1992.

Marder, Tod A. *The Critical Edge: Controversy in Recent American Architecture*. New Brunswick, N.J.: Rutgers University Press, 1980.

Rosen, Randy, and Catherine C. Brawer, eds. *Making Their Mark: Women Artists Move into the Mainstream, 1970–1985*. New York: Abbeville, 1989.

Rush, Michael. *New Media in Art*. 2d ed., New York: Thames & Hudson, 2005.

Sandford, Mariellen R., ed. *Happenings and Other Acts*. New York: Routledge, 1995.

Sayre, Henry M. *The Object of Performance: The American Avant-Garde since 1970*. Chicago: University of Chicago Press, 1989.

Schneider, Ira, and Beryl Korot. *Video Art: An Anthology*. New York: Harcourt Brace Jovanovich, 1976.

Shapiro, David, and Cecile Shapiro. *Abstract Expressionism: A Critical Record*. New York: Cambridge University Press, 1990.

Sonfist, Alan, ed. *Art in the Landscape: A Critical Anthology of Environmental Art*. New York: Dutton, 1983.

Stiles, Kristine, and Peter Selz. *Theories and Documents of Contemporary Art: A Sourcebook of Artists' Writings*. Berkeley and Los Angeles: University of California Press, 1996.

Taylor, Brendon. *Contemporary Art: Art since 1970*. Upper Saddle River, N.J.: Prentice Hall, 2005.

Terraroli, Valerio, ed. *Art of the Twentieth Century, 1946–1968: The Birth of Contemporary Art*. Milan: Skira, 2007.

Varnedoe, Kirk. *Pictures of Nothing: Abstract Art since Pollock*. Princeton, N.J.: Princeton University Press, 2006.

Venturi, Robert, Denise Scott-Brown, and Steven Isehour. *Learning from Las Vegas*. Cambridge, Mass.: MIT Press, 1972.

Waldman, Diane. *Collage, Assemblage, and the Found Object*. New York: Abrams, 1992.

Wheeler, Daniel. *Art since Mid-Century: 1945 to the Present*. Upper Saddle River, N.J.: Prentice Hall, 1991.

Wood, Paul. *Modernism in Dispute: Art since the Forties*. New Haven, Conn.: Yale University Press, 1993.

CHAPTER 16: **Contemporary Art Worldwide**

Chilwers, Ian, and John Glaves-Smith. *Oxford Dictionary of Modern and Contemporary Art*. 2d ed. New York: Oxford University Press, 2009.

Clark, John. *Modern Asian Art*. Honolulu: University of Hawaii Press, 1998.

Enwezor, Okwui, and Chika Okeke-Agulu. *Contemporary African Art since 1980*. Bologna: Damiani, 2009.

Fineberg, Jonathan. *Art since 1940: Strategies of Being*. 3d ed. Upper Saddle River, N.J.: Prentice Hall, 2010.

Heartney, Eleanor, Helaine Posner, Nancy Princenthal, and Sue Scott. *After the Revolution: Women Who Transformed Contemporary Art*. New York: Prestel, 2007.

Hertz, Richard, ed. *Theories of Contemporary Art*. 2d ed. Upper Saddle River, N.J.: Prentice Hall, 1993.

Jencks, Charles. *The New Paradigm in Architecture: The Language of Post-Modernism*. New Haven, Conn.: Yale University Press, 2002.

Jodidio, Philip. *100 Contemporary Architects*. Cologne: Taschen, 2008.

Kasfir, Sidney L. *Contemporary African Art*. London: Thames & Hudson, 1999.

Lippard, Lucy R. *Mixed Blessings: New Art in a Multicultural America*. New York: Pantheon Books, 1990.

Mullins, Charlotte. *Painting People: Figure Painting Today*. New York: Thames & Hudson, 2008.

Norris, Christopher, and Andrew Benjamin. *What Is Deconstruction?* New York: St. Martin's, 1988.

Paul, Christiane. *Digital Art*. 2d ed. New York: Thames & Hudson, 2008.

Perry, Gill, and Paul Wood. *Themes in Contemporary Art*. New Haven, Conn.: Yale University Press, 2004.

Risatti, Howard, ed. *Postmodern Perspectives: Issues in Contemporary Art*. Upper Saddle River, N.J.: Prentice Hall, 1990.

Sandler, Irving. *Art of the Postmodern Era*. New York: HarperCollins, 1996.

Smith, Terry. *Contemporary Art: World Currents*. Upper Saddle River, N.J.: Prentice Hall, 2011.

———. *What Is Contemporary Art?* Chicago: University of Chicago Press, 2009.

Sollins, Susan, ed. *Art:21 (Art in the Twenty-first Century)*. 5 vols. New York: Abrams, 2001–2009.

Wands, Bruce. *Art of the Digital Age*. New York: Thames & Hudson, 2007.

Wines, James. *Green Architecture*. Cologne: Taschen, 2008.

ASIAN ART, GENERAL

Béguin, Giles. *Buddhist Art: An Historical and Cultural Journey.* Bangkok: River Books, 2009.

Fisher, Robert E. *Buddhist Art and Architecture.* New York: Thames & Hudson, 1993.

Leidy, Denise Patry. *The Art of Buddhism: An Introduction to Its History and Meaning.* Boston: Shambhala, 2008.

McArthur, Meher. *The Arts of Asia: Materials, Techniques, Styles.* New York: Thames & Hudson, 2005.

CHAPTER 17: South and Southeast Asia

Asher, Catherine B. *Architecture of Mughal India.* New York: Cambridge University Press, 1992.

Beach, Milo Cleveland. *Mughal and Rajput Painting.* New York: Cambridge University Press, 1992.

Blurton, T. Richard. *Hindu Art.* Cambridge, Mass.: Harvard University Press, 1993.

Chaturachinda, Gwyneth, Sunanda Krishnamurty, and Pauline W. Tabtiang. *Dictionary of South and Southeast Asian Art.* Chiang Mai, Thailand: Silkworm Books, 2000.

Craven, Roy C. *Indian Art: A Concise History.* Rev. ed. London: Thames & Hudson, 1997.

Dehejia, Vidya. *Indian Art.* London: Phaidon, 1997.

Girard-Geslan, Maud, ed. *Art of Southeast Asia.* New York: Abrams, 1998.

Hardy, Adam. *The Temple Architecture of India.* Chichester: Wiley, 2007.

Harle, James C. *The Art and Architecture of the Indian Subcontinent.* 2d ed. New Haven, Conn.: Yale University Press, 1994.

Huntington, Susan L., and John C. Huntington. *The Art of Ancient India: Buddhist, Hindu, Jain.* New York: Weatherhill, 1985.

Jacques, Claude. *The Khmer Empire: Cities and Sanctuaries from the 5th to the 13th Century.* Bangkok: River Books, 2007.

Kerlogue, Fiona. *Arts of Southeast Asia.* New York: Thames & Hudson, 2004.

McIntosh, Jane R. *A Peaceful Realm: The Rise and Fall of the Indus Civilization.* Boulder, Colo.: Westview Press, 2002.

Michell, George. *Hindu Art and Architecture.* New York: Thames & Hudson, 2000.

———. *The Hindu Temple: An Introduction to Its Meaning and Forms.* Chicago: University of Chicago Press, 1988.

Mitter, Partha. *Indian Art.* New York: Oxford University Press, 2001.

Rawson, Phillip. *The Art of Southeast Asia.* New York: Thames & Hudson, 1990.

Schimmel, Annemarie. *The Empire of the Great Mughals: History, Art, and Culture.* London: Reaktion, 2006.

Seth, Mira. *Indian Painting: The Great Mural Tradition.* New York: Abrams, 2006.

Srinivasan, Doris Meth. *Many Heads, Arms and Eyes: Origin, Meaning and Form of Multiplicity in Indian Art.* Leiden: E. J. Brill, 1997.

Stierlin, Henri. *Hindu India: From Khajuraho to the Temple City of Madurai.* Cologne: Taschen, 1998.

Welch, Stuart Cary. *Imperial Mughal Painting.* New York: Braziller, 1978.

———. *India: Art and Culture 1300–1900.* New York: Metropolitan Museum of Art, 1985.

CHAPTER 18: China and Korea

Cahill, James. *The Painter's Practice: How Artists Lived and Worked in Traditional China.* New York: Columbia University Press, 1994.

Clunas, Craig. *Art in China.* 2d ed. New York: Oxford University Press, 2009.

Fahr-Becker, Gabriele, ed. *The Art of East Asia.* Cologne: Könemann, 1999.

Fong, Wen C. *Beyond Representation: Chinese Painting and Calligraphy, 8th–14th Century.* New Haven, Conn.: Yale University Press, 1992.

Fong, Wen C., and James C. Y. Watt. *Preserving the Past: Treasures from the National Palace Museum, Taipei.* New York: Metropolitan Museum of Art, 1996.

Howard, Angela Falco, Li Song, Wu Hong, and Yang Hong. *Chinese Sculpture.* New Haven, Conn.: Yale University Press, 2006.

Kim, Kumja Paik. *Goryeo Dynasty: Korea's Age of Enlightenment, 918–1392.* San Francisco: Asian Art Museum, 2003.

Li, He, and Michael Knight. *Power and Glory: Court Arts of China's Ming Dynasty.* San Francisco: Asian Art Museum, 2008.

Nelson, Sarah Milledge. *The Archaeology of Korea.* New York: Cambridge University Press, 1993.

Portal, Jane. *Korea: Art and Archaeology.* New York: Thames & Hudson, 2000.

Rawson, Jessica. *Ancient China: Art and Archaeology.* New York: Harper & Row, 1980.

Sickman, Laurence, and Alexander C. Soper. *The Art and Architecture of China.* 3d ed. New Haven, Conn.: Yale University Press, 1992.

Silbergeld, Jerome. *Chinese Painting Style: Media, Methods, and Principles of Form.* Seattle and London: University of Washington Press, 1982.

Steinhardt, Nancy S., ed. *Chinese Architecture.* New Haven, Conn.: Yale University Press, 2002.

Sullivan, Michael. *The Arts of China.* 5th ed. Berkeley and Los Angeles: University of California Press, 2009.

Thorp, Robert L., and Richard Ellis Vinograd. *Chinese Art and Culture.* New York: Abrams, 2001.

Vainker, S. J. *Chinese Pottery and Porcelain: From Prehistory to the Present.* New York: Braziller, 1991.

Watson, William. *The Arts of China to AD 900.* New Haven, Conn.: Yale University Press, 1995.

———. *The Arts of China 900–1620.* New Haven, Conn.: Yale University Press, 2000.

Watt, James C. Y., ed. *The World of Khubiliai Khan: Chinese Art in the Yuan Dynasty.* New York: Metropolitan Museum of Art, 2010.

Whitfield, Roger, and Anne Farrer. *Caves of the Thousand Buddhas: Chinese Art of the Silk Route.* New York: Braziller, 1990.

Wu, Hung. *Monumentality in Early Chinese Art.* Stanford, Calif.: Stanford University Press, 1996.

Xin, Yang, Nie Chongzheng, Lang Shaojun, Richard M. Barnhart, James Cahill, and Hung Wu. *Three Thousand Years of Chinese Painting.* New Haven, Conn.: Yale University Press, 1997.

Zheng, Xinmiao, et al. *Masterpieces of Classical Chinese Painting.* New York: Abbeville, 2011.

Zhiyan, Li, Virginia L. Bower, and He Li. *Chinese Ceramics: From the Paleolithic Period through the Qing Dynasty.* New Haven, Conn.: Yale University Press, 2010.

Zhongshi, Ouyang, Wen C. Fong, et al. *Chinese Calligraphy.* New Haven, Conn.: Yale University Press, 2008.

CHAPTER 19: Japan

Addiss, Stephen. *The Art of Zen.* New York: Abrams, 1989.

Brown, Kendall. *The Politics of Reclusion: Painting and Power in Muromachi Japan.* Honolulu: University of Hawaii Press, 1997.

Calza, Gian Carlo. *Ukiyo-e.* New York: Phaidon, 2005.

Coaldrake, William H. *Architecture and Authority in Japan.* London: Routledge, 1996.

Elisseeff, Danielle, and Vadime Elisseeff. *Art of Japan.* Translated by I. Mark Paris. New York: Abrams, 1985.

Guth, Christine. *Art of Edo Japan: The Artist and the City, 1615–1868.* New York: Abrams, 1996.

Hickman, Money L., John T. Carpenter, Bruce A. Coats, Christine Guth, Andrew J. Pekarik, John M. Rosenfield, and Nicole C. Rousmaniere. *Japan's Golden Age: Momoyama.* New Haven, Conn.: Yale University Press, 1996.

Mason, Penelope. *History of Japanese Art.* 2d ed. New York: Abrams, 2004.

Meech, Julia, and Jane Oliver. *Designed for Pleasure: The World of Edo Japan in Prints and Drawings, 1680–1860.* Seattle: University of Washington Press, 2008.

Nishi, Kazuo, and Kazuo Hozumi. *What Is Japanese Architecture?* Translated by H. Mack Horton. New York: Kodansha International, 1985.

Nishikawa, Kyotaro, and Emily Sano. *The Great Age of Japanese Buddhist Sculpture A.D. 600–1300.* Fort Worth, Tex.: Kimbell Art Museum, 1982.

Noma, Seiroku. *The Arts of Japan: Ancient and Medieval.* New York: Kodansha, 1966.

Ohki, Sadak. *Tea Culture of Japan.* New Haven, Conn.: Yale University Press, 2009.

Okudaira, Hideo. *Narrative Picture Scrolls.* Adapted by Elizabeth ten Grotenhuis. New York: Weatherhill, 1973.

Pearson, Richard J. *Ancient Japan.* New York: Braziller, 1992.

Rosenfield, John M. *Japanese Art of the Heian Period, 794–1185.* New York: Asia Society, 1967.

Sanford, James H., William R. LaFleur, and Masatoshi Nagatomi. *Flowing Traces: Buddhism in the Literary and Visual Arts of Japan.* Princeton, N.J.: Princeton University Press, 1992.

Shimizu, Yoshiaki, ed. *The Shaping of Daimyo Culture 1185–1868.* Washington, D.C.: National Gallery of Art, 1988.

Singer, Robert T. *Edo: Art in Japan 1615–1868.* Washington, D.C.: National Gallery of Art, 1998.

Stanley-Baker, Joan. *Japanese Art.* Rev. ed. New York: Thames & Hudson, 2000.

Stewart, David B. *The Making of a Modern Japanese Architecture, 1868 to the Present.* New York: Kodansha International, 1988.

CHAPTER 20: Native America

Mesoamerica and South America

Andrews, E. Wyllys, and William L. Fash, eds. *Copán: The History of an Ancient Maya Kingdom.* Santa Fe, N.M.: School of American Research, 2005.

Bawden, Garth. *Moche.* Oxford: Blackwell, 1999.

Benson, Elizabeth P., and Beatriz de la Fuente, eds. *Olmec Art of Ancient Mexico.* Washington, D.C.: National Gallery of Art, 1996.

Berlo, Janet Catherine, ed. *Art, Ideology, and the City of Teotihuacan.* Washington, D.C.: Dumbarton Oaks, 1992.

Bruhns, Karen O. *Ancient South America.* New York: Cambridge University Press, 1994.

Carrasco, David. *The Oxford Encyclopedia of Mesoamerican Cultures: The Civilizations of Mexico and Central America.* New York: Oxford University Press, 2001.

Clark, John E., and Mary E. Pye, eds. *Olmec Art and Archaeology in Mesoamerica.* Washington, D.C.: National Gallery of Art, 2000.

Coe, Michael D. *The Maya.* 8th ed. New York: Thames & Hudson, 2011.

Coe, Michael D., and Rex Koontz. *Mexico. From the Olmecs to the Aztecs.* 6th ed. New York: Thames & Hudson, 2008.

D'Altroy, Terence N. *The Incas.* New ed., Oxford: Blackwell, 2003.

Fash, William. *Scribes, Warriors, and Kings: The City of Copan and the Ancient Maya.* New York: Thames & Hudson, 1991.

Grube, Nikolai, ed. *Maya: Divine Kings of the Rain Forest.* Cologne: Könemann, 2000.

Kubler, George. *The Art and Architecture of Ancient America: The Mexican, Maya, and Andean Peoples.* 3d ed. New Haven, Conn.: Yale University Press, 1992.

McEwan, Gordon F. *The Incas: New Perspectives.* Santa Barbara, Calif.: ABC-CLIO, 2006.

Miller, Mary Ellen. *The Art of Mesoamerica: From Olmec to Aztec.* 4th ed. New York: Thames & Hudson, 2006.

———. *Maya Art and Architecture.* New York: Thames & Hudson, 1999.

Minelli, Laura Laurencich. *The Inca World.* Norman: University of Oklahoma Press, 2000.

Morris, Craig, and Adriana von Hagen. *The Incas.* New York: Thames & Hudson, 2011.

Moseley, Michael E. *The Incas and Their Ancestors: The Archaeology of Peru.* Rev. ed. New York: Thames & Hudson, 2001.

Pasztory, Esther. *Aztec Art.* New York: Abrams, 1983.

———. *Pre-Columbian Art.* New York: Cambridge University Press, 1998.

———. *Teotihuacan: An Experiment in Living.* Norman: University of Oklahoma Press, 1997.

Pool, Christopher A. *Olmec Archaeology and Early Mesoamerica.* New York: Cambridge University Press, 2007.

Rohm, Arthur H., and William M. Ferguson. *Puebloan Ruins of the Southwest.* Albuquerque: University of New Mexico Press, 2006.

Schele, Linda, and Mary E. Miller. *The Blood of Kings: Dynasty and Ritual in Maya Art.* Fort Worth, Tex.: Kimbell Art Museum, 1986.

Sharer, Robert J., and Loa P. Traxler. *The Ancient Maya.* 6th ed. Palo Alto, Calif.: Stanford University Press, 2006.

Silverman, Helaine. *The Nasca.* Oxford: Blackwell, 2002.

———, ed. *Andean Archaeology.* Oxford: Blackwell, 2004.

Silverman, Helaine, and William H. Isbell, eds. *Handbook of South American Archaeology.* New York: Springer, 2008.

Smith, Michael Ernest. *The Aztecs.* 2d ed., Oxford: Blackwell, 2002.

Stone-Miller, Rebecca. *Art of the Andes from Chavín to Inca.* 2d ed. New York: Thames & Hudson, 2002.

Von Hagen, Adriana, and Craig Morris. *The Cities of the Ancient Andes.* New York: Thames & Hudson, 1998.

North America

Berlo, Janet Catherine, and Ruth B. Phillips. *Native North American Art.* New York: Oxford University Press, 1998.

Brose, David. *Ancient Art of the American Woodland Indians.* New York: Abrams, 1985.

Cordell, Linda S. *Ancient Pueblo Peoples.* Washington, D.C.: Smithsonian Institution Press, 1994.

Fagan, Brian. *Ancient North America: The Archaeology of a Continent.* 4th ed. New York: Thames & Hudson, 2005.

———. *The First North Americans.* New York: Thames & Hudson, 2011.

Feest, Christian F. *Native Arts of North America.* 2d ed. New York: Thames & Hudson, 1992.

Milner, George R. *The Moundbuilders: Ancient Peoples of Eastern North America.* New York: Thames & Hudson, 2004.

Nabokov, Peter, and Robert Easton. *Native American Architecture.* New York: Oxford University Press, 1989.

Penney, David W. *North American Indian Art.* New York: Thames & Hudson, 2004.

CHAPTER 21: Africa

Bacquart, Jean-Baptiste. *The Tribal Arts of Africa.* New York: Thames & Hudson, 2002.

Bassani, Ezio. *Arts of Africa: 7000 Years of African Art.* Milan: Skira, 2005.

Berzock, Kathleen Bickford. *Benin: Royal Arts of a West African Kingdom.* Chicago: Art Institute of Chicago, 2008.

Blier, Suzanne P. *Royal Arts of Africa: The Majesty of Form.* New York: Abrams, 1998.

Cole, Herbert M., ed. *I Am Not Myself: The Art of African Masquerade.* Los Angeles: UCLA Fowler Museum of Cultural History, 1985.

Connah, Graham. *African Civilizations.* 2d ed. New York: Cambridge University Press, 2001.

Drewal, Henry J., and Enid Schildkrout. *Dynasty and Divinity: Ife Art in Ancient Nigeria.* Seattle: University of Washington Press, 2010.

Drewal, Henry J., John Pemberton, and Rowland Abiodun. *Yoruba: Nine Centuries of African Art and Thought.* New York: Center for African Art, in association with Abrams, 1989.

Eyo, Ekpo, and Frank Willett. *Treasures of Ancient Nigeria.* New York: Knopf, 1980.

Fagg, Bernard. *Nok Terracottas.* Lagos: Ethnographica, 1977.

Fraser, Douglas F., and Herbert M. Cole, eds. *African Art and Leadership.* Madison: University of Wisconsin Press, 1972.

Garlake, Peter. *Early Art and Architecture of Africa.* Oxford: Oxford University Press, 2002.

Geary, Christraud M. *Bamum.* Milan: 5 Continents, 2011.

Kasfir, Sidney L. *West African Masks and Cultural Systems.* Tervuren: Musée Royal de l'Afrique Centrale, 1988.

Magnin, Andre, and Jacques Soulillou. *Contemporary Art of Africa.* New York: Abrams, 1996.

McGaffey, Wyatt, and Michael Harris. *Astonishment and Power (Kongo Art).* Washington, D.C.: Smithsonian Institution Press, 1993.

Perani, Judith, and Fred T. Smith. *The Visual Arts of Africa: Gender, Power, and Life Cycle Rituals.* Englewood Cliffs, N.J.: Prentice Hall, 1998.

Phillips, Ruth B. *Representing Women: Sande Masquerades of the Mende of Sierra Leone.* Los Angeles: UCLA Fowler Museum of Cultural History, 1995.

Phillips, Tom, ed. *Africa: The Art of a Continent.* New York: Prestel, 1995.

Phillipson, D. W. *African Archaeology.* 2d ed. New York: Cambridge University Press, 1993.

Plankensteiner, Barbara. *Benin.* Milan: 5 Continents, 2010.

Schädler, Karl-Ferdinand. *Earth and Ore: 2500 Years of African Art in Terra-Cotta and Metal.* Munich: Panterra, 1997.

Sieber, Roy, and Roslyn A. Walker. *African Art in the Cycle of Life.* Washington, D.C.: Smithsonian Institution Press, 1987.

Stepan, Peter. *Spirits Speak: A Celebration of African Masks.* New York: Prestel, 2005.

Visonà, Monica Blackmun, ed. *A History of Art in Africa.* 2d ed. Upper Saddle River, N.J.: Prentice Hall, 2007.

Walker, Roslyn A. *Olowe of Ise: A Yoruba Sculptor to Kings.* Washington, D.C.: National Museum of African Art, 1998.

Wastiau, Boris. *Chokwe.* Milan: 5 Continents, 2008.

Credits

l'Archeologia Sacra; **4-3a:** John Burge/Cengage Learning; **4-3b:** John Burge/Cengage Learning; **4-4:** Scala/Art Resource, NY; **4-5:** akg-images/Andrea Jemolo; **4-6:** Cengage Learning; **4-7:** Scala/Art Resource, NY; **4-8:** Scala/Art Resource, NY; **4-9:** Österreichische Nationalbibliothek, Vienna, Bildarchiv. folio 7 recto of the Vienna Genesis; **4-10:** Yann Arthus-Bertrand/Terra/Corbis; **4-11a:** John Burge/Cengage Learning; **4-11b:** John Burge/Cengage Learning; **4-12:** ANTHEMIUS OF TRALLES and ISIDORUS OF MILETUS, interior of Hagia Sophia (looking southwest), Constantinople (Istanbul), Turkey, 532–537.; **4-13:** Cengage Learning; **4-14:** Archivio e Studio Folco Quilici; **4-15:** Cengage Learning; **4-16:** Canali Photobank; **4-17:** Canali Photobank; **4-18:** Canali Photobank; **4-19:** Ronald Sheraton/Ancient Art and Architecture Collection Ltd; **4-20:** Scala/Art Resource, NY; **4-21:** The Art Archive/Gianni Dagli Orti/Picture Desk; **4-22:** STUDIO KONTOS/PHOTOSTOCK; **4-23:** Alinari/Art Resource, NY; **4-24:** Réunion des Musées Nationaux/Art Resource, NY; **4-25:** Snark/Art Resource, NY; **4-26:** Scala/Art Resource, NY; **UNF 4-1:** Scala/Art Resource, NY; **UNF 4-2:** Österreichische Nationalbibliothek Vienna Bildarchiv. folio 7 recto of the Vienna Genesis **UNF 4-3:** Copyright Photo Henri STIERLIN Genève; **UNF 4-4:** Canali Photobank; **UNF 4-5:** Snark/Art Resource, NY.

Chapter 5
Opener (bottom): Rosario Sanguedolce/Bhagis Stock Photography/Photographer's Direct; **(detail 1)** © Bednorz-Images; **(detail 2)** © The Bridgeman Art Library; **(detail 3)** © Bednorz-Images; **(detail 4)** © Adam Woolfit/Robert Harding Picture Library; **Map 5-1:** © Cengage Learning; **Timeline:** © Bednorz-Images; **5-2:** Moshe Shai/Encyclopedia/Corbis; **5-3:** Erich Lessing/Art Resource, NY; **5-4a:** Yann Arthus-Bertrand/Encyclopedia/Corbis; **5-4b:** Cengage Learning; **5-5:** Copyright: Photo Henri Stierlin, Geneve; **5-6:** © Bednorz-Images; **5-7:** Adam Woolfit/Robert Harding Picture Library; **5-8:** Mauritius/SuperStock. **5-9:** Toyohiro Yamada/Taxi/Getty Images; **5-10:** Copyright: Photo Henri Stierlin, Geneve; **5-11:** © The Metropolitan Museum of Art/Art Resource, NY; **5-12:** The Trustees of the Chester Beatty Library, Dublin.; **5-13:** © The Trustees of The British Museum.; **5-14:** Erich Lessing/Art Resource, NY; **5-15:** Victoria & Albert Museum London/Art Resource, NY; **UNF 5-1:** Moshe Shai/Encyclopedia/Corbis; **UNF 5-2:** Yann Arthus-Bertrand/Encyclopedia/Corbis; **UNF 5-3:** Mauritius/SuperStock; **UNF 5-4:** Erich Lessing/Art Resource, NY; **UNF 5-5:** © The Trustees of The British Museum.

Chapter 6
Opener: © The Board of Trinity College, Dublin, Ireland/The Bridgeman Art Library; **Map 6-1:** © Cengage Learning; **Timeline:** © The Board of Trinity College, Dublin, Ireland/The Bridgeman Art Library; **6-2:** © The Trustees of the British Museum/Art Resource, NY; **6-3:** Erich Lessing/Art Resource, NY; **6-4:** Kunsthistorisches Museums Wien; **6-5:** Erich Lessing/Art Resource, NY; **6-6:** The Pierpont Morgan Library/Art Resource NY; **6-7:** Thomas Robbin/Photolibrary; **6-8:** Bildarchiv Steffens/The Bridgeman Art Library International; **6-9:** akg-images; **6-10:** © Bednorz-Images; **6-11a:** Cengage Learning; **6-11b:** Cengage Learning; **6-12:** Dom-Museum, Hildesheim; **6-13:** Photo: © Rheinisches Bildarchiv Köln, rba_c000008; **6-14:** Jean Dieuzaide; **6-15:** Cengage Learning; **6-16:** Jonathan Poore/Cengage Learning; **6-17a:** Jonathan Poore/Cengage Learning; **6-17b:** Jonathan Poore/Cengage Learning; **6-18:** John Burge/Cengage Learning; **6-19:** Jonathan Poore/Cengage Learning; **6-20:** Jonathan Poore/Cengage Learning; **6-21:** Jonathan Poore/Cengage Learning; **6-22:** Jonathan Poore/Cengage Learning **6-23:** Erich Lessing/Art Resource, NY; **6-24:** Abtei St. Hildegard; **6-25:** Photograph Speldoorn © Musées royaux d'Art et d'Histoire - Brussels.; **6-26:** Canali Photobank Italy; **6-27:** Jonathan Poore/Cengage Learning; **6-28:** Jonathan Poore/Cengage Learning; **6-29:** Jonathan Poore/Cengage Learning; **6-30a:** Angelo Hornak/Corbis; **6-30b:** Cengage Learning; **6-31:** The Master and Fellows of Corpus Christi College, Cambridge.; **6-32:** The Bridgeman Art Library; **6-33:** By special permission of the City of Bayeux; **6-34:** By special permission of the City of Bayeux; **UNF 6-1:** © The Board of Trinity College, Dublin, Ireland/The Bridgeman Art Library; **UNF 6-2:** Bildarchiv Steffens/The Bridgeman Art Library International; **UNF 6-3:** © Bednorz-Images; **UNF 6-4:** Jean Dieuzaide; **UNF 6-5:** Jonathan Poore/Cengage Learning.

Chapter 7
Opener (bottom): © Marc Garanger/Encyclopedia/Corbis; **(details 1 & 2)** © Jonathan Poore/Cengage Learning; **(detail 3)** © Paul Maeyaert/The Bridgeman Art Library; **(detail 4)** © Jonathan Poore/Cengage Learning; **Map 7-1:** © Cengage Learning; **Timeline:** © Marc Garanger/Encyclopedia/Corbis; **7-2:** Jonathan Poore/Cengage Learning; **7-3:** Cengage Learning; **7-4:** Cengage Learning; **7-5:** Jonathan Poore/Cengage Learning; **7-6:** Jonathan Poore/Cengage Learning; **7-7:** Jonathan Poore/Cengage Learning; **7-8:** John Burge/Cengage Learning; **7-9:** View of the nave, begun 1194 (photo), French School, (12th century)/Chartres Cathedral, Chartres, France/© Paul Maeyaert/The Bridgeman Art Library; **7-10:** Jonathan Poore/Cengage Learning; **7-11:** The Print Collector/Photolibrary; **7-12:** Jonathan Poore/Cengage Learning; **7-14:** Jonathan Poore/Cengage Learning; **7-15:** Bridgeman-Giraudon/Art Resource, NY; **7-16:** Jonathan Poore/Cengage Learning; **7-17:** Österreichische Nationalbibliothek, Vienna.; **7-18:** The Pierpont Morgan Library/Art Resource, NY; **7-19:** Réunion des Musées Nationaux/Art Resource, NY; **7-20:** Ed-

mund Nagele PCL/SuperStock; **7-21:** akg-images/Bildarchiv Monheim; **7-22:** Werner Forman/Corbis Art/Corbis; **7-23:** Svenja-Foto/Corbis; **7-24:** Bednorz-Images; **7-25:** Bednorz-Images; **7-26:** Erich Lessing/Art Resource, NY; **7-27:** Jonathan Poore/Cengage Learning; **7-28:** Scala/Ministero per i Beni e le Attività culturali/Art Resource, NY; **7-29:** Summerfield Press/Corbis Art/Corbis; **7-30:** Scala/Art Resource, NY; **7-31:** Scala/Art Resource, NY; **7-32:** Scala/Art Resource, NY; **7-33:** Scala/Art Resource, NY; **7-34:** Canali Photobank; **7-35:** Scala/Art Resource, NY; **7-36:** age fotostock/SuperStock; **7-37:** Alinari/Art Resource, NY; **UNF 7-1:** © Marc Garanger/Corbis; **UNF 7-2:** Jonathan Poore/Cengage Learning; **UNF 7-3:** Werner Forman/Corbis Art/Corbis; **UNF 7-4:** Scala/Art Resource, NY; **UNF 7-5:** Scala/Art Resource, NY.

Chapter 8
Opener: © Scala/Art Resource; **Map 8-1:** © Cengage Learning; **Timeline:** © Scala/Art Resource, NY; **8-2:** Erich Lessing/Art Resource, NY; **8-3:** Image copyright © The Metropolitan Museum of Art/Art Resource, NY; **8-4:** Scala/Art Resource, NY; **8-5:** Erich Lessing/Art Resource, NY; **8-6:** Erich Lessing/Art Resource, NY; **8-7:** Erich Lessing/Art Resource, NY; **8-8:** Photograph © 2011 Museum of Fine Arts, Boston. 93.153; **8-9:** Scala/Art Resource, NY; **8-10:** Réunion des Musées Nationaux/Art Resource, NY; **8-11a:** Bildarchiv Preussischer Kulturbesitz/Art Resource, NY; **8-11b:** Scala/Art Resource, NY; **8-12:** Erich Lessing/Art Resource, NY; **8-13:** Scala/Art Resource, NY; **Map 8-2:** Cengage Learning; **8-14:** Erich Lessing/Art Resource, NY; **8-15:** Erich Lessing/Art Resource, NY; **8-16:** Scala/Art Resource, NY; **8-17:** Jonathan Poore/Cengage Learning; **8-18:** Jonathan Poore/Cengage Learning; **8-19:** Jonathan Poore/Cengage Learning; **8-20:** Scala/Art Resource, NY; **8-21:** Elio Ciol/Corbis; **8-22:** Erich Lessing/Art Resource, NY; **8-23:** Scala/Art Resource, NY; **8-24:** Erich Lessing/Art Resource, NY; **8-25:** Canali Photobank; **8-26:** Scala/Art Resource, NY; **8-27:** Canali Photobank; **8-28:** Scala/Art Resource, NY; **8-29:** Summerfield Press Ltd.; **8-30:** Image copyright © The Metropolitan Museum of Art/Art Resource, NY; **8-31:** Jonathan Poore/Cengage Learning; **8-32:** Alinari/Art Resource, NY; **8-33:** Jonathan Poore/Cengage Learning; **8-34:** Jonathan Poore/Cengage Learning; **8-35:** Jonathan Poore/Cengage Learning; **8-36:** Scala/Art Resource Inc.; **8-37:** Scala/Ministero per i Beni e le Attività culturali/Art Resource, NY; **8-38:** Alinari/Art Resource, NY; **8-39:** Canali Photobank; **8-40:** Scala/Art Resource, NY; **8-41:** Scala/Art Resource, NY; **8-42:** Erich Lessing/Art Resource, NY; **UNF 8-1:** Erich Lessing/Art Resource, NY; **UNF 8-2:** Scala/Art Resource, NY; **UNF 8-3:** Scala/Art Resource, NY; **UNF 8-4:** Alinari/Art Resource, NY; **UNF 8-5:** Scala/Art Resource, NY.

Chapter 9
Opener: © Institut Amatller D'art Hispànic, **(all details)** akg-Images/Electa; **Map 9-1:** © Cengage Learning; **Timeline:** akg-images/Electa; **9-2:** Erich Lessing/Art Resource, NY; **9-3:** Alinari/Art Resource, NY; **9-4:** Réunion des Musées Nationaux/Art Resource, NY; **9-5:** The Royal Collection © 2011 Her Majesty Queen Elizabeth II; **9-6:** Erich Lessing/Art Resource, NY; **9-7:** M. Sarri 1983/Photo Vatican Museums; **9-8:** Araldo de Luca/Corbis; **9-9:** Arte & Immagini srl/Corbis; **9-10:** Photo Vatican Museums; **9-11:** Bracchietti-Zigrosi/Vatican Museums; **9-12:** akg-images/Electa; **9-13:** Scala/Art Resource, NY; **9-14:** Cengage Learning; **9-15:** Guido Alberto Rossi/Photolibrary; **9-16:** Mark Edward Smith/Photolibrary; **9-17:** Cameraphoto Arte, Venice/Art Resource, NY; **9-18:** Erich Lessing/Art Resource, NY; **9-19:** Scala/Art Resource, NY; **9-20:** Scala/Ministero per i Beni e le Attività culturali/Art Resource, NY; **9-21:** Scala/Art Resource, NY; **9-22:** Scala/Art Resource, NY; **9-23:** National Gallery London/Art Resource, NY; **9-24:** Scala/Art Resource, NY; **9-25:** Scala/Art Resource, NY; **9-26:** © 2006 Fred S. Kleiner; **9-27:** Superstock/Photolibrary; **9-28:** Musée Unterlinden Colmar Musée Unterlinden Colmar Inv. 88.RP.139; **9-29:** Photograph © 2011 Museum of Fine Arts, Boston. 68.187; **9-30:** Victoria & Albert Museum, London/Art Resource, NY; **9-31a:** Bildarchiv Preussischer Kulturbesitz/Art Resource, NY; **9-31b:** Bildarchiv Preussischer Kulturbesitz/Art Resource, NY; **9-32:** © National Gallery London/Art Resource, NY; **9-33:** Jonathan Poore/Cengage Learning; **9-34:** Réunion des Musées Nationaux/Art Resource, NY; **9-35:** Uppsala University Art Collection; **9-36:** Oeffentliche Kunstsammlung Basel photo Martin Bühler; **9-37:** Bildarchiv Preussischer Kulturbesitz/Art Resource, NY; **9-38:** Kunsthistorisches Museum Vienna; **9-39:** Adam Woolfitt/Photolibrary; **9-40:** Scala/Art Resource, NY; **UNF 9-1:** Araldo de Luca/Corbis; **UNF 9-2:** Scala/Art Resource, NY; **UNF 9-3:** Scala/Art Resource, NY; **UNF 9-4:** Victoria & Albert Museum, London/Art Resource, NY; **UNF 9-5:** Kunsthistorisches Museum, Vienna.

Chapter 10
Opener: The Art Archive/Gianni Dagli Orti/Picture Desk; **(detail 1)** © Massimo Listri/Corbis; **(detail 2)** © 2011 Fred Kleiner; **(detail 3)** © Vanni/Art Resource, NY; **(detail 4)** akg-images/Gerard Degeorge; **Map 10-1:** © Cengage Learning; **timeline** © Vanni/Art Resource, NY; **10-2:** Andrea Jemolo/Corbis; **10-3:** Cuboimages/Photolibrary; **10-4:** akg-images/Joseph Martin; **10-5:** Scala/Art Resource, NY; **10-6:** akg-images/Pirozzi; **10-7:** Scala/Art Resource, NY; **10-8:** Bednorz-Images; **10-9:** Scala/Art Resource, NY; **10-10:** Scala/Art Resource, NY; **10-11:** Scala/Art Resource, NY; **10-12:** The Royal Collection © 2011 Her Majesty Queen Elizabeth II; **10-13:** Summerfield Press Ltd.; **10-14:** Wadsworth Atheneum Museum

of Art/Art Resource, NY: **10-15:** Victoria & Albert Museum, London/ Art Resource, NY; **10-16:** Erich Lessing/Art Resource, NY; **10-17:** IRPA-KIK, Brussels, www.kikirpa.be; **10-18:** Erich Lessing/Art Resource, NY; **10-19:** Réunion des Musées Nationaux/Art Resource, NY; **10-20:** Frans Halsmuseum, Haarlem; **10-21:** National Gallery of Art; **10-22:** Rembrandt Harmensz. van Rijn (166-69)/Rijksmuseum Amsterdam The Netherlands/ The Bridgeman Art Library; **10-23:** © English Heritage Photo Library/ The Bridgeman Art Library International; **10-24:** The Pierpont Morgan Library/Art Resource, NY; **10-25:** Mauritshuis, The Hague; **10-26:** Erich Lessing/Art Resource, NY; **10-27:** akg-images; **10-28:** The Royal Collection © 2011 Her Majesty Queen Elizabeth II; **10-29:** Erich Lessing/Art Resource, NY; **10-30:** Photo copyright © Philadelphia Museum of Art, E1950-2-1; **10-31:** Erich Lessing/Art Resource, NY; **10-32:** © Yann Arthus-Bertrand/Altitude; **10-33:** Massimo Listri/Corbis; **10-34:** Angelo Hornak/ Corbis; **UNF 10-1:** Scala/Art Resource, NY; **UNF 10-2:** Erich Lessing/Art Resource, NY; **UNF 10-3:** Erich Lessing/Art Resource, NY; **UNF 10-4:** The Pierpont Morgan Library/Art Resource, NY; **UNF 10-5:** Erich Lessing/Art Resource, NY.

Chapter 11
Opener: © Bridgeman-Giraudon/Art Resource, NY; **Timeline:** © Bridgeman-Giraudon/Art Resource, NY; **11-2:** akg-images/Bildarchiv Monheim; **11-3:** Scala/Art Resource, NY; **11-4:** © Wallace Collection, London, UK/ The Bridgeman Art Library; **11-5:** Image copyright © The Metropolitan Museum of Art/Art Resource, NY; **11-6:** Réunion des Musées Nationaux/ Art Resource, NY; **11-7:** Summerfield Press Ltd; **11-8:** National Gallery, London/Art Resource, NY: **11-9:** National Gallery London UK/ The Bridgeman Art Library; **11-10:** National Gallery of Canada; **11-11:** Photograph © 2011 Museum of Fine Arts, Boston, 30.781; **11-12:** Scala/ Art Resource, NY; **11-13:** Photo: Katherine Wetzel © Virginia Museum of Fine Arts; **11-14:** Réunion des Musées Nationaux/Art Resource, NY; **11-15:** Scala/Art Resource, NY. **11-16:** Jonathan Poore/Cengage Learning; **11-17:** Michael Freeman/Value Art/Corbis; **11-18:** Photo © The Library of Virginia; **UNF 11-1:** © Wallace Collection, London, UK/The Bridgeman Art Library; **UNF 11-2:** Bridgeman-Giraudon/Art Resource, NY; **UNF 11-3:** Scala/Art Resource, NY: **UNF 11-4:** Photo: Katherine Wetzel © Virginia Museum of Fine Arts; **UNF 11-5:** Jonathan Poore/Cengage Learning.

Chapter 12
Opener: © Réunion des Musées Nationaux/Art Resource, NY; **Timeline:** © Réunion des Musées Nationaux/Art Resource, NY; **Map 12-1:** © Cengage Learning; **12-2:** Scala/Ministero per i Beni e le Attività culturali/ Art Resource, NY; **12-3:** Réunion des Musées Nationaux/Art Resource, NY; **12-4:** Image copyright © The Metropolitan Museum of Art/Art Resource, NY; **12-5:** The Art Archive/Museo del Prado Madrid/Gianni Dagli Orti; **12-6:** Erich Lessing/Art Resource, NY; **12-7:** Réunion des Musées Nationaux/Art Resource, NY; **12-8:** Réunion des Musées Nationaux/Art Resource, NY; **12-9:** Bildarchiv Preussischer Kulturbesitz/Art Resource, NY; **12-10:** © National Gallery, London/Art Resource, NY; **12-11:** Museum of Fine Arts, Boston; **12-12:** Image copyright © The Metropolitan Museum of Art/Art Resource, NY; **12-13:** *The Stone Breakers,* 1849 (oil on canvas) (destroyed in 1945), Courbet, Gustave (1819–77)/Galerie Neue Meister, Dresden, Germany/© Staatliche Kunstsammlungen Dresden/The Bridgeman Art Library; **12-14:** Erich Lessing/Art Resource, NY; **12-15:** Réunion des Musées Nationaux/Art Resource, NY; **12-16:** Erich Lessing/ Art Resource, NY; **12-17:** Erich Lessing/Art Resource, NY; **12-18:** Scala/ Art Resource, NY; **12-19:** Image copyright © The Metropolitan Museum of Art/Art Resource, NY; **12-20:** Gift of the Alumni Association to Jefferson Medical College in 1878 and purchased by the Pennsylvania Academy of the Fine Arts and the Philadelphia Museum of Art in 2007 with the generous support of more than 3,400 donors, photo copyright © Philadelphia Museum of Art, 2007-1-1; **12-21:** Howard University Gallery of Art, Washington, D.C.; **12-22:** Tate, London/Art Resource, NY; **12-23:** Travel Pix/ Robert Harding; **12-24:** Roger Antrobus/Corbis; **12-25:** Private Collection/ The Stapleton Collection/The Bridgeman Art Library International; **12-26:** Louis Daguerre/Time & Life Pictures/Getty Images; **12-27:** Nadar/Bettmann/Corbis; **12-28:** New York Public Library/Art Resource, NY; **UNF 12-1:** Scala/Ministero per i Beni e le Attività culturali/Art Resource, NY; **UNF 12-2:** Bildarchiv Preussischer Kulturbesitz/Art Resource, NY; **UNF 12-3:** *The Stone Breakers,* 1849 (oil on canvas) (destroyed in 1945), Courbet, Gustave (1819–77)/Galerie Neue Meister, Dresden, Germany/© Staatliche Kunstsammlungen Dresden/The Bridgeman Art Library; **UNF 12-4:** Travel Pix/Robert Harding; **UNF 12-5:** Louis Daguerre/Time & Life Pictures/Getty Images.

Chapter 13
Opener: © Bildarchiv Preussischer Kulturbesitz/Art Resource, NY; **Timeline:** © Bildarchiv Preussischer Kulturbesitz/Art Resource, NY: **Map 13-1:** © Cengage Learning; **13-2:** Erich Lessing/Art Resource, NY; **13-3:** Réunion des Musées Nationaux/Art Resource, NY; **13-4:** © Culture and Sport Glasgow (Museums); **13-5:** Photography © The Art Institute of Chicago, 1910.2; **13-6:** The Bridgeman Art Library International; **13-7:** Photography © The Art Institute of Chicago, 1928.610; **13-8:** Georges Seurat French, 1859–1891, *A Sunday on La Grande Jatte*—1884, 1884–86, Oil on canvas, 81 3/4 × 121 1/4 in. (207.5 × 308.1 cm), Helen Birch Bartlett Memorial Collection, 1926.224, The Art Institute of Chicago. Photography © The Art Institute of Chicago; **13-9:** Yale University Art Gallery/Art Re-

source, NY: **13-10:** Digital Image © The Museum of Modern Art/Licensed by SCALA/Art Resource NY; **13-11:** Art Resource, NY; **13-12:** Photograph © 2011 Museum of Fine Arts, Boston, 36.270; **13-13:** Philadelphia Museum of Art; **13-14:** Photography © The Art Institute of Chicago, 1926.252; **13-15:** Digital Image © The Museum of Modern Art/Licensed by SCALA/ Art Resource, NY; **13-16:** © 2011 The Munch Museum/The Munch-Ellingsen Group/Artists Rights Society (ARS), NY. Photo: © Erich Lessing/ Art Resource, NY; **13-17:** Erich Lessing/Art Resource, NY; **13-18:** *The Gates of Hell,* 1880–90 (bronze), Rodin, Auguste (1840-1917)/Musee Rodin, Paris, France/Peter Willi/The Bridgeman Art Library; **13-19:** © 2008 SOFAM/architect: V. Horta, photo Bastin & Evrard sprl; **13-20:** Jonathan Poore/Cengage Learning; **13-21** Thomas A. Heinz/Corbis **UNF 13-1:** Réunion des Musées Nationaux/Art Resource, NY; **UNF 13-2:** Digital Image © the Museum of Modern Art/Licensed by SCALA/Art Resource NY; **UNF 13-3:** Digital Image © The Museum of Modern Art/Licensed by SCALA/Art Resource, NY: **UNF 13-4:** *The Gates of Hell,* 1880–90 (bronze), Rodin, Auguste (1840–1917)/Musee Rodin, Paris, France/Peter Willi/The Bridgeman Art Library; **UNF 13-5:** Jonathan Poore/Cengage Learning.

Chapter 14
Opener: © 2011 Artists Rights Society (ARS), NY/VG Bild-Kunst, Bonn. Photo © Bildarchiv Preussischer Kulturbesitz/Art Resource, NY, NG 57/61; **Map 14-1:** © Cengage Learning; **Timeline:** © 2011 Artists Rights Society (ARS), NY/VG Bild-Kunst, Bonn. Photo © Bildarchiv Preussischer Kulturbesitz/Art Resource, NY, NG 57/61; **14-2:** © 2011 Succession H. Matisse, Paris/Artists Rights Society (ARS), NY. Photo © San Francisco Museum of Modern Art.; **14-3:** © 2011 Succession H. Matisse, Paris/Artists Rights Society (ARS). Photo © akg-images; **14-4:** © The Museum of Modern Art/Licensed by SCALA/Art Resource, NY; **14-5:** © 2011 Artists Rights Society (ARS), New York/ADAGP, Paris. Photo: © Solomon R. Guggenheim Museum; **14-6:** Oeffentliche Kunstsammlung Basel, photo Martin Bühler; **14-7:** © 2011 Artists Rights Society (ARS), New York/VG Bild-Kunst, Bonn. Photo: © Erich Lessing/Art Resource, NY.; **14-8:** Pablo Pablo Picasso, Les Demoiselles d'Avignon. Paris, June-July 1907. Oil on canvas, 8′ × 7′ 8″ (243.9 × 233.7 cm). Digital Image © The Museum of Modern Art/Licensed by SCALA/Art Resource, NY. Art © 2011 Estate of Pablo Picasso/Artists Rights Society (ARS), New York; **14-9:** © 2011 Artists Rights Society (ARS), NY/ADAGP, Paris. Photo: © Bridgeman-Giraudon/ Art Resource, NY; **14-10:** Réunion des Musées Nationaux/Art Resource, NY; **14-11:** © 211 Estate of Pablo Picasso/Artists Rights Society (ARS) NY. Photo © Erich Lessing/Art Resource, NY; **14-12:** © 2011 Artists Rights Society (ARS), NY. © DACS/The Bridgeman Art Library: **14-13:** Digital Image © The Museum of Modern Art/Licensed by SCALA/Art Resource, NY; **14-14:** © 2011 Artists Rights Society (ARS), NY Photo Credit : Digital Image © The Museum of Modern Art/Licensed by SCALA/Art Resource, NY; **14-15:** © 2011 Artists Rights Society (ARS), New York/ADAGP, Paris/ Succession Marcel Duchamp. Photo: © Philadelphia Museum of Art, 1998-74-1; **14-16:** Digital Image © The Museum of Modern Art/Licensed by SCALA/Art Resource, NY; **14-17:** Photo © Philadelphia Museum of Art, 1950-134-59, © 2008 Artists Rights Society (ARS), New York/ADAGP, Paris/Succession Marcel Duchamp; **14-18:** Fisk University Galleries, University of Tennessee, Nashville; **14-19:** Digital Image © The Museum of Modern Art/Licensed by SCALA/Art Resource, NY; **14-20:** Photograph by Edward Weston. Collection Center for Creative Photography © 1981 Arizona Board of Regents; **14-21:** © 2011 Artists Rights Society (ARS), New York/VG Bild-Kunst, Bonn. Erich Lessing/Art Resource, NY; **14-22:** © 2011 Estate of Giorgio de Chirico, Licensed by Artists Rights Society (ARS), NY. Photo: © The Museum of Modern Art/Licensed by SCALA/ Art Resource, NY; **14-23:** © 2011 Salvador Dali, Gala-Salvador Dali Foundation/Artists Rights Society (ARS), NY. Digital Image © The Museum of Modern Art/Licensed by Scala/Art Resource, NY, 162.1934.; **14-24:** Digital Image © 29 Museum Associates/LACMA/Art Resource, NY; **14-25:** The Museum of Modern Art/Licensed by SCALA/Art Resource, NY; **14-26:** © 2011 Successió Miró/Artists Rights Society (ARS), NY/ADAGP, Paris. Digital Image © The Museum of Modern Art/Licensed by Scala/ Art Resource, NY, 229.1937.; **14-27:** © 2011 Mondrian/Holtzman Trust c/o HCR International, VA USA; **14-28:** © 2011 Artists Rights Society (ARS), NY/ADAGP Paris. © Philadelphia Museum of Art/Corbis, 195-134-14 15.; **14-29:** © Bowness, Hepworth Estate. Photo © Tate, London/Art Resource, NY; **14-30:** The Museum of Modern Art/Licensed by SCALA/ Art Resource, NY; **14-31:** Courtesy The Dorothea Lange Collection, The Oakland Museum of California; **14-32:** Margaret Bourke-White/Time & Life Pictures/Getty Images; **14-33:** Photography © The Art Institute of Chicago, 1942.51 Estate of Edward Hopper © The Whitney Museum of American Art; **14-34:** © 2011 The Jacob and Gwendolyn Lawrence Foundation, Seattle/Artists Rights Society (ARS) NY. Photo The Phillips Collection Washington D.C.; **14-35:** Art © Figge Art Museum, successors to the Estate of Nan Wood Graham/Licensed by VAGA, New York, NY Photography © The Art Institute of Chicago,1930.934,; **14-36:** © 2011 Banco de México Trust. Licensed by Artists Rights Society (ARS), NY. Dirk Bakker, photographer for the Detroit Institute of Arts/The Bridgeman Art Library; **14-37:** Schalkwijk/Art Resource, NY; **14-38:** © 2011 Artists Rights Society (ARS), NY/VG Bild-Kunst, Bonn. Photo © Vanni/Art Resource, NY; **14-39:** © 2011 Artists Rights Society (ARS), NY/VG Bild-Kunst, Bonn. Digital Image © The Museum of Modern Art/Licensed by Scala/Art Resource, NY.; **14-40:** Jonathan Poore/Cengage Learning; **14-41:** Jonathan Poore/Cengage Learning; **14-42:** © 2011 Frank Lloyd Wright Foundation, Scottsdale, AZ/

Artists Rights Society (ARS), NY. Photo © Peter Cook/View Pictures/Photolibrary; **UNF 14-1:** © 2011 Artists Rights Society (ARS), NY/ADAGP, Paris. Photo: © Bridgeman-Giraudon/Art Resource, NY; **UNF 14-2:** Photograph by Edward Weston. Collection Center for Creative Photography ©1981 Arizona Board of Regents; **UNF 14-3:** The Museum of Modern Art/Licensed by SCALA/Art Resource, NY; **UNF 14-4:** Schalkwijk/Art Resource, NY; **UNF 14-5:** © 2011 Artists Rights Society (ARS), NY/ADAGP, Paris. Photo: © Bridgeman-Giraudon/Art Resource, NY.

Chapter 15
Opener: © 2011 Artists Rights Society (ARS), NY/DACS, London. Photo © The Bridgeman Art Library: **Timeline:** © 2011 Artists Rights Society (ARS), NY/DACS, London. Photo © The Bridgeman Art Library: **15-2:** © 2011 Artists Rights Society (ARS), NY/ADAGP, Paris. Photo: © Des Moines Art Center; **15-3:** © 2011 The Estate of Francis Bacon/ARS, NY/DACS, London. Digital Image © The Museum of Modern Art/Licensed by Scala/Art Resource, NY, 229.1948: **15-4:** © 2011 The Arshile Gorky Foundation/The Artists Rights Society (ARS), New York. Photograph: © The Museum of Modern Art/Licensed by SCALA/Art Resource, NY; **15-5:** © 2011 The Pollock-Krasner Foundation/Artists Rights Society (ARS), NY. Photo © National Gallery of Art, 1976.37.1; **15-6:** © 2011 The Willem de Kooning Foundation/Artists Rights Society (ARS), NY. Digital Image © The Museum of Modern Art/Licensed by Scala/Art Resource, NY, 478.1953; **15-7:** © 2011 Kate Rothko Prizel & Christopher Rothko. Licensed by Artists Rights Society (ARS), NY. Photo: © San Francisco Museum of Modern Art; **15-8:** © 2011 Frank Stella/Artists Rights Society (ARS), NY. Photo © CNAC/MNAM/Dist. Réunion des Musées Nationaux/Art Resource, NY; **15-9:** Helen Frankenthaler, *The Bay*, 1963 (acrylic on canvas), 205.1 × 207.7 cms, Detroit Institute of Arts, USA/© DACS/Founders Society Purchase, Dr & Mrs Hilbert H. DeLawter Fund/The Bridgeman Art Library International. Art © 2011 Helen Frankenthaler/Artists Rights Society (ARS), New York; **15-10:** The Museum of Modern Art/Licensed by SCALA/Art Resource, NY. © Bridget Riley 2011. All rights reserved. Courtesy Karsten Schubert, London; **15-11:** Art © David Smith, Licensed by VAGA, NY. Photo by Lee Stalsworth, Smithsonian Hirshhorn Museum and Sculpture Garden; **15-12:** Art © Judd Foundation/Licensed by VAGA, NY Hirshhorn Museum and Sculpture Garden, Smithsonian Institution, photo Lee Stalsworth, 72.154; **15-13:** © 2011 Estate of Louise Nevelson/Artists Rights Society (ARS), NY. Photo © CNAC/MNAM/Dist. Réunion des Musées Nationaux/Art Resource, NY; **15-14:** Art © Louise Bourgeois Trust/Licensed by VAGA, New York, NY Photo © CNAC/MNAM/Dist. Réunion des Musées Nationaaux/Art Resource, NY; **15-15:** Art © Jasper Johns/Licensed by VAGA, New York, NY Photo: Whitney Museum of American Art, New York, USA/© DACS/The Bridgeman Art Library; **15-16:** Art © Estate of Robert Rauschenberg/Licensed by VAGA, New York, NY. Photo, Courtesy of the Sonnabend Collection; **15-17:** © Estate of Roy Lichtenstein; **15-18:** © 2011 Andy Warhol Foundation for the Visual Arts/ARS, NY. Photo © 2004 The Whitney Museum of American Art; **15-19:** Art © Copyright 1969 Claes Oldenburg. Photo: © 2009 Fred S. Kleiner; **15-20:** Photo © University of Arizona Museum, Tucson, © Audrey Flack; **15-21:** Close, Chuck "Big Self Portrait" 1967–68, acrylic on canvas Collection Walker Art Center Minneapolis. Art Center Acquisition Fund, 1969,; **15-22:** Art © Estate of Duane Hanson/Licensed by VAGA, New York, NY Photo by Anne Gold; **15-23:** © The Estate of Diane Arbus. The Museum of Modern Art, New York, New York, U.S.A./Art Resource, Inc.; **15-24:** © 2011 Judy Chicago. Licensed by Artists Rights Society (ARS), NY. Photo: © The Brooklyn Museum; **15-25:** Cindy Sherman, courtesy the artist and Metro Pictures; **15-26:** Magdalena Abakanowicz, courtesy Marlborough Gallery, NY; **15-27:** Jonathan Poore/Cengage Learning; **15-28:** © 2011 Licensed by Artists Rights Society (ARS), New York. Photo: © Jonathan Poore/Cengage Learning; **15-29:** Jonathan Poore/Cengage Learning; **15-30:** Photo Peter Aaron © Esto; **15-31:** Jonathan Poore/Cengage Learning; **15-32:** © Estate of Robert Smithson. Licensed by VAGA, New York. Photo: © George Steinmetz/Corbis; **15-33:** © 2011 Carolee Schneemann/Artists Rights Society (ARS), NY. Photo © Al Geise, Courtesy PPOW Gallery; **15-34:** © 2011 Joseph Kosuth/Artists Rights Society (ARS), NY. Digital Image © The Museum of Modern Art/Licensed by Scala/Art Resource, NY, 383.1970 a-c; 15-35 Courtesy Nam June Paik Studios, Inc.; **UNF 15-1:** © 2011 The Pollock-Krasner Foundation/Artists Rights Society (ARS), NY. Photo © National Gallery of Art, 1976.37.1; **UNF 15-2:** Art © Estate of Duane Hanson/Licensed by VAGA, New York, NY Photo by Anne Gold; **UNF 15-3:** © 2011 Judy Chicago. Licensed by Artists Rights Society (ARS), NY. Photo: © The Brooklyn Museum; **UNF 15-4:** © 2011 Licensed by Artists Rights Society (ARS), New York. Photo: © Jonathan Poore/Cengage Learning; **UNF 15-5:** © 2011 Joseph Kosuth/Artists Rights Society (ARS), NY. Digital Image © The Museum of Modern Art/Licensed by Scala/Art Resource, NY, 383.1970 a-c.

Chapter 16
Opener: Courtesy of Jaune Quick-to-See Smith (An Enrolled Salish, member of the Salish and Kootenai Nation Montana) Photo: © Chrysler Museum of Art, Norfolk, VA, Museum Purchase; **Timeline:** Courtesy of Jaune Quick-to-See Smith (An Enrolled Salish, member of the Salish and Kootenai Nation Montana) Photo: © Chrysler Museum of Art, Norfolk, VA, Museum Purchase; **16-2:** COPYRIGHT: BARBARA KRUGER. COURTESY: MARY BOONE GALLERY, NEW YORK.; **16-3:** Self-Portrait, 1980 © Copyright The Robert Mapplethorpe Foundation. Cour-

tesy Art + Commerce; **16-4:** © Shahzia Sikander. Photograph: Sheldan C. Collins, courtesy Whitney Museum of American Art; **16-5:** © 1983 Faith Ringgold; **16-6:** © 2011 Estate of Jean-Michel Basquiat/ADAGP, Paris/Artists Rights Society (ARS), New York. Photography: Douglas M. Parker Studio, Los Angeles. Image courtesy of The Broad Art Foundation, Santa Monica; **16-7:** © 2011 Estate of Jean-Michel Basquiat/ADAGP, Paris/Artists Rights Society (ARS), New York. Photography: Douglas M. Parker Studio, Los Angeles. Image courtesy of The Broad Art Foundation, Santa Monica; **16-8:** Willie Bester; **16-9:** © Shirin Neshat. Photo © The Bridgeman Art Library International; **16-10:** Copyright © Xu Bing, courtesy Chazen Museum of Art (formerly Elvehjem Museum of Art), University of Wisconsin; **16-11:** Artwork © Jenny Saville; **16-12:** Photo © Whitney Museum of American Art, © Kiki Smith; **16-13:** Museum of Contemporary Art, Chicago © Jeff Koons; **16-14:** Martin Jones; Ecoscene/Corbis; **16-15:** John Gollings/Arcaid/Corbis; **16-16:** Santiago Yaniz/Photolibrary; **16-17:** Kokyat Choong/The Image Works; **16-18:** Robert O'Dea/akg-images; **16-19:** Wolfgang Volz © 1983 Christo; **16-20:** © 2011 Andreas Gursky/Artists Rights Society (ARS), New York/VG Bild-Kunst, Bonn. Photo, Courtesy Sprüth Magers Berlin London; **16-21:** Bill Viola, photo: Kira Perov; **16-22:** Photograph by David Heald © The Solomon R. Guggenheim Foundation, NY; **UNF 16-1:** Self-Portrait, 1980 © Copyright The Robert Mapplethorpe Foundation. Courtesy Art + Commerce; **UNF 16-2:** © 2011 Estate of Jean-Michel Basquiat/ADAGP, Paris/Artists Rights Society (ARS), New York. Photography: Douglas M. Parker Studio, Los Angeles. Image courtesy of The Broad Art Foundation, Santa Monica; **UNF 16-3:** Photo © Whitney Museum of American Art, © Kiki Smith; **UNF 16-4:** Santiago Yaniz/Photolibrary; **UNF 16-5:** Wolfgang Volz © 1983 Christo.

Chapter 17
Opener: Freer Gallery of Art, Smithsonian Institution, Washington, DC. Purchase, F1949.9a-d; **Timeline:** Freer Gallery of Art, Smithsonian Institution, Washington, DC. Purchase, F1949.9a-d; **Map 17-1:** © Cengage Learning; 7-2: Steatite Pasupati seal, Mohenjodaro, 2300–1750 BC,/National Museum of India, New Delhi, India/The Bridgeman Art Library: **17-3:** Benoy K. Behl; **17-4a:** Scala/Art Resource, NY; **17-4b:** Cengage Learning; **17-5:** Richard Ashworth/Photolibrary; **17-6:** Benoy K. Behl; **17-7:** Luca Invernizzi Tettoni/Photolibrary; **17-8:** V Muthuraman/Photolibrary; **17-9:** Luca Invernizzi Tettoni/Photolibrary; **17-10:** Dinodia Photos/Alamy; **17-11:** V Muthuraman/Photolibrary; **17-12:** Bhaswaran Bhattacharya/PhotoLibrary; **17-13:** Tony Waltham/Photolibrary; **17-14:** Victoria & Albert Museum, London/Art Resource, NY; **17-15:** Freer Gallery of Art, Smithsonian Institution, Washington, D.C,. Purchase, F1942.15a; **17-16:** Kevin R. Morris/Documentary Value/Corbis; **17-17:** National Museum, New Delhi; **17-18:** ml-foto ml-foto/Photolibrary; **17-19:** Alvaro Leiva/Photo-Library; **17-20:** Charles & Josette Lenars/Corbis; **17-21:** © Christophe Loviny/Corbis; **17-22:** Stuart Westmorland; **17-23:** Ladislav Janicek/Bridge/Corbis; **UNF 17-1:** Steatite Pasupati seal, Mohenjodaro, 2300–1750 BC,/National Museum of India, New Delhi, India/The Bridgeman Art Library, **UNF 17-2:** V Muthuraman/Photolibrary; **UNF 17-3:** Bhaswaran Bhattacharya/Photolibrary; **UNF 17-4:** Victoria & Albert Museum, London/Art Resource, NY, **UNF 17-5:** Charles & Josette Lenars/Corbis.

Chapter 18
Opener: © photos12.com/Panorama Stock; **(detail 1)** © Best View Stock/Photolibrary; **(detail 2)** © View Stock/Photolibrary; **(detail 3)** © Best View Stock/Photolibrary; **(detail 4)** © Alfred Ko/CORBIS; **Map 18-1:** © Cengage Learning; **Timeline:** © Alfred Ko/Corbis; **18-2:** Asian Art Museum of San Francisco, The Avery Brundage Collection; **18-3:** Chu Yong/Photolibrary; **18-4:** © Hunan Provincial Museum, Changsa City; **18-5:** The Nelson-Atkins Museum of Art, Kansas City, Missouri. Purchase, Nelson Trust, 33-521. Photo: Robert Newcombe; **18-6:** The Trustees of the British Museum/Art Resource, NY; **18-7:** TAO Images Limited/Photolibrary; **18-8:** Cultural Relics Publishing House, Beijing.; **18-9:** Photograph © 2011 Museum of Fine Arts, Boston; **18-10:** The Art Archive/National Palace Museum Taiwan/Picture Desk; **18-11:** Cultural Relics Publishing House, Beijing.; **18-12:** Cengage Learning: **18-13:** Bruno Barbier/Photolibrary; **18-14:** Collection of the National Palace Museum; **18-15:** Collection of the National Palace Museum; **18-16:** Collection of the National Palace Museum; **18-17:** Michael DeFreitas/Robert Harding Travel/Photolibrary; **18-18:** Image © Cleveland Museum of Art, Cleveland; **18-19:** John Taylor Photography, C. C. Wang Family Collection NY; **18-20:** Audrey R. Topping; **18-21:** © DeA Picture Library/Art Resource, NY; **18-22:** iberfoto/photoaisa; **18-23:** JTB Photo/Photolibrary; **UNF 18-1:** Asian Art Museum of San Francisco, The Avery Brundage Collection; **UNF 18-2:** Photograph © 211 Museum of Fine Arts, Boston; **UNF 18-3:** Percival David Foundation of Chinese Art, B614; **UNF 18-4:** John Taylor Photography, C. C. Wang Family Collection, NY; **UNF 18-5:** iberfoto/photoaisa.

Chapter 19
Opener: Museum photograph © 206 The Brooklyn Museum. 30.1478.30; **Map 19-1:** © Cengage Learning; **Timeline:** Museum photograph © 206 The Brooklyn Museum. 30.1478.30; **19-2:** Georg Gerster/Photo Researchers Inc.; **19-3:** Toyko National Museum. Image ©TNM Image Archives.; **19-4:** Iberfoto/The Image Works; **19-5:** Fotosearch/Photolibrary; **19-6:** Kyoogokokuji (Toji), Kyoto; **19-7:** All Creation/Photolibrary; **19-8:** The Gotoh Art Museum, Tokyo.; **19-9:** Todaiji, Nara; **19-10:** Photograph © 2011 Museum of Fine Arts, Boston; **19-11:** TNM Image Archives,

Note: Italic page numbers refer to illustrations.